Sprachwissenschaft auf dem Weg in das dritte Jahrtausend
Linguistics on the Way into the Third Millennium

T0326459

LINGUISTIK
INTERNATIONAL

HERAUSGEGEBEN VON

HEINRICH WEBER
SUSANNE BECKMANN
ABRAHAM P. TEN CATE
WILFRIED KÜRSCHNER
KAZIMIERZ SROKA
INGO WARNKE
LEW ZYBATOW

BAND 8

PETER LANG

Frankfurt am Main · Berlin · Bern · Bruxelles · New York · Oxford · Wien

REINHARD RAPP (HRSG./ED.)

SPRACHWISSENSCHAFT AUF DEM WEG IN DAS DRITTE JAHRTAUSEND

LINGUISTICS ON THE WAY INTO THE THIRD MILLENNIUM

AKTEN DES 34. LINGUISTISCHEN KOLLOQUIUMS
IN GERMERSHEIM 1999

PROCEEDINGS OF THE 34TH LINGUISTICS COLLOQUIUM,
GERMERSHEIM 1999

TEIL II: SPRACHE, COMPUTER, GESELLSCHAFT
PART II: LANGUAGE, COMPUTER, AND SOCIETY

PETER LANG
Europäischer Verlag der Wissenschaften

Die Deutsche Bibliothek - CIP-Einheitsaufnahme

Sprachwissenschaft auf dem Weg in das dritte Jahrtausend :
Akten des 34. Linguistischen Kolloquiums in Germersheim 1999
= Linguistics on the way into the third millennium / Reinhard
Rapp (Hrsg.). - Frankfurt am Main ; Berlin ; Bern ; Bruxelles ;
New York ; Oxford ; Wien : Lang, 2002
   Teil 2. Sprache, Computer, Gesellschaft = Language,
   computer, and society. - 2002
   (Linguistik International ; Bd. 8)
   ISBN 3-631-39543-4

Satz und Layout: Helga Ahrens

Gedruckt auf alterungsbeständigem,
säurefreiem Papier.

ISSN 1436-6150
ISBN 3-631-39543-4
US-ISBN: 0-8204-5983-6

© Peter Lang GmbH
Europäischer Verlag der Wissenschaften
Frankfurt am Main 2002
Alle Rechte vorbehalten.

Printed in Germany 1 2 4 5 6 7

www.peterlang.de

Inhaltsverzeichnis

Teil 2: Sprache, Computer, Gesellschaft

Psycholinguistik

Soziolinguistik

Kontrastive Linguistik

Computerlinguistik

Teil 1: Text, Bedeutung, Kommunikation

Syntax

Morphologie

Theoretische Linguistik

Phonologie / Phonetik

Psycholinguistik

Brain Responses Related to Prosodic Information in Natural Speech: An Event-related fMRI Study

Kai Alter, Martin Meyer, Karsten Steinhauer,
Angela D. Friederici, D. Yves von Cramon

Traditional neuropsychological observations associated right hemisphere brain damage to disturbances of patients' capability to deal with prosodic information. Since these results are mostly based on single-case studies and fail in identifying the location of lesion in detail little is really known about the cortical representation of prosody. Language is assumed to be represented predominantly in perisylvian cortex (e.g., Broca's and Wernicke's areas) of the *left* hemisphere (LH), whereas emotions and affective prosody appear to involve particularly *right* hemispheric (RH) areas (cf. Ross 1997; Baum & Pell 1999).

This raises the question where *linguistic prosody*, e.g. the correspondence between syntactic structure, intonation, accentuation and prosodic phrasing is processed in the brain. In a recent event-related potential (ERP) study we were able to demonstrate that linguistic prosody is immediately decoded and used to guide the listener's initial sentence interpretation, as reflected by a specific brain response (Steinhauer, Alter & Friederici 1999).

Thus, the current study utilized functional Magnetic Resonance Imaging (fMRI) to localize distinct brain areas involved in the processing of linguistic prosody in natural speech. As German realizes prosody particularly by pitch *(Fundamental Frequency, or F0)*, the study focuses on the contribution of this parameter.

1   Acoustic properties of natural speech

From a simplified acoustic point of view, natural speech signals can be divided into two frequency portions – into *high* or *spectral* frequencies and into *low* frequencies. Both types of frequency information have different articulatory sources. Low frequencies are produced by the glottis whereas high/spectral frequencies result from the filtering properties of the human vocal tract. The lowest frequency in the speech signal is called Fundamental Frequency (F0) and corresponds to *pitch*, higher frequencies can be analyzed as *formant* frequencies (at least for the sonorant parts of the speech signal). Under this view, prosodic information is related to the low frequency parts of natural speech, e.g., to the F0-variation (cf. Figure 1).

In the present study we used event-related fMRI in order to identify the neural substrates of the processing of correct and incorrect prosodic information. As described below, our study deals with the manipulation of prosody, e.g., the manipulation of F0.

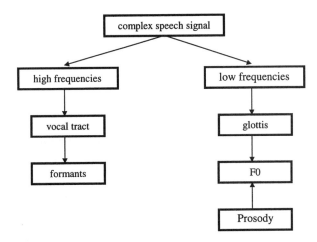

Figure 1: Associating prosodic information to F0 via dividing a complex speech signal into two frequency parts. Prosody is related to the lowest frequency in a speech signal, e.g., to the F0.

2   Material

The material consisted of 4 different conditions with either correct and illformed prosodic information.

Two conditions (cond 1 and cond 2 in Table 1) present correctly intonated sentences as originally produced by a native female speaker of German. In cond 2, however, they are narrowly focused with the main accent on the first noun phrase. In cond 3, the pitch contour was completely flattened resulting in a monotonous, artificial sounding intonation whereas lexical and syntactic information is still available. In the de-lexicalized cond 4, lexical information has been filtered out using a particular filtering procedure (Sonntag & Portele 1998). In these filtered speech signals, the general pitch contour remains unaltered (i.e., prosody was still available), however, the speech signal does not contain any spectral information.

correct condition	anomaly 1	anomaly 2
correct prosody	missing F0-excursion	missing spectral information
cond 1 & 2	cond 3	cond 4

Table 1: The four sentence conditions presented auditorily in the fMRI study containing two prosodically correct conditions (cond 1 & 2) and two conditions with illformed prosody (cond 3 & 4).

3   Method

The participants (all of them 12 right-handed German native speakers from the University of Leipzig) were asked to perform in a *prosody comparison* task. Whenever a trial was not initially marked by a beep (20% = 7 trials in each condition), subjects had to judge whether the current and the preceding sentence shared the same prosodic pattern. In the overwhelming majority of 80% of trials (= 28 in each condition), however, a trial initial beep indicated that no comparison was required.

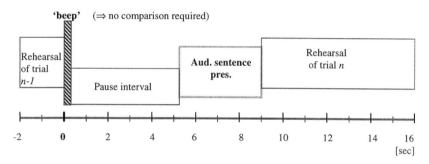

Figure 2: Time course of sentence presentation in 'Template'-Trial n. Only activation during the time interval of auditory sentence presentation is illustrated in Table 3.

The experimental design used the event-related approach. Analogous to ERP-studies, 36 sentences of each condition were presented in a pseudorandomized and unpredictable order to avoid sequence effects. So-called 'Template' trials started with a warning tone, indicating that no comparison was required. That is, subjects did not need to keep the previous prosody in working memory while listening to the current sentence. The Interstimulus Interval (ISI) lasted some 10 seconds and varied slightly dependent on the duration of the speech signal.

For each single trial 8 gradient-echo EPI T2* images (matrix 128x64, TE = 40 ms, TR = 2 sec) were obtained in eight horizontal slices (thickness = 4 mm, interslice distance = 2 mm) roughly along the bicomissural plane (AC-PC plane) using a 3.0 T Bruker 30/100 Medspec. The entire range of slices covered all parts of the perisylvian cortex and subcortical layers.

4   Data analysis and results

For data analysis the BRIAN software was used. Prior to statistical analyses, data were corrected with respect to movement and baseline artifacts and smoothed with a spatial Gaussian filter ($\sigma = 1$) (Kruggel et al. 1998). Individual functional data were analyzed by computing a pixelwise Pearson correlation of the MR signal with a 4 second delayed box car reference wave form and normalized to Z-scores. Multisubject averages of individual Z-maps (Z > 5.0) were computed in order to detect overlapping clusters.

In general, significant increase in local blood supply to all temporal and frontal brain areas which are related to speech comprehension could be observed. As a function of the prosody comparison task the right hemisphere rather than the language dominant left hemisphere was more strongly involved in the trials where no comparison was required.

In contrast to previous fMRI studies on sentence processing, we observed a stronger temporal activation of the right rather than left hemisphere. This uniform finding across all conditions points to a *significant contribution of the RH in the processing* of both affective and *linguistic prosody*.

Temporal Activation / Num of voxels	Cond1: Normal prosody	Cond 2: Narrow focus at NP1	Cond 3: Flattened pitch	Cond 4: Delexicalized sentence
LH	18793	18760	20897	17475
RH	19940	19465	24378	22069

Table 3: Cluster sizes (mm³) of significant voxels in the upper temporal lobes of both hemispheres. In each condition, activation was found to be stronger in the right hemisphere.

In addition, when *anomalous sounding speech input* (cond 3 & 4) had to be processed, *additional resources* in the left and right inferior and mid frontolateral cortices as well as in right temporal areas appeared to be allocated (cf. also Meyer, Friederici, & von Cramon 1999, for similar results). An exception is the *inferior part of Broca's area in the delexicalized condition*: in the absence of any lexical and syntactic information, this region seems not to be activated.

5   Discussion

The findings that the processing of anomalous prosodic information leads to an increased activation of right inferior and mid fronto-lateral areas can be explained by the acoustic properties of the speech signals: in the prosodically ill-formed conditions, important acoustic parameters were missing, namely the pitch variation in condition 3 and the spectral information in condition 4.

The increased right frontal activation may reflect compensatory effects for the balancing the lack of F0-variation in condition 3. As for the condition 4, these signals are reported to sound like listening to someone behind a door. In this condition, the spectral information is missed.

The increased right frontal activation may reflect compensatory effects for the balancing the lack of F0-variation in condition 3. As for the condition 4, these signals are reported to sound like listening to someone behind a door. In this condition, the spectral information is missed.

Furthermore, only in condition 4 left frontal areas seem not to be activated. Based on the present set of data, we can only speculate on the involvement of this region. First, it can be due to the lack of lexical and syntactic information. Second, following a recently discussed hypothesis on the lateralization during the processing of prosodic information (cf. Ivry & Robertson 1998), one could assume a LH-activation for the processing of high/spectral frequencies and a RH-activation for low frequencies (cf. Figure 1). The frontal LH-activation may be suppressed and/or the right frontal activation is more accentuated simply because the spectral frequencies are not available for the processing in condition 4.

For this purpose, additional experiments are needed to show how in the human brain the different functions of acoustic and prosodic information are processed in more detail.

Further evaluation employing multiple regression analyses and a universal baseline restricted to the pause interval (cf. Figure 2) is required in order to distinguish more efficiently between activation related to speech perception and activation involved in prosodic rehearsal.

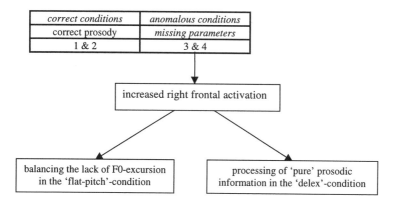

Figure 3: Explanation of the increased right frontal activation pattern. 'Pure' prosodic information is associated with F0-variation (cf. Figure 1) whereas spectral frequencies are absent.

6   References

BAUM, Shari R.; PELL, Marc D. (1999): Neural bases of prosody: Insights from lesion studies and neuroimaging. In: Aphasiology 13.8, 581-608.

IVRY, Richard B.; ROBERTSON, Lynn C. (1998): The two sides of perception. A Bradford Book. Cambridge MA, London: The MIT Press.

KRUGGEL, Frithjof; DESCOMBES, Xaver; VON CRAMON Yves D. (1998): Preprocessing of fMR datasets. In: Vemuri, B. (ed.): Workshop on Biomedical Image Analysis (WBIA). Los Alamitos CA: IEEE Computer Society, 211-220.

MEYER, Martin; FRIEDERICI, Angela D.; VON CRAMON, D. Yves (1999): Comprehension mechanisms of speech specified by event-related fMRI (Journal of Cognitive Neuroscience, Supplement 49).

ROSS, Elliott D.; THOMPSON, Robin D.; YENKOSKY, J. (1997): Lateralization of affective prosody in brain and the callosal integration of hemispheric language functions. In: Brain and Language 56, 27-54.

SONNTAG, Gerit P.; PORTELE, Thomas (1998): PURR – a method for prosody evaluation and investigation. In: Journal of Computer Speech and Language 12.4 (Special Issue on Evaluation in Language and Speech Technology), 437-451.

STEINHAUER, Karsten; ALTER, Kai; FRIEDERICI, Angela D. (1999): Brain potentials indicate immediate use of prosodic cues in natural speech processing. In: Nature Neuroscience 2, 191-196.

Towards an Anthropomorphological Semantics of Spatial Prepositions

Joachim Grabowski

1 Introduction

The use of spatial prepositions is a common means to direct the hearer's attention to a particular place, or object, by spatially relating the target to a reference object. In many cases, however, such spatial descriptions can not simply be judged correct or false; rather, their adequacy crucially depends on the underlying spatial interpretation of the respective situation. This is particularly true with dimensional prepositions and the relations they express. Therefore, the semantic description of prepositions and prepositional phrases such as *in front of*, *behind*, *to the left of*, *to the right of*, or their counterparts in other languages, poses a challenge not only for traditional linguistic semantics, but also for cognitive science in general and for cognitive psychology in particular.

On closer examination, we can differentiate the *characteristic* meaning of an expression (i.e. the 'true' semantic description) from the *referential* meaning of an utterance (Frege 1892). The second-mentioned aspect, i.e. the way dimensional prepositions are used in a given situation, has been addressed in many psycholinguistic studies (e.g., Abkarian 1982; Cox/Isard 1990; Ehrich/Koster 1983; Grabowski/Weiß 1996; Grabowski/Miller (in press); Herrmann/Grabowski 1998; Levelt 1982; Miller/Johnson-Laird 1976; Wunderlich 1981). When it comes to the theoretical underpinnings, however, the state of the art appears to be neither clear nor completely convincing. There is lack of an overarching semantic theory that would offer a well-ordered, theoretically uniform classification of the *possible* ways spatio-dimensional expressions can be used and understood. Rather, we find a great variety of theoretical constructs with different theoretical status: Some determinants relate to the cognition of spatial relations, where the physical properties of objects in the world are considered responsible for the way a spatial relation is conceived (e.g., Lang 1991, 1993). Other approaches draw on properties of linguistic elements (e.g., Talmy 1983), or concentrate on features or preferences of cognitive systems (e.g., Landau/Jackendoff 1993; Levelt 1982). We also find cognitive categories mixed with semantic categories (e.g., Herskovits 1986).

For the classification of the alternatives of dimensional interpretation, we apparently need, first, the distinction of the intrinsic versus extrinsic *frames of reference*, where the intrinsic (or object-centered) frame assumes inherent properties of the reference object. Intrinsically oriented objects, moreover, need to be distinguished according to their anthropomorphous or their facing *pattern* of the four sides in the horizontal plane, where the facing pattern is described through an inversion of the left-right poles relative to the front-back axis (Clark 1973). Next, the extrinsic frame further subdivides into the environnment centered frame and the viewer-centered, or deictic, frame. The deictic frame, in turn, varies within and between cultures with respect to the applied *strategy*, which can follow either the aligning or the vis-à-vis *principle*. (See Carlson-Radvansky/Irwin 1993; Levelt 1996; Levinson 1996; Retz-Schmidt 1988, for overviews of reference systems.) Moreover, it remains unclear with all these distinctions, which sources of variation in the use and interpretation of spatio-dimensional expressions should be integrated into the semantic description of the respective prepositions (and should therefore be considered a linguistic problem) and which should, instead, be passed on to psychology and the study of cognitive systems (beyond the range of their lexical meanings).

2   The anthropomorphous Origo as a basic space-dimensioning principle

When explaining the core meaning of spatial expressions, it is widely assumed that the dimensional conception of a spatial situation is derived from the dimensionally qualified sides of the respective reference object. Thus, if we know where, e.g., the front of object B is, we can resolve the meaning of "object A is in front of B" through the assumption that the part of the surrounding region of object B that adjoins the object's front constitutes a dimensionally specified subregion *in* which object A is located.

The concept of referential frames, then, indicates the transition from linguistic semantics to psycholinguistics: It is employed in order ro describe the principles according to which reference objects get their sides assigned. Here, the basic distinction is between the intrinsic and the deictic frame: In the intrinsic frame, the reference object has its qualified sides independent of the given situation by its inherent morphological or functional features. In the deictic frame, in contrast, the reference object has no inherent dimensioning features, or they are not used for the spatial conception of the situation; therefore, the reference object must have its sides assigned through an observer's perspective, and the dimensional qualifications of the sides change with varying positions and orientations of the observer. The principles of how sides are attributed to reference objects are elsewhere described in detail (e.g., Carlson-Radvansky/Irwin 1993; Fillmore 1971; Grabowski 1999; Levelt 1996; Miller/Johnson-Laird 1976; Retz-Schmidt 1988).

A basic assumption of the approach to the semantics of spatial prepositions presented in this paper is that we can infer a person's cognitive conception of a spatial situation from the way he or she verbally describes, or understands, a given verbal description of this situation; i.e., the cognitive conception of a spatial situation is considered a logical and process-related prerequisite of the use of linguistic expressions for this situation (cf. Tversky/Lee 1998). Therefore, in order to arrive at a uniform semantic description of dimensional prepositions, we must ask how spatial dimensions originate in our conception of a spatial situation. And the answer should be such that it overcomes the distinction between the sides of the reference object – as the basis of conceived dimensional relations – and the frames of reference which determine the assignment of sides to objects.

To achieve this, we start from the basic assumption according to which the dimensions of space, as well as their poles, are always derived from the body asymmetries of the space-conceiving human being (see as early as Stern 1936). The initial definition of the vertical line is the axis from the head to the feet, where the headward direction marks the upper pole and the feetward direction the lower pole. Only in case of the canonical erect orientation of the human body, the anthropocentric and the geocentric, gravitation-based vertical lines coincide. The first horizontal axis runs through chest and back, with the positive pole being in the direction of the privileged perceptive field of the human senses. The second horizontal axis runs perpendicular to both the vertical and the first horizontal line. It is controversial as to whether the poles of this third axis are also based on physical asymmetry. At least, left and right are distinguishable through the feature of handedness and through the location of the unpaired organs. In the tradition of Bühler (1934), the aspect of the human body that serves the space-dimensioning functions can be called an anthropomorphous *Origo*. In our case, the most important feature is the Origo's *orientation* (i.e., the directions it defines). If the Origo's spatial *position* is also considered – which at the same time provides the Origo's relative position to the object relation at issue – a viewpoint is defined as the basis of any dimensional conception of spatial contexts: the half axis that points from the positioned anthropomorphous Origo towards the positive pole of the first horizontal axis. In this view, dimensional relations are always three-place relations: An object is in a specific spatial relation to a reference object from the space-dimensioning viewpoint of an instantiated Origo.

First, we consider the case on an *actual Origo*, in which the observer (in a given situation) sets the Origo egocentrically. This is only possible in situations where the observer, the localized object and the reference object are temporally and spatially co-present. Given an actual (egocentric) Origo, there are two manners of conceiving the poles of the two horizontal dimensions (assuming that the vertical line is given.) These ways differ with respect to the Origo being either in the place of the reference object, or outside the place of the reference object. The first case shall be called *inside perspective* (or *inside Origo*), the second *outside perspective* (or *outside Origo*).

The inside perspective: The fundamental characteristic of the inside perspective is that the Origo – which is, for the moment, functionally derived from the observer's morphology in his or her actual position and orientation – is in the same place as the reference object with respect to the relevant horizontal dimensions. This situation can occur when the reference object is a container *in* which the Origo is located (e.g., inside a car or inside a garment) or when the Origo's location differs from the place of the reference object only vertically (e.g., when sitting on a chair or on a tree stump). It was already mentioned that in other theoretical contexts, the inside perspective is described such that the observer induces the reference object front and back (and with it right and left) according to the anthropomorphous pattern, thus considering the reference object as the Origo itself. However, with respect to a general and uniform account, it seems advantageous to carefully separate the space-dimensioning function of the Origo from the spatial anchoring of the localized object by the reference object (see figure 1). In localizing utterances, however, from which the underlying cognitive conception is often inferred, only the localized object and the reference object (and, of course, the spatial relation between the two) are verbally expressed, but not the space-dimensioning entity that is fundamental to the dimensional interpretation of the spatial situation. Nevertheless, it may improve the understanding of the anthropomorphological concept when it is illustrated by linguistic examples. If a speaker sits on a tree stump and uses his or her actual egocentric anthropomorphous orientation when dimensionally relating another object to the tree stump, the underlying spatial conception of the utterance "the picnic basket is behind the stump" can be described as follows: "The picnic basket is in the region of the stump, and it is in the direction from the tree stump that leads off from my back (or: that is opposite to my actual line of vision)." If a child sits in a car and says, "the ball is in front of the car," this utterance is based on the conception, "the ball is in the region of the car, and it is in the direction from the car that corresponds to my actual line of vision." Note that this case of defining the polar axis through the speaker's actual orientation does not depend on the child's relative orientation to the car: From the speaker's actual Origo in the inside perspective, *in front of the car* is always in the Origo's line of vision, whether the speaker looks through the windshield or through the rear window.

a)

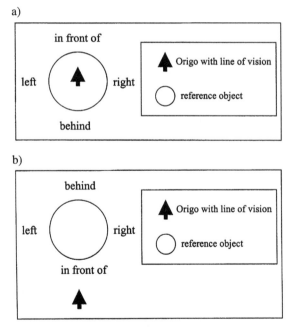

b)

Fig. 1: The conception of dimensional relations a) in the inside perspective (top) and b) in the outside perspective (bottom).

A special case of the inside perspective is when the observer conceives him- or herself as the reference object of an object relation. Again, however, there is a functional distinction between the place that the observer occupies as a physical object, and his or her body asymmetries that form the basis for the instantiation of a space-dimensioning Origo.

The *outside perspective*: If the Origo is not in the place of the reference object, as was described above, then it is always turned toward the reference object so that, from the Origo's point of view, the reference object is towards the positive pole of the first horizontal axis. This is an indispensable requirement for the conception of dimensional object relations in all cases that do not come under the inside perspective. If necessary, the observer must establish this prerequisite by a change of his or her own orientation, before an object relation is interpreted dimensionally.

In other theoretical contexts, the outside perspective is, again, described so that the observer induces the reference object with a front on the side that is facing the observer; accordingly, the opposite side of the reference object is interpreted as its back. After that, the dimensioning of space and the polarization of these dimensions is put down to these acquired sides of the reference object. This principle is often justified with reference to Clark (1973), who describes the "canonical encounter" (i.e., the face-to-face position of speaker and hearer) as the typical pattern of interaction from which other cases, in which people encounter objects, are derived. However, it appears questionable as to why the definition of front and back is derived from the hearer's facing position, but not the definition of right and left. This is because the poles of the second horizontal axis correspond, under the outside perspective, again to the anthropomorphous pattern of the Origo, and not to the intrinsic left and right of the hearer on the other side (see figure 1b)). These side-induction approaches have to assume a transposition of the left and right poles with regard to the front-back axis (cf. Wunderlich/Herweg 1991).

With a uniform description of the conception of dimensional object relations in mind, the difference between inside and outside perspective is preferably understood in a way that emphasizes as far as possible what both perspectives share in common: "right of the reference object" and "left of the reference object" are defined in both perspectives through the Origo's anthropomorphous poles on the second horizontal axis. In the face of this agreement, it is now no longer the inversion of the left-right axis that needs to be explained, but the transposition of the front and back poles on the first horizontal axis in the so-called vis-à-vis perspective compared to the anthropomorphous pattern of dimensional directions. However, the place "in front of the reference object" is characterized by the fact that it is part of the Origo's perceptual catchment area in both inside and outside perspectives. (Remember that, in the present approach, the Origo is derived from the anthropomorphous and anthropofunctional attributes of human beings.) If we take the visual sense as the most typical representative of human perception, we can say in simplified terms that "in front of the reference object" is a place on the first horizontal axis that the Origo can see; "behind the reference object" is a place on the first horizontal axis that the Origo can't see. So far, this pattern holds for both inside and outside perspective.

Both perspectives, however, differ regarding the *causes* that account for the perceptual accessibility (visibility, audibility, manipulability, etc.) of the localized object. From the inside perspective, an object is either, say, visible or (at least partially) invisible, *because* it is either in the Origo's line of vision or behind it (i.e., in the direction towards the negative pole of the first horizontal axis). From the outside perspective, an object is either visible or invisible, *because* the reference object either admits or obscures its perceptual accessibility. In the latter case, the perceptual overlap of the localized object and the reference object determines the Origo's perceptual access to the localized object. Thus, the main difference between inside and outside perspective is whether the sensory-perceptual equipment of the anthropomorphous Origo, or the position of the reference object compared to the localized object, is considered responsible for perceptual accessibility of the localized object from the Origo's point of view.

The above reconstruction of the conception of spatio-dimensional relations is solely derived from psychological conditions of human beings (and from constraints in the physical world). Now, the results generated to reach the objective of providing a general basis for the conception of all dimensional relations (with a certain emphasis on the relations in the horizontal plane) under both perspectives fulfills a central goal of linguistic semantics which is, through the analysis of the usability of dimensional prepositions, to attain core meanings that are as comprehensive and as extensive as possible or, in other theoretical approaches, to attain central prototypes of prepositional usability (Brugman 1981; Herskovits 1986; Hottenroth 1993; Vandeloise 1985).

Projected Origos: So far the discussion was restricted to Origo setting (i.e., conceiving a spatial relation from a particular Origo) via the actual position and orientation of the space-conceiving observer. However, we are capable of the cognitive processes of mental translation and mental rotation (see Shepard/Cooper 1982), i.e. we can imagine how the spatial world looks from a perspective other than our actual egocentric perspective. In other words, we can mentally project our egocentric Origo onto another position and/or orientation. For this reason, it is possible to dimension the spatial environment from a projected Origo's perspective. As with the actual egocentric Origo, projected Origos involve both position and orientation. Origo projections always follow the anthropomorphous principle, which means that the projections preserve the anthropomorphous pattern of spatial dimensions and their poles.

The necessity of the human ability to perform Origo projections follows from the very fact that a hearer, in order to comprehend a speaker's egocentric localization, must be able to imagine the speaker's point of view in all cases in which both are not co-oriented in space. No wonder the speaker, who is also hearer in many situations, also employs this ability in the course of language production.

In principle, we can put ourselves mentally in any orientation and position, thus instantiating a projected Origo. However, particularly in communicative contexts three types of projection 'recipients' are most important: canonically projected Origos, context-based projected Origos, and momentarily projected Origos.

Canonical Origo projection: Several objects are formed in such a way that people take a particular position and orientation towards these objects when using them. For such objects, asymmetry on at least one dimension is required (presupposing that the object is in its normal vertical orientation; cf. Levelt 1984). The typical position and orientation of people when handling objects of this kind can serve to define a canonical Origo's point of view, which in turn serves as a space-dimensioning entity projected by the observer. Again, an inside perspective and an outside perspective exist. Among reference objects that are typically used from the inside perspective are vehicles, garments, conference rooms, theaters, and seats. Among reference objects that are typically used from the outside perspective are grandfather clocks, closets, and TV sets.

It was already mentioned that these objects are, in psycholinguistic approaches, frequently described as having intrinsic (or inherent) fronts, backs, lefts, and rights that define spatial dimensions and their poles by themselves. In these approaches, the relation between the localized object and the reference object may be conceptualized as a three-place relation where the intrinsically directed reference object simultaneously plays the role of the Origo. In this view, the familiar problem arises that 'facing objects' need the poles of the left-right axis to be interchanged, compared to the anthropomorphous pattern of poles. Moreover – as can easily be concluded from the previous argumentation – even in the case of intrinsically directed reference objects, it appears advantageous with respect to a uniform description to not disregard the canonical, anthropomorphous interactor who defines the prerequisites for the dimensional conception of the object relation at issue. From a psychological-anthropocentric starting point, the intrinsic fronts of objects are merely derived from the typical orientation of the canonical user. The 'true' space-dimensioning principle is not the object itself, but the canonical anthropomorphous Origo.

Context-based Origo projection: Context-based projections include those cases elsewhere described as extrinsic, or environment-centered, frames of reference. Here, the observer projects the Origo into a position and orientation that people would take in a particular context because of other objects in the surroundings. For example, a house can be seen from the viewpoint of a passer-by (= outside perspective), thus conceiving a tree as being in front of the house (even if the canonical front of the house with the entrance where you typically enter it is at the side of the house that turns away from the street). Or a perfectly circular UFO may take an anthropomorphous Origo in the way a person would orientate when he or she moves in the direction of flight (= inside perspective). Or an object is presently only accessible from one particular position, which can serve as a context-based outside Origo. In contrast to the canonical perspectives, however, the context-based description of the object relation changes when the identical object constellation is put into another environment, e. g., when the street now passes the house on the other side or when the UFO changes its flight direction.

Momentarily projected Origo: The observer can mentally project the Origo into any arbitrary position and orientation which must, in the case of communication, be verbally explicated. However, people, in most cases, take perspectives that they could actually occupy; they do not conceive an object relation from the perspective of, say, somebody who is hanging under the ceiling. This projection category subdivides into real and fictitious Origos. Real Origo-recipients can be all entities that are present in the respective situation and that allow for an anthropomorphous projection, particularly, in the case of communication, the hearer or a third person.

When an object relation is imagined or recalled that is not part of the actual surroundings, the actual orientation is of no use as a space-dimensioning Origo. Particularly in such cases, it is possible, and sometimes necessary, to introduce a fictitious Origo. In route directions, for example, we hear such utterances as, "when you leave central station ...". By this phrase, a space-dimensioning Origo is introduced with respect to both position and orientation. Again, fictitious Origos are always anthropomorphous Origos and come under both inside and outside perspectives. (Consider "if you look out of my window, the bus station is right in front," as an example for the inside perspective.)

To sum it up, the most important cases of the dimensional conception of object relations vary according to two parameters:

a) Actual (i.e., non-projected, egocentric) Origo vs. canonical (or, more precisely: canonically projected) Origo vs. context-based Origo vs. momentary projection into a real or fictitious Origo, and

b) inside perspective vs. outside perspective, where the perspective parameter merely depends on the location of the Origo relative to the reference object, thus introducing different conditions for the perceptual accessibility of places.

So we get simple and theoretically uniform semantic descriptions of dimensional prepositions in the plane, for example: "A in front of B" means that A is near B and that A is perceptually accessible, from an anthropomorphous Origo's point of view. This holds for all perspectives. Which cognitive representations of an Origo language users have in which situations, is beyond the task of linguistic semantics.

3　References

ABKARIAN, G. G. (1982): Comprehension of deictic locatives: The object "behind" it. In: Journal of Psycholinguistic Research 11, 229–245.

BLOOM, P.; PETERSON, M.; NADEL, L.; GARRETT, M. (eds.) (1996): Language and space. Cambridge, MA: MIT Press.

BRUGMAN, Claudia (1981): The story of over (unpublished thesis). University of California, Berkeley.

BÜHLER, Karl (1934): Sprachtheorie: Die Darstellungsfunktion der Sprache. Jena: Fischer.

CARLSON-RADVANSKY, Laura A.; IRWIN, David E. (1993): Frames of reference in vision and language: Where is above? In: Cognition 46, 223-244.

CLARK, Herbert H. (1973): Space, time, semantics, and the child. In: Moore, T. E. (ed.): Cognitive development and the acquisition of language. New York: Academic Press, 27-63.

COX, Maureen V.; ISARD, Sarah (1990): Children's deictic and nondeictic interpretations of the spatial locatives 'in front of' and 'behind'. In: Journal of Child Language 17, 481-488.

EHRICH, Veronika; KOSTER, Charlotte (1983): Discourse organization and sentence form: The structure of room descriptions in Dutch. In: Discourse Processes 6, 169-195.

FILLMORE, Charles J. (1971): Toward a theory of deixis. In: Working Papers in Linguistics 3, 219-242.

FREGE, Gottlob (1892): Über Sinn und Bedeutung. In: Zeitschrift für Philosophie und philosophische Kritik 100, 25-50.

GRABOWSKI, Joachim (1999): Raumrelationen. Kognitive Auffassung und sprachlicher Ausdruck. Opladen: Westdeutscher Verlag.

GRABOWSKI, Joachim; MILLER, George A. (in press): Factors affecting the use of spatial prepositions in German and American English: Object orientation, social context, and prepositional patterns. In: Journal of Psycholinguistic Research.

GRABOWSKI, Joachim; WEISS, Petra (1996): The prepositional inventory of languages: A factor that affects comprehension of spatial prepositions. In: Language Sciences 18, 19-35.

HERRMANN, Theo; GRABOWSKI, Joachim (1998): Cross-linguistic differences in the use of dimensional prepositions. In: Hillert, D. (ed.): Sentence processing: A cross-linguistic perspective. San Diego: Academic Press, 265-291.

HERSKOVITS, Annette (1986): Language and spatial cognition. Cambridge: Cambridge University Press.

HOTTENROTH, Priska-Monika (1993): Prepositions and object concepts: A contribution to cognitive semantics. In: Zelinsky-Wibbelt, C. (ed.): The semantics of prepositions. Berlin: Mouton de Gruyter, 179-220.

LANDAU, Barbara; JACKENDOFF, Ray S. (1993): "What" and "where" in spatial language and spatial cognition. In: Behavioral and Brain Sciences 16, 217–265.

LANG, Ewald (1993): The meaning of German projective prepositions: A two-level approach. In: Zelinsky-Wibbelt, C. (ed.): The semantics of prepositions. Berlin: Mouton de Gruyter, 249-294.

— (1991): A two-level approach to projective prepositions. In: Rauh, G. (ed.): Approaches to prepositions. Tübingen: Narr, 127–167.

LEVELT, Willem J. M. (1996): Perspective taking and ellipsis in spatial descriptions. In: Bloom; Peterson; Nadel; Garrett: 77-107.

— (1984): Some perceptual limitations on talking about space. In: van Doorn, A. J.; van de Grind, W. A.; Koenderink, J. J. (eds.): Limits in perception. Essays in honour of Maarten A. Bouman. Utrecht: VNU Science Press, 323-358.

— (1982): Cognitive styles in the use of spatial direction terms. In: Jarvella, R. J.; Klein, W. (eds.): Speech, place and action. Studies in deixis and related topics. Chichester: Wiley, 251-268.

LEVINSON, Stephen C. (1996): Frames of reference and Molyneux's question: Crosslinguistic evidence. In: Bloom; Peterson; Nadel; Garrett: 109-169.

MILLER, George A.; Johnson-Laird, Phil N. (1976): Language and perception. Cambridge: Cambridge University Press.

RETZ-SCHMIDT, Gundula (1988): Various views on spatial prepositions. In: AI Magazine 9, 95-105.

SHEPARD, Roger N.; COOPER, L. A. (1982): Mental images and their transformations. Cambridge, MA: MIT Press.

STERN, William (1936): Raum und Zeit als personale Dimensionen. In: Acta Psychologica 1, 220-232.

TALMY, Leonard (1983): How language structures space. In: Pick, H. L.; Acredolo, L. P. (eds.): Spatial orientation. Theory, research, and application. New York: Plenum Press, 225-282.

TVERSKY, Barbara; Lee, Paul U. (1998): How space structures language. In: Freksa, Ch.; Habel, Ch.; Wender, K. F. (eds.): Spatial cognition. Berlin: Springer, 157-175.

Vandeloise, Claude (1985): Description of space in French. University of Duisburg: Linguistic Agency (Series A, Paper No. 150).

WUNDERLICH, Dieter (1981): Linguistic strategies. In: Coulmas, F. (ed.): A Festschrift for native speaker. Den Haag: Mouton, 279–296.

WUNDERLICH, Dieter; HERWEG, Michael (1991): Lokale und Direktionale. In: von Stechow, A.; Wunderlich, D. (eds.): Semantics. An internation handbook of contemporary research. Berlin: de Gruyter, 758–785.

To What Extent Can We Predict Naturalistic Slips of the Tongue?

Tapio Hokkanen

1 Introduction

One of the characteristic features of slips of the tongue in spontaneous speech is that they occur unexpectedly. If errors could be expected, speakers would be able to avoid them and reformulate their utterance before the articulation. However, there are certain structures with which we can elicitate errors and, consequently, make quite accurate predictions both on when and what kind of errors speakers will produce. These so called tongue twisters such as *Peter Piper picked a peck of pickled peppers* take advantage of repeated phonemes, homologous positions and other distracting factors in speech production.

Tongue twisters left aside, the purpose of the present study is to investigate factors that constrain slips of the tongue outside of experimental settings, in normal conversations. It is hypothesized that since certain error patterns can be elicitated and the error rate manipulated with carefully selected experimental stimuli, we have good reasons to believe that there are at least some predictable regularities that constrain errors in spontaneous speech as well. In fact, this is exactly the case: it has been pointed out in several slip studies that certain types of error are more frequent and some segments more error-prone than the others. The problem is that so far we do not know the effect of the factors behind the actual errors. It is further hypothesized that the regularities in error patterns can be used as naturalistic evidence for the strength of each constraint: the less errors, the stronger the constraint. My aim is to analyse the relative frequencies of various kinds of errors, and make conclusions on what makes us slip the way we do as well as on how the findings contribute to the theory of speech production.

The current analysis is restricted to cover only errors in phonological encoding and not e.g. lexical or morphological substitutions. Moreover, stuttering, hesitation phenomena and other disfluencies are not included in the data. The data comprises a total of 550 phonological slips of the tongue in the Finnish language collected from on-line notes and 150 hours of tape recorded unedited radio interviews as well as sportscasts. Since the number of speakers is more than 400, the effect of idiosyncrasies is minimized.

2.1 The constraints and their effect

The generalizations on the nature of slips of the tongue that have been proposed in the previous literature can be grouped into the following four classes (A to D). My classification is based on the hypothetical levels of the speech production system at which each type of error presumably has arisen.

A. Phonetic and segmental (phonological encoding)

    1) *Phonotactics.* Slips of the tongue should not violate the phonotactics of a language, or, as Wells (1951) puts it in his first law regarding errors, slips of the tongue are practically always phonetically possible noise.

    2) *Phonetic accommodation.* Secondly, in exchanges and shift errors, mislocated segments accommodate to their new environments (Garrett 1980).

    3) *Initialness effect.* Initial segments are more error-prone than the others (Meijer 1997).

    4) *Position similarity constraint.* An error and its source occupy identical word or syllable positions (Boomer & Laver 1968).

    5) *CV structure.* Movement errors do not usually change the word shape. This is referred to as Wells' (1951) second law. Despite of the error, stress pattern as well as number of syllables remain intact.

B. Syntactic (syntactic encoding)

    6) *Phrase-internalness.* An error and its source structure are rarely separated by a phrase boundary (Garrett 1980).

    7) *Word class.* Errors should not occur between open and closed class words (Garrett 1988).

C. Lexical (mental lexicon)

    8) *Lexical effect.* Errors tend to result in existing words or stems.

D. Extra-linguistic

    9) *Frequency.* The more frequent the segment is, the more resistant it is against errors.

2.2   Phonetic and segmental constraints

Phonotactics. Let us now examine these generalizations in detail. First of all, there should be no violations of phonotactics or at least they should be infrequent. One of the phonotactic characteristics of Finnish is vowel harmony, which means that within one phonological word (with the exception of compounds), there can only appear either front vowels or back vowels, while *i* and *e* are treated as neutral in this respect. In the present data there are only a few (N = 9) violations of vowel harmony. Moreover, sequences in which a segmental substitution would cause this kind of violation are further adjusted to conform their new BACK or FRONT environment (see also phonetic accommodation, below), e.g. in 1)·

    1) *opa-*   target: *epäonnen*
       \<non-word\>   bad luck + GEN
       'of bad luck'

The example above indicates an anticipation of *o* (*opa-* instead of *epäonnen*). If it were only a matter of substituting the initial *e* with *o*, the error should result in **opä-*. However, after the anticipation, the targeted *ä* is replaced by its BACK counterpart *a*. Examples like 1) indicate that vowel harmony is an automatic phonological adjustment process in the Finnish language. Other violations of phonotactics (N = 5) consist of erroneous consonant clusters. Altogether, since there are only 14 instances (2,5%) of 550 phonological errors that violate phonotactics, the first of the constraints under investigation appears to be very strong. Namely, we can argue that phonotactics holds in the remaining 97,5% of errors in the present data.

Phonetic accommodation, the second constraint, shows that sometimes the effect of a constraint may be difficult to distinguish from that of the others. For example, phonetic accommodation is related to phonotactics and shared CV structure so that phonotactics gives the guidelines on how the possible accommodation should work, and then, a possibly homologous CV structure in the immediate context further affects the resulting form. Nevertheless, phonetic accommodation is related to exchanges and shift errors, which means that since these errors are not as frequent as substitutions, the number of phonetic accommodations remains very small. Thus, there are only a few (N = 3) examples such as 2) where the effect of adjustment can be seen.

2) *muo-*   target: *mukaan   Lieksan*
                 along+ILL Lieksa+GEN
                 'along to Lieksa's'

It is worth noting in 2) that *uo* is the BACK counterpart of the opening FRONT diphtong *ie* found in the initial position of the adjacent word *Lieksan*. Let us suppose that it is the form of opening diphtong that is shifted here, irrespective of its phonetic content. Because of the immediate interruption by the speaker, we cannot be sure, however, whether the resulting structure had been an exchange of the type *muokaan Liksan* thus indicating an interplay between the diphtong and a short vowel. In any case, it is evident that this phonetically unspecified V_1V_2 sequence replaces the targeted *u* and is then accommodated in its new BACK environment. The result is convergent with the findings by Fromkin (1971b) and Berg (1986), namely that errors concern entire diphtongs rather than their constituing segments.

Initialness effect. Thirdly, initial segments are more error-prone than segments in other positions within a word. This structural constraint is referred to as initialness effect (see Dell et al. 1993). Example 3) is an indication of a substitution error in syllable-initial position:

3) *ko.mi.a lii.mi*   target: *komia liivi*
                          elegant NOM vest NOM
                          'elegant vest'

In 3), the targeted *v* of the word *liivi* is substituted by *m* from the previous word *komia*. It is essential that the targeted *v* occupies a syllable-initial position, which is in favour of initialness effect (see also position similarity constraint, below). There are errors that run counter to initialness, however. For example, 4) (anticipation of *o* in the next syllable) regards syllable nuclei and 5) features an additional *r* from a homologous syllable-final position in the previous word:

4) *u.not.to.mi.a*   target: *u.net.to.mi.a*
                                     sleepless+ Pl+PAR
                                     'sleepless'

5) *jär.vet re.her.vöi.ty.vät* target: *järvet   rehevöityvät*
                                         lake+PL   eutroficate+PRES+PL 3RD
                                         'lakes will eutroficate'

In fact, examples 4) and 5) outnumber those of the type shown in 3). The initial positions are involved only in 43 per cent (N = 236) of errors, while the remaining 57 per cent (N = 314) regard syllable rhymes, i.e. either nuclei or the codas. Shattuck-Hufnagel reports a remarkably higher proportion (78%) of onset errors in her study of English. The present result is next to chance, and consequently, it does not support initialness effect. There is one language-specific factor which might serve as a plausible explanation for the low frequency, namely that word onsets in Finnish are lightweight. The words of Finnic origin do not contain any consonant clusters in the initial position, which distinguishes Finnish from e.g. Germanic languages. This means that there would be far less opportunities for an error to occur in the initial position in Finnish (see Niemi, in press). However, this explanation is in part undermined by a finding from Spanish. Despite of the dominance of light-weight syllables in the Spanish language, García-Albea et al. (1989) report lots of phonological errors in the initial position. (For a discussion, see also Berg 1998:250-254.)

Position similarity. The position similarity constraint reminds of the initialness effect in that both are positionally defined. The major difference is that in errors indicating initialness effect, we do not need to take into account the position of the interacting segments, because the only criterion is that the error itself is in the initial position. In position similarity constraint, however, the interacting segments are homologous, i.e. by definition, they share similar positions.

6) *psosiaalipsykologina*   target: *sosiaalipsykologina*
                                      social psychologist +ESS
                                      'as a social psychologist'

7) *tunnitot muusikot*   target: *tunnetut   muusikot*
                                       well-known+PL   musician+PL
                                       'renowned musicians'

Example 6) is an anticipation of consonant cluster *ps*, most probably originating from the following identical cluster in the Finnish counterpart for 'psychologist'. This pattern speaks both for initialness effect and position similarity: the error and its source stucture appear in identical positions within the compound. On the contrary, in 7), the position similarity constraint causes the entire vowel pattern to be anticipated: in the framework of autosegmental phonology, the targeted vowel tier *u-e-u* as in *tunnetut* has been replaced as a whole by *u-i-o* from the following word, *muusikot*, while the consonant tier remains intact. The relative frequency of errors indicating position similarity is 65% (N = 360 / 550), which is far less than in Fromkin's (1971b) analysis where only 2 of 600 errors violated position similarity as well as the 96 per cent level by García-Albea et al. (1989).

CV structure. The effect of shared wordshape, or CV structure (Stemberger 1990) can be compared to that of position similarity on one hand, and of phonetic accommodation on the other. It is essential that despite of a shift or an exchange, the original CV frame of the erroneous word is retained: vowels are usually replaced by other vowels and consonants by other consonants. 8) is a typical example, in which phonetic quality, i.e. vowels *e* and *i,* are exchanged but the quantity remains intact.

8) *iseentyä*   target: *esiintyä*
                     appear INF
                     'to appear'

Errors such as 8) can be interpreted as evidence for the slots and fillers theory (Shattuck-Hufnagel 1979) as well as for views on length as a suprasegmental (Stemberger 1990). It is highly probable that in the process of phonological encoding, segmental slots are available before they are filled with the actual content. This dual representation, in fact, is found in 81 per cent (N = 445/550) of the phonological errors in the present data.

2.3   Syntactic constraints

Phrase-internalness. The first one of the syntactic constraints under investigation states that errors should not cross phrase boundaries. On the basis of the present data, however, phrase boundaries are not respected. Errors occur both within and across phrases, which suggests that in phonological encoding, phrases play little or no essential role at all. It may be the case that due to the modularity of the speech production chain, phonological encoding does not have access upwards to syntactic and morphological encoding, i.e. at the point where segmental quality is attached to the frame delivered by the upper levels, the encoding is, so to say, blind to phrase boundaries. It appears that instead of by phrases, the span of errors can be better explained by a production window (Hokkanen 1995): all phonological slips occur within a maximum span of three words from their sources. Table 1 shows the relative frequencies of errors within the production window.

Span between error and its source	Percentage of errors
Within the same phonological word	20
Between adjacent words	65
Within two word boundaries	12
Within three word boundaries	3
Total	100

Table 1: The relative frequencies of phonological errors within the production window in phonological encoding (N = 550).

Since a total of 85 per cent of all phonological errors occur within a word or between adjacent words, this constraint could be called adjacency effect. The pattern presented in Table 1 neatly fits to the theory of spreading activation as well as to the suggestion by Kempen and Hoenkamp (1987) on the incremental nature of speech production. On one hand, the activation levels of source phonemes are at their highest within the word being uttered and between it and the adjacent word. Inhibitory activation normally hinders the misselection of phonemes, but sometimes, a wrong item receives more activation and wins the competition. Since there are no errors with a span beyond three words, we may conclude that all activation levels in phonological encoding are extinguished within this limit. No errors, no activation. On the other hand, if we suppose that utterances are produced incrementally, this means that phonological encoding is to at least some extent linear, i.e. while articulating some segments, we are already planning the production of the others. Errors may then be caused by the interaction between auditory or internal feedback loops and the level of phonological encoding.

Word class. The second syntactic argument is for word classes: errors should not occur between open and closed class words (Garrett 1988). The present data (see Table 2) shows that open and closed categories can interact and participate in errors both ways: segments in closed class words serve as source structures for errors in open class words, and vice versa.

Category		Percentage of errors
No violation:	error open – source open or error closed – source closed	81
Violation:	error open – source closed or error closed – source open	19
Total:		100

Table 2: Errors with respect to open vs. closed class words (N = 550).

Here we must not forget the distributional bias: there are more errors concerning open class words just because open class words have higher textual frequency than closed class words. This bias should be taken into account and proportioned to the chances for an error to occur. However, we must bear in mind that although the division between open and closed class words constrain errors in approximately four fifths of the errors, there remains one fifth that violates this constraint.

2.4   Lexical effect

Lexical effect. Segmental errors tend to result in real words rather than in non-words. In the strictest version of lexical effect we must suppose that irrespective of how unsuitable it is in its context, an error resulting in an existing stem or word form must be regarded as contaminated by some lexical item, i.e. stem or other item in the mental lexicon. Along a less strict interpretation, we should consider these slips neither as pure phonological nor pure lexical errors. Lexical effect can be seen in roughly one fourth (N = 142/550, corresponding to 26%) of the errors in the present data, as in 9).

9) *työ*   target: *tuo*
   work NOM SG   that NOM SG
   'work'   'that'

Example 9) is an indication of the targeted BACK diphtong *uo* being substituted by its FRONT counterpart *yö*. The resulting form *työ* 'work' is an existing word and as a nominative singular definitely an item in the mental lexicon, but contextually impossible. Nevertheless, if we adopt the strict version of lexical effect, this kind of errors should not be used as waterproof evidence for phonological processes in slips of the tongue.

2.5 Extra-linguistic factors: frequency effect

Frequency. It is hypothesized that the more frequent an item is, the more resistant it is against errors. As regards the phonological errors the data should be remarkably larger in order to reveal the frequency effect in a reliable way. On the basis of the present collection, it seems plausible, however, that there are more factors than just frequency that make certain phonemes more error-prone than the others. It appears that e.g. /l/ and /r/ tend to interact with each other, and so do /m/ and /v/ as well as /a/ and /ä/, see Table 3.

Phonemes involved in errors either as targets or sources	Percentage of all phonological errors
/l/ and /r/	8
/m/ and /v/	5
/a/ and /ä/	3

Table 3: Certain single phonemes and their relative frequency of all phonological errors (N = 550).

Again, we must bear in mind the distributional bias. All of the phonemes above are relatively common in Finnish and, when proportioned to the error frequencies, none of the most infrequent phonemes outnumbered them in the present data.

It may be concluded that supposedly, the effect in question is not simply quantitative but more complex instead. Because these particular phonemes have participated in phonological changes, appear again in phonological processes, e.g. in language acquisition, and, finally, are closely related with each other in the theory of distinctive features, it may be argued that the relatively high percentages of these particular phonemes are due to specific historically and synchronically motivated interrelations as well as phonetic similarity.

3   Concluding remarks

On the basis of the present study, slips of the tongue in spontaneous speech are not random in nature but follow certain patterns. Since some patterns and certain positions are more error-prone than the others, the resulting structures in phonological errors are to at least some extent predictable. We cannot predict when an error will occur but we may, nevertheless, expect it to be of certain type. The constraints form a hierarchy in which the three most powerful constraints are phonotactics, CV structure, adjacency effect, and word class, all affecting more than four fifths of the errors. The magnitude of the initialness effect is next to chance, which runs counter to Shattuck-Hufnagel (1987) and Meijer (1997), whose results were in favour of initial positions. Lexical effect as well as phonetic accommodation do not count as effective constraints at all. Frequency may have an effect but it is difficult to distinguish it from the influence of other factors.

To sum up, it appears that both CV frame and phonotactic structure are very resistant against errors. This finding is a strong argument for lexical integrity and word-internal cohesion. As regards to the function of the speech production system, it also contributes to the slots and fillers theory by Shattuck-Hufnagel (1979). The adjacency effect further suggests that activation levels of phonemes can cause errors within a maximum span of three words. Since phrase boundaries had no effect in errors, we may conclude that phrases are not relevant units in production. Last but not least, unlike the other structurally defined constraints, the initialness effect plays no essential role in errors in the Finnish data.

4   References

BERG, Thomas (1998): Linguistic structure and change: An explanation from language processing. Oxford: Clarendon.

Berg, Thomas (1986): The monophonematic status of diphtongs revisited. In: Phonetica 43, 198-205.

DELL, Gary S., CORNELL, Juliano; GOVINDJEE, Anita (1993): Structure and content in language production: A theory of frame constraints in phonological speech errors. In: Cognitive Science 17, 149-195.

FROMKIN, Victoria (ed.) (1971a): Speech Errors as Linguistic Evidence. The Hague: Mouton. – [Reprint 1973].

— (1971b): The non-anomalous nature of anomalous utterances. In: Fromkin: 215-242.

GARCÍA-ALBEA, José E., DEL VISO, Susana; IGOA, José M. (1989): Movement errors and levels of processing in sentence production. In: Journal of Psycholinguistic Research 18, 145-161.

GARRETT, Merrill F. (1988): Processes in language production. In: Newmeyer, F. J. (ed.): Linguistics: The Cambridge Survey, vol. 3: Language: Psychological and Biological Aspects. Cambridge, MA: Cambridge University Press.

— (1980): The limits of accommodation: Arguments for independent processing levels in sentence production. In: Fromkin, V. (ed.): Errors in Linguistic Performance. Slips of the Tongue, Ear, Pen, and Hand. New York, NY: Academic Press.

HOKKANEN, Tapio (1995). Puheentuotoksen mallit ja suomen nominintaivutuksen morfosyntaktinen koodaus. [Models of Speech Production and the Morphosyntactic Encoding of Finnish Noun Inflection] (Unpublished PhL thesis, University of Joensuu, Finland).

KEMPEN, Gerald; HOENKAMP, E. (1987): An incremental procedural grammar for sentence formulation. In: Cognitive Science 11, 201-258.

MEIJER, Paul J. A. (1997): What speech errors can tell us about word-form generation: The roles of constraint and opportunity. In: Journal of Psycholinguistic Research 26, 141-158.

NIEMI, Jussi (in press): Onset + rhyme or first mora + end: Intrasyllabic structure in Finnish. Festschrift to Bruce Derwing.

NIEMI, Jussi; LAINE, Matti (1997): Slips of the tongue as psycholinguistic evidence: Finnish word-initial segments and vowel harmony. In: Folia Linguistica 31, 161-175.

Shattuck-Hufnagel, Stefanie (1979): Speech errors as evidence for a serial-ordering mechanism in sentence production. In: Cooper, W. E.; Walker, E.C.T. (eds.): Sentence Processing. Psycholinguistic Studies Presented to Merrill Garrett. Hillsdale, NJ: Lawrence Erlbaum.

SHATTUCK-HUFNAGEL, Stefanie (1987): The role of word-onset consonants in speech production planning: New evidence from speech error patterns. In: Keller, E.; Gopnik, M. (eds.): Motor and Sensory Processes of Language. Hillsdale, NJ: Lawrence Erlbaum.

STEMBERGER, Joseph P. (1990): Wordshape errors in language production. In: Cognition 35, 123-157.

— (1984): Length as a suprasegmental: Evidence from speech errors. In: Language 60, 895-913.

WELLS, Rulon (1951): Predicting slips of the tongue. In: Fromkin (1971a): 82-87.

Stem Allomorphs as Units in the Mental Lexicon

Juhani Järvikivi, Jussi Niemi

1   Introduction

The inquiry into the role of morphological units in lexical access, i.e. the process of mapping perceptual information to the mental lexicon, and their representation in the mental lexicon has been an important field of psycholinguistic research since Taft and Forster's (1975) seminal paper (see Henderson 1985; McQueen and Cutler 1998, for recent summaries). Since then, the field has seen models of visual word processing ranging from the radical de-composition model introduced by Taft and Forster (1975, 1976), which posited an obligatory de-composition procedure followed by a stem based (whether free or bound) lexical access, to equally radical holistic whole word models (Butterworth 1980), assuming a full form representation, with no need for de-composition in lexical access, for all words, whether simple or complex. Recent years have witnessed the development of an increasing number of hybrid models that combine features of de-composition and full-listing, depending on the properties of the morphologically complex words in question: The augmented addressed model (AAM) of Caramazza et al. (1988) assumes a morpheme based representation for all morphologically complex words, where the words are accessed either via their full form or via component morphemes depending on the familiarity of the word. Pinker and Prince (1991; see also Pinker 1998) argue that regular (inflected) words are processed via a rule-based (de-compositional) route, whereas all irregular words are accessed and represented as wholes. The so-called morphological race models (Frauenfelder and Schreuder 1992; Schreuder and Baayen 1995) assume a simultaneous interplay of both whole word and morphemic recognition routes, the outcome of the race depending on factors such as frequency, transparency and productivity.

Niemi and Laine have recently proposed another hybrid model, the so-called stem allomorph/inflectional decomposition model (SAID), in order to capture the empirical results obtained from a series of experiments concerning the processing and representation of Finnish nouns (Niemi et al. 1994; Laine et al. 1994). Apart from positing a semantically based difference between the processing of derivational and inflectional morphology (see also Laine *et al.* 1995; Laine 1996), the basic features of the model concerning the recognition of Finnish inflected nouns are as follows:

1) Inflected nouns (but not derived nouns) are de-composed in lexical access.
2) Bound (noun) stems (stem allomorphs) have separate representations in the input lexicon.

The evidence for the first assumption comes from a series of eye-tracking and lexical decision experiments, as well as from aphasic studies (Niemi et al. 1994; Laine et al. 1994; Laine et al. 1995). The second assumption is based on the fact that formal transparency does not seem to affect either lexical decision or aphasic reading performance (Niemi et al. 1994; Laine et al. 1994). Storing the stem allomorphs as such, would, then, eliminate the need for complex phonological operations on-line.

Apart from the psycholinguistic evidence (albeit negative) per se, there are also convincing linguistic grounds for their argument. Finnish is an agglutinating language with pervasive fusional properties and rich morphology. Finnish nouns may be morphologically marked for case (13-14 cases in active use) and number. Furthermore, nouns can also take possessive suffixes as well as clitics, for example, *vene+i+ssä+ni +kö* 'in boats?' (vene + plural + inessive + possessive + clitic). Karlsson (1983) has estimated that a Finnish noun can have as many as 2000 inflected and cliticized forms (with about 150 paradigmatic/core forms (not taking either derivation or compounding into account)), the verb morphology being even more complex, resulting in as many as 10 000 forms per verb. Derivational morphology and compounding included, the possible forms for Finnish nouns can amount to tens of thousands per noun. Furthermore, the ratio of non-zero morphs to words is 0.62 to one (based on Pajumäki and Palonen's 1984, data), and 79% of Finnish nouns have more than one stem form (based on Karlsson's 1983, data). Thus, (morpho)phonological processes and/or stem formation coupled with the highly productive inflectional morphology along with the possible possessive forms and clitics induce a heavy burden on the computational recognition system (see also Bertram et al. 1999). Along with the productive inflection, the processing load induced by the frequent many-to-one relation between phonology and morphology can be argued to be by itself reason enough to store the stem allomorphs as such, an explanation which also captures the empirically attested tendency to store most Finnish derived words as wholes[1], i.e., in this sense, all inflectional stems, whether simple or complex, tend to develop a full form representation (Järvikivi and Niemi 1999a).

The present paper discusses the results from four experiments in our attempt to characterize the nature of the Finnish (bound) stem allomorphs in more detail. The first experiment employs frequent Finnish bound stems (e.g. *anoppe < anoppeja* 'mothers-in-law' [anoppi + partitive plural], and matched non-words, e.g. *anoppo*. In order to avoid any artificial effects of orthography, especially the importance of word beginnings, the non-words were constructed so as to differ from the stems as little as possible, by changing 1-2 letters from the end of the corresponding bound stem. Thus, we expect that if the bound stems have a form representation in the visual input lexicon, as hypothesized by Niemi *et al.* (1994), the real stems should be harder to reject than the corresponding non-words, thus, eliciting longer response latencies and higher error percentages (see also Caramazza et al. 1988; Burani et al. 1995).

---

[1] Most Finnish derived forms occur in nominative singular (base) form only about 20% of the time, and most derivational affixes also exhibit more than one inflectional allomorph, thus, in effect, turning most of the derivational forms into inflectional (bound) stems (Järvikivi and Niemi 1999a).

2 Experiment 1

Participants. Forty students from the University of Joensuu were paid a 10 Fmk coffee coupon for participating in the experiment. All were native speakers of Finnish and had normal or corrected-to-normal vision.

Materials. Twenty items consisting of Finnish bound stems (e.g. *reide*) and their corresponding nominative singular forms (e.g. *reisi* 'thigh') were cross-balanced between two groups of twenty subjects, so that each subject saw only either the bound stem or the nominative singular form. An additional set of twenty non-words matched in bigram frequency with the bound stems was constructed changing 1-3 letters from the end of frequent Finnish monomorphemic nouns (e.g. *anoppo* from *anoppi* 'mother-in-law'). The experiment also included a set of twenty monomorphemic fillers.

Procedure. An ordinary lexical decision task was run using a MacIntosh Power PC running PsyScope 1.2. The subjects were to decide whether a word appearing on the screen was a Finnish word or not by pushing the corresponding 'yes' or 'no' buttons on the button box. Each word appeared in the center of the screen and remained there until a decision was made.

Results and Discussion. Table 1 summarizes the results from Experiment 1. Before the data analysis one subject was excluded due to a high error rate (56%). Overall, the analyses showed a significant difference between the three conditions both on reaction times ($F1(2,114) = 7.32$, $p<.002$, $F2(2,57) = 34.97$, $p<.0001$), and errors ($F1(2,114) = 6.34$, $p<.003$, $F2(2,57) = 4.67$, $p<.02$). Pair-wise comparisons between the bound stems and their non-word matches showed a significant difference in the RT analysis ($t1(38) = 5.02$ $p < .001$; $t2(38) = 2.97$, $p < .01$), and in the error analysis (one-tailed, $t1(38) = 1.99$ $p < .05$; $t2(38) = 1.73$, $p < .03$).

	RT	Errors (%)
Bound stems (NO)	870	5.2
Non-words (NO)	814	1.8
Nom. sg. (YES)	722	0.7

Table 1: Mean reaction times and error percentages in Experiment 1.

As expected, the stem allomorphs took both longer to reject as real words and generated more errors than the matched non-words, although the difference was kept formally as minimal as possible. The results give further support for the earlier findings that Finnish inflected nouns are decomposed in lexical access (e.g. Niemi et al. 1994). Furthermore, the prolonged latencies for the stem allomorphs are presumably due to the fact that the form in the input lexicon is activated, and the time increase is a result of checking whether the stem can occur on its own or not (see Taft and Forster 1975; Taft 1988; Caramazza et al. 1988), whereas the non-words – due to a lack of form representation – can be rejected at the early stage of lexical access. Despite the words of caution expressed by Henderson (1985, 1986) for drawing conclusions about normal processing based on experiments using non-words (see e.g., Caramazza et al. 1988; Burani et al. 1995, for a response to Henderson), it is fair to say, however, that the differences observed here would be hard to explain without admitting that the stem allomorphs have a representational reality of their own, independent of a pure form resemblance to an existing lexical item. The result is in accordance with recent findings (see e.g., Caramazza et al. 1988; Drews and Zwitserlood 1995; Allen and Badecker 1999).

However, neither the above result itself nor the earlier observed lack of phonological transparency effect (Niemi *et al.* 1994), cannot themselves tell anything about the nature of the visual representation itself. That is, the results are equally interpretable in both a framework that assumes an orthographic/visual input lexicon which encodes all combinatory morphological (morhosemantic/morphosyntactic) information with full lexical specifications (Caramazza et al. 1988), and in a framework which assumes that the visual input lexicon is purely form-based and all morphological information is represented at a separate form-independent 'intermediate' level (e.g. Günther 1988; Kelliher and Henderson 1990; Allen and Badecker 1999).

The next two experiments manipulate both the frequency of the stems (the forms), and the task (lexical decision vs. semantic decision), to further investigate the nature of the stem allomorphs.

3   Experiment 2

Participants. Twenty three students from the University of Joensuu were paid a 10 Fmk coffee coupon for participating in the experiment. None had participated in Experiment 1. All were native speakers of Finnish and had normal or corrected-to-normal vision.

Materials. Again, two sets of twenty bound stems, one for the high frequency condition and one for the low frequency condition, were selected from the Turun Sanomat lexical database (comprising 22.7 million word tokens) using Laine and Virtanen (1996) lexical search program. Both sets were matched for length in letters (5.1 and 5.2 respectively), and bigram frequency (997 and 979 respectively). The two sets of bound stems differed with respect to allomorph frequency[2] by a factor of 16.4 (0.8 and 12.6 per million respectively). A control-set of twenty non-words matched for length in letters (5.6), and bigram frequency (1048) was constructed changing one to two letters from the beginning of existing Finnish words. The experiment also included two sets of twenty monomorphemic words that were matched for lemma frequency (14 per million), length (6) and bigram frequency, differing only in the frequency of the surface form (2 and 7 per million, respectively). An additional set of 140 filler words was selected consisting of 20 monomorphemic and 40 inflected words, as well as 40 non-words with inflectional suffixes.

---

[2]   By allomorph frequency we mean the cumulative frequency of a particular (bound) stem form in all inflected words it forms a part of, e.g., *käde*+ssä 'in hand' [käsi + inessive], *käde*+llä 'on hand' [käsi + adessive], etc.

Procedure. An ordinary lexical decision task was run using a MacIntosh Power PC running PsyScope 1.2. The subjects were to decide whether a word appearing on the screen was a Finnish word or not by pushing the corresponding 'yes' or 'no' buttons on the button box. Each word was preceded by a fixation point appearing in the center of the screen for 500 msec. 500 msec after the fixation point disappeared, a word appeared in the center of the screen in black lowercase Chicago 24 point letters on a light gray background. The 200 items were presented randomized for each subject and time-out was set at 2000 msec. Each session was preceded by 20 practice trials. Additional 10 trials preceded the first experimental item in each session.

Results and Discussion. Table 2 summarizes the results from Experiment 2 (and 3). Before data analysis all incorrect responses as well as all responses longer than 3 standard deviations above the individual mean were removed. One-way ANOVA for the 'NO' responses revealed a significant difference between the three conditions in the item analysis ($F2(2,57) = 13.77$, $p<.001$) but not in the subject analysis ($F1(2,66) = 1.51$, $p>.05$). Subsequent pair-wise comparisons (a standard t-test for the items and a paired t-test for the subjects) showed no significant difference between the high and low frequency conditions, however, as expected, both the low frequency and high frequency condition differed significantly from the non-word control condition both in subject and item analyses ($t1(22) = 8.12$, $p<.001$, $t2(38) = 4.49$, $p<.01$, and $t1(22) = 6.62$, $p<.001$, $t2(38) = 4.84$, $p<.001$ respectively).

One-way ANOVA for errors showed a significant difference between the three conditions ($F1(2,66) = 5.91$, $p<.01$, $F2(2,57) = 11.79$, $p<.001$). Pair-wise comparisons did not reveal any difference between the two allomorph conditions, however, as expected, both the low frequency and the high frequency conditions differed significantly from the non-word condition (two-tailed, $t1(22) = 3.08$, $p<.01$, $t2(38) = 4.26$, $p<.001$, and $t1(22) = 4.40$, $p<.001$, $t2(38) = 4.98$, $p<.001$ respectively). There was no difference between the two monomorphemic groups either in reaction times or in errors.

Again, the overall results were similar those of Experiment 1: The allomorph conditions were rejected significantly slower than their non-word matches. However, Experiment 2 failed to produce a difference between the low frequency and high frequency allomorph conditions. As the cumulative stem frequency effect is among the most robust findings in psycholinguistics (see e.g., Taft 1979; Burani et al. 1984), the absence of any frequency effect here suggests that the stem allomorphs do not have lexical access codes in the most traditional sense (e.g., Taft and Forster 1975). Rather, they seem more like purely formal indices with no lexical properties in themselves, resembling 'lexical entering points' in the sense of Günther (1988), with a base-form centered organization of the lexicon (see also Lukatela et al. 1980). In this modified satellite approach, any frequency effect to appear would require the activation of the base-form (the nominative singular form for Finnish nouns, see Karlsson 1983; Niemi et al. 1994). A similar division into a purely form-based level of phonological/ortho-graphic representation and a form-independent level of representation where morpho-syntactic/morphosemantic information is specified has been suggested recently by, for

instance, Kelliher and Henderson (1990), Badecker et al. (1995), and Allen and Badecker (1999).

	Lexical Decision	(Exp. 2)	Semantic Decision	(Exp. 3)
CONDITION	RT	Errors (%)	RT	Errors (%)
HiF STEM (NO)	803	8.0	837	7.4
LoF STEM (NO)	811	6.7	839	8.3
Non-word (NO)	738	0.9	816	1.9
MonoH	645	3.6	691	2.6
MonoL	633	1.5	660	2.4

Table 2: Mean reaction times and error percentages in Experiments 2 and 3.

4   Experiment 3

Participants. Twenty one students from the University of Joensuu were paid a 10 Fmk
coffee coupon for participating in the experiment. None had participated in the previous experiments. All were native speakers of Finnish and had normal or corrected-
to-normal vision.

Materials. The materials were the same as those used in Experiment 2.

Procedure. The procedure was identical to Experiment 2, except that the subjects
were to respond as quickly as possible whether the word appearing on the screen had
any *meaning* or not.

Results and Discussion. Table 2 summarizes the results from Experiment 3. Before
data analysis all incorrect responses as well as all responses longer than 3 standard
deviations above the individual mean were removed. One-way ANOVA revealed no
difference between the three conditions whatsoever ($F1(2,60) < 1$, $F2(2,57) < 1$).

One-way ANOVA for errors, however, showed a significant difference between
the three conditions ($F1(2,60) = 5.37$, $p<.01$, $F2(2,57) = 5.73$, $p<.01$). Pair-wise comparisons revealed a pattern similar to Experiments 1 and 2: There was again no difference between the two allomorph conditions, however, both the low frequency and the
high frequency conditions differed significantly from the non-word condition (two-
tailed, $t1(20) = 4.15$, $p<.001$, $t2(38) = 3.49$, $p<.01$, and $t1(20) = 3.65$, $p<.001$, $t2(38) =$
2.85, $p<.01$ respectively). There was no significant difference between the two monomorphemic conditions.

Two things happened in this task: First, the response latencies for both allomorph
conditions as well as the monomorphemic (real) words were slightly elevated as compared to Experiment 2. This is an expected result in the light that the lexical decision
task taps the point in time when the word has been recognized but the meaning is not
yet accessed, whereas the response to the present task would presumably require at
least a preliminary analysis of meaning. Secondly, however, also the latencies for the
non-words were elevated almost to the level of the allomorphs. Although, at a closer

look, most of the rise in the non-word reaction times was caused by two subjects with close to average RT's for the allomorph conditions (from 840 to 880 msec), but very high Mean RT's for the non-words (1004 to 1044 respectively), the phenomenon could be an artifact induced by the type of task used.[3] It is entirely possible that the subjects developed individual strategies to deal with the question of whether the words have 'meaning' or not, which in turn is particularly reflected in the strange behavior of the non-words via task specific 'off-line' behavior.

However, at the level of errors the results are comparable to the results from the lexical decision experiment, suggesting the stem allomorphs do carry semantic information in one form or another, which is reflected in the high error percentages, whereas the error percentages for the non-words are not comparatively higher than in the lexical decision experiment regardless of the elevated response latencies. Although the results seem indicative of the activation of semantic information, as the change was most drastic in the case of the pure non-words, it is advisable to approach any interpretation of the results with caution.

The next experiment is a first attempt to inquire into the nature of the allomorphic representations themselves by employing a visual primed lexical decision task.

5   Experiment 4

Participants. Twenty two students from the University of Joensuu were paid a 10 Fmk coffee coupon for participating in the experiment. All were native speakers of Finnish and had normal or corrected-to-normal vision.

Materials. The materials consisting of prime-target pairs of the following types (see Table 3.) were selected from the Turun sanomat lexical database (comprising 22.7 million word tokens) using Laine and Virtanen (1996) lexical search program: The conditions 1, 4, and 7 included identical primes and targets, e.g. *nappi-nappi* 'button' Nom sg., *hampaa-hampaa* 'tooth', bound stem of *hammas*, *vailo-vailo* 'nonword'. The conditions 2 and 5 employed nouns in nominative singular and their oblique stems, e.g. *reisi-reide* 'thigh'. The conditions 3, 6, and 8, in turn, employed non-words (formally) unrelated to the targets as primes. Both the target items and the primes were matched for length in letters, lemma frequency (per million words), allomorph frequency (per million words, where appropriate), and bigram frequency as presented in Table 3. An additional 42 filler items consisting of word targets (e.g. juna) preceded by an unrelated word prime (e.g., käsi) were constructed in order to keep the ratio of 'yes' and 'no' responses equal.

---

[3]   See Järvikivi and Niemi (1999b) for an example of how the manipulation of the task influences the outcome of the results as compared to ordinary lexical decision.

Condition			PRIME				TARGET			
	Prime	Target	Length	Flemma	Fallo	Bigram	Length	Flemma	Fallo	Bigram
1	Word	WORD	5	15.4	*	988	5	15.4	*	988
2	Stem	WORD	5	15.4	4.5	1037	5	15.4	*	1205
3	Non-w	WORD	5.4	*	*	1066	5.2	15.4	*	1047
4	Stem	STEM	5.3	16	4.6	829	5.3	16	4.6	829
5	Word	STEM	5.2	15.2	*	1053	5	15.2	4.8	954
6	Non-w	STEM	5.2	*	*	983	5.4	15.8	4.5	932
7	Non-w (identical)	Non-w	5	*	*	1017	5	*	*	1017
8	Non-w (unrelated)	Non-w	5	*	*	842	5.2	*	*	901

Table 3. A summary of primes and targets with the respective average lengths, lemma frequencies, allomorph frequencies, and bigram frequencies for the items used in Experiment 4.

Procedure. A primed lexical decision task was run using a MacIntosh Power PC running PsyScope 1.2. The procedure was as follows: A fixation point (*) appeared in the center of the screen for 1000 msecs, followed by the prime presented in capital letters in the center of the screen for 250 msecs. Immediately after the prime a line of hashmarks (########) appeared in the center of the screen for 100 msecs followed by the target presented in the center of the screen in lower case capital Chicago 24 point letters. All stimuli were presented in black letters on a light gray background. The subject were told to decide as fast as they could whether the latter word appearing on the screen was a Finnish word or not. The 210 prime-target pairs were presented randomized for each subject and time-out for the targets was set at 2000 msec. Each session was preceded by 20 practice trials. Additional 10 trials preceded the first experimental prime-target pair in each session.

Results and Discussion. The results are summarized in Table 4. Before data analysis all incorrect responses as well as all responses longer or shorter than 2 standard deviations above/below the individual mean were removed. Furthermore, two subjects were removed from the analysis due to an error rate higher than 15%. Analyses of variance on the RT data revealed a reliable main effect of condition both by subject ($F1(7,152) = 2.86$, $p< .008$) and by item ($F2(7,160) = 41.95$ $p<.0001$). There was no difference, however, in the error analysis (for both $F1$ and $F2$, $p>.1$).

Analyses for the real word targets showed a significant difference in the item analysis ($F2(2,60) = 10.81$, $p< .0001$), but not in the subject analysis ($F1(2,57) = 1.07$ $p>.3$). There was no difference in the error analysis (both $F1$ and $F2$, $p>.2$). Pair-wise comparisons revealed a significant difference between conditions 1 and 2 ($t1(19) = 5.14$, $p<.001$, $t2(40) = 3.37$, $p<.002$) and conditions 1 and 3 ($t1(19) = 5.87$, $p<.001$, $t2(40) = 4.96$, $p<.001$).

For the non-word targets, again, the analysis showed a significant difference in the item analysis ($F2(4,100) = 6.00$, $p< .0003$), but not in the subject analysis ($F1(2,57)<1$). There was no difference in the error analysis (both $F1$ and $F2$, $p>.2$). Pair-wise comparisons between conditions 4 and 6 as well as 5 and 6 showed a significant difference by subject (one-tailed, $t1(19) = 5.32$, $p<.001$, and $t1(19) = 2.77$, $p<.007$, respectively). However, in the item analysis the difference was only marginally significant (one-tailed, $t2(40) = 1.49$, $p = .071$, and $t2(40) = 1.58$, $p = .060$, respectively). The difference between conditions 7 and 8 was significant both by subject and by item ($t1(19) = 2.50$, $p<.03$, $t2(40) = 2.30$, $p<.03$).

Condition	Prime	Target	RT (msec)	Errors (%)
1	Word	WORD	652	5.2
2	Stem	WORD	709	5.2
3	Non-word	WORD	716	2.9
4	Stem	STEM	843	10.0
5	Word	STEM	841	7.6
6	Non-word	STEM	871	11.4
7	Non-word (identical)	NON-WORD	793	6.9
8	Non-word (unrelated)	NON-WORD	827	8.8

Table 4. Mean reaction times and error percentages in Experiment 4.

In general, the experiment showed considerable variation between subjects as well as a notably high amount of errors and elevated reaction times for a priming experiment, which could be an indication of individual strategies used in relation to the type of task at hand, especially in the amount of attention paid to the primes (see also Allen and Badecker 1999, for similar tendencies). However, the identity prime conditions (1, 4, and 7 in Table 4) were uniformly significantly facilitated across all three target types as compared to the non-primed conditions, which is an indication that the task did work properly.

The most notable result is the dissociation between the stem-word and word-stem conditions (2 and 5 in Table 4): the corresponding nominative singular (e.g., *anoppi* 'mother-in-law') seems to prime the rejection of the corresponding stem allomorph (e.g., *anoppe*) as much as the allomorph itself. Furthermore, that this is indeed facilitation is shown by the fact that the earlier observed processing difference between stem allomorphs and non-words is reduced to zero if we compare the non-primed non-words with either the stem primed or word-primed stem allomorphs.[4] That this is not to be dismissed purely as a form-related effect is evident when we take into consideration the fact that the reverse condition results in no significant facilitation whatsoever. The mechanisms underlying the results may be different however. In the first case the nominative singular activates the corresponding lexical entry making the rejection of a bound stem as an independently occurring word correspondingly easier, whereas in the case of stem-stem identity priming condition, the stem simply gets a head start which results in an earlier rejection than in the non-primed condition.

---

[4]   To avoid the possible objection that the observed differences between the primed conditions directly reflect the differences between the groups of items used in those conditions, we submitted all targets used in the priming experiment to a (non-primed) lexical decision task. The results showed no significant differences within the target types (i.e., words, allomorphs, and non-words), whereas the targets differed significantly from each other across the target types (i.e., words vs. allomorphs vs. non-words).

Why, then, is there no priming in the stem-word condition? One possible answer could be sketched out by referring to the question of the nature of the orthographic/ visual input representation. On one hand, if the visual input lexicon were to carry all morphologically relevant information of the possible morphosemantic/morphosyntactic combinations of morphologically complex words, the expected outcome would predict inhibitory links between the various stem-forms (see Caramazza *et al.* 1988). On the other hand, if the input lexicon were to be a purely form-based inventory of stems and affixes with a form-neutral level of morphological representation, but the form themselves serving direct lexical access, then the outcome would predict facilitation. However, if we were to adopt the type of lexical organization where the nominative singular form serves as a nucleus and the allomorphs are sort of 'entering points' at the purely formal level of orthographic/visual representation (as in Günther 1988), the predictions would fit the outcome of the present experiment: First, the nominative singular, serving as a nucleus, would naturally activate the relevant lexical representation, and thus facilitate the rejection of the allomorph as a free form. Second, presenting a bound form without the corresponding affixal and paradigmatic links would not be enough to activate the nuclear form, i.e. the nominative singular, a result which is in accordance with the observed absence of form frequency effect in Experiment 2. Note, that this account is not interpretable in one-to-one fashion in a satellite model of Lukatela et al. (1980) (see also Günther 1988, and Laine and Niemi 1997).

6   Concluding remarks

The present experiments represent a first inquiry into the status of Finnish stem allomorphs (bound noun stems) as items in the processing and representation of Finnish inflected nouns. Niemi et al. (1994) and Laine et al. (1994) argue that stem allomorphs have separate representation at the level of the (modality specific) visual input lexicon. However, the nature of the representational level itself cannot be conclusively specified by their results alone. In general, our results provide further (positive) evidence for their claim: the undoubtedly morphological effect induced by the allomorphs across all tasks reported here indicates that Finnish inflected nouns are (prelexically) decomposed in lexical access into their morphemic constituents, and that these constituents include the stem as such (see e.g., Caramazza *et al.* 1988, and Allen and Badecker 1999, for analogical claims about the processing of Italian and Spanish inflected words respectively).

However, the question of the nature of the allomorphic representations themselves is an issue, the answer to which can only be hinted at on the basis of the present experiments. Experiments 1 and 2 provide clear indications to the effect that the stem allomorphs are units that have a representational reality over and above mere form resemblance to existing lexemes: on one hand, the (bound) stem allomorphs differ from non-words (with minimal formal difference) both qualitatively and quantitatively. On the other hand, however, we observed a dissociation between free forms and stem allomorphs both between and within tasks: Firstly, in Experiment 3, both free forms and stem allomorphs behaved similarly, i.e. the reaction times for both were elevated as compared to Experiment 2 (but see the cautionary remarks above). Secondly, in Experiment 4, we observed a dissociation between the two categories: the corresponding free form (nominative singular) clearly facilitated the responses to the stems, however, the stem allomorphs did not have any priming effect whatsoever when presented immediately before the corresponding free form.

Although any interpretation as to the results obtained must be approached with caution, and clearly further, more elaborated, experimentation is needed in order to establish any conclusions, the present results can be interpreted in a framework that adopts the base-form as a central lexical organizer. Thus, the (bound) stem allomorphs, albeit psychologically real, seem only to serve a purely formal function vis-á-vis their corresponding base-forms. Linguistically speaking, they are only formal instantiations of a paradigm with base-form as the nucleus. Consequently, linguists have always referred to the paradigm of *go*, not to the paradigm of *go, went, gone*. Furthermore, allomorphs seem to be linked via lexical-semantic connections only, and the formal associations may be totally idiosyncratic, as in suppletive paradigms. Also, they categorically either belong or do not belong to a certain paradigm, i.e., a bound form either is or is not a member of a certain lexical entry, and the semantics of a lexical entry seems to hinge upon a 'nuclear' base-form; that is, *went* means *go* plus something.

7 References

ALLEN, Mark; BADECKER, William (1999): Stem homograph inhibition and stem allomorphy: Representing and processing inflected forms in a multilevel lexical system. In: Journal of Memory and Language 41, 105-123.

BERTRAM, Raymond; LAINE, Matti; KARVINEN, Katja (1999): The interplay of word formation type, affixal homonymy, and productivity in lexical processing: Evidence from a morphologically rich language. In: Journal of Psycholinguistic Research 28, 213-226.

BURANI, Cristina; THORNTON, Anna; IACOBINI, Claudio; LAUDANNA, Alessandro (1995): Investigating morphological non-words. In: Dressler, W.; Burani, C. (eds.): Crossdisciplinary Approaches to Morphology. Wien: Verlag der Österreichischen Akademie der Wissenschaften, 37-53.

CARAMAZZA, Alfonso; LAUDANNA, Alessandro; ROMANI, Cristina (1988): Lexical access and inflectional morphology. In: Cognition 28, 297-332.

DREWS, Etta; ZWITSERLOOD, Pienie (1995): Morphological and orthographic similarity in visual word recognition. In: Journal of Experimental Psychology: Human Perception and Performance 21.5, 1098-1116.

FRAUENFELDER, Uli; SCHREUDER, Robert (1992): Constraining psycholinguistic models of morphological processing and representation: The role of productivity. In: Yearbook of Morphology 1991, 165-183.

GÜNTHER, Hartmut (1988): Oblique word forms in visual word recognition. In: Linguistics 26, 583-600.

HENDERSON, Leslie (1986): From morph to morpheme: The psychologist gaily trips where the linguist has trodden. In: Augst, G. (ed.): New Trends in Graphemics & Orthography. Berlin: Walter de Gruyter, 197-217.

HENDERSON, Leslie (1985): Towards a psychology of morphemes. In: Ellis, A. (ed.): Progress in the Psychology of Language, Vol. 1. Hillsdale, NJ: Lawrence Erlbaum, 15-72.

JÄRVIKIVI, Juhani; NIEMI, Jussi (1999a): The role of phonological transparency in morphological processing: Evidence from Finnish derived words. In: Nenonen, M.; Järvikivi, J. (eds.): Languages, minds, and brains: Papers from a NorFa summer school, Mekrijärvi, Finland, June 22-29, 1998. Studies in Languages 34, Joensuu: Joensuun yliopistopaino, 82-91.

— (1999b): Linearity and morphological structure in derived words: Evidence from category decision. In: Brain and Language 68, 340-346.

KARLSSON, Fred (1983): Suomen kielen äänne- ja muotorakenne. Juva:WSOY.

KELLIHER, Susan; Hendyerson, Leslie (1990): Morphology based frequency effects in the recognition of irregularly inflected verbs. In: British Journal of Psychology 81, 527-539.

LAINE, Matti (1996): Lexical status of inflectional and derivational suffixes: Evidence from Finnish. In: Scandinavian Journal of Psychology 37, 238-248.

LAINE, Matti; NIEMI, Jussi (1997): Reading morphemes. In: Aphasiology 11.9, 913-926.

LAINE, Matti; NIEMI, Jussi; KOIVUSELKÄ-SALLINEN, Päivi; AHLSÉN, Elisabeth; HYÖNÄ, Jukka (1994): A neurolinguistic analysis of morphological deficits in a Finnish-Swedish bilingual aphasic. In: Clinical Linguistics & Phonetics 8.3, 177-200.

LAINE, Matti; NIEMI, Jussi; KOIVUSELKÄ-SALLINEN, Päivi; HYÖNÄ, Jukka (1995): Morphological processing of polymorphemic nouns in a highly inflecting language. In: Cognitive Neuropsychology 12, 457-502.

LAINE, Matti; VIRTANEN, Patrik (1996): Turun Sanomat Computerized Lexical Database (Unpublished corpus and database program. University of Turku).

LUKATELA, Georgije; GLIGORIJEVIC, B.; KOSTIC, Aleksandar; TURVEY, Michael (1980): Representation of inflected nouns in the internal lexicon. In: Memory and Cognition 8, 415-423.

MCQUEEN, James; CUTLER, Anne (1998): Morphology in word recognition. In: Spencer, A.; Zwicky, A. (eds.): Handbook of Morphology. Oxford: Blackwell, 406-427.

NIEMI, Jussi; LAINE, Matti; TUOMINEN, Juhani (1994): Cognitive morphology in Finnish: Foundations of a new model. In: Language & Cognitive Processes 9, 423-446.

PINKER, Steven (1998): Words and rules. In: Lingua 106, 219-242.

PINKER, Steven; PRINCE, Alan (1991): Regular and irregular morphology and the psychological status of rules of grammar. In: Proceedings of the Seventeenth Annual Meeting of the Berkeley Linguistic Society, 230-251.

SCHREUDER, Robert; BAAYEN, R. Harald (1995): Modeling morphological processing. In: Feldman, L. (ed.): Morphological aspects of language processing. Hove: Lawrence Erlbaum, 131-154.

TAFT, Marcus (1988): A morphological-decomposition model of lexical representation. In: Linguistics 26, 657-667.

— (1979): Recognition of affixed words and the word frequency effect. In: Memory and Cognition 7.4, 263-272.

TAFT, Marcus; FORSTER, Kenneth (1976): Lexical storage and retrieval of polymorphemic and polysyllabic words. In: Journal of Verbal Learning and Verbal Behavior 15, 607-620.

— (1975): Lexical storage and retrieval of prefixed words. In: Journal of Verbal Learning and Verbal Behavior 14, 638-647.

Phonematische Sinnbezüge
Zu einem Problem kognitiver Sprachproduktionsmodelle

Hans Lösener

1   Semantik ohne Sprache

Ausgangspunkt der folgenden Überlegungen zur semantischen Funktionsweise phonematischer Figuren ist die Tatsache, dass die sprachliche und die semantische Dimension in einer Reihe von kognitiven Modellen zur Sprachproduktion und -verarbeitung auseinanderdriften. Dieses Auseinanderdriften von Sprache und Sinn zeigt sich etwa in der *language-of-thought*-Hypothese, also in der Annahme einer sprachfreien Organisation der Denkprozesse. Der Ausdruck *„language of thought"* selbst stammt zwar von Fodor (1975), aber das worum es geht, nämlich die Konzeption einer angeborenen, universellen semantischen Strukturierung des Denkens, ist bereits in den Postulaten der generativen Grammatik angelegt.[1] Die universelle Semantik ist das notwendige Gegenstück zur universellen Grammatik.[2] Wie diese transzendiert die universelle Semantik die Einzelsprache, oder mit den Worten von Stephen Pinker: „People do not think in English or Chinese or Apache; they think in a language of thought" (Pinker 1994:81). Das menschliche Denken findet demnach in einer Sprache hinter der Sprache statt, in einem angeborenen, universellen Mentalesisch, wie Pinker es auch nennt (Pinker 1994:478).

2   Die *language-of-thought*-Hypothese in Levelts Sprachproduktionsmodell

Die *language-of-thought*-Hypothese ist längst ein selbstverständlicher Bestandteil der kognitiven Sprachtheorie geworden.[3] Die meisten Sprachproduktionsmodelle gehen von einem metasprachlichen *message level* aus, in welchem die Sprachplanung ihren Ausgang nimmt. Als Beispiel sei hier auf das Sprachproduktionsmodell von Willem Levelt (1989, 1994) verwiesen. Grundlegend für Levelts Ansatz, wie auch für zahlreiche andere, vor allem seriell ausgerichtete Sprachproduktionsmodelle,[4] ist die Annahme unterschiedlicher Prozessorebenen, die bei der Erzeugung der Äußerung nacheinander durchlaufen werden, so bei Levelt die eines Konzeptualisieres, eines lexikali-

---

[1] Darauf haben Jerry A. Fodor und Jerrold Katz schon 1963 hingewiesen (Katz/Fodor 1963:208).

[2] „Diese These eines autonomen Syntax-Moduls zieht das Postulat einer Art von transzendentaler Semantik nach sich, für sich *seiender* Bedeutungsformen [...] Tatsächlich sind sie für die Syntax unverzichtbar. Ohne sie wäre jeder Versuch, Kombinationsregeln für syntaktische Kategorien zu formulieren, orientierungslos." (Stetter 1997: 244, Hervorhebung so im Text).

[3] Allerdings häufen sich in letzter Zeit die kritischen Stimmen. Siehe zu Fodors Konzeption etwa Putnam (1991) und zu Pinkers Ansatz das Buch von Trabant (1998).

[4] Etwa das klassische Logogen-Modell (Patterson/Shewell 1987) oder das Satzproduktionsmodell von Garrett (1990).

schen und syntaktischen Formulators und schließlich eines phonologischen Artikulators.

Bei Levelt ist die phonologische Ebene diejenige, welche von der semantischen am weitesten entfernt ist. Erst wenn der Inhalt der Äußerung semantisch festgelegt und die lexikalische und syntaktische Struktur determiniert ist, tritt der phonologische Artikulator in Aktion. Folgt man Levelts Modell, so müsste die phonologische Komponente den geringsten Anteil an der semantischen Planung der Äußerung haben. Aber so elegant Levelts Modell auf den ersten Blick erscheinen mag, so schnell stößt es in der empirischen Überprüfung auf ernste Schwierigkeiten. Denn der von Levelt angenommenen Trennung von Laut und Sinn, Signifikant und Signifikat widersprechen eine Reihe von Phänomenen, die in der tatsächlichen Sprachtätigkeit zu beobachten sind. Zu diesen Phänomenen gehören insbesondere auch die phonematischen Figuren und ihre Rolle bei der semantischen Organisation der Äußerung. Existenz und Funktionsweise der phonematischen Figuren legen den Schluss nahe, dass in der Sprachproduktion der Sinn sowenig dem Laut vorangeht, wie der Laut dem Sinn.

3   Lautsymbolische Projektionen

Die Reflexion über den Zusammenhang und das Zusammenspiel von Laut und Sinn gehört zu den ältesten Problemen des menschlichen Sprachdenkens überhaupt. Sie reicht von Platos *Kratylos* über Humboldts Überlegungen zur Buchstabenschrift bis hin zu den experimentellen Untersuchungen von Suitbert Ertel (1969) oder Stefan Etzel (1983). Wie ein roter Faden zieht sich durch diese über mehrere Jahrtausende reichende Reflexion ein fast mythisches Motiv, das Motiv des Lautsymbolismus. Der Lautsymbolismus hat nicht unwesentlich dazu beigetragen, Überlegungen zum Zusammenhang von Laut und Sinn in der modernen Linguistik, spätestens seit Saussure, zu diskreditieren. Denn die lautsymbolische Deutung sucht das Saussuresche *arbitraire du signe* außer Kraft zu setzen, indem sie einen *natürlichen* Zusammenhang zwischen phonologischer Form und semantischem Gehalt behauptet. Die Begründung der modernen Sprachtheorie durch Saussure hat der Faszination, die von lautsymbolischen Spekulationen ausgeht, allerdings keinen Abbruch getan. Ein Beispiel dafür ist die große 1997 erschienene Einführung in die Sprachpsychologie von Arnold Langenmayr, in der ein längerer Abschnitt der „expressiven Lautsymbolik" gewidmet ist (Langenmayr 1997:75-92). Gleich zu Beginn dieses Kapitels geht Langenmayr ausführlich auf die Untersuchungen von Hermann Strehle (*Vom Geheimnis der Sprache*, München 1956) ein, über deren methodische Unzulänglichkeiten er sich zwar im Klaren ist,[5] von denen er aber meint, dass sie „in nahezu genialer Weise später belegte Zusammenhänge" vorwegnehmen (Langenmayr 1997:76). So ahmen nach Strehle etwa die labiodentalen Frikative in *Wind, Fön, Wetter* oder *Taifun* das Geräusch des

---

[5]   „Auch wenn die Untersuchungen Stehles (1956) in keiner Weise den Erfordernissen entsprechen, vor allem, weil bei seinem Vorgehen dem subjektiven nachträglichen Hineininterpretieren in auffällige Zusammenhänge Tür und Tor geöffnet sind, so möchte ich doch seine Vorstellungen ausführlicher darstellen." (Langmayr 1997:75).

Windes nach (ibd.). In gleicher Weise wird der Länge der Silben ein ikonischer Charakter unterstellt:

"Kurze Silben drücken Gerafftheit (,flott', ,schnell', ,fix', ,rasch', ,stop') aus, lange Silben werden für Zähes, Gedehntes eingesetzt (,Öl', ,Teer', ,Mus', ,Brei'). Das Prinzip wird nach Strehle deutlich im Vergleich von ,schauen' (lang) und ,blicken' (kurz)." (Langenmayr 1997:77).

Auch der bekannte Vokalsymbolismus fehlt bei Strehle nicht: Dunkle Laute evozieren die Vorstellung von etwas Dunklem: *Abend, Nacht, Schlaf.* Das /u/, der Laut mit der tiefsten Bildungsstelle, signalisiert Tiefe: *Fuß, Mulde, Pfuhl.* Helle Laute werden dagegen mit der Vorstellung "hell" (*Zink, Zinn*) und "oben" verbunden: *Stirn, Gipfel, Berg* (a.a.O.). Das Prinzip, auf dem diese lautsymbolischen Interpretationen beruhen, ist einfach: Es handelt sich bei allen genannten Beispielen um eine Projektion der Wortbedeutung in die Wortform, des Signifikats in den Signifikanten. Das wird deutlich, wenn man sich diejenigen Fälle ansieht, die sich einer lautsymbolischen Deutung entziehen. Wenn das /a/ in *Abend* Dunkelheit evozieren soll, wie steht es dann mit demselben Vokal in Wörtern wie *Glanz, Flamme, Halogenlampe* oder *Strahl*? Wenn der Vokal /i/ etwas Helles evoziert, ist dann die französische *nuit* weniger dunkel als die deutsche *Nacht*? Die lautsymbolische Interpretation liebt Einzelbeispiele und muss Übersetzungen in die Fremdsprache ebenso systematisch ausblenden wie Gegenbeispiele aus der eigenen Sprache. Auch wenn sich tatsächlich mit einzelnen, isoliert geäußerten Lauten oder Lautpaaren, bestimmte Assoziationen verbinden können (/i/: klein, /u/: dunkel, /a/: groß etc.), so verliert der isolierte Laut – ich nehme den Fall der onomatopoetischen Wortbildungen aus – mit seiner Einbindung in das Wort zwangsläufig sein autonomes Bedeutungspotential. *Riesen, Titanen* oder *Giganten* haben im Deutschen nichts Kümmerliches, nur weil sie den Vokal /i/ enthalten. Die autonome Lautsemantik endet dort, wo das Phonem beginnt, nämlich bei der Geschichtlichkeit des Signifikanten, also bei der radikalen Arbitrarität der Zeichens, mit deren Anerkennung bei Saussure die Sprachtheorie beginnt.

4 Phonematische Figuren: Einige Beispiele

Mit dem Abschied von den lautsymbolischen Projektionen könnte die Frage nach der Interaktion von Laut und Sinn eigentlich ad acta gelegt werden: Da die Beziehung zwischen Signifikat und Signifikant arbiträr ist, beschränkt sich, so könnte man folgern, die semantische Funktionsweise der Phoneme darauf, durch Oppositionen das einer Sprache zugrundeliegende Phoneminventar zu bilden. Auf der Ebene des Sprachsystems trifft dies auch zu. Auf der Ebene der konkreten Äußerung sehen die Dinge allerdings anders aus. Hier gibt es tatsächlich eine semantische Funktionsweise der Phoneme. Hier können Phoneme nicht nur bedeutungsunterscheidende, sondern auch bedeutungsverbindende und damit bedeutungsschaffende Einheiten sein. Und zwar überall dort, wo phonematische Reihen und Echobeziehungen semantisch wirksam sind. Wenn man auf sie achtet, findet man sie an allen Ecken und Enden. Z.B. in Zeitungsüberschriften (*Tatwaffe Telefon, Zivilcourage und Zähigkeit, Das Beben von*

Brüssel, Leiche auf der Landstraße).[6] Neben stabreimenden Figuren trifft man häufig auch versteckte Alliterationsfiguren (*Singender Wahnsinn, Pausenkaspar für Kampftrinker*).[7] Manchmal werden mehrere phonematische Figuren miteinander kombiniert. Etwa in einer Überschrift eines Artikels über das Erscheinen einer CD mit indischer Filmmusik: „Bollywood, wie es singt und swingt." Hier werden nicht weniger als vier phonematische Figuren miteinander verknüpft: der Reim (*singt und swingt*), die aproximative Alliteration (*singt und swingt*), die phonematische Überblendung (*Hollywood + Bombay = Bollywood*) und die phonematische Analogiebildung (*leibt und lebt ⇒ singt und swingt*). Noch häufiger begegnet man in Werbeslogans solchen und ähnlichen Verfahren, z.B. Alliterationen (*Das einzig Wahre: Warsteiner – Spitzen Pilsener der Premium-Klasse*; *Mut ist der Motor des Fortschritts* [Opel]; *Wir geben ihrer Zukunft ein Zuhause* [LBS]; *Bitte ein Bit* [Bitburger]), phonematischen Echoreihen (*Felsenfrisch – Riegeler – Felsen Pils – Das Region Premium*; *Der medizinische Schutz für Zahnfleisch und Zähne* [Elmex/Aronal], Reimen, vor allem in älteren Werbetexten, häufig gekoppelt mit alliterativen Effekten (*Heute bleibt die Küche kalt, heut' gehen wir in den Wienerwald.* [Wienerwald]; *Mars macht mobil, bei Arbeit, Sport und Spiel.* [Mars]), phonematischen Überblendungen (*Tanz der Ventile* [Renault] ⇒ *Tanz der Vampire; Die Wüste bebt* [Mitsubishi Motors] ⇒ *Die Wüste lebt*). Die Werbung hat diese Verfahren weder erfunden noch für sich gepachtet. Sie finden sich auch in der Alltagssprache, so z.B. in Sprichwörtern mit Reimen (*Eile mit Weile; Probieren geht über Studieren; Sich regen bringt Segen* etc.), mit phonematischen Echos (*Es ist nicht alles Gold, was glänzt; Kleine Kinder, kleine Sorgen, große Kinder, große Sorgen* etc.) oder mit Alliterationen (*Auf einen groben Klotz, gehört ein grober Keil; Glück und Glas, wie leicht bricht das; Frisch gewagt ist halb gewonnen* etc.). Aber auch in Redewendungen sind diese Figuren anzutreffen, so etwa Reime besonders häufig in Zwillingsformeln (*kreucht und fleucht; in Hülle und Fülle; mit Ach und Krach; mit Sack und Pack* etc.); auch Alliterationen (*Händchen halten; kleine Brötchen backen; jmd. die Hölle heiß machen; mit allem Drum und Dran; gut und gerne; mit Kind und Kegel; Haus und Hof* etc.) und phonematische Paare (*Epoche machen; nicht im Sinne des Erfinders; in Schutt und Asche; mit allen Wassern gewaschen sein* etc.) sind verbreitet. Es gibt diese Figuren übrigens auch in Spontanbildungen, wie *Besserwessi, Bleifisch* (phonematische Überblendung), *wischi-waschi, fix und foxi sein, Mensch Meier, Krimskrams, Muckefuck, Remmidemmi* etc.) und in Kinderreimen (*Angeber Tütenkleber; Angsthase Pfeffernase / Morgen kommt der Osterhase; Heule, Heule, der Erwin hat 'ne Beule*)[8] und sogar, wie Freud gezeigt hat, in der Sprache des Traumes.

---

[6]   Alle Beispiele aus *Spiegel 12/1999*.

[7]   a.a.O.

[8]   Beispiele aus Rühmkorf (1981: 33).

5 Die semantische Funktionsweise phonematischer Figuren

Nach der *language-of-thought*-Hypothese dürfte es solche Erscheinungen eigentlich gar nicht geben. Geht man nämlich davon aus, dass die semantische Planung der Äußerung zunächst unabhängig von den einzelsprachlichen Signifikanten (und damit auch unabhängig von den phonologischen Gegebenheiten) erfolgt, eben in einer universellen Sprache des Denkens, dann könnten phonematische Figuren eigentlich gar nicht oder höchstens als Zufallsprodukte auftreten, in jedem Falle blieben sie von der semantischen Dimension der Äußerung getrennt. Keine der hier genannten phonematischen Figuren kann aber als Zufallsprodukt betrachtet werden, und keine ist semantisch belanglos. Im Gegenteil, wenn diese Figuren in der Sprache auftreten und sich in ihr halten können, dann deshalb, weil sie hochgradig funktional, *semantisch* funktional sind. Ihre semantische Funktionsweise kann sehr einfach sein, wie im Fall der Zwillingsformeln, wo die phonematischen Echos (Reim, Alliteration) eine Verknüpfungsfunktion besitzen. Die phonematische Verbindung verschweißt die einzelnen Wörter zu einem neuen, feststehenden Signifikanten (*Wind und Wetter, Bausch und Bogen, Luft und Liebe, Leib und Leben* etc.). Dass ihre Funktionsweise aber noch komplexer sein kann, möchte ich hier an zwei Beispielen andeuten, an einem Werbeslogan und einem Gedicht.

Quadratisch. Praktisch. Gut: Dieser erfolgreiche Werbeslogan einer Schokoladenfirma beruht nicht zuletzt auf einer raffinierten phonematischen Konstruktion. Er zeigt anschaulich, wie eine Lautfigur zu einer Sinnfigur wird, bzw. den Sinn, in diesem Fall den werbewirksamen „Witz" der Äußerung, erst ermöglicht. Diese Lautfigur besteht im wesentlichen aus der starken Reimbindung zwischen den ersten beiden Signifikanten:

Quadratisch. Praktisch. Gut.

Stark ist diese Reimbindung insofern, als nicht nur die letzten Silben identisch sind, sondern die beiden Signifikanten zusätzlich durch Echos auf /k/, /a/ und /r/ miteinander verbunden sind. Diese Reimbindung hat eine doppelte Funktion: Zum einen dient sie dazu, eine semantische Assoziation zwischen den beiden an sich völlig disparaten Signifikanten zu schaffen. Der Hinweis auf die besondere Form der Schokolade (*quadratisch*) wird verknüpft mit der Vorstellung einer gewissen Nützlichkeit (*praktisch*). Zum andern, und dies ist für die Wirkung und Wirksamkeit des Slogans noch wichtiger, schafft die starke Reimbindung einen scharfen Kontrast zum dritten Signifikanten (*gut*), der nur durch eine (schwache) Assonanz, nämlich das /t/, mit den beiden anderen verbunden ist. Tatsächlich ist das Fehlen starker phonematischer Echos hier genauso funktional wie die Reimbindung bei den ersten beiden Signifikanten. Zusammen mit den anderen phonematischen Komponenten, wie der Akzentik, die die Wortfolge in ein alternierendes Muster bringt:

Quadratisch. Praktisch. Gut

und der abnehmenden Silbenzahl pro Wort (3+2+1 Silben) wird eine superlativische Steigerungserwartung bei dem Hörer geschaffen, die durch das einsilbige, nicht-reimende Positiv *Gut* konterkariert wird. Es ist diese phonematisch-semantische Enttäuschungsfigur, auf der die Originalität und Einprägsamkeit des Slogans beruht. Die semantische Wirksamkeit resultiert hier direkt aus der phonematischen Konstruktion.

Es ist kaum möglich von phonematischen Figuren zu sprechen, von ihrer Funktionsweise und ihren verschiedenen Formen, ohne zugleich vom Gedicht zu sprechen. Nicht weil phonematische Figuren ein Privileg der Dichtung wären, sie kommen, wie wir gesehen haben, überall in der Sprache vor, aber weil ihre semantische Funktionalität in der Dichtung besonders deutlich zu Tage tritt und weil sich in der Dichtung zeigt, dass die semantische Organisation ganzer Texte auf phonematischen Figuren beruhen kann, und zwar ganz unabhängig von dem Vorhandensein metrisch vorgeschriebener Reimstrukturen. Ich möchte dies hier an einem Beispiel illustrieren, an dem Gedicht *Der alte Tibetteppich* von Else Lasker-Schüler.[9] Schon beim ersten Lesen oder Hören des Gedichtes kann man kaum umhin, die vielen Assonanzen, Alliterationen und Binnenreime zu bemerken. Man könnte darin etwas Verspieltes sehen, einen Hang zum Ornamentalen, zu ausschmückenden Klangfiguren. Tatsächlich sind die Lautfiguren des Gedichtes alles andere als eine formale Spielerei. Denn die Lautfiguren machen hier Sinn. Sie machen Sinn, weil sie zum *Sinnmachen*, zur Performativität des Gedichtes gehören. Dieser Text macht etwas durch sein Sagen und er macht, was er sagt. Darin liegt seine poetische Spezifik. Er sagt die erotische Verflechtung zwischen dem Ich und dem Du in einer Metaphorik des textilen Gewebes (*„verwirkt"*), die im Laufe des Gedichtes weiter entfaltet wird und das erotische Verwobensein auf die Welt ausdehnt (*„Tibetteppich"*, *„Teppichtibet"*, *„Maschentausendabertausendweit"*, *„buntgeknüpfte Zeiten"*).[10] Aber das Gedicht sagt diese Verflechtung nicht nur, es wird auch zu dem Ort, an dem sie sich vollzieht. Es realisiert die Verflechtung der Liebenden miteinander und mit der Welt und es realisiert sie vor allem durch die phonematischen Figuren, auf denen der Text, die semantische Organisation des Textes, beruht. Denn es sind die phonematischen Figuren, die das bewirken, was der Text behauptet: die totale Verflechtung und das vollkommene Verwobensein des Einen mit dem Anderen und Jedes mit dem Ganzen. Die wichtigsten Figuren dieser totalen Vernetzung sind:

- Binnenreime (*Deine* [...] *meine*; *Lamasohn* [...] *-pflanzenthron*; *lange* [...] *Mund / Wange bunt-*),

---

[9]   Deine Seele, die die meine liebet,
      Ist verwirkt mit ihr im Teppichtibet,
      Strahl in Strahl, verliebte Farben,
      Sterne, die sich himmellang umwarben.

      Unsere Füße ruhen auf der Kostbarkeit,
      Maschentausendabertausendweit.

      Süßer Lamasohn auf Moschuspflanzenthron,
      Wie lange küßt Dein Mund den meinen wohl
      Und Wang die Wange buntgeknüpfte Zeiten schon?
[10] Siehe auch die Textanalyse von Swantje Ehlers (1983:112).

- Wortwiederholungen, die wie identische Reime funktionieren (*die die, Strahl in Strahl, Maschentausendabertausendweit, Wang die Wange*),
- und eine Vielzahl phonematischer Echos (z.b. das siebenfache /i/ in *Ist verwirkt mit ihr im Teppichtibet*),

dazu kommen noch die auffälligen Kompositabildungen (*Maschentausendabertausendweit, Mochuspflanzenthron*) und graphemische Figuren, wie die Vokalpaare der ersten Strophe (nur <e> und <i>) oder die Häufung von Doppelkonsonanten (*Tibetteppich, himmellang*). Jede einzelne Lautfigur ist hier eine Sinnfigur, jedes einzelne phonematische Echo, jede Alliteration und jede Phonemserie trägt hier zu der totalen Verflechtung bei, die das semantische und poetische Organisationsprinzip des Textes bildet. Tatsächlich steht und fällt der gesamte Text, seine semantische Kohärenz, seine poetische Kraft, mit der Wirksamkeit der phonematischen Verflechtungsfiguren. Ohne sie bliebe von dem Text, von seiner semantischen Dimension, kaum etwas übrig; was man leicht nachprüfen kann, indem man etwa versucht, eine Inhaltsangabe des Gedichtes zu erstellen. Die Ergebnisse dürften für sich sprechen.

Was hat nun aber Else Lasker-Schüler, was haben Gedichte mit den Prämissen der kognitiven Sprachtheorie zu tun? Sehr viel, denn dieses einzelne Gedicht (man hätte ebensogut ein Gedicht von Trakl oder Celan nehmen können) zeigt die Grenzen eines Sprachproduktionsmodells auf, das ein übersprachliches *message level* als Ausgangspunkt der Äußerungsplanung annimmt. Die Funktionsweise phonematischer Figuren in der Dichtung, in der Alltagssprache und in Gebrauchstexten macht deutlich, dass die phonologische Seite einer Äußerung nicht deren äußere Form darstellt, sondern konstitutiv für die *Möglichkeit* des Sinn, des Sinnmachens ist. Überall dort, wo phonematische Figuren eine Rolle spielen, ist es unmöglich, zwischen einer inneren (mentalen) und einer äußeren (einzelsprachlich bedingten) Semantik zu unterscheiden (wie dies etwa Ray Jackendoff (1996) tut). Denn bei Äußerungen, die auf phonematischen Beziehungen beruhen, kann es ja kein zeitliches Nacheinander von semantischer Planung und phonologischer Codierung geben. Die Existenz der phonologischen Form ist ja hier Bedingung für die Möglichkeit der semantischen Planung. Aber auch von einer Vorgängigkeit der phonologischen Form vor der semantischen Planung zu sprechen macht wenig Sinn, denn die phonematische Figur ist ja kein Bestandteil des Sprachsystems selbst, sie entsteht erst in der jeweiligen Äußerung.

Die phonematische Figuren zeigen also nicht bloß die Untrennbarkeit von phonologischer und semantischer Verarbeitung, sondern auch ihre Gleichzeitigkeit im Sprachproduktionsprozess. Die semantische Funktionsweise phonematischer Figuren spricht dafür, dass die Sprachplanung mit und in der Einzelsprache beginnt und nicht in der unerfassbaren Transzendenz einer *language of thought*.

6   Literatur

BOCK, Kathryn; LEVELT, Willem (1994): Language Production, Grammatical Encoding. In: Gernsbacher.

GERNSBACHER, Morton Ann (Hrsg.): Handbook of Psycholinguistics. San Diego: Academic Press 1994.

EHLERS, Swantje (1983): Ein Spiel von Form und Inhalt. Zu Else Lasker-Schülers *Ein alter Tibetteppich*. In: Hartung, Harald (Hrsg.): Gedichte und Interpretationen. Vom Naturalismus bis zur Jahrhundertmitte. Stuttgart.

ERTEL, Suitbert (1969): Psychophonetik – Untersuchungen über Lautsymbolik und Motivation. Göttingen: Hogrefe, Verl. für Psychologie.

ETZEL, Stefan (1983): Untersuchungen zur Lautsymbolik. Diss. Frankfurt a. Main.

FODOR, Jerry A. (1975): The Language of Thought. New York: Thomas Y. Crowell.

GARRETT, M.F. (1990): Sentence processiong. In: Osherson, D.; Lasnik, H. (Hrsg): An Invitation to Cognitive Science: Language, Bd. III, Cambridge, Mass.: MIT Press.

JACKENDOFF, Ray (1996): Semantics and Cognition. In: Lappin, Shalom (Hrsg.): The Handbook of Contemporary Semantic Theory. Oxford: Blackwell 1996.

KATZ, Jerrold J.; FODOR, Jerry A. (1963): The Structure of a Semantic Theory. In: Language 39, 170-210.

LANGENMAYR, Arnold (1997): Sprachpsychologie. Ein Lehrbuch. Göttingen: Hogrefe, Verl. für Psychologie.

LEVELT, Willem (1989): Speaking. From Intention to Articulation. Cambridge, MA: MIT Press.

LEVELT, Willem; BOCK, Kathryn (1994): Language Production, Grammatical Encoding. In: Gernsbacher.

PATTERSON, K.E. / SHEWELL, C. (1987): Speak and spell: Dissociations and word-class effects. In: M. Coltheart; Sartori, G.; Job, R. (Hrsg.): The Cognitive Neuropsychology of Language. London: Erlbaum.

PINKER, Steven (1994): The Language Instinct. How the Mind Creates Language, New York: W. Morrow and Co.

PUTNAM, Hilary (1991): Repräsentation und Realität. Frankfurt a. M.: Suhrkamp.

RÜHMKORF, Peter (1981): agar agar - zaurzaurim. Zur Naturgeschichte des Reims und der menschlichen Anklangsnerven. Reinbek bei Hamburg: Rowohlt.

STETTER, Christian (1997): Schrift und Sprache. Frankfurt a. M..

TRABANT, Jürgen (1998): Artikulationen. Historische Anthropologie der Sprache. Frankfurt a. M.: Suhrkamp (Suhrkamp-Taschenbuch Wissenschaft 1386).

Zur Genese der menschlichen Kommunikation

Augustyn Mańczyk

Wahrscheinlich ist Gott ein guter evolutionärer Schöpfer, der die Welt einmal aktiviert und lebend gemacht hatte, danach aber verließ er unsere Schicksale und ließ uns
uns nach eigenen Gesetzen weiter entwickeln. Ungefähr so wie der *bricoleur* – der
Bastler formt seine gegenständlichen Entdeckungen aufs Geratewohl – scheint die
Evolution der belebten Welt auch das Ergebnis willkürlicher Ereignisse zu sein. Die
Form der Ordnung bzw. Unordnung auf der sprachlichen Ebene könnte man – aus
heutiger Sicht – als ein stabiles Paradoxon bezeichnen, denn einerseits bedienen wir
uns bestimmter, endlicher Regeln, und andererseits sind wir nicht imstande, den Kern
des Gedachten unmittelbar aufzufangen – man denke dabei an den Gebrauch von
Metaphern, Analogien u.a. Figuren, die den Stil, aber vor allem die sprachlich un-
fassbaren, komplizierten Gedankengänge in die Kommunikationsbahn bringen sollen.
   Der Ursprung und der Gebrauch der Sprache erinnern an die Evolution des Menschen und seines Bewußtseins. Als das Bewußtsein entstanden war, fand es den nächsten Weg zur Sprache – es war die einzige Möglichkeit des Ausdrucks seiner vielfältigen Funktionen. Wir wissen nicht, ob sich die Funktionen der Sprache an die Be-
wußtseinsaufträge angepaßt haben oder die Bewußtseinsfunktionen sich die Referenzen von der *Sprache im Gebrauch* ständig ausleihen. Die apriorische und aposteriorische Entstehung der Bewußtsein-Sprache verlief nicht nur parallel, sondern mehr-
schichtig und funktional, abhängig von internen (z.B. genetischen) und externen
Fakten (z.B. der Entstehung des physikalischen Stimmapparates). Organisiertes Chaos
im gesunden Hirn sowie nichtlineare Übertragung verschiedenartiger Informations-
frachten und das chemische System, dessen Funktion von der Gestalt einzelner
Eiweißteilchen abhängig ist, damit es auf die Abstraktions- und Bewußtseinsstufe
transponiert werden konnte - das ist das menschliche Gehirn.
   Vor etwa drei Millionen Jahren erschienen die ersten Hominiden mit vergrößertem
Hirn und mit anderer Zahnform. M. Sponheimer von der Rutgers University berichtet
über die neuesten Untersuchungen, die die Affenmenschen betreffen. Der *Australopithecus africanus* war öfter auf der Suche nach Nahrung in der Savanne. Er fraß vor
allem Gras, Pflanzenwurzeln und Samen aber auch kleine Säugetiere, Eidechsen und
Insekten. Besonderer Untersuchung wurde der Zahnschmelz unterworfen; man stellte
dabei eine erstaunlich hohe Konzentration des „Steppen"isotops C^{12} fest.
   Der *Australopithecus africanus* war nicht viel größer als der Schimpanse – er war
etwa 135 cm hoch und wog um die 40 kg. Ausgestattet mit einem größeren Gehirn
erinnert er an die weltbekannte Lucy (*Australopithecus afarensis*). In der Gegend von
Hader in Äthiopien wurde u.a. ein unvollständiges Skelett der kleinen Lucy aufge-
funden: drei Fuß hoch, der Körperbau noch affenähnlich, lange Arme, kurze Beine.
Lucy gehörte der gleichen Familie, aber nicht der gleichen Art und derselben Gattung
an. Sie hatte vor 3 Millionen Jahren gelebt; später, d.h. von vor 3 bis vor 1 Million
Jahren bewohnte Afrika *homo habilis* mit einem Hirnvolumen von etwa 500 bis 750
cm^3 und einer zwölfjährigen Mädchenstatur. Mit dieser Gattung entstanden die ersten

Formen einer Protosprache, die eine andere Erscheinungsbildhaftigkeit des Kommunizierens als bei Prähominiden dargeboten hatte. Vielleicht zählen diese tanz-, gestik-
und mundzeichenhaften Ereignisse zu den allerersten In-formierungen des urmensch-
lichen, sinntragenden Verstandes und der Menschwerdung überhaupt. Die Protosprach-
formen waren jedoch primitiv und arm an Inhalt, dem Bau nach gewiß reduktiv und
im allgemeinen elliptisch sowie iterativ. Ein *homo habilis*-Schädel wurde in gutem
Zustand am Turkanasee in Ostafrika entdeckt. Seine innere Fläche enthält die Spuren
des Brocazentrums, und die Gehirnhalbkugeln weisen Asymmetrie auf.

Wesentliche Anpassungsänderungen hatten sich mit dem Erscheinen des *homo
erectus* vollzogen. Seine Sprache zeichnete sich auch durch strukturelle Einfachheit
und abstraktlose Dimension aus, trotzdem stand dieses kommunikative System auf
einer höheren Stufe des Weltwortens als die der Affen und Australopithezinen. Die
Mehrheit der Paläontologen und Anthropologen ist sich darüber einig, daß der *homo
erectus* in vielen Aspekten einen bedeutsamen Platz in der evolutiven Menschenge-
schichte eingenommen hat. Sein Körperbau ähnelte mehr einem zeitgenössichen Menschen als den früheren Formen der Urmenschen. Athletische Statur mir einer schon
sichtbaren Taille, längerer Schritt, weniger hervortretende Backenknochen, größeres
Hirnvolumen u.a.. Merkmale kennzeichnen diese Zwischengattung. Während der
homo habilis sich noch in der Olduvai-Kultur des durch die zufällige Steinblockzer-
schlagung entstandenen Werkzeuges bedient hatte, schuf der *homo erectus* seine
Gerätschaften schon absichtlich für bestimmte Zwecke.

Die Schaffung wenn auch nur eines einfachsten Werkzeuges erfordert minimale
geistige Fähigkeiten. Solche Fähigkeiten besaß wahrscheinlich der *homo erectus,* aber
seine sprachlichen Errungenschaften und sein Denkvermögen waren noch auf einem
sehr niedrigen Niveau, so daß der technologische Stillstand noch in den nächsten
200.000 Jahren andauerte. Die Werkzeugformen waren eher geordnet als chaotisch
(symmetrisch, handlich); ihre Anwendung mehr oder minder bestimmt. Demzufolge
wurde eine äußere Prämisse erfüllt, damit das, was geplant und bewerkstelligt werden
sollte, auch in Worten aufgefaßt und anderen zugetragen wurde.

Vom heutigen Standpunkt war diese Zeit nicht unabänderlich vergeblich. Langsam
hatte sich der Stimmapparat formiert, der sich wesentlich von den früheren Gattungen
unterschied. Leakey hat dazu eindeutige Erklärungen u.a., daß der Mensch mehrere
Lautarten hervorbringen kann, weil sein Kehlkopf relativ tief im Hals plaziert ist.
Dies hat zu Folge, daß die Menschen unterschiedliche Lautmodulationen und Arti-
kulationsarten erzeugen können.

Der *homo erectus* (der aufgerichtete Mensch) endet mit der interaktiven Pantomi-
me, er beginnt aber eine neue Karriere als Orator. Sein Gehirnvolumen beträgt jetzt
900 cm^3, und seine neugeborenen Kinder brauchen länger als beim *homo habilis* eine
geduldige Betreuung durch die Erwachsenen. In lebensgefährlichen Situationen der
Kinder waren die Eltern und die Nachbarn gezwungen, möglichst schnelle Hilfe zu
leisten, was sicher zur Gestaltung immer engerer Beziehungen innerhalb der Gruppe
oder Gemeinschaft unter den Angehörigen geführt hat.

Man darf nicht vergessen, daß es in dieser Kulturperiode (dem sog. Acheuléen) zu
einer Weiterentwicklung der Werkzeugherstellung kam. Man produzierte u.a. Stein-
fausthammer, die mitunter auch für die Herstellung anderer Werkzeuge benutzt wur-

den. Offensichtlich kann das als ein Zeugnis einer selbstbewußten Einstellung zur Wirklichkeit betrachtet werden. Der einfachen Produktion folgt eine höhere Stufe des Angriffs, der Wirklichkeitserfassung nach.

Wahrscheinlich ging mit der Fertigung von Geräteschaften auch die Aasfleischfresserei einher. Mit einem einfachen, handlichen Steinspaltstück konnte man sogar unter der härtesten Tierhaut Fleisch herausschneiden. Diese Entdeckung, verbunden mir der Feueranwendung, hatte Epoche gemacht. Im Menu stand seit dieser Zeit gebratenes Fleisch zur Verfügung. Bickerton stellte einmal fest, daß das Sprechen den Menschen von einfachen Sinnesperzeptionen entfesselt habe und ihn in die Freiheit in Zeit und Raum geführt habe.

Vor ca. 200.000 Jahren kam das sog. Moustérien zum Vorschein, das noch keine spürbare Beschleunigung in der Werkzeugtechnologie aufwies. Es wurden dagegen Fortschritte im Bereich des Weidwerks und beim Sammeln von Pflanzenwurzeln gemacht. Die Menschen dieser Zeit schlugen gern Lagerstätten in Höhlen und im Freien auf. Charakteristische Merkmale ihrer Geräteschaften waren vor allem Schneiden mit regulärem Dreieck und rund bearbeitete Steinkerne. Diese Eigenschaften des Werkzeugs verlangten vom Projektgeber und Produzenten eine praxisbezogene Beobachtungsgabe und eine kreative Raumvorstellung. Die Praxisbezogenheit und Kreativität der Beobachtung sowie die gedankliche Räumlichkeit mußten letztendlich in eine relativ starre Gegenstands- bzw. Erscheinungsbedeutung einmünden, um in der Vorstellung in ein dem entsprechenden Lautbild umgewandelt zu werden. Dieser Vorgang, der sich über Generationen hinweg vollzog, zeigt sich z.B an einem zufällig geworfenen Stein dar, der in Stücke zerschlagen wurde. Zuerst bemerkte niemand einen brauchbaren Sinn der Steinbrocken, erst später erkannte man die Brauchbarkeit der spitzigen Steinstücke beim Stengelschneiden oder beim Herausschneiden des Aasfleisches. Tausende von Jahren haben unsere Vorfahren diesem versteinerten, harten, spitzförmigen und handlichen Gegenstand eine im Gebrauch entstandene Bedeutung gegeben. Ein unvermeidlicher Zufall bewirkte die durch Beobachtung und Erfahrung entstandene ausgeformte Bedeutung. Man kann sagen, daß eine fluktuative Ereignisfolge in einem raum-zeitlichen Moment zur qualitativen Änderung im gedanklich-kommunikativen Geschehnisfeld geführt hatte. Man könnte vermuten, der Stein vermochte mit seinen Gebrauchsmöglichkeiten den Urmenschen aufzuklären, daß das unkomplexe, praktische Bewußtsein im beschriebenen Fall mit dem Tast- und Sehsinn bewertet und bestätigt werden kann.

In der Relation Gegenstand, Mensch und Bedeutung entstand die bewußte Existenz dessen, was sich bewegte, und was unabhängig und nicht in Armweite erreichbar war. So wurde – um die vorbeilaufenden Büffel zu treffen – nicht ein Baum verwendet, sondern aus Erfahrung bewußt ein Stein, weil man schon genau wußte, diesen Gegenstand in solchen Fällen benutzen zu können. Er wurde folglich von anderen Gegenständen gedanklich abgetrennt, und jetzt erhielt unser Stein sogar zwei im Anwendungsbereich brauchbare Bedeutungen. Die Selektion und die Auswahl der Gebrauchsmöglichkeiten wurden vollzogen. Diese Tatsache hätte Edelman als Hier-und-Jetzt-Bewußtsein und als Urbewußtsein ohne Vergangenheit und ohne Zukunft bezeichnet, dessen Existenz auch bei den nichtlingualen und asemantischen Tieren anzunehmen ist.

Im Zeitraum von vor ca. 250.000 Jahren bis vor 40.000 Jahren lebte in der Eiszeit der Neandertalmensch. Nach seinem Aussterben gab es einen großen Sprung in der künstlerisch-symbolhaften Darstellung. In der Zeit des Aurignacien, Magdalénien und Solutréen entstanden die ältesten Denkmäler der Maler- und Skulpturkunst. Man beobachtet zugleich ein außergewöhnliches Streben nach Ordnung, eine Beschleunigung der Veränderungen sowie Innovationen im Werkzeugwesen.

Die Archäologen und Paläontologen sind daher – aufgrund bestimmter Befunde – der Meinung, daß es in der Epoche des oberen Paläolithikums zu einer expansiven Ausbildung einer mündlichen Sprachform kam. Es hat sich erwiesen, daß die Sprache gemeinschaftliche Vorzüge für den Menschen aufwies, zumal in kurzer historischer Zeit der Mensch die Erde eroberte, Tiere unterordnete und mit Erfolg den Acker anbaut. Die Gemeinschaftszugehörigkeit wurde deutlich gestärkt, die Zahl der Angehörigen einer Gruppe nahm zu, und es entwickelten sich spürbare Grenzen zwischen dem Eigenen und dem Fremden. Innerhalb der Gruppe verursachte die Sprache differenzierte soziale Aktivitäten. In der belebten Welt führte die Sprache zu einer Kluft zwischen den Menschen und den Tieren.

In dieser Zeit sind oft Höhlenflachreliefe und Höhlenmalereien anzutreffen. Zu Kunstgegenständen gehören gewiß anthropomorphische und zoomorphische Bilder der Bildhauerkunst, Wohnobjekte aus Mammutknochen, Riten sowie unterschiedliche Verzierungen von Werkzeug und Schmuck. Diese Kunst ist nicht nur mit weltlichen, praktischen Handlungen des Alltags verknüpft, sondern sie charakterisiert auch schamanische und andere religöse Bedürfnisse des Stammes. Reich verzierte Sanktuarien dienten religöser Zeremonie, aber auch als Ort zur Besprechung des Viehbestandes und zur Planung der Feldarbeiten. All diese Begebenheiten festigten die Beziehungen in der Gruppe und zwischen den Stämmen.

Vor 40.000 Jahren gewann der Urmensch eine Fähigkeit, die ihm eine bewußte Welt eröffnete. Diese Bewußtheit der Wirklichkeit wurde vom Menschen erzwungen und allmählich mittels des Werkzeugs, der Kunst und des Wortes wahr gemacht.

Eine künstlerische und zeichenhafte Symbolik zu schaffen, bedeutete für den Menschen zuerst eine scheinbare Entfernung vom Gegenstand, eine Distanzierung, die aber zu einem besseren Verständnis der Umgebung, der Welt führte.

Im Fruchtleben eines pränatalen Wesens entwickeln sich mehrere neuro-organische Merkmale und Fähigkeiten, die bis zum 6. Monat nach der Geburt, d.h. bis in die perinatale Periode anhalten.

Die Frage nach dem Beginn der Menschwerdung ist bis heute nicht beantwortet. Gewiß ist damit u.a. die Entwicklung der Hirnrinde verbunden, die sich durch bestimmte Kontrollfähigkeiten unterschiedlicher Bewußtseinszustände auszeichnen könnte. Ungefähr in der 7. Woche erfüllt das Hirn die ersten grundlegenden Funktionen, die denen des erwachsenen Menschen ähnlich sind, z.B. koordiniert der Impulsdurchfluß Funktionen ausgewählter Organe.

Das natürliche (im Sinne von „einfache") Bewußtsein gewinnt das Kind zwischen der 25. und 32. Lebenswoche. In dieser Zeit reagiert es in utero auf das Sprechen, es unterscheidet dieses Sprechen von anderen Tönen und weiß, was das Herzklopfen der Mutter bedeutet. Bekannt sind Experimente mit der Anwendung unterschiedlicher Tonvibrationen bei den prä- und perinatalen Untersuchungen. Dabei wurde u.a. fest-

gestellt, daß genetisch programmierte, vokale Reaktionen wie Weinen, Schreien, Lachen nach der Geburt noch aus den Erfahrungen in der pränatalen Zeit stammen.
Wenn das Maß der Menschlichkeit bzw. der Menschwerdung die Fähigkeit des
Kommunizierens ist, so sind auch die Reaktionen des noch nicht geborenen Kindes
das Maß dieser Fähigkeit. Sie haben ihren biologischen Bezug in Form von Trans-
formationen des Hirns als einer Menge einzelner Zellen in ein komplexes Netz von
gedanklichen Prozessen als zusammengesetztes Instrumentarium, das zur Bildung des
menschlichen Bewußtseins fähig ist.

In der Ontogenese ist es ziemlich einfach zu bemerken, wie sich die apriorischen
und aposteriorischen, physikalisch-gedanklichen Fakten überqueren und überlagern,
die gemeinsam ein holographisches Bild sowohl eines Kommunikationsaktes als auch
der Generierung eines neuronalen Signals darstellen können.

Der Sprecher, d.h. der Sender des Signals übermittelt die Information in Form von
z.B. sprachlichen Zeichen im entsprechenden Kanal. Dies entspricht genau dem Feu-
ern eines form- und inhaltstragenden Neurons im Hirn. Ein Kanal ist einfach ein
Axon, d.h. ein axialer Ausläufer ähnlich einem konzentrischen Fernsehkabel, in dem
Signale/Informationen schnell und auf große Entfernungen versendet werden. Für die
Qualität der Nachricht verantwortlich sind u.a. die Dendriten, die die Signale von den
umgebenden Zellen auffangen. Die Zeichenkodes in jeder Sprache entsprechen elek-
trischen Reizen, die sich außerhalb jeder Zelle befinden. Eine sprachliche Mitteilung
besteht im Grunde genommen aus Zügen von informativen Signalen, die grammatikalisiert und lexikalisiert sind. Sie bestimmen die Art und Weise der interpersonellen,
sprachlichen Kontakte. Die internervalen Bezüge bilden die Synapsen, die für den
größten Teil der neuronalen Verknüpfungen verantwortlich sind. Da die Hirntätigkeit
vor allem auf der Fähigkeit der kommunikativen Verbindungen unter den Neuronen
beruht, sind die Signale ein Schlüssel zur Erkennung der Hirnfunktionen.

Die höchste Form der Hirnaktivität ist die Gabe zur Unterscheidung zwischen *Ich*
und *Nicht-Ich*. **Zwischen** heißt hier der Weg zur Ausbildung der menschlichen Er-
kenntnisfähigkeiten sowie Überschreitung ihrer Grenzen. Auf diesem Wege scheint
die Dynamik der Selbsttranszendenz zwischen Denken und Vernunft ihren Niederschlag zu suchen, welcher in jedem Akt *des Umschaffens der Welt in das Eigentum
des Geistes* nach Bedeutung strebt. In dieser scheinbar widersprüchlichen Situation,
wo die apriorische Fähigkeit des Denkens einerseits und die aposteriorische Kenntnis
der Suche nach Bedeutung andererseits auftreten, ist der Verstand das Bindeglied
dieser Kategorien, das nicht nur die Qualität des Kommunizierens sondern auch die
Wahrheitssuche bestimmt. Arendt (1991:47) schreibt dazu:

> „Wenn das Denken und die Vernunft das Recht zur Überschreitung der Erkenntnis- und Ver-
> standesgrenzen haben, so muß man annehmen, daß Denken und Vernunft nicht dasselbe be-
> treffen, wie der Verstand (Intellekt). Antizipierend kann man kurz fassen: die Vernunft ist
> nicht durch Wahrheitssuche inspiriert, sondern durch Suche nach Bedeutung. Wahrheit und
> Bedeutung sind nicht das gleiche".

Das Fazit des bisher Gesagten könnte folgendes beinhalten:

1) Das genetische Programm setzt bestimmte Aufnahmestrukturen fest, die dem
   Kind erlauben, auf Umweltreize zu reagieren.

2) Im Lernprozeß werden die Nervenstrukturen allmählich subtiler und vollkommener. Sie bilden die Grundlage für geistige Leistungen und können sich selbst organisieren und festigen, indem sie über eigene Einschränkungen hinauskommen und neue Verhaltensmuster schaffen.

3) Diese geistigen Möglichkeiten entstehen nicht nur auf der Basis kommunikativer Gene, sondern vielmehr auf der Grundlage eines Mitwirkens der biologischen und kulturschaffenden Elemente in der Entwicklung des Kindes.

4) Philogenetische Entwicklung der Menschheit und die allmähliche Entstehung des ontischen Geistes haben zuerst im handlichen Werkzeug und dann in gedanklicher Tätigkeit ihren Ausdruck gefunden, zu der auch Sprache gehört.

5) Weder die apriorischen noch die aposteriorischen Fakten und Bedingungen haben allein die geistig-sprachlichen Leistungen des Menschen festgesetzt, sondern die Zusammenarbeit und Mitwirkung genetischer und epigenetischer Faktoren machen es möglich, daß die Australopithezinen zu Menschen geworden sind.

Literatur

ARENDT, Hannah(1991): Myślenie.Warszawa: Państwowy Instytut Wydawniczy.

BICKERTON, Derek (1990): Language and Species. Chicago: University of Chicago Press.

DIAMOND, Jarred (1996): Trzeci szympans. Warszawa: Państwowy Instytut Wydawniczy.

EDELMAN, Gerhart (1998): Przenikliwe powietrze, jasny ogień. Warszawa: Państwowy Instytut Wydawniczy.

JACOB, Francis (1987): Gra możliwości. Warszawa: Państwowy Instytut Wydawniczy.

LEAKEY, Richard (1995): Pochodzenie człowieka. Warszawa: Państwowy Instytut Wydawniczy.

PINKER, Steven (1998): Der Sprachinstinkt. Wie der Geist die Sprache bildet. München: Kindler Verlag GmbH.

Minimal Inquiries and the Acquisition of the Definite Article in Modern Greek

Theodore Marinis

1   Introduction[1]

The acquisition of definite articles has often been related to the acquisition of functional categories (see e.g. Radford 1990; Clahsen 1996; Penner & Weissenborn 1996),[2] since definite articles belong to the functional category (FC) D. Under this view, a problem that remains unsolved is why children pass through a stage in which they produce some definite articles, while at the same time there is a significant rate of definite article omission. If lack of definite articles reflects lack of FCs, the eventual presence of FCs should preclude definite article omission.

In this paper, making use of minimalist ideas concerning the feature specification of nouns and adopting Chierchia's Nominal Mapping Parameter (Chierchia 1998), I will discuss the acquisition of definite articles in Modern Greek (MG) from a rather different perspective, one which is based on the idea that the syntax-semantics mapping in the nominal system is not cross-linguistically uniform. Total and partial omission of definite articles does not pose a problem for this analysis. In contrast, this model predicts that children learning Germanic, Romance languages and MG will pass through a stage of optional use of definite articles.

2   Theoretical considerations

In the Minimalist Program, "UG makes available a set F of features (linguistic properties) and operations C_{HL} (the computational procedure for human language) that access F to generate expressions" (Chomsky 1998:12). Language acquisition involves feature selection, construction of lexical items, and refinement of the computational system.

According to standard assumptions concerning the mapping of nominal categories onto their denotations, common nouns are mapped onto predicates, they are of the type $<e, t>$, DPs are mapped onto arguments, they are of the type e (referential nominals), or $<<e, t>, t>$ (quantificational nominals). This being so, bare common nouns should not appear in argument positions because they are of the wrong type, i.e. $<e, t>$.

---

[1]   I am grateful to Anastasia Christofidou for giving me the Corpus of her son Christos. Special thanks to Susan Powers, Thomas Roeper and Thomas Hanneforth for stimulating discussions on this paper, to Paul Law, Diana Pili and the audience of the 34th Linguistic Colloquium for helpful comments. This paper is part of my Dissertation research in the Graduate Program 'Ökonomie und Komplexität in der Sprache' of the Humboldt University at Berlin and the University of Potsdam, which is supported by the DFG.

[2]   But see Pine & Martindale (1996) for a different approach to the acquisition of definite articles in English.

This line of reasoning has led to the assumption that the functional category D must be projected with a null D^0 each time a bare common noun appears in an argument position (Longobardi 1994, 1996).

Under the assumption that proper names (PNs) are universally of type e, they are of the right type to appear as bare nouns in argument positions. However, there are languages in which PNs are preceded by determiners (among others Northern Italian dialects, Swiss German, High German and Modern Greek). In order to account for this fact, Longobardi (1994; 1996), Rousou & Tsimpli (1994), Penner & Weissenborn (1996) and Marinis (1998) have claimed that definite articles used with PNs are expletives. Thus, they have argued for the distinction between substantive definite articles that turn predicates into arguments and expletive definite articles that do not have any semantic content and do not have any effect on the semantics of NPs.

Chierchia's approach, which I will adopt in this paper, treats these facts differently. Common nouns are not cross-linguistically of the type $<e, t>$. They can and sometimes must refer to kinds, i.e. common nouns can and sometimes must be of the argumental type. Thus, there is no need to assume the presence of a DP shell with a null D^0 each time bare common nouns appear in argument positions. Moreover, in this approach, the denotation of PNs, like the denotation of common nouns, is not cross-linguistically uniform: PNs may have the semantic type $<e, t>$, meaning that they are predicates true of just one individual.[3] Therefore, there is no need to stipulate two types of definite articles.

Cross-linguistic variation is expressed in this model through the use of the binary features [±arg], [±pred], which constrain the way in which nouns are mapped onto their interpretations. A [+arg] specification means that nouns can be mapped onto arguments, consequently they can appear as bare nouns in argument positions, a [-arg] one means that they cannot, thus they need a DP shell when they appear in argument positions; similarly for [+pred] and [-pred]. Accordingly, there are three combinations, which represent the possible language types, i.e. [+arg, -pred], [+arg, +pred] and [-arg, +pred][4], each one of which represents a setting of the Nominal Mapping Parameter[5] (Chierchia 1998:352-358).

Nouns have the feature specification [+arg, -pred] in languages of the Chinese type (e.g. Chinese, Japanese). In these languages, nouns are argumental (names of kinds) and their extension is mass; consequently they can occur as bare nouns in argument positions, they do not have plural marking, and they have a generalized classifier system.

Nouns in Germanic languages are [+arg, +pred]. For example, English has count nouns (CNs) and mass nouns (MNs) and allows nouns to be predicative (singular CNs) or argumental (plurals and MNs). CNs have plural marking, while a classifier system is operative with MNs. With respect to PNs, some are mapped onto argu-

---

[3] For the predicative use of PNs in Modern Greek, see Marmaridou (1982, 1989).
[4] The [-arg, -pred] specification is not a possible option, because it would prevent nouns from having any interpretation at all, i.e. nouns would be mapped neither onto arguments nor onto predicates.
[5] For alternative approaches to the typology of NPs, see e.g. Gil (1987), Löbel (1993).

ments, and appear as bare nouns in argument positions, while others are mapped onto predicates and are used with determiners (e.g. *the Gulf Stream*).

In Romance languages and MG, nouns are specified by the features [-arg, +pred]. MG has MNs and CNs, however, both are mapped onto predicates, i.e. bare nouns in argument positions are generally disallowed, as illustrated in 1) and 2). Consequently, a DP shell has to be projected each time a noun appears in an argument position. Bare nouns in argument positions are licit only in restricted environments, i.e. in positions governed by a lexical head, as in 3) or in focus, as in 4).[6]

1) *zachari   ine   ghlikia.
   'Sugar   is   sweet.'
2) *Skilia dhagonun.
   'Dogs   bite.'
3) Efagha biskota   me   to   ghalamu.
   ate   cookies   with   the   milk my
   'I ate cookies with my milk.'
4) KOTOPULO   thelo   na   fao,   ochi psari.
   CHICKEN   want   to   eat   not fish
   'I want to eat chicken, not fish.'

Apart from bare plurals, as in 3), and bare mass nouns, as in 4), MG allows bare singular count nouns (BSCN)[7] as objects of verbs of accomplishment[8] (Vendler 1967), as in 5).

5) O   Nikos   chtizi   spiti   sti   Mykono.
   The   Nikos   builds   house   in-the   Mykonos
   'Nikos is building a house in Mykonos.'

In the case of bare nouns in argument positions, I assume, following Chierchia (1998) for Italian, and Sioupi (1999) for MG, the existence of a null D,[9] which is licensed by a lexical head, as in 3) and 5) or in a Focus Phrase, as in 4). With respect to PNs, there is a clash between the (unmarked) semantics of PNs and the mapping of the syntactic category of nouns onto predicates: PNs 'want' to be argumental, but their syntactic type has to be mapped onto predicates. This clash is resolved through the use of the definite article, when PNs are arguments, as illustrated in 6).[10]

---

[6]   The same is true for Italian but not for French, in which bare arguments are disallowed altogether (Chierchia 1998).
[7]   BSCN as objects of verbs of accomplishment are licit in the same restricted environments as bare plurals and bare mass nouns are.
[8]   For an analysis of BSCN in MG, see Sioupi (1999).
[9]   Pérez-Leroux & Roeper (to appear) analyze bare nouns in argument positions in English as NPs and not as DPs. This is in line with Chierchia (1998) and this paper. Since English nouns are [+arg, +pred], bare nouns appearing in argument positions are NPs.
[10] The same is true in Northern Italian dialects. A second option is operative in Standard Italian: PNs move to an argument position (D[0]) (Longobardi 1994; 1996).

6) O   Giannis   aghapai   ti   Maria.
   the   Giannis   loves   the   Maria
   'Giannis loves Maria.'

3   Predictions for the acquisition of the definite article in Modern Greek

According to acquisition assumptions within the Minimalist Program (Roeper 1999; Powers, under review), the feature specification of lexical items may initially be non-target like. Positive evidence from the input may force children to change their feature specification. If we view the Nominal Mapping Parameter through this perspective and assume the Subset Principle, according to which children initially hypothesize the most restrictive grammar, we expect them to start with the feature specification that rules out the most, so that they may revise their hypothesis on the basis of positive evidence alone. The most restrictive feature specification is [+arg, -pred] (Chinese type), since this excludes plural morphology, definite articles and numeral quantifiers combining directly with nouns. As a consequence, children will initially omit definite articles.

Prediction 1:   – initial specification of nouns: [+arg, -pred]
*   – drop of definite articles*

Upon discovering definite articles and plural marking in the input, children should change the initial feature specification to [-arg, +pred] (Romance type), triggering the obligatory projection of a DP shell in nouns appearing in argument positions. [-arg, +pred] is the next most restrictive feature matrix, because it excludes bare nouns from argument positions altogether. However, the input to children acquiring MG contains bare plurals, bare MNs and BSCNs in lexically governed and in focus positions. Thus, children must:

a) distinguish which nouns are mass and which are count,
b) identify, in which positions bare nouns are licit, and
c) discover which verb classes allow BSCNs as arguments.

Uncertainty with respect to these aspects may result into the optional use of definite articles.

Prediction 2:   – second specification of nouns: [-arg, +pred]
*   – optional use of definite articles*

For children acquiring Germanic languages, the unrestricted occurrence of bare MNs in argument positions should lead them change the feature matrix of nouns to [+arg, +pred].[11]

---

[11]   According to Chierchia, Guasti & Gualmini (1999), children revise their initial [+arg, -pred] hypothesis to [+arg, +pred]. Positive evidence from bare partitives or overt plural indefinites trigger

Can the existence of bare arguments lead Greek children change the feature matrix to [+arg, +pred]? Are there any unambiguous triggers that nouns in MG are [-arg, +pred]?

Contexts involving PNs can provide unambiguous evidence that nouns are [-arg, +pred]. PNs are the only nouns that cannot be used as bare nouns in argument positions, irrespective of the verb class: in argument positions they must be obligatorily used with definite articles, as shown in 6), in non-argument positions, e.g. in the vocative, they must be obligatorily used without definite articles. This minimal pair can provide the relevant information for the feature specification of nouns. Importantly, PNs are very frequent in child-directed speech in both argument and non-argument positions, and we can thus be sure that children will get enough input from these two contexts.

Thus, considering this last property of MG, we predict PNs to be used with definite articles, as soon as children start using definite articles productively. This does not imply that they will use definite articles only with PNs and not with other noun classes, since having the right specification will lead them to use definite articles with all noun classes.

Prediction 3: – definite articles will appear with all noun classes simultaneously

4   The Data

This study is based on two corpora, one longitudinal, the Christofidou Corpus, and one cross-sectional, the Stephany Corpus, consisting of the recordings of 5 monolingual Greek children between the ages of 1;7 to 2;9. The ages of the children, the number of recordings and the number of utterances produced by each child are shown in Table 1.

| | *Christofidou* | *Stephany* | | | |
Child	Christos	Spiros	Janna	Meri	Maria
Age	1;7-2;8	1;9	1;11-2;9	1;9-2;9	2;3-2;9
No. of recordings	69	2	9	12	5
No. of utterances	12,383	443	1,357	4,154	3,074

Table 1: Corpora.

4.1   Stephany Corpus

All four children in the Stephany Corpus use definite articles from the first recording on, as shown in Table 2. Thus, Prediction 1, that there will be a stage in which chil-

---

the change to [-arg, +pred]. However, it is not clear, why the Subset Principle should constrain only the first hypothesis of the child, but not the second.

dren do not use any definite articles at all, cannot be falsified, since there are no previous recordings available.

The second prediction is supported by the data: all children pass through a stage in which they use definite articles optionally, as we can see in Table 2.[12]

Child	Age	MLU	definite articles present		definite articles missing	
Spiros	1;09	1.6	23 %	(n = 35)	77 %	(n = 118)
Janna	1;11	1.4	15 %	(n = 9)	85 %	(n = 50)
	2;05	2.4	93 %	(n = 67)	7 %	(n = 5)
	2;09	2.8	97 %	(n = 144)	3 %	(n = 5)
Mairi	1;09	2.0	77 %	(n = 294)	23 %	(n = 90)
	2;03	2.2	88 %	(n = 219)	12 %	(n = 31)
	2;09	2.5	91 %	(n = 258)	9 %	(n = 26)
Maria	2;03	2.3	67 %	(n = 32)	33 %	(n = 16)
	2;09	2.9	93 %	(n = 136)	7 %	(n = 11)

Table 2: Use of definite articles in obligatory contexts.

With respect to the third prediction, all children use definite articles with CNs, PNs and kinship terms (KTs) at the same time,[13] see Table 3. Thus, Prediction 3 is supported by these data.

Child	Age	MLU	with CN	with PN & KT
Spiros	1;09	1.6	21	11
Janna	1;11	1.4	5	3
	2;05	2.4	50	9
	2;09	2.8	90	38
Mairi	1;09	2.0	182	71
	2;03	2.2	110	60
	2;09	2.5	147	68
Maria	2;03	2.3	20	9
	2;09	2.9	71	33

Table 3: Use of definite articles with CNs, PNs and KTs.

4.2   Christofidou Corpus

Prediction 1 is supported by the speech of Christos. At the age of 1;7, he does not use any definite articles at all, as illustrated in Figure 1.

Between 1;8.21 and 1;11.0, he uses only a small number of definite articles (type/token = 3/12) with a restricted set of nouns (type/token = 9/12). Between 1;11.10 and

---

[12]   It should be noted that the rate of definite article omission correlates with MLU. Spiros and Janna who had the lowest MLU have the highest rate of definite article omission.

[13]   I have counted KTs with PNs, because colloquially they replace PNs, both when used in argument positions and in the vocative (see Longobardi 1996:3).

1;11.19, he does not use any definite articles at all. These facts provide evidence for a *lexically based* use of definite articles (see Pine & Martindale 1996).

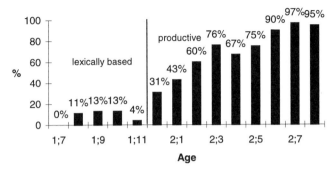

Figure 1: Use of definite articles in obligatory contexts.

From 1;11.27 onwards there is evidence for a productive use of definite articles:

a) the number of tokens increases rapidly (from 4% in 1;11 to 31% in 2;0),

b) Christos uses definite articles with more noun types than he did before, and

c) from 2;0.7 onwards, nouns that are used for the first time appear with definite articles.

However, only at the age of 2;6 does the percentage of definite articles reach 90% in obligatory contexts (Brown 1973), i.e. between 2;0 and 2;5, definite articles are used optionally, a fact that supports Prediction 2.

With respect to the use of definite articles with different noun classes, Prediction 3 is borne out. Christos uses definite articles with CNs, PNs and KTs, when he starts using definite articles productively (after 1;11), see Table 4.

Child	Age	MLU	with CN	with PN & KT
Christos	1;07	1.2	0	0
	1;08	1.1	0	2
	1;09	1.1	1	1
	1;10	1.3	3	5
	1;11	1.4	0	2
	2;00	2.0	37	45
	2;01	2.2	73	86

Table 4: Use of definite articles with CNs, PNs and KTs.

5   Discussion

The predictions deriving from the Nominal Mapping Parameter have been borne out by the data from MG. It has been shown that children start from the most restrictive hypothesis, i.e. [+arg, -pred] and upon encountering input data, they change the feature specification of nouns until they come to the one of the target language.

Prediction 1 could be tested only in the Christofidou Corpus, since all children in the Stephany Corpus have been using definite articles from the very first recording (recordings start at 1;9, lowest MLU = 1.4). However, absence of a stage, in which children do not use any definite articles is most likely an effect of sampling, for we do find some evidence of such a stage in the Christofidou Corpus, in which we have the earliest recordings (recordings start at 1;7, lowest MLU=1.2). Hence, the prediction that children initially map the features [+arg, -pred] into nouns is supported by these data.

Prediction 2 is borne out by the data from the Stephany Corpus. However, the fact that Christos initially uses a small number of definite articles followed by a period in which he does not use any definite articles at all seems to contradict our predictions. If Christos would change the feature specification from [+arg, -pred] to [-arg, +pred], we would expect a generalized and not a lexically based use of definite articles in obligatory contexts.

Does lexically based use of definite articles provide evidence against our predictions?

Obviously, it does not support them. However, since lexically based use of words along with imitations and the use of formulaic and semi-formulaic expressions is a strategy that does not characterize productive speech, it does not contradict them either. The existence of these strategies is independent from the learning algorithm that leads to productive speech, with which we are concerned in this paper. Crucial for our predictions is not the use of definite articles in such conditions but rather in productive speech. In the speech of Christos, this takes place after 1;11.27. Prediction 2 is, thus, borne out by the Christofidou Corpus as well, since Christos uses definite articles optionally from the age of 2;0 (31%) until the age of 2;5 (75%).

Prediction 3 is also supported by the data in both corpora. All five children use definite articles with CNs, PNs and KTs, as soon as they start using definite articles productively.

It remains open, how children acquire null Ds which is related to:

a) how they figure out, which nouns are mass and which are count,
b) how they identify lexically governed and focus positions, and
c) how they discover when BSCNs are licit.

With respect to the distinction between MNs and CNs, it is possible for children to use as cues the distribution of nouns with different quantifier types, e.g. *much* vs. *many* in English, as well as the use of plural marking with CNs and classifiers with MNs (for the acquisition of CNs vs. MNs in English, see Katz, Baker & Macnamara 1974; Gordon 1988). Word order and stress could provide the relevant cues for the identification of lexically governed and focus positions. The relevant cues for the identification of the class of verbs, with which bare singular count nouns are allowed might be the semantics of verbs (verbs of accomplishment).[14] [15]

In this paper, Chierchia's Nominal Mapping Parameter viewed through acquisition assumptions within the Minimalist Program has been applied to the acquisition of the definite article in MG. Crucially, the optional use of definite articles which is problematic for theories that relate definite article omission to the lack of FCs, does not pose a problem, but it is rather predicted by this model.

7   References

BROWN, Roger (1973): A first language: the early stages. Cambridge Mass: Harvard University Press.

CHIERCHIA, Gennaro (1998): Reference to kinds across languages. In: Natural Language Semantics 6, 339-405.

CHIERCHIA, Gennaro; GUASTI, Maria Teresa; GUALMINI, Andrea (1999): Early omission of articles and the syntax/semantics map. Paper presented at the GALA' 99 Conference, Potsdam, September 1999.

CHOMSKY, Noam (1998): Minimalist Inquiries: The framework. Ms MIT.

CLAHSEN, Harald (ed.) (1996): Generative perspectives on language acquisition. Empirical findings, theoretical considerations & cross-linguistic comparisons. Amsterdam: John Benjamins.

GIL, David (1987): Definiteness, Noun Phrase Configurationality, and the Count-Mass Distinction. In: Reuland, E. J.; ter Meulen, A. G. B. (eds.): The Representation of (In)definiteness. Cambridge, Massachusetts: MIT Press, 254-269.

GORDON, Peter (1988): Count/mass category acquisition: distributional distinctions in children's speech. In: Journal of Child Language 15, 109-128.

KATZ, Nancy; BAKER, Erica; MACNAMARA, John (1974): What's in a name? A study of how children learn common and proper names. In: Child Development 45, 469-473.

LÖBEL, Elisabeth (1993): Parametrization of lexical properties. In: Fanselow, G. (ed.): The parametrization of Universal Grammar. Amsterdam: John Benjamins, 183-199.

LONGOBARDI, Giuseppe (1996): The Syntax of N-Raising: A Minimalist Theory. In: OTS Working Papers.

— (1994): Reference and Proper Names: a Theory of N-Movement in Syntax and LF. In: Linguistic Inquiry 25, 609-665.

MACWHINNEY, Brian; SNOW, Catherine E. (1985): The child language data exchange system. In: Journal of Child Language 12, 271-296.

MARINIS, Theodore (in preparation): The Acquisition of the NP/DP in Modern Greek. Ph.D. Dissertation, University of Potsdam.

MARINIS, Theodore (1998): The acquisition of expletive definite articles in Modern Greek. In: Cambier-Langeveld, T.; Lipták, A.; Radford, M. (eds.): ConSole VI Proceedings. Leiden: SOLE, 169-184.

MARMARIDOU, Sophia S. A. (1989): Proper names in communication. In: Journal of Linguistics 25, 355-372.

— (1982): Diktes anaphoras sti Neoelliniki onomatiki phrasi. In: Studies in Greek Linguistics 3, 177-192.

PENNER, Zvi; WEISSENBORN, Jürgen (1996): Strong continuity, parameter setting and the trigger hierarchy: On the acquisition of the DP in Bernese Swiss German and High German. In: Clahsen, H. (ed.): Generative perspectives on language acquisition. Empirical findings, theoretical considerations & cross-linguistic comparisons. Amsterdam: John Benjamins, 161-200.

---

[14] This is in accord with the idea of Sioupi (1999) that BSCN are part of the semantics of the verb.

[15] The predictions deriving from these hypotheses are discussed in Marinis (in preparation).

PÉREZ-LEROUX, Ana T.; ROEPER, Thomas (to appear): Scope and the Structure of Bare Nominals: Evidence from Child Language. In: Linguistics.

PINE, Julian; MARTINDALE, Helen (1996): Syntactic categories in the speech of young children: the case of the determiner. In: Journal of Child Language 23, 369-395.

POWERS, Susan M. (under review): (E)merging Functional Structure. In: Lakshmanan, U. (ed.): A Minimalist Account of Language Acquisition: Functional Categories and Case Checking. Kluwer Academic Publishers.

RADFORD, Andrew (1990): Syntactic theory and the acquisition of English syntax: The nature of early grammars of English. Oxford: Blackwell.

ROEPER, Thomas (1999): Finding fundamental operations in language acquisition: Formal Features as triggers. In: Hollebrandse, B. (ed.): New Perspectives on Language Acquisition. G.L.S.A. University of Massachusetts, Amherst.

ROUSOU, Anna; TSIMPLI, Ianthi M. (1994): On the interaction of case and definiteness in Modern Greek. In: Philippaki-Warburton, I.; Nicolaidis, K.; Sifianou, M. (eds.): Themes in Greek Linguistics. Amsterdam: John Benjamins, 69-76.

STEPHANY, Ursula (1997): The Acquisition of Greek. In: Slobin, D. I. (ed.): The crosslinguistic study of language acquisition 4. Hillsdale, NJ: Erlbaum, 183-333.

Relocating the Cognitive in Sociocognitive Views of Second Language Learning

Carla Meskill, Krassimira Rangelova

1 Constructive dialogue

This work began as a conversation between the two authors: one whose work in second language acquisition leans to the sociocognitive, and one whose orientation is cognitive science. It became clear through our initial conversations that these differing orientations to second language learning could be mutually informative if we persisted in constructive dialog. Thus, our current effort to dialectically *locate* the cognitive in the currently popular sociocognitive views of language and language acquisition.

Through conversation, our goal is for each of these two traditions to reap the benefits of the other and encourage the honing and fine tuning of language learning theory and practice when both traditions mutually inform. This quest for interdisciplinary cross-fertilization is not uncommon in an age where questions regarding human learning are indeed complexifying and the urgency for mutually informative inquiry across intellectual traditions is augmenting. In the field of language learning this need for collaboration between research traditions has become particularly imperative insofar as advances within both the cognitive and sociocognitive traditions tend to be on more divergent than convergent paths at this moment in history (Bialystok 1998). There is recent movement away from what is termed *cold* cognition – from context-empty clinical views of mind – towards *hot* cognition that involves more interpretive approaches and humanistically grounded methodologies. How this may occur in the field of second language studies is our current concern.

1.1 Sociocognitive orientations

The term sociocognitive encompasses a broad range of current beliefs about learning in general, and language learning in particular. The term represents a growing attempt to reconcile the social and affective side of learning with what happens *in the black box* as it were. Within the field of linguistics, it is most closely aligned with interactionist approaches to theory and research in language acquisition. It begins with the biological predispositions of the human mind for learning and language in consort with external reality (Larsen-Freeman & Long 1991).

Within sociocognitive frameworks learners are seen as dialectically connected to social contexts in a synergistic, two-way relation. Mediating that relationship is the cognitive realm that is viewed as marshaling, routing, channeling, and generally guiding the interplay of the known and unknown; the implicit and the explicit. Meaning, in the sociocognitive sphere, is dynamic, never fixed. Its imperative is to capture and value the richness of this fluidity. Its central tenet – that learning and cognition are social, not autonomous acts – steers a great deal of current of theory, research, and practice in language and literacy education. Its central questions and research approaches focus on the social, discoursal, and affective side of the learning process; in the United States and Britain there is specific emphasis on multicultural personhood as playing a key, deterministic role in teaching and learning (Egan-Robertson 1998; Walsh 1990). That is, its position is that language, literacy, and learning are never socially nor politically neutral; these processes occur in and are guided by larger and local contextual features with which the individual interacts, transacts, and internalizes.

In language learning, major calls have come for increased emphasis on the "*social nexus*" of language learning (McGroarty 1998:596). Earl Stevik has long urged emphasis on the depth level of communicative processing with others. He has insisted that what *sticks* when learning another language is that which gets negotiated with and expressed to others (Stevik 1976). A growing number of studies that are founded on such sociocognitive views have been undertaken in the past decade. The focus of such work is on the social/physical and interpersonal dimensions of language learning environments that stimulate and support the acquisition of words and structures (Donato 1994). Such research efforts have indeed begun to demonstrate specific processes and outcomes in second language acquisition that are tied to classroom negotiation structure (Meskill, Mossop & Bates 1999; Nystrand 1997; Pica 1998).

1.2   Cognitive orientations

By contrast, the cognitive orientation to the study of learning and, by extension to language learning, has as its main imperative the quest for *a central processing unit* that is the human mind. Its frameworks and activities center on building models of mind and explicating the ways in which the mind processes and internalizes an objective reality.

A key concern of cognitive psychology and cognitive sciences in general has been the serious consideration given to human learning. Several different theories have been developed to define the determinants of learning from a cognitive perspective (Ausubel 1962, 1963; Rumelhart & Norman 1978; Anderson 1983; Kelly 1991; Kolb 1984). Although the different theoretical approaches emphasize different aspects of the multifaceted phenomenon of human learning, there is a unifying orientation that underlies all: that is, learning is a multisource phenomenon and new principles need to be forged to explain its highly interactive nature.

The cognitive orientation to learning has defined some of these new principles: e.g, learning is currently viewed as being active, constructive, cumulative, and goal oriented. There has been a shift away from the traditional focus on knowledge structures, and a strong emphasis on the mental processes for real-time co-ordination of diverse sources of learning. Emphasis now primarily lies with the crucial role of those cognitive processes and mental operations that are involved in constructing meaningful interpretations of learners' experiences. Thus, efficient learning could not be accomplished without the active conscious involvement of the learner in the process:

learners respond to events in accordance with how they perceive and interpret them (Kelly 1991). Learners are seen as active and responsible participants rather than passive responders; they make choices based on reality as they perceive it (Kohonen 1992). In this view, immediate personal experiences are seen as the focal point of learning, giving "life, texture, and subjective personal meaning to abstract concepts" (Kolb 1984:21).

Simple everyday experience, however, is not sufficient for learning to occur. The cognitive conceptions of learning emphasize that such experience must also be consciously observed and analyzed. Only experience that is reflected upon seriously will yield its full measure of learning, and reflection must, in turn, be followed by testing new hypotheses in order to obtain further experience (Sternberg 1985). Thus, knowledge structures will not become part of the learner's repertoire until they have been experienced meaningfully on a subjective level. Reflection plays an important role in this process by providing a bridge, as it were, between experience and knowledge construction. The process of learning is seen as the recycling of experience at deeper levels of understanding and interpretation (Kohonen 1992). As such, both environmental factors and factors internal to the learner contribute to learning in an interactive manner.

An important aspect of reflection is the memory system. Memory and learning, however, are often presented as different concepts and the distinction between them is preserved in many ways in psychological and psycholinguistic research (Baddeley 1976). Yet, they are inextricably linked: in fact, they are the two sides of the same coin. Memories are left behind as a result of learning, and we infer the existence of learning from memories. If memory is considered an abstract term that describes mental states which carry information, learning will then describe the transition from one mental state to a second, in which the information is in some way different. An understanding of what mental operations secure the successful transfer of information will determine efficient learning.

2   Frames of contrast

Both the cognitive and sociocognitive traditions attempt to integrate the complexities of the internal and external relationships of object and mind; sociocognitive with primacy on the interplay between context and mind; psychological on the primacy of mind. Nonetheless, there are fundamental differences between the two orientations as is reflected in Table 1.

Cognitive and sociocognitive orientations each share key concerns regarding learning in general and language learning in particular. Where they differ is in the broad notion of mind where mind is either considered in autonomous relation with an objective reality, or as manifesting a socially constructed reality in consort with the environment. This conceptual difference obviously drives the types of questions and paths of research related to each. Because we began our conversations about these different orientations around the issue of word knowledge, it is this domain to which we will restrict discussion of divergences and potential convergences of the two orientations.

Concerns	Goal of learning: knowledge	Goal of learning: membership in discourse communities
	Cognitive	Sociocognitive
Active, constructive process	in the mind	in society
Higher levels of processing involved	in the mind	through experiential transactions with others
Prior knowledge (schemata)	in the mind	through discourse, scaffolding, mentorship
Forms of representation in memory	abstract	negotiated and expressed in communication with others
Task analysis	what occurs in the mind	as the anatomy of human interchange
Instructional practices	context-free principles	context-dependent principles

Table 1: Frames of Contrast.

3　Words in a second language

The human drive for shared understandings of words evolves out of social necessity (Bickerton 1981; Pinker & Bloom 1992; Vygotsky 1978). How these shared notions become integrated into the human mind has been the focus of work in both sociocognitive inquiry and cognitive science.

3.1　Word knowledge: sociocognitive orientation

In Vygotsky's words, a word is a microcosm of human consciousness. (Vygotsky 1991). "Word meanings are dynamic rather than static formations" (Vygotsky 1991:215). This is an important notion when considering vocabulary development in another language. Learners are typically expected to internalize a meaning associated with a given word through definitions and, in more recent times, a context of use. Activity and discourse in second language learning then, aim to evoke the sense of a word, not merely its representation. Vygotsky adapts the view of Paulhan who postulated that the sense of a word is very different from its meaning. According to Paulhan, the sense of a word is the sum of all psychological events aroused in our consciousness by the word. It is a dynamic, fluid, complex whole, which has several zones of unequal stability. Meaning is only one of the zones of sense, the most stable and precise zone. Rather than being static, then, sense is a "complex, mobile, protean phenomenon; it changes in different minds and situations and is almost unlimited" (Vygotski 1991:244-245). In the Vygotskian sphere of inner speech the senses of words cojoin into an "influx of sense". Word senses converge with earlier senses and are part of and ultimately influence change on the senses of later words. A sociocognitive view of second language learning, then, approaches lexical items not as a unitary link between word and thought, but as the sense that conflates and constructs through social, discoursal activity. As such, word meanings constantly change with changes in thought and experiences. Thought, in turn, "undergoes many changes as it turns into speech" (Vygotsky 1991:219) and it is therefore through interaction with others (through the language of text or speech) that meanings get made, remade, rejected, and appropriated. Bakhtin (1981) also proposes that meaning comes into existence when two or more voices come into contact: when the voice of a listener responds to the voice of a speaker. He contends that we don't learn words from dictionaries, but from other people's mouths or pens – these words being populated by multiple meanings of others. This is what Bakhtin calls dialogicality. A living word anticipates an answer. Understanding will occur only when there is response. Primacy, in this model, lies with the response. A word will have temporary sense when it breaks through the conceptual horizon of the listener and enters into the listener's conceptual system and aperceptive background. This background is populated by objects and emotions which affect interpretation. In terms of individual lexical items, differing responses and interpretations on the part of each human being – the distance between interpretations – is viewed as a factor of both local and larger cultures (Wells 1992).

Sociocognitive frameworks see words – the sense of words – becoming conceptually and imagistically blended in the developing second language system, but that blending does not happen devoid of myriad influences beyond the words themselves and a single interlocutor's mind. Also considered in the sociocognitive framework is that the reproduction of words of others, but not necessarily the sense, is an essential component of the instructed second language acquisition process.

3.2   Word knowledge: cognitive orientation

The organization of word knowledge in permanent memory is a major psycholinguistic question as well. Most current cognitive proposals describe the representation of knowledge as involving a network of labeled associations. In this view, words become integrated into a learner's conceptual system through strings of connections, or neural networks. The integration process itself is seen as a series of stimulus-response events whereby phenomena in the environment are assigned labels. These labels and their association with the object they describe become part of an associative web in the memory system.

The network approach to human memory has been found to be a powerful way to describe memory functioning (Norman & Rumelhart 1975; Schank 1972, 1988). The claim is that memory contents are represented by patterns of activation across a wide number of nodes (Rumelhart & McClelland 1986), and that thinking about any one concept would correspond to the simultaneous activation of thousands of nodes. The specific combination of nodes, in fact, would uniquely correspond to (and thus represent) the particular concept or idea. These same nodes, in different combinations, will also be part of the patterns representing other contents. In the connectionist scheme, to know a word means to have a pattern of connections between the many nodes that together represent any one of the particular ideas or concepts that make up its meaning.

Learning, in this view, would mean to set up the pattern of connections in the network (Clark 1991; Schwartz & Reisberg 1991). As the connections within the network can be strong or weak, learning would involve adjusting the various connection strengths so that activation will *flow* in the right way. The recency and frequency with which a particular pattern of connections has been activated will influence strongly the efficiency of learning. For one thing, the more often particular links between nodes are *used*, the stronger the links become. In a complementary fashion, activation is much more likely to spread along the routes of frequently traveled connections rather than along infrequently used paths.

In learning new words, one is not just learning a collection of unrelated items. Instead, the learning is leading to a whole network of new connections. In other words, in order for the learning process to be successful the ultimate aim would be to establish a greater number of connections among what is to be learned. The better connected the knowledge structure is, the more readily accessible in memory it will be. Associations are not, however, passively stamped in; they are instead established by the learner's thinking about the items together. Good retention results from elaborate processing. In terms of the network, this form of processing aids memory by laying down retrieval paths from the context to the to-be-remembered items themselves. In essence, one is building new connections, or perhaps improving paths that already exist.

4   Convergences: some prospects for mutually informing orientations

At the broadest level, existing convergences lie in the following:

Both traditions are occupied with characterizing the intertwining of mind and its interactions with the world.

Both traditions are concerned with the complexity of word meaning and acknowledge that this complexity is laden with historical and cultural luggage. The chief desiderata that have emerged from our conversations is:

1) that cognition be viewed as it is embedded in complex social systems; and
2) that the study of meaning construction be informed by the large body of existing data on language and cognition.

At the level of word knowledge, the sociocognitive tradition may suggest that heretofore cognitive models of word knowledge – that is, networks of words and their associative links – should extend out from the autonomous individual mind to include those dialogic spaces where meaning is ultimately made through the use of language. The cognitive science tradition suggests that sociocognitively grounded research would benefit from the use of connectivity models as additional analytical lenses. This is especially promising when examining instances where language appears to be operating systematically and asystematically. Here inferences concerning predictable structures and patterns of associations can be formed through examination of the vast data derived from clinical experiments undertaken in the cognitive science tradition. Alerting sociocognitive researchers who are otherwise operating within context-based frameworks to the inferential potential such patterns and tendencies represent, how these theoretically mesh with short-term and long-term memory constructs, and how developing notions of mental schema are evident in human activity potentially informs their work.

Take the Anglicized French word *crepe* as an example. Given a random group of native English speakers, the word alone – devoid of any controlled context beyond a straight elicitation situation – evokes the sense of either a food item or a fabric. Probing for associative differences typically elicits visual, olfactory, tactile, or aural links tied to the reported recency and salience of thoughts or experiences. The sense of *crepe*, in other words, is evoked through some kind of mental association. In cognitive terms, the link between the stimulus *crepe* and an associated item in the world to which it is linked in the mind belies a structuring of words and their associates. Associated words that collocate with the word *crepe* are indicative of certain culturally induced patterns of association that extend from the mere phonetic to the conceptual in terms of the *fit* of associated words that can and cannot co-occur with *crepe*.

In sociocognitive terms, the fact that two possible senses of the word *crepe* are possible in English, and that which sense is evoked is wholly dependent on time, place, and affective state brings the associative link outside of the autonomous mind and into the arena of socio/environmental interplay. Where these two conceptual realms seem to converge is in the nature of association – the one being *in the head* could be extended to include those sociocognitively conceived considerations of context and affect – both of which may, in this convergent extension, be assisting the other: the cognitive providing the physiologically conceived link, the sociocognitive serving to *oil the connections* by virtue of affective and contextual pungency.

We believe that cognitive orientations have the potential help to fill in gaps and round out issues in sociocognitive enterprises as related to second language learning. Clinical experiments that illustrate certain architectures and tendencies of mind can and ought to be incorporated into sociocognitive theory and practices. Such established lenses can be used to gain additional perspective on learning phenomena in situ. Likewise, sociocognitive views need to be factored into cognition-based research. Issues of context, affect, and personhood can greatly inform research design and interpretation. In sum, we feel these potential convergences are valuable and perhaps worthy of further conversation.

5   Final remarks

Both the cognitive and sociocognitive traditions attempt to integrate the complexities of the internal and external relationships of object and mind; sociocognitive with primacy on the interplay between context and mind; psychological on the primacy of mind. Combining the inferential methods and assumptions of both traditions – one concerning neurophysiological functioning in the mind, the other with socially construed understandings of these same processes – can certainly aid in addressing the shortcomings of both orientations: one being exclusionarily scientific, the other often accused of lacking scientific rigor. Where differences in orientations in the *soft* and *hard* sciences have more frequently been pitted one against the other in paradigm wars, terminological battles, and the wrestling of ideologies, we suggest that through the convergence of these respective stances new metaphors can emerge.

6   References

ANDERSON, John (1983): The Architecture of Cognition. Cambridge, MA: Harvard University Press.
AUSUBEL, David (1968): Educational Psychology: A Cognitive View. New York, NY: Holt, Rinehart and Winston.
— (1962): A Subsumption Theory of Meaningful Verbal Learning and Retention. In: Journal of General Psychology, 66, 213-224.
— (1963): The Psychology of Meaningful Verbal Learning. New York: Grune & Stratton.
BADDELEY, Alan (1990): Human Memory. Hove, England: Erlbaum.
— (1976): The Psychology of Memory. New York: Basic Books.
BAKHTIN, Michael (1981): The Dialogic Imagination. In: Holoquist, M. (ed.): Four Essays by M. M. Bakhtin. Austin, TX: University of Texas Press.
BIALYSTOK, Ellen (1998): Coming of Age in Applied Linguistics. In: Language Learning 48.4, 497-518.
BICKERTON, Derek (1981): The Roots of Language. Ann Arbor, MI: Karoma Press.
EGAN-ROBERTSON, Ann (1998): Learning about Culture, Language and Power: Understanding Relationships among Personhood, Literacy Practices, and Intertextuality. Albany, NY: National Research Center on English Learning and Achievement.
ENGLE, Ron (1994): Individual Differences in Memory and their Implications for Learning. In: Sternberg, R. (ed.): Encyclopedia of Intelligence. New York: Macmillan, 700-704.
KELLY, George (1991): The Psychology of Personal Constructs. A Theory of Personality. London: Routeledge.
KOHONEN, Viljo (1992): Experiential Language Learning. In: Nunan, D. (ed.): Collaborative Language Learning and Teaching. Cambridge: Cambridge University Press, 14-41.
KOLB, David (1984): Experiential Learning. Experience as the Source of Learning and Development. Englewood Cliffs: Prentice Hall.
LARSEN-FREEMAN, Diane; LONG, Michael (1991): An Introduction to Second Language Acquisition Research. London: Longman.
MCGROARTY, Michael (1998): Constructive and Constructivist Challenges for Applied Linguistics. In: Language Learning 48.4, 591-622.
MESKILL, Carla; MOSSOP, Jonathan; BATES, Rebecca (1999): Electronic Text and English as a Second Language Environments. Albany, NY: National Research Center on English Learning and Achievement.
NORMAN, Donald; RUMELHART, David (1975): Explorations in Cognition. San Francisco: Freeman.
NYSTRAND, Martin (1997): Opening Dialogue: Understanding the Dynamics of Language and Learning in the English Classroom. New York: Teachers College Press.
PICA, Teresa (1998): Second Language Learning through Interaction: Multiple Perspectives. In: Regan, V. (ed.). Contemporary Approaches to Second Language Acquisition in Social Context. Dublin: University of Dublin Press.
PINKER, Steven; BLOOM, Paul (1992): Natural Language and Natural Selection. In: Barkow, J.; Cosmides, L.; Tooby, J. (eds): The Adapted Mind: Evolutionary Psychology and the Generation of Culture. New York: Oxford University Press, 451-493.
RUMELHART, David; MCCLELLAND, John (1986): Parallel Distributed Processing, Vol. 1. Cambridge, MA: MIT Press.

RUMELHART, David; NORMAN, Donald (1978): Accretion, Tuning, and Restructuring: Three Models of Learning. In: Cotton, J.; Klatzky, R. (eds.): Semantic Factors in Cognition. Hillsdale, NJ: Lawrence Erlbaum.

SCHANK, Robert (1984): The Cognitive Computer: On Language, Learning and Artificial Intelligence. Reading, MA: Addison Wesley.

SCHWARTZ, Barbara; REISBERG, Daniel (1991): Learning and Memory. New York: W. W. Norton & Company, Inc.

STERNBERG, Robert (1996): Cognitive Psychology. New York, NY: Holt, Rinehart and Winston, Inc.

STEVIK, Earl (1976): Memory, Meaning & Method: Some Psychological Perspectives on Language Learning. Rowley, MA: Newbury House.

VYGOTSKY, Lev (1991): Thought and Language. Cambridge, MA: MIT Press.

— (1978): Mind and Society. Cambridge, MA: Harvard University Press.

WALSH, Catherine (1990): Pedagogy and the Struggle for Voice: Issues of Language, Power, and Schooling for Puerto Ricans. NY: Bergin & Garvey.

WELLS, Gordon (1992): The Centrality of Talk in Education. In Norman, K. (ed): Thinking Voices: The Work of the National Oracy Project. London: Hodder & Stoughton.

Experimentelle Neurolinguistik
Neurobiologische Untersuchung von Sprachverarbeitungsprozessen

Horst M. Müller, Gert Rickheit

1 Einleitung

Ausgehend vom Motto des 34. Linguistischen Kolloquiums *Sprachwissenschaft auf dem Weg ins nächste Jahrtausend* soll in diesem Beitrag eine Forschungsrichtung vorgestellt werden, der für die Sprachwissenschaft der nächsten 20 Jahre eine zunehmend größere Bedeutung zukommen wird: die Experimentelle Neurolinguistik. Bei diesem neuartigen Forschungsbereich handelt es sich um den interdisziplinären Zusammenschluß von Teildisziplinen der Linguistik, Sprachphilosophie, Psycholinguistik, Neurobiologie, Medizin und Neuroinformatik. In der Kombination von Theorien und Methoden dieser Teildisziplinen steht sie im Zusammenhang mit einer neuen Gruppen-Disziplin innerhalb der Humanwissenschaften, der sogenannten *Cognitive Neuroscience,* in der kognitionswissenschaftliche Fragestellungen in neuartiger Weise gesehen und bearbeitet werden. Zu dieser humanwissenschaftlichen Gruppen-Disziplin gehört auch die Experimentelle Neurolinguistik. Für die Fach-Disziplin Linguistik bewirkt dieser Zusammenschluß zum einen ein neues Betätigungs- und Einsatzfeld, zum anderen bewirkt dieser fächerübergreifende Zusammenschluß einen Empirie- und Innovationsschub, der zu einem stark anwachsendem Wissenszuwachs auch innerhalb der Linguistik führen wird. Dabei beruht das Forschungspotential dieses Teilbereichs der Linguistik auch darauf, daß sich in den letzten Jahren äußerst innovative Zusammenschlüsse mit Nachbardisziplinen (Medizin, Neurowissenschaft, Informatik) ergeben haben, die zu neuen, erfolgreichen Kooperationen führten (Klinische Linguistik, Neurolinguistik, Computerlinguistik). Ganz allgemein ist festzustellen, daß sich das Verständnis menschlicher Kognitionsprozesse während der nächsten 20 Jahre exponentiell ausweiten wird – mit wohl noch nicht abzusehenden Konsequenzen sowohl für die Wissenschaften als auch für den Lebensalltag. Nach der *großen Zeit* der Physik, den technischen Revolutionen des Computerzeitalters und der methodisch-theoretischen Expansion der Neurowissenschaften, manifestiert z.B. in der vom amerikanischen Kongreß 1990 ausgerufenen *Dekade des Gehirns,* sieht es gegenwärtig so aus, als würde die nächste wissenschaftlich herausragende Phase die Erforschung der menschlichen Kognition und Sprachfähigkeit umfassen. In diesem Forschungsumfeld kommt der Linguistik zweifelsohne eine herausragende Rolle zu (Rickheit & Strohner 1993). Hinsichtlich der Erforschung der neurobiologischen Grundlagen der normalen und gestörten Sprachfunktion ist so innerhalb der Linguistik ein neues Spannungsfeld entstanden: die Neurolinguistik. Die Neurolinguistik besteht dabei aus drei Teilbereichen, die über unterschiedliche Nachbardiziplinen verfügen (siehe Abbildung 1).

Eine Ursache für diese Entwicklung in der Linguistik ist der große methodische Fortschritt der beteiligten Nachbardisziplinen während der letzten Jahre. In der Sprachwissenschaft verlief die bisherige Erforschung der menschlichen Sprache in methodischer Hinsicht in fünf Phasen:

1) der sprachphilosophisch orientierten Phase der Introspektion mit einer über 2000jährigen Tradition,
2) der beginnenden empirischen Erforschung anhand von vergleichenden Studien zur Typologie und Verwandtschaft von Einzelsprachen mit einer etwa 200jährigen Tradition,
3) der psycholinguistisch orientierten Phase der empirischen Verhaltensmessungen mit einer etwa 40jährigen Tradition,
4) der computerlinguistisch orientierten Simulation von einfachen Sprachvorgängen mit einer etwa 20jährigen Tradition und
5) der neurobiologisch orientierten Phase der elektrophysiologischen Untersuchungstechniken und des *Brain-Imaging* der höheren Hirnfunktionen der letzten Jahre.

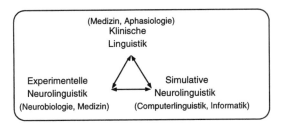

Abb. 1: Die drei Bereiche neurolinguistischer Forschung mit ihren Nachbardisziplinen (in Klammern). Die Experimentelle Neurolinguistik erforscht die Sprachfunktionen bei Gesunden, in der Klinischen Linguistik werden pathologische Sprachprozesse erforscht und therapiert. Die Simulative Neurolinguistik wird dann aus den experimentellen und klinischen Daten Modelle für die Simulation von normalen und gestörten Sprachfunktionen entwickeln, die zu ergänzenden Aussagen über die Funktion führen.

Nach der langwierigen Fundierung des gesamten sprachwissenschaftlichen bzw. sprachphilosophischen Theoriegebäudes und der sich entwickelnden Methode der Empirie ist der gegenwärtige Wissenstand der Linguistik das Ergebnis einer über 2000jährigen Forschungstradition, d.h., daß sich die Entwicklung der Sprachforschung parallel zur Entwicklung des wissenschaftlichen Denkens überhaupt entwickelt hat. Vor allem darin ist der Grund zu sehen, daß es noch nicht zu einer völligen Aufklärung der Sprachfunktion gekommen ist und in der Linguistik auch noch kein allgemeiner Konsens über die Strukturen und Prozesse der Sprachverarbeitung existiert, der sich in Form von allgemein akzeptierten Theorien und Gesetzen niederschlägt. Ein weiterer Grund liegt in der enormen Komplexität des zu untersuchenden Phänomens. Dennoch ist es erstaunlich, wie außerordentlich erfolgreich einige der Modelle und Hypothesen der sprachphilosophischen Antike waren und noch sind. Auch hier zeigt sich, daß Introspektion bzw. *einfaches Nachdenken* ebenfalls ein kognitives Werkzeug darstellt, dessen Güte auf die stammesgeschichtliche Erfahrung unzähliger Generationen zurückgeht. Dennoch hat der Einzug der Empirie die Erkenntnisfähigkeit in vielfältiger Hinsicht erweitert und gleichzeitig die Disziplin von einer unnötigen Hypothesenvielfalt befreit. Für die Linguistik bedeutete der Einzug der Feldforschung, der Komparativen Linguistik und vor allem der Psycholinguistik in den

Methodenkanon eine wesentliche Bereicherung. Nun konnten Ergebnisse von subjektiven Einflüssen gelöst betrachtet und vor allem überprüft werden. So konnte die ursprüngliche Vielfalt der Annahmen von unhaltbaren Spekulationen befreit und gleichzeitig die verbleibenden Annahmen abgesichert und zu Hypothesen ausgebaut werden. Im Zuge dieser Verdichtung und widerspruchsfreien Verknüpfung von Einzelbeobachtungen durch empirische Ergebnisse sind die gegenwärtigen Grundpfeiler linguistischer Theorie entstanden. Der überwiegende Teil linguistischen Wissens über Sprache basiert auf den Ergebnissen der Vergleichenden Linguistik und der Psycholinguistik. Auch der auf Noam Chomsky zurückgehende starke Einfluß der Generativen Grammatik basierte in methodischer Hinsicht zumeist auf Introspektion. In der nächsten Phase der methodischen Entwicklung kam es durch die Bereitstellung von Computern und entsprechenden Programmierumgebungen zur erstmaligen Implementation von Sprachverarbeitungsprozessen in einem größeren Umfang. In der Computerlinguistik war es nun möglich, die vorhandenen Hypothesen und Theorien in einer künstlichen Modellumgebung im Rahmen von computergestützten Simulationen von Sprachverarbeitungsprozessen zu überprüfen. Eng umschriebene Subprozesse der Sprachverarbeitung konnten so unter kontrollierten Bedingungen mit dem Ziel ablaufen, überprüfbare Vorhersagen zu ermöglichen. Wenngleich die Technik der Simulation auch einen sehr erfolgreichen und effektiven Ansatz darstellt, so sind zumindest gegenwärtig die Auswirkungen der Computerlinguistik auf den Wissensstand der Sprachverarbeitung noch nicht in wünschenswertem Umfang realisiert. Ein Grund für diesen Umstand kann darin gesehen werden, daß für die computergestützte Modellierung von Sprachverarbeitungsprozessen noch nicht in hinreichendem Ausmaß physiologische Eingangsdaten zur Verfügung stehen. Dabei handelt es sich um Daten zur Beschreibung der physiologischen und kognitiven Gegebenheiten des menschlichen Sprachverarbeitungssystems. Stünden genügend Daten zur Struktur, zur Funktion und zur Realisation von Sprachprozessen zur Verfügung, so könnte die Computerlinguistik wesentlich zum Wissenszuwachs beitragen. Diese Daten zur *kognitiven Realität* und vor allem zur *physiologischen Realität* von Sprachprozessen können jedoch mit den neuartigen Methoden der kognitiven Neurowissenschaft erhoben werden, die in der Experimentellen Neurolinguistik Anwendung finden. Diese neuartigen und für die Versuchspersonen ungefährlichen Techniken zur Untersuchung kognitiver Prozesse im intakten Gehirn ermöglichen es erstmals, Prozesse der akustischen Wahrnehmung, der phonologisch/syntaktisch/semantisch/pragmatischen Analyse sowie der Planung, Konstituierung und Artikulation von Sprache unmittelbar im lebenden Gehirn zu erfassen, ohne die Versuchsperson zu beeinträchtigen. Der Linguistik und Sprachphilosophie stehen somit sehr mächtige experimentelle Werkzeuge zur Verfügung.

2   Neurolinguistische Forschungsansätze

Anhand von elektrophysiologischen Untersuchungen der Hirnaktivität (Elektroenzephalographie und Magnetenzephalographie) sowie der Untersuchung mit bildgebenden Verfahren (funktioneller Kernspinresonanztomographie und Positronenemissionstomographie) können sowohl bestehende, konkurrierende Hypothesen zur Sprachverarbeitung neu beurteilt als auch vollständig neuartige Erkenntnisse erreicht werden. Die

z.T. erst seit wenigen Jahren zur Verfügung stehenden Methoden und Techniken ermöglichen einen neuartigen und äußerst innovativen Zugang der Analyse von hirn-
physiologischen Prozessen während der Sprachrezeption und Sprachproduktion. Abbildung 2 zeigt eine Methodenaufstellung der kognitiven Neurowissenschaft.

Elektrophysiologische Verfahren (Messung der direkten Neuronenaktivität)
  – Intracraniale Ableitungen
  – Elektroenzephalographie (EEG) ⎱ ereigniskorreliertes Potential (EKP, ERP)
  – Magnetenzephalographie (MEG) ⎰ Spektralanalyse (Kohärenzanalyse)

Bildgebende Verfahren (Messung anhand metabolischer Karten)
  – funktionelle Kernspinresonanztomographie (fMRI)
  – Positronenemissionstomographie (PET)

Abb. 2: Elektrophysiologische und bildgebende Verfahren der kognitiven Neurowissenschaft.

Dabei zeichnen sich die verschiedenen Methoden durch unterschiedliche Stärken aus:
PET und fMRI erreichen eine sehr hohe räumliche Auflösung im dreidimensionalen
Raum und erlauben die exakte Lokalisation von Teilprozessen im Gehirn (Liotti et al.
1994; Just et al. 1996; Binder et al. 1997). Dabei wird nicht die elektrische Aktivität
der Neuronen direkt gemessen, sondern es wird die Neuronenaktivität anhand von
Stoffwechseldaten, zumeist anhand des Sauerstoffverbrauchs ermittelt. So ergeben sich
sogenannte metabolische Karten, die für jeden Ort einen Überblick über den jeweiligen Sauerstoffverbrauch der Versuchsbedingung und der Kontrollbedingung aufzeigen. Anhand dieser Daten kann dann auf die neuronale Aktivität zurückgerechnet
werden. Allerdings ist die zeitliche Auflösung noch relativ schlecht, da die neuronale
Aktivität in dieser Form nur über einen vergleichsweise langen Zeitraum gemessen
werden kann. Beispielsweise liegt bei der PET-Untersuchung die Länge des kleinsten
möglichen Beobachtungsfensters zwischen mehreren Sekunden und einer Minute.
Auch bei der fMRI-Untersuchung, bei der in gleicher Weise die Neuronenaktivität aufgrund von Stoffwechseldaten (Sauerstoffverbrauch) ermittelt wird, ergibt sich eine methodisch bedingte Begrenzung der zeitlichen Auflösung, die gegenwärtig bei 1-2 Sekunden liegt. Erst mit der neuartigen Technik des ereigniskorrelierten fMRI, die seit
etwa 2 Jahren angewendet wird, sind Beobachtungsfenster knapp unterhalb von einer
Sekunde möglich. Weiterhin liegt die räumliche Auflösung des fMRI im Millimeterbe-
reich und ist somit noch etwas höher als die der PET-Technik. Ein weiterer Vorteil des
fMRI ist, das es wesentlich harmloser als die PET-Untersuchung ist, bei der der Versuchsperson radioaktive Substanzen über den Blutkreislauf zugeführt werden müssen.

2.1   Analyse des ereigniskorrelierten Potentials (ERP-Analyse)

Sollen jedoch Vorgänge der Sprachverarbeitung quasi on-line, während des ablaufenden Verstehensprozesses mit einer zeitlichen Auflösung im Millisekundenbereich erfaßt werden, so kommen nur nicht-invasive elektrophysiologische Verfahren wie die

EEG- oder die MEG-Analyse in Frage (Kutas 1997). Sowohl bei der EEG- als auch bei der MEG-Ableitung wird die elektrische Neuronenaktivität unmittelbar gemessen. Weiterhin sind beide Verfahren absolut harmlos und können bedenkenlos bei Versuchspersonen angewendet werden. Für die Analyse der EEG- bzw. MEG-Daten stehen zwei unterschiedliche Techniken zur Verfügung:

1) die Analyse des ereigniskorrelierten Potentials (EKP; anglo-amerikanisch *event related potential*, ERP),
2) die spektralanalytische Technik der Kohärenzanalyse.

Beide Auswerttechniken zeichnen sich durch komplementäre Analyseebenen aus und erlauben einander ergänzende Aussagen. Die ERP-Analyse zeigt anhand des zeitlichen Verlaufes von Hirnströmen wann und mit welcher Intensität sich die Versuchsbedingung von der Kontrollbedingung unterscheidet. Darüber hinaus ist auch eine grobe Beurteilung des *Wo* anhand einer Quellenlokalisation möglich. Die ERP-Analysetechnik erlaubt es, z.B. zwei kognitive Prozesse hinsichtlich ihrer Stärke und hinsichtlich ihrer Sequentialität zu dissoziieren (z.B. Rösler et al. 1993; Münte et al. 1997).

Untersuchungen von Sprachverarbeitungsprozessen mittels computergestützter EEG-Ableitungen werden seit etwa 20 Jahren durchgeführt. Grundsätzlich ist die Möglichkeit Hirnströme mit Hautelektroden abzuleiten seit etwa 70 Jahren bekannt. Jedoch erst die Bereitstellung computergestützter Analysetechniken hat der EEG-Ableitung zu ihrer zentralen Stellung innerhalb der kognitiven Neurowissenschaft verholfen. Vor allem als Folge der Entwicklungen der Informatik sind während der letzten 10 Jahre große Fortschritte in der Analyse von EEG-Signalen gemacht worden. Seit der erstmaligen Entdeckung einer sprachspezifischen Komponente im EEG, der sogenannten N400-Komponente (Kutas & Hillyard 1980) (siehe Abbildung 3), hat sich die experimentelle Untersuchung von Sprachverarbeitungsprozessen mittels EEG-Analyse rasant entwickelt.

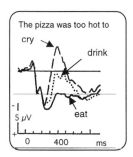

Abb. 3: Die Amplitude der N400-Komponente im ERP zeigt die Stärke der Aktivierungsprozesse im semantischen Lexikon. Liest die Versuchsperson am Ende eines Satzes wie The pizza was to hot to ... *anstelle des erwarteten Wortes* eat *ein syntaktisch passendes, jedoch semantisch unpassendes Wort (hier z.B.* drink *oder* cry*), so zeigt sich eine N400-Komponente im ERP. Die Präsentation des letzten Wortes beginnt bei 0 ms, die N400-Komponente hat ihr Maximum 400 ms nach Artikulationsbeginn dieses letzten Wortes. Mit zunehmender Stärke der semantischen Anomalie vergrößert sich die Amplitude der N400-Komponente. (Kutas & Van Petten 1994, verändert)*

Zur Beantwortung psycholinguistischer Fragen stehen nun, zusätzlich zu der bislang überwiegend genutzten Messung der Reaktionszeit elektrophysiologische Verfahren zur Verfügung, die mit einer weitaus höheren zeitlichen Auflösung einen unmittelbareren Zugriff auf die Physiologie der Verarbeitungsprozesse erlauben (z.b. Friederici et al. 1993; Mecklinger et al. 1995; Münte et al. 1998). Beispielsweise könnten meßbare Unterschiede der jeweiligen neuronalen Aktivität während der Verarbeitung unterschiedlicher Wortkategorien zu einer neuartigen Einteilung in Wortklassen führen, da es dann möglich wäre Wortkategorien auch auf ihre physiologische Realität hin zu überprüfen (Müller & Kutas 1996, 1997; Pulvermüller et al. 1996; Weiss & Rappelsberger 1996). Weiterhin ist es möglich, die mit der Analyse komplexer natürlichsprachlicher Sätze einhergehende Belastung des Arbeitsgedächtnisses zu messen und anhand dieser Daten die erfolgreiche Satzanalyse zu erfassen. So kann anhand des ERP-Verlaufs gemessen werden, ob ein Hörer wahrgenommene Relativsätze auch in der richtigen Weise verstanden hat (siehe Abbildung 4).

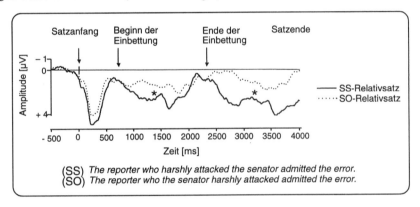

Abb. 4: Der ERP-Verlauf über 4,5 Sekunden während der Verarbeitung von zwei unterschiedlich schwierigen Relativsatzgefügen. Getestet wurden je 32 Sätz des Subjekt-Subjekt-Typs (durchgezogene Linie) gegen 32 Sätze des Subjekt-Objekt-Typs (gepunktete Linie) bei 24 Versuchspersonen. Die stärkere Belastung des Arbeitsgedächtnisses während der erfolgreichen Analyse der Satzteile der schwierigeren Sätze des SO-Typs zeigt sich anhand der unterschiedlichen Negativierung des Potentials (Sternchen). (Müller, King & Kutas 1997, verändert)

2.2   Kohärenzanalyse

Im Unterschied zur ERP-Analyse wird bei der Spektralanalyse das EEG- oder MEG-Signal in einzelne Frequenzkomponenten aufgespalten, so daß eine Transformation der Signale vom Zeitbereich in den Frequenzbereich erfolgt. Diese Transformation hat vor allem zwei Vorteile: Signalschwankungen im Analysezeitraum verlieren ihren störenden Einfluß, und es werden auch Frequenzkomponenten mit kleinen Amplituden erfaßt, die von Frequenzkomponenten mit hohen Amplituden verdeckt würden. Die Kohärenzanalyse erlaubt somit eine Beurteilung der Zunahme oder Abnahme von Synchronisationsprozessen zweier Gehirnareale im jeweiligen Frequenzband während einer kognitiven Aufgabe. Aus der Sicht der modernen Neurobiologie sind gerade diese neuronalen Synchronisationsprozesse für die Kognition von besonderer Bedeutung. Dabei wird die sogenannte Kohärenz zwischen den Signalen zweier Elektroden ermittelt (Weiss & Rappelsberger 1996), wobei die EEG-Aktivität der darunterliegenden Neuronengruppen einander ähnlicher oder einander unähnlicher werden kann. Ein Beispiel für die elektrophysiologisch ermittelte Zusammenarbeit von unterschiedlichen Hirnregionen während sprachlicher Aufgaben zeigt Abbildung 5 anhand der Verarbeitung von konkreten und abstrakten Nomina.

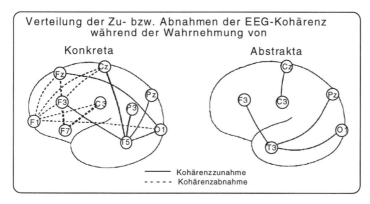

Abb. 5: Schematische Darstellungen der linken Hemisphäre und einigen Elektrodenorten. Eingezeichnet sind die signifikanten Zu- bzw. Abnahmen der EEG-Kohärenz während der Wahrnehmung natürlichsprachlicher Konkreta bzw. Abstrakta. Die Abkürzungen beziehen sich auf die im Experiment verwendeten Elektrodenpositionen. Bei der Verarbeitung von Abstrakta zeigen sich weitaus weniger Veränderungen neuronaler Synchronisationsprozesse, die sich zudem auf sprachrelevantere Regionen beschränken. (aus Weiss 1997, verändert)

Es wurde lange vermutet, daß die Analyse von konkreten Nomen mit Bezügen zu Erfahrungen in den entsprechenden Sinnesmodalitäten einhergeht und somit auch andere Bedeutungskonzepte aktiviert werden. Für die Abstrakta hingegen kann von einer kortikalen Repräsentation ausgegangen werden, die sich lediglich auf die im engeren Sinne sprachrelevanten Hirnbereiche bezieht. Beispielsweise sollte das Konkretum *Hase* mit gespeicherten Sinneseindrücken für die entsprechenden Berührungs-, Geschmacks-, Geruchs- und Gesichtssinnreize assoziiert sein, wohingegen das Abstraktum *Friede* keine Bezüge zu solchen Sinneseindrücken aufweist und sie somit auch nicht aktiviert. Anhand der EEG-Kohärenzanalyse konnten Weiss und Rappelsberger (1996) einen physiologischen Beweis für diese Annahme erbringen, da ausschließlich bei der Verarbeitung von Konkreta die entsprechenden Hirnbereiche der Sinnesmodalitäten mit den Hirnbereichen der Sprachverarbeitung kurzfristig eine engere Zusammenarbeit zeigen. Solche Ergebnisse zeigen die Verbindung der Experimentellen mit der Simulativen Neurolinguistik und der Klinischen Linguistik. Die klinische Beobachtung, daß bestimmte Patienten geringere Störungen im Zugriff auf konkrete Nomen haben, läßt sich somit anhand eines Modells aus der Simulativen Neurolinguistik erklären: Aufgrund einer viel stärkeren Redundanz im Netzwerk ist im Falle der Konkreta der Ausfall einer einzelnen Hirnregion viel leichter zu kompensieren. Somit liefern elektrophysiologische Befunde zur Sprachverarbeitung auch wichtige Hinweise für das Verständnis und die Therapie von gestörter Sprache (Rickheit 1997). In gleicher Weise unterstützen die physiologischen Ergebnisse zur Verarbeitung von Nomina propria die klinische Beobachtung einer Sonderstellung der Eigennamen bei Benennungsstörungen (Müller & Kutas 1996). Die nächsten 20 Jahre werden zeigen welchen Erkenntnisgewinn die linguistische Theorie und Modellbildung aus dem neurolinguistischen Forschungsansatz ziehen kann.

3   Literatur

BINDER, J. R.; FROST, J. A.; HAMMEKE, T. A.; COX, R. W.; RAO, S. M.; PRIETO, T. (1997): Human brain language areas identified by functional magnetic resonance imaging. In: The Journal of Neuroscience 17, 353-362.

FRIEDERICI, A. D.; PFEIFER, E;. HAHNE, A. (1993): Event-related brain potentials during natural speech processing: effects of semantic, morphological and syntactic violations. In: Cognitive Brain Research 1, 183-192.

JUST, M.A.; CARPENTER, P. A.; KELLER, T.A.; EDDY, W.F. (1996): Brain activation modulated by sentence comprehension. In: Science 274, 114-116.

KUTAS, M. (1997): Views on how the electrical activity that the brain generates reflects the functions of different language structures. In: Psychophysiology 34, 383-398.

KUTAS, M.; HILLYARD, S.A. (1980): Reading senseless sentences: brain potentials reflect semantic incongruity. In: Science 207, 203-205.

LIOTTI, M.; GAY, C.T.; FOX, P.T. (1994). Functional imaging and language: evidence from positron emission tomography. In: Journal of Clinical Neurophysiology 11, 175-190.

MECKLINGER, A.; SCHRIEFERS, H.; STEINHAUER, K.; FRIEDERICI, A. D. (1995): Processing relative clauses varying on syntactic and semantic dimensions: an analysis with event-related potentials. In: Memory and Cognition 23, 477-494.

MÜLLER, H. M.; KING, J. W.; KUTAS, M. (1997): Event related potentials elicited by spoken relative clauses. In: Cognitive Brain Research 5,193-203.

MÜLLER, H. M.; KUTAS, M. (1997): Die Verarbeitung von Eigennamen und Gattungsbezeichnungen. Eine elektrophysiologische Studie. In: Rickheit: 147-169.

— (1996): What's in a name? Electrophysiological differences between spoken nouns, proper names, and one's own name. In: NeuroReport 8, 221-225.

MÜNTE, T. F.; SCHILTZ, K.; KUTAS, M. (1998): When temporal terms belie conceptual order. In: Nature 395, 71-73.

MÜNTE, T. F.; SCHWIRTZ, O.; WIERINGA, B. M.; MATZKE, M.; JOHANNES, S. (1997): Elektrophysiologie komplexer Sätze: Ereigniskorrelierte Potentiale auf der Wort- und Satzebene. In: Zeitschrift für EEG und EMG 28, 11-17.

PULVERMÜLLER, F.; EULITZ, C.; PANTEV, C.; MOHR, B.; FEIGE, B.; LUTZENBERGER, W.; ELBERT, T.; BIRBAUMER, N. (1996): High-frequency cortical responses reflect lexical processing: an MEG study. In: Electroencephalography and Clinical Neurophysiology 98, 76-85.

RICKHEIT, G. (Hrsg.) (1997): Studien zur Klinischen Linguistik – Methoden, Modelle, Intervention. Opladen: Westdeutscher Verlag (Psycholinguistische Studien).

RICKHEIT, G.; STROHNER, H. (1993): Grundlagen der kognitiven Sprachverarbeitung: Modelle, Methoden, Ergebnisse. Tübingen: Francke (UTB 1735).

RÖSLER, F.; PÜTZ, P.; FRIEDERICI, A.; HAHNE, A. (1993): Event-related brain potentials while encountering semantic and syntactic constraint violations. In: Journal of Cognitive Neuroscience 5, 345-362.

WEISS, S. (1997): EEG-Kohärenz und Sprachverarbeitung: Die funktionelle Verkopplung von Gehirnregionen während der Verarbeitung unterschiedlicher Nomina. In: Rickheit: 125-146.

WEISS, S.; Rappelsberger, P. (1996): EEG coherences within the 13-18 Hz band as correlates of a distinct lexical organization of concrete and abstract nouns in humans. In: Neuroscience Letters 209, 17-20.

Aspects of Syntactic Development in Preteen-age Speakers of Swedish

Sinikka Niemi

1   Introduction[1]

Studies of language acquisition have predominantly been those of the early stages of language development, while only a handful of studies exist on the late stages of acquisition. A general concensus appears to be that normally developing children have acquired the basics of their first-language grammars around the ages 5-7, although rigorous experiments show that the acquisition of syntax towards adult-like mastery is relatively fast during the second ontogenetic decade (see e.g. Nippold 1998). The development of thematic roles may here serve as a relevant example: thematic role assignment by preteens and early teenagers is heavily influenced by pragmatic factors, like animacy, and canonical word order. These generalizations extend to languages as typologically dissimilar as English and Finnish (see e.g. Harris 1978, Slobin 1982, Harley 1995 for English, and Niemi and Hägg 1999 for Finnish; for processing principles/strategies associated with these and related observations, see Bever's 1970 NVN strategy; Slobin's 1973 Operational Principle C; for a cross-linguistic study of the development of sentence strategies, see Bates et al. 1984).

When pondering on the reasons for the slight interest in the late stages of first-language development, we may come up with at least two factors: one is based on our metatheoretical conceptions of language acquisition, the other on our methods:

It can be safely claimed that we are still more or less blindfolded by the Lennebergian views (Lenneberg 1967) that language, or more precisely so its grammar, has a critical, sensitive or optimal period, or periods, during which children have to receive sufficient amount of input in order to build up the core grammar of their first language. The existence of such a period, or periods, during the first few, four to five years of biological age is a fact of life. And these are also the years when the child's language proficiency develops fast, and often, in what looks like quantal leaps. Thus it is no wonder that the great majority of linguists and developmental psychologists have focused their interest on the grammatical development of these early "critical" years. However, it does not necessarily mean that at the end of this stage a child's grammar is identical to that of an adult, and that there would not exist any grammatically and processually interesting patterns during the later years.

The second biasing factor behind the emphasis on the early years is methodological. A prototypical linguistic early stage acquisition study derives its theoretical arguments from analyses of more or less spontaneous speech data. Moreover, it has to be

---

[1]   The present study has been financially supported by Academy of Finland research grants for studies of late language acquisition (1998-1999) and Genetic Language Impairment (1998-2000), recipient: Jussi Niemi, Linguistics, University of Joensuu. I am grateful to Jussi Niemi's comments for the present, concise survey of part of my PhD study. Any errors or misconceptions are, naturally enough, solely to be ascribed to the present author.

admitted that children during the latter half of their first decade do perform well in spontaneous speech tasks. However, when these same children and their older peers are put to rigorous tests they systematically fail in demanding grammatical tasks, which, however, are easy for adults and which are in everyday use by the adult population. Thus, we have to take into account the fact that in spontaneous speech children may avoid those aspects of grammar that they find, more or less subconsciously, difficult to process (cf. Herman Kolk's adaptation theory, based on the notion of selective intention, of agrammatic language production in acquired adult aphasia, e.g. Kolk and Van Grunsven 1985, Kolk et al. 1990).

2   Characteristics of Swedish syntax and aim of study

Swedish is a fixed word-order language with the SVO as the canonical order. Thus the first NP tends to be sentence-functionally the subject, and thematically the Agent:

	John	bygger	huset.
Syntactic functions:	S	V	O
Thematic roles:	Agent	Action	Undergoer
	'John builds the house.'		

Like many other Germanic languages, Swedish is not a pro-drop language in that it requires a subject marker, in e.g. its existential 1) and meteorological sentences 2):

1) a. Det finns pojkar på gården.
   b. *Finns pojkar på gården.
   'There are boys in the yard.'

2) a. Det regnar.
   b. *Regnar.
   'It rains.'

The aim of the present study is to test with rigorous off-line methods the possible changes between ages 8 and 11 in normal native speakers of (Finland) Swedish. The paper will deal with the assignment of thematic roles in active and passive sentences as well as with expletive (formal) subject sentences. In addition to these structures, in my talk in Germersheim I also discussed the acceptability of relative clause violations, such as that of subject support (e.g. *Pappa vet vem kommer hem for Pappa vet som kommer hem 'Daddy knows who som:SUBJ. SUPPORT comes home') and those of head-to-relative pronoun linkage (e.g. *Huset står där som är ditt hem for Huset som står där är ditt hem 'The house that stands there is your home') as well as experiments on negation marker and adverb placement in sentences like Emma tänker att (1) Bengt (2) har (3) ljugit (4) ('Emma thinks that Bengt has lied'), where, contrary to the expected verb-second order of Scandinavian languages, the correct intra-clausal landing-site is (2) (for details, see Niemi, in preparation).

3   Method

3.1   Subjects

The off-line tests of the present study were group-administered to Finland-Swedish normally developing children attending Swedish-language schools in the bilingual city of Vaasa/Vasa (population 56,600 out of which 25.6% Swedish-speaking). On the basis of previous studies on, e.g., English, the 71 children were chosen from two age groups: 38 children were 8-9 year old, and 33 were 10-11 year old. For sake of brevity, the first group will be refered to as the eight-year olds, and the latter as ten-year olds. On the basis of an extensive language background questionnaire covering various aspects of mastery of Swedish and Finnish and other languages the groups were further divided into strong monolinguals and weak monolinguals. In this presentation I will discuss the data on the strong monolinguals only. Of the 38 eight-year olds 26 were categorized as strong monolinguals, and the respective figure for the 33 ten-year olds is also 26. As a sidetrack on the weak monolinguals and their performance suffice it only to say that across the board they performed worse than their strong monolingual peers, which was only to be expected.

3.2   Data and procedures

The following two aspects of Swedish syntax were tested in a balanced and controlled manner.

i) Thematic role assignment in simple NVN active and passive sentences of three content words and with human or inanimate nouns

The subjects' task was to circle the word that shows who or what is doing the action described.

Active sentences:

3) Elma älskar Sixten.	'Elma loves Sixten.'
4) Elma älskar bordet.	'Elma loves the table.'
5) Bordet älskar Elma.	'The table loves Elma.'

5) is pragmatically implausible as an SVO sentence, but grammatically correct, although highly infrequent as an OVS sentence. Note that Swedish has retained oblique case-marking on pronouns only, cf. 6) and 7).

| 6) Han älskar henne. | 'He loves her.' |
| 7) Honom älskar hon. | (lit.) 'Him loves she.' |

Typical of other Indo-European languages Swedish has an agent passive, as in 8) through 10).

Passive sentences:

8) Elma älskas av Sixten.	'Elma is loved by Sixten.'
9) Bordet älskas av Elma.	'The table is loved by Elma.'
10) Elma älskas av bordet.	'Elma is loved by the table.'

ii) Acceptability of expletive subject violations

The sentences testing acceptability of expletive subject violations were created through systematically dropping the formal subject *det* corresponding to 'it, there' in infinitival subject sentences, meteorological sentences, and existential sentences (see 11) to 13)). The items were presented in one randomized set with structurally unrelated simple correct sentences as fillers (50% fillers, 50% incorrect test items). The subjects were to tick the relevant box for the correctness or incorrectness of each sentence.

a) Sentences with infinitival subjects:
 11) *[Det] är skönt att simma.   (lit.) 'Is nice to swim.'

b) Sentences with meteorological predicates:
 12) *Nu regnar [det].   (lit.) 'Now rains.'

c) Existential sentences:
 13) *[Det] finns ett bord i köket.   (lit.) 'Is a table in the kitchen.'

4   Results

4.1   Thematic role assignment

Table 1 shows the percentages of N1 assignments as Agent, and, overall, the SVO tendency permeates the active sentences in both age groups. However, there is an expected, albeit slight, ten percentage point drop in both age groups in assigning the pragmatically unlikely inanimate N1 as the Agent in the active sentences.

		ACTIVE		PASSIVE	
N Type		Age Group		Age Group	
N1	N2	8	10	8	10
Human	Human	88	97	44	16
Human	Inanimate	92	96	57	14
Inanimate	Human	80	86	36	12

Table 1: Thematic role assignment in NVN active and passive sentences with human and inanimate N's. Percentages of N1 categorized as Agent. The range of number of observations per cell: active sentences 230-256, passive sentences 110-384.

What is particularly interesting in this test is the passive set, which, like passives in many other Germanic languages, carries transparent morphosyntactic markers (here: the verbal suffixal marker -*s* and the agent prepositional phrase). A major finding here is the fast development from the younger group to the older. The eight-year olds give random responses when both noun phrases are human and they are biased in assigning the Agent role to the first noun even when it is accompanied by the implausible inanimate Agent ('Elma is loved by the table.'). (Note that in the test sentences the agent prepositional phrase never receives a locative interpretation, e.g. as would, with some stretching of one's imagination, be the case in the English sentences like *Elma is loved by* ('beside') *the table*).

The passive sentences with the inanimate N1 and human agent noun ('The table is loved by Elma') receive the most correct responses from the eight-year olds. The performance of the older group in the passives appears to be similar irrespective of sentence type. (Allowing for various test noise effects in testing young children in classrooms, we may regard a 10% incorrectness rate as being equal to the ceiling effect, or 100% correct.)

4.2 Acceptability of expletive subject violations

The younger group incorrectly accepts 62% of the expletive subject violations (of the 286 sentences categorized either correct or incorrect by the subjects), while the older group does that somewhat more rarely, viz., in 68% of the instances (out of 375). In passing, it should be said that the performance on the meteorological sentences by both groups was somewhat better than their performance on the other two sentence types, perhaps indicating that meteorological verbs with their obligatory subject *det* make up a construct, while the infinitives and the verb used in the existentials, viz., *finnas*, can also exist outside these expletive subject environments.

5 Conclusions

The present results can be embedded in the Competition Model of Bates and MacWhinney (1989), with their notions of cue validity and cue cost, as follows:

1) Assuming that normal Swedish-speaking adults would make a low number of errors, if any, in off-line tasks like the present ones, we may claim that Swedish children and adolescents have non-adult (non-normative) cue validity values in thematic role assignment and acceptance of expletive subject violations.
2) The SVO order is an overriding cue for Agent assignment in the Swedish active sentences.
3) The passive sentences show drastic signs of ontogenetic development during the few years separating the age groups: the younger group exhibits no cue priority, and they behave (semi)randomly, while the older subjects, as a group, resemble the expected adult pattern.

4) However, the grammar of the older group is not adult-like in all respects, since these subjects, quite unexpectedly, fail in the expletive subject sentences.

How are we to interpret these results? It may be the case that still as late as 8 years of age speakers of languages like Swedish have little experience with the passive. The passive (of English) is infrequent as input, and still children have to and tend to learn it by the age of 10-11. For instance, in his pioneering extensive work Brown (1973) found no full passive in the whole parent-input data he analyzed. Note also that in English, according to Horgan (1978:78), "[t]he years from 7 through adolescence appear to be important in gaining control of the passive[.]", and that these years also mark the onset of the beginning of the Piagetian stage of concrete operations.

6   References

BATES, Elizabeth; MACWHINNEY, Brian; CASELLI, Cristina; DEVESCOVI, Antonella; NATALE, Francesco; VENZA, Valeria (1984): A Crosslinguistic Study of the Development of Sentence Interpretation Strategies. In: Child Development 55, 341-354.

BROWN, Roger (1973): A First Language. London: Allen and Unwin.

HARLEY, Trevor (1995): The Psychology of Language. Hove: Psychology Press.

HARRIS, M. (1978): Noun animacy and the passive voice: A developmental approach. In: Quarterly Journal of Experimental Psychology 30, 495-504.

HORGAN, Dianne (1978): The development of the full passive. In: Journal of Child Language 5, 65-80.

LENNEBERG, Eric (1967): The Biological Foundations of Language. New York: Wiley.

KOLK, Herman; Van Grunsven, Marianne (1985): Agrammatism As a Variable Phenomenon. In: Cognitive Neuropsychology 2, 347-384.

KOLK, Herman; HELING, Geert; KEYSER, Antoine (1990). Agrammatism in Dutch. In: Menn, L.; Obler, L. (eds.): Agrammatic Aphasia, vol. 3. Amsterdam: Benjamins, 179-280.

NIEMI, Jussi; HÄGG, Minna (1999): Syntax at late stages of acquisition: Experiments with Normal and SLI children. In: Maassen, B.; Groenen, P. (eds.): Pathologies in Speech and Language. London: Whurr, 76-81.

NIEMI, Sinikka (in preparation): Swedish syntax at late stages of L1 and L2 acquisition and in familial language impairment. (PhD thesis to be submitted to the University of Joensuu).

NIPPOLD, Marilyn (1998, ed.): Later Language Development: Ages Nine through Nineteen. Boston, MA: Little, Brown and Co.

SLOBIN, Dan (1973): Cognitive prerequisites for the development of language. In: Ferguson, C.; Slobin, D. (eds.): Studies in Child Language Development. New York: Holt, Rinehart, & Winston, 175-208.

Words in the Mind:
Collocations and Cultural Connotations of Words

Krassimira Rangelova, Diane de Echeandia

1 Quantitative analysis of language

In the past decade, language corpora – large collections of authentic language use – have constituted the empirical basis for research into language, into its structure, variety and meaning (Sinclair 1993; Stubbs 1996). Through access to computational data retrieval methods for searching and pattern matching in large corpora of authentic language, it has become possible not only to evaluate actual instances of language use but also to perceive a unitary picture of the language in its lexico-grammatical structure and discover the linguistic potential through the plurality and systematicity of the collection of individual instances (Aijmer & Altenberg 1991).

1.1 Computational analysis of lexis

The corpus-based approach to language analysis has been extensively used to study the systematic distributions and patterning behavior of lexis (Sinclair 1993; Stubbs 1996). Extensive computer analysis of language use has been uncovering recurring patterns of lexical co-occurrence and has revealed the strong tendency of words to co-occur with particular words. *Collocation* has long been the name given to the relationship a lexical item has with items that appear with greater than random probability in its textual context (Firth 1957; Halliday & Hasan 1976). Thus, for example, in English, *unauthorized* collocates with *person(s)* but not with *people*, and *department* with *university*, but not with *train*, which would collocate with *compartment*, and *goal* habitually co-occurs with *kick* or *shoot* or *score* but not with *do* when used in the *sports* sense of the word. Many uses of words attract other words in strong collocations: *hard luck, hard facts, hard evidence, rancid butter, curry favour* are some examples from English.

As collocations describe specific lexical items and the frequency with which these items occur with other lexical items, they are defined along a syntagmatic, or horizontal dimension. That is, in linguistic description, a collocational unit consists of a *node* that co-occurs with a *span of words* on either side. The span consists of particular word classes filled by specific lexical items. The relationship between the node and its collocates is statistically demonstrable (Sinclair 1991; Stubbs 1996). Thus, for example, evidence from quantitative analysis of language corpora shows that the word node *problem* occurs with a span of particular words: *cause, create, pose, present,* or *address, bring up, raise,* or *confront, face, deal with.*

1.1.1 Collocational profiles of words

The computational analysis of collocations is important for the description of lexical structures in revealing the actual patterning in authentic language use. Through collocations, the specific semantic profiles of lexical items can be recognized and the different senses of a word can be identified.

The first dictionary definition of the word *job*, for instance, is 'the work that a person does regularly to earn money' (Sinclair et al 1995:902). This semantic feature of the lexical item is confirmed by some of the collocates occurring in the span of the node: *permanent, full-time, proper, well-paid*. In this sense, other common collocates in the span of *job* are: *axed, eliminated, lost, cut*. The recurring patterns of the word node reveal that the negative semantic features of *job* dominate in the meaning of the word as reflected by the span of words. Furthermore, other frequently occurring collocates include: *botched, difficult, hard, menial, stressful, thankless, unskilled*. Therefore, looking at the occurrences, it could be concluded that negative features in the meaning of *job* are prominent in the semantic profile of the word.

Current work on lexical collocations uses two ideas:

1) words have distinctive semantic profiles, and
2) the strength of association between words can be measured in quantitative terms (Stubbs 1996).

These ideas can be combined to provide comparative semantic profiles of words, which show the frequent and characteristic collocates of node words, and make explicit the semantic relations between the collocates.

1.1.2 Lexical collocations and cultural connotations

In addition to revealing the semantic profiles of words, lexical collocations also encode culture-specific information to the extent that the nature of the world around us is reflected in the organization of language, and natural language is the great matrix of cultural categories (D'Dandrade 1995). The concept of culture defined as the entire social heritage of a group, including material culture and external structures, learned actions and mental representations represent an intimate relationship between mental and physical structures. Since culture is the great storehouse of historically transmitted patterns of meanings, a system of inherited conceptions, and natural language embodies these meanings in symbols and expresses the cultural perceptions in symbolic forms by which we communicate, we would expect that the vocabulary of a language would be the best evidence of the reality of culture (Wierzbicka 1997). We could expect that, despite the massive common ground there exists between human cultures, there are also substantial differences in the way the external world is perceived and categorized by each culture. Certain aspects of the real world structures are perceived with greater salience in some cultures but not in others. In this sense, often the concept encoded in the word is culturally salient. It is this kind of inherent perceptual salience that collocational regularities often reveal. Thus, for example, the comparative computational analysis of the collocational regularities of *friend* and *friend-ship* in English reveals that certain aspects of human relations are perceived as more relevant and salient than others. The frequent collocates of *friend* include *be, make*; common collocates of *friendship* are *cement, develop, make, cherish, cultivate, destroy, ruin* (LOB Corpus). The choice of the verb *take* in *take pictures* reflects broad cultural preferences and conventions as well: in a culture where people's privacy is jealously guarded, the act of photographing is considered an aggressive act whereby you are *taking* something away from person.

1.1.3 Collocations and vocabulary knowledge

The brief overview of the nature of the patterning behavior of lexical items reveals the fact that the collocational regularities of lexis are not only statistical evidence from the quantitative analysis of language use. The recurring lexical collocations reflect important aspects of the conceptualization and categorization of the world. The relationships of a lexical item with other items is not random in the sense that it reveals how the concept connects to other concepts as well as what other concepts it is linked to.

As the statistically identifiable property of lexis is determined by the computational analysis of authentic language corpora, it can be assumed that lexical collocations reflect native speakers' intuitions about the systematic patterns of meaning relations. And indeed, native speakers of a language are sensitive to collocational links. If a native speaker of a language is given a page of authentic examples of a word in use where a blank is left each time that specific word occurs, that person would normally be able to identify the missing word with ease and accuracy, using the evidence of the context. Thus, we can assume that collocation is not only a statistical fact; it is psycholinguistically real as well.

If collocation is a phenomenon of the individual's linguistic competence then, we need to consider how collocations are recognized, and how the knowledge of collocational links is stored and accessed in memory. In other words, what is the nature of this kind of vocabulary knowledge? How is it structured in the internal lexicon of native speakers of a language? The answers to these questions have important implications for modeling vocabulary knowledge, which is a critical building block in second language learning.

Findings from language learning research further confirm the central role of collocations in language learning. Collocation is an example of a powerful link between lexical items, but the correct use of collocations is very difficult for second language learners. Language learners often make inappropriate word choices when combining commonly used words. For example, when trying to convey the meaning of *a missed appointment*, second language learners of English often use instead *lose an appointment* or *drop an appointment*. What specific place does collocation have in the memory network? If it were possible to create native-like collocations in the learner's mental lexicon, the difficulty of word combination in production would be greatly reduced.

2   The current study

The purpose of the study is to investigate the collocational patterns that occur in the semantic memory of native and non-native speakers to find out how these regularities are represented, and to understand the nature of these representations. The issues to be examined include the question of whether collocations, as a statistically identifiable property of lexis and as form and function composites, should be viewed as belonging to a theory of competence, or they are possibly psychologically real and this kind of linguistic knowledge is represented in the semantic memory of language users as well. In particular, we will look at how collocations are related to the ways in which the mental lexicon is structured and organized.

2.1   Purpose of the study

The aim of the present study was to examine native speakers' intuitions of collocations and compare them to non-native speakers' awareness of collocational links between words.

Evidence from language learning research shows that second language learners make different associational links than native speakers of a language, and this prohibits native-like speaker fluency. The word choices language learners make reveal that second language learners store information in semantic memory based on linguistic transfer across languages and according to their own cultural background knowledge. These differences in associational linkages, and storage of words lead to wrong connections and inappropriate word combinations. Thus, it is important to understand how collocations are represented in semantic memory, as well as the nature of these representations. It is hypothesized that there are differences in the mental representations of collocations in the memory system of native speakers and second language learners, and that these differences have their foundation in cultural differences. The working hypothesis for this study is that the evidence of words co-occurring together is revealing of the structure of the mental lexicon, and that the semantic network or connections between words and meanings of native and non-native speakers of a language is structured differently.

2.2   Methodology

2.2.1   Participants

The subjects for this study were a total of 50 students enrolled at the University at Albany, State University of New York. Twenty-five subjects were native speakers of English, and twenty-five subjects were non-native speakers of English who were randomly selected from the student population. The non-native speakers represented a diversity of cultures from seven different countries – European, Latin American, and Asian.

A potential disadvantage of the current sampling method is the diversity of the cultural groups. Study of one cultural group of non-native speakers of English would result in more definitive information about the cultural connotations of words.

2.2.2 Material

Twenty common English words representing the four parts of speech nouns, verbs, adjectives, and adverbs were used in the study for elicitation of collocational regularities. The words were selected from the frequency band of the 8 000 most frequent words based on the Collins Cobuild Bank of English.

After piloting the list of stimulus words, it became evident that participants from both groups were experiencing difficulties with eliciting associations for three of the stimuli – *incur*, *stiff*, and *completely* – and the three stimulus words were removed from the list.

2.2.3 Procedure

A lexical association task was used to determine language users' awareness of collocational regularities of lexical items and to uncover the frequently occurring combinations for the twenty stimulus words. For each word, subjects were asked to provide the words that immediately came to their minds when they thought about how that word was used.

Subjects were asked to respond to each word by writing down as many words as they could think of that would logically go with the target word in a specified syntagmatic order. Participants had one minute to write down the responses they elicited in the association task.

Participants received four sets of cards with the stimulus words each typed on a card. When the allowed time for elicitation of associations was over, subjects turned over the card they had been working on and continued with the next one. In this way, cross-association and priming among stimulus words and responses were controlled.

2.2.4 Results

A two-way analysis of variance was used to analyze the data collected through the association elicitation task.

Examination of the graph (Figure 1) reveals a significant interaction between native or non-native speaker and number of collocations. Examination of the means indicates that native speakers of English were able to produce a significantly greater number of collocations for the stimulus words (x = 6.22). This first finding is predictable and, and in a sense, trivial. It is not surprising that native speakers of English have an easier access to the network of connections a word node has in semantic memory as native speakers have the benefit of a life-long and extensive exposure to language use, and they can get enough experience of the way words are used. A surprising finding is the greater number of responses non-native speakers elicited for three of the stimulus words: *problem* (148 as compared with 110 for native speakers), *fast* (86 as compared with 69 for native speakers), and flexible (non-native speakers – 76; 64 native speakers). The further analysis of the specific responses elicited as collocates for the tree stimulus words, however, reveals that:

1) very few of the responses by non-native speakers can be considered as true collocates; and

2) most of the responses are incorrect and inappropriate altogether.

Thus, for example, for *problem* non-native speakers came up with *find, struggle, stop, skip, hurdle, afford, correct*. The native speakers, on the other hand, associated problem with *encounter, address, surpass, work through, ignore, circumvent, alleviate*. Non-native speakers associated *fast* with *answer, cook, communicate, jump, hike, move, handle, understand, study*; they, however, also elicit successfully some of the common associations native speakers elicit for the word: *run, write, eat, talk, walk*.

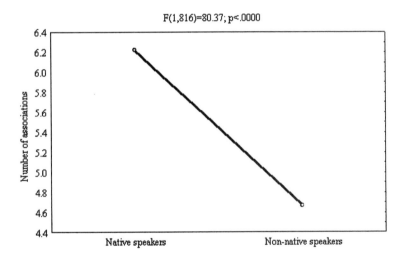

Figure 1: Number of associations elicited by subjects.

The responses elicited for each group were analyzed and compared to the statistically defined collocational profiles of the stimulus words.

The analysis of the elicited associations by subjects in the two groups shows a tendency for single occurrences of responses in the group of non-native speakers. While the total number of associations native speakers give derives from multiple occurrences of a response rather than from single associations. The comparison of these recurring associations for stimulus words shows that the patterns systematically reflect collocational regularities. Thus, corpus-based evidence shows that *achieve* is a strong collocate of *goal*. The associations native speakers give support this lexical regularity. In the group of non-native speakers, however, *achieve* occurs only once. At the same time, the systematic recurrence of *reach* as the associative response for *goal* reveals the inadequate knowledge of non-native speakers. In addition, the associations non-native speakers produce for in response to *goal* show that a frequently used sense of the word – as used in sports – is not activated in the semantic memory of non-native speakers: they fail to produce even a single association that reflects this sense of the word, e.g., *score, shoot, kick* or *miss*.

In conclusion, the findings of the analysis of the data from the lexical association task clearly show that native speakers are sensitive to collocational regularities of lexical items. On the other hand, non-native speakers show no awareness of the specific property of lexis. The evidence from the word combinations non-native speakers elicit clearly suggests that second language learners are often unaware of the collocational regularities of lexis, and are unable to actively produce native speaker-like collocations for words they obviously have 'good' knowledge of. The associations they give for stimulus words consistently reveal the inappropriacy of the combinations.

3   Discussion

The results from the analysis of the lexical association data clearly indicate that knowledge of vocabulary is organized differently in the mental lexicon of native and non-native speakers of English. Although non-native speakers have good vocabulary knowledge, that knowledge is not represented in a way that enables them to use it as efficiently as native speakers do so that they can communicate successfully. The differences between second language learners' vocabulary knowledge and native speakers' lexis often give them away as *foreigners* even if their knowledge of language is *impeccable*, i.e., they have vestiges of knowledge but it is incomplete and this makes it inadequate in language use. This implies that there are *missing connections* in the semantic network of non-native speakers which prohibit native-like fluency. As previously mentioned, words are not held in memory in isolation rather lexical units function in an integrated network. Storage of mother-tongue vocabulary involves networks of connections. Second language lexical representation, too, involves networks of associations, though second language associative links may be less firmly established, on the one hand, and, on the other hand, the connections to the *right* word nodes may not be made. *Right* in this context means those words that are typically used by native speakers in talking about that concept. If the range of connections that are established in the mental lexicon of non-native speakers when knowledge of a word is being developed is not completed, then immediate associations with first language words is likely to be set up as soon as possible.

3.1   Semantic memory: lexical and conceptual representations

A model of semantic memory that may account for the lexical choices that native speakers of a language make and the performance errors non-native speakers make would be a theoretical model which combines assumptions from linguistic theory regarding the units and structures of language with a specified encoding/retrieval mechanism based on spreading activation. The fundamental premise of such a model is the interactive activation of knowledge in an integrated network of semantic and conceptual representations. The model makes simple assumptions about the nature of the conceptual representation: its units are concepts, which appear in the lexical network connected to word nodes. The basic processing assumption is that the nodes activate through the process of spreading activation other nodes to which they are linked. The encoding and retrieval processes based on spreading activation cause the units appropriate for a given representation to become activated. This aspect of the model is very important in that just about all of its substantive predictions regarding lexical choices and word combinations derive from spreading activation. The spreading activation assumptions specify how the activated nodes affect one another: When a node is activated, it sends some proportion of its activation level to all nodes connected to it. Their activation comes about because the concepts that define them (and hence are connected to them) are part of the semantic representation. In other words, the semantic representation includes conceptual nodes that exist in the lexical network and participate in the spreading activation. The proportion of activation is not necessarily the same for each connection. Nodes that are directly connected will get the greatest level of activation. Sensitive to the activation levels of all nodes, the system then selects the node that possesses the highest level of activation.

Thus, when *appointment* enters the memory system, the corresponding node in the lexical network is activated. The other nodes to which activation spreads are the nodes that have related conceptual structures with the current node: *schedule, reschedule, keep, cancel, postpone, arrange, miss.* However, if in the second language learner's semantic network the connection to *miss* is not part of the representation, then the node will not receive the necessary level of activation, and activation will spread in directions that are different from those of a native speaker. An immediate association with the first language word node is most likely to be set up as soon as possible. Thus, the missing link with *miss* would be 'filled in' by the existing connections in the first language semantic and conceptual representation: *drop* or *lose*, as the evidence from the data analysis in the current study indicate.

3.2   Implications for second language instruction

To establish the range of reference of new words and phrases they meet and to set up the appropriate connections in the semantic network, second language learners need a great deal of exposure to authentic language input so that they can get enough experience of the ways words are used. By being familiar with collocational regularities in the lexis such as a *convenient time* and a *convenient situation* but not with ones like *a convenient person*, learners will 'realize', however, subconsciously, that the adjective *convenient* is used only with inanimate objects. Raising learners' awareness of the specific patterning behavior of lexis would provide for elaborative integration with semantic and conceptual knowledge. Furthermore, learners will also develop an understanding, subconsciously again, of the semantic differences between words which reflect the differences in cultural salience. Thus, learners will expand their semantic memory to correspond to the cultural schemata of the second language culture, and language learning will become for them shared learning and shared communication.

3.3 Implications for lexicography

The statistically identifiable property of lexical items to co-occur habitually, which is also psycholinguistically real, has strong implications for the role of dictionaries in vocabulary learning and has a great deal to offer the practice of lexicography as well. We believe that in order for dictionaries to be able to contribute beneficially to the process of putting knowledge to use, information in the lexical entries should be structured and represented in the way in which vocabulary is organized in the semantic memory of native speakers of the language.

The methods currently used are primarily intuitive. Dictionaries select lexemes among the paradigmatic, vertical axis, and treat them as individual items in a substitution relation, listing them singly and assigning them an exclusive reference. These dictionaries, however, have little to say about words along the corresponding syntagmatic axis, and present almost nothing about the collocational possibilities for individual entries. As the present study emphasizes, the meaning relations of words that occur along the syntagmatic axis also contribute to the description of the meaning of a word. Words in the span of lexical nodes contribute to its sense, and are a factor that needs to be taken account of in a description of its meaning.

If dictionaries offer information about lexical items that has no or little relevance to lexical units as they function in an integrated semantic network in memory, learners would establish the wrong connections, in the sense that they would set up the connections on the basis of their prior knowledge as stored through their first language.

4 References

AIJMER, Karin; ALTENBERG, Bengt (1991): Corpus Linguistics. Studies in Honor of Ian Svartvik. London: Longman.

BIBER, Douglas; CONRAD, Susan; REPPEN, Randi (1998): Corpus linguistics: Investigating Language Structures and Use. Cambridge: Cambridge University Press.

CARTER, Ronald (1987). Vocabulary: Applied Linguistic Perspectives. New York: Routledge

D'ANDRADE, Roy (1995): The Development of Cognitive Anthropology. Cambridge: Cambridge University Press.

FARGHAL, Mohammed; OBIEDAT, Hussein (1995): Collocations: A Neglected Variable in EFL. In: IRAL 33.4, 315-331.

FIRTH, John (1957): Papers in Linguistics. London: Oxford University Press.

HALLIDAY, Michael A. K.; HASAN, Ruqaiya (1966): Cohesion in English. London: Longman.
HASSELGREN, Angela (1994): Lexical Teddy Bears and Advanced Learners: A Study Into the Ways Norwegian Students Cope With English Vocabulary. In: International Journal of Applied Linguistics 4.2, 237-260.
MCENERY, Tom; WILSON, Andrew (1996): Corpus Linguistics. Edinburgh: Edinburgh University Press.
SCHMITT, Norbert; MCCARTHY, Michael (1997): Vocabulary: Description, Acquisition and Pedagogy. Cambridge: Cambridge University Press.
SINCLAIR, John (1991): Corpus, Concordance, Collocation. Oxford: Oxford University Press.
SINCLAIR, John et al. (1995): Collins CoBuild English Dictionary. London: HarperCollins Publishers.
STUBBS, Michael (1996): Text and Corpus Analysis. Oxford: Blackwell Publishers.
WIERZBICKA, Anna (1997): Understanding Cultures Through Their Key Words. New York: Oxford University Press.

Corpora used in the study

THE BROWN CORPUS OF AMERICAN ENGLISH, ICAME Collection of English Language Corpora. Norwegian Computing Center for the Humanities, Bergen, Norway
THE BRITISH NATIONAL CORPUS, Oxford University Computing Service, Oxford, UK.
THE LANCASTER-OSLO/BERGEN CORPUS, ICAME, Bergen, Norway
ICAME COLLECTION OF ENGLISH LANGUAGE CORPORA. Norwegian Computing Center for the Humanities, Bergen, Norway
MICROCONCORD CORPUS COLLECTION. Oxford: Oxford University Press

Soziolinguistik

Ist Deutsch noch zu retten? – Die Zukunft des deutschen Sprachgebrauchs in deutsch-amerikanischen Vereinen

Beate Benndorf

1   Einleitung

Dieser Beitrag befaßt sich mit der Frage, ob mehr als 30 Jahre nach der letzten größeren deutschsprachigen Einwanderungsbewegung die deutsche Sprache in deutsch-amerikanischen Vereinen eine Rolle spielt und wenn ja, welche. Die Analyse stützt sich auf Daten, die innerhalb der letzten drei Jahre gesammelt wurden. Dabei wurden sowohl statistische Daten durch Fragebögen erhoben als auch Vereine besucht und beobachtet. Weiterhin wurde eine Fülle schriftlicher Materialien in die Bearbeitung einbezogen.

2   Begriff des Spracherhalts

Traditionell wird Spracherhalt (*language maintenance*) als Erhalt der Muttersprache einer Sprachminderheit in einer Sprachkontaktsituation betrachtet. In den letzten Jahren haben Sprachwissenschaftler jedoch den Begriff erweitert, um den Übergangsprozeß des Sprachwechsels (language shift) mit einzuschließen. Für die Betrachtung der deutsch-amerikanischen Situation ist eine Erweiterung des Begriffs entscheidend. Die Nachkommen der Immigranten erhalten die deutsche Sprache, wenn überhaupt, nur fragmentartig (s. Fishman 1986:274). Sprach*befähigung* ist nicht mehr ausschlaggebend bei der ethnischen Gruppenbestimmung und damit für die Abgrenzung von anderen ethnischen Gruppen (s. Conklin 1983:171). Trotzdem besitzt die deutsche Sprache als solche für die Gruppenbestimmung eine hohe Wertigkeit, da die symbolische Funktion der Sprache erhalten bleibt, auch wenn die kommunikative Funktion verloren geht (Edwards 1977:263). Wie ich in diesem Beitrag zeigen will, sind besonders deutsch-amerikanische Vereine Träger dieser symbolischen Funktion der Sprache.

3   Vereine und Spracherhalt

Bei unserer Untersuchung, ob *language maintenance* eine Rolle in deutsch-amerikanischen Vereinen spielt, folge ich einer Studie von Fishman und Nahirny (1978). In dieser Studie wurden ethnische kulturelle Organisationen auf ihre Beziehung zu *language maintenance* untersucht. Dabei gingen Fishman und Nahirny (1978:157) davon aus, daß soziologische Charakteristiken wie Größe der Vereine, Alter der Mitglieder, etc. und *language maintenance* einander beeinflussen. Für die Untersuchung dieses Zusammenhangs unterscheiden Fishman und Nahirny (1978:157) zwischen *linguistically retentive organizations* (spracherhaltende Organisationen), sogenannten *positives*, und *linguistically non-retentive organizations*, sogenannten *negatives*. Die Untersuchung der soziologischen Charakteristiken sollten entscheidende Hinweise auf die Bedeutung und Intensität von *language maintenance* sowie Ethnizität in ethnischen Organisationen beider Gruppen geben.

Obwohl ich mich in der Art der Analyse stark an Fishman und Nahirnys Studie anlehne, bestehen doch auch klare Unterschiede in der Auswahl der Daten. Fishman und Nahirny unterscheiden nicht zwischen den verschiedenen ethnischen Gruppen und ihren kulturellen Organisationen, während unsere Analyse auf deutsch-amerikanische Organisationen beschränkt ist. Weiterhin endet die Datenerfassung von Fishman und Nahirny zum Ende der 1950er Jahre. Zumindestens für die deutsch-amerikanische Gruppe bedeutet der Zeitraum um 1950 und 1960 noch einmal einen gewissen Zufluß von Immigranten und damit auch eine Stärkung der deutschen Sprache in deutsch-amerikanischen Organisationen. Zu guter Letzt ergab die Art unserer Datenerfassung, daß eine Unterscheidung zwischen *positives* und *negatives* nicht ausreichend ist und eine dritte Gruppe, die sogenannten *somewhats* eingeführt werden mußte.

4   Ergebnisse

Es gibt keine genauen Angaben, wieviel deutsch-amerikanische Vereine in den USA tatsächlich noch existieren, aber meinen Schätzungen zufolge gibt es derzeit noch ca. 600. Vereine sind generell schwierig zu erreichen, da sie in der Regel kein Vereinshaus besitzen und nur über die Präsidenten erreichbar sind. Wenn ein solcher aus dem Amt scheidet, geht oft der Kontakt verloren.

Insgesamt antworteten 184 Vereine auf den ersten Fragebogen. Diese Vereine sind, basierend auf ihren Angaben zum Sprachgebrauch, als sogenannte *Usage Group* klassifiziert worden. Die *Usage Group* setzt sich dabei aus 49 *User*, 92 *Some-User* und 43 *Non-User* zusammen. *User* verwenden Deutsch zu 41-100%, *Some-User* zu 5-40% und *Non-User* zu 0-4%. Den zweiten Fragebogen beantworteten 99 Vereine, die dort auch ihre Einstellung zum Spracherhalt angegeben haben. Sie werden daher als sogenannte *Attitude Group* bezeichnet. Die *Attitude Group* umfaßt dabei 39 *positives*, 31 *somewhats* und 29 *negatives*. *Positives* haben sich entschieden, daß die Erhaltung der deutschen Sprache für sie *a top priority* oder *very important* ist, während für *somewhats* die Erhaltung *somewhat important* und für *negatives* die Erhaltung *not very important* ist oder gar kein Deutsch verwendet wird.

Unseren Ergebnissen zufolge, deren detaillierte Beschreibung den Rahmen dieses Beitrages sprengen würde, können wir genau wie Fishman und Nahirny (1978) feststellen, daß noch ein gewisser Zusammenhang zwischen soziologischen Charakteristiken und *language maintenance* besteht. Deshalb fand sich auch in unserer Analyse, daß spracherhaltende Organisationen (*positives* und *User*) eine relativ alte Mitgliedschaft besitzen (s. Tabelle 1) und bei denen die Immigranten das Vereinsleben noch dominieren (s. Tabelle 2). Diese Vereine haben nicht nur eine positive Einstellung gegenüber dem Spracherhalt, die deutsche Sprache wird auch noch weitestgehend verwendet (s. Tabelle 3). *Negatives* und *Non-User* dagegen haben eine jüngere Mitgliedschaft (s. Tabelle 1). Sie sind für spätere Generationen sehr viel interessanter, da wenig bis kein Deutsch verwendet wird.

Alter	Attitude Group				Usage Group			
	positives	some-whats	negatives	Total (100%)	User	Some-User	Non-User	Total (100%)
0-19	8 (29,6)	10 (37,0)	9 (33,3)	27	4 (14.8)	20 (74.1)	3 (11.1)	27
20-34	11 (28,9)	14 (36,8)	13 (34,2)	38	7 (18.4)	24 (63.2)	7 (18.4)	38
35-49	26 (37,1)	25 (35,7)	19 (27,1)	70	16 (22.9)	40 (57.1)	14 (20.0)	70
50-64	32 (39,5)	25 (30,9)	24 (29,6)	81	24 (29.6)	40 (49.4)	17 (21.0)	81
65+	33 (42,3)	22 (28,2)	23 (29,5)	78	23 (29.5)	40 (51.3)	15 (19.2)	78
Vereine	39	31	29	99	49	92	43	184

Tabelle 1: Altersgruppen der „Attitude" und „Usage Group" (mehr als eine Antwort möglich).

Generation	Attitude Group				Usage Group			
	positives	some-whats	negatives	Total (100%)	User	Some-User	Non-User	Total (100%)
1.	35 (40,2)	28 (32,2)	24 (27,6)	87	27 (31,0)	45 (51,4)	15 (17,9)	87
2.	31 (39,7)	27 (34,6)	20 (25,6)	78	22 (28,2)	42 (53,8)	14 (17,9)	78
3.	21 (32,3)	24 (36,9)	20 (30,8)	65	14 (21,5)	36 (55,4)	15 (23,1)	65
4.	19 (29,2)	20 (30,8)	26 (40,0)	65	13 (20,0)	35 (53,8)	17 (26,2)	65
Vereine	39	31	29	99	49	92	43	184

Tabelle 2: Generationen der „Attitude" und „Usage Group" (mehr als eine Antwort möglich).

Häufigkeit	Attitude Group				Usage Group			
	positives	some-whats	Negatives	Total (100%)	User	Some-User	Non-User	Total (100%)
None (0-4%)	4 (15,4)	9 (34,6)	13 (50,0)	26	0 (0,0)	6 (14,0)	37 (86,0)	43
Some (5-40%)	12 (30,0)	16 (40,0)	12 (30,0)	40	3 (3,5)	78 (91,8)	4 (4,7)	85
Half (41-70%)	10 (71,4)	2 (14,3)	2 (14,3)	14	16 (69,6)	7 (30,4)	0 (0,0)	23
A lot (71-100%)	13 (72,2)	4 (22,2)	1 (5,6)	18	30 (96,8)	1 (3,2)	0 (0,0)	31
Vereine	39	31	29	99	49	92	43	184

Tabelle 3: Häufigkeit der Verwendung der deutsche Sprache in Meetings.

Mit Bezug auf die Größe von Vereinen läßt sich sagen, daß 88,9% der Vereine der *Attitude Group* und 85,3% der Vereine der *Usage Group* in die Kategorie „weniger als 100 Mitglieder" fallen. Der von Fishman und Nahirny (1978,157) festgestellte Zusammenhang zwischen Spracherhalt und Vereinsgröße scheint also an Bedeutung verloren zu haben.

Interessant ist aber die Rolle von *somewhats* und *Some-User*. Obwohl diese Vereine relativ klein sind, scheinen sie bestens geeignet zu überleben. Das läßt sich z.b.
dadurch beweisen, daß *somewhats* und *Some-User* sowohl Mitglieder aus allen Altersgruppen als auch Generationen (s. Tabellen 2 und 3) einbeziehen. Meiner Meinung
nach wird in *somewhats* und *Some-User* das Bedürfnis nach symbolischer Ethnizität
und Sprache reflektiert. Die Verwendung von etwas Deutsch ist nämlich ein ausrei-
chender Marker für Ethnizität und entspricht damit, was Forscher marginale, situative
oder symbolische Ethnizität nennen (s. z.b. Salvaterra 1994:44; Brass 1996:86; Fishman und Nahirny 1978:157). Kurz gesagt bedeutet das, daß man sich selbst entscheidet, ob man seiner Ethnizität Ausdruck verleihen will oder nicht (s. Nash 1996:26).
Oft werden spezielle Situationen genutzt, um Ethnizität auszuleben, und bei solchen
Gelegenheiten fungieren z.b. Kleidung, Musik oder Sprache als Symbol der Ethnizität (s. Kreis 1996:29ff; Salvaterra 1994:44).

5   Vereine und Symbolismus

Kulturelle Organisationen sind oftmals Träger des ethnischen Symbolismus. Besonders deutsch-amerikanische Vereine verkörperten historisch gesehen die Auffassungen der Deutschen zu entscheidenden Mißverhältnissen im sozialen und kulturellen
Leben der USA (s. Conzen 1989:51), das sich grundlegend von deutschen Bedürfnissen und Vorstellungen unterschied. Vereine veranstalteten Feste, auf denen eine aufs
höchste sichtbare, sorgfältig ausgewählte und ritualisierte Kultur ausgeführt wurde (s.
Conzen 1989:45). Daher waren Vereine nicht einfach ein Nebenprodukt der Anpas-
sungsschwierigkeiten an amerikanische Verhältnisse, sondern entsprachen einem
Grundbedürfnis der Deutsch-Amerikaner nach Gesellig- und Gemütlichkeit. Vereine
stellten damit das „Kinderzimmer" für Ethnizität dar. Eine Ethnizität, die am ehesten
während eines Festes gespürt wurde. Kurz gesagt, eine Ethnizität nicht für jeden Tag,
sondern für den Feiertag (s. Conzen 1989:58). Damit werden zwei Sachverhalte erklärbar, nämlich erstens, daß Vereine in den USA noch immer vorhanden sind und
zweitens, daß die deutsch-amerikanische Gruppe am ehesten sichtbar ist während der
zahlreichen Oktober-, Mai- und Wurstfeste. Obwohl von der europäischen deutschsprachigen Kultur entscheidende Abweichungen bestehen, so besitzt die deutsch-amerikanische Kultur doch ihre Berechtigung.
Symbolismus existiert sowohl in nichtlinguistischer als auch linguistischer Form.
Beliebte nichtlinguistische Formen sind z.b. deutsche Gerichte, Trachten, Musik und
Tänze während linguistische Formen z.b. Namen und Begriffe sind.

5.1   Nichtlinguistische Symbole

5.1.1   Speisen

Spezielle deutsche Speisen und ihre Namen zählen zu den sehr sichtbaren und häufig
verwendeten Symbolen der deutsch-amerikanischen Ethnizität. Besonders bei Veranstaltungen werden diese Symbole als Teil der rituellen Kultur für unverzichtbar emp-

funden. Daher findet sich in Ankündigungen für Veranstaltungen auch eine weitreichende Verwendung dieser Namen. Beispiele sind u. a.

> „Come for a Schnitzel or Rouladen dinner between 12 - 1:30." (*Lancaster Liederkranz*)

> „Auf Zum Grössten Fest Der Schwaben – Mark your calender for this year's Volksfest! The
> 126th Volksfest will be held Labor Day Weekend ... Featuring ... Crafts, German Beer and
> Wines, German-American Singing and Dancing, Souvenirs, Shwäbische (sic!) Spezialitäten
> (Best German-American Food) – Sauer Braten * Heisser Leberkäse * Kartoffel-Salat * Maul-
> taschen * Spätzle * Bratwurst * Frankfurters * Heisser Zwiebelkuchen * Pflaumenkuchen *
> Zwetschgenkuchen * Laugenbretzeln and more!" (*Canstatter Volksfest*)"

Am häufigsten findet man Braten (einschließlich Roll-, Sauer-), Kuchen/Strudel (einschließlich Apfelkuchen, -strudel), Sauerkraut, Schnitzel (einschließlich Wiener-,
Jäger-, etc.), Spätzle (auch Spaetzle oder Spatzle), Torten (z.b. Schwarzwälder Kirsch-
torte), Wurst (besonders Brat- aber auch Knack-, Weisswurst). Natürlich darf auch
Bier (auch Weiss-, Bockbier) und Leberkäs(e) nicht fehlen.

Die Bedeutung von deutschen Gerichten wird auch dadurch deutlich, daß eine Reihe von Veranstaltungen nach deutschen Speisen benannt werden. So findet man z.b.
Wurstfest, aber auch *Schnitzel Dinner* oder *Bratwurst Essen*.

5.1.2 Kleidung

Kleidung ist wegen ihrer Sichtbarkeit eines der bedeutendsten ethnischen Symbole.
Kleidung unterscheidet Körper, die letztlich alle gleich aussehen würden, und stellt
damit eine identifizierbare Unterscheidung zwischen ihnen her (s. Isaacs 1975:43). In
den USA wird eine ganz bestimmter Kleidungsstil mit dem „Deutschtum" assoziiert.
Obwohl viele regionale Gruppen ihre eigene Festkleidung (sogenannte Trachten) besitzen, wird am häufigsten bayerische und tiroler Tracht mit Deutsch-Amerikanern in
Verbindung gebracht. Bei Veranstaltungen tragen vor allem Mitglieder von Vereinen
aber auch viele der Zuschauer Tracht als sichtbares Zeichen ihrer Zugehörigkeit zur
deutsch-amerikanischen Gruppe. Daher wird es auch nicht verwundern, wenn die
Namen für Trachten und Trachtenteile auch häufig in deutscher Sprache auftreten. Als
Beispiel ließe sich das folgende nennen:

> „Men's Tracht consists of black Lederhosen with either gold or green stickerei, traeger, (sus-
> penders), vest, blue check shirt, white shirt, knee-high stockings, stutzen (two-piece) stockings,
> hat with gamsbart, and black shoes." (*Schuhplattler Verein Alpenklang*)"

Am häufigsten wird *Dirndl*, *Lederhosen* und *Tracht* bzw. Trachten genannt.

5.1.3 Musik und Lieder

Musik verbindet die Deutschen im gemeinsamen Gefühl (s. Conzen 1989:69) und erzeugt bei Zuhörern in der Regel spezielle Gemütsbewegungen. Deswegen wurde Musik während des 1. Weltkrieges als eine der gefährlichsten Formen der deutschen Propaganda betrachtet und infolgedessen verboten (s. Finkelman 1993:184). Obwohl
nicht nur Gesang- und Musikvereine auf die Erhaltung der musikalischen Tradition

orientiert sind, so wird die Bedeutsamkeit von Musik für das deutsch-amerikanische kulturelle Erbe schon allein durch die Anzahl der Musik- (19) und Gesangvereine (44) deutlich.

Das allgegenwärtigste aller deutschen Lieder ist *Ein Prosit der Gemütlichkeit*, das bei jeder Gelegenheit auftauchen kann, wie das folgende Beispiel zeigt:

> „Following the business portion of the meetings, which last between 30 minutes to an hour and is frequently interrupted with the ‚*Ein Prosit*' song, the musicians of the club grab their instruments and the singing begins." (*Gesang-Verein of Virginia*)

Desweiteren ist Blasmusik, oder wie man in den USA sagt oompah-Musik, unverzichtbar für deutsch-amerikanische Veranstaltungen.

Wie auch bei Speisen und Kleidung, so werden auch Musiktexte und Liedtitel in der deutschen Sprache verwendet, obwohl ihr Erscheinen weniger uniform als bei Speisen und Kleidung ist. Häufiger findet man z.B. *Schneewalzer, Edelweiss, Rosamunde, O Tannenbaum* und natürlich *Ein Prosit*. Aber auch CDs und Kassetten, die von deutsch-amerikanischen Vereinen produziert werden, tragen häufig deutsche Namen wie *Ein Fest der Musik* (*Alpenfest*), *Ja das ist Blasmusik* (*Dorf Kapelle*) und *Eins, Zwei, Drei, Prost*.

5.2   Symbolische Sprache – sprachliche Symbole

Der symbolische Aspekt von Sprache bezieht sich auf die Art und Weise, wie Sprache als Symbol für Tradition, Erbe und Ethnizität fungieren kann (s. Edwards 1977: 262). Sprache besitzt ein zweifaches Potential zu symbolisieren. Zum einen kann sie andere Symbole ausdrücken und zum anderen selbst als Symbol fungieren (s. Fishman 1977:19). Als Ausdrucksform für andere Symbole wird Sprache oft verwendet wie oben für Speisen und Kleidung beschrieben. Als Symbol selbst können auch solche Dinge wie *schön sprechen* oder Vielseitigkeit der Sprache wichtig werden (s. Fishman 1977:25). In beiden Funktionen wird Sprache verwendet, um die Gruppe an das kulturelle Erbe zu erinnern und um Gruppenzugehörigkeit zu erreichen und damit andere auszuschließen (s. Giles et al 1977:307; Edwards 1977:257). Diese Funktion kann Sprache auch erlangen oder behalten, wenn kein weitreichender Sprachgebrauch mehr vorhanden ist (Edwards 1985:257). Ich behaupte, daß wenn Sprachgebrauch verloren geht, einzelne lexikalische Formen wie oben beschrieben den symbolischen Charakter der Sprache insgesamt übernehmen. Sprachbefähigung als solche ist nicht mehr relevant. Symbolische Sprache, die Verwendung einzelner Wörter und Phrasen, zieht alle Bedeutung auf sich und fungiert damit als Symbol für die Gruppenbestimmung.

5.2.1   Vereinsnamen

Namen scheinen die einfachsten, buchstäblichsten und einleuchtensten Symbole der Identitätsbestimmung (s. Isaacs 1975:46) und damit auch von Ethnizität zu sein. Namen haben etwas Magisches an sich und sind bedeutungstragend (s. Isaacs 1976:45), deshalb können Namen sowohl positive als auch negative Gefühle hervorrufen. Namen werden geändert, um sich an die *anderen* anzupassen und um eine bequeme Anonymität zu erreichen, in der wenigstens durch den Namen die Identität mit der dominanten Gesellschaft geteilt wird (Isaacs 1975:51). Gleichermaßen werden Namen verwendet, um sich von anderen abzugrenzen. Deutsch-amerikanische Vereine verwenden deshalb häufig Namen als Symbole für ihre Mitgliedschaft in der deutschamerikanischen Gruppe.

Häufig verwendete Symbole sind z.B. *Alp, Alpen* und Verbindungen mit diesen wie *Alpenröslein, Alpenland*, etc. Weiterhin finden wir auch *Enzian, Edelweiss, Liederkranz*, Verbindungen mit *Volks-* und *Rhein-*.

Die häufige Verwendung von Namen impliziert ihre Bedeutung für das ethnische Symbolsystem der Deutsch-Amerikaner. Namen besitzen Wiedererkennbarkeit, die ihnen erlaubt, als Symbol für das *Deutschtum* zu fungieren. Vereine, die aktiv einen Teil der deutschen Kultur ausüben, wie Tanz- und Gesangvereine, scheinen verstärkt solche Namen zu nutzen. Bei den von uns verwendeten Daten finden wir 12 Vereine, die *Edelweiss* in ihrem Namen tragen. Sieben dieser Vereine sind Schuhplattler. Weitere 4 tragen *Enzian* in ihrem Namen und sind ebenfalls Schuhplattler. Bei einer Betrachtung der 77 Vereine des *Gauverbands Nordamerika* stellen wir fest, daß 13 Vereine *Edelweiss*, 14 *Alpen*, 8 *Enzian* und 7 *Almrausch* in ihrem Namen tragen. Gesangvereine tragen traditionell Namen wie *Harmonie, Liederkranz, Teutonia* und *Germania*.

Interessant erscheint mir dabei, daß ein deutlicher Zusammenhang besteht zwischen der Sprache, die für den Namen verwendet wurde, und der Einstellung zum Sprachgebrauch bzw. dem Sprachgebrauch selbst. Deshalb tragen *positives* zu 41% einen rein deutschen Namen. Dasselbe gilt für 59,2% aller *User*. Auf der anderen Seite tragen *negatives* zu 51,7% und *Non-User* zu 53,5% einen rein englischen Namen.

5.2.2 Veranstaltungsnamen

Mehr noch als Vereinsnamen sind Veranstaltungsnamen ein deutlicher Beweis für die Bedeutung von symbolisch verwendeter Sprache. Veranstaltungsnamen erscheinen meistens ganz oder teilweise auf deutsch, und häufig sind sie die einzige Verwendung auf deutsch überhaupt. Typische Veranstaltungsnamen sind z.B. *Bierfest, Fasching, Oktoberfest* und *Sommerfest*. Insgesamt konnten etwa 167 verschiedene Namen gefunden werden.

Häufig verwendet werden Komposita mit *Fest* und *Abend*. Von allen 167 verschiedenen Namen konnte 42 mal *Fest* (z.B. *Alpen Fest, Gartenfest, Heritagefest)* und 21 mal *Abend* (z.B. *Gemütlichkeit Abend, Kameradschaftsabend*) gefunden werden. Bei Namen mit einem englischen Teil sind z.B. Namen mit *night* (*Polka Night, Wiener Night, Tiroler Night*) oder mit *dinner* (*Schnitzel Dinner*), aber auch Namen wie *German Fest, Hawaiian Nacht* und *Spaziergang-Picnics* zu finden.

5.2.3 Wörter mit ethnischer Bedeutung

Es gibt eine Reihe von Wörtern, die verwendet werden, um einen klaren ethnischen Bezug hervorzurufen. Viele dieser Wörter haben keinen eindeutigen *Counterpart* im Englischen, oder ihre Übersetzung umfaßt nicht das ganze Bedeutungspotential des deutschen Wortes. Beispiele sind z.b. Namen für Verantwortliche in Vereinen wie *Vortänzerin, Gaubeisitzer, Musikwart, Trachtenmutter, Gauarchivar* und *Gaurichter*.

Ein Wort, das wie kein anderes die deutsch-amerikanischen Befindlichkeiten und Bedürfnisse repräsentiert ist *Gemütlichkeit* (s. auch Bretting 1983:424; Kreis 1996: 98). Die Bedeutung dieses Wortes ist jedoch für das Individuum und für die Vereine so unklar wie nur irgend denkbar. Es beinhaltet eine vages Konzept, das es jedem Individuum erlaubt, seine eigene Bedeutung hineinzulegen (s. Cohen 1985). Der Begriff *Gemütlichkeit* wird umso dubioser, wenn man bedenkt, daß die Vorstellung, was dieser Begriff beinhaltet, sich für Deutsch-Amerikaner und Deutsche profund unterscheidet (s. z.B. Kreis 1996:99). Deutsch-Amerikaner verbinden Gemütlichkeit oft mit großen Festen und Veranstaltungen, wie die folgenden Beispiele belegen, wobei „es Besuchern aus Deutschland oft ungemütlich wird" (Kreis 1996:99):

> „Welcome to Heritagefest, a unique Old World celebration in which the entire city of New Ulm comes alive with reflections of times past. Gemütlichkeit abounds as thousands of visitors from the United States and abroad join in celebrating one of the top 100 festivals in North America." (*Heritagefest Minnesota*)

> „Oktoberfest – Held annually on the weekend after Labor Day. This event is attended by over 4,000 people on the weekend-long celebration. Many members and guest wear the traditional Lederhosen, Dirndls, Tyrolean hats. A real ‚Touch of Munich' with all of its ‚Gemütlichkeit' and fun." (*Boylston Schul-Verein*)"

Vereine sind unabdingbar mit Gemütlichkeit verbunden, da sie die Veranstaltungen ausrichten, auf denen Gemütlichkeit gefühlt und gelebt werden kann (s. z.B. Kreis 1996:8). Zusätzlich zu Gemütlichkeit finden wir auch andere Wörter wie *Kameraderie* oder *Kameradschaft, Stimmung* und *Gesellichkeit*.

Manche Wörter wie *Weihnachten* und *Volkslieder* würden ohne Probleme eine englische Übersetzung finden, trotzdem werden diese Wörter häufig auf deutsch verwendet. Diese Wörter tragen m.E. einen zusätzlichen Wert in sich. Das heißt, daß z.B. Wörter mit *Weihnacht-* nicht einfach nur auf Weihnachten (*Christmas*) hindeuten, sondern ihre Verwendung im Deutschen weist auf die Gefühlswerte hin, die mit dem deutschen Weihnachtsfest verbunden sind, „das nach landläufiger Auffassung die Deutschen am besten – stimmungsvollsten – zu feiern verstehen" (Kreis 1996:98). In gleicher Weise fängt eine Übersetzung von „Volkslieder" nicht die Bedeutung des Wortes ein. Amerikanische *folk songs* sind eben nicht vergleichbar mit Volksliedern.

6   Zusammenfassung

Vereine sind noch immer wichtige Mittler der ethnischen Kultur der Deutsch-Amerikaner, und sie sind in heutiger Zeit der einzige organisatorische Versuch, die deutschamerikanische Sprache und Kultur zu erhalten. Vereine sind damit die letzte Domäne der geschätzten Geselligkeit und Gemütlichkeit, die die Verwendung von ethnischen Symbolen bedingt. Diese Festlichkeit kann auch ohne eine weitreichende Sprachbeherrschung ausgelebt werden, was einen entscheidenden Hinweis darauf gibt, warum Vereine heutzutage noch immer eine Funktion und Überlebenschance besitzen und auch bei späteren Generationen beliebt sind. Sprache ist in ihrer symbolischen Form Bestandteil des Symbolsystems der Deutsch-Amerikaner und wird in dieser Form erhalten.

Wir haben aber auch gesehen, daß einige Vereine noch die deutsche Sprache verwenden. Ihre Überlebenschance ist jedoch begrenzt, was man an ihrer Altersstruktur und ihrer Attraktivität gegenüber späteren Generationen sieht. Die Zukunft der deutschen Sprache ist also weitestgehend auf ihre symbolische Funktion beschränkt.

7   Literatur

BRASS, Paul R. (1996): Ethnic Groups and Ethnic Identity Formation. In: Hutchinson, Smith (ed.): Ethnicity. Oxford – New York: Oxford University Press, 85-90.

BRETTING, Agnes (1983): „Little Germanies" in den Vereinigten Staaten. In: Zeitschrift für Kulturaustausch 32, 423-428.

CONKLIN, Nancy Faires; LOURIE, Margaret A. (1983): A Host of Tongues. Language Communities in the United States. New York: The Free Press.

EDWARDS, John (1985): Language, Society and Identity. Cambridge, Massachusets: Basil Blackwell.

— (1977): Ethnic Identity and Bilingual Education. In: Giles: 252-282.

FISHMAN, Joshua A. (1986): Demographische und institutionelle Indikatoren für die Erhaltung der deutschen Sprache in den USA 1960-1980. In: Trommler, Frank (ed.): Amerika und die Deutschen. Bestandsaufnahme einer 300-jährigen Geschichte. Opladen: Westdeutscher Verlag, 263-278.

— (1977): Language and Ethnicity. In: Giles: 15-57.

FISHMAN, Joshua A.; NAHIRNY, Vladimir C. (1978): Organizational and Leadership Interest in Language Maintenance. In: Fishman, J. (ed.): Language Loyalty in the United States. New York: Arno Press, 156-189.

GILES, H. (ed.) (1977): Language, Ethnicity and Intergroup Relations. London – New York – San Francisco: Academic Press.

ISAACS, Harold R. (1975): Basic Group Identity: The Idols of the Tribe. In: Glazer, Moynihan (ed.): Ethnicity. Theory and Experience. Cambridge and London: Harvard University Press, 29-52.

KREIS, Markus (1996): Von Einwanderern und Feierabenddeutschen. Forschungsbericht zur Geschichte und Gegenwart der Deutschamerikaner in Buffalo, N. Y. Dortmund: Fachhochschule Dortmund.

SALVATERRA, David L. (1994): Becoming American. Assimilation, Pluralism, and Ethnic Identity. In Walch, Timothy (ed.): Immigrant America. European Ethnicity in the United States. New York – London: Garland Publishing, Inc., 29-54.

Die Femininbildung der nomina agentis im Französischen und Italienischen zwischen Normierung und Varianz: aktuelle Tendenzen

Gabriele Birken-Silverman

Zu einem wichtigen Gegenstand der Sprachpolitik in Frankreich und Italien hat sich seit Mitte der 80er Jahre die Frage der sprachlichen Gleichstellung der Geschlechter entwickelt: mit dem Ergebnis einer Reihe ministerieller Erlasse und Empfehlungen, die Regelungen zur Beseitigung asymmetrischer Bezeichnungen im Bereich der Berufe, Funktionen und Titel beinhalten. Nach der durch die Ministerin für die Rechte der Frauen Roudy 1984 unter dem sozialistischen Premierminister Fabius verfügten Einsetzung einer *Commission ministérielle de terminologie pour la féminisation de titres* unter dem Vorsitz von Benoîte Groult – entgegen den Bedenken der Académie française – erfolgte am 11.3.86 die Veröffentlichung des vom Premierminister unterzeichneten *Circulaire relative à la féminisation des noms de métier, fonction, grade ou titre*, ein Dekret, das präskriptiv für die Verwaltungssprache sein sollte, allerdings nicht konsequent befolgt wurde. Am 6.3.98 folgte ein *Circulaire* des Bildungsministers Allègre und der Unterrichtsministerin Royal mit Feminisierungsregeln für Titel- und Funktionsträger im Bereich des Unterrichtswesens. Eine endgültige Entscheidung über die Feminisierungsregeln behielt man sich indessen bis zur Vorlage eines Abschlußberichts der *Commission* und der Ausarbeitung eines *Guide* durch das INaLF vor. In jüngster Zeit zeichnet sich nun in Frankreich ein rückwärts gerichteter Trend zur „Neutralisierung" in Form der Rückkehr zum generischen Maskulinum ab, eingeleitet durch den *Lettre sauveteur à la nation* der Académie Française (8.1.98) und ausgeführt in dem *Rapport sur la féminisation des noms de métier, fonction, grade ou titre* der *Commission générale de terminologie et de néologie* vom Oktober 1998, gefolgt vom Jahresbericht der Académie Française. Abgesehen von mehreren Schreiben an die zuständigen Ministerien gegen die Feminisierungsbestrebungen opponierender politisch rechtsstehender Senatsmitglieder[1] erhielt die Frage zunehmende Polemik mit dem erneuten Intervenieren der Académie Française durch Stellungnahmen ihres Sekretärs Druon (in *Le Figaro* 21.4.99) und das Erscheinen des *Guide* im Juni 1999 (Becquer et al. 1999) .

In Italien sollen laut Tavonis Ausführungen zum Thema *Sessismo e lingua italiana: nomi femminili di professioni e cariche* zunächst in den 50er Jahren sporadisch feminine Bezeichnungen wie *senatrice, deputatessa* in Gebrauch gekommen sein, worauf die Frauenbewegung in einem ersten Schritt mit Beanspruchung der – angeblich bis heute vorherrschenden – maskulinen Bezeichnungen reagierte und erst in einer zweiten Phase die Feminisierung der Bezeichnungen forderte, mit dem Resultat,

---

[1] Anfrage No. 05659 (29.1.98) von Serge Mathieu (Républicains et Indépendants) an das Ministère de Culture und No. 07102 (19.3.98) von Georges Gruillot (Rassemblement pour la République) an den Premier Ministre mit Anwortschreiben, ohne Antwort das Pro-Feminisierungsschreiben von Marie-Claude Beaudeau (CRC) (No. 09842) vom 23.7.98 an das Ministère de l'Education, in dem gefordert wird „que cette action doit encore gagner d'autres textes et investir de nouveaux espaces" (www.senat.fr./airs-cgi/dispatch).

daß 1986 und 1993 die *Presidenza del Consiglio ministeriale* die *Raccomandazioni per un uso non sessista della lingua italiana* von A. Sabatini herausgab, die im *Vocabolario della lingua italiana* von Zingarelli umgesetzt wurden. Indessen plädieren die Beiträge von Linguisten wie Lepschy (1987), Serianni (1997) und Tavoni (1998) für das „generische" Maskulinum und gegen präskriptive Feminisierungsregeln, während Fiorittos *Manuale di Stile* (1997) mit einem *Guida alla redazione dei documenti amministrativi* von M. E. Piemontese, hervorgegangen aus dem Projekt *Semplificazione del Linguaggio amministrativo* des Ministerrats, explizit für die Sichtbarmachung des weiblichen Geschlechts eintritt, u.a. durch Gebrauch der Titel statt *signora* und durch Splitting. Diesen sprachplanerischen Eingriffen gegenüber stehen der aktuelle Sprachgebrauch mit ausgeprägter Varianz: Akzeptanz oder aber Resistenz gegenüber den Innovationen (v.a. seitens der *Académie française*), eigene Entwicklungstendenzen sowie Vermeidungsstrategien. Im folgenden gilt das Interesse dem Abbau des generischen Mask., wie es sich in genusinvarianten Bezeichnungen manifestiert. Die Diskrepanz zwischen den sprachlenkenden Maßnahmen und ihrer Durchsetzung wird anhand eines Korpus aus der Pressesprache der Jahre 1996 bis dato untersucht (*Le Monde* (LM), *Le Figaro* (LF), *Corriere della Sera* (CS), *la Repubblica* (R)), und zwar im Hinblick auf die erscheinenden Varianten in Abhängigkeit von ideologischem Standort, Textsorte und Sprecherperspektive (d.h. Äußerungen Betroffener über sich selbst gegenüber. Mitteilungen über Betroffene). Zusätzlich werden die Internetseiten des fr. Senats, der *Assemblée nationale* und der *Camera dei Deputati* mit Informationen zu den einzelnen Volksvertretern und Sitzungsprotokolle herangezogen.

Die sprachplanerischen Initiativen in Frankreich und in Italien konstituieren den linguistischen Aspekt der Bestrebungen zur Durchsetzung der *parité des femmes* (vgl. das *Manifeste de la parité* 1996) bzw. der *pari opportunità*. Symptomatisch für die aktuellen soziokulturellen Rahmenbedingungen mögen folgende Verhältnisse sein: In Frankreich ging von 1992/93 bis 1996 der Anteil der mit höchsten politischen Ämtern beauftragten Frauen von 5,7% in der Nationalversammlung auf 5,5% zurück, d.h., unter den EU-Staaten nahm Frankreich in dieser Hinsicht den letzten Platz ein, während sich die Situation in Italien etwas besser darstellte (1992 Frauenanteil in der *Camera dei Deputati* 8%, im Senat 9,5%). Neuesten Daten für 1998 zufolge beträgt der Anteil der fr. Frauen im Senat 5%, in der Nationalversammlung 10,9%. Der linguistischen Debatte, bes. in bezug auf Berufe, Ämter und Titel an der Spitze der sozialen Hierarchie, kommt in Frankreich (u.a. im Mediendiskurs) ein zentraler Stellenwert zu, während das Problem in Italien nicht im Brennpunkt des öffentlichen Interesses steht.

Die zur Beseitigung der asymmetrischen Personenbezeichnungen ausgearbeiteten Regelungen beinhalten jeweils drei Lösungswege (s. Tab. 1):

1) Opposition durch f. Genusmarker.

Dieses Verfahren, im It. in Form der f. Genusendung *-a*, ist dort relativ unproblematisch unter der Voraussetzung des m. Genusmarkers *-o*, wirft hingegen Schwierigkeiten auf bei m. *-e*, da neben der Opposition mit dem f. Genusmarker *-a* zwei wietere Möglichkeiten offenstehen (Differentialgenus, Suffigierung mit *-essa*). Ähnlich problematisch ist dieser Fall im Fr., wo -e als oppositioneller Marker des Fem. fungieren kann, und zwar bei konsonantisch auslautendem Mask. mit je nach lautlicher Umgebung ggf. phonetischenVeränderungen des Basislexems und bei auf -é auslautendem Mask. mit lediglich graphematischer Funktion. Zusätzlich markiert hier indessen ggf. der Art. das Genus.

2) Die geschlechtsspezifische Differenzierung erfolgt mit den Mitteln der Wortbildung (Suffixe):

a) innovative Bildungen nach althergebrachten Mustern,

b) Tilgung von althergebrachten Verbindungen mit negativ konnotiertem Suffix.

	fr. Regelung		Sprach-gebrauch	it. Regelung		Sprach-gebrauch
1)	m.	f.	m./f.	m.	f.	m./f.
1) Opposition Genus- marker	-K président conseiller	-e présidente conseillère	président conseiller	-o segretario deputato	-a segretario deputata	segretario deputato
	-é député	-e députée	m./ f. député	-e	-a	
				-tor-e	-a	
2) Suffigie- rung	-(t)eur contrôleur chercheur	-(t)euse contrôleuse chercheuse	m./ f. contrôleur chercheur	-e dottore	-essa dottoressa	dottore, admin. dottoressa
	-teur directeur conservateur	-trice directrice conservatrice	m./ f. directeur conservateur	-tore direttore procuratore	trice direttrice procuratrice	direttore procuratore
				-tore	-essa	
3) Differen- tialgenus	le -K médecin	la chef		il/lo INVARIA- BILIA	la	il leader
	le -eur professeur	la	prof			
	le la -e ministre	la	le ministre	il/ lo presidente, -e	la docente	il presidente, il docente

Tabelle 1: Feminisierung der nomina agentis: Normierung und divergierender Sprachgebrauch.

Bes. die fr. Regelung ist hier auf Eliminierung des -esse-Suffix bedacht, während im It. im traditionellen Sprachgebrauch verankerte Fem. auf -essa offiziell erhalten bleiben, indessen besonders in der Verwaltungssprache als invariable Mask. auftreten. Ansonsten stellt fr. -(t)euse die f. Entsprechung der von Verbalstämmen abgeleiteten m. Bezeichnungen auf -(t)eur dar, vorausgesetzt t gehört zum Basisvb., oder dieses ist erkennbar. Ist diese Voraussetzung nicht gegeben, so entspricht dem m. -teur das f. -trice, im Falle -eur wird indessen Lösungsweg 3 (Differentialgenus) eingeführt. Im It. gilt als dominantes Prinzip Suff.-Wechsel -tore/ -trice, neben Abweichungen mit Suff.-Wechsel zu -essa oder reiner Genusmarkeropposition mit m. - tor-e und f. -tor-a.

Die Möglichkeit der Genusmarkierung durch Suff. ist dabei eingeschränkt durch die negativen Konnotationen etlicher f. Suff., die zwar referentiell genusspezifische Eindeutigkeit und Eigenständigkeit markieren, aber gleichzeitig konnotativ semantische Abwertung implizieren. Daher gilt es hier, solche vielfach im allgemeinen Sprachgebrauch übliche suffigierte Bildungen durch andere, nicht negative Assoziationen beinhaltende zu ersetzen.

3) Die Geschlechtsspezifizierung erfolgt lediglich mit grammatischen Mitteln durch attributive Modifikatoren im Syntagma (Differentialgenus).

Differentialgenus wird im Fr. für bestimmte Bezeichnungen eingeführt, deren m. Formen auf Konsonant, -eur oder -e muet enden. Im It. gilt es für Bezeichnungen auf -e und invariable Lehnwörter, überschneidet sich aber mit der Möglichkeit der Suffigierung. Als Lösungsmöglichkeit eliminiert wird der Gebrauch lexikalischer Mittel, d.h. von Attributen wie femme/donna. Gleichfalls nicht beschritten wird der etwaige Weg lexikalischer Neuschöpfungen.

Bemerkenswerterweise erfolgt eine Orientierung am traditionellen Sprachgebrauch in den im Internet veröffentlichten Informationen zu den Mitgliedern des fr. Senats und der *Camera dei Deputati*. Z.B.: it. *segretario della commissione parlamentare* (Maria Carazzi), *sottosegretario di Stato per il tesoro, il bilancio e la programmazione economica* (Laura Maria Pennacchi), *avvocato* (Maria Teresa Armosino) (vgl. *avvocata* (Bibelsprache mit Bezug auf die Gottesmutter), *avvocatessa* (negativ konnotiert)), *magistrato* (Tizia Parenti), *direttore didattico* (Valentina Aprea; Piera Capitelli), *ricercatore universitario* (Rosy Bindi), *dirigente politico* (Fulvia Bandoli), *docente universitario* (Maria Carazzi). Für sämtliche it. Abgeordnete weiblichen Geschlechts gilt ggf. der Hinweis: *già deputato nella legislatura XII*.

Eine Begründung für die Verwendung des generischen Mask. ist Serianni (1997: §57) zu entnehmen, die allerdings mit den Regeln im Zingarelli kontrastiert:

„L'uso di lasciare invariato al maschile il nome di professione si ha invece quando il significato della funzione o della carica, in senso astratto o onorifico, prevale rispetto alla designazione del sesso di chi la esercita."

Analoges trifft auch für das Fr. zu, so daß hier ein pragmasemantisches Kriterium zur Begründung der Varianz eingeführt wird. Explizit differenziert der fr. Rapport der *Commission* vom Oktober 1998 gegenüber den vorangegangenen Regelungen zwischen personenbezogenen Berufsbezeichnungen einerseits und auf juristische Personen bezogenen Bezeichnungen von Titel, Funktion und Grad in der Weise, daß lediglich erstere m. und f. Formen zur Referenz auf Individuen hätten, letztere hingegen Neutra darstellten, die durch das generische Mask. repräsentiert seien. D.h., entsprechend dem in Frankreich in die Debatte eingeführten Argument soll eine Unterscheidung zwischen natürlichen Personen einerseits und juristischen Personen andererseits gelten, derart daß letztere durch invariantes Neutrum – also generisches Mask. – sprachlich zu bezeichnen seien. Diesem in dem Rapport geregelten institutionellen und juristischem Sprachgebrauch folgt der fr. Senat (Frauenanteil 1998: 5%) in seinem Mitgliederverzeichnis mit Vitae (http://www.senat.fr): *vice-président* (Marie-Madeleine Dieulongard), *conseiller général* (Annick Bocardé), *conseiller municipal* (Josette Durieu), *adjoint* (Marie-Madeleine Dieulongard). Bemerkenswerterweise erfolgt weniger konsequente Orientierung an den traditionellen Normen seitens der *Assemblée Nationale* (Frauenanteil 1998: 10,9%): *présidente de droit* bzw. *présidente de la commission des lois* (Catherine Tasca), *conseillère des services de l'Assemblée Nationale* (Corinne Luquiens), *conseillère des services du Sénat* (Camille Mangin), aber: *représentant de la Commission des affaires étrangères* (Michèle Alliot-Marie), *représentant de la commission des affaires sociales* (Annick Bocandé). Aus den Sitzungsprokollen: *En réponse la ministre a apporté les éléments suivants/En réponse aux intervenants, la ministre a donné les éléments d'informations suivants* (4.5.99), *Présidence de Mme Nicola Catala, vice-présidente/ Mme la présidente/ Mme la ministre* (Catherine Trautmann, ministre de la culture et de la communication) (20.5.99). Dieser Sprachgebrauch entspricht der in der offiziellen Sprachregelung reflektierten Präferenz der Betroffenen, dem Wunsch nach Beseitigung der Asymmetrie und Sichtbarmachung des Geschlechts,[2] während die Einstellung der betroffenen it. Frauen gerade umgekehrt ist.

Die Untersuchung der Akzeptanz der Richtlinien und Empfehlungen im Sprachgebrauch der Medien, denen eine besondere Rolle für die Implantation der Regelungen zukommt, ergibt als Parameter der auftretenden Variation

1) den ideologischen Standort,
2) die Textsorte,
3) die Sprecherperspektive und
4) die Erörterung eigener Wege und Vermeidungsstrategien.

In bezug auf den ideologischen Standort zeichnet sich ab, daß zwar in allen sondierten Printmedien Schwankungen auftreten, doch primär LM weitgehend bemüht ist, die neuen Normen umzusetzen, während der konservativ orientierte LF tendenziell an der traditionellen Asymmetrie der Personenbezeichnungen festhält bzw. alte und neue Varianten nebeneinander verwendet; d.h., in Abhängigkeit von der ideologischen Ausrichtung variieren hier die nomina agentis je nach Tageszeitung.

Le Monde: Christa Randzio-Plath [...] a été longtemps *avocate* (2.3.99), Hélène Arnaud-Roueche, *avocate* de formation (2.3.99), Gloria Alfred, *avocate* spécialisée dans les conflits (17.8.97); *la présidente* Biljana Plavsic (6.9.97), *la présidente* du Parlement, Nicole Fontaine (30.8.99); *conseillère* municipale (4.6.97); Yvette Roudy, *député* PS (27.8.97) – Angela Eagle, *députée* travailliste et secrétaire d'Etat (13.9.97); Maija Runcis, *chercheur* au département d'histoire (27.8.97); Margaret Maruani est *directrice* de recherche (9.3.99); *le secrétaire d'Etat* américain, Madeleine Albright (1.9.97) – *la secrétaire d'Etat* américaine, Madeleine Albright (2.3.99); *la commissaire* européenne, Emma Bonino (31.7.99) – *le commissaire* européen, Emma Bonino (30.9.97; 4.7.97); *la juge* Marie-Odile Bertella-Geffroy (7.6.97) – *le juge* Susan Webber Wright (24./25.8.97), *le juge* Christine Schlumberger (7.6.97), les étranges déboires *du juge* Eva Joly (9.9.97)
Le Figaro: *l'avocat général*, Evelyne Lesieur (25.2.99) – *l'avocate* Gisèle Halimi a remis ses propositions pour féminiser le monde politique (7.3.97), Marie-Hélène Mattei, *avocate* de la Cuncolta (15.5.97); Sophie d'Hélias, *président* de Franklin Global Investor Services (30.5.97) – Marie-José Forissier, *présidente* d'Initiative Media Worldwide (23.5.97), Mary Robinson, *présidente* de l'Irlande (9.3.97); Marie-Aimée Latournerie a été nommée membre *conseiller d'Etat* (28.2.99),

---

[2] „La cause de la féminisation des titres et fonctions avait progressé lorsque les femmes du gouvernement Jospin avaient demandé à être nommées *„Madame la ministre'."* (Bernard 1.7.98, 32).

conseiller municipal (2.5.97), *conseiller géneral* (7.3.97, 17.8.97) – Sophie Berrogain, *conseillère* hors classe de la chambre régionale (28.2.99), cette militante de Seine-Maritime, *conseillère* d'insertion en milieu pénitentiaire (11.7.97); Emmanuelle Bouquillon, 35 ans, *député* UDF (7.3.97), Marie-Josée Roig, le maire RPR d'Avignon, *député* (28.5.97), *député* européen en 1979 (Emma Bonino) (9.3.99) – *députée* européenne (9.3.97) – *le député* RPR Nicole Catala (10.3.99) – Nicole Catala, *députée* RPR sortante (30.5.97); Michèle Ressi (...) est (...) *chercheur* au CRS (21.5.97) – May Chartoni-Dubarry, *chercheuse* à l'Ilfri [Institut français des relations internationales] (23.2.99); Suzan Michelson, *directeur* de recherche (...) à l'Institut Pasteur (25.2.99); *le secrétaire d'Etat* américain Madeleine Albright (17.2.99, 22.2.99, 24.2.99) – les entretiens de *la secrétaire d'Etat* (2.3.99); *le commissaire* européen (Emma Bonino) (9.3.99), Edith Cresson (...) *commissaire* européen (29.5.96); *le juge* d'instruction, Chantal Perdrix (21.5.97)

Ein Vergleich der Belege von 1996-1999 zeigt, daß LM – mit wenigen Ausnahmen – die Regeln der Feminisierung umsetzt, während LF in den Jahren 1996/97 noch ausgeprägte Tendenzen zur Verwendung des generischen Mask. aufwies, die nunmehr allerdings weitgehend den Richtlinien angepaßt worden sind – ausgenommen einige wenige Fälle, die symbolisch die politische Couleur repräsentieren: der Sprachgebrauch *le ministre* zeichnet den politisch Rechtsstehenden gegenüber *la ministre* der Linken aus. Im it. Bereich hingegen sind sowohl CS als auch R durch das jeweilige Variantenspektrum bis hin zum heterogenen Gebrauch verschiedener Formen innerhalb eines Beitrags gekennzeichnet.

La Repubblica: la nipote del duce, *deputata* napoletana (25.4.96) – Alessandra Mussolini, *deputato* di An (2.8.96) – Franca Gambato (...) *la deputata* più giovane (9.5.96, 4), Nilde Iotti, *deputata* del Pds (15.8.96), Maria Rita Lorenzetti, *deputata* di Foligno (19.5.96), *deputata* della X legislatura (Anna Finocchiaro) (18.5.96), il testo presentato dalla *deputata* progressista (Giovanna Melandri) (2.8.96); *la presidente* della Camera Irene Pivetti (22.4. 96, 23.4.96) – *il presidente* delle comunità ebraiche in Italia Tullia Zevi (26.4.96), *il nuovo presidente* della Liberia (Ruth Perry) (19.8.96), *il presidente* dei giovani industriali della Confindustria, Emma Marcegaglia (10.7.96); Husniya Jabarra (...) *docente universitario* (20.5.99) – il caso *della docente* che lascia la cattedra (25.5.96); Pamela Harriman, *ambasciatore* americano (23.4.96)

Corriere della Sera: Alessandra Mussolini, *deputato* di Alleanza Nazionale (1.4.96), Cristina Matranga, rieletta *deputato* di Forza Italia (10.5.96), Laura Pennacchi, *deputato* (13.6.96), eletta per la prima volta *deputato* (Livia Turco) (18.5.96) – *deputata* del PCI (Anna Finocchiaro) (18.5.96), *deputata* ds (Giovanna Melandri) (3.2.99); *la presidente* della camera Irene Pivetti (4.4.96, 8.5.96), *la presidente* della Camera ha preso parte a una cena (14.4.96) – *il presidente* della Camera Irene Pivetti (14.4.96, Bildtitel) – *la presidente* (della Rai, Letizia Moratti) (4.4.96), *dalla presidente* dell'associazione (Federcasalinghe), Federica Rossi Gasparrini (18.4.97), lo scontro fra *la presidente*, cioè Biljana Plavsic, (3.7. 97), il cancello della residenza *del presidente* Mary Robinson (3.4.96), Maria Teresa Salvemini, *docente* universitaria, 60 anni, tre figli ed un marito (23.5.96), *ambasciatrice* della Gran Bretagna (Diana) (18.4.96)

Die scheinbar disparate Varianz wird in der Grammatik von Serianni (1997: §58) folgendermaßen kommentiert:

„Raramente però iniziative politiche del genere hanno poi una reale influenza sul comportamento linguistico collettivo. Le numerose oscillazioni nell'uso per i nomi di professione femminile sono dovute al fatto che, qui più che in altri casi, la lingua riflette la situazione di una società in movimento. Càpita dunque che in uno stesso articolo di giornale chi scrive adotti soluzioni differenti a seconda del nome da trattare al femminile."

Indessen zeichnen sich bei der Sondierung einer genügend großen Zahl von Belegen doch gewisse Tendenzen des Sprachgebrauchs in den beiden Printmedien ab: Soll herausgestellt werden, daß es sich um Funktionsträger weiblichen Geschlechts handelt, erscheint *deputata* (nahezu durchgängig in R), steht die Funktion im Vordergrund, *deputato* (fast durchweg im CS). Umgekehrte Verhältnisse scheinen im Falle *il/la presidente* vorzuliegen: R stellt die Funktion mit männlichem Geschlecht heraus, während CS das weibliche Geschlecht als bemerkenswerte Abweichung hervorhebt – ausgenommen, es handelt sich um das höchste Staatsamt. Das f. Genus wird besonders dann markiert, wenn die Funktionsträgerin in negativem Kontext erscheint, während in neutralem Kontext das „neutrale" generische Mask. verwendet wird, z.b. *la proposta che la commissaria europea lancia a Romano Prodi* (CS 14.5.96), *la polemica della commissaria* (Emma Bonino) (CS 22.4.97), *Emma Bonino, commissario europeo* (CS 14.5.96) (Bildtitel). Invariabel bleiben generell: *ministro,*[3] *sindaco,*[4] *giudice, magistrato, arbitro, dirigente, avvocato.* Ironische und abwertende Konnotationen werden in diesen (wie in anderen Fällen) durch Suffigierung mit *-essa* ausgedrückt. Die Resistenz gegenüber den neuen Regelungen äußert sich ferner durch Festhalten an der Markierung durch *donne* bzw. *femme*: it. *l'arbitro donna* (CS 3.4.96), *donne leader* (R 8.5.96), *donne soldato, capo di Stato donna* (R 19.8.96), *la donna-notaio star* (Vincenza Ardito) (CS 21.4.97), *una donna magistrato* (R 25.8.96), fr. *première femme pilote d'un bombardier B-52 de l'US Air-Force, le lieutenant Kelly Flinn* (LF 21.5.97), *une femme policier* (LM 4.7.97). Ironische Konnotationen vermittelt *signora* + Funktion: *la signora sottosegretario* (CS 3.6.96).

In bezug auf die Textsorten zeichnet sich zum einen entsprechend der ideologischen Ausrichtung des LF die Resistenz gegenüber den Neuerungen gleichermaßen in den publizierten Leserbriefen ab. Nach domänenspezifischen Bereichen sind es hier wie auch im it. CS vor allem Wirtschaft und Politik, die in erheblichem Maße an den traditionellen asymmetrischen Bezeichnungen festhalten. Eine besondere Rolle spielen dabei die im CS publizierten öffentlichen Bekanntmachungen als die Verwaltungssprache, die den ministeriellen Erlassen praktisch keine Beachtung schenkt.

Während die Regelungen auf die Implementation von Wortbildungsmustern zur Beseitigung der Asymmetrie der Bezeichnungen, zur Sichtbarmachung der Frauen und zur Tilgung abwertender Suff. zielen, stellt sich jedoch beim Sprachgebrauch den Betroffenen das Problem semantischer Konnotationen in gleicher Weise bei einem Großteil der als Fem. markierten Varianten, d.h., die Marker werden als Indices für Zweitklassigkeit und Abwertung aufgefaßt, so daß mit diesem Argument auch betr. Frauen für Genusinvarianz, d.h. traditionellen Gebrauch des Mask. plädieren. Z.B heißt es über die Schlichterin („le premier médiateur") der Electricité de France in LF Economique (22.4.99,VII): „Au risque de susciter la colère de Ségolène Royal, elle tient à ce qu'on l'appelle ‚le' médiateur. „Le nom de la fonction est neutre et indépendant de la personne qui l'exerce; explique-t-elle. Féminiser les titres est une querelle qui me

---

[3] Aber vgl.: *il radoppio delle donne Ministro in questo Governo* in einem Grußwort der Präsidentin der *Commissione Nazionale per la Parità e le Pari Opportunità*, Silvia Costa, (Todi, 7 Nov. 98) (http://www.palazzochigi.it/istituzionale/todi.html)
[4] Aber vgl.: dalla sindaca di Todi, Katiuscia Marini (ibid.)

semble vaine. Ce n'est pas un enjeu." Diese Haltung dient wiederum in den Medien der Legitimation des Festhaltens an den traditionellen Varianten.

Eigene Entwicklungswege deuten sich insofern an, als Genusinvarianz oder aber symmetrisch verteilte m. und f. Formen bei ein- und demselben Lexem mit semantischer Differenzierung verbunden werden: *le secrétaire* für die höchste Kategorie, *la secrétaire* (selten hingegen *le secrétaire*) für eine Bürokraft. Weitere Beispiele: fr. *Kathleen Domange, directeur de l'UFR de langues [Unité de formation et de recherche de l'Université nouvelle de Clergy-Pontoise]* (LF.3.97) – *Anny Laroche, directrice de Point Math* (LF 5.3.97), it. *Lucia Annunziata, direttore del Tg3* (CS 10.4.97) – *Irene Pizzimenti, direttrice del circolo didattico* (CS 18.4.96), *Bia Sarasini, direttrice della rivista Noidonne* (CS 16.7.97).

Weitere eigene Lösungswege bietet die graphische Darstellung, mittels derer besonders LF und CS ironische Konnotationen einführen: Gebrauch von Klammern im Fließtext, Gebrauch des bestimmten Artikels in Anführungszeichen, die metasprachliche Informationen beinhalten, gleichermaßen mit Fragezeichen versehene Einschübe in Klammern.

Nach diesem kurzen Ausschnitt aus dem Status Quo der Feminisierung der Bezeichnungen für Berufe, Funktionen, Titel und Grade in Frankreich und Italien stellt sich abschließend die Frage nach einer Zukunftsprognose der sprachlichen Entwicklungen. Für Frankreich, wo das Problem ein wahres Politikum darstellt, deutet sich an, daß das zunächst die sprachliche Gleichstellung fördernde staatliche Eingreifen nun vielmehr umgekehrt diese Entwicklung zu bremsen trachtet, indem zum einen differenziert wird zwischen Berufsbezeichnungen im engsten Sinne und höhere Qualifikationen implizierenden Bezeichnungen, die auch Titel, Grad und Funktion implizieren können, darunter besonders solche, die in Beziehung zum Staat stehen; zum anderen wird unterschieden zwischen offizieller Sprachnorm und *langage familier*. Dabei gilt die Feminisierung grosso modo für solche Berufe, die nicht etwa in Bezug zum Staate oder zu Institutionen stehen und eine Karriere implizieren sowie für die *langage familier*. In Italien wirkt weiterhin die Ideologie der freien Entwicklung des Sprachgebrauchs auf der Basis der mit höherem Prestige behafteten „generischen" männlichen Berufsbezeichnungen.

Literatur

BECQUER, Annie et al. (1999): Femme, j'écris ton nom. Guide d'aide à la féminisation des noms de métiers, grades et fonctions. Paris: La documentation française.

BERNARD, Philippe: L'éducation nationale féminise les intitulés des ses titres et fonction. In: Le Monde 1.7.98, 32.

DRUON, Maurice: Lettre ouverte à M. le premier ministre sur la langue française. L'Italie mussolinienne, l'Allemagne hitlérienne, la Russie stalinienne ont connu de ces tentatives de changements arbitraires de leur langue nationale. In: Le Figaro 21.4.99, 32.

LA LANGUE FRANÇAISE. Extrait du rapport de la commission générale de terminologie. Résumé des observations et des recommandations de la commission, http://www.culture.fr./culture/dglf/rapport/rap-act-98/extrait-termino.html.

FIORITTO, Alfredo (1997): Manuale di stile. Bologna: Mulino.

HOUSSIN, Monique (1997): Le féminin entre crochets. Entretien avec Benoîte Groult. (http://www. regards.fr/archives/1997/199702/199702cit.06.html)

LEPSCHY, Giulio (1987): Sexism and the Italian Language In: The Italianist 7, 158-169.

— (1989): Lingua e sessismo. In: Lepschy, Giulio: Nuovi saggi di linguistica italiana. Bologna: Mulino, 61-84.

REY-DEBOVE, Josette (1999): Féminisation de la langue: une affaire d'usage. In: Le français dans le monde 304, mai-juin 1999.

ROUSSEAU, Jean (1998): „Madame la Ministre". La féminisation des noms en dix questions. (http://www.ciep.fr/chroniq/femi/femi.htm)

SAINT-CRIQ, Régine; Prévost, Nathalie (1993): Vol au-dessus d'un nid de machos. Paris: Michel.

SERIANNI, Luca (1997): Italiano. Grammatica, sintassi, dubbi. Milano: Ed. Torinese.

SGROI, Salvatore Claudio (1998): Una questione di democrazia linguistica ovvero come semplificare il linguaggio burocratico-amministrativo. In: Bolletino di Atteneo 1, http://www-lex.sistemia.it/ bdahtml/boll 1-98/linguaggio.htm.

TAVONI, Mirko (1998): La norma dell'italiano oggi: Frequently Asked questions, http://www.italica. rai.it/01txt/5livello/facolta/lingua/tavoni).

Quintilians Einstellung gegenüber seiner Muttersprache
Ein Kapitel zum Sprachbewußtsein in der römischen Antike

Thorsten Fögen

1   Vorbemerkungen

Kaum ein anderer lateinischer Autor hat sich nach Cicero so ausführlich über den Stellenwert seiner Muttersprache geäußert wie Quintilian. Zwar ist seine *Institutio oratoria*, deren Abfassung und Veröffentlichung Adamietz (1986:2247f) überzeugend auf den Zeitraum zwischen 86 und 96 n. Chr. datiert, auf Rhetorik und deren Vermittlung ausgerichtet, dabei insbesondere auf die Ausbildung des vollkommenen Redners; jedoch werden im Verlauf dieses Werkes zahlreiche Aspekte gestreift, die über rein rhetorische Belange hinausgehen, so z.B. die grammatische Unterweisung des Rhetorikschülers sowie pädagogische Prinzipien. Es werden zusätzlich immer wieder sprachliche Fragen thematisiert, die höchst aufschlußreiche Einblicke in Sprachbewußtseinsformen der Epoche Quintilians vermitteln. Dabei greift der Autor verständlicherweise vielfach auf Überlegungen zurück, die in ähnlicher Form bereits von Cicero formuliert worden waren (zu Cicero cf. Fögen 2000a, aber auch Fögen 1999). Andererseits wird rasch deutlich, daß Quintilian trotz solcher Anlehnungen an sein großes Vorbild dessen Blickwinkel nicht nur erweitert, sondern in zentralen Punkten überdies zu einer anderen Einschätzung kommt, vor allem in Hinblick auf die Bewertung der Elaboriertheit und Leistungsfähigkeit der lateinischen Sprache.

2   Der Sprachvergleich in *Inst. orat.* 12.10

Die ausführlichste zusammenhängende Gegenüberstellung von Charakteristika der lateinischen und griechischen Sprache findet sich im zehnten Kapitel von Buch 12 der *Institutio oratoria*. Eigentliches Thema von *Inst. orat.* 12.10 sind die Stilgattungen der Rede. Deren Verschiedenheit sei in erster Linie dadurch bedingt, daß die Kunstfertigkeiten der Redner keineswegs einheitlich ausgeprägt seien und daß sich auch beim Publikum kein uniformer Geschmack ausmachen lasse. Statt dessen herrsche eine bunte Vielfalt, die das immer wieder thematisierte Konzept des *orator perfectus* letztlich als reine Utopie erscheinen lassen (12.10.2). Mit dem Hinweis auf die regional unterschiedlichen Verhältnisse, die für die Geschmacksbildung verantwortlich sein können, ist ein zentraler Punkt angedeutet, der schon ganz zu Beginn erwähnt worden war und im weiteren Verlauf des Kapitels zugespitzt wird: So wie sich griechische und etruskische Statuen deutlich voneinander unterschieden, so wichen auch asianische Redner von ihren attischen Fachkollegen ab (12.10.1). Im Anschluß an einen überleitenden Überblick über die Entwicklung der griechischen Malerei und Bildhauerkunst (12.10.3-9) folgt eine Betrachtung über die einzelnen Epochen zunächst der römischen und dann ansatzweise der griechischen Rhetorik (12.10.10-26). Die römischen Redner

unterteilt Quintilian nach drei Gruppen: In die Frühphase, die trotz gewisser Rauh-
heiten bereits hervorhebenswerte Qualitätsmerkmale aufweise, gehörten z.b. Laelius,
die Scipionen, Cato und die Gracchen. Als Vertreter der *media forma* werden Crassus
und Hortensius genannt, bis schließlich die eigentliche Blütezeit der römischen Rhetorik mit Größen wie Caesar, Caelius, Calidius, Pollio, Messala, Calvus, Brutus, Sul-
picius und Cassius einsetze, die dann später durch Seneca, Africanus, Afer und andere
weitergeführt worden sei (12.10.10f). Eine Sonderstellung müsse trotz aller Kritik
Cicero zugeschrieben werden, da er alle für einen Redner denkbaren Vorzüge in seiner Person vereine (12.10.12-15). Vor allem solche Redner, die sich selbst den At-
tikern zurechneten, hätten mit ihrem überzogenen Stilideal – in Wirklichkeit einer
Pervertierung der Forderung nach einem einfachen und gesunden Stil (*sanitas*) – die
strahlende Redekraft Ciceros abgelehnt (12.10.14f).

Dieser Einschub dient als Überleitung zu einer Erörterung der unterschiedlichen
Wesenszüge attischer und asianischer Beredsamkeit, in deren Rahmen auch die her-
ausragenden griechischen Redner kurz charakterisiert werden: Während sich die *Attici* durch gesunde Knappheit und Verzicht auf überflüssiges Beiwerk auszeichneten,
fielen am asianischen Stil dessen Schwulst und Hohlheit, also das Fehlen des richtigen Maßes, auf (12.10.16). Es folgt nun eine aufschlußreiche Erklärung für die historische Entwicklung dieser beiden Stilrichtungen, die insbesondere der spätrepublika-
nische Philologe Santra vertreten zu haben scheint: Als sich das Griechische in Klein-
asien auszubreiten begann, hätten dortige Einwohner, die sich trotz ihrer fehlenden
ausreichenden Sicherheit in der griechischen Sprache mit der Redekunst auseinander-
setzten, mangels Kenntnis treffender, „eigentlicher" Wörter (*ea, quae proprie signari
poterant*, also κύρια ὀνόματα) zu Umschreibungen ihre Zuflucht genommen; diese
ursprünglichen Notlösungen seien aber im kleinasiatischen Raum trotz längst konso-
lidierter Griechischkenntnisse allmählich zu einem festen Stilmerkmal der dortigen
Redner geworden (12.10.16). Quintilian selbst hält jedoch eine andere Deutung für
wahrscheinlicher: Der Unterschied zwischen den beiden Stilrichtungen liege in den
diametral entgegengesetzten regionalen Wesensarten der Bewohner Attikas und
Kleinasiens begründet. Es kennzeichne die attische Mentalität mit ihrem verfeinerten
Gespür, daß ihr ein hohles Wortgeklingel fremd sei. Die *Asiana gens* dagegen sei von
Hause aus aufgeblasener und neige zu Prahlerei, was sich auch in Sprache und Stil nie-
derschlage (12.10.17). Bestimmte Charaktereigenschaften, die zusammengenommen
die Mentalität einer regional begrenzten Gruppe von Sprechern konstituieren, werden
also hier für das Vorhandensein typischer Stilmerkmale verantwortlich gemacht. Die
gleiche Denkweise liegt dann auch zugrunde, wenn die Stilart, die zwischen Asianis-
mus und Attizismus anzusiedeln sei, als „rhodische" (*genus Rhodium*) bezeichnet wird
(12.10.18f). Im weiteren Verlauf (12.10.20-26) räumt Quintilian mit der These auf,
daß die von ihm eindeutig bevorzugten attischen Redner einen gänzlich einheitlichen
Stil aufwiesen: Die Begabungen griechischer Rhetoren manifestierten sich in zahlreichen Stilformen. Attische Züge fänden sich auch bei solchen Rednern, die man allgemein nicht zu den Attizisten im engeren Sinne rechne. Zu rigorose Aufteilungen ver-
kennten, daß die Wendung „attisch reden" nichts anderes besage als „aufs beste reden" (12.10.26, zuvor schon 12.10.21).

Soweit zum Hintergrund des nun folgenden, für unsere Fragestellung eigentlich interessanten Abschnitts, der sich über *Inst. orat.* 12.10.27-39 erstreckt: Attischen Vorbildern, so heißt es zu Beginn des weiteren Gedankenganges, im Medium der lateinischen Sprache nachzueifern, sei aus verschiedenen Gründen nur sehr schwer möglich. Dies sei vor allem durch die lautlichen Eigenarten des Lateinischen bedingt, die eine Nachahmung griechischen Wohlklangs ausschlössen. Bestimmte griechische Buchstaben wie υ und ζ[1], die einen unvergleichlichen lautlichen Genuß beim Hörer evozierten, existierten im Lateinischen nicht, während wiederum andere klanglich düstere und ungeschliffene Buchstaben (12.10.28: *tristes et horridae*) nur in der lateinischen, nicht aber in der griechischen Sprache aufträten[2]. Das Defizit des Lateinischen ist also ein doppeltes: Zum einen entbehrt es zwei euphonische Buchstaben, zum anderen besitzt es – gleichsam als kläglichen Ersatz dafür – zwei Ungetüme, die das Griechische nicht kennt. In der Forschung ist es nach wie vor umstritten, um welche beiden Buchstaben es sich bei der letzteren Gruppe handelt: Hahn (1941:31) vertrat die Auffassung, Quintilian meine *f* und das konsonantische *u* (F), auf die er im anschließenden Passus ausführlicher eingehe. Austin (1943:11f; wiederholt in 1946: 20) dagegen plädierte zunächst für *f* und *q* und sah den eingeschobenen Hinweis Quintilians auf das konsonantische *u* lediglich durch seine graphische Nähe zum griechischen Digamma (F) begründet. In seinem Kommentar zum 12. Buch der *Institutio oratoria* verwirft er jedoch diese Position und schließt sich der Meinung Hahns unter Ergänzung folgender Begründung an: *f* sei im lateinischen Alphabet der sechste Buchstabe, ganz so wie das ζ im griechischen. Das gleiche gelte für das konsonantische *u*, das wie das griechische υ die zwanzigste Position im Alphabet einnehme (dagegen aber Coleman 1963:12); gegen das *q* als solches Stellung zu beziehen, könne nicht Quintilians Absicht gewesen sein, da dieses im Griechischen als Buchstabe κ ebenfalls auftrete (1948:237f). Coleman (1963:10-18) hat einige Zeit danach die komplizierte Frage wieder aufgenommen und gewichtige Argumente dafür vorbringen können, daß Quintilian mit den als *tristes et horridae* umschriebenen Buchstaben durchaus *f* und *q* gemeint habe, die anders als das dem Digamma entsprechende konsonantische *u* nicht im Griechischen vorkämen.

Die einzelnen Aspekte der zum Teil sehr verwickelten Debatte hier im Detail erneut zu verfolgen, kann nicht unsere Aufgabe sein. Wir begnügen uns daher mit der folgenden Feststellung: Quintilian spricht der griechischen Sprache deshalb einen hö-

---

[1] Daß es sich bei den *iucundissimas ex Graecis litteras* eindeutig um υ und ζ handeln muß und nicht etwa, wie früher vermutet, um υ und φ, haben die Arbeiten von Hahn (1941) und Austin (1943) gezeigt. Cf. zuvor aber schon den Hinweis bei Sturtevant (1940:121 n. 49).

[2] *Inst. orat.* 12.10.27f: *namque est ipsis statim sonis durior, quando et iucundissimas ex Graecis litteras non habemus (vocalem alteram, alteram consonantem, quibus nullae apud eos dulcius spirant, quas mutuari solemus, quotiens illorum nominibus utimur. quod cum contingit, nescio quo modo velut hilarior protinus renidet oratio, ut in 'zephyris' et 'zopyris': quae si nostris litteris scribantur, surdum quiddam et barbarum efficient), et velut in locum earum succedunt tristes et horridae, quibus Graecia caret.* Der hier zitierte Text ist von Austin (1943:9) übernommen, der im Anschluß an erste dahingehende Schritte Madvigs den in Klammern gesetzten Text als Parenthese auffaßt und damit für das Verständnis der beiden Paragraphen einen entscheidenden Fortschritt erbrachte.

heren ästhetischen Stellenwert zu, weil sie sowohl durch das Vorhandensein als auch durch das Fehlen bestimmter Laute klangliche Merkmale aufweise, über die das Lateinische nicht verfügt. Kennzeichnend für das Lateinische seien neben den schon erwähnten Merkmalen ferner Wortschlüsse mit dem nach einem Kuhlaut klingenden -*m*, für das das Griechische das ungleich lieblichere v setze (12.10.31). Einen ähnlich rauhen Klangeindruck böten Wortendungen auf -*b* oder -*d*, die man bereits in der römischen Frühzeit auf verschiedene Weise abzumildern versucht habe (12.10.32).

Daß es den Prinzipien der modernen Linguistik widerspricht, einer Einzelsprache aufgrund bestimmter phonetisch-phonologischer Eigenschaften einen Vorrang gegenüber anderen Sprachen zuzuweisen, versteht sich von selbst. Es ist ebensowenig die Aufgabe der Sprachwissenschaft, die Wirkung zu beschreiben, die sprachliche Laute auf den Hörer ausüben (cf. Desbordes 1989:276 [= 1994:200]; allgemeiner Stanford 1943:3); dies könnte allenfalls die literarische Ästhetik wagen, wenngleich sie sich damit auf ein sehr problematisches, weil in höchstem Maße der Subjektivität unterworfenes Terrain begäbe. Auch die Art und Weise Quintilians, den Lautbestand des Griechischen und Lateinischen zu skizzieren, weist aus heutiger Perspektive insbesondere den Mangel auf, die Phänomene „Graphem" und „Phonem" nicht auseinanderzuhalten. Andererseits steht Quintilian mit seinen Bemerkungen innerhalb der Antike in einer langen Tradition (dazu Stanford 1967: bes. 1-73), die mindestens bis in das 6. Jahrhundert v. Chr. zu Lasos von Hermione zurückreicht und unter den erhaltenen Texten ihren ausführlichsten Niederschlag in dem Traktat *De compositione verborum* des Dionysios von Halikarnassos (1. Jh. v. Chr.) findet[3].

Das Lateinische und Griechische werden in diesem Kapitel nicht ausschließlich nach *phonetisch-phonologischen Aspekten* miteinander verglichen; zusätzlich werden Sprachebenen berücksichtigt, die schon in früheren Kapiteln der *Institutio oratoria* als Anhaltspunkte für eine Differenzierung zwischen beiden Sprachen dienten: die *Wortbetonung* (Bereich der Suprasegmentalia), der *Wortschatz* (Lexikon) und die Existenz von *Dialekten* (ausgeprägte diatopische Variation).

Für die Akzentuierung griechischer und lateinischer Wörter wird in 12.10.33 vom Gehalt her im wesentlichen das wiederholt, was Quintilian bereits in 1.5.29-31 formuliert hatte, dort allerdings ohne die hier sehr ausgeprägte Abwertung des Lateinischen, das sich angesichts seiner Betonungsregeln den Vorwurf einer gewissen Starrheit (*rigore quodam*) gefallen lassen müsse. Daher griffen lateinische Dichter auf griechische Wörter zurück, um die ästhetische Wirkung ihrer Verse zu erhöhen und nach griechischem Vorbild ein *dulce carmen* zu produzieren (cf. Herescu 1948:243f). Gravierender als dieser Nachteil des Lateinischen sei jedoch das Fehlen von Bezeichnungen für zahlreiche Sachverhalte, also die im Vergleich zum Griechischen auffällige Lücke im Wortbestand, die man durch Metaphern oder Umschreibungen schließen müsse (cf. auch 8.3.30 37, 8.6.4-18) Erschwerend komme hinzu, daß auch unter den existierenden Wörtern die Auswahl alles andere als groß sei – die Rede ist hier von

---

[3] Wichtig sind in diesem Zusammenhang vor allem *De compositione verborum*, Kap. 14, aber auch Kap. 11 (122.11-124.9 und 124.20-126.2 Rhys Roberts), Kap. 12 (130.15-132.3) und Kap. 16 (158.1-160.20). Zu Dionysios Halikarnassos und seinen euphonischen Theorien gibt Stanford (1967:49-73) einen hilfreichen Überblick.

der „höchsten Armut" (*summa paupertas*) – und man daher bei der Suche nach Synonymen immer wieder auf dasselbe lexikalische Material zurückgreifen müsse (12.10.34). Das Griechische zeichne sich demgegenüber nicht nur durch einen größeren Wortbestand aus, sondern überdies durch das Vorhandensein von unterschiedlichen Dialekten (12.10.34, cf. auch 1.5.29).

Im Anschluß an diese Feststellungen wird die Betrachtung zurückgelenkt auf das anfänglich diskutierte Problem der Stilarten: Quintilian unterstreicht, daß es aus den genannten Gründen unfair sei, von der lateinischen Sprache die Anmut des Attischen (*gratiam sermonis Attici*) zu verlangen. Dieser fehle sowohl der klangliche Liebreiz (*iucunditas*) als auch die Wortfülle (*copia*) des Attischen. Gleichwohl gebe es Möglichkeiten, diese Defizite auszugleichen, da schließlich auch das Lateinische über Vorzüge verfüge, die man nur richtig nutzen müsse. Ein nicht allzu differenzierter Wortschatz verlange inhaltliche Erfindungskunst (12.10.36f). Zwar seien die Griechen in der attischen Stilgattung die unübertreffbaren Meister, jedoch bedeute dies nicht, daß ein Römer sich in dieser Stilart gar nicht versuchen solle. Er müsse dabei nur andere Schwerpunkte setzen als sein griechischer Kollege, vor allem durch Einhaltung des erforderlichen Maßes und durch sein Urteilsvermögen; zudem könne er zur Würze seines Vortrags auf genügend andere rhetorische Mittel zurückgreifen, die seine Muttersprache ihm biete (12.10.38). Jedenfalls habe es genügend römische Redner gegeben, die die Umsetzbarkeit dieser Empfehlungen überzeugend bewiesen hätten (12.10.39).

3   Zusammenfassung und Ausblick

Daß die Einstufung des Lateinischen als einer gerade gegenüber dem Griechischen „armen" Sprache schon in der Zeit der späten Republik verbreitet war, läßt sich bereits einigen Stellen bei Lukrez und Cicero entnehmen (cf. Fögen 2000a: bes. 17-19, 22f; ausführlich Fögen 2000b). Auch in der frühen Kaiserzeit setzt sich diese Auffassung offenbar mehrheitlich fort: Allein der Umstand, daß Quintilian erst gar nicht den Versuch unternimmt, die Position Ciceros aufzugreifen und durch weitere Argumente zu verteidigen, legt die Vermutung nahe, daß er sich mit seiner Hintanstellung des Lateinischen gegenüber dem Griechischen der damaligen *communis opinio* anschließt. Sowohl durch ihre Möglichkeiten der Wortbildung (Morphologie) als auch durch den Umfang des Wortschatzes (Lexikon) und nicht zuletzt aufgrund ihrer klanglichen Schönheit (Phonetik) sei die griechische Sprache eindeutig im Vorteil.

So sehr sich Quintilian bei seiner Vermittlung des rhetorischen Handwerkszeugs inhaltlich an Cicero anlehnt, so augenfällig ist der Unterschied zwischen beiden Autoren in der Bewertung der Leistungsfähigkeit und Elaboriertheit des Lateinischen. Geht es beispielsweise um Fragen des Wortschatzes, so diskutiert auch Quintilian wie sein Vorgänger die Möglichkeit des Sprachausbaus durch Metaphern; wenn er jedoch eine Entscheidung darüber zu treffen hat, ob sich zur Bezeichnung eines bestimmten Sachverhalts das zur Verfügung stehende griechische oder lateinische Wort besser eignet, so fällt sein Urteil eindeutig zugunsten der griechischen Termini aus. Betont wird von Quintilian immer wieder die Härte lateinischer Lehnübersetzungen griechischer Fachbegriffe, wohingegen Cicero gleich an mehreren Stellen dem lateinischen Vokabular vor allem aufgrund seines angeblich größeren semantischen Differenzierungspotentials einen Vorteil gegenüber dem griechischen Wortschatz zuschreibt (cf. Fögen 2000a: bes. 18f, 22-24, 28-30).

Während Cicero sich bei der Begründung seiner Einschätzung des Lateinischen nahezu ausschließlich auf lexikalische Aspekte beschränkt, erweitert Quintilian in seiner Argumentation den Blickwinkel beträchtlich: Insbesondere im ersten Buch der *Institutio oratoria*, das der Grammatik gewidmet ist, kontrastiert er systematische Unterschiede zwischen dem Lateinischen und Griechischen auf morphologischer und – in geringerem Umfang – syntaktischer Ebene. Darüber hinaus widmet er seine Aufmerksamkeit den Eigenarten beider Sprachen im suprasegmentalen Bereich, wenn er auf deren anders geartete Betonungsregeln eingeht. Überhaupt nicht bei Cicero vertreten ist Quintilians phonetisch-phonologische Betrachtung des Lateinischen und Griechischen, die er untrennbar mit einer – aus heutiger Sicht unzulässigen – ästhetischen Bewertung verknüpft: Das Griechische sei nicht allein in Morphologie, Syntax und Lexikon dem Lateinischen überlegen, es könne auch durch seinen weit größeren Wohlklang, seine ihm von Natur aus innewohnende Euphonie den Vorrang beanspruchen. Andererseits bestünden durchaus gewisse Möglichkeiten für den Römer, die Defizite seiner Muttersprache auszugleichen, indem er sich in durchdachter Weise ihre Stärken zunutze mache und mit anderen, aber nicht weniger effektiven sprachlich-rhetorischen Mitteln arbeite, als sie das Griechische aufweise. Es ist also nicht so, daß Quintilian dem Lateinischen den Status einer Kultursprache gänzlich aberkennen will; gleichwohl ist es unbestreitbar, daß er seiner Muttersprache auf allen sprachlichen Ebenen einen geringeren „Reichtum" als dem Griechischen zuschreibt.

Anders als bei Cicero in seinen philosophischen Schriften bestand für Quintilian nicht die Notwendigkeit, seinen Landsleuten den Sinn und Zweck seiner Tätigkeit, also die Darstellung eines dem Ursprung nach griechischen Lehrgebäudes in lateinischer Sprache, zu erläutern. Cicero selbst hatte – neben anderen Autoren – ihm auch für die Rhetorik den Weg geebnet, so daß das Lateinische als Medium seiner Darstellung nicht erst den Lesern schmackhaft gemacht werden mußte. Folglich kann Quintilian gegenüber seiner Muttersprache eine ungleich kritischere Haltung einnehmen und ist nicht gezwungen, aus Gründen der Eigenwerbung einer offenbar allgemein vertretenen Auffassung von einem defizitären Charakter des Lateinischen zu widersprechen.

Die Abwertung der Muttersprache zugunsten einer angeblich elaborierteren Sprache, wie wir sie bei Autoren der römischen Antike einschließlich Quintilian finden, ist eine Konstante, die sich unter ähnlichen sprachgeschichtlichen Voraussetzungen für verschiedene Sprachräume nachweisen läßt, so z.B. für die Einstellungen gegenüber dem Deutschen im Vergleich zum Französischen und Lateinischen im 17. Jahrhundert, aber auch später (cf. dazu kurz mit besonderem Bezug auf Leibniz Stickel 1999, allgemeiner Schlieben-Lange 1992 und ganz besonders Straßner 1995). Die zeitgenössische Spracheinstellungsforschung hat nachgewiesen, daß Vorstellungen über den Wert und Unwert einer Einzelsprache eine Art Universale darstellen, von dem sich gerade linguistisch ungeschulte Sprecher kaum befreien können. Im europäischen

Raum verbindet man vielfach mit bestimmten Sprachen entsprechende Eigenschaften wie Klangfülle, Eleganz und lexikalischen Reichtum oder deren Gegenteil (cf. zuletzt Giles; Niedzielski 1998: spez. 85). In der modernen Soziolinguistik wird es jedoch abgelehnt, einer Sprache einen inhärenten Wert zuzusprechen (*inherent value hypothesis*); statt dessen geht man von der *social connotations hypothesis* aus, die besagt, daß Einstellungen gegenüber einer Einzelsprache oder einer Sprachvarietät einschließlich der damit verbundenen ästhetischen Wertungen durch konkret faßbare politische, soziale und kulturelle Entwicklungen beeinflußt werden (Giles; Niedzielski 1998:88-91, mit weiterer Literatur). Verschiedene Sprachen oder Varietäten nach ihren phonetisch-phonologischen Qualitäten oder aufgrund anderer Kriterien auf einer Werteskala anzuordnen, ist damit ausgeschlossen, sofern es um eine wissenschaftlich motivierte Einzelsprachbeschreibung oder Kontrastierung von Sprachen geht. Gerade wegen ihres subjektiven Charakters stellt jedoch die Ermittlung und Dokumentation von Spracheinstellungen für die Sprachwissenschaft wie auch für die Soziologie und Sozialpsychologie ein überaus wichtiges Untersuchungsfeld dar, das gesellschaftliche Verhältnisse und Prozesse in anschaulicher Weise widerspiegelt.

Für die von uns betrachtete Epoche ließe sich dabei folgendes Resultat formulieren: Die Selbstverständlichkeit, mit der die Römer ihren politischen Machtbereich mehr und mehr ausweiten, findet auch im ersten nachchristlichen Jahrhundert keinen direkten Niederschlag in ihrem kulturellen und dabei vor allem sprachlichen Selbstbewußtsein (cf. Rochette 1993: spez. 233f). Es ist dabei besonders auffällig, daß von Quintilians Seite wie auch von anderen Autoren außer Cicero nicht der geringste Anspruch auf Ebenbürtigkeit des Lateinischen mit dem Griechischen erhoben wird, sondern daß man statt dessen der eigenen Muttersprache einen geringeren Wert zuschreibt. Dies mag man zum Teil durch die in der frühen Kaiserzeit ausgeprägte Zweisprachigkeit gerade in gebildeteren Kreisen erklären. Dennoch ist gerade bei Quintilian die Identifikation mit seiner Muttersprache offensichtlich nicht so stark ausgeprägt, daß er sie dem Griechischen vorziehen würde; die gesamte *Institutio oratoria* läßt zudem erkennen, wie sehr er der griechischen Sprache und Literatur verhaftet ist, auch wenn er in seiner Vertrautheit mit der griechischen Welt sicherlich nicht mit Cicero konkurrieren kann.

Abschließend sei eine kurze Bemerkung zur antiken terminologischen Erfassung der Einstellungen zur lateinischen Sprache angefügt: Zwar scheint sich die bei Lukrez geprägte Formel der *patrii sermonis egestas* weder bei Cicero noch bei Quintilian begrifflich als Stereotyp verfestigt zu haben; wenn Quintilian seine eigenen oder andere Einschätzungen des Lateinischen substantivisch zu fassen versucht, so spricht er nämlich nicht von der *egestas*, sondern von der *paupertas* der lateinischen Sprache (so z.B. 8.3.33, 12.10.34). Gleichwohl läßt es sich nicht bestreiten, daß sich auch ohne die Herausbildung eines einzigen festen Schlagwortes zur Erfassung des Sachverhalts in Quintilians *Institutio oratoria* die überwiegend negative Einstellung der Römer gegenüber ihrer Muttersprache in der frühen Kaiserzeit deutlich widerspiegelt.

Ein wenig anders nimmt sich die Situation für weitere frühkaiserzeitliche Autoren wie Seneca (*Ep.* 58.1) oder Plinius d. J. (*Ep.* 4.18.1) aus: Zwar sind beide Autoren nicht auf einen alleinigen Begriff zum Ausdruck ihrer Einstellung gegenüber dem Lateinischen festgelegt, sondern bieten dem Leser zusätzlich zu *egestas* jeweils ein Synonym – *paupertas* bzw. *inopia* – zur Auswahl an; dennoch wird zur Umschreibung der persönlichen Wertung der Muttersprache in beiden Fällen dem Begriff der *egestas* der Vorzug gegeben, bei Plinius sogar unter ausdrücklicher Berufung auf Lukrez. Der eigentliche Urheber dieser Prägung ist also mehr als hundert Jahre nach ihrem Aufkommen durchaus noch im Bewußtsein lateinischer Autoren, auch wenn Quintilian selbst nicht auf diesen Terminus zurückgegriffen hat.

4   Literatur

Nachfolgend werden aus Platzgründen nahezu ausschließlich die im Laufe des Aufsatzes zitierten Werke aufgeführt. Die Bibliographie erhebt somit nicht den Anspruch auf eine erschöpfende Erfassung der relevanten Sekundärliteratur. Ausführliche Zusammenstellungen wichtiger Literatur zum Thema „Spracheinstellungen in der griechischen und römischen Antike" finden sich in den Arbeiten von Fögen (1999, 2000a, 2000c und besonders 2000b).

ADAMIETZ, Joachim (1986): Quintilians „Institutio oratoria". In: Aufstieg und Niedergang der römischen Welt II/32.4, 2226-2271.

AUSTIN, R.G. (1948): Quintiliani Institutionis oratoriae Liber XII. Oxford. – [Repr. 1965]

— (1946): Quintilian XII.10.27-8: A postscript. In: Classical Review 60, 20.

— (1943): Quintilian XII.10.27-8. In: Classical Review 57, 9-12.

BARWICK, Karl (1936): Quintilians Stellung zu dem Problem sprachlicher Neuschöpfungen. In: Philologus 91, 89-113.

COLEMAN, Robert (1963): Two linguistic topics in Quintilian. In: Classical Quarterly 57, 1-18.

DESBORDES, Françoise (1989): L'idéal romain dans la rhétorique de Quintilien. In: Ktema 14, 273-279. [= Desbordes (1994). In: Dangel, Jacqueline (ed.): Grammaire et rhétorique: notion de Romanité. Paris: AECR (Université des Sciences Humaines de Strasbourg: Contributions et travaux de l'Institut d'Histoire Romaine 7), 197-203.]

FÖGEN, Thorsten (2000a): Sprachbewußtsein in der römischen Antike. Ciceros Stellungnahme zum Problem der *patrii sermonis egestas*. In: Deminger, Szilvia; Fögen, Thorsten; Scharloth, Joachim; Zwickl, Simone (Hrsg.): Einstellungsforschung in der Soziolinguistik und Nachbardisziplinen – Studies in Language Attitudes. Frankfurt am Main etc.: Lang (VarioLingua 10), 13-39.

— (2000b): *Patrii sermonis egestas*: Einstellungen lateinischer Autoren zu ihrer Muttersprache. Ein Beitrag zum Sprachbewußtsein in der römischen Antike. München – Leipzig: Saur (Beiträge zur Altertumskunde 150).

— (2000c): Quintilians Einschätzung der lateinischen Sprache. In: Grazer Beiträge 147-185.

— (1999): Spracheinstellungen und Sprachnormbewußtsein bei Cicero. In: Glotta 75, 1-33.

— (1998): Bezüge zwischen antiker und moderner Sprachnormentheorie. In: Listy filologické 121, 199-219.

GILES, Howard; NIEDZIELSKI, Nancy (1998): Italian is beautiful, German is ugly. In: Bauer, Laurie; Trudgill, Peter (Hrsg.): Language Myths. London – Harmondsworth: Penguin, 85-93.

HAHN, E. Adelaide (1941): Quintilian on Greek letters lacking in Latin and Latin letters lacking in Greek (12.10.27-29). In: Language 17, 24-32.

HERESCU, N. I. (1948): Poétique ancienne et moderne au sujet de l'euphonie. In: Mélanges de philologie, de littérature et d'histoires anciennes offerts à Jules Marouzeau par ses collègues et élèves étrangers. Paris: Les Belles Lettres, 221-247.

ROCHETTE, Bruno (1993): La diversité linguistique dans l'Antiquité classique. Le témoignage des auteurs de l'époque d'Auguste et du 1er siècle de notre ère. In: Isebaert, Lambert (ed.): Miscellanea linguistica Graeco-latina. Namur: Société des Études Classiques (Collection d'Études Classiques 7), 219-237.

SCHLIEBEN-LANGE, Brigitte (1992): Reichtum, Energie, Klarheit und Harmonie. Die Bewertung der Sprachen in Begriffen der Rhetorik. In: Anschütz, Susanne R. (ed.): Texte, Sätze, Wörter und Moneme. Festschrift für Klaus Heger zum 65. Geburtstag. Heidelberg: Heidelberger Orientverlag, 571-586.

STANFORD, William B. (1967): The Sound of Greek. Studies in Greek Theory and Practice of Euphony. Berkeley – Los Angeles: Univ. of California Press (Sather Classical Lectures 38).

— (1943): Greek views on euphony. In: Hermathena 61, 3-20.

STICKEL, Gerhard (1999): Deutsch als Wissenschaftssprache und Gottfried Wilhelm Leibniz. In: Sprachreport 15.2, 16-19.

STRASSNER, Erich (1995): Deutsche Sprachkultur. Von der Barbarensprache zur Weltsprache. Tübingen: Niemeyer.

STURTEVANT, Edgar Howard (²1940): The Pronunciation of Greek and Latin. Philadelphia.

Das Fremde im Eigenen
Zum Problem der Mehrsprachigkeit

Renata Horvat-Dronske

Verstehen Sie eigentlich Kroatisch? Möglicherweise Kajkawisch, einen der drei konstitutiven Dialekte des Kroatischen?[1] Auch nicht? Dann möchte ich versuchen, Ihnen das Gegenteil zu beweisen.

Serbus/Servus!
Kistijant/Kistihant!
Ober, gemišt!
Bedinerica klofa tepihe u lihthofu.
Ibercuk od zica je znucan.
Peglam veš.
Šos je plisiran od hintergrunda.
Narihtaj vekericu na frtalj 8.
Ivica je feš i ledik.
Darfst nihz reden, halts Maul.
Ferdamani trotlin!

Auch wenn in den gerade zitierten Beispielen, die aus wirklich vollzogenen kommunikativen Situationen, bzw. aus der in einem Teil des kajkawischen Areals erscheinenden Faschingszeitung *Zvonec*[2] entnommen worden sind, nicht jedes Wort, jede Partikel oder jedes Morphem bekannt waren, können wir uns darüber einigen, dass wir es doch noch geschafft haben, sie zu dekodieren, zu entziffern, also zu verstehen. Auch wenn dies nicht oder nicht vollständig der Fall gewesen ist, muss zumindest der Eindruck entstanden sein, dass hier jemand, wenn es so etwas überhaupt gibt, ein *komisches Deutsch* spricht/schreibt. Dabei handelt es sich um Beispiele, die in einer, Ihnen eigentlich unbekannter regionalen Varietät des Kroatischen, formuliert wurden.

An dieser Stelle möchte ich zunächst kurz versuchen, das besondere Sprachbild des bereits erwähnten kajkawischen Dialektes und die damit verbundene sprachliche Kompetenz seiner SprecherInnen darzustellen.

---

[1] Das Kroatische besteht außer dem gerade genannten Kajkawischen, aus zwei weiteren Dialekten: dem Stokawischen und dem Cakawischen. Die Bezeichnungen für diese regionalen Varietäten des Kroatischen leiten sich von der in dem jeweiligen Dialekt gebrauchten Fragewortes *was* ab: Im Kajkawischen lautet diese Form folglich *kaj*, im Stokawischen *što* und im Cakawischen *ča*.

[2] Die Zeitung *Zvonec* (Die Glocke), die mit einigen Unterbrechungen seit 1906 jährlich zur Faschingszeit erscheint, ist nur lokal verbreitet – im Kajkawischen Areal nordwestlich der kroatischen Hauptstadt Zagreb. Die in der Zeitung gebrauchte sprachliche Varietät ist – abgesehen von wenigen in der standardsprachlichen Varietät verfassten Artikel und Gedichte – das Kajkawische. Der sprachliche Ausdruck der Zeitungsartikel ist zwar schlicht, jedoch sehr lebensnah und dementsprechend authentisch: Gerade deshalb eignet sich diese Zeitung als eine legitime Quelle, auf die auch in dieser Arbeit zurückgegriffen wird.

In der Beschreibung des Kajkawischen werden als Besonderheiten dieser regionalen Varietät im Hinblick auf die anderen Dialekte des Kroatischen (das Stokawische und das Cakawische) unterschiedliche phonetische (wie das Vorhandensein von Diphtongen etwa), morphologische (der Gebrauch älterer Flexionsformen), vor allem aber lexikalische Merkmale hervorgehoben. Auf der lexikalischen Ebene zeichnet sich das Kajkawische im Unterschied zu den anderen Dialekten dadurch aus, dass eine Vielzahl älterer Ausdrücke noch immer verwendet wird. Insbesondere gehört zum lexikalischen Korpus des Kajkawischen eine große Anzahl aus dem Ungarischen sowie aus dem Deutschen bzw. dem Österreichischen stammender Lehnwörter, wobei die aus dem deutschsprachigen Raum entlehnten Wörter deutlich überwiegen. (Vgl. Težak-Babić 1994:22-25) Ein solches Erscheinungsbild des Kajkawischen hängt im Falle des Ungarischen mit den geographischen, im Wesentlichen aber mit den historisch-politischen Faktoren zusammen. Im Falle des Deutschen sind nur die zuletzt genannten Faktoren von Bedeutung, da Kroatisch, somit auch Kajkawisch und Deutsch/Österreichisch keine unmittelbar aneinander grenzenden Sprachen sind. Als Bestandteil der Österreichisch-ungarischen Monarchie wurde das kajkawische Areal zu einem politisch bedingten Sprachberührungsraum für die Sprachen und sprachlichen Varietäten der Monarchie. Wenn man die Auswirkungen dieser Sprachkontakte auf das Kajkawische rein deskriptiv auffasst, lässt sich Folgendes festhalten: Die als Folge der sprachlichen Kontakte aufzufassenden Entlehnungsprozesse haben sehr früh angesetzt (laut Žepić 1995 noch weit vor der Gründung der Monarchie, im 13. Jahrhundert etwa) und dauern bis zum heutigen Tag an. Dieses soll durch nur zwei Beispiele illustriert werden: die Replik *farbati* entspricht auf der semantischen Ebene vollständig der aktuellen lexikologischen Definition des Modells *färben*. Jedoch ist in der Replik, laut dem Grimmschen *Deutsches Wörterbuch*, die mhd. Bedeutung „fälschen, teuschen, beschönigen, schmücken, triegen, entstellen" auch vorhanden. Die Replik hat also die Bedeutung des Modells, die es zum Zeitpunkt des Entlehnens beinhaltet hat, konserviert, während in der Gebersprache, durch Sprachwandelprozesse, darunter auch durch den Bedeutungswandel, diese Bedeutung teilweise oder gar vollständig verschwunden ist. Zu den aktuelleren Entlehnungen gehört, unter anderem, die Replik *Kinderjaje* (Kind +kr. jaje [Ei]), die wiederum einen besonderen Status hat: Für diese Replik gibt es im Deutschen kein direktes Modell, dafür aber existiert auf dem (nicht nur) deutschen Markt ein konkretes Produkt – das Kinder-Überraschungsei.

Weiterhin lässt sich feststellen, dass das gesamte aus dem Deutschen stammende Lehngut einen wichtigen Teil des von den SprecherInnen des Kajkawischen in der alltäglichen Kommunikation gebrauchten Wortschatzes ausmacht. Es ist in vielen Situationen, beim Bezeichnen von Werkzeug oder anderen Gerätschaften etwa, wie auch im Küchenjargon oder im Haushalt allgemein fast unentbehrlich. Wie weit das aus dem deutschsprachigen Raum stammende Lehnwortgut den kajkawischen Dialekt durchdringt lässt sich u.a. auch daran absehen, dass selbst im Bereich des Schimpfens, der an und für sich überreichlich durch eigensprachliches Material abgedeckt ist, deutsche Wörter und Wendungen benutzt werden (z.B. *ferfljuhta* - verflucht, *ferdaman* - verdammt).

Es gibt einen in diesem Zusammenhang interessanten autobiographischen Roman von Pavao Pavličić, von einem der bekanntesten zeitgenössischen Autoren Kroatiens also, unter dem Titel *Šapudl*. Im Lichte der jüngsten tragischen Kriegsereignisse in Kroatien erscheint dieser literarische Text als ein Versuch Pavličićs das durch den Krieg Verlorengegangene wiederzufinden, das durch den Krieg Zerstörte wiederherzustellen. Die literarische Suche nach der vernichteten Welt, nach der Vertrautheit des ursprünglich Eigenen, geschieht in diesem Text durch Spracharbeit, nämlich durch die einfache begriffliche Auflistung der „Dingwelt". Sie mündet folglich in der Konstruktion eines – heimatlichen – Sprachfeldes, auf dem der Autor sich sein eigentliches Zuhause vergegenwärtigt: Die wiedergewonnene Präsenz der verlorengegangenen Heimat erscheint hierbei

> „als Effekt der Aufrufung von Wörtern wie *jauzna* (Mahlzeit), *serbus* (Servus), *vajndling* (Weitling), *snenokle* (Schneenockerl), um hier nur einige der aus dem Österreichischen stammenden Wörter zu nennen." (Dronske 1997),

also durch die Benennung von deutschsprachigen Lehnwörtern, in deren Aura der verloschene Glanz des Eigenen, der verbrannten Heimat sich neu (re-)präsentiert oder neu (re-)präsentieren soll.

Šapudl spielt in Ostslawonien, genauer gesagt in Vukovar, also in einem Sprachgebiet, dessen dialektale Varietät in einem etwas geringeren Umfang als das Kajkawische von deutschen Lehnwörtern geprägt ist. Dennoch finden wir hier in der literarischen Inszenierung Pavao Pavličićs denselben Mechanismus der Identifizierung des Eigenen durch das Fremde, der eigenen Sprachwelt durch das eigentlich fremde Lehnwort wieder, der in noch höherem Maße für das Kajkawische wirksam sein müsste. Dies macht u.a. die Studie des amerikanischen Linguisten Magner (1966) über die in der kroatischen Hauptstadt Zagreb gesprochene Varietät, die zugleich dem kajkawischen Dialekt angehört, deutlich. Hier wird vom Autor festgestellt, dass das Besondere an dem sprachlichen Ausdruck der ZagreberInnen ihr eigenständiger Wortschatz sei. Diesen Wortschatz präsentiert nun Magner durch eine ausführliche Liste von für Zagreb, also auch für das Kajkawische typischen Wörtern, die – und hier überschneiden sich die linguistischen und die literarischen Diskurse – überwiegend aus deutschen Lehnwörtern besteht. Das Vorhandensein von Lehnwörtern im lexikalischen Korpus einer Sprache/sprachlichen Varietät ist selbstverständlich kein Spezifikum des Kajkawischen: Ohne diese Spuren der Sprachkontakte sind viele Sprachen oder ihre regionalen Varietäten vor allem aber die durch die technisch-elektronische, wissenschaftliche und kulturelle Entwicklung und durch den internationalen Austausch bedingten funktionalen/fachlichen Lekte fast nicht mehr vorstellbar. Das Besondere an der Situation im Kajkawischen ist also die Tatsache, dass sich hier die Prozesse der Selbstidentifikation oder der Legitimierung einer sprachlichen Varietät und ihrer SprecherInnen u.a. anhand eines Sprachmaterials vollzieht, das nicht zum ursprünglichen „eigenen" Wortbestand gezählt werden kann. Mit anderen Worten, das, was in den zitierten wissenschaftlichen Arbeiten als das Charakteristische oder zumindest als ein zentrales Charakteristikum des Kajkawischen aufgefasst wird, das also, was das Authentische dieser Varietät des Kroatischen konstituiert und folglich ihr Eigenes definiert, ihre Eigenheit ausmacht, stammt aus einer anderen, einer fremden Sprache. Fremdheit und Eigenheit, Eigenes und Fremdes sind hier folglich in einer Form miteinander verflochten, in der sich das Eigene als Effekt des Fremden zu erkennen gibt, in der der kajkawische Dialekt, die Varietät des Kroatischen also, durch das Fremde, besser: das Fremdsprachliche, nämlich durch die aus dem deutschsprachigen Raum stammenden Lehnwörter, wesentlich bestimmt zu sein scheint.

Lipczuk hat in seinem Artikel *Deutsche Einflüsse im Polnischen und deren Reflexion in Polen* (1999) auf die nicht unbedeutende Anzahl an deutschen Lehnwörtern hingewiesen, die im Polnischen vorhanden seien und in der alltäglichen Kommunikation, folglich vor allem in der gesprochenen Sprache eine wichtige Rolle spielten. Die Germanismen gehörten dabei „zum Zentrum der polnischen Lexik" und seien „so geläufig, daß man sich – abgesehen von Linguisten – bei weitem auch nicht allen – ihrer fremden Herkunft gar nicht bewußt ist" (Lipczuk 1999: 292).

Das Fremde des aus dem deutschen Sprachraum stammenden Lehnwortschatzes scheint sich demzufolge in Polen weitgehend oder vollständig aufgelöst zu haben, wenn das dort vorhandene normale Sprachbewusstsein das artikulierte Lehnwort nicht mehr in seiner Differenz zu muttersprachlichen Merkmalen wahrnimmt.

Genau dies ist im untersuchten kajkawischen Areal nicht der Fall. Die hier vorhandenen Repliken sind zwar morphologisch, phonologisch, semantisch und syntaktisch adaptiert. Dies bedeutet etwa im Bereich der Phonologie, dass die für die deutsche Sprache spezifischen Lautwerte durch entsprechende kajkawische ersetzt worden sind, sodass der Lautkörper des deutschen Modells sich überall dort in entsprechender Weise transformiert, wo er von dem kajkawischen phonologischen System abweicht: *zurück* lautet folglich *curik*, *Möbel* wird als *mebljin* realisiert, *öffnen* wird zu *ofnuti*.

Trotz dieser für den größten Teil des Lehnwortbestandes geltenden vollständigen Adaption ist bei den SprecherInnen des Kajkawischen ein zumindest rudimentäres Bewusstsein über die Besonderheit dieser Repliken vorhanden. Bei meinen Untersuchungen zum Lehnwortbestand in der im kajkawischen Sprachraum gesprochenen Sprache war fast jede/r SprecherIn in der Lage eigenständig ihm bekannte Lehnwörter zu benennen. Dieses Bewusstsein von der Fremdheit selbst der vollständig adaptierten Repliken ergibt sich dabei weniger aus den vielfältigen Kontakten mit dem deutschen Sprachraum, wie sie sich im Zusammenhang mit Tourismus, Migration, DAF-Unterricht in der Schule und deutschsprachigen Fernsehprogrammen für einen Großteil der SprecherInnen auch aktuell notwendig einstellen. Die besondere Markierung des deutschsprachigen Lehnwortgutes, seine noch in der vollständigen Angleichung an den kajkawischen Sprachbestand registrierbare Spezifik resultiert weit eher aus der Differenz zwischen kroatischer Standardsprache und kajkawischer Varietät denn aus seiner Übereinstimmung mit dem Deutschen.

Wir haben hier also dasselbe Spiel zwischen dem Fremden und dem Eigenen, wie wir es oben bereits beobachtet haben: ein Fremdes, das in der Differenz zur hochsprachlichen Varietät als Eigenes imaginiert wird, ein Fremdes, das gerade in dieser Abweichung zur sprachlichen Selbstidentifizierung dient und die Intimität des Dialekts in seinem Abstand zur offiziösen/offiziellen Standardsprache unterhält. Dabei ist der deutsche Ursprung nicht ausgelöscht, viele der Lehnwörter sind im Bewusstsein der SprecherInnen durchaus in ihrem Status als Lehnwörter präsent, es existiert folglich ein Wissen darüber, dass diese Wörter ein deutsches Modell zur Grundlage haben. Aber dieser Tatbestand wird überlagert von dem Unterschied zwischen Dialekt und Hochsprache, innerhalb dessen gerade das entlehnte Wort als zentrales Zeichen für die eigene sprachliche Heimat fungieren kann.

Damit kommen wir zum letzten Teil meines Referates. In den soziolinguistischen Abhandlungen scheint die Diskussion über den Begriff der Mehrsprachigkeit noch nicht eindeutig abgeschlossen zu sein. Generell lässt sich behaupten, Mehrsprachigkeit ist die Fähigkeit eines Individuums an zwei oder mehreren sprachlichen Systemen zu partizipieren. Allerdings sind in diesem Kontext weder der Begriff des Sprachsystems, noch – bezogen auf die erforderliche Partizipation des Individuums – die Qualität dieser Fähigkeiten klar definiert. Die Definition der Mehrsprachigkeit bezieht sich dabei bei manchen Autoren nicht mehr auf zwei unterschiedliche standardsprachliche Systeme, vielmehr wird die Fähigkeit des Individuums unterschiedliche Varietäten/Lekten (regionale, soziale, funktionale oder individuelle) innerhalb ein und derselben Sprache zu beherrschen als Mehrsprachigkeit angesehen. Insofern ist Mehrsprachigkeit ein universelles Phänomen, an dem alle SprecherInnen in der einen oder anderen Weise teilhaben.

Immerhin wird hier davon ausgegangen, dass diese unterschiedlichen Lekten von den SprecherInnen verstanden und auch aktiv beherrscht werden. Dies betonen einige Autoren auch im Hinblick auf einen Begriff der Mehrsprachigkeit, der auf Kompetenzen in verschiedenen Sprachen angewendet wird. Einer weiteren Auffassung der Mehrsprachigkeit nach, ist diese bereits beim bloßen Verstehen einer fremden Sprache gegeben, also nicht erst dann, wenn eine sichere Beherrschung der fremden Sprache vorhanden ist, die es ermöglicht, in dieser Sprache sinnvolle Äußerungen zu formulieren. Das Verblüffende am Kajkawischen besteht nun in einer sprachlichen Selbstidentifizierung anhand eines fremden sprachlichen Materials, ohne dass diese mit einer sprachlichen Kompetenz korrespondieren würde, die es den SprecherInnen ermöglichte, sich innerhalb des linguistischen Systems, aus dem die Entlehnungen stammen, auf eine wie auch immer begrenzte Weise zu verständigen. Dies gilt, obwohl gleichzeitig ein Bewusstsein über die Herkunft auch der vollständig adaptierten Lehnwörter und damit ein Gefühl für das fremde sprachliche System vorhanden ist.

Das für das Kajkawische typische Spiel des Fremden im Eigenen bewegt sich deshalb außerhalb der Mehrsprachigkeit, aber es berührt dessen äußerste Grenzen, und zwar in einer produktiven Weise. Indem das Fremde hier zum Medium der Selbstidentifikation wird, sperrt sich das Kajkawische gegen alle Formen des Sprachpurismus. Und indem Elemente einer anderen Sprache einen – sowohl quantitativ wie symbolisch – signifikanten Bestandteil des eigenen Dialekts ausmachen, müssten gute Voraussetzungen gegeben sein, die Grenze der Mehrsprachigkeit aktiv zu überschreiten. Dies aber erfordert, dass man sich konkret die Frage stellen muss, wie der Lehnwortschatz des Kajkawischen und die im Kajkawischen eingeschlossenen Vorerfahrungen mit dem Deutschen in einem DAF-Unterricht fruchtbar gemacht werden können.

Literatur

BECHERT, Johannes; WILDGEN, Wolfgang (1991): Einführung in die Sprachkontaktforschung. Darmstadt: Wissenschaftliche Buchgesellschaft (Die Sprachwissenschaft).

DRONSKE, Ulrich (1997): Das Lehnwort als Heimat. Zu Pavao Pavlicic' Roman *Sapudl*. In: Muhr, R.; Schrodt, R. (Hrsg.): Österreichisches Deutsch und andere nationale Varietäten plurizentrischer Sprachen in Europa. Wien: Hölder-Pichler-Tempsky, 379-386.

GLOVACKI-BERNARDI, Zrinjka (1993): Österreichische und süddeutsche Elemente in der Agramer Mundart. In: Muhr, R. (Hrsg.): Internationale Arbeiten zum österreichischen Deutsch und seinen nachbarsprachlichen Bezügen. Wien: Hölder-Pichler-Tempsky, 76-78.

GRIMM, Jakob; GRIMM Wilhelm (1991): Deutsches Wörterbuch. München: Deutscher Taschenbuch Verlag.

HORVAT-DRONSKE, Renata (1999): Zu den lexikalischen Auswirkungen des deutsch-kroatischen Sprachkontakts auf den kajkawischen Dialekt der kroatischen Sprache. Repliken ohne Modelle. In: Spillmann; Warnke: 101-104.

— (1995): Die Übernahme von Lehnwörtern aus dem österreichisch-deutschen Sprachraum im kajkawischen Dialekt von Hrvatsko zagorje (Kroatien). In: Muhr; Schrodt, Wiesinger: 374-380.

LIPCZUK, Ryszard (1999): Deutsche Einflüsse im Polnischen und deren Reflektion in Polen. In: Spillmann; Warnke: 291-297.

LORENZ, Kruno (1988): Das Eigene und das Fremde im Dialog. In: Matusche: 122-129.

MAGNER, Thomas (1966): A Zagreb Kajkavian Dialect. In: The Pennsylvania University Studies 18.

MATUSCHE, Petra (Hrsg.) (1988): Wie verstehen wir Fremdes? Aspekte zur Klärung von Verstehensprozessen; Dokumentation eines Werkstattgesprächs des Goethe-Instituts München vom 24.-26. November 1988. München: Goethe-Inst., Referat 42/AWD etc.

MUHR, R.; SCHRODT, R.; WIESINGER, P. (Hrsg.) (1995): Österreichisches Deutsch. Linguistische, sozialpsychologische und sprachpolitische Aspekte einer nationalen Variante des Deutschen. Wien: Hölder-Pichler-Tempsky.

OKSAAR, Els (1988): Problematik im interkulturellen Verstehen. In: Matusche: 7-20.

PAVLIČIĆ, Pavao (1995): Šapudl. Zagreb: Znanje.

SPILLMANN, Hans Otto; WARNKE, Ingo (Hrsg.) (1999): Internationale Tendenzen der Syntaktik, Semantik und Pragmatik. Akten des 32. Linguistischen Kolloquiums in Kassel 1997. Frankfurt a. M.: Peter Lang (Linguistik international 1).

TEŽAK, Stjepko; Babić, Stjepan (1994): Gramatika hrvatskoga jezika. Zagreb: Školska knjiga.

ŽEPIĆ, Stanko (1995): Das österreichische Deutsch in Zagreb und Osijek: Zur Geschichte der deutschen Sprache in Kroatien. In: Muhr; Schrodt; Wiesinger, 354-374.

Social Reality and Perceptions of French in Senegal

Omar Ka

1 Introduction

Terms such as *English-speaking Africa*, *French-speaking Africa*, and *Portuguese-speaking Africa* are commonly used to designate African countries that have been colonized, respectively by Great Britain, France or Belgium, and Portugal. However, these terms are highly misleading because less than 30% of Africans speak such colonial languages in any given country. Although they have been declared official languages in the great majority of African countries, their domains of use are quite limited, even among the minority that claims to speak them. This is indeed the case in the West African country of Senegal, which was the first French colony in Sub-Saharan Africa.

At the time of Independence in 1960, Senegal – along with most other former French colonies in Africa – declared French the sole official language, this in the very first article of the new Constitution. Almost fourty years later, and despite a number of proposals for reform (for an account of those proposals, cf. Sylla 1987; Ka 1993a, 1993b), French is still the language of administration and government, the exclusive medium of public education, and the language of the urban elite. This is in contrast with a sociolinguistic situation in which multilingualism is the norm, with Wolof as the *de facto* lingua franca, spoken by about 70 to 80% of the population. French is spoken as a first language by less than a quarter of one per cent of school-age children. About 80% of the population cannot read or write French; according to a *Haut Conseil de la Francophonie* Report (HCF 1990).

This paper will attempt to describe the well-defined contexts in which French is used in Senegalese society, the contrasting socioeconomic statuses of those who claim to use French and those who do not, and the images of the French language carried in each group. This will show the correlation in Senegal between socioeconomic status and knowledge of French; the correlation between the perceptions of French and its official status as the *de facto* major means of economic advancement and national political power; the contradiction between the official language policy and the social reality of the country; and the impact of such a policy on development goals.

2 Ethnic and linguistic distribution

According to the results of the 1989 National Census, the distribution of the main ethnic groups in Senegal is the following:

Wolof	43.7%
Fulbe	23.2%
Seereer	14.8%
Joola	5.5%
Manding	4.6%

This can be compared to results from the same census concerning the distribution of the main languages:

Wolof	70.9%
Pulaar	24.1%
Seereer	13.7%
Joola	5.7%
Manding	6.2%
Soninke	1.4%

The ethnic and linguistic distribution figures clearly show that Wolof is the lingua franca in Senegal; it is spoken by at least 70% of the population (other reliable estimates put that percentage at 80%: cf. Baker 1980; CONFE.M.E.N 1986), although the percentage of persons claiming Wolof ethnicity is only 43%.

In addition, earlier figures (Verrière 1965) show that French, the official language, is spoken as a first language by less than 0.25% of school-age children. Within the general population, about 80% cannot read or write French; according to the Haut Conseil de la Francophonie's 1990 Report, 10% are "real" speakers, and 14% "occasional" speakers.[1] This contrasts with the privileged status that French enjoys in Senegal.

3   The status of French

As stated earlier, French is the sole official language; as such, it is the language of administration and government, the exclusive medium of public formal education from elementary school to the university. This is the same status that already existed during the colonial period, when the French colonizer decided to impose its language in all domains of public life (see for instance Crowder 1962; Turcotte 1983). At Independence, the new Senegalese government chose to continue the same language policy, despite the poor results of a century of colonization on the rate of literacy in French (Dumont 1983). According to the typology of language policies in Africa by Heine (1990), the language policy in Senegal would be that of an official exoglossy (i.e., the use of a foreign language as the official language) in a traditionally multilingual context. Such a policy contradicts the accepted consensus that an official language should guarantee access and participation in the political, economic and educational system of a country (Kellman 1972).

Within the Senegalese educational system, less than half of school-age children enter school, despite the clear progress made since 1960 when the percentage was only about 10% (Verrière 1965). Although there are obvious demographic, social and economic factors accounting for the low literacy rate, one cannot underestimate the negative impact of the present language policy on that rate (Dumont 1983; Sylla

---

[1] "Real" speakers are defined in HCF (1990:28) as those who are able to express themselves, understand and be understood in French in all contexts. "Occasional" speakers are those who have a rudimentary or specialized mastery of the language, and who make a strictly utilitarian use of it.

1987; Djité 1991). In the next section, I will examine how such a policy is in direct relation with the specific contexts in which French is used in an urban environment.

4 Contexts of use

The data for this section is derived from a survey of speakers of French residing in Dakar, the capital city of Senegal (Blondé 1975a, Dumont 1983). To the question about the contexts in which they used French, the following answers were obtained:

- 5% of respondents spoke French with their parents;
- 20% with their children;
- 23% with a friend;
- 37% with another Senegalese whom they meet for the first time;
- 63% with a co-worker;
- 90% with an African who is not from Senegal;
- 92% with their supervisor.

The data clearly show that French is the language of power and social distance, the language of international communication, the language of the workplace.

In contrast, French is not the language of the private sphere: it is rarely used at home or with friends, domains in which Senegalese languages are almost always used.[2] However, Senegalese languages are still entirely excluded from the public sphere, despite a few attempts at changing the status quo (cf. Ka 1993a, 1993b; Sylla 1987).

The data also show that French is used in very specific domains – such as the workplace, international communication –, despite the fact that it is the official language; after a century of colonization and fourty years of Independence, one would have expected it to have made more inroads, for instance in the private sphere. One strong reason for this lack of progress is the vitality of Wolof in the urban context: this language has witnessed a rapid and continuous expansion during and after the colonial period (for a description of the socioeconomic and sociolinguistic factors behind this expansion, cf. C.L.A.D. 1966).

5 Contrasting socioeconomic statuses

Blondé (1975a, 1975b) describes two sociolinguistic surveys, one among respondents literate in French, and the other among respondents illiterate in that same language.[3] The results of the surveys show a marked contrast between the two groups of respondents in terms of their respective socioeconomic status.

---

[2] One might note that, in the urban environment and in these same domains, varying degrees of code-switching may occur between those languages and French.

[3] Due to space limitations, I refer the reader to Blondé (1975a, 1975b) for a complete description of the sampling and the methodology used in the two surveys.

Among the illiterate respondents:

- about 43% work in the primary economic sector (they are farmers, herders or fishermen);
- about 19% are unemployed;
- 10% are housewives.

However, among the literate respondents:

- about 33% are civil servants or office workers;
- 19% are students;
- 16% are teachers.

Thus, as could be expected, about 68% of those literate in French are involved in the administration, the tertiary sector, or the educational system, domains in which the use of French is required. In Senegal, those domains are primarily urban or semi-urban. As in most other former French colonies (cf. Bourhis 1982), the knowledge of French constitutes one of the dividing lines between urbanized and western-oriented elites and the majority of the population, which is still constituted by rural workers and the urban poor.[4]

6   Images of French

The surveys in Blondé (1975a, 1975b) include attitudinal aspects related to the perceptions of French in both the literate group (Blondé 1975a) and the illiterate group (Blondé 1975b). Given the paucity of language attitude research data in Africa (Adegbija 1994), these surveys yield precious information on the reasons why illiterate respondents would or would not like to learn French, and on the reasons why literate respondents learned the language.[5]

According to the surveys, 86.6% of the respondents who are illiterate in French would like to learn the language. The reasons given are pragmatic in nature:

- almost half (49.1%) think that knowing French "allows one to have a good job";
- 28.2% view French as a "means of communication among Africans";
- 21.8% think that the language "allows one to be educated";
- a very small minority (0.9%) would learn French because "it is the official language."

The figures above show that French is viewed by these respondents essentially as a tool for economic advancement and education. This view mirrors the functions offi-

---

[4]   60% of the population is rural and 40% urban, with the majority of the latter concentrated in Dakar, according to the 1989 National Census.

[5]   It is worth noting that among those who are illiterate in French, almost half (40%) have gone to Koranic School (90% of the Senegalese population is Muslim), and therefore has some degree of literacy in Arabic.

cially assigned to it. However, the fact that French is the official language plays almost no role in the respondents' desire to learn the language; this might point to a certain disconnect between government and the governed: the latter do not seem to identify with the laws and regulations made in their name, especially given the fact that those are written in a language they do not know. French is also perceived as a communication link with Africans from other former French colonies; this is particularly true given the fact that there is no widely spoken West African language shared by all these countries. One might still keep in mind that French is a language known by only a minority in each country (HCF 1990).

Interestingly, 13.4% of the persons surveyed express no desire to learn French, because for the majority of them (64.7%), French is "the language of white people." This clearly reveals a negative view of French as the language of the former European colonizer, and therefore an instrument of domination and oppression.

The responses given by persons literate in French as to why they learned the language show a marked contrast with those given by the illiterate group:

- 42% learned French because "it is the official language";
- only 8% learned the language "to have a good job."

This group shows a much greater awareness of the law, and the implications of declaring French the official language of the country. As we have seen in section 5, most of its members are civil servants, office workers, teachers, or students; as such, they have to use the official language in their daily activities at work or at school. The low percentage of those who claim to have learned the language "to have a good job" might be due to the fact that most of the respondents already enjoy good positions in the workplace, and do not consider this as a primary reason for them to have learned French. Conversely, they might also be aware that knowing French is no longer the sole guarantor of economic success (Sylla 1987). Other reasons given for learning French include:

- professional obligations (38.5% of the respondents);
- the possibility to communicate with other Africans (36.5% of the respondents);
- cultural reasons: French is seen as a "moyen de culture" by 20% of the respondents;
- more subjective reasons: according to 5% of the respondents, "it is good to speak French."

Here also, practical needs – professional or communicative – are cited, this time by more than 35% of the respondents in each case. However, more ideological motivations also appear: 20% view French as a medium to access "culture", understood here as meaning "high culture." This shows the high prestige associated with French, which itself results from the colonial ideology of considering French language, culture and civilization as superior to any other (for the consequences of such an ideology on French colonial policies in Africa, see for instance Crowder 1962; Calvet 1987; Treffgarne 1986).

7   Conclusion

The examination of the data shows a clear correlation between the socioeconomic status of the respondents and their knowledge of French: the more one is educated in French, the higher his/her position is in the social and economic structure of the country. Knowing French gives access to power, since the executive, legislative and judicial branches of Government all use that language as the sole official language.

There also exists a strong correlation between the perception of French by the respondents and its official status: since mastering French is a major means of economic advancement, it is not surprising that most of those respondents feel the need to learn it, this despite the colonial baggage that the language carries.

One may note the contradiction between the Senegalese government's policy, aimed in effect at maintaining political, economic and cultural ties with the former colonizer through the use of French as the official language, and the social reality of the country: the majority of Senegalese citizens cannot participate effectively in the political and economic system because of their lack of knowledge of French. This reinforces the linguistic and cultural dependency on France, and represents a major obstacle in the process of political and economic democratization. It also has a negative impact on the related goals of social and economic development, which imply the democratization of knowledge (Sylla 1987).

Major proposals were made in the mid eighties, aimed at reforming the educational system of the country, including the current language policy (CNREF 1984; Ka 1993a, 1993b). Even though they still have not been put in force by the present Senegalese government, the success of such language status planning efforts will crucially depend on the recognition and use of Senegalese languages as instruments of socioeconomic advancement.

8   References

ADEGBIJA, Efurosibina (1994): Language Attitudes in Sub-Saharan Africa: A Sociolinguistic Overview. Clevedon: Multilingual Matters.

BAKER, Paul (1980): Inventaire provisoire des langues principales et de l'utilisation des langues dans les Etats indépendants de l'Afrique au sud du Sahara. Paris: UNESCO - IAI.

BAMGBOSE, Ayo (1989): Issues for a Model of Language Planning. In: Language Problems and Language Planning 13.1, 24-34.

BLONDÉ, Jean (1975a): Analyse des résultats d'un premier essai de sondage sociolinguistique effectué en milieu lettré. Dakar: C.L.A.D (Le français au Sénégal: enquêtes et recherches 1).

— (1975b): Résultats d'un sondage sociolinguistique effectué en milieu analphabète. Dakar: C.L.A.D. (Le français au Sénégal: enquêtes et recherches 3).

BOURHIS, Richard Y. (1982): Language Policies and Language Attitudes. Le Monde de la Francophonie. In: Ryan, E. B.; Giles, H. (eds.): Attitudes towards Language Variation. London: Edward Arnold. 34-62.

CALVET, Louis-Jean (1987): La guerre des langues et les politiques linguistiques. Paris: Payot.

C.L.A.D. (CENTRE DE LINGUISTIQUE APPLIQUÉE DE DAKAR) (1966): L'expansion du wolof au Sénégal. Dakar: C.L.A.D. XI.

C.N.R.E.F. (COMMISSION NATIONALE DE RÉFORME DE L'ENSEIGNEMENT ET DE LA FORMATION) (1984): Rapport général, 2 vol.. Dakar: Imprimerie Occident Africain.

CONFE.M.E.N. (CONFÉRENCE DES MINISTRES DE L'EDUCATION DES ETATS D'EXPRESSION FRAN-
ÇAISE) (1986): Promotion et intégration des langues nationales dans les systèmes éducatifs. Bilan
et inventaire. Paris: Champion.
CROWDER, Michael (1962): Senegal: A Study of French Assimilation Policy. London: Oxford Uni-
versity Press.
DJITÉ, Paulin (1991): Langues et développement en Afrique. Language Problems and Language
Planning 15.2, 121-138.
DUMONT, Pierre (1983): Le français et les langues africaines au Sénégal. Paris: Karthala – A.C.C.T.
H.C.F. (HAUT CONSEIL DE LA FRANCOPHONIE) (1990): Etat de la francophonie dans le monde: Rap-
port 1990. Paris: La Documentation Française.
HEINE, Bernd (1990): Language Policy in Africa. In: Weinstein, B. (ed.): Language Policy and Po-
litical Development. Norwood, NJ: Ablex. 167-184.
KA, Omar (1993a): Senegalese Languages in Education: the First Congress of Wolof. In: Fishman, J.
(ed.): The First Congress Phenomenon: The Earliest Stage of Language Planning. The Hague:
Mouton. 305-320.
KA, Omar (1993b): Une nouvelle place pour le français au Senegal? In: The French Review 67.2,
276-290.
KELMAN, Herbert (1972): Language as an aid and barrier to involvement in the national system. In:
Fishman, J. (ed.): Advances in the Sociology of Language II. The Hague: Mouton. 185-212.
PHILLIPSON, Robert (1992): Linguistic Imperialism. Oxford: Oxford University Press.
SÉNÉGAL (République du), MINISTÈRE DE L'ECONOMIE ET DES FINANCES (1989): Principaux ré-
sultats provisoires du recensement général de la population et de l'habitat du Sénégal (avril-mai
1988). Dakar: Bureau National du Recensement.
SYLLA, Abdou (1987): L'école future pour qui? Dakar: ENDA.
TREFFGARNE, Carew (1986): Language Policy in Francophone Africa: Scapegoat or Panacea? In:
Language in Education in Africa. Published Seminar Proceedings, Centre of African Studies.
Edinburgh University Press. 141-170.
TURCOTTE, Denis (1983): Lois, règlements et textes administratifs sur l'usage des langues en Afrique
Occidentale Française (1826-1959). Québec: Presses de l'Université Laval.
U.N.E.S.C.O.-BUREAU RÉGIONAL POUR L'EDUCATION EN AFRIQUE (1985): Les langues communau-
taires africaines et leur utilisation dans l'enseignement et l'alphabétisation. Dakar: UNESCO-
BREDA.
VERRIÈRE, Louis (1965): La population du Sénégal. Aspects quantitatifs. Dakar: Faculté de Droit et
des Sciences Economiques, Université de Dakar.
WEINSTEIN, Brian (1984): Francophonie: Language Planning and National Interests. In: Kramarae, C.
et al. (eds.): Language and Power . London: Sage. 227-242.

Diglossia and Codeswitching Structure: Implications for Syntactic Constraints on Intrasentential Codeswitching

Nkonko M. Kamwangamalu

1 Introduction

In recent years much progress has been made concerning certain aspects (e.g. discourse, syntax, pragmatics) of language contact and codeswitching in multilingual communities around the world (e.g. Kachru 1983; Myers-Scotton 1993; Milroy & Muysken 1995; Auer 1997). From a syntactic point of view, these and several other studies have shown that languages or grammars in contact interact at all levels of linguistic structures (e.g. nouns, verbs, phrases, etc.). This interaction is not random, but it is rule-governed. The question, however, has often been raised of how codeswitching is structured (Clyne 1987). For instance, is codeswitching structure determined by the grammar of one of the participating languages in a given speech situation; or is it the case that it is determined evenly by all the participating languages?

This paper examines these issues in the light of codeswitching (hereafter CS) data involving English with selected African languages; and against the backdrop of the diglossic relationship that exists between English and these languages. In this relationship English is the High (H) language and African languages are the Low (L) languages in the sense of Ferguson (1959) as revised in Fishman (1967). Accordingly, in their linguistic behaviors African bilingual speakers tend to draw linguistic items from English when speaking an African language. I argue that structurally the resulting CS speech is almost exclusively governed by the syntactic structure rules of the African language with which English is involved in CS. Elsewhere I have referred to the participating African language as the host or matrix language; and have described English as the guest or embedded language (Kamwangamalu 1989). The concept of matrix language has been defined from various angles in the literature. Some researchers (e.g. Bhatt 1997) describe the ML as the language of the INFL, that is, the language which generates inflectional morphology, as well as related microlinguistic features, such as word order, agreement, tense marking, etc. Others (e.g. Myers-Scotton 1993:232) describe the the matrix language as "the language with the higher frequency of morphemes in a discourse sample in which CS occurs". Others still define the matrix language as the one that a bilingual speaker is most fluent in (e.g. Bentahila & Davies 1997). In this paper, I argue that the criteria for determining the matrix language (e.g. inflectional morphology, word order, frequency of morphemes, etc.) all fall out from the diglossic situation in which CS takes place; and that diglossia provides a basis against which the matrix language and constraints in CS can be determined. It is not surprising, then, that in a diglossic situation only the language identified as L supplies the rules according to which CS is structured. This point is in tune with the Matrix Language Principle, which I have proposed previously to account for syntactic constraints in CS (Kamwangamalu 1989). Briefly, what this principle says is that in CS one language, the matrix language, is structurally more dominant than the

other, the embedded language; it determines what constituents of the embedded language can and where they should be used in a CS utterance. Before I present evidence
for this principle, I shall first describe the language situation in Africa, with a focus on
diglossia, to provide the background against which intrasentential constraints on CS
will be discussed. This will be followed by an overview of some of the proposed universal constraints in CS. I shall demonstrate that these constraints are not as universal
as they have been claimed to be. Considering that diglossia is universal, I shall suggest
that these constraints should be abandoned, for they hardly take into account the diglossic situation in which most CS takes place.

2   Diglossia in Africa

Ferguson (1959) uses the term *diglossia*[1] to refer to a situation where two genetically
related varieties of a language, one identified as the *H(igh)* variety and the other as the
L(ow) variety, have clearly distinct functions in the community. The H variety is used
in formal settings; whereas the L variety is used in informal interactions with family,
friends, colleagues (Ferguson 1972:236). Ferguson (1972:245) defines diglossia as

> "a relatively stable language situation in which, in addition to the primary dialects of the lan-
> guage (which may include a standard or regional standards), there is a very divergent, highly
> codified (often grammatically more complex) superposed variety, the vehicle of a large and
> respected body of written literature, either of an earlier period or in another speech commu-
> nity, which is learned largely by formal education and is used for most written and formal
> spoken purposes but is not used by any sector of the community for ordinary conversation."

Fishman (1967) has extended the definition of diglossia to include situations where
two genetically unrelated languages are used in the community, one in formal settings
and the other in informal settings. This extended or broad diglossia as it has come to
be known, best describes the relationship that holds between African languages and
former colonial languages, English, French and Portuguese. This relationship is diglossic: English, French, and Portuguese are the H languages; and the African languages are the L languages.

The concept of diglossia has received considerable attention in the literature (e.g.,
Berger 1990, Fishman 1983, Timm 1981, Schiffman 1997). Studies of diglossia, including those that have attempted to associate diglossia with CS (e.g. Mkilifi 1978,
Scotton 1986; Wald 1986), have discussed this concept mostly from a functional perspective. For instance, Mkilifi (1978) discusses the triglossia Vernacular-Swahili-
English in Tanzania in terms of the functional dependency that exists among these
languages. He shows that each of these languages is assigned to certain domains in
the community: the vernacular is used as an intra-group language and is associated
with rural African culture-related activities; Kiswahili is associated with pre-industrial,
non-technological urban type of African culture; English is associated with technology and official business. In a sense, then, these languages are in complementary distribution; a point that Wald (1986) also makes about the Yakoma (L) - Sango (H) di-

---

[1]   Harold Schiffman (1997:214) notes that the phenomenon of *diglossia* was mentioned earlier, as
     diglossie, in the work of Marcais (1932-3).

glossia in Bangui, Central African Republic. In this diglossia, as in the Vernacular-Swahili-English triglossia in Tanzania, CS is very common and is dependent on the variables of the context of situation: the topic, the setting, and the interlocutors. Like Mkilifi and Wald, Scotton (1986) examines CS and diglossia from a functional perspective, but with a focus on the applicability of her markedness model in narrow and broad diglossic communities. In particular, Scotton explores whether the functions of CS proposed in the markedness model (e.g. CS as marked choice, CS as unmarked choice, CS as sequential choice, CS as exploratory choice) obtain in both types of communities. She concludes (1986:414) that narrow diglossic communities differ most distinctly from other bilingual communities in not allowing CS as an overall unmarked choice. It is explained that two conditions underpinning CS as unmarked choice are not met in narrow diglossic communities. These are:

"(1) Gradient domain complementarity and/or differential allocation of the varieites in the community's repertoire across groups in the community such that role models for the unmarked use of more than one variety for the same conventionalized exchange exist" (Scotton 1986:414)

and

"(2), Positive evaluation of the indentity associated with the unmarked choice of both varietes in the same exchange" (Scotton 1986:414)

To my knowledge, and as is evident from the studies examined above, diglossia has hardly been used to explain syntactic patterns in CS; to explain the role of each participating language in structuring CS; nor to describe intrasentential constraints on CS. Ferguson himself has considered the place of CS in diglossia but on a smaller scale and much less central place (Wald 1986:426) and mostly from a functional perspective. The closest that Ferguson comes to describing CS structure in a diglossic situation is when he says that "H stems [occur] with L grammatical encoding" (Ferguson 1962:77). In this paper I argue that diglossia is a very powerful theoretical construct for the study of CS structure: the distinction between H and L parallels the distinction between the matrix language (ML) and the embedded language (EL). The language identified as L is usually the matrix language; while the one identified as H is usually the embedded language. This distinction between H and L or ML and EL is crucial in any attempts to describe CS structure and attendant intrasentential constraints. The language identified as L, I shall argue, is also the one imposing constraints on CS structure.

3   Constraints on codeswitching: an overview

Research into the syntax of CS has come a very long way. Earlier studies of the syntax of CS claimed that CS was a random mixture of languages, that is, bilingual speakers engage in CS because there are no constraints on what they can or cannot mix in their speech (Espinosa 1917; Lance 1975). Over the years, however, several studies have shown that there exist structural constraints in CS. Some of these constraints have been claimed to be language specific; while others have been claimed to be language universal.

Language specific constraints are those that apply to CS in a particular multilingual community. Language universal constraints are those that are assumed to apply to CS structure cross-linguistically. Many such constraints have been proposed, among them the Government Constraint (di Sciullo et al 1986), the Dual Structure Principle (Sridhar & Sridhar 1980), the Stand-Alone Principle (Azuma, 1996), the Equivalence Constraint (Poplack 1981), the Switch Alpha Constraint (Choi 1991), to list but a few. Several studies have shown that, like grammars, the proposed constraints leak; that is, none of these constraints are as universal as they have been claimed to be (e.g. Bentahila & Davies 1983; Clyne 1987; Bhatt 1997). Due to space limitation, I shall review only one of the most popular of these constraints, the Equivalence Constraint (Poplack 1981), together with a related constraint, the Switch Alpha Constraint (Choi 1991).

3.1   The equivalence constraint

Codeswitches will tend to occur at points in discourse where juxtaposition of L1 and L2 elements does not violate a syntactic rule of either language that is, at points around which the surface structure of the languages map onto each other.

The Equivalence Constraint has been challenged in several studies (e.g. Bentahila 1983; Bhatt 1997; Kamwangamalu 1987; Choi 1991, Myers-Scotton 1993). The conclusions that emerge from these studies is that the Equivalence Constraint is inadequate for it focuses on the linear order of items rather than on their structural relations. This constraint perhaps holds for structurally similar languages such as those on the basis of which it was formulated, viz. Spanish and English; but it fails to account for cross-linguistic structural patterns in CS. In order to remedy the inadequacies of the Equivalence Constraint, Choi (1991) proposes what he calls the Switch Alpha Constraint.

3.2   The switch-alpha constraint

"*Switch-alpha* means switch anything anywhere, that is, any element can be switched in any place in a structure so long as the particular-language-pair integrity is maintained" (emphasis in the original) (Choi 1991:896).

Choi claims that switch-alpha is an unspecified universal rule in CS grammar. It is similar to move-alpha in generative grammar in that like move-alpha, which results from the interaction of several factors such as case, morphological properties and so on. switch-alpha, too, is a consequence of the interaction of several facts, such as language-particular integrity, particular-language-pair integrity, and specific-language-pair constraints.

In a recent study (Kamwangamalu 1994), however, I have demonstrated that switch-alpha is a replica rather than an alternative to the constraint it was intended to supersede, the Equivalence Constraint (Poplack 1981). The main claim of both switch-alpha and the Equivalence Constraint is that in CS the syntactic integrity of either of the languages involved should not be violated. The data in (1) challenges this claim. It shows that in siSwati-English CS, CS inside the NP (e.g. *conversation yabo* 'lit.: conversation their') does not require syntactic equivalence between the structures of siSwati and English, as would be required by the Equivalence Constraint; nor does it require that the syntactic integrity of the language-pair involved be preserved, as Choi suggests. It is evident that the order of elements in the noun phrase *conversation yabo* 'conversation their' is definitely not English. This suggests that only the syntactic integrity of one language, siSwati, is preserved; while that of the other language, English, is violated.

1) *siSwati-English*
   Kule **CONVERSATION** *yabo* **ba-ADDRESS-a** *liciniso* **CONCERNING** *le*
   SITUATION
   in conversation their 3AGR-address-FV truth concerning this situation
   "In their conversation they address the truth concerning this situation"

4 The Matrix Language Principle

As I have observed elsewhere (e.g. Kamwangamalu 1999), the idea that in code-switching one language is structurally more dominant than the other has appeared in various guises in recent literature (e.g. Azuma 1993; Grosjean 1988; Joshi 1985; Forson 1988). Here, however, I will focus on one of these guises, the *Matrix Language Principle*, which I have proposed in previous works on constraints in CS (Kamwangamalu 1987, 1989, 1994). In its original form, the *Matrix Language Principle* stipulates that

> "In every code-mixed discourse (D) involving language X (L$_x$) and language Y (L$_y$), where L$_x$ is identified as the host (or matrix) language and L$_y$ as the guest (or embedded) language, the morphosyntactic structure rules of L$_y$ must conform to the morphosyntactic structure rules of L$_x$, the language of the discourse (Kamwangamalu 1989:132)."

Put simply, the Matrix Language Principle requires that in CS a distinction be made between two types of languages, the ML and the EL. In recent literature the ML and the EL have also come to be known as *absorbing code* and *absorbed code* (Pandey 1996), or as *waxing language* and *waning language* (Myers-Scotton 1997), respectively. Second, the Matrix Language Principle requires that the ML licenses the switchability of the linguistic elements drawn from the EL. Against this background, I argue that in CS involving English, French or Portuguese with an African language, the African language is almost exclusively the matrix language; that is, the African language determines where in a CS structure linguistic items of the embedded language, English (French or Portuguese) should be used. What this means is that the matrix language and the embedded language participate unequally in structuring CS, with the matrix language being structurally more dominant than the embedded language.

Similar ideas have independently been proposed in Myers-Scotton (1993). In her approach, which she calls the *Matrix Language Frame Model*, Myers-Scotton says that two interrelated hierarchies direct the structuring of sentences containing CS. These are:

a) *The Matrix Language vs Embedded language hierarchy.* Of the two or more languages involved in CS, one plays the more dominant role. It is labelled the *Matrix Language,* with the other language(s) labelled the *Embedded Language(s).*

b) *The system vs content morpheme hierarchy.*

The hierarchy in b) is built on two principles, i) *The Morpheme Order Principle* and ii) *The System Morpheme Principle.* The former principle says that in a codeswitched constituent, morpheme order will be that of the matrix language; while the latter claims that productive system morphemes, that is function words, inflectional affixes and auxiliary verbs must come from the matrix language. Except for its psycholinguistic orientation, sociolinguistically Myers-Scotton's model is essentially the same as Kamwangamalu's (1989) model (see above), which claims that "in a codeswitched structure only the matrix language will determine the acceptability/unacceptability of any participating constituent [from the embedded language]" (Kamwangamalu 1994: 74).

Due to space limitation, the discussion that follows provides only one piece of evidence, inflectional morphology, for the proposed Matrix Language Principle. Additional evidence can be seen in Kamwangamalu (1994).

4.1   Inflectional morphology

In CS involving English (or French, Portuguese) with an African language, an English verb can take on an inflectional morpheme of the African language involved. This can be seen from verbal inflections on the verbs *discuss, lose, overturn,* and *reach* in the data in 2) - 4). These verbs have one feature in common: they display the form of what Boeschoten (1991:101) has termed *telegraphic switching,* that is, they lack some obligatory grammatical information, in this case the *ed* morpheme, required in their language of origin, English.

2) *siSwati-English*
   Tennis association i-discuss-ile (*i-discuss-ed) le-problem ku **meeting** yabo ye kugcina.
   (The tennis association discussed that problem at their last meeting)

3) *Swahili-English* (Mkilifi 1978:140)
   Ile **accident ilitokea alipo-lose (*alipolost) control** na **aka-overturn (*aka-overturned) and landed into a ditch.**
   (The accident occurred when he lost control and overturned and ...)

4) *Zulu-English* (Kieswetter 1995:63)
   Ungasho *my friend*, sesi-*reach*-e i-*point of no return*
   (You don't say my friend, we have reached a point of no return.)

This data shows that the English verbs *discuss, lose, overturn,* and *reach* lack the obligatory English past tense morpheme -*ed* because past tense is already accounted for by the past tense morphemes of the respective African languages with which English is involved in CS: the siSwati -*ile* in 2), the Swahili -*li*- and -*aka* in 3), the Zulu -*si*- in 4). The prevalence in this data of the syntax of the African languages over that of English results in codeswitches that Appel & Muysken (1987) describe as 'suspension of grammar', that is codeswitches that maintain the syntactic integrity of one language (here, an African language) but not of the other language (e.g. English).

5 Conclusion

Over the past years several attempts have been made to define intrasentential constraints in CS (Poplack 1981; Sridhar and Sridhar 1980; di Sciullo et al 1986; Clyne 1987; Myers-Scotton 1993; Azuma 1996). These and related studies have indeed contributed significantly to our understanding of CS. However, most of them have tended to overlook the macrolinguistic context in which CS takes place. In this paper I have argued that diglossia is a useful macrolinguistic construct for the study of intrasentential CS. Diglossia determines the sociolinguistic status, H or L, of each of the participating languages in CS. It thus serves as a basis on which the distinction between the matrix language and the embedded language can be made. With this distinction in mind, I have proposed that constraints in CS can be defined in terms of the Matrix Language Principle. What this principle says is that in CS two types of language need to be distinguished, the matrix language on the one hand; and the embedded language on the other. In a diglossic situation, the matrix language is usually the one identified as L. It is this language, L, but not H, that determines CS structure, as the evidence presented in this paper has shown.

Additional evidence for the Matrix Language Principle comes from studies of CS across languages; e.g. Forson (1988) on Akan-English CS in Ghana; Khati (1992) on Sotho-English CS in Lesotho (and South Africa); Kamwangamalu and Lee (1991) on Chinese (Mandarin)-English CS in Singapore; Haust (1995) on Wolof-English and Mandinka-English CS in the Gambia; and Boeschoten (1991) on Turkish-Dutch CS in the Netherlands.

For instance, in his study of Akan-English CS Forson (1988:90) points out that the Akan grammatical system and grammatical items are preferred in Akan-English CS. This, Forson argues, supports the claim that, no matter how much English is found in Akan-English CS, the sociolinguistic setting indicates that the speakers consider themselves as speaking Akan, or the relevant Ghanaian language. Within the approach proposed in the present study, Akan would qualify as the matrix language. It is, thus, the language in terms of which constraints in Akan-English CS would have to be defined.

Similarly, in his study of Turkish-Dutch CS in the Netherlands Boeschoten (1991) provides yet additional evidence for the Matrix Language Principle. In particular, Boeschoten remarks that "with respect to the Turkish-Dutch data, it is important to note that the nature of switches is asymmetrical, i.e. the integrity of the Turkish syntax is maintained, but not of the Dutch". Boeschoten does not explicity refer to the role of diglossia in determining Turkish-Dutch CS structure. However, his following conclusions are telling:

i) a model of CS should be related to the sociolinguistic setting of varieties in a given society; and, more importantly,

ii) it should pay attention to social asymmetry (i.e. the strong tendency to unidirectionality of code-switches which cannot be accounted for by formulating post-hoc constraints).

I would like to argue that the social asymmetry is indeed a result of the diglossic relationship of Turkish to Dutch in the Netherlands, a relationship where Turkish is L and Dutch is H. Consequently, Turkish licenses the switchability of Dutch elements in Turkish-Dutch CS.

The facts presented here and throughout this paper suggest strongly that, in a diglossic situation, L determines CS structure and attendant intrasentential constraints.

6   References

APPEL, Rene; Muysken, Pieter (1987): Language Contact and Bilingualism. Baltimore, MD: Edward Arnold.

AUER, Peter (ed.) (1997): Codeswitching in conversation. London: Routledge.

AZUMA, Shoji (1996): Free Morpheme Constraint revisited. In: World Englishes 15.3, 361-68.

— (1993): The frame-content hypothesis in speech production: Evidence from intrasentential code-switching. In: Linguistics 31, 1071-93.

BERGER, Marianne R. (1990): Diglossia within a general theoretical perspective: Charles Ferguson's concept 30 years later. In: Multilingua 9.3: 285-95.

BENTAHILA, Abdelali; DAVIES, Eirlys E. (1997): Codeswitching: an unequal partnership. In: Jacobson, Rodolfo (ed.): Codeswitching Worldwide. Berlin: Mouton, 25-50.

— (1983): The syntax of Arabic-French code-switching. In: Lingua 59.4, 301-30.

BOESCHOTEN, Hendrik (1991): Asymmetrical code-switching in immigrant communities. In: Papers for the workshop on constraints, conditions and models. ESF Scientific Networks, 85-100.

CHOI, Jae Oh (1991): Korean-English codeswitching: switch-alpha and linguistic constraints. In: Linguistics 29, 877-902.

CLYNE, Michael G. (1987): Constraints on code-switching: How universal are they? In: Linguistics 25, 739-64.

COULMAS, Florian (ed.) (1997): The Handbook of Sociolinguistics. Cambridge, Mass.: Blackwell.

DI SCIULLO, Anne Marie; Muysken, Pieter; Singh, Rajendra (1986): Government and codemixing. In: The Journal of Linguistics 22, 1-24.

Espinosa, Aurelio (1917): Speech mixture in New Mexico: the influence of the English language on New Mexican Spanish. In: Stephens, H. M.; Bolton, H. E. (eds.): The Pacific Ocean in History. New York: Macmillan, 408-28.

FERGUSON, Charles A (1959 [1972]): Diglossia. In: Word 15, 325-40.

FISHMAN, Joshua (1983): Epistemology, methodology and ideology in the sociolinguistic enterprise. In: Language Learning 33.5, 33-47.

— (1967): Bilingualism with and without diglossia; diglossia with and without bilingualism. In: The Journal of Social Issues 23.2, 29-39.

FISHMAN, J. A. et al. (eds.) (1986): The Fergusonian Impact, ii. Berlin: Mouton de Gruyter.

FORSON, Barnard (1988): Codeswitching, our third tongue? In: Universitas 10, 180-94.

HAUST, Delia (1995): Codeswitching in the Gambia: Eine soziolinguistische Untersuchung von Mandinka, Wolof und Englisch in Kontakt (with an English summary). Köln: Köppe (Sprachkontakt in Afrika 1).

KACHRU, Braj B. (1983): On mixing. In: The Indianization of English: The English language in India. New Delhi: Oxford University Press, 193-207.

KAMWANGAMALU, Nkonko M. (1999): The state of codeswitching research at the dawn of the new millennium. In: The South African Journal of Linguistics 17.4.

— (1994): siSwati-English codeswitching: the matrix language principle and linguistic constraints. In: The South African Journal of African Languages.

— (1989): Codemixing across languages: Structure, functions, and constraints (Doctoral dissertation, University of Illinois) Urbana, Illinois.

— (1987): French/Vernacular Code-Mixing in Zaire: Implications for Syntactic Constraints. In: Chicago Linguistic Society 23.1, 166-80.

KAMWANGAMALU, Nkonko M.; LEE Cher Leng (1991): Chinese-English codemixing: A case of matrix language assignment. In: World Englishes 10.3, 247-61.

KHATI, Thekiso (1992): Intra-lexical switching or nonce borrowing: Evidence from Sotho-English performance. In: Herbert, Robert (ed.): Language and Society in Africa, Johannesburg: Wits University Press, 181-96.

KIESWETTER, Alyson (1995): Codeswitching amongst African high school pupils. Johannesburg: University of the Witwatersrand Occasional Papers in African Linguistics 1.

LANCE, Donald (1975): Spanish-English code-switching. In: Hernandez-Chavez, C.; Beltramo. A. (eds.): EL Lenguaje de los Chicanos. Arlington, VA: Center for Applied Linguistics, 138-53.

MARCAIS, W. (1930): La diglossie Arabe. In: L'Enseignement Public 97, 20-39.

MKILIFI, Abdoulaziz M. (1978): Triglossia and Swahili-English bilingualism in Tanzania. In: Fishman, Joshua (ed.): Advances in the study of societal multilingualism. The Hague: Mouton, 129-149.

MYERS-SCOTTON, Carol (1997): Codeswitching. In: Coulmas: 217-37.

— (1993): Duelling languages: Grammatical structure in codeswitching. Oxford: Oxford University Press.

MILROY, Lesley; Pieter Muysken (eds.) (1995): One speaker, two languages: Cross-disciplinary perspectives on codeswitching. Cambridge: Cambridge University Press.

PANDEY, Anita (1996): The pragmatics of code alternation in Nigerian English. In: Studies in the Linguistic Sciences 24.2.

POPLACK, Shana (1981): Sometimes I'll start a sentence in Spanish y termino en Espanol: Toward a typology of code-switching. In: Linguistics 18, 581-618.

SCHIFFMAN, Harold (1997): Diglossia as a sociolinguistic situation. In: Coulmas: 205-16.

SCOTTON, Carol Myers (1986): Diglossia and codeswitching. In: Fishman et al.: 403-15.

SRIDHAR, S. N.; SRIDHAR, Kamal K. (1980): The syntax and psycholinguistics of bilingual codemixing. In: The Canadian Journal of Psychology 34, 407-16.

TIMM, Leonora A (1981): Diglossia old and new – a critique. In: Anthropological Linguistics 23.8, 356-367.

WALD, Paul (1986): Diglossia applied: Vernacular mixing and functional switching with Bangui Yakomas. In: Fishman et al.: 417-30.

Linguists and Public Linguistics in the 21st Century

Robert D. King

It is stating the obvious to say that modern linguistics is heavily weighted toward theoretical linguistics – toward formal theory. Theory is the center of the enterprise, and the other things that linguists do – sociolinguistics, applied linguistics, acquisition, historical linguistics – are situated on the periphery. Whether one likes this set of priorities or not, it is a fair statement of the way things are and have been for most of modern linguistics.

I do not think the primacy of theory is a priori a bad thing. I want to be emphatic about that because I will be arguing here for the importance of what I call "public linguistics" – linguistics in aid of a better society – but to say that public linguistics is important does not mean that it should be the heart of the linguistics venture. It is a question of balance. Theory needs no defenders. Public linguistics does. My intention is to refresh our collective memory of a time when public linguistics played a larger role in linguistics than it does today. I want to make the case that we should bring public linguistics in from the cold. The next millennium will need a more sophisticated understanding of language.

The drift of the center of gravity of linguistics toward formal theory is heavily evident to anyone whose involvement in the field predates the 1970s. I got into linguistics at the beginning of the 1960s – more than a generation ago. I cannot remember ever asking myself in the 1960s and 1970s what the "relevance" of my research in linguistics might be. The thing was good in itself: knowledge for the sake of knowledge was a positive good. Research was its own reward. Linguistic theory was and is its own justification. These things one felt.

Nevertheless, there was a sentiment that I shared along with most of my pre-Chomsky cohort – that linguistics was important beyond itself, that we were in the vanguard of a movement that would bring enlightenment to the "larger" community in matters of language. Language mattered, linguistics mattered; therefore "public linguistics" was part of our mission. Our discipline was "extroverted" in the Jungian sense of "connectedness to the outside world": concerned beyond itself.

Linguistics, like any science or social science, intrinsically has two dimensions: the dual aspect of looking inward and looking outward. There have always been physicists there to mediate between their academic field and the affairs of government – to engage in "public physics." J. Robert Oppenheimer comes to mind, as does Werner Heisenberg though in a quite different aspect. You can be a physicist without being an Oppenheimer, but it is good that an Oppenheimer was there to explain physics to non-physicists. It is never good for an academic discipline to define itself so narrowly and to so design its reward structures as to discourage the deployment of its knowledge around the problems of society.

Public linguistics was an important constituent of earlier American linguistics. This was notably true of the two giants of American linguistics, Edward Sapir and Leonard Bloomfield. The bibliography of Sapir's writings selected by David Mandelbaum (1985) shows the exceptional reach of the man – far beyond those theoretical writings of his that are classics in linguistics. Sapir wrote prolifically on non-theoretical topics and for non-linguistic audiences: "Wanted, a World Language"; "The Function of an International Auxiliary Language"; "Speech as a Personality Trait' (speech delivered before the Illinois Society for Mental Hygiene." And, as a student of Franz Boas, there were many essays attacking the fallacies of "race": "Let Race Alone"; "Racial Superiority"; "Undesirables – Klanned or Banned." Dell Hymes' *Epilogue* to the 1985 reprinting of Sapir's *Selected Writings* stresses his contribution past the narrow limits of academic linguistics and anthropology (Mandelbaum 1985:598-600). One notices how prolific a contributor Sapir was to *non-academic* journals: *The American Mercury* and *Nation*, two of his favorite publication outlets, were leading general journals of intellectual opinion in the 1920s and 1930s.

Leonard Bloomfield, while an altogether different personality type from Edward Sapir – he was much more shy and withdrawn – took his public obligations as linguist very seriously. In his obituary of Bloomfield Bernard Bloch wrote:

"His absorbing interest in linguistics as a science did not prevent him from devoting himself also – more diligently than the majority of linguists – to its practical applications, especially in the teaching of reading and the study of foreign languages. In opposition to many scholars ... he felt that scientific inquiry was by no means wholly its own justification, which lay rather in the hope that it might lead us ultimately 'toward the understanding and control of human events.' Among the more utilitarian products of this conviction are ... his English primer, a complete course for teaching school-children to read and write." (Hockett 1970:527)

The tradition of "public linguistics" continues today in American linguistics but less prominently, it is clear, than in the early days. It is a shrunken presence. As a discipline we have become, to use Jungian terminology a final time, more "introverted": "the state or tendency toward being wholly or predominantly concerned with and interested in one's own mental life."

It is an interesting question what has led to the demise of public linguistics as a respected part of our mission. It is a trend, a bias, widespread in the social sciences – in sociology, economics, anthropology, psychology. Surely the linguistic mindset that goes back to Chomsky and before him to Bloomfield bears some responsibility for what has happened in our field. It is not necessarily a single direct step from Bloomfield's "Postulates" and Chomsky's declaration that "Linguistics is a branch of the study of the mind" to "Nothing matters much but formal linguistic theory," but it has been an easy progress. And I think on the whole that this has been an unfortunate development, the eclipse of public linguistics.

I have been talking about linguistics in America, but most schools of linguistic theory have had a "public" aspect that was felt to be an important part of their mission. Certainly linguistics in Germany was this way. I am thinking of the *Deutscher Sprachatlas*, the Institut für deutsche Sprache and other such "public" manifestations – institutions – of the discipline. I leave it to observers closer to the current scene to judge how public a countenance linguistics has in contemporary Germany.

The public function was an important part of the "British School" associated with J. R. Firth. Firth had worked in India, and he brought to his linguistics a keen perception of the practical need for linguists to apply their expertise to social and political questions in which language plays a part, as did and do so many problems in India.

Firth was also a gifted popularizer of linguistics. His books *The Tongues of Man and Speech*, written in the 1930s for the public, are models of their kind (Firth 1964). Public linguists is very nearly the last thing that comes to mind when one thinks of the Prague School, but here is Mathesius, one of the founders of the Prague Linguistic Circle, writing about its activities in the early 1930s:

> "After the Prague Congress of Slavists we were increasingly conscious of our duty not to neglect ... propaganda for our ideas at home. We could attempt to do this propagandist work with a good conscience because our approach to language and its functions had never for us been a purely linguistic affair ... [T]he consequences implied by our conception of the functions of the standard language impinged ever more intensely on the issue of our cultural life ... [W]e presented ourselves to the wider public of Czech educated circles in a series of meetings, the purpose of which was not to celebrate but to fight." (Mathesius 1966:145)

The "fight" that Mathesius alludes to was the battle over Standard Czech after Czechoslovakia had gained its independence at the end of the First World War. During Habsburgian hegemony the Czech language had retreated to the countryside and yielded its place among the urban intelligentsia to German. In such a situation, when a language is being reforged after a period of neglect or suppression, linguists can rarely afford not be "public" linguists. Ordinary people want to know how to write their language and which words and constructions to use, and if linguists do not help supply the answers then others less suited to the task will. We see this in the Baltic countries today, their languages emerging from the domination of the Russian language as the countries themselves emerge from the domination of the Soviet Union (Levin 1999). Under such circumstances linguists cannot claim the indulgence of introversion, nor can they look down their noses at linguistic prescriptivism (as we linguists normally do, almost reflexively).

I doubt seriously whether Panini and his associates ever stopped to ask themselves whether what they were doing was "formal linguistics" or "public linguistics" in my sense. A question like that simply could not arise. Linguistics in ancient India was the core of tradition – it possessed an intellectual centrality and scholarly hegemony that beggars belief today. Philosophy occupied center stage in ancient Greece, as law and public administration did in imperial Rome. In classical India, however, it was *language* – the study of Sanskrit grammar – that the intellect worshipped. The study of language in ancient India required no apologists. Linguistics was suffused with the light of sanctity, endowed with religious purpose. Panini and Patanjali and later Indian grammarians conceived their ministrations on behalf of the Sanskrit language as a devotional. Their activity was more akin to a priesthood, a calling, than it was the writing of a grammar of Sanksrit.

This merging of grammar and linguistics with religion and public life is alien to the Western mind – it is a dualism almost impossible for Westerners to grasp. The Western mind, left to itself, always drifts toward monism: we venerate the "Either-Or" and anathematize the "Both-And." Consequently we come to think of our discipline not as a house of many rooms but as a discipline in which formal theory is the central enterprise and the most worthy, and the rest perches on the periphery.

It seems to me that this inward-turning in linguistics comes at a particularly unfortunate time, for public policy in country after country badly needs the advice and counsel of linguists. For example, the very existence of minority languages is threatened as never before. We do not know precisely how many languages there are in the world today, but even setting aside the usual niggling questions of "language" versus "dialect" there are several thousand, and some linguists believe that there are more than 6,000. (These data and the accompanying discussion are taken from *The Washington Post*, 9 August 1999, A1, A8.)

At least one of these languages disappears on an average of every two weeks: its last native speaker dies – a shocking and saddening statistic. And the velocity of language loss is accelerating. Michael Krauss, director of the Alaska Native Language Center and one of the linguists most involved in language-preservation, says: "The only [languages] that are safe have some kind of power or state support, or have sheer numbers on their side. That's less than 200 languages." Krauss believes that 95% of the other remaining languages will disappear during the next century or become "moribund" – spoken by a few elders, but untaught and unknown among children. Krauss is possibly more pessimistic than other linguists, but even the optimists believe that half of the languages that are not made safe by numbers and state power will disappear in a hundred years.

Let us not harbor the illusion that loss of languages could be reversed if only governments were willing to listen to linguists for once. Too many forces at work in our world today conspire to condemn minority and regional languages to extinction. It sometimes seems to me as if every single development in modern times has had the unintended consequence of working against the retention of minority languages: radio, television, film, the global economy, air travel, automobiles, the spread of English as a world language, pop culture, Big Macs, Quarter Pounders with Cheese, Coca Cola, Pepsi, the Internet, hot dogs, french fries. Not *one* of these things encourages the preservation of a threatened language.

Above all, marginal languages are condemned to a slow death by the Cult of Youth that has completely eclipsed Veneration for Elders in society after society. Speakers of endangered languages are always older people, often very old people. If society respects its elders, then young people learn their language; if not, not.

There is no magic simplification of the problem of preserving threatened languages, but it is heartening to see what can be done. A language restoration program in Hawaii suggests possibilities for bringing back a threatened language from the brink of extinction. This program started in 1984 with twelve preschoolers being taught in their ancestral language, Hawaiian, and took them into high school, adding a year of curriculum in Hawaiian at a time. The first eleven seniors graduated in 1999, and there are now almost 2,000 students enrolled in the program, including 200 in preschool and 500 in kindergarten. This is a small success story of public linguistics in an otherwise almost empty book, and every bit of it required close cooperation between school officials, parents, organizations like the PTA (Parent Teacher Association – a staple of the American school system), and linguists.

At the very least linguists have the public obligation to preach from every rostrum that it is a tragic thing to lose a language. One of the saddest aspects of this situation is that the speakers of a threatened language are so often indifferent to its fate, as are government officials who might be in a position to do something about it. "So what if Choctaw, or Navajo, or Catalan in the French département of the Pyrénées-Orientales, or Irish, or Yiddish, or whatever disappears? Money talks: there is no economic reason to keep these languages alive." Such attitudes are more widespread, even among speakers of those languages, than we like to admit even privately. If nothing else we owe it to ourselves as linguists to rail against this point of view and to gain adherents of language preservation.

To lose a language is to lose a culture. It is as tragic as the loss of a species. We – we linguists – need to construct a climate of opinion that equates the two: the loss of a language and the loss of a species. The movement to save the whale did not "just happen." It was the result of an organized movement led by people resolved to make the disappearance of a species unacceptable.

Can linguists do any less? As Krauss (1992:10) has written:

"To what extent are endangered languages a priority in modern linguistics? Which languages of the world receive the most attention? Are graduate students encouraged to document moribund or endangered languages for their dissertations? How much encouragement is there to compile a dictionary of one? How many academic departments encourage applied linguistics in communities for the support of endangered languages? How many departments provide appropriate training for speakers of these languages who are most ideally suited to do the most needed work? Obviously we must do some serious rethinking of our priorities lest linguistics go down in history as the only science that presided obliviously over the disappearance of 90% of the very field to which it is dedicated."

Peculiar things have been going on in my own country in the sphere of language politics. Language has almost never been a major political issue in American life. The idea of language as a political force – as something that might threaten the unity of a country – is alien to our way of thinking and to our cultural traditions. The need for public linguistics has been correspondingly low, but this has changed for the worse in recent years (because of large-scale immigration). An ill-advised effort to have English declared the official language of the United States began in the 1980s.

I did my "public-linguistics" part to defang the Official English movement by writing an article for the American mass-circulation journal of intellectual opinion *The Atlantic Monthly* (April, 1997). (On this article and the often bizarre reactions to it see King 1999. One of the lessons of public linguistics I learned is this: you had better grow a thick skin if you enter the public arena.)

In my piece I limited my concern to just the one question I saw and still see as most fundamental, the question that lies at the root of most of the uneasiness: Is the unity of America threatened by the preservation on its soil of languages other than English? I argued in the usual ways familiar from introductory linguistics classes that we should remain supine and reduce the decibel level about language: the less said about it the better; and above all the less *done* about legislating language (like passing laws making English official) the better. We have – we *still* have – a clear and *strong* national identity, a transcendent "Unique Otherness" (as I called it) that inoculates us against the linguistic illnesses that bore from within the body politic of Canada, Belgium, Sri Lanka, and other countries with weakly fused national identities. Switzerland, for example, is stable past the point of boredom in spite of its multiple languages – because it has a strong national identity. I also believe, contrary to much opinion, that India with its some nineteen official languages is no longer threatened by language

(King 1997). India, as different from Switzerland as two countries can possibly be, too has a strong sense of national identity, for all its political problems. The thrust of my article was that language diversity poses no threat to American unity, that we are not close to any kind of danger point in this regard, and I am optimistic enough to believe that we never will be. I suggested that we relax and luxuriate in the richness of our linguistic diversity and our traditional tolerance of language differences. To pass a law is to ask for trouble. The Law of Unintended Consequences – Sod's Law the British call it – always comes into play when laws are passed, and who can say where a law making English the official language would take us? Wise governments stay as far away from language legislation as they possibly can.

I am happy to say that the movement to make English the official language of the United States has now stalled and is, barring unforeseen events, dead in the water. I would love to leave the impression that I single-handedly defeated it by my article – the picture of St. George slaying the dragon sways before me – but, alas, I am afraid my article had less than nothing to do with it. Politics has done Official English in. There are simply too many immigrants in America who, whether they keep their language or not – and they usually do not past the first generation – mistrust language legislation. It sounds threatening, atavistic, unfriendly, anti-immigrant, xenophobic – all of which it of course in fact is. And these people vote. Politicians may be deaf to the disquisitions of linguists, but they are neither deaf nor stupid when it comes to counting votes. So I think that America is safe for the time being from ill-advised state meddling with language.

The big news in Europe of course is the European Union. That its creation – along with the Internet and the rise of English as the default auxiliary world language – has altered the linguistic landscape of Europe dramatically is to put it far too feebly. Applied linguistics in particular has been the great beneficiary. I quote from one of the Webpages created for this conference: "FASK (Faculty of Applied Linguistics and Cultural Studies) of the Johannes Gutenberg University Mainz ... is dedicated to training and research in the fields of translation and interpreting, with more than 800 of its 2300 students coming from 70 different foreign countries." Those are extraordinary numbers, and they speak more loudly than any words of the degree to which linguistics has become a player in the marketplace of the EU.

Current developments in the European Union call for a greater involvement of linguists in public affairs than ever before, and I mean more than in the training of interpreters and translators. Part of the price of admission to the EU is acceptance of the *Charte européenne des langues régionales et minoritaires*. This Charter requires member countries to respect their regional and minority languages and to undertake measures for the preservation and enhancement of these languages. If speakers of a minority language want instruction in that language, the Charter mandates that they can obtain it. Documents and road signs must be printed in the minority language under certain circumstances. There is going to be a lot more bilingual education and schooling in minority languages than before in Europe and elsewhere – and therefore a greater need for linguistic expertise.

Such matters, bilingual education and the rights of minority languages in a majority culture, always touch exposed nerves. Linguistic tolerance is no more common than tolerance itself. Bilingual education has become a major lightning rod of discontent in the United States. In June 1998 California passed overwhelmingly its Proposition 227 which in effect bans bilingual education. But it is not only in America that linguistic diversity is thought to be a problem by many ordinary citizens. French public opinion is much divided on the *Charte européenne des langues régionales et minoritaires*. Prime Minister Lionel Jospin supported it, President Jacques Chirac opposed it on the grounds that "on peut parfaitement reconnaître aux langues régionales leur place dans notre patrimoine culturel ... sans remettre en cause l'unité de la Nation" (*Le Monde*, 8 May 1999; *Le Figaro*, 24 June 1999).

One must resist the temptation to see this in terms of the muddled simplicities of conventional politics: the Left is good, i.e. on the right side of linguistic issues; the Right is bad, i.e. on the wrong side. I was living in France when all of this came to a head in June, 1999, and many members of Jospin's left-of-center coalition, even one of his ministers, openly and clamorously opposed the Charter. Prime ministers normally sack ministers who publicly oppose them. The fact that Jospin did not says eloquently how queasy many of Jospin's supporters feel about agreeing to anything that appears to demote the position of "la belle langue" in France. In America the novelist and cultural critic Gore Vidal, who is anything but a conservative, was one of the early supporters of U.S. English, the organization behind the movement to make English the official language.

Language issues and controversies abound in the countries that have arisen from the ashes of the Soviet Empire: Lithuania, Estonia, Latvia, Moldova, Kazakhstan, Ukraine, Belarus, and on and on. Africa has always had its share of language problems, as does South America. Language is never far from the surface of things in India (King 1997). The ethnic conflicts that disfigure our world today usually have a linguistic subtext – think of the countries created out of the former Yugoslavia.

Let me close by restating the principal themes of this paper. I have always thought that linguistics is a marvelous discipline to work in. One can be as abstract, as pure, as formal as one wants to be; but one can also contemplate the infinitely fascinating – if untidy – exchanges between language and society, between language and nationalism, between language and ethnic identity, between language and public policy. And consistency is not a virtue here: do one now, do the other later. This flexibility is one of the attractions of our discipline for me.

We can do 'public linguistics' if we want to, but nobody says that we have to. Indeed, not everyone is suited to it. To do public linguistics is to enter a world of politics that is inherently nasty, demeaning, and deeply unsatisfying to most of us who have chosen academic careers. Politics is a mare's nest of compromise and accommodation, of raised voices and deal making, a world in which rational considerations count for less than nothing against the power of the ballot box. Not everyone is suited for the political arena.

However, it will be a great tragedy if we should all remain aloof from the public fray. If linguistic public-policy decisions are made without the contribution of linguists, then bad decisions are going to be made. We have as a profession an obligation to educate, to convey something of the importance of linguistics to wider publics. We must continue to try to bring the same kind of enlightenment to the public understanding of language that others have brought in areas of human activity such as sex, mental illness, alcoholism, and ecology.

The need for wise linguistic input into questions of public policy – the need for a "public linguistics" – has never been greater. It should be a prominent part of linguistics in the new millennium.

References

FIRTH, John R. (1964): The Tongues of Man; and Speech. London: Oxford (reprint).
HOCKETT, Charles F. (1970): A Leonard Bloomfield Anthology. Bloomington: Indiana.
KING, Robert D. (1999): Lessons of Public Linguistics. In: Southwest Journal of Linguistics 18, 1-14.
— (1997): Nehru and the Language Politics of India. Delhi: Oxford.
KRAUSS, Michael E. (1992): The world's languages in crisis. In: Language 68.1, 4-10.
LEVIN, Jules (1999): Slavic as a Sign in the Development of Lithuanian. In: Shapiro, M.; Haley, M. (eds.): The Peirce Seminar Papers: Essays in Semiotic Analysis, 4. New York: Berghahn, 77-86.
MANDELBAUM, David G. (1985): Edward Sapir: Selected Writings in Language, Culture, and Personality. Berkeley: California. [Originally published 1949.]
MATHESIUS, Vilém (1966): Ten Years of the Prague Linguistic Circle. In: Vachek, J. (ed.): The Linguistic School of Prague. Bloomington: Indiana, 137-51. [The original of this article first appeared in Czech in 1936.]

Sprachplanung in der Diaspora – Soziolinguistische Aspekte bei der Normierung der standardjiddischen Aussprache

Ane Kleine

Es ist bis heute umstritten, ob ‚Standardjiddisch' überhaupt existiert. Und dennoch: Es gibt in Lehr- und Wörterbüchern detaillierte Beschreibungen dieser Varietät des modernen Jiddisch. Wenn nun diese Beschreibungen einen Spiegel der Realität darstellen und wir von der Gegenwart einer jiddischen Standardsprache ausgehen dürfen (Kleine 1998), so bleibt offen, wie sie sich herausbilden konnte. Schließlich war Jiddisch nie (lange genug)[1] Nationalsprache, keine staatliche Instanz konnte je eine Norm ausrichten.

Hier soll nun ein wenig in die komplexen Zusammenhänge bei der Herausbildung einer standardjiddischen Sprache hineingeleuchtet werden. Dabei habe ich mir die Frage gestellt, inwiefern sich die Diasporasituation auf die Herausbildung einer standardisierten Varietät ausgewirkt hat.

1   Jiddisch

Lassen Sie mich zunächst, für alle diejenigen, die mit dieser Sprache nicht vertraut sind, einen ganz knappen Abriß des Jiddischen geben, bzw. für diejenigen, die möglicherweise die Streitigkeiten um die Ursprünge des Jiddischen mitverfolgt haben, meinen Standpunkt darlegen.

Jiddisch ist die, den mittel- und oberdeutschen Mundarten anfangs nahestehende, aber von vornherein nicht mit ihnen identische Sprache der nichtassimilierten aschkenasischen Juden Mittel- und Osteuropas. Es ist nicht die einzige, aber die größte Gruppenverkehrssprache der Juden in der Diaspora. Sie entstand etwa im 9. Jahrhundert und war von Anfang an eine Sprache, die hebräisch-aramäische Elemente, sowie romanische und germanische Elemente in sich vereinte.

Das größte zusammenhängende Ausdehnungsgebiet des Jiddischen in Europa belegt den Raum: Deutschland, die Schweiz, Österreich, Oberitalien, Polen, Ungarn, Rumänien, die Baltischen Länder, Westrußland, die Ukraine und Weißrußland und zählte vor Ausbruch des Zweiten Weltkrieges etwa 12 Millionen Sprecher. Damit war Jiddisch die drittgrößte Germanische Sprache.

---

[1]   Um 1930 wurde von sowjetischer Seite der Versuch zur Schaffung eines autonomen jüdischen Siedlungsgebietes in Biro-Bidschan unternommen, mit Jiddisch als Landes- und Verwaltungssprache, doch das Projekt scheiterte.

1.1 Herausbildung jiddischer Mundarten durch *Interlingualen Sprachkontakt*

Natürlich kam es mit der Ausdehnung des jiddischen Sprachgebiets zur Herausbildung verschiedener Mundarten; ein Fakt, der wohl kaum erklärungsbedürftig scheint. Hervorzuheben ist jedoch eine Besonderheit der jiddischen Sprache, die zwar nicht unbedingt einzigartig ist, aber einen Grundpfeiler meiner Überlegungen darstellt: Von Anfang an war das Jiddische immer in engem Kontakt mit mindestens einer koterritorialen Fremdsprache, wobei die Sprecher und Sprecherinnen nicht *neben* sondern *inmitten* der anderen Sprachen lebten.

Anfangs waren es die Dialekte des genetisch verwandten Deutsch, die auf das Jiddische einwirkten. Bald kamen auch schon italienische Mundarten hinzu, als größere Gruppen aschkenasischer Juden nach Norditalien auswanderten. Mit den großen Migrationsbewegungen nach Osteuropa während der Pogrome, die die Pest und die Kreuzzüge für die Juden mit sich brachten, kamen schließlich in ganz erheblichem Maße slawische Elemente hinzu. Der Einfluß des Slawischen betrifft dabei alle Ebenen der Sprache: Wortschatz ebenso wie Syntax, Formenlehre und das Lautsystem. Und zwar desjenigen Jiddisch, welches nun in Osteuropa gesprochen wird. Das Westjiddische macht diese Veränderungen natürlich nicht mit.

Doch die Frage war ja nicht: Wie kommt es bei einer Sprache, die ein so großes Sprachgebiet einnimmt, zur Herausbildung von Mundarten, sondern – im Gegenteil: Warum lassen sich eigentlich, und zwar in jedem Entwicklungsstadium des Jiddischen – Ausgleichstendenzen feststellen?

1.2 Ausgleichstendenzen im Jiddischen durch *Intralingualen Sprachkontakt*

Innerhalb des großen historischen Stammgebiets des Jiddischen scheint es nicht nur zu dialektalen Ausdifferenzierungen gekommen zu sein, sondern gleichzeitig auch zu überregionalen Ausgleichstendenzen. Die treibenden und hemmenden Kräfte bei der Herausbildung einer Standardsprache für das Jiddische sind vielfältig; auch ist innerhalb der Forschung die Standardisierung des Jiddischen noch kaum, die Regulierung der Aussprache gar nicht aufgearbeitet worden. Hier möchte ich nun kurz einige Faktoren aufzählen, um der Problematik gerecht zu werden und aufzuzeigen, wo ein Vergleich mit den meisten anderen Sprachen nicht möglich ist.

Zunächst ist durch die größere Mobilität der jüdischen Bevölkerung ein intensiver Kontakt von Sprecherinnen und Sprechern unterschiedlicher Mundarten gewährleistet. Durch zahlreiche Vertreibungen und damit verbundene Umsiedlungen, wie auch durch die Bindung an spezielle Berufe, unter denen der des mobilen Händlers recht häufig war, war natürlich auch die Notwendigkeit präsent, sich ohne große Schwierigkeiten untereinander verständigen zu können. Die Pflicht, in der Diaspora über die weiten Entfernungen miteinander zu kommunizieren, wird als ein weiteres Erklärungsmodell angeführt; und das gilt übrigens auch schon für die frühere Zeit und bezieht sich dabei natürlich vornehmlich auf eine *schriftliche Ausgleichssprache*. Für das ältere Jiddisch hat Weinreich (1973:80) die Prozesse bei der Herausbildung einer gemeinsamen Schreibsprache zusammengetragen und bezeichnete sie als *Shraybshprakh A.*

Ich möchte hier vor allem die neuere, die moderne jiddische Sprache, betrachten. Zumal ich mich auf die Aussprache konzentriere, über die natürlich nur in der neueren Zeit gesicherte Erkenntnisse vorliegen. Mein Betrachtungszeitraum beginnt mit der Wende vom 19. ins 20. Jahrhundert. Ich unterscheide dabei zwei Epochen: die Zeit vor der Shoah und die Zeit nach dem Zweiten Weltkrieg.

2   Sprachliche Entwicklungen des Jiddischen in neuerer Zeit

2.1   Der Einfluß der modernen Sprachwissenschaft

Zu Beginn des 20. Jahrhunderts beginnt die moderne Sprachwissenschaft auch das Jiddische zu betrachten. War vormals das Augenmerk hauptsächlich auf die nichtgermanischen Elemente der Sprache der aschkenasischen Juden – und auf jede beobachtete ‚Andersartigkeit' vom Deutschen – gerichtet, so geschah dies häufig um das Jiddische zu diskreditieren oder als ‚verderbtes Deutsch' darzustellen (M. Weinreich 1923).

Nun aber begann man das Jiddische als eigenständige Sprache, nach Methoden der diachronen und synchronen Sprachwissenschaft, zu betrachten (Kleine 1999). Die genetischen Sprachbeziehungen rückten ins Zentrum der Aufmerksamkeit. Die Nähe zum Deutschen war ein so augenfälliges Merkmal, daß sich daraus ein Bedürfnis nach Abgrenzung ergeben mußte.

„Eine [...] weitverbreitete gesellschaftliche Sicht der Sprache ist diejenige, die sich mit ihrer Autonomie befaßt, d.h. mit der Einzigartigkeit und Unabhängigkeit des sprachlichen Systems oder zumindest einer Varietät innerhalb dieses Systems. Für Sprachgemeinschaften, deren Sprachen sehr deutlich voneinander unterschieden sind, ist die Autonomie oft von geringer Bedeutung. [...] Wo Sprachen einander ziemlich ähnlich zu sein scheinen und zwar phonologisch, lexikalisch und grammatisch, kann es hingegen sehr wichtig sein, ihre Autonomie oder zumindest die Unabhängigkeit der schwächeren von der stärkeren zu beweisen. [...] Ein Hauptmittel zur Pflege der Autonomiegedanken bezüglich einer Sprache ist ihre Standardisierung" (Fishman 1975:29).

Die dialektalen Unterschiede innerhalb des Jiddischen traten in den Hintergrund, beim Blick auf die überregionalen Gemeinsamkeiten der Sprache, die sie wiederum von der Nahsprache Deutsch gemeinschaftlich absetzten.

2.2   Das Vorhandensein einer gewachsenen Hochsprache

Und tatsächlich mußte man Gemeinsamkeiten im Sinne einer Hochsprache nicht aus dem Hut zaubern.

„Eine der am besten bekannten gesellschaftlichen Verhaltensweisen gegenüber der Sprache ist die Standardisierung, d.h. die Kodifizierung und Billigung eines formalen Katalogs von Normen innerhalb einer Gemeinschaft von Sprechern, die den ‚richtigen' Sprachgebrauch definieren [...] Die Standardisierung ist keine Eigenschaft irgendeiner Sprache als solcher, sondern eine charakteristische gesellschaftliche Behandlung der Sprache [...]" (Fishman 1975:28).

Wie oben beschrieben, hatte es zu allen Zeiten Ausgleichstendenzen gegeben, war man sich der Prägung, die eine überregionale Ausgleichssprache haben müßte, weitgehend bewußt (Katz 1993:52-55). Ende des 19. Jahrhunderts hatten zudem die sogenannten Klassiker der modernen jiddischen Literatur – Sholem Aleykhem, Mendele Moykher Sforim und Yitshkhok Leybush Perets – zumindest eine moderne *schriftliche Hochsprache*, die sogenannte *Shraybshprakh B* geformt.

Mit der Literatur einher geht ein Schreibusus, der für die, in der jiddischen Dialektologie so wichtigen Vokale, als ‚konservativ' bezeichnet werden kann. Er bildet mit dem Zusammenfall bestimmter Vokale, bzw. der Distinktion bestimmter anderer Vokale, die in manchen südostjiddischen Mundarten zusammenfallen, am ehesten den Lautstand des Nordostjiddischen ab. Nach dieser schriftlichen Hochsprache bezeichnet man auch die korrespondierende Aussprache als *literale Aussprache*. Sie war vor allem von der intellektuellen Oberschicht Litauens, den ‚Litvakes' geprägt. Innerhalb des osteuropäischen Judentums gab es damals ein deutliches Prestigegefälle von Norden nach Süden, weshalb man sich eher der nördlichen Aussprache anpaßte, als einer südlichen. Das Phonemsystem der standardjiddischen Sprache unterscheidet sich daher nur wenig vom litauischen Jiddisch (Katz 1993:49f, 57).

2.3 Das Vorhandensein einer Bühnenhochsprache

Auch auf der Bühne war ein ‚Standard' gewachsen. Doch diese sogenannte *Bühnenaussprache*, die als südlich geprägte überregionale Ausgleichssprache für das jiddische Theater und in der jiddischen Filmproduktion Geltung erlangt hatte, konnte sich, im Gegensatz zur nordjiddisch orientierten *literalen Aussprache*, nicht durchsetzen. Dies ist um so bemerkenswerter, als die südjiddischen Mundarten viel mehr Sprecherinnen und Sprecher besaßen, demographisches Übergewicht hatten. Festzuhalten bleibt aber, daß der *literale Standard* als Gegenspieler zur Bühnenhochsprache in die Diskussion eingeht.

2.4 Das jiddisch-weltliche Schulsystem als Multiplikator

Das Engagement jiddisch-weltlicher Schulen zu Beginn des 20. Jahrhunderts trug darüber hinaus wesentlich zur Verbreitung dieses Standards bei, hatte er sich erst einmal als Unterrichtssprache durchgesetzt (Katz 1993:48). Seinen Siegeszug antreten konnte er vor allem, weil die Lehrerseminare im Norden, bei den ‚Litvakes' saßen, die Impulse zu einem weltlichen Schulsystem vom Norden ausgingen, wo die eben erwähnte *literale Aussprache* entstand.

2.5 Das YIVO-Institut und moderne Lehrbücher des Jiddischen

Ein weiterer Multiplikator mit Vorbildfunktion war auch das YIVO, das ‚jüdische wissenschaftliche Institut', welches an allen wissenschaftlichen Entscheidungen beteiligt war und durch dessen Arbeit überregionale Konventionen diskutiert und festgelegt wurden;[2] engagiert wirkte es an der Ausbildung der Lehrkräfte für jiddischweltliche Schulen mit und nimmt so eine wichtige Funktion sowohl in Phase 1, also vor der Shoah, als auch in Phase 2, d.h. nach dem Zweiten Weltkrieg, ein. Als sichtbares Produkt des hier erwähnten Stichwortes *„Aufkommen der modernen sprachwissenschaftlichen Beschäftigung mit dem Jiddischen"* wurde es 1925 gegründet und siedelte 1941 von Wilna nach New York über.

Nach dem Schockzustand, den es mit der Umsiedlung der Sprachgemeinschaft – oder, um es deutlich zu sagen: dem überlebenden Rest der Sprachgemeinschaft – zu überwinden galt, trug es nach dem Zweiten Weltkrieg wesentlich zur immensen Beschleunigung bei der Herausbildung des Standards, v.a. einer Standardaussprache bei. Hier wurde zu Ende geführt, was in Osteuropa begonnen hatte (Mark 1951:7). Das anerkannteste und am weitesten verbreitete Lehrbuch, ‚College Yiddish' von U. Weinreich, entstand; 1949 wird es erstmals gedruckt, seither erlebte es über 20 Wiederauflagen. Da es auch als Lehrbuch zur Erlernung des Jiddischen als Fremdsprache konzipiert ist, findet sich in ihm die erste detaillierte Beschreibung jener standardjiddischen Aussprache, die ganz ohne Zweifel ein Resultat dieser Diskussionen verkörpert.[3] Nahezu alle Darstellungen der Aussprache des modernen Jiddisch, die sich heute in anderen Lehrbüchern finden, basieren auf diesem Lehrbuch – ich habe das nachgeprüft.

2.6 Jiddisch als Zweit- bzw. Fremdsprache in den neuen Exilgemeinden

In den neuen Exilgemeinden kommt es ferner zu einer rasanten Anpassung an die Umgebungssprache. Vor allem die jüngere Generation erlernt häufig nur – oder zunächst nur – die Sprache der neuen Heimat. Jiddisch wird von der nachkommenden

---

[2] Im Bereich der Grammatik einigte man sich etwa auf drei grammatische Genera, in der Lexik entschied man sich im Wesentlichen zu einer akkumulativen Anerkennung von Wörtern unterschiedlicher Provenienz. Der größte Schritt wurde 1937 gemacht, als mit den *Takones* die Orthographie festgeschrieben wurde. Zwar war es im Zuge der Orthographieregelung auch nötig gewesen, sich über einen gemeinsprachlichen Aussprachestandard zu verständigen, ganz besonders, wenn es um die lateinschriftliche Transkription ging, doch kann auf keine, mit den *Takones* vergleichbare, Publikation zurückgegriffen werden.

[3] Wie groß jedoch die Unsicherheit über eine Aussprache geblieben war (und ist) zeigen Publikationen aus späteren Jahren, in denen die Frage nach der Standardlautung noch als völlig offen gilt und von grundsätzlichen Problemen angefangen bis zu Detailfragen von Grund auf diskutiert werden. So werden 1951 in Yiddishe Shprakh die Artikel von U. Weinreich und Mark zur Diskussion um die Aussprache des Jiddischen herausgebracht. Die Standardwerke zur jiddischen Sprache von Birnbaum der Jahre 1974 und 1979 lassen das Problem um eine genormte Hochsprache weiterhin sehr akut erscheinen.

Generation oft erst als Zweitsprache oder gar als Fremdsprache erlernt. Jiddisch ist, über Nacht, nicht mehr die Sprache der Familie und des Alltags, sondern Unterrichtsfach an Schulen und Hochschulen. Das wiederum leistet dem schulisch-akademischen Sprachgebrauch und dem Rückgriff auf Lehrbücher, wie etwa ‚College Yiddish' Vorschub; selbstredend wird meist nicht ein Dialekt, sondern Standardsprache unterrichtet.

2.7 Neue Ballungszentren in Übersee und engster Kontakt von Dialektsprechern

In den neuen Exilgemeinden in Übersee treffen darüber hinaus nun Sprecher verschiedener Mundarten aufeinander; sie leben unmittelbar nebeneinander. Die Sprecherin aus Wilna ist schon im Hausflur konfrontiert mit der jiddischen Aussprache ihrer Nachbarin aus Odessa; hier ist keine geographische Zuordnung einer Mundart mehr möglich. Die selbstregulierenden Restriktionen der einzelnen Mundarten zerfallen mit der Zerschlagung der gewachsenen Dialektgebiete. Die sprachsoziologisch-historische Realität bot die Optionen ein Dialektgemisch entstehen zu lassen und/oder ein neues, allgemeines Regelwerk auszuarbeiten. Der *intralinguale Sprachkontakt* ist hier auf seinem Hochpunkt. Um der Eindeutigkeit und Verständlichkeit Willen wuchs das Bedürfnis nach einer einheitlichen, normierten Aussprache (U. Weinreich 1951: 27).

3 Zusammenfassung

3.1 Standardjiddisch

Unter Bezugnahme auf den ersten Satz dieses Beitrags möchte ich es wagen, zu behaupten, daß es tatsächlich einen Standard in der Aussprache des Jiddischen gibt; manche Leserin und mancher Leser wird möglicherweise kategorisch gegen meine These stimmen ... Doch es ist mittlerweile aus der Diskussion um den Standard ein klares Bild von der ‚richtigen' Aussprache hervorgegangen.

> „The intriguing questions in this respect are not so much the extent to which corpus planning has penetrated into widespread written/spoken usage (which by all general indicators could be expected to be relatively negligible [...]), but the extent to which it is known, liked and, used in even the most specialized circles" (Fishman 1981b:752).

So ist der Standard Realität geworden. Paradoxerweise haben Befürworter wie Gegner gleichermaßen dazu beigetragen, dieses Bild zu festigen. Selbst Aussagen, die sich vehement gegen den – im Entstehen begriffenen oder vermeintlich schon festgelegten – ‚Standard' richten, bekräftigten damit die Vorstellung über die Gestalt dieses ‚Standards'; sie stützten die Vorstellung, daß das, was da als ‚Standard' kritisiert wird, tatsächlich ‚der Standard' ist.

Vermittelt wird dieser formal kodifizierte Sprachgebrauch durch Lehrbücher, Grammatiken, Wörterbücher, usw. Das kulturelle Establishment fördert insgesamt die Akzeptanz dieser Varietät. Dies bedeutet aber nicht, daß die jiddischen Mundarten verpönt oder gar aufgegeben werden. Hervorgegangen ist aus diesem Prozeß lediglich die Einigung auf eine überregionale Hochsprache v.a. des Sprachunterrichts.

> „The ‚spread of language' does not always entail gaining new speakers or users […] Frequently it entails gaining new functions or uses, particularly ‚H' functions (i.e. literacy related functions in education, religion, ‚high culture' in general, and, in modern times, in econotechnology and government too) for a language that is already widely known and used in ‚L' functions (i.e. everyday family, neighborhood, and other informal/intimate, intragroup interaction) […].The last century has witnessed the rise and fall (but not the complete elimination) of such efforts on behalf of Yiddish" (Fishman 1981a:370f).

3.2 Die zwei Typen des Sprachkontakts und ihr Einfluß auf die Entwicklung des Jiddischen

Ich habe versucht das ganz Spezifische des Jiddischen in Hinblick auf die Standardisierung der Sprache allgemein und der Aussprache im Besonderen auf wenigen Seiten anzudeuten. Wichtig war dabei der ständig auf das Jiddische einwirkende Sprachkontakt. Ich denke, es bringt tatsächlich ein wenig Licht ins Dunkel, wenn man vor allem für das Jiddische folgende zwei Typen des Sprachkontakts unterscheidet: den *interlingualen Sprachkontakt* und den *intralingualen Sprachkontakt*.

Mit anderen Worten heißt das: Sprachkontakt einerseits als das Aufeinandertreffen von Sprechern unterschiedlicher Sprachen und andererseits als Begriff für Kontaktsituationen, in denen Sprecherinnen und Sprecher verschiedener Mundarten zusammenkommen. Beide Typen des Sprachkontakts sind auch jeweils in ihrem zeitlichen Kontext zu gewichten. Folge dieses *interlingualen Sprachkontakts* für das Jiddische war also: eine Ausdifferenzierung, eine Untergliederung in Mundarten. Warum? Nicht zuletzt auch, weil es sich bei diesem riesigen Ausdehnungsgebiet des Jiddischen um verschiedene koterritoriale Sprachen handelte, die jede auf ihre Weise, Einfluß auf das Phonemsystem, wie alle anderen Ebenen des Jiddischen hatten.

Hier kann ein Hochpunkt in etwa gesetzt werden, nachdem das Westjiddische, im Zuge der Aufklärung und Assimilation in Deutschland aufgegeben wurde, das Ostjiddische sich hingegen, als eigenständige Sprache endgültig emanzipierte. Wir haben in der ersten Hälfte des 20. Jahrhunderts in Osteuropa Städte wie Warschau mit 34% jiddischsprachiger Bevölkerung, Bialystok sogar mit 76%, Berditschew in der Ukraine mit 80%; Ballungszentren in Osteuropa, die es sich sozusagen ‚leisten' konnten, eine klar regional gefärbte Varietät zu benutzen. Für das Überleben der Sprachgemeinschaft war es nicht mehr existentiell, einen dialektalen Ausgleich zu schaffen. Selbstredend spielten die modernen, multimedialen Kommunikationssysteme wie Radio oder gar Fernsehen noch keine Rolle.

Als Gegenpol dazu setze ich nun den *intralingualen Sprachkontakt*. Gruppen verschiedener dialektaler Provenienz treffen hierbei aufeinander. Exemplarisch für die frühere Zeit hatte ich innerhalb dieses Rahmens genannt: die große Mobilität (ob freiwillig oder unfreiwillig), und die Notwendigkeit einer Minderheitsgruppe, sich über weite Distanzen miteinander verständigen zu können.

In Phase 2, also nach der Entwurzelung der Sprachgemeinschaft und dem Ausge-
löschtwerden der jüdischen Gemeinden in Europa ist alles anders. In Übersee entstehen neue Ballungsräume. Die Überlebenden finden sich zusammen in neuen Zentren
in den USA (dort vor allem in New York), in Melbourne (Australien), in Johannesburg (Südafrika), Buenos Aires (Argentinien), in Mexiko, Uruguay usw. Es kommt zu
unmittelbarer Präsenz verschiedener Mundarten auf einem engen Raum. Man kann
sich verständigen – die jiddischen Mundarten waren nie so weit von einander entfernt,
daß sie Kommunikation ernsthaft verhindert hätten. Doch spätestens die nachkom-
mende Generation wird – sofern sie das Jiddische nicht völlig zugunsten der Koterri-
torialsprache aufgibt – nicht mehr über eine sichere regionale Varietät verfügen.
Selbstverständlich kommt es auch ganz unspektakulär zu Dialektmischungen und dem
Entstehen neuer Exildialekte. Aber – jener *intralinguale Sprachkontakt* – und das ist
hier Gegenstand – bewirkt auch etwas anderes: Seine Dynamik kann als gegenläufige
Tendenz zu den Prozessen des *interlingualen Sprachkontakts* begriffen werden. Er
führt eben nicht zur Ausdifferenzierung in Untermundarten, sondern zu einem Ausgleich im Sinne eines Standards, einer gemeinsamen Hochsprache.

4   Literatur

BIRNBAUM, Salomo, A. (1979): Yiddish – A Survey and a Grammar. Toronto: University of To-
    ronto.
— (1974): Die jiddische Sprache. Ein kurzer Überblick und Texte aus acht Jahrhunderten. Hamburg:
    Buske.
FISHMAN, Joshua A. (1981a): Attracting a Following to High-Culture Functions for a Language of
    Everyday Life: The Role of the Tshernovits Language Conference in the 'Rise of Yiddish'. In:
    Cooper. Robert. L. (Hrsg.): Language Spread: Studies in Diffusion and Social Change. Arlington
    1981. [Zitiert nach der überarbeiteten und erweiterten Fassung in: Fishman (1985c): 369-394.]
— (1981b): Epilogue: Contributions of the Sociology of Yiddish to the General Sociology of Lan-
    guage. In: The Field of Yiddish 4, 1980, 475-498. [Zitiert nach der überarbeiteten und erweiterten
    Fassung in: Fishman (19885c): 739-756]
— (1985c): Never Say Die! A Thousand Years of Jewish Life and Letters. The Hague etc.: Mouton.
    (Contributions to the Sociology of Language 30)
— (1975): Soziologie der Sprache. Eine interdisziplinäre sozialwissenschaftliche Betrachtung der
    Sprache in der Gesellschaft. München: Hueber.
KATZ, Dovid (1993): *tikney takones. fragn fun a yidisher stilistik.* [Amended Amendments. Issues in
    Yiddish stylistics] Oxford: *oksforder yidish.*
KLEINE, Ane (1999): Florilegium zur jiddischen Phonetik. Eine Zeitreise. In: Jiddische Philologie.
    Röll, W; Neuberg, S. (Hrsg.): Festschrift für Erika Timm. Tübingen: Niemeyer 1999, 51-63.
— (1998): Toward a 'Standard Yiddish Pronunciation'. An Instrumentally Aided Phonetic Analysis.
    In: Schmid, M. S; Austin, J. R., Stein, D. (Hrsg): Historical Linguistics 1997. Selected papers
    from the 13th International Conference on Historical Linguistics, Düsseldorf, 10-17 August 1997.
    Amsterdam: John Benjamins, 201-211.
MARK, Yudl (1951): *vegn a klalishn aroysreyd.* [On the Standard Pronunciation of Yiddish.] In:
    yidishe shprakh, Bd. XI, 1951, 1-25.
TAKONES FUN YIDISHN OYSLEYG. YIDISHER VISNSHAFTLEKHER INSTITUT. ROYM (= Rom) 1947[4] –
    [[1]1937].

WEINREICH, Max (1923): Studien zur Geschichte und dialektischen Gliederung der jiddischen Sprache. 1. Teil: Geschichte und gegenwärtiger Stand der jiddischen Sprachforschung. (Diss. Univ. Marburg). Nachdruck 1993 u. d. T.: Geschichte der jiddischen Sprachforschung. (hrsg v. J.C. Frakes). Atlanta: Univ. of South Florida.

— [= Vaynraykh, Maks] (1973): *geshikhte fun der yidisher shprakh. bagrifn, faktn, metodn.* New York: YIVO. [= Weinreich, Max (1980): History of the Yiddish Language (übers. v. S. Noble und J. A. Fishman). Chicago, London: University of Chicago.

WEINREICH, Uriel (1951): *tsu der frage vegn a normirter oysshprakh* [= How to Standardize Yiddish Pronunciation]. In: yidishe shprakh, Bd. XI/1951. 26-29.

— (1949): College Yiddish. An Introduction to the Yiddish Language and to Jewish Life and Culture. New York: YIVO.

Italo-Albanians and Albanians: A Problematic Case of (Socio-)Linguistic Contact

Marta Maddalon, Giovanni M. G. Belluscio

The aim of our research is to investigate a type of sociolinguistic contact that we consider peculiar because of the nature of the two languages involved and their particular relationship, i.e.

1) they are genetically related;
2) Arbëresh is an example of a further development of a NEW variety, used by a minority group, living in a foreign country;
3) linguistic and cultural contacts between Albanians and Italo-Albanians have always been scarce, complex, and one way mainly: Arbëresh → Albanian.

From this starting point, in our present paper, we tackle some very general problems, on the one hand from a more 'social orientated' point of view, we consider in particular the cultural attitude towards Italy, and its influence on linguistic and socio-linguistic behaviour; on the other hand, we describe and comment some interesting examples of different developments in Arbëresh, showing a more or less precise chronology of certain structural and lexical changes in Albanian itself. This may well be another good example of "using the past to explain the present", as also the contrary. Finally, we present and discuss the more linguistically and socio-linguistically relevant events, at all pertinent levels of linguistic analysis, including a tentative description of the CS and CM models used by our speakers. The very last point involves the way in which many *young* Albanians learn Italian, no longer by direct contact but through the mass media, and how this determines performance as distinct from erstwhile acquisition by direct contact with native speakers.

In our paper we describe some of the more interesting problems noted, as well as attempting a general comparison between the two systems in contact (Albanian and Arbëresh), pointing out the differences and the principal elements passed from one to the other, wittingly or not. Some tentative conclusions will be made to focus ethnic attitudes between the two groups involved, and the role of lingustic performance in this process. The other interesting aspect is the way in which many Albanians have learned Italian. In the past, when Albania was an Italian colony, many Albanians spoke Italian, but after World War Two, during the last regime, the international political relations with western countries were practically forbidden. Most people learned Russian at school. If we make an exception for older people who know Italian because of former Italian domination, most young people have learned it from Italian TV programmes that are very popular in the country. The role of television programmes in second languages acquisition is becoming more relevant at the present. From an oral communication from Uruguayan sources we learn that it is quite common for people in many South American countries to use Spanish + Portuguese at home because they have learned Portuguese watching Brasilian television.

Arbëresh/Italian: the first kind of sociolinguistic contact

The first migratory trend from Albania towards Italy approximatively four houndred and fifty years ago was provoked by the Turkish invasion that obliged Albanians to leave their Country and look for a new place to live peacefully. There were many successive migratory waves in the immediately following period and the social composition of the participants, as well as their different settlements, is connected with the complex history of Albanian migration in Italy.

Generally, from a linguistic point of view, it is important to consider the geographical distribution and the provenance of the majority of the first groups that arrived in Italy. As we know, in fact, Albania is linguistically divided in two main groups, Geg and Tosk, and of course in this case it is important to remember that the Albanians that left for Italy belonged to the Tosk group. The successive development of Italo-Albanian dialects is based on this variety. Of course, the knowledge and general use of Arbëresh differ from community to community, and depends on the age of speakers.

The repertoire

The main varieties posessed by Italo-Albanian speakers are Italian and Arbëresh, in the case of communities in which the language, as well as cultural traditions (i.e. the Orthodox rite from a religious point of view), are still vital. It would be more precise to use 'regional Italian', instead of 'Italian' tout court, and to add to those codes the local dialect, as well, genetically 'akin' to Italian in a broad Romance sense but in a strict phylogenic sense and structurally 'more akin' to Roumanian and Sardinian etc. Since the Italo-Albanian problem is bedded into the more general one of the overall Italian repertoire, it would be easier to schematize the two sociolinguistic situations and make a rapid comparison:

Italian repertoire (spoken)
Regional Italian (H): formal, some degree of standardization, etc.
Regional Italian (L): informal, less standardized, especially if a regional (or sub-regional) koiné does not exist.
Dialect (1): more or less Italianized, especially in big towns.
Dialect (2): less Italianized and more local, especially in more isolated places and small villages.

Arbëresh repertoire (spoken)
Regional Italian (H): formal, some degree of standardization, etc.
Regional Italian (L): informal, less standardized, especially if a regional (or sub-regional) koiné does not exist .
Dialect (1) more or less Italianized, especially in big towns.
Dialect (2) less Italianised and more local, especially in more isolated places and small villages.
Arbëresh: there may be relevant differences, both linguistically and in the different degree of Italianization.

(Scheme 1)

Considering the time and the kind of contact between Albanians and Italians, it is quite clear that the first and main linguistic relationship is an Albanian / local Calabrian dialect type. We can summarize the mutual linguistic exchange as follows:

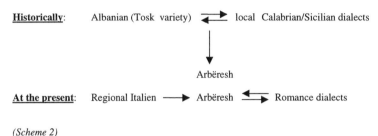

(Scheme 2)

The particular situation of Arbëresh with respect to Italian as Dachsprache (with which it has no genetic relationship, unless in a broad I.-E. sense), together with no mutual understanding between their Albanian code and Italian, must be taken into account. In the case of Arbëresh the way in which they consider and use their language or Italian is based on the fact that Arbëresh is a "we code" and Italian is a "they code" in everyday, normal conversation[1]. A further 'complexity' is due to the fact that, as already stated, their repertoire is completed by regional Italian and Calabrian dialect, that in its local varieties plays the role of "we code" vis-à-vis Italian, considered the "they code" in many linguistic exchanges.

'we code' - 'they code' scheme

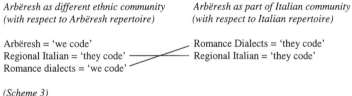

(Scheme 3)

Determining what must be considered 'we code'/'they code' is always complicated because, apart from general considerations about common feelings towards a particular code, many other factors must be taken into account, a fact sometimes not completely clear to the speakers involved, either. Much field-work on very complex sociolinguistic situations, mainly because of the number and typology of relationships between the codes involved, has shown that a static definition is neither the more appropriate nor the most useful (cf. McLure-McLure 1988: passim). In our case, in fact, if we take into account the sociolinguistic position of Italo-Albanians, we can surely apply to their situation the well known Gumperz addage:

---

[1] It is interesting to note that in many Arbëreshë villages the speaker say *'fjasmi (alla) si na'* to indicate the Arbëresh code, i.e. 'let's speak as we (do)'.

"The tendency is for the ethnically specific minority language to be regarded as 'we code' and become associated with in-group and formal activities, while the majority language serves as 'they code' associated with the more formal, stiff and personal out-group relations" (Gumperz, 1976:8).

However, they share living and social space with Italians and they share their repertoire as well, so local Romance dialects may become 'we code' and regional Italian 'they code', following general sociolinguistic Italian behaviour.

Social identity: some remarks

All problems involved in *every* kind of social and linguistic contact are 'peculiar', in some way or another. Starting from this quite obvious consideration, we tackle, in particular, some problems of determining ethnic identity, as far as some linguistic phenomena (in the widest sense) will guide us in that task; further on, we consider the different feeling towards Italian and its culture, whether shared or not by the two groups.

For Arbëresh Communities, in fact, it is quite obvious that one of the main problems was, and still is, the maintenance of their cultural identity. The way in which this happens, in every contact situation with minority groups living in a foreign country, is interesting in itself, and may enable us to find and comment the more useful strategies applied in such cases. In particular, for the Arbëreshë, we claim that the maintenance of their cultural identity, as well as of their language, the main medium for this maintenance, may well be their capacity to adapt, plus the acceptance of having to give up part of the so-called 'pureness' of their language and tradition, in favour of Italian culture and language (in Calabrian or Sicilian terms, etc.). "Tutto cambia perché nulla cambi", to summarize, in Gattopardo terms, is often a good survival strategy in an unfavourable situation.[2]

The choice of coming to Italy is surely due to the political crisis after the fall of Hoxha's regime and to the geographical proximity of Italy, but a great part of the decision is based on the hope of starting a new life exactly like the one they see on television. This is a case of complex interplay between cultural and linguistic aspects. In fact, the image of Italy they have from TV sources determines a positively biased attitude in general, even though grounded on false presuppositions; such a positive attitude usually encourages and facilitates language learning.

The sample

Our sample is composed of 12 speakers, males and females, 6 Italo-Albanians, from 28 to 65 years of age, living from birth in the Arbëresh village of Spezzano Albanese (in the province of Cosenza), and 6 Albanians, coming from different parts of Albania (see map 1), aged from 25 to 42, resident in Italy for different lengths of time.

Many factors may have influenced communicative exchanges analysed, in particular the different degree of acquaintanceship between participants[3], the difference

---

[2]   G. Tommasi di Lampedusa, *Il Gattopardo*, Feltrinelli 1957.
[3]   In a longer version we describe the social networks in which they participate.

in sex, age and social position, notwithstanding the tendentially artificial nature of the situation, a sort of an 'interview', even if topics were undirected. From a diastratic point of view, at any rate, the sample is quite homogeneous since all the informants share a good cultural level; as already said, diatopic differences must be taken into account, as explained.

(Map 1)

Linguistic phenomena

We group together and comment conversations on the basis of the length of Albanian speakers' residence in Spezzano, as well as on their knowledge of the codes involved. We have taken into account all levels of linguistic analysis (that will be commented in a longer version): the present paper, however, concentrates on the phonetic and the lexical levels, considering dialectal differences internal to Shqip (Albanian). We make a first distinction between general observations on the similarity and the differences between Albanian and Arbëresh, and the mutual influence when they are used in the same linguistic exchange. On the other hand, we must take into account, and try to insert our consideration on CS examples in a more general analytical model for this phenomenon. Both aspects are very complex to analyse; in particular in the second case, considering recent developments in CS definition and analysis, we limit ourselves to a general description of some examples. We group together and comment conversations on the basis of the length of Albanian speakers' residence in Spezzano, as well as on their knowledge of the codes involved.

Lexical level

a) Verbs remodelled on the Calabro-Italian form, and conjugated according to the Arbëresh/Albanian model, i.e.: *e kapirte* (= e kuptove 'I understood'), *sa të sistemarem* (= për të u rregulluar ~ sistemuar, 'to settle down'), *abituarmi* (= mësohemi 'we get used'*) sa të guadhanjar* (= sa të fitoj 'to earn'), or typical Arbëreshë verbs: *shërbej* (= punoj 'to work'), *i kalluan* (= i vodhëtin 'they stole')[4];

b) Arbëreshë nouns or Italian arbëreshized nouns: *katund* (= fshat 'village'), *ftigë* (= punë 'job, work'), *purtun* (= derë e madhe 'door'), *domandet* (= pyetjet 'questions'), *me komunën* (= me bashkinë 'with the Town Council'), *kriaturët* (= fëmijët 'the children'), etc.;

c) Arbëreshë adjectives or Italian arbëreshized adjectives: *një cik* (= pak 'a little, some'), *pakund* (= shumë 'many, much, a lot of'), *më diversu* (= më i ndryshëm 'more different'), *më pexhu* (= më keq 'worse'));

d) Arbëreshë adverbs or Italian arbëreshized adverbs: *papanë* (= edhe një herë 'again'), *njëmend* (= tani 'now'), *nani* (= tani 'now'), *ndëç* (= nëqoftë se, 'if'), *mai* (= kurrë 'never'), *mungu* (= as 'neither'), etc.;

e) phrases such as: *një xhoj shpi* (= një shtëpi tepër të bukur 'a very nice house'), *shpi me afit* (= shtëpi me qirà 'a house to let), etc.

In some cases, words whose precise Italian equivalent is not known are rendered by words not understood by the Arbëresh, who use other lexical items in their stead (*kocka* 'bone', Arbëresh: *asht*); the form *asht* is common to both Albanian and Arbëresh, while the first is not, so in this case the lexical choice works (apparently) against mutual understanding. Other phenomena found in our interviews are false starts, in the case of Albanians mainly, but not exclusively; the direction is more often Italian → Albanian and the reasons are linked to the difficulty in finding the right Italian word, but in many cases it is also a sign of 'good will' and cooperation: to go back to a common linguistic source or 'common Albanian', which includes Diaspora varieties, notwithstanding obvious differences and historical distance, as an ethnically significant act. This consideration seems to contrast with the observation on the use of Italian as a 'lingua franca', already commented. It is worth noting that in some cases speakers decide to translate elements from Italian into Albanian or to present

---

[4]   On the role and the differences in the usage of past tense and present perfect in Arbëresh, cf. Altimari (1994). We think that a contrastive analysis on the differences between their use in different regional Italians (differences exist also among different parts of Calabria region) and Italo-Albanian varieties would be very useful.

together the Albanian and the Arbëresh version of the same word (see below). In some cases, it is clearly a choice based, more or less consciously, on a shared ethnicity.[5]

The heart of the matter is that in this case a great anomaly exists in the relationship between a language and one of its varieties, developed not in the same sociolinguistic context, but far away in time and space, a variety that has, moreover, an evident diglossic relationship with *another* language (Arbëresh repertoire). We think that, if we are going to talk about old and new ethnicity[6] (cf. Gumperz 1982) and to discuss conversational cooperation strategies[7] (Heller 1982, 1988), we must take into account many factors, some of which are new and different vis-à-vis the classical situation investigated.

Since the way in which a people or a group calls itself is internally meaningful, it will be useful to observe the relationship between the different names adopted to indicate themselves or the *others*; the words used are: *Shqiptar – Arbëresh – Albanez* (only in one case was there an explicit request by an Arbëresh speaker (conversation 2) to point out the exact origin of the word 'gjegji'[8]). Arbëreshë never use the term *Shqiptar* to call Albanians (it is the common Albanian word for 'Albanian'; it must have become 'common' for 'inhabitant of Albania' after the Diaspora). The Arbëreshë extensively use *Albanez*, and the same Albanians agree to adopt this name to indicate themselvs, as a sort of cooperation signal, as an alternative to *Shqiptar*. There are no problems in the opposite direction, because Abanians always use *Arbëresh* for Italo-Albanians, never *Gjegji*, either because it would be a pointless phatic expression, without sense for them, or they would have already grasped its cultural, ergo negative, valency.

Code choices, code-switching and code-mixing examples

Apart from clearly defined situations, in which code choices are, for example, due to external factors such as the need for mutual understanding, or to 'declare' a certain ethnic *belonging*, in most cases it is very difficult to elicit not only the reasons for a particular phenomenon, but also to have a complete picture of what is actually going on in conversational exchanges. The unequal knowledge of the codes surely plays a

---

[5] Similar situations are often described by authors, cf. Scotton (1983 and 1988) inter alia.

[6] On the argument of differences between old and new ethnic ties, we may compare the description given in Gumperz (1982), where he points out the change of focus: "the old ethnic ties found their linguistic expression in loyalty to a language other than that of the major society. The new ethnic identities rely on linguistic symbols to establish speech conventions that are significantly different." (Ibid.:6). This seems to be very appropriate in the case of the relationship between Arbëresh and regional Italian, as is quite clear observing the code-mixing phenomena between the two.

[7] As observed by Heller (1982:109) "it [sc. negotiation] is made up of implicit and explicit strategies for seeking the kind of information that seems necessary in order for the participants to hold a conversation, and that information is information not only about what a persons's mother tongue is, but also *what his or her ethnicity is*" (our italics).

[8] It is the autocthonous term used to indicate Italo-Albanians by Calabrians and Sicilians: it would appear to be the imperative of the *gjegjënj* 'listen' verb used phatically (*gjegj këtu* 'listen here!') as an explicit incipit to conversation, or *gje'*! (for *gjegjinj/gjegjem*) to answer for a call.

role in the choice and adds some complexity to our analysis. We limit our considerations to few examples, but not without bringing attention once again to the fact that
Arbëresh *is* the historical result of a (socio-) linguistic contact and that, as noted in
Gardener-Chloros (1995:69): "Any mixture sooner or later is associated with a new
identity". Arbëresh is in itself a 'living' source of the main phenomena we are dealing with, such as borrowings, code-switching, code-mixing, interferences etc.

Commenting Albanians' performance, taking into account their lack of knowledge
of Italian, in some cases, we notice a certain trend towards a clear separation between
the two codes in most conversations. For Arbëresh, the situation appears more complex, considering the number and the role of the codes in their repertoire. In their performance we often find whole clauses in Italian, mixed with Albanian words.

Text 1.
(A=Albanian speaker, B=Arbëresh speaker; Italian words are underlined)

Po, e martuar.	**A.**	Yes, married.
Ë!	**B.**	*Ë!*
E ... quan ... kur filloi guerra lufta in Al-bania	**A.**	And ... whe ... when started the war the war in Albania
Ah!	**B.**	*Ah!*
Là ... atje ishte mot...	**A.**	There, there it was time...
Text 1.		

Ah ... In Grecia sono ... ho sentito io al ... nel telegiornale, kuando era...kur isha në Albania, që jan më shum albanez në Grecia se në ... se in Italia. Però, mia cognata për shembull, per esempio ... për shembull, shkoj in Albania, shkoj in Grecia perché lei c'ha due ... tre sorela là. Una sorela e ka in Italia, due sorela sono in Grecia, che c'hano cinque ani che lavorano.	**A.**	Ah ... In Greece there are ... I heard it at the ... at the telegiornale (= news pro-gramme), when I was ... when I was in Albania, that there are many more Alba-nians in Greece ... than in Italy. But, my sister in law, for example ... for example for example went to Albania, went to Greece because she has two ... three sis-ters there. One sister she has in Italy, two sisters are in Greece, that have five years that work (i. e. = they work there since five years).
Lavorano anche in Grecia.	**B.**	*They work in Greece, too.*
Eh! ... Çë shërbejn in Grecia. Kështu që ajo vajti tek sorelat e sua, e io ... un erdha tek mia mama.	**A.**	Yes! ... That work (Arbër.) in Greece. So she went to her sisters', and I ... I came to my mum.

- Considering most of the examples of translation and repetition, they seem to indicate that Italian is often choosen by speakers as a linguistic 'common ground',
to guarantee understanding, especially when Albanian or Arbëresh might fail
(feedback function). This happens following two possible directions: the first
'internal' or functional: to be sure that the message has been understood properly; the second, an external one, that concerns conversational cooperation: of-
fering the participants a wide gamut of code choices.

- Shqip (Albanian) speakers in general were often worried about the possibility of
not being understood; this, of course, favours Italian.

- Passing from one code to another, using alternative forms for the same term, etc. favours metalinguistic comments, that make the speakers more conscious of linguistic differences between Albanian and Arbëresh.[9]
- The problem of ethnic sharing between the two groups and the degree of reciprocal social acceptance are not easy to comment, but are also very interesting from a sociolinguistic point of view. In our conversation samples, we found some showing what Italo-Albanian communities feel towards new incoming Albanians, e.g.:

Text 2.
(D=Albanian speaker, C=Arbëresh speaker)

Doja t'ju bëja un tani një pyetje. E … çfar opinioni keni ju për shqipëtarët që … jetojn këtu në Spixan me ju?.	**D.**	I'd now like to ask you a question. What's your opinion about Albanians who are now living in Spezzano with you?
Nëng të kapirte!	**C.**	*I didn't understand!*
Allora te lo traduco. *[Sì].* E…cosa pensate voi per gli albanesi che vivono qua a Spezzano tra di voi?	**D.**	Then I'll translate it (for you). *[Yes].* Er … What do you think about Albanians who are now living in Spezzano among you?
Allora … u penxarinj se … jan persone come noi, che hano bisogno di aiuto…[hm] *e che* [in albanese] *kam i ndihmi,* [hm…] *però … non t … non tutti e … pënxarnjën kështu* [hm hm]. *U njoh pa … pakund albanesi,* [hm hm] *shurbenjin puru me mua e son … jan delle brave persone, e … tutte istruite. Io questo penso pënxarinj këtë. E … non ho trovato hm … per esempio, un albanese che … non … cioè non era socievole,* [hm hm] *e … No …*	**C.**	*Well … I think that … they are people like us, who need help…*[hm] *and that* [In Albanian, please] *we have to help them* [hm…] *but … not a … not all people do … think so* [hm hm]. *I have met a lo … many Albanians,* [hm hm] *they work with me and are … are decent people, and … all with a good educational level. This is what I think this is what I think. And … I've never met hm … for example, an Albanian who wasn't … I mean, who wasn't very*

---

[9] This is an example of a linguistic exchange in which the speakers use alternatively the Arbëresh and Albanian word for 'October'. Beyond the comments on the different usage, it is interesting to notice the graduality among codes: 1) ['meze o'tobre] = Italian but with Arbëresh phonetic realization, plus a partial morphological adaptation '(il) mese (di) ottobre'; 2) ['muaji o'tobrit] = Arbëresh 'month + October + gen' (but the genuine form would had been 'muaji shën mitrit'); 3) ['muaji te'tor] = Albanian.

Text 3.
(F=Albanian speaker, E=Arbëreshe speaker)

…im shoq ka … ha … në tetor bën katër vjet *[hm…]*, e kam pure…	**F.**	My husband, has … has … in October, IT IS four years (that he has been here) *[hm…]*, and I have also …
Ttetor … ç'ësht' tetor?	**E.**	*Tetor … What is tetor?*
Tetor është otobre.	**F.**	Tetor is October.
Mese (/'meze/) tobre, mese (/'meze/) otobre, muaji otobrit.	**E.**	*The month of October, the month of October, the month of October*
Muaj … muaj neje…	**F.**	The month … the month we….
Na thomi otobre se, ormai [sì] *e thomi si italiano.* [Sì, italiano; ne i themi…] *Tetor* [tetor] *Tetor* [muaj tetor.]	**E.**	*We say October because now* [yes] *we say it like in Italian* [Yes, Italian, we say …] *Tetor* [tetor] *Tetor* [month 'tetor'].

| *non mi so ... non mi so spiegare, nëng di* *t'spiegarem, comungue* *sono...hm...aspetta. Non so dire ...* | *sociable* [hm hm] *and ... No...I don't know* *... I don't know how to explain myself, I* *don't know how to explain, however* *I'm...hm...hang on ... I can't say ...* |

As already stated, the analysis of the contact studied needs more indepth treatment, since the situation types seem to be still fluid and change still ongoing. Our research along the lines indicated continues.

References

ALTIMARI F. (1994): La distribuzione del passato presuntivo nell'albanese d'Italia. In: Altimari, F; Savoia, L. (eds.): I dialetti italo-albanesi, Bulzoni Editore, Roma, 211-21.

— (1991): Alcuni etnici di origine albanese nei dialetti della Calabria. In: Zjarri XX.33, 151-6.

AUER, P. (1988): A conversation analytic approach to code switching and transfer. In: Heller: 187-213.

BLOM, J. P.; GUMPERZ, J. J. (1968): Fattori sociali determinanti del comportamento verbale. In: Rassegna Italiana di Sociolinguistica IX, 301-328.

GARDNER-CHLOROS, P. (1995): Code-switching in community, regional and national repertoires: the myth of the discreteness of linguistic systems. In: Milroy, L.; Muysken, P. (eds.): One speaker, two languages. Cambridge: Cambridge University Press, 68-88.

GUMPERZ, J. J. (1982): Discourse strategies. Cambridge: Cambridge University Press.

— (ed.) (1982): Language and social identity. Cambridge. Cambridge University Press (Studies in interactional sociolinguistics 2).

— (1976): The sociolinguistic significance of conversational code-switching. In: Cook-Gumperz; Gumperz (eds.): Papers on language and context. Working Paper 46, Language Behaviour Research Laboratory, Berkeley.

HELLER , M. (ed.) (1988): Code Switching. Anthropological and Sociolinguistic Perspective. Berlin: Mouton – De Gruyter.

MCCLURE, E.; MCCLURE, M. (1988): Macro-and micro- sociolinguistic dimensions of code-switching. In: Heller: 25-51.

ROMAINE, S. (1989): Bilingualism. Oxford: Blackwell.

SCOTTON, C. M. (1988): Code Switching as indexical of social negotiation. In: Heller, 151-186.

— (1983): The negotiation of identities in conversation: a theory of markedness and code choice. In: International Journal of Sociology of Language 44, 115-136.

TRUMPER, J. B. (1984): Language variation, code switching, S. Chirico Raparo (PZ) and the migrant question (Konstanz). In: Auer, P.; Di Luzio, A. (eds.): Interpretive Sociolinguistics. Tübingen, 29-54.

TRUMPER, J. B.; Maddalon, M. (1988): Converging divergence and diverging convergence. The dialect – language conflict and contrasting evolutionary trends in Modern Italy. In: Auer, P.; Di Luzio, A. (eds.): Variation and convergence: studies in social dialectology. Berlin-New York: Mouton de Gruyter, 217-259.

Les relations bilingues (?) entre Suisses allemands et Romands

Luzian Okon

1 Remarques générales

J'insiste beaucoup sur le point d'interrogation dans le titre de ma contribution, puisqu'il renferme le problème épineux dont il faut traîter.

Je pense aboutir à quelques vérités de fait et, surtout, à des suppositions et des hypothèses. Je ne serais pas en mesure de résoudre les problèmes de contacts linguistiques entre les deux ethnies, les germanophones et les francophones. La Suisse quadrilingue (où l'on parle l'allemand, le français, l'italien et le romantsch, plus le schwyzerdütsch et les dialectes tessinois, c'est-à-dire le ticines) a souvent été considérée comme un véritable « laboratoire des langues en contacts » (Lüdi 1989:405), comme un pays où règne la paix linguistique et où le contact des langues se réalise et se manifeste sans conflits. Cela n'est pas tout à fait le cas. Selon le professeur Nelde, d'ailleurs, il n'y aurait jamais de contacts entre les langues sans conflits. On a baptisé cet axiome « Nelde's Law ». Certes, on ne trouve pas les hostilités, quelquefois atroces, qui existent entre les deux ethnies en Belgique, les Flamands et les Wallons, mais il y a des animosités, souvent sous-jacentes, qu'on n'arrive pas à faire disparaître. S'il ne s'agit pas d'une paix linguistique proprement dite en Suisse, il s'agit d'un respect mutuel et d'une cohabitation de plusieurs ethnies et de leurs cultures, acceptable et satisfaisante. Lors du Festival internazionale del Film à Locarno de l'année 1999 (4 - 14 août), le régisseur (grisonnais) Daniel Schmid a accordé une interview aux journalistes dans laquelle il a précisé son point de vue, en formulant la réponse à la question:

> « Ha ancora senso la Svizzera? » (parce qu'elle n'est toujours pas membre de l'Union européenne): « è un modello per come quattro culture differenti possono vivere insieme senza amarsi, ma rispettandosi », et encore « quel colore speciale di questo paese unico, dove le identità culturali ci fanno diversi, ma non nemici. »(Helbling, LaRegione Festival Ticino, 7 agosto 1999, 13)

Et ce respect mutuel suppose des efforts constants et réciproques, et c'est dans ce sens que le nouvel article sur les langues, datant du 6 octtbre 1995 et voté par le peuple, veut être utile. L'article serait « un impegno », comme précisait le message du Conseil fédéral. Et les efforts continuent à se manifester: tout récemment, LaRegione parle d'un projet de loi du Canton de Fribourg qui précise ceci:

> « In un prossimo futuro tutti gli allievi e gli studenti friburghesi dovranno essere in grado di comprendere e parlare la seconda lingua ufficiale del cantone. È l'obiettivo di un disegno di legge promosso in prima svizzera dalle autorità cantonali » (LaRegione, 24 agosto 1999:5)

Mais tous ces efforts et les visions optimistes n'excluent pas le scepticisme, la polémique et même, mais rarement, l'aversion. Du côté romand, la peur de la germanisation est bien forte et quasiment éternelle. Il faut la prendre au sérieux, même si elle n'est pas toujours légitime. Roland Brachetto, journaliste romand qui collabore avec le Basler Zeitung, où il publie chaque semaine un article, en français, sur la Romandie, donne libre cours à son scepticisme qu'il exprime tout de même poliment, mais impérativement, en posant la question ancienne et saillante: « Y a-t-il un problème linguistique en Suisse? Oui, mais il n'a pas atteint le degré de virulence qu'il a en Belgique. Il reste à l'état larvé » (Brachetto, 1 août 1992:9). Donc, malgré la législation existante qui protège les communautés linguistiques, il faut se méfier, il faut lutter pour sauvegarder son identité romande, même s'il faut apprécier les progrès qui ont été atteints. Le principe de territorialité n'était pas satisfaisant, est-ce que le nouvel article sur les langues sera plus utile, plus avantageux? Et pourquoi Jacques Chessex, le numéro un de la littérature romande qui a remporté le Prix Goncourt pour son roman « L'Ogre » (1973), n'a-t-il pas participé à la Foire du Livre de Francfort, en 1998, à côté de ses collègues suisses allemands? Est-ce qu'il y a un fossé entre les hommes de lettres suisses allemands et romands? Et encore: lorsque le professeur Joseph Deiss, bilingue, de Fribourg, a été élu conseiller fédéral (comme successeur du Tessinois Flavio Cotti), il y avait le commentaire méchant d'un Genevois. « In ogni caso si tratta di un falso romando » (Stojanovic, Giornale del Popolo, 24 marzo 1999:2). C'est un renseignement choquant et hostile qu'on n'attendait pas dans un pays démocratique et officiellement plurilingue, un acte d'arrogance, cette fois-ci du côté romand.

2   La Suisse, un pays bilingue et plurilingue

Il y a trois cantons bilingues, Berne, Fribourg et le Valais, et aussi trois villes bilingues: Biel / Bienne, Fribourg / Freiburg et Sierre / Siders. Mais c'est seulement à Bienne que l'on trouve la diglossie, que la cohabitation de l'allemand et du français est officiellement reconnue et pratiquée, où même les inscriptions des rues sont bilingues, où l'administration municipale est bilingue et fait des publications dans les deux langues.

L'École d'ingénieurs de Bienne, récemment devenue une Haute École spécialisée, est officiellement bilingue. On a l'habitude d'engager de préférence des professeurs bilingues, et les cours des matières techniques sont donnés partiellement en allemand et en français, selon la langue maternelle des professeurs, et cela peut mener, dans le meilleur des cas, à un processus constant d'immersion. Abstraction faite de l'enseignement bilingue dans les matières techniques, nous avons aussi des leçons des langues maternelles allemande et française (langue, littérature et civilisation) et des leçons d'allemand et de français, comme première langue étrangère. Une étudiante étrangère de l'École de musique de Bienne a été interrogée sur sa vie à Bienne, et elle a donné spontanément la réponse élogieuse: la vie à Bienne est un cours permanent de langues. Statistiquement et démographiquement, le pourcentage des deux ethnies, à Fribourg et à Bienne, est le même, mais à l'inverse, dans les deux villes. Kolde donne des chiffres précises, en tirant la conclusion suivante:

„Seit Beginn dieses Jahrhunderts sind die Anteile der beiden Sprachgruppen an der Gesamtbevölkerung beider Städte fast stabil: 1970 wurden in Freiburg 57% Französischsprachige und 28% Deutschsprachige gezählt, in Biel waren es genau umgekehrt 57% Deutschsprachige und 27% Französischsprachige." (Kolde 1980:246).

Dans les deux villes, on a laissé de côté les italophones. C'est à Bienne que presque tout le monde parle alternativement les deux langues, sans différence sociale, tandis qu'à

Fribourg, selon une acception ancienne (et pas encore périmée), ce sont les « couches basses » et normalement les germanophones immigrés de confession protestante qui parlent l'allemand, notamment sous la forme du Schwyzerdütsch, tandis que les « couches élevées » et catholiques parlent le français. Les deux groupes ethniques, à Fribourg, habiteraient aussi dans des quartiers différents, tandis que Bienne donne l'image d'une habitation mixte. Les germanophones à Fribourg représentent une minorité qui se trouve, socialement parlant, à l'écart, tandis que la minorité romande de Bienne est seulement une minorité statistique. Sur les plans politique, social et moral, les Romands biennois sont considéres pleinement comme les égaux des habitants Suisses allemands: c'est que la ville de Bienne a résolu le mieux la paix linguistique et sociale, en pratiquant l'intégration des deux ethnies dans une seule et même communauté et en faisant preuve de beaucoup de tolérance (Kolde 1980:247).

Selon Rougemont, philosophe et homme de lettres romand et, surtout, Éuropéen avant la lettre (dans les années cinquante déjà), le problème des minorités ne devrait pas se poser dans un État démocratique et fédéraliste. C'est quelque chose de honteux, de scandaleux, d'indigne, c'est l'apanage des dictatures qui persécutent les minorités. Il a formulé six thèses sur la Suisse et l'Europe et considère la Suisse comme modèle d'une Europe future. Il proclame catégoriquement:

troisième thèse: « Le fédéralisme ne connaît pas le problème des minorités. »

cinquième thèse. « Le fédéralisme repose sur l'amour de la complexité, par contraste avec le simplisme brutal qui caractérise l'esprit totalitaire. » (Rougemont 1994:35-38).

Il semblerait que la ville de Bienne a résolu le problème de la cohabitation linguistique de deux ethnies dans un sens absolument très positif, selon les revendications de Rougemont.

3 Le bilinguisme, ses définitions et son côté à la fois idéal, pragmatique et esthétique

Les publications sur et les définitions du bilinguisme, depuis Uriel Weinreich (1952) et Georges Mackey, en passant par John Gumperz et jusqu'à nos jours, sont extrêmement nombreuses. Retenons-en deux, dont la première se veut systémique et idéale et la deuxième, par contre, fonctionnelle et pragmatique:

Bloomfield propose (en 1933) la définition systémique: « ... bilingualisme, native-like control of two languages. » (Bloomfield 1933:56). Très peu de gens disposent de cette possibilité, il s'agit surtout de ceux qui ont appris deux langues parallèlement dans leur enfance ou leur jeunesse.

Grosjean propose une définition fonctionelle, plus large et moins absolue. « Le bilingue est la personne qui se sert de deux langues dans la vie de tous les jours » (Grosjean 1982:2) et encore: « ... for the bilingual individual, bilingualism is a fact of life, as normal as sleeping and eating. » (Grosjean 1982:268).

Cette deuxième définition implique aussi la tendance au code-switching, dont il y a trois types, selon Gumperz: situational, relational et metaphorical (Gumperz 1982:75). C'est l'emploi de deux (ou plusieurs) langues sans réserve, sans restriction idéologique, selon le besoin, dans la vie de tous les jours. Je pense qu'il s'agit là du bilinguisme suisse, pragmatique, disposé à aider celui qui ne comprend pas ou pas suffisamment ma langue, ce qui m'entraîne à parler la sienne. Pour cela, il ne faut même pas maîtriser parfaitement les deux langues (« native like »), il faut seulement être apte à communiquer. Selon Lüdi (1989), la plupart des Suisses maîtrisent suffisamment les deux langues, l'allemand et le français, ils peuvent donc communiquer entre eux: « Il est vrai que la majorité des Suisses n'est pas plurilingue au sens fort du terme.» Et encore: « Chaque Suisse alémanique dispose (donc) au moins d'une maîtrise rudimentaire du français, et, vice versa, chaque Romand possède des connaissances de base en allemand.» (Lüdi 1989, VII:406). Mais il faut préciser tout de même qu'il s'agit plutôt d'une formule par trop optimiste. Selon Windisch, tout de même, le Suisse allemand serait plus fort dans l'autre langue, il arriverait plus près de la perfection. « Le Latin parfaitement bilingue est un oiseau rare ». (Windisch 1992, I: 120). C'est ce qu'il constate au cours d'une longue recherche « sur place », mais les Suisses allemands (et aussi les Tessinois) n'apprennent et ne parlent pas seulement le français, ils sont bilingues aussi dans le sens de Ferguson: ils parlent la langue standard, mais aussi leur dialecte (ou plutôt plusieurs dialectes alémaniques). (Ferguson 1959:325-340). Pour le Tessin, c'est moins le cas; le dialecte est en train de disparaître dans les centres urbains et se parle surtout dans les zones rurales (Bianconi 1979:25). Pour les Suisses allemands, en revanche, le dialecte représente une langue proprement dite et se parle indépendamment des couches sociales, et c'est ici que réside le problème de la situation asymétrique de l'emploi de l'allemand et du français en Suisse.

4   Pourquoi, donc, les Romands parlent-ils moins souvent et aussi moins volontiers la langue des compatriotes Suisses allemands?

Mes réponses sont empiriques et restent souvent des suppositions:

4.1   Il semblerait que les Romands ont peur de perdre leur identité linguistique et sociale, dans le sens de Gumperz (1990). Refuser la langue de l'autre signifie également « to create social distance » (Grosjean 1982:136).

4.2   Le(s) dialecte(s) suisse(s) allemand(s) représentent une barrière. Les Romands, apprennent la langue standard et sont confrontés avec les dialectes, lorsqu'ils se dèplacent en Suisse allemande.

4.3   La peur de la germanisation est au moins sous-jacente, sinon présente, même si des Romands contestent cette germanisation. Par exemple, un conférencier romand, Jean-François Maire, a contesté cette germanisation, lors du Congrès AILA de Sidney (1989): « Frenchspeaking Switzerland is monolingual; despite what the pessimists say, French is not all threatened by German, and is not a minority language in the sense in which that term is used elsewhere. » C'est-à-dire p.ex., le Polonais aux États-Unis. (Halliday 1990, II:43).

4.4 Le français est une langue mondiale, universelle, l'allemand ne l'est pas. On apprend certainement moins volontiers une langue qui n'est pas universelle.

4.5 Est-ce que l'allemand, du point de vue sonore, ne paraît pas assez beau aux Romands? Donc, une raison esthétique?

4.6 La morpho-syntaxe de l'allemand est compliquée et dure à apprendre, il y a donc une raison didactique à énumérer:

- les déclinaisons des substantifs et des adjectifs sont compliquées: der Mann, die Männer, die schönen Männer, den schönen Männern.
- les verbes irréguliers sont nombreux (die starken Verben): essen - ass - gegessen, fallen - fiel - gefallen.
- la place du verbe à la fin de la subordonnée est insolite: ... weil er nicht genug Geld hatte.
- l'expression de la modalité est difficile à apprendre: « devoir » signifie à la fois: müssen, sollen, dürfen;
- « wollen » dans le sens de la supposition: er will gestern um 10 Uhr zu Hause gewesen sein (= il prétend avoir été ...).
- certains déictiques posent des problèmes: hier, da, dort.
- certains particules énonciatives (interjections) sont difficiles à traduire: Was hat er denn bloß? So setzen Sie sich doch!

Mais ma liste est incomplète. Voilà seulement quelques suggestions!

5 Références bibliographiqes

BIANCONI, Sandro (1979): Comportamento linguistico e riuscita scolastica dei giovani ticinesi. Bellinzona: Ufficio cantonale di statistica.

BLOOMFIELD, Leonard (1933): Language. New York: Henry Holt

BRACHETTO, Roland (1992): Une bouffée d'air de Romandie. Ici on parle français. Dans: Basler Zeitung, 1. August.

FERGUSON, Charles (1959): Diglossia, Word 15.

GROSJEAN, François (1982): Life with two languages. An introduction to bilingualism. Cambridge, Mass.: Harvard University Press.

GUMPERZ, John J. (1990): Language and social identity. Cambridge. Cambridge University Press.

— (1982): Discourse strategies. Cambridge. Cambridge University Press.

HELBLING, Gianfranco (1999): Daniel Schmid il contrabbandiere. Dans: La Regione Festival Ticino, 7 agosto.

KNECHT, Pierre (1979): Le français en Suisse romande: aspects linguistiques et sociolinguistiques. Dans: Valdman, A.: le français hors de France. Paris. Champion.

KOLDE, Gottfried (1980): Vergleichende Untersuchungen des Sprachverhaltens und der Spracheinstellungen von Jugendlichen in zwei gemischtsprachigen Schweizer Städten. Dans: Zeitschrift für Dialektologie und Linguistik. Beihefte, Heft 32: Sprachkontakt und Sprachkonflikt. Wiesbaden: Steiner.

LÜDI, Georges (1989): Aspects de la conversation exolingue entre Suisses romands et alémaniques. Dans: Actes du XVIII Congrès international de linguistique et de philologie romanes (Trèves 1986), t. VII. Tübingen: Niemeyer.

MAIRE, Jean-François (1990): Les mots régionaux, c'est du « chenit » (or what to do with regionalism in the teaching of French as a foreign language). Dans: Halliday, Michael A. K.; Gibbons, John; Nicholas, Howard (eds.): Learning, keeping and using language. II, 43. Amsterdam – Philadelphia: John Benjamins.

ROUGEMONT, Denis de (1994): Écrits sur l'Europe, vol. I, 1948 - 1961. Paris: la Différence.

STOJANOVIC, Nenad (1999): Pericolo etnico in Svizzera? Dans: Giornale del Popolo, 24 marzo.

WINDISCH, Uli (1992): Les relations quotidiennes entre Romands et Suisses allemands; les Cantons bilingues de Fribourg et du Valais, 2 volumes. Lausanne: Payot

Möglichkeiten der Erhaltung und Revitalisierung bedrohter Sprachen

Laura Sacia

1   Einleitung

Nach Krauss (1992) werden etwa 90% aller Sprachen innerhalb des nächsten Jahrhunderts als bedroht gelten oder gar aussterben. Er definiert bedrohte Sprachen als

> „languages which, though now still being learned by children will – if the present conditions continue – cease to be learned by children during the coming century" (Krauss 1992:6).

Obwohl nicht mit letzter Sicherheit von der Richtigkeit seiner Prognose ausgegangen werden kann, zeigt sie doch zumindest eine besorgniserregende Tendenz auf. Kann diese Entwicklung aufgehalten werden?

Folgende Punkte sollen hier behandelt werden: Erstens, was ist bislang getan worden, um bedrohte Sprachen zu erhalten oder zu revitalisieren? Zweitens, wie erfolgreich waren die Revitalisierungs- oder Erhaltungsprogramme für bedrohte Sprachen bisher? Drittens, was können Linguisten zur Revitalisierung oder Erhaltung bedrohter Sprachen beitragen?

2   Spracherhaltungs- und Revitalisierungsprogramme

2.1   Spracherhaltung – Fallbeispiel Pohnpei

Ich benutze den Begriff *Spracherhaltung* für die Erhaltung einer Sprache die noch relativ gesund ist, welche aber künftig bedroht sein könnte. Die Programme sollen Sprechern helfen, kompetent in ihrer Sprache zu bleiben, indem sie Sprechen, Lesen und Schreiben gelehrt werden.

Pohnpei liegt in den Föderierten Staaten von Mikronesien (FSM). Sie ist eine der vier Hauptinseln von Mikronesien. Sie ist auch der Regierungssitz der FSM. Nach der Volkszählung von 1994 sprechen 89% der pohnpeianischen Bevölkerung Pohnpeianosch (die einheimische Sprache). Von diesen 89% sprechen 19,498 Pohnpeianisch als erste Sprache und 4,494 als Zweitsprache (Rehg 1998:338). Pohnpeianisch ist noch relativ gesund, jedoch gibt es Anzeichen dafür, daß die Situation sich verschlechtert. Nach Rehg (1998:324ff) hat die Zahl der Menschen, die sehr fortgeschrittenes Englisch sprechen, zugenommen. Auch die Zahl der englischen Lehnwörter nahm zu, sogar bei älteren Sprechern, welche typischerweise kein gutes Englisch sprechen. Darüber hinaus haben ältere Sprecher darauf hingewiesen, daß jüngere Pohnpeianer Mängel in der Verwendung des numerischen Klassifikatorensystems wie auch in der Verwendung des Honorificumsystems zeigen. Englisch ist die Amtssprache der FSM und der größte Teil der zwischenstaatlichen Kommunikation findet auf Englisch statt. Der Grund hierfür ist, daß die vier Hauptsprachen der FSM (Yapesisch, Trukesisch, Kosraianisch, Pohnpeianisch) sehr verschieden sind. Mit Englisch können Mikronesier außerdem auf internationaler Ebene kommunizieren. Selbst der Großteil der Korrespondenz innerhalb der pohnpeianischen Regierung läuft auf Englisch, obgleich Pohnpeianisch die Muttersprache der Beamten ist (Andreas 1998:9). Es scheint, daß Englisch in immer mehr Bereichen benutzt wird, womit gleichzeitig die Bereiche abnehmen, die traditionell pohnpeianisch waren. Englisch ist nicht nur die Wahlsprache der Regierung, sondern auch in einem Großteil der Medien. Die Mehrheit der Fernsehprogramme in Pohnpei ist beispielsweise amerikanisch, und diese werden nicht synchronisiert (Rehg 1998:325). Es gibt einige Fernsehprogramme auf pohnpeianisch, aber diese haben ein erheblich geringeres Budget und sind deswegen für die Zuschauer nicht so attraktiv gestaltet wie ihre amerikanischen (oder in einigen Fällen japanischen) Gegenstücke (Rehg 1998:329).

Eine der wichtigsten Domänen für die Anwendung einer Sprache ist die Schule. Leider ist Englisch auch die Wahlsprache für das Bildungssystem. Wie Rehg feststellt:

> „English is highly regarded on Pohnpei because, at present, it is seen as a necessary prerequisite for educational success. Because so little has been written in Pohnpeian, it is impossible for a speaker of this language to obtain a modern education without learning English or some other cosmopolitan language." (1998:337)

Es ist selbstverständlich, daß Kinder darauf vorbereitet werden sollten, in einem globalen Wirtschaftsgefüge zu leben und sich mit ihren Nachbarn zu verständigen. Doch es scheint, als ob die Verwendung von Englisch überproportional zu seiner Bedeutung wächst. Obwohl der pohnpeianische Lehrplan vorschreibt, daß Pohnpeianisch vom ersten bis zum dritten Schuljahr Unterrichtssprache und vom vierten bis zum achten Schuljahr Pflichtfach ist, sieht die Praxis anders aus. Sobald Schüler fließend Englisch können, werden sie automatisch versetzt, unabhängig von ihrer Kompetenz in Pohnpeianisch (Andreas 1998:5)

Kann man gegen diese Entwicklung ankämpfen, und wenn ja, wie? Nach Andreas (1998:6) gibt es zwei Faktoren, die eine erfolgreiche Sprachpolitik und -planung bedingen. Der erste Faktor ist das Bewußtsein und die Mitsprache der Sprachgemeinschaft. Dies ist sehr wichtig für den Erfolg eines jeden Spracherhaltungsprogramms. Andreas schlägt vor, Workshops zu bilden, welche die gegenwärtige linguistische Situation beschreiben und sowohl die Menschen auf die bestehende Gefahr des Verlustes ihrer Sprache aufmerksam macht, als auch darauf, was dieser Sprachverlust für ihre Kultur bedeuten würde. Damit erhofft er den Dialog zwischen den Sprachgemeinschaften Pohnpeis zu fördern und ihren Input und Vorschläge zu erhalten – nicht nur auf der Ebene der Programmausführung, sondern auch auf der Ebene der Programmplanung. Der zweite Faktor, den Andreas erwähnt, die Einbeziehung der traditionellen Führer der Gesellschaft (im Falle Pohnpeis – die *Nahnmwarrki*) ist ebenfalls wichtig für die Spracherhaltung, da die traditionellen Führer von Pohnpei immer noch große Autorität besitzen. Wie Andreas feststellt:

> „It is almost impossible to plan and execute any state development project without the consent of the traditional leaders. Although [they] do not participate in the creation of laws for the State, they play a major and powerful role that often supersedes the power of the leaders and officials elected or appointed under Pohnpei's democratic system of government." (Andreas 1998:9)

Zu diesem Zeitpunkt ist es schwierig vorherzusagen, ob die Spracherhaltungspro-
gramme greifen werden. Doch die Einbeziehung der Gemeinschaft und der traditionellen Führer darf nicht unterschätzt werden.

2.2 Sprachrevitalisierung: Ein Vergleich von Gälisch und Hebräisch

Ich verwende den Begriff Sprachrevitalisierung (engl.: *language revitalization*) zur
Beschreibung der Revitalisierung einer Sprache, welche eine Anzahl ihrer Sprecher
verloren hat und welche als „bedroht" aufgefaßt werden muß. Es existieren verschiedene Grade der Sprachgefährdung, weshalb Sprachrevitalisierungsprogramme in ihrer
Gestaltung und in ihrer Ausführung variieren. Während einige Programme sich an
Menschen richten, welche die bedrohte Sprache als ihre Muttersprache gelernt haben,
sind andere Programme für Menschen gedacht, welche keine Vorkenntnisse der bedrohten Sprache haben, bevor sie ins Programm einbezogen werden. Einige Programme beginnen, während die Kinder noch sehr jung sind, andere, wenn die Sprecher
schon älter sind. Im folgenden soll die Situation von Gälisch, häufig *Irisch* genannt,
beschrieben werden, welche die einheimische Sprache von Irland ist. Nach Grimes
(1993:801f) gibt es 260.000 Menschen in Irland, welche entweder fließend Gälisch
sprechen, oder Gälisch-Muttersprachler sind. Diese Information basiert auf einer
Volkszählung von 1983. Diese Zahl könnte sich deshalb bis heute geändert haben.
Nach Fishman (1996:196f) sprechen 3% der irischen Bevölkerung Gälisch als erste
Sprache. Englisch ist die dominante Sprache in Irland seit über einem Jahrhundert.
Dies ist größtenteils auf die Industrialisierung zurückzuführen, welche eine Veränderung in der Demographie und Sozialstruktur verursachte, indem die Menschen vom
Lande in die Städte abwanderten. In den Städten ist Englisch schon seit Jahrhunderten die dominante Sprache gewesen. Es stammt von den Anglo-Normannischen Er-
oberungen des Mittelalters. Darüber hinaus bewirkten die Ausfälle der Kartoffelernte
in den vierziger Jahren des letzten Jahrhunderts, daß die irische Landbevölkerung,
besonders die Sprecher des Gälischen, in großer Zahl auswanderten oder verhunger-
ten.

Die Gebiete in Irland, in denen Gälisch noch Muttersprache ist, werden *Gaeltachtai*
genannt. Die *Gaeltachtei* liegen weit entfernt von den Städten. Das Land ist arm an
natürlichen Ressourcen. Die *Gaeltachtei* sind bäuerliche Gemeinden mit geringer
Industrialisierung und einer hohen Arbeitslosenquote. Der Großteil der Jugend emi-
griert von der *Gaeltachtai* und wechselt deshalb zu Englisch. Nach Carnie (1996:106f)
betrachten viele junge Leute Englisch als eine

> „kind of economic liberator. Speaking English well benefits the young person in his or her
> quest for a job outside the *gaeltacht*, where the bulk of jobs are to be found."

Ein weiteres Problem ist, daß Gälisch historisch als Sprache von geringem Ansehen
betrachtet wurde. Wer Irisch sprach, galt als ungebildet und arm. Selbst heute noch
halten viele Irischsprachige ihre Sprache für nutzlos im Vergleich zu Englisch (Carnie
1996:108).

Eine Sprachrevitalisierungsbewegung ist seit dem Ende des 19. Jahrhunderts in Irland aktiv. Dabei wurde die Sprache auch ein Symbol der repuplikanischen Bewe-

gung. Irisch wurde 1937 offiziell zur ersten Sprache in der Verfassung des irischen Freistaates deklariert. Zu dieser Zeit wurde begonnen, Irisch auch in Schulen außerhalb der Gaeltacht für Nicht-Muttersprachler zu unterrichten. Trotz alledem waren Revitalisierungsversuche aus verschiedenen Gründen relativ erfolglos: Erstens waren die hierfür benutzten Methoden antiquiert, d.h., die Lehrer stützten sich primär auf die *grammar-translation* Methoden statt auf mehr kommunikative Herangehensweisen. Zweitens fühlten sich viele Schüler gezwungen, Gälisch zu lernen, da sie bis in die 70er Jahre unseres Jahrhunderts eine obligatorische Gälisch-Prüfung bestehen mußten, um ein Hochschulzertifikat erhalten zu können. Drittens ist Gälisch allgemein auf das Klassenzimmer beschränkt, was den Lernenden dieser Sprache nur begrenzte Bereiche gewährt, in welchen sie ihre sprachlichen Fähigkeiten üben können. Viertens gibt es wenige Medien, z.B. Bücher, Zeitungen oder Fernsehprogramme auf Gälisch, und wenn sie verfügbar sind, so sind sie teurer oder von geringerer Qualität als die englischen, oder ihre Zielgruppen sind eher ältere Leute (Carnie 1996:108ff).

Betrachten wir den Versuch, Gälisch den Status einer Muttersprache zu geben – was Sprachrevitalisierer beabsichtigten, als sie mit den Revitalisierungsprogrammen begannen –, muß festgestellt werden, daß diese Versuche erfolglos blieben. Doch kann auch eine optimistischere Haltung eingenommen werden, indem hervorgehoben wird, was bereits erreicht wurde. Obwohl in 75 Jahren die Zahl der Muttersprachler von 5% auf 3% gesunken ist, sprechen jetzt ungefähr zwei Drittel der irischen Bevölkerung Gälisch als Zweitsprache (Fishman 1996:197).

Zahlreiche Autoren haben die gälische Situation mit der hebräischen verglichen, da Hebräisch revitalisiert wurde, nachdem es Jahrtausende praktisch ausgestorben war. Das ist nur zum Teil richtig. Es ist wahr, daß Hebräisch für fast zweitausend Jahre nicht als Muttersprache gesprochen wurde, doch wurde es weiterhin in geschriebener Form benutzt, und z.T. auch in gesprochener Form – meistens als *Lingua Franca* (Fellman 1973:12f). Die Revitalisierung des Hebräischen sollte deshalb eher als ein Fall von *Revernacularization* betrachtet werden als ein Fall von Revitalisierung. Es ist beachtenswert, daß Hebräisch heute die Muttersprache von etwa 4.500.000 Menschen in Israel und 100.000 in den Vereinigten Staaten ist (Grimes 1993:646).

Warum war die Revitalisierung des Hebräischen so erfolgreich während der Revitalisierungsversuch mit Gälisch erfolglos blieb? Beide Versuche begannen etwa gleichzeitig (spätes 19. Jahrhundert), und beide Sprachen hatten Gemeinden, welche eine feste ethnische Identität besaßen. Warum waren also die Ergebnisse so verschieden? Zu allererst sollte der Status beider Sprachen berücksichtigt werden. Wie schon erwähnt, war Gälisch eine Sprache von niedrigem Ansehen, und es mußte mit Englisch konkurrieren, welche die Muttersprache der Mehrheit aller Iren ist. Hebräisch, auf der anderen Seite, war eine Sprache mit hohem Ansehen für die jüdische Gemeinschaft für Jahrtausende. Der Übergang von Englisch zu Gälisch wäre ein Übergang von einer Prestige-Sprache zu einer Sprache mit niedrigem Ansehen (Slomanson 1996:118). Mit Hebräisch, auf der anderen Seite, verlief der Übergang häufig von einer Sprache mit niedrigem Ansehen, wie z.B. Jiddisch, zu einer Sprache mit hohem Ansehen. Zweitens sollte die Sprachgemeinschaft betrachtet werden. Die Bevölkerung von Irland ist linguistisch sehr homogen, während die Menschen in der hebräischen Bewegung verschiedenen sprachlichen Ursprungs waren, welche im späten 19. Jahrhundert nach Israel, damals Palästina, immigrierten. Hebräisch konnte deshalb als *Lingua Franca* von hohem Ansehen fungieren.

2.3 Sprachrevitalisierung: Fallbeispiel Hawaiianisch

Vor etwa hundert Jahren wurde Hawaiianisch, damals eine Sprache, die sowohl in gesprochener als auch in geschriebener Form, sowohl innerhalb als auch außerhalb der Schule florierte, von der Regierung der Hawaiianischen Republik verboten, um nicht-hawaiianische Mächte zusammenzuschließen und die Annexion Hawaiis durch die Vereinigten Staaten zu fördern, welche im Jahre 1898 stattfand. Ein territoriales Gesetz wurde 1919 verabschiedet, welches verlangte, daß Hawaiianisch in der Lehrerausbildung und in den Oberschulen gelehrt werden mußte. Trotzdem verminderte sich die Zahl der Sprecher von Hawaiianisch bis in die späten 70er Jahre dramatisch, als der Bundesstaat Hawaii Bestimmungen verabschiedete, die deklarierten, daß Hawaiianisch neben Englisch als Amtssprache des Bundesstaates Hawaii anerkannt wurde. Zu dieser Zeit wurde die Zahl der Muttersprachler des Hawaiianische auf weniger als 2000 geschätzt, mit einer Mehrheit von älteren Sprechern (Schütz 1992:349ff).

Fast ausgestorben, erwachte in den späten 70er Jahren ein erneutes Interesse an der hawaiianischen Sprache und Kultur. Am wichtigsten für die Revitalisierung des Hawaiianischen war die Einrichtung von privaten, gemeinnützigen *Immersion Preschools*, bekannt geworden als *Punana Leo* (wörtlich „Sprachnester") im Jahre 1984. Die *Punana Leo* wurden in Anlehnung an die erfolgreichen *Kohanga Reo* Maori Sprachnester in Neuseeland konzipiert. In diesen Kindergärten werden die Kinder im Alter von drei bis fünf Jahren ausschließlich auf Hawaiianisch angesprochen und sprechen selbst zehn Stunden am Tag, fünf Tage pro Woche ausschließlich Hawaiianisch (Schütz 1992:356ff).

Während der letzten 15 Jahre haben sich die hawaiianischen *Immersion Schools* etabliert, die Zahl ihrer Schüler ist gestiegen und damit auch die Akzeptanz der Gemeinschaft und der Regierung. Diese Schulen hatten viele Hürden zu nehmen, wie z.B. den Mangel an ausgebildeten Lehrern, zeitgemäßen Lesematerialien oder aber auch Auseinandersetzungen mit naiven Bedenken seitens einiger Beamte, für die solche *Immersion* Programme eher anti-englisch als pro-bilingual sind (Schütz 1992:361).

Trotz alledem sind die Mitglieder der hawaiianischen Revitalisierungsbewegung sehr einsatzbereit gewesen, und haben große Mühen auf sich genommen, um Hawaiianisch eine lebendige Sprache werden zu lassen. Der Mangel an Lesematerialien wurde z.B. zum Teil ausgeglichen mit der Einführung von Internetquellen auf hawaiianisch, welche die geographisch isolierter liegenden hawaiianischen Schulen zu leichterer Kommunikation befähigt. Diese Internetquellen bieten eine Fülle von Nachrichten und Literatur in hawaiianischer Sprache an. Hawaiianisch in der technologischen Domäne verwendet zu sehen, gibt Sprechern den Eindruck, daß ihre Sprache tatsächlich nützlich und sehr lebendig ist. Diese Tatsache macht Hawaiianisch auch für jüngere Sprecher attraktiv.

2.4   Zusammenfassung

Gibt es also ein Patentrezept für Spracherhaltung und -revitalisierung? Leider nicht. Die Forschung hat gezeigt, daß der Erfolg von Spracherhaltung und -revitalisierung multifaktoriell beeinflußt wird. Spracherhaltungs- und Sprachrevitalisierungsprogramme in den Schulen sind zwar hilfreich, doch sind sie nicht fähig, die gesamte Last der Umkehrung eines Sprachwechsels allein zu tragen. Die Verantwortung muß auf der gesamten Sprachgemeinschaft liegen, um ausreichend viele Domänen für die Sprache zu erhalten. Medien, welche sich an junge Sprecher richten, sind ebenfalls wichtig, denn junge Leute sind jene, welche entscheiden, ob sie ihre Sprache an ihre eigenen Kinder weitergeben oder nicht. Vielleicht ist ein gewisser Stolz der Sprecher auf ihre Sprache und Kultur am wichtigsten, denn ohne diesen gäbe es keinen Antrieb, die Sprache zu erhalten.

3   Unsere Rolle als Linguisten

Es gibt einige Beiträge, die Linguisten leisten können um bei der Erhaltung und Revitalisierung einer Sprache mitzuhelfen. Linguisten können z.B. bei der Erstellung von Lehrplänen und bei der Entwicklung von effektiven und spannenden Lehrmethoden mitarbeiten. Vielleicht der wichtigste Beitrag, den Linguisten leisten können, ist die Dokumentation bedrohter Sprachen. Selbst rudimentäre Wörterbücher oder auch Grammatik-Nachschlagewerke und Audioaufnahmen von bedrohten Sprachen zusammenzustellen, ist nicht nur hilfreich für die Sprachgemeinschaft, sondern auch für die Linguistik. Daten über weniger bekannte oder bedrohte Sprachen sind essentiell für die Entwicklung linguistischer Theorien und können helfen, gegenwärtige Hypothesen zu stützen oder zu widerlegen. So ist z.B. nicht auszuschließen, daß Sprachen existieren, welche sich syntaktisch derart abweichend verhalten, daß sie die gegenwärtigen Ansichten über die *Universal Grammar* widerlegen. Mit der Dokumentation bedrohter Sprachen fördern wir ein besseres Verständnis der historischen Linguistik und der Frühgeschichte.

Trotz alledem scheint es, daß die Dokumentation bedrohter Sprachen im allgemeinen sehr wenig Aufmerksamkeit von Linguisten erhält. Wie Krauss (1992:10) feststellt:

> „To what extent are endangered languages a priority in modern linguistics? Which languages of the world receive the most attention? Are graduate students encouraged to document moribund or endangered languages for their dissertations? How much encouragement is there to compile a dictionary of one? Obviously we must do some serious rethinking of our priorities, lest linguistics go down in history as the only science that presided obliviously over the disappearance of 90% of the very field to which it is dedicated."

Die Situation der pazifischen Sprachen spiegelt dieses Argument sehr gut wider. Im Pazifik werden circa 1400 Sprachen gesprochen. Das entspricht etwa einem Viertel aller Sprachen (Lynch 1998:25). Viele dieser Sprachen werden von weniger als 5000 Menschen gesprochen, und ein Teil dieser Sprachen hat weniger als 200 Sprecher. Nur ein geringer Prozensatz dieser Sprachen ist bisher dokumentiert. Ein gutes Beispiel hierfür ist Western Oceanic, eine Sprachfamilie mit 242 Sprachen. Für lediglich

15 Sprachen in dieser Familie existieren Wörterbücher, für nur 23 Sprachen sind Grammatik-Nachschlagewerke erarbeitet worden (Liao 1999). Diese Zahlen zeigen auf, daß noch ein großer Teil Dokumentationsarbeit geleistet werden muß. Als Linguisten müssen wir uns bewußt sein, daß sprachliche Diversität das Rückgrat unserer Disziplin ist. Obwohl wir wenig Einfluß haben auf Sprachwechsel, welcher größtenteils von sozio-ökonomischen Faktoren, Politik, Sprachstatus und der Einstellung der Sprecher zu ihrer eigenen Sprache beeinflußt wird, können wir doch zumindest helfen, diese Sprachen für künftige Generationen durch Dokumentation zu erhalten.

4 Literatur

ANDREAS, Robert (1998): Language Planning in the Federated States of Micronesia: The Status of Planning in Pohnpei. (Unpublished).

CARNIE, Andrew (1996): Modern Irish: A Case Study in Language Revival Failure. In: MIT Working Papers in Linguistics 28, 99-114.

FELLMAN, Jack (1973): The Revival of a Classical Tongue: Eliezer Ben Yehuda and the Modern Hebrew Language. The Hague: Mouton.

FISHMAN, Joshua (1996): Maintaining Languages – What Works? What Doesn't? In: Cantoni, Gina (ed): Stabilizing Indigenous Languages. Flagstaff: Center for Excellence in Education, Northern Arizona University.

GRIMES, Barbara (1993): Ethnologue: Languages of the World. Dallas: Summer Institute of Linguistics.

KRAUSS, Michael (1992): The World's Languages in Crisis. In: Language 68.1, 4-10.

LIAO, Hsiu Chuan; Isozaki, Yoshiko; Rutter, Kenji (1999): The Need for the Documentation of Minority Languages: The Example of Oceanic Languages. (Presentation by Hsiu Chuan Liao at the Forum of the Endangered Languages Issue, University of Hawai'i at Manoa, 15 April, 1999). (Unpublished).

LYNCH, John (1998): Pacific Languages: an Introduction. Honolulu: University of Hawai'i Press.

REHG, Kenneth (1998): Taking the Pulse of Pohnpeian. In: Oceanic Linguistics 37, 323-345.

SCHÜTZ, Albert (1992): The Voices of Eden: A History of Hawaiian Language Studies. Honolulu: University of Hawaii Press.

SLOMANSON, Peter (1996): Explaining and Reversing the Failure of the Irish Language Revival. In: MIT Working Papers in Linguistics 28, 115-135.

Importing and Exporting Linguistic Material – Exchanging Expertise

Thomas M. Sengani

African languages have since the days of the missionaries been taught as second or even foreign languages to mother-tongue speakers. The reason has of course been the system of the day which did not only discriminate against the speakers but also relegated the languages themselves. Academics and language planners were almost entirely non-mother tongue speakers, most of whom could not communicate in the languages and as such they concentrated on issues such as pure articulatory phonetics, the so-called regular and irregular sound changes, internal structures of words, sentence structures, their grammaticality and the meaning of words, usually out of context. The focus was on book grammar rather than on grammar use and this left students poorly equipped to deal with language issues in the context of their professional lives. As a result, these languages have been looked down upon, even by their speakers, and are today rarely used in government and professional services, more to the further detriment of millions of these speakers. With the change of government has come an enormous need for the use of these languages, as services are better delivered in and through them. Although the government now supports the further development of these languages, funding is limited and there is a need for more linguistic expertise to improve the status of these languages.

Although some students and scholars have studied at institutions in Germany and students and scholars in Germany have done research in our country, there is a visible lack of organised working co-operation between scholars in Germany and South Africa. While the system of language teaching is changing in South Africa, areas needing attention include the understanding and application of language concepts, curriculum development, diversified teaching methods especially involving cultural, research approaches, publication culture context, etc. A closer working relationship between German and South African scholars can help bridge the gap.

Scholars in the first world have been involved in research for decades. Just as first world expertise in the field of business has enriched us tremendously, it would likewise be enriching to import linguistic expertise from the first world, especially the provision of training programmes, exchange for students and teaching personnel. In South Africa, African language practitioners stand to gain from scholars in Germany if we can establish proper co-operation and the initiation of the exchange of scholars, concepts, theories, teaching and research methods, data and human resources. Both scholars and students in South African institutions would be more productive if they applied linguistic knowledge to business, law, medicine, education, religion, the media, science and technology, etc. Skills and expertise in these fields would help them to create jobs and improve the delivery of services, which have become critical issues in South Africa today.

1.0   Introduction

In our daily lives we interact through and by language. The arrival of a child at birth is announced through language and communication with him or her in all spheres of life is through language. The songs we sing, the poetry we chant and the art we design are all facilitated through language. The friendships we establish, the enmity we create, the business we engage in, the legal tangles we get trapped in, the therapy we receive in bad times and our relationship with God, all have language at the centre stage. All these take place in a two-way stream, an exchange of expertise.

1.1   Missionary ventures

The first process in exchanging expertise began with the missionaries since they were the first to teach African languages. Most of them could not communicate in the languages and as such they taught them as foreign languages to their mother-tongue speakers. The main aim was to teach Africans to read and write so that the propagation of the gospel could be facilitated (Mathivha1985; Satyo 1988; Milubi 1998). In this way, they introduced Africans to reading, the written word, printing houses etc. While the expertise was relevant, their process was therefore imposing because their partners, who happened to be Africans, had no choice but to take whatever material they were offered without giving anything in return. This was rather a one-way traffic as the teachers rarely tried to understand the people's culture, politics, education system, religion etc. so as to integrate these within the educational system. This new lifestyle created another community within a community, i.e. a community of the learned which divorced itself from the others. The new educational system had as such no African philosophical foundation.

The study and teaching of African languages resulted in the division of language groups, as people from different linguistic background were rarely accommodated in one school. Areas and schools were set aside for particular language groups. This was a practice to deny the African people social interaction which had for years enriched their exchange of expertise. However, traditional schools among Africans continued to flourish and there was what one could call cultural and linguistic integration as the peoples lived in harmony.

1.2   The emergence of non-mother tongue intellectuals

Another dimension in the teaching of these languages came with the involvement of academics, especially linguists. Most of these scholars influenced the curriculum of African languages in schools and even at tertiary level because they and not Africans were the planners of the subjects, curricula and advisors to government, examiners and writers of grammar books. Most of the African students were encouraged to pursue their studies in literature since the teachers were not conversant with the languages. Linguistics was reserved for mostly non-mother tongue speakers because it had always been regarded as being scientific and as such difficult for Africans whose talents allegedly lay in relating stories. This process did not do the exchange of expertise any good. Linguistic material was then largely directed at second and/or third language speakers instead of first language speakers. Since the planners and teachers lacked proficiency in these languages, mother-tongue students continued to be taught in either English or Afrikaans.

The other problem has been the underdevelopment of these languages. Whilst the establishment of Language Committees and later Language Boards was a good gesture, the policy on these languages was not clearcut. Firstly they have always been referred to as 'first' languages but have been taught as second or third languages. Most former members of the established committees, and boards now confess that rules on grammar, borrowing etc. were imposed by the authorities. For instance they point out that they were encouraged to borrow more from Afrikaans than English and were forbidden from borrowing from related languages to their own languages and that those members who resisted this move were ignored. The language committees and boards could have been a challenging platform for exchanging ideas. Critical debates could have produced critical thinkers thus making an exchange of expertise a profitable one.

1.3   The rise of African scholars

During the 70's, 80's and early 90's the frustration in the teaching of African languages led a number of African language university educators to introduce these languages as media of instruction at some of their university departments. This move was criticised by most European and African scholars. The main issue was that the use of African languages as media of instruction would lower the standard of these languages and that lecturers would encounter problems when they interacted with their counterparts in the United States of America and Britain. Another reason given was that there were no grammar books written in the languages for use at university level and also that there was no ready terminology in the languages to explain linguistic concepts.

However, the major underlying reason for the rejection of African languages as media of instruction especially at historically white universities with first language students, was to protect non-mother tongue educators since most of them could not and, even now, cannot communicate in the languages of which they are said to be experts. Teaching in these languages in class would be an embarrassment for them. How do you teach a language in which you can hardly converse? How do you convince students or put your views across to them? What if he or she asks you a question in that very language?

In exporting and importing products there is giving and taking, but in the teaching of African languages this has not been the case, as the language speakers have been made to import stale products. There has not been any fair exchange of expertise because African languages have for decades been taught out of context to first language speakers. Grammar books appear far removed from the daily language of communication. People often come up with questions such as, "Do African languages offer any bread? Are they relevant in today's world?" When university students are asked why they do not opt to study an African language, their answer has generally been, "For what purpose? What do you do with African languages?" This is an uninformed reaction academically but it reflects on the failure of the exchange of expertise in the system of African language teaching.

2   African languages and other disciplines

African language scholars today find themselves on the defensive because of the rate at which student numbers are decreasing. This spells doom for some departments at some universities. The communities need professionals with expertise in the languages to help in solving language-related problems, but these are hard to come by. If these languages are relevant, then the question is, "What is their position in the curriculum of a university?" Such a question was posed by King (1980) when the position of Linguistics in the United States was being threatened. He went on to allege that, "[t]here are no good prophets in higher education" (ibid:6) because in both the 60's and 70's scholars could not predict that many departments could close down because of decreasing numbers of students. In South Africa too, changes found most scholars unprepared.

A number of scholars have expressed concern about the manner in which these languages are being taught because very little has been seen in terms of addressing problems in the communities. Burling (1970:2) complains that:

"The scholar who calls himself a linguist differs from his colleagues in other disciplines in examining language for its own sake rather than as an instrument by which to seek an understanding of other matters. The results of linguistic investigation may be of interest to its sister disciplines, but solving their problems has not been the linguist's major goal. In fact, it is reasonable to suggest that real progress in learning about the structure and organization of language only came when a few men began to narrow their interest down to language itself and to set aside any concern for the uses to which language is put."

He goes on to indicate that linguists tend to deal with language as just a system with its internal logic, rules and features. To him this has minimized their concern and narrowed their focus thus simplifying their task. Hubbard (1995) has gone on to remark that phonology is barren if not linked to real practical issues. Kuno (1972) has in the same vein criticised syntactitians for being too rigid in that they deal with very small data coming up with generalizations which are far removed from reality. Having researched more in language policy, Cluver (1979) saw the dawn of the inter-disciplinary era and commented that linguists could be reaching the end of a syntactic era. The curriculum at the schools and tertiary level has focussed on the identification of speech sounds, sound changes, word-units, sentence construction, and word meaning with no link to daily communicative language. The views expressed by these scholars call for a serious link between language and the society in which it is used. This suggests a working relationship between the language teacher and the speaker which can be considered an exchange of expertise.

African languages are indeed relevant and offer 'bread' provided those of us who are practitioners can learn to be relevant too. There is a dire need to link the two major branches, of linguistics namely linguistics and applied linguistics. However, doing this will be a tough task because these two, according to Mey (1993:286) "… do not seem to speak to each other." Theoretical Linguistics has been viewed as being 'real', 'proper', 'genuine', 'legitimate' and 'a science' indeed whereas applied linguistics has been found to be improper, 'illegitimate and almost the soft underbelly of linguistics' (Mey 1993). In this impasse, pragmatics should be brought into the picture to forge relations between the two important branches. In order to make them relevant, theories should be tested or applied in the real spoken language. In fact many other disciplines became more practical by mining material in the linguistic golden field whilst we were still practising traditional grammar. It cannot be denied that in our daily use of language we employ phonetics, phonology, morphology, syntax and semantics and these can be linked to other disciplines to help solve many societal problems.

A serious issue that scholars would have to handle with courage is the belief that scientific concepts can only be expressed in European languages. African languages have been undermined by many influential but uninformed scholars as being almost 'handicapped'.

What cannot be denied is that when speakers of a language identify an object and its function they are able to coin terms for it. This means that research should be conducted amongst the language users themselves and, according to Milubi (1998:8), in order to accomplish their goal, scholars will in some cases end up borrowing, adapting and incorporating terms into their languages.

3   The significance of exchange programmes

The political changes in South Africa have heralded a new era not only in the lives of the indigenous people of the country, but also in the educational system. African languages have been upgraded to the status of official languages. They are protected by the constitution and every person has the right to be heard in his or her own language. The new government has been making promises to better the lives of millions by delivering services in their own languages and thus proving that they do recognise these languages. What liberating news. We have seen the employment of the services of translators, interpreters, speech writers, etc. For the first time speakers of the languages are being consulted on issues involving their languages and are contributing towards their development. Provincial language boards are in the process of being established in all the provinces and under them are specific language committees that focus on individual languages so as to involve people at grassroots level. This is a clear indication that a proper exchange of expertise can now take place between the language developer and its user.

Universities have now seen the need to revamp and in some cases completely overhaul the curriculum of African languages. Courses are being designed to be career-oriented leading students not only into teaching but also into other related fields.

It is now clear that the focus has to be interdisciplinary and the target market is among others, researchers, writers, journalists, policy-makers, language advisors, consultants, translators, interpreters, mediators, managers, facilitators etc.

The picture looks good and promising. It opens up new but unknown avenues with streams of specializations for students. There is also a dire need for African language practitioners to acquire expertise in the field. In this way they can be aware not only of the linguistic issues concerning the languages but they also should be able to collect data, organise and analyse information in order to translate linguistics as a science for consumers so as to solve the social, political, educational, medical, legal, economic, cultural problems etc. and contribute towards the development of their communities.

Much of what is being done is home-grown and is promising, however, there is a need to import some of the ideas in order to build a strong foundation. South Africa is gaining a lot from exchange programmes that have been initiated with many foreign countries in business and cultural relations. It is now time to introduce another dimension, that of forging bilateral relations, i.e. introducing exchange programmes between universities. I take the cue from Wolff (1991) in a paper entitled, "Prospects and limits of bilateral cooperation among university institutions in Africa and the Federal Republic of Germany". Among others, Wolff mentions staff and student exchange, research training and publication support. From this paper, it is possible that certain countries in Africa are benefiting from the cooperation. We, too, in South Africa would like to join for the same reasons.

3.1   Language development

African languages are characterized by variations in orthographies, spelling systems, vocabularies etc. that need attention because they have not been unified.

The Department of Arts Culture, Science and Technology is in the process of establishing National Language Units to be based at some universities and these units will concentrate on lexicographical and terminological work. There is thus a need for skilled manpower in both areas and it is in such areas that we need experts to train staff, i.e. lexicography and terminography, either at home universities or abroad .

3.2   Language for specific use

There is also a big gap between the language of the professionals and that of the ordinary person. Professionals have been blamed for keeping the language of their professions to themselves and inaccessible to the ordinary person thus making things difficult. Many believe that the worlds of medicine, law, business etc, are far removed from the public they are supposed to serve. There is thus a strong feeling that professionals have a responsibility to make their knowledge and language accessible to the people around them.

There is a great need to train people in translation and interpretation as language consultants, publishers etc. Professionalization should also be directed towards language and education, religion, medicine, law, business, labour, civil service, etc.

3.3 Curriculum development

The development of any subject depends largely on the curriculum on which it is based. The designing of a curriculum in African languages would need to redress the imbalances of the past thus taking into account the culture of the people and the goal it aims to achieve.

Another academic step we need to take is to hold discussions with scholars in disciplines such as economic management, health sciences, law, business etc. because while they focus on other issues, they eventually sell their products in languages and in our case the African languages.

There is thus a real need to link African language curriculum to the professions so as to make them relevant. The curriculum should be directed towards performing a service in the community which uses the languages. This means that the curriculum should be linked with professional services. In order to strengthen the position above, universities need to co-operate at least on staff and student exchange, research training and library support.

4   Conclusion

The adventures of both the missionaries and the non-mother tongue intellectuals in the teaching of African languages were based on the demonstration of power and the subjugation of the people and as such did not achieve their goal. The teaching of African languages was based on a one-way traffic road because the planning and designing of the curriculum, the writing of books and academic debates were solely the luxury of the foreign teacher. African people were in most cases used as guinea pigs except in very few cases as among these foreigners were men of integrity. Neither parties could gain since the teachers lacked proficiency in the languages they were teaching and the students remained unchallenged. What could have been an academic milestone in terms of exchange of expertise in the teaching of African languages failed.

The way forward came out of protest by mother tongue teachers who, despite difficulties such as the lack of published mother tongue literature, decided to embark on the new path of teaching through African languages. This was also made possible because of the emergence of democracy.

At the moment much in terms of planning has been achieved. Exchanges of ideas with fellow language teachers within African language departments across universities is happening, a feat that was unheard of during the apartheid days. The workshops and seminars run by visiting scholars have for the first time placed us on speaking terms with colleagues from especially European languages, a very rare feat indeed. Consequently there is now unparalled enthusiasm to hold talks with colleagues from other disciplines in business, law, science and technology etc. thus placing African languages on a path of success. We would welcome scholars from foreign countries to come and improve on what we have thus far been doing. Organized bilateral co-operation will help with the training of staff and students in many spheres to tackle the challenges in the new millennium. Of course in any exchange of expertise based on understanding and respect both parties stand to gain. Foreign scholars stand to gain in terms of research material, the marketing of their institutions and countries and the creation of job opportunities in both countries.

5   References

ATLATIS, J. E.; TUCKER, G. R.(1979): Language in Public life.Washington. Georgetown University Press.

BURLING, R.(1970): Man's many voices-Language in it's cultural context. New York. Holt, Rinehart and Winston, inc.

CLUVER, A.D. de V. (1979): Die toepaste linguistiek. Inaugral Lecture: University of South Africa.

GRINDSTED A.; WAGNER, J. (eds.) (1992): Communication for Specific Purposes. Fachsprachliche Kommunikation. Tübingen. Gunter Narr Verlag (Kommunikation und Institution 21).

HERBERT, R. K. (1980): Linguistics in human service Education in Hudson, G. (ed): Linguistics and the University Education in the 80's. Michigan: East Lansing.

HUBBARD, E. H. (1995): Development Discourse. Applied Linguistics and Academic Empowerment.

HUDSON, G. (1980): Linguistics and the University Education. Michigan. East Lansing.

KING, R.D. (1980): Linguistics and a University Education in the 80's. In Hudson, G. (ed): Linguistics and the University Education in the 80's. Michigan: East Lansing.

KUMALO, M. B.: First Language Teaching at Tertiary Institutions.What are the objectives. In: SAALT 23.1, 60-71

KUNO, S. (1979): Functional Syntax. In: Moravesik, A.; Wirth, J. H.: Syntax and Semantics, vol. 13. New York: Academic Press.

LO BIANCO, J. (1996): Language as an economic resource. Language planning report, no. 5.1.

MATHIVHA, R. N.1985. The Berlin Missionary Venture in Education at Tshakhuma, Venda. 1872-1954 (Unpublished M.A diss.). Pietersburg, University of the North.

MEY, J. L. (1993): Pragmatics – An introduction. Oxford: Blackwell.

MILUBI, N. A (1998): The Role of language in the New South Africa-A quest for relevance. Inagural lecture: University of the North.

— (1997): Aspects of Venda Poetry. Pretoria: J. L. van Schaik.

MIRJALIISA, C. (1996): Business negotiations.Interdependence between Discourse and the Business Relationship. In: English For Specific Purposes 15.1, 19-36.

Satyo, C. S (1988): The apartheid context of African language studies. Inaugural lecture: University of Cape Town.

STRAUSS, G et al. (1996): The Economics of language-Language planning report, no 5.2.

TOMIC, O. M; SHUY, R. W, (1987): The Relation of Theoretical and Applied Linguistics. New York: Plenum Press.

WOLFF, E. (1991): Prospect and limits of bilateral cooperation among university institutions in Africa and the Federal Republic of Germany. In: Cyffer, N. et al. (eds): Language standardization in Africa = Sprachstandardisienrung in Africa = Standardisation des langues en Afrique. Hamburg. Helmut Buske Verlag.

War After the War – the North and the South in Competition for Linguistic Domination in Vietnam

Jacek Świercz

In 1885, Vietnam finally became a French colony. In practice, since 1945, and officially since the withdrawal of French troops in 1954, the country had been divided into two parts: communist North and capitalist South. The two countries were at war and maintained no contact with each other. And so, for 30 years the Vietnamese language had been developing in two totally different directions.

In the North, standardisation works combined with a large-scale anti-illiteracy campaign had been carried out already since 1945-1954. After 1966, under the banner of "preserving the purity and clarity of the Vietnamese language", the rulers began implementing a very rigorous language policy with clear nationalist elements. This policy, no matter how we perceive it, produced serious effects. Special language commissions were appointed. The authorities ordered "Vietnamisation" of the language and significant reduction of the number of borrowings. A spelling reform was carried out and first Vietnamese language dictionaries were compiled. However, the majority of those works had a distinct political and ideological context and the language was to a great extent dominated by the communist new-speak.

In the South, fewer changes were introduced into Vietnamese. Partially, it was connected with cultivating the beliefs and traditions forgotten or prosecuted in the North. By contrast to the North, less importance was attached to the care over the purity of the language while adopting Chinese vocabulary and borrowing words from French and English took place much more often.

In the Far East, such double-track language development can still be found in Korea (Korean language in North Korea and in South Korea) and in China (for example Mandarin Chinese in the People's Republic of China and in Taiwan).

All of the politically divided countries are characterised as having of what Paul Kratochvil has called "divided languages" (Kratochvil 1973). According to his definition a divided language is "any language spoken by a community a large section of which splits away and becomes physically separated from its matrix."

In the case of Vietnam, I find the terms "South-Vietnamese language" and "North-Vietnamese language" fully justified. In my speech they will relate to the official varieties of Vietnamese language used between 1945-1975 in the Republic of Vietnam (being the official name of the South) and in the Democratic Republic of Vietnam (being the official name of the North), respectively.

As a result of the North's victory in 1975 the country united and, in 1976, the Socialist Republic of Vietnam, with Vietnamese as the official language, was founded.

Although in principle we now consider Vietnamese a unified language (let us describe it – in correspondence to Kratochvil's (1968) Modern Standard Chinese – by the term Modern Standard Vietnamese), in fact we distinguish between three major Vietnamese dialects: the northern one (with the main city of Hanoi), the middle one (Hue), and the southern one (Saigon, in 1975 renamed Ho Chi Minh City). The differences between these dialects relate mainly to phonetics and vocabulary and some of them are significant.

Upon receiving an invitation to participate in the 34th Colloquium of Linguistics, I began thinking about a possible topic of my speech. It was only then that I noticed I had never come across any information concerning the impact of South-Vietnamese language on North-Vietnamese language and on Modern Standard Vietnamese after the country's unification in any of the numerous books and articles published after 1975. Quite intrigued, I decided to carry out an instant "research". After many weeks of searching for materials in Europe and Vietnam it turned out such an issue does not exist in Vietnamese linguistic literature. At this point, I have to stress that a huge number of publications on linguistics appeared in Vietnam in those days, and numerous linguistic books are still published there today.

Therefore the lack of relevant materials seemed strange to me, especially as, in my opinion, the above-mentioned phenomenon deserves attention and possibly description.

Bearing in mind authentic Vietnamese "prosecution" of words of Chinese origin that took place during the period of bad relations between Vietnam and China and knowing who the winner was in 1975, I decided to search further.

I looked through the books on dialects. Relatively few such publications appeared. I must mention here that in Vietnam local country speeches and the languages of numerous national minorities inhabiting the country are also considered dialects and the majority of books are devoted to these very languages-speeches. As far as the differences between the dialects of the North and the South are concerned, Vietnamese grammar books are limited to the detailed description of phonetic differences and a trite mention about lexical ones. As a rule, the differences are illustrated by two or three typical examples, such as hoa/N – bong/S (a flower) or qua/N – trai/S (a fruit), and that's it. In time, the chapters devoted to borrowings become more and more extensive (with lots of information on words taken from Chinese, French, English, Russian, etc.) but there is nothing about the borrowings from South Vietnamese.

At the same time, when I was looking through the materials, I came across a very intriguing text by the leading linguist from the North, Nguyen Kim Than, written in 1966, that is to say, many years before the country united.

This is what he wrote:

> "The basic dialect must be that of the region which is the most developed culturally and which often is also the most developed politically and economically, also the region which has played the greatest part in the historical development of the nation – also the dialect enjoying the most prestige among the people and representing the direction in which the national language is moving". (Nguyen Kim Than 1966:14)

For an expert in Vietnamese language, such words wrote by a North-Vietnamese linguist leave no doubt as to which "dialect" was to be binding after the country's unification. It was, of course, the northern dialect of Hanoi, which had been not only the cradle of Vietnamese civilisation but also a communist capital.

Looking through other Nguyen Kim Than's works I found that in 1975 he said the aim of the new state's language policy will be to make Vietnamese the „weapon of the revolution after it was liberated by that revolution". (Nguyen Kim Than 1975:14)

Who will be fighting against whom was officially formulated in the article „The Unity of the Vietnamese language" published in April 1976:

"The development of literary Vietnamese through several centuries has proved that it is based on the language spoken in the very cradle of the nation and representative of the language of cultural Thang Long. We can clearly see this through the poems by Nguyen Trai, Doan Thi Diem and down to Nguyen Du, and from our first works of prose down to the most famous prose texts in Vietnamese literature within the past few decades. We can also see this particularly significant phenomenon whereby the "quoc ngu" script which had been first used in Saigon, actually did not become widely used among the nation until the Dong Kinh Nghia Thuc school in Hanoi disseminated it as the new system of writing. Newspapers and novels, also born in Saigon, did not become firmly rooted in the cultural and intellectual life of the nation and did not positively influence the national language until those products got published in Hanoi, that is to say, in the unified literary language of the entire country." (Nguyen Kim Than 1976:10-12)

That's the end. It was exactly at this point that the issue of South-Vietnamese language officially came to its end, at least in Vietnamese linguists' works.

I managed to get the one and only book published in 1200 copies in October 1993 by Ho Chi Minh City Publishing House (that is not in Hanoi, which is an important fact). The title of the book written by Phung Nghi was "One hundred years of Vietnamese language development" (Phung Nghi 1993). I was fascinated by the very first sentence in the preface from the publishing house: "Still not everything was unified and standardised in the Vietnamese language". (Phung Nghi 1993:7) So, after nearly twenty years, still something wasn't all right!

Unfortunately, I found no more reasons to be happy with these materials. It was the first book that contained some important information about the differences between the dialects of the North and the South. It contained an invaluable table showing the effects of different ways of neologisms creation in the North and in the South (Phung Nghi 1993:23):

a) from 1945 to 1975 (as much as four examples!),
b) from 1975 until today (17 examples).

However, while presenting Vietnamese language development, the author described the period 1975 - 1993 in the following way (Phung Nghi 1993:22):

1) Several new words appeared: cassette, fax, video, karaoke, SIDA, compact disc;
2) After the unification, the South "acquainted oneself" with many new words that had been used in the North for a long time (a long list of the communist newspeak words follows).

And what about the North which also "acquainted oneself" with many new words which had been used in the South for a long time? Not even a word.

This is where my scientific research ended. All that was left for me to do was to look through dictionaries and to talk with people.

Looking through the dictionaries produced hardly any effects. It was enough for me to take a book or a dictionary published in Saigon before 1975 to realise how enormous the differences between South-Vietnamese and North-Vietnamese languages were: many words were just incomprehensible to me (I speak the Northern dialect of

Modern Standard Vietnamese). Still, all Vietnamese dictionaries published after 1975 were written in North-Vietnamese (even if they were published in Saigon). Even if I came across a dialect word in a dictionary, it was not described as dialectal – it just appeared as some further item in an entry. In the latest Vietnamese-English dictionary compiled by Bui Phung, all the words mentioned by Phung Nghi were accompanied by an abbreviation meaning "dated" (Bui Phung 1995).

Of course, it was the discussions with people that I most benefited from. Unfortunately, the material gathered this way is not scientific and reliable enough to allow me to give you any figures or percentage data at this time. However, there is just one thing that should be said here: the older generation in the South still speaks South-Vietnamese while the younger one speaks it less and less. The mass media and teachers use Modern Standard Vietnamese in its North-Vietnamese form. Just after the country's unification the authorities did their best to make it impossible for the former teachers from South Vietnam to get the job. Many of them emigrated or escaped from the country.

However, reading a best seller illegally translated in Saigon or taking a look on the packaging of the goods manufactured in the South by private companies is enough to find many words which do not officially exist or are described in the dictionaries as dated.

After 1986, Vietnam, just as communist China, began to introduce market economy (while the political system remained unchanged). In the new economic environment, it was the open and enterprising South that became the driving force of Vietnamese economy. The vast majority of foreign investments are focused there. This is also the place where all the novelties, including the linguistic ones, begin their Vietnamese life. By contrast to the North, which plunged into stagnation, and by contrast to – which I regret to say – provincial Hanoi, the South is flourishing and Saigon is slowly regaining its name of the "Pearl of Indochina". For the young generation of Vietnamese Saigon is a synonym of dynamism, modernity, luxury and a better tomorrow and therefore a wide acceptance accompanies the penetration of the Southern dialect to the rest of the country – especially among teenagers.

Vietnam is on the threshold of great changes and the centre of cultural and economic life is slowly but steadily moving southwards. If we agree with the theory of Nguyen Kim Than (Nguyen Kim Than 1966:14), the country is going to go through great linguistic changes and the odds are that it is the South that will win this battle. Personally, I still carefully examine the process whose existence I told you about today. I hope to present the results of my research in the near future.

Literature

BUI PHUNG (1995): Tu dien Viet-Anh, Hanoi-Ho Chi Minh, NXB The Gioi.
KRATOCHVIL, Paul (1973): The Norm and Divided Chinese. In: Journal of the Chinese Language Teachers Association 8.2, 62-69.
— (1968): The Chinese Language Today, Features of an Emerging Standard. London.
NGUYEN KIM THAN (1976): Tinh thong nhat cua tieng Viet. In: Van hoa Nghe thuat 56 (April1976), 10-12.

NGUYEN KIM THAN (1975): Thu nhin lai chang duong lich su cua tieng Viet trong 30 nam qua. In: Ngon ngu 25 (September 1975), 1-14.

— (1966): Ren luyen ve ngon ngu, Hanoi, Khoa hoc.

PHUNG NGHI (1993), 100 nam phat trien cua tieng Viet, Ho Chi Minh, NXB TP Ho Chi Minh.

Achieving Meaningful Interaction in Native / Non-Native Service Encounters – The Negotiation of a Base Code

Maria-Carme Torras i Calvo

1   Introduction[*]

Over the last few years, the issue of establishing the *base code* of bilingual conversations has received a lot of attention in the language contact literature. However, establishing the base code of a bilingual conversation is not just the analyst's concern but also the participants' themselves. This paper seeks to contribute to research on the base code by analysing participants' code choice activities in a corpus of service encounters. In my analysis, I adopt the participants' own perspective through the study of *sequentiality* (Auer 1984, 1998) in order to explain their processes of negotiation of meaning. My approach draws upon the conversation-analytic perspective developed by Auer (1984, 1998) and Gafaranga (1998 forthcoming a, forthcoming b) for the study of bilingual interaction.

In talk-in-interaction between speakers who do not share the same degree of competence in the same languages, the base code question arises right at the beginning of the encounter. The goal-oriented nature of service interaction requires participants to engage in conversational work that ensures the understanding necessary for the successful accomplishment of the service. The joint selection of a base code is one of the tasks that crucially contributes to successful communication.

The data on which this study is based consists of a trilingual corpus of 822 service encounters audio-recorded at five settings in the Barcelona area, namely two 'Anglo' pubs, a university Erasmus office, a Chamber of Commerce, and an airline company head office. The data includes both face-to-face and telephone service interactions. As the data was gathered in Barcelona, Catalan and Castilian constitute equally legitimate choices in public interaction by virtue of the official status they share. In addition, the international or foreign nature of the settings chosen implies a third possible code, namely English. Participants thus have a choice in terms of the code in which they can carry out their interaction. On the other hand, the data analysed very often involves first-time encounters between strangers who do not know about each other's *language preference* (Auer 1984, 1998). Service participants come from different speech communities and sociolinguistic backgrounds and, as a result, they are not equally competent in the same languages and do not share linguistic expectancies about their encounter.

This presentation is organised into two parts. First, I will provide a brief characterisation of service encounters as an *activity type* (Levinson 1992). Second, I will discuss how the base code is negotiated by the service participants in the data.

[*] I gratefully acknowledge the support of the Direcció General de Recerca, Autonomous Government of Catalonia, for grant no. 1998BEAI200015.

2   Characterisation of the Service Encounters

Service encounters can be defined as an instance of *activity type* (Levinson 1992:69). They are a culturally recognised activity, partially constituted by talk, which consists of goal-defined bounded events. Levinson divides the structure of an activity into a number of subparts or *episodes*. Drawing upon the work of systemic linguists such as Ventola (1983, 1987) and Halliday and Hasan (1989), the overall episode structure of a generic service encounter can be outlined as follows:

(greeting) >   **request > compliance > sale > purchase**   > (closure) > (goodbye)

The schema above shows that not all the episodes of a service encounter have the same status in the structure. Whereas the request, compliance, sale, and purchase episodes constitute the *nuclear service*, the episodes in brackets may not occur at all.

3   Negotiation of the Base Code

In first-time service encounters, the service seeker and giver cannot rely on previous shared experience in order to decide a code for their interaction. The data reveals that, in the absence of such experience, they engage in implicit and explicit negotiations to settle the code choice issue. The negotiation of a base code is not only affected by considerations of the participants' *language preference* but also by the episode structure outlined in the previous section.

3.1   Implicit Base Code Negotiation

In many first-time encounters in the data, service participants are seen to engage in the implicit *language negotiation sequences* described by Auer. As schematised in Figure 1,[1] implicit code negotiation in the data generally spans over three turns.

A - L1, B - **L2**, A - **L2**, B - **L2**, A - **L2** ...

Figure 1: Convergence to a co-participant's code choice.

Participant A converges to Participant B as soon as Participant A has evidence of Participant B's language preference, typically in turn 03. Through their respective turns, service participants display their own language preference and attend to the language preference of their co-participants. An instance of immediate convergence is provided in example 1.

---

[1]   A and B are the participants in a given exchange. L1 and L2 stand for languages or codes.

EXAMPLE 1[2]

This conversation corresponds to the beginning of a service encounter at Pub 2. A Spanish musician (MUS) is talking to a customer (CUS) at the bar while waiting to be served. A British waiter (BA1) approaches them.

01 *MUS:	copa de whisky i: endavant [=! laughs] !
%eng:	a glass of whisky and: let's carry on [=! laughs] !
%add:	CUS
02 *CUS:	[=! laughs].
03 *BA1:	què vols?
%eng:	what would you like?
04 *MUS:	*erm uh one* **chupito** *of Jameson and some water please.*
%eng:	erm uh a shot of Jameson and some water please.
05 *BA1:	*sure thanks.*

It is interesting to note that the waiter (BA1), who opens the encounter in turn 03, orients to the musician's (MUS) language preference right from the start. He relies on contextual information in order to decide on a code to initiate the service. Waiter BA1 is British and only has a basic command of Catalan. However, he overhears the musician and the customer (CUS) talking in this language and this contextual information leads him to formulate the service bid in Catalan. He assumes that Catalan is the musician's preferred language. However, in turn 04, the musician reveals his preference for English and the waiter immediately switches to this language in turn 05. English is then adopted for the rest of the encounter.

In the data under analysis, convergence to the other participant's code choice takes the form of *compliance* (Burt 1990, 1992, 1994). Compliance consists in choosing the code the interlocutor is speaking at a given moment independently of whether this is the interlocutor's native language or not. In the majority of encounters examined, service providers adopt the language in which they are addressed. This is the case in example 1. Exceptions to this pattern are usually related to cases where the service seeker considers the service provider's competence in a given language to be limited or non-existent. Such exceptions will not be dealt with in this paper.

In order to fully understand how implicit code negotiation works in the service data examined, it is necessary to take into account the notion of *episode*. As described in Section 2, service encounters are not monolithic conversational units. Rather, they consist of a flexible conversational structure that is integrated by a number of subparts. More specifically, episode structure allows us to explain why implicit language negotiation sequences can actually occur more than once in the same service encounter. In example 1, participants engage in implicit code negotiation while accomplishing the first episode of the encounter (i.e. the service request) and then stick to

---

[2] The data has been transcribed following the guidelines set out in the *LIDES Coding Manual* (LIPPS Group, forthcoming). Participants' utterances are reproduced on a main tier using standard orthography. Each main tier begins with a turn number, an asterisk, the speaker's codename and a colon. A free English translation of the utterances is provided below the main line on the dependent tier %eng. See Section 6 for a more detailed explanation of the transcription conventions used in this paper.

the code selected, that is English, throughout the encounter. However, service participants can also initiate a new implicit negotiation process at some later episode in the encounter as in example 2. This example shows a service encounter where implicit negotiation sequences occur at two different points in the interaction. In each case, implicit negotiation occurs at the beginning of an episode, namely the sale episode starting in turn 08 and the second service request episode starting in turn 13.

EXAMPLE 2

This encounter occurs at Pub 1. The participants are a British waitress (BA2) and a Spanish customer (CU1).

01 *CU1:	una cervesa rossa petita # una Guinness # petita # feu cafès?
%eng:	one small lager # one Guinness # small # do you serve coffee?
02 *BA2:	0 [=! shakes her head].
03 *CU1:	doncs ja està.
%eng:	that's it then.
%sit:	BA2 serves the drinks while talking to another waiter.
04 *CU1:	**una Carlsberg pequeña?**
%eng:	one small Carsberg?
%sit:	BA2 comes back with the two beers.
05 *BA2:	**MMM MMM.**
06 *CU1:	**que no [/] no es negra no?**
%eng:	it isn't [/] it isn't stout is it?
07 *BA2:	**no # es este.**
%eng:	no # it's this one.
%sit:	pointing at the half-pint on the bar
08 *CU1:	VALE XXX # quant és?
%eng:	OK xxx # how much is it?
10 *BA2:	**tres treinta y cinco.**
%eng:	three thirty-five.
11 *CU1:	**y estas?**
%eng:	and these?
12 *BA2:	**tres treinta y cinco.**
%eng:	three thirty-five.
%sit:	CU1 gives BA2 the money and leaves.
13 *CU1:	posa'm una aigua d'aquestes.
%eng:	can I have one of those waters?
%sit:	BA2 comes back to CU1.
14 *BA2:	**una # qué sabor quieres?**
%eng:	one # which flavour would you like?
15 *CU1:	XXX.
16 *BA2:	UNA?
%eng:	one?
17 *CU1:	SI.
%eng:	yes.
%sit:	BA2 gives CU1 the drink.

No obvious negotiation goes on in the first service request (turns 01 through 03). The customer (CUS) uses Catalan but the waitress (BA2) responds non-verbally to her request in turn 01 by shaking her head. Once the request has been formulated, the waitress leaves and comes back after a while with the drinks. In turn 04, the customer opens the compliance episode in Castilian. She asks the waitress about one of the beers she has just left on the bar for her. The compliance episode (turns 04 through 07) is carried out entirely in Castilian. No period of divergent talk occurs.

The first language negotiation sequence involving divergent talk turns occurs in the sale episode (turns 08-12). The customer initiates this episode in Catalan (turn 08). In turn 09, the waitress tells her the amount due in Castilian and the customer converges to this language in the subsequent turn. The sale episode is completed in Castilian. After the sale episode, the waitress leaves for a while.

A new implicit negotiation sequence starts in turn 13, which coincides with a second service request by the same customer. The customer places her order in Catalan and, in the following turn, the waitress uses Castilian. Although the subsequent turns contain unintelligible material and lexical items which can equally belong to both Catalan and Castilian, the fact that speech proceeds smoothly with no orientation to code problems indicates that Castilian has been taken up by the participants. In fact, the sale and purchase sequences that occur after turn 17 are in Castilian. Selection of Castilian in this encounter seems to be based on considerations of language competence. The customer seems to prefer Catalan since she initiates most of the episodes in this language. However, since the waitress is a foreigner, she is probably not expected to know Catalan and thus the customer converges to the language chosen by the waitress, namely Castilian.

As illustrated by example 2, the corpus shows that new implicit negotiations at the beginning of a new episode do not tend to result in the adoption of a new code when this new episode is nuclear to the service (see Section 2). This pattern indicates that code selection between unacquainted service participants is influenced by immediate experience acquired in earlier stages of the service, just as code selection between acquainted parties is influenced by experience gained in previous encounters. Renegotiatons are typically triggered by interruptions of the service (e.g. a telephone call) and serve the purpose of updating the code. Summing up, participants show preference for accomplishing the nuclear episodes in the same code. By contrast, adoption of a new code occurs when the renegotiation takes place at the beginning of optional or peripheral episodes such as small talk episodes and goodbyes.

3.2 Explicit Base Code Negotiation

In the data, explicit negotiation sequences make up an independent episode of the type described by Codó (1998). Codó identifies this sequence as the *language negotiation episode*. The episode begins with a request in which one party, usually the information seeker, asks about the other party's language preference. In the data, the language negotiation episode occurs in the initial stages of the encounter as in example 3. The service provider (SEC) suspends the service compliance in turn 03 to initiate a language negotiation episode.

EXAMPLE 3

This conversation takes place at the Erasmus office between a Spanish secretary (SEC) and a British Erasmus student (STU). The student has handed in her registration form to SEC, who is examining it.

01 *SEC:	**hola** # *it's all right* **no** # MMM # *I need the [/] the signature of your coordinator.*
%eng:	hello # it's all right isn't it # mmm # I need the [/] the signature of your coordinator.
02 *STU:	**ah: bien # sí.**
%eng:	uh: OK # yeah.
03 *SEC:	MMM # *here* # *important* # *the [/] once you [/] you have your [/] your signature mmm* # *your* /0.3# **te puedo hablar en español no** /0.25# **o prefieres en inglés**?
%eng:	mmm # here # important # the [/] once you [/] you have your [/] your signature mmm # your /0.3# I can talk to you in Spanish can't I /0.25# or do you prefer English?
04 *STU:	ah # **inglés** [=! laughs].
%eng:	uh # English [=! laughs].
05 *SEC:	**inglés** # *once you have your signature you only have to give me the piece mmm* # *it doesn't have [/] it's not necessary to wait.*
%eng:	English
06 *STU:	ah.
07 *SEC:	*or if I'm not here you have to give me by the [/] the door [/] under the door [/] you pass it by the door [/] under the door* # *mmm*?
08 *STU:	*so do I need the erm [/] the English*?

SEC initiates the service with a greeting in Castilian and then, within the same turn, shifts to English. In turn 02, the student (STU) uses Castilian. This language is not adopted initially by SEC in turn 03. However, halfway in the turn, SEC interrupts himself and after a pause, he switches to Castilian to ask whether he can speak to STU in this language. This request initiates a language negotiation episode. Through his self-interruption, the pause and the actual request, SEC reveals that he is aware of STU's choice of Castilian in turn 02. In other words, the use of Castilian in turn 02 leads SEC to hesitate his previous use of English and thus decides to reassess the situation with STU. Through his request in turn 03, SEC tries to determine whether the old relevance, that is English, still holds. He explicitly puts forth both Castilian and English as possible choices, which can be seen as a neutrality strategy that allows the service provider to proceed with the interaction without imposing any code on the service seeker.

STU's reply in turn 04 and SEC's acknowledgement in turn 05 show that the language negotiation episode is entirely accomplished in Castilian, even though the code that is negotiated explicitly turns out to be English. This pattern points to the independent status of the language negotiation episode as an optional subtask in service encounters between bi/multilingual strangers. In turn 05, SEC switches to English after acknowledgement of the new code, that is to say, after completing the language negotiation episode. Subsequently, he reformulates the utterance he left unfinished in turn 03. The interaction proceeds in English.

An obvious question that the occurrence of explicit and implicit processes rises is why participants go all this length to negotiate a code for their interaction. Under Gafaranga's (1998, forthcoming a) approach, these negotiation processes demonstrate that the need for *order* is the speakers' own concern.

From an ethnomethodological perspective, the concept of *order* in social action is inseparable from that of *social norm* (Garfinkel 1967; Heritage 1988). Working as landmarks with respect to which social action is made intelligible, social norms account for the orderliness and thus the possibility of social life. Social norms are shared background expectancies that inform members' activities. If they have not been established by members through previous experience, they must be established on the spot, as in the case of the first time encounters under analysis. Bilingual participants take the trouble to negotiate a code for their conversation so as to realise order in their talk. They need a *social norm* with respect to which they can make sense of what is going on in their interaction. Once the code of interaction has been selected, it works as a *scheme of interpretation* (Garfinkel 1967:120) in relation to which whatever is done is interpreted.

Gafaranga argues that schemes of interpretation can be phrased in terms of the concept of *preference*. For example, on the level of topic organisation, talk follows an organisational principle one may refer to as preference for same topic talk. On the level of speech acts, preference for agreement and preference for acceptance after an invitation have been widely documented by conversation analysts. Likewise, on the level of code choice, there is a *preference for talk in the same code*.

4 Conclusion

The study of native/non-native service interaction shows that the negotiation of a base code is one of the key pieces of conversational work that must be accomplished to ensure mutual understanding. Negotiation processes provide participants with a scheme of interpretation with respect to which their interaction can be interpreted. In first-time encounters, the base code is negotiated through implicit or explicit sequences, whereby the service parties attend to each other's language preference.

A fundamental feature of code selection in the service encounters analysed is that negotiation processes, both implicit and explicit, are closely related to the notion of *episode*. As regards implicit negotiation, two different patterns may obtain. Participants can negotiate a code in the initial episode of the service and adopt it for the rest of their encounter. Alternatively, they can renegotiate the code at different points in the course of their interaction. These points correspond structurally to the initiation of a new episode. Renegotiation usually leads to a new code when the new episode is non-nuclear. On the other hand, explicit negotiation is dealt with in an episode specifically devoted to this job, namely the *language negotiation episode* identified by Codó (1998). The language negotiation episode can be regarded as an optional episode within the generic structure of bi/multilingual service encounters. Its independent status is demonstrated by the fact that a different code can be selected to carry out this episode. In short, code negotiation is part and parcel of bilingual service encounters, to the extent that it can become a service episode in its own right. Code choice is therefore a significant aspect of the organisation of talk as argued in Gafaranga (1998).

To finish, it must be noted that the fact that bilingual participants show preference for talk in the same code does not mean that a particular base code will always be adhered to. Social norms are not rules which must be followed but schemes of interpretation. Thus a norm can apply or be deviated from, but deviance will still be identified and interpreted in terms of that relevant norm. It is precisely because of the assumption that talk is normatively conducted in the same code that one can speak of code alternation as a meaningful conversation activity. Further research should investigate the conversational role that code alternation, that is deviation from the base code into another code, plays in native-nonnative service interaction.

5   References

AUER, Peter (ed.) (1998): Code-Switching in Conversation. London: Routledge.
— (1984): Bilingual Conversation. Amsterdam: Benjamins.
BURT, Susan Meredith (1994): Code Choice in Intercultural Conversation: Speech Accommodation Theory and Pragmatics. In: Pragmatics 4, 535-559.
— (1992): Codeswitching, Convergence and Compliance: The Development of Micro-Community Speech Norms. In: Journal of Multilingual and Multicultural Development 13, 169-185.
— (1990): External and Internal Conflict: Conversational Code-Switching and the Theory of Politeness. In: Sociolinguistics 19, 21-35.
CODÓ, Eva. (1998): Analysis of Language Choice in Intercultural Service Encounters (Unpublished M.A. Thesis. Departament de Filologia Anglesa i de Germanística. Universitat Autònoma de Barcelona).
GAFARANGA, Joseph (forthcoming a): Language Choice as a Significant Aspect of Talk Organisation: The Orderliness of Language Alternation (to appear in: Text).
— (forthcoming b): Medium Repair vs. Other-Language Repair: Telling the Medium of a Bilingual Conversation (to appear in: International Journal of Bilingualism).
— (1998): Elements of Order in Bilingual Talk: Kinyarwanda-French Language Alternation (Unpublished PhD dissertation. Department of Linguistics and Modern English Language. University of Lancaster).
HALLIDAY, Michael; HASAN, Ruqaiya (1989): Language, Context, and Text: Aspects of Language in a Social-Semiotic Perspective. Oxford: Oxford University Press.
LEVINSON, Stephen (1992): Activity Types and Language. In: Drew, P.; Heritage, J. (eds.): Talk at Work. Interaction in Institutional Settings, Cambridge: Cambridge University Press, 66-100.
LIPPS Group (forthcoming): LIDES Coding Manual: A Document for Preparing and Analysing Language Interaction Data (to appear in: International Journal of Bilingualism).
TORRAS, Maria-Carme (1999): Selection of Medium in Conversation: A Study of Trilingual Service Encounters (Unpublished MA thesis. Departament de Filologia Anglesa i de Germanística. Universitat Autònoma de Barcelona. Universitat Autònoma de Barcelona).

6   Transcription Conventions

Catalan	Plain type stands for stretches of talk in Catalan.
Castilian	Boldface stands for stretches of talk in Castilian.
English	Italic type stands for stretches of talk in English.

UPPER CASE	Use of upper case corresponds to stretches of talk that cannot be clearly identified as Castilian, Catalan or English.
%add:	This dependent tier specifies the addressee.
%sit	This dependent tier specifies contextual information relevant to the interpretation of a given utterance.
:	Lengthened syllable
#	Pause
\figure#	Length of pause in seconds (e.g. \0.5#)
xxx	Unintelligible material (e.g. because of background noise)
0	Action not accompanied by speech
[/]	Retracing
[=! text]	Paralinguistic material (e.g. laughing)

Doing Gender in Political Discourse: A Case Study of the 1997 City and County Magistrate Elections in Taiwan

Jennifer M. Wei

1 Introduction

This paper argues that simplistic gender expectations and gender roles can do harm to women in politics, and cites examples from negative campaign ads to make the case in point. During the 1997 election, there were five female candidates, out of a total of eighty, and this six-percent of female candidacy constituted the highest number in Taiwan history. Three out of five female candidates were elected as county magistrates, all of them had long histories serving at important government posts, developing grass roots connections, and participating as political activists. Despite their socio-political track record, the election rhetoric directed on these female candidates still centered on traditional female qualities of caring and congeniality as well as being seen as a moral paragon. But such qualities also tended to make a candidate seem to be incompetent, unfit, or uncompromising in a political arena where patriarchal values rule. Moreover, in what was to a large extent a negative campaign, stereotypical female qualities such as female sexuality and domesticity were highlighted to attack female candidates. In short, simplistic gender distinction and gender roles were important disadvantages for female candidates when seeking political office. Knowing when to play which role and the possible constraints and limitations that came with switching roles, was very important for female candidates.

Data for analyses were collected from newspapers, the Internet, and propaganda disseminated by candidates during the election period, roughly from September 1997 till December 1997. This paper tries to answer how unequal gender relations are enacted and maintained in political discourse and how the available models for gender studies in sociolinguistics contribute to such relations. The paper is outlined as

1) issues concerning women running for public office;
2) dominant models in sociolinguistics studies;
3) analyses of examples;
4) conclusions.

2 Running as a woman

Witt et al. (1994) has identified a number of differences in female candidates that pose specific campaign problems for women. These range from women's marital status – either the presence or the absence of a husband – to children, credentials, and the ability to put across campaign messages (ibid.:9f). Each of these may evoke an image of female superiority in domesticity and moral conscience when it comes to serving the country; yet at the same time such virtues may doom them to condescension when it comes to leading the country. For example, motherhood may be revered within the family, but it is not considered a credential for holding political office. Moreover, if a candidate is married, her husband and the rest of the family members have to show that they have visible means of support so that she is seen to be sacrificing her primary obligations for political ambitions. And an unmarried woman, who is seen as an even more serious problem in Chinese society (a point that we will take up later), is advised to find a male escort for campaign events, perhaps a brother, uncle, or a grown son, in order to avoid any sexual innuendo or hint of impropriety.

The reason why merely running for office would cause such extra concerns, if not troubles might be that women are still the minority in politics, and since politics is still very much dominated by men, how a candidate is judged, seen, and evaluated is based on patriarchal norms. Women who try to run for public office are actually blurring the lines between the private domain or the domestic domain, in which women have been socialized to belong, and the public domain or the politics domain in which men have been socialized to belong. Being a female political candidate certainly requires crossing the boundary between the private domain and the public domain. Despite her individual drive and political aspirations, a female political candidate, at least in Taiwan is still seen, judged, and evaluated as woman first, political candidate second. In fact, stereotypes, such as female sexuality and conventional gender roles are so powerful and entrenched in the culture that they almost work against those who try to make a difference.

Another complication for female political candidates is therefore that the expectations for women who are political candidates are, in most situations, contradictory. Stivers (1993) argues that the images of expertise, leadership, and virtue that are vital for administrative power contain gender dilemmas. Qualities such as bravery, independence, tough-mindedness, and vision are not what is expected of a woman, namely, softness, dependence, submissiveness, and subordination. The supposedly masculine features of leadership not only perpetuate gender stereotypes but also bestow political and economic privileges on men.

In addition to an imbalance in power relation between men and women, contradictory expectations, female candidates also experience the problem that their political credentials and aspirations are as well as easily dismissed by certain extremely negative sexual terms and cultural symbols. In a video entitled *Running mate: gender and politics in the editorial cartoons,* Miller (1993), the director examines the gender stereotypes which hounded Geraldine Ferraro on the Mondale/Ferraro ticket from the moment she was chosen as Mondale's running partner in the 1988 election. Ferraro's nomination was compared to the selection of winners in the Miss America pageant. Moreover, she was depicted in domestic, romantic, or explicitly sexual contexts, and as the campaign progressed, Mondale and Ferraro became a "couple" in the traditional sense of husband and wife.

In short, those portrayals confirmed the conventional expectations that women are passive, weak, and domestic and that a female candidate's strengths are dismissed in domestic and sexual terms. What Ferraro faced was not an isolated case, for similar charges were made against female candidates in the 1997 Taiwan election. For example, female candidates were criticized for their marital status, for their families' alleged misconduct, and for sacrificing their family for political advancement. In any case, Miller's findings will help put our later analysis in perspective and further a cross-cultural comparison of systematic obstacles that female candidates will have to face during elections.

3 Dominant models on gender in sociolinguistics

In the section, we will examine the assumptions of the dominant models in sociolinguistics and argue that our conventional ways of talking about gender, that is, seeing the difference between men and women as complementary, and talking about them in socio-cultural terms that are stereotypical have consequences for women who seek public office. In sociolinguistics, gender study has received a lot of scholarly attention and has helped readers understand the relationship between gender and language to a certain extent. However, as we will see from the following analyses, most of the dominant models, namely, the difference/deficiency model (Lakoff 1975, 1979; Jesperson 1922), the dominant/power model (Fishman 1980) and the cultural difference model (Gumperz 1982; Tannen 1990) take gender as a starting point, predetermined by either anatomy, or social roles prescribed by society. Thus, individuals who participate in daily discourse have little control of what is prescribed and expected of them, and the social contexts which are crucial to how and when differences between men and women arise are to a large extent unexamined.

The difference/deficiency model assumes that men and women speak differently and that such difference is the results of early socialization and the different expectations that society has for each gender (Lakoff 1975, 1979).

Another influential model that explains why men and women speak differently is the dominant/power model. It points out that the reason women speak differently from men is because of their inferior social status and lack of social resources. Thus, women feel they need to use standard language to lend authority to their speech, emphasize correct grammar to add to their confidence, and favor more polite language for fear of offending those who have power over them (Fishman 1990, West & Zimmerman 1983).

Criticisms for these two models are that the difference/deficiency model is taking gender as a preconceived social category, that is, static, invariable, and diametric, whereas the dominant/power model is criticized for taking power as an all pervasive category, and is too simple to explain the dynamism of real social interaction between men and women (Uchida 1992).

The last model under review is the cultural difference approach, based on Gumperz (1982) for studying problems in interethnic communication. Members from different speech communities bring their own roles, assumptions, and expectations of communication to their conversations with others. And miscommunications and misinterpretations are likely to arise since speakers rely on their own intentions, assumptions, and expectations to interpret and understand what is going on. Likewise, men and women carry their respective rules, norms and expectations into conversations, and so miscommunication results (Tannen 1986, 1990). Criticisms for this model are mainly that it is not quite applicable to forms of miscommunication between men and women, since members of language and culture groups obviously have access to, information about, and contacts with each other, which contribute greatly to understanding. Men and women, however, are not segregated at school, at work, and in most places and social gatherings, and there is a lot of socio-cultural overlap between men and women. In short, we need a more dynamic model to help us examine the social contexts in which so-called differences between men and women are constructed and enacted for personal and political gains, and to make us critically reconsider the consequences of such simplistic thinking.

Connell (1995) proposes a "social construction" perspective of gender, which suggests that the social contexts in which individuals participate help redefine the meaning of gender, and that individuals make use of linguistic resources to "act out" gender or gender roles for personal or political gains. That is, the new research explores the remaking of conventions in social practice itself, rather than treating the public conventions about masculinity as preexisting norms that are passively internalized and enacted (Connell 1995:35). Crawford (1995) further argues that such a model maintains that speakers make use of whatever linguistic resources are available to them and are constantly "acting out" gender in a contested political discourse. In brief, the socio-cultural construction view sees gender as an ongoing social process that is dependent upon systematic restatement, a process that is variously referred to as "performing gender," or "doing identity work." The three female politicians in the 1997 Taiwan election, for example, in acting out the expected familial roles, such as cooking, caring for children and the weak affirmed the socially constructed images of what women should be.

If doing gender is an on-going process, and both men and women have a stake in this dialectic relationship, then this process has important implications for the way in which we theorize the question of difference. What cannot be overlooked is that gender "performances" will certainly involve men and women in drawing upon socio-cultural resources, such as popular cultural terms, which they perceive to be appropriate. The task is not without complications. On the one hand, as we have seen from previous examples, female politicians play the expected female roles and embody the so-called feminine qualities in order to set foot in politics. On the other hand, as we will see from examples of the negative campaign rhetoric, such "feminine" qualities and gender roles are the means by which a female candidate is attacked. What needs to be remembered is the underlying patriarchal norms used to evaluate politicians' performance. The right questions should be: How are gender relations enacted and maintained in political discourse? And what are the contributing factors to the pervasiveness of metaphors or images used to describe a female political candidate?

The above findings and questions are especially important since we will encounter how, in negative advertisements, a female candidate's strength and potential are dismissed in domestic or negative sexual terms, and how domestic responsibilities, and marital status of a woman become the target of criticism for female politicians in Taiwan.

4   The three elected female magistrates

In this section, we will look into the terms used against the female candidates in negative advertising during the 1997 Taiwan County and Magistrate Election. The question is how are they attacked? Attacks against Lu were provoked by the quick change she made in the cabinet during her tenure, her goal to model Taoyuan after Western cities, her single marital status, lack of competence, and the amount of money she spent on remodeling her office. *Bianlian*, or "sudden change of face," *hennuren*, or "vicious woman," and *yangbaozi*,[1] or "foreign bun" were among the terms used. *Bianlian*, or "sudden change of face," not only shows a swift change of expression or intention but also indicates a change of heart. This term thus refers to Annette Lu's emotional and psychological state, and suggests that she was neither trustworthy nor stable.

Attacks as such were directed at Lu as a person, which had little to do with what her camp proposed. However, the effects of these terms were not diminished by their triviality, since they tap into the subjects such as marital status, and female psychology, two juicy topics that draw the public's attentions easily.

As we have pointed out at the beginning of the paper, an unmarried female candidate, who is seen as a serious problem in Chinese society, is advised to find a male escort for campaign events, in order to avoid any sexual innuendo or hint of impropriety. Annette Lu has never been married, and has been a strong advocate for feminine liberation in Taiwan. She chose not to marry in order to devote more time and energy to her rising political career, and she didn't follow the advice suggested in the first section. Her decisions, sound and strong as they were, didn't spare her from strong attacks.

In Chinese society, women have long taken the subordinate, submissive, and supportive roles, and their virtues exist only after they have become mothers. Single women are seen as commodity to their fathers when they are young, dangerous to men when they have reached puberty, and a disgrace to their family if they remain unmarried. As a matter of fact, unmarried women are such a disgrace to their family that after they die their name will not be recorded in the family genealogy.[2] Thus, attacks on Lu's single status and independence are rooted in conventional expectations of women. Problems arise when individuals break away from the conventional gender expectations. In short, the deeply entrenched notions of women as being dependent

---

[1]   *Baozi*, or "bun" is one of the most popular foods in Taiwan. People eat it on all kinds of occasions and at various times in the day. It is usually stuffed with vegetables, meat, or bean paste to add to the taste. By adding a prefix, *yang*, or "foreign" to *baozi*, this phrase becomes an oxymoron, which connotes exclusion and dismissal. The label *yangbaozi*, or "foreign bun" thus ostracized Lu. The use of popular food to refer to candidates is one of the common linguistic strategies used in elections. In the 1998 Taipei mayoral election, Ma Ying-jeou was referred to as pizza while Chen Shui-bian as *baozi* (*United Daily*, July 20th, 1998, section 4).

[2]   The spirits of unmarried women are considered *lah-sap* or *bo-chheng-khi*, or "dirty," or "polluted," in traditional Han society, according to the study done by Shih in 1996. That is why their names are not recorded in the family genealogy, nor will they receive proper burial with other family members. Here, treating their spirits as dirty or polluted further proves how a patriarchal society uses folk religion to maintain a dominant male ideology and to rid itself of "inappropriate" elements.

on either men or their families are so strong that any deviation from them excites moral outrage and public scorn.

Parallel examples are found in Taichung City mayor, Chang Wen-ying. Attacks were made against Chang regarding the number of her husband's previous marriages, her family's political connections, and her father-in-law as being an incompetent former Taichung mayor. All of these attacks portrayed Chang as an inauspicious omen to avoid, an instigator to blame, or a victim to pity. In one attack ad, subtitled, *yinanwunu,* or "one man with five women," Chang's husband was ridiculed for his relations with girlfriends and ex-wives. Chang's marriage was interpreted as an inauspicious omen to Taichung because her husband's first girlfriend died in a motorcycle accident, the second one moved out after years of cohabitation, his first and second marriages ended in divorce, and his marriage to Chang resulted in the birth of twin boys after only six months of their marriage. The advertisement ended with a Confucius maxim: *yishizhibuzhi, heyitianxia guojiawei,* which can be translated as "If one is not capable of handling domestic affairs, how can one be able to handle national affairs?" Thus, Chang's competence and potential as the next possible mayor of Taichung was tarnished by her husband's marriage record. As a consequence, Chang had to shoulder the blame and suspicion. Like the attack on Annette Lu in Taoyuan as being vicious and immoral because of her single status, and the one on Ferraro blaming her for her husband's alleged tax fraud, Chang was not only another blame but was also seen as being unfit to govern.

In short, marital status and the alleged misconduct of immediate family members were the focus of the attacks on Annette Lu and Chang Wen-ying. Whether single or married, they were still to blame for not living up to patriarchal cultural expectations. It is true that men are also required to be faithful to their spouses and be responsible for their families, but they are not held to such impossibly high standards as to be criticized for the misconduct of their wives or mothers-in-law, or condemned for not being able to find a suitable mate, thus making it very unlikely that they will be able to enter the political race.

Finally, there was the Chia-yi mayor, Chang Po-ya. As far as the researcher knows, Chang was probably one of the very few lucky female candidates who was spared from being attacked for her status as a woman. She comes from a family which possesses strong ties with the local elite, and she marries into a wealthy family, which have lots of resources and connections in the city. During the campaign, her husband, and mother-in-law were seen to lobby for her, a must that was mentioned in the previous section of how married female candidates should rely on family supports to prove that they not only can manage a family, but have strong backups from family members. It is beyond the current paper to further investigate the roles of political clout and family backups in how a female candidate is attacked. Nevertheless, it will be interesting to probe into issues such as whether strong family political connections, and strong visible backups from family members, especially one's husbands, and in-laws will protect a female candidate from receiving attacks directed on domestic responsibilities and sexual improprieties.

5   Conclusions and suggestions

This paper has attempted to illustrate how simplistic thinking about gender and gender roles takes a toll on the quality of political discourse in Taiwan. Drawing on data from election rhetoric and negative political advertisements, the paper has tried to demonstrate that conventional gender roles and feminine qualities might work for female candidates in differentiating themselves from male candidates, but they also worked against female politicians in a fierce political election. That is, the three elected female city and county magistrates successfully marketed themselves as caring, congenial, and responsible, all supposed feminine qualities that not only helped the weak and the disadvantaged, but also differentiated the candidates from their male counterparts who, in general, were perceived as insensitive, uptight and corrupt.

Nevertheless, female politician's political aspirations and potential are still measured against conventional patriarchal rules. Worse, the expectations for a woman and those for a political leader are conflicting. Female candidates, at least in Taiwan, are still seen as women first, and political candidate last. Thus, female candidates are facing an up-hill battle in getting elected to political office. In addition, our conventional ways of talking about gender and gender roles have consequences on how power relations between men and women are enacted. A more dynamic model, such as the socio-construction model, is needed in order to emphasize the importance of the context, which renews the meaning of gender, and the agency of individual's who actively try to adopt available linguistic and cultural sources at hand to "perform" gender, or gender roles for personal or political gains.

Conflicting expectations of gender appropriateness and managerial effectiveness often leave women in an unbreakable, untenable double bind. Such is the strategy perennially used by those with power against those without (Jamieson 1995), and our findings from the negative advertising against the three elected women in Taiwan prove that the double bind strategy might have a cross-cultural potency. That is, we have seen that in both the Ferraro's case in the States, and in the three elected female candidates in Taiwan, couching a female candidate's performance in domestic terms, and using male standards to judge her as deficient or deviant prove to be an effective strategy to dismiss the aspirations and contributions of a female candidate.

6   References

CONNELL, R.W. (1995): Masculinities. Oxford: Polity Press.
CRAWFORD, Mary (1995): Talking difference: On gender and language. London: Sage Publications.
FISHMAN, Pamela (1990): Conversational insecurity. In: Cameron, Deborah (ed.): The feminist critique of language: A reader. New York: Routledge, 234-241.
GUMPERZ, J. (1982): *Discourse Strategies*. Cambridge: Cambridge University Press.
JAMIESON, Kathleen Hall (1995): Beyond the double bind: Women and leadership. New York: Oxford University Press.
JESPERSEN, Otto (1922): Language: Its nature, development and origin. New York: Henry Holt.
LAKOFF, Robin (1979): Women's language. In: Butturff, D.; Epstein, E. L. (eds.): Women's language and style. Akron, OH: University of Akron Press.
LAKOFF, Robin (1975): Language and woman's place. New York: Harper and Row.

MILLER, Elaine K. (1993): Running mate: Gender and politics in the editorial cartoons. New York: First Run/Icarus Films.

SHIH, Fan-lung. (1996): "The Inappropriate Elements in Belief and Social Construction – a Case Study of the Three Temples in Northern Taiwan," presentation at Women and Religion Seminar, Ethnology Institute at Academic Sinica, Taipei, Taiwan.

STIVERS, Camilla. (1993): Gender images in public administration: Legitimacy and the administrative state. London: Sage Publications.

TANNEN, Deborah (1990): You just don't understand: Women and men in conversation. New York: William Morrow, Ballantine.

— (1986): That's not what I meant: How conversational style makes or breaks your relations with others. New York: William Morrow, Ballantine.

UCHIDA, Aki (1992): When "difference" is "dominance": A critique of the "anti-power-based" cultural approach to sex differences. In: Journal of Language in Society 21, 547-568.

WEST, Candace; FENSTERMAKER, Sarah (1993): Power, Inequality, and the Accomplishment of Gender: An Ethnomethodological view. In: England, Paula (ed.) Theory on Gender/Feminism on Theory. New York: Aldine De Gruyter, 151-74.

WITT, Linda; PAGET, Karen M.; MATTHEWS, Glenna (1994): Running as a Woman: Gender and Power in American Politics. New York: The Free Press.

Language Planning and the Hegemony of the Nation-State: The Case of Singapore

Andrew Wong

0   Introduction

Researchers often cite Singapore as a prime example of how language planning can be used for promoting racial harmony. Since it was discovered in 1819, Singapore has developed into a multiracial society. The various waves of immigrants have contributed to the ethnic diversity of Singapore's population – 77% Chinese, 15% Malay, 6% of Indian origins, and 2% of other ethnic definitions in 1980. However, the major ethnic groups in Singapore did not always co-exist peacefully. Since Independence in 1965, the People's Action Party (PAP), the ruling party in Singapore, has taken an active role in promoting harmony among ethnic groups. With its policy of multiracialism and four official languages (Mandarin Chinese, English, Malay, Tamil), the Singapore Government has transformed the speech and writing behavior of all of its citizens. Riney (1998) points out that in the next few decades, Singapore will become more linguistically homogenous than it has ever been. For the Singapore Government, this linguistic homogeneity, which is regarded as essential to racial harmony, is what it has been aiming to achieve for many years.

Unlike its role in maintaining racial harmony, the role of language planning in legitimizing Chinese dominance in Singapore has received little attention. In recent years, several critics of classical language planning (e.g. Tollefson 1991) have shown that language planning often reproduces sociocultural inequalities. One of the most poignant examples is the use of language planning to oppress minority groups. In Singapore, however, power is not exercised in the form of overt oppression; rather, it is manifested through *hegemony* – that is, "the consensual basis of an existing political system within civil society" (Adamson 1980:171). As Gramsci (1971) points out, only weak states need to rely on the use of force in their domination. Strong states rule almost exclusively through hegemony. To truly understand how hegemony is created, it is essential to explore:

1) how nation-states gain the consent of the general public; and
2) how they strengthen the structural position of the elite.

In the remainder of the paper, I explain how the Chinese-dominated Government in Singapore uses language planning as one of its strategies to affirm its control of the nation-state. By gaining the consent of the Malays and the Indians and strengthening the Chinese community, it succeeds in ruling Singapore through hegemony.

1   Promoting racial harmony: Manufacturing consent

One of the main goals of language planning in Singapore is to promote racial harmony. In view of racial tensions among various ethnic groups, the Singapore Government has been promoting the policy of multiracialism since Independence. The official goal is to create a multiracial and multilingual society. This point has been expounded by key officials in the Government since the 60s. In a speech to Malay Singaporeans, for instance, the current Prime Minister, Goh Chok Tong, states:

"Singapore is a multi-racial, multi-lingual and multi-religious society. It requires a fine balance of interests to keep every community at ease. Every community has an equal place in Singapore. *To give practical meaning to this, we have made English the common working language, so that no community has any unfair advantage.* English must always be the dominant administrative and economic language, to *give all races equal chances in education and jobs.*" Prime Minister Goh Chok Tong, Tabung Amal Aidilfitri '97 Launch (emphasis added)

The main tenet of the principle of multiracialism is that while ethnic communities are encouraged to mingle with each other, they should be allowed to develop their own cultures. Following this principle, the Singapore Government designated English as the language for interethnic communication, while the three "Mother Tongues" – Mandarin Chinese, Malay and Tamil – are used to represent the three major ethnic groups. Officially, all four languages have the same status. Singaporean children are also required to learn at least English and their respective "Mother Tongues" at school.

In addition, recognizing the symbolic value of language, Singapore declared Malay as the national language after Independence. In a sense, this was the result of Singapore's short history as part of the Federation of Malaysia from 1963 to 1965. However, it was also a gesture to acknowledge the significant role that Malay plays in the region. Although Singapore was expelled from Malaysia, the symbolic status of Malay has remained unchanged. The National Anthem of Singapore is sung and military commands are given in Malay. Until 1981, a person applying for citizenship was also required to pass a simple oral Malay language test (Kuo 1984).

Realizing the importance of the policy of multilingualism for gaining the consent from the Malay and the Indian communities, the Singapore Government refused to make Chinese the sole official language, even after its separation from the Federation of Malaysia in the mid 60s. When Singapore declared its independence, Chinese-educated elites asked the Prime Minister to institute Chinese as the official language of Singapore. However, the Government reiterated its policy of multilingualism. The policy of multilingualism is important for maintaining friendly relations with Malaysia and Indonesia, and it is also needed to show that the Singapore Government endorses multiracialism. By promoting the policies of multiracialism and multilingualism, the Singapore Government has succeeded in gaining the consent of the other two ethnic groups.

2 The creation of a unified Chinese identity

"Once upon a time, there was a father with ten sons who never got along with one another. One day when he was on his death bed, he summoned his sons to his side. He told one of his sons to bring him twenty chopsticks. He gave one to each of them and asked them to break it. The individual chopsticks snapped easily. Then he put the remaining ten chopsticks together and told his sons to try breaking them, but none of them managed to. The old man said, "One chopstick breaks easily, but ten of them together are indestructible. If you are united, no one can harm you." (A Traditional Chinese Story)

Nevertheless, underneath the surface of multiculturalism and bilingual education is the contestation among the four official languages. Although Mandarin Chinese, English, Malay and Tamil are supposed to have the same status, this is not true in reality. Judging from the language-related policies of the Singapore Government, it appears that although multiracialism is encouraged, the Government has made a more concerted effort at creating a unified Chinese Identity than at dealing with the language issues of the other two major ethnic groups.

The Chinese in Singapore are often divided into several dialect groups (Cheng 1985). Hokkiens, Teochews, Cantonese, Hakkas, and Hainanese are the five major dialect groups. Dialect differences were also marked by differences in customs and character (Purushotam 1998:43). Before independence, the perpetuation of "dialect" identities caused a great deal of interdialect rivalry in Singapore (Yen 1976; Song 1967: 402). Given the fact that language is often equated with cultural identity in Singapore, it is understandable that the myriad of Chinese dialects spoken in Singapore were usually blamed for the divisiveness of the Chinese community. This point is illustrated by the following excerpt from Senior Minister Lee Kuan Yew's speech (quoted in Newman 1988:443):

"The choice for Singapore is simple – continue with [Chinese] dialects, and we will end up using only [Chinese] dialects and English. We will continue to have a fractured multilingual society."

As a result of the rivalry among various Chinese dialect groups, the Singapore Government chose Mandarin, a relatively neutral dialect, as the "Mother Tongue" of the Chinese community. The promotion of Mandarin has little to do with the search for a *lingua franca* for the Chinese community. Before Independence, many Chinese Singaporeans who claimed to speak a dialect would also be familiar with another Chinese dialect, Bazaar Malay, and sometimes English and/or Mandarin (Platt 1980). With a repertoire like this, it would be unusual to find two Singaporean Chinese not being able to find some common means of communication.

In fact, the promotion of Mandarin has more to do with the need for a unified Chinese Identity. The Chinese-dominated Government realized that to maintain its survival, it would be essential to consolidate the support from the Chinese population in Singapore. The promotion of Mandarin as the designated language for the Chinese community is an essential component of a program that encourages the creation of a unified Chinese Identity in Singapore. Government officials, including the current Prime Minister, Goh Chok Tong, have emphasized the importance of Mandarin on many different occasions. For example:

"For the Chinese community, our aim should be a single people, *speaking the same primary language,* possessing a distinct culture and a shared past, and sharing a common destiny for the future. Such a Chinese community will then be tightly knit ...." (PM Goh Chok Tong 1991 Speak Mandarin Campaign Launch; emphasis added)

In what follows, I discuss two important language-related policies that target the Chinese community in Singapore: the *Speak Mandarin Campaign* and the SAP (Special Assistance Plan) Schools Project. The goals of these two policies are to encourage the learning and the use of Mandarin instead of dialects and to create a unified Chinese Identity in Singapore. In addition, I compare the efforts that the Singapore Government has made to address the language issues pertinent to the Chinese community, on the one hand, and the Malay and Indian communities, on the other.

2.1   Speak Mandarin Campaign

The Speak Mandarin Campaign was an attempt by the Singapore Government to elevate the status of Mandarin in the Chinese community. Although Mandarin was chosen as the official language associated with the Chinese community in Singapore, it is not the native language for the majority of Chinese Singaporeans, nor was it used as a strong *lingua franca* in the Chinese community (Kuo 1984a). The Singapore Government realized that to improve the status of Mandarin, it would be necessary to create a more conducive environment for the use of Mandarin. To encourage the learning and the use of Mandarin instead of dialects in both public and private domains, the Singapore Government launched the first Speak Mandarin Campaign in the late 70s.[1] The message of the Campaign – to replace dialects with Mandarin – was emphasized in various areas: the media, school, and public service.

At the early stage of the Speak Mandarin Campaign, the government had already decided to eradicate the use of dialects in the media. As early as 1978, the Singapore Broadcasting Corporation (SBC), a semi-governmental statutory board, decided to phase out commercials in Chinese dialects. Soon after the launching of the Campaign, it also started dubbing popular Cantonese drama serials from Hong Kong into Mandarin. Although many Chinese Singaporeans expressed their dissatisfaction with the eradication of Chinese dialects in the media, SBC decided to go ahead with the implementation of the policies and to complete the conversion (Kuo 1984a, 1984b).

SBC Television also made important contributions to the learning of Mandarin. A new conversational Mandarin course was launched in late 1979. Dialogue sequences extracted from the course were shown between television programs as "fillers". Furthermore, slides were used between television programs to teach the correct use of Mandarin for standardized food items. The Promote Mandarin song was also sung, with Chinese subtitles, by local singers to bring home the message of the Campaign. School is another arena in which the message of the Speak Mandarin Campaign has been underscored. To encourage the learning and the use of Mandarin, the Singapore Government provides special incentives to schools that teach students English and Chinese at first language level (see Section 2.2). It also suggested various measures to

---

[1]   Since then, the Speak Mandarin Campaign has become an on-going event.

eradicate the use of dialects. One of these measures is the use of the designated romanized phonetic system – *Hanyu Pinyin* (based on Mandarin) – instead of dialect transliterations in English, to spell and document the names of school students. The main reason was that standardizing Chinese names by using *Hanyu Pinyin* would make it impossible to tell which dialect group a pupil belonged to by simply looking at his or her name.

The Speak Mandarin Campaign has also affected the linguistic practices of those in the public service. Since the Speak Mandarin Campaign was launched, any transactions with government departments, if done in Chinese, are required to be conducted in Mandarin. As a result, conversational Mandarin courses were offered to Chinese officers in the public service. Furthermore, the government encouraged the use of *Hanyu Pinyin* names instead of dialect transliterations in English for food items on signboards, new companies, and new street names. All these measures are in line with the Speak Mandarin Campaign, and they have maximized the use of Mandarin in the public arena.

2.2 SAP (Special Assistance Plan) schools project

While for the most part, the Speak Mandarin Campaign focuses on *status planning*, the establishment of SAP (Special Assistance Plan) schools is concerned with *acquisition planning* (Cooper 1989). The SAP project was initiated in 1980. It aimed to convert nine established Chinese secondary schools into bilingual institutions and to bolster the learning of Mandarin.[2] SAP schools serve the main purpose of allowing good students (the top 8% of those passing the Primary School Leaving Examination) to learn both English and Chinese at first language level. These schools are provided with special incentives and financial assistance. In 1989, the Singapore Government also announced the "seed schools" scheme. This scheme would allow ten primary schools to teach Chinese at first language level as well. "Seed schools" would also be given additional financial resources, including good bilingual teachers.

2.3 How about the Indian and the Malay communities?

As mentioned previously, the explicit goal of the two language-related policies discussed previously is to encourage the learning and the use of Mandarin, while the implicit goal is to create a unified Chinese Identity in Singapore. Judging from the 1990 census, the Singapore Government has succeeded its explicit goal. Table 1) shows that the percentage of Singaporeans using Mandarin increased by more than 15%, while the percentage of those using Chinese dialects decreased by at least 22%.

---

[2] It was announced in January 1999 that an additional school (Nan Hua Secondary) will participate in the SAP Project.

Language	1980	1990
Mandarin	10.2%	26.0%
Chinese Dialects	59.5%	36.7%

Table 1: Predominant Household Language 1980, 1990. (Source: Census of Population, 1990).

It is possible that under the influence of the Speak Mandarin Campaign, Chinese Singaporeans might over-report their use of Mandarin as the predominant household language. However, using observations to understand the actual language-choice behaviors of Chinese Singaporeans, Xu et al. (1998) found results similar to those reported in the census. With the implementation of the Speak Mandarin Campaign and other cultural and educational policies, the Government has also succeeded in emphasizing the importance of a cohesive Chinese community. In recent years, the distinction among various Chinese dialect groups has been blurred (Purushotam 1998).

Compared to the Chinese community, the other two ethnic groups (the Malay and the Indian communities) have not received as much attention from the Singapore Government. Table 2) shows that there has been a significant shift from Malay or Tamil (the two "Mother Tongues") to English: in both communities, the percentage of children speaking English increased by at least 5%.

Ethnic Group/Language Spoken to Siblings	1980 (per cent)	1990 (per cent)
Malay Households	100.0	100.0
English	3.1	8.1
Malay	96.3	91.8
Others	0.6	0.1
Indian Households	100.0	100.0
English	32.2	40.3
Tamil	48.9	38.6
Others	10.4	5.6

Table 2: Persons aged five years and over in private households by ethnic group and language spoken to siblings 1980 and 1990. (Source: Lau 1993:8).

Unlike the Chinese community, the Indian and the Malay communities have not received any substantial support from the Government for the maintenance of their respective Mother Tongues. There has been no "Speak Malay Campaign" or "Speak Tamil Campaign". Ironically, although the Singapore Government believes that the use of "Mother Tongue" is essential to the transmission of "core values," it does not make any significant attempt to reverse the shift from Malay or Tamil to English. In fact, in some of the promotional materials for the "Speak Mandarin Campaign," it is claimed that "[t]he Malay and Indian communities have less problems with dialects as they each have their own common language to communicate in" (quoted from the web-site for the "Speak Mandarin Campaign", http://www.gov.sg/pkmandarin/history/history.htm). Especially for the Indian community, the common language has become English instead of Tamil. Interestingly, while the Singapore Government insists on the use of Mandarin within the Chinese community, it does not see any problem with the increasing importance of English for intra-ethnic communication in the Indian community. In terms of the language varieties allowed to be taught at school, the Indian community has also received different treatment from the Government. Students of Chinese origin are required to learn Mandarin Chinese. On the other hand, Indian children are recently allowed to study their own Indian languages (e.g. Hindi, Punjabi, Gujarati, Urdu and Bengali) as their "Mother Tongue" (Purushotam 1998:94; Riney 1998). Why have Indians been treated differently? Does it mean that English is inappropriate for the conveyance of Chinese values, but it is appropriate for the transmission of "core values" of Indian culture?

In addition, with regard to the teaching of "Mother Tongues", the Singapore Government established SAP Schools, so that top students of Chinese origin can learn both English and Chinese at first language level. However, there are no schools similar to the SAP schools where Malay or Indian traditions and culture could be taught (Abdullah and Ayyub 1998). Consequently, unlike their Chinese counterparts, top Malay and Indian students do not have access to SAP schools with better resources.

3   Conclusion

The above analysis shows that there is a contradiction in the language policies of the Singapore Government. To promote racial harmony and social cohesion, certain language policies encourage multilingualism and multiracialism. On the other hand, other policies benefit one ethnic community at the expense of the other two. Through these policies, the Singapore Government is able to create hegemony. The Singapore Government does not oppress minority languages. Rather, it gives lip service to the language needs of minority groups, while at the same time, it strengthens the Chinese community through language and other social policies.

Departing from the traditional focus of language planning research, which stresses the suppression of minority languages, this study shows that the strongest form of language planning is one that empowers the ruling elite through the consent of subordinate groups. If the goal of language planning is to study various sociological factors which influence language change, it is impossible to ignore the question of who formulates and implements language policies. The issue of power can no longer be overlooked in language planning research.

4   References

ABDULLAH, Kamsiah; AYYUB, Bibi Jan (1998): Malay Language Issues and Trends. In: Gopinathan; Pakir; Kam; Saravanan: 179-190.
ADAMSON, Walter (1980): Hegemony and Revolution: A Study of Antonio Gramsci's Political and Cultural Theory. Berkeley and Los Angeles: University of California Press.
AFRENDRAS, Evangelos; KUO, Eddie (eds.) (1980): Language and Society in Singapore. Singapore: Singapore University Press.
CHENG, Lim Keak (1985): Social Change and the Chinese in Singapore: A Socio-economic Geography with Special Reference to Bang Structure. Singapore: Singapore University Press.

COOPER, Robert (1989): Language Planning and Social Change. Cambridge: Cambridge University Press.

FISHMAN, Joshua (1994): Critiques of Language Planning: A Minority Language Perspective. In: Journal of Multilingual and Multicultural Development 15, 91-9.

GOPINATHAN, Saravanan (1998): Language Policy Changes 1979-1997: Politics and Pedagogy. In Gopinathan; Pakir; Kam; Saravanan: 19-44.

GOPINATHAN, Saravanan; PAKIR, Anne; KAM, Ho Wah; SARAVANAN, Vanithamani (eds.) (1998): Language, Society and Education in Singapore. Singapore: Times Academic Press.

GRAMSCI, Antonio (1971): Selections from the Prison Notebooks of Antonio Gramsci. New York: International Publishers.

HARRISON, Godfrey (1980): Mandarin and the Mandarins: Language Policy and the Media in Singapore. In: Journal of Multilingual and Multicultural Development 1/2, 175-180.

KUO, Eddie (1984a): Television and Language Planning in Singapore. In: IJSL 48, 49-64.

— (1984b): Mass Media and Language Planning: Singapore's "Speak Mandarin" Campaign. In: Journal of Communication 34, 24-35.

LAU, Kak En (1993): Singapore Census of Population 1990: Literacy, Languages Spoken and Education. Statistical Release 3. Singapore: Department of Statistics.

LUKE, Allan; MCHOUL, Alec; MEY, Jacob (1990): On the Limits of Language Planning: Class, State and Power. In: Baldauf, R.; Lukes. A. (eds.): Language Planning and Education in Australasia and the South Pacific. Clevedon: Multilingual Matters, 25-44.

NEWMAN, John (1988): Singapore's Speak Mandarin Campaign. In: Journal of Multilingual and Multicultural Development 9.5, 437-449.

PAKIR, Anne (1994): Educational Linguistics: Look to the East. In: Georgetown University Roundtable on Languages and Linguistics, 370-383.

PLATT, John (1980): Multilingualism, Polyglossia and Code Selection in Singapore. In: Afendras; Kuo: 63-83.

PURUSHOTAM, Nirmala (1998): Negotiating Language, Constructing Race: Disciplining Difference in Singapore. Berlin and New York: Mouton de Gruyter.

RINEY, Timothy (1998): Toward More Homogeneous Bilingualism: Shift Phenomena in Singapore. In: Multilingua 17.1, 1-23.

SCOTTON, Carol M. 1993. Elite Closure As a Powerful Language Strategy: The African Case. In: International Journal of the Sociology of Language 103, 149-63.

SONG, Ong Siang (1967): One Hundred Years' History of the Chinese in Singapore. Singapore: University Malaya Press.

TOLLEFSON, James (1991): Planning Language, Planning Inequality. London: Longman.

XU, Daming; CHEW, Cheng Hai; CHEN, Songcen (1998): Language Use and Language Attitudes in the Singapore Chinese Community. In: Gopinathan; Pakir; Kam; Saravanan: 133-154.

YEN, Ching Huang (1976): The Overseas Chinese and the 1911 Revolution with Specific Reference to Singapore and Malaya. Kuala Lumpur: Oxford University Press.

Angewandte Sprachwissenschaft

Bridging the Gap Between Grammar and Usage

Tatyana Chirko, Tatiana Lomova

1   Why a new grammar?

For centuries a grammar book and a dictionary have been a sufficient kit for learners as *recipients* of a foreign language, a satisfactory aid to *reading* and *understanding*. Grammars equipped students with structures, which they learned to recognize in texts depending on dictionaries for the meanings of individual words and on the context for just one meaning out of few.

The advent of the communicative approach to TFL, with its heavy emphasis on productive language skills, changed the situation drastically. Today learners are eventually measured by the ability to *produce* competent language i.e. by their actual output. It has become obvious now that rules of grammar and lexis, if learned separately, do not meet naturally in the head of a person wishing to give meaningful and accurate messages. To learn the skill, students need guidance on how concrete words are arranged in a sentence to express a particular meaning in a particular situation.

In order to meet this need the authors of newly created (or revised) grammars and dictionaries try to bring them closer together: grammars tend to provide lists of words to which the rules apply, while dictionaries offer grammatical comment on their lexical entries.

Another answer to the requirement is a new type of reference tools, called usage books, which are voluminous sets of notes on individual words, arranged alphabetically and involving different aspects of meaning, grammar, collocation and idiom, variety and purpose. This is, undoubtedly, a valuable source of information concerning the individual details of *usage*. However, usage books do not show (and, of course, cannot show) how the separate points fit together. Besides, in order to refer to them learners should be aware of what their problems of usage are. As such learners are few and far between, these books are mainly teachers' resource. But what is more important still is that there remains a considerable gap between the generalities of grammar and the individuality of expression, on which this reference tool, understandably, concentrates.

2   What kind of grammar?

The missing link can be produced by a grammar of word classes or *lexico-grammar*[1], built on the following assumptions:

---

[1] This term has been devised to make it distinct from the word-oriented theories such as Lexical-Functional Grammar or Word Grammar, which are built as systems of rules defining Language Competence and "rather than being aimed at the description of particular languages, concentrate on universal laws and tendencies" (Droste and Joseph 1991:18)

a) the meaning of the word includes the relations it forms with other words; so the choice of one word in a structure entails the choice of another;
b) the meaning of the word should be compatible with the role it is to play in the semantic structure of a sentence built on a certain syntactic pattern.

From this perspective, to know a foreign word means to know, among other things, its *combinatorial potential* within the sentence patterns of the language. This potential is comprised of the word's ability to open positions for other words, as well as the ability to fill in the positions opened by other words. So it can be said one knows the word *available* in English only if one can use it in every possible position within every possible sentence pattern (following a copula as in *Some parking room is available*; following a noun in an existential structure *There's / We have some parking room available;* preceding a for- phrase in its transform *There's / We have some room available for parking,* etc.) and if one is aware of what constraints the categorical semantics of the whole sentence containing *available* imposes on the choice of the word for its Subject (to fit the idea of the Opportunity – existent or non – existent – the words should denote some Limited Resources, such as funds, space, equipment, etc.).

There are three main factors that determine the word's combinatorial potential. Traditional grammar books have successfully dealt with the first two, namely, the grammatical class the word belongs to and the grammatical form it takes when used in a certain sentence pattern. The news with *Lexico-Grammar* is that it is primarily concerned with the third factor, which is the lexico-semantic grouping the word enters when it occurs in a definite position and performs a definite function. The new grammar undertakes to reveal those more or less *covert* semantic categories, which govern combinability of words as sentence elements.

Some of these categories come naturally, as a result of *conceptual agreement* between the words joined in a structure. It is natural, for instance, that when talking about the way things *taste,* we use adjectives describing the sense: *acidic, sweet, bitter, salty, spicy, vinegary, lemony, fruity,* but when talking about the way things *feel* we turn to a different range of adjectives: *hard, soft, rough, smooth, silky, velvety, mossy, hairy, furry.*

However, other semantic categories can only be discovered through corpus research. Thus, if a learner wishes to know what adjectives are used with the copula *go,* a traditional grammar and even a usage book would be of little help, because they can offer only examples, while a lexico-grammar would be prepared with the word type under the categorial umbrella of Adjectives of Failure/Decay. The corpus indicates that shoes *go hard* (if you put them to dry close to the fire); telephones *go dead*; batteries *go flat* and so do beer and champagne; bread and chocolate *go stale*; meat and fish *go funny* or *bad*; milk *goes sour*; cheese *goes mouldy,* jam – *sugary.* As regards people, there is no end to unwanted things that they can go – *bald, blind, deaf, pale, tense, blank, blurred, bitter, grave, crestfallen, peculiar, batty, potty, unsane, senile ...*

2.1   The format for a lexico-grammar

The task of describing the above-mentioned properties of the language vocabulary for teaching purposes may not seem feasible at all unless an appropriate format is found to describe them. The format offered in this paper is the one the authors chose for their research-based, corpus-driven Handbook of Lexico-Grammar of English for Russian Learners (Chirko et al. 1998). In it an attempt is made to provide a consistent and systematic description of the word-classes fitting each position in the major sentence patterns of the English language.

As the title of the book suggests, the description is laid out as a series of learning activities and practices, many of which are inductive, i.e. moving from the language facts to the rules, so that students can formulate the grammatical statements by themselves.

Because the handbook is meant to be used in monolingual classes, Russian-English correspondences are dealt with on a regular basis. Attention is focused on the differences in the predicate argument structure of the outwardly similar sentence patterns and in the grammatical behaviour of the words treated as equivalents in Russian-English and English-Russian dictionaries.

It is the authors' firm belief that the starting point and the core of a lexico-grammatical description *must* be the Verb, as the most syntax sensitive type of word, which sets the sentence pattern itself. Each chapter of the book is therefore assigned to one nuclear sentence pattern, e.g. Subject – Verb – Subject Complement or Subject – Verb – Direct Object, within which lexico-semantic subclasses of the Verb are distinguished and indicated by type designations.

From this point the description moves on to the verb dependent word types, first those that stand closest to the verb (directly related to it), then those that are the farthest from it in the structure.

The chosen format allows the division of the broad grammatical classes of words found in traditional grammar, such as *transitive* verbs or *uncount nouns,* into subclasses, then sub-subclasses and ultimately down to the usage-end.

2.2   A case for ditransitives

Ditransitive verbs, for example, which set the model with two objects, fall into several main types, including the *Pass*-type, the *Bring*-type, *Tell*-type, the *Pay*-type, etc. Each of them is represented by a different range of lexical items in Russian. This is particularly true of the *Make*-type, restricted to a fairly closed group of verbs: *make somebody a cup of tea, cook/prepare somebody a meal, fix somebody a plate of food, mix somebody a drink, pour somebody some wine, cut or carve somebody a slice of roast beef* and a few others. The Russian language, in which ditransitive verbs form a very wide class, also allows *wash somebody a shirt, *dig somebody a garden, *comb somebody hair, *bandage somebody a wound, etc. Minimising the interference from the patterns of usage of the native language is a prime concern of the lexico-grammatical component of an EFL course.

The semantics of the verb lays constraints on the noun type used in the direct object position. So lists of such nouns are compiled for each semantic grouping of ditransitives and even for some individual verbs, e.g. *cause/spare* somebody *trouble, bother, difficulty, inconvenience, pain, suspense, embarrassment, unpleasant moments, etc.*

Furthermore, when a group of the nouns or a noun needs to be extended, a list of appropriate adjectives or other word-types used as attributive modifiers, is supplied e.g. *give* somebody a *sidelong look, a passing, flicking, appraising, calculating, reflective, dazed, quizzical, roguish, rueful* or *murderous look ....*

The utmost periphery of the description is predictably constituted by intensifying adverbs such as *totally, completely, perfectly, fully, utterly, thoroughly, intensely, highly, deeply* and others, each with its own combinatorial preferences.

As some of the above-given examples show, alongside the items that are joined in accordance with the general rules of syntax and therefore freely allow substitution, Lexico-Grammar also deals with recurrent, fixed combinations of words and even idioms like *give* somebody *the go-ahead, the brush-off, the slip, the creeps,* etc.

3 A usage-biased grammar

To sum up: the lexico-grammar of this kind offers students lists of words that

a) fit a particular syntactic position within a particular sentence pattern;
b) occur regularly whenever another word or other words are used;
c) relate to a semantic grouping (thematically centred or situationally-bound);
d) make up a productive set or a frozen entity.

So one can speak here about a grammar that is heavily biased towards usage. Indeed, lexico-grammar leads to the point where a teacher can choose to put a finishing touch by commenting on the pragmatic and stylistic acceptability of a word or a word combination and on the difference between American and British English.

4 How does regular grammar fit in?

It goes without saying that dealing with the arrangement of words in the syntactic context, one cannot ignore the points of regular grammar. They are treated in the book as they occur and interact in the sentences built on the same pattern. This means that one problem, e.g. articles or agreement between subject and verb, can be studied in its different aspects in more than one chapter in the book. On the other hand, one pattern can offer an ideal framework for overall study of a problem, as does, for instance, the pattern There VS for all sorts of quantifiers and place adverbials.

The section detailing grammatical peculiarities of sentences build on the given pattern is preceded by the Map of Contents, drawn for learners to visualise the full potential of the positional scheme of the sentence type (the constituents of the sentence interrelated and ordered in a certain way) and also the grammatical problems a learner normally faces when using the pattern to produce meaningful utterances.

Thus, the handbook in lexico-grammar can be used together with other practice materials and students can turn to any traditional reference book for the rules explaining further grammatical points.

5   References

CHIRKO, Tatyana; LOMOVA, Tatyana; RYBAKOVA, Svetlana (1998): Making a Message in English. A Handbook in Lexico-Grammar of English for Russian Learners, Vol. 1. Voronezh: Russkaya Slovestnost.

DROSTE, Flip; JOSEPH, John (1991): Introduction: Linguistic Theory and Grammatical Description. In: Droste, Flip; Joseph, Joseph (eds.): Linguistic Theory and Grammatical Description. Amsterdam – Philadelphia: John Benjamins, 1-21.

Language Awareness and TEFL

Tadeusz Danilewicz

Language awareness has become a trendy concept in recent years. Awareness of language as grammatical code was central to language learning in grammar translation methodology but its role was diminished in both structural and communicative language teaching. Speaking very loosely, one might say that the language awareness movement aims to foster, in various sections of society, a sensitivity to the nature of language and its importance in everyday life. Most authors provide a necessarily vague and imprecise definition of the concept of language awareness hoping for the notion to clarify itself in time. They talk about finding things about language, becoming conscious about one's own and other's use of it in speech and in written forms, developing a sensitive relationship to it, being able to talk explicitly about one's insights into it. It appears then that the notion of language awareness has many uses and senses, and therefore, it must remain vague.

Dictionaries provide the following definitions of the phrase *to be aware*:
Cambridge International Dictionary of English (CIDE) defines the phrase as:

"i knowing that something exists, or having knowledge or experience of a particular thing.
ii Aware also means having special interest in or experience of something and also being well informed of what is happening in that subject at the present time." (CIDE 1995:86)

Longman Dictionary of English Language and Culture (LDELC) gives the following three senses of the phrase:

"i having knowledge or understanding ii having knowledge or consciousness of the stated type, e.g. politically aware / artistically aware; iii showing understanding of oneself, and other people; SENSITIVE, eg. She's a very aware person." (LDELC 1993:68)

In Collins Cobuild English Usage (CCEU), the entry for *aware of* includes the following explanation: "If you are aware of something, you are conscious of it, or you know that it exists." (CCEU 1993, 80)

Longman Language Activator (LLA) defines the phrase as part of the verb *to know* in the following way: "to be aware is to know that a serious situation exists." (LLA 1993, 732) thus distinguishing it from the phrase *to be conscious* which is defined as: "to know that a particular situation exists and to have it in your mind." (ibid:1993, 732)

The above definitions imply that being aware is an active process that involves some *attention* in order to have *control* over one's actions. It would appear then that the third sense of the phrase to be aware presented in LDELC above: "showing understanding of oneself, and other people." (LDELC 1993:68) though far from precision, describes best the concept of being linguistically aware, i.e. being sensitive to one's own and other people's use of language.

The next question is whether people really need to become more linguistically aware? If we take a closer look around, we are bound to notice confusing instructional

leaflets, strangely worded signs in shops or absurd or even incomprehensible translations into foreign languages. The Polish parliament has just passed a law trying to
protect the Polish language against unnecessary foreign influence. It appears then that
the nature and role of language is not generally appreciated therefore, people should
become more aware of the influence of language on our lives and raising such awareness should be a part of general education.

Sharwood Smith (1997) observes that most people accept language as we accept
the air we breathe. We cannot get along without it, and we take it for granted almost
all the time. We become very aware of language when trying to communicate abroad,
we all sometimes look for the right word or have problems finding appropriate linguistic forms to express our attitude toward the surrounding world. However, such
awareness is still at a relatively low level. Only few people are fully conscious of the
ways, subtle or not so subtle, in which our use of language may affect others. Very
few people are aware of the extent to which language is used dishonestly to mislead
and manipulate. Still fewer of us recognize that our very perceptions of the world are
influenced, and our thoughts are mostly shaped by language. Therefore, if it is true
that we are all in some sense prisoners[1] of language, it is equally true that liberation
begins with an awareness of that fact.

There seems to exist a distinction between the conscious, analytic, technical knowledge of the language system, and the intuitive knowledge of language that drives
spontaneous language performance. Johnson-Laird in his two books "Mental Models"
(1983) and "The Computer and the Mind: An Introduction to Cognitive Science"
(1988) stresses the fact the human mind is capable of parallel processing of information which means that millions of processes take place simultaneously. Therefore, we
are not aware of most of them. This implies that cognitive processes of which we are
conscious or aware are rather limited. Furthermore, Jackendoff in his book "Consciousness and the Computational Mind" (1987) observes that the cognitive processes of
which we are conscious or aware constitute *the results* of computations rather than the
computations themselves. In other words, we cannot consciously investigate the rapid
way words and structures are computed in our heads. A conscious analytic introspec-
tion shows that *the actual* computations or conceptualisations – to use a more familiar
term from cognitive linguistics – are inaccessible to our conscious minds. This implies that cognitive processes of which we are conscious hardly ever dictate, *directly*,
the way in which we solve linguistic or other problems.

Sharwood Smith poses three issues that need to be considered in connection with
raising language awareness:

"a) which people are supposed to become aware (teachers, learners, government officials, the
media, the general public);
b) which out of the many aspects of language that may be distinguished they are supposed to
become aware of (accent, grammar, communicative function, language loyalty, etc.,); and
c) which people, or other agencies, are to be responsible for bringing about the awareness."
(Sharwood Smith 1997:26)

---

[1] Roman Kalisz has observed that we can equally well say that language is our prisoner.

If language awareness is a movement that aims to make as many people as possible sensitive to the influence of language on our lives, then *all* efforts directed towards raising language awareness seem to be highly recommendable activities as, in principle, they should lead to a more effective and responsible use of language.

In 1945, George Orwell in his essay on "Politics and the English Language" said that "What is above all needed is to let the meaning choose the word, and not the other way out." (Orwell 1945:35) Orwell's observation is not only valid for the English language as it is used by native speakers but it can obviously refer also to the domain of teaching English as a foreign language (TEFL).

The search for the "best" or "ideal" way to teach languages is always associated with some background assumptions or dogma until more facts about what goes on in learners' heads are revealed. In late seventies and early eighties, Krashen (1983) introduced the so-called natural method or approach to language teaching and learning. The method was based on a certain amount of empirical research which showed an unchangeable natural order of acquisition of some aspects of morphosyntax, holding for all learners regardless of their native language. This fact was used to diminish the role of conscious language analysis in second language acquisition. The teachers' explanations of grammar intricacies, or complex language functions contribute only to the language learner's technical knowledge of language. Sharwood Smith (1997) observes that this kind of knowledge plays as minimal a role in the actual development of language skill as, for example, driving school theory contributes to the learner driver's ability to corner, brake on icy roads, and drive a car effortlessly in a busy city centre. In this sense, language awareness in language learning would have a general educational value as technical knowledge, but would appear to have little value with respect to the facilitation of the learner's progress in the development of language skill.

The computer analysis of actually occurring language has revealed that a lot of what is presented in language textbooks does not correspond with the "real" language of native speakers. John Sinclair observed that

> "We are teaching English in ignorance of a vast amount of basic fact. This is not our fault, but it should not inhibit the absorption of new material." (Sinclair 1985:252)

Although Sinclair is talking about English in particular hoping to bring about changes in the syllabus of English, it is quite obvious that his remarks could apply to the teaching of any foreign language. In other words, the findings of corpus analysis can help specify the objectives of learning based on an awareness of actual language usage.

For a foreign language teacher, language awareness can rightly be claimed to constitute an essential intellectual framework which has to be in place before effective teaching and learning can even begin. In other words, the foreign language teacher must be aware of how the particular language she is teaching is actually put to use by its users. Language awareness then appears to be a sine qua non condition to be satisfied by any professional foreign language teacher. The more the foreign language teacher is aware and knows about the target language system, its usage and cultural background, the more likely she is to experience success in her teaching practice.

Hymes (1972) proposed that to be communicatively competent in a language you had to be capable of making four kinds of judgement about a particular instance of use, namely:

1) Whether and to what degree it was possible.
2) Whether and to what degree it was feasible.
3) Whether and to what degree it was appropriate.
4) Whether and to what degree it was actually done (performed, attested).

The four judgements refer to the objectives of learning as specified by a syllabus which takes the communicative facts of language into account. The judgements or criteria can also be said to measure language awareness. The first judgement is based on the parameter relating to grammaticality, i.e. whether the performed structure follows the accepted system of grammatical or lexical rules. The second one deals with cognitive intelligibility, i.e. how far the encoded message is accessible. In the structural syllabus, grammatical, i.e. possible items were selected and ordered in ways to make them easy to process. Judgements 3 and 4 refer to appropriateness and attestedness, respectively. It should be noted, however, that while parameters 1 and 2 can be satisfied by probably any professional non native English language teacher, judgements 3 and 4 will undoubtfully cause some problems not only to non native but also to native professional English language teachers. Therefore, while 1 and 2 are the judgements which are verifiable against some agreed upon set of rules or norms, 3 and 4 are subject to answers which need to be qualified by phrases like ... *to a certain extent / degree ... or ... there is a tendency ...* which indicate their fuzzy and temporary character.

Communication as the contextually appropriate use of language is bound up with culture. According to Widdowson,

"To learn a language is clearly not just to pick up the most common patterns of usage but to realise these as appropriate use, to know what communal and cultural significance they carry as social action. Language awareness in respect to appropriateness, therefore, involves cultural factors of a complex and subtle kind." (Widdowson 1997:36)

The attestedness judgement or condition has to do with teaching the language as actually attested in real life. If you are claiming to be teaching the ability to communicate, you need to be aware of the patterns of language which people actually produce when they communicate, rather than some invented version of them. Here, a corpus analysis will indicate patterns of texts, their frequency of occurrence and attested features of the language that people have actually produced. All this implies that ideally, teachers of a foreign language should have an awareness of the language they are teaching as it is used in normal social circumstances by its users.

However, even this kind of awareness is not enough as teachers have first of all to define their pedagogic objectives and secondly, specify the route of achieving these objectives. This means that teachers need to consider the foreign language not only for what it is to its users, but also for what it is to the learners. According to Widdowson (1997), the foreignness of the language to be learned is not only that it is a different language from the mother tongue, in that it represents an alternative grammatical code, but in that it appears to be quite a different phenomenon in that it consists of linguistic forms whose communicative potential remains unrealised. For example, Polish and English linguistic forms expressing politeness are quite different and hence Polish speakers of English who are unaware of that fact sometimes appear impolite to native speakers of English and conversely, unaware English speakers of Polish seem ironical, i.e. also impolite to native speakers of Polish.

The four judgements which characterise a communicatively competent person in a language in Hymes' (ibid.) terminology, can also be said to define a representative example of a person who is linguistically aware. The question is how this ideal example of language awareness can be put to work in teaching.

There has been a tendency in the past to assume that features of usage and use which are revealed by linguistic description must necessarily constitute the content to be taught in language classes. However, as Widdowson put it "descriptive validity does not directly transfer to pedagogy." (Widdowson ibid.) Learners know from their experience of instruction in other subjects that teaching progresses through half-truths and partial generalisations which are gradually reformulated and revised. This is the necessary consequence of the fact that you cannot learn everything at once. Learners must recognise that what they do in class has a temporary instructional character.

Kasper claims that language learners need to be introduced into different kinds of pragmatic knowledge:

> "The learner's task is not very different from that of the pragmaticist: she has to discover the contextual (situational) and co-textual (linguistic) constraints governing SA (Speech Act) selection and modes of realisation in the target language and culture. In Hymes' terms, she has to discover what is possible, feasible, appropriate and done in carrying out SAs in L2." (Kasper 1989:42)

However, the learner's role is not exactly like that of the pragmaticist in that the learner's task is not only to analyse language but first of all to engage with it. Furthermore, it is not only a matter of knowing about the linguistic constraints governing SAs, but also of knowing how far they can be effectively acted upon. In other words, how is awareness of language an enabling condition for learning and use; how far can students access it and act upon it in the process of learning.

In what follows, I present fragments of in-service students' task at Gdansk University Teacher Training College. The aim of the task was to raise language awareness by improving effectiveness of teacher-student communication in the classroom. The in-service students were first briefly introduced to the classical now Grice's Co-operative Principle and the four maxims which govern most verbal exchanges (Grice 1975). The co-operative principle was formulated by Grice in the following way:

> "Make your conversational contribution such as is required, at the stage at which it occurs, by the accepted purpose or direction of the talk exchange in which you are engaged." (Grice 1975:45)

The four maxims are:

a) The maxim of quantity, which is paraphrased as:

1) Make your contribution as informative as is required (for the current purposes of the exchange).
2) Do not make your contribution more informative than is required.
b) The maxim of Quality, under which falls a "super-maxim" – "try to make your contribution one that is true". This is paraphrased as:
1) Do not say what you believe to be false.
2) Do not say that for which you lack adequate evidence.
c) The maxim of relation, which Grice paraphrases simply as "be relevant".
d) The maxim of manner, which is paraphrased as:
1) Avoid obscurity of expression.
2) Avoid ambiguity.
3) Be brief (avoid unnecessary prolixity).
4) Be orderly.

The students observed that any violation of at least one of these maxims must result in growing tension between those who are involved in the conversation.

Next the students were asked to tape their lessons, then prepare scripts of their conversations with their pupils and finally, apply Grice's implicatures to their lesson scripts.

What follows is an original fragment of a typical analysis prepared by one of the students:

"English lesson – 13th May 99
Primary school children
1. Greeting the students & checking the attendance list.
T. – Hello.
Sts .- Hello.
T. Let's see if everybody is here. / QUALITY – I've already noticed that some students are missing / Marta ... Marika ... Sławek ...
S. – Absent!
T. – Absent? / MANNER – suggests unjustified surprise / What's wrong with him? Is he on a trip? / QUANTITY – too many questions & QUALITY – lack of adequate evidence & RELATION – what I need to know is who is absent, any additional information is irrelevant at this stage /
S.- No. (one of the students) He is sleeping. / MANNER – obscurity of expression, which causes confusion /
T. – Sleeping? is he ill?
S. – Yes.
T. – Michal ...Krystian – absent. He has broken his leg, hasn't he?
S. – Yes.
2. Presentation and practice.
T. – Michal, how many signs of the zodiac do you know?
S. – Twenty.
T. – Are you sure? This is twenty:20 (writing the number on the blackboard) / RELATION – the number of the signs is irrelevant; nevertheless, to some extent asking the question was justified – it functions as a link to the next & main part of the lesson / ....
I think we can write the subject of our lesson today and the subject is: The signs of the zodiac. / MANNER – prolixity /
S. – (copying the subject)

T. – Ready? Good. Now I would like you to take your pencils and draw the symbols of the zo-
diacal signs. Start with the first one. / MANNER – the phrase: 'the first one' causes confusion
– what I said wasn't clear / ..."

After completing the task, the students exchanged their scripts with comments among themselves for comparison and discussion. The discussion led to the following conclusions:

- teachers speak too much in class; their contributions are often more informative than required, it's difficult for teachers to be brief in their verbal exchanges with pupils;
- there is a clear tendency for the maxims of quantity and manner to be broken most often by teachers. In result the teachers felt that some of the class time had partly been wasted;
- the discussion also indicated that the maxims which were most often broken by pupils turned out to be the maxims of manner: there were many cases of obscurity of expression and ambiguity.

In the end, the students were asked to evaluate the task. Most of them found the activity very useful as it made them more aware of the kind of language used in the teacher student verbal exchange. Therefore, it appears that at least some tools developed by pragmatics and cognitive linguistics can successfully be used in TEFL to increase language awareness.

References

GRICE, Henry P (1975): Logic and Conversation. In: Cole, P.; Morgan, J. L. (eds.): Syntax and Semantics, vol. 3: Speech acts New York – San Francisco – London: Academic Press, 41-58.

HYMES, Dell (1972): On Communicative Competence. In: Pride, J.; Holmes, J. (eds.): Sociolinguistics. London: Penguin Books, 269-293.

JACKENDOFF, Ray (1987): Consciousness and the Computational Mind. Cambridge, Ma: MIT Press.

JOHNSON-LAIRD, Philip N. (1988): The Computer and the Mind: An Introduction to Cognitive Science. Cambridge, Ma: Harvard University Press.

— (1983): Mental Models. Cambridge, Ma: Harvard University Press.

KASPER, Gabriele (1989): Variation in Interlanguage Speech Act Realisation. In: Gass, S. C. et al. (eds.): Variation in Second Language Acquisition. Clevedon: Multilingual Matters, 37-58.

KRASHEN, Stephen D. (1983): The Natural Method. Hayward, Ca: Alemany Press.

ORWELL, George (1945): Politics and the English Language. In: Escholz, P.; Rosa, A., Park, V. (eds.): Language Awareness. New York: St. Martin's Press, 23-35.

SHARWOOD SMITH, Michael (1997): "Consciousness-raising" Meets "Language Awareness". In: Fremdsprachen Lehren und Lernen 26, 24-32.

SINCLAIR, John M (1985): Selected Issues. In: Quirk, R.; Widdowson, H. (eds.): English in the World, Cambridge: University Press, 248-254.

WIDDOWSON, Henry (1997): The Pedagogic Relevance of Language Awareness. In: Fremdsprachen Lehren und Lernen 26, 33-43.

Dictionaries:

PROCTER, Paul et al. (eds) (1995): Cambridge International Dictionary of English. Cambridge: Cambridge University Press.

SINCLAIR, John et al. (eds.) (1993): Collins COBUILD English Usage. London: Harper Collins Publishers.

SUMMERS, Della et al. (eds.) (1993): Longman Language Activator. Harlow: Longman Group UK Limited.

— (eds.) (1992): Longman Dictionary of English Language and Culture. Harlow: Longman Group UK Limited.

Apprentissage précoce de langue étrangère: interférences de traitement entre langue et musique

Christelle Dodane

1   Introduction

L'imprégnation naturelle d'une langue se fait d'abord par les éléments prosodiques (rythme et intonation), avant les caractéristiques segmentales. Dans le langage émergent (Konopczynski 1991), l'enfant restitue d'abord les patrons intonatifs de base et les caractéristiques rythmiques de sa langue (mise en place progressive de l'allongement final pour le français). N'ayant pas encore accédé à la parole, il analyse le flux langagier par contours de hauteurs. De même, lorsqu'un locuteur s'exprime dans une langue étrangère pour l'auditeur, c'est d'abord la prosodie de cette langue que ce dernier décèle, incapable qu'il est de la segmenter en unités linguistiques porteuses de sens. La mise en place des structures prosodiques apparaît donc comme un véritable pré-requis dans l'apprentissage d'une langue étrangère, qui favorise une meilleure prononciation: les schémas rythmiques et intonatifs d'une langue constituent la véritable charpente à partir de laquelle le système phonologique pourra s'organiser. La prosodie constitue en cela « la structure d'accueil de tous les autres éléments de la parole, qui sans elle, restent vides de signification » (Konopczynski 1999): les langues sont des musiques en elles-mêmes. D'ailleurs, le terme même de prosodie provient du mot grec *ôdê*, qui veut dire chant. Les éléments musicaux que sont le rythme et l'intonation sont en quelque sorte les composantes du *chant* de la langue. Ce qu'exprimait avec élégance Companys dans ses cours de correction phonétique lorsqu'il remarquait que « toutes les langues chantent, mais pas sur le même air ».

2   Traitement de la langue et de la musique

2.1   Traitement global

Dès le début la vie, l'enfant traite l'information auditive de manière globale, en extrayant les contours de hauteur des mélodies et des expressions verbales. Ces contours fonctionnent comme des *unités élémentaires de traitement*, qui semblent constituer un important mécanisme d'organisation perceptif, lequel va diriger la segmentation de patterns plus complexes (Trehub 1984). Intuitivement, les mères adoptent une « pédagogie » parfaitement adaptée à ces capacités de traitement. Dans le *Langage Adressé aux Enfants* (L.A.E. ou *baby talk*), les éléments prosodiques sont exagérés aux dépens de l'information segmentale, afin d'inculquer à l'enfant le patron intono-accentuel de sa langue maternelle. On suppose en effet que la prosodie contient de nombreux indices sur les unités ou les frontières linguistiques importantes. Ainsi, les contours de hauteur sont simplifiés, le rythme est plus lent et plus régulier, les répétitions sont nombreuses, la hauteur est plus élevée de 3 à 4 demi-tons, les voyelles sont prolongées comme dans une chanson et accentuées par une tessiture plus étendue

(Fernald 1989). Ces caractéristiques confèrent des qualités musicales au baby talk. De même, les berceuses possèdent des propriétés différentes des autres chansons (tempo lent, rythme régulier, nombreuses répétitions, voyelles allongées sur lesquelles module la ligne mélodique). On retrouve ce type d'adaptation en L2 dans ce que Giacomi et Hérédia (1986) appellent la *coopération exolingue*: le professeur de langue étrangère exagère l'intonation et marque plus le rythme lorsqu'il s'adresse à un apprenant. L'ensemble de ces ajustements vocaux censé s'adapter aux capacités de traitement de l'apprenant dans un but d'acquisition peut être qualifié de *pédagogie inconsciente*.

2.2   Traitement local

Les similitudes entre la langue et la musique paraissent d'autant plus fortes que l'environnement exerce sur elles les mêmes types de contraintes. Jusqu'à 6 mois, l'enfant est une sorte de *super-discriminateur* capable de percevoir une multitude de contrastes phonétiques et musicaux. Mais, au contact de sa langue et de son système musical maternel, son attention perceptuelle va progressivement se fixer sur des événements acoustiques simples, des *points de repère* faciles à traiter: les *prototypes* (Rosch 1973). En fait, l'enfant se focalise uniquement sur les représentations qui lui seront utiles pour l'acquisition de sa langue et de son système maternel; il augmente ainsi sa performance et sa rapidité de traitement. Ainsi, à 6 mois, l'enfant connaît une première réorganisation perceptuelle autour des contrastes vocaliques de sa langue maternelle (Kuhl 1994) et, entre 10 et 12 mois, une seconde période de réorganisation centrée sur les contrastes consonantiques (Best 1993). En ce qui concerne les contrastes musicaux, la réorganisation se fait également vers 10 à 12 mois autour des *bons intervalles* que sont la quinte et l'octave largement présents dans les voyelles (Eilers 1991). Une fois ces prototypes acquis, le système perceptuel va évaluer tout événement sonore en fonction de la structure de ces représentations internes, quitte à les filtrer ou à les déformer. C'est ce que Troubetskoy appelle le *crible phonologique*. Les travaux de Eilers (1991) semblent montrer qu'il existe également un *crible musical*. Ce processus d'*acculturation linguistique et musicale* est capital dans les processus d'acquisition et tout aussi nécessaire à l'adaptation de l'enfant à son milieu. Pendant les premiers mois de la vie, la parole et la musique seraient ainsi dominées par des tendances communes de traitement et des mécanismes de perception liés à une capacité cognitive générale.

3   Transfert de compétence de l'écoute musicale à l'écoute linguistique

La perception verbale et musicale de l'enfant étant dominée par un traitement en contours de hauteur (traitement global), une analogie entre l'analyse musicale et la perception d'une langue étrangère peut être établie. Le processus de *va-et-vient* caractéristique de l'écoute musicale devrait être transférable et utile en situation d'écoute d'une séquence parlée. Les capacités d'écoute développées lors d'un apprentissage musical pourraient être transférables à l'apprentissage du système intono-accentuel d'une langue étrangère. Nous essaierons de savoir si les capacités *analytiques* caractéristiques d'une oreille musicienne *experte,* utilisées dans la détection des intervalles sont transférables au traitement des rapports de fréquence des sons de la parole et au traitement des unités segmentales (traitement local). Nous ferons une analogie entre l'analyse de la forme musicale et celle de la forme verbale à deux niveaux: global (prosodie) et local (segmental). Ainsi, une oreille entraînée par l'expérience musicale pourrait être plus efficace pour percevoir et produire:

- l'intonation d'une langue étrangère (traitement global);
- les contrastes phonologiques d'une langue étrangère (traitement local). Elle pourrait être efficace aussi en établissant une analogie entre l'analyse des différentes composantes des intervalles musicaux (rapport entre fréquence des notes) et des phonèmes (rapport entre les formants).

L'association d'un apprentissage musical à l'apprentissage d'une langue étrangère devrait être bénéfique en raison d'une interaction entre la pédagogie de la langue et celle de la musique. Une telle association permettrait une *ouverture de l'oreille* et empêcherait une spécialisation trop prégnante du système perceptuel sur le système maternel linguistique et musical.

4   Expérimentation

4.1   L'âge et l'apprentissage d'une langue étrangère

L'âge joue un rôle déterminant dans les processus d'acquisition. Avant 10 ans, on sait que l'apprentissage d'une langue seconde, notamment au niveau intono-accentuel est relativement aisé en raison de la plasticité cérébrale de l'enfant. En revanche, après 10 ans environ, le cerveau se comporte auditivement en fonction de la première langue (Luria 1974) car la plasticité cérébrale se détériore. C'est ce que montraient déjà les travaux de Penfield et Roberts (1959), en constatant qu'après un traumatisme cérébral, les possibilités de récupération des fonctions langagières étaient fort différentes avant et après 10 ans. Il est donc fondamental de commencer l'apprentissage d'une langue seconde avant ce *seuil fatidique* (Hagège 1996). Mais quand exactement? Comme Garabédian (1996) le souligne, le plus tôt serait le mieux afin de mettre à profit les grandes capacités de l'enfant. Pour des raisons institutionnelles, il est difficile de commencer cet apprentissage avant l'école maternelle, tous les enfants n'étant pas concernés. Nous avons réalisé notre première expérimentation. Dans le cadre du programme d'Initiation aux Langues Vivantes (réforme effective dès la rentrée scolaire de 1995 qui fixe une première sensibilisation à une langue étrangère à partir du CE1). Mais, actuellement, l'enseignement des langues étrangères a été reporté au CM1, c'est-à-dire au moment où les enfants sont âgés de 9 ans. Or, il est déjà presque trop tard quand on sait que l'âge idéal pour débuter un apprentissage précoce se situe entre 4 et 8 ans. Pendant cet *âge heureux* (Guberina 1991), l'enfant fait en effet preuve d'excellentes capacités d'imitation.

4.2   La musicalité de l'anglais

Dans l'étude de la prosodie, confronter l'anglais au français, deux langues prosodiquement très différentes est intéressant. L'anglais est une langue musicale, caractérisée par de fortes variations de hauteur et couvrant une large tessiture. Il utilise principalement les variations de hauteur et d'intensité. Les tons mélodiques sont très difficiles à acquérir pour les français dont la tessiture est plus restreinte. D'autre part, l'organisation rythmique de l'anglais est complètement différente de celle du français. L'anglais est une langue à tendance *stress timed* (Pike 1947) où la place de l'accent n'est pas prédictible, mais l'espace perceptuel entre deux pics accentuels est à peu près stable. A l'inverse, la place de l'accent tonique en français est prédictible puisqu'elle affecte toujours la dernière syllabe du mot prosodique. A partir de là, il nous paraît intéressant d'étudier la restitution de l'intonation et du rythme spécifique de l'anglais par des enfants francophones.

4.3   Le corpus

Notre corpus est constitué des productions de quatre enfants scolarisés en CE1, apprenant l'anglais. Nous avons enregistré ces enfants dialoguant avec un locuteur natif, qui n'est pas l'enseignant habituel de la classe. Notre corpus est constitué d'énoncés spontanés, d'énoncés en répétition différée (vocabulaire appris en classe) et d'énoncés en répétition immédiate (inconnus des enfants). Sur les quatre enfants, deux sont musiciens (ils suivent des cours d'instrument et de solfège en conservatoire). Les deux autres ne font pas de musique et sont issus de milieux non musiciens.

5   Premiers résultats

5.1   Traitement global de la langue étrangère: la prosodie

5.1.1 En répétition différée du vocabulaire appris en classe, nous avons remarqué chez les enfants musiciens un comportement d'exagération des paramètres prosodiques. La figure 1 représente la courbe intonative du mot *blue* produite par un enfant musicien et par le locuteur natif.

La structure globale de la courbe est bien imitée; elle respecte le pattern *en cloche* typique de l'anglais (contour montant, puis descendant). L'enfant perçoit et restitue l'ampleur tonale de l'anglais, bien que ces larges glissements de hauteur soient très difficiles à reproduire par les français (tessiture du français restreinte à une octave). La courbe semble être trop exagérée par rapport à celle du locuteur natif, notamment sur la descente. montée de 9 demi-tons et descente de 18 demi-tons alors que le locuteur natif ne monte que de 7 demi-tons et descend de 7 demi-tons. La voyelle [u:] qui a tendance à se diphtonguer légèrement en anglais n'est pas reproduite par l'enfant qui, à la place, produit la voyelle française non diphtonguée [u], très allongée: elle dure en effet 358 ms sur un énoncé total de 586 ms alors que la diphtongue du locuteur natif dure 319 ms sur un total de 603 ms. Par rapport à la durée totale des énoncés, la voyelle de l'enfant est très longue.

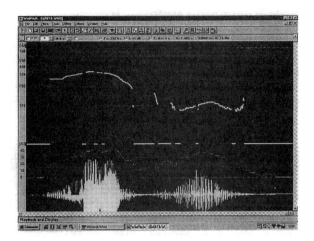

Figure n°1: courbe intonative du mot « blue » produite par une enfant musicien à gauche et le locuteur natif à droite (échelle logarithmique)

L'enfant musicien joue donc avec les paramètres de durée et de hauteur. Il manipule, transforme la substance sonore pour mieux la dominer et l'assimiler. Il montre par là qu'il est en pleine phase d'acquisition. Le comportement d'*imitation-jeu* décrit par Piaget (1937) nous semble adéquat pour expliquer ce phénomène. Les non musiciens produisent des contours descendants et plats caractéristiques du français. Ils appliquent la prosodie du français aux énoncés anglais. La prosodie de leur langue maternelle semble fonctionner comme un filtre, un *crible prosodique*.

5.1.2 En répétition immédiate de mots qu'ils ne connaissent pas, les deux enfants musiciens changent de comportement. Ils ne peuvent plus jouer avec les contours de mots qu'ils n'ont jamais entendus: ils se contentent de les imiter scrupuleusement, souvent au demi-ton près, manifestant ainsi un comportement d'*imitation-copie* (Piaget 1937). Nous pensons que ces deux types d'imitation sont essentiels pour que l'enfant s'adapte à la prosodie d'une langue étrangère. Dans un premier temps, il reproduit exactement les contours prosodiques et ensuite, il les manipule pour les assimiler graduellement. Est-ce que ces comportements sont caractéristiques d'une oreille musicale?

5.2   Traitement local de la langue étrangère: les contrastes vocaliques

Que se passe-t-il à sept ans lorsqu'un enfant, déjà fortement influencé par sa langue maternelle, reproduit les contrastes d'une langue seconde? Après avoir été traitées de manière globale, les séquences verbales et musicales sont traitées de manière analytique. Une oreille musicale est entraînée à l'écoute analytique. Est-ce qu'il y aura un transfert de compétences de la musique à la langue? L'auditeur analyse en effet les rapports entre les différentes composantes sonores. Pour la musique, il va décoder les intervalles (relation entre les fréquences des notes) et, pour la langue, les contrastes phonétiques (relation entre les fréquences des formants). Aujourd'hui, on sait que l'information essentielle pour l'identification des voyelles réside dans la forme globale du spectre et plus précisément dans la localisation des maxima spectraux correspondant aux deux ou trois premiers formants. Malgré toutes les variations inhérentes à la production de la parole, un locuteur reconnaîtra toujours les phonèmes de sa langue maternelle, ainsi que le patron caractéristique qui lui permet d'identifier le son correspondant. Quel est ce patron? Qu'est-ce qui reste invariable malgré les différences de physiologie, l'âge, le sexe, l'origine sociolinguistique? L'identité perceptuelle d'une voyelle est peut-être justement constituée par la distribution des rapports entre ses trois premiers formants.

5.2.1 Les voyelles

Selon Kuhl (1994), il existe une représentation de l'espace vocalique adaptée à la langue maternelle. L'espace acoustique initial est divisé en frontières psycho-acoustiques correspondant aux caractéristiques phonémiques de la langue maternelle. Ces représentations internes, constamment générées par le cerveau, comparent leur propre structure aux formes qui se présentent dans l'environnement linguistique. Ainsi, les contrastes non-natifs seront filtrés en fonction de la structure des contrastes natifs. Les valeurs formantiques sont-elles distribuées de la même manière que dans le modèle anglais ou, au contraire, filtrées par les contrastes maternels? Les valeurs des trois premiers formants des productions en anglais ont été déterminées pour le locuteur natif et pour les quatre enfants. Les résultats ne montrent pas de différence entre les enfants musiciens et les enfants non musiciens. Ils rencontrent tous les mêmes problèmes: les contrastes vocaliques de l'anglais sont filtrés en fonction de leurs contrastes vocaliques maternels. Plus les voyelles de la langue cible sont proches des voyelles de la langue maternelle, plus l'enfant a des difficultés à les reproduire. Il les assimile au prototype de voyelle le plus proche de sa langue maternelle. Les enfants de notre échantillon assimilent tous les contrastes vocaliques de l'anglais [e] au contraste français [ɛ] comme dans les mots *red* et *yellow*, alors que le son produit devrait être plus fermé. De même, la voyelle [ɒ] dans un mot comme *orange* est assimilé au contraste français beaucoup plus central [œ]. La voyelle [I] n'existe pas en français; elle est assimilée à la voyelle [ɛ], plus ouverte. Les problèmes rencontrés avec la voyelle [ə] ne relèvent pas uniquement de l'assimilation, mais également de la structure rythmique de l'anglais. En effet, les syllabes sont plus ou moins dilatées ou au contraire comprimées, voire supprimées, selon le temps qui sépare deux pics accentuels. En syllabe inaccentuée, le timbre de la voyelle [ə] sera en conséquence très neutre et sa durée, très courte. Le français, au contraire, possède une rythmicité syllabique: les enfants ont donc tendance à trop allonger et à trop mettre en relief le timbre de la voyelle [ə] en position inaccentuée.

5.2.2 Les diphtongues et triphtongues

Les enfants n'arrivent pas à reproduire les diphtongues de l'anglais et ils produisent plutôt une succession de deux voyelles. C'est le cas pour [i:] et [u:] qui sont légèrement diphtongués en anglais. Ils produisent les voyelles correspondantes [i] et [u] du français, mais sans diphtongaison. De même, au lieu de la diphtongue [aɪ] dans un mot comme *violet*, les enfants produisent une séquence de deux voyelles trop ouvertes; la transition est trop lente pour produire une diphtongue. Dans le cas de la diphtongue [au] dans un mot comme *brown*, ils produisent une seule voyelle [ʌ], mais celle-ci est très allongée. Tous les enfants échouent à reproduire les diphtongues à cause de leur articulation trop tendue. En effet, la vraie diphtongaison s'explique physiologiquement par une inaptitude à maintenir les organes articulatoires en place pendant l'articulation d'une voyelle longue. Sur un spectrogramme, une diphtongue se caractérise par une grande instabilité des trois premiers formants et par leurs trajectoires divergentes. Nous pouvons observer cette configuration spécifique sur le spectrogramme de l'énoncé *violet*, produit par le locuteur natif (figure n°2) où les formants de la triphtongue [aɪə] sont très instables. Au contraire, sur la figure n°3, les trois formants sont parfaitement stables et caractéristiques de la prononciation de tous les enfants de notre échantillon.

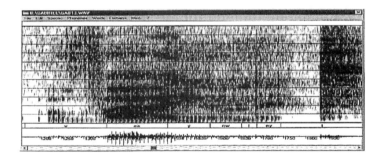

Figure n°2: spectrogramme mot violet *produit par le locuteur natif*

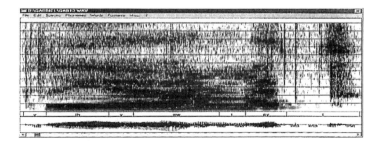

Figure n°3: spectrogramme mot violet *produit par une enfant musicien*

L'enfant ne reproduit par la triphtongue ; par contre, il semble la percevoir, car il compense par une durée allongée le groupe de voyelles correspondant: l'enfant produit à la place de la triphtongue [aɪə], le groupe [ijɔ] qui dure 470 ms, alors que la triphtongue, produite par le locuteur natif, ne dure que 306 ms. Après cette production approximative de l'enfant, le locuteur natif intervient pour le corriger et lui demande de répéter le même mot. Après cette correction, l'enfant réussit à produire une diphtongue, la seule de notre échantillon. La durée de la diphtongue s'est abaissée à 409 ms. L'enfant a réussi à atteindre l'énoncé cible, il est moins dépendant des paramètres prosodiques. La prosodie a joué son rôle de structure d'accueil: une fois qu'elle est en place, l'enfant peut se focaliser sur les contrastes phonétiques. Dans ce cas, nous pensons qu'il y a interférence entre le niveau global et le niveau local. Mais, un seul cas n'est de toute évidence pas suffisant pour conclure; le hasard a pu amener cette unique production correcte.

6   Discussion et conclusion

Ces premiers résultats ne concernent que quatre enfants et ne peuvent bien sûr pas être généralisés, mais montrent des tendances intéressantes. Certains enfants, et spécialement les enfants musiciens, font preuve de grandes capacités à copier la prosodie d'énoncés qu'ils n'ont jamais entendus et ensuite à jouer avec leur contour de hauteur et leur durée afin de les assimiler. Une fois les patterns prosodiques acquis, l'enfant pourra se concentrer sur les contrastes phonétiques. La prosodie semble donc être une étape fondamentale dans le processus d'acquisition d'une langue étrangère. Elle pourrait aider l'enseignant à baliser le *parcours acquisitionnel* de l'apprenant en lui révélant l'état de sa progression (imitation ou jeu). La mise en place des structures prosodiques devrait intervenir avant tout travail de perfectionnement des éléments segmentaux.

En revanche, il n'y a pas de différence significative entre les productions des enfants musiciens et des enfants non musiciens en ce qui concerne les contrastes phonétiques. Ils rencontrent les mêmes problèmes: les contrastes anglais sont assimilés à la structure des contrastes français et les enfants ne peuvent restituer les diphtongues. Pourtant, un des enfants musicien manifeste un comportement intéressant: il exagère les paramètres prosodiques lorsqu'il rencontre une diphtongue. Tout se passe comme s'il percevait le phénomène, mais n'ayant pas les bonnes habitudes articulatoires pour le reproduire, il compense par la durée et la hauteur. Ce phénomène de compensation est-il caractéristique d'une oreille musicale? Nous confronterons ces tendances à une population plus large ultérieurement.

7   Références bibliographiques

BEST, Catherine T. (1993): Learning to Perceive the Sound Pattern of English. Lipsitt: Ablex Publ.
EILERS, Rebecca E.; LYNCH, Michael P.; OLLER, Kimbrough D.; URBANO, Richard C.; WILSON, Paul (1991): Children's perception of native and nonnative musical scales. In: Music Perception 9.1, 121-132.

FERNALD, Anne (1989): Intonation and communication intent in mother's speech to infant's: Is the Melody the Message? In: Child Development 60, 1497-1510.

GARABEDIAN, Michèle (1996): Apprendre les langues étrangères le plus tôt possible à l'école primaire: pourquoi? Pourquoi faire? In: Les Langues à l'Ecole, un Apprentissage? Actes du Colloque. Dijon: IUFM, 13 et 14 mars.

GIACOMI, Alain; HEREDIA, Christine de (1986): Réussites et échecs dans les communications linguistiques entre locuteurs francophones et locuteurs immigrés. In: Langages, décembre, 84, 9-24.

GUBERINA, Pierre (1991): Rôle de la perception auditive dans l'apprentissage précoce des langues. In: Le Français dans le Monde, Recherches et Applications: numéro spécial Enseignants / Apprentissages Précoces des Langues, août-septembre, 65-70.

HAGEGE, Claude (1996): L'Enfant aux Deux Langues. Paris: Odile Jacob.

KONOPCZYNSKI, Gabrielle (1999): L'acquisition du système prosodique de la langue maternelle et ses implications pour l'apprentissage d'une L2. In: Delcloque (ed.): Speech Technology Applications in C.A.L.L., Eurocall'99.

— (1991): Le Langage Emergent: Aspect Vocaux et Mélodiques. Hambourg: Buske Verlag.

KUHL, Patricia (1994): Introduction to Communication Sciences and Disorders. San Diego: Singular Publishing Group Inc.

LURIA, Alexander R. (1974): L'Enfant Retardé Mental. Paris: Privat.

PENFIELD, WILDER; Roberts L. (1959): Speech and Brain Mechanisms. Princeton: Princeton University Press.

PIAGET, Jean (1937): La Construction du Réel chez l'Enfant. Paris: Delachaux et Niestlé.

PIKE, Kenneth (1947): Phonemics. University of Michigan Press, Ann Arbor.

ROSCH, Eleanor H. (1973): Natural categories. In: Cognitive Psychology, mai, 4/3, 328-350.

TREHUB, Sandra E.; BULL, Dale; THORPE, Leigh A. (1984): Infant's perception of melodies: the role of melodic contour. In Child Development 55, 824-830.

TROUBETSKOY, Nicolas S. (1949): Principes de Phonologie. Paris: Klinsieck.

The Accessibility of Universal Grammar to Turkish Adults Learning English as a Second Language: Head-complement Parameter Resetting

F. Özden Ekmekci, Cem Can

Introduction

Regarding the role of Universal Grammar (UG) in L2 acquisition, three logical possibilities have been articulated:

- The first is the *no access* hypothesis, which claims that no aspect of UG is available to the L2 learner.
- The second is the *direct access* (*full/continuous access*) hypothesis, which claims that UG in its entirety constrains L2 acquisition (Flynn 1988; Schachter 1988; White 1985, 1990; Towell & Hawkins 1994) .
- According to the third, called the *indirect access* (*partial access*) hypothesis, only L1-instantiated principles and parameter-values of UG are available to the learner.

Like most of the researchers in the related field, we reject the first hypothesis because we believe that UG provides an answer to the poverty-of-stimulus argument in L2 as well as in L1 acquisition (White 1989). Therefore, we will be investigating the validity of the last two hypotheses on Turkish adults learning English.

English and Turkish have some mismatching values considering the parametric variations like the *Pro-drop Parameter, Governing Category Parameter*, and *Head-direction Parameter*. Since the head-direction parameter has not received a comparative in-depth study, this particular study aims at contributing the current debate on the issue by investigating the accessibility of UG in the acquisition of the head-direction parameter in Turkish adult learners learning English as an L2. According to the head-complement parameter, languages are classified as left and right branching. Figure 1 illustrates this parametric variation between English and Turkish.

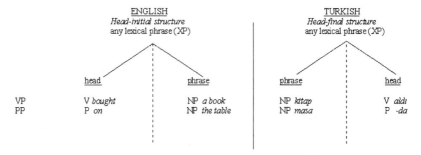

Figure 1: Head-direction Parameter in English and Turkish.

Turkish learners, equipped with the head-last value of the parameter, need sufficient positive evidence to discover the head-first value employed in English during the acquisition process. Whether or not such a parametric conflict between L1 and L2 causes difficulties in the construction of L2 grammar is an open and controversial question in SLA (see White 1989, 1996; Eubank 1991, 1994; Gass & Selinker 1994; Tarone et al. 1994; Towell & Hawkins 1994; Cook 1995; Clashen 1996; Ritchie & Bhatie 1996; Ellis 1997; Flynn et al. 1998). Most of these studies, however, focus either on different principles and parameters other than head-direction parameter or on L2 learners of different languages other than the Turkish. Moreover, these studies are methodologically limited in that they rely, in large, on the grammaticality judgement tasks (GJT), which are criticised by many researchers (Lakshamanan & Teranishi 1994; Munnich et al. 1994) for lacking validity in indicating the learners' actual competence in L2. Therefore, to increase the validity of our study, we have employed two other types of tasks aside from GJT.

Methodology

Subjects

A total of 45 subjects were randomly chosen from high school and university level students and grouped under three levels (15 subjects in each) according to their proficiency levels obtained from the University of Michigan placement test. Since the age is a crucial consideration, the subjects chosen were all above the critical age period ranging from 16 to 20. The following precautions have been taken to eliminate the extraneous variables:

- none of the subjects have lived in a country where English is spoken as a native language;
- subjects speaking an L1 (such as Arabic and Kurdish) other than Turkish have been excluded from the study to avoid any interference which might stem from parametric similarity between that language and English;
- the teachers of subjects are native speakers of Turkish;
- since gender is not taken as a variable in this study, subjects have been randomly chosen regardless of their sexes.

Instruments

As instruments, three tasks namely Grammaticality Judgement (GJT), Elicited Imitation (EI), and Jigsaw (JT) were utilized. Just a week before the assessment, the subjects have been provided with the meanings of all unknown lexical items in the three tasks in a two two-hour training session to prevent any failure in their judgements originating from misconception. Moreover, the instructions in English for the tasks have been orally translated to Turkish in order to clear any ambiguity regarding the performance of the task.

a) *The GJT*

The GJT is given in a multiple-choice format to examine the subjects' grammaticality judgement ability by choosing the right value of the head-complement parameter for the complements embedded in VPs and NPs in the total of 92 sentences.

Phrase	Head	Complement	Phrase	Head	Complement
NP	N	PP	VP	V	NP
		S			D.O.
		that-clause			I.O.
		whether-clause			PP
		for-clause			AP
		wh-clause			S
		Red.Rel.-clause			*that-clause*
					if-clause
					infinitive-clause (+ subj.)
					infinitive-clause (- subj.)
					causative
					bare infinitive-clause
					ing participle-clause(+ sbj.)
					-ing participle-clause (- sbj.)
					-ed participle-clause
					whether-clause (- subj.)
					whether-clause (+ subj.)
					wh-clause
					wh-clause, to infinitive

Table 1: The distribution of the types of complements included in tasks

The subjects were allotted approximately 15-seconds per sentence to judge the grammaticality of a task item using their intuition rather than relying on prescriptive grammar. Two days after the assessment of the GJT, subjects were interviewed one by one to understand on what basis they have made their correct judgements of their Not OK sentences. If no explanation of any modification of the Not OK sentences was provided, these items were evaluated as incorrect in spite of their correct judgements previously made.

b) *The EIT*

In the EIT subjects have been asked to repeat 50 sentences (18 with NPs and 32 with VPs) designed to tap data on their current state regarding the acquisition of the head-complement parameter in English. These sentences were chosen from a corpus created from the printed materials prepared by native speakers, and were controlled as much as possible in terms of length (not more than 15 words) due to the restriction imposed on the short term memory (Eubank 1989; Flynn 1989; Bley-Vroman & Chaudron 1994; Munnich, Flynn and Martohardjono 1994).

c) *The JPT*

JPT comprises the same sentences introduced in EIT only with the words scrambled in each sentence. The subjects were asked to formulate a grammatical sentence out of these scrambled words. Their failure to rewrite the sentences correctly would suggest the probability of L1 transfer, and the correct formulation would be an indication of their access to UG.

Data Analysis and Conclusion

The data collected from the three tasks was analyzed focusing on the use of NPs and VPs in three different tasks.

NP in GJT, EIT, and JPT: Tables 2 and 3 display the ANOVA results of judgements of the OK and Not OK sentences that include various complements implemented in NPs in the GJT. According to Table 2, the correct judgements of all the OK sentences except 22 and 90, which are in the form of reduced relative clauses, are not statistically significant among groups. In the Not OK counterparts of these sentences (see Table 3), however, there is no significant difference among the learners in different groups. There is a gradual increase in the correct judgements of these sentences parallel to the increase in their language proficiency.

(Red. Rel. Cl.)

22. The rules *allowing public access to wilderness areas* need to be reconsidered.
90. I come from a city *located in the southern part of the country.*

	Mean			Standard Deviation			
Item #	Beginner	Intermediate	Advanced	Beginner	Intermediate	Advanced	* F
22	.40	.80	.93	.50	.25	.41	.0024
90	.60	1.00	1.00	.50	0	0	.0004

*Table: 2 ANOVA results of the each NP items according to the levels (OK) [Note: Score range = 0-1, N = 45, df = 2, *Statistically significant (p ≤ .05)]*

	Mean			Standard Deviation			
Item #	Beginner	Intermediate	Advanced	Beginner	Intermediate	Advanced	* F
29	.06	.33	.46	.51	.48	.25	.0480
79	.13	.40	.66	.50	.48	.35	.0098

*Table 3: ANOVA results of the each NP items according to the levels (Not OK) [Note: Score range = 0-1, N = 45, df = 2, *Statistically significant (p ≤ .05)]*

The correct judgements for sentences 29 and 79, on the other hand, reflect a statistically significant difference between the beginner group and the intermediate and advanced groups. These two sentences include PP complements embedded in NPs violating the English value of the head-complement parameter.

(PP)

29. *Nobody can guess *about the future* his dreams.

79. *None of his friends knew his *electronics* interest in.

Regarding PP complements, the rate of both OK and Not OK judgement increase among the groups parallel to their level of proficiency. In the GJT, the other complements included in the NPs in both OK and Not OK sentences to be judged reveal no significant difference across the groups of different language proficiency. A similar increase is observed in the number of statistically significant correct judgements in NPs in the EIT. For instance, items 9-14 (see table 4) yield statistically significant results among the groups with a gradual increase from the beginner group towards the advanced one. The distribution of wh-words in these wh-clauses in the NPs are as follows:

Item #	Mean			Standard Deviation			* F
	Beginner	Intermediate	Advanced	Beginner	Intermediate	Advanced	
9	.46	.80	.93	.51	.41	.25	.0100
10	.66	1	.93	.48	0	.25	.0157
11	.53	.73	1	.51	.45	0	.0098
12	.40	.80	.93	.50	.41	.25	.0002
13	.53	.73	.93	.51	.25	.45	.0460
14	.40	.60	.86	.50	.50	.35	.0288

*Table 4: ANOVA results of the each NP items in EIT according to the levels [Note. Score range = 0-1, N = 45, df = 2, *Statistically significant ($p \leq .05$)]*

(Wh-clause)

9. I do not remember the name of the girl *who made a speech at the meeting yesterday.*
10. The students *who had been absent from the class for a month* were dismissed.

Items 11 and 12 have wh- clauses starting with *which.*

11. The music *which my girl friend and I listened to last night* was very good.
12. The meeting *which we will attend tonight* is organised by my university.

Items 13 and 14 have wh-clauses starting with *whose.*

13. My sister teaches a class for students *whose native language is not English.*
14. I have to call the man *whose umbrella I accidentally picked up after the meeting.*

Items 15 and 16 comprising *whom* as complementizer have not been found significantly different among the groups. This may be due to the specific wh-word (whom) utilized as a complementizer in the wh-clause.

We see an increase in the number of statistically significant items across groups. In fact, all the items except items 3 (that-clause), 7 (for-clause), 10 (wh-clause) in JPT results regarding the NPs reflect statistically different results. We observe similar results in the counterparts of these three items.

Item #	Mean Beginner	Mean Intermediate	Mean Advanced	Standard Deviation Beginner	Standard Deviation Intermediate	Standard Deviation Advanced	* F
2	0	.06	.40	0	.25	.50	.0038
4	.66	.93	1	.48	.25	0	.0157
5	.66	1	1	.48	0	0	.0024
6	.53	1	.93	.51	0	.25	.0007
9	.80	1	1	.41	0	0	.0393
12	.40	.53	.86	.50	.51	.35	.0254
13	.60	1	1	.50	0	0	.0004
14	.60	1	1	.50	0	0	.0004
15	.53	.93	.93	.51	.25	.25	.0051
16	.40	.80	1	.50	.41	0	.0003
17	.13	.66	.80	.35	.48	.41	.0002

*Table 5: ANOVA results of the each NP items in JPT according to the levels [Note. Score range = 0-1, N = 45, df = 2, *Statistically significant (p ≤ .05)]*

VP in GJT, EIT, and JPT

Tables 6 and 7 display the ANOVA results of judgements of the OK and Not OK sentences with various complements embedded in VPs in the GJT. The ANOVA results of each VP item according to different levels (see table 6), subjects' judgements on sentences 53, 13, 16, 59, 72, and 26 demonstrate statistically significant differences across groups. Among these sentences, 53 (This academic appears *unintelligent*.) includes an AP as a complement embedded in VP; in 13 a that-clause is embedded in VP (The White House spokesman says *that crisis between those two countries will end soon*.); in 16 VP comprises an if-clause (An aerosol spray can will explode *if you throw it into a fire*.); in 59 an infinitive-clause with a subject is included in VP (They allow *people to fish at this lake*.); in 72 there is an –ing participle clause with a subject placed in VP (The children listen *to the birds singing early in the morning*.); in 26 a wh-clause with a to-infinitive is embedded in VP (They always discuss *how much to pay the waiter*.).

Item #	Mean Beginner	Mean Intermediate	Mean Advanced	Standard Deviation Beginner	Standard Deviation Intermediate	Standard Deviation Advanced	* F
53	.66	1	1	0	0	.48	.0024
13	.73	1	1	.45	0	0	.0105
16	.13	.33	.66	.35	.48	.48	.0079
59	.66	.60	1	.48	0	.50	.0222
72	.60	1	1	.50	0	0	.0004
22	.40	.80	.93	.50	.25	.41	.0024
26	.53	.86	.86	.51	.35	.35	.0491

*Table 6: ANOVA results of the each VP items according to the levels (OK) [Note. Score range = 0-1, N = 45, df = 2, *Statistically significant (p ≤ .05)]*

Although the judgements on these sentences reveal significant differences among groups, judgements of their counterparts with similar structures, on the other hand, have been found insignificant (see Table 7 and 8). In GJT, regarding the Not OK of VP items, only 81, which has an AP as a complement in VP (*These apples strange smell), and 37, which has a –ed participle clause embedded in VP (*My sister her dress cleaned needs to get) are statistically significant across the groups.

Item #	Mean			Standard Deviation			* F
	Beginner	Intermediate	Advanced	Beginner	Intermediate	Advanced	
81	0	.13	.40	0	.35	.50	.0122
37	0	0	.20	0	.41	0	.0393

Table 7: ANOVA results of the each VP items according to the levels (Not OK) [Note. Score range = 0-1, N = 45, df = 2, *Statistically significant (p ≤.05)]

The ANOVA results regarding the VP items in EIT (see table 8) indicate that we see that the results of learners' judgements on sentences 20, 23, 24, 25, 26, 27, 32, 35, 36, 38, 40, 42, 43, 44, 45, 46, 47, and 50 are found significant as opposed to GJT. As in the other tasks, the number of the sentences revealing significance increases gradually across groups.

Item #	Mean			Standard Deviation			* F
	Beginner	Intermediate	Advanced	Beginner	Intermediate	Advanced	
20	.53	.93	.93	.51	.25	.25	.0051
23	.53	.86	1	.51	.35	0	.0031
24	.46	.86	.93	.51	.35	.25	.0041
25	.40	.93	.86	.50	.25	.35	.0008
26	.40	.66	.93	.50	.48	.25	.0065
27	.40	.86	.93	.50	.35	.25	.0008
32	.46	.60	1	.51	.50	0	.0032
35	.53	.93	1	.51	.25	0	.0007
36	.53	.80	1	.51	.41	0	.0068
38	.33	.66	.86	.48	.48	.35	.0079
40	.33	.60	.93	.48	.50	.25	.0020
43	.40	.60	.86	.50	.50	.35	.0288
44	.53	.93	.80	.51	.25	.41	.0332
45	0	.20	.93	0	.41	.25	.000
46	.40	.80	.93	.50	.41	.25	.0024
47	0	.13	.66	0	.35	.48	.000
50	.26	.73	.93	.45	.45	.25	.00202

Table 8: ANOVA results of the each VP items in EIT according to the levels [Note. Score range = 0-1, N = 45, df = 2, *Statistically significant (p ≤.05)]

In Table 9, the types of complements embedded in VPs are presented.

Phrase	Head	Complement	Item #
NP	N	N	1, 2
		S	
		that-clause	3, 4
		whether-clause	5, 6
		for-clause	7, 8
		wh-clause	9-16
		red.Rel.-clause	17, 18
NP total			18
VP	V	NP	
		direct object	19, 20
		indirect object	21, 22
		PP	23, 24
		AP	25, 26
		S	26, 27
		NP + PP	27, 28
		that-clause	29, 30
		if-clause	31,. 32
		infinitive-clause (+ subject	33, 34
		infinitive-clause (- subject	35, 36
		causative	37, 38
		bare infinitive-clause	39, 40
		wh-clause, to infinitive	41, 42
		-ing participle-clause (+ subject	43, 44
		-ing participle-clause (- subject	45, 46
		-ed participle-clause	47, 48
		whether, to infinitive	49, 50
VP total			32
TOTAL			50

Table 9: NP item numbers and the corresponding complements in EIT and JP

Table 10 presents the ANOVA results of the VP items in JPT. In this task, similar to EIT, there is an increase in the number of sentences among the groups.

Item #	Mean			Standard Deviation			* F
	Beginner	Intermediate	Advanced	Beginner	Intermediate	Advanced	
19	.66	1	1	.48	0	0	.0024
22	0	.33	.33	0	.48	.48	.0393
23	.40	.86	1	.50	.35	0	.0001
24	.80	1	1	.41	0	0	.0393
25	.60	.93	1	.50	.25	0	.0038
26	.80	1	1	.41	0	0	.0393
27	.66	1	1	.48	0	0	.0024
28	.60	1	1	.50	0	0	.0004
29	.60	1	1	.50	0	0	.0004
32	.26	.80	1	.45	.41	0	0
33	.53	.80	. 93	.51	.41	.25	.0332

Item #	Mean Beginner	Mean Intermediate	Mean Advanced	Standard Deviation Beginner	Standard Deviation Intermediate	Standard Deviation Advanced	* F
34	.60	1	1	.50	0	0	.0004
36	.60	1	1	.50	0	0	.0004
37	.60	1	.86	.50	0	.35	.0122
38	.73	1	1	.45	0	0	.0105
41	.46	.93	1	.51	.25	0	.0001
43	.53	.93	1	.51	.25	0	.0007
48	.20	.86	.86	.41	.35	.35	0
49	.73	1	1	.45	0	0	.0105
50	.73	1	1	.45	0	0	.0105

*Table 10: ANOVA results of the each VP items in JT according to the levels [Note. Score range = 0-1, N = 45, df = 2, *Statistically significant (p ≤.05)]*

These sentences are namely 19, 23, 24, 25, 26, 27, 28, 29, 32, 33, 34, 36, 37, 38, 41, 43, 48, 49, and 50. These items and their corresponding types of complements are also presented in Table 9.

Conclusion

As can be deduced from the analysis of the instruments, data obtained from each task, namely GJT, EIT, and JPT, yielded different results due to the nature of the performance each task evaluates. For instance, while the GJT task evaluates the knowledge of (un)grammaticality, the EIT and the JPT measure the subjects' performances on the reconstructions. GJT is not adequate enough to yield a reliable result. The other tasks, namely EIT and JPT, prove to be better indicators since errors can be traced to the grammatical abilities of the subjects and not left out to chance.

When we evaluate the data in terms of the accessibility to UG in adult L2 acquisition, we arrive at the following conclusions:

- The learners do not have a direct access to UG in the L2 acquisition process. If they had a direct access, the head-complement parameter setting would operate in their L2 acquisition exactly as it does in L1. That is, learners would pick up the L2 value of the head-complement parameter when they are exposed to the L2 input that displays the position of that value. In this case the Turkish adult learners would start out with the correct L2 parameter value and not accept any interference from their L1. In other words, L2 acquisition process would take place automatically, and the subjects' native language would not interfere. The obtained results, however, indicate that the errors of the learners reflect their adoption of the Turkish value for the head-complement parameter in most cases.
- The overall analysis of the data obtained from the three tasks support the hypothesis that adult L2 learners have an *indirect access* to UG in their acquisition of the head-complement parameter. This hypothesis predicts that learners transfer their L1 value to the L2 under the assumption that this value also applies to the L2 data. Thus, they initially produce incorrect sentences, but as their learn-

ing proceeds, they gradually reset their parameter to accord with the value of the L2.

Accordingly, we might claim that Turkish L2 learners first transfer their head final L1 value to English, but, as their learning proceeds, they eventually switch from their L1 value to the correct English value. At this point, we face a problem regarding the interpretation of our obtained data. How can we decide on the reason of this eventual attainment of the correct parameter value? Is it an outcome of the general learning strategies or is it an outcome of the parameter resetting process? In our opinion, in order to answer this question, the acquisition process of English as a first language should be looked into from this perspective.

Regarding the head-complement parameter setting in the acquisition of English as L1, Radford (1990) states that

"given parameters are categorically based, once a child is able to parse an utterance such as 'Close the door!', he will be able to infer from the fact that the verb *close* in English precedes its complement *the door*, that *all verbs* in English precede their complements (since Universal Grammar excludes the possibility that some verbs may precede and others follow their complements). If we further assume that (in the unmarked case, i.e. 'normally') a given parameter has the same value across categories, then the child will also be able to hypothesize that not just verbs, but all other categories (adjectives, nouns, categories, etc.) likewise precede their complements in English" (Radford 1990:61).

According to Radford (1990), setting the head-complement parameter *requires minimal linguistic experience*, which means once the head-initial value is set for a given phrase, it will automatically be set for all phrases at the same time.

Under the light of the above discussion, it might be claimed that only a revealed parallelism between L2 data and L1 data (both English in this case) could support the resetting hypothesis. In other words, if the Turkish adult learners of English were observed to assign the head-initial value correctly to complements in the phrases under discussion (NP and VP) in a statistically equal manner, resetting view would be supported. In this study, we find the evidence of an unequal distribution of the assignment of the head-initial value across complements within NP and VP phrases. Consequently, basing our claim on the Window of Opportunity Hypothesis proposed by Schachter (1988), we might argue that, after a certain age L2 acquisition takes place in terms of certain nonlinguistic problem-solving and learning strategies such as analogising, hypothesis testing.

References

ELLIS, R. (1997): SLA research and language teaching. Oxford: Oxford University Press.

EUBANK, L. (ed.). (1991): Point counterpoint: Universal Grammar and second language acquisition. Amsterdam: John Benjamins.

COOK, V. J. (1985): Chomsky's Universal Grammar and second language learning. In: Applied Linguistics 6, 2-18.

CLASHEN, H. (ed.) (1996): General perspectives on language acquisition. Amsterdam: John Benjamins.

FLYNN, S. (1987): A parameter setting model of L2 acquisition: Experimental studies in anaphora. Dordrecht: Reidel.

FLYNN, S.; MARTOHARDJONO, G.; ONEIL, W. (eds.): (1998). The generative study of second language acquisition. London: Lawrence Erlbaum.

GASS, S.; SELINKER, L. (1994): Second language acquisition. London: Lawrence Erlbaum.

LAKSHMANAN, U.; TERANISHI, K. (1994): Preferences versus grammaticality judgements: Some methodological issues concerning the governing category parameter in second-language acquisition. In Tarone; Gass; Cohen: 185-206.

MUNNICH, E.; FLYNN, S.; MARTOHARDJONO, G. (1994). Elicited imitation and grammaticality judgement tasks: What they measure and how they relate to each other. In Tarone; Gass; Cohen: 207-226.

RADFORD, A. (1990). Syntactic theory and the acquisition of English syntax. London: Blackwell.

RITCHIE, C. R.; BHATIA, T. K. (eds.) (1996): Handbook of Second Language Acquisition. New York: Academic Press.

SCHACHTER, J. (1988): Second language acquisition and its relationship to Universal Grammar. Applied Linguistics 9, 219-235.

TARONE, E. E.; GASS, S. M.; COHEN, A. D. (eds.) (1994): Research methodology in second-language acquisition. London: Lawrence Erlbaum.

TOWEL, R.; HAWKINS, R. (1994): Approaches to second language acquisition. Bristol: Multilingual Matters.

WHITE, L. (1996): Universal Grammar and second language acquisition: Current trends and new directions. In Ritchie, C. R.; Bhatia, T. K. (eds.): Handbook of Second Language Acquisition. New York: Academic Press, 85-116.

— (1990): Universal Grammar and second language acquisition. Amsterdam: Benjamins.

— (1985): The acquisition of parameterised grammars: Subjacency in second language acquisition. In: Second Language Acquisition 1, 1-17.

How is Communication Achieved by a Second Language Learner?[1]

Ana Paulina Peña Pollastri

1   Introduction

Language is a feature unique to human beings. Its acquisition in childhood, as a mother tongue or first language, has led to a variety of theories and interesting research projects. On those bases, second language acquisition theories have tried to determine, among other things, whether the two processes are alike in nature and sequence, which are the personal factors that contribute to the process, which are the external influences more likely to affect acquisition, what are the effects of instruction in learning a second language, and which are the optimal conditions for instruction to contribute to learning. Considering that the acquisition of a language is, in its own right, an extremely complex process, it seems reasonable to consider that all those factors have a share in the success of a second language learner's goal, which is to be able to communicate effectively with native speakers. As to the elements that make up communicative competence, the sources cited by Larsen-Freeman and Long (1994) seem to agree in the fact that communicative competence refers to the ability to produce grammatically correct and meaningful language, to act according to generally agreed social patterns, to engage in a conversation, and to use non-linguistic, besides linguistic, strategies to achieve communication. It is along the lines of communicative competence that I undertook this research project. It was geared towards analyzing the factors operating in a second language learner which contribute to make the learner able to communicate in a second language environment. My attention was focused, accordingly, on the developmental state of the language, and on the strategies used for interaction together with the influence of a native-speaker counterpart.

2   The study

The study was carried out with the help of Makiko, 19 years old, Japanese native speaker, OPIE (Ohio Program of Intensive English) and Anthropology student at Ohio University, with a six-month length of residence in the United States. Being a foreign student myself, I counted on the cooperation of Jan, US undergraduate Linguistic student at Ohio University, in most of the study sessions. The research methodology was chosen according to the purpose pursued in each section of the project. The data evaluation was done on the bases of stated criteria from different sources, and the conclusions were drawn accordingly.

---

[1]   This is a revised version of a paper written in the Winter 1996 for the Department of Linguistics, Ohio University. I am grateful to Dr. Beverly Olson Flanigan of Ohio University for her valuable comments on its earlier versions.

Considering Makiko, she fitted Corder's (1974) adult learner's characterization in that she had her maturational process complete, her language behavior developed, and particular motivations (namely, pursuing an academic degree in a US university) stimulating her acquisition process, I hypothesized that she should be an active learner, not only in formal instruction but also in social interaction, and thus truly involved in her own language development. It was yet to be discovered which areas of communicative competence she was strong in.

3   The spoken language

3.1   Data collection

To find out the extent to which Makiko had acquired grammatical patterns in her oral production, my methodological approach was cross-sectional: I used the data collected in one particular session, almost at the beginning of the study period. I was a participant observer and used a *semi-structured* natural communication task, a category in between Dulay, Burt, and Krashen's (1982) extremes. I provided the subject with four pictures depicting a girl, a young man, several women doing outdoor activities, and a group of men and a woman holding a business meeting. No particular questions were prepared to go along with the pictures, although they had been selected to elicit some grammatical features in which problems were assumed to arise: irregular plurals, masculine/feminine pronouns, use of adjectives and progressive tenses (present and hopefully past). She was asked to look at the pictures, and then comment on the appearance, feelings and activities of the people portrayed. The session was recorded and later transcribed for analysis.

3.2   Qualitative assessment

The error analysis was carried out by identifying errors by means of Corder's (1971) procedure and categorizing them according to Richards' (1974) classification. It rendered an inventory of errors, the most outstanding of which are included in Table 1, and proved useful to identify the problem categories: Makiko showed problems mainly for producing verbs (present progressive, third person singular, *be* singular and plural, and present progressive instead of simple present), plurals, and pronouns. She also failed to use articles and was confused about prepositions (which was not surprising for a beginner), among other errors.

  Although these data truly represented the profile of a learner in rather early stages of grammatical development, I felt somewhat uncertain as to whether they should be considered problem areas on fair grounds – considering errors may represent items in the process of being acquired – since most of the items were alternately produced right and wrong, and this kind of analysis did not provide me with the clue.

3.3   Quantitative assessment

The other alternative was to perform a quantitative analysis by scoring the same speech sample using the *Bilingual Syntax Measure* (Burt, Dulay, Hernández Chávez 1976) test, considered at the time as the only tool that allowed a comparison of the errors produced by one learner against his or her own complete language sample. It renders a *Syntax Acquisition Index* (SAI), which

> "reflects the degree of grammaticality of the subject's total speech corpus, or of a randomly selected sample of utterances ... at a given point in time" (Dulay, Burt, Krashen 1982:253)

and indicates one of three levels of proficiency, all of which are matched to a table in which grammatical items are ordered in a seemingly developmental sequence proposed by the test designers.

Category	Error Type	Examples
Errors in prod. of verb groups	*be* omitted before *verb-ing*	Somebody skating. She just looking up.
	verb stem for *be + verb-s*	She really look happy. She have a Christmas present.
	Wrong form of *be*	These shoes is for running. Four persons is, are running ....
Errors in the use of articles	Omission of *the*	she might be boss ... ... wear same clothes ...
	Omission of *a*	She has video tape. I have strong muscle pain.
Errors in the use of plural	Irregular plural for both singular and plural	This men is handsome. This women hiking ...
	Irregular plural + *s*	The mens have ties ... Two of the mens are ...
	Mass nouns + *s*	I can see a lot of natures, trees, waters, ... In this picture there are trees and soils.
Errors in the use of prep.	*in* instead of *to*	One more people attended in this conference I came in Athens last year.
	Omission of preposition	... looks his own notes. ... attending some clubs.

Table 1: Error analysis outcome for Makiko.

To perform the test, after downsizing the original speech sample by taking every third meaningful utterance from the transcript, I scored the resulting 28 utterances according to the *Bilingual Syntax Measure* procedures. Makiko's SAI was 81, which put her in Level 3, though apparently not far from Level 4. By placing her score on the Burt, Dulay, and Hernández Chávez' (1976) scale (Table 2), it is possible to see that she was assumed to have already acquired word order and the use of pronouns, which she roughly had. It is also evident that she would have had to acquire seven additional structures before completing Level 4. In order to know how far she was from there, I analyzed the scores further categorizing her errors, counting the points she had lost in each category and working out a percentage by category against the total points the analyzed samples had lost (56.5 points). The resulting percentages, added to Table 2, show that almost 72 per cent of those errors were concentrated on the grammatical items included in Level 4. A couple of conclusions were drawn as a result of this. First, although the learner did not master completely the items included in her SAI level, she was well into the way of acquiring the items that would take her into the intermediate level. Second, the acquisition order reflected in the table, though not strict, is representative of the degree of difficulty that each item poses to a second language learner, and can be reliable.

On the whole, Makiko's second language seemed to be undergoing a more or less predictable development, although at the time of the study there seemed to be no specific item acquired but a series of items under active acquisition. It is significant that for those items being developed there was a constant self-correction (evidence of her consciousness on the whole process), while there was systematic avoidance of the ones which were beyond her capabilities.

Grammatical categories (as to acquisition order)	Level	Subject errors
Word order	Level 3 (Survival)	5.3%
Pronoun case	SAI 45-84 (*81* for Makiko)	13.3%
Progressive -*ing*		14.2%
Copula singular		5.3%
Short plural	Level 4 (Intermediate)	10.6%
Auxiliary singular		14.2%
Article	SAI 85-94	11.5%
Copula plural		5.3%
Auxiliary plural		10.6%
Past regular		0.0%
Present indicative	Level 5 (Proficient)	2.6%
Possessive -*s*		0.0%
Long plural	SAI 95-100	0.0%
Conditional auxiliary		0.0%
Past irregular		1.8%
Perfect auxiliary		3.5%
Past participle		1.8%

Table 2: Acquisition order and SAI levels against Makiko's performance (adapted from Burt, Dulay, Hernández Chávez 1976:20).

4   The strategies

4.1   Data collection

To focus on the communication strategies Makiko used for interaction and the way in which interaction with a native speaker could influence her language performance, I used a longitudinal approach comparing the data from five one-hour sessions carried out during four weeks (January 24 to February 21). During those sessions, my native-speaker colleague's participation was crucial, but no communication task was structured, since the goal of the study was to observe the spontaneous language produced by both participants. I was an observer and sometimes a participant in the conversations, during each of which one half-hour segment was recorded and later transcribed for analysis.

4.2   Non-native speaker communication strategies

Tarone, Cohen, and Dumas (1983:5) define a communication strategy as

"a systematic attempt by the learner to express or decode meaning in the target language, in situations where the appropriate systematic target language rules have not been formed".

Out of the categories typified by Tarone (Larsen-Freeman; Long 1996), Makiko resorted mostly to simplifying the syntax of her utterances, miming, appealing for assistance, avoiding a topic, or abandoning a message by semantic interference. Her attitude in using those resources, however, evolved throughout the study period. Table 3 shows some of those examples.

Makiko used syntactic simplification most of the times she found herself urged to give details about a certain topic throughout the study period. Her assistance appeal strategies, however, were varied, becoming more elaborate by the end of the study period. During the first conversation, she mimed to elicit specific vocabulary and repeated the new word in order to learn it. Later on, she silently appealed for assistance, and again repeated the new lexical item. In the latest instances, however, she was able to turn those appeals into explicit requests for information. It is apparent that she chose to avoid the topic whenever she lacked the specific English vocabulary for a particular topic, although she improved in this as well. In the first session she could not talk about stray dogs and cats in Japan and she simply put an end to the topic. On the last conversation, however, she acknowledged at the very beginning that she did not know about tea ceremonies in Japan, but later on she made an effort to make herself understood: she struggled to express the abstract concept of family traditions for which she clearly did not have the appropriate vocabulary, until she got to the concreteness of the ceremony itself and indirectly explained why she did not know about it. In the early conversation sessions she directly abandoned a topic which was not semantically clear for her. These examples show Makiko as an attentive and active participant in the conversation. She profited from her interaction with her conversation partners to enlarge her vocabulary and acquire new conversation strategies, thus shifting form gesticulative to linguistic strategic resources during the study period.

Communication Strategy		Example
Syntactic simplification		J: What's the name of that? M: Uhm ... uhm ... an entrance exam. Many senior student take entrance exam to go university. Just February. You have to take February or March. I don't know exactly the name, so kind of ... We call just entrance exam.
Appeal for assistance	Mime	M: ... and keep them [dogs] with ... (mime) J: Collar M: Collar, and, with the name and number. P: And how do you get that number? M: Uhm ... when they got the ... (mime) P: Vaccination? M: Yeah, the vaccinations ...
	Implicit appeal for assistance	M: I can't bring the fruit from the ... uhm P: The supermarket? M: No, no, uhm ..., uhm ..., the ..., the ... P: The dining-room! M: Yeah! From dining-room.
	Explicit appeal for assistance	M: What's a quiz team?
Topic avoidance	End topic	P: Do you have that problem in Japan? M: Uhm ...,uhm ..., I don't know.
	Make effort to continue	M: It's very special and uhm ... I cannot ... how to, how to ...uhm ... how to work on this ceremony ... uhm ... I don't know! (same conversation, later) M: There are a couple ... families. It's ... which are ... say ... they are ... and they just as ... good ... to send ... the tea ... Ah! How to say it! Uhm ... There are couple families and they trace ... uhm ... kind of a ... rules tea ceremony and if I want to know about tea ceremony, how to do that, I have to belong to one of the families, so ...
Topic abandonment		P: Do they use it [bike] for going to work? M: Uhm ... P: For going to work. M: Going to work ...? P: By bike, by motorbike. M: Uhm ... P: Do they use a motorbike instead of a car to go downtown? M Uhm ... I think both very useful to go ... to go anywhere because ... uhm ... Japan is very narrow, so ...

Table 3: Makiko's communication strategies in interaction with a native speaker.

4.3   Native speaker strategies

As regards the tactics Jan used, she very much resembled the native speaker characterized by Long (1983) in that she was not at all concentrated on speech modifications (she actually sounded completely natural) but rather on adjusting herself to a conversation pattern that would enhance comprehension in her non-native partner, which can be observed in some examples included in Table 4.

The native speaker basically concentrated on comprehension checks and used several tactics at the suspicion that there was a lack of understanding. There were instances in which she clarified utterances, either her own or from the other conversation partner. She generally tried, however, to include explanations or to offer choices that would help her listener follow the conversation. It is noticeable that in all cases, Jan tried to make Makiko understand what the conversation was about so as to keep it going, and she was successful in doing it most of the times. She was a positive counterpart for an alert non-native speaker developing a second language.

Native Speaker Strategy	Example
Comprehension check	J: Do you elect class officers? M: Class officers? J: Do you know what that is? M: Ehm ..., I don't. J: Every class in high-school elect three or four kids to represent them ... M: Ah ..., but in Japan usually two people, so ...
Clarification of other's utterance	P: When do you do the tea ceremony? M: When ...? J: Do you do this every ⌈day, M: ⌊No ...⌋ or once ⌈a week, J: M: ⌊No ...⌋ J: or ... M: No, we call tea ceremony, but it not actually ceremony ...
Clarification of own utterance	J: Is there a certain age that you have to be [to get a driver's license]? M: What's age? J: A certain age before you can go to driving school? M: A certain age? J: Because in the US we have to be at least ⌈sixteen M: ⌊Ah, yes!⌋ J: before you can go to driving school. M: Ah, yes! Eighteen ... in Japan.

Table 4: Native speaker tactics in interaction with non-native speaker.

4.4   Conversational routines

Conversational routines, as defined by Richards and Sukwiwat (1983:114) are those utterances that

> "recur, are predictable, and are associated with particular social situations and with particular types of interaction."

Their acquisition by a non-native speaker is, thus, a significant step towards fluency. At the time of the study, Makiko still used simple routines, such as: *Ah, I know* to show comprehension; *how do I say?*, or *how to say?* to allow herself time to think (which she actually adopted after hearing Jan using it); or *it's cool* to express liking or admiration.

She lacked, however, many of the routines produced by native speakers in everyday social situations, such as the additional remarks upon meeting someone or saying good-bye, or the spontaneous comments that any given situation generates. Because of the strong association between these routines and each particular culture (Richards, Sukwiwat 1983), it is fair to assume that she had not been immersed in our western culture long enough to acquire and produce them spontaneously and unconsciously.

Considering that both learner strategies and influence from conversation partners play a critical role in the pursue of communication, it was worthwhile to analyze this non-native speaker' s ability for interaction and conversational routines in an English speaking environment concurrently with the native-speaker tactics. It was observed that all the factors considered here – strategies, tactics and routines – interact in the second-language learner and enable her to communicate with native speakers of the language she is acquiring.

5   Conclusion

Having considered that communicative competence was not a matter of language alone, but rather, a combination of many different factors interacting and influencing reciprocally the performance of a second language speaker, I centered this study on the acquisition process that a college Japanese learner had been undergoing in the United States. Of the many factors considered to make up communicative competence, my attention was focused, on the one hand, on the language this learner was able to produce, and on the other, on the communicative strategies she was able to use, together with her receptiveness to examples set by her interaction partners.

Regarding the matter of which component of communicative competence was stronger in her person and made her interact efficiently, a clear difference was perceived between her language level and the strategies she used. Her language, in fact, was found in an early stage of development, struggling to evolve, but not yet quite accomplished. Her strategies, conversely, were numerous and effective, ranging from mimic and gestures at the beginning of the study, to direct questions at its conclusion. It can be safely inferred from these facts that her communicative competence at that time relied heavily on interactional and learning strategies, which she exploited to the fullest. Regarding the prospects of her success in learning the language, she had faced the process with the right attitude. Thus, it is possible to predict a favorable outcome.

6   References

BURT, Marina; DULAY, Heidi; HERNÁNDEZ CHÁVEZ, Eduardo (1976): Bilingual Syntax Measure. New York: Harcourt Brace Jovanovich.

CORDER, S. Pit (1974): The significance of learner's errors. In: Schumman, J.; Stenson, J. (eds.): New Frontiers in Second Language Learning. Rowley, Mass: Newbury House, 90-99.

— (1971): Idiosyncratic Dialects and Error Analysis. In: IRAL 9, 147-159.

DULAY, Heidi; Burt, Marina; Krashen, Stephen (1982): Aspects of L2 Research Methodology. In: Dulay, H.; Burt, M.; Krashen, S. (eds.): Language Two. New York: Oxford University Press, 244-260.

LARSEN-FREEMAN, Diane; LONG, Michael H (1994): An Introduction to Second Language Acquisition Research. London: Longman.

LONG, Michael H. (1983): Native Speaker/Non-Native Speaker Conversation and the Negotiation of Comprehensible Input. In: Applied Linguistics 4.2, 126-141.

RICHARDS, Jack C. (1974): A Non-Contrastive Approach to Error Analysis. In: Richards, J. (ed.): Error Analysis. London: Longman, 172-188.

RICHARDS, Jack C.; SUKWIWAT, Mayuri (1983): Language Transfer and Conversational Competence. In: Applied Linguistics 4.2, 113-125.

TARONE, Elaine; COHEN, Andrew D.; DUMAS, Guy (1983): A Closer Look at Some Interlanguage Terminology: A Framework for Communication Strategies. In: Faerch, C.; Kasper, G. (eds.): Strategies in Interlanguage Communication. London and New York: Longman, 4-14.

Parameter Setting, Linguistic Clusterings, and L2 Acquisition

Yolanda Ruiz de Zarobe

1   Introduction

One of the aims of recent research within the framework of Universal Grammar has been to articulate more precisely the nature of parameter setting in language acquisition. Much of this research has been devoted to constraining the theory of parameter setting, while seeking to offer a unitary explanation for a number of phenomena. From the perspective of second language acquisition, one of the most controversial areas is that of parameters. Parameters represent different options permitted by Universal Grammar that interact with the universal principles to form the grammar of the individual languages. Furthermore, these parameters, which show the ways in which languages may vary, can represent a clustering of grammatical properties. These properties are tightly related: once one structure has been acquired, the acquisition of the others will proceed naturally. Thus, for any particular parametric selection, a variety of superficial effects will result.

One such parameter is the *pro*-drop parameter, or null subject parameter, which has a number of attributed properties, such as the ability to omit subject pronouns, inversion of subjects and verbs in declarative sentences, and apparent *that*-trace violations, where the subject is extracted out of a clause that contains a complementizer. Languages like Italian and Spanish are [+*pro*-drop], and have all these associated properties, while French and English are [-*pro*-drop], and do not show this clustering of characteristics. These differences are illustrated in the examples below:

1) a. Es una chica muy guapa.
   b. She is a very beautiful girl.
      *Is a very beautiful girl.
2) a. Ha llegado Juan
   b. Juan has arrived
      *Has arrived Juan.
3) a. ¿Quién dijiste que iba a venir?
   b. Who did you say was going to come?
      *Who did you say that was going to come?

The aim of this research is to test the behaviour of these properties in second language acquisition, to see whether the same relationship holds in the acquisition of English as a second language.

2 The study

2.1 Subjects

The study reported in this paper used data from 150 adult Spanish speakers learning English at the Public University of Navarre, in Spain. The subjects were placed in five different levels of English proficiency, based on their results from the Placement Test administered by the Public University of Navarre in Spain. Nevertheless, to ensure that they were correctly classified, they were asked to perform two tasks: a cloze test, which controls their overall proficiency,[1] and a questionnaire, where they included information about their knowledge of English, amount of time spent in English-speaking countries, proficiency in other languages, and related questions. Subjects who did not complete any of the tasks as requested were disqualified. After undergoing both tests, subjects were divided in five levels: 29 students in Level 1, 29 in Level 2, 34 in Level 3, 20 in Level 4, and 18 in Level 5.

All the subjects in our research were studying within an autonomous-learning programme, which consisted of class attendance three times a week and the possibility of working autonomously in a self-access centre.

2.2 Instruments

In order to investigate the acquisition of these related properties, our subjects were asked to translate into English twelve sentences that exemplified the properties clustering with the *pro*-drop parameter, namely missing referential subjects:

4) a. Me gusta mucho Nueva York.
   'Like very much New York'
   I like New York very much.
   b. Cuando tenía veinte años, estuve un verano en esa ciudad.
   'When I was twenty, spent a summer in that city'
   When I was twenty, I spent a summer in that city.

subject-verb inversion:

5) a. Cuando te fuiste llegó Pedro.
   'When you left arrived Peter'
   When you left Peter arrived.
   b. No irá Juan a tu casa.
   'Won't go John to your home'
   John won't go to your home.

and the *that*-trace effect:

6) a. ¿Quién piensas que trabaja en ese colegio?
   'Who do you think that works in this school?'

---

[1] These tests have been reported effective as a supplementary placement procedure for entering language programs.

Who do you think works in this school?
b. ¿Quién piensas que no vendrá a la fiesta?
'Who do you think that will not come to your party?'
Who do you think will not come to your party?

In the case of the missing subjects and the subject-verb inversion, there was an equal number of affirmative, negative, interrogative and embedded clauses. The sentences exemplifying the *that*-trace effect included the same number of affirmative and negative questions. Furthermore, sentences were controlled both for vocabulary choice and length.

2.3   Results and discussion

Results are summarized in table 1 and table 2. The former reports on the total number of errors commited in the acquisition of English as a second language, the latter describes the percentages of errors.[2]

	L1	L2	L3	L4	L5
Referential subjects	8	12	5	0	0
Subject-verb inversion	20	26	4	2	0
That-trace effect	85	118	65	28	19

Table 1: Number of errors in ESL

	L1	L2	L3	L4	L5
Referential subjects	0.28	0.24	0.15	0.00	0.00
Subject-verb inversion	0.69	0.53	0.12	0.10	0.00
That-trace effect	2.93	2.41	1.91	1.40	1.06

Table 2: Percentages of errors in ESL

Our results show that there is a gradual improvement with level with respect to the three properties. If we look at two of these properties, missing subjects and subject-verb inversion, we see how there are no errors in the late stages of acquisition, suggesting that these structures have eventually been mastered. Nevertheless, the number of errors differs, being higher in the case of postverbal subjects. This may be due to the interpretation of these sentences. Although we only used intransitive sentences in order to avoid any kind of ambiguity,[3] students may still be considering the postverbal

---

[2]   Errors refer to omissions of referential subjects in obligatory contexts, use of postverbal subjects, and extraction of the subject out of a clause containing the complementizer *that*.

[3]   As suggested by Liceras (1988, 1989), the noun phrases in sentences such as
1) a. Telefonearon mis padres para preguntármelo.
        'Phoned my parents to ask about it'
        My parents phoned to ask about it
    b. Ya han llamado mis hermanos.
        'Already have phoned my brothers'
        My brothers have already phoned.

noun phrases as direct objects, due to two factors: the pressure of the task and the limitation of time.

Nevertheless, despite the differences in acquisition, both structures seem to follow a similar development, something that does not happen with the final *pro*-drop structure tested here: the *that*-trace effect.The Spanish subjects seemed to have a problem in using these constructions, and although there was improved accuracy with level of proficiency, the number of violations is high, even in the latest stages of acquisition.

There are a number of points to be made about these results. First, these structures involve questions where the subject of the embedded clause has been extracted, and they are clearly more complex than the other two structures under consideration. Thus, our subjects may be producing ungrammatical sentences due to a lack of mastery in extractions out of embedded questions. Moreover, these complex structures may force the Spanish speakers to transfer the information from their first language, where violations of the *that*-trace effect are permitted. Although interference with the first language[4] may also explain the errors found in constructions with missing subjects, the Spanish subjects eventually perceive the necessity of subject pronouns in declarative sentences, while failing to notice that extractions out of embedded clauses do not require the presence of *that* in English.

These results suggest that the three properties traditionally attributed to the *pro*-drop parameter behave in a different way in second language acquisition.[5] Of the three structures that we have analyzed, subject-verb inversion and missing subjects seem to be more closely related, while there is no connection between these two structures and the *that*-trace effect. Speakers of Spanish identify both properties as being structurally related, because both of them have to do with the *freedom of subjects* (whether or not they are overt and the extent to which their position in the sentence is free) (Gass 1995). They seem to notice the relationships between these structures but are not able to make connections between these two forms and *that*-trace sequences, which seem to have a different status in their interlanguage.

---

can be interpreted as direct objects by those learners who have not acquired the verb morphology in Spanish or have not internalized the *a* marking of Spanish direct objects when they have the feature [+human, +definite].

[4]   The influence of the native language in the acquisition of a second language cannot be disputed. Although some researchers (Martohardjono and Flynn 1995, among others) claim that learners do not rely primarily on their first language grammars in the construction of the target language, "there is suggestive evidence that differences due to the NL typology are systematically attested in a given IL, at least in the case of early null subjects in the Spanish IL of our learners" (Liceras and Díaz 1998:334).

[5]   Authors such as White (1985, 1986) and Lakshmanan (1986) have investigated the acquisition of the properties related to the *pro*-drop parameter in second language acquisition. Both of them claimed that learners of English did not recognize these three structures as belonging to a unified parameter. According to White, the order of acquisition was:

• subject-verb inversion - missing subjects - *that*-trace effects

This hierarchy of difficulty was different from the one found by Liceras (1989), which was:

• missing subjects - subject-verb inversion - *that*-trace effects

As can be seen, both authors' results were similar in the case of the *that*-trace effect. Learners of English seem to have everlasting problems interpreting these sentences.

3 Conclusions

We have discussed the behaviour of some properties traditionally attributed to the *pro*-drop parameter: missing referential subjects, postverbal subjects and the *that*-trace effect. These three structures do not behave in a similar way in second language acquisition. Although these differences may be partly due to the effect of the native language in the interlanguage, there is evidence that indicates that the Spanish learners of English tend to make connections between those properties that are structurally related. Thus, we find a similar development in the case of missing subjects and subject-verb inversion, than with the *that*-trace effect. *That*-trace sequences, that are not superficially related to the other properties, will be the last to be acquired.

4 References

GASS, Susan (1995): Universals, SLA and Language Pedagogy. In: Eubank; Selinker, Sharwood Smith.

EUBANK, L; SELINKER, L.; SHARWOOD SMITH, M. (eds.): The Current State of Interlanguage. Amsterdam: John Benjamins.

LAKSHMANAN, Usha (1986): The Role of Parametric Variation in Adult Second Language Acquisition: A Study of the "Pro-drop" Parameter. In: Papers in Applied Linguistics 2, 97-118.

LICERAS, Juana M. (1989): On some Properties of the Pro-drop Parameter: Looking for Missing Subjects in Non-native Spanish. In: Gass, S.; Schachter, J. (eds.): Linguistic Perspectives on Second Language Acquisition. Cambridge: Cambridge University Press.

— (1988): Syntax and Stylistics: More on the Pro-drop Parameter. In: Pankhurst, J.; Sharwood Smith, M.; van Buren, P. (eds.): Learnability and Second Languages. Dordrecht: Foris.

LICERAS, Juana M.; DÍAZ, Lourdes (1998): On the Nature of the Relationship between Morphology and Syntax: Inflectional Typology, *f*-Features and Null/Overt Pronouns in Spanish Interlanguage. In: Beck, M. (ed.): Morphology and its Interfaces in Second Language Knowledge. Amsterdam: John Benjamins.

MarTohardjono, Gita; FLYNN, Suzanne (1995): Language Transfer: What do we Really Mean. In: Eubank; Selinker; Sharwood Smith (eds.).

WHITE, Lydia (1986): Implications of Parametric Variation for Adult Second Language Acquisition: An Investigation of the Pro-drop Parameter. In: Cook, V. J. (ed.): Experimental Approaches to Second Language Acquisition. Oxford: Pergamon.

— (1985): The Pro-drop Parameter in Adult Second Language Acquisition. In: Language Learning 35, 47-62.

Übersetzungswissenschaft

Internet und World Wide Web – Neue Kommunikationstechnologien für Sprachwissenschaftler und Translatoren

Helga Ahrens

0 Einleitung

In zahlreichen Berufszweigen ist heute immer mehr von den sog. „Neuen Medien", insbesondere dem Internet, die Rede. Sie prägen die berufliche Tätigkeit des Einzelnen in den unterschiedlichsten Bereichen, was sich – oberflächlich – z.b. schon auf der Visitenkarte zeigt: Dort ist neben Telefon- und Faxnummer meist auch eine E-Mail-Adresse zu finden.

Dolmetschen/Übersetzen, Sprach- und Translationswissenschaft sind für die sog. Telearbeit oder sogar Tele*heim*arbeit geradezu prädestiniert. Die Vorbereitung auf einen Dolmetscheinsatz, die Übersetzung eines Textes und/oder wissenschaftliches Arbeiten erfordern z.B. umfangreiche Recherchen. Diese Informationsbeschaffung wird durch die weltweite Vernetzung im „Global Village" erleichtert. Mittels eines leistungsfähigen Computers und eines Netzanschlusses werden Recherchen durchgeführt, die früher nur schwer oder in der Kürze der Zeit auch gar nicht möglich waren. Die Ergebnisse der Arbeit (Übersetzungen, Forschungsergebnisse etc.) können schnell in elektronischer Form übermittelt werden. Ein weiterer Vorteil: Die Arbeitszeit kann an persönliche Bedürfnisse angepaßt werden.

Die Fähigkeiten mit der weltweiten Datenvernetzung und ihren „Auswirkungen" umzugehen, müssen schon in der beruflichen Ausbildung gefördert werden. Dabei sind vor allem zwei Aspekte zu berücksichtigen:

- *Informationsrecherche* und
- *Kommunikationsmöglichkeit* im und über das Internet.

Letztere wird immer mehr zu einem wesentlichen Bestandteil der *Berufsorganisationstechniken*. Kommunikation meint hier nicht „nur" Korrespondenz im Sinne der elektronischen Post (E-Mail), sondern die Abwicklung von Geschäften, Aufträgen etc. im *Global Village*.

Ein weiterer Punkt ist die *Öffentlichkeitsarbeit*. Sie gehört ebenfalls zu den genannten Berufsorganisationstechniken. Web-Präsenz stellt eine weitere Art der Kommunikation dar: Es geht z.B. um die Darstellung eigener beruflicher Tätigkeiten zu geschäftlichen Zwecken. (Ein Beispiel: Ein Translator ist durch eine Homepage im Internet vertreten, die potentielle Auftraggeber animieren soll, Aufträge an ihn zu vergeben.)

Ich möchte in meinem Beitrag zunächst kurz auf den Bereich der Informationsrecherche über das Internet zu sprechen kommen und aufzeigen, welche Möglichkeiten sich hier bieten. Im Anschluß daran soll die Kommunikation im und über das Internet näher betrachtet werden.

1   Informationsrecherche

Als Grundlage für die Informationsrecherche dient der *Auftrag*. Er dient als erster Anhaltspunkt für die Frage: Wer (Auftraggeber) benötigt was (welche Informationen) wo (in welchem Kontext), warum (zu welchem Zweck), wie (in welcher Form) und wann (zu welchem Zeitpunkt)? (Vgl. auch die Lasswell-Formel bei Lasswell 1964:37.)

Dabei ist aufgrund der Vielfalt der im *Global Village* angebotenen Informationen ökonomisches Vorgehen gefragt.[1] Denn angesichts der Fülle der im Internet angebotenen Informationen und der täglich steigenden Zahl der *Web Sites* ist es schwierig und mitunter auch zeitaufwendig, bei einer Recherche tatsächlich brauchbare Ergebnisse zu erzielen. Zwar wird die Beschaffung von Informationen einerseits durch die *elektronische Abrufbarkeit* beschleunigt – teils sogar erst ermöglicht – und somit erleichtert.[2] Doch müssen zunächst neue Recherchetechniken eingeübt werden. Läßt man sich ziel- und orientierungslos auf das Abenteuer Internet ein, so ist vielleicht anfangs das Staunen groß über Menge und Vielfalt der Informationen. Doch kann auch bald die Lust vergehen. Denn nicht alles ist auch brauchbar. Und: Ebenso vielfältig wie die Informationen sind die möglichen Suchstrategien. Ohne diesbezügliche Kenntnisse ist eine effektive Nutzung des Internets nicht möglich. So führt die einfache Eingabe eines Suchbegriffs zu einer derart hohen Zahl von Ergebnissen, daß man vermutlich Jahre bräuchte, um allen nachzugehen (und – wie erwähnt –, es ist nicht einmal gesagt, daß alle Ergebnisse auch relevant sind.). Eine Retrievalsprache muß erlernt werden (z.B. die Verknüpfung von Suchbegriffen durch Boolesche Operatoren (*und*, *oder*, *nicht*) etc. Die Suche nach Informationen kann über Suchprogramme, die Eingabe eindeutiger sogenannter URL-Adressen (URL = *Uniform Ressource Location*), oder auch durch Raten und Kombinieren durchgeführt werden.

Gefragt ist auch eine *neue Art des Lesens*. Texte im Internet setzen sich zum einen aus zahlreichen Elementen wie geschriebenen Texten, Graphiken, Audio-, Videosequenzen etc. zusammen und entsprechen außerdem dem Prinzip der *Hypertextstruktur*, d. h., in den Text sind Verweise (*Links*) zu anderen Dokumenten eingebettet. Diese Links sind als Verbindung zu weiteren Informationen interessant, erfordern jedoch klare Entscheidungen, ob der Leser ihnen nachgehen muß, kann und/oder sollte.

Doch welche Informationsquellen sind für Sprachwissenschaftler und Translatoren relevant?

Im Rahmen einer kurzen Aufzählung lassen sich hier vor allem folgende *Angebote* aufzählen:

---

[1]   Ich habe in diesem Zusammenhang früher den Terminus „pfadfinderisches Spurenlesen" gebraucht und vom Translator auch als „Transmowgli" im Internet-Dschungel gesprochen in Anlehnung an Rudyard Kiplings Dschungelbuch, in dem der unter den Tieren aufgewachsene Junge Mowgli von seinen Freunden systematisch in die Gesetze der Wildnis eingeweiht wird. So ist er in der Lage, sich im Dschungel zurechtzufinden und zu überleben. Ähnlich wie Mowgli muß der Translator die Gesetze des Internet-Dschungels kennen und befolgen lernen, wenn er sich dort zurechtfinden will. (Vgl. Ahrens 1999.)

[2]   Dazu kommt: Informationen sind „rund um die Uhr", 24 Stunden täglich, abrufbar. Ein weiterer Vorteil des *Electronic Publishing*: Aktualisierungen, Korrekturen etc. lassen sich noch „in letzter Minute" – oder auch nach der eigentlichen Publikation – in regelmäßigen Abständen vornehmen.

1) Ein häufig genutztes Angebot sind z.b. Online-Bibliothekskataloge. Fast alle großen Bibliotheken verfügen heute über einen *Online Public Access Catalogue* (OPAC). Doch nicht nur Literaturquellen können recherchiert werden, auch Quellentexte selbst sind abrufbar. In Archiven und virtuellen Bibliotheken werden Texte elektronisch gespeichert. Werke der Weltliteratur, wie z.b. Shakespeare, sind über das Internet abrufbar. (Vgl. z.b. das 1971 initiierte Gutenberg-Projekt, in dessen Rahmen Weltliteratur der Öffentlichkeit in elektronischer Form zugänglich gemacht wird.) Und vieles mehr.

2) Berufsorganisationen, Ausbildungsstätten, Dokumentationsdienste etc. bieten Informationsmaterial an. Fachliche Informationen jeder Art werden auf diese Art zur Verfügung gestellt.

3) Eine wichtige Informationsquelle sind ein- oder mehrsprachige Wörterbücher und Terminologiedatenbanken. Dadurch wird der Zugriff auf wertvolles Arbeitsmaterial ermöglicht. Die translatorische Tätigkeit besteht z.b. – Schätzungen zufolge – zu bis zu 60% aus terminologischen Recherchen.

4) Weltweit können Zeitungen in der jeweiligen Landessprache gelesen werden.

5) Immer mehr Fachzeitschriften „entdecken" das Internet und stellen ihre Beiträge ins Internet. Dabei bieten Publikationsorgane die Beiträge für jedermann zugänglich an oder regeln den Zugang z.b. durch Benutzerkennungen und Passwörter (letzteres ist mit einem Abonnement vergleichbar).
Andere Web-Site-Betreiber weisen auf gedruckte Zeitschriften hin. Diese sind besonders dann interessant, wenn sie z.b. Inhaltsverzeichnisse enthalten, um eine möglichst optimale Beurteilung seitens des/r Interessenten zu ermöglichen. Die Tendenz zum *Electronic Publishing* steigt, und immer mehr Zeitschriften geben diesem Trend nach. (Beispiele sind: Trans, Internet-Zeitschrift für Kulturwissenschaften: http://www.adis.at/arlt/institut/trans/, Transst: http://spinoza.tau.ac.il/~toury/transst/index.html).

6) Wissenschaftliche Beiträge einzelner Autoren, die früher als Print-Version publiziert wurden, und dadurch nur einem „eingeschränkten" Adressatenkreis zur Verfügung standen, können nun – in elektronischer Form – einem größeren Publikum zugänglich gemacht werden.

7) Auch berufsbegleitende Aktivitäten (Hotelbuchungen, Nachschlagen von Zugfahrplänen, Kongreßankündigungen etc.) lassen sich über das Internet vornehmen.

2 Kommunikation im Internet

Das Internet fördert die direkte Kommunikation insofern, als die am Kommunikationsprozeß Beteiligten unmittelbarer miteinander in Beziehung treten können, als dies z.b. auf dem Postweg möglich war und ist.

Die bereits dargestellte (Fach-)Informationsrecherche ist *eine* Art der Kommunikation. Dabei handelt es sich häufig um „*einseitige*" Kommunikation, da jemand Kontakt zu einer Informationsquelle (z.b. einer Bibliothek oder einer Datenbank) aufnimmt, um dort Informationen abzurufen.

Doch geht es in zunehmendem Maße nicht mehr *nur* um Informationsbeschaffung auf Anfrage, sondern um tatsächliche Interaktion zwischen Kommunikationspartnern. Im Fall einer Translation beispielswiese wird Kooperation zwischen Auftraggeber und Translator und Translator und Kollege(n) für die professionelle und skoposgerechte Auftragsausführung vorausgesetzt .

Auftragsabwicklung inklusive *Kommunikation* mit dem Auftraggeber wird heute immer stärker mit Hilfe von Datenübertragungsdiensten (z.b. FTP = *File Transfer Protocol* etc.) abgewickelt. Das Handling von E-Mails mit und ohne Attachments, die Nutzung von Hilfsanwendungen für den Datentransport (z.b. Anwendungen zur Datenkomprimierung) etc. müssen eingeübt werden. Voraussetzung ist eine entsprechende technische Ausrüstung und die Bereitschaft, mit dieser Ausrüstung professionell umgehen zu können.

Auch die Unternehmen erkennen diesen Trend: So bekam ich z.b. von einem (Telekommunikations-)Unternehmen ein Anschreiben inklusive Fragebogen zugeschickt, in dem nach Übersetzern und Dolmetschern (im Bereich des Telefon-Dolmetschens) gesucht wurde, die an einer Auftragsübernahme oder Festanstellung interessiert seien. Technische Voraussetzung: ein leistungsfähiger Computer und ein ISDN-Anschluß. Übersetzungen sollen via Internet übertragen werden, die Telefon-Dolmetscher werden per Konferenzschaltung mit den jeweiligen Gesprächspartnern verbunden. Arbeiten vom „Home-Office" aus.

Gleichzeitig Recherche- und Kommunikationsmöglichkeit ist z.B die Möglichkeit eines Auftraggebers, sich online einen Translator zu suchen. Translatoren sind häufig in verschiedenen Berufsorganisationen und Übersetzungsagenturen vertreten. Diese Organisationen wiederum stellen ihre Dienste im Internet zur Verfügung, indem sie z.B. die Nutzung von Datenbanken anbieten, über die ein Auftraggeber sich einen Translator nach verschiedenen Kriterien, wie Arbeitssprache und/oder Wohnort, oder auch gezielt nach einem empfohlenen Translator suchen kann. Auch die Vermittlung von Translatoren durch nationale und internationale Übersetzungs- und Dolmetschagenturen ist über das Internet möglich.

In bezug auf die *Kommunikation unter Kollegen* geben Berufsverbände Hilfestellung. Sie bieten eigene Web-Sites und Foren an, über die eine Kommunikation unter den Mitgliedern möglich ist. Für viele Berufsgruppen gibt es Diskussionsforen – *Mailing Lists* (z.B. Lantra-L, ein Forum für übersetzungsrelevante Fragen) und *News Groups* – über die ein Erfahrungsaustausch möglich ist.

Eine kleine Zwischenbemerkung: Vom sozialen Standpunkt aus wird bisweilen die Befürchtung ausgesprochen, die Kommunikation über das Internet würde die *spontane* (informelle) Kommunikation unterdrücken, da „[d]er Gebrauch von elektronischen Kommunikationsmedien [...] dazu führen [kann], daß der persönliche Kontakt formaler Kommunikationsabläufe kontinuierlich zurückgeht" und zu einer Eingrenzung der sozialen Kontakte führen (Höfels 1997). Dies scheint mir jedoch zu verallgemeinernd. So kann z.B. die Homepage eines Translators auch dazu führen, daß ein Kontakt zu einem Kollegen, der – zufällig oder auf eine gezielte Suche hin – auf diese Homepage gestoßen ist, überhaupt erst geknüpft wird.

Letzten Endes liegt es natürlich auch am Einzelnen selbst, wie er mit dem neuen Medium Internet ungeht.

Unter dem Aspekt der Informationsrecherche habe ich auf die steigende Tendenz des *Electronic Publishing* hingewiesen. Texte im Internet werden aus demselben Grund wie gedruckte Texte publiziert. Sie sollen gelesen werden, eigene Erkenntnisse einem Publikum mitteilen – und auch andere vom eigenen Standpunkt überzeugen. Web-Sites werden auch dazu genutzt, sich und seine Tätigkeit(en) vorzustellen, um z.b. das eigene Auftragsvolumen zu steigern. Diese Entwicklung hat Auswirkungen: Der Trend zur eigenen Homepage setzt sich immer mehr durch. Dies betrifft zum einen Organisationen, Unternehmen und Verbände, zum anderen immer stärker auch die *private Homepage.*

Ob die Homepage nun als „Publikationsorgan" oder „Kontaktmittel" dienen soll – wichtig ist eine *skoposgerechte Aufbereitung der Information(en).* Das Lese- und Rezeptionsverhalten in bezug auf Online-Texte folgt anderen Regeln als die Rezeption gedruckter Texte. Allein das Kommunikationsmedium erfordert eine andere Strukturierung des Textes. So ist es z.b. ermüdender, lange Texte am Bildschirm zu lesen als ein Buch vor den Augen zu haben.

Um eine *wettbewerbs- und „kommunikations"fähige* Homepage zu erstellen, müssen Regeln für Organisation und Struktur von Web-Sites beachtet werden. Dies beginnt bei der Internet-Adresse der jeweiligen Web-Site und setzt sich bei der Textproduktion fort. Die Textstruktur ist – aufgrund des Hypertextcharakters von Online-Texten – eine andere: Man hat es nicht mehr mit „Fließtext" zu tun, sondern mit vielen kleine(re)n Texten, die durch eine Link-Struktur miteinander verbunden sind. Regeln und Kenntnisse der Textgestaltung von Online-Texten müssen berücksichtigt werden. Ein wesentlicher Faktor ist z.B. die Farbgestaltung: Die Hintergrundgestaltung beispielsweise bietet mehr Möglichkeiten als ein Print-Medium, in dem die Farbkombination „schwarze Schrift auf weißem Hintergrund" vorherrscht. Regeln wie „Informationen gleicher Art sollten auf gleiche farbliche Weise gestaltet werden" etc. finden hier Anwendung. Doch schon die Frage, welche Farben benutzt werden, ist wesentlich. (Hier können Erkenntnisse der Farbpsychologie weiterhelfen.)

Es ist auch auf *Suchmaschinentauglichkeit* der Seite zu achten. Sie muss Meta-Informationstags enthalten, über die die Seite bei Eingabe entsprechender Suchbegriffe gefunden wird. Sonst geht sie in der Informationsflut des Web leicht verloren.

Eine ständige Pflege der Seite(n) ist unabläßlich. Sie fördert das Interesse und animiert den Besucher der Seite „öfter mal hineinzuschauen", ob es etwas Neues gibt.

Auch wenn Sprachwissenschaftler und Translatoren ihre Seite(n) nicht selbst erstellen, sondern die Textgrundlage liefern und andere mit der eigentlichen Erstellung der Site(s) beauftragen, sollten sie ihre Web-Site(s) ständig im Auge behalten und auf regelmäßige Wartung achten. Schließlich geht es auch um die Wahrung der eigenen Interessen.

Eine beliebte Angewohnheit ist es, auf einer Homepage *persönliche Bookmarks* (d.h. Sites, die für den Betreiber der Seite und dessen anvisierte Zielgruppe von besonderem Interesse sind) aufzulisten. In diesem Zusammenhang ist allerdings darauf hinzuweisen, daß eine *organisierte* Bookmark-Sammlung wertvoller ist, als die bloße Auflistung. Persönliche Linksammlungen stellen häufig eine solche Auflistung dar, die lediglich eine thematische Anordnung bzw. Strukturierung aufweist. Dies ist natürlich die einfachste Art, eine Web-Site der „persönlichen" Links zu erstellen.

(Man trifft auf eine Seite, die als interessant eingestuft wird, fügt sie über einen simplen Befehl „Add Bookmark" in die eigene Sammlung ein und stellt diese Sammlung ins Internet.) Professioneller – und sicherlich von größerer positiver Resonanz – wäre es hingegen, die einzelnen Sites z.b. mit einem Kommentar zu versehen, der es dem Besucher der Web-Site auf den ersten Blick ermöglicht zu erkennen, ob die betreffende Seite auch für ihn relevant sein kann.

Eine seriöse Homepage mit relevanten Informationen und weiteren Hilfen zur Nutzung möglicher Informationsquellen dient auch der *Anerkennung* der eigenen beruflichen Tätigkeit. Dieser Aspekt scheint mir besonders für Translatoren relevant zu sein, die häufig darüber klagen, daß die Bezeichnung Übersetzer keine geschützte Berufsbezeichnung ist. Nach wie vor müssen Translatoren noch *Aufklärungsarbeit* leisten um klar zu machen, was Übersetzen tatsächlich bedeutet und welche vielfältigen Aspekte es beinhaltet.

Abschließend kann in diesem Zusammenhang gesagt werden: Einer privaten Homepage kommt insofern eine besondere Bedeutung zu, als sie in drei Bereichen eine Rolle spielen kann:

1) Sie fördert die Kommunikation, indem sie *weltweiten* Kontakt zu Kollegen und Auftraggebern ermöglicht.
2) Sie kann bei der Recherche von Nutzen sein, da der jeweilige Besitzer der Homepage häufig Links zu verwandten Themen aufführt.
3) Sie dient der Öffentlichkeitsarbeit, da sie Aufschluß gibt über Tätigkeit, Interessen und Dienstleistungen und dadurch nicht zuletzt den Status von Sprachwissenschaftlern und Translatoren in der Gesellschaft verbessern kann.

Eine ausgezeichnete Möglichkeit der Recherche und Kommunikation wäre die *gezielte Organisation* persönlicher Homepages. Entscheiden sich immer mehr Sprachwissenschaftler und Translatoren für solch eine Homepage kann dadurch ein „Netz" entstehen, das Kontakt und Kommunikation untereinander fördert. Werden dort auch eigene Publikationen zur Verfügung gestellt, würden Wissenschaftsaustausch und Kontaktaufnahmen über Ländergrenzen hinweg wesentlich erleichtert.

3   Literatur

AHRENS, Helga (1999): „Der Translator im Dschungel des Internet oder: Pfadfinderausbildung für Translatoren?, in: TEXTconTEXT 13 = NF 3.1, 25-47.
ALANEN, Anukaisa (1996) The translator and the current services of the Internet [Proseminar paper], http://www.uta.fi/~tranuk/prosemc.htm).
BÖLTER, Birgit (1995): Telearbeit, http://www.igp.uni-stuttgart.de/ep/html/bbc-tele/telearbeit.html [Stand 1999].
LIBRARY & INFORMATION SCIENCE: Citation guides for electronic documents (1999), http://www.ifla. org/I/training/citation/citing.htm.
HAUENSCHILD, Christa + HEIZMANN, Susanne (Hrsg.) (1997): Machine translation and translation theory. Berlin – New York: Mouton de Gruyter (Text, translation, computational processing 1).
LASSWELL, Harold (1964): The structure and finction of communication and society. In: Bryson, Lyman (Hrsg.): The communication of ideas. A series of addresses. New York: Cooper Square Publ. (Religion and civilization series), 37-51.

MÜNZ, Stefan (1998): *Die Energie des Verstehens: HTML-Dateien selbst erstellen. SELFHTML* [Version 7.0], http://www.teamone.de/selfhtml/ (Stand: 27.4.1998). – Gedruckte Version: Münz, Stefan + Nefzger, Wolfgang (1998) *HTML 4.0 Handbuch: HTML 4.0 – JavaScript – DHTML – Perl* [+ CD-ROM]. Feldkirchen: Franzis-Verlag (Professional Series). – Version 8.0 v. 27.10.2001, http://selfhtml.teamone.de/.

PROJECT GUTENBERG. *Fine Literature Digitally Re-Published* [© 1971-2001], http://www.gutenberg.net.

RISKU, Hanna (1998): *Translatorische Kompetenz. Kognitive Grundlagen des Übersetzens als Expertentätigkeit.* Wien: Dissertation (1995). Tübingen: Stauffenburg (Studien zur Translation 5).

SANDRINI, Peter (1995): „Übersetzer auf der Datenautobahn. Online Ressourcen für Sprachmittler", in: *Mitteilungsblatt des österreichischen Übersetzer- und Dolmetscherverbandes Universitas* 3, 2-5.

SCHELLER, Martin et. al. (1994): *Internet: Werkzeuge und Dienste von „Archie" bis „World Wide Web",* http://www.ask.uni-karlsruhe.de/books/inetbuch/all.html – Gedruckte Version: *Internet: Werkzeuge und Dienste. Von „Archie" bis „World Wide Web"* [hrsg. von der Akademischen Software Kooperation]. Berlin etc.: Springer1994.

VERMEER, Hans J. (1983): „interaktionsdeterminanten. ein versuch zwischen pragma- und soziolinguistik", in: Vermeer, Hans J.: *Aufsätze zur Translationstheorie.* Heidelberg: Selbstverlag, 12-32. – Repr. aus: Nickel, Gerhard + Raasch, Albert (eds.) (1974): *IRAL-Sonderband. Kongreßbericht der 5. Jahrestagung der Gesellschaft für Angewandte Linguistik GAL e. V.* Heidelberg: Julius Groos 1974, 297-321.

Interaktionsforschung im kontrastiven Vergleich: einige synergetische Ansätze

Cornelia Feyrer

1   Einleitung

Die kontrastive Beschreibung von Modalität (M) zeigt, daß modale Ausdrucksweisen in der Interaktion eine gewichtige Rolle spielen und auch für den Übersetzer unter funktionaler Perspektive relevant sind. Im folgenden Beitrag sollen Ansätze aus der Interaktions- und Markerforschung zum Französischen (F) auf die Beschreibung von Modalpartikeln (Mpn) im Deutschen (D) angewandt werden. Als Beispiel wird die MP *doch* im Sprachvergleich D-F herausgegriffen.

2   Französische Marker-, deutsche Partikelforschung und translatorische Relevanz

Während die deutsche Sprache über relativ gut voneinander abgrenzbare eigene Kategorien von Lexemen zum Ausdruck von M verfügt, übernehmen im F unterschiedliche ‚Marker' diese Funktion bzw. erfolgt der Ausdruck von M auf verschiedenen sprachlichen und außersprachlichen Ebenen. Eine signifikante translationsrelevante Besonderheit modaler Strukturen liegt im Wechselspiel von Implizitem und Explizitem in der kommunikativen Interaktion. MPn fungieren oft – z.B. in der Argumentation – als Marker für die implizite Ebene der sozialen Interaktion. Insofern kann von einer Interrelation zwischen M und Argumentation bzw. Interaktion gesprochen werden. Die MP *doch* zeichnet sich aufgrund ihrer adversativen Funktion durch ein besonders starkes interaktives Potential und damit interaktionsstrategischen Gehalt aus. Für die kontrastive Analyse dieses Potentials sind u.E. Ansätze aus der Interaktionsforschung zum F, wie sie aus Genf[1] vorliegen, interessant. Ziel der Genfer Forschungen ist es, aus konversationsanalytischer Perspektive zu Themen der kommunikativen Interaktion Stellung zu nehmen. Es geht dort um ‚interaktive Marker', die definitorisch wie folgt umrissen werden können: „Un marqueur indique de manière univoque la fonction interactive de l'acte" (Auchlin/Zenone 1980:33). Auch die von Moeschler und Reboul (1994:465) beschriebenen *connecteurs pragmatiques* leisten Ähnliches, ihre Funktion besteht darin „d'une part de relier des segments de discours (les énoncés), et d'autre part de contribuer à la constitution d'unités discursives complexes à partir d'unités discursives simples".

---

[1] Wir beziehen uns hier auf Studien in den *Cahiers de linguistique française* (Genf).

3   Zur kontrastiven Betrachtung von Ausdrucksformen von Modalität

Berührungspunkte zwischen Partikel- und *Marqueur*-Forschung, die auch Übersetzungsrelevanz aufweisen, ergeben sich insofern, als unter konversationsanalytischem
Gesichtspunkt die starke Kontextabhängigkeit von Sprechakten aufgezeigt wird. Dazu zählt die Einbeziehung des Interaktionskonzepts in den sprechakttheoretischen
Rahmen (cf. Auchlin, Zenone 1980), in welchen dann *marqueurs* oder Partikeln eingebettet werden können (cf. Spengler 1980), oder die Betrachtung von *marqueurs* im
Hinblick auf ihre Rolle im Interaktionsgeschehen (cf. Roulet 1980).

3.1   Die Dichotomie zwischen ‚Illokution' und ‚Interaktion'

Roulet (1980) unterscheidet z.B. zwischen ‚Illokution' und ‚Interaktion'. Überträgt
man diese Differenzierung auf die deutschen MPn, so wird deren interaktionsmodifi-
zierendes Potential transparent. *Es ist doch wirklich warm hier.* könnte z.B. mit *Ne
crois-tu pas qu'il fait trop chaud ici?* übersetzt werden. Nach Roulet (1980:89) ergibt
sich hier auf der Ebene der „valeur illocutoire littérale" ein informationsermittelnder
Sprechakt, auf der Ebene der Interaktion jedoch eine abgeleitete Aufforderung, ein
durch den „marqueur de dérivation illocutoire" *ne crois-tu pas* von der reinen Illokution abweichender oder dazu sogar konträrer „valeur dérivée de requête", oder – je
nach Kontext – eine höfliche Zurückweisung. In Zusammenhang mit der Zurückweisung unterscheidet auch Moeschler (1980) zwischen *illocution* und *interactivité* und
erstellt eine Typologie interaktiver Funktionen, worunter er die Klassifikation von
Sprechakten nach dem Bezug zum vorhergehenden bzw. nachfolgenden Sprechakt
versteht. Für den Übersetzer sind v.a. die *valeurs interactives* maßgeblich und nicht
unbedingt die *valeurs illocutoires*. Daraus erklärt sich auch der in der Übersetzung
häufig stattfindende Satztypwechsel als Entsprechung für Modales im Ausgangstext
(AT). Bezeichnenderweise sieht Roulet (1980:91) auch in den Satzarten „marqueurs
d'orientation illocutoire", die die Relation zwischen den Interaktanten verdeutlichen.
Récanati (1981) beschäftigt sich seinerseits mit der pragmatischen Äquivalenz zwischen Satztypen. Er untersucht das assertive illokutionäre Potential von Deklarativ-
sätzen und zeigt, daß mittels indirekter illokutiver Akte auch andere kommunikative
Funktionen wahrgenommen werden können. Die etwas erweiterte Sichtweise von
Illokution und Interaktion erleichtert es auch, die auftretenden Entsprechungsformen
für *doch* in einen translationsrelevanten Rahmen zu bringen. Differenziert man zwischen Illokution und Interaktion bzw. zwischen Satztyp und Satzmodus, so kann man
auch dem Interaktionspotential einer Aussage mehrere Erscheinungsformen zugestehen. Die auf der Ebene der Interaktion auftretenden Entsprechungen für den Ausdruck von M können demnach als *marqueurs d'actes interactifs* mit *valeur modale*
angesehen werden, wodurch auch Rückschlüsse auf das Funktionieren von M im D
ermöglicht werden.

3.2 Interaktiv-illokutives Potential und der Ausdruck von Modalität

Um die durch das Textganze bzw. die Kommunikationssituation als übergeordnete Größe transportierte M erfassen zu können, muß der Übersetzer den Gesamttext auf seine interaktive, modale Kohärenz hin prüfen. Dieses Postulat vertreten auch Auchlin und Zenone (1980:25-27) bei der Analyse von Aufbau und Struktureinheiten von Kommunikation im F. Wie sich aus einem Frage-Antwort-Schema in der Interaktion eine Konversation ergibt, so ergibt sich M durch das Zusammenwirken der Aktionen und Reaktionen aller Beteiligten am Interaktionsgeschehen. Was Auchlin und Zenone anhand von Beispielsätzen über Illokutionen ableiten, gilt auch für Fragen der M. Wird z.b. die Frage *A: Tu viens demain?* als Aufforderung verstanden, könnte B *Bon d'accord* antworten, wird die Frage als Versicherungsfrage interpretiert, wäre *Oui oui, je n'ai pas oublié* als Antwort denkbar. Der Rezipient muß in einem Schlußverfahren die beabsichtigte Illokution aus dem Zusammenspiel von Sprachlichem und Außersprachlichem inferieren, wobei es durchaus auch zum Mißglücken der Kommunikation kommen kann. Auchlin und Zenone (ibid.) nennen als Beispiel: *A: Tu viens demain? B: Bon d'accord. A: Mais ce n'était qu'une question!* Hier wird durch adversatives *mais* in der Replik A's B's falsche Interpretation deutlich. Für B wird seine falsche Schlußfolgerung aber erst in der zweiten Aussage A's erkennbar. Im D hätten wir in beiden Aussagen A's ein modales *doch*, jedoch handelt es sich im ersten Fall um ein schwach adversatives *doch* der Versicherungsfrage und im zweiten Fall um ein stark adversatives *doch* der Zurückweisung, wodurch Funktionsvarianten (FVn) von *doch* sichtbar werden. Ebenso wird fakultativer und obligatorischer Gebrauch von argumentativen Markern erkennbar. Die Übersetzung der rückversichernden, initiativen bzw. zurückweisenden, reaktiven Aussage A's könnte lauten: *A: Du kommst doch morgen? ... A: Aber das war doch nur eine Frage!* Beide *doch*-Varianten determinieren die Folgesequenzen des Gesprächspartners und können interaktionsstrategisch eingesetzt werden. Wenn Auchlin und Zenone (1980:32) von „fonction réctroactive" und „fonction proactive" sprechen, so ergeben sich Parallelen zum reaktiven bzw. initiativen Charakter einzelner FVn des modalen *doch*. Wir meinen daher, daß die Ergebnisse der Genfer Interaktionsforschung im Hinblick auf überselzungsorientierte Betrachtungen weitgehend auf die Partikelfrage im Sprachvergleich D-F übertrag- und anwendbar sind. Daher erscheint es auch sinnvoll, in bezug auf die dem Übersetzer zur Translaterstellung im F zur Verfügung stehenden Marker von *marqueurs de modalité* in Zusammenhang mit einer „fonction interactive de l'acte" (ibid.:33) zu sprechen. Letztere wiederum erfährt eine bestimmte Ausrichtung in der Interaktion. Dics gilt auch für die initiativ oder reaktiv ausgerichteten deutschen MPn.

3.3 Das Konzept der ‚*valeurs*‘ und ‚*fonctions*‘

Auchlin und Zenone (1980) schließen aus der Kontextdeterminiertheit der Interpretation von Aussagen bzw. aufgrund der aufscheinenden *marqueurs* auf unterschiedliche *valeurs* einer Aussage im Sinne von unterschiedlichen Interpretationsmöglichkeiten und grenzen diese gegenüber der *fonction* im Sinne der „relation actuelle et unique d'une occurrence avec un autre constituant" (ibid.:28) ab. In Analogie dazu läßt sich der Schluß auf unterschiedliche, kontextabhängige modale *valeurs* ziehen. Im Fall von *doch* können nach der adversativen Graduierung FVn beschrieben werden. Führt man den Analogieschluß in bezug auf die Unterscheidung zwischen *valeur* und *fonction* weiter, so kann man sagen, daß es im Hinblick auf modale Aussagen zwar viele *valeurs*, die FVn, gibt, aber nur eine *fonction*, diejenige, M auszudrücken. Dementsprechend zeichnen sich die FVn durch unterschiedliche *valeurs interactives* aus, was auch Auchlin und Zenones Definition für *valeur interactive* entspricht:

> „Par *valeur interactive* nous entendons le type de caractérisation qui permet une identification suffisante d'un acte d'après la relation qu'il entretient avec une autre occurrence" (ibid.:43).

Wenn also Marianne in den *Geschichten aus dem Wiener Wald* auf einen Vorwurf von Alfred mit einer stark adversativen Zurückweisung (*Ich mach dir doch keine Vorwürf*) reagiert, dann aber gleich eine schwach adversative Beschwichtigung (*Du kannst doch nichts dafür.* ÖH:143-144) anfügt, wofür sich in der Übersetzung für das zurückweisende *doch* ein argumentatives *mais* findet, das schwach adversative *doch* aber mit einer idiomatischen Wendung übertragen wird (*Mais je ne te fais pas de reproches, ce n'est pas de ta faute.* ÖH':48), so werden im Translat sowohl unterschiedliche FVn wie auch die adversative Graduierung deutlich.

3.4   Die *face*-Konzeption

Gehen wir nochmals auf die Differenzierung zwischen Illokution und Interaktion von Roulet (1980) zurück, so wird z.B. die Zurückweisung mit *doch* zu einem interaktiven Schachzug, mit dem der Sprecher versucht, sein Gesicht zu wahren. Roulet geht in Anlehnung an Goffman, Brown und Levinson (cf. ibid.:80ff) davon aus, daß generell in der sozialen Interaktion das Bedürfnis vorhanden ist, den eigenen Interaktionsbereich und den des Gegenübers zu schützen, und unterscheidet zwischen *face négative*, dem Bestreben, den eigenen Interaktionsbereich zu schützen, und *face positive*, dem Bedürfnis, vom Gegenüber anerkannt und geschätzt zu werden.[2] Roulet (1980) klassifiziert die illokutiven Akte – entgegen den Ansätzen von Austin und Searle – nach Bedrohung der einen oder anderen *face*-Seite von oder durch den Sprecher oder Hörer. Wendet man diese Konzeption auf die Vorkommensvarianten der MP *doch* an, so wird ersichtlich, daß nach der jeweiligen *face*-Bedrohung stark oder schwach adversative FVn der MP, die auch in der Übersetzung unterschiedliche translatorische Strategien erfordern, unterschieden werden können. Kritik oder Vorwurf richten sich so gegen die *face positive* des Hörers (*Der Leopold, das bin doch ich!* ÖH:184 / *Mais Leópold, c'est moi.* ÖH':85), wie sich Entschuldigung oder Geständnis (*Ich mach dir doch keine Vorwürf.* s.o.) gegen die *face positive* des Sprechers und Angebot oder Versprechen gegen dessen *face négative* richten.

---

[2]   Zur näheren Bestimmung der *face*-Konzeption verweisen wir auf Langner (1994:25ff).

3.4.1 Die *face*-Konzeption und interaktive Marker

Roulet (1980) nimmt weiters eine Einteilung interaktiver Marker nach den diversen Strategien der Interaktion und den Arten impliziter Kommunikation vor. Ausgehend von der *face*-Konzeption wird jeder illokutive Akt zu einem potentiell aggressiven und gegen die *face positive* oder *négative* gerichteten interaktiven Zug. Dies führt zur *figuration (face-work)*, dem Bestreben, diese Angriffe zu neutralisieren. Das Bedürfnis, die eigene *face* zu schützen, äußert sich auf zwei Ebenen: einerseits in der Art des Aufbaus der einzelnen Gesprächszüge, also der Strukturierung der Interaktion, und andererseits in der Ausführung der einzelnen Akte. Zur Formulierung eines solchen Aktes der Bedrohung einen modalisierenden Ausdruck zu setzen, wäre eine Entscheidung für eine bestimmte Ausführung eines solchen Zuges in der Interaktion. Dies gilt für die Interaktion im AT genauso wie für die Erstellung der Übersetzung, wo die entsprechenden Entscheidungen für die eine oder andere Übersetzungsvariante getroffen werden müssen: Bei Horváth findet sich z.B. auf Valeries Frage *Waren Sie noch Soldat?* ein verneinendes *Leider nein* von Erich, zu welchem ein begründendes *ich bin doch Jahrgang 1911* (ÖH:134) angefügt wird. Die Begründung kann als Schutz der eigenen *face* gesehen werden, im F bleibt dieses *doch* unübersetzt, da es schwach adversativ ist: *Non, hélas ... je suis de la classe de 1911.* (ÖH':38). Wollte Erich hingegen mit einer stark adversativen Zurückweisung reagieren, was einem Angriff gegen die *face positive* des Gesprächspartners gleichkäme, würde das Translat eine Entsprechung verlangen, z.B. eine konjunktionale Wendung: *Non, hélas ... puisque je suis de la classe de 1911.* Vieles der in der Interaktion ablaufenden „communication par sous-entendus", wie sich Goffman ausdrückt (Roulet 1980:82), äußert sich in der Übersetzung. Dies gilt im besonderen für die Arten der *figuration*, da das hier in der Ausgangssprache transportierte Implizite und Ambigue nicht immer in derselben Art und Weise in die Zielsprache übertragen werden kann, gerade das Ambigue ist aber für das *ménagement* der eigenen *face* und der des Gegenübers in der Interaktion von zentraler Bedeutung: „Être ambigu, c'est le meilleur moyen de ne pas s'imposer, de laisser à l'autre le choix de l'interprétation qui lui convient le mieux [...]" (ibid.:82). Der Ausdruck von M wäre also ein *ménagement de la face*. Es kommt zu „implicitations conversationnelles" (ibid.:84), d.h. zu kontextgebundenen impliziten Zusatzinformationen.[3] Den einzelnen Arten der Interaktion werden Marker zugewiesen (cf. ibid.:86). Expliziter Ausdruck wäre z.B. mittels performativer Verben realisiert, und impliziter Ausdruck (*implicitations conversationnelles*) wäre durch bestimmte Marker, die *marqueurs indicatifs d'acte illocutoire*, gekennzeichnet. Dabei handelt es sich vielfach um Ausdrucksformen von M, z.B. um die modale Verwendung von *quand-même* (*Er ist doch ein sehr erfahrener Chirurg. Il est quand même un chirurgien très expérimenté*). Versucht der Übersetzer, die Struktur der *conversations par sous-entendus* zu entschlüsseln, so erleichtert dies der Kohärenzbildung im Zieltext.

---

[3] Im Gegensatz dazu sieht Roulet die *implicitations conventionnelles*, d.h. kontextungebundene, konventionalisierte Ausdrucksformen, dies würde z.B. modale Ausdrucksformen im Höflichkeitskontext wie *Sie trinken doch noch ein Glas Bier? / Vous boirez bien encore un verre de bière?* betreffen.

3.4.2 Die *face*-Konzeption und modale Funktionsvarianten

Die FVn der MP *doch* lassen sich in schwach und stark adversative Varianten untergliedern,[4] diese Untergliederung entspricht auch in etwa der Unterscheidung nach Angriffen gegen die jeweilige *face*. U. E. können diese Klassifizierungsmöglichkeiten dem Übersetzer dienlich sein, Entsprechungsmöglichkeiten in der Zielsprache faßbar und systematisierbar zu machen. Die stark adversative Zurückweisung, der Vorwurf bzw. die Kritik an der Aussage des Gegenübers entsprechen Angriffen gegen die *face positive* des Gesprächspartners (*Die Gerechtigkeit kann man doch nicht kaufen!* DB:45 / *Mais on ne peut pas acheter la justice!* DB':46-47). Schwach adversative FVn wie Vorschlag, Bestätigung oder beruhigende Versicherung entsprechen Angriffen gegen die *face négative* des Gesprächspartners (*Du kannst doch nichts dafür.* s.o.). Die Aufgabe des Übersetzers besteht darin, diese impliziten Interaktionsstrukturen faßbar zu machen und ein in der Interaktion kohärentes Translat herzustellen. Mit Hilfe der Ansätze aus der Interaktionsforschung können Illokution und Interaktion insofern in einen translationsrelevanten Bezugsrahmen gestellt werden, als die Relationen zwischen den einzelnen Zügen in der Interaktion transparent werden und so ersichtlich wird, wie stark interaktive Komponenten die Dimension von Übersetzungseinheiten determinieren.

3.4.3 Die *face*-Konzeption und interaktive Kohärenz im Translat

Bei Dürrenmatt wird ein zurückweisendes *doch* im F mittels Satztypwechsel wiedergegeben: DER POLIZIST: *Passen Sie mal auf, Ill. Eine Anstiftung zum Mord liegt nur dann vor, wenn der Vorschlag, Sie zu ermorden, ernst gemeint ist. Das ist doch klar.* (DB:63-64) / L'ADJUDANT: *Attention, Ill, attention. Il n'y aurait provocation au meurtre, que si le projet de vous faire assassiner avait été pensé sérieusement. C'est clair?* (DB':69). Dadurch wird die argumentative Grundhaltung des Sprechers wie auch das Interaktionsgeschehen im Translat verändert. Das deklarative *Das ist doch klar* wird zur Frage *C'est clair?* bzw. die Replik *Meine ich auch* zu *Il me semble.* Dies entspricht zwar der Interrogationsstruktur im Translat, aber nicht der des AT. Betrachtet man diese Interaktion von der face-Konzeption ausgehend, so stellt im AT die erste Aussage des Polizisten eine Zurückweisung gegen die *face positive* Ills dar. Die im Translat aufscheinende Versicherungsfrage *C'est clair?* richtet sich jedoch gegen die *face négative* des Hörers und entspricht daher nicht der interaktiven Kohärenz des Textes. Ill reagiert in der Folge mit einem *Der Vorschlag bedroht mich, Polizeiwachtmeister, ob die Dame nun verrückt ist oder nicht. Das ist doch logisch*, also auch mit einer Zurückweisung gegen die *face positive* des Polizisten. Die Übersetzung mit *C'est pourtant logique* für Ills *Das ist doch logisch* entspricht wieder der *face*-Ausrichtung im AT. Es zeigt sich somit, daß eine Anwendung der *face*-Konzeption vor translationsrelevantem Hintergrund dem Übersetzer Hilfestellung bei der Aufrechterhaltung interaktiv-textueller Kohärenz geben kann. Für den Übersetzer können solche Ansätze zur Herstellung von Kohärenzbeziehungen dienlich sein, d.h., er

---

[4] Eine dementsprechende Typologisierung findet sich bei Feyrer (1998).

kann umso leichter Entsprechungen finden oder erkennen, je intensiver er versucht, die erwähnten Interaktions- und Argumentationsstrukturen im AT zu erfassen und im Translat zu berücksichtigen.

4 Interaktive Marker

4.1 Explizite und implizite Marker

Was im D oft implizit durch eine Partikel an M eingebracht wird (*Ich liebe dich doch!* DB:39), wird im F oft um einiges expliziter, z.b. durch ein Verb, wiedergegeben (*Tu sais: je t'aime!* DB':39). Solche Verben klassifiziert Roulet (1980) als *marqueur dénominatif d'interaction*. Was im F als interaktiver Marker beschrieben wird, kann im D zum Isolieren einer FV der MP dienen, nämlich hier z.b. der des expliziten Erinnerns an bekannte Sachverhalte mit Hilfe von Verben des Wissens. Dem Expliziten und dem Impliziten entsprechen nach Roulet (1980:86) eigene Arten von illokutiven *marqueurs*, zu denen er die performativen Verben im expliziten Bereich (*marqueurs dénominatifs d'acte illocutoire*) und z.b. Adverbialformen wie *quand même* im impliziten Bereich (*marqueurs indicatifs d'acte illocutoire*) zählt. Auch hier sind nach der Einteilung nach Markern FVn auszumachen. So gesehen zählen argumentatives *mais* oder emphatisches *bien* oder *donc* zu den impliziten *marqueurs*, da hier implizite Argumentationsstrukturen vermittelt werden, wohingegen z.b. Konjunktionen wie *puisque* oder *car* zu den expliziten *marqueurs* gerechnet werden können. Im Bereich der argumentativen *marqueurs* hat Spengler (1980) eine Gliederung dieser Marker vorlegt, welche deren argumentative Funktionen aufzeigt. So werden z.b. *mais, quand même* oder *pourtant* (*C'est pourtant logique.* s.o.) als kontrastive *marqueurs* von adverbiellem *bien* (*Sie sind doch Wienerin* ÖH:154 / *Vous êtes bien viennoise* ÖH': 57) als konfirmativem *marqueur* abgegrenzt. Dies entspricht der MP *doch* in unterschiedlicher kommunikativer Funktion, wobei schwach und stark adversative bzw. reaktiv oder initiativ angelegte und dissens- oder konsensmarkierende FVn unterschieden werden können.

4.2 Obligatorische und fakultative Marker

Roulet (1980:96) unterscheidet weiters zwischen obligatorischen und fakultativen Markern, auch *doch* weist FVn auf, bei denen eine Entsprechung für den modalen Ausdruck obligatorisch und andere, bei denen er fakultativ ist. Wenn z.b. bei Dürrenmatt der Bürgermeister Ills *Was schart ihr euch um mich?* empört mit einem *Wir scharen uns doch gar nicht um Sie* zurückweist (DB:83), so wird die Übersetzung *On ne vous entoure pas* (DB':94) weder der impliziten Argumentation noch dem Ausdruck der Zurückweisung gerecht, ein interaktiver Marker (*Mais on ne vous entoure pas!*) wäre hier wohl angebracht. Roulets Einteilung der *marqueurs* ist generell für die Einteilung der französischen Entsprechungen für deutsche MPn hilfreich. Roulet (1980:97) beschreibt prosodische und morphologische *marqueurs* und sieht auch die syntaktische Emphase als *marqueur* an. Gerade auf Syntaxebene finden sich oft Entsprechungen für Modales: *Aber bei einem Herrn sieht man doch in erster Linie auf das Inne-re...* (ÖH:132) / *Mais chez un homme, ce qu'on regarde d'abord, c'est l'intérieur...* (ÖH':36).

4.3   Pragmatische Konnektoren: *quand même* als Beispiel

Auch die Beschreibung einzelner *marqueurs* ist für die translationsrelevante Analyse hilfreich. *Quand même* wird z.b. von Moeschler und Spengler (1981) als kontrastiver Marker mit implizitem Potential beschrieben, dazu zählt z.b. das Insistieren auf eine Tatsache (*Mais on ne peut quand même pas acheter la justice!* s.o.). Spengler (1980:136) stellt fest, daß *quand même*, im Gegensatz zu *mais* einen Bruch mit dem vorhergehenden Sprechakt anzeigt. Dies macht ersichtlich, warum in der Übersetzung die Kombination von *mais* und *quand même* die Adversativität und das Insistieren auf bekannte Sachverhalte von *doch* in der Zurückweisung gut verdeutlichen kann. *Quand même* signalisiert – wie *mais* und *pourtant* – i.d.R. eine Zurückweisung und wird daher bei Moeschler (1980:71) auch als „marqueur interactif de réfutation" be-zeichnet. Diese Adverbien dienen häufig als Entsprechungen für modales *doch*, da sie im F als kontrastiv-argumentative Marker auf interaktiver Ebene dieselbe Leistung erbringen wie die MP im D. *Quand même* ist also in hohem Maße dazu geeignet, Im-plikaturen auszulösen. Dies verweist uns wieder auf Roulet (1980) und seine Kon-zeption der *figuration* bzw. des *ménagement de la face*, da *quand même* in der Inter-aktion die Möglichkeit bietet, „de refuser et d'accepter à la fois la situation, le com-portement ou l'acte linguistique de son interlocuteur" (Moeschler/Spengler, 1981:93), was wiederum Parallelen zur Verwendungsweise von *doch* in seinen FVn zeigt. So entsprechen die von Moeschler und Spengler (1981) differenzierten Verwendungs-weisen von *quand même* auch den folgenden FVn von modalem *doch*: „emplois absolu dans un contexte directif" (ibid.:94/97) in der höflichen Bitte mit Rückversi-cherung (*Sie kommen doch mit zur Gerichtsverhandlung? / Vous m'accompagnerez quand même aux débats judiciaires, non?*), oder „emplois réfutatif" (ibid.:103) in der Zurückweisung, wobei je nach Kontext Implikaturen ausgelöst werden können (*Er ist doch ein sehr erfahrener Chirurg / Il est quand même un chirurgien très expérimen-té*).

5   Evaluierung und Schlußfolgerungen

Da im D manche MPn starken argumentativen Gehalt haben können und die Interak-tion mitdeterminieren, eignen sich aus übersetzungsrelevanter Perspektive Ansätze aus der Markerforschung zum F, um Verbindungen zu Funktionsbeschreibungen der deutschen Partikeln herzustellen. Die vergleichende Betrachtung von Ergebnissen aus der Partikel- und der Markerforschung ist insofern translationsrelevant, als die unter-suchten französischen Marker und Konnektoren vielfach die Funktion der Partikel in der Übersetzung wahrnehmen oder als Teiläquivalent im Zusammenspiel mit anderen Ausdrucksweisen für M in der Interaktion agieren können und die Analyse interaktiver Marker im Translat auch zu Rückschlüssen über das Funktionieren der MPn im D zuläßt. Als auf die translationsrelevante Betrachtung anwendbare Konzepte aus der Marker- und Interaktionsforschung wurden die Dichotomie zwischen Illokution und Interaktion, die *face*-Konzeption, das Konzept der *valeurs* und *fonctions* und einige Ansätze zur Beschreibung der *marqueurs interactifs* herausgegriffen. Es hat sich gezeigt, daß ein derartiger Ansatzpunkt die Herausarbeitung von FVn im D erleichtert, v.a. aber auch zur Herstellung und Evaluierung interaktiver Kohärenz im Translat herangezogen werden kann. Zu den im Vorhergehenden angesprochenen Synergien zwischen der deutschen Partikelforschung und der *marqueur*-Forschung zum F ließen sich noch zahlreiche weitere hinzufügen, die wir hier nicht mehr nennen können. Wir hoffen jedoch, exemplarisch die reziproke Anwendbarkeit der unterschiedlichen Ansätze aus Interaktions- und Partikelforschung und deren Relevanz und Nutzen für die übersetzungsorientierte Analyse von MPn und *marqueurs* illustriert zu haben.

6 Literatur

AUCHLIN, Antoine; ZENONE, Anna (1980): Conversations, actions, actes de langage: éléments d'un système d'analyse. In: Cahiers de linguistique française 1, 6-41.

FEYRER, Cornelia (1998): Modalität im Kontrast: Ein Beitrag zur übersetzungsorientierten Modalpartikelforschung anhand des Deutschen und des Französischen (Diss. Innsbruck 1997). Frankfurt: Lang (Europäische Hochschulschriften: Reihe 21, Linguistik 202).

LANGNER, Michael (1994): Zur kommunikativen Funktion von Abschwächungen. Pragma- und soziolinguistische Untersuchungen (Diss. Freiburg i. Br. 1993). Münster: Nodus (Studium Sprachwissenschaft, Beiheft 23).

MOESCHLER, Jacques (1980): La réfutation parmi les fonctions interactives marquant l'accord et le désaccord. In: Cahiers de linguistique française 1, 54-78.

Moeschler, Jacques; REBOUL, Anne (1994): Dictionnaire encyclopédique de pragmatique. Tours: Éditions du Seuil.

MOESCHLER, Jacques; SPENGLER, Nina de (1981): *Quand même*: De la concession à la réfutation. In: Cahiers de linguistique française 1, 93-112.

RÉCANATI, François (1981): Le potentiel illocutionnaire des phrases déclaratives. In: Cahiers de linguistique française 2, 23-40.

ROULET, Eddy (1980): Stratégies d'interaction, modes d'implication et marqueurs illocutoires. In: Cahiers de linguistique française 1, 80-127.

SPENGLER, Nina de (1980): Première approche des marqueurs d'interactivité. In: Cahiers de linguistique française 1, 128-155.

Quellen

DB = Dürrenmatt, Friedrich (1985): Der Besuch der alten Dame. Eine tragische Komödie. Neufassung 1980. Zürich: Diogenes.

DB' = Dürrenmatt, Friedrich (1985): La Visite de la vieille dame. Tragi-comédie en trois actes. Paris: Flammarion.

ÖH = Horváth, Ödön von (1994): Geschichten aus dem Wiener Wald (in drei Teilen). In: Krischke, T. (Hrsg.): Ödön von Horváth. Gesammelte Werke. Frankfurt am Main: Suhrkamp, 101-208.

ÖH' = Horváth, Ödön von (1992): Légendes de la forêt viennoise. Pièce populaire en trois parties. Paris: Actes Sud-Papiers.

Die implizite Theorie erfolgreicher Literaturübersetzer
Eine Auswertung von Interviews

Rainer Kohlmayer

1 Einleitung

Die LiteraturübersetzerInnen kommen in der Übersetzungstheorie wenig vor, obwohl

- ihre Produkte oft und gerne kritisch analysiert werden bzw. als Belege irgendwelcher theoretischer Konzepte dienen,
- ihre Theorieresistenz oft und gerne bemängelt wird,
- ihnen von Seiten einiger Theoretiker immer wieder bestimmte Verfahrensweisen präskriptiv verordnet werden.

Mein eigener Ansatz besteht darin,

- reduktionistische Theorieansätze kritisch zu hinterfragen (Kohlmayer 1988, 1997),
- die Übersetzungsarbeit als Konsequenz eines individuellen semantischen und empathischen Kompetenzgefüges zu deuten (Kohlmayer 1996a, 1996b),
- die Selbstaussagen von Literaturübersetzern auszuwerten und literatursemiotisch zu beschreiben.

Letztere Aufgabe setzt repräsentative Sammlungen solcher Selbstaussagen voraus (Honig 1985; Klein 1986; Börsenblatt-Serie 1994/1995). Bei der Suche nach derartigen Quellen stößt man ständig auf die eingangs erwähnten Paradoxien der modernen Übersetzungswissenschaft: Der Vielzahl theoretischer Äußerungen von Nichtpraktikern steht eine Minimalzahl von Werkstattberichten der Praktiker gegenüber, wobei die einen die jeweils anderen zu ignorieren scheinen.

2 Selbstaussagen von sechs erfolgreichen Literaturübersetzern

In den folgenden Ausführungen werte ich hauptsächlich eine Sendereihe aus, die Ende 1996 vom Deutschlandfunk unter dem Titel „Die Kunst des Übersetzens" ausgestrahlt, von mir aufgenommen und weitgehend transkribiert wurde. In der Sendereihe wurden sechs bekannte LiteraturübersetzerInnen, drei Frauen und drei Männer, von Lerke von Saalfeld in halbstündigen Einzelinterviews über ihre Arbeit befragt. Es handelte sich um Swetlana Geier, die vor allem durch ihre Dostojewski-Neuübersetzungen bekannt wurde, um Helmut Scheffel, der vor allem französische *nouveau-roman*-Autoren und Semiotik-Gurus (z.B. Roland Barthes) verdeutschte, um Ragne Maria Gschwend, die z.B. Italo Svevo neu übersetzte, um Willi Zurbrüggen, der vor allem lateinamerikanische Autoren übersetzt, Reinhard Kaiser, der Sachbücher und Literatur aus dem Englischen und Amerikanischen übersetzt und auch selbst als

Schriftsteller hervorgetreten ist, Hildegard Grosche, die für die Vermittlung ungarischer Literatur wichtig war. Es handelt sich also um recht erfolgreiche Übersetzer mit sechs verschiedenen Sprachen, die mehr oder weniger genau über ihren Werdegang, ihre Arbeitsmethoden und ihre spezifischen Probleme Auskunft gaben.

Ich versuche im Folgenden, die in den Interviews angeschnittenen Themen unter wenigen Oberbegriffen zu bündeln. Dabei wähle ich aus der Fülle der möglichen Gesichtspunkte hier nur drei aus:

- Welches *Ziel* setzen sich diese Literaturübersetzer?
- Was sagen sie über das Problem der *Sprachunterschiede*? (Das Problem der kulturellen Unterschiede im weiteren Sinne lasse ich beiseite).[1]
- Was sagen sie über ihr übersetzerisches *Verhalten*?

2.1 Zur Zielsetzung der Literaturübersetzer

Die meisten erwähnen den von Schleiermacher formulierten Zielkonflikt, ob man also den Leser zum Autor oder aber den Autor zum Leser hinbewegen solle, ohne jedoch eine Entweder-Oder-Position einzunehmen. Der Tenor ist, dass Übersetzer nun einmal zwischen dem fremdkulturellen Original und dem deutschen Lesepublikum *vermitteln* müssen. „Ich versuche, beiden gerecht zu werden", fasst Frau Grosche die allgemeine Kompromissbereitschaft zusammen. Scheffel nuanciert: Wenn der Originalautor in seiner Sprache bis an den Rand der Möglichkeiten gehe, dann müsse dies auch der Übersetzer in seiner Sprache nachvollziehen, damit ein Rest von Fremdheit erhalten bleibe. Aber es dürfe „kein holpriges Deutsch" (Scheffel) entstehen. Die „stilistischen Eigenarten des Autors müssen rüberkommen", aber es müsse sich „wie ein guter deutscher Text lesen", formuliert Frau Gschwend ihren übersetzerischen Kompromiss.

In diesem Punkt stimmen alle überein. „Das muttersprachliche Ohr entscheidet", der „Spaß am Formulieren im Deutschen" sei ausschlaggebend bei dem Beruf (Kaiser). Das Fremde solle nicht „mit der Holzhammermethode" gezeigt werden, alles müsse im Deutschen „lebendig" bleiben, solle „mit Genuss" lesbar sein (Zurbrüggen). Derselbe „Lesegenuss" wird von mehreren als Ziel genannt. Scheffel, offensichtlich der theoretisch reflektierteste und emotional distanzierteste dieser Übersetzer (gewis-

---

[1] Das Thema Kultur wird in der Diskussion oft über- und unterschätzt. Zur Zeit ist Literaturübersetzung – analog den sonstigen Güter- und Dienstleistungsverkehr – überwiegend ein Transfer zwischen Großstadtkulturen, d.h. zwischen kulturell relativ homogenen Lesergruppen. Die kulturellen Ähnlichkeiten zwischen den Bücher und Zeitungen lesenden Großstadtbewohnern der Welt sind relativ groß. Und für diese Menschen wird in der Regel übersetzt. Unterschätzt wird dagegen wohl eher die kulturelle Distanz zwischen nationalen Zentren und Rändern, also zwischen dörflicher und Großstadtkultur. Die Distanz kann Jahrhunderte betragen. Vgl. das kulturelle Gefälle zwischen Latein und Althochdeutsch: 300 Jahre lang war die deutsche Schreibkultur eine nahezu reine Übersetzungskultur. – Die meisten der im Folgenden behandelten Übersetzer trennen nicht zwischen sprachlichen und kulturellen Problemen. Sie gehen von einem kulturbestimmten oder mentalitätsorientierten Sprachbegriff aus (sehr deutlich bei Geier und Gschwend).

sermaßen also der ideale *nouveau-roman*-Übersetzer), möchte, dass die „ästhetischen Qualitäten" erhalten bleiben.

Die allgemeine Zielvorstellung der Übersetzer – auf jeden Fall „lebendiges Deutsch", nur ja kein „Übersetzerdeutsch" zu schreiben – enthält also die schlichte Prämisse, dass die literarischen Übersetzer vor allem im Deutschen bzw. in der jeweiligen Zielsprache gewandt und findig sein müssen.

2.2 Zum Problem der Sprachunterschiede

Alle Übersetzer sprechen lexikalische, syntaktische und pragmatische Unterschiede zwischen den Sprachen als ihre normalen Alltagsprobleme an. So spricht Frau Gschwend etwa von den vielen italienischen Partizipialkonstruktionen, die im Deutschen in Nebensätze verwandelt werden müssten, von der italienischen Häufung links- und rechtsseitiger Adjektivattribute, die im Deutschen so nicht möglich seien, von der größeren Vagheit und tautologischen Rhetorik des Italienischen, wo man im Deutschen terminologisch präzise sein müsse, vom Wegfall der Personalpronomina in italienischen Sätzen usw.

Kaiser weist darauf hin, dass der englische Satzbau völlig anders sei als der deutsche, dass da in der Regel die Satzteile völlig umgewälzt werden müssten; dass gerade die lexikalische Nähe zum Englischen eine Gefahr darstelle, wie man sie im Deutschen sonst nur aus diachronischen Übersetzungen kenne: Mittelhochdeutsch „vrouwe" sei ja auch nicht einfach „Frau". Für ihn seien die Übersetzungen aus dem Mittelhochdeutschen im Rahmen seines Germanistikstudiums eine gute Vorbereitung auf den Beruf gewesen.

Die literarischen Übersetzer erweisen sich in diesen Interviews als ausgesprochen reflektiert hinsichtlich der Sprachkontraste, die sie auch präzise benennen können, ob es um das Fehlen der Hilfs- und Modalverben im Russischen (Geier) oder um die Pragmatik der Anredeformen geht, dass z.B. das höfliche deutsche „Sie" nicht nur *förmlicher* sei als das frz. „vous", sondern auch vom Klangmaterial her ganz anders wirke, wenn es in einem Text ständig wiederholt werden müsse (Scheffel).

Mehrere erwähnen, dass sie gar nicht genug Wörterbücher und Nachschlagewerke haben können. Die meisten sind aber völlig davon überzeugt, dass die deutsche Gegenwartssprache flexibel genug ist, um praktisch alle Nuancen jeder Ausgangssprache nachzubilden.

So gibt Zurbrüggen zwar zu, dass das Deutsche, verglichen mit dem Spanischen und Lateinamerikanischen, auf den ersten Blick nicht gerade eine „sinnliche Sprache" zu sein scheine, fügt dann aber hinzu, dass er gerade beim Übersetzen „die Sinnlichkeit des Deutschen" entdeckt habe, und zwar beim Nachschlagen in Synonymwörterbüchern, beim Suchen „unterhalb des aktiven Wortschatzes". *Übersetzen sei ein Entdeckungsprozess.* Meiner Meinung nach ist diese Maxime Zurbrüggens eine großartige Botschaft aus der kreativen Praxis an die Theorie – ein Stück fröhlicher Übersetzungstheorie gegenüber dem Grauschleier zahlreicher theoretisch-didaktischer Äußerungen.[2]

Nur bei einem einzigen pragmatischen Problem werfen die interviewten Übersetzer das Handtuch der Resignation: Bei der Übersetzung von Dialekten. Fremde Dialekte könne man grundsätzlich nicht mit deutschen Dialekten wiedergeben, behaupten Scheffel und Gschwend, die dazu ausführlich befragt wurden. Scheffel bedauert, dass es im Deutschen keine überregionale Umgangssprache gebe (wie im Französischen), in die man ausweichen könne; die deutsche Umgangssprache sei zwar sehr farbig, aber eben immer stark regional geprägt. Man könne Faulknersche Figuren nicht schwäbeln lassen, obwohl manche Übersetzerkollegen für derartige Lösungen plädierten.

Die wenigen Punkte, die ich hier aus der Fülle der metasprachlichen Bemerkungen der Übersetzer angeführt habe, zeigen jedenfalls, wie unverzichtbar mikroskopische Sprachreflexion für anspruchsvolle Übersetzer zu sein scheint.

Dabei spielten in diesen Interviews textlinguistische Probleme der literarischen Gattungen keine große Rolle. Das lag wohl vor allem daran, dass die Interviewerin des Deutschlandfunks nicht danach fragte. In der Praxis muss der literarische Übersetzer selbstverständlich Bescheid wissen über unterschiedliche Erzählperspektiven, also z.B. über erlebte Rede, inneren Monolog, auktoriales Erzählen und dgl.

2.3 Zum übersetzerischen Verhalten

Ich habe diese komplexe Frage in fünf Punkte untergliedert, die aber insgesamt unter dem Schlagwort „holistische Verkörperung" zusammengefasst werden könnten.

2.3.1 Subjektivität

Gehen wir aus vom Selbstverständnis der Übersetzer. Allen literarischen Übersetzern ist klar, dass ihre Arbeit subjektiv geprägt ist, dass das Übersetzen ein Interpretieren ist; alle legen Wert darauf, ihren Interpretationsspielraum zu betonen, auszunutzen, bewusste Interpretations-Entscheidungen zu fällen. Für das Selbstverständnis und Selbstbewusstsein der erfolgreichen Literaturübersetzer scheint dieses Bewusstsein von interpretatorischer Freiheit eine wichtige Rolle zu spielen. Verstehen und subjektives Reproduzieren sehen sie als kreative, künstlerische Tätigkeit an.

Zurbrüggen spricht enthusiastisch von einem „Leidenschaftsberuf". Swetlana Geier bringt das Ethos der Subjektivität einleuchtend auf den Punkt: In der Kunst gäbe es keine Objektivität, kein Loslösen vom eigenen Geschmack. Man könne ja auch nicht „den objektiven Bach" spielen. Offensichtlich sind alle stolz darauf, Interpreten bedeutender Menschen und Werke sein zu dürfen.

---

[2]　Der Zwang zur Aktivierung passiver Sprachkenntnisse macht den großen pädagogischen Wert des Übersetzens auch schon im Sprachunterricht aus. Das gilt auch für die Übersetzung in die Muttersprache. Übersetzen sei die beste Art von *kreativem* Schreiben, die man sich vorstellen könne, meint auch Wechsler (1998).

2.3.2 Sympathie

Zwischen literarischem Übersetzer und Autor bzw. Autoren herrscht in der Regel eine große Sympathie, wie aus den Interviews von fünf der sechs Übersetzer hervorgeht. Lediglich Swetlana Geier lässt durchblicken, dass Solschenitsin ihr nicht besonders sympathisch gewesen sei, von dem sie auch nur ein einziges Buch übersetzt habe. Alle anderen sehen sich als eine Art Partner der Autoren, deren Nähe sie suchen. Selbst wenn der ursprüngliche Übersetzungsauftrag nur per Zufall kam, was die Regel zu sein scheint (!), so wollen sie die Autoren doch als ganze Menschen in ihrem ganzen Kontext kennenlernen. Frau Gschwend sagt es am deutlichsten: Die Autoren „prägen" die Übersetzer; man denke notgedrungen über andere Themen nach, lese andere Bücher, lese die Lieblingsbücher der Autoren, die Briefwechsel, versuche, sich „in sie reinzudenken". Auch Zurbrüggen legt auf das persönliche Kennenlernen großen Wert, er glaubt, die Autoren dann „intuitiv besser zu verstehen", wenn er sie, wie er sagt, „sinnlich" erlebt habe.

2.3.3 Empathie

Fast alle Übersetzer erwähnen mehr oder weniger deutlich, sie hätten beim Übersetzen ein ganzheitliches Bild von den sprechenden Figuren.

Die Sprechweise der Personen sei von Dostojewski festgelegt, die Sicht der Person durch den Übersetzer sei entscheidend, sagt Swetlana Geier. Dabei seien – unter Anspielung auf Bachtins Romantheorie, wonach in Dostojewskis Romanen ein Gegeneinander von Stimmen und Ideen herrsche – auch die einzelnen Figuren selbst polyphon, bis auf Fürst Myschkin im „Idiot", dessen Sprache nicht individuell, sondern abstrakt sei, da er als „Mensch an sich" entworfen sei. Diese Abstraktheit sei besonders schwer zu übersetzen gewesen.

Helmut Scheffel erwähnt die Bedeutung des Subtextes, der „sous-conversation" bei Nathalie Sarraute, wo eben – zu erschließen aus winzigen Andeutungen – unterhalb der eigentlichen Verbalsprache „ein ganzer Film" persönlicher Einstellungen und Gefühle ablaufe, den man erhalten müsse.

Zurbrüggen spricht vom „Reinfinden in die Person", besonders in Dialogen: „[W]ie spricht er jetzt genau, grinst er oder lächelt er dabei, wenn er das sagt, oder schubst er ihn oder stupst er ihn?" Aber im Prinzip müsse man sich auch bei normalen langen Prosasätzen seine Gedanken machen, was also wohl bedeutet, sich ein ganzes Bild machen, eine Art Film im Kopf haben.

Reinhard Kaiser ist sich am explizitesten dieser geistigen Schauspielerei bewusst, als was man diese empathischen Identifikations- und Rollenspiele etwas burschikos bezeichnen könnte. Wörtlich sagt er (entsprechend meiner Transkription):

> „Und ich meine, man könnte das auch so formulieren – und ich – mir kommt es ja so vor, als wenn das Übersetzen 'ne ganze Menge – auf sprachlicher Ebene natürlich, nicht auf gestischer oder körperlicher, aber auf sprachlicher Ebene – mit Schauspielerei zu tun hat. Also verschiedene Rollen spielen, verschiedene Rollen *sprachlich* spielen, inszenieren und zum Klingen

bringen. Da ist der Reiz eben auch der, nicht nur eine Rolle und immer wieder denselben Typus zu spielen, sondern ganz unterschiedliche."

Also: „Schauspielkunst" (Güttinger 1963:41; Levý 1969:66), „Kopftheater" (Kohlmayer 1996a:75-88) oder „Film im Kopf", wie Helmut Scheffel und andere sagen. Diese These vom Übersetzen als schauspielerischem Rollenwechsel ist aus vielen anderen Übersetzeraussagen zu belegen. Dabei scheint mir die Behauptung Kaisers, die „Schauspielerei" beschränke sich auf das rein Sprachliche, sei nicht gestisch und körperlich, falsch oder untertrieben zu sein. Der Literaturübersetzer setzt den Körper ein – mimisch, gestisch, stimmlich. Bei Bühnentexten ist dies ohnehin offensichtlich, bei narrativen Texten scheint es mir ebenso naheliegend zu sein – und wird auch aus vielen Quellen bestätigt. So merkt Klaus Birkenhauer in einer Zusammenstellung von Charakteristika der literarischen Übersetzer die laufbahntypische Besonderheit an, dass „ein gar nicht geringer Prozentsatz der Übersetzer [...] früher einmal beim Theater" gewesen sei (Klein 1986:507).

2.3.4 Ton und Atmosphäre

Das ganzheitliche Verhalten der Literaturübersetzer zeigt sich auch darin, dass sie gerne vom „Ton des Ganzen" (Scheffel) oder vom Erhalten der „Atmosphäre" (Geier) eines Buches sprechen. Scheffel, der ansonsten am wenigsten emotional oder nebulös argumentiert, ist hier am nachdrücklichsten: Es komme weniger auf einzelne Fehler an als darauf, den „Ton des Ganzen" zu finden, der für den jeweiligen Autor typisch sei; bei bedeutenden Kunstwerken habe der Text tatsächlich einen bestimmten Ton. In der französischen Übersetzertradition, in der Scheffel zu Hause ist, wird die mündliche, rhetorisch-körpersprachliche Seite des Übersetzens immer wieder betont (Barthes 1974). Ein neueres Beispiel dafür ist das Buch des bedeutenden Übersetzers Henri Meschonnic über die Poetik des Übersetzens: „Il en découle clairement que, dans un texte littéraire, c'est l'oralité qui est à traduire" (Meschonnic 1999:54). Die deutsche Literatur- und Übersetzungsgeschichte kann hier nachdrücklich auf Herders „Ästhetik des Gehörs" (Poltermann 1987:49) und Nietzsches Medienphilosophie (Fietz:1992) verweisen, die sich ausführlich über die Bedeutung des „Tons" in der Literatur geäußert haben (Kohlmayer 1996a:75f.).[3]

Diese intensive Orientierung an der individuellen Machart der Texte, an der „handwerklichen Komponente", die in der Schriftstellerei ebenso vorhanden sei wie beim Übersetzen (Kaiser), das Achten auf die individuelle Sprechweise der Figuren, das psychologische Interesse am Kennenlernen der einzelnen Autoren ist vermutlich der Grund, weshalb literarische Übersetzer so wenig Interesse an abstrakteren translationstheoretischen Überlegungen haben, während ihnen etwa sprachlich-grammatische und lexikalische Dinge sehr wichtig sind.[4]

---

[3] Im Unterricht zeigt sich meist schon beim lauten Lesen einer Passage, wie gut jemand übersetzen wird. Lesen ist immer auch eine körpersprachliche und semantische Analyse.

[4] Kein einziger der sechs literarischen Übersetzer spricht vom Publikum oder vom Auftraggeber und dergleichen Marketing-Kategorien, mit denen heute die ‚nichtliterarischen' Übersetzerstu-

2.3.5 Doppelbindung

Im übersetzerischen Verhalten der Literaturübersetzer zeigt sich somit ein eigentümliches und vermutlich unauflösbares Paradox bzw. eine für Literaturübersetzer wohl typische „Doppelbindung" (Watzlawick et al. 1969): Fast bei allen Autoren schimmert mehr oder weniger deutlich die Auffassung durch, dass die *Satzeinheit* des Originaltextes möglichst zu respektieren sei. Jedenfalls klingt das bei Scheffel deutlich an, und auch Ragne Maria Gschwend wendet sich ausdrücklich gegen das Glätten und Zerschneiden der langen Sätze des Originals. Aber andererseits sollen die Satzeinheiten aus der Zielsprache heraus, also aus dem Deutschen heraus neu geschaffen werden, entsprechend dem Ton und der Atmosphäre des *Ganzen*. Orientierung am Satz *und* Orientierung am Ganzen also.

Diese paradoxe Doppelbindung zwischen bottom-up und top-down-Prozessen (wie die Psycholinguistik das nennt) – bzw. zwischen analytischem und synthetischem Vorgehen, zwischen linker und rechter Gehirnhemisphäre, wie manche vermuten – schlägt sich z.B. in dem außerordentlich nützlichen übersetzerischen Motto von Swetlana Geier nieder: „Nase hoch beim Übersetzen!" Womit sie ausdrücken will, dass nicht die syntaktische Reihenfolge auf dem Papier nachgebaut, sondern der Satz nach dem Verstandenhaben aus dem Gedächtnis heraus zielsprachlich neu geformt werden soll. Das körpersprachliche Motto „Nase hoch beim Übersetzen" wiegt einige Kilo übersetzungsdidaktische Lektüre auf.

3 Literaturübersetzen als Verkörperung

Aus diesen Selbstaussagen relativ erfolgreicher LiteraturübersetzerInnen, die natürlich durch weitere Analysen verfeinert und ergänzt werden müssen, ergeben sich meiner Meinung nach einige Rückschlüsse auf Theorie und Didaktik des Literaturübersetzens.

Die fiktionale Welt und die erzählten Inhalte können anscheinend *nicht körperlos* weiter gegeben werden, der literarische Text bindet seine Botschaften immer an bestimmte Sprechweisen und Figuren. Die Semantik eines literarischen Textes ist gebunden an die Präsenz eines Körpers, einer Stimme, eines „Tons", eines Ich. Der Text ist als Verbalsprache nur die Spitze des Eisbergs, der Übersetzer bzw. Leser nimmt aber nicht nur die Verbalsprache mit ihren semantischen Informationen wahr, sondern auf Grund zahlloser Andeutungen wird er gezwungen, eine Art „Film im Kopf" ablaufen zu lassen, den aggressiven, ironischen oder bitteren oder gemütlichen Ton des Erzählers oder der Figuren zu erschließen. Für den Übersetzer und Leser ist alles Verbale Symptom eines ganzen Menschen.

---

denten traktiert werden und – im Hinblick auf ihre spätere Funktion im Dienstleistungssektor – durchaus auch traktiert werden müssen. In der Literaturübersetzung gilt eher, dass der besorgte Blick aufs Publikum den Text ans jeweilige Publikum bindet, wodurch die Verfallszeit des Textes verkürzt wird (vgl. Kohlmayer 1988).

Der gesamte Aufwand an literarisch-handwerklichem Material – Rhythmus, Reim, Pausenzeichen und sonstige Satzzeichen, Wortstellung, Stilebenen, rhetorische Figuren usw. – dient dazu, *bestimmte Sprechweisen möglichst lebendig, unverwechselbar, symptomatisch, materiell zu fixieren.* Satzbau, Klang, Atemführung, Rhythmus usw. sind das Baumaterial der Literatur, mit dem die Botschaften auf spezifische Art verschmolzen sind.

Der Literaturübersetzer muss den symptomatischen *Sprachgestus* erfassen können – die Einheit aus materieller und geistiger Sprachform. Was die oben genannten Literaturübersetzer als „Ton", „Sprechweise", „Stil" usw. bezeichneten, ist genau diese Qualität des literarischen Textes: Die Suggestion einer Ganzheit, die aus einzelnen Sprachelementen zu ergänzen ist.

Ich nenne diese *abduktive*[5] Fähigkeit der verstehenden Ergänzung oder Vervollständigung und der zielsprachlich produktiven Neuschaffung „empathische Kompetenz", also das verstehende Erschließen eines stimmlichen, gestischen, körperlichen, emotionalen Gesamtbildes aus verbalen Andeutungen und das entsprechende zielsprachliche Reproduzieren. Ähnlich wie man beim Telefonieren mit Freund oder Freundin die Gestik und Körperlichkeit des Anderen geistig präsent hat und anhand zahlloser sprachlich-stimmlicher Kleinigkeiten immer wieder aufs Neue vor sich sieht, muss der Literaturübersetzer eine bestimmte Sprechweise als Gesamtbild reproduzieren bzw. produzieren.

Literaturübersetzen ist also Literaturinszenieren und intensivstes Leben in anderen Personen. Ich könnte hier viele einschlägige Zitate vorlegen (vgl. Kohlmayer 1996a: 87f). Es mehren sich die Anzeichen, dass sich die Literaturübersetzer derzeit mit größerem Selbstbewusstsein auf die theoretische Besonderheit ihrer Übersetzweise besinnen: Das 1998 erschienene Buch des amerikanischen Übersetzers Robert Wechsler trägt gleichsam als Fanal den programmatischen Titel: „Performing without a Stage. The Art of Literary Translation".

Ich will zum Schluss noch ein Beispiel zitieren, das vor wenigen Jahren in einem Interview vorkam. Die Germersheim-Absolventin Karin von Schweder-Schreiner, die über 40 Bücher aus dem Portugiesischen ins Deutsche übersetzte, antwortete auf die Frage, wie sie sich nach der Fertigstellung eines Buches fühle, folgendermaßen:

> „Ich habe in diesem Buch [= Jorge Amado, „Tocaia Grande"] gelebt, mit den Personen gelebt. Als ich fertig war, war ich tieftraurig. [...] Ich habe mit diesen Personen so intensiv Umgang gehabt, sie waren mir so ans Herz gewachsen, daß ich das Gefühl hatte, ich muß mich von lieben Freunden verabschieden und weiß, daß ich sie lange, lange nicht wiedersehen werde. Das berührt mich jetzt noch immer. Das fand ich einfach unglaublich! Ich fand es phantastisch, wie lebendig er diese Figuren geschaffen hatte!" (Börsenblatt-Serie, 9.12.1994:13)

Nun kann man natürlich einwenden, diese Einfühlerei sei noch lange kein Beweis für die Qualität einer Übersetzung. Richtig. Ich würde aber erwidern, dass literarisches Übersetzen *ohne* starke Empathie von vornherein unmöglich ist. Die Fähigkeit zum

---

5   Diese Ergänzung ist keine Deduktion und keine Induktion, sondern im Peirceschen Sinn eine *Abduktion*: Hypothesenbildung auf der Basis von vorläufigem, unvollständigem Material, wie bei der detektivischen Hypothesenbildung (Rohr 1993).

Kopftheater, Gefühlstheater, Körpertheater ist die Voraussetzung für das Literaturübersetzen. Daraus ergibt sich dann die interessante Folgefrage, wie eine entsprechende Didaktik des Literaturübersetzens sinnvoll zu gestalten wäre.

4 Literatur

BARTHES, Roland (1974): Die Lust am Text. Frankfurt: Suhrkamp.

BÖRSENBLATT-SERIE (1994/1995): Kunst, Wissenschaft und Praxis des Übersetzens. 26. August 1994 bis 7. Februar 1995 (11 Folgen).

FIETZ, Rudolf (1992): Medienphilosophie. Musik, Sprache und Schrift bei Friedrich Nietzsche. Würzburg: Königshausen & Neumann.

GÜTTINGER, Fritz (1963): Zielsprache. Theorie und Technik des Übersetzens. Zürich: Manesse.

HONIG, Edwin (1985): The Poet's Other Voice. Conversations on Literary Translation. Amherst: University of Massachusetts Press.

KLEIN, Nikolaus (1986) (Hrsg.): Übersetzer – Kuriere des Geistes. Vom Übersetzen ins Deutsche. In: Zeitschrift für Kulturaustausch 36.4, 504-644 (24 Werkstattberichte).

KOHLMAYER, Rainer (1997): Was dasteht und was nicht dasteht. Kritische Anmerkungen zum Textbegriff der Übersetzungstheorie. In: Fleischmann, E. et al. (Hrsg.): Translationsdidaktik. Grundfragen der Übersetzungswissenschaft. Tübingen: Gunter Narr, 60-66.

— (1996a): Oscar Wilde in Deutschland und Österreich. Untersuchungen zur Rezeption der Komödien und zur Theorie der Bühnenübersetzung. Tübingen: Niemeyer (Theatron 20).

— (1996b): Wissen und Können des Literaturübersetzers. Bausteine einer individualistischen Kompetenztheorie. In: Kelletat, Andreas F. (Hrsg.): Übersetzerische Kompetenz. Beiträge zur universitären Übersetzerausbildung in Deutschland und Skandinavien. Frankfurt am Main etc.: Lang (Publikationen des Fachbereichs Angewandte Sprach- und Kulturwissenschaft der Johannes-Gutenberg-Universität Mainz in Germersheim, Reihe A: Abhandlungen und Sammelbände 22), 187-205.

— (1988): Der Literaturübersetzer zwischen Original und Markt. Eine Kritik funktionalistischer Übersetzungstheorien. In: Lebende Sprachen 33.4, 145-156.

LEVÝ, Jiří (1969): Die literarische Übersetzung. Theorie einer Kunstgattung. Frankfurt am Main: Athenäum (Athenäum Bücher zur Dichtkunst).

MESCHONNIC, Henri (1999): Poétique du traduire. Paris: Verdier.

POLTERMANN, Andreas (1987): Die Erfindung des Originals. Zur Geschichte der Übersetzungskonzeptionen in Deutschland im 18. Jahrhundert. In: Schultze, B. (Hrsg.): Die literarische Übersetzung. Fallstudien zu ihrer Kulturgeschichte. Berlin: Schmidt, 14-52.

ROHR, Susanne (1993): Über das Schönheit des Findens. Die Binnenstruktur menschlichen Verstehens nach Charles S. Peirce: Abduktionslogik und Kreativität. Stuttgart: Metzler & Poeschel.

SAALFELD, Lerke von (1996): „Die Kunst des Übersetzens". Deutschlandfunk 8. September bis 13. Oktober 1996 (Interviews mit den ÜbersetzerInnen Swetlana Geier, Helmut Scheffel, Ragne Maria Gschwend, Willi Zurbrüggen, Reinhard Kaiser, Hildegard Grosche).

WATZLAWICK, Paul et al. (1969): Menschliche Kommunikation. Formen, Störungen, Paradoxien. Bern etc.: Hans Huber.

WECHSLER, Robert (1998): Performing without a Stage. The Art of Literary Translation. North Haven: Catbird Press.

Übersetzungswissenschaftliche Minima in einem allgemeinen russistischen Sprachkurs

Cornelia Mannewitz

Ein Erlebnis, das ich einmal mit einer ausländischen Studentin hatte, soll illustrieren, worum es geht: Diese Studentin studierte neben Germanistik in ihrer Heimat auch Russisch und wollte es während ihres Auslandsaufenthalts nicht ganz vergessen. Daher kam sie zu mir und wollte sich für einen Übersetzungskurs einschreiben. Auf meine Frage, warum sie gerade einen so anspruchsvollen Kurs wähle, antwortete sie sehr erstaunt, Übersetzung sei doch das A und O des Fremdsprachenlernens – mit Übersetzung beginne es, und ohne Übersetzung sei auch ein Weiterlernen doch überhaupt gar nicht vorstellbar.

Man kann wahrscheinlich noch immer niemandem einen Vorwurf machen, der so denkt. Er hat die Vorstellungen von der Rolle der Übersetzung übernommen, die ungeachtet aller zurückliegenden Jahrzehnte der Existenz einer Übersetzungswissenschaft und entsprechender didaktischer Überlegungen (vgl. dazu ausführlich Krings 1995) noch in manchem Fremdsprachenunterricht existieren. Übersetzung dient im Verständnis vieler hauptsächlich dazu, sprachliche Korrektheit zu überprüfen, Fehler aufzuzeigen; das scheint auch das Anliegen der Übersetzung (noch dazu mit einsprachigem Wörterbuch) als Prüfungsform zu sein, wie sie in vielen Ersten Staatsprüfungen in Deutschland von Lehramtskandidaten verlangt wird.

Selbstverständlich kann das Übersetzen auch auf diesem Gebiet Funktionen haben. Ein falsch verstandener kommunikativ orientierter Fremdsprachenunterricht lehrt zum Beispiel mitunter Vermeidungsstrategien: Bestimmte Wörter und Konstruktionen, die einem Studenten zu schwer erscheinen, kann er meiden, wenn ihm nur synonyme Ausdrucksmittel zu Gebote stehen – darunter leiden die Sprachsystemkenntnisse, aber auch die Methodenkenntnisse (z.B. der Wörterbuchbenutzung) bleiben rudimentär, und an ihnen zu arbeiten, ist auch gerade auf dem fortgeschrittenen Niveau, das die Studenten im Hauptstudium erreicht haben, sinnvoll. Allerdings gibt es dafür Übungen an einzelnen Sätzen und womöglich noch kleineren syntaktischen Einheiten. Was hingegen eigentlich in einem Übersetzungkurs geschehen sollte, möchte ich im folgenden darlegen. Dabei gehe ich von der curricularen Situation eines konkreten von mir geleiteten Kurses aus:

Die Studenten sind keine Übersetzer- bzw. Dolmetscherstudenten (deshalb „allgemeiner russistischer Sprachkurs"). Sie absolvieren ein Magister- oder ein Lehramtsstudium. Der Kurs hat einen Umfang von drei Semesterwochenstunden und ist Teil der sprachpraktischen Ausbildung im Hauptstudium. Nach Wahl kann in ihm ein benoteter Schein erworben werden; sollten die Studenten im Nebenfach studieren, müssen sie den Kurs aber nicht besuchen, weil im Hauptstudium nicht so viele Stunden für sie obligatorisch sind (der Kurs konkurriert zur Zeit mit einem fachsprachlichen und einem Konversationskurs). Dies sind die Rahmenbedingungen, unter denen minimale Einsichten in die Problematik des Phänomens Übersetzung vermittelt werden sollen.

Um das zu erreichen, müssen folgende Aufgaben gelöst werden:

- Übersetzen wird als Sprachtätigkeit dargestellt; es ist neben Hören, Sprechen, Lesen und Schreiben eine selbständige Fertigkeit, die noch dazu durch ihren sprachübergreifenden Charakter ausgezeichnet ist
- das Wesen der Übersetzung (oder eigentlich, genauer, unter Einbeziehung des Dolmetschens – der Translation) wird erläutert
- innerhalb der objektiv gegebenen Grenzen wird ein gewisses übersetzerisches Problembewußtsein entwickelt.

Als Ausgangspunkt dienen dabei folgende Grundannahmen (gleichzeitig die oben apostrophierten Minima):

1) Bei der Übersetzung handelt es sich um einen komplizierten Prozeß mit vielen Parametern. Die Übersetzung transportiert eine Information aus einer Sprache A in eine Sprache B, und zwar so, daß die in Sprache B erhaltene relevante Informationsmenge mit jener in Sprache A identisch ist. (Im vollen Bewußtsein der Tatsache, daß es andere Möglichkeiten gibt, gehe ich dennoch hier von diesem informationstheoretisch inspirierten Verständnis der Übersetzung aus, wie es von Vernay (1991:27ff) in Anlehnung an Mounin formuliert worden ist. Aus ihm ergeben sich nämlich Anknüpfungspunkte für weitere Fragen: zum Sender, zum Empfänger und zur Art der Information. Der Übersetzer muß sowohl die Intentionen des Senders als auch die Erwartungen des Empfängers berücksichtigen. Damit und mit der zu transportierenden Information hängen Problemkomplexe wie soziale Unterschiede zwischen Sender und Empfänger, Textsortenerfahrungen und der Kulturspezifik des zu Übersetzenden generell zusammen, die somit ebenfalls zum Gegenstand übersetzungstheoretischer Überlegungen werden und sich ja auch in entwickelten Konzeptionen niederschlagen (etwa in der Skopos-Theorie; vgl. dazu Reiß/Vermeer 1991). Hönig definiert 1995 das Übersetzen sogar in diesem Sinne: „(Übersetzen ist) die Fähigkeit, zielsprachlich und -kulturell unauffällige Texte auf der Grundlage einer ausgangssprachlichen Textvorlage erstellen zu können" (Hönig 1995:26-17). Und: Bei der Übersetzung stoßen Sprachen zusammen. Diese Tatsache gerät bei den vorangegangenen Überlegungen fast aus dem Blickfeld der Betrachtung, ist aber natürlich ein wesentliches Merkmal der Übersetzung. Es ist bereits deutlich, daß es mit einer Arbeit an den Reflexionen struktureller Unterschiede zwischen Ausgangs- und Zielsprache dabei nicht sein Bewenden haben kann.)

2) Was übersetzt wird, ist der Text, nicht der Satz und schon gar nicht das einzelne Wort. (Ohne dies zu postulieren, können wir der Komplexität der Information nicht gerecht werden. Einige grundlegende Überlegungen dazu finden sich übrigens in einem älteren, aber noch immer sehr instruktiven Beitrag von Dressler mit dem Titel „Der Beitrag der Textlinguistik zur Übersetzungswissenschaft" (Dressler 1991), unter anderem auch der Gedanke, daß Textlinguistik und Über-

setzungswissenschaft selbst sowohl hinsichtlich ihres Alters als auch ihres Status im Kanon der sprachwissenschaftlichen Disziplinen miteinander verwandt sind; inwieweit hieraus auf Präferenzen für Synergieeffekte zwischen beiden geschlossen werden kann, soll hier dahingestellt bleiben.)

3) Ein Übersetzer trifft ständig sowohl mikro- als auch makrostrategische Entscheidungen (zu diesem Begriff vgl. Hönig 1995:50ff). Diese Annahme verwundert nicht nach den beiden vorausgegangenen; sie wird auch unten, anhand der Beispiele, noch weiter expliziert.

Die genannten Minima bauen auf übersetzungswissenschaftlichen Erkenntnissen auf und sind außerdem, wenn man ehrlich ist, gar nicht so weit entfernt vom gesunden Menschenverstand. Trotzdem sind sie für Studenten zunächst oft schwer zu akzeptieren. Studenten kommen mit unterschiedlichen Erwartungen in den Kurs, aber meist mit den befürchteten: Sie wollen üben; sie wollen sprachliche Fehler korrigieren; sie fragen nach jedem übersetzten Satz, ob die Übersetzung so akzeptabel ist; in einem extremen Fall begann eine Studentin stets sofort und prima vista zu übersetzen, noch ehe sie selbst den Satz auch nur ansatzweise überblickt hatte.

Es ist daher erforderlich, aus den vereinbarten Minima Grundprinzipien für das Arbeiten im Kurs abzuleiten:

1) Es werden Texte übersetzt. Die kleinste Einheit des Übersetzungsvergleichs und der Übersetzungskritik ist der Absatz. Einzelne lexikalische oder grammatische Schwierigkeiten werden anhand einzelner kontextloser Sätze abgehandelt.

2) Ziel ist nicht die „ultimative", perfekte Übersetzung; am wichtigsten ist die Diskussion über Probleme.

3) Die Überschrift des Textes wird zuletzt übersetzt. Das mag wie ein unnötiger Gag wirken, trägt aber nur der Tatsache Rechnung, daß Überschriften von Texten in besonderem Maße kulturspezifisch sind. Man vergleiche etwa die Filmtitel „The Money Pit" und „Полосатый рейс" mit den zumindest im ersten Fall erstaunlicherweise „reißerischeren" deutschen Verleihtiteln „Geschenk ist noch zu teuer" bzw. „Nun schlägt's dreizehn!" oder die Restitution des Dostojewskischen Originaltitels «Преступление и наказание» für das im deutschen Sprachraum Usus gewordene moralisierende „Schuld und Sühne" durch die neue Übersetzung von Swetlana Geier mit dem Titel „Verbrechen und Strafe".

Die im folgenden vorgestellten Texte – zugegebenermaßen Extreme, Herausforderungen und mitunter auch eine Zumutung für den sich treulich in der Sprache übenden Studenten – und ihre Übersetzungsvarianten spiegeln einiges von dieser Arbeit:

1) Die Studenten bekamen einen Text über Sicherheit und Brandschutz aus einer Gebrauchsanweisung für einen Heizlüfter zur Übersetzung. Die Gebrauchsanweisung stammte noch aus sowjetischer Zeit, aus den 80er Jahren, und die Studenten hatten die Aufgabe, den Text so zu übersetzen, daß dieses Gerät in den 90er Jahren in Deutschland verkauft werden könnte – eine Aufgabe, die nicht frei ist von Science-Fiction-Elementen, denn sowohl der Ort als auch die Zeit

der Rezeption dieses Textes sollten verändert werden (ein Fall einer „overt translation" nach House – vgl. House 1977:66ff und, besonders zur didaktischen Bedeutsamkeit dieses Begriffs, House 1997:167 –, bei der der Ausgangstext offensichtlich nicht für denjenigen geschaffen ist, der seine Übersetzung rezipiert). Zum Vergleich wurde ein moderner deutscher Text einer Gebrauchsanweisung für eine Waschmaschine herangezogen. Natürlich wurden Unterschiede festgestellt: Im russischen Text fielen besonders rigorose Formulierungen wie „внимательно ознакомьтесь с настоящим руководством по эксплуатации" (statt einfach nur „ознакомьтесь") und die vielfache Wiederholung von „запрещается" (sogar in Großbuchstaben) auf; insgesamt wurde eine starke Orientierung auf die technischen Aspekte des Geräts deutlich, die sich übrigens außerdem in verschiedenen technischen Zeichnungen und im allgemeinen anspruchslosen Design dieser Gebrauchsanweisung sowie auch im Gebrauch techniksprachspezifischer Maßangaben zeigte, so zum Beispiel in der Angabe einer Entfernung bei einer Aufstellungsempfehlung für Wohnräume in Millimetern. Im deutschen Text dagegen war das Gerät sogar personifiziert (das Gerät sprach von sich in der ersten Person – unschwer zu erraten, daß die Studenten in ihrer Übersetzung so weit nicht gingen), begegnete recht häufig das Wort „bitte" oder wurde statt des Imperativs der Konjunktiv gebraucht; insgesamt herrschte eine Orientierung auf den Käufer vor (zumal den technisch nicht versierten). Vgl. Formulierungen wie „Spritzen Sie keinesfalls mein Äußeres mit einem Wasserstrahl ab!"; „Sollten Sie mich eines Tages endgültig außer Betrieb nehmen und durch ein neues Gerät ersetzen, dann sorgen Sie bitte für die Zerstörung meines Türschlosses" u.ä. Es folgen Beispiele für Formulierungen des Originaltextes und Übersetzungsvarianten für sie (mit Kursivdruck sind offensichtliche Fälle einer Angleichung an das Muster der deutschen Gebrauchsanweisung, mit Fettdruck dagegen Übernahmen aus dem Original bezeichnet, die hinsichtlich ihrer Angemessenheit im deutschen Text diskutiert werden könnten):

„4.1. Перед включением электротепловентилятора внимательно ознакомьтесь с настоящим руководством по эксплуатации." – „Lesen Sie vor dem Einschalten des Elektroventilators **aufmerksam** die vorliegende Bedienungsanleitung!", „Vor Inbetriebnahme des Heizlüfters *bitte* **aufmerksam** Gebrauchsanweisung durchlesen." „4.2. ПОМНИТЕ, что в электротепловентиляторе применяются открытые нагревательные элементы, поэтому он должен работать ПОД НАДЗОРОМ." -*„Denken Sie daran, daß im Elektroventilator offene Heizelemente vorhanden sind, deshalb sollte er nur unter Aufsicht arbeiten.", „Bitte beachten Sie: Im Heizlüfter befinden sich offenliegende Heizstäbe. Gerät nur unter Aufsicht betreiben." (…) „4.8. КАТЕГОРИЧЕСКИ ЗАПРЕЩАЕТСЯ прислонять и навешивать на электротепловентилятор бытовые вещи для сушки во время его работы." – „Es ist strikt verboten, während des Betriebs an den Elektroventilator Gegenstände zum Trocknen anzulehnen bzw. zu hängen.", *„Achtung!* Bei der Benutzung des Heizlüfters *auf keinen Fall* Sachen zum Trocknen auf das Gerät hängen/legen." „4.9. Не устанавливайте электротепловентилятор близко к стенам, шкафам, портьерам и другим бытовым предметам. Расстояние от вышеуказанных предметов должно быть не менее 200 мм." – „Stellen Sie den Elektroventilator nicht in der Nähe von Wänden, Schränken, Portieren oder anderen Gegenständen auf. Der Abstand von den obengenannten Gegenständen *sollte* nicht weniger als *20 cm* betragen.", „Heizlüfter nicht zu dicht an Wände, Schränke, Vorhänge oder andere Einrichtungsgegenstände stellen. Der Abstand zu den oben genannten Gegenständen *sollte* nicht weniger als *20 cm* betragen."

Als begleitende Übungen dienten übrigens nicht nur solche zur Übersetzungskritik und die Übersetzungen selbst, sondern auch „einfache" im Schreiben eines Textes einer festgelegten Textsorte (zum Beispiel einer Grußadresse) in beiden Sprachen unter Beachtung der entsprechenden Textgestaltungsnormen.

2) Diese Übersetzung verlangte von den Studenten bereits eine hinreichende „Wurstigkeit" im Umgang mit dem Sprachmaterial. Trotzdem war die Aufgabe, ein Lied zu übersetzen, noch anspruchsvoller für sie (es handelte sich um das Lied „Я верю, друзья" von V. Vojnovič/Text und O. Fel'cman/Melodie). Die formalen Kriterien sind hier sogar strenger als bei einem Gedicht, denn Versmaß und Reim müssen genau eingehalten werden, und gleichzeitig darf die inhaltliche Entfernung vom Original nicht zu groß sein. Nachfolgend Übersetzungsvarianten für die erste Strophe und den Refrain:

(Original:)

„Заправлены в планшеты / Космические карты. / И штурман уточняет / В последний раз маршрут. / Давайте-ка, ребята, / Споемте (в другом варианте: Закурим – К.М.) перед стартом. / У нас еще в запасе / Четырнадцать минут. / Я верю, друзья, / Караваны ракет / Помчат нас вперед / От звезды до звезды. / На пыльных тропинках / Далеких планет / Останутся наши следы." -

A)

„Hineingesteckt in die Kartentasche//Eingesteckt in die Kartentasche
die kosmischen Karten.//die kosmischen Karten.
Und der Steuermann/Pilot präzisiert//Der Pilot präzisiert ein
ein letztes Mal den Kurs.//letztes Mal den Kurs.
Kommt, Kinder,//Los, Kinder, auf denn, kommt, laßt
laßt uns singen vor dem Starten.//uns singen vor dem Starten.
Wir haben noch Zeit/Es ist noch Zeit,//Ein Vorrat an Zeit bleibt uns,
die letzte Viertelstund.//die letzte Viertelstund.
    Ich glaube daran/vertraue darauf, Freunde,//Ich glaube daran,
daß unendlich viele Raketen//daß unendliche Raketen
uns in die Zukunft tragen//uns tragen in die Zukunft
zu den Sternen hinauf.//zu den Sternen hinauf.
Auf staubigen Pfaden//Auf staubigen Pfaden
weit entfernter Sterne//entfernter Sterne
werden unsere Spuren zurückbleiben.//zurückgeblieben die Spuren.",

B)

„Die Weltraumkarten **stecken**
schon in der Karten**tasche**.
Der Kaptain präzisiert/überprüft noch
das letzte Mal den **Kurs**.
Kommt, Freunde, laßt uns **rauchen**
vor unserm Start ins **Weltall**.
Noch zehn Minuten warten,

dann geht es endlich **los**.
Ich glaube daran,
daß Millionen **Raketen**
vorantragen uns
von Gestirn zu **Gestirn**.
Auf staubigen Pfaden
entfernter **Planeten**
sind dann unsre Spuren **zu sehn**."

Variante A zeigt deutlich den Kampf der Studentin mit dem Text (links der doppelten Schrägstriche kann man eine Art Interlinearversion, rechts eine elaboriertere Übersetzungsvariante erkennen), der allerdings trotz allem nicht zu einer eigenen, souveränen Lösung geführt hat. Variante B ist wesentlich gelungener; die Fragen des Inhalts und auch der Metrik sind hier durchaus befriedigend gelöst, nur einige Reime sind nicht berücksichtigt (sie sind allerdings auch im Original nicht präzise; mit Fettdruck sind die nötigen Reime bezeichnet, zusätzlich unterstrichen sind die in der Übersetzung tatsächlich realisierten). Fast am interessantesten war übrigens die der Übersetzung vorausgehende Diskussion über das Lied. Hierbei zeigte sich, daß heutige Studenten in Deutschland Schwierigkeiten haben, sich in den Charakter eines typischen sowjetischen Massen- und Jugendliedes einzufühlen. Die Studenten reflektierten über einzelne Aspekte des Textes – teilweise interpretierten sie die häufige Erwähnung von „Raketen" als eine verschleierte Lobpreisung der sowjetischen Aufrüstung – und bezweifelten die Notwendigkeit der Einhaltung der strengen Formforderungen, offensichtlich mit dem Vorbild eines individuell zur Gitarre vorgetragenen Liedes im Hinterkopf. Man wird nicht fehlgehen, hierin einen Beleg für die Höhe der Barrieren zu sehen, die die Kulturspezifik von Texten mitunter für die Übersetzung baut.

3) Beispiel 3 könnte auch an erster Stelle stehen. Es enthält eine ganze Palette von Aspekten, die für die Entwicklung übersetzerischen Problembewußtseins wichtig sind. Der russische Text stammte aus dem Internet. Bei allen daraus resultierenden möglichen Zweifeln an seiner Reputation ist er ein typisches Beispiel moderner russischer Belletristik mit der in ihr enthaltenen Auswahl an Sprachvarietäten (die ebenfalls ein Ausweis seiner Kulturspezifik sind). Dieser Text sollte in erster Linie die Grundannahme stützen, daß der Gegenstand der Übersetzung der Text ist; zweitens sollte er deutlich machen, welche Rolle Sprachvarietäten in einem modernen russischen Text spielen, und Methodenkenntnisse zum Umgang mit ihnen entwickeln. Das Hauptaugenmerk galt dem besonders frequenten und den Studenten bis dato unbekannten Wort „ништяк". Slangwörterbücher des Russischen, mit denen (und mit deren mitunter strittiger lexikographischer Qualität) die Studenten sich hierbei zwangsläufig auseinandersetzen mußten, führen (mindestens) zwei Bedeutungen dieses Wortes an: ‚gut' (genauer gesagt, eine positive Bewertung, evtl. stärker emphatisch) und ‚Essensrest'. Es entstand eine echte Semantisierungssituation, in der makrostrategisch argumentiert und Textkohäsionsmittel zu Rate gezogen werden mußten. Bald wurde aus den Kontexten klar, daß das Wort hier in beiden Bedeutungen verwendet ist (die entsprechenden Indikatoren sind im Text durch Kursivdruck her-

vorgehoben). Es folgt ein Auszug aus dem Text mit einer Übersetzung (in dieser Übersetzung sind durch Kursivdruck die Wörter und Konstruktionen hervorgehoben, die das stilistische Kolorit des Ausgangstextes im Deutschen wiedergeben, sowie durch Fettdruck mit Unterstreichen die beiden Äquivalente von "ништяк"):

(„Сказка про мышу") „А вот история из жизни старого растамана. Просыпается, короче, старый растаман у себя на хате и думает две мысли. Первая мысль: о, *ништяк*. Ну, это чисто абстрактная мысль, это он по сезону всегда так думает, как проснется: о, *ништяк*. Потому что *ништяк* в натуре. *Тело как перышко, крыша как друшляк, внутри желудка пустота*. А вот вторая мысль, он думает: а неплохо бы вот подняться и что-нибудь из *ништяков вчерашних заточить* неплохо бы. Потому что там *ништяков нормально осталось, типа банка тушонки, булка хлеба, картошки пол-казана*, короче ни фига себе *ништяков* осталось. И вот он встает и идет их *заточить*. А *ништяков*, короче, нету. Пустой казан стоит, и все. Даже хлеба не осталось. Нету вобще ничего, короче. И вот растаман громко думает: а кто это мои *ништяки* все *захавал*? А из-под шкафа отзывается стремный загробный голос: ЭТО Я *НИШТЯКИ* ТВОИ *ЗАХАВАЛ*!!!" –

(„Das Märchen von der Maus") „Hier *also* eine Geschichte aus dem Leben eines alten Rastamannes. *Okay*, ein alter Rastamann wacht bei sich in der *Bude* auf und denkt zwei Sachen. Erstens: oh, *klasse*. *Na ja, also* das *is* ein rein abstrakter Gedanke, das denkt er immer, wenn er aufwacht: oh, *klasse*. Denn es ist tatsächlich alles *klasse*. Der Körper wie eine Feder, der *Kopf wie ein Sieb*, im Magen eine einzige Leere. Und da plötzlich der zweite Gedanke, er denkt: *wär* eigentlich nicht schlecht, aufzustehen und sich was von den **Resten** von gestern *reinzuziehen*. *Weil da is* noch *'n bißchen was* übrig, *so in Richtung Fleischdose, Stückchen Brot, 'n halber Topf Kartoffeln*, also alles mögliche *is* noch da. Also steht er auf und will sich *'n bißchen was reinziehen*. *Und was is – nichts übrig*. Alles, was da steht, *is 'n leerer Topf. Nich mal* Brot *is* da. Wirklich überhaupt nichts. Und der Rastamann denkt laut: *Mann*, wer hat meine *ganzen **Reste*** weggespachtelt? Und da kommt *von unter dem Schrank 'ne* drohende tiefe Stimme: ‚Ich war das, der deine **Reste** *weggespachtelt* hat!'"

Man kann annehmen, daß auch dieser Text die Komplexität der übersetzerischen Aufgabe recht gut veranschaulicht hat. Wenn der letzte eigentlich noch notwendige Schritt, nämlich der zur Suche nach einem gemeinsamen Äquivalent für „ништяк", in diesem Fall zwar noch nicht gegangen, aber als Problem und Desiderat erkannt wurde, hat auch er seine Rolle bei der Durchsetzung der übersetzungstheoretischen Minima eines allgemeinen russistischen Sprachkurses erfolgreich gespielt.

Literatur

DRESSLER, Wolfgang (1991): Der Beitrag der Textlinguistik zur Übersetzungswissenschaft. In: Kapp: 61-71.

HÖNIG, Hans G. (1995): Konstruktives Übersetzen. Tübingen: Stauffenburg (Studien zur Translation 1).

HOUSE, Juliane (1997): Translation quality assessment. A model revisited. Tübingen: Narr (Tübinger Beiträge zur Linguistik 410).

— (1977): A model for translation quality assessment. Tübingen: Narr (Tübinger Beiträge zur Linguistik 88).

KAPP, Volker (Hrsg.) (³1991): Übersetzer und Dolmetscher. Theoretische Grundlagen, Ausbildung, Berufspraxis. Tübingen: Francke (UTB 325).

KRINGS, Hans P. (³1995): Übersetzen und Dolmetschen. In: Bausch, Karl-Richard; Christ, Herbert; Krumm, Hans-Jürgen (Hrsg.): Handbuch Fremdsprachenunterricht. Tübingen – Basel: Francke (UTB für Wissenschaft), 325-332.

REISS, Katharina; VERMEER, Hans (²1991): Grundlegung einer allgemeinen Translationstheorie. Tübingen: Niemeyer (Linguistische Arbeiten 147).

VERNAY, Henri (1991): Elemente einer Übersetzungswissenschaft. In: Kapp: 26-37.

Abgrenzung und Brauchbarkeit des ‚Key-Word'-Konzepts im Lichte der Übersetzungstheorie und -praxis (Sprachenpaar Deutsch <> Spanisch)

Arturo Parada

Der Semantik- und Semtheorie fällt es außerordentlich schwer, sich auf Universalien festzulegen. Dies darf nicht verwundern insofern es hier ja um wesentliche Probleme von – temporal und lokal bedingter – Abgrenzung, Festlegung und Definition von Bedeutungen vor dem Hintergrund konstanter und stets zu verifizierender sprach- und sprecherspezifischer Wandelbarkeit geht. Sinn im Wort ist nur als abstrakte, von allen anderen sie wesentlich modifizierenden und determinierenden Gegebenheiten ‚entleerte' Größe vorstellbar. Das Substrat, das übrigbleibt, macht Wörterbücher möglich und legt zur gleichen Zeit ihre zeitlich-räumliche Beschränktheit fest. Vor diese Tatsache gestellt, kann man nun als Anhänger der Gebrauchstheorie der Bedeutung Wittgensteins mittlerweile geflügeltem Wort den Rang einer praktisch erfahrbaren Tatsache zugestehen: „Die Bedeutung eines Wortes ist sein Gebrauch in der Sprache." Andererseits kann man an der Hypothese Wotjaks festhalten, der die kleinsten Bedeutungseinheiten, also die Seme, als „begrifflich noetische Abstraktionselemente, als Grundelemente der Widerspiegelung der Realität im menschlichen Bewußtsein" auffaßt und ihr höchstwahrscheinlich universelles Wesen behauptet (Stolze 1982:80). Die Wortfeldforschung hat ihrerseits versucht, einer beziehungsreichen Vielschichtigkeit, von der sie auszugehen hatte, Rechnung zu tragen, indem sie lexikalische Basen oder Grundraster gruppierte und somit Wortgruppen oder eben Wortfelder schuf, in denen die Seme als signifikative Differenzierungsmerkmale fungierten. Dieses Verfahren der Komponentenanalyse erlaubte nun zwar v. a. durch den Rekurs auf Oppositions- und Komplementärrelationen die *durchschnittliche* Bedeutung der Wortfeldmitglieder zu präzisieren und festzulegen. Doch zeigten bald darauf folgende Untersuchungen, daß die Aktualisierung der Wortfeldelemente die im Wortfeld vorgenommene Definition relativierte, in Frage stellte oder sogar aufhob. Der Text, Ko- und Kontext erwies sich als sinnmodifizierender und sinnkonstituierender Handlungs- und Spielraum der nun neue Relationen eingehenden Elemente.

Dies brachte die Notwendigkeit mit sich, zu dynamischen Beschreibungsmethoden vorzustoßen und die für das Gleichgewicht zwischen Permanenz und Variabilität verantwortlichen, sagen wir, ‚Regulierungsenzyme', welche ja überhaupt Kommunikation möglich machen, zu entdecken und zu erforschen. Vor diesem Hintergrund ist wohl die Sprechakttheorie in ihrer semantischen und pragmatischen Ausrichtung (Referenzsemantik) oder die Propositionsbedeutungsanalyse zu beurteilen.

Nun kommt aber bei der Übersetzung ein großes und zur gleichen Zeit großartiges Problem hinzu, und zwar daß es der Übersetzer mit – mindestens – zwei Sprachen zu tun hat. Es geht also nicht nur darum, ‚Bedeutungen' in einer Sprache, also in einem in dieser Sprache verfaßten Text, in ihrer Übersummativität zu eruieren und festzulegen, sondern auch zu entscheiden, welche pragmatisch-funktionellen, kommunikativen und semantischen Entsprechungen oder Korrespondenzen den noch zu verfassenden Zieltext auszumachen haben. Hönig und Kußmaul haben diese Notwendigkeit folgendermaßen definiert:

> „Im Abwägen zwischen Kontext-Determination und Sem-Determination besteht das Geschäft des Übersetzers. Dabei übersetzen wir nicht mit einer maximal möglichen semantischen Genauigkeit, sondern nach der Maxime vom notwendigen Differenzierungsgrad mit der im Kontext ausreichenden semantischen Genauigkeit." (Hönig/Kußmaul 1996:96)

Die Tatsache, daß nicht Wörter, vielleicht auch gar nicht mehr hauptsächlich Texte, sondern Sprechintentionen, Funktionen, Absichten, Informationsangebote usf. aus einer Sprachkultur in eine oder mehrere andere Sprachkulturen übersetzt werden und daß sowohl im Ausgangs- als auch im Zieltext Sinn aus einem Zusammenspiel sprachlicher und außersprachlicher Elemente resultiert, läßt jedwede Allgemeinheit anstrebende Beschreibungsversuche, die den Anspruch erheben, für die Übersetzungstheorie und -praxis relevant zu sein, als ein praktisch unmögliches Unterfangen erscheinen. Mehr denn je erweist sich hier Sprache als „dynamisches Polysystem" (Wandruzska), das der notgedrungenen Statik der Wissenschaft zuwider läuft. Schon Nida hatte feststellen müssen, daß es beim Übersetzen primär um eine Art von Kulturverständigung geht, die weit über den linguistischen Rahmen hinausreicht:

> „Because translating always involves communication within the context of interpersonal relations, the model for such activity must be a communication model, and the principles must be primarily sociolinguistic in the broad sense of term. As such, translating becomes a part of the even broader field of anthropological studies." (Nida 1976)

Was hat uns nun tatsächlich die anthropologische Linguistik, die wir zum großen Zweig der „cultural studies" zählen mögen, in dieser Hinsicht heute anzubieten?

Die in Australien tätige Sprachkulturforscherin Wierzbicka geht von der unmittelbaren, im Grunde traditionsreichen und theoretisch eindeutigen Feststellung aus,

> „that the meanings of words from different languages don't match (even if they are artificially matched, faute de mieux, by the dictionaries), that they reflect and pass on ways of living and ways of thinking characteristic of a given society (or speech community) and that they provide priceless clues to the understanding of culture." (Wierzbicka 1997:4)

Da sich aber die Forscherin der ‚Wirklichkeit' durch Sprache nähert, greift Wierzbicka zu dem 1976 von Raymond Williams als Grundlage für seine sprachkulturellen Studien benutzten Begriff von „Key word", der von ihr folgendermaßen definiert wird:

> „‚Key words' are words which are particularly important and revealing in a given culture. […] There is no finite set of such words in a language, and there is no ‚objective discovery procedure' for identifying them. To show that a particular word is of special importance in a given culture, one has to make case for it." (Wierzbicka 1997:15ff)

Die weiteren Ausführungen Wierzbickas zum Begriff „Key word", die m.E. zum Teil wenig ergiebig, z. T. sehr problematisch sind, sollen hier nicht weiter erläutert werden, da es ihr ausschließlich um kulturelle „patterns", uns aber um diese in Beziehung zu übersetzungsrelevanten Aspekten geht. Festzuhalten ist, daß sich der Begriff auf Wörter bezieht, die sinn- und symbolgeladene anthropologisch-kulturelle Identität der jeweiligen Sprachgemeinschaft beinhalten und vermitteln.

Demzufolge ist ein „Key Wort" ein Lexem, das den *Text* in sich trägt, ein Wort also, das komplexe historisch gewachsene Bedeutungszusammenhänge und sich mehr oder weniger automatisch einstellende Analogien beinhaltet, ein also einerseits besonders polysemisches, aber andererseits auch eng umgrenztes Wort. Trotz dieser potentiellen Bedeutungsvielfalt unterliegen „Key Wörter" im geringeren Maße der Wandelbarkeit, und weisen somit eine Bedeutungsstabilität auf, die auf einem gemeinschaftlichen (Hintergrund-)Konsens beruhen mag (z. B.: deutsch: ‚Bildung', spanisch: ‚sobremesa'). Die entsprechenden symbolischen diastratischen, diaphasischen, diatopischen usw. Bedeutungsvariationen und -varianten bilden sich komplementär oder im Gegensatz zu diesem Konsens, der in seinen Fundamenten kaum oder wenig erschüttert wird. Dies mag auch die Ursache dafür sein, daß Key Wörter zusammen mit ihrem ganzen Netz von Bedeutungsrelationen definitiv ‚erstarren' können. Man denke nur an das deutsche Wort ‚Mietskaserne', von dem weiter unten noch die Rede sein wird.

Zweisprachige, herkömmliche Wörterbücher geben keinen Aufschluß über den Bedeutungsreichtum dieser Wörter. Aber einsprachige normalerweise auch nicht. Wiedergegeben wird Unmittelbares, Vordergründiges, nie der jeweilige aktuelle Sinnreichtum und noch weniger die Potentialität, die Key Wörter innerhalb eines – wahrscheinlich – regulierten Subsystems innehaben. Der Muttersprachler braucht meistens keine zusätzlichen Erklärungen, um ‚Key Kultur' vollständig auszuschöpfen, denn der Hintergrund ist gegeben, er ist einfach *da*, er erklärt sich von selbst und versteht sich also auch von selbst, so daß Gruppen- und Gemeinschaftsidentität aufgrund von verschwiegenem, doch geteiltem Wissen entstehen kann.

Der nicht bikulturelle, keinen kulturkundigen Muttersprachler zur Hand habende Übersetzer hat nun kaum Chancen, an dieses Wissen zu gelangen. Vor das Problem gestellt, kann er sich für eine schlußfolgernde, immer gewagte Interpretation, für die resignierende, unprofessionelle Tilgung oder zugunsten einer wortwörtlichen Übersetzung entscheiden. Letzteres Prozedere ist, so meine ich, das Übliche und bringt normalerweise völlig sinnentstellte oder unfreiwillig komische Passagen hervor.

Erschwerend kommt hinzu, daß „Key Wörter" ein geschlossenes und ein offenes Inventar aufweisen und daß kontextgebundene, also sofort vergängliche „Key-Kommunikation" auftreten kann. Auch scheint mir die Möglichkeit gegeben, daß ein Key Wort in bestimmten Kontexten neutralisiert wird, also diesen Rang verliert. In dieser Hinsicht weist das Key-Wort-Konzept sicherlich auf ein komplexes, sprachgemeinschaftsspezifisches „Fuzzy System" hin.

Ein Beispiel soll dies verdeutlichen. Wir können uns folgende Dialogsituation vorstellen. Es treffen sich in Dortmund zwei gute Bekannte auf der Straße. Der eine fragt: „Na, wie läuft Dein neues Geschäft?" Die Antwort lautet: „War heut' mal wieder bei Aldi einkaufen …!"

Kein heute gängiges einsprachiges oder zweisprachiges Wörterbuch gibt Aufschluß über die Bedeutungsvielfalt, die das Wort „Aldi" sozial- und kontextgebunden hier hineinträgt, und zwar, daß die Supermarktkette Aldi in Deutschland heutzutage als eine der preisgünstigsten Einkaufsmöglichkeiten gilt – im Gegensatz z.B. zu Spanien, wo die Kette unter gleichem Namen ebenfalls vertreten ist, ohne daß ihr diese Wertung zukäme. Das Wort „Aldi" kann, muß aber nicht als Key Wort fungieren, denn obwohl es einen weiten, allgemein akzeptierten Bedeutungshintergrund aufzuweisen hat, der eben solche komplizenhafte Kommunikation ermöglicht, ist die Analogie noch nicht automatisch – kontextabhängig kann sie vom Sprecher evoziert werden, oder auch nicht.

Es bleibt nun dem Interpreten, sprich dem Übersetzter überlassen, durch sein Kultur-, Welt- und Sprachwissen Sinnpotential zu aktivieren, um durch sich gegenseitig ausbalancierende Begrenzungen den Text auf eine interpreten- und zeitgebundene Weise zu ‚entgrenzen', d.h. zu fixieren. Das Ergebnis des Erschließungsverfahrens hängt nicht zuletzt von Quantität und Qualität des sozio-kulturellen Hintergrundwissens des Interpreten ab. Denn es gehört zur *Kultur*, wenn Andeutungen verstanden werden und nicht alles expliziert wird. Das ist der Rahmen, in dem sich Key Wissen und Key Kultur oft bewegt, ein Rahmen der infiniten Potentialität, der ironischen Anspielungen, ein auf eine ganze Sprachgemeinschaft ausgedehntes Betätigungsfeld einer entproblematisierten, doch zur gleichen Zeit oft stillen und für den außenstehenden Interpreten kryptischen Kommunikation: ein geteiltes Wissen, das keiner zusätzlichen Erläuterung bedarf. Daher auch, daß auf diesem Gebiet die größten Anforderungen an den Übersetzer gestellt werden, und dies sowohl hinsichtlich der Erschließungsleistung als auch der – um es mit Wotjak zu sagen – „Anpassung des Inhalts des Gesagten/Gemeinten an den Vorwissensstand des in einer abweichenden Sprach- wie Kulturgemeinschaft aufgewachsenen Empfängers" (Wotjak 1991:182).

Es gilt nun die Regel: je offener, unpräziser, im Sinne von nicht eindeutig determiniert, der Text ist, um so mehr werden Inhalte angesprochen, die nicht verbalisiert sind, sondern als geschichtlicher Erfahrungs-/Handlungshintergrund mitgegeben werden. Dies hat zur Folge, daß mikro- und makrostrukturelle Netzerschließungsverfahren (Gerzymisch-Arbogast 1994:75f) nur sehr bedingt anwendbar sind, weil:

1) auf die jeweiligen *Frames* und *Scenarios* stillschweigend angespielt wird, diese vorausgesetzt werden;

2) nicht immer ein Informant hinzugezogen werden kann, da es oft um kaum beschreibare Realia (?) und Spezifika geht, die im Rahmen eines flexiblen, nicht eindeutigen, aber vorherrschenden Konsens doch individuell wahrgenommen und verstanden werden;

3) es sich nicht (immer) um sozial geregelte Abläufe oder Vorgehensweisen handelt;

4) aus den erwähnten Gründen kein ausgangssprachliches oder zielsprachliches Wörterbuch, keine Lexika hinzugezogen werden können;

5) sich Bedeutung im Text aktualisiert und somit verändert;

6) und m. E. sehr wichtig, Profile und Definitionen oft nur durch einen Vergleich/ Kontrast auf gleicher Ebene mit den gleichen, also ähnlichen Spezika einer anderen Kultur deutlich und möglich werden.

In welchen Texten tritt nun dieses Plurale, Aufgeladene und Angereicherte, dieser bachtinsche „plurilingüisme", „discours bivocal", diese „décentralisation verbale" (Bachtin 1978, 1979, 1987) vornehmlich auf? Natürlich in literarischen Texten, vor denen die Übersetzungswissenschaft eine allgemeine und nur zu verständliche Scheu zeigt, denn:

„The extent to which a text is translatable varies with the *degree* to which it is embedded in its own specific culture, also with the distance that separates the cultural background of source text and target audience in terms of time and place." (Snell-Hornby 1988:41)

Wir wollen diese Problematik nun in Beziehung zum Key-Word-Begriff setzen und anhand literarischer Texte beleuchten.

Juan Ramón Jiménez' Gedicht „Desnudos" beginnt:

„Por el mar vendrán
las flores del alba
– olas, olas llenas
de azucenas blancas –,
el gallo alzará
su clarín de Plata."

Es ist ein Gedicht, das auf Sinneswahrnehmung, auf geteilter Wirklichkeit fußt, ein also sehr ‚publikumsorientiertes' Gedicht. „Mar", Meer, könnte durchaus als ein Key Wort für die Halbinsel Spanien gelten. Die spanische Geschichte und Kultur weiß natürlich immer wieder vom Meer zu berichten, über das Meer zu schreiben. Auf irgendeine Weise ist das Meer für sehr viele Einwohner Spaniens immer präsent, was sich natürlich auch in der Sprache niederschlägt: „había la mar de gente", „estaba la mar de guapa", „estoy hecho un mar de confusiones" sagt man, wenn man berichtet, daß irgendwo ein wahres ‚Gewimmel' von Leuten war, daß ein Mädchen, eine Frau besonders hübsch aussah oder daß man nicht weiß, wo einem der Kopf steht. Es dient auch als euphemistischer Fluch: „¡la mar serena …!" usw. Im Gedicht wird die Präsenz des Meeres durch die „olas", Wellen, noch einmal verstärkt, während die Blumen, konkret die Lilien, „azucenas", Farben evozieren und die Naturpräsenz unterstreichen. Jeder mittelmäßig gebildete Spanier kann, andererseits, kaum das Wort „alba", Morgengrauen, hören, ohne eine Beziehung zu Cervantes' *Quijote* herzustellen, wo es heißt: „La del alba sería cuando don Quijote salió de la venta tan contento …" usw. (*Quijote* I, IV). Spanien war viele Jahrhunderte hindurch und bis vor kürzester Zeit ein Agrarland, so daß der „gallo", der Hahn, sozusagen auch zur ‚Familie' gehört; „Clarín" deutet auf die militärische Tradition Spaniens hin, und so manche spanische und lateinamerikanische Zeitung trägt auch heute noch diesen Namen. Das Wort „Plata", Silber, kann neutral als Farb-Metallbild oder auch in Beziehung zum lateinamerikanischen Silber, Beute der spanischen Eroberungsfeldzüge – „Por el mar vendrán" –, interpretiert werden, usw.

Jedes der hier erläuterten Wörter, sogar die phonetisch-syntaktischen Muster, evozieren also sofort für den muttersprachlichen Leser, und natürlich in verschiedenem Maße und auf individuelle subjektive Weise, eine aus einem Netz von Bedeutungsrelationen gebildete Wirklichkeit, aus dem dieses Gedicht *bewußt* schöpft und in welche es sich somit absichtsvoll einbettet. Das Gedicht selbst ‚lebt' von dieser Einheit der Vielfalt.

Wotjak drückt dieses Phänomen – eine Eigenschaft natürlicher Sprachen – sehr prägnant aus:

„Dabei ist davon auszugehen, daß sich kulturspezifische Wissenskomponenten auch sememisiert als Bestandteil der vergesellschafteten und usualisierten Bedeutungen von Einzellexe-

men, Komposita wie – phraseologischen – Mehrwortkomplexen synchron relativ invariant und
anteilig perspektiviert eingefroren finden und damit kulturell Divergierendes sememisch – semantisch und damit direkt sprachlich – lexikalisiert relevant bzw. transportiert wird." (Wotjak,
1991:186)

Hier nun eine aus einer Anthologie spanischer Lyrik übernommene deutsche Übersetzung.

Juan Ramón Jiménez

„Entblösst
Die Blumen des Morgengrauns
kommen über das Meer
– Wellen und Wellen von
weißen Lilien –.
Der Hahn bricht aus in seinen
Trompetenruf von Silber."
(Rose aus Asche [2]1992:13)

Ist diese Übersetzung von Erwin Walter Palm eine im üblichen Sinn getreue Übersetzung? Ohne Zweifel: man vergleiche und man wird sehen, daß kein Wort fehlt und
daß nur geringfügige Änderungen vorgenommen worden sind (Zeiten!).

Doch für den durchschnittlichen deutschsprachigen Leser sind die Bezeichnungen,
wenn auch die gleichen, doch ganz andere als für den spanischen Leser, und das bedeutet, daß sich völlig verschiedene Analogien einstellen, die letztendlich über den
Sinn des Textes entscheiden. Oder wird etwa Literatur sogleich auf eine entfremdende
Art gelesen? Hier wird deutlich, daß Konnotationen eben viel mehr sind als einfache
Anhängsel: sie entscheiden auf determinierende Weise über den Kommunikations-
rahmen, in dem sich Verständigung abzuspielen hat.

Ein bekanntes Gedicht von Arno Holz beginnt mit den Versen:

„Phantasus I

Ihr Dach stieß fast bis an die Sterne,
Vom Hof her stampfte die Fabrik,
Es war die richt'ge Mietskaserne
Mit Flur-und Leiermannsmusik!
Im Keller nistete die Ratte,
Parterre gab's Branntwein, Grog und Bier,
Und bis ins fünfte Stockwerk hatte
das Vorstadtelend sein Quartier."

Bei Arno Holz' Gedicht handelt es sich um eine realistische Schilderung des deutschen Mietskasernenelends Ende des 19. Jhs., eine Beschreibung, die durch ihre unmittelbare Bezogenheit zu einer streng definierten Realität für uns hier von Interesse
ist. „Mietskaserne", „Leiermannsmusik", ja sogar „Hof" oder „Fabrik" sind ge-
schichts-soziokulturell sehr stark aufgeladene Begriffe, die v.a. für die älteren Generationen Deutschlands wahre Key Wörter darstellen. Andererseits entdeckt der in der
Geschichte der deutschen Literatur Sachkundige hier eine ganze Reihe von Vorweg-
nahmen und Beziehungen zu der späteren Kunst des Expressionismus, so daß der
Text, wie jeder bedeutende literarische Text auch, in mehrfacher Hinsicht dynamische
Bedeutungsbeziehungen herzustellen weiß.

Eine spanische, im Prinzip rein Instrumentale Version dieses Gedichtes lautet folgendermaßen:

„Phantasus I

Su tejado rozaba casi las estrellas;
a través del patio llegaba el machacar de la fábrica.
Era una auténtica hospedería
¡con música en el pasillo y pianola!
En la bodega anidaba la rata;
aguardiente, ron y cerveza había en el principal
y hasta la quinta planta defendía
su guarida la miseria suburbana."
(In Acosta 1997:719)

Wiederum steht in der spanischen Fassung so gut wie alles, was im deutschen Original vorkommt. Man erkennt durchaus, worum es geht: Vorstadtelend. Hierin können spanische Leser dem Gedicht folgen. Doch scheint gerade das, was Übersetzung und Original hier verbindet, und zwar der Bezug zu einer materiellen objektiven Beschaffenheit, in diesem Fall am unwichtigsten zu sein. Wichtig ist der Anteil an menschlicher Erfahrung, den hier die Wörter in sich tragen und der erlaubt, ein Referenzgewebe zu aktivieren, das vielfältige und verschiedenartige vernunft- und gefühlgeleitete Beziehungen zu Kultur als historisch-synchronischer Gesamtkomplex unterhält, projiziert oder als Potentialität anbietet. Die Evokationen, die von den angeführten Übersetzungen hervorgerufen werden, decken sich aber kaum mit denen der jeweiligen Originale. An mangelnden Fähigkeiten der Übersetzer dürfte es nicht liegen. Die Frage ist vielmehr: Wie läßt sich *Erfahrung* über-setzen, wie unterscheidet man Konnotation von Notation von ‚Essenz'? Welchen Bewertungsmaßstab setzt man an?

Aus Vorangehendem könnte man durchaus den Eindruck gewinnen, daß Sprache nicht ausreicht, um kulturspezifische Erfahrungshorizonte sinn- und funktionsgerecht in die eigene Sprachkultur zu übertragen. Dabei kann es natürlich nicht darum gehen, Nivellierungen vorzunehmen, die das Fremde zugunsten des Eigenen aufheben, im Gegenteil: Es geht um *erfassen* und *mitteilen* von erlebter Wirklichkeit, die sich in Sprache ausdrückt. Da aber von der übersetzungswissenchaftlichen und -praktischen Perspektive die Analyse und Erarbeitung von Texten traditionell eher linguistisch determiniert war, stellt sich die Frage, ob nicht ein anderer, kulturbezogener Zugang zu Texten zu einem besseren Verständnis und somit zu besseren Übersetzungsleistungen führen könnte. In dieser Hinsicht sind *kulturelle Wörterbücher* bzw. kulturelle Datenbanken als dringendes Anliegen zu betrachten, deren Anfertigung kaum ohne Hinzuzichung einer historisch-synchronischen Kulturkomparatistik möglich sein wird.

Vorab sollten aber diese Schlußfolgerungen auf ihre Richtigkeit überprüft werden:

1) Ein grundlegendes Problem besteht darin, daß die entsprechenden Kulturen ihre ‚señas de identidad', ihre ‚Kulturmerkmale' nicht systematisch erfaßt haben. Die Gründe hierfür haben als Arbeitshypothesen zu gelten: Isolation/Abgrenzung/ einseitige Beziehungen, nicht entwickelte bzw. beschränkte Selbstwahrnehmung, keine kulturelle und ökonomische Notwendigkeit usw.

2) Die Oberflächenübersetzung ist nicht imstande, semantisch-kulturell sehr stark aufgeladene Texte kommentarlos zu transferieren.

3) Es ist ein auf Konsens beruhendes Umdenken in der Beurteilung von Transferleistungen vonnöten: der Übersetzer wird mehr und mehr als hochqualifizierter, (im allgemeinen) vertrauenswürdiger Kulturexperte zu betrachten sein.

Es ist bekannt, daß der spanische Dichter García Lorca ein großes Ansehen und eine große Verbreitung in Rußland genießt, welches zum großen Teil hervorragender kommunikativer Übersetzungen zu verdanken ist. Ein großes Ansehen genießt Lorca auch in Deutschland, doch hauptsächlich auf Grund des kultur-literarischen Renommees, das dem Dichter aus Granada vorangeht. In dieser Hinsicht beklagt der Romanist Tietz, „daß sich das Fehlen einer langen Tradition des Übersetzens, wie sie bei Texten aus dem Englischen oder Französischen besteht, bei Übertragungen aus dem Spanischen noch immer negativ bemerkbar macht." (Tietz 1990:17) Mit Tradition ist hier wohl nichts anderes als sprachlich-kulturelle Erfahrung, also Nähe zur fremden und auch, und v.a., zur eigenen Kultur gemeint.

Für die Übersetzungswissenschaft und -praxis kann diese Nähe nur aus einer offenen, jeweils festzulegenden interdisziplinären und interkulturellen Verfahrensweise entstehen.

Literatur

ACOSTA, Luis (Hrsg.) (1997): La literatura alemana a través de sus textos. Madrid: Cátedra.

BACHTIN, Michail (1987): Rabelais und seine Welt. Volkskultur als Gegenkultur. (Aus dem Russischen von Gabriele Leupold) Frankfurt a. M.: Suhrkamp.

— (1979): Die Ästhetik des Wortes. Frankfurt a. M.: Suhrkamp (Edition Suhrkamp 967)

— (1978): Esthétique et théorie du roman. (Traduit du russe par Daria Olivier) Paris: Gallimard.

GERZYMISCH-ARBOGAST, Heidrun (1994): Übersetzungswissenschaftliches Propädeutikum. Tübingen – Basel: Francke Verlag (UTB 1782).

HÖNIG, Hans G.; KUSSMAUL, Paul (⁴1996): Strategie der Übersetzung. Ein Lehr- und Arbeitsbuch. Tübingen: Gunter Narr (Tübinger Beiträge zur Linguistik 205).

NIDA, Eugene A. (1976): A Framework for the Analysis and Evaluation of Theories of Translation. In: Brislin, R. W. (Hrsg.): Translation: Applications and Research. New York: Garder Press, 47-91.

PALM, Erwin Walter (Hrsg.) (²1992): Rose aus Asche. Spanische und spanisch-amerikanische Gedichte 1900 - 1950. Frankfurt a. M.: Suhrkamp (Bibliothek Suhrkamp 734).

SNELL-HORNBY, Mary (1988): Translation Studies. An Integrated Approach. Amsterdam – Philadelphia: John Benjamins.

STOLZE, Radegundis (1982): Grundlagen der Textübersetzung. Heidelberg: Julius Groos Verlag (Sammlung Groos 13)

TIETZ, Manfred (Hrsg.) (1990): Die spanische Lyrik der Moderne. Frankfurt a. M.: Vervuert/Iberoamericana.

WIERZBICKA, Anna (1997): Understanding Cultures through their Key Words – English, Russian, Polish, German, and Japanese. New York: Oxford University Press.

WOTJAK, Gerd (1993): Interkulturelles Wissen und zweisprachig vermittelte Kommunikation. In: Revista de Filología Alemana 1, 181-196.

Stellung der literarischen Personennamen im Übersetzungsprozeß[*]

Eliza Pieciul

1 Einführung

„Eigennamen in der Übersetzung" – diese Verbindung bedeutet Schwierigkeiten. Dies ergibt sich daraus, daß man von Übersetzung nur dann sprechen kann, wenn Bedeutung vorhanden ist. Ein Wort hat einen Sinn, den es zu bewahren gilt. Und wie verhalten sich die Eigennamen? Wir wissen, daß beim Gebrauch der Eigennamen eine Bedeutung im Sinne von Gattungsnamen keine Rolle spielt, da die primäre Funktion der Eigennamen in ihrer Referenz liegt. Man kann von einem Namen – anders als beim Wort – nicht sagen, daß man ihn „versteht", pragmatisch jedoch läßt sich eine gewisse Bedeutung bestimmen (vgl. Bauer 1985:220), die *Bedeutsamkeit* genannt wird. Die Bedeutsamkeit der Eigennamen wird als Summe der Konnotationen verstanden, an die gedacht und die vermittelt wird, wenn man einen Eigennamen nennt. Die Bedeutsamkeit[1] ist eine Größe, die assoziativ wirkt, die nicht nur auf den Namensträger hinweist, sondern ihn auch charakterisiert.

2 Bedeutsamkeit der Eigennamen und Übersetzung

Wenn man über die Bedeutsamkeit der Eigennamen reflektiert, so stellt sich die Frage, inwiefern der assoziative Wert der Eigennamen übersetzt (besser wiedergegeben[2]) werden muß. In Schriftstücken amtlich-öffentlichen Charakters (in Urkunden, Dokumenten etc.) kommt es nur auf die primäre Funktion der Identifikation an, und die Bedeutsamkeit spielt somit keine Rolle. Darüber hinaus werden Personennamen nicht übersetzt, damit es nicht zu einer Spleißung kommt, bei der zwei verschiedene Namen für einen Namenträger stehen.

Anders muß man literarische Namen behandeln, deren Bedeutsamkeit von den Schriftstellern bewußt genutzt wird. Man versteht literarische Namen als „poetische Mittel besonderer Art" (Gutschmidt 1981:494), die die „Namenlandschaft" eines fiktionalen Textes bilden. Sie sind so eng mit den häufig vermutbaren Intentionen des Namengebers verknüpft, daß die Leser einen Personennamen als ein aufgegebenes

---

[*] Eine Analyse im Rahmen des vorbereiteten Dissertationsprojekts: „Literarische Namen in deutsch-polnischer Translation. Eine kontrastive Studie am Beispiel der Prosawerke von Thomas Mann"

[1] Die Notwendigkeit, einen neuen Terminus zu gebrauchen, geht auf die Unterscheidung zwischen dem engen und weiten Bedeutungsbegriff zurück: „Die enge Bedeutungsauffassung erkennt nur die begrifflichen Merkmale eines Gegenstandes beziehungsweise einer Erscheinung als ‚Bedeutung' an, während die weite auch die nichtbegrifflichen, die konnotativen Bewertungskomponenten und situativen Komponenten der Gesamtbedeutung einbezieht." (Walther 1988:54)

[2] Man spricht von der Wiedergabe, und nicht der Übersetzung von Eigennamen, da die Übersetzung nur eine von unterschiedlichen Wiedergabemöglichkeiten eines EN darstellt (neben Adaptation, Substitution usw.).

Rätsel empfinden und erwarten, „er müsse Bedeutsamkeit haben" (Seibicke 1982:92). Die Analyse der Namen kann auch Stütz- und Schlüsselfunktion für die Interpretation gewinnen (vgl. Kunze 1998:197). Namen sind so wichtig, „daß wir meinen, mit dem Namen auch schon die Figur zu haben" (Bachmann 1978:247).

Bei der Übersetzung eines literarischen Werkes sind die Eigennamen nicht nur in ihrer Referenz beizubehalten, sondern auch ihre Bedeutsamkeit ist ein Wert, den man gleichermaßen wiedergeben muß, damit die Intention des Autors auch in der Übersetzung sichtbar ist. Um die Möglichkeiten einer adäquaten Wiedergabe der Bedeutsamkeit von PN im Übersetzungsprozeß darzustellen, soll die Stellung der Personennamen in konkreten literarischen Texten (Original und Übersetzung) verglichen werden. Dies soll am Beispiel von Thomas Manns Prosa geschehen.

3   Personennamen in Thomas Manns Prosa und ihre Wiedergabe im Polnischen

Thomas Manns Namenschöpfung hat Beachtung bei vielen Literaturkritikern und Namenforschern gefunden. Das Interesse an seinen literarischen Namen ist durchaus nicht verwunderlich, da Mann, ein außerordentlicher und äußerst fruchtbarer Namenschöpfer, seine Figuren bewußt und sorgfältig benannte[3]. Bachmann bezeichnet ihn daher als den letzten großen „Namenserfinder", einen „Namenzauberer" (Bachmann 1978:247). Die Funktion der Namen in Manns Werken geht weit über die Grundfunktion der Namenwahl – die Referenz – hinaus. Seine Namen dienen natürlich der Benennung der Figuren, aber man wird zugleich bemerken müssen, daß sie eher typisierend als individualisierend eingesetzt werden. Sie erfüllen zwar die Funktion, jede Gestalt als ein Individuum hervorzuheben, gleichzeitig jedoch machen sie die Figur zu einem gewissen Typus und verleihen ihr die zu erfüllende Rolle. Im Extremfall werden sie zur Formel (vgl. Tyroff 1975:9).

Man muß sich fragen, wie diese Rollen in der Übersetzung der Prosa Manns ins Polnische bewahrt werden oder zu bewahren wären, da es für die Frage der äquivalenten Übersetzung von großer Bedeutung ist, ob der Name auch im übersetzten Text seine Funktion realisieren kann oder nicht. In der Analyse werden die redenden und klassifizierenden Namen aus Manns Werk dargestellt.

3.1   Redende Namen

Redende Namen, d.h. Namen mit einer sinnhaltigen Charakterisierungsfunktion, gehören zu den verbreitetsten Kunstgriffen dichterischer Namengebung (vgl. Birus 1978:30). Thomas Manns Prosa ist ein gutes Beispiel dafür, daß redende Namen mit ihrer durchsichtigen und eindeutigen Motiviertheit nicht nur in älterer Literatur vorzufinden sind.

---

[3] Wie wichtig die Personennamen für den Autor waren, kann man den sorgfältigen Aufzeichnungen in seinen Notizbüchern entnehmen.

In den „Buddenbrooks" haben wir das bekannte Schulkapitel, wo die wilhelminische Schule „zur Institution der Verdrehung der Wertmaßstäbe" wird (Grau 1971: 234). Dies erreicht Mann u.a. durch seine gesinnungslosen Lehrertypen des wilhelminischen Zeitalters, deren Namen zur Steigerung der grotesken und bedrohlichen Atmosphäre beitragen:

Doktor *Mantelsack*; Professor *Hückopp*, Spinne genannt; der geistreiche Doktor *Mühsam* (man beachte das Zusammenspiel von „geistreich" und „mühsam"), der „feine" Oberlehrer, Doktor *Goldener*; Kandidat *Modersohn*, Doktor *Marotzke* (der „ständig ungewaschen aussah").

Auch die Patienten des Kurhauses „Berghof" führen solche Namen, daß man zwangsläufig glauben muß, dort „oben" herrsche eine andere Ordnung: *Blumenkohl, Kleefeld, Iltis, Düstmund, Rotbein*. Es gibt auch eine gewisse *Leila Gerngroß*, die früh sterben muß; *Frau Stöhr*, bei deren Schilderung mehrmals das Adjektiv „störrisch" vorkommt, oder *Herrn Ferdinand Wehsal*, die Verkörperung des inneren Leides.

Besonders eklatant sind die redenden Namen im Spätwerk „Doktor Faustus", wo die beschriebene Gesellschaft „ein Aquarium voll phantastisch geformter Fische" sein sollte (Mann an Agnes E. Meyer. In: Mann 1992:222). So konvenieren die Grotesk-Schilderungen der deutschen Gesellschaft mit einer grotesken Namengebung, z.B.: *Rollwagen, Radbruch, Schuh, Unruhe, Zwitscher, Breisacher, Edelmann, von Gleichen-Rußwurm, Nackedey, Ölhafen, Riedesel, Rosenstiel, Schlaginhaufen, Zur Höhe, Knöterich, Kranich* und *Kürbis*.

Redende Namen dienen als Etikette einer oder mehrerer Eigenschaften, und „machen den Träger zu etwas weniger als einem Menschen, nämlich zur bloßen Verkörperung der betreffenden Eigenschaft" (Güttinger 1963:77). Gerade in diesem Punkt stellt sich die Frage der Wiedergabe von redenden Namen. Ihre Funktion im literarischen Werk setzt voraus, daß sie vom Rezipienten verstanden werden, sonst „haben sie ihren Zweck verfehlt" (Thies 1978:133).

Laut heutiger Übersetzungsnorm werden in Prosawerken die Familiennamen nicht substituiert, da die Fremdheitsatmosphäre wegen der einheimischen Formen gefährdet wäre. Wenn man bemüht wäre, alle redenden Namen semantisch zu übersetzen, müßte die Substitution zur falschen Annahme führen, daß es sich bei den Trägern der eingebürgerten Namen um Vertreter der ZS-Welt handelt.

Die konsequente Transkription der redenden Namen bedeutet aber die Nivellierung der lexikalisch zu bestimmenden Wortteile der Namen, und, was damit zusammenhängt, die Nivellierung der Funktionen, die sie im Werk erfüllen. In den meisten Fällen kann der Leser nicht bewußt wahrnehmen, daß er etwas von der Autorenbotschaft vermißt. Die Verluste machen sich dann eher auf der allgemeinen Ebene bemerkbar, in der die ironischen, komischen und satirischen Inhalte „gedämpft" werden oder ganz verlorengehen. Oft aber sind redende Namen Bestandteile von Wortspielen. Ihre inhaltliche Seite wird dann doppelt „zum Sprechen" gebracht, da der semantische Gehalt der Namen in einem Wortspiel thematisiert wird. Hier wird der ZS-Leser bemerken, daß ihm eine gewisse Information abhanden kommt. In solchen Fällen kommt es zu Verlusten, und es entsteht der Eindruck von Inhaltslücken oder Mangel an Logik.

„Immer willst du mein Schweigen haben. Ich bin doch nicht von der Familie Schweigestill."
(Mann 1975:231)

„Rüdiger Schildknapp, der Übersetzer, (...) gehörte zu der Runde ... Aus seinem Namen
schloß er, daß seine Vorfahren reisige Begleiter von Edlen und Fürsten gewesen waren, ..."
(Mann 1975:166-170)

„Ferner gedenke ich (...) der Verwalterin des Molkereiwesens, Frau Luder, einer haubentra-
genden Witwe, deren ungewöhnlich würdevoller Gesichtsausdruck zu einem Teil wohl der
Verwahrung gegen ihren Namen galt ..." (Mann 1975:26)

Alle diese Stellen aus „Doktor Faustus" und ähnliche sind in der Übersetzung unverständlich, da sich das übersetzerische Verfahren auf die Transkription beschränkt und
die Namen in keiner Weise erläutert werden. Man kann den Eindruck gewinnen, daß
man es allzu oft als selbstverständlich hinnimmt, daß die bloße Transkription die einzig mögliche Lösung ist. Gerade dort aber, wo Unverständlichkeit droht (und beim
Lesen der Mannschen Meisterprosa sollte dies doch nicht geschehen), muß man nach
anderen Möglichkeiten der Wiedergabe suchen. Wenn der Name eine Information
enthält, so muß man versuchen, diese Information auch dem ZS-Leser zu vermitteln.
Man sollte die Information explizieren, z.b. das Adjektiv „schweigsam" in den Satz
einflechten, damit der Satz: „ich bin doch nicht von der Familie Schweigestill" auch
in der ZS wirken kann.

Redende Namen sind ein schwieriges Übersetzungsproblem. Ihre semantische
Durchsichtigkeit spielt eine bedeutende Rolle im Werk, ihre Transkription in der
Übersetzung macht sie zu leeren Referenzzeichen. Die Wiedergabe ihrer Bedeutsamkeit muß aber nicht unbedingt die semantische Übersetzung des Namens selbst einbeziehen, nur müssen die Kompensationsmittel (ratsam sind dann textinterne Kommentare) vorsichtig und geschickt eingesetzt werden.

3.2 Lokale Zuordnung

Ein ähnliches Verfahren kann man bei den lokal klassifizierenden Namen anwenden,
wobei es möglich wäre, die Unübersetzbarkeit der mundartlichen Formen teilweise
aufzuheben. Die lokale Zuordnung der Namen dient der antithetischen Thematik in
Manns Prosa. In den „Buddenbrooks" wird das norddeutsche Element dem süddeutschen entgegengestellt und durch Platt ausgedrückt, wobei z.B. Christian Budden-
brook *Krischan* genannt wird. Die Verkörperung des süddeutschen Elements, *Alois
Permaneder* (Vorname und Nachname typisierend urbayrisch) spricht Dialekt und
nennt seine Frau aus der Ostseehafenstadt nicht Tony, sondern *Tonerl*, was im Text
explizite betont wird:

„Was er aber dann (...) seiner Gattin gesagt hatte, war dies: „Tonerl" - er nannte sie Tonerl -
„Tonerl, mir war's gnua" (Mann 1987:310)

„... oznajmił małżonce: - Tońka - nazywał ją Tońką - Tońka, mamy dosyć." (Mann 1988:266)

Die dialektale Sprachvariante kann nicht in der Zielsprache bewahrt werden, was auf
die bekannte Erscheinung der Unübersetzbarkeit von Mundarten hinweist. Der deutsche Leser weiß, was der Rufname „Tonerl" konnotiert – der polnische Leser muß

sich mit einer Kompensation begnügen, die eher eine sozial markante Sprachschicht evoziert (*Tońka* als stark umgangsprachliche Verkürzung des Vornamens *Antonia*).

Auch hier ist jedoch die Sache nicht ganz verloren: Warum sollte der polnische Leser die implizite (und für den AS-Leser durchaus verständliche) Information nicht in Form einer expliziten Bemerkung bekommen, bspw.: „er nannte sie – *auf seine süddeutsche Art* – Tonerl". Auch die plattdeutschen Formen müssen nicht prinzipiell vermieden werden. So könnte die Bemerkung: „Krischan, *wie er auf Platt genannt wurde* ...", die mundartliche Färbung und damit das Lokale und das Antithetische bewahren.

3.3 Historische Zuordnung

Ein noch anderes Verfahren würde sich bei dem Versuch bieten, die historisch klassifizierenden Namen zu bewahren, die ein ausgesprochen einzelsprachliches Phänomen darstellen. Die Einsetzung von Namen, die eine bestimmte Epoche evozieren sollen, bezieht sich auf die historische Sprachentwicklung und die historischen Namensgebungskonventionen, die nur in einer Sprache in der gegebenen Form existieren. Dieses Problem wird in „Doktor Faustus" besonders deutlich, wo ganze Textpassagen auf Lutherdeutsch geschrieben sind. Dies betrifft auch speziell die Personennamen: viele sind Quellen des ausgehenden Mittelalters entnommen (vgl. Voss 1975:131). Sie stammen zum großen Teil aus Luthers Briefen. Es sind oft Namen, die von zahlreichen Reformationsführern getragen wurden, z.B. waren Baworinski Senior der böhmischen Brüder, Bullinger Nachfahre Zwinglis in Zürich, Hubmeyer und Schappeler Anführer der Wiedertäuferbewegung. Die Auswahl der Reformationsnamen hat eine ideologische Funktion und betont Manns Einstellung, daß Reformation die deutsche Geistesgeschichte determiniert und die Gegenwart beeinflußt hat.

Die Transkription der Namen in der Übersetzung ist auch hier einerseits die einzig mögliche Lösung. Die Namen weisen zwar auch in der Übersetzung auf dieselben Vorbilder hin, weswegen auch ZS-Leser die zitierten Namen als historisch belegt entziffern oder einfach diesen Aspekt der Weltkreierung ignorieren können. Andererseits ist es unmöglich, den auffallenden, archaischen Charakter der Namen, die in der AS-Rezeption als alt empfunden werden (bspw. Deutschlin, Teutleben), auch im ZS-Text zu bewahren. In der ZS-Empfindung sind das zeitgeschichtlich neutrale Namen, die nur den nationalen Charakter zum Ausdruck bringen. Die vordergründige Funktion der historischen Zuordnung wird nicht realisiert.

Hier könnte man ein Verfahren anwenden, das den Schwerpunkt der Erklärung ausschließlich auf die Metaebene verschiebt – der ideologische Aspekt ist so wichtig, daß man das kommentierte Übersetzen anwenden sollte (als umfangreiche Erläuterungen im Anhang verstanden). Die Lektüre der schöngeistigen Literatur kann nämlich auch Wissen vermitteln, so daß man vor Kommentaren nicht zurückschrecken sollte. Auch die Tatsache, daß die Kommentare in einem textexternen Anhang verfaßt wären, würde die metasprachliche Störung verringern.

4   Schlußfolgerungen

Die Analyse der Werke von Thomas Mann läßt die enorme Rolle der PN in der stilistischen, aber auch ideologischen Dimension erkennen. Die Stellung der PN in den besprochenen Werken zeigt deutlich, daß es sich bei den literarischen Namen um keine „leeren Zeichen" handelt. Sie wurden bewußt und sorgfältig eingesetzt und erfüllen eine Vielzahl von Rollen. Bedenken wir die Situation eines polnischsprachigen Lesers, der zum großen Teil auf Namen stößt, die er bloß in ihrer Referenzfunktion aufnimmt und lediglich als Hinweis auf ihre deutsche Herkunft erkennt. Die redenden Namen (Modersohn, Grobleben, Gosch, Nackedey, Breisacher, Luder, Schweigestill, Schleppfuß etc.) sind für ihn leer, ganz zu schweigen von der Symbolik vieler anderer (Ellen Brand, Peeperkorn, Leverkühn, Ziemßen).

Eine Übersetzungsanalyse zeigt, daß die Übersetzer zu oft die Unübersetzbarkeit der Personennamen als selbstverständlich betrachten, wobei sie ihre doch nicht zufällige Bedeutsamkeit in den meisten Fällen außer acht lassen. Obwohl die Transkription (also nicht etwa die – wie es früher war – semantische Übersetzung der Namen) als einzig mögliche Lösung zu betrachten ist, so ist die Aufgabe des Übersetzers damit noch nicht erfüllt – er kann (und muß) versuchen, die Bedeutsamkeit der Personennamen auf anderen Wegen zu bewahren. Wie gezeigt, muß man oft die Präsuppositionen explizit machen, dem Leser in einer textinternen Anmerkung die Bedeutsamkeit näherbringen und notfalls einen Anhang verfassen. Natürlich sind das immer Fragen, die am konkreten Beispiel zu lösen sind. Obwohl man Verluste in Kauf nehmen muß, so kann man gleichzeitig behaupten, daß die Wiedergabe der Personennamen nicht nur möglich, sondern auch durchaus erforderlich ist – wenn sie auch im übersetzten Werk „poetische Mittel besonderer Art" bleiben sollen.

5   Literatur

BACHMANN, Ingeborg (1978): Der Umgang mit Namen. In: Werke. Bd. 4: Essays, Reden, Vermischte Schriften, Anhang. München – Zürich: Piper.

BAUER, Gerhard (1985): Namenkunde des Deutschen. Bern – Frankfurt a. M. – New York: Peter Lang (Germanistische Lehrbuchsammlung 21).

BIRUS, Hendrik (1978): Poetische Namensgebung: Zur Bedeutung der Namen in Lessings Nathan der Weise. Göttingen: Vandenheock & Ruprecht (Palaestra 270).

GRAU, Helmut (1971): Die Darstellung gesellschaftlicher Wirklichkeit im Frühwerk Thomas Manns. (Dissertation Freiburg i. Br.).

GUTSCHMIDT, Karl (1981): Aspekte der poetischen Onomastik. In: Rymut, K. (Hrsg.): Proceedings of Thirteenth International Congress of Onomastic Sciences, Cracow, August 21-25, 1978, Vol 1. Wrocław – Warszawa – Kraków – Gdańsk – Łódź: Ossolineum.

GÜTTINGER, Fritz (1963): Zielsprache. Theorie und Technik des Übersetzens. Zürich: Manesse.

KUNZE, Konrad (1998): dtv-Atlas Namenkunde. Vor- und Familiennamen im deutschen Sprachgebiet. München: Deutscher Taschenbuchverlag (dtv 3234: dtv-Nachschlagewerke).

MANN, Thomas (1992): Selbstkommentare: „Doktor Faustus" und „Die Entstehung des Doktor Faustus" (hrsg. v. Hans Wysling). Frankfurt a. M.: Fischer (Fischer-Taschenbücher 6893 = Informationen und Materialien zur Literatur).

MANN, Thomas (1987): Buddenbrooks. Verfall einer Familie. Frankfurt a. M.: Fischer (Gesammelte Werke/ Thomas Mann).

— (1975): Doktor Faustus. Das Leben d. dt. Tonsetzers Adrian Leverkuehn, erzählt von e. Freunde Frankfurt a. M.: Fischer (Das erzählerische Werk / Mann, Thomas 9).

MANN, Tomasz (1988): Buddenbrookowie. Warszawa: Książka i Wiedza.

SEIBICKE, Wilfried (1982). Die Personennamen im Deutschen. Berlin – New York: Walter de Gruyter (Sammlung Göschen 2218).

THIES, Henning (1978). Namen im Kontext von Dramen. Studien zur Funktion von Personennamen im englischen, amerikanischen und deutschen Drama (Diss. Regenburg 1977). Frankfurt a. M. – Bern – Las Vegas: Lang (Sprache und Literatur 13).

TYROFF, Siegmar (1975): Namen bei Thomas Mann in den Erzählungen und den Romanen Buddenbrooks, Königliche Hoheit, Der Zauberberg (Diss. Salzburg 1972). Frankfurt a. M. – Bern: Peter Lang (Europäische Hochschulschriften: Reihe 1, Deutsche Literatur und Sprache = Langue et littérature allemandes 102).

VOSS, Lieselotte (1975): Die Entstehung von Thomas Manns Roman >Doktor Faustus<. Dargestellt anhand von unveröffentlichten Vorarbeiten. Tübingen: Niemeyer (Studien zur deutschen Literatur 39).

WALTHER, Hans (1988): Historisch-gesellschaftliche Determinanten in Benennungsakten. In: Benennung und Sprachkontakt bei Eigennamen. Beiträge zur Namenforschung, Beiheft 27, 52-67.

Zur Semantik literarischer Namen

Sprechende Namen in der Komödie „Zemsta" [Die Rache] von Aleksander Graf Fredro

Małgorzata Sieradzka-Kulasa

Namen zu geben ist nicht so leicht wie man denkt (Goethe)

1 Vorbemerkungen

Der vorliegende Beitrag setzt sich zum Ziel, auf die Bedeutsamkeit der Namensgebung für die Drameninterpretation aus der Sicht des Lesers hinzudeuten. Die Namen dienen einerseits als Mittel zur Kennzeichnung von Personen, Tieren, Orten u.ä., andererseits sind sie Mittel zur Erzeugung von Stimmung, die von den Schriftstellern meistens mit einer bestimmten Überlegung gebraucht werden. (vgl. Eis 1970:59) In grober Einteilung unterscheidet man zwischen authentischen Namen und literarischen Namen. Die literarischen Namen werden von den Autoren für literarische Zwecke gewählt. Unter zahlreichen Arten von Namen, die in der Literatur zu finden sind, erregen die sogenannten „redenden Namen" die meiste Aufmerksamkeit beim Rezipienten, d.h. allgemein gesagt solche Namen, bei denen die lexikalische Bedeutung besonders wichtig ist und die nach Zimmer (1981:96) „per definitionem nur für nicht-existierende Personen gelten".[1] Obwohl die sprachwissenschaftliche Forschung, darunter in erster Linie die Namenskunde, seit langem bestrebt ist, den Namen zu definieren und sein Wesen zu bestimmen, werden redende Namen nicht als eine der Namenskategorien, sondern meistens am Rande der Überlegungen zum Namen behandelt. Laut Thies (1978:10) stehen sie bei der Drameninterpretation im Vordergrund, denn sie geben dem Empfänger zusätzliche Signale. Es obliegt dem Rezipienten, um Thies weiter zu folgen, sei er Leser oder Zuschauer, die innere Beziehung zwischen sprechenden Namen und Namensträgern wahrzunehmen – sich der Tatsache voll bewußt zu werden, daß auf diese Art und Weise auf die für den Namensträger charakteristischen Eigenschaften und auf deren Wichtigkeit hingewiesen werden kann.

Gegenstand meiner Überlegungen ist die Interpretation von ausgewählten Namen, die in der Komödie „Zemsta" von Aleksander Graf Fredro (1793-1876) vorkommen.[2] Da dieser Aufsatz keinen Anspruch darauf erhebt, diese Eigennamen unter allen denkbaren Gesichtspunkten systematisch zu betrachten, werde ich im folgenden nur

---

[1] Der Begriff „redender Name" wurde erstmals von Lessing (1963:350) gebraucht. In diesem Aufsatz werden die Termini: „redender Name" und „sprechender Name" als Synonyma behandelt und austauschbar verwendet.

[2] Einer der besten und bekanntesten polnischen Dramatiker, dessen Komödien neben Słowackis und Mickiewicz' Stücken zu den bedeutendsten Werken der polnischen Theaterliteratur im 19. Jh. gehören. Die wichtigsten Komödien: „Mąż i żona" (1822; dt. „Mann und Frau" 1955), „Cudzoziemszczyzna" (1822; [Fremdtümelei]), „Damy i huzary" (1825; dt. „Damen und Husaren" 1954), „Pan Jowialski" (1833; dt. „Familie Jowialski" 1969), „Śluby panieńskie" (1833; dt. „Mädchenschwüre" 1955), „Wielki człowiek do małych interesów" (1866; dt. „Herr Genialski" 1972).

versuchen, „redende Namen" als sprachliche Phänomene und literarische Erfindungen darzustellen. Daher werde ich meine Aufmerksamkeit nur auf einige bedeutende Fragen der Namensforschung, wie z.b. Funktion, Etymologie und Bedeutung der Namen, richten, und diese stichwortartig behandeln. Im Mittelpunkt des Interesses stehen die redenden Namen, mit denen die vier Helden der Komödie „Zemsta" (1834) versehen wurden: *Raptusiewicz, Milczek, Papkin* und *Dyndalski*. Es sei an dieser Stelle angemerkt, daß die Namen nicht allein als Sprachformen, sondern im Kontext des Gesamtwerks betrachtet werden. Zum Schluß soll untersucht werden, was der Rezipient der deutschsprachigen Fassung der Komödie anstelle der redenden Namen im Zieltext vorfindet, wobei die Frage nach der Übersetzbarkeit von sprechenden Namen (mit)behandelt wird.

2   Zur Funktion sprechender Namen

Den Überlegungen zur Funktion redender Namen will ich eine sehr allgemeine Feststellung vorausschicken: die Meinungen über die Bedeutung der Eigennamen sind geteilt. Die Frage, ob Eigennamen Bedeutung haben oder nicht, ist ein immer wiederkehrender Streitpunkt, der kontrovers diskutiert wird. Die einen, wie z.b. der Logiker Mill (1856: Bd. 1:33), sind der Meinung, daß aus dem Namen nicht auf das Wesen des Namensträgers zu schließen sei.[3] Laut seiner Feststellung hätten Eigennamen keine Bedeutung, sie seien nur Bezeichnungs- und Erkennungsmarken, dagegen keine Prädikate des Namensträgers. Die anderen, wie z.b. zahlreiche Interpreten literarischer Namen, vertreten eine entgegengesetzte Ansicht und billigen sowohl realen als auch fiktiven Namen die Kategorie „Bedeutung" zu. Der Linguist Jespersen (1963: 64-71) ist der Auffassung, daß Eigennamen die bedeutungsträchtigsten sprachlichen Elemente sind. Meines Erachtens sind literarische Namen Bezeichnungs- und Erkennungsmarken, denen zugleich eine bestimmte Bedeutung zugeordnet ist.

In den folgenden Passagen des Aufsatzes will ich nur in wenigen Grundzügen darstellen, welche Funktionen sprechenden Namen zugeordnet werden. Redende Namen bilden zweifellos eine besondere Art der Eigennamen. Wenn sie als Namen gebraucht werden, haben sie lexikalische Bedeutung und erfüllen in erster Linie die Aufgabe, die Namensträger zu bezeichnen und zu kennzeichnen. Darüber hinaus dienen sie zur Anrede der betreffenden Personen.[4] Generell gesehen haben Namen auch eine individualisierende Funktion. Laut Maync (1917/18:658) ist jede Namensgebung aus der Sicht des Namensgebers eine Art Belebung, Beseelung und Individualisierung. Durch Verleihung eines Namens läßt sich die Identität des Namensträgers leichter erkennen. Das gilt auch für literarische Namen, mithin für sprechende Namen. Es wurde bereits erwähnt, daß den Namen, die zugleich Bezeichnungsfunktion haben, eine lexikalische Bedeutung zugeordnet wird. Solche Namen, die eine der wichtigsten Charaktereigenschaften der fiktiven Figuren benennen, sind nicht nur redende, sondern auch de-

---

[3] Näheres: vgl. Thies (1978:39f).
[4] Zur Diskussion über die Rolle der einzelnen Funktionen, die sprechende Namen haben, welche in der bisherigen Forschung zur linguistischen und literarischen Onomastik geführt wird, vgl. bei Thies (1978:40f).

skriptive Namen, die laut Thies (1978:56) als typisch literarisch angesehen werden. Für die Zwecke des vorliegenden Beitrags ist die Tatsache von Bedeutung, daß sprechende und somit deskriptive Namen auf der einen Seite die Andersartigkeit ihrer Träger erkennen lassen und auf der anderen Seite ihr eigenartiges Wesen schildern.

Wie gesagt, dienen Namen zur Benennung von Personen, außerdem werden sie benutzt als literarisches Mittel zur zusätzlichen signalisierenden Charakterisierung bzw. Typisierung ihrer Träger. Diese Funktionen üben sprechende Namen aus, die aus Wörtern gebildet werden, die im täglichen Umgang gebraucht werden. Durch diese Namen werden die Bezeichneten nicht nur charakterisiert, sondern auch individualisiert, d.h. aus der Masse der anderen herausgehoben.[5] Thies (1978:106) unterstreicht in Anlehnung an Binder (1961/62:95), daß die Namensträger nicht nur gekennzeichnet, sondern eigentlich gezeichnet werden. Zimmer (1981:70) dagegen hebt folgendes hervor: bei redenden Namen tritt die primäre Funktion des Namens, nämlich die Identifizierung, zugunsten der charakterisierenden Funktion in den Hintergrund. Nach seiner Auffassung sind sprechende Namen stark „durchsichtig".

Wie bereits erwähnt wurde, sind redende Namen deskriptiv und üben Suggestionswirkung aus. Da durch einen deskriptiven Namen eine hervorstechende Charaktereigenschaft z.B. einer dramatischen Gestalt hervorgehoben und bezeichnet wird, so wird dadurch auch der Namensträger gekennzeichnet. Zur Veranschaulichung dieser These sei im folgenden auf die Charakterzüge von vier männlichen Figuren aus „Zemsta" hingewiesen, die sprechende Namen tragen.

3   Name und Wort: die Deutung sprechender Namen am Beispiel der Komödie „Zemsta"

Aus der Spezifik der literarischen Einbettung der sprechenden Namen ergeben sich einige Konsequenzen. Wenn wir aus dem gerade Gesagten ein Fazit ziehen, dann erweist sich, daß redende Namen unmißverständlich die Eigenart ihrer Träger beschreiben und ein Bild der Namensträger evozieren. Ihre Bedeutung hängt nicht nur von der Form des Namens ab, sondern auch vom literarischen Kontext, in den sie eingebettet werden. Diese Behauptung trifft auf die Komödie zu, aus der die sprechenden Namen stammen, mit denen ich mich im folgenden befassen werde. Überdies ist zu unterstreichen, daß die redenden Namen der Helden in „Zemsta" an Bedeutung gewinnen, wenn sie im sozio-kulturellen Kontext analysiert werden. Die Namensträger repräsentieren eine soziale Gruppe, nämlich die der Sarmaten. Sie sind die letzten Vertreter der Epoche, die als „sarmatyzm" [Sarmatismus, Sarmatentum] bezeichnet wurde und die am Ende des 18. und Anfang des 19. Jahrhunderts nach und nach in den Hintergrund tritt.[6]

---

[5] Laut Głowiński (1996:152) lenken sie die Aufmerksamkeit des Rezipienten auf die Wesensart des den Bezeichneten bestimmenden Charakterzug. Sprechende Namen, deren Etymologie leicht durchschaubar ist und gewisse Assoziationen weckt, suggerieren bestimmte Eigenschaften des Namensträgers (Wilpert 1989:605) und weisen auf deren Wichtigkeit hin.

[6] Es besteht die Annahme, daß die Polen sarmatischer Abstammung sind, wovon bei Długosz in den „Annales" die Rede ist. Laut dieser These hätten die Sarmaten Gebiete in Europa bewohnt. (Błoński 1992:127). Zum ersten Mal wurden die Polen im 10. Jh. von einem französischen Chro-

An dieser Stelle soll hervorgehoben werden, daß der Leser des Dramas im Gegensatz zum Zuschauer die (vorteilhafte) Möglichkeit hat, alles, was er nicht erfaßt hat, bzw. das Versäumte, durch wiederholtes Verfolgen der Handlung, erneute Interpretation von Anspielungen, Vor- und Zurückblättern nachzuholen. Das bezieht sich auch auf die sprechenden Namen. In einem Lesetext sind sie im Unterschied zu den Namen auf der Bühne von wesentlicher Bedeutung. Während der Schauspieler über eine breite Palette von Bühnenmitteln[7] oder theatralischen Konventionen verfügt, mit denen er die für den Namensträger typischen Charaktereigenschaften hervorkehrt, sind redende Namen in einem Lesetext tatsächlich als eine der wenigen Charakterembleme zu behandeln.

Wie oben erwähnt, sollen die sprechenden Namen im literarischen Kontext untersucht werden. Die Handlung der Komödie „Zemsta", der ich die redenden Namen entnommen habe, spielt wahrscheinlich am Ende des 18. Jahrhunderts, im süd-östlichen Teil Polens. Ihre Thematik ist dem Leben des galizischen Landadels entnommen. Einige der Helden repräsentieren typische Eigenschaften des Sarmatismus.[8] Das sind vor allem die Hauptpersonen der Komödie: Cześnik[9] *Raptusiewicz* und Rejent[10] *Milczek*, sein Nachbar und Gegner zugleich, wie auch zwei Nebenfiguren: *Dyndalski*, Haushofmeister bei Cześnik und *Papkin*, ein alter Diener. Sie repräsentieren eine Kultur, die allmählich in Vergessenheit geraten ist. Die Komödie ist so konzipiert, daß sich die eigentümliche Atmosphäre und das Kolorit der zu Ende gehenden Epoche der Adelsrepublik, d.h. der Zeit unter der Herrschaft des Königs Stanislaus August,[11] im Werk niederschlagen. Einzelne Repräsentanten der im damaligen Polen zahlreichen und ein Schmarotzerleben führenden Sarmaten werden bildhaft dargestellt. Das Kolorit der früheren Zeiten und der einstigen Realien wird gewissermaßen als unwiederbringliche Vergangenheit und darum nachsichtig geschildert. Das wird durch den Einsatz von entsprechenden sprachlichen Mitteln erreicht. Eines von ihnen zeigt sich darin, daß Fredro einige Figuren der Komödie mit sprechenden Namen ausstattete, die auf Charakterzüge ihrer Träger hindeuten. (Inglot 1968:189f)

Die bisherigen Überlegungen zur Funktion der Namen sollen mit anschaulichen Beispielen untermauert werden. Die Tatsache, daß einige Gestalten der Komödie sprechende Namen tragen, ist zweifelsohne für die Interpretation des Stücks von Bedeutung. *Raptusiewicz, Milczek, Papkin* und *Dyndalski* sind die Namen fiktiver litera-

---

nisten als Sarmaten bezeichnet. Aus der Bezeichnung „Sarmatien", die sich erst im 17. Jh. durchsetzte, wurden zwei andere Begriffe, nämlich „Sarmatismus" und „sarmatisch" abgeleitet. Nach Suchodolski (1986:103) wurden sie „zu Synonymen für besondere Werte, hauptsächlich für ritterlichen Geist, Moral, Patriotismus und Frömmigkeit, denen die Schlachta huldigte und die sie gegenüber anderen Völkern und auch gegenüber den anderen sozialen Schichten der Adelsrepublik verteidigte."

[7] Levý (1969:158) unterstreicht z.B. die Rolle des Satzakzents und der Satzintonation, d.h. der akustischen Mittel, die im Text nicht erfaßbar sind, deren sich der Schauspieler bedienen kann, um stilistische Fehler des Übersetzers zu korrigieren.

[8] Dieser Begriff bezieht sich nicht nur auf die Ideologie der Schlachta, worauf oben eingegangen wurde, sondern auch auf Lebensstil, Mentalität und Sittlichkeit der Adeligen, ihre Vorliebe für Traditionalismus, Konservativismus, reaktionäre Gesinnung, Ungeniertheit und Heftigkeit.

[9] Cześnik = Mundschenk, Ehrentitel der Adeligen in der Zeit der Adelsrepublik.

[10] Rejent = Notar, früher: Verwalter der gerichtlichen Kanzlei und des Gerichtsarchivs.

[11] vornehmlich während der zweiten Hälfte seiner Regentschaft

rischer Figuren. Alle vier sind sprechende Namen, d.h. Namen, die von gewöhnlich
in der Umgangssprache gebrauchten Wörtern abgeleitet wurden und zugleich auf die
wichtigste Charaktereigenschaft, die das Wesentliche der betreffenden Gestalt kennzeichnet, hinweisen. Sie sind als Paradebeispiele anzusehen, mit denen demonstriert
werden kann, wie die Benennung fiktiver Gestalten als literarisches Mittel zu ihrer
zusätzlichen Typisierung verwendet wird. Es sei noch folgendes angemerkt: Die genannten Namen sind Familiennamen, d.h. Appellativa, deren Bedeutungen üblicherweise als wenig attraktiv empfunden werden, so z.B. bei Eis (1970:22).[12] Diese Familiennamen sind aufschlußreich, denn hier erscheinen sie als redende Namen, daher
besitzen sie eine gewisse Anziehungskraft, erregen die Aufmerksamkeit des Rezipienten und wirken nicht so farblos wie gewöhnlich gebrauchte Familiennamen.

Im folgenden werde ich mich auf die Etymologie der sprechenden Namen, mit denen die vier Helden in der Komödie „Zemsta" versehen wurden, konzentrieren.

Cześnik [Mundschenk], ein durchaus zänkischer, dabei offenherziger Charakter,
heißt *Raptusiewicz*, was ein psychologisches Merkmal dieser Figur ausdrückt, denn
raptus bedeutet „Hitzkopf", „Jähzorniger". Wenn man die Handlung des Stücks verfolgt hat, kann nicht bezweifelt werden, daß *Raptusiewicz* ein jähzorniger Charakter
und Händelsucher ist. Da Cześnik von der Neigung zur Heftigkeit übermannt wird,
gerät er leicht in Erregung, und dann verhält er sich unbeherrscht, unbesonnen. Er
verkörpert adeligen Hochmut, lebhaftes Temperament und Neigung zur Waghalsig-
keit (Inglot 1971:147). Das sind typisch sarmatische Merkmale.

Rejent [Notar] ist ein heuchlerischer, habgieriger, verlogener, ruhiger und listiger
Rechtsgelehrter. Seine Charaktermerkmale und berufliche Genauigkeit passen zu seinem introvertierten Nachnamen *Milczek*, was im Polnischen einen schweigsamen
Menschen bezeichnet. Sinko (1918:17) charakterisiert ihn durchaus prägnant und zutreffend als einen im Stillen heimtückischen, bösartigen und bissigen Menschen.

Papkin ist in der Komödie eine Figur, mit der die Komik am meisten gesteigert
wird. Er ist schwächer als andere, deshalb wird er ständig von den übrigen Personen
ausgenutzt. *Papkin* ist eine für den Übergang vom 18. ins 19. Jh. typische Figur, ein
komisch-sympathischer Schmarotzer, der sich durch kleine Dienste bei Cześnik und
Rejent einschmeichelt. Somit ist er Parasit, d.h. jemand, der vom herrschaftlichen
Tisch Speisereste sammelt, z.B. *papka*, d.h. „Brei".[13] Wahrscheinlich ist sein Name
von dem Wort *papanie*, als Synonym für „Essen", abgeleitet, das im Sinne der alt-
polnischen Redewendung, daß man „papką i czapką", also mit gutem Essen und
Hochachtung, Menschen für sich gewinne, gebraucht wird (Sinko 1918:17). Es gibt
aber noch eine Erklärung für den Namen *Papkin*, die auf das Diminutivum *papka*,
d.h. „Brei" bzw. „Kinderbrei" zurückzuführen ist. Diese Bezeichnung könnte sich auf
Personen beziehen, die leidenschaftlich gern, auch bei anderen, essen. Da *Papkin*
gutem Essen und Trinken nicht abgeneigt ist, besonders wenn er sie nicht auf eigene

---

[12] In der einschlägigen Literatur wird darauf hingewiesen, daß die Namen aus Appellativen entstanden sind. Nach Fleischer (1992:13) sind sie auch sprachliche Zeichen und erfüllen dieselbe Kom-
munikationsfunktion wie Appellativa. Zwischen Namen und Appellativum bestehen grundsätzliche Funktions- und Gradunterschiede. Vgl. hierzu Fleischer (1992:23), der folgendes betont: das
Appellativum charakterisiere und der Name identifiziere. Diese Bemerkung trifft auch auf sprechende Namen zu.

[13] *Papkin* wird von Sinko (1918:1) dem Typus „Parasitus-gloriosus" zugeordnet.

Kosten genießt, trifft auch diese Interpretation auf seinen Namen zu. Sinko (1918:17) verweist in seinen Überlegungen zur Bedeutung der sprechenden Namen noch auf die von Kucharski vorgeschlagene Deutung des Namens, der *papka* als „Mundwerk", „Maul" im Sinne „Prahler", „Aufschneider" versteht. *Papkin* ist folglich ein unglaublich redefreudiger, schlagfertiger und großsprecherischer Mensch. Obwohl Sinko (1918:17) diese Interpretation in Zweifel zieht und sie für wenig wahrscheinlich hält, scheint mir diese Deutung des sprechenden Namens *Papkin* besonders zutreffend zu sein.

Dyndalski, ein alter Diener, steht mit Cześnik auf vertrautem Fuße. Im allgemeinen aber zollt *Dyndalski* seinem Herrn Respekt, er ist ihm gegenüber ein loyaler Diener. Die von Cześnik geäußerten Meinungen nimmt er immer ernst. Nicht selten wird der ergraute alte Hofdiener von seinem Herrn geringschätzig behandelt. Im Gegensatz zu den anderen besprochenen Namen findet der Name Dyndalski in der einschlägigen Literatur keine Beachtung. Deswegen soll er an dieser Stelle einem Deutungsversuch unterzogen werden. Im Vergleich zu den voranstehenden Namen erweckt dieser Name nicht viele Assoziationen und enthält ein anderes komisches Element. Es handelt sich um das der Umgangssprache entnommene Verb *dyndać* („baumeln"), von dem der Name hergeleitet wurde. In bezug auf diese Person ist es im übertragenen Sinne zu verstehen: der Diener ist allzu nachgiebig und schwankend. Dyndalski verkörpert also einen willensschwachen, energielosen, weichlichen Menschen, der unaufmerksam und langsam ist.[14] Bereits Sinko (1918:17) bezeichnete ihn kurz aber überzeugend als einen „baumelnden Waschlappen". Es ist außerdem zu bemerken, daß nur dieser Name unter allen Eigennamen in der Komödie eine typisch polnische Namensendung -*ski* hat.

Wenn man die Deutung „des wahren Sinnes" redender Namen betrachtet, kann man sich folgende Feststellung erlauben: Alle analysierten suggestiven Eigennamen sind direkt sprechende literarische Namen, die beim Rezipienten eine bestimmte Vorstellung von den Namensträgern evozieren. Während *Raptusiewicz* und *Milczek* ihren Hintersinn direkt offenbaren, kann man *Papkin* und *Dyndalski* als „feiner getönte" redende Namen bezeichnen. Der Einsatz dieser Namen verleiht den Figuren der Komödie eine besondere Aura. Chrzanowski (1917:290) hebt hervor, daß diese vier Gestalten Cześnik *Raptusiewicz*, Rejent *Milczek*, *Papkin* und *Dyndalski* in der polnischen Literatur des 19. Jahrhunderts als Meisterstück in Bezug auf die Charakterisierung der Personen anzusehen sind. Meiner Ansicht nach verdanken wir diese Suggestivität teilweise auch den sprechenden Namen, die auf den Rezipienten wie ein Bild wirken.[15]

---

[14] Die Analyse hat gezeigt, daß die untersuchten redenden Namen suggestive Personennamen sind. Zum Wesen der Personennamen äußert sich Eis (1970:9) sehr treffend: „Wenn man einen Personennamen hört, pflegt man sich von seinem Träger eine Vorstellung zu bilden, auch wenn man ihn nicht kennt. Namen können farblos wirken oder aufhorchen lassen, sie können dem Träger Sympathie und Respekt oder Abneigung und Spott eintragen". Diese Beschreibung gilt auch für die analysierten sprechenden Namen, die direkt darauf hinweisen, was man von ihren Trägern zu gewärtigen hat.

[15] Darüber hinaus stuft Chrzanowski (1917:176-179) drei der vier mit sprechenden Namen Bezeichneten in die von Fredro entwickelten acht Haupttypen ein. *Milczek* verkörpere den Typ des

Nach der Analyse der Semantik der redenden Namen soll noch ein Problem angegangen werden. Die genannten Namen dienen nicht nur zur Identifizierung, Typisierung und vordergründigen Charakterisierung ihrer Träger, sondern erzeugen auch eine komische Wirkung. Komik durch Namensgebung entsteht nicht willkürlich. Laut Lamping (1983:90) kann man sie interpretieren als „ein Verfahren komischer Darstellung, eine im Werk angelegte, vom Autor intendierte, vom Leser zu realisierende oder zu aktualisierende Komik." Gerade in der Bedeutung der analysierten sprechenden Namen liegt die Namenskomik, die erst dann wirksam ist, wenn ihr semantischer Gehalt mit den Charakterzügen ihrer Träger konfrontiert wird. *Raptusiewicz* und *Milczek* sind Menschen mit unterschiedlichen Charakteren, der eine ist genau der Gegensatz zum anderen, was schon ihre Namen signalisieren. Durch diese zwei antithetischen redenden Namen wird ein komisch wirkender Kontrast angedeutet und ausgedrückt. Im Falle der Namen *Dyndalski* und *Papkin* entspringt die Komik den Assoziationen, die diese Personenbezeichnungen wachrufen.

Die Aussagekraft der angeführten Eigennamen ist offensichtlich unbestritten. Sie wird noch größer, wenn ihre Symbolik mit den Charaktereigenschaften der Namensträger konfrontiert wird. Meines Erachtens ist noch eine These aufzustellen: Die symbolische Bedeutung der sprechenden Namen und die für ihre Träger typischen Charakterzüge bedingen sich gegenseitig. Einerseits vermitteln sie dem Rezipienten ein bestimmtes Vorwissen über die Bezeichneten und signalisieren, was für einen Charakter der jeweils Bezeichnete hat. Andererseits wird durch die Namenswahl gerade diese Charaktereigenschaft hervorgehoben, die sein Wesen in bedeutendem Maße bestimmt. Sprechende Namen erlangen somit ihre Bedeutung im literarischen Kontext: erst die Kenntnis von den sich in der Komödie abspielenden Ereignissen ermöglicht dem Leser oder dem Zuschauer, sich zu vergewissern, ob der redende Name sowie der damit unterstrichene Charakterzug tatsächlich auf den Namensträger zutrifft oder die individuelle Charakterisierung – was mitunter auch passiert – den Rezipienten auf eine falsche Fährte lockt.

4   Sprechende Namen in der deutschsprachigen Fassung der Komödie

Diese Konfrontation wie auch die komische Wirkung, wie sie sprechende Namen zu zeitigen vermögen, werden dem Empfänger der deutschsprachigen Fassung der Komödie vorenthalten, denn alle Namen, darunter auch die sprechenden Namen, werden nicht übersetzt. Die Frage, ob die Eigennamen in die Zielsprache übertragen werden sollen, ist eines der brisanten Probleme, die in der einschlägigen Literatur von Linguisten, Logikern und auch Übersetzungswissenschaftlern angeschnitten werden. Laut Dymacz (1997:366) plädieren die meisten dafür, daß die Namen im Zieltext in der Form des Originals gebraucht werden sollen. Dieser Ansicht ist z.B. auch Fleischer (1992:23), der die Übersetzung eines Namens in eine fremde Sprache bzw. die Schaffung eines sinngemäßen Äquivalents für unnötig hält. Diese Stellungnahme erweist sich jedoch meiner Meinung nach als zu kategorisch. Ich würde deswegen eine an-

---

Heuchlers und ist der polnische Tartuffe. *Cześnik* repräsentiere den Typ des Heißsporns, während *Papkin* einen prahlerischen Feigling vertrete.

dere Position einnehmen und einfach die Frage stellen: Gilt dieses Verfahren auch für
Fälle, wo ein Name schon die Charakteristik der Person beinhaltet? Die bereits skizzierten Eigenschaften, die die Charaktere der vier Figuren ausmachen, beweisen, daß
die Namen als „Visitenkarten" ihrer Träger zu betrachten sind. Sowohl ihr semantischer Gehalt als auch der sozio-kulturelle Kontext, in den sie eingebunden werden,
liefern einen Nachweis dafür, daß sie nicht zufällig oder willkürlich gewählt und
konkreten Personen zugeordnet wurden. Fredro versuchte beim Empfänger eine bestimmte Reaktion hervorzurufen, denn sprechende Namen implizieren die Affektivi-
tät: Humor oder Ironie, Verachtung oder Sarkasmus. Redende Namen sind in „Zemsta" kein Selbstzweck, sie kennzeichnen das Verhalten, Wesen und Gemüt der Figuren und wirken erheiternd. Umso bedauerlicher, daß sie in der deutschen Fassung
nicht übersetzt wurden, wodurch ihr Signalwert verlorengegangen ist. Der deutschsprachige Rezipient ist deswegen außerstande zu beurteilen, ob sie sympathie-
heischend, abstoßend oder erschreckend wirken. Die nicht übersetzten Namen lassen
keine Rückschlüsse auf die Personen zu, klingen ihm nur exotisch im Ohr und
erwecken somit nicht die gleichen humoristischen Assoziationen, wie sie dies beim
Leser des Originals tun. Für den Rezipienten der deutschen Fassung sind sie unverständlich und bleiben wohl nichts anderes als gehaltlose, nichtssagende, wahrscheinlich abschreckende „Zungenbrecher". Dadurch, daß die Namen unübersetzt bleiben,
wird der Zieltext da verfremdet, wo er im Original ganz natürlich klingt. An dieser
Stelle drängt sich, ganz zu Recht, folgende Frage auf: wie sollte man mit sprechenden
Namen in der Übertragung umgehen? Die beste Lösung wäre gewiß, sie zu übersetzen oder in der Zielsprache so nachzubilden, daß das Spiel mit Bedeutungen und Assoziationen beibehalten werden kann.[16] Für redende Namen erscheint mir die Übersetzung als eine geeignete Strategie. Ich will mich der Meinung von Güttinger (1963:
77) anschließen, der behauptet: „Sprechende Namen müssen auch im Deutschen sprechen." Sie müssen, Güttinger (1963:76) weiter folgend, „zweckentsprechend übersetzt werden, um zu wirken." Eine ähnliche Position bezieht auch Zimmer (1981:99),
der in einer schematischen Darstellung der Übersetzbarkeit von Namen, auch von Namen fiktiver Personen, darunter die redenden/suggestiven Namen, diese eindeutig den
übersetzbaren zuordnet. Als Kriterium für die Übersetzung der Namen stellt er die
Kategorie „Charakterisierung" auf. Zimmer (1981:116) schreibt: „Literarische Namen sind meist charakterisierend, was bei redenden Namen zwangsläufig zu Übersetzung führt, falls dies der Kontext zuläßt." In der Komödie „Zemsta" ist die Übertragung der Namen somit unbedingt geboten.

Da Reiß (1971:12f) hinsichtlich konstruktiver Übersetzungskritik es für unabdingbar erklärt, einer beanstandeten Übersetzung einen Gegenvorschlag gegenüberzustellen, will ich nun Beispiele für mögliche deutsche Entsprechungen redender Namen vorschlagen.[17] Die Wiedergabe des appellativischen Gehalts der Namen ist durch-

---

[16] Dieses Postulat wird in die übersetzerische Praxis umgesetzt, wovon beispielsweise die Übertra-
     gungen der Komödie „Der zerbrochene Krug" von Heinrich von Kleist zeugen. In beiden polni-
     schen Fassungen entsprechen auch in der Form den redenden Namen polnische Äquivalente. Das
     sind die Namen *Adam* und *Eva*, also redende Namen der einfachsten Art und die nachgebildeten:
     Lampka, Jasnotka, die für den deutschen Namen *Licht* gebraucht werden.

[17] Dabei postuliert Reiß: Es sei dem Leser die Entscheidung überlassen, ob er die gerade kritisierte
     Übersetzung oder den vom Kritiker formulierten Gegenvorschlag vorzieht.

aus denkbar, entsprechend könnten die Helden die folgenden deutlich sprechenden Namen mit bewußt gewählten durchsichtigen Etyma erhalten: Cześnik *Raptusiewicz* – *Heißsporn* bzw. *Hitzkopf*, Rejent *Milczek* – *Schweiger*, *Papkin* – *Herumdreher* bzw. *Schmarotzer* und *Dyndalski* – *Baumelski*[18] bzw. *Baumler*. Es zeigt sich, daß die Eigennamen auch in der deutschen Fassung das ausdrücken können, was ihre Träger darstellen oder wodurch sie sich auszeichnen.

Als Schlußfolgerung kann folgendes festgehalten werden: der redende bzw. suggestive Charakter der Namen verlangt nach Übersetzung. Wenn aber infolge der Systemdifferenzen oder Abweichungen im Bereich der Bildungskonventionen ein solches „Rekonstruieren" nicht zustande kommen kann, sollte sich der Übersetzer anderer Mittel bedienen. Mika (1954) hätte mindestens angemessene kompensatorische Strategien anwenden können, um die Aussagekraft der Namen zu markieren. Mein Vorschlag wäre, die sprechenden Namen z.B. in einer Einleitung oder in einem Nachwort, wo kulturspezifische Realien beschrieben werden, einzuführen und ihre Bedeutung zu erklären. Im „Notfall" könnte man ausgangssprachlichen redenden Namen Anmerkungen mit erforderlichen Umschreibungen anschließen. Meines Erachtens würde eine derartige Notlösung dem Zieltext einen geringeren Schaden zufügen als die vorhandene übersetzerische Entscheidung. Dadurch, daß die sprechenden Namen in „Zemsta" nicht übertragen wurden, wird die gewünschte künstlerische Wirkung der Komödie wesentlich beeinträchtigt und die Namenskomik geht verloren. Das zeugt davon, wie wichtig eine gattungsspezifische Übersetzung ist. Abschließend läßt sich also die Richtigkeit wie auch Aktualität der anfangs angeführten Sentenz von Goethe nur bestätigen: „Namen zu geben ist [wirklich] nicht so leicht wie man denkt."

5   Literatur

BINDER, Wolfgang (1961/62): Hölderlins Namenssymbolik, Hölderlin-Jahrbuch 12, 95-204.

BŁOŃSKI, Jan (1992): Sarmatismus – zur polnischen Adelskultur. In: Kobylińska, E. et al. (Hrsg.): Deutsche und Polen. 100 Schlüsselbegriffe. München: Piper, 127-133.

CHRZANOWSKI, Ignacy (1917): O komedyach Aleksandra Fredry. Kraków: Akademja Umiejętności.

DYMACZ, Monika (1997): Ach, Pereira – czyli o tłumaczeniu nazwisk. In: Filipowicz-Rudek, M. et al. (Hrsg.): Między oryginałem a przekładem III. Kraków: Universitas, 366-368.

EIS, Gerhard (1970): Vom Zauber der Namen. Berlin: Erich Schmidt.

FLEISCHER, Wolfgang (1992): Zum Verhältnis von Name und appellativum im Deutschen. In: Fleischer, W. (Hrsg): Name und Text. Ausgewählte Studien zur Onomastik und Stilistik (zum 70. Geburtstag hrsg. und eingel. von Irmhild Barz et al.). Tübingen: Max Niemeyer, 3-24.

GŁOWIŃSKI, Michał et al. (1996): Podręczny słownik terminów literackich. Pod redakcją J. Sławińskiego. Warszawa: Open.

GÜTTINGER, Fritz (³1963): Zielsprache. Theorie und Technik des Übersetzens. Zürich: Manesse.

JESPERSEN, Otto (⁹1963): The Philosophy of Grammar. London: Allen & Unwin.

LAMPING, Dieter (1983): Der Name in der Erzählung. Zur Poetik des Personennamens. Bonn: Bouvier.

LESSING, Gotthold Ephraim (²1963): Hamburgische Dramaturgie. Stuttgart: Kroener (Kroeners Taschenausgabe).

---

[18] In dieser Form könnte der Name eine für polnische Nachnamen typische Endung haben.

LEVÝ, Jiři (1969): Die literarische Übersetzung. Theorie einer Kunstgattung. Frankfurt a. M: Athenäum.

MAYNC, Harry (1917/18): Nomen et omen. Von bürgerlicher und dichterischer Namengebung. In: Westermanns Monatshefte 123, 653-664.

MILL, John Stuart (⁴1856): A System of Logic. London: Parker.

REISS, Katharina (1971): möglichkeiten und grenzen der übersetzungskritik. kategorien und kriterien für eine sachgerechte beurteilung von übersetzungen. München: Max Hueber (hueber hochschulreihe 12).

SINKO, Tadeusz (1918): Genealogia kilku typów i figur Aleksandra Fredry. Kraków: Akademja Umiejętności.

SUCHODOLSKI, Bogdan (1986): Geschichte der polnischen Kultur. Warszawa: Interpress.

THIES, Henning (1978). Namen im Kontext von Dramen. Studien zur Funktion von Personennamen im englischen, amerikanischen und deutschen Drama (Diss. Regenburg 1977). Frankfurt a. M. – Bern – Las Vegas: Lang (Sprache und Literatur 13).

WILPERT, Gero von (⁷1989): Sachwörterbuch der Literatur. Stuttgart: Alfred Kröner.

ZIMMER, Rudolf (1981): Probleme der Übersetzung formbetonter Sprache. Ein Beitrag zur Übersetzungskritik (Habil.-Schr. Marburg/Lahn). Tübingen: Max Niemeyer (Zeitschrift für romanische Philologie, Beiheft 181.).

Quellen

FREDRO, Aleksander (¹⁰1971): Zemsta. Bearb. und Nachwort von M. Inglot. Wrocław u.a.: Zakład im. Ossolińskich, Biblioteka Narodowa. XXXIII.

— (1954): Die Rache des Verschmähten. Deutsch von Mika, Viktor. In: Sinn und Form. Beiträge zur Literatur 3. Berlin, 355-436.

Warum soll man Sprachlehrbücher nicht übersetzen?

Zygmunt Tęcza

Die im Titel meines Beitrags gestellte Frage, die von vornherein präsupponiert, *dass* man Sprachlehrbücher nicht übersetzen soll, will ich sogleich beantworten, denn die Antwort scheint mir durchaus einfach: Man soll nämlich Sprachlehrbücher nicht übersetzen, weil man sie oft genug nicht übersetzen kann.

Dies wäre also die eigentliche These meines Referats: *Man kann Sprachlehrbücher grundsätzlich nicht übersetzen, oder genauer: sich auf die schlichte Übersetzung im herkömmlichen Sinne beschränken, will man die Intention des Originalautors wahren und zugleich den Anforderungen des Zielpublikums gerecht werden.* Es sei hier nur an die fünf Äquivalenztypen von Koller (1979) sowie an die Skopostheorie von Reiß und Vermeer (1984) erinnert.

Ich wäre nie auf die Idee gekommen, mir die Frage nach der Möglichkeit oder Unmöglichkeit der Übersetzung von Sprachlehrwerken zu stellen, wäre mir nicht das Angebot gemacht worden, eines von ihnen aus dem Deutschen ins Polnische zu übersetzen – und hätte ich jenes Angebot nicht angenommen. Das Ergebnis meiner Arbeit lässt sich nun kaum als zufrieden stellend bezeichnen.

Es handelt sich dabei um den kompakten Sprachkurs „Französisch in 30 Tagen", zuerst 1995 im Humboldt-Taschenbuchverlag (in Zusammenarbeit mit Langenscheidt) erschienen, in seiner polnischen Ausgabe aus dem Jahre 1998. Der erwähnte Titel ist Bestandteil einer Reihe, in der auch Lehrwerke für weitere Sprachen wie Englisch, Spanisch, Italienisch (allesamt in 30 Tagen zu erlernen!) herausgebracht wurden, alle mit analogem Aufbau und gleicher drucktechnischer Gestaltung. In meinen weiteren Ausführungen will ich gelegentlich auch auf Beispiele aus dem Englisch-Lehrbuch zurückgreifen. Hauptgegenstand der Analyse bleibt jedoch „Französisch in 30 Tagen" in deutscher und polnischer Fassung.

Der Sprachkurs beginnt mit einem Vorwort, wo u.a. sein Titel ‚entzaubert' wird, indem es heißt: „Vermeiden Sie Lernstreß! Das Buch müssen Sie nicht in dreißig Tagen durchackern" (S. 11). Dennoch wird dem Benutzer ein schneller Lernerfolg in Aussicht gestellt:

> „Die dreißig Lektionen dieses Selbstlernkurses vermitteln Ihnen solide Grundkenntnisse der französischen Alltagssprache und versetzen Sie in die Lage, sich in Französisch korrekt und idiomatisch zu verständigen" (ibid.).

Dieser Kommentar, der übrigens eher vom Verlag als von den Autoren stammt – er ist in verblüffend ähnlicher Gestalt auch in „Englisch in 30 Tagen" zu finden –, kann dem Leser gewiss einen ersten Eindruck über die Natur der betreffenden Lehrbücher verschaffen.

Auf das Vorwort folgt ein kurzes Kapitel über die Aussprache des Französischen. Einzelne Phoneme bzw. Laute werden innerhalb von Wortformen präsentiert und anschließend durch Analogien zu deutschen Lauten erläutert.

Gerade bei diesem französisch-deutschen Vergleich wird der polnische Übersetzer von „Französisch in 30 Tagen" mit ersten Schwierigkeiten konfrontiert, denn viele

Erläuterungen kann er in seine Fassung des phonetischen Kommentars nicht einfach übernehmen (Tab. 1). Für einen polnischen Französisch-Lerner, der des Deutschen nicht mächtig ist, würden solche Erklärungen eher nutzlos sein; sie durften daher nicht übersetzt, sondern mussten durch anders geartete phonetische Hinweise substituiert werden.

franz. Laut	+ Vorkommensbeispiele	Ausspracheerläuterung
e	*tenir*	wie kurzer deutscher ö-Laut
	léger	wie geschlossenes deutsches e
u	*rue*	wie deutsches ü
r	*rue, barre, verve*	meist wie deutsches Gaumen-r

Tab. 1: Ausgewählte phonetische Erläuterungen aus „Französisch in 30 Tagen"

Umgekehrt gibt es aber auch Fälle, wo das Polnische im Bereich der Aussprache bessere Analogien zum Französischen parat hat als das Deutsche (Tab. 2).

Phonetische Erklärung in „Französisch in 30 Tagen"	Phonetische Analogie im Polnischen
Nasales ä: *vin, impossible, sympa, un, lundi, parfum*	ę wie in *kęs, pięta*
Nasales o: *bonjour, pompe, ton*	ą wie in *pąk, mąka*
Stimmhafter sch-Laut: *jour, cage, gilet*	ż wie in *żaba, nożyce*

Tab. 2: Französisch-polnische Analogien im Bereich der Aussprache

Auch wenn die hier genannten polnischen Phoneme mit den französischen nicht absolut identisch sind, so stehen sie den letzteren dennoch sehr nahe und eignen sich relativ gut zur Erklärung der französischen Aussprache – zumal in einem Lehrwerk mit eher begrenzten Ansprüchen auf linguistische Akribie. Auf jeden Fall eignen sie sich dazu wesentlich besser als der deutsche Originalkommentar, der übrigens ziemlich lakonisch geraten ist.

Noch weniger übersetzbar zeigt sich das nächste Kapitel des zur Debatte stehenden Buches, in dem „grammatische Fachausdrücke" dem Leser erklärt werden. Es handelt sich hierbei um ein einsprachiges deutsches Glossar, das mit nur wenigen Ausnahmen internationalisierte grammatische Termini lateinischer Herkunft einerseits und deren schulgrammatische Entsprechungen andererseits aufführt (Tab. 3).

Grammatische Fachausdrücke	
Adjektiv	Eigenschaftswort
Adjektivisch	in der Funktion eines Eigenschaftswortes
Adverb	Umstandswort
Akkusativ	Wenfall, 4. Fall
Akkusativergänzung	direkte Objektergänzung
Aktiv	Tätigkeitsform
Artikel	Geschlechtswort

Tab. 3: Anfang der Liste grammatischer Termini in „Französisch in 30 Tagen"

Da das Polnische grundsätzlich eigene Fachausdrücke für grammatische Erscheinungen entwickelt und die lateinischen Termini nur in seltenen Fällen übernommen hat (*deklinacja, koniugacja* und *ortografia* sind die einzigen Beispiele aus dem untersuchten Verzeichnis), würde bei einer Übersetzung dieser Wortliste ins Polnische deren linke Spalte entfallen und sie selbst ihre Eigenschaft als Glossar einbüßen.

Will nun der Übersetzer das Kapitel „Grammatische Fachausdrücke" überhaupt aufrechterhalten, muss er eigene Erläuterungen für die einzelnen polnischen Termini geben (bzw. bereits vorhandene fremde Definitionen zitieren). Dies ist auch tatsächlich geschehen: in der polnischen Fassung wurde das Verzeichnis grammatischer Fachausdrücke praktisch neu zusammengestellt.

Unmittelbar nach jenem Verzeichnis beginnt der Hauptteil des Lehrbuchs, der aus 30 Lektionen besteht. Jede Unterrichtseinheit ist nach dem gleichen Muster aufgebaut und umfasst grundsätzlich drei Teile:

1) einen französischen Dialog mit anschließend folgender deutscher Übersetzung,
2) einen grammatischen Kommentar samt Übungen,
3) eine Wortschatzliste sowie „landeskundliche Tips".

In Anlehnung an diese Struktur will ich nun translatorische Schwierigkeiten, die sich bei dem Transfer der einzelnen Lektionen ins Polnische ergeben, in drei Schritten besprechen, die der Reihe nach: 1. Morphosyntax, 2. Lexik und 3. Landeskunde thematisieren.

1 Morphosyntax

Ein erstes schwerwiegendes Problem grammatischer Natur taucht bereits in der ersten Lektion auf. Dort werden nämlich die Formen des französischen Artikels eingeführt.

Wie Tab. 4 zeigt, wird im Original das Wissen um die Existenz der Wortart Artikel sowie die Kenntnis deren grammatischer Eigenschaften und Funktionen beim deutschen Leser offenbar stillschweigend vorausgesetzt. Dies ist insofern berechtigt, als die Muttersprache des Lehrbuch-Benutzers, das Deutsche, ebenfalls eine Artikelsprache ist, und zwischen dem französischen und dem deutschen Artikelsystem unübersehbare Parallelen bestehen. So kann man sich – zumindest in einem Lehrwerk wie dem hier besprochenen – auf die Nennung wesentlicher Unterschiede beschränken (etwa: die Pluralform des unbestimmten Artikels, kein Neutrum im Französischen).

Die Übernahme des fraglichen Kommentars in die polnische Fassung – sprich: seine einfache Übersetzung, die hier auch tatsächlich erfolgt ist – führt hingegen zwangsläufig zu Verstehensschwierigkeiten bei einem polnischen Rezipienten, der es bisher mit keiner Artikelsprache zu tun hatte. Was ist ein Artikel? Und wieso gibt es davon gleich zwei verschiedene, einen bestimmten und einen unbestimmten? Wozu sind sie überhaupt da? – dies sind Fragen, die sich ein Pole, der Französisch innerhalb von 30 Tagen erlernen will, gleich am ersten Tag stellen – und leider keine Antwort bekommen wird.

„Französisch in 30 Tagen"			„Francuski w 30 dni"		
Der bestimmte und der unbestimmte Artikel			Rodzajnik określony i nieokreślony		
bestimmter Artikel		unbestimmter Artikel	rodzajnik określony		rodzajnik nieokreślony
maskulin	feminin	maskulin feminin	męski	żeński	męski żeński
Singular			liczba pojedyncza		
le sac	la gare	un sac une gare	le sac	la gare	un sac une gare
Plural			liczba mnoga		
les sacs les gares		des sacs des gares	les sacs les gares		des sacs des gares
l' steht anstelle von le/la vor Substantiven, die mit Vokal oder stummem h anfangen: l'hôtel m (das Hotel) l'arrivée f (die Ankunft)		Im Gegensatz zum Deutschen gibt es im Französischen eine Pluralform des Artikels: un sac (eine Tasche), des sacs (Taschen); une gare (ein Bahnhof), des gares (Bahnhöfe)	l' pojawia się w miejsce le/la przed rzeczownikami zaczynającymi się od samogłoski lub niemego h: l'hôtel m (hotel) l'arrivée f (przyjazd)		Francuski posiada formę liczby mnogiej tego rodzajnika: un sac (torba), des sacs (torby); une gare (dworzec), des gares (dworce)
Merke: Im Französischen sind alle Substantive maskulin oder feminin. Es gibt kein Neutrum!			Zapamiętaj: We francuskim wszystkie rzeczowniki są rodzaju męskiego lub żeńskiego. Nie ma rodzaju nijakiego!		

Tab. 4: Informationen zum franz. Artikel in deutscher und polnischer Lehrbuchfassung

Am zweiten Tag wird er übrigens erfahren, dass es im Polnischen keine Entsprechung für den französischen Teilungsartikel gibt – denn es gibt im Deutschen keine Entsprechung für den französischen Teilungsartikel, und die betreffende Information wurde auch diesmal einfach aus dem Deutschen ins Polnische übersetzt (Lektion 2). Ob sie nun dem polnischen Französisch-Lerner weiterhilft, ist eher zweifelhaft, da ihm vor allem eine grundlegende Erläuterung der in seiner Sprache nicht vorhandenen grammatischen Erscheinung *Artikel* fehlt.

Wünschenswert wäre in der polnischen Ausgabe auch eine kurze Schilderung des Zusammenhangs zwischen der Funktion des französischen Teilungsartikels und der polnischen Kasusopposition von Akkusativ und Genitiv bei Mengenangaben mit transitiven Verben, weil an dieser Stelle eine deutliche Funktionsähnlichkeit vorliegt. Da jedoch eine diesbezügliche Information im deutschen Original (verständlicherweise!) fehlt, hat man sich auch hier auf die bloße Übersetzung des grammatischen Kommentars beschränkt.

Ähnliche Defizite liegen in der polnischen Fassung ebenfalls dort vor, wo dem Leser der Bau der französischen analytischen Tempusformen erläutert wird (Lektion 4, 7). Bei dem deutschen Rezipienten wird auch in diesem Falle die Kenntnis von Erscheinungen wie Perfekt mit den Hilfsverben *haben* und *sein*, regelmäßige und unregelmäßige Verben etc. vorausgesetzt, und zwar mit gutem Recht, denn er kennt sie alle aus seiner Muttersprache. Eine schlichte Übersetzung des betreffenden Kommentars ins Polnische muss man hingegen wieder als einen Fehlschlag bewerten.

Bisweilen ist es auch nicht möglich, Beispiele für grammatische Erscheinungen zu übersetzen; sie müssen eher ausgetauscht werden, und zwar in der Regel dort, wo im

Original französisch-deutsche Vergleiche vorkommen. Ein solcher Fall wird in Tab.5 präsentiert.

Grammatische Erläuterung in „Französisch in 30 Tagen"	Polnische Entsprechungen der französischen Beispiele (ebenfalls reflexiv)
„Nicht jedes Verb, das im Französischen reflexiv ist, ist es auch im Deutschen, z.B. *s'appeler* (heißen), *se promener* (spazierengehen), *se debrouiller* (zurechtkommen)." (Lektion 13)	nazywać *się* przechadzać *się* radzić *sobie*

Tab. 5: Französische reflexive Verben mit nichtreflexiven deutschen Äquivalenten

Da ausgerechnet im Polnischen zumindest zwei von den drei hier aufgezählten französischen Verben ebenfalls reflexiv sind, muss im Translat (wenn es nicht ein Missbrauch ist, in diesem Falle von einem *Translat* zu reden) nach geeigneteren Exempeln gesucht werden.

Gelegentlich erweist es sich als notwendig, einen grammatischen Kommentar völlig zu beseitigen, da er für das Deutsche, nicht aber für das Polnische zutrifft:

> „Die Konjunktion *que* (dass) leitet im Französischen Objektsätze ein. Im Deutschen kann die Konjunktion *dass* auch wegfallen: Er sagt, Sabine ist (sei) krank." (Lektion 22)

Im Polnischen ist nämlich die Subjekt- und Objektsätze einleitende Konjunktion *że* unter keinen Umständen eliminierbar.

Relativ selten kommt es vor, dass eine grammatische Information in der polnischen Ausgabe überflüssig ist, da eine Analogie diesmal nicht zwischen der zu erlernenden Fremdsprache und dem Deutschen, sondern zwischen der zu erlernenden Fremdsprache und dem Polnischen vorliegt. Ein Beispiel aus „Englisch in 30 Tagen" (Lektion 19):

> „*When* und *if* werden oft verwechselt, haben jedoch eine unterschiedliche Bedeutung: *when* = wenn, wann – etwas geschieht zu einem bestimmten Zeitpunkt, während eines bestimmten Zeitraums (es steht fest, dass etwas geschehen wird); *if* = wenn, falls – etwas wird geschehen, wenn eine bestimmte Bedingung erfüllt ist (es ist nicht sicher, ob etwas geschehen wird)."

Die im Original signalisierte Verwechslungsgefahr besteht nun lediglich in Bezug auf den deutschen Muttersprachler, da er das deutsche *wenn*, das mit dem englischen *when* genetisch gleich und ihm formal immer noch sehr ähnlich ist, sowohl temporal als auch konditional zu gebrauchen gewohnt ist. Das Polnische verfügt hingegen über zwei verschiedene Konjunktionen: *kiedy* bzw. *gdy* und *jeśli* bzw. *jeżeli*, deren Anwendungsbereich ziemlich genau dem der englischen *when* und *if* entspricht. Die in der Lizenzausgabe reproduzierte Information, dass *when* und *if* oft verwechselt werden, hat also wenig Rückhalt in der polnischen Wirklichkeit.

2   Lexik

Beherrscht der Übersetzer nur das Deutsche, die im jeweiligen Lehrbuch didaktisierte Fremdsprache aber nicht – oder er beherrscht sie, zieht sie aber bei der Übertragung ins Polnische nicht zu Rate –, so können gelegentlich auch Wortschatzlisten zur Quelle potenzieller Fehler werden, und zwar in erster Linie dort, wo das deutsche Äquivalent des gegebenen französischen (oder englischen) Wortes semantisch plurivalent ist; vgl. Tab. 6.

Fremdspr. Vokabel	dt. Äquivalent im Lehrbuch	gemeintes Semem des dt. Wortes
campagne	Land (Lektion 2)	Dorf
crois (croire)	glauben (Lektion 8)	einer Meinung sein
lac	See (Lektion 2)	der See
engl. *dish*	Gericht (Engl. Lektion 25)	Speise

Tab. 6: Wortschatzlisten als Falle für den Übersetzer

Da die meisten Vokabeln jedoch im Dialog der jeweiligen Lektion verwurzelt sind, hält sich das o.g. Fehlerrisiko in Maßen.

Ein augenfälliges lexikalisches Defizit liegt in der polnischen Fassung hingegen dort vor, wo dem Lerner (in der Lektion 7) ausgewählte Ländernamen und die dazugehörigen Bezeichnungen für Nationalitäten präsentiert werden. Außer Frankreich und Deutschland finden sich in diesem Verzeichnis u.a. auch Schweden, Argentinien, Japan und Portugal – Polen aber fehlt (im Englisch-Lehrbuch übrigens auch). Ob hier durch die bloße Übersetzung die Funktion des Lehrbuchs aufrechterhalten wurde, dem Lernenden das notwendigste Vokabular zu vermitteln, ist eher zweifelhaft.

Ähnlich wie es bei vielen grammatischen Erklärungen der Fall ist (s.o.), kann auch ein auf die Lexik bezogener metasprachlicher Kommentar des Autors schier unübersetzbar sein. Dass der Übersetzer dieses Problem gelegentlich schnell lösen kann, indem er eben nicht übersetzt, sondern eigentlich das Gegenteil des im Original Gesagten formuliert, zeigt ein amüsantes Beispiel aus dem Englisch-Lehrbuch (Tab. 7).

„Englisch in 30 Tagen"				„Angielski w 30 dni"			
Monatsnamen				*Nazwy miesięcy*			
Beim Lernen der Monatsnamen haben Sie es relativ leicht, denn die meisten sind auf Englisch und Deutsch sehr ähnlich:				Nauczenie się nazw miesięcy nie jest takie łatwe, gdyż nie są one podobne do nazw w języku polskim [„Das Erlernen von Monatsnamen ist gar nicht so leicht, denn sie sind den polnischen (Monats-)Namen nicht ähnlich."]:			
January	Januar	*July*	Juli	*January*	styczeń	*July*	lipiec
February	Februar	*August*	August	*February*	luty	*August*	sierpień
March	März	*September*	September	*March*	marzec	*September*	wrzesień
April	April	*October*	Oktober	*April*	kwiecień	*October*	październik
May	Mai	*November*	November	*May*	maj	*November*	listopad
June	Juni	*December*	Dezember	*June*	czerwiec	*December*	grudzień
							(Lektion 14)

Tab. 7: Englisch-Lehrbuch: Monatsnamen samt metasprachlichem Kommentar

3 Landeskunde

Bei den landeskundlichen Informationen, die im zur Debatte stehenden Franzö-
sischkurs enthalten sind, wird immer wieder – mehr noch als bei Grammatik und
Wortschatz – auf deutsche Gegebenheiten, in diesem Falle auf die deutsche außersprachliche Realität Bezug genommen. Die Sache ist relativ unproblematisch, solange es sich etwa um Vorwahlnummern beim Telefonieren ins Heimatland handelt
(es reicht hier 19 49 durch 19 48 zu ersetzen), oder um Größen der Damenbekleidung
(das Größensystem ist in Deutschland und in Polen gleich). In den meisten Fällen ist
jedoch der jeweilige Vergleich zwischen Frankreich und Deutschland durch die feh-
lende Analogie zu Polen nicht mehr relevant und muss bei der Übertragung möglichst
geschickt umgangen werden (Tab. 8).

Kommt also mancherorts wegen der vorhandenen Bezugnahme auf Deutschland
eine Übersetzung nicht in Frage, so wird entweder – wo es nur möglich ist – das Adjektiv *deutsch* einfach durch *polnisch* ersetzt oder es wird auf den reichlich ver-
schwommen wirkenden Vergleich mit „anderen Ländern" ausgewichen –, oder aber
der Vergleich wird völlig eliminiert.

Dass die schlichte Substitution von *deutsch* durch *polnisch* bei der Übernahme lan-
deskundlicher Informationen keinesfalls eine ungefährliche Prozedur ist, zeigt das in
Tab. 8 an letzter Stelle angeführte Beispiel. Wer als Pole nur einmal mit dem französischen TGV oder dem deutschen ICE gefahren ist, wird wissen, dass es in Polen
(noch?) keinen analogen Zugtyp gibt – allein vom Aussehen und von der Geschwin-
digkeitsleistung her.

Französisch in 30 Tagen"	„Francuski w 30 dni"
„Grunsätzlich wird *Mademoiselle* häufiger verwendet als *Fräulein* im Deutschen." (Lektion 1)	„Zasadniczo określenie *Mademoiselle* stosowane bywa częściej niż w innych językach." [Grundsätzlich wird die Bezeichnung *Mademoiselle* häufiger verwendet als in anderen Sprachen.]
„Grundsätzlich haben alle Läden in Frankreich länger geöffnet als in Deutschland." (Lektion 4)	„Generalnie wszystkie sklepy we Francji otwarte są dłużej aniżeli w innych krajach europejskich." [Grundsätzlich haben alle Läden in Frankreich länger geöff-net als in anderen europäischen Ländern.]
„Es gibt für berufstätige Frauen mehr Möglichkeiten, ihr Kind in einer Krippe unterzubringen als in Deutschland." (Lektion 3)	„Kobiety czynne zawodowo mają stosunkowo duże możli-wości umieszczenia swego dziecka w żłobku." [Berufstätige Frauen haben relativ viele Möglichkeiten, ihr Kind in einer Krippe unterzubringen.]
„Der französische *TGV* entspricht dem deutschen ICE." (Lektion 12)	„Francuski *TGV* odpowiada ICE (Inter City Express) w Polsce." [Der französische *TGV* entspricht dem ICE (Inter City Ex-press) in Polen.]

Tab. 8: Ausgewählte landeskundliche Informationen aus dem Französisch-Lehrbuch

Auf der anderen Seite sind jedoch gelegentlich unübersehbare Parallelen zwischen
der französischen und der polnischen Realität vorhanden, die bestimmte landeskundliche Erläuterungen überflüssig machen; als redundant betrachte ich demgemäß In-

formationen wie die über das Wesen des Namenstages (Lektion 5), aber auch die Er-
läuterung, dass man bei der Begrüßung den Namen des Gesprächspartners nicht nennt
(Lektion 1), oder dass *Bonjour* sowohl „Guten Tag" wie „Guten Morgen" heißt (ibid.;
Bonjour hat ja im Polnischen auch nur *ein* Äquivalent).

Spätestens an dieser Stelle wird mir der Leser eine durchaus schizofrene Haltung
vorwerfen; denn ich beanstande vielerorts zielsprachliche Lösungen – allen voran die
vorbehaltlose Übernahme origineller Inhalte, wo adaptierendes Eingreifen vonnöten
gewesen wäre – und übersehe dabei, dass ich selbst Autor jener Lösungen bin. Dieser
Widerspruch lässt sich aber objektiv erklären: die endgültige Beschaffenheit von
„Francuski w 30 dni" ist nämlich durch zwei außersprachliche Gegebenheiten in ent-
scheidendem Maße beeinträchtigt worden, und zwar:

1) Eine bedeutende Einschränkung drucktechnischer Natur. Das deutsche Original
   musste von Anfang an quasi als Matrize für die polnische Ausgabe benutzt werden; die Seitenzahl ist in beiden Büchern gleich, identisch sind auch der Gehalt
   und die technisch-formale Gestaltung jeder einzelnen Seite. Von vornherein
   ausgeschlossen war also die Möglichkeit, eine Textstelle auf die nächste Seite
   überlaufen zu lassen, wenn man eine zusätzliche, sei es auch die kürzeste Information etwa über das Wesen des deutschen Artikels in die polnische Fassung
   hätte einbauen wollen.
   Einen skurrilen Beweis dafür, dass es sich bei den Lizenzausgaben um eine
   treue Wiedergabe der jeweiligen deutschen computerhergestellten Druckvorlage
   handelt, liefert die polnische Version von „Englisch in 30 Tagen", wo mitten in
   einer grammatischen Übung (Lektion 24) plötzlich ein kurzer Kommentar in
   deutscher Sprache erscheint – er wurde von den Übersetzern aus Versehen nicht
   beseitigt, bzw. nicht durch die polnische Entsprechung substituiert. An sich
   hätte ja in der polnischen Ausgabe von „Englisch in 30 Tagen" kein einziges
   deutsches Wort vorkommen dürfen. Auch zahlreiche Druckfehler, die im fran-
   zösischsprachigen Teil des Originallehrbuchs „Französisch in 30 Tagen" vorhanden sind, tauchen in der polnischen Ausgabe wieder auf.
2) Unzureichende Absprache zwischen Verlag und Übersetzer. Hätte ich in der
   Rolle des Letzteren von Anfang an meinen Spielraum gekannt oder auch nur ge-
   wusst, dass ich ein notwendiges Minimum an Ergänzungen im grammatischen
   Kommentar und im Vokabular vornehmen darf und soll, so wäre gewiss die
   eine oder andere Textstelle noch zu retten gewesen. Ursprüngliche Anweisungen des Verlages befolgend, habe ich mich indes auf die bloße Übersetzung des
   deutschen Lehrbuchteils beschränkt – und nachher keinen Einfluss mehr auf den
   polnischen Text gehabt. Eine Adaptation an die Bedürfnisse polnischer Rezipienten sollte vom Verlag selbst und ggf. von einem Fachgutachter vorgenommen werden. Dass die Resultate jener Adaptation eher enttäuschend sind, dürfte
   aus den obigen Ausführungen ersichtlich sein.

Aber auch ungeachtet der beiden außersprachlichen Faktoren sehe ich die von mir
zuvor aufgestellte These, dass Sprachlehrbücher nicht einfach übersetzt werden sollen, bestätigt. Will man den Begriff der Übersetzung nicht übermäßig strapazieren, so
ist das im Falle der besprochenen Lehrwerke insgesamt anzuwendende Verfahren

eher als eine (mehr oder weniger weitgehende) Adaptation zu betrachten denn als eine Spielart der Übersetzung.

Literatur

KOLLER, Werner (1979): Einführung in die Übersetzungswissenschaft. Heidelberg: Quelle & Meyer (UTB 815).

REISS, Katharina; VERMEER, Hans J. (1984): Grundlegung einer allgemeinen Translationstheorie. Tübingen: Niemeyer (Linguistische Arbeiten 147).

Quellen

BROUGH, Sonia; Wittmann, Carolyn (1995): Englisch in 30 Tagen. München: Humboldt/Langenscheidt.

BROUGH, Sonia; WITTMANN, Carolyn (1996): Angielski w 30 dni. Tłum. A. Krzemińska, St. Janowski. Warszawa: Humboldt/Langenscheidt/Rea.

FUNKE, Micheline (1998): Francuski w 30 dni. Tłum. Z. Tęcza. Warszawa: Humboldt/Langenscheidt/ Rea.

— (1995): Französisch in 30 Tagen. München: Humboldt/Langenscheidt.

Stereotyp als translationswissenschaftliche Größe und die kulturelle Kompetenz des Translators

Lew Zybatow

0   Einstimmung

Wenn man durch den Paradigmendschungel der jungen, aber wuchernden Translations-wissenschaft streift, so kann das, wenn nicht abenteuerlich, so doch mitunter recht amüsant sein. So kann man nicht umhin, sich zu wundern über die nicht explizit zuge-gebene, jedoch unverkennbare gegenseitige Inakzeptanz zwischen den eher linguistisch und den eher funktional orientierten Vertretern der übersetzungswissenschaftlichen Zunft. Dieser beidseitige Ausschließlichkeitsanspruch ist jedoch nicht nur amüsant, sondern leider auch für Selbstverständnis und Entwicklung der Disziplin nicht gerade förderlich. Denn was zu welchem Zweck wie übersetzt werden soll (wofür sich haupt-sächlich die funktionalistisch orientierte Translationswissenschaft interessiert) und wie das Übersetzen/Dolmetschen dann im einzelnen vor sich geht (womit sich die linguistisch orientierte Translationswissenschaft vornehmlich befaßt) sind zwar zwei unterschiedliche Fragestellungen, jedoch zwei Seiten einer Medaille, die beide von der Translationswissenschaft behandelt werden müssen. So habe ich mich z.B. gefragt, wieso angesichts des immer wiederkehrenden Satzes, daß Translation ein kultureller Transfer sei, – dieser Transfer jedoch wohlgemerkt immer und notwendig über das zeichensprachliche Material realisiert wird – in der Translatologie – soweit ich sehen kann – noch kein einigermaßen systematischer Versuch unternommen wurde, die Kultur bzw. das kulturelle Wissen zu Sprache in Beziehung zu setzen. Denn die be-kannte Problematik der sog. Realia bzw. nulläquivalenten Lexik greift zu kurz, um das komplexe Beziehungsgeflecht Sprache - Kultur - Translation auf eine systemati-sche Weise aufzudröseln und aufzuzeigen, was von der Kultur wie an der Sprache hängt und welche translationstheoretischen wie -praktischen Konsequenzen sich dar-aus ergeben.

   Man muß allerdings einräumen, daß eine soche Aufgabe ein sehr weites Feld ist. Deshalb möchte ich im folgenden an einer kleinen Parzelle dieses Feldes eine inter-disziplinäre Vorgehensweise demonstrieren und zeigen, wie man mittels einer lingui-stischen Theorie kulturspezifische Inhalte einfangen und translationstheoretisch wie -praktisch bewältigen kann. Zugleich soll sich zeigen, daß damit auch ein wichtiger Bereich der kulturellen Kompetenz des Translators erschlossen werden kann. Dazu wende ich mich dem interdisziplinären Begriff des Stereotyps zu.

1   Der interdisziplinäre Begriff des Stereotyps aus linguistischer Sicht

Der Begriff des Stereotyps erfreut sich in letzter Zeit einer gewissen Renaissance – und zwar in verschiedenen Wissenschaftsdisziplinen, wie z.B. Soziologie, Sozialpsycholo-

gie, Politikwissenschaft, Kulturwissenschaft, Ethnologie, Literaturwissenschaft, die –
soweit ich sehen kann – alle mit dem an Lippmann (1922) orientierten, d.h. einem
recht weiten Verständnis des Stereotyps operieren. Danach sind Stereotypen – etwas
verallgemeinert ausgedrückt – Denkschemata bzw. stabile kognitive Vorstellungs-
strukturen, mit deren Hilfe wir die Welt sehen und interpretieren.

Aus Platzgründen muß ich auf eine Zusammenschau interdisziplinärer Stereotypen-
auffassungen verzichten, um direkt zu meinem Entwurf der Stereotypen aus linguistischer Sicht zu kommen. Auf die Idee zu diesem Entwurf brachte mich seinerzeit die
Klassifizierung der Stereotypen aus linguistischer Sicht in Gülich (1978:6) – vgl. 1).

1)

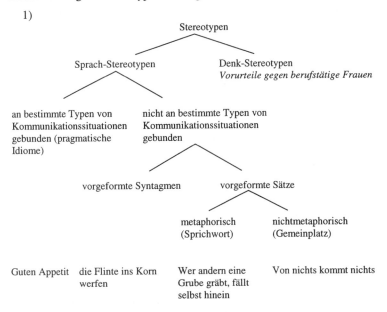

Hieraus ist – erstens – ersichtlich, daß der Stereotyp-Begriff in der Linguistik ambig
ist und in Sprach- und Denkstereotyp zerfällt. Genauer gesagt, das (Alltags)Verständ-
nis von Stereotyp als etwas Festgestaltigem (griechisch ‚stereos‘ gleich fest und ‚ty-
pos‘ gleich Gestalt), also Stereotyp als etwas Festgestaltiges, Vorgeprägtes, Schablo-
nenhaftes, wird in der Sprachwissenschaft zum einen auf die sprachlichen Strukturen
und zum anderen auf die kognitiven, gedanklichen Strukturen bezogen, woraus sich
die Zweiteilung in Sprach- und Denkstereotypen ergibt.

Zweitens ist an dem Schema in 1) auffällig, daß einer doch ziemlich weitverzweig-
ten Einteilung der Sprachstereotypen (also phraseologischer Einheiten im engeren und
weiteren Sinne) – vgl. Sie bitte die Einteilung links – eigentlich ein weißer Fleck auf
Seiten der Denkstereotypen – also rechts – gegenübersteht.

So war die Versuchung da, sich dieses weißen Fleckes anzunehmen und zu fragen,
was sich wohl hinter den sog. Denkstereotypen aus linguistischer Sicht verbergen und

wie ihre Beziehung zur natürlichen Sprache sein mag. Denn die Denkstereotypen sind zwar kognitive Größen, werden aber durch Sprache geprägt und begegnen uns in sprachlichen Formulierungen.

2 Denkstereotypen in Wort und Text

Stereotypen sind „Bilder in den Köpfen", sagt Lippmann (1964:27), und das leuchtet auch ein, wenn man z.b. bei Koeppen (1973:198) in seiner Novelle „Nach Rußland und anderswohin" am Anfang liest:

> 2) „Es war ein kleiner, ein gar nicht seriös aussehender Brief ... Die Botschaft der proletarischen UdSSR erkundigte sich sehr liebenswürdig bei mir, einem Bürger der BR, ob ich eine Einladung in die Sowjetunion annehmen würde."
>
> a) „Sogleich sah ich mich, in Pelze gehüllt, eine Pelzmütze auf dem Kopf, zusammen mit Polewoi in einem Schlitten sitzen. In einer Troika glitten wir durch die winterliche Weite. In der Luft klirrte der Frost. Die Leiber der Pferde dampften. Schellen läuteten an ihrem Geschirr. Märchenkirchen hoben sich aus dem Schnee – gebrochene goldene Kreuze. Wölfe begleiteten unsere Fahrt, Reif im gesträubten Fell und hungrig die roten Zungen. Der heilige Marc Chagall schwebte über sturmschiefen Holzhäusern, die wir am Abend erreichten. Wir schliefen zur Nacht in schweren Betten, die auf breite warme Kachelöfen geschichtet waren. Wir löffelten roten Borschtsch, in dem weiß und fett die Sahne versank. Wir aßen Töpfe voll Kaviar leer und Pfannen mit gerösteter Grütze. Wir tranken süßen Tee und scharfen Wodka und lauschten schwermütigen Balalaika-Klängen."
>
> b) „Es gibt Leute, die mich schelten werden. Aber hat Dante nicht die Einladung in die Hölle angenommen? Und die Hölle auf Erden? Ist sie ein geographisch zu erfassender Ort, ein begrenztes Territorium? Gibt es irgendwo ein Schild: Hier beginnt die Hölle, hier endet das Paradies? Und wenn es dieses Schild geben sollte, – wer hat es aufgestellt? Darf man ihm trauen? Ich halte nichts von Schildern. Ich reiste in die Sowjetunion."

Diese Bilder wurden also bei Koeppen allein durch eine Einladung in die Sowjetunion „angerufen". Imaginationen, die sich mit dem Wort Sowjetunion verbanden, die er noch vor der Erfahrung mit diesem Lande in seinem Kopf trug und die er in 2a) direkt versprachlicht hat. Unter 2b) wird auch eine Vorstellung ausgedrückt – diesmal aber indirekt: in die Sowjetunion fahren – heißt: in die Hölle fahren.

Diese Vorstellung ist nicht explizit verbalisiert, sondern aus den Äußerungen unter 2b) ableitbar, und hier kommen textuell aufgebaute, indirekte, implizite sprachliche Ausdrucksweisen von Stereotypen zum Tragen. Auf diese Art von Stereotypen – ich nenne sie textbezogene Stereotypen – gehen wir später ein, denn zunächst möchte ich mich den mit einem Wort in Verbindung stehenden Stereotypen – den sog. wortbezogenen Stereotypen – zuwenden.

3 Wortbezogene Stereotypen

Meine Überlegungen dazu (vgl. Zybatow 1995) resultieren aus der Auseinandersetzung mit linguistischen Arbeiten zum Stereotyp von Quasthoff (1973), mit den sprachphilosophischen Stereotypen-Auffassungen von Putnam (1979), dem psychologischen Prototypen-Diskurs von Rosch (1977) sowie dem anschließenden linguistischen Diskurs zur Stereotypen- und Prototypensemantik, auf die ich hier ebenfalls im einzelnen nicht eingehen kann.

Summa sumarum lassen sich aus der Diskussion in der Literatur zur linguistischen Stereotypensemantik m.E. zunächst z w e i grundsätzliche Arten der Beziehung zwischen Stereotyp einerseits und der Wortbedeutung andererseits ableiten:

a) Stereotypen als Inhalt von Bedeutungsbeschreibungen – ich nenne sie Bedeutungsstereotyp und

b) Stereotypen als mit einem Wort verbundene Assoziationen – ich nenne sie Assoziationsstereotyp.

Bedeutungsstereotypen beinhalten jene typischen Merkmale, die in der Alltagsvorstellung der Sprachbenutzer begriffliche Kategorien voneinander abgrenzen lassen (d.h. z.b. die Kategorie der Vögel von der Kategorie der Nichtvögel oder eine Tasse von einer Nicht-mehr-Tasse, nämlich einem Krug). Assoziationsstereotypen hingegen beinhalten Merkmals- bzw. Eigenschaftszuschreibungen, die nicht die Zugehörigkeit eines Exemplars X zu einer bestimmten Kategorie determinieren, sondern die in einer Kultur als typisch erwartete Eigenschaften von X beinhalten. Assoziationsstereotypen sind somit für die denotative Bedeutung nicht konstitutiv. D.h., X ist über semantische Merkmale eindeutig definiert und kann darüber hinaus – in einem abgeleiteten Sinne – mit stereotypen Eigenschaftszuweisungen verbunden werden. Dies zusammen ergibt die Gesamtbedeutung eines Wortes, was wir uns anhand der Bedeutung des Wortes „Vater" klarmachen wollen. So hat in 3) – nach Harras (1991:34) das Wort „Vater" zwei Lesarten.

3)   Gesamtbedeutung von *Vater*

Relationale Bedeutung	Stereotyp
x ist Vater von y →	‚sorgt für y'
Zwischen x und y	‚erzieht y'
besteht ein Abstammungs-	”
verhältnis ∧	”
das Abstammungs-	
verhältnis ist	
dezent von x zu y ∧	
x ist männlich	

.

Lesart 1	Lesart 2
‚Verwandtschaftsbeziehungen'	‚soziale Rolle'

Während die Lesart 1 die Zugehörigkeit eines X zur Kategorie Vater hinreichend bestimmt, prädiziert die 2. Lesart – das Assoziationssterotyp – die in der Gesellschaft typischen Erwartungshaltungen, wie: X sorgt für Y usw. Doch jemand, der nicht für sein Kind sorgt und es nicht erzieht usw., ist zwar ein schlechter Vater, bleibt aber trotzdem im Sinne der Lesart 1 ‚Vater‘, d.h., die Assoziationsstereotypen können zur Bestimmung der Kategorienzugehörigkeit nicht verwendet werden.

Des weiteren scheint mir wichtig hervorzuheben, daß nicht alle Sprachteilnehmer die mit einem Wort in einer Sprachgemeinschaft verbundenen Stereotypen teilen, diese aber beim Textverstehen trotzdem einkalkulieren müssen. D.h., es gilt zwischen dem Kennen und dem Teilen von Stereotypen zu unterscheiden.

Und gerade das Kennen von kulturellen Stereotypen (ohne sie unbedingt teilen zu müssen) ist eine essentielle Komponente der kulturellen Kompetenz eines guten Übersetzers bzw. Dolmetschers.

Als Illustration für die translatorische Relevanz des Assoziationsstereotyps nehmen wir den deutschen Satz ‚Pole blieb Pole‘, aus dem Auszug in 4) aus dem „Tod in Rom" von Koeppen (1975:31). Vgl. Sie bitte 4), wo im Bewußtseinsstrom eines deutschen Generals die Tautologie ‚Pole bleibt Pole‘ vorkommt. Wenn wir den deutschen AT und die entsprechenden Übersetzungen ins Slowakische, Russische und Englische vergleichen, so stellen wir fest, daß alle ZS-Texte – im Vergleich zu der völlig nackten Tautologie des deutschen AS-Textes zusätzliche Hinweise des jeweiligen Übersetzers enthalten. Der deutsche AT dagegen setzt das Verständnis von ‚Pole blieb Pole‘ (sprich: des Polenstereotyps) einfach voraus.

4) „und dann würde sich's zeigen, was für ein feiner Kerl er war, mit Achtung, denn er bewunderte sich als fairen Krieger, als tötenden Sportsmann sozusagen, würde er vom Tommy sprechen und vom Ami und vielleicht sogar von den polnischen Legionären der Anders-Armee, aber das war nicht sicher, denn *Pole blieb Pole*, und auf dem Soldatenfriedhof würde man mit allseitig heerem Gefühl sich selber und die Toten ehren. Die Toten lachten nicht, sie waren tot."

Slovakisch:
Lebo Poliak je len Poliak

Russisch:
Poljak èto, v konce koncov, tol'ko poljak.

Englisch:
because Polacks were still Polacks

Rückübersetzungen:
Denn ein Pole ist *nur* ein Pole   ein Pole ist *schließlich nur* ein Pole   Pol*acken* sind *nach wie vor* Pol*acken*

Die übersetzerische Herausforderung liegt nun gerade darin zu entscheiden, ob und wenn ja, wieviel von dem impliziten Inhalt hier sprachlich zu explizieren und mit welchen sprachlichen Mitteln dieses delikate Problem zu lösen ist – nur mit Synsemantika – wie in der slowakischen und russischen Version, oder – expliziter – mit morphologisch markierten pejorativen Spitznamen – wie in der englischen Version?

Soviel zu den Assoziationsstereotypen und insbesondere zu ihrer Übersetzungsrelevanz.

Die nächste Stereotypenart in meiner Taxonomie wortbezogener Stereotypen sind die sog. Interpretationsstereotypen, die ebenfalls die Aufmerksamkeit eines jeden Übersetzers verdienen.

Grob gesagt, handelt es sich dabei um bestimmte kultur- oder diskursgebundene stereotype Interpretationen offener soziokultureller Begriffe. Zumeist sind diese Wörter Abstrakta, die auch als soziokulturelle Schlüsselwörter bezeichnet werden. Diese Art von Lexikoneinheiten können auch als offene Begriffe im Wittgensteinschen Sinne angesehen werden, die keine klar umgrenzten, eindeutig zu beschreibenden Einheiten benennen, also so etwas wie z.B. *Liebe, Freiheit, Demokratie* u.ä. Da ich der Auffassung bin, daß die Bedeutungen von lexikalischen Einheiten nicht alle nach einem durchgängigen Prinzip organisiert sind, d.h., die Bedeutungsbeschreibung eines Wortes wie *Haus, Stuhl, Tisch, Schrank* usw. unterscheidet sich von der Bedeutungsrepräsentation von *Freiheit, Gleichheit* usw., und sich dementsprechend auch nicht alle Lexikoneinheiten nach einem Muster beschreiben lassen, erscheint mir für offene Begriffe die Beschreibung im Rahmen der Zweistufensemantik (im Sinne von Manfred Bierwisch – vgl Bierwisch/Schreuder 1992) als vorteilhaft. Eine solche Bedeutungsbeschreibung stellt eine Struktur dar, die aus einer Mischung von Konstanten und Variablen besteht, welche in verschiedenen Diskursen oder in verschiedenen Kulturen, in welchen das Wort verwandt wird, unterschiedlich belegt werden können.

Was ist dann das Interpretationsstereotyp? Das ist eine bevorzugte Belegung der Variablen in dieser offenen Bedeutungsstruktur, die dadurch als Normalbelegung in einem Diskurs oder in einer Kultur gilt, solange der Kontext nichts anderes nahelegt.

Besonders relevant für Übersetzer ist die Kenntnis der Interpretationsstereotypen in relativ weit voneinander entfernten Kulturen. Dazu kann ich aus Platzgründen nur verweisen auf Nordenstamm (1993), der auf eine spannende Weise seine Untersuchungen von und seine Schwierigkeiten mit den arabischen Begriffen ,*ird, sharaf, karama*' für *Ehre, Würde* und *Anständigkeit* beschreibt.

Erst durch eine ausgedehnte und umfassende Informantenbefragung lüftete Nordenstamm die Geheimnisse bzw. die sehr spezifischen (Be)deutungen dieser Moralbegriffe. (Wenn man z.B. bedenkt, daß die Bewahrung der Anständigkeit der weiblichen Familienmitglieder *(ird)* eine notwendige Bedingung dafür ist, um die Familienehre *(sharaf)* aufrechtzuerhalten; oder z.B., daß Frauen in der arabischen Welt aufgrund der dort getroffenen Voraussetzung, daß die weibliche Natur schwach ist, als Menschen ohne *karama* – sprich ohne Würde – betrachtet werden usw.).

Nordenstamm meint zu Recht, daß erst ein adäquates Verstehen dieser Schlüsselbegriffe – die eben nicht gleich *Würde, Anstand* usw. in einer anderen Kultur sind – die Voraussetzung für das Verstehen der arabischen Kultur überhaupt und natürlich für eine richtige Übersetzung entsprechender arabischer Texte ist, für die die in Wörterbüchern angebotenen Äquivalente für diese Begriffe – wie z.B. die englischen Wörter *honor, dignity, respect, nobility* u.ä. nur höchst unzureichend und u.U. auch irreführend sind. D.h., auch bei den Interpretationsstereotypen sind glückliche übersetzerische Lösungen gefragt, die der Kompetenzerweiterung der ZS-Leser dienen sollen.

Vom Interpretationsstereotyp nun zu der letzten wortbezogenen Stereotypenart in meiner Taxonomie – zum Abbildungsstereotyp.

Seit der kognitiven Wende in der Linguistik wird man zunehmend auf metaphorische Vorstellungswelten einer Sprach- und Kulturgemeinschaft aufmerksam (wozu die in einer Kultur üblichen metaphorischen Standardvorstellungen über Sachverhalte, Problemsituationen und ihre Lösungswege gehören).

Und eben die in einer Kultur mit verhältnismäßiger Konstanz auftretenden metaphorischen Modelle, auf die kulturell relevante Sachverhalte in systematischer Weise abgebildet werden, fasse ich (vgl. Zybatow 1995) als Abbildungsstereotypen einer Sprach- und Kulturgemeinschaft. Abbildungsstereotypen sind Basismetaphern, die stereotype Sichtweisen prägen, wie z.b. das Begreifen der Politik als Krieg, der Zeit als Geld, des Fortschritts als eine Bewegung nach vorn oder oben usw.

Das Wesen der Metaphorisierung besteht darin, daß ein bestimmter kognitiver Bereich, auch Frame genannt, wie z.b. der Bereich „Geld" auf einen anderen kognitiven Bereich – z.b. den Bereich der Zeit – projiziert wird. Denken Sie etwa an die metaphorischen Kollokationen mit „Zeit" in verschiedenen Sprachen, die alle auf wörtliche Kollokationen mit „Geld" zurückführbar sind. D.h., bei der Metapher handelt es sich nicht um ein rein poetisches Mittel der Steigerung der Bildhaftigkeit der Sprache, sondern hinter den Metaphern stehen kognitive Strukturen, die die Wahrnehmung der Wirklichkeit durch eine Sprach- und Kulturgemeinschaft bestimmen.

Unter diesen neuen kognitiven Aspekten stellt sich eine aus interkultureller Sicht sehr interessante Frage, ob sich die Einzelsprachen in ihren Alltagsmetaphern unterscheiden oder eher ähneln.

Genau diese Frage wird zum erstenmal auf eine systematische Weise in bezug auf zwei Kulturen in dem Forschungsprojekt „Interkultureller Vergleich der Struktur kollektiver Vorstellungswelten anhand von metaphorischen Modellen in den Printmedien Rußlands und Deutschlands" durch ein deutsch-russisches Forschungsteam untersucht, dessen Ergebnisse von großer Relevanz u.a. auch für die translatologische Forschung sein werden.

4   Textbezogene Stereotypen

Die Denkstereotypen spielen nicht nur – wie bereits vorgestellt – bei der Interpretation lexikalischer Bedeutungen eine Rolle, sondern auch textbezogen – als Wissenshintergrund zur Interpretation von Texten.

Diese „textbezogenen" Stereotypen (vgl. Zybatow 1995) konstituieren das Norm- und Wertesystem einer Sprach- und Kulturgemeinschaft und werden als solche (selbst wenn sie nicht geteilt werden) natürlich gekannt. Deshalb müssen die textbezogenen Stereotypen nicht immer explizit ausgedrückt werden, sondern sie werden in der Tat häufiger implizit angerufen oder bleiben überhaupt verbal unausgedrückt. In diesen Erscheinungsformen sind sie an verschiedenen Stellen im Text präsent und spielen beim Verstehen des Ausgangstextes bzw. bei der Stiftung von textuellen Bewertungszusammenhängen eine wichtige Rolle.

5   Zusammenfassung: Überblick und Ausblick

Zunächst möchte ich, gewissermaßen im Überblick, den Gesamtentwurf meiner Stereotypen als sprach- und kulturübergreifende slots einer übersetzungsrelevanten Kultursemantik Revue passieren lassen: erstens, Gülichs Sprachstereotypen, zu denen ich zusätzlich noch verschiedene Arten der Intertextualität hinzufügen würde, die als kulturell bedingte textuelle Mehrdimensionalität (Text im Text) vom Übersetzer erkannt werden müssen. Zweitens, die Denkstereotypen, zunächst die wortbezogenen Assoziations-, Interpretations- und Abbildungsstereotypen, auf die ich ausführlicher eingehen konnte, und schließlich die textbezogenen Denkstereotypen, die im AT explizit, meist jedoch nur implizit (durch Präsuppositionen, Implikationen, Allegationen) ausgedrückt oder aber sprachlich ganz und gar nicht ausgedrückt werden, jedoch unsichtbar aber notwendig dem AT innewohnen als kulturell verbindliche Verstehens- und Bewertungsmaßstäbe.

Alle diese Stereotypen – ob Sprachstereotypen, die alle nicht einfach syntaktisch-semantisch kompositionell zu verarbeiten sind, – oder verschiedene kulturell vorgeprägte und sprachlich unterschiedlich verpackte Denkstereotypen sind sprachlich identifizierte und kulturell bedingte Kristallisationspunkte verdichteter Sinnstiftung. D.h., bei allen diesen Stereotypen als sprach- und kulturübergreifende slots, die jeweils kulturspezifisch inhaltlich ausgefüllt werden, hat es der Übersetzer mit übersetzerischen Herausforderungen zu tun: er muß die jeweiligen Stereotypen kennen, im AT erkennen, ob ihrer Relevanz im AT bzw. für den ZT einschätzen und glückliche Lösungen zur Überwindung der jeweiligen kultursemantischen Diskrepanzen finden können.

Soweit einige Bausteine der hier skizzierten translationsrelevanten Kultursemantik im Überblick. Als Ausblick bleibt zu hoffen, daß die in der Translationswissenschaft angestrebte Interdisziplinarität nicht nur proklamiert, sondern auch praktiziert wird. Dies bedeutet u.a., daß die Sprachwissenschaft interdisziplinär natürlich unbedingt dazugehört, da die Translation immer eine Operation über Sprache(n) ist und bleibt. Die Interdisziplinarität der Translationswissenschaft bedeutet auch, daß diese nicht hinter den bereits gewonnenen Erkenntnissen der Sprachwissenschaft zurückbleiben darf, die in den letzten Jahrzehnten sehr viel über die Beziehung zwischen Sprache, Kultur und Gesellschaft nachgedacht hat. Besonders aussichtsreich erscheint mir dabei die kognitive Wende in der Sprachwissenschaft, deren Fruchtbarkeit für die Translationswissenschaft – trotz einiger Versuche in diese Richtung – noch lange nicht erkannt zu sein scheint.

6   Literatur

BIERWISCH, Manfred; SCHREUDER, P. (1992): From concepts to lexical items. In: Cognition 42, 23-60.

GÜLICH, Elisabeth (1978): ‚Was sein muß, muß sein. Überlegungen zum Gemeinplatz und seiner Verwendung (Antrittsvorlesung an der Fakultät für Linguistik und Literaturwissenschaft der Universität Bielefeld am 4. Februar 1977). Bielefeld: Uni. (Bielefelder Papiere zur Literaturwissenschaft 7).

HARRAS, Gisela (1991): Zugänge zu Wortbedeutungen, in: Harras, Gisela; Haß, Ulrike; Strauß, Gerhard (Hrsg.): Wortbedeutungen und ihre Darstellung im Wörterbuch. Berlin – New York: de Gruyter (Schriften des Instituts für Deutsche Sprache 3), 1-96.

KOEPPEN, Wolfgang (1992): Death in Rome. London.

KOEPPEN, Wolfgang (1981): Smrt' v Rime. Bratislava.
— (1980): Smert' v Rime. In: Koeppen, W.: Golubi v trave. Moskva: Progress.
— (1975): Der Tod in Rom. Roman. Frankfurt a. M.: Suhrkamp (Suhrkamp-Taschenbuch 241).
— (1973): Nach Rußland und anderswohin: empfindsame Reisen. Frankfurt a. M.: Suhrkamp (Suhrkamp-Taschenbücher 115).
LIPPMANN, Walter ([1922] 1964): Public Opinion. London.
NORDENSTAM, Tore (1993): Kulturelle Übersetzbarkeit in pragmatischer Sicht, in: Frank, A. P. et al. (Hrsg.): Übersetzen, verstehen, Brücken bauen. Geisteswissenschaftliches und literarisches Übersetzen im internationalen Kulturaustausch. Berlin: Schmidt (Göttinger Beiträge zur internationalen Übersetzungsforschung 8), 192-203.
PUTNAM, Hilary (1979): Die Bedeutung von „Bedeutung". Frankfurt a. Main: Klostermann (Klostermann-Texte: Philosophie).
Quasthoff, Uta (1973): Soziales Vorurteil und Kommunikation. Eine sprachwissenschaftliche Analyse des Stereotyps. Ein interdisziplinärer Versuch im Bereich von Linguistik, Sozialwissenschaft und Psychologie. Frankfurt a. Main: Athenäum Fischer Taschenbuch Verl. (Fischer-Athenäum-Taschenbücher 2025 : Sprachwissenschaft)
ROSCH, Eleonore (1977): Human categorization, in: Warren, E. (Hrsg.): Advances in Cross-Cultural Psychology, Vol. 1. London, 3-49.
ZYBATOW, Lew (1995): Russisch im Wandel. Die russische Sprache seit der Perestrojka. Wiesbaden: Harrassowitz (Osteuropa-Institut <Berlin> / Abteilung für Slavische Sprachen und Literaturen: Veröffentlichungen der Abteilung für Slavische Sprachen und Literaturen des Osteuropa-Instituts (Slavisches Seminar) der Freien Universität Berlin 80).

Kontrastive Linguistik

Der Einfluß des Angloamerikanischen auf das Deutsche und Neugriechische

Panagiota Balanga

1   Einleitung

Unser Zeitalter ist das Zeitalter der Globalisierung und Internationalisierung, ein Zeitalter, in dem der Gedanke an eine Weltgesellschaft konkreter ist als je zuvor. Doch die Frage, die sich aufdrängt, ist, ob wir damit auch der Verständigung näher kommen, ob wir sprachlich immer mehr zusammen wachsen. Die Begriffe Globalisierung und Internationalisierung sind nicht nur für den Weltwirtschaftsmarkt von Bedeutung. Auch die Linguisten sprechen von Globalisierung, die Globalisierung der englischen Sprache nämlich, die zur Lingua Franca geworden ist und für deren globale Verbreitung es viele politische und ökonomische Gründe gibt.

Anglizismen im Deutschen sind seit dem 2. Weltkrieg Gegenstand wissenschaftlicher Untersuchungen und Evaluierung[1]. Carstensen (1965; 1980) ist hier besonders herauszustellen. Im Vergleich dazu wurde einer englisch-neugriechischen Interferenzforschung kaum Bedeutung beigemessen. Ziel der vorliegenden empirischen Untersuchung ist, die Tendenzen des englischen Einflusses auf die deutsche und neugriechische Pressesprache am Beispiel zweier überregionaler Wochenzeitungen aufzuzeigen und die Übernahmeart des englischen Wortgutes in das entsprechende Sprachsystem zu untersuchen.

2   Vorgehensweise

Untersucht wurden die zwei überregionalen Wochenzeitungen DIE ZEIT und TO BHMA ΤΗΣ ΚΥΡΙΑΚΗΣ. Auf den angloamerikanischen Spracheinfluß bezogen, wurde den untersuchten Medien ein gewisser Anspruch im Sinne der von ihnen dargebotenen Themen und deren Darstellung unterstellt, ebenso wie ein gewisser Grad an Überlegtheit und Verantwortungsbewußtsein bei der Verwendung englischen Wortgutes. Für die Untersuchung sollte die geschriebene Sprache auf überregionaler Ebene im Vordergrund stehen, um regionale Eigenheiten eines Sprechers auszuschließen. Das Material setzt sich zusammen aus 118 DIN-A 2 Seiten der Wochenzeitung DIE ZEIT vom 3. und 10.7.1999 und 250 DIN-A 3 Seiten der Wochenendausgaben von TO BHMA ΤΗΣ ΚΥΡΙΑΚΗΣ vom 1. und 8.8.1999. Obwohl eine genaue statistische Auswertung nicht im Vordergrund der Untersuchung stand, erschien es sinnvoll, eine annähernd gleiche Seitenanzahl des Quellenmaterials als Ausgangsbasis für den Vergleich heranzuziehen. Analysiert wurde ausschließlich redaktionelles Quellenmaterial. Werbliches Quellenmaterial, eingeschlossen der „Rubrik Stellenangebote", das

---

[1]   Zum Stand der Forschung vgl. auch Fink et al. (1997).

bei der ZEIT insgesamt 78, bei der TO BHMA 68 Seiten ausmacht, blieb von vornherein unberücksichtigt. Ebenfalls nicht berücksichtigt wurden Anglizismen in Gestalt von Eigennamen (Orts- und Personennamen, Namen von Institutionen, Firmennamen, Währungsangaben, Automodelle, Rundfunk- und Fernsehprogramme). Mehrfachnennungen blieben ebenfalls unberücksichtigt. Als englisches Wortgut zählen Worte, die der Leser auf den ersten Blick als englisches Wortmaterial identifiziert. Vollsubstituierte Anglizismen, d.h. Wörter, die als englische nicht mehr erkennbar sind, wurden weggelassen.

Das gefundene Wortgut wurde in folgende Bereiche unterteilt:

- Politik (Innen- und Außenpolitik)
- Wirtschaft (Wirtschaft, Finanzwirtschaft, Börse)
- Neue Technologien (Computer, Telekommunikation)
- Kultur (Literatur, Kunst)
- Medien (Musik, Film- und Fernsehen)
- Sonstiges[2] (Freizeit, Tourismus, Reisen, Sport, Mode, Umwelt u.a.)

3   Erfassung der Daten

Die englischen Entlehnungen des untersuchten Quellenmaterials wurden zunächst quantitativ nach Sachgebieten erfaßt.

Sachgebiete	DIE ZEIT	TO BHMA ΤΗΣ ΚΥΡΙΑΚΗΣ
Politik	3	0
Wirtschaft	29	25
Neue Technologien	42	13
Medien	31	14
Kultur	6	1
Sonstiges	72	24
Gesamt	183	77

Bei der nahezu gleichen Anzahl von Seiten, fanden sich im Deutschen 183, im Neugriechischen 77 englische Wörter, deren Aufnahme in das deutsche bzw. griechische Sprachsystem auf unterschiedliche Weise erfolgte. Die Ergebnisse zeigen, daß im Deutschen die Verwendung des Englischen mehr verbreitet ist als im Neugriechischen. Der Grund ist offensichtlich: Das Griechische ist später mit der englischen Sprache in Kontakt getreten als das Deutsche. Obwohl im Lehrplan griechischer Gymnasien Englisch als Fremdsprache angegeben wird, wird es häufig nicht gelehrt. Folglich kann man davon ausgehen, daß nur ein sehr geringer Teil der griechischen Bevölkerung Englisch spricht und versteht. Erschwerend für einen englischlernenden Griechen ist auch das Erlernen eines neuen Schriftzeichensystems, das sich von dem Griechischen unterscheidet. So kommt es häufig vor, daß in Texten, die für ein großes Publikum

---

[2]   Es wurde auf Grund eines besseren Überblicks darauf verzichtet, den Bereich „Sonstiges" weiter zu unterteilen.

bestimmt sind und für jeden verständlich sein müssen, bei der Verwendung von Anglizismen auch die griechische Übersetzung, bzw. bei Fachvokabular eine griechische Übersetzung mit dem entsprechenden englischen Begriff, der dann in Klammern steht, geliefert wird:

των βασικών δεδομένων της οικονομίας (των fundamentals)

Anders ist die Situation im Vergleich dazu in Deutschland. Es ist davon auszugehen, daß ungefähr ein Drittel der deutschen Bevölkerung Englisch spricht, ein weiteres Drittel könnte sich im Notfall durchaus verständigen, und nur ein Drittel kann überhaupt kein Englisch.

4 Erklärungen der Beobachtungen

Die Bereiche *Kultur (6/1)*[3] und *Politik (3/0)* weisen im untersuchten Quellenmaterial wenig Anglizismen auf, was für beide Sprachen gleichermaßen zutrifft. Dem gegenüber stehen die Bereiche *neue Technologien (42/13), Wirtschaft (29/25)* und *Medien (31/14)*, die mehr als die Hälfte der gefundenen Anglizismen beinhalten (Dt.: 101 v. 183 / Ngr.: 52 v. 77). In den Bereichen *neue Technologien* und *Wirtschaft* handelt es sich hauptsächlich um Wörter, die übernommen wurden, um sprachliche Lücken zu schließen. So haben sich beispielsweise im Finanzwesen über die klassischen Aktien hinaus neue Produkte wie *bonds* oder *financial futures* herausgebildet, im Bereich *neue Technologien* kam es zu Errungenschaften, wie *Computer, Scanner, Display* für die eine Bezeichnung nötig war. In diesen Fällen wurden Wörter mit der Sache, die sie bezeichnen, aus dem amerikanischen Englisch entlehnt.

Für die globale Verbreitung des Englischen gibt es noch einen weiteren Grund. Die englische Sprache wird oft zum Träger von Prestige, Statussymbol und Gruppenzugehörigkeit. Mit dem Gebrauch des Angloamerikanischen geht die Hoffnung auf Modernität und Fortschritt einher. Nicht anders ist die Verwendung der englischen Sprache bei der Modeschöpferin Jil Sander zu erklären, die in einem FAZ-Interview (1996) äußerte, ihr Leben sei eine „giving story", für ihren Erfolg sei ihr „coordinated concept" entscheidend, und „die Idee, daß man viele Teile einer collection miteinander combinen kann. Aber die audience hat das alles von Anfang an auch supported" (Zitiert nach Fink 1997:54).

Ein anderes Beispiel ist der englische Wortgebrauch im Geschäftsbericht der deutschen Telekom von 1998, wo sich der Vorstandsvorsitzende Ron Sommer wie folgt äußerte: „Nach der zehnten Minute gewähren wir mit dem Tarif für Regio Call, German Call, Global Call einen Preisnachlass." (Der Stern 36/99). Regio Call wird hierfür anstelle von Ortsgespäch, German Call anstelle von Ferngespräch, Global Call anstelle von Auslandsgespäch verwendet. Die entsprechenden Ausdrücke heißen in englischsprachigen Ländern *local call, distance call* und *international call*. Hierin

---

[3] Die erste Zahl gibt die Anzahl der gefundenen englischen Worte im Deutschen, die zweite im Neugriechen an.

zeigt sich ganz besonders, daß der Gebrauch englischen Wortgutes einen reinen Werbe-
zweck erfüllt und somit durchaus als eine Art „lexikalischer Eintagsfliegen" zu charakterisieren ist.

5   Substitutionstypen und grammatische Wortarten

Im folgenden soll noch kurz der Frage nachgegangen werden, wie die Aufnahme
englischen Wortguts in das deutsche bzw. neugriechische Sprachsystem erfolgt. Das
aus den Ausgaben der beiden Wochenzeitungen entnommene Wortgut wurde in Ent-
lehnungstypen[4] unterteilt. Dabei wurde unterschieden zwischen:

a) *Nullsubstitution*
   Wortgut, bestehend nur aus englischsprachigen Wortelementen. Hierzu zählen
   Übernahmen mit und ohne Veränderungen in lexikalischer, semantischer, mor-
   phologischer Hinsicht, ebenso wie die Schöpfung neuer Wörter aus englischem
   Wortmaterial mit eigener semantischer Bedeutung.

b) *Teilsubstitution*
   Kompositionelles Wortgut bestehend aus englischsprachigen und anderssprachi-
   gen[5] Wortelementen.

Im Neugriechischen kommt die Nullsubstitution als Übernahme ohne lexikalische,
semantische und morphologische Veränderungen vor, wie beispielsweise *corporate
banking, web, comic strips, fitness* oder *happening*. Darüber hinaus gibt es Übernahmen ohne lexikalische und semantische aber mit morphologischer Veränderung. Die
morphologische Veränderung besteht in der Wiedergabe des englischen Wortes durch
das griechische Zeichensystem, da sich das Grapheminventar der Ausgangssprache
Englisch von dem der Zielsprache Neugriechisch unterscheidet. So finden sich Beispiele wie *μπίζνεσμαν, φαξ, σίριαλ, τσάρτερ, ριμπάουντ, σασπένς*.
Alle Nullsubstitutionen verändern im Neugriechischen die semantische Bedeutung
der Gebersprache Englisch nicht. Was die Schreibvarianten anbetrifft, so stehen beide
gleichberechtigt nebeneinander. Es herrscht hier keine Einheitlichkeit, so daß es dem
Ermessen des Autors unterliegt, welche Schreibweise er vorzieht. Der Gebrauch ist
abhängig vom Sprachgebrauch und den Fremdsprachenkenntnissen des jeweiligen
Autors und denen der Leserschaft. Ob mit griechischen oder lateinischen Schriftzei-
chen, die Aufnahme in das griechische grammatische System erfolgt meist in Form
eines Substantivs, das mit dem Genus des Neutrums versehen wird. Es erfährt jedoch
keine Formveränderung, d.h., das Substantiv wird nicht dekliniert. Unter dem gefundenen Wortgut wurde nur ein Adjektiv (*stoned*) gefunden. Übernahmen von Adver-

---

[4]   Zur Terminologie vgl. Carstensen/Galinsky (1963).
[5]   Andersprachige Elements sind nicht nur deutsche Elemente. So kommt beispielsweise häufig die
      Kombination mit französischen Elementen vor.

bien und Verben wurden nicht gefunden[6]. Ganz anders verhält es sich im Deutschen, welches bei der Übernahme englischen Wortmaterials in das deutsche Sprachsystem eigene Wege geht. Auch gibt es hier Übernahmen ohne lexikalische, semantische und morphologische Veränderung. So erscheinen Wörter wie *Government, Joint-Venture, Casting, Charter, Fairness* und *Shopping*. Die einzige Veränderung hier ist die Groß-schreibung, die allerdings nicht stark ins Gewicht fällt.

Am häufigsten kommt im Deutschen die Übernahme mit lexikalischer und seman-tischer Veränderung vor. So existieren Wörter, bei denen die Bedeutung im Deut-schen nicht mit der Bedeutung im amerikanischen bzw. britischen Englisch überein-stimmt:

City
Dt.: Innenstadt
AE: downtown   BE: city center

Publicitymanager
BE: publicity agent

Auch gibt es zahlreiche Wörter, die morphologischen Veränderungen unterliegen, indem sie entgegen dem englischen Gebrauch

a) im Deutschen zusammengeschrieben werden, wie
Dt.: *Touchscreen, Shoppingcenter, Hairconditioner, Hometrainer*
BE: *touch screen, shopping center, hair conditioner, home trainer*
b) oder ebenso wie deutsche flektierbare Wortarten den Flexionsregeln des deut-schen grammatischen Systems unterstellt werden:

BE	$\Rightarrow$	Dt.
to scan	$\Rightarrow$	ge*scann*t
to pierce	$\Rightarrow$	ge*pierc*t
hobby (-ies)	$\Rightarrow$	Hobby*s*
to shop	$\Rightarrow$	shop*pen*

Eine besondere Eigenart des Deutschen im Bereich der Nullsubstitution ist die Schöp-fung neuer Wörter aus englischem Wortmaterial jedoch mit eigener Semantik[7]. Hierzu zählen Wörter, wie das im Deutschen häufig verwendete Wort *Handy* (BE: *mobile phone*).

Zusätzlich zu den Nullsubstitutionen gibt es auch, wie oben erwähnt, die Teilsub-stitutionen. Das Neugriechische verbindet hier englisches mit griechischem Wortma-terial, das der grammatischen Kategorie Substantive angehört: *offshore εταιρίες, dis-count κατάστημα, leader της αγοράς, τιμές fixing*. Im Deutschen lassen sich hier Kom-posita, bestehend aus einem Deutschen und einem englischen Bestandteil finden:

---

[6]   Das bedeutet nicht, daß sie nicht existent sind. In einem größeren Korpus wäre ihr Vorkommen durchaus möglich. So kennt das Neugriechische Bildungen mit der Endung -άρω/-αρω, wie z.B. παρκάρω vom Englischen *to park*.

[7]   Gemäß Carstensen (1980) ist dies eine Art semantischer Scheinentlehnung.

Investmentgesellschaft, High-Tech-Sitzgelegenheit, Medienjunkie, Sonntagstrip, Radlerdress[8], *Shoppingausbeute*. Im Bereich der Verben und Adjektive gibt es ebenfalls kompositionelles Wortgut: *einscannen, computergestützt.*

6   Schlußfolgerungen

Das Neugriechische gebraucht, bezogen auf das gefundene Wortgut, die englische Sprache als reine Funktionssprache, um neue Sachverhalte zu benennen. Daß eine wirkliche Integration in das griechische Sprachsystem nicht erfolgt zeigt sich

a) in der nominalen Verwendung des englischen Wortschatzes, der nicht dekliniert wird,

b) in der uneinheitlichen Schreibung,

c) in dem Nebeneinanderexistieren von griechischer Übersetzung und englischen Begriffen. Im großen und ganzen erweist sich das Sprachsystem des Neugriechischen als besonders widerstandsfähig bei der Übernahme und Einverleibung von Anglizismen[9].

Das Deutsche gebraucht die englische Sprache wie das Griechische auch einerseits als Funktionssprache, andererseits ist die Verwendung auch eine Prestigefrage. Als solches wird der Versuch einer Assimilation unternommen, mittels der erwähnten Arten der Übernahme, wie

a) Nominale und verbale Verwendung des englischen Wortschatzes,

b) Angleichung an das deutsche Flexionsschema (Konjugation und Deklination)

c) Bildung neuer Wörter aus deutschem und englischem Wortmaterial (Affigierung und Kompositionen),

d) Wortschöpfungen.

An dieser Stelle sei noch einmal darauf verwiesen, daß die erweiterte Aufnahme englischen Wortgutes in der deutschen Sprache auch in der bereits längeren intensiveren Übung der Deutschen in der englischen Sprache, zum Teil natürlich auch in den intensiveren Kontakten zu England und Amerika, begründet ist.

7   Literatur

CARSTENSEN, Broder (1980): Semantische Scheinentlehnungen des Deutschen aus dem Englischen. In: Viereck, W. (Hrsg.): Studien zum Einfluß der englischen Sprache auf das Deutsche. Tübingen: Narr, 77-100.

---

[8]   Interessant bei diesem Beispiel ist, daß das englische Wort *dress* die Bedeutung *Kleid* hat, entgegen dem deutschen Gebrauch, wo *dress* die Bedeutung von Kleidung einnimmt.

[9]   Apostolou-Panara (1985) spricht in ihrer Dissertation von „inneren Widerständen, die nichts anderes sind, als das, was wir ´Sprachgefühl´ nennen." (Zitiert nach Karvella 1993).

CARSTENSEN, Broder (1965): Englische Einflüsse auf die deutsche Sprache nach 45. Heidelberg: Winter.

CARSTENSEN, Broder; GALINSKY, Hans (1963): Amerikanismen der deutschen Gegenwartssprache. Entlehnungsvorgänge und ihre stilistischen Aspekte. Heidelberg: Winter.

FINK, Hermann (1997): Von *Kuh-Look* bis *Fit for Fun:* Anglizismen in der heutigen Allgemein- und Werbesprache. Frankfurt a. Main: Peter Lang (Freiburger Beiträge 3).

FINK, Hermann, FIJAS, Liane, SCHONS, Danielle (1997): Anglizismen in der Sprache der Neuen Bundesländer. Frankfurt am Main: Peter Lang (Freiburger Beiträge 4).

KARVELLA, Ioanna (1993): Das Fremde und das Eigene. Zum Stellenwert des Fremdwortes im Deutschen und Griechischen. Frankfurt am Main: Peter Lang. (Europäische Hochschulschriften 21).

Restrictive and Non-restrictive Relative Clauses in Japanese

Yoko Collier-Sanuki

1 Introduction

Despite their syntactical, morphological, phonological and semantic differences from English relative clauses (RCs), Japanese RCs have been analyzed analogously to those of English in most research including Kuno (1973), Inoue (1976) and Masuoka (1997). Furthermore, Miyake (1995) claims that the distinction between restrictive and non-restrictive RCs in Japanese is not only crucial but also syntactically explainable even though they are indistinguishable in any way at the surface level. This paper, on the contrary, argues that the distinction between restrictive and non-restrictive RCs in Japanese depends strongly on the contexts in which they are used and are not structurally motivated. In so doing, I will point out, following Haan (1987), the problems of classifying RCs in indefinite noun phrases (NPs). Then I will divert from Haan and show how context and shared knowledge about head NPs can affect interpretations between restrictive and non-restrictive RCs in Japanese. These discussions will support the speculation raised by Andrews (1985:29) that

> "Japanese speakers report considerable difficulty in distinguishing between the two types of clauses, which suggests more strongly that Japanese has no syntactic differentiation between the two types".

2 Definitions of restrictive and non-restrictive relative clauses

2.1 Conventional definitions of restrictive and non-restrictive relative clauses

Traditionally, RCs are divided into two types, restrictive and non-restrictive, depending on the types of head NPs that they modify and their associated functions of modification. Below are the definitions given in Quirk (1972:858):

> "Modification can be restrictive and non-restrictive, that is, the head can be viewed as a member of a class which can be linguistically identified only through the modification that has been supplied (*restrictive*). Or the head can be viewed as unique or as a member of a class that has been independently identified (for example, in a preceding sentence): any modification given to such a head is additional information which is not essential for identifying the head, and we call it *non-restrictive*."

According to these definitions, the functions of restrictive and non-restrictive RCs are distinctive and exclusive of each other. A RC is non-restrictive when its head NP is uniquely identifiable without it: consequently, the information that the RC provides is merely additional and not essential. On the other hand, RCs that modify head NPs that are not identifiable by their own virtue are restrictive. They function to identify their head NPs. The table below summarizes the definitions by Quirk:

Relative clauses	Head NPs	Functions
Restrictive	Identifiable only with RC	Identification
Non-restrictive	Identifiable without RC	Additional information

1) Conventional definitions of restrictive and non-restrictive RCs

2.2   Supplementary definitions of restrictive and non-restrictive relative clauses

Haan (1987:172) points out that

> "[the] distinction that is usually made between restrictive and non-restrictive RCs appears to be based in most cases on the distinction between modifiers in definite NPs".

Since indefinite NPs are not identifiable by virtue of their *indefiniteness*, no RCs that modify them can be non-restrictive. For the same reason, no RCs can help make indefinite NPs identifiable. Consequently, RCs that modify indefinite NPs have no place in Quirk's functional definitions. The table given above, thus, actually is incomplete, missing entries concerning indefinite NPs as seen below:

Relative clauses	Head NPs	Functions
Restrictive	Identifiable only with RC	Identification
Non-restrictive	Identifiable without RC	Additional information
?	Indefinite	?

2) Missing entries of indefinite head noun phrases

In the case of English, however, the deficiencies in the definitions are safeguarded by the use of phonological characteristics between restrictive and non-restrictive RCs. A summary from Quirk (1957) below, quoted in Haan (1987:101), explains these supplementary definitions:

> "Leaving considerations of meaning aside, there are three features which mark off what are here called 'non-restrictive' clauses from the 'restrictive' ones: these are juncture, intonation, and prominence. Restrictive clauses (as in 'you're living in a world which is in the main stream') are linked to their antecedents by close syntactic juncture, by unity of intonation contour, and by continuity of the degree of loudness. In contrast, non-restrictive clauses are characterized by open juncture (recognized, together with the following features, by a comma in written materials), a fresh intonation contour, and a change (especially a diminution) in the degree of loudness."

Notice that the head NP of the restrictive RC example given in the quote above is indefinite. The example is repeated below:

3) *a world* [which is in the main stream].

While the indefinite head NP cannot be identified as discussed above, the RC is nonetheless categorized non-restrictive "by close syntactic juncture, by unity of intonation contour, and by continuity of the degree of loudness". The fact that the example phrase does not make sense without the RC as shown below supports the conclusion that the RC in (3) is used restrictively:

4) *you're living in a world

We may thus fill in the gaps of the previous table as below:

Relative clauses	Head NPs	Functions
Restrictive	Identifiable only w/RC	Identification
Non-restrictive	Identifiable w/o RC	Additional information
Restrictive	Indefinite	Identification

5) Supplemented definitions of restrictive and non-restrictive RCs

3 Problems in interpreting restrictive and non-restrictive relative clauses in Japanese

3.1 Problems with non-restrictive relatives in Japanese

According to the definitions given in the previous sections, non-restrictive RCs are those that modify head NPs that are uniquely identifiable. Primary examples of such uniquely identifiable head NPs include personal pronouns and names, as shown below:

6) *John*, [who came yesterday], was here again.

Because the head NP, John, is uniquely identifiable, the RC that modifies it is non-restrictive and not needed for identification of the head NP. In other words, non-restrictive RCs only provide additional information and can be omitted without affecting the rest of the sentence semantically. The example below, which is (6) without the RC, is equal to its original in meaning:

6') John was here again.

However, these definitions do not account for the behavior of RCs in Japanese. An example of RCs that modify personal pronouns *I* is given below:

7) Demo,   sore   wa,   boku   no   sei   ja-arimsen.
   However   that   TOP   I   GEN   cause   not
   'That, however, is not my fault.'

   [Muttsu   no   toki,   otona   no   hito tachi   ni,   ekaki   de
   six-years-old GEN   when   adult   GEN   people-plural   by   painter   by

   mi-o-tateru-koto   o   omoikirasareta   okage-de,   uwabami   no   uchigawa
   make-living   ACC   made-to-give-up   due-to   boa   GEN   inside

   to   sotogawa   no   e   o   kaku   yori   hoka   wa,   marukiri
   and   outside   GEN   drawing   ACC   draw   than   other   TOP   completely

e	o	kaku-koto	o	shinakatta]	*boku*	nan-desu	kara.
Drawing	ACC	draw-ing	ACC	did-not-do	I	COP	because

'Because it was I [who had never drawn anything, except boas from the outside and boas from the inside, since six years old due to the fact that I was discouraged by the grown-ups to become a painter].'

According to the definitions discussed previously, the RC in the example above is non-restrictive and could be omitted freely without altering the meaning and grammaticality of the entire sentence that contains it. However, this is not the case: the sentence would not make sense at all without the RC, as seen below.

7') *Boku   nan-desu   kara.
    I   COP   because
    *'Because it was I.'

Similarly, as Masuoka (1997) pointed out, a RC that modifies *jibun* 'self' in the example below cannot be deleted even though the head NP *jibun* 'self' is co-indexed with Shuichi (a Japanese male first name) and its referent is unique:

8) Shuichi   wa   [dooyoo suru]   *jibun*   o   kanji-nagara   itta.
    Shuichi   TOP   upset do   self   ACC   feel-ing   said

'Shuichi, feeling *himself* [who was upset], said.' (Masuoka 1997)

8') *Shuichi   wa   jibun   o   kanji-nagara   itta.
     Shuichi   TOP   self   ACC   feel-ing   said

     *'Shuichi, feeling himself, said.'

The observations above show that some non-restrictive RCs in Japanese, or RCs that modify uniquely identifiable head NPs, do not merely provide additional information but are an essential part of their head NPs. This, in turn, indicates that the functional definitions of non-restrictive RCs that have been developed for English are not useful in the case of Japanese. The next section will discuss problems with restrictive RCs.

3.2   Problems with restrictive relative clauses in Japanese

3.2.1 Indefinite head noun phrases in Japanese

In addition to having no syntactical, morphological or phonological indications that distinguish restrictive and non-restrictive RCs, Japanese does not employ an article system. Therefore, we must depend on context to judge the information status of head NPs. This makes it even more complex to determine if a Japanese RC is restrictive or non-restrictive. Consider the example below:

9) Soko   e,   [kirakira-to   akari   no   tsuita]   *tokkyuu*   ga,   kaminari   no
    there   to   brilliantly   light   GEN   on   express   NOM   thunder   GEN

    yooni,   gogo-to,   tentetsugoya   o   furuwasete   yukimashita.
    Like   roaring   switchman's-cabin   ACC   shake   went-away
    (Hoshi, p. 117)

'At that time *an express* [which was brilliantly lighted] passed by, shaking the switchman's cabin like thunder.'

Although the lack of an article system in Japanese does not morphologically indicate the information status of *tokkyuu* 'express' in the sentence above, the context clearly indicates that it is an indefinite NP: it was mentioned only once in the story and does not refer to any particular express train. It is just a train that happened to pass by at that moment. In fact, the translation of the same sentence from its original French into English utilizes the indefinite article as below:

9E) And *a* brilliantly lighted express train shook the switchman's cabin as it rushed by with a roar like thunder. (Prince, p. 71)

Thus, we may safely determine that the head NP, *tokkyuu* 'express', is indefinite. According to the definitions given in 2.2, the RC that modifies it, then, should be restrictive.

3.2.2 Restrictive relative clauses that modify indefinite head noun phrases do not identify

Having determined that the head NP in 9), *tokkyuu* 'express', is indefinite, the definitions given in 2.2 predict that the RC that modifies it will be restrictive and, thus, function to identify the head NP. However, this is not the case with 9): the RC merely describes what the train was like and can be deleted without changing the meaning of the original sentence. Compare 9) with 9'), which is 9) without the RC:

9') Soko   e, tokkyuu ga,   kaminari   no   yooni, gogo-to,   tentetsugoya
     there   to express NOM   thunder   GEN   like   roaring   switchman's-cabin

     o   furuwasete yukimashita.
     ACC   shake   went-away
     'At that time an express passed by, shaking the switchman's cabin like thunder.'

A comparison of the two versions does not show crucial differences in meaning, indicating that the content of the RC is mere additional information. The sentences that follow 9) support this speculation. Examine the two sentences below, which follow 9) in the original story:

10) Suruto, mata,   moo-hitotsu   no   [kirakira-to akari no   tsuita] *tokkyuu* ga, ...
    then   again   another   GEN   brilliantly light GEN on   express NOM
    'Then, another *express* [which had brilliant lights on,] ... .'   (Hoshi, p. 117)
11) Suruto, [kirakira-to akari no   tsuita] *sanban-me no*   *tokkyuu*   ga, ...
    then   brilliantly light GEN   on   the-third GEN   express NOM
    'Then, the third *express* [which had brilliant lights on,] ... .'   (Hoshi, p. 118)

Not only does the deletion of the RC from 9) not affect the meaning and grammaticality of the entire sentence, no significant changes occur even if the RCs are removed from 10) and 11). The RCs in them merely describe how the trains were brilliantly lighted, and this information does not help the readers to identify the trains as unique objects. In other words, these RCs function non-restrictively. Below is another example of a RC that modifies an indefinite head NP.

12) Momoiro   no   renga   de   dekite-ite,   mado   ni jeranium   no   hachi
    pink-color   GEN   brick   by   be-made-of   window at geranium   GEN flower-pot

    ga   oite-atte,   yane no   ue   ni hato no   iru,   kireina   uchi   o
    NOM   put-out   roof GEN   top   on dove GEN   exist   beaturiful house   ACC

    mita   yo.
    saw   Interjection (Oojisama, p. 24)
    'I saw a beautiful house that was made of pink bricks, had geranium flower pots by the windows and doves on the roof.'

As indicated by the use of an indefinite article in the translation, the house in the example above is not a particular, unique house. This is clear from the context: the house was mentioned only once with neither reference to other entities in the story nor any relation to the story itself. Since the head NP is indefinite, the definitions given in 2.2 predict that the RC that modifies it will be restrictive and function to identify the head NP. However, as in the previous examples, the RC does not help the reader identify a specific house. It merely describes what the house looks like, or more specifically in what way the house was beautiful. Consequently, it is possible to reconstruct the RC as a separate sentence as seen below, without changing the meaning of the original sentence:

13) kireina   uchi   o   mita yo.
    beautiful   house   ACC   saw   Interjection
    'I saw a beautiful house.'

    Momoiro   no   renga de   dekite-ite,   mado   ni jeranium   no   hachi
    pink-color GEN   brick by   be-made-of   window at geranium   GEN flower-pot

    ga   oite-atte, yane no   ue   ni hato ga   ita   yo.
    NOM   put-out   roof GEN   top   on dove NOM   exit   Interjection
    'It was made of pink bricks, has geranium flower pots by the windows and had doves on the roof.'

In summary, the examples discussed in this section demonstrate that restrictive RCs that modify indefinite head NPs in Japanese do not always function to identify them. Rather, they often simply describe head NPs, giving additional information.

4   Effect of knowledge about head nouns on restrictive and non-restrictive interpretations

Smith (1964) and Ross (1967) proposed that universal quantifiers preceding a common noun are followed only by restrictive RCs in English. Inoue (1976) claimed that this constraint holds in Japanese also and, thus, the example below must be interpreted restrictively:

14) [Eigo   o   naratte-iru]   *nihon-juu   no   subete   no   gakusei*
    English   OBJ   learn-ing   Japan-all   GEN   all   GEN   students

    kara   iken   o   kiku   hitsuyoo   ga   aru.
    from   opinion   OBJ   solicit   need   NOM   exist
    'We must solicit opinions from every student in Japan [who studies English].'
    * 'We must solicit opinions from *every student in Japan*, [who studies English].'

However, I argue that the distinction between restrictive and non-restrictive RCs in Japanese depends strongly on the common knowledge about their head nouns. Consequently, although I agree that the example above given by Inoue should be interpreted non-restrictively, I claim that the restraint is not due to the quantifier scope but rather is due to knowledge regarding the head noun. Compare 14) with 15) below:

15) [Eigo   o   naratte-iru]   *nihon-juu   no   subete   no   chuugakusei*
    English   OBJ   learn-ing   Japan-all   GEN   all   GEN   Junior-high-students

    kara   iken   o   kiku   hitsuyoo   ga   aru.
    from   opinion   OBJ   solicit   need   NOM   exist
    *'We must solicit opinions from every Junior-high student in Japan [who studies English].'
    'We must solicit opinions from *every Junior-high student in Japan*, [who studies English].'

Notice that the two examples are syntactically identical and that the only differences between the two are their slightly different head NPs: *gakusei* 'students' in 14) is replaced by *chuugakuesei* 'junior-high students' in 15). Yet, the grammaticality of their restrictive and non-restrictive interpretations is opposite as seen in the accompanying translations. Based on the Japanese education system where English is compulsory for Junior-high but not other levels of students, the RC in 14) is interpreted restrictively while that in 15) is interpreted non-restrictively.

Similarly, stereotypes can also affect restrictive and non-restrictive interpretations of RCs, as in the following two examples:

16) [Yoku hataraku]   *kanada-jin*   wa   home-rareru.
    Hard   work   Canadians   TOP   be-praised
    '*The* Canadians [who work hard] are praised.'

17) [Yoku hataraku]   *nihon-jin*   wa   home-rareru.
    hard   work   Japanese   TOP   be-praised
    '*Japanese*, [who work hard], are praised.'

As in the previous pair of examples, 16) and 17) are structurally identical. However, as the corresponding translations indicate, 16) is interpreted restrictively but 17) non-restrictively by most, if not all, native speakers of Japanese. The difference in interpretations is due to the shared stereo types that Japanese are industrious but Canadians are not. Of course, not everyone shares all common knowledge and stereo types even among people of the same cultural background. Consequently, restrictive and non-restrictive interpretations of RCs such as 16) and 17) may not be the same for everyone. Furthermore, restrictive and non-restrictive interpretations may change if the nature of head NPs change with time.

The observations discussed in Section 3 present how the distinctions between restrictive and non-restrictive RCs do not depend on the identifiabilities of their head NPs as defined in the definitions discussed in Section 2. It has also been shown that the distinction between restrictive and non-restrictive RCs in Japanese depends strongly on the contexts in which they are used, which, in turn, provides further evidence that the distinctions are not structurally motivated.

5 Summary

This paper pointed out how the conventional definitions of restrictive and non-restrictive RCs must be supplemented by phonological information and, thus, cannot be applied to Japanese, which lacks phonological distinctions between restrictive and non-restrictive RCs. It also showed how Japanese RCs are heavily governed by context and shared knowledge and, thus, cannot be structurally motivated. In summary, the present paper has shown why it is difficult for native speakers of Japanese to distinguish between restrictive and non-restrictive RCs.

6 References

ANDREWS, Avery D. (1985): Studies in the syntax of relative and comparative clauses. Outstanding dissertations in linguistics. New York: Garland Pub.

HAAN, Pieter de (1987): Relative Clauses in Indefinite Noun Phrases. In: English Studies: A Journal of English Language and Literature 68.2, 171-190.

INOUE, Kazuko (1976): Henkeibunpo to nihongo-Joo [Transformational Grammar and Japanese-part1] 1. Tokyo: Taishukan.

KUNO, Susumu (1973): Nihon bunpo kenkyu. Tokyo: Taishukan Shoten.

MASUOKA, Takashi (1997): Fukubun. 2, Shin nihongo bunpo sensho. Tokyo: Kuroshio shuppan.

MIYAKE, Tomohiro (1995): Nihongo fukugoo meishiku no koozo-seigenteki/hiseigenteki rentai-shuushokusetsu o megutte. In: Gendai nihongo kenkyuu 2, 49-66.

QUIRK, R. (1957): Relative clauses in educated spoken English. In: English Studies 38, 97-109.

QUIRK, Randolph, GREENBAUM, Sidney; LEECH, Geoffrey; SVARTVIK, Jan (1972): A Grammar of Contemporary English. London: Longman.

ROSS, John Robert (1967): Constraints on Variables in Syntax (Ph.D. dissertation, Massachusetts Institute of Technology, Boston).

SMITH, C. S. (1964): Determiners and relative clauses in a generative grammar of English. In: Language 40, 37-53.

Data Sources

SAINT-EXUPÉRY, Antoine de (1961): The little prince (transl. by Katherine Woods). New York: Harcourt Brace Jovanovich.

SAINT-EXUPÉRY, Antoine de (1966): Hoshi no ojisama. (transl. by Aro Naito). (ed.). Tokyo: Iwanami Shoten.

Die deutschen Modalpartikeln und die spanischen *conectores*, oder: deutsche Konnektoren und spanische Modalpartikeln?
Stand der Forschung Deutsch-Spanisch

Hang Ferrer Mora

1   Einleitung

Nach der pragmatischen Wende der 70er-Jahre hat sich das linguistische Interesse einigen Themen zugewandt, die in der linguistischen Tradition entweder ignoriert oder kaum behandelt worden waren. Das ist der Fall bei den dt. Modalpartikeln (MPn). Die dt. MPn werden in erster Linie der mündlichen Sprache, insbesondere auch der Umgangssprache zugeschrieben. Das bedeutet aber nicht, dass sie nicht in geschriebenen Texten vorkommen, ihre Domäne ist aber v.a. das Gespräch in seinen vielfältigen Formen, wobei die Gesprächspartner dadurch ihre Einstellungen dem Gesagten gegenüber zum Ausdruck bringen. Nicht nur werden sprachliche Sachverhalte dadurch bewertet, sondern auch außersprachliche Situationen wie der Kontext. Diese pragmatische Diskurswelt, die aus Präsuppositionen, Schlussfolgerungen, Mitgemeintem und Allgemein- und Weltwissen besteht, kann von den Sprechern nicht während des Gesprächs explizit gemacht werden, denn dies würde den natürlichen Ablauf bzw. den diskursiven Redefluss so beeinträchtigen, dass die mündliche Kommunikation, durch ihre Lebhaftigkeit gekennzeichnet, kaum möglich wäre und daher ihren Zweck verfehlte. MPn dienen weiterhin dazu, die Äußerung im Kontext zu verankern.

2   Kontrastive Studien Deutsch-Spanisch: Stand der Partikelforschung

Da es im Sp. keine in der Linguistik festgelegte Wortklasse gibt, die den dt. MPn entspricht, gehen die meisten kontrastiven Studien Deutsch-Spanisch über MPn von der linguistischen Beschreibung der dt. MPn aus.

2.1   Zierer (1978)

In seiner Arbeit von 1978 *Las partículas ilocativas del idioma alemán y sus equivalentes en el idioma español* (Die illokutiven Partikeln der dt. Sprache und ihre Entsprechungen in der sp. Sprache) versucht Ernesto Zierer, Ausdrücke als Äquivalente für die dt. MPn anhand zahlreicher Beispiele und deren Übersetzung ins Spanische zu bieten. Im Inhaltsverzeichnis stehen die Einzellexeme, die nach dem Autor der Wortklasse MPn angehören: *aber, auch, bloß, denn, doch, eben, halt, eigentlich, einfach, etwa, ja, mal, noch, nur, schon, vielleicht* und *wohl*. Verwirrend ist aber, dass Zierer noch einmal die Liste der MPn auf Seite 12 aufführt, dabei aber einige von ihnen weglässt, nämlich *doch, einfach* und *noch*. Trotzdem werden sie dabei als MPn behandelt und dementsprechend erläutert.

Die Bedeutung der einzelnen MPn wird auf der pragmatischen Ebene angesiedelt und von anderen Funktionen abgegrenzt. Zierer beschreibt die verschiedenen illokutiven Funktionen (Sp. *función ilocativa*[1]) der MPn, d.h., für den Autor fungieren diese Partikeln als MPn, wenn sie eine illokutive Funktion haben.

In der Arbeit wird keine Quelle für die Beispiele angegeben. Daraus kann man schließen, dass Zierer die Beispielsätze selbst kreiert hat. Diese Beispielsätze werden meistens isoliert, d.h. ohne Kontext vorgeführt. Beerbom (1992:97-98) stellt sowohl die Akzeptabilität als auch den Status der Partikeln bei einigen Beispielen in Frage. Dies kann man auch anhand von anderen Beispielen beweisen (vgl. Zierer:1978:19).

Was die Übersetzungen der Beispiele und v.a. der Partikeln anbelangt, erwähnt Zierer im Vorwort seine Frau, eine Peruanerin, deren Muttersprache Spanisch ist, die deshalb als Informantin agiert hat. Weitere Angaben über ihre Deutschkenntnisse oder Sprachkompetenz sind nicht zu finden, was eine entscheidende Rolle bei der Analyse und Bewertung der sp. Entsprechungen spielt.

Für fast alle dt. MPn gibt Zierer eine spanische Entsprechung an. Da die dt. MPn in seinen Beispielen unterstrichen werden, in den sp. Übersetzungen aber nicht, ist dadurch nicht immer genau zu erkennen, welche sprachlichen Mittel der Autor als Entsprechungen für die jeweilige dt. MP ansieht. Die von ihm vorgeschlagenen Mittel im Sp. und ihre Gebrauchsbedingungen werden auch nicht weiter kommentiert. Es wird keine linguistische Analyse der vorgeschlagenen spanischen Entprechungen durchgeführt. Diese Tatsache führt zu erheblichen Schwierigkeiten bei einer eventuellen Etablierung von direkten Entsprechungen zwischen den dt. MPn und ihren sp. Analogen.

2.2   Acosta Gómez (1984)

In seinem Aufsatz mit dem Titel *Las partículas modales del alemán y del español* (Die Modalpartikeln der deutschen und spanischen Sprache) hat sich Luis A. Acosta Gómez von einem linguistisch-kontrastiven Ausgangspunkt aus mit den MPn beschäftigt.

Im ersten Teil seiner Arbeit werden die Charakteristika der MPn erläutert. Im zweiten Teil werden die Bedeutungen der dt. MPn analysiert und anhand einiger Beispiele veranschaulicht, wobei es sich um selbst kreierte Beispielsätze handelt.

Acosta befasst sich in seiner Studie mit den MPn *aber, auch, bloß, denn, doch, eben, eigentlich, einfach, etwa, halt, ja, mal, nur, ruhig, schon, wohl*; umstritten sind die Partikeln *einmal* und *gerade*, die bei der Distribution der MPn nach Satzmodi erwähnt, jedoch nicht als solche besprochen werden; hingegen ist *vielleicht* nicht aufgelistet, wird aber erläutert, und zwar als MP.

Acosta stellt im letzten Teil nach seiner Analyse der dt. MPn die Hypothese auf, dass es im Sp. auch Lexeme gibt, die als MPn betrachtet werden können. Als erste Annäherung schlägt er die Einzellexeme *bien, conque, pero, pues, si, y* und *ya*, von denen die möglichen Funktionen als MP beschrieben werden.

Am Ende wird auf verschiedenen Ebenen ein Vergleich zwischen den dt. und den sp. MPn angestellt, wobei Acosta feststellt, dass die dt. MPn den sp. gegenüber Un-

---

[1]   Da in der spanischen Forschung der Begriff ‚*ilocativa*‘ kaum zu finden ist oder sich nicht durchgesetzt hat, gehen wir davon aus, dass ‚*ilocativa*‘ bei Zierer dem Terminus ‚*ilocutivo*‘ gleichgesetzt wird.

terschiede auf der phonologischen und syntaktischen Ebene aufweisen, doch auch viele Gemeinsamkeiten auf dem semantischen und pragmatischen Niveau haben. Auch wenn sich die von Acosta angeführten Lexeme als mögliche MPn im Sp. erweisen, so gibt es leider in seiner Arbeit keine Beispiele aus kontrastiver Sicht Dt.-Sp., die als Beweismaterial für Äquivalente der dt. MP im Spanischen fungieren könnten. Trotzdem stellt der Aufsatz Acostas die erste Arbeit überhaupt dar, in der die Existenz einer besonderen Wortklasse von MPn im Sp. postuliert wird.

2.3 Beerbom (1992)

1992 hat Christiane Beerbom ihre Dissertation *Modalpartikeln als Übersetzungsproblem. Eine kontrastive Studie zum Sprachenpaar Deutsch-Spanisch* veröffentlicht. Wie aus dem Titel zu ersehen ist, beschäftigt sich die Autorin mit den dt. Modalpartikeln aus einer kontrastiven Perspektive und deren translationsbedingten Problemen bei ihrer Wiedergabe in anderen Sprachen wie dem Sp., in denen es offensichtlich weder eine ähnliche Wortklasse noch direkte Äquivalente gibt.

Nach den ersten Kapiteln, in denen Beerbom eine Einführung in die Partikelforschung sowohl im Dt. als auch im Sp. und in die Rolle zweisprachiger Wörterbücher bei der Etablierung der Äquivalente gibt, werden die MPn *doch, eben/halt, ja* und *schon* ausführlich analysiert. Darüber hinaus versucht sie mit zahlreichen Beispielen vor allem aus der deutschen Literatur und deren „professioneller" Übersetzung die Sprachmittel im Sp. zu bestimmen, die als Äquivalente der dt. MPn fungieren. Die ermittelten sp. Entsprechungen werden beschrieben und mit den dt. MPn verglichen. Am Ende der Studie befasst sich die Autorin mit den dt. MPn, die in tendenziösen und rhetorischen Fragen vorkommen.

Um die vielfältigen Bedeutungen der vorerwähnten MPn zu präzisieren, nimmt Beerbom Bezug auf die Ergebnisse aus den dt. linguistischen Arbeiten, die sich mit der Partikelforschung intensiv befasst haben.

Cárdenes Melián (1997:15) kritisiert an den von Beerbom angeführten Beispielen, dass das Zitat meist sehr kurz ist und folglich das gesamte Umfeld der Äußerungen unberücksichtigt bleibt. Damit verstößt die Autorin gegen ihre eigene Behauptung, dass „die Übersetzungsmöglichkeit (der MPn) je nach Kontext variiert" (Beerbom 1992:457).

Als Ergebnis der Untersuchung wird festgestellt, dass „den dt. MPn im Sp. keine Eins-zu-eins-Entsprechungen gegenüberstehen" (ibid.). Im Gegensatz zu Acosta meint Beerbom, dass es keine den dt. MPn entsprechende Wortklasse im Sp. gebe, obwohl zahlreiche Mittel zu finden seien, die die Funktionen der dt. MPn im Sp. wiedergeben.

Problematisch scheint mir die Behauptung Beerboms zu sein, dass die wichtigsten durch die Korpusanalyse ermittelten Entsprechungen als nur partielle Äquivalente gelten. In ihrer Arbeit werden stets die Begriffe *Entsprechung* und *Äquivalent* verwendet, aber weder genügend definiert noch diskutiert.

Auch wenn Beerbom die Existenz einer Wortklasse von MPn im Sp. ausschließt, untersucht sie in der sp. Linguistik den Gebrauch von Partikeln wie *pero, si, ya, pues, sí (que), y, acaso* und andere Sprachmittel wie *es que* u.a. Nachdem sie feststellt, dass nur in 30 % der Fälle die MPn in ihrem Korpus als ein (Teil)Äquivalent für eine dt.

MP erkennbar ist, hält sie die Übersetzung jeder MP im Text für unangemessen; die Autorin betrachtet dies sogar als „Verstoß gegen die Norm des Spanischen" (Beerbom 1992:461).

Abgesehen von den oben angeführten kritischen Anmerkungen ist Beerboms Studie die erste wissenschaftliche Arbeit, die sich ausführlich mit den MPn und ihren Übersetzungsmöglichkeiten aus kontrastiver Sicht befasst, wobei die Ergebnisse, nämlich die sp. Äquivalente, auch linguistisch analysiert und diskutiert werden.

2.4   Prüfer (1995)

Irene Prüfer untersucht in ihrer Arbeit *La traducción de las partículas modales al español y al inglés* die Übersetzungsmöglichkeiten der dt. MP im Spanischen und im Englischen. Als Ausgangspunkt für die Studie nimmt die Autorin die Forschungsergebnisse der zahlreichen Arbeiten über dt. MPn.

Ihre Untersuchung stützt sich auf einen theoretischen Rahmen innerhalb der Pragmatik und der angewandten Sprachwissenschaft, bei dem Postulate der Übersetzungswissenschaft und der Textlinguistik mit einbezogen werden. Das Hauptanliegen Prüfers ist, einen Beitrag zur Lexikografie im Bereich der angewandten Linguistik zu leisten.

Um die Entsprechungen für zwanzig dt. MPn[2] im Spanischen und Englischen zu bestimmen, geht Prüfer methodisch ebenso vor wie Beerbom. Mögliche Partikelkombinationen werden hier auch berücksichtigt.

Anhand einer Beispielsammlung wird ein Korpus aus dt. literarischen Originalwerken und deren Übersetzungen hergestellt. Dieses Belegmaterial wird durch selbst kreierte Beispiele und Beispiele aus anderen Korpora ergänzt. Die Autorin verweist darauf, dass sie viele von den angeführten Beispielen selbst übersetzt hat, sogar Übungen von ihren Schülern werden eingeschaltet, wenn bestimmte Verwendungen oder Partikelkombinationen in ihrem Korpus nicht auftauchen. Damit stoßen wir auf die Frage der Sprachkompetenz. Diese Tatsache und die subtilen Nuancen der dt. MPn lassen manchmal Zweifel an den englischen und sp. Übersetzungen aufkommen, z.B. wird die MP *vielleicht* von Prüfer im Sp. durch Ausrufe wie ‚*tontito*' (‚Dümmchen') wiedergegeben, was meines Erachtens nicht akzeptabel ist.

Leider sind in ihrer Studie wenige Kommentare zu der Angemessenheit der Übersetzungen zu finden, die höchstens als Nebenbemerkungen in den Fußnoten vorkommen. Auf diese Weise werden alle Sprachmittel aufgelistet, die aus fremden und eigenen Übersetzungen gewonnen werden. Eine linguistische Auseinandersetzung mit den ermittelten Entsprechungen findet nicht statt. Die im theoretischen Teil angeführte wissenschaftliche Vorgehensweise wird nicht konsequent in die Praxis umgesetzt.

Abgesehen von einer Unmenge vielfältiger Ausdrücke, die Prüfer als Entsprechungen bietet, betrachtet die Autorin folgende Lexeme im Sp. als Partikeln: *acaso, en-*

---

[2]   Die von Prüfer untersuchten MPn sind: *aber, auch, bloß, denn, doch, eben, eigentlich, einfach, einmal, etwa, halt, ja, mal, noch, nur, ruhig, schon, überhaupt, vielleicht* und *wohl.* Die betonten Varianten von *bloß, ja* und *nur* werden auch eingeschlossen. Auffällig ist die separate Behandlung von *einmal* und *mal* (vgl. Prüfer 1995:31ff)

tonces, pues, pero, si, sí und *ya*; die Frage aber, ob sie eine Wortklasse von MPn bilden, wird nicht diskutiert.

Aufgrund der mangelnden linguistischen Analyse lassen sich die Ergebnisse kaum lexikografisch verwerten oder didaktisch anwenden.

Interessant an Prüfers Studie ist zum einen die theoretische Perspektive, die aber leider nicht konsequent genug durchgeführt wird, zum anderen die Inklusion von Partikelkombinationen und ihren Äquivalenten im Sp.

2.5 Cárdenes Melián (1997)

Im Unterschied zu den anderen besprochenen Studien hat José Cárdenes Melián in seinem Buch *Aber, denn, doch, eben und ihre spanischen Entsprechungen. Eine funktional-pragmatische Studie zur Übersetzung deutscher Partikeln* nur diese vier dt. Partikeln und ihre äquivalenten Ausdrucksmittel im Sp. detailliert untersucht. Ein weiterer Unterschied, der sofort ins Auge fällt, ist die Bezeichnung *Partikeln* im Untertitel: Es handelt sich dabei nicht nur um die Funktion *Modalpartikel*, sondern auch um andere Funktionen innerhalb der Partikel-Klasse.

Die Arbeit von Cárdenes Melián hat mit denen Beerboms und Prüfers gemeinsam, dass die dt. Partikeln unter der Perspektive der Übersetzung analysiert werden. Seine Vorgehensweise ist die gleiche: Zunächst werden aufgrund dt. Forschungsergebnisse die Verwendungen der Partikeln erläutert und dann anhand eines selbst erstellten Korpus aus dt. literarischen Werken und deren Übersetzungen und aus Transkriptionen von anderen Korpora die aufgesuchten spanischen Äquivalente analysiert.

Cárdenes Melián legt bei den angeführten Beispielen besonderen Wert auf den Kotext und den Kontext, um die Bedeutung der jeweiligen Partikel und die illokutive Funktion der Äußerung zu bestimmen. Leider hat er das nicht konsequent genug durchgeführt, denn bei den meisten Beispielen steht ein längerer Abschnitt der dt. Originalversion, doch bei der sp. Übersetzung steht normalerweise nur der Satz, der die mögliche Entsprechung enthält. Typografisch sind einige Beispiele (z.B. auf S. 77) verwirrend, weil der Text in beiden Sprachen ohne besondere Markierung angeführt wird.

Die linguistische Auseinandersetzung mit den sp. Entsprechungen und deren Verwendungen geschieht meistens durch die Übersetzungen. Es wäre geeigneter, sich auf die sp. Linguistik bzw. auf sp. Originaltexte als Beweismaterial zu stützen.

Cárdenes Melián zieht den Schluss, dass es im Sp. nicht eine eigene Wortklasse von MPn gibt, weil die sp. linguistische Sprachforschung sich nicht lange und intensiv genug damit beschäftigt hat. Die scheinbare Armut des Sp. liegt also im Fehlen einer gründlichen pragmatischen Forschung (vgl. Cárdenes Melián 1997:188).

Die Arbeit von Cárdenes Melián leistet einen interessanten Beitrag zur kontrastiven Linguistik, weil die Entsprechungen und ihre Gebrauchsbedingungen diskutiert werden. Der Autor geht neue Wege, indem er behauptet, dass es irrelevant ist, in welchem Grad die Partikeln in beiden Sprachen morphosyntaktische Gemeinsamkeiten aufweisen.

2.6   Ferrer Mora (1999)

In seiner Dissertation mit dem Titel *Las partículas modales alemanas en el modo interrogativo y sus equivalencias en español como criterio para una taxonomía de preguntas* (Die dt. MPn im interrogativen Satzmodus und deren Entsprechungen im Sp. als Kriterium für eine Taxonomie von Fragen) hat sich Hang Ferrer Mora mit den MPn auseinandergesetzt, die in formellen Fragesätzen vorkommen können. Ziel der Arbeit ist einerseits die sp. Entsprechungen für die ausgewählten MPn zu bestimmen, andererseits ihre Rolle als potenzielle illokutive Indikatoren in Bezug auf Fragesätze zu überprüfen.

Nach der ausführlichen Beschreibung des Interrogativmodus in beiden Sprachen nach formellen und funktionellen Kriterien werden die Entsprechungen anhand der Forschungsergebnisse aus den dt. und sp. kontrastiven Studien über MPn linguistisch analysiert. Die pragmatische Bedeutung der sp. Äquivalente werden mithilfe eines sp. Korpus aus authentischen Gesprächen bestimmt und mit anderen Funktionen kontrastiert. Die zahlreichen vielfältigen Ausdrücke werden nach verschiedenen Kriterien eingeteilt.

Ferrer Mora stellt fest, dass die sog. *conectores*, mit denen sich die sp. linguistische Forschung seit den 80er Jahren intensiv beschäftigt hat, viele Gemeinsamkeiten mit den dt. MPn aufweisen. Einige dieser Lexeme sind *pero, pues, y, que, acaso, entonces, ya* und Ausdrücke wie *es que*. Der Autor verteidigt als Schlussfolgerung die Existenz von MPn im Sp. und betont die Notwendigkeit einer weiteren Auseinandersetzung mit dem Thema in der sp. linguistischen Forschung.

2.7   Ergebnisse

Aus den kontrastiven Forschungsergebnissen geht hervor, dass es zweifelsohne im Sp. Sprachmittel gibt, die den dt. MPn entsprechen. Nun ist die Frage, ob diese Sprachmittel als MPn oder nur als pragmatische Ausdrücke und Anweisungen betrachtet werden können. Im Allgemeinen lassen sich diese heterogenen Sprachmittel in sieben Großgruppen einteilen:

1) Konnektoren (Konjunktionen), z.B. *pero, pues, y*
2) Adverbien, z.B. *acaso, entonces, ya*
3) Interjektionen, z.B. *hombre*
4) Ausdrücke, (die aus mehr als einem Wort bestehen), z.B. *es que*
5) Tags (Vergewisserungsfragen), z.B. *¿no?, ¿verdad?*
6) Grammatikalische Mittel, z.B. Tempora und Modi des Verbs, usw.
7) Prosodische Merkmale, z.B. Betonung, Intonation, emphatische Akzente, usw.

Die in den Studien am meisten erwähnten Lexeme im Sp. werden der Übersichtlichkeit halber tabellarisch dargestellt:

	Zierer	Acosta	Beerbom	Prüfer	Cárdenes	Ferrer
acaso	+	-	+	+	+	+
entonces	+	-	-	+	-	+
pero	+	+	+	+	+	+
pues	+	+	+	+	+	+
si	-	+	+	+	+	-
ya	+	+	+	+	-	+
y	+	+	+	o	+	+

3 Die sp. *conectores* als Wortklasse und im Einzelnen

3.1 Die *conectores* als Wortklasse in der sp. Linguistik

Die in der kontrastiven Forschung Dt.-Sp. gefundenen Entsprechungen für die MPn und ihre Funktionen sind in der sp. Linguistik ab den 80er, viel intensiver und ausführlicher jedoch in den 90er-Jahren beschrieben worden. Ihre Werte und Funktionen wurden am Anfang für Einzellexeme erläutert, erst in den letzten Jahren werden diese Partikeln als Einheiten unter derselben Wortklasse behandelt.

Martín Zorraquino verfolgt den Begriff *partícula* in den Grammatiken des Sp. Unter anderen Partikeln befinden sich in ihrem Aufsatz die Lexeme *bien*, *ya*, *que*, *pues*, *si*, *no*, *y*, *pero*, *sí que*, denen andere Funktionen als die rein syntaktischen zugeschrieben werden. Martín Zorraquino plädiert für die Bezeichnung *partícula* anderen Begriffen gegenüber wie *marcadores de discurso*, *enlaces extraoracionales*, *operadores discursivos*, *operadores pragmáticos*, *apéndices*, usw. (vgl. Martín Zorraquino 1992:118ff).

In den 90er-Jahren scheint der Begriff *conector* im Rampenlicht der sp. Partikelforschung im Bereich der Umgangssprache zu stehen (vgl. u.a. Briz Gómez 1993, 1994, 1998; Pons Bordería 1998; Portolés Lázaro 1994). Anders als in der deutschen Partikelforschung werden diese Partikeln in der sp. Linguistik als Sprachmittel aufgefasst, die innerhalb einer dialogischen Makrostruktur der Gliederung bzw. Markierung zwischen kleineren Gesprächseinheiten dienen.

Conector ist ein gemeinsamer Nenner für eine Reihe von Lexemen bzw. Ausdrücken, deren Hauptfunktion in der Verbindung zwischen gleichwertigen oder heterogenen Teilen besteht. Die Art und Weise dieser Verbindung wird durch unterschiedliche modalisierende Nuancen determiniert, die sich sowohl aus der Grundbedeutung dieser Lexeme als auch aus anderen Faktoren, wie dem Kontext, herleiten lassen. Da diese Basisfunktion eines Konnektors zu allgemein ist, wird der Begriff durch Adjektive wie *argumentativo* oder *pragmático* präzisiert. Im Unterschied zu den in den meisten Grammatiken ausführlich beschriebenen *Konjunktionen*, deren Funktion auf der syntagmatischen oder Satzebene angesiedelt wird, agieren die *conectores* auf der pragmatischen Ebene.

3.2 Analyse von einzelnen *conectores*: *pero*

In diesem Punkt wird bewiesen, dass einige *conectores* wie *pero* die gleichen Funktionen wie die dt. MPn erfüllen und dass sie in der sp. Umgangssprache relativ häufig vorkommen, im Gegensatz zu den Schlussfolgerungen Beerboms.

Anhand von Ergebnissen in der sp. linguistischen Partikelforschung und mit Belegen für die verschiedenen Anwendungsmöglichkeiten der mutmaßlichen sp. MPn aus einem Korpus der gesprochenen spanischen Standardsprache möchte ich die Grundlage für eine funktionale Wortklasse von PMn schaffen.

Der Konnektor *pero* wird in der sp. Grammatik als *conjunción coordinante adversativa* (adversative koordinierende Konjunktion) eingestuft. Nach der Konjunktion *y* ist *pero* die am häufigsten verwendete Konjunktion im heutigen Spanischen (vgl. Beerbom 1992:306).

Einige linguistische Beschreibungen von *pero* befassen sich mit emotionalen oder konnektiven Aspekten: So wird *pero* auch als *'emphatic emotional adjunt'* (Steel, 1976:17), *'enlace coloquial'* (Vigara Tauste, 1980: 66), *'partícula expletiva o enfática'* (María Moliner 1982), *'partícula modal'* (Acosta Gómez 1984), *'conector (pragmático) de antiorientación'* (Briz Gómez 1994:380) bezeichnet; der Partikel *pero* werden andere emotionale Werte zugeschrieben, wie Überraschung (*RAE* 1986:511; Vigara Tauste 1992:124ff), Protest (Acín Villa 1994:220-221) oder Ärger (Pons Bordería 1998:25). *Pero* gilt als MP-Äquivalent für *aber, bloß/nur, denn, doch* und *eigentlich* (Ferrer Mora 1999:229).

Als Konjunktion verbindet *pero* Propositionen oder bestimmte Satzteile; als Konnektor nimmt die Partikel Bezug auf eine Präsupposition, auf eine Vorgängeräußerung oder auf den Kontext, indem der Sprecher seiner Äußerung Emphase verleiht, die normalerweise mit einem Vorwurf oder mit einer Kritik zu tun hat, d.h., der Sprecher bringt ein Gegenargument zum Ausdruck.

In 1) zeigt Sprecher T3 mit seiner von *pero* eingeleiteten Frage an, dass er nicht wusste, dass E1 ein Landhaus besitzt. Dadurch wird seine Unkenntnis über eine Präsupposition der Äußerung von E1 zum Ausdruck gebracht:

1) E1: A Benidorm tenemos que ir / Hemos de ir de acampada a mi chalet
   T3: ¿A tu chalet...? *Pero* ¿tú tienes un chalet en Benidorm? (Briz Gómez 1993a:171)

Nicht immer ist eine Äußerung mit *pero* als Konnektor mit dem Ausdruck von Überraschung verbunden. In einigen Antworten signalisiert *pero* Kritik oder Vorwurf. In 2) wird die Bitte von A mit Hilfe von *pero si* zurückgewiesen:

2) A: ¿puedes decirme la hora? B: ¡*pero* si llevas reloj! (Briz Gómez 1998:170)

B findet es unlogisch, dass A nach der Uhrzeit fragt, weil er selber eine Armbanduhr trägt. Implizit ist eine negative Antwort dabei. In diesem Beispiel kommt *pero* in Kombination mit der MP *si* zusammen vor. Auf diese Weise zeigt Sprecher A die Anknüpfung seiner Erwiderung an die Vorgängeräußerung.

4   Deutsche MPn als Konnektoren und sp. *conectores* als MPn

Abgesehen von der Tatsache, dass die bisher analysierten Lexeme als Äquivalenten von einigen dt. MPn fungieren, werden die Gemeinsamkeiten zwischen beiden Partikelgruppen darüber hinaus kurz erläutert:

1) Beide (MPn und *conectores*) sind morphologisch unflektierbar.

2) Beide sind bis auf Einzelfälle unbetont.

3) Beide sind auch meistens weglassbar (fakultativ) auf der propositionalen Ebene; hingegen vertreten wir die Meinung, dass sie auf der pragmatischen Ebene nicht weglassbar sind, ohne die pragmatische bzw. argumentative Bedeutung einer Äußerung zu verändern.

4) Beide sind mit gewissen Beschränkungen untereinander kombinierbar.

5) Beide können nicht allein als Antwort stehen.

6) Beide sind nicht erfragbar.

7) Beide können nicht negiert werden.

8) Beide sind meistens satzmodusabhängig.

In Bezug auf die syntaktische Distribution stehen die dt. MPn fast immer im Mittelfeld; hingegen stehen die meisten sp. Konnektoren am Anfang des Satzes, aber andere Lexeme wie *acaso* oder *entonces* können auch relativ frei verschoben werden.

Auf der phonetischen und morphologischen Ebene weisen die dt. MPn und die sp. Konnektoren Gemeinsamkeiten auf; dagegen verhalten sie sich anders auf der syntaktischen. Auf der pragmatischen Ebene bzw. im illokutiven Bereich haben sie auch viel gemeinsam: Sie drücken die Einstellung des Sprechers zum Gesagten aus und können auf je unterschiedliche Weise die Illokution modifizieren. Darüber hinaus können die dt. und sp. MPn dazu dienen, eine Äußerung im Interaktionszusammenhang zu verankern, auf das gemeinsame Wissen der Gesprächspartner zu verweisen oder einen bestimmten Bezug zu einer vorangegangenen Äußerung anzuzeigen (vgl. Thurmair 1989:2). Betrachtet man das von Thurmair postulierte Merkmal <KONNEX> für viele der dt. MPn, dann lässt sich unmittelbar daraus ableiten, dass starke Ähnlichkeiten zwischen ihnen und den sp. Konnektoren bestehen.

Wir setzen uns für die Existenz einer funktionalen Klasse von MPn im Sp. ein und schließen uns damit der Meinung von Cárdenes Melián an,

„derartige Schlussfolgerungen, dass also das Spanische keine vergleichbare Klasse von Wörtern hat, die diese Funktionen auf so subtile Weise ausdrücken können, (…) hängen einzig und allein mit dem derzeitigen Stand der Forschung der spanischen Sprache zusammen" (Cárdenes Melián 1997:188).

Wir haben hier versucht zu beweisen, dass es im Sp. jenseits der bloßen Entsprechungen eine funktionale Wortklasse von MPn mit spezifischen Charakteristika gibt. Die Klasse der sp. MPn bleibt noch offen. Eine sprachwissenschaftliche Auseinandersetzung mit allen sp. Entsprechungen ist leider in diesem Rahmen nicht möglich. Es wäre aber wünschenswert, dass dieses brennende Thema innerhalb der sp. Linguistik wieter erforscht wird.

5   Literatur

ACÍN VILLA, Esperanza (1994): Sobre pero enfático. In: Cuadernos de Investigación Filológica XIX-XX (1993-1994), Universidad de la Rioja, 219-233.

ACOSTA GÓMEZ, Luis Ángel (1984): Las partículas modales del alemán y del español. In: Studia Philologica Salmanticensia, Universidad de Salamanca 7-8, 7-41.

BEERBOM, Christiane (1992): Modalpartikeln als Übersetzungsproblem. Eine kontrastive Studie zum Sprachenpaar Deutsch-Spanisch (Diss. Heidelberg 1991). Frankfurt a. M. etc.: Peter Lang (Heidelberger Beiträge zur Romanistik 26).

BRIZ GÓMEZ, Antonio (1998): El español coloquial en la conversación. Esbozo de prag-magramática. Ariel: Barcelona.
— (1994): Hacia un análisis argumentativo de un texto coloquial. La incidencia de los conectores pragmáticos. In: Verba 21, 369-395.
— (1993): Los conectores pragmáticos en español coloquial (I): su papel argumentativo. In: Contextos XI 21-22, 145-188.
CÁRDENES MELIÁN, José (1997): Aber, denn, doch, eben und ihre spanischen Entsprechungen. Eine funktional-pragmatische Studie zur Übersetzung deutscher Partikeln. Münster – New York – München – Berlin: Waxmann (Mehrsprachigkeit 3).
FERRER MORA, Hang (1999): Las partículas modales alemanas en el modo interrogativo y sus equivalentes en español como criterio para una taxonomía de preguntas. (Diss. Universitat de València).
FUENTES RODRÍGUEZ, Catalina (1987): Enlaces extraoracionales. Sevilla: Alfar.
María Moliner (1990): Diccionario de uso del español, 2 vols.. Madrid: Gredos.
MARTÍN ZORRAQUINO, María.Antonia (1992): „Spanisch: Partikelforschung (Partículas y modalidad)". In: Holtus, G.; Metzeltin, M.; Schmitt, C. (Hrsg.): Lexikon der Romanistischen Linguistik. Tübingen: Niemeyer, 111-125.
PONS BORDERÍA, Salvador (1998): Conexión y Conectores. Estudio de su relación en el registro informal de la lengua. Universitat de València.
PORTOLÉS LÁZARO, José (1994): „La distinción entre los conectores y otros marcadores del discurso en español". In: Verba 20, 141-170.
PRÜFER, Irene (1995): La traducción de las partículas modales al español y al inglés. Frankfurt am Main etc.: Peter Lang.
RAE (1986): Esbozo de una nueva gramática de la lengua española. Madrid: Espasa-Calpe.
STEEL, Brian (1976): A Textbook of Colloquial Spanish. Madrid: SGEL.
THURMAIR, Maria (1989): Modalpartikeln und ihre Kombinationen. Tübingen: Niemeyer (Linguistische Arbeiten 223).
VIGARA TAUSTE, Ana María (1992): Morfosintaxis del español actual. Madrid: Gredos.
— (1980): Aspectos del español hablado. Madrid: SGEL.
ZIERER, Ernesto (1978): Las partículas ilocativas del idioma alemán y sus equivalentes en el idioma español. Universidad de Trujillo.

Die Mehrheit als Sonderfall?

Bildung und Verwendung von Bezeichnungen für Frauen im Niederländischen und ein Vergleich zum Deutschen, Englischen und Französischen

Madeline Lutjeharms

1 Einleitung

Während im Deutschen und seit kurzem auch im Französischen eine Feminisierung von Berufsbezeichnungen für Frauen bevorzugt wird, steht eine Entscheidung für das Niederländische noch aus. Es ist fraglich, ob es überhaupt zu Empfehlungen mit Bezug auf eine Feminisierung kommen wird. Dies hat mehrere Ursachen, die mit der Bildung der Bezeichnungen und mit dem Sprachempfinden Niederländischsprachiger zusammenhängen.

2 Zur Bildung von Bezeichnungen für Frauen im Niederländischen

2.1 Genus im Niederländischen

In den indoeuropäischen Sprachen gab es ursprünglich vermutlich zwei Genera, ein sächliches Genus und ein Genus, aus dem später das Maskulinum und das Femininum entstanden sind (Corbett 1991:309). Sprachen mit mehr als drei Genera sind keine Seltenheit, aber es kommen auch Sprachen vor, in denen die Kategorie Genus nicht vorhanden ist, so beispielsweise Finnisch oder Chinesisch. Von einer direkten Beziehung zwischen Genus und Sexus kann also nicht die Rede sein (vgl. Sieburg 1997; Lutjeharms 1987).

Während im Deutschen die drei Genera der indoeuropäischen Sprachen noch realisiert sind, ist das Genus bei englischen Substantiven verschwunden. Auch im Niederländischen wird bei den Substantiven nicht mehr von Genus gesprochen, obwohl beim bestimmten Artikel noch zwei Formen vorkommen: *de* und *het*. Für den unbestimmten Artikel gibt es nur eine Form (*een*). Der Artikel *de* ist ursprünglich die Form für Maskulinum und Femininum (und für die Mehrzahl), *het* die für Neutrum. Heute wird in der niederländischen Grammatik allerdings nur noch von *de*- und *het-woorden* gesprochen. Psychologisch gesehen wäre das sehr häufige *de* als die unmarkierte Form und das seltenere *het* als die markierte Form zu betrachten (vgl. Deutsch; Wijnen 1985). Es könnte also behauptet werden, dass im Niederländischen bei den Substantiven die Kategorie Genus verschwunden ist. Allerdings ist der Unterschied weiblich/männlich in der flämischen Variante der niederländischen Umgangssprache unter dem Einfluss der Dialekte zum Teil noch an einer Endung beim Artikel oder Demonstrativpronomen hörbar. Auffällig ist jedoch, dass sich die Sprechenden dessen im Allgemeinen nicht bewusst sind, wie ich bei meinen Studierenden immer wieder feststelle. Für den Deutscherwerb ist es eine große Hilfe, wenn man noch weiß, ob ein Substantiv mit dem Artikel *de* ursprünglich männlich oder weiblich ist. Der Unterschied männlich/weiblich kann inzwischen nur noch in der Sprache einer Minderheit der Studierenden beobachtet werden, vielen von ihnen muss jedoch erst erklärt werden, woran sie es hören können.

Bei den Personal- und Possessivpronomina ist die Situation dem Deutschen ähnlich. Bei den Relativ- und Demonstrativpronomina werden Formen verwendet, die *de* und *het* entsprechen (*die/dat; deze/dit*).

In der letzten Ausgabe der offiziellen Wortliste des Niederländischen (Woordenlijst Nederlandse taal 1995) wird bei den Substantiven angegeben, ob es *de-* oder *het-woorden* sind. Bei den meisten – aber nicht bei allen – *de-woorden* wird noch *(m.)* für männlich und *(v.)* für weiblich angegeben. Im Vorwort heißt es allerdings, die Sprachverwendung zeige, dass die Unsicherheit bei der Wahl des grammatischen Geschlechts immer größer werde und dass eine umfangreiche Untersuchung dringend erforderlich wäre (53). Diese Unsicherheit ist im Norden des Sprachgebietes (in den Niederlanden) noch viel größer als im Süden (in Flandern).

2.2   Movierung und Differentialgenus im Niederländischen

Im Deutschen ist die Bildung movierter Formen durch die Produktivität der Nachsilbe *-in* an sich unproblematisch. Diese Nachsilbe wird sogar verwendet, wenn eigentlich schon eine (andere) weibliche Nachsilbe vorhanden ist, wie in *Prinzessin*. Die Nachsilbe *-in* kommt im Niederländischen zwar vor, allerdings nicht sehr häufig und nur bei sehr alten Bezeichungen (wie *boerin* - Bäuerin -, *heldin*), denn sie ist seit langem nicht mehr produktiv. Auch die Nachsilben *-es* (aus dem Französischen, wie in *prinses, lerares* - Lehrerin) und *-a* (Differentialgenus bei Substantiven aus dem Lateinischen, wie *politica* neben *politicus*, aber **technica* neben *technicus* ist nicht möglich) sind nicht mehr produktiv. Movierte Formen können nur noch mit *-e* und *-ster* gebildet werden, allerdings unter bestimmten Bedingungen (für eine Beschreibung der Bildungsmöglichkeiten im Niederländischen siehe Van Santen 1998, von der verschiedene der hier verwendeten Beispiele stammen).

Für die Komplexität der Bildung movierter Formen können mehrere Gründe angeführt werden, die einerseits mit der Bildung von Personenbezeichnungen im Allgemeinen und andererseits mit dem Vorhandensein vieler weiblicher Nachsilben zusammenhängen.

Die Bildung von Personenbezeichnungen ist im Niederländischen komplizierter als im Deutschen. Im Deutschen werden Deverbativa ziemlich konsequent mit *-er* gebildet, die movierten Formen dann mit *-in*. Im Niederländischen wird zum Stamm eines Verbs am häufigsten ein Differentialgenus auf *-er/ster* gebildet, wobei *-ster* die weibliche Nachsilbe ist (*schrijven* -schreiben-, *schrijfster schrijver / spreken, spreekster, spreker*). Neben der produktiven Nachsilbe *-ster* kommen aber auch movierte Formen auf *-es* vor (*dichten, dichter, dichteres / lezen, lezer, lezeres*). Die Endung *-ster* wird zudem nicht nur zur Bildung eines Differentialgenus verwendet, sondern auch zur Bildung movierter Formen zu männlichen Bezeichnungen auf *-aar*, die ebenfalls zum Stamm eines Verbs gebildet werden können (*twijfelen* - zweifeln -, *twijfelaar, twijfelaarster*). Die Endung *-ster* wird außerdem noch benutzt für Femininbildungen zu den männlichen Denominativa auf -ier (*avonturier - Abenteurer -, avonturierster*) und auf -*aar* (*kluizenaar - Eremit -, kluizenaarster*). Doch auch bei Denominativa kommt Differentialgenus vor (wie bei *wetenschapper - Wissenschaftler-, wetenschapster*). Die noch sehr produktive Nachsilbe -*ster* wird also sowohl zur Bildung des Differentialgenus – bei Verbalstämmen – wie zur Bildung movierter Formen verwendet und in letzterem Fall zur Movierung von Bezeichungen mit unterschiedlichen (männlichen) Nachsilben.

Die produktive Nachsilbe -*e* zur Bildung von Bezeichnungen für Frauen kommt vorwiegend bei Fremdwörtern vor (*psychologe, laborante, miljonaire*). Sie ist allerdings nur möglich bei betonter Endsilbe der männlichen Bezeichnung. Zu Bezeichnungen wie *consul, minister, notaris* oder *psychiater* mit Betonung der vorletzten Silbe ist daher keine Movierung möglich. Bei germanischen Bezeichnungen ist die Movierung auf -*e* nur möglich bei den Substantiven auf -*ling* (anders als im Deutschen, wo bei Substantiven auf -ling keine in-Movierung möglich ist), -*genoot, verwant* (*vreemdelinge* - weiblicher Fremdling -, *lotgenote* - Schicksalsgenossin -, *geestverwante* - Geistesverwandte -, vgl. Van Santen 1998:48).

2.3 Geographische Personenbezeichnungen

Bei Bezeichnungen für Nationalitäten kann die Bildung männlicher Formen sehr variieren (*Duitser, Nederlander, Fin, Engelsman, Fransman, Belg, Italiaan, Spanjaard, Vlaming* usw. zu jeweils *Duitsland, Nederland, Finland, Engeland, Frankrijk, België, Italië, Spanje, Vlaanderen*). Die Bezeichnungen für Frauen werden sehr systematisch mit Hilfe der geographischen Adjektive gebildet (*Duitse, Nederlandse, Finse, Engelse, Belgische, Italiaanse, Spaanse, Vlaamse* usw., wobei *Française* – zum französischen Adjektiv – eine Ausnahme bildet). Eine Mehrzahlbildung ist bei diesen Bezeichnungen für Frauen allerdings sehr unüblich (bis auf: *Françaises*).

2.4 Weibliche Bezeichnungen sind oft nicht möglich

Bei vielen Personenbezeichnungen ist es nicht möglich, ein Femininum zu bilden. Dies ist beispielsweise bei den substantivierten Adjektiven und Partizipien der Fall, bei denen die Nachsilbe -*e* generische Bedeutung hat (*deskundige* - Experte/in -, *gelovige* - Gläubige/r - *bediende* - Angestellte/r -, *afgevaardigde* - Abgeordnete/r), bei – ursprünglich männlichen – Zusammensetzungen mit -*bode* (*postbode* - Briefträger/in), bei aus dem Englischen übernommenen Substantiven wie *manager, accountant*, bei vielen anderen Bezeichnungen wie *ruiter* - Reiter/in -, *premier* - Ministerpräsident/in -, *wijsgeer* - Philosoph/in - u.ä.

Bei aus dem Französischen übernommenen Bezeichnungen auf -*(t)eur* herrscht große Unsicherheit. Van Santen (1998:49) fand Formen wie: *grimeuse, grimeurster, grimeerster, grimeurse* zu *grimeur*. Diese Unsicherheit zeigt die Probleme im Niederländischen, hängt aber wohl auch mit der Situation im Französischen zusammen.

Im Französischen ist die Femininbildung der Substantive auf *-eur* ziemlich komplex, auch wenn sie sich auf feste Regeln stützt. Deverbativa werden mit Hilfe der Nachsilben *-eur/euse* gebildet (*chercheur/ chercheuse*), also ein Differentialgenus (zur Bildung von Bezeichnungen für Frauen im Französischen siehe Delbecque 1998). Bei Substantiven auf *-eur* ohne Bezug zu einem Verb ist eine movierte Form auf *-e* möglich, aber auch die Verwendung nur des weiblichen Artikels (*le/la professeur, la professeure*). Mit der Nachsilbe *-teur* gilt für Deverbativa die allgemeine Regel für *-eur* (*le rapporteur, la rapporteuse*), aber ohne Bezug zum Verb kommt hier die weibliche Form *-trice* vor (*directeur/ directrice*). Trotz dieser Regeln herrscht Verwirrung bei der Bildung (so verweist die *Communauté française de Belgique* 1994:28 nicht nur auf *auteur*, sondern auch auf *auteure* (Quebec) und *autrice* (Schweiz) als weibliche Formen). Bezeichnungen auf *-teur/-trice* kommen im Niederländischen vor (*acteur/actrice*, aber zu *auteur* ist im Niederländischen ein Femininum ausgeschlossen), doch die ursprünglich männliche Form wird häufig generisch verwendet (so beispielsweise *directeur*).

2.5   Neutrale Personenbezeichnungen

Wie im Deutschen kommen auch im Niederländischen echte generische Personenbezeichnungen vor, bei denen das Genus keine Bedeutung hat, wie die Zusammensetzungen mit *-kracht* (-kraft, wie *leerkracht, werkkracht*) oder *-hoofd* (*diensthoofd* - Abteilungsleiter/in oder *schoolhoofd* - Schulleiter/in) und vor allem die größere Gruppe der substantivierten Adjektive (*taalkundige* - Sprachwissenschaftler/in oder *deskundige* - Experte/in) und Partizipien (*verkozenen* - Gewählte/Abgeordnete). Letztere Gruppe wird jedoch anders als im Deutschen nicht bewusst erweitert, wohl weil danach kein Bedürfnis besteht, da die ursprünglich nur für Männer verwendeten Bezeichnungen im Niederländischen wenigstens auf der grammatischen Ebene keine sehr starke männliche Konnotation haben.

3   Zur Verwendung weiblicher Personenbezeichnungen im Niederländischen

3.1   Neutralisierung oder Differenzierung?

Grammatikalisch betrachtet sind Personenbezeichnungen im Niederländischen weder männlich noch weiblich (es sind *de-woorden*), es sei denn, es handelt sich um Zusammensetzungen mit *-vrouw/-man* wie *zakenman/-vrouw* (Geschäftsmann/-frau) oder es existiert entweder eine eingebürgerte movierte Form oder ein Differentialgenus. Einerseits ist aus grammatischen Gründen eigentlich kein Bedürfnis nach einer besonderen Form für Frauen zu erwarten. Andererseits sind alte movierte Formen wie die Bezeichnungen auf die nicht mehr produktiven Endungen *-in* und *-es* sehr geläufig. Daraus ergeben sich unterschiedliche Tendenzen. Aus dem Bedürfnis nach Parallelität mit den vorhandenen Bezeichnungen kann der Wunsch nach neuen Femininbildungen entstehen. Häufig ist das Problem dann, welche Nachsilbe für die Neubildung gewählt werden soll. Sehr oft ist eine weibliche Form gar nicht möglich, wie bei *minister* oder *professor*. Diese Probleme legen es nahe, auf eine Femininbildung zu verzichten. Das impliziert aber auch eine Ungleichheit im System der Personenbezeichnungen.

BefürworterInnen neuer Femininbildungen führen als wichtigste Argumente an, dass sie Frauen sichtbar machen wollen, dass sie wissen wollen, ob sie es mit einer Frau oder einem Mann zu tun haben und dass sie auch von sich selbst in der Berufsbezeichnung zeigen wollen, dass sie eine Frau sind. Bei einem Kolloquium im März 1998 zu diesem Thema (Lutjeharms 1998) zeigte sich, dass vor allem junge Frauen (Akademikerinnen, aber vorwiegend Nicht-Linguistinnen) die Feminisierung fordern. Die BefürworterInnen der Neutralisierung empfinden die weiblichen Bezeichnungen, besonders die Neubildungen, oft als abwertend, eine Empfindung, die gelegentlich auch noch im deutschen Sprachgebiet vorkommt. Eine typische Reaktion war die der sehr bekannten niederländischen Schriftstellerin Connie Palmen während eines Interviews im Deutschland-Funk am 19.09.99. Sie bestand darauf, dass sie ein „Schriftsteller" sei, nicht eine „Schriftstellerin", weil schreiben eine „maskuline" Beschäftigung sei. Im Niederländischen kann sich eine Frau sowohl als *schrijver* wie als *schrijfster* bezeichnen, beide Formen klingen korrekt und sind üblich.

Die große Mehrheit der LinguistInnen befürwortet die Neutralisierung, weil sie dazu neigen, das ganze Sprachsystem zu berücksichtigen. Dabei werden mehrere Argumente angeführt. Die Verwendung weiblicher Formen ändere das Denken nicht (De Caluwe 1998, vgl. Gathercole 1989 und Khosroshahi 1989). Im Falle movierter Formen habe die ursprüngliche männliche Bezeichnung prototypischen Wert. Die Bildung weiblicher Formen sei oft nicht möglich, diese Formen seien nicht immer gleichwertig und wir brauchten auf jeden Fall auch neutrale Bezeichnungen (mehrere Autorinnen in Lutjeharms 1998).

Doppelformen sind umständlich, zudem rufen sie das Problem der Reihenfolge hervor. Sobald über eine Gruppe von Menschen im Allgemeinen gesprochen oder geschrieben wird, taucht doch wieder das generische Maskulinum auf. Sogar wenn von nur einer Frau die Rede ist, wird oft durcheinander mal eine weibliche Bezeichnung mal das generische Maskulinum (oder soll man sagen: die geschlechtsneutrale Bezeichnung?) verwendet. Im Deutschen dagegen werden in Bezug auf eine einzelne Frau heute fast ausschließlich movierte Formen verwendet.

3.2   Das Problem der Zusammensetzungen

Mit alten movierten Substantiven sind Zusammensetzungen zum Teil möglich, wenn auch unüblich, wie in *boerinnenleven* (Bäuerinnenleben). Normaler klingt aber *het beroep van lerares* (der Beruf einer Lehrerin) während *het lerarenberoep* (Lehrerberuf) durchaus geläufig ist, wie ähnlich *vereniging van schrijfsters* gegenüber *schrijversvereniging*. Formen wie **docenteschap* (*docentschap*) oder **biologescongres* (*biologencongres*, Beispiele nach Van Santen 1998:54) sind nicht gut möglich, was u.a. daher rührt, dass die Mehrzahlform (auf -s) der Movierungen auf -e ziemlich ungebräuchlich ist.

3.3   Sind für das niederländische Sprachgebiet Richtlinien zu erwarten?

In Flandern wurden 1994 einige Richtlinien zur nicht-sexistischen Sprachverwendung
veröffentlicht, so die des „Rates für Chancengleichheit zwischen Männern und
Frauen" – so lautet der offizielle Name auf Deutsch – mit der Empfehlung der Neutralisierung (Van Varenbergh 1998) oder die der *Vlaamse Overlegcommissie Vrouwen
(VOV)*, die auf Wunsch des Bildungsministers verfasst wurde. Die Richtlinien der
VOV enthalten eine sehr vorsichtige Empfehlung der Neutralisierung, ohne die Formen mit weiblichen Nachsilben abzulehnen. Die Verwendung von Doppelformen
sollte nicht auferlegt werden. Die VOV empfiehlt jedoch die Verbreitung von Listen
mit neutralen, männlichen und weiblichen Berufsbezeichnungen (1998:111). Der
(belgische) „Rat für Chancengleichheit zwischen Männern und Frauen" hat sich im
Übrigen für die sprachliche Gleichbehandlung im Französischen dem Erlass der französischen Gemeinschaft in Belgien (1993) angeschlossen, in dem Feminisierung empfohlen wird (Van Varenbergh 1998; *Communauté française de Belgique* 1994). Für
das Deutsche – die dritte Amtssprache in Belgien – verweist der Rat auf die in Deutschland geltenden Richtlinien. In den Richtlinien, die im deutschen Sprachgebiet entstanden sind, werden Differenzierung und die Verwendung von Doppelformen empfohlen.

Im niederländischen Sprachgebiet, d.h. in den Niederlanden und Belgien, besteht
eine offizielle Instanz für Beratung und Entscheidungen bei Sprachproblemen, die
Taalunie (Sprachunion), die auch für die oben erwähnte Wortliste (2.1) zuständig ist.
Die *Taalunie* hat entschieden, keine Richtlinien mit Bezug auf die Verwendung von
Bezeichnungen für Frauen herauszugeben. Es werden aber Listen mit weiblichen,
männlichen und neutralen Bezeichnungen – soweit sie im Niederländischen regelkon-
form sind – aufgestellt. Diese Listen sind als Orientierungshilfe gemeint. Die Entscheidung soll dann den einzelnen Sprechenden überlassen werden. Dies ist aufgrund
der komplexen sprachlichen Situation wohl auch die einzige vernünftige Haltung. Es
ist zu erwarten, dass sich das heutige Mischsystem mit alten weiblichen Bezeichnungen, mit gelegentlichem Gebrauch neuer movierter Formen und mit vielen neutralen
– teilweise ursprünglich generisch verwendeten männlichen – Formen weiterhin halten wird.

4   Sprachvergleich

4.1   Niederländisch und Englisch

Das Niederländische ist mit dem Englischen vergleichbar, insofern als es bei den
Substantiven – jedenfalls in der Standardsprache – kaum noch eine Opposition
männlich-weiblich gibt. Zudem kann bei vielen Substantiven das biologische Geschlecht wie im Englischen nur mit Hilfe lexikalischer Mittel verdeutlicht werden
(*lady doctor/vrouwelijke arts*). Die Seltenheit der Verwendung eines männlichen Adjektivs hängt nicht mit dem Sprachsystem, sondern mit gesellschaftlichen Entwicklungen zusammen (vgl. *male nurse*, hier im Niederländischen Differentialgenus: *ver-
pleegster/verpleger*). Oft werden im Niederländischen auch dann lexikalische Mittel

verwendet, wenn eine movierte Form möglich ist (*female students, vrouwelijke studenten*), besonders bei den unüblichen Mehrzahlformen. Doch anders als im Englischen verfügt das Niederländische auch noch über viele alte weibliche Bezeichnungen, und es ist manchmal möglich, neue weibliche Berufsbezeichnungen zu bilden.

4.2   Niederländisch und Französisch

Wie das Französische hat das Niederländische viele Derivationssuffixe für die Bildung weiblicher Bezeichnungen. Das führt zu Unsicherheiten bei der Bildung von Bezeichnungen für Frauen, weshalb ein Bedürfnis nach Listen mit Femininbildungen entsteht. Die Uneinheitlichkeit der Lösungen, die im viel größeren französischen Sprachgebiet existiert (siehe das – zwar extreme – Beispiel *auteur*, 2.4, doch es gibt andere Beispiele, wie die vielen Anmerkungen in der Liste der *Communauté française de Belgique* 1994, zeigen), möchte man im niederländischen Sprachgebiet vermeiden. Die Entwicklung im französischen Sprachgebiet ist nicht synchron verlaufen. Sprachliche Gleichbehandlung durch die Verwendung weiblicher Personenbezeichnungen wurde unter amerikanischem Einfluss zuerst in Quebec gefordert. Dann folgten die anderen Randgebiete und mit großer Verzögerung auch Frankreich. Die Situation ist inzwischen mit der des deutschen Sprachgebiets vergleichbar. Ähnlich wie im Deutschen und anders als im Niederländischen hat das Französische eine grammatische Opposition weiblich/männlich, die sich nicht nur bei den Substantiven und den Artikeln zeigt, sondern die auch bei der Adjektivdeklination, im Französischen sogar in der Mehrzahl, hör- und sichtbar ist. Dadurch und durch die Opposition weiblich/männlich beim Personalpronomen in der dritten Person Mehrzahl ist die nicht-sexistische Sprachverwendung in der Mehrzahl im Französischen schwieriger als im Deutschen.

Für das Französische hat sich also die Hypothese von Hellinger (1990:119f) schließlich bestätigt:

„SprecherInnen einer Sprache mit der grammatischen Opposition m/f werden die Strategie der Feminisierung wählen, wenn die Opposition m/f durch eine ausreichende Anzahl von Kongruenzregeln fest im morphosyntaktischen System der Sprache verankert ist, wenn die Sprache über feminine Wortbildungsmuster verfügt, die noch produktiv sind oder wieder produktiv gemacht werden können und wenn die semantische Zweitrangigkeit persönlicher Feminina nicht als zu hoher Preis für die sprachliche Sichtbarkeit von Frauen empfunden wird."

4.3   Niederländisch und Deutsch

Ähnlich wie im Deutschen existieren im Niederländischen weiterhin verbreitete movierte Formen, allerdings bei sehr viel weniger Personenbezeichnungen. Im Deutschen sind heute zur Bezeichnung einzelner Frauen fast ausschließlich grammatisch weibliche Formen erlaubt. Dies kommt im Niederländischen nur in einigen wenigen Fällen vor. Wenn aber differenziert wird, hat das Niederländische bei den Zusammensetzungen mit einer Personenbezeichnung dasselbe Problem wie das Deutsche: Zusammensetzungen mit movierten Formen wirken komisch oder sind auf jeden Fall

sehr unüblich. Die Problematik bei der Verwendung der Doppelformen ist vergleichbar. Sobald es nicht um eine bestimmte Frau oder Frauengruppe geht, werden die
Femininbildungen meist vergessen und setzt sich die generische Verwendung der
männlichen Bezeichnungen wieder durch. Dies wird aufgrund der Umständlichkeit
der Doppelformen gelegentlich sogar empfohlen (Dietrich 1996). Dabei ist allerdings
zu berücksichtigen, dass sich im Deutschen die männliche Konnotation der grammatisch männlichen Bezeichnungen durch die Verallgemeinerung der -in-Movierungen
verstärkt hat, während die ursprünglich männlichen Bezeichnungen im Niederländischen sich eher in die Richtung der verstärkten generischen Bedeutung entwickeln.
Die Notwendigkeit neutraler Formen gilt für beide Sprachen, wie auch im Französischen, wenn der Artikel nicht zur Differenzierung reicht (wie in *le/la journaliste*).
Sonst kann man Doppeldeutigkeit nicht vermeiden in Sätzen wie: „Sie ist die Beste
der Assistentinnen". Wird hier mit allen Assistierenden verglichen oder nur mit den
weiblichen?

5   Abschließende Überlegungen

Ob sich das Niederländische eher in die deutsch-französische oder in die englische
Richtung entwickeln wird, ist noch nicht absehbar. In der flämischen Variante des
Niederländischen ist die Opposition männlich/weiblich zum Teil noch hörbar, was
erklärt, dass es in Flandern mehr BefürworterInnen einer Feminisierung gibt als im
Norden.
      Beide Lösungen – Differenzierung und Neutralisierung – haben Vor- wie auch
Nachteile. Im Deutschen ist die individuelle Frau durch die Verwendung movierter
Formen in der Sprache sichtbarer gemacht worden. Es ist jedoch sehr fraglich, ob das
auch für die Frauen als Gruppe gilt. Zudem haben die movierten Formen den Nachteil, dass das männliche Basiselement prototypischen Wert hat und daher als Normal-
fall betrachtet wird. Eine befriedigende Beseitigung der sprachlichen Benachteiligung
von Frauen ist im Deutschen und Französischen schwieriger als im Niederländischen
– teilweise aus unterschiedlichen Gründen –, aber im Niederländischen ist sie schwieriger als im Englischen. Das Niederländische befindet sich nicht nur geographisch, sondern auch grammatisch zwischen dem Englischen und dem Deutschen.

6   Literatur

COMMUNAUTÉ FRANÇAISE DE BELGIQUE (1994): Mettre au féminin. Guide de féminisation des noms
     de métier, fonction, grade ou titre. Conseil supérieur de la langue française, Service de la langue
     française.
CORBETT, Greville (1991): Gender. Cambridge etc.: Cambridge University Press.
DE CALUWE, Johan (1998): Vervrouwelijking of niet? Over de (on)macht van de taal over het den-
     ken. In: Lutjeharms: 57-61.
DELBECQUE, Nicole (1998): Feminisering in Romaans perspectief: Structurele en functionele analyse
     van de Franse en Spaanse functie- en beroepsnamen. In: Lutjeharms: 19-33.
DEUTSCH, Werner; WIJNEN, Frank (1985): The article's noun and the noun's article: explorations
     into the representation and access of linguistic gender in Dutch. In: Linguistics 23, 793-810.

DIETRICH, Margot (1996): Grundsätze für die geschlechtergerechte Gestaltung von Gesetzestexten. In: Der Sprachdienst 40, 163-167.

GATHERCOLE, Virginia C. (1989): The acquisition of sex-neutral uses of masculine forms in English and Spanish. In: Applied Psycholinguistics 10, 401-427.

HELLINGER, Marlies (1990): Kontrastive feministische Linguistik: Mechanismen sprachlicher Diskriminierung im Englischen und Deutschen. München: M. Hueber Verlag.

KHOSROSHAHI, F. (1989): „Penguins don't care, but women do": A social identity analysis of a Whorfian problem. In: Language in Society 18, 505-525.

LUTJEHARMS, Madeline (ed.) (1998): Feminisering van beroepsnamen: een juiste keuze? Studiereeks Instituut voor Taalonderwijs, nr. 6, Vrije Universiteit Brussel.

— (1987): „Liebe Leser" oder „liebe Leserinnen und Leser": Zum Verhältnis von Genus und Sexus im Deutschen. In: Germanistische Mitteilungen 26, 33-41.

SIEBURG, Heinz (Hrsg.) (1997): Sprache Genus/Sexus. Dokumentation Germanistischer Forschung 3. Frankfurt a. M.: Peter Lang.

Van Santen, Ariane (1998), Vorming en betekenis van vrouwelijke beroepsnamen. In: Lutjeharms: 47-56.

VAN VARENBERGH, Myriam (1998): Advies N° 2 over het geslacht van beroeps- en functienamen van 9 december 1994. In: Lutjeharms: 99-102.

VLAAMSE OVERLEGCOMMISSIE VROUWEN (SERV) (1998): Advies over de feminisering van beroepsnamen. In: Lutjeharms: 103-112.

WOORDENLIJST NEDERLANDSE TAAL (samengesteld door het Instituut voor Nederlandse Lexicologie in opdracht van de Nederlandse Taalunie (1995). Den Haag – Antwerpen: Sdu Uitgevers/Standaard Uitgeverij.

Konvertierung ungarischer DPs ins Deutsche nach dem Kriterium der Definitheit und der Spezifiziertheit

Márton Méhes

1 Einführung

Die Konvertierung der ung. Artikel in ihre dt. Entsprechungen ist sowohl für den Sprachunterricht als auch für die kontrastive Forschung ein interessantes Problem. Einen aktuellen Beitrag insbesondere zum Problem der Verschmelzungen aus Präposition und Artikel und ihren Korrelaten im Ungarischen bildet Canisius (1995). Aus diesem Beitrag geht u.a. hervor, warum die beiden ung. Phrasen *a moziba* bzw. *moziba* gleichermaßen mit *ins Kino* übersetzt werden, wobei *ins Kino* jedoch zwei verschiedene Fälle in sich vereint. Wir werden auf der Basis von Canisius (1995) weiterfragen und erforschen, warum z.B. die kursiv gesetzten Phrasen in den ung. Sätzen 1) und 2) mit den kursiven Phrasen in den dt. Sätzen 1') und 2') übersetzt werden.

1) *Motorkerékpárral* ütközött egy személygépkocsi tegnap Iharosberénynél.
2) *Egy motorkerékpárról* áradozott nekem.
1') Ein PKW kollidierte gestern *mit einem Motorrad* bei Iharosberény.
2') Er schwärmte mir *von einem Motorrad* vor.

Es ist nämlich erstaunlich, daß die ung. Phrase in 1) mit dem Nullartikel steht und in 2) mit dem unbestimmten Artikel (*egy*), wohingegen der dt. Ausdruck sowohl in 1') als auch in 2') den unbestimmten Artikel (*einem*) benutzt. Wie ist dieser Unterschied zu erklären? Kann man für solche Unterschiede Regeln formulieren?

In der vorliegenden Arbeit wird der Versuch unternommen, die Skizze eines generellen Modells für die Konvertierung der ung. Artikel (im Kontext) ins Deutsche zu entwerfen. Das Ziel ist, für jede beliebige ung. DP – mit dem bestimmten, dem unbestimmten und dem Nullartikel – die dt. Entsprechung vorauszusagen.

2 Die Merkmale DEF und SPEC

Wir gehen davon aus, daß alle DPs des Ungarischen und des Deutschen als eine einfache Merkmalkombination der Merkmale [+/-DEF] (Definitheit vs Indefinitheit) und [+/-SPEC] (Spezifiziertheit vs Nicht-Spezifiziertheit) zu beschreiben sind. Nach unserer Hypothese sollte eine ung. DP mit einer beliebigen Kombination dieser Merkmale mit einer DP der gleichen Kombination ins Deutsche übersetzt werden. Die Kombination der Merkmale wird im Ungarischen durch eines der drei determinierenden Elemente (definiter Artikel, indefiniter Artikel oder Null-Artikel) realisiert. Da sich die Artikelwahl im Ungarischen und im Deutschen nicht deckt, ergibt sich die Frage, was für ein Artikel für eine bestimmte Merkmalkombination im Deutschen steht und warum (s. dazu Kap. 3).

Zuerst sollten jedoch die Merkmale DEF und SPEC näher definiert werden. Diese Merkmalpaare tragen eindeutig *semantische* Informationen.

2.1   Das Merkmal +/-DEF

Referenziell *definit* ist ein „identifizierter" Gegenstand (vgl. Heger 1983:101) als Einzelobjekt oder eine homogene Menge von Objekten mit der gleichen Eigenschaft, wo die Bezeichnung in ‚alle x' konvertiert werden kann (generische Ausdrücke). Hier wird eine bestimmte Menge aus der Menge der Mengen referenziell identifiziert. *Indefinit* ist ein referenziell nicht identifizierter Gegenstand.

2.2   Das Merkmal +/-SPEC

„Das Merkmal SPEZIFIZIERT gilt für Gegenstände, von deren realer und individueller Existenz der Sprecher/Schreiber weiß, auch wenn er sie nicht eindeutig identifizieren kann oder will" (Grimm 1989:97). Mengentheoretisch formuliert heißt das, daß der Sprecher/Schreiber eine Präkonzeption über eine Menge von Gegenständen besitzt (z.b. auf Grund von Vorerwähnung), doch keiner der Gegenstände in der Menge wird als Einzelobjekt in seiner „individuellen Existenz" identifiziert.

„Das Merkmal UNSPEZIFIZIERT gilt für (beliebige) Gegenstände, die zwar über die für ihre Klasse typischen Eigenschaften verfügen, von deren tatsächlicher und individueller Existenz der Sprecher aber unter Umständen nichts Genaues weiß. Für seine Kommunikationsabsicht genügt – falls vorhanden – ein beliebiger Gegenstand mit diesen für die Klasse typischen Eigenschaften." (Grimm 1989:96f)

3   Die ungarischen und die deutschen Artikel

Im Ungarischen stehen insgesamt drei Artikeltypen zur Verfügung: der bestimmte Artikel (*a, az*), der unbestimmte Artikel (*egy*) und der Nullartikel. Die Artikel sind – da es viel mehr morphosemantische Inhalte und syntaktische Funktionen gibt als drei – polyfunktionale Morpheme. Untersuchen wir dazu als Beispiel die Ambiguität des Satzes 3):

3) Issza a kávét.

Die Übersetzung dieses Satzes ins Deutsche erfolgt gemäß den zwei Bedeutungen von 3) einmal mit dem Nullartikel, einmal mit dem definiten Artikel:

3') Er trinkt den Kaffee (, der gerade in seine Tasse ausgeschenkt wurde).

3'')Er trinkt Kaffee. (Er pflegt Kaffee zu trinken.)

Auf den Grund für die dt. Artikelwahl kommen wir noch zurück. Wir sollten jetzt zeigen, welche Artikelformen in dt. DPs oder PPs in Frage kommen. Der bedeutendste Unterschied zwischen Ungarisch und Deutsch ist der, daß am dt. Artikel im Gegensatz zum Ungarischen die nominalen Kategorien Genus, Kasus und Numerus markiert werden. Wenn wir die (aus Ágel 1996:20 übernommenen) Sätze 4), 5) und 6) vergleichen, sehen wir, aus welchen Bestandteilen sich der dt. Artikel zusammensetzt, und in welchem Zusammenhang die Bestandteile zum determinierten Nomen stehen:

4) Ich muß zum Arzt gehen.
5) Ich muß zu einem Arzt gehen.
6) Ich muß zu dem Arzt (in der Josephstraße) gehen.

Wie Ágel (ebd.) schreibt, ist „das Flexiv *-(e)m* [in *zum* verantwortlich] für die Aktualisierung, der Artikel *ein-* für die Partikularisierung und der Artikel *d-* für die Individuierung".
Der sog. definite oder bestimmte Artikel besteht also aus der Kombination zweier Elemente, aus einem *d*-Element, das für die Individuierung des Nomens im Kontext verantwortlich ist, und aus einem Flexiv, dem Genus/Kasus/Numerus-Marker (*-(e)s* in *des*, *-(e)m* in *dem*), der für die Aktualisierung des Nomens zuständig ist. Da die Artikelformen also selbst segmentiert werden können, besteht für das Deutsche die Möglichkeit, die einzelnen Elemente auch unabhängig voneinander zu verwenden. Dadurch entsteht der zweite wichtige Unterschied zwischen den beiden Sprachen. Einerseits kennt das Deutsche neben den Vollformen des Artikels reduzierte Formen mit neuer Funktion, andererseits können reduzierte Formen mit Präpositionen verschmolzen werden (*beim, im, vom, zum, ins* etc.). Die „schwachen Artikel" (Harweg 1989) weisen eine enklitische und eine proklitische Version auf (vgl. Canisius 1995:122), die zueinander in Opposition stehen:

7) Er geht aufs Gymnasium.
8) Ich geh' auf s'Adalbert-Stifter-Gymnasium.

In 7) wird *aufs Gymnasium* „pseudogenerisch" gebraucht, es „bezeichnet nämlich eine Art von – individualisierter – Institution" (Harweg 1989:18). In 8) ist *auf s' A.-S.-Gymnasium* „semideiktisch", und zwar insofern, als das Denotat dieses Ausdrucks „nicht direkt (...), sondern indirekt, nämlich dadurch, daß Sprecherin und Adressat sich in einem Revier befinden, (...) deiktisch determiniert ist" (Harweg 1989:3). Zu diesem Revier zählt auch das betroffene Gymnasium.
Insgesamt sprechen wir im Fall des Deutschen über vier mögliche Artikelformen – von denen die vollen Formen noch polyfunktional sind -, die als Äquivalente der drei ungarischen Artikel bei einer Übersetzung zur Verfügung stehen:

a.   der starke bestimmte Artikel („Vollform")
b.   der schwache bestimmte Artikel
b.1 der (pseudogenerische) enklitische schwache Artikel
b.2 der (semideiktische) proklitische schwache Artikel
c.   der unbestimmte Artikel
d.   der Nullartikel.

4   Die einzelnen Fälle der ungarisch-deutschen DP-Konvertierung

I   [+D, +S]

I.1 a/az → *der/die/das*

9) A kutya még nem evett semmit.

9') Der Hund hat noch nichts gefressen.

Fangen wir mit dem klarsten Fall an. Satz 9) und seine dt. Entsprechung setzen voraus, daß der in Rede stehende Hund aus dem Kontext bekannt oder deiktisch erreichbar ist. Es wird ein konkretes Objekt benannt aus einer Menge ähnlicher Objekte. Die Identifizierbarkeit (Heger 1983:101) als Bedingung der Definitheit ist gegeben. Damit verbunden ist die reale Existenz des Gegenstandes ebenfalls gegeben, was per definitionem Spezifiziertheit gewährleistet.

I.2   *a/az* → proklitisches, semideiktisches *s'*

10) Az Adalbert Stifter Gimnáziumba járok.

10') Ich geh auf s'Adalbert Stifter Gymnasium.

Semideiktische Artikelreste unterscheiden sich von Vollformen dadurch, daß sie ausschließlich die Merkmalkombination [+D, +S] aufweisen, wogegen die vollen Formen nichtspezifizierte Inhalte determinieren können (s. Punkt II). Die Ersetzung des semideiktischen Artikelrests durch die Vollform ist in vielen Fällen – so auch in 10) – angebracht.

Die Identifizierbarkeit à la Heger (s.o.) ist gewährleistet, es wird ein konkretes Objekt benannt. Die Spezifiziertheit ist durch die Semi-Deixis gewährleistet.

II   [+D, -S]

II.1 a/az → *der/die/das*

11) A kutya emlősállat.

11') Der Hund ist ein Säugetier.

In neutralen generischen Sätzen verwendet das Ungarische den definiten Artikel. Das entspricht dem dt. Artikelgebrauch. Die Definitheit ist dadurch gegeben, daß der generische Ausdruck auf eine Menge von Objekten referiert, und in dieser Menge sind alle Exemplare eines Genus vorhanden. *A kutya* bzw. *der Hund* ist generisch durch *minden kutya* bzw. *alle Hunde* zu paraphrasieren. An diesem Punkt scheint die bisherige Auffassung über Definitheit ins Schwanken zu kommen. Laut Heger (1983) sind nämlich generische Ausdrücke am wenigsten definit, da referenziell kaum identifiziert werden kann. Das ist auch richtig, wenn man als Denotat des Ausdrucks weiterhin ein Einzelobjekt nehmen will, und nicht eine homogene Menge. Doch wenn man die Menge aller Hunde als konkretes Objekt behandelt, sieht man, daß für die Menge die referenzielle Identität herzustellen ist. Die tatsächliche Identität der Denotate (in der Menge) ist dem Sprecher nicht bekannt, ausschließlich die Eigenschaft, nach der die Menge definiert ist. Der Ausdruck ist also nicht spezifiziert.

Generische Ausdrücke werden auch mit Hilfe des indefiniten Artikels gebildet:

12) Egy kutyának négy lába van.
12') Ein Hund hat vier Beine.

In diesem Fall weisen die indefiniten Phrasen in beiden Sprachen die Merkmale [-D, -S] auf. Diese Sätze drücken eine Norm aus, die durch die Paraphrase *Ein Hund hat normalerweise vier Beine* wiederzugeben ist. Die deklarative Bedeutung des generischen Satzes in 11) wird hier durch eine zusätzliche Information ergänzt. Der indefinite Artikel ist berechtigt, weil wir die Zugehörigkeit eines beliebigen Exemplars zur Menge der Hunde thematisieren.

II.2 *a/az* → $\emptyset$

13) Az arany fém.
13') Gold ist ein Metall.

Aus der Sicht des Ungarischen besteht zwischen den Sätzen 11) und 13) überhaupt kein Unterschied. Interessant ist nur, daß im Deutschen statt des definiten Artikels 11) der Nullartikel erscheint 10). In diesem Fall haben wir es mit einem „fixierten Artikelgebrauch" (Heger 1989:103) zu tun. Auf völlig arbiträre Weise verwenden das Ungarische und das Französische vor Stoffnamen den bestimmten Artikel, während das Deutsche und das Englische das nicht tun. Das heißt aber nicht, daß das im Deutschen gar nicht möglich wäre. Statt 13') kann man auch den korrekten Satz

13'') Das Gold ist ein Metall.

verwenden. In diesem Fall ist eine „sekundäre Artikelfunktion" (ibid.) anzutreffen, die Unterscheidung eines Genus.
    Wenn der bestimmte Artikel in diesen Ausdrücken erlaubt ist und sonst der Nullartikel ein fixierter Artikelgebrauch zu sein scheint, ist es kein Wunder, daß die Merkmale [+D, -S] mit denen der Sätze 11) und 11') übereinstimmen. Die Ausdrücke *az arany/Gold* referieren hier wiederum auf eine Menge von Objekten, nämlich auf alle Objekte der Welt, die aus Gold sind. Es wird auf eine konkrete Menge referiert (= Definitheit), ohne weitere Informationen über die tatsächliche Existenz der Exemplare (= Nichtspezifiziertheit).
    Als Zwischenergebnis können wir festhalten, daß sich I.2 genau so zu I.1 verhält wie II.2 zu II.1. M.a.W., die reduzierten Artikelformen – und in diesem Zusammenhang betrachten wir auch den Nullartikel als reduzierte und zwar als „maximal" reduzierte Form – weisen hier die gleichen Merkmale auf wie die vollen Formen. Das ist auch nicht verwunderlich, da die schwachen Formen u.U. durch die Vollformen ersetzt werden können, ohne daß die Grammatikalität der Phrase beeinflußt würde. Der Unterschied innerhalb der reduzierten Formen zeigt uns, daß auch die vollen Formen unterschiedlicher Art sein müssen, und das wird mit dem Unterschied in der Spezifiziertheit erklärt.

III [-D, -S]

III.1 $\emptyset$ → pseudogenerisches, enklitisches *-s*

14) Moziba megyünk.

14') Wir gehen ins Kino.

Canisius (1995) untersucht u.a. die ung. Ausdrücke *moziba* (*ins Kino*) und *a moziba* (*in s' Kino*), und bringt folgendes Ergebnis: „[Die] artikellose ungarische Form steht da, wo die deutsche Verschmelzung pseudogenerische Bedeutung hat. [Die] artikelhaltige ungarische Form steht da, wo die deutsche Verschmelzung indirekt deiktische, semideiktische, Funktion hat" (117).

Letzterer Fall lag in I.2 vor. Die fragliche PP in Satz 14) und ihr dt. Äquivalent sind pseudogenerisch, sie referieren auf „eine Art von – individualisierter – Institution" (Harweg 1989:3). Der springende Punkt ist dabei, daß Ausdrücke wie *moziba megy* und *ins Kino gehen* nicht auf eine Phrase mit dem unbestimmten Artikel zurückzuführen sind. Sie übernehmen vielmehr die Bedeutung eines komplexen Verbs.

> „Mit dem *mozi* [in 14)] ist kein bestimmtes Kino gemeint: [14)] meint vielmehr soviel wie *Ich habe mir gestern einen Kinofilm angesehen* bzw. *Ich war gestern in einem Film*" (Canisius 1995:107).

Weitere Beispiele für solche pseudogenerischen Gefüge gibt es sowohl mit Verschmelzung/Präposition (*színházba megy* und *ins Theater gehen, iskolába jár* und *zur Schule gehen*) als auch ohne Präposition (*autót vezet* und *autofahren/Auto fahren, kerékpározik* und *radfahren/Rad fahren*).

Nicht spezifiziert sind die pseudogenerischen Ausdrücke aus dem gleichen Grunde wie die generischen Ausdrücke in II. Indefinit sind sie deswegen, weil die genannten Objekte (Kino, Theater etc.) weder ein referenziell identifiziertes Objekt noch eine konkrete, scharf umrissene Menge darstellen (sie beziehen sich nicht auf *ein* Kino oder *ein* Theater).

III.2 ∅ → ein/eine

15) Apáca érkezett.

15') Eine Nonne ist angekommen.

Wieder eine Konstruktion mit dem Nullartikel im Ungarischen, wie in Punkt III.1, nur wird dieser Ausdruck mit dem indefiniten Artikel übersetzt. Der Unterschied zu III.1 ist der, daß Satz 15) in der Tat ohne Änderung der ursprünglichen Bedeutung auf einen Satz mit dem indefiniten Artikel zurückgeführt werden kann:

15'') Érkezett egy apáca. = 15) Apáca érkezett.

Die pseudogenerischen Ausdrücke, die ja im Ungarischen nicht auf einen Satz mit dem indefiniten Artikel zurückgeführt werden können, erscheinen auch im Deutschen ohne den indefiniten Artikel und werden – falls möglich – mit dem pseudogenerischen enklitischen Artikel realisiert. Alle Phrasen hingegen, die selbst mit dem indefiniten Artikel stehen oder auf eine solche Konstruktion zurückgeführt werden können, werden ins Deutsche mit dem indefiniten Artikel übersetzt.

Die Indefinitheit solcher Ausdrücke ist dadurch begründet, daß sie keine referenziell identifizierten Objekte oder eine konkrete Menge, sondern ein unbestimmtes Denotat bezeichnen. Sie sind nicht spezifiziert, weil die konkrete Existenz vom Sprecher und Hörer nicht wahrnehmbar sein muß. M. a. W., die Existenz des Objektes ist in Zeit und Raum nicht festgelegt, wir haben keine Vorkenntnisse über das Denotat.

III.3 egy → *ein/eine*

16) Egy apáca érkezett.

16') Eine Nonne ist angekommen.

Da 16) – wie in III.2 gezeigt – mit 15) äquivalent ist, gelten die gleichen Bedingungen für die dt. Übersetzung und für die Erklärung der Indefinitheit und der Nichtspezifiziertheit.

IV [-D, +S]

egy → *ein*/eine

17) *Egy* apáca megérkezett.

17') *Eine* Nonne ist schon angekommen.

Zu 17) und 17') sollten wir uns die Situation vorstellen, daß wir in einem Zimmer sitzen und fünf Nonnen erwarten. Plötzlich stürzt jemand ins Zimmer und äußert 17) bzw. 17') mit Akzent auf *egy* und *meg-/eine* und *an-*. Die Verwendung des indefiniten Artikels ist korrekt, weil wir aus einer (momentan konkreten) Menge ein Exemplar herausnehmen. Der Unterschied zu den Fällen in Punkt III ist die Spezifiziertheit der indefiniten Ausdrücke. Die läßt sich dadurch erklären, daß die konkrete Existenz des bezeichneten Objektes von Sprecher und Hörer wahrgenommen wird; sie haben eine Präkonzeption über die Menge, zu der auch das herausgegriffene – jedoch nicht identifizierte – Exemplar gehört.

5 Einige Konsequenzen

5.1 Erklärung einer ungarischen Ambiguität

Auf der Basis des bisher Gesagten kehren wir nun zu dem – wie die Übersetzungen gezeigt haben – ambigen Satz 3) und seinen möglichen dt. Entsprechungen zurück. Die Erklärung der ung. Ambiguität durch den dt. Artikelgebrauch bereitet im Sinn von Kapitel 4 keine Schwierigkeiten mehr. Satz 3') entspricht der Konvertierung nach der Merkmalkombination [+D, +S], genau wie im Fall I.1. Interessanter ist Satz 3''), der regelgerecht die Merkmale [+D, -S] aufweist und in dem *Kaffee* als Stoffname zu interpretieren ist; sonst ist der Nullartikel kaum erklärbar (vgl. Fall II.2). Und tatsächlich: Im Ungarischen ist diese Bedeutung des Satzes eindeutig darauf ausgerichtet, daß derjenige, der den Kaffee trinkt, dieses nicht nur regelmäßig tut, sondern diesen Stoff (Kaffee) auch problemlos verträgt. Das Nomen steht in dem Satz offensichtlich als Stoffname. Daher ist die dt. Übersetzung mit dem Nullartikel korrekt.

Wenn jemandem diese Erklärung von 3'') keine ausreichende Antwort liefern sollte, kann der Nullartikel und die allgemeine, die Gewohnheit des Kaffetrinkens ausdrückende Bedeutung auch anders erklärt werden. Dazu werden wir den Ausdruck *Kaffee trinken* als ein komplexes Verb behandeln, in das ein Nomen inkorporiert ist.

5.2   Inkorporierung

Im Zusammenhang mit Fall III.1 haben wir pseudogenerische Gefüge mit Verschmelzung (Präposition) und ohne Präposition untersucht. Gemeinsam ist diesen Gefügen erstens, daß sie sowohl im Ungarischen als auch im Deutschen der Merkmalkombination [+D, -S] entsprechen. In den Verschmelzungen werden die nominalen Flexive enklitisch an die Präposition gefügt. In den Ausdrücken ohne Präposition ist diese Enklitisierung nicht möglich und auch nicht nötig, da der Nullartikel die genannte Merkmalkombination ohnehin ausdrücken kann. Zweitens ist den Gefügen gemeinsam, daß sie im Gegensatz zu den [-D, -S]-Phrasen in III.2 und III.3 in keinem Fall auf einen Satz mit unbestimmtem Artikel zurückzuführen sind. Sehen wir uns dazu die Beispiele 18), 19) an:

18)   ohne Präposition:
      a. autót vezet (= Auto fahren) ≠ vezet egy autót (= ein Auto fahren)
      b. kávét iszik (= Kaffee trinken) ≠ iszik egy kávét (= einen Kaffee trinken)
19)   zwei weitere Beispiele mit Präposition:
      a. fodrászhoz megy (= zum Friseur gehen) ≠ elmegy egy fodrászhoz (= zu
         einem Friseur gehen)
      b. kinevez vkit igazgatónak (= jn zum Direktor ernennen) ≠ *kinevez vkit
         egy igazgatónak (= *jn zu einem Direktor ernennen)

Die Ausdrücke autót vesz (= ein Auto kaufen) und autót vezet (= Auto fahren) scheinen sich auf den ersten Blick sehr ähnlich zu sein. Unsere Regel der gemeinsamen Merkmale in III.2 besagt jedoch, daß für die Übersetzung der Phrase ins Deutsche mit dem unbestimmten Artikel auch der ung. Satz auf eine Phrase mit dem ung. unbestimmten Artikel egy zurückführbar sein muß, und autót vesz ist in der Tat auf die Phrase vesz egy autót (= ein Auto kaufen) zurückzuführen. Die Merkmalregeln halten einander ähnliche Phrasen – wie autót vezet und autót vesz – eindeutig auseinander und erklären uns die dt. Äquivalente.

Nach der alten dt. Rechtschreibung wurden inkorporierende Verben wie autofahren oder radfahren zusammengeschrieben. Nach unserer Überlegung ist das eine absolut berechtigte Schreibweise gewesen, da sie die Inkorporierung abbildet und z.B. eindeutig ausdrückt, daß ein ung. Verb wie kerékpározik auch im Deutschen einem einzigen Verb entspricht.

6   Literatur

ÁGEL, Vilmos (1996): Finites Substantiv. In: Zeitschrift für Germanistische Linguistik 24, 16-57.
CANISIUS, Peter (1995): Moziban, a moziban und im Kino: Verschmelzungen aus Präposition und
    Artikel im Deutschen und ihre Korrelate im Ungarischen. In: Studien zur Germanistik 3, 103-142.
GRIMM, Hans-Jürgen (²1989): Lexikon zum Artikelgebrauch. Leipzig: Enzyklopädie.
HARWEG, Roland (1989): Schwache und starke Artikelformen im gesprochenen Neuhochdeutsch. In:
    Zeitschrift für Dialektologie und Linguistik 56.1, 1-31.

HEGER, Klaus (1983): Was ist ‚Definitheit'? In: Faust, M. et al. (Hrsg.): Allgemeine Sprachwissenschaft, Sprachtypologie und Textlinguistik. Festschrift für P. Hartmann, Tübingen: Narr (Tübinger Beiträge zur Linguistik 215), 99-104.

HEIM, Irene (1991): Artikel und Definitheit. In: Stechow, A. et al. (Hrsg.): Semantik. Ein internationales Handbuch der zeitgenössischen Forschung. Berlin – New York: W. de Gruyter (= HSK 6), 487-535.

Konsonantenäquivalenz im Jakutischen und Deutschen

Natalja Popova

1   Einleitung

Jakutisch sprechen die im Nord-Osten Sibiriens lebenden Jakuten.
Jakutisch wird der grammatischen Struktur und teilweise dem Wortschatz entsprechend zur türkischen Sprachfamilie gerechnet. Bekanntlich umfaßt die türkische Sprachfamilie etwa 30 Sprachen. Von den anderen Vertretern dieser zur Turksprachfamilie gehörenden Sprachen sind die Jakuten durch mehrere Tausende Kilometer getrennt.

Kein Problem löst heute derart lebhafte Diskussionen in der russischen Turkologie aus wie die Suche nach einer Klärung der Herkunft der Jakuten und ihrer Sprache: Wo kommen die Jakuten in Jakutien eigentlich her, und welche Sprache haben sie mitgebracht? Aber nicht dies ist die Fragestellung meines heutigen Referates, sondern die Konsonantensubstitution anhand der konfrontativen Analyse des Deutschen und des Jakutischen.

Die konfrontative Analyse ist heute nicht mehr Prärogative der Sprachwissenschaftler, sondern gewinnt immer mehr an Gewicht für Fremdsprachendidaktiker. Kenntnisse, die sich auf die Feststellung, Beschreibung und Erklärung von aufgetretenen Fehlern bei Lernenden beziehen, könnten der Fremdsprachendidaktik eine methodisch und didaktisch bezogene Unterrichtshilfe zur Verfügung stellen.

Der fremde Akzent wird in der Regel durch den negativen Transfer von muttersprachlichen Gewohnheiten, die in der Zielsprache keine Entsprechung haben, erklärt. Wenn ich [ˈkafaril] statt [gavaˊril] höre, bin ich mir sicher, dass ein Deutscher russisch spricht. Durch die Zerlegung des im Russischen unbekannten Lautes [ŋ] in [n] und [g], einem schwachen Geräusch beim [ʃ] und das Zungenspitzen-R im Wort [ʃprɪŋn] ist die Aussprache eines Russen erkennbar. Typisch jakutisch wäre es, auf Deutsch [sɪmeʀ] statt [tʂimɐ] zu sagen.

2   Zum Begriff der Äquivalenz

Ich möchte heute auf die phonologischen Ähnlichkeiten der jakutischen und der deutschen Sprache eingehen. Der zu untersuchende Gegenstand des Referates soll das Konsonantensystem des Jakutischen und Deutschen und die mittels der kontrastiven Analyse festgestellte Konsonantenäquivalenz in diesen Sprachen sein. Unter Äquivalenz wird hier die Substitution des Lautes der Fremdsprache durch den gleichen oder ähnlichen der Muttersprache verstanden.

Es wird logischerweise erwartet, daß die Ähnlichkeit der Laute der Muttersprache mit denen der Zielsprache für die Lernenden kein besonderer Auslöser für einen Verstoß gegen die korrekte Aussprache ist.

Es ist bekannt, daß es in den Sprachen, die in der Welt gesprochen werden, keine zwei identischen Laute gibt. Laute, die akustisch und physiologisch ähnlich sind, können in absolut unterschiedlichen phonologischen Systemen organisiert sein. Um dies zu prüfen, nehmen wir beispielsweise das Wort „Park", das man in jedem Wörterbuch des Deutschen finden kann. Alle vier Phoneme (p), (a), (r) und (k) sind auch im Phonemsystem des Jakutischen vorhanden.

Der jakutische Plosiv (p) wird im Unterschied zum deutschen stark aspirierten, medial implosiv und final explosiv erzeugten (p) sehr schwach aspiriert und immer implosiv artikuliert. Der Vokal [a] ist im Deutschen ein Mittelzungenvokal, im Jakutischen ein Hinterzungenvokal. Der uvulare Vibrant (R) wäre bei einer deutschen Aussprache des gegebenen Wortes als stimmhafter Frikativ realisiert, bei einer jakutischen Aussprache dagegen als apiko-alveolarer Vibrant und je nach der Stellung des Wortes im Satz zwei- oder dreischlägig. Der jakutischen Phonotaktik entsprechend kommt das Phonem (p) nie in der initialen Position, und das Phonem (k) nie in der finalen Position vor.

3 Konsonantensystem des Jakutischen

Im Jakutischen gibt es 31 Konsonantenphoneme, von denen 14 den Konsonantenphonemen des Deutschen ähnlich sind. Die jakutischen Phoneme sind im folgenden *kursiv* gedruckt. Die Konsonanten der beiden Sprachen sind im wesentlichen ähnlich systematisiert.

3.1 Konsonantenäquivalenz des Deutschen und des Jakutischen

	bilabial	labio-dental	Alveolar	palato-alveolar	palatal	velar	uvular	glottal	pharyn-gal
Plosiv	p *p p:*		t *t t:*			k *k k:*		ʔ	
	b b		d *d d:*			*g g g:*			
Frikativ		f	s *s s:*	ʃ	ç *j*	x	χ *χ:*	h	
		v	z		*ŭ j*		*ɦ*		*ħ*
Affrikate		pf	tʃ ts		*č ĵ*				
Nasal	m *m m:*		n *n n*	*ñ*		ŋ *ŋ ŋ:*			
Lateral			l *l l:*						
Vibrant			r				R		

Der obigen Tabelle kann man entnehmen, daß die Systemäquivalenz im wesentlichen in den Bereichen von Plosiven, Nasalen, Lateralen und Vibranten auftritt: jedem Phonem des betroffenen Bereiches des Deutschen entspricht ein Phonem des Jakutischen.

Die Gegenüberstellung von Stimmhaftigkeit und Stimmlosigkeit hat Entsprechungen in drei Fällen:

t - d   p - b   k - g
t - d   p - b   k – g

Eine genaue Analyse der im Deutschen und im Jakutischen äquivalenten Phoneme macht jedoch die Unterschiedlichkeit deutlich, die die phonetischen Spezifika der beiden Sprachen bestimmt. Zu betonen wäre noch einmal, dass Äquivalenzphoneme bei ihrer Realisation beim Sprechen kein Missverstehen hervorrufen.

Den Merkmalen, die den äquivalenten Konsonantenphonemen des Jakutischen und Deutschen ihre Spezifika geben, liegen die starke Muskelspannung der deutschen Konsonanten und die stärkere Aspiration der Plosive zugrunde. In der initialen Position werden die jakutischen Plosive ganz leicht behaucht und in der finalen Position implosiv erzeugt (Djatschkowskij 1977:11). Alle Plosive mit Ausnahme von *(p)* und *(s)*, alle Nasale, *(l)* und *(r)* werden vor und nach den jakutischen Vorderzungenvokalen *(i)*, *(ə)*, *(γ)*, *(θ)* palatalisiert (*t'iir'* – *tɪɪr:* ausdehnen – aufschneiden; *k'ə l'* – *tɪk:* Imp. Komm - schnippen, *s'ir* - *suorat*: Land - Joghurt).

Neben den Differenzen in der Relevanz der Besonderheiten in der Artikulation lassen sich Differenzen in der Distribution erkennen.

Distributionelle Beschränkungen betreffen im Jakutischen die initiale und die finale Position, in der einige Konsonanten entweder nicht vorkommen z.B. *(r)*, *(j)*, *(ŋ)* und *(b)*, *(d)*, *(g)*, *(ĉ)* entsprechend, andere sehr selten, z.B. initiale *(g)* und *(p)*. Im Deutschen erscheint das zu den äquivalenten Konsonanten gehörende (ŋ) im Anlaut ebenfalls nicht, das Vorkommen von (j) ist auf diese Position beschränkt. Das Auftreten von verschiedenen Konsonanten im Deutschen ist durch Kurz- und Langvokale eingeschränkt, für andere gibt es kombinatorische Varianten (Meinhold, Stock 1980: 177).

Die deutsche Phonotaktik ermöglicht es, dass bis zu drei anlautende Konsonanten aufeinander folgen wie in „Strumpf" und bis zu fünf auslautende wie in „kämpfst".

Im Anlaut von jakutischen Wörtern gibt es keine Doppelkonsonanten. Dies betrifft auch den Auslaut mit Ausnahme der Konsonantenverbindungen *[lt]* und *[rt]* (*bult* – Beute; *t'üör't* - vier), während im Inlaut das Maximum der Kombination meist zwei Konsonanten beträgt. Deswegen tritt in Fremdwörtern ein Vokal, der die Ansammlung von Konsonanten zerteilt. Z. B. „*χaatĉɪstɪba*" - russisch: katschestwo – Qualität, auf.

Die Konsonantenkombination des Jakutischen ist im wesentlichen auch qualitativ beschränkt. Z.B. können die stimmlosen Konsonanten nicht neben den stimmhaften Konsonanten oder nach den Sonoranten (m, n, ŋ, r) stehen. Im Deutschen ist die Folge Nicht-Sonor/Sonor (meistens Liquid oder Nasalkonsonant) im Anlaut und im Auslaut in umgekehrter Abfolge möglich (Meinhold; Stock 1980:181).

4   Plosive

Im Bereich der Plosive hat jedes Phonem des Deutschen außer des Knacklautes einen Äquivalent im Jakutischen. In bezug auf die Artikulationsmerkmale unterscheiden sich die Phoneme durch die explosive – implosive Realisation in Auslaut. Wegen der schwachen Muskelspannung des Sprechapparats tendieren die Plosive *(b)* und *(g)* zu den entsprechenden Frikativen. Differenzen gibt es auch in der Relevanz der physikalischen Merkmalen und in der Distribution. Die Phonotaktik des Jakutischen ist dadurch gekennzeichnet, dass *(p)* im Anlaut und *(k)* im Auslaut sowie *(d)* und *(g)* im Auslaut nicht vorkommen, während dies im Deutschen möglich ist. *I*m Unterschied zum entsprechenden deutschen Phonem wird das jakutische *(k)* nur in der finalen Position mit schwacher Aspiration erzeugt z.B. *k'iħi – balιk'*: Mensch – Fisch.

P	*bilabial, plosiv, oral, stimmlos, ungespannt, obstruent, schwach aspiriert, final implosiv*
p	bilabial, plosiv, oral, stimmlos, gespannt, obstruent, stark, aspiriert, final explosiv
b	*bilabial, plosiv, oral, stimmlos, gespannt, obstruent, schwach aspiriert, final nicht vorkommend*
b	bilabial, plosiv, oral, stimmlos, gespannt, obstruent, stark aspiriert, final, explosiv
t	*alveolar, plosiv, oral, stimmlos, ungespannt, obstruent, schwach aspiriert, final implosiv*
t	alveolar, plosiv, oral, stimmlos, gespannt, obstruent, stark aspiriert, final explosiv
d	*alveolar, plosiv, oral, stimmlos, ungespannt, obstruent, schwach aspiriert final nicht vorkommend*
d	alveolar, plosiv, oral, stimmlos, gespannt, obstruent, stark aspiriert, final explosiv
k	*velar, plosiv, oral, stimmlos, ungespannt, obstruent, final schwach aspiriert, final implosiv*
k	velar, plosiv, oral, stimmlos, gespannt, obstruent, stark aspiriert, final explosiv
g	*velar, plosiv, oral, stimmlos, ungespannt, obstruent, schwach aspiriert, final nicht vorkommend*
g	velar, plosiv, oral, stimmlos, gespannt, obstruent, stark aspiriert, final implosiv

5   Nasale

Die deutschen Nasale können durch äquivalente Nasale des Jakutischen ersetzt werden.

m	*bilabial, nasal, sonorant, ungespannt, dauernd, final explosiv*
m	bilabial, nasal, sonorant, gespannt, dauernd, final explosiv
n	*alveolar, nasal, sonorant, ungespannt, dauernd*
n	alveolar, nasal, sonorant, gespannt, dauernd
ŋ	*Velar, nasal, sonsorant, ungespannt, dauernd*
ŋ	Velar, nasal, sonsorant, gespannt, dauernd

6   Laterale

Das Phonem (l) gibt es in beiden Sprachen.

l *alveolar, lateral, sonorant, ungespannt, dauernd*
ł   alveolar, lateral, sonorant, gespannt, dauernd

Das jakutische *(l)* hat 4 Allophone:

• nichtpalatalisiert vor und nach den Hinterzungenvokalen z.b. *la:ħ, oul*
• palatalisiert vor und nach den Vorderzungenvokalen z.b. *l'θk'θö, kuθ l'*
• velarisiert in der Kombination Vokal + l + Konsonant z.b. *ałtan, s ı łtaħ.*
• palatalisiertes Mittelzunge – l vor *č* und *ĵ* z.b. *bul čut , ı alĵ ı t.*

7   Vibrant

Das Konsonantismus der jakutischen Sprache verfügt über den apiko – alveolaren Vibrant *r,* der den deutschen uvularen Vibrant R und seine Allophone (stimmhafter und stimmloser Frikativ sowie vokalisiertes r) substituieren kann, ohne die Kommunikation zu stören.

Es ist bekannt, dass in Deutschland zwei Varianten des Phonems (r) – das Zäpfchen - r und das Zungenspitzen - r – gängig sind und je nach regionaler Herkunft des Sprechers frei gegeneinander ausgetauscht werden können. Der apikalalveolare Vibrant der jakutischen Sprache hat drei positionsbedingte Realisationsarten: die einsschlägige Realisierung kommt in der intervokalen Position vor, die zwei- oder dreischlägige je nach der Stellung des Wortes im Satz.

r *apikal , alveolar, vibrant, sonorant, gespannt, initial nicht vorkommend*
R   uvular, vibrant, sonorant, gespannt

8   Frikative

Der frikative Bereich ist im Jakutischen schwach belegt. Nur zwei Phoneme des Jakutischen sind hier als Äqiuvalente des Deutschen zu nennen:

s *alveolar, frikativ, oral, stimmlos, gespannt, nicht obstruent, dauernd*
s   alveolar, frikativ, oral, stimmlos, gespannt, obstruent, dauernd

In der Phonologie der jakutischen Sprache gibt es zwei Phoneme, die ungefähr dem deutschen (j) entsprechen: *(j)* und *(ŭ).*

$ŭ$ *palatal, frikativ, oral, stimmhaft, gespannt, nicht obstruent, dauernd*
ĵ   *palatal, frikativ, nasal, stimmhaft, gespannt, nicht obstruent, dauernd*
j   palatal, frikativ, oral, stimmhaft, gespannt, kein obstruent, dauernd

9   Affrikate

Die Affrikatenäquivalenz ist durch das Paar (tʃ) - *(č)* belegt:

č   *alveolar, affrikate, oral, stimmlos, gespannt, obstruent, dauernd*
ʧ   alveolar, affrikate, oral, stimmlos, gespannt, nicht obstruent, dauernd

10   Konsequenzen für den Phonetikunterricht

Jene in beiden Sprachen scheinbar gleich oder ähnlich artikulierten Laute, die beim Ausspracheerwerb häufig außer acht gelassen werden, können die korrekte Aussprache erschweren. Die Überwindung der durch die Konsonantenäquivalenz verursachten Ausspracheunzulänglichkeiten sollte zunächst durch die Beherrschung des eigenen Sprechapparats, durch bewußte Artikulationsbewegungen und schließlich durch Kenntnisse der phonologisch – allophonischen Ähnlichkeiten der Ausgangs- sowie der Zielsprache ermöglicht werden. Die konfrontative Analyse weist auf mögliche Fehler hin, läßt den Studierenden die Muttersprache als Hilfsmittel beim Lernen einer Zielsprache verwenden und gibt dadurch dem Lehrenden und dem Lernenden Mittel in die Hand, um mit weniger Energie- und Zeitaufwand das erwünschte Resultat zu erzielen.

11   Literatur

BARASCHKOV, P. (1953): Swukowoj sostav jakutskogo jasyka. Jakutsk: Jakutskoje knishnoe isdatelstwo.

DJATSCHKOWSKIJ, N. (1977): Swukowoj stroj jakutskogo jasyka. Tschast II. Konsonantism. Jakutsk: Jakutskoje knishnoe isdatelstwo.

KRUGER, J.-R. (1962): Yakut Manual. Area Handbook, Grammar, Graded Reader and Glossary. Project N 63.

KHARITONOV, L. (1987): Samoutschitel jakutskogo jasyka. Jakutks: Jakutskoje knishnoe isdatelstwo. Jakutsk.

MEINHOLD, G.; STOCK, E. (1980): Phonologie der deutschen Gegenwartssprache. VEB Bibliographisches Institut Leipzig.

Substantiv-Verb-Kollokationen im deutsch-ungarischen Kontrast

Anna Reder

1   Relevanz der Kollokationen im Sprachunterricht

Der Fremdsprachenerwerb erfordert vom Lerner bekanntlich Kompetenzen auf phonetisch-phonologischer, morphologischer, syntaktischer und lexikalischer Ebene. Bestimmen wir etwas näher, was der Begriff „lexikalische Kenntnisse" beinhaltet. Der Lerner hat sich in diesem Bereich zuerst einmal Vokabeln anzueignen, die ihm in Form von Simplizia, Derivaten und Zusammensetzungen sowie Wortverbindungen (WVB) begegnen. Einen Typ von Wortverbindungen bilden die syntagmatischen Wortverbindungen, die sich bekanntlich weiter untergliedern lassen:

syntagmatische Wortverbindungen

freie syntagmatische WVB   Kollokationen   Phraseologismen

Kollokationen sind im weitesten Sinne Kombinationen von Wörtern, die aufgrund ihrer semantischen Verträglichkeit eine Einheit bilden. Es sind Wortgruppen, die in Texten öfter als statistisch zu erwarten ist, vorkommen. Kollokationen bilden ein spezielles Problem bei der Aneignung lexikalischer Kenntnisse.

Betrachtet man die Kollokationen kontrastiv, sind vor allem die strukturellen Unterschiede auffallend, die aber nicht den Untersuchungsgegenstand bilden. Diese Unterschiede ergeben sich größtenteils dadurch, daß das Ungarische im Vergleich zum Deutschen eher eine agglutinierende und das Deutsche mehr eine flektierende Sprache ist. Kollokationen können auch unter lexikologischem Aspekt sprachspezifisch sein. Beim diesbezüglichenVergleich läßt sich feststellen, daß die äquivalenten Kollokationen durchaus nicht immer aus äquivalenten Elementen bestehen. Ein Vergleichsmodell aus zweigliedrigen Kollokationen könnte wie folgt aussehen. Ich verwende bei den Beispielen Wortartensymbole, die in der einschlägigen Fachliteratur als Bezeichnungen für die Kollokationsbeschaffenheit üblich sind. (a - b steht symbolisch für zweigliedrige Kollokationen)

	a'- b'	*Aufsehen erregen* (S - V) = *feltünést kelt* (S - V)
		Aufsehen (S) = *feltünést* (S), *erregen* (V) = *kelt* (V)
a - b:	a'- c	*einen Kurs belegen* (S - V) = *kurzust felvenni* (S - V)
		Kurs (S) = *kurzust* (S), *belegen* (V) ≠ *felvenni* (V) (= *aufnehmen*)
	e - f	*reichlicher Genuß von Whisky* (A - S -S) = *nem veti meg a whiskyt* (S – V)
		Whisky = *whiskyt*
		reichlicher Genuß ≠ *nem veti meg* (= *nicht verachten*)
	A'	*im Sterben liegen* (S - V) = *haldoklik* (V);

Es gibt Wortkombinationen, die in beiden Sprachen aus den gleichen Bestandteilen bestehen, z.B:

Aufsehen erregen = feltünést kelt, wobei *Aufsehen = feltünés, erregen = kelt.*

Es gibt auch zahlreiche Kollokationen, die sich in einer oder sogar in mehreren Komponenten unterscheiden. Ein ungarischer Deutschlerner kann, beeinflußt durch seine Muttersprache, erklärbare idiomatische Fehler begehen, wie z.B.

*einen Kurs aufnehmen (= szemináriomot felvesz) anstatt *belegen*;

Die Kollokationen, die erst durch einen Wortartenwechsel übersetzbar sind, werden im Modell der Kategorie des völligen Fehlens der Äquivalenz zugeordnet, z.B:

reichlicher Genuß von Whisky = nem veti meg a whiskyt (= Whisky nicht verachten)

Aus der deutschen affirmativen A-S-S-Kollokation wird im Ungarischen eine aus einem negierten Verb und einem Substantiv bestehende Kollokation. Eine selbständige Klasse bilden im Modell des deutsch-ungarischen Vergleichs diejenigen Kollokationen, denen in der jeweils anderen Sprache keine Kollokation entspricht, sondern ein Simplex, z.B:

im Sterben liegen (S - V)= haldoklik (V);

2   Identifizierungsmatrix für Kollokationen

Im folgenden beschäftige ich mich sprachvergleichend mit Substantiv-Verb-Kollokationen und primär mit den Kombinationsmöglichkeiten und Selektionsbeschränkungen ihrer Elemente.

Welche sprachlichen Entitäten als Kollokationen zu bezeichnen sind, dafür gibt es in der germanistischen Linguistik diverse Definitionen. Wenn man die ungarische Literatur zu Rate zieht, bemerkt man, daß der Terminus „Kollokation" nicht verwendet wurde und heute immer noch kaum verwendet wird, sondern lediglich der Oberbegriff „Wortverbindung" („szókapcsolat") oder „Syntagma" existiert. Der Terminus „szókapcsolat" entspricht etwa dem deutschen „Phraseologismus". Gemeinsamkeit in der Terminologie ergibt sich dadurch, daß die phraseologischen Einheiten entweder ins Zentrum oder in die Peripherie eingeordnet werden. Kollokationen, die stabile Wortverbindungen sind und keine Idiomatizität aufweisen, fallen in den Bereich der peripheren phraseologischen Einheiten.

Für die Identifizierung der Kollokationen habe ich auf der Basis der Fachliteratur eine Merkmalmatrix abgeleitet, mit deren Hilfe ich versuche, die Kollokationen von freien Wortverbindungen und von zentralen phraseologischen Einheiten abzugrenzen (Lehr 1998; Feilke/Feilke 1996):

    i)   Mehrgliedrigkeit
    ii) Analysierbarkeit

iii) Asynthetisierbarkeit

iiii) semantische Eigenwertigkeit des Gesamtausdrucks

Die Abgrenzung gegenüber verwandten Kategorien mit Hilfe der obigen Merkmale scheint eine zuverlässige Methode zu bieten, birgt aber in manchen Fällen Identifizierungsschwierigkeiten, erzeugt fließende Grenzen.

„Mehrgliedrigkeit" bezieht sich auf die Formseite der Kollokationen. Sie ist einerseits ein Merkmal zur Abgrenzung von Komposita (Eingliedrigkeit). Andererseits ermöglicht dieses Kriterium, daß Kollokationen, im Sinne von „collocation" bei Firth (1957), auch aus mehr als zwei Komponenten bestehen können. Die heutzutage übliche Verwendung des Terminus „Kollokation" in der Lexikologie rechnet mit zwei Bestandteilen, wie z. B. Basis und Kollokator bei Hausmann (1993). Mit der Kategorie der Mehrgliedrigkeit kann die Zweigliedrigkeit als ein unterer Grenzwert festgelegt werden. Lediglich zweigliedrige Entitäten als Kollokationen zu bezeichnen würde zahlreiche Ausdrücke von der Kategorie der Kollokationen ausschließen, wie z.B. *mit der Maus klicken, die Ehe geht in die Brüche.* Wenn wir die Kollokationen als Realisierungen der Valenz der Verben betrachten, reicht die Zwiegliedrigkeit bei jenen Wortverbindungen auf keinen Fall aus, bei denen ein Bestandteil ein Verb mit einer Präpositionalrektion ist. Wir schließen uns zwar der Subklassifizierung der Kollokationen von Hausmann an und analysieren die Substantiv-Verb-Kollokationen, wobei wir aber einräumen, daß die Binarität lediglich für die autosemantischen Bestandteile der Kollokationen zur Bedingung gemacht wird.

Bei der Inhaltsseite der Kollokationen verwenden wir in Anlehnung an Lehr (1998) das Charakteristikum der Analysierbarkeit. Kollokationen sind analysierbar. Ihre Gesamtbedeutung kann unter Berücksichtigung der syntaktischen Regeln aus den Bedeutungen der einzelnen Komponenten erschlossen werden.

Etwas ausführlicher soll hier auf die Asynthetisierbarkeit eingegangen werden, denn dieses Charakteristikum macht die Kollokationen zu einem fehlerträchtigen Bereich für DaF- Lerner.

Kollokationen sind asynthetisierbar. Das Ersetzen der Komponenten durch Synonyme kann zu ungebräuchlichen Wortkombinationen führen. Nehmen wir das Beispiel *Interesse wecken.* Wenn wir die Kollokation *Interesse wecken* auf das Kriterium der Asynthetisierbarkeit hin überprüfen, kommen wir zu folgendem Ergebnis: Die Synonyme *erwecken, aufwecken* verhalten sich bei der Substitutionsprobe unterschiedlich; *erwecken* ist nämlich verbindbar mit *Interesse,* wobei *aufwecken* Inkompabilität mit *Interesse* aufweist. Wenn wir dieselbe Substitutionsprobe in der äquivalenten ungarischen Kollokation vornehmen, stellen wir fest, daß im Ungarischen auch *aufwecken* als Kollokant auftritt, sogar mit hoher Frequenz. Dieser Unterschied kann eine Erklärung für den oft zu beobachtenden idiomatischen Interferenzfehler **Interesse aufwecken* abgeben.

	Interesse		érdeklődést
wecken	+	kelt	+
erwecken	+	kelt	+
aufwecken	-	felkelt	+

Mit dem vierten Merkmal wird die semantische Funktion der Kollokationen zum Ausdruck gebracht, die von Firth (1957:190) „meaning by collocation" genannt wird. Mit der semantischen Eigenwertigkeit des Gesamtausdrucks (Feilke/Feilke 1996:117) als Kriterium läßt sich die Reichweite des Kollokationsbegriffs über die semantische Determination im Sinne einer Basis-Kollokator-Relation hinaus ergänzen. Als Beispiel hierfür dienen Kollokationen, die redundante Elemente enthalten, wie z.b. *zu Fuß gehen = gyalog megy.*

3   Kontrastiver Ansatz

Bei einer kontrastiven Untersuchung, wie ich sie bis jetzt durchgeführt habe, gehe ich davon aus, daß sich äquivalente Verben im Deutschen und im Ungarischen darin unterscheiden können, mit welchen Substantiven sie kollokieren. Einige deutsche Verben und ihre ungarischen Äquivalente habe ich in bezug darauf analysiert, inwieweit die Elemente des Paradigmas der in der einen Sprache kollokablen Substantive in der anderen Sprache Entsprechungen haben. Die Hypothese lautet, daß ungarische Verben im allgemeinen dem Bereich kollokabler Substantive weniger Restriktionen auferlegen als deutsche Verben. Diese Hypothese wird mit Hilfe der von Leisi (1971:77) übernommenen Dichotomie ‚rational' vs. ‚expressiv' genauer formuliert (das Begriffspaar wurde von Leisi eingeführt in freier Anlehnung an Begriffe, die Bally für einen ähnlichen Unterschied in Morphologie und Syntax verwendet).

Leisi unterscheidet Verben mit und ohne Objektbedingungen. Bei den Verben mit Objektbedingungen gibt es graduelle Unterschiede. Leisi nennt ein Verb in dem Maße rational, wie es von Subjekt- und Objektbedingungen unabhängig ist; ein Beispiel ist *kommen.* Ein Verb ist nach Leisi in dem Maße expressiv, wie sein Gebrauch von Subjekts- und Objektsbedingungen abhängt; ein Beispiel ist *pflücken.* Zum Verb *pflücken* gibt es lediglich eine kleine Auswahl von objektfähigen Gegenständen.

Als „rational" sind solche Verben zu bezeichnen, die ein großes Substantivparadigma, als „expressiv" solche Verben, die nur ein begrenztes Substantivparadigma zulassen. In diesen Termini formuliert, lautet die Hypothese, daß deutsche Verben im Vergleich zu ungarischen eher als expressiv zu bewerten wären, während das Ungarische mehr rationale Verben enthält[1].

Die Auswahl der kontrastiv zu beobachtenden Substantiv-Verb-Kollokationen kannn nicht auf einem Wörterbuch basieren, denn es gibt noch kein deutsch-ungarisches oder ungarisch-deutsches Kollokationswörterbuch. In den allgemeinen zweisprachigen und einsprachigen Wörterbüchern sind die Kollokationen auch nur sporadisch aufgeführt und gelegentlich in den Beispielsätzen integriert. Auch die Vokabellisten für Sprachprüfungen enthalten kaum explizit aufgeführte Kollokationen. Als Grundlage des Vergleichs mit dem Ungarischen dienen mir in den folgenden fünf Punkten die deutschen Beispiele von Leisi (1971). Bei den ungarischen Äquivalenten

---

[1] Leisi hat deutsche und englische Verben miteinander kontrastiert. Er kam zu der Feststellung, daß das Basic English wesentlich mehr rationale Verben enthält als das Deutsche. In Leisis Sinne ist das Französische rationaler als das Deutsche oder das Englische (Leisi 1971:78).

berufe ich mich auf das neue Deutsch-ungarische Großwörterbuch sowie auf das Lexikon „Ungarische Wortschatzkammer" (Kiss 1999).

Die Verben, bei denen der Bereich der kollokablen Substantive in den beiden Sprachen zusammenfallen, bleiben unberücksichtigt, denn sie sind in bezug auf die Rationalität oder Expressivität der Verben unter kontrastivem Aspekt neutral. Im folgenden werden rationale deutsche Verben mit ihren ungarischen Entsprechungen verglichen.

a) Menschen vs Tiere als Subjekt im Deutschen – keine Restriktion im Ungarischen:

<Menschen> essen
<Tiere> fressen   *eszik*

Die Verben der Nahrungsaufnahme sind im Deutschen durch das Subjekt bedingt, indem sie entweder für Menschen (*essen*) oder für Tiere (*fressen*) gebraucht werden können. Das ungarische *eszik* ist klassematisch indifferent.

b) Bedingtheit der Verben der Kochprozesse durch das Objekt im Deutschen – keine Restriktion im Ungarischen

kochen   *főz*
braten <Fleisch>
backen <Teigware>
rösten <Kastanien>   *süt*
schmoren <Braten>
dünsten <Gemüse>   *párol*

Das Deutsche scheint auch in diesem Bereich mehr zu differenzieren. Solange nicht gesagt wird, was gekocht wird, gibt es eine völlige Äquivalenz in den beiden Sprachen. Bedingt durch das Objekt gibt es für das eine ungarische Verb *süt* drei Verben (*braten, backen, rösten*) im Deutschen. Nicht das Objekt, sondern die Art und Weise des Kochens ist ausschlaggebend bei der Wahl zwischen *schmoren* und *dünsten*. Für die deutsche kochkunstspezifische Bezeichnung (*schmoren* = ‚Fleisch kurz anbraten und dann in Brühe in einem zugedeckten Topf langsam gar werden lassen'), die zu den Realia gehört, kann auch kein äquivalentes ungarisches Verb gefunden werden.

c) Menschen vs Naturerscheinungen als Subjekt im Deutschen – keine Restriktion im Ungarischen

<Wind> weht
blasen <Horn>
pusten <ins Feuer>   *fúj*
<Katze> fauchen
sich <die Nase> putzen

Eine bewegte Luft wird im Deutschen nur dann mit dem Verb *wehen* bezeichnet, wenn sie von einer Naturerscheinung ausgelöst wird. Wird der Luftausstoß von einem Menschen verursacht, bezeichnet man die Bewegung, je nach Kürze, mit den Verben *blasen* oder *pusten*. Im Ungarischen gibt es keine derartige Bedingung. Alle (nicht idiomatischen) Wortverbindungen, wie z. B. *<ins Feuer> <ein Lied> <jm Rauch ins Gesicht> blasen* etc., die die Verben *wehen, blasen* und *pusten* eingehen, werden im Ungarischen mit *fúj* gebildet. Auch die Verben in den Wortverbindungen *<Katze> fauchen, sich <die Nase> putzen* werden mit *fúj* übersetzt. Diese Übersetzung ist nachvollziehbar, denn bei *fauchen* und *sich die Nase putzen* ist der gemeinsame Bedeutungskern mit dem Verb *fúj* ,Luft ausstoßen' feststellbar. Das lautmalende Verb *fauchen* ist weiter differenziert als *fúj*, denn es bringt außer dem Atemausstoß auch noch das dabei entstehende zischende Geräusch des Tieres zum Ausdruck. Die ungarische Kollokation **Nase blasen* läßt sich damit erklären, daß der Luftstrom bei *fúj* nicht unbedingt wie bei *blasen* im Deutschen durch die Lippen strömen muß.

d) Tiere vs Wildtiere als Subjekt im Deutschen – keine Differenzierung im Ungarischen

<Haustiere> weiden
<Wildtiere> äsen   *legel*
<Tiere> grasen

Der Gebrauch der Verben *weiden* und *äsen* hängt im Deutschen von den Tiergattungen ab. Bei *grasen* hat das Objekt *(Gras)* einen Einfluß auf die Wortwahl. Im Ungarischen gibt es keine Einschränkungen, weder durch die Tiergattung noch durch das Objekt.

e) Der Objektbereich ist im Deutschen primär von der Form des Objektes abhängig
   Im Ungarischen hingegen gibt es auch formunabhängige Bezeichnungen

	Deutsch	Ungarisch
etwas/jn an eine bestimmte Stelle bringen und dort in stehender Haltung lassen	*stellen*	*állít*
etwas/jm in eine „sitzende" Position bringen	*setzen*	*ültet*
etwas/jn an eine bestimmte Stelle bringen und dort in liegender Haltung lassen	*legen*	*fektet*
etwas/jn an eine bestimmte Stelle bringen und dort lassen	*tun* (gespr.)	*rak*
		tesz
		helyez

Die Verben verlangen in beiden Sprachen sowohl ein direktes Objekt als auch eine weitere, auf das Ziel referierende Ergänzung. Der korrekte Gebrauch der drei deutschen Verben *stellen, legen, setzen* bereitet den Lernern nicht deshalb Schwierigkeiten, weil es keine Entsprechungen im Ungarischen gäbe, sondern deshalb, weil parallel dazu auch Verben in der ungarischen Standardsprache existieren, die durch die Form des Objektes nicht bedingt sind und deren Gebrauch bevorzugt ist. Die Kollokationen, z. B zu *setzen <eine Flöte, ein Glas> <an den Mund>* oder *<einen Punkt>*, werden nicht mit dem ungarischen „Äquivalent" *ültet* übersetzt, sondern mit den formunabhängigen generellen Verben *tesz, rak, helyez*.

f) Beschränkung auf engste Objektklassen im Deutschen – keine Beschränkung im Ungarischen

Es geht hier um Verben, die ein Objekt von so genau bestimmter Art erfordern, daß es dafür nur ein einziges Substantiv oder sehr wenige Substantive gibt.

pflücken <Obst > <Blumen> <Baumwolle>   *szed*

Das deutsche Verb *pflücken* ist auf *Obst* und *Blumen* beschränkt, obwohl diese Greif- und Zupfbewegung zweifellos auch bei anderer Ernte vorkommen kann. Das äquivalente ungarische Verb *szed* hat keine derartige Objektbeschränkung. Ein hohes Maß an Objektbeschränkung weist das Verb *fällen* auf. Historismen wie *einen Helden fällen* (in der Bedeutung von *zu Fall bringen*) sind im Laufe des Sprachwandels aus dem Deutschen ausgeschieden. Die Kollokation *fällen* *<Baum>* findet ihr Äquivalent in der ungarischen Wortverbindung *kivág <fát>*. Der Gebrauch dieses Verbs ist nicht beschränkt auf *Baum*, sondern kollokiert mit jeglicher Pflanzenbezeichnung und diversen Gegenstandsbezeichnungen.

In den angeführten Beispielen wurden expressive Verben des Deutschen mit ihren ungarischen „Äquivalenten" verglichen. Es läßt sich eindeutig feststellen, daß die „äquivalenten" ungarischen Verben eher rational sind. Die Beispiele untermauern also unsere Hypothese. Eine weitere Aufgabe zur Überprüfung der Hypothese ergibt sich aus dem inversen Ansatz, nämlich expressive ungarische Verben mit ihren deutschen „Äquivalenten" zu konfrontieren. Erst nach diesem Verfahren kann die Hypothese in eine stichhaltige Aussage umgewandelt werden.

4 Folgen für den Sprachunterricht

Abschließend soll auf mögliche Folgerungen für den Fremdsprachenunterricht und speziell für den Erwerb des Deutschen durch ungarische Muttersprachler eingegangen werden. Wie versucht der Lerner die arbiträre Divergenz bei den phraseologischen Einheiten in der Zielsprache und in der Muttersprache zu bewältigen? Studien zum Transferverhalten im Rahmen der Zweitsprachenerwerbforschung (Kellermann 1977) haben gezeigt, daß Lerner – wenn es sich um Idiome handelt – mit einer Nichttransferierbarkeitshypothese operieren. Bei Kollokationen arbeiten die Lerner demgegenüber – wie die Vielzahl der Interferenzfehler zeigt – mit einer Transferierbarkeitshypothese.

Die folgenden Vorschläge gelten der Schulung der Kollokationskompetenz:

a) Um dem Transferverhalten der Lerner entgegenzuwirken, bedarf es einer bewußten Kollokationsschulung. Sie kann realisiert werden, indem die Lerner für die Kollokationen sensibilisiert werden sowie in der Form von diversen gezielten Kollokationsübungen.

b) Expressive Verben sollten zusammen mit ihren kollokablen Substantiven behandelt und gelernt werden.

c) Bei der Vermittlung der Vokabelbedeutung sollten die Bedeutungsunterschiede zu den ungarischen „Äquivalenten" angegeben werden, sowohl im Semantisierungsprozeß als auch in zweisprachigen Wortgleichungen.

d) Bei der Erschließung der Bedeutung von Kollokationen kann das Verfahren des entdeckenden Lernens effizient eingesetzt werden. Das Erkennen der Motivation der Bedeutung einer Wortverbindung kann für Fremdsprachenlerner lernerleichternd wirken, begründet aber die Selektion nicht immer ausreichend.

5   Literatur

AGRICOLA, Erhard (1992): Wörter und Wendungen. Wörterbuch zum deutschen Sprachgebrauch. Mannheim: Duden.

FEILKE, Helmuth, FEILKE, Lena (1996): Sprache als soziale Gestalt: Ausdruck, Prägung und die Ordnung der sprachlichen Typik. Frankfurt am Main: Suhrkamp.

FIRTH, John Rupert (1957): Papers in Linguistics 1934-1951. London: Oxford University Press.

GÖTZ, Dieter; Haenesch, Günther; Wellmann, Hans (Hrsg.) (1993): Langenscheidts Großwörterbuch Deutsch als Fremdsprache. Das neue einsprachige Wörterbuch für Deutschlernende. Berlin: Langenscheidt.

HALÁSZ, Előd; FÖLDES, Csaba; UZONYI, Pál (1998): Deutsch-ungarisches Großwörterbuch. Budapest: Akadémiai Kiadó.

HALÁSZ, Előd; FÖLDES, Csaba; UZONYI, Pál (1998): Ungarisch-deutsches Großwörterbuch. Budapest: Akadémiai Kiadó.

HAUSMANN, Franz Josef (1993): Ist der deutsche Wortschatz lernbar? Oder: Wortschatz ist Chaos. In: Info DaF 20, 471-485.

KELLERMANN, Ernst (1977): Towards a characterization of the strategy of transfer in second language learning. In: Interlanguage Studies Bulletin 2, 58-145.

KISS, Gábor (Hrsg.) (1999): Magyar szókincstár. Rokon értelmű szavak, szólások és ellentétek szótára. Budapest: Tinta (Ungarische Wortschatzkammer). Wörterbuch der sinnverwandten Wörter, der Redewendungen und der sprachlichen Gegensätze).

LEHR, Andrea (1998): Kollokationen in Langenscheidts Großwörterbuch Deutsch als Fremdsprache In: Wiegand, Herbert Ernst (Hrsg.): Perspektiven der pädagogischen Lexikographie des Deutschen. Untersuchungen anhand von „Langenscheidts Großwörterbuch Deutsch als Fremdsprache". Tübingen: Niemeyer (Lexicographica / Series maior 38), 256-279.

LEISI, Ernst ([4]1971): Der Wortinhalt. Seine Struktur im Deutschen und Englischen. Heidelberg: Quelle & Meyer (UTB 95).

MUHR, Rudolf (1994): Österreichisches Sprachdiplom. Lexikalische Ausdrücke und Kollokationen. Sprechhandlungen – Formulierungen – Strukturen. Österreichisches und deutsches Deutsch. Wien: Hölder – Pichel – Tempsky.

Phraseologische Einheiten mit Vogelbezeichnungen
Ein Vergleich Deutsch-Russisch

Veronika Savtschenko

Die Sprache spiegelt alte Traditionen, Sitten und Bräuche ihres Trägers, geschichtliche Fakten, Erscheinungen des gesellschaftlichen, politischen Lebens, sozioökonomische Verhältnisse sowie Besonderheiten der Natur wider. In der Sprache findet auch die Mentalität eines Volkes ihren Niederschlag.

Eines der aktuellen Probleme der Gegenwartslinguistik ist die Erforschung der Beziehungen zwischen der Sprache und der Mentalität eines Volkes. In der Sprache ist die innere Welt des Menschen, ihre kognitive Sphäre, deutlich dargestellt. Deswegen ist die Sprache eines der Objekte der Analyse bei der Mentalitäts-Forschung. Die Kursker Linguisten Chrolenko und Petrenko meinen: „Die Mentalität objektiviert sich am besten in der Sprache durch das ethnische Weltbild" (Chrolenko; Petrenko 1996:145).

Die Träger jeder Sprache haben ihre Stereotype und ähnliche Assoziationen. Aber die „Weltansichten" (Terminus W. von Humboldts) der Träger verschiedener Sprachen sind unterschiedlich. Nach der Meinung von Dobrovol'skij und Piirainen kommt in der Idiomatik „die Spezifik der wertend-modalen Einstellung zur Realität, die in der jeweiligen Sprache als eine übliche, überlieferte ‚volkstümliche' Sicht der Welt festgehalten ist" (Dobrovol'skij; Piirainen 1992:141) zum Ausdruck. Nur beim Vergleich kann man die Spezifik der ethnischen Sicht der Welt feststellen.

Ziel meiner Forschung ist zu zeigen, wie sich die Mentalität des deutschen und des russischen Volkes im phraseologischen Weltbild widerspiegelt.

Das Objekt dieser Forschung sind deutsche und russische Phraseologismen mit Substantiven, die Vögel bezeichnen, und Phraseologismen mit den Adjektiven, die von den Vogelbezeichnungen abgeleitet sind. Diese Phraseologismen nenne ich im Folgenden „Vogelphraseologismen".

Für die Analyse habe ich 85 deutsche und 133 russische phraseologische Einheiten aus den Wörterbüchern „Duden. Redewendungen und sprichwörtliche Redensarten" (1998), „Moderne deutsche Idiomatik" von Friederich (1995), „Deutsch-russisches phraseologisches Wörterbuch" von Binovitsch und Grischin (1975) und „Fraseologitscheskij slowar' russkogo jasyka" von Molotkow (1986) herangezogen.

In den russischen und deutschen Vogelphraseologismen sind folgende Kenntnisse und Vorstellungen über die Vogelwelt zum Ausdruck gekommen:

1) Charakteristik des Verhaltens der Vögel, zum Beispiel: *sich benehmen wie der Vogel Strauß* (*den Kopf in den Sand stecken wie der Vogel Strauß*) ‚Augen vor etwas Unangenehmem verschließen'; *strausowaja politika* (wörtl.: Straußpolitik) ‚ein feiges Streben, Entscheidungen zu entgehen');

2) Beziehungen des Menschen zu der Vogelwelt: *gusej draznit'* ironisch (wörtl.: Gänse reizen) ‚j-n absichtlich kränken, reizen';

3) Hören von Vogellauten durch die Menschen: *beim ersten Hahnenschrei aufstehen* usw. ‚ganz früh am Morgen aufstehen usw.'; *petucha dawat' (pustit')* ugs. (wörtl.: den Hahn geben (lassen)) ‚beim Singen einen Quietschlaut ausstoßen';

4) äußere Erscheinung der Vögel: *schwarz wie ein Rabe / die Raben* ugs ‚1. sehr dunkel, tiefschwarz; 2. oft scherzhaft (meist von Kindern) sehr schmutzig'; *kak woron tschjornyj'* (wörtl.: schwarz wie ein Rabe); *kak woronowo krylo* (wörtl.: wie der Rabenflügel) ‚tiefschwarz';

5) die Rolle der Vögel in verschiedenen Bräuchen: z.b. *kak s gusja woda* (wörtl.: wie von der Gans das Wasser) ‚j-m ist alles egal'. Felizyna und Mokienko (1990) meinen, dass dieser Vergleich sich darauf bezieht, dass das Gänsegefieder das Wasser nicht durchlässt: es rollt hinunter. Diesen Ausdruck gebrauchte man früher in den Zaubersprüchen. Abergläubische meinten, dass die Worte *kak s gusja woda, s menja suchota* (wörtl.: wie von der Gans das Wasser, von mir die Krankheit) den Menschen heilen konnten. Diese Redewendung gebrauchen heutzutage die Mütter häufig beim Baden der kleinen Kinder als einen scherzhaften Ausdruck (Felizyna, Mokienko 1990:45).

Meine Untersuchungen haben auch ergeben, dass in der deutschen Phraseologie etwa 35 verscheidene Vogelarten vorkommen, in der russischen 30. Lediglich 21 dieser Arten werden in beiden Sprachen verwendet. Zu den Vogelarten, die in beiden phraseologischen Systemen Verwendung finden, gehören: der Adler, die Elster, die Ente, die Gans, der Geier, der Hahn, das Huhn, die Krähe, der Kuckuck, die Meise, die Nachtigall, der Papagei, der Pfau, der Rabe, der Reiher, die Schwalbe, der Schwan, der Spatz, der Strauß, die Taube und der Truthahn. Die Gattungsbezeichnung „Vogel" wird auch in beiden phraseologischen Systemen gebraucht. Es gibt aber eine Reihe von Vogelarten, die entweder nur der deutschen oder nur der russischen Phraseologie eigen sind. Die Arten, über die nur die deutsche Phraseologie verfügt, sind u.a. die Eule, der Goldfasan, die Heidelerche, der Rohrspatz, das Rotkehlchen, die Turteltaube und die Wachtel. Nur in russischen Phraseologismen sind unter anderem folgende Vogelarten vertreten: die Bläßweihe, der Birkhahn, die Dohle, die Drossel, der Kanarienvogel, die Tauchente, der Specht und der Habicht.

Am häufigsten kommt in der deutschen Phraseologie die Gattungsbezeichnung „Vogel" vor, gefolgt von den Arten Kuckuck, Hahn, Huhn. Im Russischen taucht ebenfalls der Vogel an sich am häufigsten auf, gefolgt von Huhn, Hahn und Gans.

Jedes Volk verleiht bestimmten Vögeln symbolische Bedeutungen oder bestimmte Eigenschaften. Die Linguistin Tscherdanzewa (1977) hat die Phraseologie der Tierwelt im allgemeinen erforscht und ist dabei zu folgendem Ergebnis gekommen:

> „Die Symbolik fällt gewöhnlich in verschiedenen Sprachen nur im Großen und Ganzen zu sammen, in Einzelheiten und im Funktionieren der Symbole kann es große Unterschiede geben" (Tscherdanzewa 1977:160).

So symbolisiert zum Beispiel die Nachtigall in beiden Sprachen dasselbe, nämlich einen Menschen mit schöner Stimme. Die Deutschen singen wie eine Nachtigall, während sich die Russen auf „Kursker Nachtigall" (*kursker solowej*) beziehen. Die Nachtigallen in der Umgebung von Kursk sind in ganz Russland durch ihren besonders schönen Gesang berühmt, was die Entstehung der Redewendung erklären könnte. Darüber hinaus versteht man unter einer Kursker Nachtigall einen Menschen, der gern und viel spricht. Neben der Nachtigall benutzen die Deutschen einen weiteren Vogel mit schöner Stimme. Sie singen wie eine Heidelerche. Im russischen phraseologischen System fehlt die Heidelerche dagegen gänzlich.

Auch der Pfau symbolisiert sowohl im Deutschen als auch im Russischen dasselbe, Eitelkeit und Überheblichkeit: *wie ein Pfau (ein) Rad schlagen; sich wie ein Pfau spreizen; stolz wie ein Pfau; chodit' pawlinom* (wörtl.: sich wie ein Pfau gehen). Im nächsten Beispiel geht es auch um Eitelkeit. Auch der Truthahn symbolisiert in beiden phraseologischen Systemen einen eitlen Menschen: *herumstolzieren wie ein Truthahn, sich gebärden (aufblasen) wie ein Truthahn,* identisch auf russisch *nadut'sja, kak indjuk* (wörtl.: sich aufblasen wie ein Truthahn). Außer Pfau und Truthahn wird auch der Hahn in der deutschen und in der russischen Phraseologie mit Eigenschaften wie Eitelkeit und Übermut versehen: *stolz wie ein Hahn; einherstolzieren wie ein Hahn auf dem Mist; chodit' petuchom* (wörtl.: gehen wie der Hahn). Im Russischen stehen darüber hinaus Kranich und Tauchente für Eitelkeit. Man kann wie ein Kranich auf dem Rain einherstolzieren (*wystupat' slowno schuravl' na meshe*) oder wie eine Tauchente gehen (*chodit' gogolem*). Zur Etymologie der letzteren Redewendung meint der russische Sprachforscher Mokienko (1975), dass sie sich darauf bezieht wie eine Tauchente schwimmt, nämlich „den Kopf schneidig erhoben". Mokienko zitiert dabei ein russisches Volkslied:

„Auf dem Flüsschen schwimmt ein Tauchentlein
Und trägt das Köpfchen höher als das Ufer" (Mokienko 1975:60).

Der deutschen Phraseologie hingegen ist die Tauchente unbekannt.

Die Elster verkörpert sowohl im deutschen als auch im russischen phraseologischen System einen diebischen Menschen: *stehlen wie eine Elster; eine diebische Elster; soroka-worowka* (wörtl.: die Elster – eine Diebin). Es scheint, beide Völker hätten bemerkt, dass Elstern gerne glänzende Dinge in ihrem Nest verstecken. Außerdem versinnbildlicht die Elser in beiden phraseologischen Systemen einen geschwätzigen Menschen: *wie eine Elster schwatzen, trestschat' kak soroka* (wörtl.: e-e Elster schwatzen). Die Russen bezeichnen auch einen redefreudigen Menschen als *sorotschij jasyk* (wörtl.: eine Elsterzunge).

Es gibt eine ganze Reihe von russischen und deutschen phraseologischen Einheiten, die zum Ausdruck bringen, dass das Huhn ein dummes Wesen ist: *ein dummes (albernes) Huhn; da lachen ja die Hühner*!; identisch auf russisch *kuram na smech; kurinye mosgi* (wörtl.: Hühnergehirn)*, kurinaja golowa* (wörtl.: Hühnerkopf). Im „Duden. Redewendungen und sprichwörtliche Redensarten" (1998) wird die Herkunft der Redewendung *Da lachen ja die Hühner!* auf folgende Weise erläutert:

„Die Redensart geht wohl davon aus, daß Hühner für dumme, einfältige Tiere gehalten werden. Wenn also selbst die Hühner aufmerksam werden und zu lachen (gackern) beginnen, muß etwas schon unsinnig oder lächerlich sein" (Duden 1998:352f).

Nach all diesen Gemeinsamkeiten kann es nicht verwundern, dass ein und derselbe Vogel in beiden Sprachen auch andere verschiedene Funktionen erfüllen kann. Während man im Deutschen z.B. von einer „*dummen Gans*" redet, bezeichnen die russischen Redewendungen mit dem Substantiv *gus'* ‚Gans' *gus' laptschatyj* (wörtl.: eine Gans mit Schwimmfüßen); *chorosch gus'* (wörtl.: eine gute Gans); *gus' porjadotschnyj* (wörtl.: eine recht gute Gans) einen hinterlistigen pfiffigen spitzbübischen Menschen. Die Gans wird im Russischen außerdem mit Wichtigkeit assoziiert: *washnyj gus'* (wörtl.: eine wichtige Gans).

In der russischen Folklore ist der Rabe der Vorbote der Not, des Unglücks und des Todes: z.B. sagt der Volksmund „*Woron na dwore k pokojniku w isbe*" (wörtl.: Ein Rabe im Hof prophezeit einen Verstorbenen im Haus) usw. Man glaubt auch, wenn der Rabe krächzt, sagt er Not voraus. In der russischen Malerei (z.B. das Gemälde von Wasnezow W. M. „Ein Recke am Scheideweg"), in der russischen Literatur (z.B. das Märchen über den Raben und den Adler in Puschkins Erzählung „Die Hauptmannstochter") symbolisiert der Rabe einerseits Ewigkeit und Weisheit, aber andererseits Tod und Unglück. In der russischen Phraseologie hat der Rabe auch symbolische Bedeutung „etwas Böses, Finsternis, Tod, Unglück": z.B. *woron slowestschij* (wörtl.: ein unheildrohender Rabe). So bezeichnet man denjenigen, der Not oder Misserfolg voraussagt.Die Redewendung *tschjornyi woron* (wörtl.: ein schwarzer Rabe) steht für das Gefängnisauto für den Transport der Verhafteten in der Zeit von Stalins Repressalien.

Dobrovol'skij und Piirainen meinen aber:

> „Nur relativ wenige Tierkonstituenten weisen im Phraseologismus eindeutig das Merkmal einer symbolischen Funktion auf, manche lassen sich sowohl symbolisch als auch metaphorisch interpretieren, und viele sind ohne symbolischen Bezug" (Dobrovol'skij; Piirainen 1996:159).

So erscheint z.B. der Rabe in weiteren russischen Phraseologismen nicht in symbolischen Funktionen. In den Phraseologismen *kak woron tschjornyj* (wörtl.: schwarz wie ein Rabe); *kak woronowo krylo* (wörtl.: wie ein Rabenflügel) wird die Farbe seines Gefieders charakterisiert. In den deutschen Phraseologismen bezeichnet der Rabe einen diebischen Menschen: *stehlen wie die Raben*. In dem Phraseologismus *schwarz wie ein Rabe* ist seine Charakteristik die schwarze Farbe seines Gefieders; ebenso in der russischen Phraseologie. Im Phraseologismus „ein weißer Rabe" wird das Substantiv „Rabe" metaphorisch gebraucht.

Ich fasse also zusammen. In der Sicht auf die Vogelwelt haben Deutsche und Russen sowohl viel Gemeinsames als auch viel Trennendes. Im deutschen und russischen phraseologischen Weltbild fallen die durch Vogelbezeichnungen ausgedrückten Symbole teilweise zusammen. Häufig sind aber diese Symbole nationalspezifisch. Die Parallelen in der Wahrnehmung der Vögel bei Deutschen und Russen könnte man durch kulturelle Kontakte und auch dadurch erklären, dass beiden Völkern dieselben Vogelarten bekannt sind. Die Differenzen in der Sicht der Vogelwelt sind durch die spezifische deutsche und russische Denk- und Interpretationsweise, tief in der Vergangenheit verwurzelte traditionelle Symbolik, Aberglaube, Literatur, Folklore und ethnokulturelle Traditionen zu erklären.

Literatur

CHROLENKO, Alexandr Timofeewitsch; PETRENKO, Olga Alexandrowna (1996): Etnitscheskoe swoeobrasie semantiki narodno-poetitscheskoj retschi. In: Duchownoe obustrojstwo Rossii. Kursk: GUIPP, 145-162.

DOBROVOL'SKIJ, Dmitrij Olegowitsch; PIIRAINEN, Elisabeth (1992): Zum Weltmodell einer niederdeutschen Mundart im Spiegel der Phraseologie. In: Niederdeutsches Wort. Beiträge zur niederdeutschen Philologie 32, 137-169.

DOBROVOL'SKIJ, Dmitrij Olegowitsch; Piirainen, Elisabeth (1996): Symbole in Sprache und Kultur. Studien zur Phraseologie aus kultur-semiotischer Perspektive. Bochum:Universitätsverlag Dr. N. Brockmeyer.

FELIZYNA, Wera Petrowna; MOKIENKO, Walerij Michailowitsch (1990): Russkie fraseologismy. Moskva: Russkij jasyk.

MOKIENKO, Walerij Michailowitsch (1975): W glub' pogoworki. Rasskasy o proischoshdenii krylatych slow i obrasnych wyrashenij. Moskva: Proswestschenie.

TSCHERDANZEVA, Tamara Sacharowna (1974): Jasyk i ego obrasy. Otscherki po italjanskoy fraseologii. Moskva: Meshdunarodnye otnoschenija.

BINOWITSCH, Leonid Eduardowitsch; GRISCHIN Nikolai Nikolaewitsch ([2]1975): Deutsch-russisches phraseologisches Wörterbuch. Moskva: Russkij jasyk.

DUDEN. Redewendungen und sprichwörtliche Redensarten (1998): Wörterbuch der deutschen Idiomatik (bearb. v. Günter Drosdowskij und Werner Scholze-Stubenrecht). Mannheim – Leipzig – Wien – Zürich: Dudenverlag (Der Duden in 12 Bänden 11.)

FRIEDERICH, Wolf (1995): Moderne deutsche Idiomatik.. Ismaning: Max Hueber Verlag.

MOLOTKOW, Alexandr Iwanowitsch (Hrsg.) (1986): Fraseologitscheskij slowar' russkogo jasyka. Moskva: Russkij jasyk.

The Syntactic Origin of English and Spanish Verbal Compounds
Exploring the Interface between Morphology and Syntax

Margarita Vinagre

1   Introduction

The aim of this paper is to present some aspects of the interface between morphology and syntax through the study of English and Spanish verbal compounds. Over the last thirty years, many linguists have tried to explain the generation of verbal compounds by means of syntactic transformations, lexicalist principles and argument structures (cf. Lees 1960, Halle 1973, Aronoff 1976, Roeper and Siegel 1978, Allen 1978, Selkirk 1982, Lieber 1983, Anderson 1992). Nowadays, it has been widely accepted that compounds are created in the lexicon by means of lexical rules and principles, since they are seen as lexical items formed by a mere concatenation of words. As we shall see in this study, verbal compounds are not simple lexical items but complex lexical items with syntactic structure and therefore, it is necessary to postulate a change in the locus where these elements originate.

2   On the definition of compounds

In general terms, a compound has been defined as

> "the result of the fixed combination of two or three free forms or words that have an otherwise independent existence. These items, though clearly composed of elements, have the identifying characteristics of single words." (Adams 1973:30).

Other authors (Katamba 1993:54) define a compound as "the one which contains at least two bases which are words or at any rate root morphemes." As we can gather from these definitions, even though authors differ in their terminology, they seem to agree in that compounds are formed by linking words or lexemes. This type of formal definition is applicable to some extent, since it seems to me that other considerations of a syntactic and semantic nature need to be considered as well if an adequate definition of compounds is to be postulated. However, since in many cases formal aspects have been given priority over syntactic and semantic ones, it is not surprising that according to many linguists, compounds are to be entered directly into the lexicon. In addition, from a semantic point of view, they often present lexicalized meanings and idiosyncrasies which are better handled within the lexicon. This lexicalist proposal could be accepted as an explanation for root compounds but not for verbal compounds, since the latter are generated in syntax as we shall see. The distinction between root and verbal compounds is crucial, since completely different approaches are necessary for their interpretation. Root or primary compounds are terms whose elements are not deverbal. As regards the category of each one of the elements, in English a compound noun can be formed by a noun, adjective, particle or verb on the left and a noun on the right. A compound adjective can be formed by a noun, adjective or particle on the left and an adjective on the right. A compound verb can have a particle or verb followed by a verb. The resulting compound noun, adjective or verb functions as such in syntactic structures: e.g. Although the situation is not looking good, there is no need to be *downhearted*. In English words such as *high school, head strong, icy cold, skin head* are all root compounds. In Spanish, there are two main types of compound nouns. The first type are N'→N-A compounds (*aguardiente* [*eau-de-vie*, clear brandy distilled from fermented fruit juice], *bomba atómica* [atomic bomb]). The second type are N'→ N-N where we have two co-ordinated elements (e.g. *carricoche* [covered wagon], *cama nido* [truckle bed])[1]. There are also compound adjectives of the A'→ A-A type such as *tonticiego* [silly-and-blind] although they are not very common.

As we have mentioned above, from a formal point of view, these terms are the result of the concatenation of words and as the lexicalist proposal suggests, all these primary compounds can be formed in the lexicon since they are easy to account for. All that is needed in order to generate them is a lexical device that concatenates words (i.e. word Formation Rules) such as the following:

$[[X]_N+[Y]_N]_N$ *casa cuna* [children's home]/ *apron string*
$[[X]_N+[Y]_A]_A$ *headstrong*
$[[X]_N+[Y]_A]_N$ *hierbabuena* [mint]
$[[X]_A+[Y]_A]_A$ *tonticiego* [silly-and-blind] /*icy cold* etc.

Root compounds can also be created by analogy, based on the above-mentioned structures. Regarding their semantic interpretation, we need to consider the degree of lexicalization of the term under analysis. It is possible to find terms whose meaning is the result of the sum of the meanings of the elements which form the compound (semantic compositionality). Thus, *químico-físico* [chemist-physicist] and *vagón-cisterna* [tank wagon] in Spanish and *apron string* or *music box* in English can be interpreted this way. There are other compounds such as *aguardiente* [lit. burning water], *hierbabuena* [lit. good herb] in Spanish, *dead centre* and *goldfish* in English, whose full meaning cannot be deduced from the meaning of the elements which form the compound. They are partly lexicalized and therefore it is possible to understand that *aguardiente* is some kind of *agua* and *hierbabuena* is some kind of *hierba*. In the same way, *dead centre* refers to the absolute centre of a place. However, the final interpretation has to be left to the dictionary where all the idiosyncratic information is stored. Exocentric compounds make semantic interpretation even more complex, since they have no semantic head. We have compounds such as *piel roja* [red skin] in Spanish and *pickpocket* or *lazybones* in English which are hyponyms of the head which is not overtly expressed (for instance 'person' in the case of *pickpocket, lazybones* and *piel roja*). For their interpretation, the use of the dictionary may be necessary in order to

---

[1]   A third type of compound (N' → N-PP) should be treated in the same way as verbal compounds due to its syntactic structure. We are referring to compounds such *as bomba de neutrones* or *caja de Pandora*.

identify the head. For instance, a *hunchback* is "a person who has a large bump on their back"[2]. Finally, we have fully lexicalized compounds such as *caradura* [lit. hard face, cheeky], *perrito caliente* [hot dog] or *deadline, dead man's handle* whose meaning is not related at all to the meaning of the elements which form the compound. We can only understand these terms by checking their meaning in the dictionary and in many cases, pragmatic considerations have to be considered.

Once we have analyzed the formal, syntactic and semantic aspects to be considered when interpreting root compounds, I will focus on the analysis of verbal compounds where some crucial differences can be observed. These differences will lead us to postulate a syntactic explanation for the generation of verbal compounds.

Verbal compounds are formed from deverbal heads and the non-heads fulfil the function of argument of the verb from which the head is derived. In this type of compounds, the subcategorization of the head will allow us to determine the syntactic and semantic relations that can be established between the head and the non-head. We are referring to terms such as *triturador de carne* [crushing machine], *calentador de aire* [fan heater], *echadora de cartas* [fortune-teller] in Spanish and *truckdriver, heartbroken, music lover* in English. The deverbal heads (*triturador, calentador, echadora* in Spanish and *driver, broken* and *lover* in English) are derived from a verb (*triturar, calentar, drive, break,* etc.) and the non-heads (*carne, aire, cartas, truck, heart* and *music*) function syntactically as direct object of the head in sentences such as *Calentamos el aire, Echa las cartas* or *He drives a truck, She loves music.* From a semantic point o view, the non-heads are either patient, that is the entity that undergoes the effect of the action, often undergoing some change in state (*carne, aire, heart, music*) or theme, the entity which is moved by an action or whose location is described (*cartas, truck*).

As we can see, a first difference between root and verbal compounds in Spanish (if not in English) refers to its morphological structure. Spanish verbal compounds are formed by more than two words and it is frequent to find that some of these words also form a phrase within the compound. In the above-mentioned examples (*triturador de carne, echadora de cartas, calentador de aire*), the underlined elements are all prepositional phrases. From a syntactic point of view, we have already mentioned the fact that there is a head which behaves in the same way as a head does in syntactic structures. The identifying feature of heads in both syntax and morphology is that the properties of the head are those of the whole; in general, there is complete agreement of features between the head and the whole. In compounds, the role of the head is clear: it determines the category, plurality, gender (in Spanish) and other general features of the compound. For instance, the compounds *devoradoras de hombres* [man-eaters] in Spanish and *head strong* in English can be represented as follows:

1) a. [[devoradoras]]$_N$ [de hombres]$_{PP}$] $_N$
   b. [[devoradoras]$_{PL}$[de hombres]$_{PL}$] $_{PL}$
   c. [[devoradoras]$_{FEM}$[de hombres] $_{MASC}$]$_{FEM}$

---

[2] Cf. Collins-Cobuid English Language Dictionary.

2) a. $[[head]_N[strong]_A]_A$
   b. $[[head]_{SG}[strong]_{SG}]_{SG}$

As we can see, the role of the head is the same as in syntax, it carries the grammatical information that will percolate to the whole compound. As regards the non-head of the compound, this element fulfils the argument structure of the verb from which the head is derived and it has to be a word which could appear immediately after the verb in the corresponding verb phrase. Thus, even though we say *quick-fried* (from *fry quickly*), we cannot say **slow-killer* (from *kill somebody slowly*).

From a semantic point of view, the non-heads of verbal compounds receive a theta-role from the head in the same way a sentence-level argument does. For instance, if we take examples such as those in 3), 4) and 5):

3) taxi driver
4) driving of trucks
5) *taxi driving of trucks

It is clear that there is theta-marking in compounds. In 3) the theta-role is assigned by *drive* to its subcategorized complement *taxi* and to *trucks* in 4). However, 5) is a violation of the theta-criterion since it is not possible to assign the same theta role (theme in this case) to two arguments. As we can see, there are differences of a morphological, syntactic and semantic nature between root and verbal compounds that would call for a change in the treatment given to the latter. In addition, the lexicalist principles which have been postulated within generative morphology to explain compound-formation are inadequate to deal with verbal compounds as we shall see below.

3　　Compound-formation in lexicalist morphology

When we analyze the different proposals which have been postulated within lexicalist morphology to explain compound-formation (e.g. Roeper and Siegel's (1978) Transformation Theory, Allen's (1978) Overgenerating Morphological Theory, Selkirk (1982) Word-formation Grammar and Lieber's (1983) Argument-Linking Theory, we realize that they take as the basis for their postulate the following principles:

6) a. The No Phrase Constraint: syntactic phrases cannot be involved in compound-formation (Botha 1983);
   b. The Righthand Head Rule: endocentric compounds are always headed on the rightmost element of the compound (Williams 1981b);
   c. Only irregular inflection is found within compounds, e.g. *teeth-marks* but **nails-marks*.

If we think of the type of Spanish verbal compounds under consideration, we realize that all the above-mentioned principles need to be rejected if we are to consider them

as such. Verbal compounds such as *devoradoras de hombres* present the following
structure:

7) X' → X-Y''

Formal: [[[devora]$_V$ d-oras]$_N$ [de hombres]$_{PP}$]$_N$
            [[devorador-a-s]$_{FEM,PL}$ [de hombre-s]$_{MASC, PL}$]$_{FEM,PL}$
Syntactic: [[devoradoras] $_{Suj}$ [de hombres]$_{Dir Obj}$
            [[devoradoras]$_{head}$ [de hombres]$_{non-head}$
Semantic: [[devoradoras]$_{Agent}$ [de hombres]$_{Patient}$

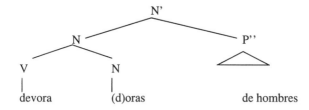

As we can see, these compounds are clearly formed from the concatenation of a word
and a phrase which means that they do not comply with the No Phrase Constraint.
These compounds also have their head on the left which means that they do not comply with William's Righthand Head Rule. Finally, they present inflectional affixes
within the compound (i.e. gender and/or plural affixes), a fact that goes against the
lexicalist principle stated in 6c). All the lexicalist principles stated in 6) are formulated as constraints and conditions in order to generate verbal compounds in the lexicon. Most of these principles are of a syntactic nature and their introduction in the
lexicon merely duplicates the principles and conditions already existent in syntax. The
need to formulate these constraints derives from the specific interpretation lexicalist
morphology gives to the relationship between the lexicon and syntax. Therefore,
many inconsistencies which result from applying the above-mentioned principles to
verbal compounds can be avoided if we can offer a different explanation (a syntactic
one) to the way the lexicon and syntax interrelate.

4   The interface between morphology, syntax and the lexicon:
       an alternative proposal

In order to postulate a theory that provides a syntactic approach to verbal compound-
formation, it is crucial to understand that morphology represents an interface between
different components of the grammar: the lexicon, syntax and phonology[3]. Thus, I
belief that compound-formation lies in the boundaries between the lexicon and syntax. Compounds exhibit properties that are of a clear syntactic (as well as lexical) nature. These properties are meant to pose problems for a lexicalist theory in which com-

---

[3]   Although I will not go into details about this last component.

pound-formation processes take place solely in the lexicon. Only when a proposal that considers a mapping of both components is postulated, is it possible to deal with verbal compound-formation in a more satisfactory way. According to this proposal, verbal compounds are generated in syntax and agree to syntactic principles. Later, some of them may be introduced in the lexicon in order to undergo further derivational processes[4] or in order to deal with their idiosyncratic properties. Thus, we have phrasal words[5], which are finally checked by morphology in order to ensure that they are well-formed, grammatical verbal compounds. There is also an interface between morphology and the lexicon. Thus, morphology should not be identified with the lexicon itself. There are various morphological processes which take place at the lexical level and thus are defined purely over the lexically listed objects. I would suggest that derivational morphology, together with lexical compounding take place here[6] whereas verbal compounding takes place in syntax. In any case, independently of whether the compound-formation process has taken place in syntax or in the lexicon, the morphology will make sure that they are well-formed terms.

4.1   A syntactic proposal for the generation of verbal compounds

The lexicalist principles analyzed above strongly state the following: "No syntactic rule can refer to a morphological category feature", that is to say, syntactic rules are rejected as inadequate in the generation of verbal compounds. However, the syntactic parallelism which can be observed between a compound and its corresponding verb phrase should be represented by incorporating aspects of the syntactic structure into the lexical representation of the compound. In addition, the analysis of the morphological, syntactic and semantic properties of verbal compounds calls for a new definition of compound which stresses the complex nature of verbal compounds as opposed to that of primary compounds. A definition of this type could be as follows:

> A verbal compound is a complex term of level X' in the X-bar hierarchy, formed by a head of level X^0 and a non-head which can belong to either level X^0 or Z'' in the above-mentioned hierarchy. The head is always deverbal and the non-head holds a syntactic and/or semantic relationship with the head. The syntactic relations which can be held between the elements of the compound are stated in terms of grammatical functions whereas the semantic relations are stated in terms of argument structure.

In addition, two syntactic principles already existent in syntax, the Theta Criterion 8) and the Projection Principle 10) apply in the generation of verbal compounds:

---

[4]   For instance, the suffix =s at the end of some Spanish verbal compounds (e.g. *echadora de cartas, promotor de ventas*, etc.) is a lexical affix (it does not have plural meaning and it does not play a syntactic role in the compound) and as such is attached to the component structure in the lexicon. The same could be said of English verbal compounds which present a plural morpheme in the middle (attached to the non-head) of the compound. This morpheme is also of a lexical nature for the same reasons mentioned above.

[5]   I have taken this term from Spencer (1991:454). Phrasal words are "syntactically formed phrases which enter the lexicon".

[6]   Primary or root compounds would therefore be the result of a lexical compounding process.

8) The Theta Criterion (Chomsky 1981): If a verb has theta roles in its theta grid, then they must be assigned an argument position.

According to this principle, it is possible to have a compound *matasuegras* in Spanish [(it) kill(s) mothers-in-law, party blower] but not *suegrasmata. The verb *matar* (to kill) obligatorily requires the presence of a subject/agent (who performs the action), and an object/patient (who undergoes the effect of the action). These two arguments have to appear within the compound whose representation would be as follows:

9) matasuegras

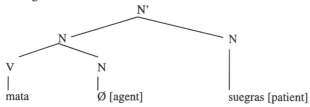

The first element of the compound is a verb which presents a lexicalized theta-role (agent). It is clear that there is theta-role assignment, since it is not possible to create compounds such as *suegrasmata, *hijosmata, *madresmata, *padresmata etc. The agent theta-role has already been filled and is not possible to find another argument agent within the compound.

As regards the Projection Principle, it can be defined as follows:

10) The theta grid of the verb is projected to all syntactic levels: D-structure, S-structure and L(ogical) F(orm).

According to this principle, the forms in 11a) and b) should be derived from an underlying representation which resembles 11c):

11) a. music lover
    b. music loving
    c. love music: love[+agent][+patient]

Thus, the theta-grid of the verb from which the head is derived has to be projected at all syntactic levels, in order to create grammatical verbal compounds.

I am suggesting that syntactic rules have access to the internal structure of verbal compounds and that their structure is generated by Word Structure Rules which reside in syntax. These rules are similar to phrase structure rules but have different properties with respect to the notions of the X-bar theory as we shall see below.

4.2 Word-structure rules

As it has been suggested, the process of compounding involves the combination of words into a syntactic structure. It is clear that the principles governing the internal relations of these elements are syntactic in a way which is somewhat different from other aspects of morphology. Thus, compounds, unlike affixed words, provide motivation for assigning internal structure to words, and it is my assumption that they are generated by Word-Structure Rules (WSRs) distinct from Word-formation Rules. These rules reside in syntax and would have the following features:

12) a. They generate complex words whose structure belongs to level X' in the X-bar hierarchy (i.e. X' → X-Y''/ X' → X-Y);

b. WSRs can create structures in which the sisters to the head may be lexical categories: X' → X-Y (*cazamariposas* [butterfly net]); X' → Y-X (*flamethrower*);

c. They state that the head (whether it is overtly expressed or not) is on the left in the case of Spanish compounds, whereas it is on the right in the case of their English counterparts (e.g.English: X' → Y-$\underline{X}$ (*air conditioning*) Spanish: X' → $\underline{X}$(Ø)-Y(*engañabobos* [swizz]); X' → $\underline{X}$-Y''(*lanzamiento de jabalina* [javelin throwing]);

d. They comply with the Theta-Criterion and the Projection Principle.

WSRs would create structures like the following:

-heartbreaker
break[+agent][+patient]
Formal: N' → N-$\underline{N}$; [[heart]$_N$[breaker]$_N$]$_N$
Syntactic: [[heart]$_{non-head}$[breaker]$_{head}$]; [[heart]$_{object}$[breaker]$_{subj}$]
Semantic: [[heart]$_{patient}$[breaker]$_{agent}$]
-guardacoches
guarda[+agent][+theme]
Formal : N' → $\underline{N}$-N; [[[guarda]$_V$ Ø]$_N$ [coches]$_N$]$_N$
Syntactic: [[guarda]$_{head}$[coches]$_{non-head}$];[[guarda]$_{subj}$ [coches]$_{object}$]
Semantic: [[guarda]$_{agent}$ [coches]$_{theme}$]
-triturador de carne
tritura [+agent][+patient]
Formal : N' → $\underline{N}$-P''; [[tritura]$_V$ d-or]$_N$ [de carne]$_{PP}$]$_N$
Syntactic: [[triturador]$_{head}$[de carne]$_{non-head}$]; [[triturador]$_{subj}$ [de carne]$_{object}$]
Semantic: [[triturador]$_{agent}$ [de carne]$_{patient}$]

WSRs would therefore generate the structures of verbal compounds in syntax and once generated they are introduced in the lexicon where they may undergo further lexical processes. Finally, all idiosyncrasies are dealt with in the lexicon. It seems to me that only when morphological, syntactic, semantic (and pragmatic) aspects are considered, is it possible to fully understand the complexities and problems that verbal compounds pose for a lexicalist approach to verbal compound-formation and to offer a more suitable explanation for their generation.

5   References

ADAMS, Valerie (1973): An introduction to modern English word-formation. London: Longman.
ALLEN, Margaret (1978): Morphological Investigations (Ph. D Dissertation, University of Connecticut).
ANDERSON, Stephen (1992): A-morphous morphology. Cambridge: Cambridge University Press.
ARONOFF, Mark (1994): Morphology by itself. Mass: MIT Press.
— (1976): Word formation in generative grammar. Mass: MIT Press.
BOTHA, Rudolph (1983): Morphological mechanisms. Oxford: Pergamon Press.
CARSTAIRS, Andrew (1992): Current morphology. London: Routledge.
DI SCIULLO, Anna Maria; WILLIAMS, Edwin (1987): On the definition of word. Cambridge, Mass: MIT Press.
HALLE, Morris (1973): Prolegomena to a theory of word-formation. In: Linguistic Inquiry 4, 3-16.
JACKENDOFF, Ray (1977): X-bar syntax: a study of phrase structure. Linguistic Inquiry Monograph 2. Cambridge, Mass: MIT Press.
— (1972): Semantic interpretation in generative grammar. Cambridg, Mass: MIT Press.
KATAMBA, Francis (1993): Morphology. London: The Macmillan press Ltd.
LEES, Robert (1970): Problems in the grammatical analysis of English nominal compounds? In: Bierwisch, M.; Herdoph (eds): Progress in linguistics. The Hague: Mouton (Ianua linguarum, Series maior 43), 174-186.
— (1960): The grammar of English nominalizations. The Hague: Mouton.
LIEBER, Rochelle (1983): Argument linking and compounds in English. In Linguistic Inquiry 14, 251-285.
— (1981): On the organization of the lexicon. Indiana: University Linguistic Club.
PESETSKY, David (1985): Morphology and logical form. In: Linguistic Inquiry 16, 193-246.
ROEPER, Thomas; SIEGEL, Mark (1978): A lexical transformation for verbal compounds. In Linguistic Inquiry 9, 199-260.
SINCLAIR, John (general ed.) (1991) *The Collins-Cobuild English language dictionary*. London: Collins ELT.
SCALISE, Sergio (1984): Generative morphology. Dordrecht: Foris.
SELKIRK, Elisabeth (1982): The syntax of words. Cambridge, Mass: MIT Press (Linguistic Inquiry Monograph 7).
SPENCER, Andrew (1991): Morphological theory. Cambridge, Mass: Basil Blackwell Ltd.
VINAGRE, Margarita (1999): Análisis contrastivo de los compuestos ingleses y españoles: la aplicación de principios sintácticos en la generación de términos léxicos. In: Estudios de Lingüística Descriptiva y Comparada. III Simposio Andaluz de Lingüística General. Universidad de Sevilla, Kronos, 469-478.
— (1996): The interface between syntax and morphology: a study of English and Spanish verbal compounds. Ph. D. dissertation, University of Seville.
WILLIAMS, Edwin (1981a): Argument structure and morphology. In: Linguistic Review 1, 81-114.
— (1981b): On the notions 'lexically related' and 'head of a word'. In: Linguistic Inquiry 12, 245-74.

Pragmatik

Wordplay and Implicatures

Philippe De Brabanter

1   Introduction

In this paper, I would like to throw a bridge between a metalinguistic and a neo-Gricean account of puns. The metalinguistic dimension is highlighted by a number of writers (e.g. Sobkowiak 1991 *passim*; Delabastita 1993:68; Attardo 1994:168) but, to my knowledge, there has been no thoroughgoing attempt at formalising the metalinguistic semantics and pragmatics of puns. On the other hand, several linguists have brought – or suggested bringing – Grice's Cooperative Principle and implicatures to bear on verbal humour (Raskin 1985: esp. 103; Attardo 1994:271-92). Sobkowiak goes so far as to contemplate the benefits of "considering metalinguistic manipulation [...] as one type of *flouting* or *exploitation* of the Gricean maxims, e.g. that of relevance or manner (avoid ambiguity)" (1991:20), but he does not proceed to deliver the suggested analysis. However, his insight is certainly worth investigating at greater length, and this paper is conceived as a tentative step in that direction.

Any discussion of puns in terms of implicatures presupposes that puns are acts of verbal communication. It may seem odd to raise the issue, but a quick look at some of the relevant literature shows that puns are often considered to *disrupt* communication. Grice for one claims that the intention to amuse, which can be assumed to underly a majority of puns, can never give rise to 'non-natural meaning,' which is widely viewed as a necessary condition for communication (1989:92; Levinson 1983:101). Other writers who hold similar views are Sobkowiak (1991:1) and Guiraud (1979:86). Raskin and Attardo only grant jokes (and puns) the status of '*non-bona-fide* communication'. It can nevertheless be shown (see De Brabanter, in preparation) that puns may be included within acts of communication, but lack of space prevents me from discussing this any further here. The reader is therefore requested to suspend any disbelief s/he might experience.

In the analyses that follow, I shall avail myself of the division between 'sentence-meaning' and 'utterance-meaning' as worked out by Lyons (1995). Sentence-meaning is meaning that depends exclusively on grammatical and semantic competence, owing nothing to the co-text, context, or the act of uttering. Usually, formal semanticists reduce it to propositional content, but like Lyons I take it to cover also 'thematic meaning,' which derives from the way the theme of the utterance is articulated to its rheme, and 'characteristic use,' which accounts for the fact that a grammatically declarative sentence will preferentially be read as a statement, an interrogative one as a question, and an imperative one as an injunction – the relevant point being the relation between a grammatical form and a default interpretation. Utterance-meaning, on the other hand, adds to sentence-meaning whatever depends on the context of utterance, notably implicatures, whether conventional or conversational, and deixis. Thus, a proposition, in which all the referential expressions of the propositional content are given a referent, pertains to utterance-meaning. It is useful to note that those utterances that are not matched with a sentence have no meaning other than their utterance-meaning.

I would like to insist on the difference between sentence, propositional content, and proposition. Propositional content is in the same relation to the sentence as lexical meaning is to the lexeme: a potentiality waiting to be fleshed out in discourse. As to the proposition, it must not be confused with the sentence. Lyons remarks that

> "[t]he vast majority of sentences in the most familiar natural languages can be used, on particular occasions of utterance, to assert, to query or to deny indefinitely many propositions, each of which has a constant truth-value which is independent of that of each of the others that may be expressed by uttering the same sentence" (1995:143).

Besides, in the same way as a sentence can be used to convey however many propositions, it is also well-known that one and the same proposition can be expressed by a large number of (synonymous) sentences.

2   The various configurations

On the basis of the above distinction, four different cases can be delineated:

   a) [+ sentence-meaning, + utterance-meaning]
   b) [+ sentence-meaning, - utterance-meaning]
   c) [- sentence-meaning, + utterance-meaning]
   d) [- sentence-meaning, - utterance-meaning]

We can eliminate two from the outset: d) is irrelevant here because it captures a situation in which no meaning is communicated at all. b) can be left aside as well because it attaches to cases where everything is encapsulated in the sentence-meaning. This automatically rules out any possibility of double-entendre in which the second(ary) meaning would be captured at the utterance-level. The only b) cases I can think of are general assertions such as *All men are mortal*, but even these are likely to yield implicatures in contexts other than strictly regimented syllogisms.

2.1   Puns embedded in non-sentences

We shall first look into c), i.e. puns occurring in utterances that are unacceptable grammatically or semantically:

> 1) "'BRITAIN TO BEET THE WORLD!' a page-five headline in the Daily Express had declared above a photograph of Albert and a government agriculturist standing proudly in front of their 'experimental' acres." (Fry, 1995: 211)

To avoid needless complications induced by the presence of several utterers, only the headline in capitals will retain our attention. Strictly speaking, 1) is not a sentence: it is ungrammatical because an N is wrongly used instead of a V. Alternatively, it could also be said to be a-lexical since it is not the 'right' lexeme *beat* that has been used. The utterance, therefore, is devoid of sentence-meaning. But it has utterance-meaning, the 'emergence' of which can be accounted for by means of conversational implicatures. Indeed, it is easy to see what motivates such inferences: one of the maxims of Manner is flouted: the utterance is 'obscure' precisely because it is grammaticaly ill-formed. Therefore, the reader will be prompted to calculate such implicatures as:

The author of the headline wanted to convey information concisely and strikingly. S/he used the N *beet* in such a way as to conjure up the V *beat*, which is the expected word in this co-text. Thus, I infer that what s/he meant was: "Britain will defeat the rest of the world thanks to its beets".

It is worth noting that the implicatures derived from 1) include a metalinguistic operation on *beet*, which can be labelled as 'metalinguistic connotation.' This concept developed from Rey-Debove's 'autonymic connotation' (1997:251-91) consists in the conjuring up (connotation) of a whole sign by another sign which already has a denotative meaning. In the end, the connoted sign forms the connotative meaning of said sign, a pattern that can be represented by the formula E_1 (C_1 (E_2 (C_2))), where:

> E = Expression and C = Content, i.e. Hjelmslev's terms for Saussure's *signifiant* and *signifié* respectively.
> E_1 = b-e-e-t
> C_1 = "an edible plant of the goosefoot family"
> E_2 = b-e-a-t
> C_2 = "defeat"

Such a metalinguistic operation is a necessary condition for 'getting' the pun. The possible objection that the operation is so automatized as to be barely conscious is not, however, any more damaging here than it is in the case of a great deal of the ordinary implicatures calculated by hearers/readers on a daily basis.

Let us scrutinise a further example:

> 2) "Why is a deceptive woman like a seamstress? Because she is not what she seems! ('Not bad,' the friendly reader may remark, button the hole perhaps it's sewnly sew-sew; a-hem! and a needles(s) addition to our work." (quoted in Augarde, 1984: 209)

This is another example of a non-sentence. Yet, with the help of implicatures the following proposition can be reconstructed, one which is homophonous with the initial one "but on the whole, perhaps it's only so-so, ahem, and a needless addition to our work".

Clearly, the implicata in 2) carry less meaning and information than in 1). They contribute nothing to the whole reconstructed proposition. They are purely local and thoroughly gratuitous phenomena: the punster seems to have got carried away with his own playing and his only aim is to maximise the number of punning opportunities.

I believe the differences between 1) and 2) warrant the differentiation of two planes: a narrow local one, and one that extends to the whole utterance (not to be confused with utterance-meaning):

- in 1), the local phenomenon, which neatly fits metalinguistic connotation, suffuses a more informative proposition with additional meaning on the utterance plane;

- in 2), local phenomena, which are also analysable as instances of metalinguistic connotation, are ends in and of themselves. The proposition reconstructed is a mere pretext, witness its weak informativeness.

In other words, 1), which is not merely gratuitous but endeavours to convey some information as well, contains a pun that is central to the utterer's informative intention, whereas in 2) the puns tend instead to disrupt or nullify this intention. It could be inferred that gratuitous puns, of which 2) offers several illustrations, fulfil only one of the two (or more) functions of punning utterances, viz. the intention to amuse.[1] This is reflected in the twofold observation that the central implicatures calculated on the basis of a gratuitous pun are 'local' in character, and are preferentially realised as metalinguistic connotation. By contrast, in those puns where the informative function is in the foreground, local implicatures also play a role on the extended utterance plane: they are necessary steps on the way to establishing the overall implicatum that is the reconstructed proposition integrating the contribution of the pun(s) present.

These observations throw some light on some hitherto rarely investigated aspects of conversational implicatures. We shall return to these at the close of the next section.

2.2   Puns embedded in sentences

We can now turn to configuration a). This pattern concerns a vast number of puns, e.g.:

3) "Once Nora had set the ball rolling, other couples took the floor." (Carter 1991:218)

The pun is on *set the ball rolling*, an idiom in which *ball* means "a hollow or solid spherical body used in a game or sport". Yet, the co-text of 3) mentions a *ball* in the sense of "an occasion for formal dancing". The first *ball* conjures up the second in spite of the fact that the latter is not usually regarded as capable of *rolling*. What the pun brings to the utterance-meaning is encapsulated in the proposition "Nora got the ball under way". Since the two *balls* are homonyms, it can in principle be assumed that what is connoted is a whole sign rather than just a sense or a signified, as in ordinary connotation. Hence the formula:

$E_1 (C_1 (E_1 (C_2)))$, with
C_1 = "spherical body used in a game"
C_2 = "an occasion for formal dancing"

Analysis is not always that straightforward, however. Difficulties are a function of the degree of gratuitousness of the pun. In the following example, police superintendent San-Antonio is having a chat with his boss, a greying, balding man:

---

[1]   The intention to amuse may arguably not be central to all puns. It is not impossible to distinguish between that intention and a 'humorous' intention, whose sole purpose would be to generate something recognisable as humour (with or without amusement). These questions are discussed in De Brabanter (in preparation).

4) "– Qu'avez-vous? s'informe le déplumé en s'efforçant de maintenir son sérieux.
– Je crois, patron, que nos pensées sont aussi parallèles qu'une voie ferrée...
– C'est-à-dire?
Déjà, l'homme chauve sourit.
– C'est-à-dire que [etc.]" (San-Antonio 1961:42)

A fairly close translation (that loses the humour):

– What's up? The featherless one asks trying hard to remain serious.
– I think, boss, that our thoughts are running along perfectly parallel lines...
– Which means?
Already, the bald man is smiling.
– It means that [...]

We shall concentrate on *Déjà, l'homme chauve sourit*. This is a sentence, a fairly innocuous-looking one at that. However, it made this writer laugh because of the assumed presence of a pun. The latter's existence is unprovable; there can at best be only a suspicion, but one that is countenanced by the following insights: the adventures of superintendent San-Antonio are riddled with bullet-holes *and* puns, and there seldom elapse more than a few lines without new plays on words. This particular expectation will help identify a pun on *chauve sourit*, which is homophonous with the connoted *chauve-souris* ("bat"). Once again, metalinguistic connotation provides an accurate account, and can be held to occur in one of the implicata derived from the utterance.

It is likely that those readers liable to calculate implicatures on *Déjà, l'homme chauve sourit* will do so because they assume that failing these implicatures one or the other conversational maxim will be breached, in this case the maxim of Relation: some readers may take it that the sentence-meaning of the utterance is in itself insufficiently relevant precisely because its narrative contribution is close to nil. A pun therefore warrants the presence of the utterance by making it relevant.

If it is accepted that there is a conversational implicature, then the next question to ask is "what is the nature of the resulting implicatum?". Some implicata clearly have the form of propositions, i.e. their standard appearance in most of the literature. Two remarks are in order: 1. the difference between implicatures (inference mechanisms) and implicata (the outcome of these mechanisms) is often neglected.[2] This is unsurprising if we remember that the very term *inference* is often used indifferently for both process and product. 2. Most authors do simply not thematise the question of the nature of implicata. That is why the inference that they are propositions is often based on indirect evidence. Here are the main clues: the standard symbols for propositions, p and q, are used to identify implicata (Bussmann 1996:221; Sebeok 1986:339); implicatures are presented as (non-truth-conditional) inference mechanisms, and it is standard in logic for inferences to manipulate and produce propositions (Auroux 1990:1248; Bouissac 1998:302-03; Levinson 1983:102 sq.; Horn 1992:261). None the less, there are several writers who define implicata explicitly as propositions: Grice (1975 *passim*); Wilson & Sperber (1979:86 sq.); Gazdar (1979:38); Leech (1981:296; 1983:9); Ducrot & Schaeffer (1995:476). Among the writers consulted,

---

[2] Gazdar (1979:37) explicitly draws his readers' attention to his (and others') 'sloppy' use of Grice's term.

Lyons (1977) is the only one to address the nature of implicata in any detail. After suggesting that they are propositions (1977:593), he goes on to qualify this assertion (1977:605). Unfortunately, the idea that implicata are not necessarily propositions remains unexplained and unexemplified.

The present study, however, suggests that there is a type of implicatum that cannot easily be regarded as a proposition. Taking up again the distinction made above between a local and a wider plane, it appears that 4) does not lend itself to reconstructing an overall proposition integrating the meaning supplied locally by the pun. Such propositions as "Already, the man is a bat" or "Already, the man has become a bat" are scarcely relevant, contrary to the propositions rebuilt in 1) and 3), respectively "I'll be a man in his grave = a dead man", "Britain is to beat the world thanks to its beets" and "Nora got the ball under way".

In 4), as in 2), certain implicata seem to be confined to the local plane. In other words, they should not be conceived of as full-fledged propositions but rather as bare instances of metalinguistic connotation. Actually, forcing them into a proposition as in 1) and 3) would amount to denying their gratuitousness.

Furthermore, 4) presents us with an extra paradox compared to 2): the implicature that we are concerned with in 4) seems to be going in the wrong direction: it generates extra nonsense (a non-proposition) rather than extra sense. Ordinary conversational implicatures, in assuming the utterer's observance of the Cooperation Principle, increase the amount of meaning or the informativeness of utterances. For the case in hand to comply with this general trend, it should then be concluded that nonsense can be meaningful. This may look like something of a truism, especially to those who are fond of Lewis Carroll's *Jabberwocky* or, in a less linguistic vein, the humour of Boris Vian or the Monthy Pythons. However, it cannot be overemphasised that 4) involves the opposite process to these examples: rather than meaning being squeezed out of nonsense, it is nonsense that springs out of an utterance that initially makes sense (it has sentence-meaning). One way of saving the day is to assume that the process under discussion breaks down into two stages: from sense to nonsense, and from nonsense to sense. The latter stage would be reached as a result of the putative pun increasing the relevance of an otherwise all-too-ordinary statement.

3   Puns that do not lend themselves to a Gricean analysis

What I have in mind are so-called 'polysemous' puns (Guiraud 1976:11). Here are a few examples:

5) "(The CHAIRMAN has hurriedly wiped the board clean and is putting his underpants back into his brief case.)
FRENCH: What is that?
WITHENSHAW: Pair of briefs
FRENCH: What are they doing in there?
WITHENSHAW: It's a brief case." (Stoppard 1976:43)

(6) "[The dictator gets up and pays his harem a visit:] Le Polonais enfila son peignoir (pour commencer) et prit l'ascenseur qui le hissa d'un étage." (San-Antonio 1996:23) [translation: The Pole slipped on his dressing gown (for a start) and rode the lift to the upper floor.]

7) "– [the doctor:] Otherwise he'll be fine. I'm sure he's a good healer.
– You speak truer than you know [...]" (Fry 1995:306)

In all three examples it seems more sensible to assume that the connotative content is not a whole sign but just another sense of the same sign. Hence, the appropriate formula is E_1 (C_1 (C_2)), or rather E_1 (C_{1a} (C_{1b})) to show that the two Cs are contextual actualisations of the same potential signified. Contrary to cases of homonymy, the two Cs are linked to the same signifier within a single sign. In 5) *brief case* has a twofold signified (denotative + connotative[3]), i.e. "a case for carrying documents" and "a case for pairs of briefs". In 6) the denotative and connotative contents of *enfila* are "slip sth on" and "shag". In 7), *good healer* has a subjective meaning in the doctor's mouth, "someone who heals easily", then an objective one in his addressee's reply: the addressee knows about the secret healing powers of the young man who has just been hurt and who is "a great healer of animals".

What is interesting is that these puns should rather not be analysed in terms of implicatures either. Lyons indicates that in cases of grammatical ambiguity and polysemy (and perhaps also certain cases of homonymy within the same word-class), an utterance is likely to be the form of more than one sentence. Usually, co-textual and contextual clues allow selecting the 'right' sentence. Here, the opposite obtains: in 6) for instance the interpolated clause, *pour commencer*, forces the utterance to be the form of two sentences at the same time, each one of which selects one of the two senses of *enfila*. This cannot normally fit into the theoretical framework of implicatures, since the additional meanings these supply are part of the utterance-meaning and are always calculated on the basis of a single sentence (when there is a sentence).

4 Conclusion

By way of conclusion, I shall suggest that the distinction made by many a writer between pun and play on words *stricto sensu* (see Augarde 1984:204-05) finds another confirmation here: the two verbal acts do not display the same semantic and pragmatic behaviour, since the pun admits of implicatures – one of which takes the shape of metalinguistic connotation – while the play on words does not.

Several problems could not be tackled here. First, what is the meaning level where the metalinguistic connotation of puns belongs? It straddles sentence-meaning and utterance-meaning, and E_2 (C_2) results from an implicature. Now, in Rey-Debove's canonical examples for 'autonymic connotation' – e.g. "They've taken industrial action, as it is called nowadays" – the *whole* configuration pertains to sentence-meaning. This is a discrepancy that deserves further investigation.

Second, metalinguistic connotation certainly does not display one of the typical features of conversational implicatures as inventoried by Grice in "Logic and Conversation" (1989:39; point 2): non-detachability. Any other utterance with the same meaning as the initial one should normally permit the same implicatures, whatever its

---

[3] Contrary to what Rey-Debove (1997:253) implies, it is often difficult to determine which is which.

form. This is clearly not the case here as formal likeness is essential. The detachability of these implicatures also needs to be explored at greater length.

5   References

ATTARDO, Salvatore (1994): Linguistic Theories of Humor. Berlin – New York: Mouton de Gruyter.
AUGARDE, Tony (1984): The Oxford Guide to Word Games. Oxford – New York: Oxford University Press.
AUROUX, Sylvain (1990): Encyclopédie philosophique universelle. Les notions philosophiques, vol. 1. Paris: PUF.
BOUISSAC, Paul (1998): Encyclopedia of Semiotics. New York – Oxford: Oxford University Press.
BUSSMANN, Hadumod (1996): Routledge Dictionary of Language and Linguistics (transl. and ed. by G. Trauth; K. Kazzazi). London – New York: Routledge.
CARTER, Angela (1991): Wise Children. London: Chatto & Windus.
DE BRABANTER, Philippe (in preparation): Jeux de mots et communication.
DELABASTITA, Dirk (1993): There's a Double Tongue. An investigation into the translation of Shakespeare's wordplay with special reference to Hamlet. Amsterdam – Atlanta: Rodopi.
DUCROT, Oswald; SCHAEFFER, Jean-Marie (1995): Nouveau dictionnaire encyclopédique des sciences du langage. Paris: Seuil.
FRY, Stephen (1995): The Hippopotamus. London: Arrow books.
GAZDAR, Gerald (1979): Pragmatics. Implicature, presupposition, and logical form. New York – San Francisco – London: Academic Press.
GRICE, Herbert Paul (1989): Studies in the Way of Words. Cambridge, Mass. – London: Harvard University Press.
GUIRAUD, Pierre (1976): Les Jeux de Mots. Paris: PUF, collection que sais-je?
HORN, Laurence (1992): Pragmatics, implicature and presupposition. In: Bright, W. (ed.): International Encyclopedia of Linguistics, vol. 3. New York – Oxford: Oxford University Press, 260-66.
LEECH, Geoffrey (1983): Principles of Pragmatics. London – New York: Longman.
— (1981): Semantics. The study of meaning. Penguin Books.
LEVINSON, Stephen C. (1983): Pragmatics. Cambridge: Cambridge University Press.
LYONS, John (1995): Linguistic Semantics. An introduction. Cambridge: Cambridge University Press.
— (1977): Semantics, Vol. 1. Cambridge: Cambridge University Press.
RASKIN, Victor (1985), Semantic Mechanisms of Humor. Dordrecht – Boston – Lancaster: Reidel.
REY-DEBOVE, Josette ([2]1997): Le Métalangage. Etude linguistique du discours sur le langage. Paris: Armand Colin.
SAN-ANTONIO (1996): De l'antigel dans le calbute. Fleuve noir 167.
— (1961): San-Antonio chez les Mac. Fleuve noir 18.
SEBEOK, Thomas A. (1986): Encyclopedic Dictionary of Semiotics, Vol. 1. Berlin – New York – Amsterdam: Mouton de Gruyter.
SOBKOWIAK, Wlodzimierz (1991): Metaphonology of English Paronomasic Puns. Frankfurt a. M. etc.: Peter Lang.
STOPPARD, Tom (1976): Dirty Linen. New York: Grove Press Inc.
WILSON, Deirdre; SPERBER, Dan (1979): Remarques sur l'interprétation des énoncés selon Paul Grice. In: Communication 30, 80-94.

Sprachwandel und Sprechereinstellungen im Russischen Ergebnisse einer Umfrage

Andrea Dettmer

1 Einleitung

Der Wandel der russischen Sprache seit Beginn der Perestrojka ist allgegenwärtig; nicht erst seit gestern machen sich eklatante Veränderungen im Sprachgebrauch der Medien bemerkbar. Aus linguistischer Sicht manifestiert sich dieser Wandel auf allen Ebenen der Sprache; ausführlich erforscht wurden bisher aber lediglich Morphologie und Lexik. Insbesondere lexikalischen Neuerungen wird große Aufmerksamkeit zuteil, was u.a. in zahlreichen Wortsammlungen und anderen rein deskriptiv gehaltenen Werken zum Ausdruck kommt (vgl. Duličenko 1994; Rathmayr 1991; Zemskaja 1996). Die Veränderungen auf pragmatischer Ebene – d.h. der Wandel der kommunikativen Handlungsmuster (Textsorten) – wurde jedoch in der Russistik bisher stark vernachlässigt, obwohl gerade auf diesem Gebiet tiefgreifende Veränderungen stattfinden, die ihrerseits den Sprachwandel auf anderen Ebenen erklärbar machen.

Dieser so verstandene pragmatische bzw. Textsortenwandel wurde in der gegenwärtigen Entwicklung der slawischen Sprachen, vor allem des Russischen und Bulgarischen, erstmals durch Zybatow (1995a, 1995b) in das wissenschaftliche Blickfeld gerückt und als systematischer methodisch-theoretischer Ansatz erprobt. Damit lassen sich Auslösung, Verbreitung und Geltung von sprachlichen Wandelerscheinungen verfolgen und erklären.

Neben fremdsprachlichen Interferenzen finden sich in der russischen Gegenwartssprache vor allem solche sprachlichen und stilistischen Neuerungen, die auf den wachsenden Einfluß bestimmter sozialer Varietäten des Russischen zurückzuführen sind, wie z.B. des Jugendjargons oder des *mat* – einer vulgären, doch jedem Russen vertrauten Schimpf- und Fluchsprache. Dabei fällt auf, daß solche der niederen stilistischen Ebene zuzuordnenden Elemente häufig Eingang finden in Textsorten, die normalerweise durch normgerechten Gebrauch der russischen Hochsprache charakterisiert sind bzw. es bis vor Beginn der Perestrojka waren. Zu diesen Textsorten gehören z.b. Berichte über offizielle politische, wirtschaftliche oder gesellschaftliche Sachverhalte in den Printmedien. Diese machen zudem durch extensive Verwendung eines durch Mündlichkeit geprägten Stils auf sich aufmerksam. Insbesondere vor dem Hintergrund des während des totalitären Sowjet-Regimes propagierten, stark normierten und hölzern und gestelzt klingenden Stils des sogenannten Newspeaks fallen die sprachlichen Veränderungen im postsozialistischen Russisch sofort ins Auge. Journalisten wurden damals durch Zensur und unmißverständliche Vorgaben von oben gezwungen, sich eben jenen unpersönlichen, jedoch mit den ideellen Grundsätzen des Marxismus konform gehenden Sprachgebrauch zu eigen zu machen. Mit dem Zerfall der Sowjetunion fiel auch die Zensur und mit ihr die Überwachung der publizistischen Aktivitäten durch sogenannte Sprachideologen und vermeintliche Sprachpfleger. Die geänderten politischen Rahmenbedingungen ermöglichten nun eine freie

Meinungsäußerung sowie einen dem Einfluß sprachpuristischer Instanzen entzogenen Sprachgebrauch. Die Folgen waren – und sind – nicht zu übersehen: Die auf den Seiten der Zeitungen und Zeitschriften lange Zeit unterdrückten Anglizismen, Jargonismen, Vulgarismen (z.b. aus dem *mat*) sowie Elemente der einfachen, vor allem im städtischen Gebiet gesprochenen, etwas derben Umgangssprache (des sogenannten *prostorečie*) werden nun extensiv genutzt. Somit werden die bis dato geltenden stilistischen Normen weitestgehend außer Acht gelassen, ja, vorsätzlich verletzt, u.a. mit dem Ziel, Aufmerksamkeit zu erregen und eine in jeder Hinsicht freie Gesinnung zu demonstrieren. Dies markierte den Anfang einer mit Vehemenz geführten Diskussion über Vor- und Nachteile dieses modernen Sprachgebrauchs. Wissenschaftler wie Laien äußerten sich in Aufsätzen, Leserbriefen und Interviews zu dem vermeintlichen Verfall der russischen Literatursprache.

Dieser öffentlich geführte Metadiskurs hat mich dazu veranlaßt, die Attitüden und Einstellungen russischer Muttersprachler zum Wandel ihrer Sprache einmal selbst näher zu untersuchen. Dies geschah im Rahmen einer soziolinguistischen Feldstudie während eines Forschungsaufenthaltes in Sibirien. Die Ergebnisse der Befragung von 158 russischen Muttersprachlern im Mai 1998 sollten vor allem zwei Fragen beantworten:

1) Wie nehmen russische Muttersprachler die Veränderungen in ihrer Sprache wahr?
2) Wie bewerten sie diese Veränderungen?

Die Beschäftigung mit einer Fremdsprache setzt natürlich profunde Kenntnisse in derselben voraus; doch dem Nicht-Muttersprachler hapert es meist trotzdem an der notwendigen Intuition, dem Sprachgefühl. Jegliche Bewertung, jede Beurteilung der Fremdsprache erfolgt deshalb immer unter dem Blickwinkel der eigenen, in diesem Fall eben der deutschen, Sprache und Mentalität. Aus eben diesem Grunde sollte der Standpunkt der Muttersprachler nicht ignoriert werden.

2   Ergebnisse der Umfrage

Zunächst einige Anmerkungen zur Methodik: Es wurden 158 russische Muttersprachler ab 18 Jahren befragt. Es handelt sich um eine zweidimensional quotierte Stichprobe, d.h., die Stichprobe spiegelt den Bevölkerungsdurchschnitt im Hinblick auf Geschlecht und Alter wider. Die Probanden mußten russische Muttersprachler sein sowie Leser von Zeitungen und / oder Zeitschriften. Die Umfrage in Form von persönlichen Interviews (face-to-face) wurde vom 2. bis zum 20. Mai 1998 in der Stadt Tomsk (Sibirien) an wechselnden Standorten (öffentlichen Plätzen) durchgeführt.

2.1   Dimension des Sprachwandels

Insgesamt ist jeder vierte russische Muttersprachler der Auffassung, daß sich der Sprachgebrauch in den Printmedien innerhalb der letzten zehn Jahre (also seit der

Perestrojka) *sehr stark* verändert habe (ca. 25 %). Eine *starke* Veränderung hat mehr als die Hälfte der Befragten konstatiert (ca. 51 %). Lediglich knapp 18 % bezeichnen die Veränderungen in der Sprache der Printmedien als geringfügig, ca. 6 % wollen keinen Unterschied zum publizistischen Sprachgebrauch vor der Perestrojka festgestellt haben. Es fällt auf, daß Frauen wesentlich sensibler auf derartige Erscheinungen reagieren, denn im Vergleich zu den russischen Männern schätzen sie die Dimension des Sprachwandels deutlich größer ein: Während mehr als 85 % der Frauen der Ansicht sind, der Sprachgebrauch der Printmedien habe sich *stark* oder sogar *sehr stark* verändert (Kategorie 1 und 2 addiert), schließen sich dieser Meinung nur gut zwei Drittel der Männer an (ca. 67 %).

In Abhängigkeit vom Alter der Probanden lassen sich weitere signifikante Unterschiede feststellen: Vor allem jungen Erwachsenen zwischen 25 und 39 Jahren sowie Senioren (55 Jahre und älter) sind die sprachlichen Veränderungen im postsozialistischen Russisch aufgefallen, denn in diesen Segmenten finden sich mit jeweils ca. 83 % der Nennungen überdurchschnittlich hohe Werte (Kategorien *stark* und *sehr stark* addiert). Zum Vergleich: Jugendliche kommen hier nur auf rund 64 %.

Wie zu erwarten ist, spielt auch die Bildung eine Rolle im Hinblick auf die Bewertung der Sprache: Mit steigender Bildung nimmt die Zahl derer, die den Sprachwandel als sehr tiefgreifend bezeichnen (Kategorie *sehr stark*), kontinuierlich von ca. 8 % (Probanden mit Hauptschulbildung) auf gut 39 % (mit Hochschulbildung) zu. Diese Zahlen lassen vermuten, daß besser gebildete Personen infolge ihres Vorsprungs im Bereich kognitiv-intellektueller Fähigkeiten sensibler sind für derartige Veränderungen, da sie sich offenbar intensiver mit der Sprache – z.B. über die Nutzung von Printmedien – auseinandersetzen. Ob sich dieser Wissensvorsprung auch auf das Textverständnis auswirkt, wird sich im Zusammenhang mit den Fragen 4 und 5 herausstellen, welche sich auf einen den Testpersonen vorgelegten Ausschnitt eines authentischen Interviews beziehen.

2.2 Wichtigste Veränderungen

Auch wenn der Wegfall der Zensur und die sich dadurch entwickelnde Meinungs- und Themenvielfalt nicht primär zu den Veränderungen im Sprachgebrauch zu rechnen sind, so haben sie sich doch ganz erheblich auf ihn ausgewirkt. Aus diesem Grund wurde bei den Antworten auf die Frage nach den wichtigsten Veränderungen im Sprachgebrauch der Medien (offene Frage!) auch die Kategorie *Themenvielfalt, Meinungsfreiheit, Wegfall der Zensur* aufgenommen, denn diese wurde am häufigsten genannt: Knapp 37 % der russischen Muttersprachler halten dies für eine der wichtigsten Wandelerscheinungen. Mit äußerst knappem Abstand folgen die zahlreichen fremdsprachlichen Ausdrücke, im wesentlichen Entlehnungen aus anderen Sprachen (ca. 36 %). Mehr als ein Drittel der Befragten führt den veränderten Sprachgebrauch der Journalisten und Redakteure also auf deren Vorliebe für Fremdwörter zurück. Probleme mit dem Verständnis gibt jeder Fünfte an: Viel Unverständliches, Unsinn und auch Überflüssiges sei in den Zeitungen und Zeitschriften aufgetaucht. Ebenso häufig wird aber auch ein positiver Aspekt hervorgehoben, nämlich die Tatsache, daß die Sprache seitdem lockerer, interessanter, lebendiger geworden sei.

Neologismen – also neue Wortschöpfungen, neue Lexik – bezeichnen rund 16 % der Befragten als wichtigste Veränderungen im Sprachgebrauch der Printmedien; ein fast ebenso hoher Anteil verweist auf die gestiegene Frequenz von Jargonismen und Slangismen in Zeitungen. Frauen nennen diesen Aspekt dreimal so häufig wie Männer, was darauf zurückzuführen sein könnte, daß eine derbe Ausdrucksweise bei Männern immer noch eher gesellschaftlich akzeptiert wird als bei Frauen, welche offensichtlich stärker auf derartige Abweichungen achten.

In Zusammenhang mit dem Jargon ergibt sich ein weiteres interessantes Detailergebnis: Der Aussage, daß Printmedien sich heute vielfach einer unverständlichen Ausdrucksweise bedienen, stimmen die Befragten mit steigendem Alter um so häufiger zu. So pflichten lediglich knapp 8 % der Jugendlichen dieser Aussage bei, unter den Senioren sind es hingegen rund 36 %. Umgekehrt identifizieren mit steigendem Alter immer weniger Menschen die sprachlichen Veränderungen als Jargon- oder Slang-Ausdrücke. Dies könnte darauf hinweisen, daß die Jargonismen für ältere Menschen häufig nicht als solche zu erkennen sind und statt dessen für unverständlich, unsinnig gehalten werden.

Je älter die Probanden sind, desto seltener können sie dem modernen Sprachgebrauch etwas Positives abgewinnen: Mit steigendem Alter sinkt der Anteil derjenigen, die glauben, daß die Sprache der Medien insgesamt lockerer, interessanter und vielseitiger geworden ist. Höher gebildete Personen stimmen dieser Aussage übrigens deutlich häufiger zu als jene mit Hauptschulbildung bzw. mittlerer Bildung. Letzteren fallen nämlich vor allem die zahlreichen fremdsprachlichen Ausdrücke (50 % bzw. 47 %), die neue Lexik (40 % bzw. 23 %) sowie der insgesamt unverständliche Sprachgebrauch in den modernen Printmedien auf (30 % bzw. 23 %). Aus diesen Ergebnissen könnte man schließen, daß die Zeitungslektüre Personen mit niedriger Schulbildung zunehmend Schwierigkeiten bereitet, da sie in der Regel nicht über die notwendigen Fremdsprachenkenntnisse verfügen, um die entsprechenden Ausdrücke zu verstehen.

2.3 Bewertung der Veränderungen

An dieser Stelle wurden die befragten Muttersprachler aufgefordert, die von ihnen zuvor konstatierten Veränderungen zu bewerten, d.h., diese Frage gibt Aufschluß über die Einstellung russischer Muttersprachler zum Wandel ihrer Sprache. Das Ergebnis fällt eindeutig aus: Mehr als die Hälfte der Befragten beurteilt die Veränderungen negativ, lediglich gut ein Viertel bezeichnet sie als Bereicherung für die russische Sprache. Für weitere 21 % spielen die Veränderungen keine Rolle.

Frauen signalisieren eine etwas positivere Einstellung als Männer, denn sie bewerten die Veränderungen häufiger als Bereicherung für die Sprache. Männer hingegen demonstrieren häufiger Gleichgültigkeit gegenüber den sprachlichen Wandelerscheinungen.

Die Einstellung zum Sprachwandel scheint eindeutig altersabhängig zu sein, was meines Erachtens auch leicht nachzuvollziehen ist: So bewertet die Mehrheit der Jugendlichen (rund 56 %) die Veränderungen eher als Bereicherung, Senioren hingegen sehen dies nur in 14 % der Fälle so. Mit steigendem Alter nimmt daher auch die Zahl derjenigen kontinuierlich zu, die die Veränderungen im Sprachgebrauch negativ bewerten.

Negative bis gleichgültige Äußerungen stammen vor allem von Personen mit niedriger Schulbildung. Nur jeder Zehnte dieser soziodemographischen Untergruppe ist der Auffassung, daß die russische Sprache durch die Neuerungen und Veränderungen bereichert worden ist. In der Gruppe der Probanden mit mittlerer Schulbildung sind es sogar nur knapp 7 %, während Personen mit höherer Bildung (Berufsfachschule/ Technikum bzw. Universität) diesbezüglich auf deutlich höhere Werte kommen (39 % bzw. 33 %).

2.4 Textverständnis

Nach Vorlage des Ausschnittes aus einem Interview der Zeitung *Argumenty i Fakty* – wurden die Testpersonen gebeten anzugeben, ob ihnen alle der im Text benutzten Ausdrücke bekannt sind oder nicht. Der vorgelegte Text wurde bewußt aufgrund seiner hohen Zahl an Jargonismen und Anglizismen ausgewählt. Dementsprechend eindeutig fiel das Ergebnis aus: Acht von zehn Muttersprachler verneinen die Frage nach dem Verständnis sämtlicher Ausdrücke. Vor allem Frauen haben deutliche Schwierigkeiten mit der entsprechenden Ausdrucksweise, denn ihr Anteil liegt mit gut 87 % spürbar höher als der der männlichen Testteilnehmer (ca. 71 %). Dieses Ergebnis stützt erneut meine obige These, daß eine derbe, zumindest jedoch von Jargonismen geprägte Sprache tendenziell eher eine Domäne der männlichen Sprecher ist, während Frauen möglicherweise stärker auf eine angemessene Ausdrucksweise achten. Die These, daß ein geschlechtsspezifischer Sprachgebrauch existiert, ist natürlich nicht neu, doch sie beweist sich an dieser Stelle aufs Neue, was zweifellos für die Qualität der erhobenen Daten spricht. Nicht gänzlich auszuschließen ist natürlich auch eine bewußt *geschönte* Antwort der weiblichen Probanden gemäß der bereits angesprochenen gesellschaftlichen Erwartungshaltung.

Wie zu erwarten ist, nehmen die Probleme beim Textverständnis mit steigendem Alter zu, d.h., während Jugendliche vielfach überhaupt keine Schwierigkeiten haben, gibt es in der Altersgruppe der ab 55jährigen niemanden, der ausnahmslos alle benutzten Ausdrücke versteht. Ein Zusammenhang ergibt sich auch mit der Bildung: Je höher die Schulbildung, desto geringer ist die Zahl derjenigen, die bestimmte Wörter und Ausdrücke nicht deuten können. Die numerische Auswertung macht das Ausmaß der Schwierigkeiten deutlich: Mit zunehmendem Alter verlagert sich der Schwerpunkt immer weiter in Richtung der Kategorie *6 und mehr (unbekannte) Wörter*.

2.5   Bewertung der Ausdrucksweise

Die Bewertung der Ausdrucksweise sollte mithilfe des russischen Schulnotensystems erfolgen, d. h. die beste Note ist die 5, die schlechteste die 1, wobei die Note 3 (eigentlich formaler Mittelwert) erfahrungsgemäß eher negativ aufgefaßt wird.

Faßt man jeweils die beiden besten bzw. die beiden schlechtesten Noten zusammen, so zeigt sich, daß die Bewertung insgesamt deutlich negativ tendiert. Zwei Drittel aller Befragten vergeben eine 1 bzw. eine 2, geben also ihrem Mißfallen Ausdruck. Mit steigendem Alter nimmt die Zahl derer, denen die Ausdrucksweise nicht gefällt, von 22 % (Jugendliche) auf 95 % (Senioren) zu. Auf den ersten Blick überraschend mag die Tatsache erscheinen, daß sich nicht – wie zu vermuten – in erster Linie die höher gebildeten Muttersprachler über den Sprachgebrauch entrüsten bzw. ihn negativ bewerten, sondern vor allem jene mit niedriger bzw. mittlerer Schulbildung. Wirft man jedoch einen Blick in die Statistik, so wird ersichtlich, daß diese Korrelation auf die Altersverteilung zurückzuführen ist: So sind unter den höher gebildeten Muttersprachlern mehrheitlich Personen zwischen 18 und 39 Jahren zu finden, die ja, wie bereits erwähnt, den Veränderungen im Sprachgebrauch der Medien generell aufgeschlossener gegenüberstehen.

2.6   Gründe für eine negative Bewertung

Gefragt nach den Beweggründen für eine schlechte Benotung, werden zuallererst die vulgäre Sprache, die Jargon- und Slang-Ausdrücke angeführt (55 %). Hier ergeben sich kaum altersabhängige, wohl aber geschlechtsspezifische Differenzen: Frauen bemängeln die vulgäre Sprache mit 59 % etwas häufiger als Männer (50 %). Drei von zehn Muttersprachlern halten die Ausdrucksweise nicht für druckreif, da sie nicht der literatursprachlichen Norm entspricht. Einem Fünftel mißfällt das niedrige sprachliche Niveau, welches für sie primitiv und ungebildet anmutet.

Die Tatsache, daß der Text sinngemäß nicht vollständig zu erschließen ist, bietet gut 17 % einen Anlaß für eine schlechte Note. Diesbezüglich ist jedoch zu berücksichtigen, daß es sich bei dem vorgelegten Text lediglich um einen Ausschnitt handelt, welcher gezwungenermaßen aus dem Gesamtzusammenhang gerissen wurde. Trotz der Anweisung der Interviewer an die Probanden, sich lediglich auf die Sprache zu konzentrieren, kann dies ein Grund gewesen sein, wieso der Sinn insgesamt als unverständlich bezeichnet wurde. Das Ergebnis ist dahingehend zu relativieren. Die unbekannte Lexik sowie die fremdsprachlichen Entlehnungen sind jedem Neunten ein Dorn im Auge.

2.7   Fazit

Die vorliegende Fragebogenstudie, die meines Wissens in dieser Form im russischen Sprachraum bisher noch nicht durchgeführt worden ist, hat vor allem eines geleistet: Anstatt die bereits eingehend diskutierten Meinungen und Einstellungen professioneller Sprachforscher und -experten auf ihre Legitimation hin zu untersuchen, spiegeln die erhobenen Daten die Attitüden jener Sprachträger wider, die sich – weitgehend unbelastet von der vorherrschenden wissenschaftlichen Auffassung – zum Zustand und zur Entwicklung der russischen Sprache geäußert haben. So gelang es, ein realistisches Bild der aktuellen Meinungslage zu zeichnen, auch wenn die Ergebnisse eher den Charakter einer Fallstudie tragen.

Daß diese Umfrage aufgrund ihrer im Hinblick auf die Grundgesamtheit eher geringen Fallzahl nicht als repräsentativ gelten kann, wurde bewußt in Kauf genommen; begrenzte zeitliche und organisatorische Kapazitäten wirkten sich jedoch erschwerend auf den Befragungsprozess aus und haben eine Erhöhung der Fallzahl behindert. Dennoch tragen die Ergebnisse dieser Studie dazu bei, die Einstellungen russischer Muttersprachler zum Wandel ihrer Sprache zu erhellen. Sie erlauben einen Einblick in die Beurteilung bestimmter Tendenzen in der Sprachentwicklung und die Akzeptanz verbindlicher Sprachnormen.

Es ist wahrscheinlich, daß die Studie – würde sie erneut an einem anderen Ort (z.B. in Moskau) durchgeführt werden – andere Ergebnisse liefert als die hier erhobenen Daten. Dies ist im wesentlichen auf die soziodemographische Zusammensetzung der Bevölkerung in den unterschiedlichen Regionen der Russischen Föderation zurückzuführen. Unterschiede in Abhängigkeit vom Einkommen, Bildungsniveau, Lebensstandard und nicht zuletzt auch vom Grad der Öffnung bzw. der räumlichen Nähe zum Westen wirken sich möglicherweise auf die Einstellungen zum Wandel des Kulturgutes Sprache aus. Ich sehe daher mit Spannung allen künftigen Untersuchungen dieser Art entgegen, die neue Erkenntnisse über den Sprachwandel und die damit verbundenen Sprechereinstellungen im russischen Sprachraum generieren.

3   Literatur

DULIČENKO, Aleksandr Dimitri (1994): Russkij jazyk konca XX stoletija. München: Otto Sagner.

RATHMAYR, Renate (1991): Von komersant bis džast-in-taim: Wiederbelebungen, Umwertungen und Neubildungen im Wortschatz der Perestrojka. In: Jachnow, H. (Hrsg.): Slavistische Linguistik 1990. München: Otto Sagner.

ZEMSKAJA, Elena Aleksandrowna (1996): Aktivnye processy sovremennogo slovoproizvodstva. In: Zemskaja, Elena Aleksandrowna (Hrsg.): Russkij jazyk konca XX stoletija. Moskva: Jazyki Russkoj Kul'tury, 90-41.

ZYBATOW, Lew Nikolaevič (1995a): Das Sichtbare der „unsichtbaren Hand". Zu Innovationen in der russischen und bulgarischen Sprache der Gegenwart. In: Junghanns, U. (Hrsg.): Linguistische Beiträge zur Slawistik aus Deutschland und Österreich. II. JungslawistInnen-Treffen Leipzig 1993. Wien (Wiener Slawistischer Almanach, Sonderband Nr. 37) 277-293.

— (1995b): Russisch im Wandel. Die russische Sprache seit der Perestrojka. Wiesbaden: Harrassowitz.

How to Spill the Beans in Idiom Processing and not to Kick the Bucket in the Attempt

Bárbara Eizaga Rebollar

Until recently, the study of idioms and fixed expressions had been regarded as a phenomenon *on the margin of language*. It has only been during the last two decades that the analysis of this sort of expressions has been considered a central issue in language, as everyday language contains many thousands of idiomatic, slang and proverbial phrases whose figurative interpretations differ from their literal meanings. Therefore, two main theories have arisen: the compositionality theory, which argues that the figurative meaning of an idiom is a function of the meanings of their individual parts, and the classical or noncompositionality theory, which holds the opposite view, i.e. that idioms are expressions whose overall meaning cannot be derived from the meaning of their individual parts. But, let us analyse both theories in more detail.

1   Compositionality

This theory, as I have mentioned above, argues that the literal meanings of the parts of an idiom contribute independently to its overall figurative meaning, although it recognizes different degrees of analizability (see Gibbs 1994; Nunberg, Sag and Wasow 1994).

According to this view, some idioms are highly decomposable because their idiomatic meanings – while conventional – are distributed among their parts like *pop the question,* which means "to propose marriage". In this example, very much used by the defenders of the approach such as Gibbs or Nunberg, it is *easy* to know that *"'question' in 'pop the question' refers to 'marriage proposal' when the verb pop is used to refer to the act of uttering it"* (Gibbs and Nayak 1989). Furthermore, this kind of idiom can be lexically and syntactically modified, without altering its semantic meaning, as it can be seen in the next example:

John popped the difficult question and Mary accepted.

Other idioms are abnormally decomposable, i.e. their individual components have a more metaphorical relationship with their literal meanings. For instance, the meaning of the idiomatic phrase *spill the beans* can be related with that mental image of beans contained in the HEAD or in the MIND and being spilled accidentaly all over the floor. This sort of images explains "some of the metaphorical knowledge that motivates the meanings of the idiomatic phrases (Gibbs 1994)". Idioms belonging to this group may undergo some modifications.

Sam didn't spill a single bean.[1]

---

[1]   An anecdote regarding the flexibility of this idiom is that according to British English speakers this expression cannot undergo any modification without losing its figurative sense. The example

The last idiomatic category is formed by nondecomposable idioms, which cannot undertake any type of lexical, syntactical or semantical modification, such as *kick the bucket*:

> *Old Mrs. White kicked the bucket four days before her ninety-fourth birhday.*

In those idioms it is difficult to see the relationship between a phrase's individual components and the idiom's figurative meaning. Their origin is cultural and, as such, unknown in most of the cases; for this reason, these idioms are frozen metaphors.

Apart from this classification, Gibbs further distinguishes between correctly-formed idioms, those with a literal and a figurative meaning, and ill-formed idioms, which are semantically more decomposable and syntactically more productive.

However, when analysing the compositional approach, some considerations need to be taken into account:

1) Where can we draw the division between literal and figurative meaning? In my opinion, the differences between the normally decomposable and the abnormally decomposable idioms are not very clear, because the lexical components of the so-called NORMALLY DECOMPOSABLE idioms such as *pop the question* have also a relative degree of metaphoricity with their figurative meanings. Hence, it is very difficult to make this type of classification, according to the definition of compositionality given by Gibbs and others.

2) Another problem of compositionality is ambiguity. If an idiom's overall meaning depends on the literal meanings of the individual components and on how these components are combined, we will not be able to distinguish between the literal and figurative meaning. Imagine we hear the utterance, *John spilled the beans.* Unless we have a context to process this utterance, we will never be able to know whether the speaker is meaning that *John revealed a secret* or *John literally spilled the beans.* What we know for sure is that John is going to have problems in both cases, either for having a big mouth or for being clumsy. Hence, we, hearers, need a CONTEXT, in which we can process the idiomatic phrases in order to resolve ambiguities and to assign a sense (literal or figurative) to the utterance.

3) With regards to the semantical and syntactical inflexibility of the nondecomposable idioms as a determining feature of this group of phrases, it can be argued that the same degree of rigidity can be found in the nondecomposable phrase *cool one's heel* (wait impatiently) or *kick the bucket* (die) as in the abnormally decomposable idiom *blow one's stack*, whose syntactic structure is analogue to the structure of the former.

4) The last remark I want to point out is related to the Gibbs's distinction between correctly-formed and ill-formed idioms. First of all, this classification is only grounded on the idiom's pragmatic feature, because the ill-formed ones are, according to Gibbs, those which lack a logical sense like *crack a joke, swallow one's pride, etc.*, and those correctly-formed are the logical ones, such as *ring*

---

shown above is considered incorrect by native English speakers, whereas for American speakers it is perfectly right, keeping its idiomatic sense.

the bell, pull the strings, lift a finger, etc. What is not clear to me is whether we can consider such an expression right or wrong, basing our study only on a pragmatic issue. Secondly, I do not see the relation between being ill-formed and decomposable, and correctly-formed and nondecomposable. But supposing that we would accept this classification, something that I doubt, we can still find idioms which are decomposable and correctly-formed at the same time like *miss the boat.* Therefore, this argument is not a concluding one when analysing idiomatic phrases.

So, as shown above, the compositional theory needs to explain some flaws or weaknesses if it wants to account for a proper analysis of idiomaticity. However, I entirely agree with this theory in the statement that idioms are of very diverse types, ranging from expressions that undergo nearly all grammatical transformations without losing their idiomatic meanings (e.g., *lay down the law*) to idioms that cannot undergo even the simplest transformation without losing their figurative meaning (e.g., *face the music*) and this makes their classification very difficult indeed.

2   Noncompositionality

The other main view is the noncompositional theory that states that idioms are expressions whose overall meaning cannot be derived from the meaning of their individual parts. This definition suggests that idioms cannot be processed in the same way as expressions with literal meanings and, as many experiments have proved, the idiomatic meaning of these expressions is processed faster than their literal one (Cacciari & Tabossi 1988; Gibbs, Nayak & Cutting 1989; Vonk & Van de Voort 1989; Colombo 1993). This view holds that their figurative meanings are stored in the mental lexicon as a single lexical entry, that is in the same way the meanings of individual words are listed in a dictionary. Hence, retrieving the figurative meaning of the whole phrase is much faster than accessing the literal meaning of each individual word and then computing a literal meaning of that phrase. However, there has been much discrepancy when addressing the issue of how and when the meaning of these phrases becomes available to the hearer in discourse comprehension.

3   A cognitive approach

Following the noncompositionalist hypothesis that idioms are stored in the memory as single lexical entries, I wish to offer an approach based on the cognitive theory of Relevance proposed by Sperber and Wilson, because in my opinion it explains more clearly how we, human beings, process the information we receive in a given context. The role context plays in idiom processing and acquisition is a central issue in this view, because it helps to resolve possible ambiguities (not explained by the compositional analysis, as we have seen before) and to attach a specific sense to a given expression. Thus the idiomatic phrase *kick the bucket* will have the literal meaning of *struck the pail with his foot* or the figurative sense of *die,* depending on the context in which the idiom appears.

According to Sperber and Wilson (1995), when processing information, the hearer accesses the various types of information stored in the long-term memory at that address.

The information the hearer accesses and which is stored in the memory at a certain address are of three different types: logical, encyclopaedic and lexical. The logical entry for an idiom consists of a set of deductive rules which apply to logical forms of which the concept expressed by the idiom is a constituent. The encyclopaedic entry contains the information about the extension and denotation of the object, that is the information gained through experience. The lexical entry contains information about the phrase of natural language which expresses it. On this approach, a conceptual address is thus a way of accessing the logical, encyclopaedic and linguistic information which is needed in the processing of an idiom. The *lexical* entry, then, includes information about its syntactic category, co-occurrence possibilities, phonological structure, etc. It is a representation with a linguistic form.

The *encyclopaedic* entry contains information about the objects, events and/or properties associated with the concepts expressed by the phrase. For example, the encyclopaedic entry for the concept *kick the bucket* would contain a set of assumptions which will vary across speakers, time and cultures because we do not share the same assumptions about concepts. Furthermore, they are always open because new information may always be added to them; that is, there is no point at which an encyclopaedic entry can be said to be complete and no minimum without which one would not say that the associated concept has not been mastered at all. The information of this type of entries is thus representational: it consists of a set of assumptions which may undergo deductive rules.

The *logical* entry consists of a set of deductive rules, each with a set of input and output assumptions, that is a set of premises and conclusions. Sperber and Wilson assert that

"the only deductive rules which can appear in the logical entry of a given concept are the elimination rules for that concept. According to them, they apply only to sets of premises in which there is a specific occurrence of that concept, and yield only conclusions from which that occurrence has been removed" (Sperber & Wilson 1995:86).

For example, the logical rule of *and-elimination* takes as input a simple coordinated premise and yields as output one of its constituents:

And-elimination
1) *Input:* (X and Y)
   Output: X
2) *Input:* (X and Y)
   Output: Y

That is, it applies only to premises containing *and,* and yields conclusions where *and* has been removed. The rule *modus ponendo ponens* takes as input a pair of premises, a conditional and its antecedent, and yields as output the consequent of the conditional:

Modus Ponendo Ponens:
Input: (a) X
        (b) (If X then Y)
Output: Y

That is, it applies only to premises containing a designated occurrence of the concept *if ... then*, and yield conclusions from which this occurrence has been removed. Exactly the same phenomenon happens with the rule *modus tollendo ponens*, whose input is a pair of premises, one a disjunction and the other the negation of one disjunct, and yields as output the other disjunct:

Modus tollendo ponens:
1) Input: (a) (X or Y)
           (b) (not X)
   Output: Y
2) Input: (a) (X or Y)
           (b) (not Y)
   Output: X

That is, it applies only to premises containing a designated occurrence of the concept *or*, and yields conclusions from which that occurrence has been eliminated Then, the content of an assumption is constrained by the logical entries of the concepts it contains, whereas the context in which it is processed is partly determined by the encyclopaedic entries.

But let us apply this approach to the examples mentioned above. I will begin with the first example used, *pop the question*.

Ex. John popped the difficult question to Mary.

When we hear this utterance, our mental device activates the lexical entries of the concepts that appear in the phrase[2]:

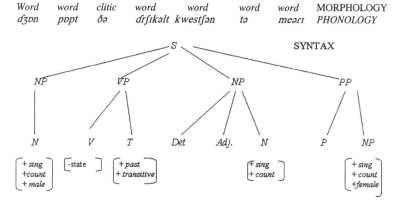

---

[2]   The following schema pretends to be a full specification of how the lexical entries might be accessed, distinguishing therefore between the morphological, phonological and syntactical level.

Then, the hearer will retrieve from the long-term memory the encyclopaedic entries of the concepts that appear in the phrase. In this case, as the idiom has not got any literal reading and as idioms are stored as single entries in the mental lexicon, we would have the following assumption:

- propose marriage to someone

The device applies the deductive rules of the logical entries to the encyclopaedic entry above. In this case, the rule applied is *modus ponendo ponens*, as shown below:

1) a. If somebody pops the question to someone, he/she proposes marriage to her/him.
   b. John popped the question to Mary
   c. John proposed marriage to Mary

Logical entry: somebody proposes marriage to someone.
Suppose now that we take the example of an idiom ABNORMALLY DECOMPOSABLE, according to Gibbs classification, such as the one mentioned before:

John's friends wanted a surprise party for him, but Tom spilled the beans.

Here, as in the example analysed above, the process is the same. First of all, we activate the lexical entries of the concepts that appeared in the phrase:

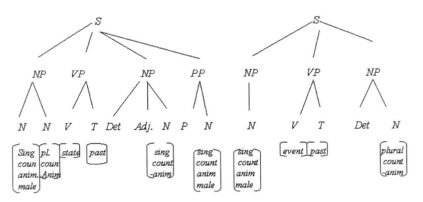

Then, the encyclopaedic entries of the concepts of the idiom would be accessed[3]. For instance, I would have the following set of assumptions:

- someone has revealed a secret to someone

---

[3] This set of assumptions would vary from one person to another, because they depend greatly on experience.

- someone has thrown out some food because she/he did not like it or she/he felt sick, etc.
- someone is a big mouth.

In this example we can have both readings: the literal and the figurative one. Hence, we need the context to disambiguate it and to be able to attach a sense to this sentence. As we did in the former example, we apply now the logical entries to the encyclopaedic ones in more or less the following way[4]:

1) a. *If somebody wants to have a surprise party for someone, it must be something unexpected.*
   b. *John's friends want to have a surprise party for him.*
   c. *John must not be told about it.*
2) a. *If someone does not tell something to somebody, then it is a secret.*
   b. *John must not be told about it.*
   c. *Then it is a secret.*
3) a. *If somebody tells the secret, the party will not be a surprise for John.*
   b. *Tom has told the secret.*
   c. *The party will not be a surprise for John.*
4) a. *To spill the beans can mean to "reveal a secret" or "to throw out some food all over the floor".*
   b. *The meaning of "throwing out the food onto the floor" does not fit into the context with that which has been deduced above.*
   c. *Therefore, the meaning in this context is "to reveal a secret".*

Logical entry for spilling the beans: to reveal a secret.

4   Conclusion

As I hope to have shown, following this cognitive approach, we can explain, on the one hand, the processing of idioms without having to classify them as the compositionalist view does, something which has made many researchers *kick the bucket* (and which will continue to do so), due to the enormous variety of idiomatic phrases existing in any language and the problem that this fact represents for any classification. This approach also offers a solution to the problem of ambiguity, set by the literal and figurative meaning that some idioms can have. On this view, the context is the frame in which all the received information is processed and retrieved.We cannot process any information out of context, because the moment we utter a sentence, we process it unconsciously in a specific context. Therefore, the context is a central feature of our mental device.

However, there are still a lot of features to improve and to research within this account such as the mobility of some idioms (something yet to be discussed) or the role

---

[4]   The number of deductive rules the mental device does is very large, but for the time´s sake, I will not name all of them, only the ones I have considered more relevant for this paper.

that culture plays in the acquisition of these phrases, which may determine the perception of the speakers with regards to the mobility and flexibility of this sort of expressions (see footnote 1).

5   References

EVERAERT, M.; VAN DER LINDEN, E.; SCHENK, A.; SCHREUDER, R. (1995): Idioms. Structural and psychological perspectives. Hillsdale, NJ etc.: Erlbaum.

GIBBS, Raymond W. (1994): Poetics of Mind. Figurative thought, language and understanding. Cambridge: Cambridge University Press.

— (1990): Psycholinguistics. Studies on the Conceptual Basis of Idiomaticity. In: Cognitive Linguistics 1, 417-51.

JACKENDOFF, R. (1997): The architecture of the Language Faculty. MIT Press

NUNBERG, G., SAG, I.; WASOW, T. (1994): Idioms. In: Language 70, 491-538.

SPERBER, Dan; WILSON, Deirdre (^{2}1995): Relevance: Comunication and Cognition. Oxford: Blackwell.

Ikonizität und die endogene Konstruktion von Ähnlichkeit

Peter Godglück

In den meisten Zeichenklassifikationen sind *Ähnlichkeit* und *Analogie* konstitutiv für den Begriff des sprach- oder nichtsprachlichen Ikons. Nur selten aber ist *Ähnlichkeit* selber Reflexionsgegenstand. Sie spielt vielmehr die Rolle eines selbstevidenten Definiens oder gar eines selber nicht erklärungsbedürftigen Explanans (Keller 1995:113ff). Aber ganz so wie die großen Geschwister des Ikons – Index und Symbol – mit *Kausalität* und *Konventionalität* nach einer theoretisch-begrifflichen Klärung ihres je eigenen Definiens verlangen, muß auch die Ähnlichkeitsrelation in ihren logisch-strukturellen und dynamisch-kognitiven Aspekten sowie in ihren sowohl alltäglich variierenden als auch in ihrer standardisierten sprachlichen Ausdrucksform reflektiert werden.

Eine solche Reflexion interpretiert Ähnlichkeit in einem konstruktivistischen Modell und macht

1) Aussagen über die Vor- und Nachbereiche (VB, NB) der Ähnlichkeitsrelation, sie markiert
2) die Subjekte bzw. Agens der Ähnlichkeitskonstruktion und macht schließlich
3) Angaben zu Art und Komplexität der Kriterien, nach deren Maßgabe das Ähnlichkeitsräsonnement vollzogen wird.

Die linguistische Rede über Ähnlichkeit kann hiernach durch eine standardisierte Form des Ähnlichkeitsurteils diszipliniert werden, und unterschiedlichste Erscheinungsformen von Ähnlichkeit und den ihnen zugrunde liegenden Räsonnements – seien sie explizit geäußert oder in umfassenderen Handlungszusammenhängen implizit – können auf diese Standardform bezogen werden. Eine solche Form kann konzipiert werden in Anlehnung an Darstellungsweisen der generativen Semantik. Sie umfaßt das standardisierte Prädikat ‚*ähnlich*' mit seinen beiden Argumenten ‚*Vorbereich*' und ‚*Nachbereich*' (VB, NB) und ein höher geordnetes Prädikat ‚*erzeugen*', womit alle Arten der Konstruktion, sei es in Wahrnehmung, Denken u. a. angesprochen sind. Die Argumente des Prädikats ‚*erzeugen*' sind zum einen das ‚*AGENS*' der Konstruktion und zum andern die gesamte Proposition ‚ähnlich [VB, NB]', die als ein vom jeweiligen AGENS hergestellter ‚ZUSTAND' kategorisiert werden kann. Die gesamte, nun über eine Einbettung verfügende Proposition ‚erzeugen [AG, ähnlich [VB, NB]]' nenne ich Ähnlichkeitskonstruktion. Diese wiederum ist in den Argumentrahmen eines ‚Cause'-prädikats aufgenommen. Das zweite Argument im Rahmen dieses Prädikats bilden die ‚KRITERIEN' verschiedenster Art und Komplexität, die ‚*machen, daß*' die Ähnlichkeitskonstruktion zustande kommt. So ergibt sich für die Standardversion eines Ähnlichkeitsurteils die folgende in Figur 1 dargestellte Form (Godglück 1998:21ff).

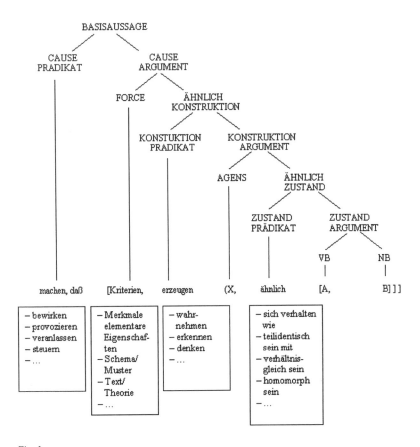

Fig. 1

Es ist offenkundig, daß in dieser Struktur die Positionen VB und NB, AGENS und KRITERIEN variabel gehalten sind und mit ihren Erfüllungsmengen bzw. den hieraus gewählten Konstanten, die auf komplizierte Weise miteinander agieren, große Spielräume in der Genese von Ähnlichkeitsurteilen eröffnen. Als wichtigster Spielraum in der Ähnlichkeitsgenese kann dabei der Übergang von elementaren oder komplexen Eigenschaftsprädikationen zu sekundären Ähnlichkeitsprädikationen gelten. Die Notwendigkeit, einen solchen Übergang zu vollziehen, ist es, die Ähnlichkeitsurteile (‚Kanaries ähneln Zitronen‘) von Eigenschaftsprädikationen (‚Kanaries sind gelb‘; ‚Zitronen sind gelb‘) unterscheidet und sie diesen systematisch nachordnet. Der Übergang selber aber ist nicht restringiert und die Kür von (im einfachsten Falle) elementaren Eigenschaftsprädikaten zu KRITERIEN einer Ähnlichkeitskonstruktion ist ein nur durch Tradition, kollektiven Druck und unterschiedlichste Interessen mitbestimmter, prinzipiell aber freier und arbiträrer Akt.

Die Standardform des Ähnlichkeitsurteils und ihre Variablen können nun auch genutzt werden, um eine erste Begriffsbestimmung des Ikons zu geben und nach dieser Vorgabe zu untersuchen: In der Diktion der Standardform zählen all jene Erscheinungen zu den Ikonismen, die die Stelle des Vorbereichs besetzen, damit in Ähnlichkeitsbeziehung zum Nachbereich treten, mit diesem also Gemeinsamkeiten aufweisen und schließlich aufgrund dieser Ähnlichkeitsbeziehung einen Verweischarakter haben, mithin Zeichen sind. Dabei können sowohl die Varianten des Vor- als auch des Nachbereichs sprachlicher oder nichtsprachlicher Art sein, allerdings nicht in allen Kombinationen. Beispiele für nichtsprachliche Vorbereiche sind alle (ab)bildhaften Zeichen und ihre Bildgegenstände; Beispiele für sprachliche Vorbereiche lassen sich auf allen sprachlichen Ebenen auffinden, so im lautlichen und lexikalisch-onomastischen Bereich mit zumeist onomatopoetischen Effekten, in der Syntax, z.B. im Verhältnis von Klammerstrukturen und den mit diesen Strukturen realisierten Inhalten oder auch im Verhältnis der textuellen Nenn- zur realen Abfolge von Ereignissen, Handlungen usw. in Erzählungen, Kochrezepten oder Wegbeschreibungen (Godglück 1998:133ff).

Solche Ikonismen entstehen – oder können in ihrer Entstehung rekonstruiert werden – auf der Grundlage unterschiedlicher Kriterien. Man kann sie – nun nicht nur hinsichtlich der Ikonismen, sondern für alle Ähnlichkeitsräsonnements und Analogien – in drei Gruppen unterscheiden, und jede dieser Gruppen kann zusätzlich nach der Provenienz der Kriterien – endogen oder exogen – unterschieden werden.

Die erste und gleichsam einfachste Kriteriengruppe bilden die elementaren Eigenschaften. Sie können repräsentiert werden durch Prädikate oder Verknüpfungen von Prädikationen. Auf ihnen gründende Ähnlichkeiten sind z. B. die zwischen Singular- und Pluralformen einerseits und ihren Denotaten andererseits, sofern die Pluralformen z.B. reduplizierend gebildet sind. Exogenes Kriterium dieses Ikonismus ist das ‚Mehr‘ an morphologischem Aufwand zur Produktion einer Pluralform, was dem ‚Mehr‘ des durch diese Form denotierten Inhalts entspricht. Es ist z. B. auch die oft besprochene Ähnlichkeit zwischen Ausdrücken wie ‚S-Kurve‘ und ‚no U-turn‘, deren Ähnlichkeitskriterium in der Linienführung des ‚S‘ bzw. ‚U‘ im Vorbereich und der entsprechenden realen Straßenverläufe im Nachbereich liegt.

Die zweite Gruppe faßt komplexere, zu Schemata und Mustern verdichtete Eigenschaften zusammen. Dazu zählen z. B. Satz- und Textschemata und die damit verbundenen Ikonitäts- und Ähnlichkeitsempfindungen. Auch diese Kriterien sind als Eigenschaften der jeweilig in Ähnlichkeit stehenden Vor- und Nachbereiche auszumachen und fokussierbar, mithin exogen.

In einer dritten Gruppe sind Kriterien zusammengefaßt, die als Texte und als Texte spezifischer Ordnung, als Theorien rekonstruiert werden können. Sie liegen Ähnlichkeitsräsonnements zugrunde, durch die etwa die Analogie zwischen gotischer Architektur und scholastischer Philosophie (Panofsky 1989) konstruiert werden kann. Sie sind auch die Grundlage für politische Diskurse wie beispielsweise die Kampagne amerikanischer Politiker und Medien zur ‚Hitlerisierung‘ Saddam Husseins und damit zur Rechtfertigung der amerikanischen Militärintervention am persischen Golf (Holyoak/ Thagard 1996:101ff). Der Status solcher komplexer Kriterien als endogen oder exogen ist ontologisch unbestimmt und muß diskursiv bzw. dialogisch ausgehandelt werden.

Idealtypisch aber läßt sich der Unterschied zwischen exo- und endogenen Kriterien, gleichgültig welcher Gruppe sie angehören, umschreiben:

Exogene Kriterien von Ähnlichkeitskonstruktionen sind all jene, die aus substantiellen oder akzidentiellen Eigenheiten der in Frage stehenden Vor- und Nachbereiche hervorgehen. Als solche markieren exogene Kriterien objektive Eigenschaften. Daß sie aber auch Ergebnis von Auswahl und Fokussierung sind, gibt den nach Maßgabe dieser Kriterien gefällten Urteilen ihren Charakter als Konstruktionen.

Endogene Kriterien und die ihnen folgenden Ähnlichkeitsurteile erhalten dagegen ihren konstruktivistischen Charakter durch die partielle Selbständigkeit der Räsonnements und ihrer Unabhängigkeit von den Objekten. Ich nenne solche Teilverfahren der analogischen kognitiven Prozesse *Simulfakter* oder Ähnlichmacher. Simulfakterkriterien funktionieren gleichsam wie Stempel, die, von ihren Benutzern selbst hergestellt, beliebigen Objekten aufgedrückt werden können, um sie dann als Simulakren wahrzunehmen und auf der Grundlage der ‚selbstgemachten' Kriterien als ähnlich zu begreifen (Godglück 1998:190ff). Dabei sind die Verfahren zur Herstellung solcher Stempel langen historischen oder evolutionären Prozessen zu verdanken. Die sogenannten Allgemeinqualitäten (Ertel 1969), die jedem Objekt noch vor einer bewußten und kategorisierenden Prädikation zukommen, können so interpretiert werden. Endogene Ähnlichkeit kann aber auch entstehen als Resultat interessegeleiteter und völlig bewußter ‚Abstempelung'. Simulfaktor fungieren dann als Text/Theoriekriterien, die eine spezifische Ähnlichkeitskonstruktion nahelegen. Beispiele hierfür sind etwa die Leittexte zur Konstruktion von Epochen oder die Erklärungs- und Begründungsdiskurse zur Analogie von Farben und Klängen, Sprache und Bildern oder (Programm)- musik und Erzählung (Godglück 1998:214ff).

Natürliche Ähnlichkeitsräsonnements durchlaufen zwar alle Positionen der Standardform in all ihren Varianten, sie sind aber nur selten in ihrer Gesamtheit geäußert und nicht erkennbar an der sprachlichen Oberfläche des Urteils. Selbst der Ähnlichkeitszustand, in der Notation der Basisform also ‚ähnlich [VB, NB]' muß nicht expliziert werden und kann innerhalb verschiedener Domänen und Zwecke analogischen Räsonnements wirken als ‚tacit knowledge'.

Dies gilt auch für Ikonitätsempfindungen, insbesondere, wenn sie endogenen Kriterien zu verdanken sind. Sie finden ihren Ausdruck gemeinhin nicht in einem mehr oder minder expliziten Ähnlichkeitsurteil, sondern in einer Äußerung zum *Passen* oder der *Angemessenheit* sprachlichen Ausdruckes. So passen Namen zu ihren Trägern, Logos zu Produkten und Firmen, Gedichte zu einer Landschaft oder einem Bild, und eine Beschreibung ist einem Verhalten, einer Einstellung oder einem Gedanken angemessen. Die Ähnlichkeitsräsonnements, die solchen Angemessenheitsempfindungen zugrundeliegen, reichen aber auch über Sprache und sprachliche Vorbereiche von Analogien, die in der Rhetorik seit der Antike in der Theorie des Aptums behandelt werden (Godglück i.V.), hinaus und erfassen nichtsprachliche, wohl aber als Ikonismen interpretierbare Ähnlichkeiten: so etwa im Räsonnement, das entscheidet, ob ein Kleid, eine Robe zu einer Soirée paßt, ob eine Strafe einer Tat angemessen (Günther 1988) ist, oder ob kurze Hosen zu Helmut Kohl passen. In all diesen Fällen, den sprachlichen wie den nichtsprachlichen, wirken schwer dingfest zu machende, prinzipiell arbiträr, in Geschichte konstruierte Kriterien. In den meisten Fällen sind sie endogen, historisch sedimentiert und nur un- oder vorbewußt. Sie sind in Kollektiven verbreitet und gelten dann zumeist als *natürlich*. Ihr Charakter als Konstruktion ist undurchsichtig und sie wirken *quasi-objektiv*.

Gegenüber solchen Arten kollektiven, zumeist nur unterschwelligen Wissens von Ähnlichkeitskriterien, stehen aber auch individuelle, oft ebenso ‚verschwiegene‘ Formen der Kriterienkonstruktion, die als Varianten des „mainstreams“ der Angemessenheitsvorstellung toleriert, ausgegrenzt, bisweilen gar pathologisiert werden können. Beide Arten der Ähnlichkeitskonstruktion, die kollektiv-konventionelle wie die individuell-singuläre, fokussieren oder generieren (per Simulfakter) ihre Kriterien arbiträr. Dies macht auch Ikonismen, die immer wieder gegen eine allgemeine Arbitraritätsthese in Anspruch genommen werden, zu Fällen einer im Prinzip willkürlichen Semiose.

Diese These von der Existenz ikonischer, auf verdeckten endogenen Kriterien aufruhender Ähnlichkeitskonstruktion erfordert unterschiedlichste, konzeptionell-theoretische wie auch empirische Verfahren des Nachweises von Simulfaktern und ihrer möglichen Wirkungsweise. Wichtige konzeptionelle Einsichten dazu lassen sich aus einem Kontaktbereich zwischen Theorien künstlicher Intelligenz und Kognitionswissenschaften gewinnen, wie sie von der ‚Fluid Analogies Research Group‘ (den ‚FAR-Gonauten‘) erarbeitet worden sind (Mitchell 1993; Hofstadter et al. 1996). Ihr Gegenstand ist der seit der Antike wichtigste Typus der Analogie, Proportionen der Form ‚A : B = C : D‘ (A verhält sich zu B wie C zu D). Über die bei der Konstruktion solcher Proportionen wirksamen Ähnlichkeitskriterien versuchen die ‚FARGonauten‘ Aufschluß zu gewinnen, indem sie verschiedene, systematisch variierte Vorbereiche (die Terme A und B) und vom Nachbereich nur Term C vorgeben und dann von Versuchspersonen verlangen, die Aufgabe ‚A : B = C : D‘ zu lösen, bzw. einen Term D anzugeben, durch den die Proportion vervollständigt wird.

So kann die folgende Proportionsgleichung sowohl durch exogene wie auch endogene Kriterien gelöst werden:

Term A	:	Term B	≡	Term C	:	Term D
eqe	:	qeq	≡	abbbc	:	?

Eine Lösung aufgrund eines exogenen Kriteriums könnte z. B. D = bbbacbbb lauten, und das Kriterium, nach dem sie zustande kommt, könnte wie folgt formuliert werden:

Kriterium$_1$:
‚Der Mittelteil (das sind alle Buchstaben, die einen linken und rechten Nachbarn haben) der Terme A und C wird sowohl als Type wie auch als Token zum Rechts- bzw. Linksaußen der Terme B und D‘.

In diesem Kriterium sind damit eindeutig Eigenschaften des Vorbereichs der Proportion fokussiert, zu denen es, wie bei allen Merkmalselektionen, Alternativen gibt,

Eine Alternative führt zu der Lösung: D' = babcb. Diese Lösung wird möglich, wenn man hinsichtlich des Types und der Tokens der jeweiligen Buchstaben in A, B und C keine Restriktionen formuliert. ‚qeq' geht nämlich aus ‚eqe' hervor durch eine Umstellung des Buchstabentypes, während ‚babcb' aus ‚abbbc' hergestellt werden kann durch eine Tokenverschiebung von zwei der im Mittelteil von Term C enthaltenen ‚b'. Die erste Lösung der Proportion war nur möglich, weil Type und Tokens der Terme A und C in den entsprechenden Positionen von B und D übereinstimmen. Für die Lösung D' kann also folgendes Ähnlichkeitskriterium formuliert werden:

> Kriterium$_2$:
> ‚Ein Type oder Token des Mittelteils (definiert wie in Kriterium$_1$) der Terme A und C wird zum Links- bzw. Rechtsaußen der Terme B und D'.

Diesen Lösungen können durch die subjektive, möglicherweise auch unscharfe Ausschöpfung des Fokussierungsspielraumes weitere hinzugefügt werden. Sie sind aber immer Kriterien, die über abstrakten oder konkreten, substantiellen oder akzidentiellen Eigenschaften der gegebenen Terme und der Verhältnisse, in denen sie stehen, formuliert sind.

Die endogene Konstruktion von Kriterien durch einen Simulfakter kann nun die Menge der Lösungen der Proportionsgleichung entscheidend erhöhen. Dazu ist es nötig, dem Vor- und Nachbereich der Analogie eine Struktur zuzuordnen. Wählt man dazu eine einfache Zahlenfolge, z. B. ‚1, 3, 1', so erhält man so etwas wie ein Modell der ursprünglichen Analogieaufgabe (vgl. Figur 2).

$$e\ q\ e \quad : \quad q\ e\ q \quad = \quad a\ bbb\ c \quad : \quad ?$$
$$1\ 3\ 1 \quad : \quad 3\ 1\ 3 \quad = \quad 1\ 3\ 1 \quad : \quad 3\ 1\ 3$$

Fig. 2

Die beliebige Zuordnung der Zahlenfolge ‚1, 3, 1' zum Term A = eqe erlaubt die Modellierung des Vorbereichs der Ausgangsproportion, also ‚1, 3, 1 : 3, 1, 3'. Da nun das Modell dieselbe analogische Struktur haben soll wie die Ausgangsproportion, muß auch dem Term C = abbbc die Zahlenfolge ‚1, 3, 1' zugeordnet werden und für den vierten Term des Modells D ist dann wieder die Folge ‚1, 3, 1' anzusetzen. Diese ist gleichsam die Maske des vierten, in der Ausgangsproportion gesuchten Terms. Durch die Zuordnungen, wie sie in Figur 2 vorgenommen wurden, ergibt sich durch die Folge ‚3, 1, 3' eine Vorschrift zur Gestaltung des gesuchten vierten Terms der Ausgangsproportion. Nach dieser Vorschrift bleiben die Buchstabentypes von Term C an ihrem Platz, nur die Anzahl der Token wird im Sinne der Zahlenfolge verändert. Type a und Type c, die nur mit je einem Token repräsentiert sind, werden nun vertreten von je 3 Token, und der dreifach repräsentierte Buchstabentype c kommt in Term D nur noch einmal vor. Die durch das Simulfakterkriterium gewonnene Lösung der Proportionsgleichung lautet also: D'' = aaabccc. Es ist leicht zu erkennen, daß durch dieses Verfahren eine Menge weiterer Lösungen der Proportionsgleichung möglich ist, da jede beliebige Folge von Zahlen, die auf ‚eqe' abgebildet wird, eine neue Lösung erzeugt. So ergibt die Folge ‚1, 2, 3' die Lösung ‚aaabbc' oder die Folge ‚2, 1, 2' die Lösung ‚abbc' (vgl. Figur 3):

```
e q e   :   q e q   ≡   a bbb c   :   aaa bb  c
| | |       | | |       | ∨ |       ∨ ∨ |
1 2 3   :   3 2 1   ≡   1 2 3   :   3 2 3

e q e   :   q e q   ≡   a bbb c   :   a bb  c
| | |       | | |       | ∨ |       | ∨ |
2 1 2   :   1 2 1   ≡   2 1 2   :   1 2 1
```

Fig. 3

Die Zuordnungen der jeweiligen Simulfakterkriterien, z. B. also ‚1, 2, 3' oder ‚2, 1, 2', zu den Termen der Ausgangsproportion, können auch auf andere Weise vorgenommen werden. Bei gleichem Kriterium, z. B. ‚1, 2, 3', aber anderer Zuordnungsvorschrift, entsteht dann auch eine andere Lösung der Ausgangsproportion. So z. B. in Figur 4:

```
A           B   ≡   C           :  D
e q e   :   q e q   ≡   a bbb c   :   aaa bbb c
| | |       | | |       | ∨ |       ∨ ∨ |
1 2 3   :   3 2 1   ≡   1 2 3   :   3 2 1
```

Fig. 4

In Term C werden die ‚2' und das mittlere ‚b' einander zugeordnet. Der so erfaßte Type ‚b' wird dann in Term D durch zwei Tokens repräsentiert und den beiden unverändert erhalten gebliebenen hinzugefügt. Simulfakterkriterien bestehen also gleichsam aus zwei Komponenten. Zum einen aus dem Kriterium selber, hier einer Zahlenfolge, und zum anderen einer genauen Vorschrift der Abbildung der Zahlenfolge auf die bekannten Terme der Proportion. Erst hieraus ergibt sich die Lösung der Analogieaufgabe.

Diese Beispiele sind artifiziell. Demnach sind sie nützlich bei der Klärung von transkategorialen, nicht an Objekteigenschaften orientierten Ähnlichkeitsräsonnements, mithin für die Erörterung des Begriffes ‚Simulfakter'. Sie geben einen vereinfachten, weil formal-schematischen, dennoch aber wesentlichen Einblick in Elemente und Prozeduren zur Konstruktion „unsinnlicher" (Benjamin 1991a, b) Ähnlichkeiten. Zu diesen Bestandteilen und Prozeduren gehören vor allem

1) mögliche Vor- und Nachbereiche von Ähnlichkeitsrelationen (im formalen Beispiel die jeweiligen Verhältnisse zwischen Buchstabenfolgen, darstellbar als Proportion);

2) Verfahren zur Gewinnung von objektunabhängigen Kriterien (im Beispiel Zahlen und ihre spezifische Syntaktifizierung). Solche Verfahren können (nicht nur) im Falle der einfachen Zahlenfolgen durch Produktionssysteme und generative Mechanismen verschiedenster Komplexität simuliert werden. Dazu gehören notwendig

3) Verfahren der Zuordnung, Abbildung oder Projektion der objektunabhängigen Kriterien auf die Objekte der jeweiligen Vor- und Nachbereiche (in den Beispielen sind sie repräsentiert durch eine einfache graphische Darstellung mit Zuordnungsgeraden oder -dreiecken).

Mit diesen drei Komponenten, den in möglichen Vor- und Nachbereichen repräsentierten Weltausschnitten, den davon unabhängigen Kriteriengeneratoren und Kriterien und den Abbildungsverfahren, operieren urwüchsig-natürliche Simulfakter – in welcher Komplexität und welchem Bewußtseinsmodus auch immer – über den Spielräumen einer jeden Ähnlichkeitskonstruktion, und sie können sie endogen und arbiträr nutzen zur Erzeugung von Ikonismen.

Literatur

BENJAMIN, Walter (1991a): Lehre vom Ähnlichen. In: Benjamin, Walter: Gesammelte Schriften Bd. II, 1. Frankfurt a. M.: Suhrkamp, 204-210.

— (1991b): Über das mimetische Vermögen. In: Benjamin, Walter: Gesammelte Schriften Bd. II, 1. Frankfurt a. M.: Suhrkamp, 210-213.

ERTEL, Suitbert (1969): Psychophonetik. Untersuchungen über Lautsymbolik und Motivation, Göttingen: Hogrefe.

GODGLÜCK, Peter (in Vorbereitung): Aptum und Ikon. Rhetorische und semiotische Aspekte sprachlicher Angemessenheit].

— (1998): Sprache – Zeichen – Analogie. Philologische Aspekte von Ähnlichkeit (Habil.-Schr. Saarbrücken).

GÜNTHER, Klaus (1988): Der Sinn für Angemessenheit. Anwendungsdiskurse in Moral und Recht. Frankfurt a. M.: Suhrkamp.

HOFSTADTER, Douglas R. und die FLUID ANALOGIES RESEARCH GROUP: Die FARGonauten (1996): Über Analogie und Kreativität, Stuttgart: Klett-Cotta.

HOLYOAK, Keith J.; THAGARD, Paul (1996): Mental Leaps. Analogy in Creative Thought, Cambridge: MIT Press.

KELLER, Rudi (1995): Zeichentheorie. Tübingen – Basel: Francke.

MITCHELL, Melanie (1993): Analogy-Making as Perception. A Computer Model, Cambridge: MIT Press.

PANOFKY, Erwin (1989): Gotische Architektur und Scholastik. Zur Analogie von Kunst, Philosophie und Theologie im Mittelalter. Köln: DuMont.

Deixis im Überschneidungsbereich von Situation, Grammatik und Lexik

Friedrich Lenz

1   Einleitung

Die Deixis ist ein universales sprachliches Phänomen, dessen Erklärung an die Situativität von Äußerungen geknüpft ist. Deshalb wird sie vor allem im Rahmen der linguistischen Pragmatik untersucht (vgl. etwa Levinson 1983 oder Yule 1996). Auf der anderen Seite ist sie auch Gegenstand grammatischer Beschreibungen, da deiktische Ausdrücke in hohem Maße grammatikalisiert sind. In diesem Beitrag soll gezeigt werden, dass der Umgang mit Deixis nicht nur auf situativen Informationen und der Kenntnis der Grammatik basiert, sondern dass sie vielfach nur im Zusammenhang mit lexikalischen Informationen zu interpretieren ist. Es gibt Formen der Deixis, etwa die Diskursdeixis, die nur über bestimmte lexikalische Elemente vollständig zu erklären sind.

2   Der Deixisbegriff

Deiktische Ausdrücke sind bekanntlich solche Ausdrücke, die erst in der Gebrauchssituation ihre kommunikative Bedeutung entfalten. Sie haben also, wenn überhaupt, wenig kontextunabhängige Denotation oder Sinn im Verständnis von Lyons (1977). Ihre Beschreibung scheint dementsprechend besser in die Grammatik als in das Lexikon zu passen. Diese Einschätzung wird nun noch dadurch bestärkt, dass es sich um eine begrenzte Zahl von Ausdrücken handelt, mit denen Deixis ausgeübt wird. Im Gegensatz zu den Elementen des Lexikons sind Deiktika offenbar Elemente einer geschlossenen Klasse von sprachlichen Ausdrücken. Diese Auffassung vertritt etwa Hanks (1989), dessen Deixisdefinition zunächst als Grundlage für die Diskussion dienen soll. Für ihn ist Deixis

> „a special variety of reference (…) which is limited both formally and functionally. Formally (…) deictics in the present sense are morphemes (or strings of morphemes) that in most languages make up a closed paradigmatic set (…). Their basic communicative function is to individuate or single out objects of reference or address in terms of their relation to the interactive functions in which they occur." (Hanks 1989:104f)

Bei den Deiktika handelt es sich also um eine geschlossene Klasse von Morphemen bzw. Ausdrücken. Dass Deixis als spezielle Form der Referenz zu betrachten ist, ist erst in jüngster Zeit verstärkt beachtet worden (vgl. Lenz 1997) und hat natürlich damit zu tun, dass der Referenzbegriff selbst erst mit dem Aufkommen der linguistischen Pragmatik zunehmend verwendet wird bzw. neu gefasst worden ist. Ansonsten wird meistens auf die Zeigemetapher – Deixis kommt ja vom griechischen Wort für Zeigen – zurückgegriffen, um zu verdeutlichen, dass man mit den Deiktika Entitäten in der Situation identifiziert. Zeigen kann man aber genau genommen nur auf Dinge im Raum. Mit den Deiktika identifizieren wir durchaus auch andere Entitäten. Insofern ist der Referenzbegriff in der Tat adäquater.

Referenz ist im Gegensatz zu Denotation und Sinn an den Äußerungsakt gebunden. Gerade bei den deiktischen Ausdrücken ist es offensichtlich, dass sie keine Referenz an sich haben, sondern sie erst im Äußerungsakt bekommen. Die deiktischen Ausdrücke lassen sich am besten durch die Regeln für ihren richtigen Gebrauch in der Kommunikationssituation beschreiben. Diese Regeln betreffen nicht nur grammatische Morpheme, wie etwa die Tempusmorpheme, sondern auch andere deiktische Ausdrücke, die man eher im Wörterbuch als in der Grammatik findet. Ein treffliches Beispiel[1] für die Angabe einer Gebrauchsregel wäre etwa der Eintrag für *here* im Collins Cobuild English Dictionary (1995:798): „You use *here* when you are referring to the place where you are."

Vor dem Hintergrund, dass es sich bei den Deiktika um eine geschlossene Klasse von Ausdrücken mit keiner oder wenig kontextunabhängiger Bedeutung handelt, ist es dennoch nicht verwunderlich, dass der Begriff Deixis zum ersten Mal in der Grammatik auftaucht. Soweit wir wissen, benutzt ihn der alexandrinische Philologe Appolonius vor etwa 2000 Jahren zum ersten Mal, um in seiner Grammatik die Wortklasse der Pronomen zu definieren, deren lexikalischer Gehalt unbestreitbar äußerst gering ist.[2]

Im übrigen hat auch Bühler, der als der Begründer der modernen Deixistheorie gelten kann, die Deiktika zum Ausgangspunkt einer neuen Wortklasseneinteilung machen wollen, als er die Deiktika, die er *Zeigwörter* nannte, von den Nennwörtern trennte. Die Bedeutungskonstitution der Nennwörter vollzieht sich innerhalb des Symbolfeldes in, wie er sagt, „herkömmlicher Weise", indem sie als Symbole fungieren, die in bestimmten, wie man heute sagen würde, Sinnrelationen zu anderen Symbolen des Feldes stehen. Die Nennwörter haben somit eine konstante Bedeutung, indem sie „ihren Gegenstand als ein so und so Beschaffenes charakterisieren" (Bühler 1934:119).

Die Zeigwörter haben dagegen keinen konstanten Symbolcharakter, sondern fungieren eher als Signale, die innerhalb des Zeigfeldes fallweise bestimmte „Feldwerte" erhalten. Das Charakteristische der Zeigwörter ist ihre situationsabhängige, aufmerksamkeitssteuernde Funktion, weshalb sie außerhalb des Zeigfeldes keine wirkliche Bedeutung hätten. Bühler schränkt jedoch ein, dass die Zeigwörter dennoch einen quasi abgeschwächten lexikalischen Gehalt hätten. Sie seien zwar in erster Linie Signale, aber in zweiter Linie auch Symbole. Immerhin nennen sie nämlich den Aufmerksamkeitsbereich – den lokalen, temporalen und personalen Bereich – innerhalb dessen wir uns orientieren.

---

[1] Solche Beispiele sind allerdings selten. Meistens finden sich keine Gebrauchsregeln, sondern Paraphrasen, die wiederum auf andere deiktische Ausdrücke zurückgreifen. So lautet etwa der Eintrag für *here* sowohl im LDCE (1995:491) als auch im OALD (534) „at, in or to this place."

[2] Die betreffende Stelle lautet (in der Übersetzung von Buttmann 1877:77) folgendermaßen: „Demnach ist Pronomen alles dasjenige, was mittelst Hinweisung [Deixis i.O.] und Zurückweisung [Anaphora i.O.] die Stelle der Nomina vertritt und keinen Artikel annimmt."

3 Deiktische Dimensionen

Der Ausgangspunkt der deiktischen Orientierungshandlung ist die Origo, die durch die Zeigwörter *hier, jetzt, ich* repräsentiert ist. Das Zeigfeld setzt sich damit aus drei Orientierungskategorien zusammen, die in der heutigen Deixisforschung meist als deiktische Dimensionen bezeichnet werden. Bühler selbst verwendet den Dimensionsbegriff nicht. Man darf sich sein Zeigfeld auch keinesfalls als dreidimensionalen Raum vorstellen.

Nur die lokale Dimension kann man räumlich, d.h. dreidimensional, auffassen, die zeitliche ist dagegen linear, und die personale setzt sich aus diskreten Einheiten zusammen, die über Kommunikationsrollen bestimmt sind. Letztlich ist der ontologische Status der Referenzobjekte, nämlich ob es sich um pysikalische Entitäten im Raum, temporale Entitäten in der Zeit oder personale in der Kommunikation handelt, entscheidend für die jeweils zu benutzende Ausdrucksklasse. Damit haben die Deiktika zumindest soviel kontextunabhängige Bedeutung, dass aus ihnen der Status der Referenzobjekte oder die Dimension hervorgeht, in der der deiktische Referenzakt von statten geht.

Im folgenden sollen nun einige dimensionsspezifische Deiktika herausgriffen und darauf eingegangen werden, über welche weitere kontextübergreifende Bedeutung sie verfügen und was vielleicht in der ein oder anderen Weise in einem Wörterbuch stehen müsste.

3.1 Lokale Deiktika

Die paradigmatischen lokaldeiktischen Ausdrücke im Englischen sind die Adverbien *here* und *there*.[3] Wir hatten schon die in Collins-Cobuild aufgeführte Regel, für den richtigen Gebrauch von *here* erwähnt: „you use here when you are referring to the place where you are." Bei *here* fällt die lokale Origo, der Sprecherstandpunkt, mit dem zu identifizierenden Ort zusammen. Insofern ist die Regel adäquat. Man muss jedoch vorsichtig sein, denn das heißt keineswegs, dass die beiden Orte identisch sind. Der exakte Bezug auf den Sprecherstandpunkt wie in 1a) ist eher die Ausnahme.

Normalerweise ist der zu identifizierende Raum größer und umfasst auch die Umgebung des Sprechers. Die Ausdehnung dieses Umgebungsraums hängt von der Situation und dem sprachlichen Kontext ab. Wenn ich 1b) in der freien Natur äußere, ist der Umgebungsraum etwa die klimatische Region, in der ich mich befinde. In einem Zimmer wäre der Umgebungsraum, auf den ich mich beziehe, eben dieses Zimmer. Abhängig vom sprachlichen Kontext kann er aber auch viel größer sein, z.B. bei 1c).

1a) I am standing here and don't move an inch.

---

[3] Wenn ich mich hier in erster Linie auf das Englische konzentriere, hat das vor allem damit zu tun, daß ich mich in der linguistischen Beschreibung des Englischen am besten auskenne. Prinzipiell ist aber zu erwarten, daß die Aussagen zumindest auf vergleichbar aufgebaute Sprachen, wie etwa das Deutsche, in ähnlicher Weise zutreffen.

1b) It is hot here.

1c) It is warmer here than on Mars.

Offenbar ist der zu identifizierende Raum relativ zur Situation und zum Gesprächs-gegenstand. Vermutlich ist bei *here* so etwas wie eine lokale Gricesche Relevanz-maxime anzusetzen. Der relevante Umgebungsraum hängt von unserer Wahrnehmung der Situation und des Themas ab, und dementsprechend präsupponieren kooperieren-de Gesprächspartner einen adäquaten Raum. Eine solche pragmatische Regel steht selbstverständlich nicht im Lexikon, scheint aber auch für andere Deiktika eine Rolle zu spielen.

Bei Lokalisationen mit *there* ist dies offensichtlich, denn auch hier ist der relative Umgebungsraum entscheidend. Bei *there* liegt nämlich der zu identifizierende Raum außerhalb der Sprecherregion. *There* ist zudem noch in seinem deiktischen Gebrauch (es kann ja auch anaphorisch gebraucht werden und ist dann unabhängig von der ak-tuellen Kommunikationssituation) zwangsläufig mit einer Zeiggeste verbunden. Man will ja nicht den ganzen Raum außerhalb der Sprecherregion, der ja unendlich groß ist, identifizieren, sondern nur einen Bereich in ihm. Deshalb brauchen wir eine Zeig-geste oder ein Äquivalent (vgl. Harweg 1990), etwa eine Kopfbewegung, Blickrich-tung o.ä.[4]

Zur Lokalisierung im Raum haben wir noch eine zweite Klasse von deiktischen Adverbien zur Verfügung. Dieses Referenzsystem ist immer gerichtet und an den Di-mensionen des Raums orientiert. Es kommt also nicht nur auf die Position der Origo an, sondern auch auf seine Richtung. Dieses dimensionale oder gerichtete Referenz-system ist im Englischen repräsentiert durch *left/right*, *above/below* oder *front/back*. Was rechts vom Sprecher ist, kann man nur wissen, wenn man weiß, in welche Rich-tung er ausgerichtet ist. Entscheidend ist meistens die Blickrichtung.

Die Regeln für den richtigen Gebrauch der Lokaldeiktika sind ungleich komplexer, als hier angesichts des knappen Raums dargelegt werden konnte, und auf die Demon-strativa musste ganz verzichtet werden. Dennoch dürfte klar geworden sein, dass es in der Tat nur eine begrenzte Klasse von lokaldeiktischen Ausdrücken gibt, und dass ihr Gebrauch jeweils vom Kontext und der Kommunikationssituation, speziell vom Spre-cher, abhängt.

3.2   Personale Deiktika

Situationsabhängigkeit und Grammatikalisierung ist bei den Personaldeiktika noch deutlicher ausgeprägt. Deiktisch sind die Personalpronomen der 1. und 2. Person, im Englischen also *I*, *you* und *we*. Die anderen (*she, he, it und they*) sind anaphorisch und

---

[4]   Auch *here* kann mit einer Geste verwendet werden. Dann wird ein Ort innerhalb des Sprecher-raumes identifiziert. So kann ich auf eine Stelle des unmittelbar vor mir stehenden Tischs zeigen und sagen *the pencil is here*. Dann meine ich nur den Ort, an dem sich der Bleistift befindet. Da dieser Ort aber in meinem Umgebungsraum liegt, kann ich auf keinen Fall sagen *the pencil is there*. Auf der anderen Seite kann ich nicht sagen *it is raining here* und aus dem Fenster zeigen.

bleiben hier unberücksichtigt. Der Referent der deiktischen Pronomen ändert sich mit der Sprecher- bzw. Adressatenrolle im jeweiligen Gesprächsbeitrag. Will der Sprecher auf sich selbst referieren, verwendet er *I*, will er einen oder mehrere Adressaten referieren, verwendet er *you*. *We* ist adäquat, wenn er sich auf sich selbst und die Adressaten bezieht. Der einzig etwas kompliziertere Fall ist das exklusive *we*, das deiktisch und anaphorisch ist. Es sind nämlich außer dem Sprecher nicht die in der Kommunikationssituation anwesenden Adressaten gemeint, sondern Personen, auf die im sprachlichen Kontext schon referiert wurde. In 2) referiert der Sprecher mit *we* also deiktisch auf sich selbst und anaphorisch auf John und Henry.

2) Yesterday I met John and Henry. We had a great time.

Im Grunde ist das System der personalen Deiktika aber relativ unkompliziert und in jeder Grammatik ausreichend beschrieben.[5]

3.3 Temporaldeiktika

Ähnlich verhält es sich zumindest teilweise bei der Temporaldeixis. Der richtige Gebrauch der Tempora ist zwar ungleich komplizierter, aber auf jeden Fall bilden sie in der Grammatik ein zentrales Thema. Schließlich ist hier die Grammatikalisierung besonders weit fortgeschritten, was man schon daran sieht, dass sie vor allem mit gebundenen, d.h. grammatischen Morphemen realisiert werden. Comrie (1985:9) kann deshalb die Tempuskategorie folgendermaßen definieren: „Tense is gramaticalised expression of location in time." Dass sie deiktische Ausdrücke sind, erklärt er damit, dass die Lokalisation auf der Zeitachse von einem deiktischen Relatum ausgeht. Die Tempora drücken eine Zeitrelation aus, die in der temporalen Origo, dem Sprechzeitpunkt, ihren Ursprung hat. Auf die komplexen Zeitrelationen, die dabei letztlich eine Rolle spielen, kann hier nicht eingegangen werden (vgl. aber Lenz 1997).

Weitere temporaldeiktische Ausdrücke sind die Klasse von Zeitadverbien, die – ebenfalls von der temporalen Origo ausgehend – eine Position auf der Zeitachse spezifizieren. Sie sind vergleichbar mit den Ortsadverbien, nur dass die Positionen, die sie lokalisieren, nicht im dreidimensionalen Raum, sondern in der eindimensionalen Zeit liegen. *Now* entspricht dabei *here*. Es spezifiziert die direkte Umgebung um den Sprechzeitpunkt. Aber auch hier hängt die Ausdehnung vom Kontext ab, wie die folgenden Beispiele zeigen.

3a) Press the button now.
3b) He is now working on his PhD.
3c) The average temperature in the Stone Age was three degrees higher than it is now.

---

[5] Komplizierter wird es allerdings, wenn man wie etwa Levinson (1983) eine eigene sozialdeiktische Dimension einführt, die dann auch die sogenannten *honorifics* beinhaltet und sich mit der personalen zumindest partiell überschneidet.

Die Zeitspannen in den drei Sätzen unterscheiden sich erheblich und hängen vor allem mit dem lexikalisch ausgedrückten Situationstyp zusammen. Wenn etwas erfahrungsgemäß in Sekundenbruchteilen geschieht, wie ein Knopfdruck, ist die Umgebung um den deiktischen Verankerungspunkt geringer als bei einem langwierigen Prozess, dem Schreiben einer Dissertation oder gar einer Klimaveränderung. Wesentlich ist, dass die Ausdehnung relativ zu den betreffenden Situationstypen ist, und diese werden primär lexikalisch ausgedrückt.

Auch bei der Interpretation temporaldeiktischer Adverbien, die keine Simultaneität mit der Sprechzeit ausdrücken, kommt es zwangsläufig auf die lexikalischen Einheiten im Kontext und unser Weltwissen über Dauer, Häufigkeit und Umstände der damit ausgedrückten Situationen an.

4a) I will soon eat my sandwich.
4b) I will soon buy a house.

Soon gibt eine relative Zeitrelation an. Deshalb können wir erwarten, dass die in 4a) ausgedrückte Situation früher eintreten wird als die in 4b). Absolut sind dagegen deiktische Adverbiale zu verstehen, die kalendarische Zeiteinheiten enthalten. Die Einheiten – Jahre, Monate, Wochen, Tage, Stunden etc. – sind an astronomischen Zyklen festgemacht, deren Dauer im lexikalischen Gehalt definiert ist. Insofern sind diese Zeitangaben nicht abhängig vom Kontext. Tabelle 1 gibt exemplarisch einen Überblick.

anterior zur Sprechzeit	simultan zur Sprechzeit	posterior zur Sprechzeit
kalendarisch: n calendaric units *ago* *last* calendaric unit (n=1) *yesterday* (cal. unit = day)	kalendarisch: *this* calendaric unit *today* (cal. unit = day)	kalendarisch: *in* n calendaric units *next* calendaric unit (n = 1) *tomorrow* (cal. unit = day)
nicht-kalendarisch: *formerly - recently - just*	nicht-kalendarisch: *now – currently – nowadays*	nicht-kalendarisch: *immediately – soon – later*

Tab.1: Temporaldeiktische Adverbiale

4   Diskursdeixis

In der Literatur zur Deixis werden heute auch andere deiktische Dimensionen erwähnt, vor allem die Diskursdeixis. Fillmore (1975:70) war einer der ersten, der sie behandelt. Er beschreibt sie folgendermaßen: „Discourse deixis has to do with the choice of lexical or grammatical elements which indicate or otherwise refer to some portion of the ongoing discourse." Beispiele für Diskursdeixis wären etwa:

5a) We have just been discussing time deictics.

5b) I will explain the nature of discourse deixis later.

Mit solchen Äußerungen bezieht sich der Sprecher eindeutig auf eine „Portion" des ablaufenden Diskurses. Ich glaube nun, dass es nicht lexikalische *oder* grammatische Elemente sind, die für die Realisation der Diskursdeixis verantwortlich sind, sondern dass es immer lexikalische *und* grammatische Elemente sind. Die Diskursdeixis ist nämlich eine besondere Form der Deixis, genau genommen der Temporaldeixis, aber keine eigenständige Dimension (vgl. Lenz 1997). Es gibt keine speziell diskursdeiktischen Ausdrücke. Vielmehr haben wir es primär mit temporaldeiktischen Ausdrücken zu tun – in den Beispielen die Adverbien *just/later* und die Tempora (present perfect/future). Das ist auch nicht weiter erstaunlich, denn ein Diskurs und natürlich auch seine Teile sind temporale Entitäten, auf die man schließlich auch mit temporaldeiktischen Ausdrücken referieren kann.

Darüber hinaus muss noch angezeigt werden, dass es sich um reflexiven Sprachgebrauch handelt, dass man sich auf den Diskurs selbst bezieht, also in eine Metakommunikation eintritt. Dies geschieht mit lexikalischen Mitteln, in erster Linie mit kommunikativen Verben, in unseren Beispielen mit *discuss* und *explain*. Es können auch relativ unspezifische Kommunikationsverben sein, etwa *say* oder *talk* bzw. spezifische Sprechaktverben wie *apologise* oder *resign*. Dazu kommen Verben, die im übertragenen Sinne zur Referenz auf Diskurssituationen verwendet werden können, z.B. Verben, die propositionale Einstellungen ausdrücken (*believe, think* aber auch *despise, loathe* etc.) oder Wahrnehmungsverben (*see, realise, understand* etc.) oder Verben, die Ereignisse bezeichnen, die solche Wahrnehmungen hervorrufen (*show, demonstrate, indicate* etc.). Man kann also auf eine im Prinzip offene Liste von kommunikativen Verben zurückgreifen,[6] um sich auf den ablaufenden Diskurs zu beziehen. Selbstverständlich kann man dazu auch deverbale Nomen verwenden. 6a) und 6b) sind ebenso diskursdeiktisch wie 5a) und 5b), wobei das temporaldeiktische Element hier in *preceding* und *following* steckt:

6a) the preceding discussion
6b) the following explanation.

Lokaldeiktische Ausdrücke kommen im Rahmen der Diskursdeixis eigentlich nur in schriftlichen Texten vor, und auch dort transformieren wir den dreidimensionalen Raum in einen eindimensionalen, womit wir dieselbe lineare Ordnung schaffen, in der wir die Zeit begreifen. Die drei räumlichen Dimensionen werden auf die vertikale reduziert. Wir referieren auf Diskursteile in einem Text in der vertikalen Dimension, also auf Teile oben oder unten:

7a) the discussion above
7b) the explanation below.

---

[6] Dass es eine Vielzahl und nicht klar zu begrenzende Liste von Sprechaktverben im weiteren Sinne gibt, zeigen etwa die beiden Wörterbücher von Wierzbicka (1987) und Ballmer/Brennenstuhl (1981).

Dabei lassen sich *above* und *below* ja auch temporal interpretieren, als vorher oder nachher vom ‚jetzt' innerhalb des ablaufenden Produktions- oder Rezeptionsprozesses.[7] Das schlägt sich auch in der Kompatibilität mit den Tempora nieder. Wie 8) zeigt kann *above* nicht mit einem Zukunftstempus, *below* nicht mit Vergangenheitstempora gebraucht werden.

8a) I explained Bühler's sign theory above.
8b) I will explain Bühler's sign theory below.
8c) *I explained Bühler's sign theory below.
8d) *I will explain Bühler's sign theory above.

Ansonsten lokaldeiktisch gebrauchte Ausdrücke fungieren also im Rahmen der Diskursdeixis quasi temporaldeiktisch. Dass lokale Ausdrücke verwendet werden, um Temporalität auszudrücken, ist im übrigen gar nicht so ungewöhnlich. Dies hängt wohl mit unserer lokalistischen Zeitkonzeption zusammen (vgl. Lyons 1977). Es ist im Grunde nicht möglich, sich über Entitäten in der Zeit zu unterhalten, ohne auf (Zeit-) Punkte, Achsen, Räume zurückzugreifen.

5   Fazit

Wir haben es bei den Deiktika mit einer (mehr oder minder) geschlossenen Klasse von Ausdrücken zu tun, die gemäß der drei deiktischen Dimensionen dazu verwendet werden, um auf personale, lokale und temporale Entitäten zu referieren. Die deiktische Referenz basiert dabei auf Ausdrücken, die traditionell sowohl grammatisch als auch lexikalisch beschrieben werden. In etlichen Fällen – bei der Diskursdeixis sogar notwendigerweise – müssen wir auf eine Kombination von grammatischen und lexikalischen Einheiten zurückgreifen.

6   Literatur

BALLMER, Thomas; BRENNENSTUHL, Waltraud (1981): Speech Act Classification. A Study in the Lexical Analysis of English Speech Activity Verbs. Berlin: Springer.
BÜHLER, Karl (1934): Sprachtheorie. Die Darstellungsfunktion der Sprache. Stuttgart: Fischer.
BUTTMANN, Alexander (1877): Des Appolonius Dyskolos vier Bücher über die Syntax. Berlin: Dümmler.

---

[7] *Above* oder *below* sind lokaldeiktische Ausdrücke, die lediglich in schriftlichen Texten vorkommen. Das ebenfalls lokaldeiktische *here* ist dagegen auch im mündlichen Diskurs zu finden. Ein Satz wie „*I am talking/writing about deixis here*" kann mündlich und schriftlich geäußert werden. Dabei ist jeweils eine lokaldeiktische Interpretation möglich, wenn auch nicht wahrscheinlich. In dieser lokaldeiktischen Lesart referiert der Autor auf den Ort, an dem er die Äußerung hervorbringt. Die näherliegende Interpretation ist jedoch diskursdeiktisch. *Here* dient dann zur temporalen Lokalisierung eines Diskursteiles innerhalb des Gesamtdiskurses, wobei der eigentliche lokale Ort bzw. Raum, in dem der Referenzakt stattfindet, irrelevant ist. *Here* heißt dann so etwas wie ‚an dieser Stelle im ablaufenden Diskurs', also *now*.

COLLINS-COBUILD (1995): Collins-Cobuild English Dictionary. London: Harper-Collins.

COMRIE, Bernhard (1985): Tense. Cambridge: Cambridge University Press.

FILLMORE, Charles (1975): Santa Cruz Lectures on Deixis. Indiana University Linguistics Club.

HANKS, William (1989): The Indexical Ground of Deictic Reference. In: Papers from the Annual Regional Meeting of the Chicago Linguistic Society 25, 104-122.

HARWEG, Roland (1990): Studien zur Deixis. Bochum: Brockmeyer (Bochumer Beiträge zur Semiotik 25).

LENZ, Friedrich (1997): Diskursdeixis im Englischen. Sprachtheoretische Überlegungen und lexikogrammatische Analysen (Habil.-Schr. Passau 1996). Tübingen: Niemeyer (Linguistische Arbeiten 369).

LEVINSON, Stephen (1983): Pragmatics. Cambridge: Cambridge University Press (Cambridge textbooks in linguistics).

LDCE (1995): Longman Dictionary of Contemporary English. London: Longman.

LYONS, John (1977): Semantics, Vols. 1, 2. Cambridge: Cambridge University Press.

OALD (1995): Oxford Advanced Learner's Dictionary. Oxford: Oxford University Press.

WIERZBICKA, Anna (1987): English Speech Act Verbs. A Semantic Dictionary. Sydney: Academic Press.

YULE, George (1996): Pragmatics. Oxford: Oxford University Press (Oxford introductions to language study).

Einige Bemerkungen zur Bedeutung der Satzelemente für Textverständnis und Textqualität

Robert Ruprecht

1 Das Problem

Napoleon I. soll es, so wird berichtet, nie fertig gebracht haben, die englische Sprache zu erlernen, was ihm das Verständnis für seinen Erzgegner verschlossen habe. Zwar war er sich des voltairischen Rats bewusst, dass es gut sei, ‚die Akten des Gegners‘ zu studieren, er habe es auch zu verschiedenen Malen versucht, sei aber immer wieder daran gescheitert, dass er zwar die Strukturen des Englischen ohne weiteres begriffen habe, aber nie dazu gekommen sei, auch die Wörter zu erlernen. Die Wörter zu kennen, gilt landläufig als das A und O des Spracherwerbs. Wörter verstehen ist auch die erste Hürde des Sprachverstehens. Die Strukturen einer Sprache zu kennen, hat aber einen mindest ebenso hohen Stellenwert. Dass sie von den bloßen Sprachbenützern aber nicht ganz so hoch eingeschätzt werden, mag damit zusammenhängen, dass man die Strukturen nicht ganz so bewusst erwirbt wie die Wörter. Darin mag die geringe Beliebtheit der Beschäftigung mit Grammatik bei den Lernenden begründet sein: Wörter sind zählbar und lassen sich erwerben; Strukturen sind nicht ganz so leicht greifbar und werden, zumindest in der eigenen Sprache, oft unbewusst angewandt.

Diese Bemerkungen sind trivial. Schaut man sich aber in der wissenschaftlichen Literatur um, gerade auch in derjenigen unseres direkten Interesses, müssen wir feststellen, dass solche Trivialitäten vielleicht doch einige Aufmerksamkeit verdienen. Immer wieder stößt man auf Texte, die den Eindruck vermitteln, der Autor, die Autorin habe die ganze Mühe des Formulierens an die Wörter gewandt und halte sich nur widerwillig an die Rahmenbedingungen, die ihr Gebrauch voraussetzt. Damit beeinträchtigen sie das Verstehen beim Leser, der ein Gleichgewicht zwischen Strukturen und Wörtern wohl vorauszusetzen geneigt ist und aus seiner allgemeinen Lese-Erfahrung stillschweigend voraussetzen kann.

Es stellt sich die Frage, ob hier ein Optimum erreicht werden könne und woran allenfalls zu denken sei, wenn es darum gehe, einen Text möglichst verstehbar zu machen. Schaut man sich in gängigen stilistischen Grammatiken um (z.B. Heringer 1989; Reiners 1991; Schneider 1988), wird einem geraten, man solle kurze und klare Sätze schreiben. Das ist eine eingängige Formel, die auch das zu vermitteln scheint, was in Schulen und volkstümlichen Kursen gelehrt wird. Dass sich kaum jemand wirklich daran hält, kann als Chance begriffen werden, denn sie stimmt einfach nicht. Mit diesem Rezept wollen wir uns also nicht aufhalten. Es lässt sich übrigens zeigen, dass es keinen Zusammenhang zwischen der Länge eines Satzes und seiner Verständlichkeit gibt (Ruprecht 1999).

Es gibt aber einen Zusammenhang zwischen der Art, wie ein Satz strukturiert ist, und seiner Verständlichkeit. Damit ist nicht die Frage gemeint, ob man eher einfache oder komplexe Sätze schreiben soll, denn diese kann kaum schlüssig beantwortet werden: Es ist auf jeden Fall wesentlich schwieriger, einen guten Text zu schreiben, der nur aus einfachen Sätzen besteht (ibd.).

2 Der Begriff des Satzelements

Die Frage, die uns hier beschäftigen soll, ist diejenige nach der Füllung der einzelnen Satzelemente. Satzelemente sind, im Unterschied zu Gliedsätzen, die als Haupt- oder Nebensätze unvollständig sein können, als vollständige Haupt- oder Nebensätze definiert. (Ruprecht 1993) Der Begriff Satzelement geht also nicht auf das logische Gefüge im Satz ein sondern nur auf die Füllung seiner Haupt- und Nebensätze. Konsequenterweise heißen Haupt- oder Nebensätze, die ein oder mehrere Satzglieder mit einem neben- oder übergeordneten Satz gemeinsam haben, halbe Satzelemente. Der folgende Satz

[1] „Er schenkte ihr ein Glas Burgunder ein, den sie liebte, von dem sie aber nur trank, wenn der Herr sie dazu einlud, obgleich sie die Kellerschlüssel führte." (Keller 1944)"[1]

hat die Struktur HS NS1 NS1 NS2 NS3 und enthält somit fünf Satzelemente von den Längen 7, 3, 6, 6, 5. Das bedeutet: Die Füllung der Satzelemente meint, wieviele Wörter in einem Satzelement enthalten sind. Es ist durchaus möglich, dass ein ganzes Satzelement kürzer ist als ein halbes, wie das folgende Beispiel zeigt, dessen halbes Satzelement wegen der Konjunktion ein Wort länger ist als das ganze:

[2] „Dann nahm er das Waldhorn von der Wand und blies eine ihrer Lieblingsmelodien auf den Greifensee hinaus." (Keller 1944)

Die Längenunterschiede können mitunter beträchtlich sein. Die Frage ist also: Wie steht es mit dem Zusammenhang zwischen der Füllung von Satzelementen mit Wörtern und der Verstehbarkeit eines Textes?

Es gibt, soweit ich sehe, keine Ratschläge dazu, wieviele Wörter in einem Satzelement untergebracht werden dürfen. Stilistische Anweisungen, kurz, klar und knapp zu schreiben, können bestenfalls als indirekte Hinweise gedeutet werden; Hinweise allerdings, denen mit einigem Misstrauen zu begegnen ist, da sie letztlich auf eine Verarmung des Sprachgebrauchs hinzielen. (Ruprecht 1999)

Der folgende Satz enthält 23 Wörter und besteht aus einem Satzelement:

[3] Sie sind gestern abend bei strömendem Regen und totaler Dunkelheit zuhause in der Aarbergergasse 27 im dritten Stock in Bern vollständig erschöpft angekommen.

Dass er problemlos zu verstehen ist, hängt sicher auch damit zusammen, dass er von uns keine besonderen Leistungen fordert: Wir müssen weder irgendwelche ungewöhnlichen Begriffe kennen noch auf unvertraute Vorstellungswelten eingehen.

Der folgende ist gut doppelt so lang.

[4] „Sie, Hans und Luise und ihre vier Kinder, Michael, Sabine, Simon und Kathrin sind gestern abend nach vierzehnstündiger von mehreren Staus unterbrochener Fahrt von Portugal aus quer durch Spanien und Frankreich bei strömendem Regen und totaler Dunkelheit zuhause in der Aarbergergasse 27 im dritten Stock in Bern vollständig erschöpft angekommen.

---

[1] Die Beispielsätze, sofern nicht frei erfunden, stammen aus Heringer (1989), Keller (1944) und Menke-Eggers (1988).

Er ist noch durchaus verständlich, aber nicht mehr wirklich übersichtlich. Er enthält zwei Probleme: Es ist sicher schon im Beispiel [3] aufgefallen, dass die Ortsangabe „in Bern" unglücklich positioniert ist. Die Information kommt eigentlich zu spät. Folgerichtiger schiene die Angabe unmittelbar nach „zuhause", da alles Weitere dann eine Präzisierung ist von „in Bern" ist. So, wie die Angabe da steht, ist sie ein Nachtrag, der den Lesefluss behindert. Der Satz [4] enthält als zusätzliche Schwierigkeit, dass die Zuordnung von „bei strömendem Regen" nicht mehr eindeutig ist. Bezieht sich diese Angabe auf die Wetterbedingungen unterwegs, bei der Ankunft, oder auf beides? Es scheint also so zu sein, dass die Gefahr der Unverständlichkeit eines Satzes mit der Anzahl der Satzglieder wächst.

Wo, stellt sich die Frage, liegt der Punkt der Unverträglichkeit? Wieviele Satzglieder oder Wörter darf ein Satzelement maximal enthalten, ohne unverständlich zu werden?

Die Antwort ließe sich vielleicht ermitteln, sie wäre aber kaum viel wert, nicht nur, weil es ja nicht darum gehen kann, immer an der Limite zu formulieren, sondern auch, weil gerade diese Frage der Anordnung der Satzglieder im Satz von nicht zu unterschätzender Bedeutung ist, da ja z.B. genau die gleichen Wortgruppen je nach Anordnung ganz Verschiedenes bedeuten können:

[5] Das ist ein Problem für Linguisten – Für Linguisten ist das ein Problem.

Verunklärung lässt sich nämlich durch eine lockere, aber, streng genommen, immer noch logische Anordnung der einzelnen Satzglieder sehr leicht erreichen:

[6] Hans und Luise, sie sind in Bern vollständig erschöpft zuhause bei strömendem Regen und totaler Dunkelheit gestern abend im dritten Stock in der Aarbergergasse 27 angekommen.

Solche Beispiele müssen allerdings künstlich hergestellt werden, denn eine ungeschickte Anordnung der Satzglieder findet man in gedruckten Texten eigentlich nicht sehr häufig, außer bei den unechten Satzgliedern, den Attributen. Das probateste Mittel der Verunklärung liegt allerdings in der Möglichkeit, Satzglieder durch Attribute zu ergänzen. Da Attribute die Eigenschaft haben, ihr Beziehungswort zu präzisieren, schränken sie auch ein. Jedes zusätzliche Attribut nimmt seinem Beziehungswort etwas von seiner Bedeutung weg, was bedeutet, dass große Attributfügungen gegen null hin tendieren, in der Praxis null allerdings kaum erreichen, weil ein Bedeutungsrestchen übrigbleiben muss, wenn man nicht ausdrücklich Bedeutungslosigkeit erreichen will. So lässt sich das folgende Beispiel, das darauf verzichtet, irgendwelche schwer verständlichen Begriffe zu brauchen, im übrigen aber eine möglichst logische Anordnung der Wörter beachtet, praktisch nicht mehr überblicken:

[7] Der am Anfang der letzten Woche von Fritz für diese längst geplante Wanderung in den Alpen extra ausgeliehene, seinerzeit von ihm zur Erinnerung an eine Klassenzusammenkunft in der alten Heimat aus dem kleinen Weiler Mühleberg zwischen Langenthal und Affoltern in den Wynigenbergen heimgebrachte inzwischen auch schon etwas mitgenommene aber immer noch wertgehaltene Hut des Vaters des Bruders seines Freundes und ehemaligen Schulkollegen Karl Heinz Wagenbach, jetzt Lehrer an der sechsten Klasse an der Volksschule Niederbipp, ging auf der nicht ungefährlichen aber sehr lohnenden, stellenweise sogar spektakulären und bei allen einigermassen sicheren Berggängern seit Jahren äußerst beliebten Wanderung auf dem gut gesicherten Weg zwischen dem östlich über dem Mattertal gelegenen und in der letzten Zeit, vor allem während des Tourismusbooms, stark gewachsenen aber leider nicht autofreien Walliser Bergort Grächen mit seinen ausgedehnten Skipisten und Wanderwegen

und der vor allem im Ausland berühmt gewordenen Grächen-Dollars, einer die deutsche Mark dem Schweizer Franken gleichsetzende Währung, und dem klassischen und autofreien aber per Auto und Postautokurs leicht erreichbaren Begkurort Saas Fee, also von Nordwest über den Bergkamm nach Südost, verloren.

Das alles, um zu sagen, dass ein Hut verloren ging. Das Beispiel ist extrem. Man muss sich aber nicht sehr bemühen, um echte zu finden:

[8] „Selbst die sich von den Grenzen der Ästhetik des Wahrscheinlichen befreiende Konzeption des Fiktionalen als Phantastisches denkt das Verstehen fiktionaler Rede noch im Rückbezug auf die Regeln der Modifikation unserer Wirklichkeit, die ihren verstehensermöglichenden Rahmen bilden." (Menke-Eggers 1988)

Ohne solche Formulierungen kritisieren zu wollen, zeigen sie doch, dass der große denkerische Aufwand, den sie von beiden Seiten fordern, mitunter auch den Autor überfordern kann, dass er den Überblick über die grammatischen Zusammenhänge verliert. So steht „Phantastisches" verloren im Satz und kann in ihn nur eingefügt werden, wenn die richtige Genitivendung gesetzt wird. Der so in einer attributiven Fügung geäußerte Gedanke könnte einsichtiger werden, wenn das Attributgefüge in ein Satzgefüge übergeführt würde. Etwa:

[9] Selbst eine Konzeption, die das Fiktionale als Phantastisches versteht, sich also von den Grenzen befreit, die die Ästhetik des Wahrscheinlichen setzt, denkt das Verstehen fiktionaler Rede noch dadurch, dass sie sich auf die Regeln bezieht, nach denen wir die Wirklichkeit modifizieren. Sie bilden den Rahmen, die sie erst verstehbar machen.

Diese Version ist allerdings vierzehn Wörter bzw. Eine knappe halbe Zeile länger, dafür scheint die Formulierung durchsichtiger. „Verloren" ist allerdings der indirekte Hinweis auf gedankliche Dichte, den die originale Version enthält. Und es muss darauf hingewiesen werden, dass Durchsichtigkeit nicht notwendig ein absoluter Richtwert guten Formulierens ist. (Ruprecht 1999)

3   Wie viele Wörter gehören in ein Satzelement?

Diese Frage kann nicht normativ beantwortet werden. Beispiel [4] zeigt aber, wie dehnbar die Grenzen sind; es zeigt, dass, durchsichtige Füllung vorausgesetzt, in einem einzigen Satzelement erstaunlich viele Wörter respektive Satzglieder untergebracht werden können, ohne dass die Verstehbarkeit der Aussage wesentlich beeinträchtigt wird. So lassen sich denn in der schönen Literatur immer wieder Satzelemente antreffen, die dreißig und mehr Wörter enthalten, ohne dass der Leser das überhaupt wahrnimmt.

Es scheint allerdings sozusagen optimale Durchschnittswerte zu geben, deren Respektierung der Verstehbarkeit eines Textes aufhelfen könnte. Diese zu ermitteln, ist jedoch ein etwas mühseliges Unterfangen, ob man sie nun über Tests oder aufgrund der Analyse vorhandener Texte herausbekommen will. Auf rein spekulativem Wege lassen sich keine Ergebnisse gewinnen. Man ist auf Empirie angewiesen, will man sich nicht der Versuchung hingeben, „einleuchtende" Behauptungen im Stil von „Die Hauptsache gehört in den Hauptsatz" zu verkünden. Da es problematischer ist, Versuchsreihen durchzuziehen, als Texte zu analysieren, ist letztere Methode angewandt worden.

Ohne den entsprechenden Nachweis geben zu können, sei auf eine seinerzeit im Auftrag des Schweizer Radios durchgeführte Untersuchung hingewiesen, die gezeigt haben soll, dass ein substanzieller Prozentsatz von Leuten angebe, Sätze, die mit „obwohl" eingeleitet sind, nicht verstehen zu können. Das hat zur Direktive geführt, die Konjunktion „obwohl" aus dem mündlichen Repertoire zu streichen. Wollte man nach solchem Muster vorgehen, müsste am – allerdings in weiter Ferne liegenden – Ende eigentlich Sprachlosigkeit stehen.

Ausgangspunkt unserer Überlegung ist die Beobachtung, dass es offenbar Werte gibt, die für gewisse (allerdings nur grob eingegrenzte) Textsorten spezifisch zu sein scheinen. Dichterische Prosa scheint sich um den Wert sieben herum zu bewegen, journalistische Texte scheinen ungefähr elf Wörter pro Satzelement zu enthalten, und das weitgehend ohne Rücksicht darauf, was für eine Verbreitung bzw. Niveauanspruch das Medium hat, in dem sie erscheinen. Der Niveauanspruch drückt sich in der durchschnittlichen Satzlänge aus (Ruprecht 1998).

Diese Mittelwerte sind allerdings nicht sehr vielsagend. Man kann aus ihnen nicht viel mehr gewinnen als die Aussage, dass sich Dichter und Schriftsteller offenbar bemühen, nicht sehr viele Wörter in ihren Haupt- bzw. Nebensätzen unterzubringen, während es problemlos scheint, ihren Standard für Gebrauchstexte deutlich zu übertreffen, ohne dass die Leser Mühe haben, die Texte auch zu verstehen. Daraus ließe sich immerhin der praktische Schluss ziehen, mit dem Auffüllen von Satzelementen mit Wörtern vorsichtig umzugehen. Anders herum: Beim Redigieren eines Texts darauf zu achten, die Satzelemente möglichst schlank zu halten.

Das darf allerdings nicht so weit getrieben werden, dass man versucht, alle Sätze möglichst dem Mittelwert anzunähern, weil, wie jedermann gleich einsieht, das stetige Einhalten eines Mittelwerts zu langweiligen Resultaten führen muss, also letztlich zur Unlesbarkeit führt. Damit stellt sich die Frage, wie sich die Längen der Satzelemente verteilen.

Um zu einer Antwort hierauf zu kommen, steht wieder nur der etwas mühselige Weg der Analyse von möglichst vielen Sätzen offen.

Vergleichen wir zwei Autoren miteinander, deren Schreiben als vorbildlich gilt, die aber auf ganz verschiedenen Gebieten tätig gewesen sind, so zeigt sich das in Fig. 1 dargestellte Ergebnis. Die Kolonnen beziehen sich auf je hundert Sätze, rechts auf Gottfried Keller: *Der Landvogt von Greifensee* (1944) und links auf Ernst Mach: *Die Mechanik in ihrer Entwicklung* (1988). Aufgelistet sind die ganzen Satzelemente nach ihrer Verteilung. Satzelemente mit nur einem Wort kommen keine vor, Satzelemente mit mehr als 24 Wörtern sind in den gewählten Textstellen nur bei Mach anzutreffen. Die beiden Kolonnen zeigen deutliche Übereinstimmungen, aber auch ganz klare Unterschiede. Beide Autoren haben ihr Hauptgewicht ungefähr am gleichen Ort und den größten Anteil beim selben Wert (6 Wörter pro Satz), allerdings ist die Streuung bei Keller harmonischer, die Grenzen sind nicht so scharf abgesetzt wie bei Mach, der dafür bei den höheren Werten einen längeren Auslauf zeigt. Denkt man sich die Zahlenwerte in eine Kurve umgesetzt, so verläuft diejenige rechts (Keller) recht regelmäßig, während diejenige Machs einige Ausschläge aufweist, woraus man auf die größere sprachliche Meisterschaft des Dichters schließen könnte. Weiter sei bemerkt, dass Keller offenbar wesentlich komplexere Strukturen braucht, da er auf hundert

Sätze gut 170 Satzelemente mehr hat (Keller 1944:397, Mach 1988:207, also nur gut zwei pro Satz).

1		
2	2	10
3	4	22
4	8	34
5	21	39
6	26	50
7	20	41
8	15	43
9	14	42
10	14	23
11	15	14
12	16	20
13	7	13
14	7	8
15	4	7
16	9	3
17	6	3
18	3	1
19	3	3
20	3	2
21	1	
22	3	1
23	1	
24	1	
Mehr	4	

Fig. 1: Vergleich Mach – Keller

Es ist nun zu bedenken, dass es durchaus möglich ist, sich bei der Füllung der Satzelemente eine gewisse Disziplin aufzuerlegen und im Interesse der Verstehbarkeit eines Textes darauf zu achten, Verstopfungen zu vermeiden. Darin liegt der praktische Nutzen dieser Untersuchung. Man könnte, will man das Ergebnis des Vergleichs in einen stilistischen Ratschlag umsetzen, darauf hinweisen, dass es nicht nötig sei, in kurzen und möglichst simplen Sätzen zu schreiben, wenn man optimale Verständlichkeit anstrebe, dass man seinen eigenen Schreibneigungen durchaus Raum geben könne, solange man daran denke, seine Satzelemente nur selten mit zwölf und mehr Wörtern zu füllen; wenn man es so weit bringt, auch auf eine gute Streuung zu achten, kann das der Verstehbarkeit der Texte nur aufhelfen. Dagegen solle man sich auch nicht wehren, mitunter über die Schnur zu hauen, sofern man die Sache so weit im Griff hat, dass man auch bei über dreißig Wörtern pro Satz eine optimale Anordnung findet. Ein Nebenrat wäre dabei, komplexe Attributgefüge vorsichtig zu behandeln. Keineswegs kann es aber darum gehen, Satzgefüge um jeden Preis in einfache Sätze zu verwandeln, da die andere grammatische Form meist auch eine inhaltliche Veränderung impliziert:

[10a] „Es war einmal ein Schloss, das stand auf einem Berg."
[10b] „Auf einem Berg stand einmal ein Schloss". (Heringer 1989)

Der erste Fall lenkt dahin, dass im folgenden Satz vom Berg die Rede ist, der zweite deutet an, dass der Text mit einem Hinweis auf das Schloss fortfährt. Satzgefüge möglichst eliminieren zu wollen, ist ein Versuch, die Sprache zu reduzieren.

Interessant ist es nun, dass sich, je hundert Sätze genommen, charakteristische Bilder zeigen, die autorenspezifisch zu sein scheinen. (Dieser Frage soll an einem anderen Ort nachgegangen werden.) Das kann insofern nicht erstaunen, als eine Kontrolle der Verteilung der Satzelemente in einem Text praktisch undenkbar ist. Wer zählend und messend schreibt, wird kaum einen guten Text produzieren: Wer schreibt, drückt sich aus. Offenbar hat er auch in Bezug auf die Strukturen und – wie sich zeigt – die Satzelemente seinen eigenen, allerdings nicht einfach von vornherein gegebenen, Sprachstil.

Noch interessanter scheint aber die Tatsache, dass sich mit der Zeit ein Ausgleich zu ergeben scheint. Schon fünfhundert Sätze genügen, um eine harmonische Folge der Werte zu erlangen (vgl. Fig. 2). Der Verlauf einer gedachten Kurve ist bei Keller (rechts) allerdings etwas harmonischer als bei Mach. Trotzdem ist der Ausgleich, der durch die Zusammenfassung von fünfhundert Sätzen entsteht, verblüffend. Sie erklärt sich allerdings, wenn man beobachtet, dass die jeweiligen Hundertereinheiten, die hier berücksichtigt sind, ihre Spitzenwerte immer an einem anderen Ort haben, währenddem die Einzelwerte bei Keller recht konstant verteilt sind. Auch darin kann ein Hinweis auf seine größere sprachliche Meisterschaft gesehen werden.

1	2	
2	20	38
3	39	89
4	72	147
5	100	193
6	112	198
7	106	193
8	96	183
9	77	152
10	73	112
11	81	65
12	66	60
13	62	37
14	38	30
15	36	26
16	35	19
17	19	15
18	10	8
19	12	8
20	11	5

Fig. 2: Vergleich 500 Sätze Mach – Keller

Nimmt man ein Sammelsurium von Texten journalistischer Art, ergibt sich, was man erwarten kann. Die Verteilung ist flacher, die Satzelemente mit höheren Werten als 10 sind deutlich häufiger vertreten. Auch große Mengen von Sätzen ergeben nicht wirklich ein harmonisches Bild.

Die Konstanz der Mittelwerte quer durch die Palette der Tageszeitungen (mit Ausnahme wohl der Boulevardblätter, deren Werte eher in der Gegend der dichterischen (!)
zu liegen scheinen) lässt vermuten, dass sich hier doch eine Art praktikables Optimum
anbietet. Dichterisches Schreiben erfordert hohe sprachliche Disziplin. Gutes wissenschaftliches Schreiben vermutlich nicht viel weniger. Liegen wir also bei einem Mittel von etwa zehn Wörtern pro Satzelement und erlangen eine einigermaßen passable
Streuung der Werte, so dürften wir erreicht haben, was von uns verlangt werden
kann. Alles andere bleibt selbstverständlich vorausgesetzt.

Bei Keller liegt der Mittelwert „Wörter pro Satzelement" etwas tiefer als bei Mach.
Für einen Dichter ist Kellers Wert verhältnismäßig hoch, Mach hält etwa die Mitte zwischen dichterischer und journalistischer Prosa.

4   Schlussbemerkung

Müssen wir also in einem von uns dem Publikum zugemuteten Text einen mühsam erarbeiteten und nach verschiedenen Seiten überprüften komplexen Sachverhalt in Sätzen möglichst unübersichtlicher weil alles in eins werfender attributiver Konstruktion
und damit schwer überblickbarer Gestalt ausdrücken?

Oder wäre es zweckmäßig, dass wir dem Publikum Texte offerieren, die einen von
uns erarbeiteten Sachverhalt darlegen, den wir nach verschiedenen Seiten überprüft
haben, indem wir die komplexe Materie in möglichst übersichtlicher, wenn auch durchaus komplexer Form vorstellen, die auch schwer Verständliches in nachvollziehbarer
Gestalt ausdrückt?

5   Literatur

HERINGER, Hans Jürgen (1989): Grammatik und Stil. Praktische Grammatik des Deutschen. Frankfurt: Cornelsen.
REINERS, Ludwig (1991): Deutsche Stilkunst. Ein Lehrbuch deutscher Prosa. München: Ch. Beck
RUPRECHT, Robert (1999): Verstehst du auch, was du liesest? In: Wirkendes Wort 3, 462-482.
— (1998): Kontinuität oder Entwicklung? Zur Frage nach der Veränderung der deutschen Syntax in
den letzten hundert Jahren. In: Strässler, Jürg (Hrsg.): Tendenzen europäischer Linguistik. Tübin-
gen: Niemeyer, 190-195.
— (1993): Die Syntax als Metrik der Prosa. Bern: P. Lang.
SANDERS Willy (1992): Sprachkritikastereien und was der „Fachler" dazu sagt. Darmstadt: Wiss.
Buchgesellschaft.
SCHNEIDER Wolf (³1988): Deutsch für Kenner. Die neue Stilkunde. (Bearb. von M. Leier). Hamburg:
Gruner und Jahr.

Quellen

HERINGER, Hans Jürgen (1989): Grammatik und Stil. Praktische Grammatik des Deutschen. Frank-
furt: Cornelsen.
KELLER, Gottfried (1944): Der Landvogt von Greifensee. In: Sämtliche Werke, Band 9 (hrsg. v. Carl
Helbling). Bern: Francke.

MACH, Ernst (1988): Die Mechanik in ihrer Entwicklung. Nachdruck 1988 Hgg v. Gereon Wolters, Darmstadt : Wiss. Buchgesellschaft.

MENKE-EGGERS Christoph (1988): Die Souveränität der Kunst. Frankfurt a. M.: Athenäum.

Gibt es einen biozentrischen Sprachgebrauch?

Wilhelm Trampe

1   Ökolinguistische Pragmatik

Wie beziehen wir uns in unseren Äußerungen auf die (durch Tradition, Erziehung, Erfahrung vermittelte) Realität von Natur? So lässt sich die allgemeine Fragestellung eines pragmatischen Ansatzes innerhalb der Ökolinguistik formulieren (vgl. Trampe 1990; Fill 1993). Damit greift die ökolinguistische Pragmatik eine der grundlegenden Fragestellungen der linguistischen Pragmatik auf, wie sie Anfang der 70er-Jahre im seinerzeit viel beachteten Funk-Kolleg Sprache von Dieter Wunderlich für diesen damals noch jungen Wissenschaftszweig formuliert worden war (Wunderlich 1973:102). Mit der eingangs aufgeführten Fragestellung sollte ein Teil des Aufgabenfeldes angesprochen werden, dessen Bearbeitung als dringend erforderlich erschien. Obwohl der Club of Rome ebenfalls 1973 den Friedenspreis des Deutschen Buchhandels für die Studie „Grenzen des Wachstums – Bericht des Club of Rome zur Lage der Menschheit" erhielt und die Ausbeutung und Zerstörung natürlicher Ressourcen sich spätestens seitdem bis in die 80er-Jahre zu einem zentralen Thema öffentlicher Diskussion entwickelte – sodass am Ende des 20. Jahrhunderts die ökologische Bedrohung als die Bedrohung schlechthin empfunden wurde –, blieb es der ökologischen Linguistik vorbehalten, sich mit der anfangs genannten Frage systematisch auseinander zu setzen. Eine Erklärung dafür, dass erst nach zehn Jahren erstmals Finke (1983) innerhalb der Linguistik eine erste Skizze einer ökologischen Sicht auf unseren sprachlichen Umgang mit Natur und auf Sprache im Allgemeinen entwickelte, mag darin liegen, dass sich linguistische Pragmatik traditionellerweise mit der Untersuchung und Beschreibung der Wirkung sprachlicher Mittel auf den Menschen und des Nutzens sprachlichen Verhaltens für den Menschen beschäftigt (vgl. z. B. Levinson 1994)[1].

Der Ansatz einer ökolinguistischen Pragmatik erweitert die pragmalinguistische Perspektive insofern, da es hier auch um die Frage nach den Auswirkungen des jeweils realisierten oder realisierbaren Sprachgebrauchs im Umgang mit Natur auf unsere natürliche Mitwelt im Rahmen unserer gesellschaftlich-kulturellen Lebensform und um die Gefahren eines ausschließlich auf menschlichen Nutzen bedachten Sprechens über Natur geht. So soll in dieser Untersuchung auch der Frage nachgegangen werden, ob es und wenn ja, wie es uns möglich sein kann, eine anthropozentrische sprachliche Perspektivierung zugunsten einer öko- bzw. biozentrischen Perspektivierung zu überwinden.

Mit der Verwendung des Begriffs der „sprachlichen Perspektivierung" wird hervorgehoben, dass ein bestimmter Sprachgebrauch immer auch eine bestimmte Weltsicht (Humboldt) im Sinne einer Weltanschauung (Goethe) beinhaltet, denn mit der Vorstellung von Sprache kann immer die Vorstellung von einer Lebensform (Witt-

---

genstein) verbunden werden. Damit erscheint Sprache als interdependentes Element der Kultur der Gesellschaft, das durch seine lexikalischen und syntaktischen Strukturen und Prozesse bestimmte Erfahrungen begünstigt oder behindert.

> „Wie wir die Natur aufgliedern, sie in Begriffen organisieren und ihnen Bedeutungen zuschreiben, das ist weitgehend davon bestimmt, dass wir an einem Abkommen beteiligt sind, sie in dieser Weise zu organisieren – einem Abkommen, das für unsere Sprachgemeinschaft gilt und in den Strukturen unserer Sprache kodifiziert ist. Dieses Übereinkommen ist natürlich nur ein implizites und unausgesprochenes, *aber sein Inhalt ist absolut obligatorisch*; wir können überhaupt nicht sprechen, ohne uns der Ordnung und Klassifikation des Gegebenen zu unterwerfen, die dieses Übereinkommen vorschreibt." (Whorf 1963:12).

Diese von Benjamin Lee Whorf im Jahre 1956 formulierte Aussage zum Verhältnis von Sprache, Denken und Wirklichkeit der Natur lässt die Kernthese des von ihm und Edward Sapir begründeten „linguistischen Relativitätsprinzips" erkennbar werden. Bezogen auf die erkenntnisleitende Fragestellung im Titel dieser Abhandlung hätte die rigide Auslegung dieses Prinzips zur Folge, dass ein nicht-nichtanthropozentrisches Weltbild innerhalb eines anthropozentrischen sprachlichen Weltbildes undenkbar wäre. Von einer Art mentalen Gefangenschaft, bedingt durch eine sprachliche Weltsicht, kann allerdings aus der Sicht einer Ökologischen Linguistik nicht gesprochen werden, denn die sprachliche Kreativität ermöglicht ein unbegrenztes Schaffen von Beziehungen und Bedeutungen – und damit auch Naturzugängen (vgl. Trampe 1990:105f). So erscheint es durchaus möglich, die Perspektivierung, die eine Sprache einer Sprachgemeinschaft auf lexikalischer und syntaktischer Ebene vorgibt, zu beschreiben, zu hinterfragen und über Alternativen nachzudenken. Die Übereinstimmung in der Lebensform, die sich im sprachlichen Verhalten zeigt, gründet allerdings nicht nur in der sozialen und kulturellen Praxis, sondern auch in der genetischen Ausstattung. Aufgrund des gattungstypischen genetischen Potenzials kann Sprache nicht-nichtanthropozentrisch sein in dem Sinne, dass das Stiften von Beziehungen und Bedeutungen durch Sprache immer an bio- und tradigenetische Voraussetzungen des Menschen gebunden bleibt. Wie bezogen auf Wissen und Wissenschaft ein epistemischer Anthropozentrismus unvermeidbar ist, denn jedes Erkennen bleibt an unsere menschlichen Möglichkeiten gebunden (Groh/Groh 1996:112), so können wir – als Naturwesen – einem natürlichen Anthropozentrismus nicht entkommen, der uns als Gattungswesen ausweist.

Mit Blick auf die moderne „Naturwissenschaft" bemerkt bereits Whorf (1963) kritisch:

> „…, dass kein Individuum Freiheit hat, die Natur mit völliger Unparteilichkeit zu beschreiben, sondern eben, während es sich am freiesten glaubt, auf bestimmte Interpretationsweisen beschränkt ist." (Whorf 1963:12)

Und an anderer Stelle heißt es: „… dass Sprachen die Natur in vielen verschiedenen Weisen aufgliedern, …" (Whorf 1963:13). Im Prozess der gesellschaftlich-kulturellen Praxis entstehen im Medium der Sprache somit spezifische Lebensformen im Umgang mit Natur. Wittgenstein, für den die Vorstellung von Sprache als Lebensform innerhalb seiner Spätphilosophie als Schlüsselbegriff bezeichnet werden kann, benutzt zur Kennzeichnung der ideologischen Basis der Lebensformen ebenfalls den Begriff des „Weltbildes" (Wittgenstein 1984:139 (ÜG 94); zur Modellvorstellung von Sprachen als Lebensformen bei Wittgenstein vgl. Trampe 1996). Innerhalb des natürlichen Anthropozentrismus entstehen somit zwangsläufig Weltbilder, die Naturbilder enthalten.

Bezogen auf die sprachliche Perspektivierung von Natur lassen sich mehr oder weniger komplexe Fragestellungen anschließen, die sich sowohl auf das Sprachsystem (Ebene der langue) als auch auf die Ebene des Sprachgebrauchs beziehen (Ebene der parole): Wie gliedern unterschiedliche Sprachen die Natur auf? Welches Naturbild zeigt sich in unserem Sprachsystem? Welche Bedeutung räumen wir in unserem Sprachgebrauch der Natur ein? Wie stellt sich unser Sprachgebrauch den biologischen/ökologischen Gegebenheiten der Welt?

Obwohl es sicher notwendig ist, dass eine ganzheitlich orientierte Ökologische Linguistik, die sich grundlegend mit dem Verhältnis von Sprache und Natur beschäftigt, weiter gehen muss, als sich nur mit einer linguistischen Analyseebene zu beschäftigen, beschränke ich mich hier auf einen kleinen Ausschnitt aus dem umfassenden Aufgabenbereich einer Ökologischen Linguistik: auf die Klassifizierung der Wortwahl im Sprachgebrauch zur Perspektivierung unseres sprachlichen Naturverhältnisses.

Bezogen auf unsere sprachliche Beziehung zur Natur können als Teil unserer Lebensform zunächst unterschiedliche Definitionen und Vorstellungen von dem, was als Natur bezeichnet wird, unterschieden werden, die wiederum bestimmte Weltbilder widerspiegeln. An dieser Stelle sei lediglich auf die umfassende Darstellung zur Geschichte der Naturvorstellungen von Gloy (1995/1996) verwiesen. Für die hier verfolgten Zwecke werde ich folgende Begriffsbestimmung zugrunde legen: „Natur" wird aufgefasst als etwas, was unabhängig vom willentlichen Wirken des Menschen existiert oder so gedacht werden kann. Damit wird eine Perspektive eröffnet, die den Menschen selbst als Natur- und Kulturwesen sieht. Gleichzeitig wird es möglich, naturnahe von naturfernen Aktivitäten sprachlich zu unterscheiden.

2   Anthropozentrismus und Biozentrismus

Bei der Untersuchung unserer derzeitigen Lebensform im Hinblick auf den Umgang mit Natur erweist sich eine anthropozentrische Perspektive als dominierend, die sich in unterschiedlichen Graden sprachlich zeigen kann. In diesem dualistischen Weltbild, das einer eindimensionalen technisch-ökonomischen Rationalität verhaftet ist, ist zunächst Natur immer das Äußere – Nicht-Menschliche. Anthropozentrismus degradiert Natur zu einem Objekt, das der Mensch technisch und ökonomisch zur Verfügung hat – ein Objekt, das nur einen Wert besitzt in Bezug auf menschliche Werte. Diesem sog. „engen" anthropozentrischen Ansatz steht ein weiter Anthropozentrismus zur Seite, der auch dort, wo z.B. die Rechtsordnung ökologischen Gütern einen „Eigenwert" einräumt, dieses um des Menschen willen geschieht.

Demgegenüber betont eine bio- oder auch ökozentrische Perspektive den Subjektcharakter von Natur und die Naturverbundenheit des Menschen. Nach Taylor (1997:93ff) beinhaltet diese Sicht auf Natur und ökologische Gefüge vier Ideen: Menschen erwerben die Mitgliedschaft in der Lebensgemeinschaft der Erde zu den gleichen Bedingungen wie nicht menschliche Mitglieder; die Ökosysteme der Erde sind durch ein komplexes Netz miteinander verknüpft, sodass das gesunde Funktionieren eines Elements von dem des anderen abhängig ist; jeder Einzelorganismus wird als teleologisches Zentrum von Leben aufgefasst, das sein individuelles Wohl auf seine eigene Weise anstrebt; die Vorstellung, Menschen seien aufgrund ihrer genetischen Ausstattung anderen Spezies überlegen, stellt lediglich ein irrationales Vorurteil dar. Die sich aus diesen vier Ideen ergebende Haltung der Achtung vor der Natur kann mehr oder weniger konsequent vertreten werden.

Im Folgenden sollen nun Formen des anthropozentrischen Sprachgebrauchs unterschieden und herausgestellt werden. Allerdings soll hier damit begonnen werden, diesen Formen der sprachlichen Anthropozentrik systematisch Alternativen gegenüberzustellen oder zumindest anzudeuten. Andere Elemente ökolinguistischer Sprachkritik bleiben an dieser Stelle außen vor (vgl. dazu z.B. Trampe 1998).[2] Der Versuch, dem anthropozentrischen Vokabular ein alternatives gegenüberzustellen, beinhaltet z.T. Konstruktionen. D.h., die Antwort auf die in der Überschrift gestellte Frage – „Gibt es einen biozentrischen Sprachgebrauch?" – kann erst dann mit ja beantwortet werden, wenn sich die o.g. biozentrischen Ideen der Achtung vor der Natur tatsächlich in der Sprachpraxis niedergeschlagen haben. Von einem alternativen Sprachgebrauch im Umgang mit Natur sind wir allerdings noch weit entfernt.

Aus zwei Gründen erscheint es mir sinnvoll, nicht nur bei einer Auflistung der Formen anthropozentrischen Sprachgebrauchs und bei einer ökolinguistischen Sprachkritik stehen zu bleiben.

Erstens: Der Streit um Wortbedeutungen und um die „richtige" von mehreren möglichen Bezeichnungen ist typisch für die ökologische Diskussion (Strauss et al. 1989:97). Politiker wissen, dass die „Besetzung von Begriffen" wichtig ist, um Perspektiven anzudeuten. Alternative Zugangsweisen zu Natur – wie beispielsweise eine biozentrische – können sich nur durchsetzen, wenn ein Bewusstsein für Alternativen vorhanden ist.

Zweitens: Die Erfahrungen der feministischen Linguistik haben gezeigt, dass die Richtlinien zur Vermeidung des sexistischen Sprachgebrauchs (Trömel-Plötz et al. 1981) eine große und kritische Resonanz gefunden haben. Der Feminismus als Bewegung wird im Gegensatz zur Ökologiebewegung auch mit einer sprachkritischen Einstellung verbunden (vgl. Schiewe 1998:270ff). Inzwischen finden sich die o.g. Richtlinien in Lehrbüchern im Unterrichtsfach Deutsch und dienen als Anregung für sprachdidaktisch motivierte Reflexionen über Sprache.

So sind auch mit den folgenden Richtlinien zur Vermeidung eines anthropozentrischen Sprachgebrauchs Veränderungsvorschläge angesprochen, die es möglich erscheinen lassen, einen sprachlichen Zugang zur Natur zu finden, dem eine andere sprachliche Weltsicht entspricht: ein bio- oder ökozentrisches Weltbild. Mit der Veränderung des Sprachgebrauchs wäre bereits ein Schritt zur Veränderung unserer Lebensform, die die ökologische Krise erzeugte, getan.

---

[2]   Dabei geht es einer ökolinguistischen Sprachkritik nicht darum, eine Art ‚Ecological Correctness' zu kreieren.

3 Richtlinien zur Vermeidung eines anthropozentrischen Sprachgebrauchs

Sprache ist kein Abbild der Wirklichkeit. Sprache als Medium anthropozentrischen Selbstverständnisses erweist sich als Vehikel einer naturfernen Beziehungs- und Bedeutungsstiftung im Umgang mit Natur.

Das Ziel dieser nun folgenden Richtlinien ist es zunächst, anthropozentrischen Sprachgebrauch identifizierbar zu machen und damit Anlässe zu schaffen, mit Hilfe der sprachlichen Kreativität eine alternative biozentrische Sprachpraxis zu entwickeln, die die naturfeindliche Sprachpraxis und damit die sie begleitende ökologische Krise überwinden hilft.

Grundsätzlich sind mindestens acht Arten anthropozentrischen Sprachgebrauchs zu unterscheiden. Diese werden anhand von Beispielen veranschaulicht. Einige Beispiele lassen sich durchaus mehreren Klassen zuordnen. Den unterschiedlichen Formen und Merkmalen eines anthropozentrischen Sprachgebrauchs, die Hilfen für dessen Identifizierung liefern sollen, werden Alternativen gegenübergestellt, die einem biozentrischen sprachlichen Weltbild zugeordnet werden können.

1) *Utilitarisierung von Natur.* Merkmale: Der Nutzen ist entscheidend für die Benennung, diese gibt Informationen über die Art und den Grad der Brauchbarkeit für den Menschen.

Anthropozentrischer Sprachgebrauch	*Alternativen*
Pelztier	Wiesel, Ozelot etc.
Honigbiene	Biene
Seidenraupe	Raupe
Ödland	Moor, Bruch etc.
Fleischrasse/Fleischtier	Limousin, Hochlandrind etc.
Nützling/Nutztier/Schädling	Marienkäfer, Esel, Kohlweißling etc.

Merkmale der Alternativen: Wegfall der Nutzenaspekte in der Benennung, Achtung des Selbstwertes der Natur. Konkretisierung bei der Benennung der Natursubjekte.

2) *Diskriminierung von Natur.* Merkmale: Natur wird sprachlich zum unwerten Leben, da ein Nutzen nicht gesehen wird; über Tiere und Pflanzen wird abwertend gesprochen.

Anthropozentrischer Sprachgebrauch	*Alternativen*
Unkraut	Kräuter (z.B. Giersch, Wicke)
Ungeziefer	Insekten (z.B. Mücke, Fliege)
Ungräser	Gräser (z.B. Quecke, Weiche Trespe)
Viecher	Kühe, Schafe etc.

Merkmale der Alternativen: Achtung des Selbstwertes aller Lebewesen; Wegfall der Vorsilbe „Un-"; Konkretisierung bei der Benennung, Verwendung des Gattungsnamens.

3) *Technokratisierung von Natur.* Merkmale: Natur wird vom Standpunkt der Technik und Verwaltung und des Funktionierens der Abläufe bezogen auf den Menschen betrachtet; die „Beherrschung" der Natur ergibt sich aus der Überzeugung von der Überlegenheit des Menschen gegenüber den anderen Lebewesen; damit verbunden ist eine emotionale Distanzierung

Anthropozentrischer Sprachgebrauch	*Alternativen*
Verschmutzungsrecht	durch Geldleistungen gekauftes Recht, Natur zu schädigen
Umweltschutztechnik	Versuch des Schutzes der natürlichen Mitwelt durch den Einsatz von Technik
Grünordnungsplan	Landschaftsumgestaltungspläne
Ökosystemmanagement	Eingriff in ökologische Gefüge
Naturmanagement	Versuch der Beherrschung von Natur
Tierproduktion	Tierzucht und –mast
Maisproduktion	Maisanbau
Umweltverträglichkeitsprüfung	Abschätzung der Schäden für die natürliche Mitwelt
Fleischproduzent/Fleischproduktionsanlage	Tierhaltung zum Zweck der Tötung und Verwertung der Tierkörper

Merkmale der Alternativen: Aufgabe der Fiktion von der Beherrschbarkeit der Natur; Wegfall des Produktionsbegriffs (ökologisch gesehen bleibt der Mensch im Naturhaushalt Konsument, diese bescheidene Rolle kann er lediglich durch sprachliche Fiktion überwinden!).

4) *Objektivierung/Mechanisierung von Natur*. Merkmale: Natur wird sprachlich zum leblosen Etwas, das behandelt werden kann wie Sachen und Maschinen.

Anthropozentrischer Sprachgebrauch	*Alternativen*
Erneuerung von Birken	Fällen und Anpflanzen von Birken
Austausch von Grünzeug	Ersatzbepflanzung
Auswechselung von Bäumen	Fällen und Anpflanzen von Bäumen
Ferkelmaterial	Ferkel
Empfängermaterial	Kühe, Sauen usw.
Landschaftsverbrauch	Betonierung von Landschaft etc.
Flächenstilllegung	Aufgabe der Bewirtschaftung
Entwässerungsobjekte	Feuchtwiesen etc.

Merkmale der Alternativen: Jeder Organismus wird als teleologisches Zentrum von Leben aufgefasst; Lebewesen werden weder als leblose Dinge noch als Maschinen aufgefasst; Vermeidung eines mechanistischen Vokabulars.

5) *Anthropomorphisierung von Natur*. Merkmale: Naturgeschehen wird und Verhaltensweisen anderer Lebewesen werden nach menschlichen Maßstäben bezeichnet und kategorisiert.

Anthropozentrischer Sprachgebrauch	*Alternativen*
Raubvogel	Greifvogel
Raubtier	Fleischesser, fleischverzehrendes Tier
Naturgesetze	Gesetze zur Erklärung und Beherrschung von Naturgeschehen
Umwelt	soziale, natürliche etc. Mitwelt
Umweltverschmutzung	Vermüllung, Zerstörung und Vergiftung von sozialen, natürlichen etc. Mitwelten
Vorfluter	Abwasserkanal

Merkmale der Alternativen: Einsicht, dass nichtmenschliches Leben eigenen Werten unterliegt (Selbstwertcharakter) und dass sich der Mensch von natürlichen Prozessen prinzipiell nicht isolieren kann; „Objektivität" bleibt menschliche Intersubjektivität.

6) *Tabuisierung*. Merkmale: Alles, was mit von Menschen ausgehenden Naturzerstörungen und Tötungen von Pflanzen und Tieren zusammenhängt, wird sprachlich ausgeblendet; ungewollte Lebewesen werden sprachlich – mit dem Ziel der emotionalen Immunisierung – ignoriert und ausgeschlossen; z. T. durch Euphemisierung.

Anthropozentrischer Sprachgebrauch	*Alternativen*
Aussterben	Ausrottung durch den Menschen
Artenrückgang	Ausrottung einer Lebensform
Das Verschwinden des Grüngürtels	Zerstörung eines Lebensraumes
Keulen	Töten seuchenkranker Tiere
Pflanzenbehandlung/-smittel	Töten von unerwünschten Pflanzen; Einsatz
Pflanzenschutz/-mittel,	von Pflanzengiften
Ackerfreihaltung, Spritzung von Getreide	
Umweltverschmutzung	Vermüllung, Zerstörung und Vergiftung von natürlicher Mitwelt

Merkmale der Alternativen: sprachliche Aufhebung der Tabus; differenzierte Darstellung der Zerstörungspotentiale; Herausstellung des Agens.

7) *Dichotomisierung/Distanzierung*. Merkmale: Distanzierung von anderen Lebewesen durch unterschiedliche Bezeichnung für die gleichen Sachverhalte; bei Übertragung der für Tiere oder Pflanzen geltenden Bezeichnungen auf den Menschen bekommen diese einen pejorativen Charakter.

Anthropozentrischer Sprachgebrauch	*Alternativen*
Tiere fressen/Menschen essen	Lebewesen essen
Tiere werfen Junge/Menschen	Lebewesen gebären Kinder
Tiere verenden/Pflanzen gehen ein/Menschen sterben	Lebewesen sterben
Tieren werden geschlachtet/ Menschen werden getötet	Lebewesen werden getötet

Merkmale der Alternativen: Aufhebung der sprachlichen Unterschiede, menschliche Bezeichnungen auch für Tiere und Pflanzen (oder umgekehrt).

8) *Nivellierung von Natur*. Merkmale: Andere Lebewesen werden zur namenlose Masse, zum namenlosen Etwas; Namensgebung für Individuen mit Eigennamen entfällt, statt dessen werden Nummerierungen o.ä. eingeführt

Anthropozentrischer Sprachgebrauch	*Alternativen*
Grünpflanzen	Atlaszeder, Schildfarn etc.
Straßenbegleitgrün	Bergahorn, Weißdorn etc.
Bäume	Rotbuche, Traubeneiche etc.
Stellplatznummer 245 (zur Kennzeichnung einer Kuh)	„Eigenname"
Käfigzeile 98/Mitte/5 (zur Kennzeichnung eines Huhnes)	„Eigenname"

Merkmale der Alternativen: Jeder Organismus wird als teleologisches Zentrum von Leben aufgefasst; Benennung mit Eigennamen; Schaffung von Nähe durch Konkretisierungen; der natürlichen Diversität soll die sprachliche Diversität Rechnung tragen.

Der hier vorgelegte Beispielkatalog ist sicherlich unvollständig. Wenn in Einzelfällen keine überzeugende sprachliche Alternative angegeben wurde, so aus dem trivialen Grund, dass es nicht darum gehen kann, etwas Gezwungen-Wirkendes zu konstruieren. Wenn auch in der Regel bei Personen, die im besonderen Maße mit der sprachlichen Referenz auf Natur zu tun haben wie „Natur- und Umweltschützer", eine Sensibilisierung für die ökologische Relevanz der Sprache nicht besonders ausgeprägt ist, so sind dennoch einige kritische Bestrebungen zur Vermeidung eines anthropozentrischen Sprachgebrauchs feststellbar. Neben den oben dargestellten alternativen Verwendungsweisen ist das Bemühen zu beobachten, Neologismen zu kreieren, um sich deutlich von einer naturfeindlichen Sprachpraxis abzusetzen, indem statt von „Unkraut" von „Ackerwildkraut" oder statt von der „Erschließung von Bauland" von der „Zersiedlung von Landschaft" gesprochen wird.

Neben der sprachlichen Kreativität, die sicherlich zur Entwicklung eines biozentrischen Sprachgebrauchs vonnöten ist, werden in einigen Texten zur Kennzeichnung der anthropozentrischen Perspektive bereits Worte oder Aussagen in Anführungszeichen gesetzt, um dadurch die Problematik dieser Bezeichnung deutlich zu machen.

Eine weitere Strategie zeigt sich darin, dass Paraphrasierungen benutzt werden, um den anthropozentrischen Sprachgebrauch zu vermeiden, wie es hier auch in einigen Fällen in dem Beispielkatalog für einen alternativen Sprachgebrauch versucht wurde.

Über einen anderen Sprachgebrauch nachdenken heißt auch, über eine andere gesellschaftlich-kulturelle Lebensform nachdenken. Anthropozentrische Sprache verwenden bedeutet, Natur nicht zur Sprache kommen zu lassen und damit die ökologische Krise zu manifestieren und die Überlebensbedingungen der gesamten Vielfalt aller Kreaturen auf diesem Planeten zu verschlechtern. Die Entwicklung und Verwendung eines nicht-anthropozentrischen Sprachgebrauchs sind erste Schritte in Richtung einer gesellschaftlichen Veränderung auf dem Weg zu einem nachhaltigen Naturschutz.

Aus einer lebensweltlichen Perspektive darf man erwarten, dass der Gegenstandsbereich der Sprachwissenschaft sich auch den drängenden Problemen der gesellschaftlich-kulturellen Praxis öffnet. Ein solches drängendes Problem stellt unser derzeitiger anthropozentrischer Umgang mit Natur im Medium der Sprache dar. Die Linguistik könnte ihren Beitrag zur Erhaltung einer vielfältigen natürlichen Mitwelt als Selbstwert leisten. Eine Verbreitung und Diskussion der vorgelegten Prinzipien zur Vermeidung eines anthropozentrischen Sprachgebrauchs könnte ein Schritt in diese Richtung sein. Nicht nur aus einer ökolinguistischen Perspektive dürfte ein solcher Schritt eine wesentliche Aufgabe der Sprachwissenschaft auf dem Weg ins nächste Jahrtausend darstellen.

4   Literatur

FILL, Alwin (1993): Ökolinguistik. Eine Einführung. Tübingen: Gunther Narr (Narr-Studienbücher).

FINKE, Peter (1983): Politizität. In: Finke; Peter (Hrsg.): Sprache im politischen Kontext. Tübingen: Niemeyer, 15-75.

GLOY, Karen (1995-1996): Das Verständnis der Natur, 2 Bde. München: Beck.

GROH, Ruth; GROH, Dieter (1996): Die Außenwelt der Innenwelt. Frankfurt: Suhrkamp (Suhrkamp-Taschenbuch Wissenschaft 1218).

LEVINSON, Stephen C. (1994): Pragmatik. Tübingen: Niemeyer.

SCHIEWE, Jürgen (1998): Die Macht der Sprache. Eine Geschichte der Sprachkritik von der Antike bis zur Gegenwart. München: Beck.

STRAUSS, Gerhard; HASS, Ulrike; HARRAS, Gisela (1989): Brisante Wörter von Agitation bis Zeitgeist. Ein Lexikon zum öffentlichen Sprachgebrauch. Berlin/New York: De Gruyter.

TAYLOR, Paul W. (1997): Die Ethik der Achtung für die Natur. In: Birnbacher, D. (Hrsg.): Ökophilosophie. Stuttgart: Reclam, 77-116.

TRAMPE, Wilhelm (1998): Against Ecological Correctness. In: Brinkhuis, F.; Talmor, S. (Hrsg.): Memory, History and Critique. European Identity at the Millennium. Proceedings of the 5. Conference of the International Society for the Study of European Ideas. 19 - 24 August 1996. Cambridge M.A.: MIT Press, 187/V-1-4.

— (1996): Language as a Part of a 'Form of Life'. In: 11. World Congress of Applied Linguistics. 4 - 9 August 1996. Jyväskylä, Finland.

— (1990): Ökologische Linguistik. Grundlagen einer ökologischen Sprach- und Wissenschaftstheorie (zugl.: Diss. Lavesloh / Bielefeld 1988 u.d.T. „Aspekte einer ökologischen Linguistik"). Opladen: Westdeutscher Verlag.

TRÖMEL-PLÖTZ; Senta; GUENTHERODT, Ingrid; HELLINGER, Marlis; PUSCH, Luise F. (1981): Richtlinien zur Vermeidung sexistischen Sprachgebrauchs. In: Linguistische Berichte 71, 1-7.

WHORF, Benjamin Lee (1963): Sprache – Denken – Wirklichkeit. Reinbek: Rowohlt.

WITTGENSTEIN, Ludwig (1984): Über Gewissheit. Gesammelte Schriften. Bd. 8. Frankfurt a. M.: Suhrkamp.

WUNDERLICH, Dieter (1973): Referenzsemantik. In: Funk-Kolleg Sprache. Frankfurt a. M.: Fischer. 102–112.

Contextual Triggers for English Equative Tautologies

Tomoko Tsujimoto

1 Introduction

The importance of contextual factors in the interpretation of tautological expressions, in the form of 'A is A', has been discussed by a number of researchers. However, how contexts affect our understanding of tautologies has not been fully explored. One of the reasons for this neglect is that most of the previous studies center around idiomatic and lexicalized tautologies, such as *War is war* and *Business is business* whose surrounding contexts have little influence on their interpretations. In this paper, after reviewing some representative studies, I examine non-idiomatic tautologies in the interpretation of which the context plays a vital role. I claim that the categorical unstableness of an entity triggers tautology. Tautology must be treated as a formula to object to a categorical view presented, or hidden, in the previous utterances. It will be shown that when 'a particular entity E is not included in a category A' or 'E should not be considered A' is implied or openly claimed from the context, and the recipient does not share that view, a tautology 'A is A' can be triggered. Tautology is metalinguistic in that it comments on the way we categorize things with words.

2 Previous studies

How do tautological expressions, which, truth-conditionally, ought to carry no new information, come to have communicative significance? How can a discourse participant come to reach, for instance, 1b) from 1a)?

1) a. War is war.
   b. Terrible things always happen in war, that's its nature and it's no good lamenting on that particular disaster.

To answer these questions, a number of approaches have been proposed. A Gricean approach claims that the source of tautology's communicative significance lies in its user's flouting of the maxim of Quantity. Thus Levinson (1983:111) explains:

2) Since this [maxim] requires that speakers be informative, the asserting tautologies blatantly violate it. Therefore, if the assumption that the speaker is actually co-operating is to be preserved, some informative inference must be made.

He then points out the important role a particular context plays in the interpretation of a tautological expression. However, as he himself admits, how the appropriate implicature is to be extracted remains quite unclear in this approach. Wierzbicka's (1987) semantic approach, in contrast to the pragmatic one, emphasises the language specific

and context independent aspects of tautologies and classifies the types of their communicative imports according to their sentential forms as in 3).

3) a. A sober attitude toward complex human activities
       N (abstr) is N (abstr)   e.g. War is war.   Business is business.
   b. Tolerance for human nature
      N (hum. pl.) are N (hum. pl.)   e.g. Boys are boys.   Kids are kids.
   c. Tautologies of obligation
      (art) N is (art) N   e.g. A rule is a rule. A deal is a deal.

Wierzbicka (1987) admits that some tautologies are ambiguous and that a tautology
can have two or more different communicative imports depending on the context of
utterance. However, her account gives us no clue how they are derived and how the
context is involved in bringing forth different implications a particular tautology may
have.

The third approach, proposed by Fraser (1988), summarized in 4), assigns the
hearer the task of inferencing what the speaker intends to convey with a particular
tautology.

4) An English nominal tautology signals that the speaker intends that the hearer
   recognize:
   i) that the speaker holds some view towards all objects referenced by the NP;
   ii) that the speaker believes that the hearer can recognize this particular view;
   iii) that this view is relevant to the conversation.

According to Fraser, *Business is business* may convey the idea that business is cut-
throat, that business is money-making, or that business is enjoyable, unpredictable
etc. depending on the utterance context. And the hearer is expected to pick up the
most relevant one in the current context. Fraser's account attempts to cover non-idiomatic tautologies as well as idiomatic ones. But at the same time the details of contextual factors are left unspecified. Although he assumes that speaker and hearer
share some view about the object referred to by the NP, any views can be held about
it. And we cannot be sure which is the right one, especially when it comes to non-
idiomatic tautologies.

Ward and Hirschberg (1991) present a revised pragmatic approach. They analyze
the interpretation process of a tautology as follows.

5) – S has affirmed a tautological utterance of the form 'a is a', which appears to
     add nothing to our mutual beliefs in general, and, in particular, nothing to
     our mutual beliefs about 'a';
   – Assuming that S is observing the Cooperative Principle, then, by the maxims
     of Quantity and Relation, S has said as much as s/he truthfully can that is
     relevant about 'a';
   – S might have produced utterances of a similar form, say 'a is b', (where 'a'
     and 'b' are distinct, modulo referring expressions), which could have added
     something to our mutual beliefs about 'a';
   – S chose not to utter such alternatives;

– thus S implicates that these alternatives are not relevant for the purposes of the exchange.

In 6) below, they explain, from the 'a is a' expression *Vodka is vodka*, 'a is b' can be worked out as '(some) vodka is Russian'. By the fact that this expression has not been chosen, the speaker implies that she believes that is not relevant to the current exchange.

> 6) Stolichnaya vodka has been a slow mover, though, said restaurant manager Bill Leung. But not because of politics. 'Hardly anybody orders it. In a small town, people don't know the difference between vodkas. Vodka is vodka,' he said. (Ward & Hirschberg 1991:514)

This revised pragmatic approach is quite viable in that it puts in the picture the un-uttered message, i.e., 'a is b'. Even if it is not actually uttered, the deliberately avoided utterance can be implied and conveyed to the hearer by the extra-linguistic or tonal property of the surrounding utterances. To work out the communicative import packed in a tautology, it is essential that we should look into the unuttered message, hidden in the discourse. Still, there remain a few points to be made clear in this analysis. First, there should be some particular kind of irrelevancy which triggers tautologies. Secondly, if 'a is b' is irrelevant, what is the speaker's own idea about 'a'? Not just implying that the 'a is b' is irrelevant, a tautology also carries the speaker's idea about 'a' which is relevant in the current discourse.

In the following sections, the key to reach the speaker's idea about 'a' will be sought in the contextual patterns. It will be discussed that tautology essentially conveys the speaker's own categorical understanding of a particular entity when she finds it is not shared with the other discourse participants.

3   Contextual triggers for tautologies

The surrounding contexts of tautological expressions have some definite patterns. To see what they are, it is essential to examine those surrounding non-idiomatic tautologies, for the contexts in which idiomatic tautologies appear are largely irrelevant to the extent that they have little influence on their interpretations. Studies based only on those idiomatic examples would lead to the oft-repeated account that tautologies are to confirm the prototype of the category or the immutability of the category. That this is only half true will be discussed below.

It is observed based on the 60 attested examples of non-idiomatic tautology that the one who utters a tautology does not agree with her recipient on the categorization of an entity in focus (E). Before illustrating this with examples, however, we need to have a clear view on what a category is.

3.1   Prototype view of category and hedges

The account I propose here is in line with the prototype view of categories (cf. Taylor 1995). It is assumed that

i)   elements of a category are assigned membership in virtue of their similarity to the prototype;

ii) there are degrees of membership according to their closeness to the prototype;

iii) attributes of a category may be differently weighed in different contexts;

iv) category boundaries are not necessarily clear-cut. In this framework, one entity may be more central in a category than others; category boundaries may be fuzzy.

For example, a robin is more central an element of the category BIRD than, say, a penguin. And a bat is not usually classified as a bird. However, when the attributes [possession of wings] and [ability to fly] are highly evaluated as criteria in a particular context, even a bat can be labelled as a bird as in 7a).

7) a. Loosely speaking, a bat is a bird.
   b. Strictly speaking, a bat is not a bird.

Hedges, as Taylor (1995:75-77) notes, make use of this flexibility and even have power to restructure a category. They may extend or narrow category boundaries. When category boundaries are extended as in 7a), what is normally considered a falsehood can be regarded as true in a restricted sense. On the other hand, 7b), since the boundary of the category BIRD is viewed from a technical point of view, a bat is not allowed to sneak into it.

'Expert' categories (cf. Taylor 1995:72) are often supposed to have all-or-nothing membership and clear-cut boundaries. Even so, since some words have both expert and folk definitions, their boundaries may become fuzzy in the everyday use of the words. Thus the category KILLING, which appears to be most clearly defined in legal discourse, can be easily extended using a hedge as in 8).

8) He killed Alice in that he did nothing to keep her alive.
   (Herrmann 1975 cited from Taylor 1989:78)

The speaker of 8) considers what 'he' did an instance of KILLING, though it is not a prototypical one. She gives the reason for the loose categorization using a hedge *in that*. It may be said that the hedge *in that* is a means to justify the speaker's categorization. Of course, not everyone may be convinced of her way of categorizing this particular event. In fact, one might argue that his act should not be called killing at all.

So far, we have seen that categories are not as strictly regimented as the classical theory of category claims and as has been widely believed. Category boundaries may be extendible or narrowable; category membership may be gradient according to the closeness to the prototype; attributes may be variously evaluated in each context. Hedges reveal these quite clearly. They are called for when the speaker becomes conscious of the difference of her categorization from others', to justify her own categorization.

3.2 Categorical disagreement and tautology

3.2.1 Overview

In the last section, we have seen that hedges are to justify speaker's categorization. Tautologies are, on the other hand, to say no to such justification by opposing the other's, often unusual, way of categorization. This oppositional nature of tautology explains the frequent appearance of adversative conjunctions such as 'but' or 'still' accompanying tautologies as in 9a) and 9b).

9) a. Nevertheless, marriage is marriage. (Cf. Takeda 1998:91)[1]
   b. Language is still language, whether it is realized as the product of speech or of writing.

The dismissive phrases such as 'this is the end of it' also frequently follow tautologies. This is also understood as a result of the speaker's oppositional attitude to her recipient's preceding remark. Gibbs and McCarrell (1990) report that tautologies in negative contexts are found more comprehensible than in positive contexts[2]. This also suggests the oppositional aspect of tautology. Tautologies are thus triggered by the categorical disagreement between speaker and hearer[3]. There are two major types of categorical disagreements found as triggers for tautologies. One is concerned with a particular entity: whether an entity (E) should be included in a category (A). The other concerns the attributes of A. The relative importance of each attribute may differ from person to person. Some may add an attribute or two, while others may delete some from the whole attributes. In fact, these two types can be seen as two sides of the same coin. The difference lies in which is in focus: a particular entity (E) or a category (A) as a whole.

---

[1] Takeda (1998) notes that adversative conjunctions often co-occur with proverbs. He sees this as evidence of the fact that proverbs are used as a persuasive means to oppose the other's argument and, at the same time, reinforce speaker's.

[2] For example, the positive and negative contexts for 'Carrots are carrots' are (1) and (2) below respectively.
   1) Carrots are great sources of vitamin A. They have just enough sugar in them to give you an energy boost but not much in the way of calories and fat. The ideal munchie food.
   2) Carrots are ultimately boring. They don't even have enough sugar in them to give you a real boost and even the taste is raw. The ideal food for rabbits but not for people.

[3] There are examples in which categorical disagreement is found in the speaker himself. This is the case in the example cited in Fraser (1988:219). *My son is My son* uttered by the father when his son has just won a scholarship reconfirms an attribute [academic excellence] of the category MY SON for him.

3.2.2 Tautologies of category elements

Let us now start with the examples of the former type, which mostly trigger non-idiomatic tautologies. In 10) below, the defense is trying to narrow the category boundary of MURDER to win a favourable verdict.

10) The defense claimed White had asked him to kill her. The prosecution countered with the claim 'Murder is murder'. (Ward & Hirschberg 1991:512)

By 'White had asked him to kill her', the defense argues that it is not the accused but White who wanted to kill the victim. And the hidden message here is that what the accused did (E) should not be seen as an instance of MURDER (A), or at least as 'the prototypical murder', since he only followed White's order. Note that the hidden message can be rephrased as below, using a hedge.

11) E is not an instance of A in that somebody else had asked the accused to kill the victim.

The prosecution of course does not accept such an arbitrary reorganization of the category MURDER and is urged to set forth the one that he believes is right. He then put forward a counterargument with a tautology: E should be classified as an instance of A. A tautology is thus triggered from this categorical disagreement.

Understatement can also be seen as an attempt to narrow a category boundary and put an entity out of the category in question. In 12), Henry and Spencer, the narrator, are praising Paul, a boy of weak frame, for having benched 105 pounds. Paul is too shy to be proud of that and tries to underestimate his achievement.

12) I picked Paul up at the Harbour Health Club.
"He benched one-oh-five today on the Universal," Henry said.
"Not bad," I said.
Paul nodded, "The Universal is easier," he said.
"One-oh-five is one-oh-five," I said. (Robert B. Parker, *Early Autumn*)

By 'The Universal is easier', Paul is implying that the weight he benched (E) was not as heavy as 105 pounds (A) would normally be thought. This could be rephrased again from a categorical point of view as below.

13) E is not an element of A in that the machine he used is easier.

Spencer then counters Paul's categorization with a tautology: E should be included in A, whatever machine he may use. The tautology 'One-oh-five is one-oh-five' thus shows Spencer's idea that the weight Paul benched on the Universal should be included in the category of 105 pounds, though it may not be felt as heavy as would be on other machines.

The categorical account also explains why non-nominals can take the A position in an equative tautology, A is A. In 14), an extract from a detective story, the adjective 'brown' occurs as A. Here a detective is looking for a girl with chestnut hair (girl 1). He found a girl (girl 2) who seems to know the girl 1. Since the chestnut hair is the only clue to find the girl 1, it is quite vital for the detective to get the word 'chestnut' out of girl 2.

14) 'How was her hair dressed?'
'In the Indian style when I saw it. Combed straight back from the forehead and plaited.'
'And dark?'
'Quite brown.'
'Any particular shade?'
'Brown is brown to me.'
It was too much to hope that she would say chestnut.
(P. Lovesay, *Bertie and the Crime of Passion*)

The detective-narrator here tries a few leading questions. From them, we can read that he is trying to put the colour of the girl 1's hair (E) in the category of CHEST-NUT or something darker than usual BROWN (A). But the girl 2 does not share this categorical view and answers E should be included in A.

A particular entity (E) is highlighted in each of the examples above: what the accused did in 10), the weight Paul benched in 12), and the colour of the girl's hair in 14). The preceding context tells us in which category the other party believes the entity E should be included. A tautology raises an objection to that and at the same time tries to confirm the legitimacy of the speaker's own understanding about E. The communicative import of a tautology must thus be worked out from this categorical viewpoint. What is the stake is not the prototypical categorization, but the speaker's own, whether it is prototypical or not. It is true that in many cases the speaker tries to maintain more or less a prototypical view of the category to which E is supposed to belong. But a tautology may also express a non-prototypical view. For instance, few would share what the speaker claims in 15).

15) A: She isn't Lizzy, if you please, she is Her Imperial Majesty.
B: Lizzy is Lizzy (to me).[4]

And nobody would be sure which side to stand in 16) .

16) A: This isn't Champagne. This is sparkling wine.
B: Champagne is Champagne.

We must not take the frequent occurrence of one type as the unique and intrinsic property of tautology. Non-prototypical views may also be claimed as in 15) and 16).

---

[4]   This is a constructed example from an example cited in Horn (1985:133).

3.2.3 Tautologies of category attributes

There is another type of categorical disagreement in which a particular attribute is focused on. The attribute highlighted in 17) is reworded by the speaker himself, i.e., 'pretty hopeless'. The speaker here reinforces with a tautology this attribute, which he thinks is forgotten or paid less attention to than should be.

17) "... Sometimes a physician just strolls in for a chat – slack moment. A good many of the young chaps come in for veganin or aspirin when they've got a hangover – and occasionally, I'd say, for a flirtatious word or two with one of the girls if the opportunity arises. Human nature is always human nature. You see how it is. Pretty hopeless." (Agatha Christie, *Hickory Dickory Death*)

The categorical disagreement does not manifest itself clearly here, but the speaker himself assumes there is. He thinks an attribute of the category HUMAN NATURE, [pretty hopeless], is ignored or forgotten by his recipient. And that triggers a tautology. The disagreement is presented more explicitly in the next example.

18) 'Don't you think, Mr Cubbit,' he said at last, 'that your best plan would be to make a direct appeal to your wife, and ask her to share her secret with you?' Hilton Cubbit shook his massive head. 'A promise is a promise, Mr Holmes. If Elsie wished to tell me, she would. If not, it is not for me to force her confidence.' (C. Doyle, *The Dancing Men*)

Mr Cubbit had made a promise, when he married Elsie, not to ask her about her past. Holmes' suggestion that he should ask her about her trouble leads him to break his promise. Holmes ignores the attribute [should not be broken] of the category PROMISE. Mr Cubbit in turn tries to remind him of that attribute; he has to keep his promise.

The 'meaning' of idiomatic tautologies are often described as obligation, tolerance, or reassurance. However, idiomatic tautologies are also based on the difference in categorical understanding between speaker and hearer just as non-idiomatic ones are. Therefore 'obligation' , 'tolerance' or 'reassurance' are more appropriately considered implications we derive from tautologies by pragmatic inference.

5 Conclusion

It is concluded that English equative tautologies are triggered by a categorical disagreement over a particular entity or a particular attribute, i.e., whether the entity is categorized as A or not, and how important the attribute is for A. When speaker and hearer disagree over the categorization of E, that can trigger a tautological utterance, A is A, conveying that E should be included in, or called, A. The fact that adjectives can form an A is A tautology also supports this analysis. When speaker and hearer disagree over the weighting of an attribute of A, that can trigger an A is A, conveying the speaker's idea about the attribute's special importance in A. Idiomatic tautologies tend to be of the latter type; non-idiomatic ones tend to be of the former. Taylor

(1995:76) characterises 'hedges as linguistic expressions which speakers have at their disposal to comment on the language they are using'. Likewise, we can characterize tautologies as expressions which speakers and listeners have at their disposal to comment on the way we categorize things.

6   References

FRASER, Bruce (1988): Motor oil is motor oil: an account of English nominal tautologies In: Journal of Pragmatics 12, 215-220.

GIBBS, Jr. Raymond; McCarrell, Nancy (1990): Why boys will be boys and girls will be girls: understanding colloquial tautologies. In: Journal of Psycholinguistic Research 19.2, 125-145.

HORN, Lawrence (1990): Metalinguistic negation and pragmatic ambiguity. In: Language 61.1, 121-174.

LEVINSON, Stephen (1983): Pragmatics. Cambridge: Cambridge University Press.

TAKEDA, Katsuaki (1998): The usage of "A is A" formulas. In: The working papers of the department of education of University of Wakayama.

TAYLOR, John (1989): Linguistic categorization. Oxford: Oxford University Press.

TSUJIMOTO, Tomoko (1998): Tautologies in Context, a paper read at the 16th annual meeting of the English Linguistic Society in Japan.

WARD, Gregory; HIRSCHBERG, Julia (1991): A pragmatic analysis of tautological utterances. In: Journal of pragmatics 15, 507-520.

WIERZBICKA, Anna (1987): Boys will be boys: 'radical semantics' vs. 'radical pragmatics'. In: Language 63.1, 95-114.

Schreiben mit und in *mental spaces*
Medial bedingte *blends* in text-basierten MOOs

Michaela Zitzen

1   Einleitung

Im Mittelpunkt der nachstehenden Untersuchung soll das von Fauconnier und Turner (1994) entwickelte Konzept der *mental blends* stehen. Obwohl sich die Konstruktion von *mental blends* sowohl auf der semantischen[1] als auch auf der pragmatischen Ebene widerspiegelt, kann im Rahmen dieses Beitrages nur auf pragmatisch relevante Teilaspekte von *blends* eingegangen werden.

In einem ersten Schritt soll aufgezeigt werden, welche Funktion *mental blends* in mündlichen und schriftlichen Gesprächskontexten zukommt. Vor diesem Hintergrund soll in einem zweiten Schritt diskutiert werden, welche Art von *blends* in den synchron ausgerichteten text-basierten MOOs erzeugt wird. Aus pragmatischer Sicht stellt sich in diesem Zusammenhang die Frage, ob es sich bei dieser Form des Kommunizierens, die begrifflich als *Computer-mediated Communication* (CMC) gefaßt wird, um Kommunikation *am* Bildschirm oder vielmehr um Kommunikation *im* Bildschirm handelt.

2   *Mental blends* in mündlichen und schriftlichen Gesprächssituationen

Sowohl in mündlichen als auch in schriftlichen Gesprächssituationen dienen *blends* dazu, den räumlichen und zeitlichen Rahmen des physischen Kontexts, in welchem sich der Sprecher (und der Hörer) derzeitig befinden, mental durch die Einbettung eines virtuellen Gesprächskontexts zu erweitern. In schriftlichen Gesprächssituationen wird dies offensichtlich, wenn wir in Texten Zitate einbauen, indem wir ehemals zu einem bestimmten Zeitpunkt in der Vergangenheit geäußerte Worte vergegenwärtigen, etwa in der Form von: „Ich kann Person X nur zustimmen, die hervorhebt …". Durch den Gebrauch des Präsenz wird eine Nähe zwischen den zwei räumlich und zeitlich voneinander getrennten Sprechern hergestellt, die innerhalb des *blends* eine dialogische Auseinandersetzung führen. Wie die Einbettung eines *blends* innerhalb einer *face-to-face* Situation aussieht, veranschaulicht Fauconnier (1997) anhand ihres berühmten Beispiels *The Great Debate*, in welchem sich ein Philosophieprofessor mit den folgenden Worten an seine Klasse richtet:

[1] I claim that reason is a self-developing capacity. [2] Kant disagrees with me on this point. [3] He says it's innate, [4] but I answer that that's begging the question, [4] to which he counters, in *Critique of Pure Reason*, that only innate ideas have power. [5] But I say to that, what

---

[1]   Innerhalb der Domaine des Computers ist das Phänomen *Computervirus* eines der jüngsten und von Fauconnier (1997) diskutierten Beispiele für die Konstruktion eines *mental blend,* welches sich auf der semantischen Ebene widerspiegelt.

about neuronal group selection? [6] And he gives no answer. (Fauconnier 1997:157; Durch-
nummerierung M. Z.)

Diesen monologischen an ein physisches Publikum gerichteten Beitrag präsentiert der
Philosophieprofessor in Form eines *blends*, in welchem er mit Kant eine *face-to-face*
Diskussion führt.

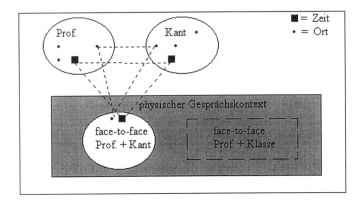

Abb. 1: The Great Debate

Von diesem *blend* bleiben die Zuhörer allerdings ausgeschlossen, so daß nur der Professor scheinbar unmittelbaren Zugang zu Kants Worten hat, die er für die Klasse in
indirekter Rede bzw. als diegetische Zusammenfassung wiedergibt. Letzteres trifft auf
die beiden Äußerungen „Kant disagrees with me on this point." und „And he gives no
answer" zu, die insofern eine besondere Form von indirekter Redewiedergabe darstellen, als daß es sich bei ihnen jeweils um „only the bare report that a speech event
has occured without any specification of what was said or how it was said" (McHale:
in Fludernik 1993: 289) handelt.

Neben der Aufhebung der räumlichen und zeitlichen Trennung, die den Professor
und den Philosophen Kant innerhalb des *blends* als zwei kopräsente Gesprächsteilnehmer erscheinen lassen, führt die in Äußerung [4] explizit genannte Referenz auf *Critique of Pure Reason* darüberhinaus zu einer Verblendung von medial schriftlichen
und medial mündlichen Gesprächskontexten. Angesichts der Tatsache, daß es sich bei
Kant um einen längst verstorbenen Philosophen handelt, kann sich der Professor nur
auf dessen hinterbliebene Schriftstücke stützen. Innerhalb des *blends* werden diese allerdings ihrer medialen Schriftlichkeit enthoben, indem der Professor diese als konzeptuell mündlich konzipierte Dialogsequenzen präsentiert. Der Philosophieprofessor
spricht somit mit Kant und gleichzeitig zu einem physisch anwesenden Publikum, das
aber nur die tatsächlich gesprochenen Worte des Professors mitverfolgen kann.

2.1 Medial bedingte *blends* in CMC-Kontexten

Bedingt durch den medien- u. kommunikationstechnischen Fortschritt des 20sten Jahrhunderts, stellt der Computer das Hypermedium schlechthin dar, der sich von dem ursprünglichen *Personal Computer* zu einem *Interpersonal Computer* entwickelt hat, indem er uns neben seiner Funktion als Arbeitsmittel zugleich neue Formen der Informationsbeschaffung und der Telekommunikation ermöglicht. Im Hinblick auf seinen telekommunikativen Einsatz eröffnet sich sowohl auf medialer als auch auf konzeptueller Ebene ein neuer Kommunikationsmodus, der innerhalb der Forschung begrifflich als Computer-mediated Communication (CMC) gefaßt wird. Der Begriff CMC bezieht sich zunächst einmal auf ein schriftliches Kommunizieren zwischen zwei oder mehreren Leuten, das über die Tastatur und am Bildschirm vollzogen wird. Hierbei stellt der Bildschirm, an dem wir Texte lesen und schreiben, nicht nur das elektronische Äquivalent zum konventionellen Papierschriftverkehr dar. Vor diesem Hintergrund sollen nachstehend die medialen und linguistischen Faktoren, die eine Konzeptualisierung der 2-dimensionalen Bildschirm(schreib)fläche als begehbare Orte bzw. als *common places* (vgl. Bolter 1991) evozieren, anhand von text-basierten MOOs und unter Einbezug der in Kapitel 2 dargelegten diskursorganisatorischen Funktion der *mental blends* aufgezeigt werden.

3 Text-basierte MOOs[2]

MOOs gehören neben Chats zu den wichtigsten synchron ausgerichteten Kommunikationstechnologien, die beide gleichermaßen ein schriftliches Kommunizieren mit Leuten aus aller Welt über die Tastatur in Echtzeit ermöglichen. Damit ist die medialschriftlich determinierte Gesprächssituation in MOOs und Chats – ähnlich wie in oralen Kommunikationssituationen – durch eine annähernd zeitdeiktische Simultanität im Hinblick auf Sprachproduktion und -rezeption gekennzeichnet. Vereinzelte Aussagen, wie z.B. die eines MOO-Sprechers: „If you use the to-command then everyone can hear you!" zeigen, daß das MOOen und Chatten, obwohl es sich jeweils um eine schriftliche Form des Kommunizierens handelt, weniger als Schreib- und Lesevorgang empfunden wird, sondern vielmehr als oral geprägte Prozesse des Sprechens und Hörens. In diesem Zusammenhang spielt die Konzeptualisierung der Schreiboberfläche eine entscheidende Rolle. Im Gegensatz zu dem traditionellen Papier-Schriftverkehr, bei welchem das einmal Geschriebene – selbst wenn es in hohem Maße mündlich ausgerichtet ist (wie es z.B. bei kurzen Notizen der Fall ist) als fixiert und stabil konzeptualisiert wird, ist wie Bolter (1991:11) hervorhebt, „the conceptual space of electronic writing on the other hand, ( ) characterized by fluidity and an interactive relationship between writer and reader". Besonders als Anfänger kann einem beim erstmaligen Versuch zu Chatten oder zu MOOen das *Hören und Sehen* oder zumindest das Sehen vergehen. Denn mit jedem eingetippten und über die Enter-Taste ab-

---

[2] Neben den textbasierten MOOs gibt es auch graphisch ausgerichtete MOOs, in welchen die einzelnen Gesprächsteilnehmer als animierte Comic-Figuren auf dem Bildschirm erscheinen.

geschickten Gesprächsbeitrag, der in Bruchteilen von Sekunden auf den Bildschirmen aller eingeloggten Gesprächsteilnehmer erscheint, bewegt sich die Textfläche zeilenweise nach oben. Dies bedeutet, daß die Schreiboberfläche (es sei denn keiner ‚redet') stets in Bewegung ist, so daß wie Bolter (191:71) anführt: „In electronic texts both the reader's eye and the writing surface are in motion." Ähnlich wie beim Telefonieren wird die räumliche Trennung zwischen den Gesprächsteilnehmern durch die unmittelbare Interaktionsmöglichkeit zwar reduziert, aber nicht aufgehoben.

3.1   Medial bedingte blends in text-basierten MOOs

Die für virtuelle Gesprächskontexte typische Trennung zwischen unmittelbarer Interaktion und Kopräsenz (vgl. Rasmussen 1997) wird in MOOs – und dies unterscheidet sie von Chats – aufgehoben. In Anlehnung an Chafe (1994:45), welcher herausstellt, daß „Copresence and interaction together define a property that can be called situatedness", soll aufgezeigt werden, mit welchen linguistischen Mitteln in text-basierten MOOs eine virtuelle *face-to-face* Kommunikationssituation evoziert wird.

Analog zu konventionellen *face-to-face* Kommunikationssituationen beginnt dies zunächst mit der Schaffung einer gemeinsamen text-basierten Umgebung. Während es sich bei den meisten Homepages von öffentlichen Einrichtungen um eine abstrakte Darstellungsweise von Raum handelt, die oft auf die sich hinter einer Institution verbergenden Organisationsstrukturen beschränkt ist, stellen MOO-Umgebungen virtuelle Replikationen von Klassen- bzw. Konferenzräumen, Institutionen oder sogar ganzer Städte dar. Wenn ich beispielsweise das Anglistische Institut der Heinrich-Heine-Universität (HHU) im Internet besuche, klicke ich mich durch die verschiedenen Homepages der jeweiligen Lehrstühle, die den internen Aufbau des Instituts widerspiegeln. Wäre die HHU als ein MOO angelegt, würde ich mich in textuell eingeschriebenen Seminar- und/oder Büroräumen wiederfinden, die mit für mich typischen Gegenständen, wie Tischen, Stühlen, Tafeln, Büchern etc. ausgestattet sind, und wo ich darüber hinaus auf andere MOO-Besucher stoße. Das entscheidene Charakteristikum eines MOOs – welches ihm als Kommunikationsmedium letztendlich auch seinen Namen (MUD object-oriented)[3] verleiht – ist seine inhärente objekt-orientierte Pragmatik, die es dem MOO-Besucher ermöglicht, mittels bestimmter im MOO-Server eingebauter Befehle über Objekte in der MOO-Umgebung Handlungen auszuführen. Alle MOO-Besucher können die textuell vorgenommenen Veränderungen in Echtzeit mitverfolgen und auf diese in einem weiteren Schritt wiederum sofort über sogenannte *communication commands* verbal oder nonverbal reagieren oder antworten. Wie das Zusammenspiel zwischen verbalen und nonverbalen Interaktionen im Rahmen von MOO-basierten Telekonferenzen aussieht, soll anhand einiger mitgeschnittener logfiles[4] näher veranschaulicht werden.

---

[3]   Für nähere Erläuterungen zur Geschichte und der MOO-spezifischen Pragmatik verweise ich an dieser Stelle auf: http://cinemaspace.berkeley.edu/~rachel/moolist/moolist.yeehaw.com

[4]   Die Namen der Gesprächsteilnehmer in Textausschnitt 1 wurden meinerseits anonymisiert. Orthographische und sonstige Fehler entsprechen dem Originaltext.

1 ◆ Linda turns recorder on.
2 ● Linda smiles ...
3 *Linda says, "I would like to welcome you all here to our Librarians' Online Support team"*
4 *pia [to Paul]: yes*
5 *Linda says, "THis session is being held in conjecture with the DU conference being held at*
6 *Eastern Kentucky University"*
7 *Linda says, "perhaps we should intoduce ourselves"*
8 *Linda says, "stary with Joe?"*
9 *Linda says, "oops start"*
10 *Paul [to pia]: thanks -just testing here ...*
11 ● Joe smiles
12 *Joe says, "I'm Joe, I teach in the school of Library and information Science at the Unvier-*
13 *sity of Southern Mississippi – glad to meet you all"*
14 *Linda introduces herself, I am a reference librarian at the Wethersfield Public library*
15 ◆ Iris stands up from blue table ...
16 ◆ Iris sits down at pink table...
17 *pia [to Iris]: welcome*
18 --(snipped)--
19 ● Karin wave to claudia
20 *Linda says, "I thought that today we would share whatever teaching experience we have*
21 *here today"*
22 *Claudia says, "I am CLaudia, a doc student in Technology Education and an associate prof*
23 *at a community college"*
24 ● Linda smiles.. and turns to Joe
25 doris has disconnected.
26 ● Joe smiles agian and waves to everyone
27 ● Claudia sits down at pink table. . .
28 *Joe says, "perhaps I can start the talk rolling?"*
29 ● pia smiles at claudia
30 ● pia takes a look at Claudia.
31 --(snipped)--
32 Linda says, "the MOO allows you to program, customize the environmen t"
33 ● pia raises her hand
34 Linda says, "pia?"
35 ● Joe nods agreement with Linda

(Textausschnitt 1: libteach)

Beim ersten Überfliegen erinnert der Auszug dieses MOO-Gesprächs eher an einen schriftlichen Entwurf eines noch aufzuführenden Theaterstücks, der sich analog zu der von Hermann (1996) vorgenommenen Charakterisierung von dramatischem Diskurs in Primär- und Sekundärtext unterteilen läßt. Der Primärtext umfaßt die in dem Textausschnitt 1 kursiv gesetzten direkten verbalen Handlungen, die die einzelnen MOO-Sprecher über den *say-command* vollzogen haben. Der durch die Symbole (●, ◆) markierte Sekundärtext beschreibt ähnlich wie Regieanweisungen alles, was sich sonst noch neben dem Dialog ereignet.

Im Unterschied zu Chat-Konversationen, sind die einzelnen Gesprächsbeiträge in MOOs nicht nur einem (fiktiven) *nickname* zugeordnet, sondern auch mit einem redeeinleitenden Verb versehen und durch Anführungstriche typographisch als direkte Rede abgesetzt. Darüber hinaus wird das redeeinleitende Verb – in diesem Fall „say" –

von dem MOO-Server durch das Hinzufügen des 3rd Person Sg-S automatisch in die dritte Person Singular umgewandelt, so daß die Quelle der tatsächlich gesprochenen Worte, die explizit als wörtliche Rede markiert sind, zunächst als die einer dritten Person erscheinen, die personendeiktisch gesehen weder die Rolle des Sprechers noch die des Hörers einnehmen kann. Allerdings zeichnen sich MOOs gerade dadurch aus, daß die einzelnen MOO-Besucher alternierend die Rolle des Sprechers und Hörers einnehmen können. Vor diesem Hintergrund und unter Einbezug meiner vorhin genannten These, daß MOOs medienpsychologisch darauf ausgerichtet sind, eine virtuelle *face-to-face* Gesprächssituation zu erzeugen, dient diese Art der Rededarstellung dazu, die MOO-Sprecher in einen gemeinsamen dritten Raum, sprich in einen medial bedingten *blend* (siehe Abildung 2), hineinzuprojizieren.

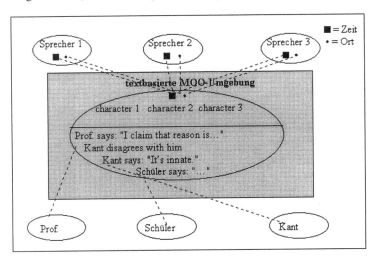

Abb. 2: Medial bedingter blend/ The Great Debate *in textbasierten MOOs*

Im Unterschied zu Fauconniers *The Great Debate*, in welchem der seitens des Philosophieprofessors konstruierte *mental blend* dazu dient, den fiktiven Dialog mit Kant als unmittelbares Geschehen in den derzeitigen physischen Gesprächskontext der Klasse einzubetten, zielt der medial bedingte *blend* in MOOs in genau umgekehrter Richtung darauf ab, einen *blend* außerhalb der jeweiligen physischen Umgebungen der einzelnen räumlich voneinander getrennten MOO-Gesprächsteilnehmer herzustellen. Während der Professor in *The Great Debate* sein *origio* als derzeitiger Sprecher beibehält, also die Rolle als agierendes Subjekt, das sowohl mit Kant als auch zu der Klasse spricht, handelt es sich bei der Rededarstellung in MOOs um eine doppelte Perspektivierung, die jeden MOO-Sprecher als Subjekt und gleichzeitig als Objekt auf dem Bildschirm erscheinen läßt. Jeder MOO-Besucher ist insofern immer Subjekt, als er medial schriftliche Sprachhandlungen vollzieht, welche auf dem Bildschirm durch die typographische Markierung seiner Worte als direkte Rede zur Geltung kommen. Indem die Worte automatisch durch den MOO-Server den jeweiligen Charakter-Doubles zugeordnet werden, sieht sich der vor dem PC sitzende Sprecher gleichzeitig auch als Objekt, er wird zum Beobachter seiner eigenen Handlungen, die er in der Rolle seines Charakter-Double und zusammen mit allen anderen Charakteren innerhalb des durch die MOO-Umgebung erzeugten *blends* ausführt. In Anlehnung an Bardini (1997) werden MOO-Besucher – sobald sie einmal textuell als Charaktere eingeschrieben sind – zu *interface agents*, welche wechselseitig als kopräsente Akteure innerhalb der MOO-Umgebung repräsentiert werden, die zusammen Tele-Gespräche und Tele-Handlungen durchführen.

Die textuelle Repräsentation von Tele-Handlungen, wie z.B. in Zeile 1 oder in Zeile 15 und 16, wo Iris den Wechsel ihres Sitzplatzes textuell präsentiert, verleiht MOO-Gesprächen einen durchaus theatralischen Charakter, allerdings mit dem entscheidenden Unterschied, daß die duale Existenz von Theaterstücken als Text und Bühnenperformanz in text-basierten MOOs zusammenfällt: Der Text ist die Performanz, der von den Gesprächsteilnehmern interaktiv und in Eigenregie gestaltet wird.

Ein besonders hervorstechendes Charakteristikum kommunikativen Verhaltens in MOOs ist die textuelle Einschreibung nonverbaler Kommunikationsmittel, wozu Blickkontakt (Zeile 29-30), gestische Handlungen (Zeile 19, 29, 33) und schließlich auch Mimik und Körperzuwendung gehören, die in dieser Kombination in Zeile 25 auftreten. Bei all diesen nonverbalen Kommunikationsmitteln handelt es sich um Gesprächsaktivitäten, deren kommunikative Funktion aber nur dann gegeben ist, wenn Sprecher und Hörer kopräsent sind. Wie bereits im Hinblick auf die Art und Weise der Rededarstellung und in Gegenüberstellung mit Fauconniers *The Great Debate* veranschaulicht wurde, werden die in der physischen Welt räumlich voneinander getrennten Gesprächsteilnehmer innerhalb der MOO-Umgebung als kopräsente Akteure in den medial erzeugten *blend* hineinprojiziert, die dort eine virtuelle *face-to-face* Kommunikation führen. Liddell (1998:290) hebt in diesem Zusammenhang hervor, „once the blend is established, the speaker operates within that space as an integrated unit". Ist der medial bedingte *blend* und die damit einhergehende Evozierung einer virtuellen *face-to-face* Gesprächssituation einmal hergestellt, so läßt sich dieser beliebig erweitern, was seitens der MOO-Sprecher mit jeder textuellen Einschreibung von nonverbalen Kommunikationsmitteln auch vorgenommen wird. Die innerhalb der MOO-Umgebung evozierte virtuelle Kopräsenz bzw. Telepräsenz manifestiert sich in einem weiteren Schritt darin, daß die einzelnen Gesprächsteilnehmer auf die textuell repräsentierten nonverbalen Handlungen reagieren. Solche Reaktionen finden sich in Textausschnitt 1 in Zeile 28, wo Joe auf die von Linda in Zeile 24 textuell in Szene gesetzte Körperzuwendung als *turn-taking* Signal reagiert, und in Zeile 34, wo die Moderatorin auf die Vorabankündigung eines Gesprächsbeitrags in Zeile 33 mit dem namentlichen Aufrufen von pia reagiert. Indem die MOO-Sprecher den textuell in Szene gesetzten nonverbalen Handlungen analog zu konventionellen *face-to-face* Konversationen eine diskursorganisatorische Funktion beimessen, erhalten diese gleichzeitig einen performativen Charakter. Ähnlich wie bei performativen Sprechakten, wird jede textuelle Repräsentation in dem Moment, wo sie auf dem Bildschirm erscheint, als tatsächlich stattfindende Handlung konzipiert. Abweichend von konventionellen Performativa, die in der 1. Ps. Präsens und im Indikativ stehen, handelt es sich in MOOs um Semi-Performativa, da die jeweiligen Aktionen durch den medial bedingten *blend* auf die jeweiligen Charakter-Doubles in der 3. Ps. Sg. Präsens Indikativ übertragen werden (vgl. Cherny 1995).

4   Ausblick

In text-basierten MOOs wird ein virtuelles Raumerlebnis interaktiv und ausschließlich über textuelle Kommunikation hergestellt. Durch den medial bedingten *blend* in MOOs bewegen sich die in der physischen Welt räumlich voneinander getrennten Teilnehmer als kopräsente Akteure auf einer virtuellen Bühne, auf welcher sie textuell verbale und nonverbale Handlungen durchführen. Verbunden mit der im Rahmen des voranstehenden Beitrags herausgestellten MOO-spezifischen Textualität, eröffnet sich für die Pragmatik ein völlig neues Forschungsfeld, denn in den durch MOOs erzeugten Gesprächssituationen gestaltet sich der Kontext nicht mehr aus nicht-verbalen und verbalen bedeutungserzeugenden Anteilen, sondern lediglich aus verbalen Anteilen. Folglich muß sich eine pragmatisch ausgerichtete Untersuchung medial bedingter Gesprächskontexte fortan mit der Strukturierung von verbalen und den verbalisierten nicht-verbalen Anteilen unter Berücksichtigung der 2-dimensionalen Bildschirm(schreib)fläche beschäftigen.

5   Literatur

BARDINI, Thierry (1997): Bridging the Gulfs: From Hypertext to Cyberspace. In: Journal of computer-mediated communication 3.2 [available online], http://www.ascusc/jcmc/vol3/issue2/bardini. html.

BOLTER, Jay D. (1991): Writing space. The Computer, Hypertext, and the History of Writing. Hillsdale, NJ: Lawrence Earlbaum.

Chafe, Wallace (1994): Discourse, Consciousness, and Time. The Flow of Conscious Experience in Speaking and Writing. Chicago – London: The University of Chicago Press.

CHERNY, Lynn (1999): Conversation and Community: Chat in a Virtual World. Cambridge University Press.

— (1995): The Modal Complexity of Speech Events in a Social Mud. In: EJC/REC 5.4 [available online].

COULSON, Seana (1996): Menendez Brothers Virus: Blended Spaces and Internet Humor. In: Goldberg, A. E. (ed.): Conceptual Structure, Discourse and Language. Stanford, California: CSLI Publication, 67-81.

FAUCONNIER, Gilles (1997): Mapping in Thought and Language. Cambridge, MA: CUP.

— (²1994): Mental Spaces. Cambridge, MA: MIT Press.

FAUCONNIER, Gilles; Mark Turner (1994): Conceptual Projection and Middle Spaces. UCSD Cognitive Science Technical Report.

FLUDERNIK, Monika (1993): The Fictions of Languages and the Languages of Fiction. London, USA, Canada: Routledge.

HERMAN, Vimala (1996): Space in Dramatic Discourse. In: Pütz; Dirven: 553-569.

HERRING, Susan (ed.) (1996): Computer-Mediated Communication. Linguistic, Social and Cross-Cultural Perspectives. Amsterdam: Benjamins.

LAUREL, B. (1993): Computers as Theatres. Reading, MA: Addison-Wesley.

LIDDELL, Scott K. (1998): Grounded Blends, Gestures, and Conceptual Shifts. In: Cognitive Linguistics 9.3, 283-314.

MONDALA, Lorenza (1996): How Space Structures Discourse. In: Pütz; Dirven: 571-590.

PÜTZ, M.; DIRVEN, R. (eds.). The Construal of Space in Language and Thought. Berlin – New York: Mouton de Gruyter (Cognitive Linguistics Research 8),

RASMUSSEN, Terje (1997): Social Interaction and the New Media. The Construction of Communicatice Contexts. In: Nordicon Review 18.2, 63-76.

Lexikologie / Lexikographie

L'application d'un outil statistique à la classification d'unités lexicales: locutions grammaticales, toutes des adverbes?

Marie-Hélène Antoni

1 Introduction

1.1 Classification

Un des problèmes classiques de la description des unités linguistiques est celui de leur classification, de leur catégorisation: il s'agit de faire émerger des régularités, des propriétés communes, qui conjointes, amènent des regroupements possibles; c'est sur le partage de propriétés par un certain nombre d'unités que l'on fait émerger des notions telles que celles de verbe, nom, etc ... On sait que ce travail, qui semble faire l'objet d'un consensus pour les grandes « parties du discours », est loin d'être achevé et que les interrogations méthodologiques fondamentales sont toujours d'actualité, comme en témoignent par exemple les réflexions d'un Nolke (1990) sur la classification des adverbes.

1.2 Par des outils informatiques

Le travail présenté ici est né de la rencontre entre plusieurs univers, dans un contexte applicatif particulier de la linguistique informatique: ici, les choses se sont renversées, si l'on peut dire, et l'outil informatique a été utilisé à des fins d'analyse de phénomènes linguistiques: il s'agissait de classifier des unités suivant leurs propriétés, afin de pouvoir coder ce qui s'avérerait nécessaire dans un dictionnaire informatisé, destiné a priori à une utilisation par la machine. Ce contexte particulier fournit des outils et contraintes qui lui sont propres, les contraintes concernant le grand degré de formalisation nécessaire à tout traitement, la liberté résidant en ceci que ces mêmes outils permettent de traiter massivement des données, et de tester rapidement diverses hypothèses.

1.3 D'unités lexicales complexes

Les unités qui ont retenu notre attention sont des « composés ». Le nombre de travaux en cours et de colloques qui se tiennent autour de la composition et de la terminologie témoignent de ce que cette zone de la lexicographie est peu à peu apparue comme déterminante dans les contextes d'applications industrielles en traitement de l'information: qu'il s'agisse de détecter l'information clé, de la traduire de façon pertinente ou d'améliorer les résultats des analyseurs syntaxiques, l'identification de ces unités de taille supérieure au mot s'est avérée essentielle.

1.4   Qui commencent par une préposition

Nous nous sommes concentrée sur les composés qui commencent par une préposition
(à l'insu de, à l'évidence, en l'occurrence …). Dans le contexte d'indexation, il s'agit
en effet d'éliminer les prises en compte d'unités qui ne sont pas dans un emploi re-
cherché, (différence de valeur entre « une occurrence et en l'occurrence »), ou encore
de trouver de spécifieurs particulier. Quoiqu'il en soit, il s'est agi de les encoder dans
un dictionnaire, et il est très vite apparu que nous n'avions pas une idée suffisamment
claire des propriétés de ces unités pour en faire une description cohérente et stable.

Après avoir rappelé les principes devant présider à une démarche classificatoire et
présenté les descriptions existantes des unités lexicales que nous étudions, nous pré-
senterons les critères de description retenus, l'outil statistique utilisé et la méthodolo-
gie employée lors des diverses opérations de description/classification.

2   Méthodologie en classification

La démarche classificatrice impose de clarifier les critères qui permettront d'assigner
telle ou telle catégorie à telle unité, ou encore ceux qui, apparaissant conjointement
chez un certain nombre des unités étudiées, justifient l'apparition d'une classe. L'évidence de cette proposition ne s'assortit pas aussi aisément de clarté et de cohérence
dans la mise en œuvre de cette démarche. Dans un article tout à fait percutant, Nolke
(1990) va jusqu'à reformuler radicalement la question des méthodes en classification,
en posant explicitement ces quatre questions, dont on s'étonne qu'elles ne préexistent
pas à toute tentative de classification:

1) Que classifier?
2) Pourquoi classifier?
3) Comment classifier?
4) Quels critères appliquer?

Primordiale est évidemment la question de savoir quelle est la nature de ce qu'on se
propose de classifier. Se basant sur l'observation des classifications d'adverbiaux
qu'il discute, Nolke souligne que:

> « La distinction fondamentale entre unité lexicale et fonction syntaxique ne paraît jamais très
> nette chez les auteurs cités. En fait, ceux-ci font semblant de classer les adverbes, mais ce
> qu'il font réellement, c'est classer leurs occurrences. »

Ils se concentrent en fait sur leurs emplois, sans se soucier de voir dans quelle mesure
ces emplois sont réservés à des adverbes. Or:

> « Un même adverbe peut avoir des fonctions fort différentes. (…). Dans cette optique, on doit
> admettre la possibilité que des unités formelles autres que les adverbes puissent assumer la
> fonction d'adverbial. »

Nolke met ici l'accent sur le fait que, si l'on souhaite se servir de tests comme critères
dans le travail classificateur, il faut préalablement chercher à savoir quelles sont les
propriétés véritablement testées. Et les exemples sont nombreux, où il semble que la
confusion règne entre un test de fonctionnement syntagmatique, et une propriété caté-

gorielle[1]. Ce manque de définition de l'objet à classifier et de ce qui est testé remet en cause la pertinence de la classification. Un autre facteur peut la compromettre: que le projet classificatoire, le pourquoi et le comment, ne soient pas assez clairement posés. En effet, il ne suffit pas d'exiger d'une classification qu'elle soit une taxinomie exhaustive, qu'elle contienne des classes homogènes et en nombre limité, il faut aussi qu'elle soit intéressante. Il est donc important de déterminer avec soin quels sont les objectifs de la classification, ce qui déterminera le choix des tests, c'est à dire les propriétés que devront partager les éléments des classes, leur définition intensionnelle. Ce point implique un long travail d'élaboration des propriétés testées. En effet pour qu'un test puisse servir à une classification, il faudra:

> « 1. qu'il soit pertinent; 2. qu'il soit reproductible; 3. qu'il s'applique sans problème à n'importe quel élément de l'ensemble étudié; 4. qu'il fournisse une réponse claire »

C'est à ce prix seulement que l'on pourra interpréter de façon cohérente les résultats de la classification, chose impossible si l'on ne dispose pas d'outils de mise en perspective, c'est-à-dire de construction du sens à partir des observations révélées par la classification. De plus Nolke souligne qu'on devrait réfléchir sur le statut des tests retenus, ainsi que sur leurs relations mutuelles (définitoire ou descriptifs), et considérer la possibilité de les hiérarchiser. C'est à ce stade qu'entrent en ligne les test formels. En effet, ayant assuré l'autonomie du critère définitionnel par rapport aux tests formels, on pourra appliquer ceux-ci en vue de vérifier l'homogénéité distributionnelle de la classe établie, dont on ancrera les propriétés dans la forme linguistique:

> « Une classe d'unités liguistiques définie à l'aide d'un critère sémantico-pragmatique n'a pas grand intérêt, si elle n'a pas aussi une réalité syntaxique et/ou relationnelle. Les résultats des tests sont ainsi susceptibles d'acquérir une valeur explicative. »

Dans un tel contexte, un comportement « atypique » d'unités appartenant par ailleurs ostensiblement à une classe devient tout à coup porteur de sens. Cette méthode permet même de prévoir dans quelles conditions ces tests ne fonctionnent pas.

2.1 Définition du « quoi »: les composés introduits par une préposition

Cet ensemble (environ 2500) d'unités lexicales complexes pose en effet un certain nombre de problèmes qui lui sont propres.

2.1.1 Irrégularité de leur description

Leur description est très irrégulière, non seulement d'un ouvrage à l'autre, mais souvent à l'intérieur d'un seul dictionnaire.

Certaines de ces unités ont la particularité de pouvoir être fermées par un fonctionnel (préposition ou conjonction): *à l'exclusion de, à l'époque de, à la merci de*. Les

---

[1] Les tests de reprise pronominale en font par exemple partie: s'il est vrai que *jean est malade* ou *pierre est petit* peuvent se pronominaliser en *il l'est*, il n'est pas vrai que cela tienne au statut adjectival de *malade* ou *petit*. Ainsi, *pierre est le fils de ma meilleure amie* se pronominalise en *il l'est*, ce qui ne montre en rien que *le fils de ma meilleure amie* est un adjectif.

descriptions de cette particularité sont loin d'être homogènes, indépendamment du fait que seule une des formes soit attestée (comme c'est le cas pour *à l'improviste, à l'insu de*) . Le composé avec fonctionnel peut être présenté soit comme une unité lexicale à part entière soit comme une variante de l'emploi « absolu » (ou inversement), s'il est présenté comme variante, le fonctionnel peut soit faire partie du composé, soit introduire un complément de la tête du groupe prépositionnel; enfin, elles sont parfois présentées comme partie d'une forme verbale figée. Ainsi, on trouve dans le DNT:

- à l'intérieur et à l'intérieur de (les deux formes)
- à l'extérieur mais pas *à l'extérieur de (l'une des deux)
- aux alentours de mais pas *aux alentours
- (une seule des deux, malgré le changement de sens)
- être à la merci de qqn (un syntagme verbal, présenté comme un synthème)

2.1.2 Quelle partie du discours?

Ces unités semblent déroger à la règle qui veut qu'on puisse attribuer au composé une « étiquette grammaticale » ou « partie du discours » (et aux entrées d'un dictionnaire en général). Seuls 30% d'entre eux sont étiquetés dans le DNT, et de façon parfois un peu contestable: on désigne leur fonction dans l'exemple donné, mais rien de plus. Enfin, et c'est la conséquence logique de ce qui précède, cette attribution varie d'une description à l'autre: selon les travaux, on trouve *de bonne humeur* parmi les adjectifs ou parmi les adverbes;

2.1.3 Quelle homogénéité sémantique?

Au delà d'une très grande hétérogénéïté apparente: *au fur et à mesure, à gauche, à tue-tête, à discrétion, à la bonne franquette, à toute berzingue*, l'observation que nous avons faite de ces unités lorsque nous avons décrit leur structure syntaxique interne (le pattern qui les décrit) a montré qu'elles présentaient en fait une grande homogénéïté sémantique.

2.1.4 Quelle fonction syntaxique ou textuelle?

Leur étude se justifie par le fait qu'exprimant très largement le temps (*à l'époque*), le lieu (*à gauche*), le degré (*à peu près*), l'organisation argumentative (*en conclusion*) et des précisions sur le cadre de l'énonciation (*au dire de*), ces unités sont susceptibles d'apparaître dans tous les types de textes.

2.2 Objet et méthode de la description

Il s'agit ici de cerner leurs propriétés afin d'en faire une description cohérente et stable; nous avons donc construit un ensemble de critères descriptifs permettant

- de déterminer pourquoi on ne leur attribue pas systématiquement de catégorie syntaxique
- de chercher des corrélations entre des descripteurs syntaxiques et sémantiques.

C'est sur le premier point que nous nous arrêterons dans le cadre imparti ici.

Pour ce faire, nous avons décidé de recourir à une méthode de classification utilisant le critère de Condorcet pour faire émerger les grandes tendances qui sont difficilement perceptibles lorsqu'on observe la masse des unités et de leurs propriétés particulières. Le recours à un outil automatique de classification statistique permet de battre en brèche les impossibilités classiques, liée à la manipulation de masses de données: si l'ensemble qu'on désire classifier est d'une certaine taille, on ne peut vérifier directement ni l'exhaustivité, ni l'homogénéité des classes. Ici, l'organisation rapide des classes et les possibilités d'observer divers regroupements permettent de veiller à la cohérence des recoupements effectués.

Les critères définitoires de la classe se construisent en quelque sorte après coup, émergeant des classes comme des éléments élucidant d'une observation empirique de ressemblance quant aux propriétés.

3 Principes de classification

L'analyse de données a pour objet de mettre en évidence l'organisation ou la structure d'un ensemble d'éléments, appelé corpus. Dans notre cas, le corpus est formé d'unités lexicales caractérisées par plusieurs descripteurs de propriétés syntaxiques et/ou sémantiques. Il s'agit ensuite de donner une représentation fiable des propriétés globales des unités lexicales en fonction des descripteurs. Les méthodes d'analyse de données employées à cette fin sont donc des méthodes de réduction de dimensions qui permettent de représenter les relations d'un grand nombre d'éléments entre eux en fonction des descripteurs que l'on a choisis. La méthode de classification utilisée ici est une méthode non hiérarchique dont l'objet est d'extraire du corpus des groupes homogènes, appelés classes, d'éléments qui se ressemblent entre eux et se distinguent des autres.

3.1 Classification statistique en analyse relationnelle des données

Chaque unité lexicale étant associée à une séquence de descripteurs, on peut procéder à une classification des données, c'est-à-dire à un regroupement des éléments lexicaux d'après la similarité de leurs descripteurs. La mesure de cette ressemblance est ici calculée à l'aide du critère de Condorcet. Les éléments sont comparés par paire, plus exactement, ce sont les descripteurs associés aux données qui sont comparés. On procède d'une part au comptage des descripteurs que les unités ont en commun, d'autre part au comptage des descripteurs que l'une des unités a et l'autre pas.

Prenons deux éléments (des mots notés M) et la séquence de descripteurs (notés D) qui les caractérisent: M1 (Dl, D2, D5, D7, D8) M2 (D1, D3, D5, D6, D8)

On peut représenter cette information sous forme d'une matrice faisant apparaître les éléments en ordonnée et les descripteurs en abscisse. Dans le cas où le descripteur est pertinent, on note sa présence par '1' dans le cas où il ne l'est pas, on note son absence par '0'. On obtient alors un tableau de la forme suivante:

	D1	D2	D3	D4	D5	D6	D7	D8
M1	1	1	0	0	1	0	1	1
M2	1	0	1	0	1	1	0	1

Le but du calcul est alors

- de maximiser le nombre de ressemblances, c'est-à-dire de cas où les deux unités présentent le même descripteur: couples (1,1)
- de minimiser le nombre de dissemblances, c'est-à-dire de cas où l'une des unités a un descripteur que l'autre n'a pas: couples (0,1) et (1,0).

Peu à peu émergent des classes auxquelles on associe des descripteurs (les descripteurs qui la caractérisent), et pour chaque unité, on calcule la classe dont elle est la plus proche, classe à laquelle elle est alors intégrée. Il arrivera que l' attribution de certaines unités à des classes ne nous semble pas pertinente d' un point de vue linguistique. L'interprétation de cette « erreur d'attribution » a toujours pu faire l'objet d'une explication cohérente[1]. Ces cas sont suffisamment rares et leur explication suffisamment simple pour que le principe même de la classification se justifie pleinement.

Pour obtenir une classification plus ou moins fine, on peut aussi jouer sur le « seuillage » du critère, c'est-à-dire faire varier le degré de similarité nécessaire pour que l'unité soit attribuée à une classe. Ainsi, si l'on décide que seules les unités ayant tous leurs descripteurs en commun doivent être regroupées, on voudra une similarité de 100% (identité absolue de tous les descripteurs), on choisira le seuil de valeur 1. Afin de regrouper des unités qui ont des ressemblances sans avoir exactement le même comportement, on abaisse le seuil: pour avoir une idée très grossière des liens entre les unités, on mettra le seuil très bas. Qu'il soit dès lors bien clair que pour tout seuil inférieur à 1, l'affectation d'une unité à une classe ne signifie ni qu'elle a tous les descripteurs de la classe, ni que tous les siens sont des descripteurs de la classe.

Nous avons ici observé la structuration progressive des classifications à 50%, 60%, 70%, 80% de similarité des descripteurs, afin de pister le parcours des unités et de comprendre finement leur regroupement

3.2   Descripteurs retenus

Les propriétés testées qui seront évoquées ici correspondent aux relations de la séquence décrite avec les autres éléments de la phrase: nous voulons en effet comprendre pourquoi l'attribution d'une catégorie syntaxique n'est ni systématique ni homogène. La structure syntaxique interne des locutions a par ailleurs fait l'objet d'une classification permettant de faire émerger des patterns de structures, patterns identifié par un code et présent comme descripteur associé à chacune des unités décrites. On note en outre dans les descripteurs la présence ou l'absence du fonctionnel de fin de groupe (*de, où, en, que,...*)., l'observation des parties semi-figées des composés, toutes variations qui pourraient avoir une incidence sur les compatibilités externes des unités au niveau syntaxique comme au niveau sémantique.

Variation de déterminant: *à cet (tous les, certains) égard(s), à peu de choses près*
Répercussion sur les compatibilités externes:

> *c'est à peu près pareil / c'est à peu de choses près pareil*
> *à peu de choses près, je pense qu'il a tort / *à peu près, je pense qu'il a tort*
> *il a râté son examen à peu de choses près / *il a râté son examen à peu près*

Présence du fonctionnel: *aux alentours (de)*
Répercussion sur les propriétés sémantiques:

> *aux alentours de la maison*: emploi locatif
> *aux alentours de huit heures*: emploi temporel
> *aux alentours, c'était le désert*: emploi locatif; **aux alentours (+temps)*

Combinaison de propriétés:

> *A fleur de peau* mais pas **à fleur*
> *A son aise* mais pas **à l'aise de Pierre*
> *A l'époque de (x)* → *à cette/son époque*
> *A moment de (x)* → *à ce/*son moment*
> *Au détriment de (x)* → *à *ce/son détriment*

Pour chacune des unités, on a testé si elle pouvait apparaître comme

> *modifieur de constituant (adverbe, adjectif, nom, verbe), avec ou sans collocation; modifieur de groupe syntagmatique; modifieur d'énoncé; modifieur d'énonciation.*

3.3 Présentation de résultats

La première des classifications, à 50% de similarité, fait apparaître deux grandes classes qui seront affinées par les classifications suivantes:

La première de ces classes est caractérisée essentiellement par le fait qu'elle permet d'exprimer la manière à tous les niveaux de l'organisation syntagmatique. Une autre de ces caractéristiques est d'être très fortement marquée par le figement sémantique, tant interne (non-autonomie ou emploi figuré d'un constituant), qu'externe (collocation). Cette classe se sous-catégorisera en expression d'un mode de réalisation (manière, manière intense, vitesse), en expression de l'intensité péjorative et de la quantité. Des exemples en sont: *à la bonne franquette, à toute vitesse, à foison, à volonté, à prix d'or.* Les unités qui la composent semblent appeler majoritairement la catégorisation adverbiale. Il s'agit avant tout d'adverbes de constituant apparaissant très fréquemment en collocation, extrêment figés, et dont le degré d'intégration à l'énoncé ne fait aucun doute.

La seconde de ces classes est caractérisée par sa spécialisation spatio-temporelle, contextuelle et argumentative. Elle fait elle aussi immédiatement penser à une partie du lexique très fortement marquée par la notion d'adverbe. On peut isoler sans difficulté des adverbes spécifiant ce qu'on appelle habituellement le cadre de l'énonciation, c'est-à-dire ici principalement le cadre spatio-temporel (*à gauche, aux calendes grecques*), et des adverbes de manières pouvant eux aussi porter sur les modalités de l'énoncé (*au hasard*), des adverbes d'énonciation proprement dits, qui portent sur le dire (*à mon avis*), des adverbes exprimant les modalités du cadre de l'énonciation et la structure argumentative, l'organisation logique d'un énoncé étant donné un certain contexte, textuel ou non. Des exemples en sont: *à savoir, à propos, au dire de, au demeurant, à l'instar de.*

Les indicateurs spatio-temporels, qui participent à l'expression des « circonstances globales » et sont partie intégrante du contenu du dit, supportent peu de modifications. Seule est autorisée l'intériorisation du repère, par reprise de l'expansion. On trouve des démonstratifs, des possessifs, et l'article défini (qui est le « standard » lors de l'enregistrement dans les dictionnaires de la forme « canonique » de la locution) peut être vu comme la forme la plus indéterminée de la reprise anaphorique par un démonstratif « pauvre ». *A gauche de la maison / A sa gauche / A gauche; A l'époque de la Régence / A cette époque / A l'époque.*

Les indicateurs de manière ne peuvent être modifiés, ou plus exactement, la modification implique la désynthémisation, qui ne pose aucun problème. On se trouve alors sur la ligne de partage entre un adverbe et un circonstanciel . Nous les distinguons des adverbes dits « contextuels » qui apportent des informations sur le produit linguistique et participent de toute autre façon à la création du contenu de l'énoncé. Eux sont modifiables, et leur degré de cohésion avec le contenu des énoncés est très variable.

4   Problèmes d'attribution d'une catégorie

L'attribution de la partie du discours « adverbe » à l'ensemble des unités ne va cependant pas sans soulever un certain nombre de problèmes, qui légitiment les hésitations ou incohérences que nous avons relevées lors de notre étude sur l'existant, tant au niveau d'analyses spécifiques qu'au niveau de la pratique dictionnarique

- bon nombre d'entre eux ne portent pas sur le verbe (*à dire vrai, au fond, au plus tôt*)
- certains apparaissent de façon privilégiée ou fréquente comme modifieurs du nom (*à dormir debout, à huis clos*)
- le statut du fonctionnel de fin, qui amène les catégorisations classiques à distinguer entre adverbe (sans fonctionnel), préposition (le fonctionnel est une préposition) ou conjonction (le fonctionnel est une conjonction).

Dans le premier grand groupe, qui exprime « la manière », les formes avec fonctionnel sont suffisamment rares pour être absorbées par les classes sans. La seule différence que l'on peut faire dans leur fonctionnement réside en ceci qu'il leur faut une expansion. Pour ce qui est de l'autre groupe, qui exprime les propriétés du cadre contextuel, les choses sont différentes: un grand nombre d'individus peut apparaître avec un fonctionnel (la préposition *de*, majoritairement), et sera identifié comme l'ensemble des locutions prépositionnelles. Les classes se trouvent en quelque sorte dupliquées, l'une présentant les adverbes, l'autre les prépositions. La similitude des listes d'éléments présents dans les classes amène à s'interroger sur le bien fondé de cette distinction, basée sur des habitudes descriptives venues des « mots simples ». Ainsi, on peut faire correspondre aux prépositions spatiales de base des adverbes spatiaux de base et opposer *sur* à *dessus*. Pour les composés, on opposera *à l'intérieur de* et *à l'intérieur*. Mais nous avons vu que leur enregistrement n'est pas systématique dans les dictionnaires. Leur cohérence formelle laisse parfois à désirer mais les « incohérences » de codage semblent ici plutôt être l'expression d'une intuition linguistique solide: il n'y a qu'une unité, il ne s'agit donc pas de l'enregistrer plusieurs fois. Il ne s'agit pas d'un simple gain de place. Par ailleurs, il y a de réelles difficultés à distinguer « *à gauche de* la maison » de *à gauche*, puis à éviter soigneusement toutes les formes du type *à sa gauche*. Le problème ne vient-il pas tout simplement de ce que la tradition française récuse fermement que l'adverbe puisse avoir un complément?

Notre hypothèse sera que les groupes décrits ici (hormis les syntagmes adjectivaux apparaissant dans des termes techniques *à arbre à came, à pied télescopique* et ne pouvant porter que sur des substantifs, mis dans une classe à part dès la classification à 50%) sont tous des adverbes. Ils peuvent par ailleurs être analysés différemment en contexte: ils sont susceptibles d'assumer diverses fonctions syntaxiques. Le problème est bien sûr délicat dans les cas où la forme sans fonctionnel n'est pas attestée (*à l'exclusion de; au dire de*), et c'est sans doute l'une des raisons de cette persistance à les traiter comme des prépositions. Mais il nous semble cohérent d'envisager trois types de schémas de complémentation

1) des adverbes « protoypiques », n'acceptant pas de compléments, comparables en quelque sorte à des verbes intransitifs: *A discrétion / Aux anges*
2) des adverbes qui acceptent un complément; ces compléments peuvent le plus souvent être « anaphorisés », par un possessif ou un démonstratif. Dans ce cas, la préposition est absorbée par le pronom, un peu comme *y* absorbe *à* et *en* absorbe *de*. On observe alors un bouleversement de la linéarité de surface, l'expansion étant intégrée à l'unité lexicale. *A sa gauche / A cette époque*.
   a) complément obligatoire, l'adverbe n'apparaissant jamais sans son expansion: A l 'exclusion de X, *A l 'exclusion; Au dire de X, *Au dire; A la manière de X ,*A la manière
   b) complément facultatif, l'adverbe pouvant avoir un emploi absolu: *A gauche de X, A gauche; A l'époque de la X, A l'époque*

Dans le cas où le complément n'est pas réalisé, on peut avoir des modifications des propriétés. C'était le cas par exemple pour le couple *Aux alentours/Aux alentours de*. C'est aussi le cas pour des unités telles que *au fond* ou *à l'opposé* qui, sans expansion, prennent un sens plus abstrait et fonctionnent dans le système de l' argumentation. Là encore, on peut tenir la comparaison avec le système verbal, *rire de* et *abuser de* se distinguant de *rire* et d'*abuser*, comme on peut tenir la comparaison avec toutes les « catégories majeures »: les adverbes sont comme elles tout à fait susceptibles d'accepter des compléments la présence peut être obligatoire ou non, son optionnalité pouvant avoir des incidences sémantiques: les formes « absolues » n'ont pas toujours le même sens que les formes « saturées ».

5   Références bibliographiques

ANTONI-LAY, Marie, Hélène; ZAYSSER, Laurence (1994): A Generic Model for Reusable Lexicons; The GENELEX Project. In: Linguistics and Literary Computing 9.1,47-56.

BENZECRI, Jean-Pierre (1980): Pratique de l'analyse des données: Analyse des correspondances. Paris: Dunod.

BORILLO, Andrée (1990): A propos de la localisation spatiale. In: Langue Française 86, 75-85.

CERVONI, Jean (1990a): Prépositions et compléments prépositionnels. In: Langue Française 86, 85-90.

— (1990b): La partie du discours nommée adverbe. In: Langue Française 88, 5-11.

FRANCKEL, Jean-Jaques; MARANDIN, Jean-Marie; MILNER, Jean-Claude (1992): L'individualité lexicale. In: Cahiers de Lexicologie 61.2, 6-57.

GROSS, Gaston (1989): Typologie des adjectivaux, Rapport LLI, Université Paris XIII.

— (1988): Degré de figement des noms composés. In: Langages 90, 57-72.

GROSS, Maurice (1990): La caractérisation des adverbes dans un lexique-grammaire. In: Langue Française 86, 90-103.

— (1986): Grammaire transformationnelle du français: syntaxe de l'adverbe. Paris: ASSTRIL.

— (1988): Les adjectifs composés. In: Grammaire et histoire de la grammaire [Texte imprimé]: hommage à la mémoire de Jean Stéfanini. (recueil d'études rassemblées par Claire Blanche-Benveniste, André Chervel et Maurice Gross). Aix-en-Provence: Université de Provence.

LAY, Mari-Hélène (1990): Les mots multiples: critères d'identification, CS Paris, Etude F.150, IBM.

MARANDIN, Jean-Marie (1984): Distribution et contexte dans une description lexicale. In: Cahiers de Lexicologie 44, 3-17.

MARCOTORCHINO, Jean-François; WARNESSON Isabelle (1983): Pertinence synonymique – Recherche algorithmique par agrégation de similarités. In: Cahiers de Lexicologie 42, 28-62.

MARTINET, André (1985): Syntaxe Générale. Paris: Armand Colin.

— (1979): Grammaire Fonctionnelle du Français. Paris: Crédif.

— (1970): Eléments de linguistique générale. Paris: Armand Colin.

MOREAU, René; WARNESSON, Isabelle (1983): Ordinateur et lexicographie. In: Lexique 2: le dictionnaire. Lille: Presses Universitaires de Lille, 121- 130.

NEF, Frédéric (1990): Problèmes de classification des adverbes d'un point de vue logique. In: Langue Française 88, 51-59.

NOLKE, Henning (1990): Les adverbiaux contextuels: problèmes de classification. In: Langue Française 88, 12-27.

PINCHON, Jaqueline (1980): Syntagme prépositionnel et adjectif de relation. In: Cahiers de Lexicologie 37.2, 91-100.

VAN BAARDEWIJK-RESSEGUIER, Josette (1983): non-alternance entre syntagme prépositionnel et adjectif de relation. In: Cahiers de Lexicologie 43, 73-84.

Dictionnaires:

Le DICTIONNAIRE de notre temps (1992). Paris: Hachette.
Le petit Robert, Dictionnaire (1987). Paris: Le Robert, Paris.
Larousse de la langue française Lexis (1979). Paris: Librairie Larousse.

The Past Participle in the Nominal Phrase: Observations from Italian

Chiara Frigeni

1   Topic and structure of the paper

The topic of this paper is the Italian Past Participle (Pastp) in the Nominal Phrase (NP), i.e. the "status" of a participle whose function is to modify a head noun (N). Since the element that normally modifies a head noun is an adjective (A), the main question of this paper is: *How can a PastP with this function be distinguished from an A?* In other words: Which parameters can be found in order to distinguish a PastP from an A?

The verbal origin and nature of a PastP can be more successfully captured in a structure such as the NP, which employs only one of its potential functions, that being the adjectival. In other words, a contrastive analysis of PastPs and As in NPs reveals the verbal nature of the PastPs.

The main idea is that the differences between PastPs and As are to be found in the analysis of the nature of the relationship between the modifiers in question and their head N. The relationship established between a N and its participial modifier is not the same which occurs between a N and its adjectival modifier.

This difference is traced by first beginning the analysis on the syntactic and semantic level, then considering the problem which emerges when the morphological negation of (adjectival-) PastP is discussed.

Thus, the paper will discuss the following points:

- the object of the analysis will be defined by investigating what kind of PastP are allowed to modify a N in Italian;
- it will be shown what kind of syntactic relationship becomes established between a N and its participial modifier and a set of syntactic tests, collected from various literature, will be proposed, which are able to distinguish between a PastP and an A;
- this relationship will be discussed on the semantic level as well as by observing the different meaning of the adverbs *bene* ('well') and *appena* ('just', 'already') and whether they modify a PastP or an A. Also, the observations about the gradation of PastPs and As through the superlative morpheme *-issimo* are of interest;
- the question of the morphological negation will be presented and a solution proposed.

2   Object of the analysis

In order to identify the object of the analysis, Burzio's Verb Classification (1986) is adopted, which distinguishes the verbs using the parameter of the auxiliaries they need.

Thus, the following verbal classes are defined: transitive verbs (whose auxiliary is *avere*, 'to have') (*distruggere, capire, invitare, piegare*, etc.); intransitive verbs whose auxiliary is *essere* ('to be'), which Burzio calls unaccusative (*arrivare, partire, comparire/scomparire*, etc.); intransitive verbs whose auxiliary is *avere*, called unergative verbs (*telefonare, dormire, morire, camminare*, etc.); finally verbs which can be used like transitive or unaccusative verbs, which are classified as ergative (*aumentare/diminuire, migliorare/peggiorare, affondare, cambiare*, etc.).

In Italian, the only Past Participles which can appear in NPs are derived:

(i)   from transitive verbs, whose PastP has a passive meaning (PPP):
      V: distruggere (Agent, Patient/Theme) > PPP: *distrutto*
      NP: *la casa distrutta (dall'incendio)*

whose paraphrasis through a relative sentence (RS) is: *la casa che l'incendio ha distrutto*;

(ii) from unaccusative verbs, whose PastP has an active meaning:
      V: *arrivare* (Theme)   > PastP: *arrivato*
      NP: *il pacco arrivato*
      RS: *il pacco che è arrivato*

(iii) from ergative verbs, whose PastP has an active meaning in its unaccusative use and a passive one in its transitive use:
      V: *affondare* (Agent, Theme or Theme)> PastP active/passive: *affondato*
      NP: *la nave affondata/ la nave affondata (dal cacciabombardiere)*
      RS: *la nave che è affondata/la nave che il cacciabombardiere ha affondato*

PastPs derived from unergative verbs (intransitive verbs with auxiliary *avere*) cannot be used to modify a head N[1].

---

[1]   The following NPs are questionable:
      a. Le *lingue parlate* nella Confederazione svizzera sono quattro
      b. I *dialetti parlati* nelle valli bergamasche sono fonologicamente differenti
      where the PastP *parlato* is derived from an unergative verb (*parlare*, 'to speak'). However the verb *parlare* in these NPs is used as a transitive in the sense of *parlare una lingua/un dialetto*, where the presence of a direct object changes its meaning and the class to which it belongs.
      A similar observation can be made by considering other NPs in which the PastP in question is derived from another unergative verb, *chiacchierare* ('to gossip') (as shown by d) and e)):
      c. Il *film più chiacchierato* del momento è "La vita è bella" di Roberto Benigni.
      d. *L'argomento chiacchierato ieri al telefono con Valeria
      e. L'argomento di cui ho chiacchierato ieri al telefono con Valeria
      In (c) the meaning of the whole NP is "a much talked about film", in which case the N *film* is the expression of the object to which it has been discussed. Here, *chiacchierare* is synonymous to the transitive verb *discutere* ('to discuss') and therefore can be used in the participial form as modifier of a head N.

3   Syntactic tests

"The NP of which the adjectival passive is predicated must be thematically related to the base verb; that is, it must be an argument of this verb" (Levin & Rappaport 1986:626).

Since every verb class distinguished has a different argument structure, their various PastPs have different relationship to the head N.

Thus, a PPP (derived from a transitive verb or from an ergative verb in its transitive use) is related to the head N like the base verb is related to its internal argument (identified by the functional category of direct object, DO). This can be made clear by considering the corresponding relative sentences 1b) and small clauses (SC) (1c):

1) a. NP: la ricerca condotta dal nostro gruppo
   b. RS: la ricerca$_i$ che(DO)$_i$ il nostro gruppo ha condotto
   c. SC: [$_F$ PRO$_i$ [$_V$ [condotta] [la ricerca]]], il nostro gruppo$_i$ ne pubblicò i risultati

An active PastP (derived from an unaccusative verb or from an ergative verb in its unaccusative use) is related to the head N in the same way the base verb is related to its external argument (identified by the functional category of subject, S):

2) a. NP: la notizia giunta ieri
   b. RS: la notizia$_i$ che(S)$_i$ è giunta ieri
   c. SC: [$_F$ [$_V$ [giunta] [la notizia]]], Saverio esultò.

Such a syntactic net, resulting from the verbal nature of the PastP, is not shown by any adjectival modifier of a head N.

In order to show that a PastP, contrary to an A (examples are always marked as c) in the series below), retains some of its verbal nature when also inserted in an NP, we have collected several syntactic tests[2]:

i) compatibility with clitics (Guasti 1991):

3) a. la notizia comunicata (PPP) > la notizia comunicata*gli*
   b. il pacco arrivato (active PastP) > il pacco arrivato*le*
   c. il ragazzo fedele (A) > *il ragazzo fedele*le*/ il ragazzo a lei fedele

ii) compatibility with a by-phrase (valid only for PPP) (Gaatone 1987, 1998; Lenz 1996):

4) a. il raccolto distrutto *dalla grandine*
   b. il ritardo causato *dallo sciopero dei macchinisti*
   c. il raccolto abbondante (**dalle provvidenziali piogge*)

test i) and ii) can be applied inside the NP;

iii) compatibility with the auxiliary *venire* ('to come') (valid only for PPP) (Guasti 1991):

---

[2]   Unfortunately we have not the possibility here to discuss every test and the way it works (for a more detailed explanation, see Frigeni 1999:91-95).

5) a. Stefano è salutato > Stefano *viene* salutato
   b. la riunione è posticipata > la riunione *viene* posticipata
   c. la riunione è inderogabile > *la riunione *viene* inderogabile

iv) possibility of impersonal constructions (valid only for PPP) (Gaatone 1987, 1998):

6) a. tali incontri erano previsti > *si erano previsti tali incontri*
   b. il dibattito era concluso > *si era concluso il dibattito*
   c. tali incontri erano utili > **si erano utili tali incontri*

Tests iii) and iv) must be applied outside the NP.

4   Semantic tests

In addition to these standard syntactic tests, PastPs also retain their verbal characteristics with respect to adverb modification. Some adverbs display different semantics according to whether they are attached to a PastP or to an A.

> „C'est plutôt donc le sémantisme commun aux pp et aux verbes correspondants qui doit être tenu pour responsable de leur compatibilité avec certains adverbes, que le statut syntaxique de pp et des adjectives" (Gaatone 1998:60).

Concerning this, the behaviour of the adverb *bene* ('well') is exemplary (for a similar analysis of the French adverb *bien* cf. Rivière 1990:132-137); similar interesting observations can be made by considering the behaviour of the temporal adverb *appena* ('just', 'already') (Frigeni 1999:99).

Thus, if *bene* modifies an A, its only function is to increase the degree of the quality expressed by the A. In this case *bene* is considered to be a degree-functor, i.e. it has a augmentative function, and has as potential synonymy to the quantitative adverb *molto* ('very') and therefore its antonym is *poco* ('(a) little'):

7) a. È *ben/molto contento* di sposarsi   vs   *poco* contento
   b. Sarai *ben/molto stanco* di fare avanti e indietro!   vs   *poco* stanco
   c. Un *tipo ben/molto ambizioso*: non lo facevo così! vs   *poco* ambizioso

But if *bene* modifies a PastP, its function is to predicate in which way the action expressed by the PastP is realized. *Bene* has an evaluative function, it can be paraphrased as an explicit qualitative judgement about the result of the action/process expressed by the PastP and its antonym is the adverb *male* ('bad'):

8) a. È una relazione *ben scritta*[3] (= buona/ efficace/ ecc.)   vs scritta *male*
   b. Un *piano ben studiato* (= *realizzato secondo buoni criteri)* vs studiato *male*
   c. Un appartamento *ben arredato* (= con gusto)   vs arredato *male*

---

[3] The reverse order (*scritta bene, studiato bene, arredato bene*) is also possible and corresponds more clearly to the sequence verb-adverb (*Ha scritto bene la relazione*, etc.). Concerning the position of *bene* with the A, it should be noted that *bene* always precedes the A, as all other adverbs do, which modify the degree of the quality expressed by A.

Further evidence of the different meanings of *bene*, whether it occurs with an A or with a PastP, is given by the fact that the two antonyms (*poco* and *male*) are not interchangeable: *poco* as degree-functor is allowed only with A (with PastP it would have a pure quantitative interpretation, thus *poco arredato*, for example, means 'with little furniture'): *male* is allowed only with PastP. Furthermore, the comparative forms of *bene* also show this difference (Frigeni 1999:98).

The comparative form of the augmentative *bene* is *più* (which is also a simple degree-functor), while the comparative form of the evaluative *bene* is *meglio* (which is itself intrinsically evaluative):

9) a. la *relazione più valida* di quella di Fulvia è quella di Silvana
   b. *la relazione *meglio valida* di quella di Fulvia è quella di Silvana
10) a. la *relazione scritta meglio* di quella di Fulvia è quella di Silvana
    b. *La relazio»ne *più scritta* di quella di Fulvia è quella di Silvana

Also *appena* ('just', 'already') shows a different meaning when modifying an A or a PastP. If it occurs with an A, then its original temporal interpretation gets lost and it behaves as a simple functor that lowers the degree of the quality expressed by the A:

11) è appena *(appena)*[4] stanco/godibile/utile/efficace/sufficiente/etc.

But if *appena* modifies a PastP, it retains its temporal meaning which is made possible by the verbal nature of the PastP.

12) a. il latte *appena munto* ha un altro sapore
    b. cosa ne pensi del concerto *appena ascoltato*?
    c. la donna appena *comparsa* sulla soglia è mia zia

According to Guasti (1991:331) PastPs can not be modified as As can be: i.e. with degree-functors as *molto/assai* ('very') and the superlative suffix *-issimo*. A few comments and clarifications can be made to this statement.

First, the PastPs that can appear with the degree-modifier *molto/assai* are often forms which have been strongly lexicalised as As (particulary PastPs of so-called psychological verbs, such as *molto* or *assai attratto/commosso/disgustato/impaurito*, etc.): Therefore, the possibility to be modified by *molto/assai* can be adopted to test the degree of lexicalisation of a PastP as an A.

Second, the possibility for a PastP to form a superlative through the suffix *-issimo* is not excluded, but it is restricted by a specific semantic condition regarding the base verb (Rainer 1983:56-58). The base verb must express either a recursive action/process or an action which can be completed by more than one agent (it is often the case that a verb that shows both the semantic possibilities: *citare, vendere/comprare, studiare, discutere*, etc.).

This means that the suffix *-issimo*, if attached to a PastP derived from such verbs, has a frequentative and/or pluriagentive meaning, for example:

13) un autore citatissimo/lettisimo/vedutissimo/compratissimo/etc.

---

[4] In its reduplicated form, *appena appena*, it means a very low degree (which tends towards zero).

Where *citatissimo/lettissimo/*etc. can mean either 'often quoted/read/etc.' or 'quoted/ read/etc. by many'.

Third, the degree-functors in question can modify a PastP with the pragmatic function that Rainer defined „affirmative" as well[5]. In this use, the suffix *-issimo* increases the power of the affirmation that a certain entity is in a certain state (which is expressed by A or by PastP). As a pragmatic function it does not undergo any restrictions, as shown from these examples, which from a pure semantic view could be almost paradoxical:

14) è proprio morto, *mortissimo/* è proprio chiusa, *chiusissima*

5   The puzzle of morphological negation

With respect to morphological negation the PastP presents a puzzle.

The Italian negative prefixes *iN-* and *dis-/s* attach to A directly[6]. The derivational rules are very simple and do not violate the morphological principle that a prefix does not change the syntactic category of the base to which it has been attached (Scalise 1990, 1994)[7]:

15) [iN- A]A and [dis-/s- A]A

The morphological negation of PastP with the prefix *iN-*, on the other hand, appears to cancel out the verbal properties of the PastP discussed above. This contrast is explained by hypothesizing that *iN-* can be attached a PastP just in case this PastP is reanalyzed as an A, in a formula:

16)   [iN- [pp]A]A

Such an analysis is supported by applying the syntactic tests we have collected in section 3 to these negative forms: *iN*-As (i.e. *iN*-As and [*iN-* [pp]A]As) which obviously do not show any verbal properties, they are straighforward As. There are no counterexamples because Italian [iN-pp]As are always derived from a finite set of verbs (see 17) for the formula and 18) for exhaustive list of them), derived from *iN*-prefixed adjectives:

17) [iN-[A]]V

18) inattivare, impossibilitare, impazientire, immunizzare, immobilizzare, inabilitare, indisporre

---

[5] Relational adjectives (such as *italiano*, 'italian') allow gradation through *molto/assai* and *-issimo* only if these elements express the "affirmative" function (*italianissimo*, 'really italian').

[6] Examples of this derivations do not need to be listed, because they are quite well-known.

[7] "Per esprimere il fatto che i prefissi, contrariamente ai suffissi, non cambiano la categoria sintattica della loro base", si può ricorrere a questa rappresentazione[Pre+ [ ]ax]ax". (Scalise 1990:130)

The negative prefix *dis-/s-* does not cancel the verbal properties of the PastP. The simplest explanation is that the prefix *dis-/s-* is not attached to the PastP, but rather to its verbal base:

19) [[dis-/s- V]pp]A

In short, this means that a *dis-/s-*-PastP is derived from a *dis-/s-*-verb and can be inserted in an NP as a modifier of the head N retaining all its verbal features. This can be demonstrated by applying the syntactic tests: every [*dis-/s-*-pp]A can always appear in verbal syntactic frames.

A difference between the two negative prefixed PastPs exists also in the meaning: the *iN*-forms designate a "zero state", i.e. the entity it predicates is not altered by the action/process expressed by the base verb (*inatteso, insepolto, inapplicato*, etc.); the *dis-/s-*-forms express a "cancelled state", the reverse negation (Grossman 1994) of the state obtained by the action/process expressed by the base verb (*disatteso, dissepolto, disapplicato*, etc.).

In other words, the *dis-/s-* forms presuppose the "positive state" expressed by the positive PastP, while the *iN*-forms do not.

6   Proposals

In this paper, several and often heterogeneous observations were made about the nature and state of PastPs inserted into NPs by differing the levels of the analysis: syntactic, semantic and morphological. But as noted, it is always difficult to keep them completely separated and this is the most interesting feature of PastPs.

Further research is needed in explaining the interaction between adverbs and PastPs inside NPs in order to capture the nature of the PastP-modifiers and the relations between modifying function and meaning of the base verbs (in particular their aspect). Such an inquiry could also offer a new perspective in the field of studying adverbs.

7   References

BELLETTI, Adriana (1981): Frasi ridotte assolute. In: Rivista di Grammatica Generativa 6, 3-32.
BRIANTI, Giovanna (1992): Périphrases aspectuelles de l'italien. Le cas de andare, venire et stare + gérondif (Thèse présentée à la Faculté des lettres de l'Université de Gèneve pour obtenir le grade de docteur èn lettres) Berne: Peter Lang S.A..
BURZIO, Luigi (1986): Italian syntax.. Dordrecht: D. Reidel Publishing Company, 20-84.
FRIGENI, Chiara (1999): Il participio passato all'interno del sintagma nominale alla prova dei prefissi negativi. Pavia: Tesi di Laurea in Lettere Moderne, Facoltà di Lettere e Filosofia dell'Università di Pavia (MS.).
GAATONE, David (1998): Le passif en français. Paris: Duculot.
— (1987): Préfixes négatifs. Adjectifs et noms verbaux. In: Cahiers de Lexicologie 50.1, 79-90.
GRIMSHAW, Jeane (1990): Argument Structure. Cambridge, MA: The MIT Press.
GROSSMANN, Maria (1994): Opposizioni direzionali e prefissazione. Analisi morfologica e semantica dei verbi egressivi prefissati con des- e es- in catalano. Padova: Unipress.

GUASTI, Maria Teresa (1991): La struttura interna del sintagma aggettivale. In: Renzi; Salvi: Vol. II, Chapter VI.

HASPELMATH, Martin (1994): Passive Participles across Languages. In: Fox, Barbara A.; Hopper, Paul J. (eds.): Voice: Form and Function. Amsterdam: Benjamins (Typological studies in language 27), 151-177.

MILAN, Carl (1985): Das Passiv im Deutschen und Italienischen. Die Partizipialkonstruktionen mit werden/sein und essere/venire. Heidelberg: Carl Winter Universitätsverlag.

LENZ, Barbara (1996): Sein, bleiben und werden im Negations- und Partizipial-Kontext. In: Linguistische Berichte 162, 161-182.

LEVIN, Beth; RAPPAPORT, Malka (1986): The Formation of adjectival Passives. In: Linguistic Inquiry 17.4, 623-661.

RAINER, Franz (1983): Intensivierung im Italienischen. Salzburg: Salzburger Romanistische Schriften VII.

RENZI, Lorenzo; SALVI, Gian Paolo (eds.) (1988-1995): Grande grammatica italiana di consultazione, 3 Vols. [(vol. I, 1988; vol. II, 1991; vol. III, 1995)]. Bologna: Il Mulino.

RIVIÈRE, Nicole (1990): Le Participe Passé est-il Verbe ou Adjectif?. In: Travaux de Linguistique et de Philologie XXVIII. Strasbourg-Nancy: Librairie Klincksieck, 131-169.

SCALISE, Sergio (1994): Morfologia. Bologna: Il Mulino.

— (1990): Morfologia e lessico. Bologna: Il Mulino.

SCHEPPING, MarieTheres (1997): Die Negation der Wortbildung am Beispiel der italienischen Präfixe s-/dis-. Konstanz: Universität Konstanz (MS.)

WASOW, Thomas (1977): Transformation and the Lexicon. In: Culicover, Peter W. et al. (eds.): Formal Syntax. Proceedings of the 1976 MSSB irvine Conference on the Formal Syntax of Natural Language, June 9 - 11, 1976. New York: N.Y. Academic Press, 327-360.

Typologie und Übersetzbarkeit von Eigennamen in einem elektronischen Wörterbuch Deutsch-Französisch

Thierry Grass

Sowohl bei der automatischen, halbautomatischen als auch der manuellen Übersetzung stellen die Eigennamen ein besonderes Problem dar. In dieser Studie wird von einer Typologie der Eigennamen ausgegangen, aus der Anweisungen für die Übersetzung abgeleitet werden (*„übersetzen"*, *„nicht übersetzen"*, *„transkribieren"*), die dem Lexikographen bei der Erstellung eines Wörterbuchs helfen sollen. Grundlage ist die pragmatisch orientierte Typologie Gerhard Bauers, die die Eigennamen in fünf Grundtypen unterteilt: *Anthroponyme, Toponyme, Ergonyme, Praxonyme* und *Phänonyme*. Aus diesen fünf Grundtypen werden Subtypen abgeleitet, die sich bei der Übersetzung mehr oder weniger homogen verhalten. Besondere Aufmerksamkeit wird polylexikalischen Sequenzen vom Typ N + N gewidmet (in denen N kein Vorname ist), die aus einem gemischten Zeitungskorpus stammen, der von Franz Guenthner vom *Centrum von Informations- und Sprachverarbeitung (CIS)* in München extrahiert wurde. Weitere Schwierigkeiten bei der Übersetzung der Eigennamen werden ebenfalls unter Berücksichtigung morphosyntaktischer, semantischer und pragmatischer Kriterien erläutert. Näher eingegangen wird auf die Frage der Übersetzung oder der Nichtübersetzung englischer Eigennamen innerhalb eines deutschen Textes in die Zielsprache Französisch. Ferneres Ziel dieser Arbeit ist die Erstellung eines zweisprachigen, elektronischen Wörterbuchs der Eigennamen Französisch-Deutsch.

1   Einleitung

Die *Onomastik* oder das „Studium der Eigennamen" hat lange Zeit nur zwischen den Namen von Personen, den *Personennamen* bzw. *Anthroponymen*, und den Namen von Orten, den *Ortsnamen* bzw. *Toponymen*, unterschieden. Diese klassische Unterscheidung, die man noch in den meisten Wörterbüchern der Sprachwissenschaft finden kann, ist sehr beschränkt, da sie z.B. den Terminus *Person* nur für natürliche Personen verwendet, während es auch Rechtspersonen, ethnische oder kulturelle Gruppen und Stiftungen gibt, die ebenfalls in diese Kategorie passen. Auch der Terminus *Ortsname* kann Verwirrung stiften, da er sich tatsächlich nur auf die Namen von Orten bezieht. Flüsse sind zum Beispiel keine Orte, gehören jedoch trotzdem zu den Eigennamen.

§ 59 der *amtlichen Regelung zur deutschen Rechtschreibung* definiert Eigennamen wie folgt: „Eigennamen sind Bezeichnungen zur Identifizierung bestimmter einzelner Gegebenheiten (eine Person, ein Ort, ein Land, eine Institution usw.)." Der *Petit Robert* auf CD-ROM gibt eine ähnliche Definition: „Mot ou groupe de mots servant à désigner un individu et à le distinguer des êtres de la même espèce."

Die Definition des *Duden Wörterbuchs* auf CD-ROM, ist sehr ähnlich: „Name, der ein Individuum (Person, Gruppe, Sache usw.) bezeichnet u. als einmaliges von allen gleichartigen Individuen unterscheiden soll."

Es ist sehr schwierig, ein ontologisches Kriterium zu finden, das der ganzen Vielfalt der Eigennamen gerecht wird, in dem sowohl die Individualität wie auch die kulturelle Identität berücksichtigt wird. Die Klassifikation, die in dieser Arbeit berücksichtigt wird, beruht auf pragmatischen Kriterien, es handelt sich um die Klassifikation von Bauer (1985:51), die den Referenten als Bezugspunkt nimmt:

> „Die Einteilung der Eigennamen richtet sich nach der Bewertung der den Namen als Referenten zugrunde liegenden Bestandteile der objektiven Realität."

Diese Klassifikation, die ihre Rechtfertigung aus der extralinguistischen Realität holt, beruht auf einer Unterteilung in fünf Hauptgruppen, deren zwei erste bereits akzeptiert sind: es handelt sich um *Anthroponyme, Toponyme, Ergonyme, Praxonyme* und *Phänonyme.*

Diese Studie soll eine Grundlage für die Erstellung eines elektronischen deutsch-französischen Wörterbuchs liefern. Sie wird im Rahmen des internationalen Forschungsprojektes *Prolex*[1] geführt, welches zum Ziel hat, Eigennamen in einem Text automatisch zu identifizieren, zu ordnen und bei Bedarf auch zu übersetzen.

Die Grundlage der vorliegenden Arbeit besteht aus einem gemischten Korpus[2], der zum Teil aus Zeitungsartikeln bestand, und der uns vom *CIS (Centrum für Informations- und Sprachverarbeitung)* der Universität München zur Verfügung gestellt worden ist. Er besteht aus 28.709 Einträgen vom Typ N1 + N2, wobei N1 und N2 Nomina sind, die mit einem Großbuchstaben anfangen. Jeder dieser Einträge hat die Frequenz 10 oder mehr, d.h., sie kommen wenigstens 10 Mal in den Zeitungsartikeln vor. Um Sequenzen vom Typ *Vorname + Nachname* auszuschließen, wurden mit Hilfe eines elektronischen Vornamenwörterbuch (fast) alle Vornamen ausgesondert. Durch die grammatische Kategorie des Kasus im Deutschen können jedoch manche Sequenzen mehrmals auftauchen.

2   Die Typologie der Eigennamen nach Bauer

Die *Anthroponyme* bezeichnen ein oder mehrere Individuen, die durch das Sem [+menschlich] charakterisiert werden. Dazu gehören Einzelnamen (*Familien-* und *Vornamen*), aber auch Sammelnamen wie die Völkernamen, die sog. *Ethnika (die Deutschen = les Allemands*), und die Namen von Institutionen (*die UNO = l'ONU, die Europäische Union = l'Union européenne*), Parteien (*die SPD = le, la SPD, die Demokratische Partei = le parti démocrate*), Verbänden und Vereinen (*der VfB Lübeck = le FC Lübeck*). In dieser Gruppe findet man besonders häufig Akronyme, wie die aufgeführten Beispiele zeigen. Die Namen von künstlerischen Truppen, Orchestern oder Bands (*New Yorker Philharmoniker = orchestre philharmonique de New York, die Toten Hosen = les Tote Hosen*) zählen ebenso zu den Anthroponymen wie

---

[1]   Homepage von *Prolex* unter http://www.li.univ-tours.fr/FRLI/BdChm/Projet1.htm
[2]   Als Grundlage diente u.a. die *Süddeutsche Zeitung.*

Pseudonyme und *Hypokoristika* (Kosenamen). Namen von übernatürlichen Wesen gelten auch als Anthroponyme. Es handelt sich dabei um die Namen von Gottheiten: *Gott* (in politheistischen Religionen kann diese Bezeichnung nicht mehr als Eigenname angesehen werden), *Zeus, Krishna,* usw.

Völkernamen, obwohl sie sich direkt auf Ortsnamen beziehen, werden ebenfalls in diese Gruppe eingegliedert.

Zu den *Toponymen*, oder geographischen Namen, gehören nicht nur Namen von Ländern und Städten (*die Vereinigten Arabischen Emirate = les Emirats arabes unis, New Jersey = le New Jersey, Bad Kreuznach = Bad Kreuznach*) sondern auch Subgruppen wie Orte, sog. *Microtoponyme* (*der Kreis Groß-Gerau = le district de Gross-Gerau*), Wasserläufe, sog. *Hydronyme* (*der Rio Grande = le Rio Grande*) und Gebirge, sog. *Oronyme* (*die Rocky Mountains = les Rocheuses*). Auch die Namen von Straßen (*die Frankfurter Straße = la Frankfurter Strasse*), Seen (*das Kaspische Meer = la mer Caspienne*), Inseln (*die Kanarischen Inseln = les îles Canaries*), von Wüsten (*die Wüste Gobi = le désert de Gobi*) und schließlich von Gebäuden (*das Weiße Haus = la Maison-Blanche, das Café Giesing = le Café Giesing, das Landgericht Frankfurt = le Tribunal de grande instance de Francfort, die Kirche St Paul = l'église Saint-Paul, das Schloß Auerbach = le château d'Auerbach*) werden zu den Toponymen gezählt.

Grévisse und Goosse sind der Meinung, daß die Himmelsrichtungen als Toponyme behandelt werden können (1986:117), falls keine Umstandsbestimmung des Ortes dabei steht (*Nordfrankreich = le Nord oder le nord de la France*).

Die *Bewohnernamen* sind eng mit Toponymen verbunden. Da sie das Sem [+menschlich] besitzen, werden sie zu den Anthroponymen gezählt.

Ergonyme (vom griech. *ergon*: Arbeit, Kraft) sind Waren und Produkte. Die Produktionsstätten zählen auch zu den Ergonymen. Bauer spricht ebenfalls von Fabriknamen, was jedoch zu einschränkend ist, es wäre vielleicht besser von Betrieben oder Unternehmen zu sprechen (*Microsoft® Corporation = Microsoft Corporation*). Man schließt dabei auch die Genossenschaften, die Forschungs- und Lehranstalten, sowie die militärischen Einrichtungen[3] ein. Neben Bezeichnungen von Produkten findet man auch Titel von Büchern sowie die Namen von anderen Veröffentlichungen und Kunstwerken.

Praxonyme (vom griech. *praxis*: Tätigsein) werden von Bauer wie folgt definiert (1985:55):

„alle Namen, die zur Bezeichnung von Ereignissen und Geschehnissen benutzt werden, als deren Auslöser, Träger, Teilnehmer und betroffene Menschen gelten können."

In dieser Gruppe finden wir historische Ereignisse (*der Dreißigjährige Krieg = la Guerre de Trente Ans*) und einige Krankheitsnamen (*Alzheimer Krankheit = maladie d'Alzheimer*). Es sind im Grunde Phraseologismen, die zu geschichtlichen, ärztlichen und anderen Fachsprachen gehören

Auch kulturelle Ereignisse (*Berliner Filmfestspiele = Festival du film de Berlin, Bayreuther Festspiele = Festival de Bayreuth*) werden zu dieser Gruppe gezählt.

---

[3] Diese gehören eher zu den Toponymen, da sie primär durch den Ort bestimmt werden: *das Pentagon = le Pentagone, die Maginotlinie = la Ligne Maginot.*

Phänonyme (vom griech. *phainómenon*: das Erscheinende) umfassen Naturkatastrophen und Orkane (*der Hurrikan Mitch = le cyclone Mitch*), Hoch- und Tiefdruckgebiete sowie Gestirne und Kometen (*der Halleysche Komet = la comète de Halley*).
Die Kategorisierung von Bauer ist vollständig, obwohl sie die Appellativa für Haustiere ignoriert (wir schlagen die Bezeichnung *Zoonyme* vor). Einige von diesen sind quasi lexikalisiert (*Rex, Waldi, Wolf / Médor*). Grévisse und Goosse fügen eine weitere Kategorie hinzu (1986:119), die von Bauer ebenfalls nicht erwähnt wurde. Es sind Namen, die bestimmten mythischen Objekten gegeben wurden: z.b. *Durandal* oder *Excalibur* für Schwerter in Heldenliedern. Um keine zusätzliche Klasse zu kreieren, werden die *Zoonyme* mit den Anthroponymen, *mythische Objekte* mit den Ergonymen aufgeführt.

3   Polylexikalische Eigennamen

Meistens, aber nicht immer, bestehen polylexikalische Eigennamen aus einem Syntagma, dessen Basis aus einem Eigennamen gebildet wird. Polylexikalische Eigennamen kommen ebenso oft in einem Text vor wie monolexikalische Eigennamen, so Kolde (1995:400f):

„Nur wenige EN [Eigennamen] sind so einfach wie Otto, Köln oder Rhein strukturiert ... / ... Ein Blick auf EN wie *lac Léman, Mont Blanc, Place Neuve, Tour Eiffel, (Université) Paris III* zeigt, daß die Struktur komplexer EN durchaus den für die betr. Sprache gültigen Regeln wie der der Prä- bzw. Postdeterminierung entspricht."

Im allgemeinen sollten Namen von Firmen und von Produkten nicht übersetzt werden, wenn sie alleine stehen. Bei Eigennamen wie *Microsoft Deutschland* wird nur *Deutschland* übersetzt.
Die englischen Akronyme der bekanntesten Organisationen werden von der deutschen Sprache übernommen, wobei sie in der französischen Sprache systematisch übersetzt werden (*die NATO = l'OTAN, die UNO = l'ONU, die Champions League = la Ligue des Champions*).
Historische Ereignisse werden als Träger nationaler Identität systematisch übersetzt.

4   Morphosyntaktische Betrachtungen

Einige morphosyntaktische Regelmäßigkeiten werden hier in Hinblick auf die Automatisierung der Übersetzung zusammengefaßt.

4.1   Genus

Im untersuchten Korpus sind die Einträge, die extrahiert wurden, ohne Artikel aufgeführt. Eine automatische Verarbeitung des Korpus setzt unter anderem eine Zuweisung des Genus voraus, um die flektierten Formen zuweisen zu können. Im Allgemeinen gibt es keine Übereinstimmung des Genus zwischen der deutschen und der französischen Sprache. Die Regeln können den entsprechenden Grammatiken entnommen werden.

4.2 Kasusreduktion

Wenn es keine Übersetzung für einen Eigennamen gibt, wird die deutsche unflektierte Form des Nominativs übernommen. Diese Rückbildung anderer Fälle auf den Nominativ Singular oder Plural nennen wir mangels eines besseren Begriffes *Kasusreduktion.*

- *Er wohnt in der Alten Bergstraße = il habite dans la Alte Bergstrasse, il habite la Alte Bergstrasse, il habite Alte Bergstrasse*
- *Ich habe es in der Neuen Zürcher Zeitung gelesen = je l'ai lu dans le Neue Zürcher Zeitung*

Im zweiten Beispiel haben wir es nicht nur mit einer Kasusreduktion sondern auch mit einem Genuswechsel zu tun: *Neue Zürcher Zeitung* bezieht sich auf frz. *journal* und nimmt den Maskulinum des Oberbegriffs ein[4].

Bezüglich eines informatisierten Korpus ist es von Vorteil sog. *kanonische Formen* eines Eigennamen zu definieren: z.B. *Wiener Kongre-* pour *Wiener Kongress, Wiener Kongreß, Wiener Kongresses*

4.3 Numerus

Im Gegensatz zum Deutschen sind Familiennamen im Französischen in der Mehrzahl unveränderlich und tragen keine Pluralendung. Nach Kolde (1995:415f) kennzeichnet die Mehrzahl auf -s, im Deutschen relativ selten, die Zugehörigkeit zweier Personen zur gleichen Familie. Die unmarkierte Pluralform zeigt dagegen, daß zwei Menschen den gleichen Namen tragen, ohne zur gleichen Familie zu gehören (*die beiden Schulzes sind wieder da ≅ les deux [de la famille] Schulze sont revenus / die beiden Schulze sind wieder da ≅ les deux Schulze [de deux familles différentes] sont revenus*).

Paradoxerweise dient eine seltenere Form zum Ausdruck der Verwandtschaft, wobei die üblichere Form das Fremde charakterisiert. Die Pluralform auf -s kann auch für Toponyme verwendet werden (*In Deutschland gibt es drei Neustadt(s) ≅ en Allemagne, il y a trois [communes du nom de] Neustadt*)[5]. Im allgemeinen jedoch ist die Pluralform als Hauptform für Eigennamen selten (*die Vereinten Nationen / les Nations Unies*).

---

[4] Bei französischen Germanisten besteht dennoch die Tendenz (oder der Snobismus), den ursprünglichen Genus zuzuweisen: z.B. je l'ai lu dans *la Zeit* (vs. *le journal*).
[5] Beim Übersetzen ins Französische kann das Fehlen der Pluralmarke durch eine Erweiterung wiedergegeben werden.

4.4   Großschreibung und Graphie

Auf deutsch ist die Großschreibung kein entscheidendes Merkmal des Eigennamens, da die Substantive schon durch die Großschreibung gekennzeichnet werden. Wenn auch die Regeln bezüglich der Großschreibung der Nomina im Deutschen einfach sind, gilt das nicht für Adjektive. Für die Großschreibung von Adjektiven im Deutschen gibt uns die *amtliche Regelung zur deutschen Rechtschreibung* Regeln[6] (§§ 59-62), auf die in diesem Rahmen nicht weiter eingegangen werden soll. Für das Französische führt *Le bon usage* eine vollständige, jedoch unklare Synthese auf, wann was groß oder klein geschrieben werden soll (1986:117-134).

Ein weiteres Problem besteht darin, Eigennamen zu transkribieren, die ursprünglich in einem anderen Alphabet als dem lateinischen geschrieben wurden. Die Transkriptionsregeln für Namen arabischer, chinesischer, russischer oder sonstiger fremder Herkunft sind im Deutschen und Französischen verschieden, so daß bei der Übersetzung eine Umtranskribierung stattfinden muß.

Der ehemalige Premierminister Israels *Benjamin Netanjahu* wird im Französischen *Nétanyahou* oder *Netanyahou*[7] geschrieben, was zeigt, daß selbst bei der Transkription in eine Sprache schon unterschiedliche Versionen auftauchen können.

4.5   Komposita

Die Bildung von Komposita ist eine Eigenart der deutschen Sprache und ermöglicht die Schaffung von stets neuen monolexikalischen oder polylexikalischen Einheiten.

In Frankreich wird unterschieden (Schanen/Confais 1986:362f) zwischen Komposita hypotaktischer Struktur (*Bezirksausschuß Obergiesing* ≅ *commission du district d'Obergiesing*), deren Elemente gebunden oder ungebunden sind (*Filmzentrum Bären* = *Centre cinématographique Bären, Filmfest München* = *Festival du film de Munich*), und Komposita parataktischer Struktur, die mit Bindestrich gebunden werden (*Mercedes-Benz C-Klasse* = *classe C de chez Mercedes[-Benz]*, Rennstall *McLaren-Mercedes* = *écurie McLaren-Mercedes*) oder graphisch getrennt sind (*Toyota Celica Turbo* = *Toyota Celica Turbo, Rote Armee* = *Armée rouge*).

5.   Übersetzen oder nicht?

Diese Studie wurde durchgeführt, um ausgehend von bestimmten Typen von Eigennamen Übersetzungsregeln zu definieren. Der Schwerpunkt wurde darauf gelegt zu bestimmen, ob ein Eigenname zu übersetzen ist oder nicht. Folgende Tendenzen für die Übersetzung der einzelnen Typen konnten zusammengefaßt werden:

---

[6]   Im WWW unter: http://www.ids-mannheim.de/grammis/reform/inhalt.html
[7]   Mit dem Akzent in *Le Monde*, ohne in *Libération* vom 17. Mai 1999.

- Anthroponyme gelten als Mischtyp: Vornamen und Nachnamen, Pseudonyme, „moderne" Orchesternamen werden meistens nicht übersetzt, Ethnika, Partei-, Vereins- und „klassische" Orchesternamen werden meistens übersetzt.
- Toponyme werden nur dann übersetzt, wenn in der Kultur der Zielsprache sie von Bedeutung sind. Ländernamen, bedeutende Flüsse, große Gebirgsketten werden übersetzt, kleinere Ortschaften nicht.
- Ergonyme werden nie übersetzt, wenn sie monolexikalisch sind und selten, wenn sie polylexikalisch sind.
- Umgekehrt werden Praxonyme quasi immer übersetzt, außer wenn sie in der Zielsprache lexikalisiert sind, wie z.B. *der Anschluß* [von 1938]: *l'Anschluss.*
- Monolexikalische Phänonyme werden meistens nicht übersetzt, bei den polylexikalischen wird der Kern (der Eigenname an sich) unübersetzt gelassen und die Umgebung übersetzt.

In der folgenden Tabelle werden die Grundtendenzen detaillierter aufgeführt. Anhand dieser Tabelle werden formale Anweisungen gegeben, die sowohl für die automatische, als auch für die manuelle Übersetzung gelten. Die Ausnahmen können im Falle einer Implementierung separat in einem Ausnahmewörterbuch erfaßt werden. Die Implementierung setzt natürlich voraus, daß in einem elektronischen Wörterbuch der Eigennamen diese verschiedenen Typen berücksichtigt werden.

	Teilgruppe	Übersetzungsanweisung	Anmerkungen
Anthroponyme	Familiennamen	nicht übersetzen	außer bei besonderer Absicht in einer Fiktion
	Vornamen	nicht übersetzen	eventuell transkribieren
	Pseudonyme	nicht übersetzen	außer bei einer Kurzform, die vom Familiennamen oder Vornamen abgeleitet wird
	Bewohnername[8]	nicht übersetzen	außer bei Ableitungen aus einer „bekannten" Stadt, z.B. Vienne/Viennois
	„Ethnika"[9]	übersetzen	z.B. die Franzosen
	Hypokoristika	übersetzen	z.B. Häschen = mon lapin
	„Moderne" Bands	nicht übersetzen	z.B. Simple Minds
	„Klassische" Orchester und Truppen	übersetzen	z.B. Wiener Philharmoniker = orchestre philharmonique de Vienne
	Parteien und Organisationen, Sportvereine[10]	übersetzen	außer bei bestimmten eigentümlichen Formen, z.B. Likud
	Zoonyme	übersetzen	z.B. Milou = Struppi

---

[8] Suffix –er od. seltener -aner = *les habitants de ...*
[9] Diese Subklasse wird von Bauer nicht erwähnt.
[10] Selbst Akronyme sollten, soweit es geht, übersetzt werden: VfB Stuttgart = FC Stuttgart

	Teilgruppe	Übersetzungsanweisung	Anmerkungen
Toponyme	Länder	übersetzen	z.b. Österreich = l'Autriche
	Städte	nicht übersetzen	außer bei einer bekannten Stadt, z.b. Neapel = Naples
	Mikrotoponyme, Straßen	nicht übersetzen	z.b. Bad Godesberg
	Hydronyme	nicht übersetzen	außer bei einem bekanntem Fluß, z.b. die Donau = le Danube
	Oronyme	nicht übersetzen	außer bei einem bekanntem Berg, z.b. das Matterhorn = le Cervin
	Militärische Einrichtungen[11]	übersetzen	z.b. die Maginotlinie = la Ligne Maginot
Ergonyme	Marken	nicht übersetzen	eventuell transkribieren
	Unternehmen	nicht übersetzen	außer für bestimmte Elemente, die nicht zur polylexikalischen Grundform gehören
	Bildungs- und Forschungseinrichtungen	übersetzen	z.b. Max Planck Institut = Institut Max Planck
	Titel von Büchern, Spielfilmen und Kunstwerken	übersetzen	Gibt es eine französisch-sprachige Fassung des Werkes?
	Mythische Objekte	übersetzen	z.b. das Schwert *Excalibur*
Praxonyme	Historische Ereignisse	übersetzen	z.b. Wiener Kongreß = Congrès de Vienne
	Krankheiten	übersetzen	außer der Basis, bestehend aus einem Familienname
	Kulturelle Ereignisse	übersetzen	z.b. Berliner Filmfestspiele = Festival du film de Berlin
Phänonyme	Stürme, Orkane	übersetzen	außer der Basis, bestehend aus einem Vornamen z.b. Hurrikan Mitch = cyclone Mitch
	Hoch- und Tiefdruckgebiete	nicht übersetzen	
	Gestirne und Kometen	übersetzen	z.b. der Halleysche Komet = la comète de Halley

6   Schlußbetrachtungen

In dieser Studie wurde die Komplexität bei der Übersetzung von Eigennamen verdeut-licht: die Übersetzung von Eigennamen ist nicht einfacher als die von anderen Nomi-na, auch wenn dies vielfach angenommen wird. Einige der Gründe sollen hier noch einmal kurz zusammengefaßt werden:

Konnotationen spielen bei der Übersetzung von Eigennamen eine wesentlich grö-ßere Rolle als bei der Übersetzung von anderen Nomina, da sich Eigennamen oft auf nationale Ereignisse, Personen oder Orte beziehen. Für die Übersetzung von Film-

---

[11] Bauer zählt diese zu den Ergonymen.

oder Buchtiteln muß zum Beispiel überprüft werden, ob es eine Fassung des jeweiligen Werkes in Landessprache gibt. Morphosyntaktische Besonderheiten stellen eine weitere Schwierigkeit bei der Übersetzung von Eigennamen dar. Und letztendlich muß im Vorfeld der Übersetzung geklärt werden, ob eine Übersetzung gemäß den oben zusammengefaßten Tendenzen sinnvoll erscheint oder nicht. Hinzu kommt, daß Eigennamen oft polylexikalisch sind, und sie daher zum Teil komplett übersetzt oder nicht übersetzt, aber manchmal auch nur teilübersetzt werden.

Ein zweisprachiges Wörterbuch der Eigennamen Deutsch-Französisch, das bisher noch nicht im Handel erhältlich ist, hätte damit vieles zu berücksichtigen.

7   Literatur

BAUER, Gerhard (1985): Namenkunde des Deutschen. Bern etc.: Lang (Germanistische Lehrbuchsammlung 21).

DROSDOWSKI, Günther (1984): Grammatik der deutschen Gegenwartssprache. Mannheim: Bibliographisches Institut.

GREVISSE, Maurice; GOOSSE, André (1986): Le bon usage. Paris: Duculot.

Helbig Gerhard; Buscha, Joachim (1979): Deutsche Grammatik. Leipzig: VEB Verlag Enzyklopädie.

Kolde Gottfried (1995): Grammatik der Eigennamen (Überblick). In: Eichler, E.; Hilty, G.; Löffler, H.; Steger, H.; Zgusta, L. (Hrsg.): Namenforschung. Ein internationales Handbuch zur Onomastik. Berlin: Walter de Gruyter, 400-408.

SCHANEN, François; CONFAIS, Jean-Paul (1986): Grammaire de l'allemand – formes et fonctions. Paris: Nathan.

Sprichwörter im onomasiologischen Wörterbuch

Tamás Kispál

1 Einleitung

Sprichwörter sind satzwertige feste Verbindungen, die nach einer Definition von Röhrich/Mieder (1977:3) „eine Lebensregel oder Weisheit in prägnanter, kurzer Form ausdrücken". Sprichwörter sind im weiteren Sinne der Phraseologie zuzurechnen, da sie – wenn auch nicht alle – die phraseologischen Merkmale „Polylexikalität", „Festigkeit", „Idiomatizität" und „Lexikalisierung" aufweisen. Polylexikalität und Festigkeit sind dabei unumstritten, das idiomatische Merkmal wird jedoch von einigen Phraseologen den Sprichwörtern nicht zuerkannt. Während Feilke (1996) die „idiomatische Prägung" auch auf Sprichwörter bezieht, argumentiert Fleischer (1994) in seiner Ablehnung damit, daß die Idiomatizität in seiner Interpretation nur auf lexikalische Einheiten bezogen werden kann, und Sprichwörter betrachtet er nicht als lexikalische Einheiten, sondern als Texte. Lexikalisierung ist ein anderes umstrittenes Charakteristikum von Sprichwörtern. Ruef (1995:6ff) faßt Sprichwörter wie andere feste Wortverbindungen als lexikalische Einheiten auf.

In der Lexikologie wird „die anhaltend zu erörternde Frage der Integration der phraseologischen Elemente in den Wortschatz" (Lutzeier 1996:124) immer mehr diskutiert. Lutzeier (1995:33ff) zählt auch die phraseologischen Einheiten zum Gegenstand der Lexikologie. In seinen Ausführungen werden jedoch Sprichwörter nicht erwähnt, und ohne explizit darauf einzugehen werden Sprichwörter von ihm m.E. nicht in den Gegenstandsbereich der Lexikologie miteinbezogen. Ähnlich verhält es sich auch bei Schindler (1996), der nur die zur Lexik gehörenden Ein- und Mehrwortlexeme zum zentralen Gegenstand der Lexikologie rechnet. Sprichwörter als Teile der zitierten Einheiten, der Textemik lassen sich laut Schindler (1996:122) nur peripher der Lexikologie, in seiner Terminologie dem Sprachschatz zuordnen. Ebenso wird in der Wortfeldtheorie die Aufnahme der phraseologischen Einheiten thematisiert (z.B. Schindler 1993). Phraseologismen als Benennungen können und sollten auch im Rahmen der Wortfeldtheorie untersucht werden. Sprichwörter können jedoch nicht als Nominationen betrachtet werden und bei diesen Minitexten ist die Einordnung in Wortfelder m.E. auszuschließen (siehe Kap. 3).

2 Sprichwörter in allgemeinen onomasiologischen Wörterbüchern

In drei prominenten onomasiologischen Wörterbüchern (Sanders; Dornseiff; Wehrle/ Eggers) habe ich die Behandlung von Sprichwörtern untersucht. Die drei Wörterbücher benutzen drei teilweise verschiedene Gliederungen. Alle diese Wörterbücher betrachten jedoch das onomasiologische System von *Roget's Thesaurus of English words and phrases* (1852) mehr oder weniger als vorbildlich. Das englische Wörterbuch ließ sich von einem einheitlichen Weltbild leiten. Es gliedert sich in sechs Groß-gebiete mit 1000 Begriffen. Wehrle/Eggers ist seit 1961 „genau dem englischen Ge-genstück von Rogets Thesaurus angeglichen" (S. V). Sanders hat die 1000 Begriffe Rogets auf 687 reduziert. Das Gliederungsprinzip von Roget hat er allerdings beibe-halten. Dornseiff hat den deutschen Wortschatz in 20 Sachgruppen aufgeteilt, die je-weils in 20-90 Begriffe zerfallen.

    Sprichwörter und Redewendungen werden in allen drei Wörterbüchern aufgenom-men.[1] Schon in den Vorworten wird darauf hingewiesen (Wehrle/Eggers VIIf.; San-ders XLVIII; Dornseiff 5). Der Sprichwortbestand der onomasiologischen Wörterbü-cher unterscheidet sich erheblich. Während Dornseiff nach meiner Zählung nur 29 Sprichwörter, Sanders 48 Sprichwörter enthält, sind in Wehrle/Eggers 190 Sprich-wörter zu finden. Dornseiff kodifiziert Sprichwörter („Redensarten, Formeln, Sprich-wortartiges, Zitate" laut der „Anweisung zum Gebrauch des Buches") im Wörter-buchartikel unter den Verben und verbalen Ausdrücken. In Sanders kommen sie mal in der Gruppe „Substantiva" (z.b. *Wer andern eine Grube gräbt, fällt selbst hinein* – 502 a), mal unter „Zeitwörter" (z.B. *Eine Hand wäscht die andere* – 111 b) vor.[2] Mit-unter wurden satzwertige feste Verbindungen in Sanders unter einem eigenen Punkt kodifiziert (z.B. 55 f, 377 p, 544 k). In Wehrle/Eggers werden „Sprichwörter und sprichwörtliche Redensarten (...) unter d) an den Schluß der Artikel gestellt" (S. XIV).[3] Eine klare Abtrennung der satzwertigen festen Verbindungen erfolgt in Wehrle/ Eggers auch dadurch, daß sie mit großen Anfangsbuchstaben geschrieben werden. Alle drei untersuchten Wörterbücher haben sowohl einen systematischen als auch einen alphabetischen Teil. Die Aufnahme der Sprichwörter in den alphabetischen Teil der Wörterbücher kann beim Nachschlagen sehr vorteilhaft sein. Wehrle/ Eggers merkt in der „Einführung für den Benutzer" an, daß der alphabetische Teil u.a. als Verzeichnis der Redewendungen zu verwenden ist (S. XV). In Wehrle/Eggers sind Sprichwörter in diesem Teil eingeordnet, „soweit es gelang, ihren Inhalt auf eine knapp andeutende Formel zu verkürzen" (XIII). Aus diesem Grund sind z.B. folgende verkürzte Andeutungen im Wörterbuch zu finden: *gebranntes Kind; grober Klotz; der dümmste Bauer; viele Köche; Sperling in der Hand; Taube auf dem Dach; das Eisen schmieden; ein Häkchen werden; sich früh üben; sich lieben; geschenktem Gaul ...; aus den Augen; wer A sagt; wo Rauch ist ...* Einige Wörterbuchbenutzer haben dabei wohl eine harte Nuß zu knacken. Viele Sprichwörter im systematischen Teil wurden in den alphabetischen Teil nicht aufgenommen (z.B. *Was Hänschen nicht lernt, lernt Hans nimmermehr* (129) – *Der Apfel fällt nicht weit vom Stamm* (11, 167) – *Man soll den Tag nicht vor dem Abend loben* (67, 125) – *Der Krug geht so lange zum Wasser, bis er bricht* (327) – *Wo ein Wille ist, da ist auch ein Weg* (600) – *Morgenstunde hat*

---

[1]   In Roget (1988) konnte ich nur Redewendungen, aber keine Sprichwörter finden.

[2]   Die Buchstaben *a, b, c* usw. markieren hier keine Wortartengruppen. Die mikrostrukturelle Ein-ordnung der WB-Artikel erfolgt hier allerdings in der wortartenspezifischen Reihenfolge Sub-stantive, Verben, Adjektive und Adverbien wie in Wehrle/Eggers. Auf eine ausführliche Dis-kussion der Mikrostruktur der Wörterbücher kann der vorliegende Beitrag nicht eingehen.

[3]   Redewendungen sind nicht immer unter d), sondern gelegentlich unter den anderen Punkten (a), b), c)) eingeordnet.

Gold im Munde (125)), obwohl ähnliche gelungene oder weniger gelungene andeutende Formeln wahrscheinlich auch bei ihnen hätten gefunden werden können. Umgekehrt ist es in Dornseiff, in dem viele Sprichwörter nur im Register vorkommen. Am angegebenen Ort im systematischen Teil werden sie nicht aufgezeichnet (*Eile mit Weile – Gewalt geht vor Recht – Eine Hand wäscht die andere – Lügen haben kurze Beine – Ende gut, alles gut – Gegensätze ziehen sich an – Gesagt, getan – Je eher, je lieber – Ruhe ist die erste Bürgerpflicht – Würde bringt Bürde – Alles hat seine Zeit*). Auch im Register von Dornseiff (z.b. *das dicke Ende; wie du mir*) und im alphabetischen Teil von Sanders (z.b. *bis der Krug bricht etc.; der Geist ist willig, aber etc.; ein Sperling in der Faust etc.*) tauchen einige verkürzte Sprichwortandeutungen auf.

Onomasiologische Wörterbücher leisten dem Nachschlagenden vor allem bei der Textproduktion Hilfe, wie auch der Untertitel von Wehrle/Eggers besagt: „ein Wegweiser zum treffenden Ausdruck". In einer Situation, wo man einen passenden Ausdruck sucht, kann man oft tatsächlich Sprichwörter anwenden. Sie sind jedoch nicht mit Benennungen gleichzusetzen. Statt ein Wort oder eine Redewendung anzuwenden, kann man nicht einfach ein Sprichwort einsetzen. Die Wörterbuchfunktion der Wortfindung (Reichmann 1990:1063) bewährt sich bei Sprichwörtern nicht. Statt „dumm" lassen sich die Redewendungen *ein Brett vor dem Kopf haben; die Weisheit nicht gerade mit Löffeln gegessen haben; nicht alle Tassen im Schrank haben* (Wehrle/Eggers: 499) verwenden – obwohl Redewendungen und Einzellexeme auch nicht ohne weiteres miteinander auszutauschen sind –, aber die Sprichwörter *Die Dummen werden nicht alle – Alter schützt vor Torheit nicht – Der dümmste Bauer hat die dicksten Kartoffeln* (Wehrle/Eggers: 499) beim Begriff „Dummheit" in Wehrle/ Eggers können natürlich das Wort „dumm" keinesfalls ersetzen. Den Inhalt von Redewendungen durch Begriffe zu bestimmen, ist ein nützlicher und vielversprechender Versuch (siehe Kap. 3). Den Sinn von Sprichwörtern durch Leitbegriffe wiederzugeben ist aber ein ziemlich zweifelhaftes Unterfangen (vgl. auch Hose 1993:92).

Die Einordnungen können zwar einige Bedeutungsaspekte hervorheben, aber das allein kann bei der Verwendung wohl sehr wenig helfen. Etwa 14% der in Wehrle/ Eggers aufgenommenen Sprichwörter (26 Sprichwörter) werden bei mehr als einem Begriff kodifiziert. Dabei ragt das Sprichwort *Aus den Augen, aus dem Sinn* hervor, das unter fünf Begriffen vorkommt: *Veränderlichkeit; Abwesenheit; Unsichtbarwerden; Gedankenlosigkeit; Vergessen*. In Dornseiff ist fast der Hälfte der Sprichwörter (45% – 13 Sprichwörter) mehr als ein Begriff zugeordnet. Auch in diesem Wörterbuch folgen dem Sprichwort *Aus den Augen, aus dem Sinn* fünf Begriffe im Register: *Unbeständigkeit; Unterlassen; Nachlässig; Unaufmerksamkeit; Vergessen*. Im systematischen Teil von Dornseiff erscheint es allerdings nur bei dem Begriff *Unbeständigkeit*. Durch die Mehrfachzuordnung kann man den Sinn und die Verwendungssituation eines Sprichworts zwar leichter herausfinden als wenn sie nur unter einem Begriff eingeordnet sind (z.B. *Wer A sagt, muß auch B sagen* (Wehrle/Eggers: *Wirkung*; Dornseiff: *Fortsetzung*); *Lügen haben kurze Beine* (Wehrle/Eggers: *Unwahrheit*; Dornseiff: *Rache*)), aber diese Begriffsauswahl bei einem Sprichwort stellt sich für den Benutzer nur heraus, wenn das Sprichwort im alphabetischen Teil vorhanden ist und wenn der Benutzer es evtl. in der verkürzten Form auch findet. Dabei könnten

Querverweise im systematischen Teil helfen. Bei einigen Wörtern wurde diese Methode in Wehrle/Eggers und in Dornseiff sporadisch angewandt, bei Sprichwörtern jedoch nie.[4] Sanders enthält öfter Verweise auch bei Sprichwörtern (z.B. 472 b (Gefahr): „*Der Krug geht so lange zu Wasser, bis er bricht* (510 b) etc.") Aber von einer konsequenten Anwendung von Querverweisen kann auch hier nicht die Rede sein.[5] Als eine Voraussetzung für den Nachschlageerfolg betrachtet auch Reichmann (1990: 1063) „ein für onomasiologische Wörterbücher spezifisches Verweissystem".

Die schon theoretisch umstrittene Zuordnung von Sprichwörtern zu Begriffen kann praktisch besonders schwierig sein. Einige Sprichwörter sind in Wehrle/Eggers ziemlich trivial, ohne Rücksicht auf ihre analogische Struktur eingeordnet, z.B. *Morgenstunde hat Gold im Munde* (*Tageszeiten*) – *Wo ein Wille ist, da ist auch ein Weg* (*Wille*). Der Grundgedanke von anderen Sprichwörtern wird durch den Begriff besser erfaßt, z.B. *Wenn alte Scheunen brennen, dann brennen sie lichterloh* (*Liebe*) – *Eigenlob stinkt* (*Eitelkeit*). Einige Begriffe, denen Sprichwörter in Wehrle/Eggers zugeordnet werden, können als die (eine mögliche) kommunikative Funktion der jeweiligen Sprichwörter betrachtet werden: Zweifel (485): *Trau, schau, wem – Was ich selber tu, trau ich andern zu – Es ist nicht alles Gold, was glänzt.* Warnung (668): *Durch Schaden wird man klug – Gebranntes Kind scheut das Feuer.* Ratschlag (695): *Guter Rat ist teuer – Wem nicht zu raten ist, dem ist auch nicht zu helfen.* Hoffnung (858): *Hoffnung läßt nicht zuschanden werden – Die Hoffnung grünet immerfort – Hoffen und Harren macht manchen zum Narren.* Wegen der Polyfunktionalität von Sprichwörtern könnten noch zahlreiche andere Sprichwörter bei den angeführten Begriffen angegeben werden, wie auch die zitierten Sprichwörter daneben noch andere Funktionen im Kontext haben können.

Die bei Sprichwörtern angegebenen Begriffe in den verschiedenen Wörterbüchern können einander teilweise oder völlig ergänzen: *Eile mit Weile* (Wehrle/Eggers: Langsamkeit; Vorsicht; Zurückhaltung; Dornseiff: *Langsam; *Vorsicht); *Wie du mir, so ich dir* (Wehrle/Eggers: Vergeltung; Dornseiff: Vergeltung; Vertauschung); *Der Apfel fällt nicht weit vom Stamm* (Wehrle/Eggers: Verwandtschaftsbeziehung; Nachkommenschaft; Dornseiff: *Ähnlich); *Ende gut, alles gut* (Wehrle/Eggers: Ende; Erledigung; Dornseiff: *Vollenden; *Erfolg; *Ehe, Heirat); *Not kennt kein Gebot* (Wehrle/Eggers: Notwendigkeit; Zwangslage; Dornseiff: Rechtfertigung); *Das dicke Ende kommt nach* (Wehrle/Eggers: Nachzeitigkeit; Dornseiff: *Nachteil; Unlust verursachen).[6]

---

[4] Nach den als Ausgangszeichen (als Lemmata) fungierenden Begriffen stehen aber meist Verweisbegriffe in den Wörterbüchern.

[5] Beim erwähnten Sprichwort gibt es z.B. unter *510 b* (Erfolglosigkeit; Mißerfolg; Fiasko) keinen Verweis auf *472 b*. Ähnlich: *Viel Geschrei und wenig Wolle* (377e, 450 c, 618 a). Unter *377e:* keine Verweise. Unter *450 c* Verweise auf *377 e, 618 b* (falscher Verweis!). Unter *618 a* Verweise auf *377 e, 450 c.*

[6] Das Zeichen * weist darauf hin, daß die Zuordnung in Dornseiff nur im alphabetischen Teil erfolgt.

3 Sprichwörter im phraseologischen Synonymwörterbuch von Schemann

Synonymen- und Antonymenwörterbücher werden zu den onomasiologischen Wörterbüchern gerechnet (vgl. Wiegand 1990:2177ff). Kühn/Püschel (1990:2086f) behandeln „Synonymen- und Thesauruslexikographie" in einem Kapitel. In diese Reihe gliedert sich auch das Synonymwörterbuch von Schemann (vgl. Wiegand 1990:2178f). Schemann ist ein onomasiologisches Wörterbuch der deutschen „Redensarten". Nach dem systematischen Teil enthält es – wie allgemeine onomasiologische Wörterbücher – auch einen alphabetischen Teil, in dem die aufgeführten „Redensarten" nach den Schlüsselwörtern alphabetisch geordnet sind.

Den Phraseologiebestand des Deutschen mit Hilfe des onomasiologischen Ansatzes zu ordnen versuchten auch schon Friederich (1966) und Görner (1979). Friederich (1966) enthält keine Sprichwörter, wie auch die zweite Auflage (Friederich 1976). Görner (1979) enthält als erster onomasiologische Angaben, obwohl dies in erster Linie doch ein alphabetisches Wörterbuch ist und die Schlüsselbegriffe kritisiert werden können (Hausmann 1985:107). Teilweise wird auch die Hierarchie bei den Begriffen vermißt (Möhring 1992:130).

Die Gliederung des Bestandes erfolgt im systematischen Teil von Schemann nicht nach den Prinzipien der bekannten onomasiologischen Wörterbücher.[7] Schemann (1989:XXVIII) ließ sich nicht von einem durchgehend einheitlichen Weltbild leiten. Er teilt den Wortschatz in neun „Großfelder" ein. Diese „Großfelder" gliedern sich weiter in „Einzelfelder" und „Unterfelder". Bei diesen Feldern handele es sich um Wortfelder, die „in einem theoretisch strikten Sinne" kritisiert werden können (vgl. Wolski 1993:95). Im Wörterbuch habe ich insgesamt 142 Sprichwörter gezählt. Bei den Sprichwörtern erhebt sich die Frage, wie sie als Mini-Texte (und keine Wortschatzeinheiten) überhaupt in ein Wortfeldsystem passen können. Obwohl „unter onomasiologischem Aspekt keine strenge Grenze zwischen Lexik und Phraseologie zu ziehen ist" (Piirainen 1990:216), gilt dies wohl für die Sprichwörter nicht.

Die meisten Sprichwörter kommen im Großfeld „Stellung zur Welt", die wenigsten im Großfeld „Leben - Tod" vor. Bei einigen (nicht wenigen) Einzelfeldern sind keine Sprichwörter zu finden. Vergleicht man die Zuordnung von einigen Sprichwörtern in Schemann mit ihrer Zuordnung in allgemeinen onomasiologischen Wörterbüchern, kann man sehen, daß neben Ähnlichkeiten auch manche Unterschiede zu beobachten sind. *Kommt Zeit, kommt Rat* wurde z.B. in Schemann (1989) und in Wehrle/Eggers (1993) ähnlich eingeordnet. Ein Unterschied liegt jedoch z.B. beim Sprichwort *Lieber einen Spatz/(einen Spatzen/ den Spatzen) in der Hand als eine/(die) Taube auf dem Dach*[8] in den Wörterbüchern vor. In Schemann (Gb 3): „Kritische Lage • Gefahr • Auseinandersetzung – Haltung in der Gefahr – vorsichtig; sicher ist sicher". In

---

[7] Schemann (1989:XXXIff.) vergleicht allerdings sein Wortfeldsystem mit dem von Roget, Sanders und Casares (Julio Casares: Diccionario Idéologico de la Lengua Espanola, Barcelona (G. Gili) 1959).

[8] In Wehrle/Eggers in der Form *Ein Sperling in der Hand ist besser als zwei Tauben auf dem Dach.* In Sanders: *Ein Sperling (Vogel) in der Hand (Faust) ist besser als zehn (als eine Taube, ein Kranich) auf dem Dach.*

Wehrle/Eggers (777): „Gebiet des Wollens – Besitzverhältnisse – Vermögenslage – Inhaberschaft". In Sanders (544k): „Besitz, Eigenthum". Während Schemann die Vorsichtigkeit betont, legen Wehrle/Eggers und Sanders auf den Besitz Wert. *Wie du mir, so ich dir* kommt sowohl in Schemann (Gc 14) als auch in Sanders (502), in Dornseiff (16.80) und in Wehrle/Eggers (718) ins Unterfeld „Vergeltung". *Wie man in den Wald ruft, so schallt es heraus* ist in Wehrle/Eggers in demselben Wortfeld (718). In Schemann ist es jedoch unter „Haltung zu den Mitmenschen – Umgang – gutes Benehmen, Form" (Ea 11). Betont Schemann hier die positive Konnotation, hebt Wehrle/Eggers die negative Haltung hervor. Und beides stimmt, denn dieses Sprichwort kann im Deutschen, so wie *Wie du mir, so ich dir*, sowohl positiv als auch negativ konnotiert sein.

4   Die Synonymität von Sprichwörtern

Die syntaktische Synonymität oder die Synonymität oberhalb der Wort-, Wortschatz-ebene wird im allgemeinen meist abgelehnt. Ebenso kann die Synonymität von Sprichwörtern als inakzeptabel betrachtet werden. Dennoch kann die gemeinsame lexikographische Aufführung von Sprichwörtern mit ähnlichem Sinn als nützlich er-scheinen.

    In Schemann sind die „Redensarten" in den „Unterfeldern" zu „semantischen Blöcken" zusammengefaßt, in denen sich die synonymen oder bedeutungsähnlichen „Redensarten" befinden. Daß die Synonymität ganz unterschiedlich aufgefaßt werden kann, räumt auch Schemann (1989:XXIV) ein. Je nach dem Grad der Bedeutungs-differenzierung stehen zwischen den Blöcken ein- bis vierfache Abstände. „Der ge-ringste, einfache Abstand drückt aus, daß der Bedeutungsunterschied verhältnismäßig gering, der größte, vierfache Abstand, daß er beträchtlich ist." (Schemann 1989:XXV)

    Das Wörterbuch von Schemann ist beim Nachschlagen von synonymen Redewen-dungen gut zu verwenden. Die Sprichwörter können jedoch mit Redewendungen nicht als synonym betrachtet werden. Sprichwörter können höchstens für die Veranschauli-chung der lexikographierten Felder einigermaßen nützlich sein. Um Feststellungen von der Sprichwortsynonymität zu machen, gibt es ziemlich wenige kodifizierte Sprich-wörter im Wörterbuch. Einige Sprichwörter mit ähnlichem Sinn lassen sich in den Unterfeldern doch entdecken.

    Es wird nicht/nichts so heiß gegessen, wie es gekocht wird und *Ein toter Hund beißt nicht mehr* sind in demselben Unterfeld (Gb 7: Formeln der Ermutigung), aber sie sind keine synonymen Sprichwörter. Sie wurden natürlich auch nicht im gleichen semantischen Block aufgeführt (Gb 7.12 bzw. Gb 7.21). *Gleich und gleich gesellt sich gern* und *Bei Nacht sind alle Katzen grau.* (If 1.17 bzw. 1.18) bzw. *Wie der Herr, so's Gescherr/so's Geschirr/so der Knecht* und *Der Apfel fällt nicht weit vom Stamm* (If 2.8 bzw. 2.9) sind zwar nicht im gleichen semantischen Block, aber ihr Sinn ist je-weils sehr ähnlich. *Vorsicht ist besser als Nachsicht!* und *Vorsicht ist die Mutter der Porzellankiste!* (beides Gb 3.6) bzw. *Gut Ding will Weile haben* und *Kommt Zeit, kommt Rat* (beides Aa 10.8) sind in der Einteilung von Schemann jeweils in demselben „semantischen Block", also eigentlich synonym.

Auch in Wehrle/Eggers (z.b. unter *Dummheit* (499), *Vergeltung* (718)) und in Sanders (z.b. unter *Besitz; Eigenthum* (544), *Geld; Geldbeziehungen* (559)) sind bei einigen Begriffen mehrere Sprichwörter aufgeführt. Dies bedeutet hier meist nicht, daß diese Sprichwörter synonym wären. Als Sprichwortauswahl zu einer bestimmten Thematik können sie allerdings verwendet werden.

5   Zusammenfassung

Nach einer Auffassung seien Sprichwörter keine Wortschatzeinheiten, sondern sie bilden eine eigene Textsorte. Anhand dieser Theorie hätten Sprichwörter keinen Platz in den Wörterbüchern, die die Elemente des Wortschatzes in onomasiologischer Gliederung aufführen. Sprichwörter können jedoch zur Peripherie des Wortschatzes gezählt werden. Dementsprechend ist ihre Kodifikation in onomasiologischen Wörterbüchern begründet. Da sie aber im Gegensatz zu Wörtern und Redewendungen keine Nominationseinheiten sind, ist ihre Einordnung in ein Begriffssystem ziemlich problematisch.

Dornseiff und Sanders enthalten verhältnismäßig wenige Sprichwörter (29 bzw. 48 Sprichwörter). In Wehrle/Eggers wurde eine größere Zahl von Sprichwörtern (190 Sprichwörter) aufgenommen. Nicht nur die Zahl der Sprichwörter, sondern auch die aufgenommenen Sprichworteinträge unterscheiden sich in den drei Wörterbüchern in hohem Maße. Die unterschiedliche Zuordnung der Sprichwörter zu den Begriffen zeigt sich auch bei denselben Sprichwörtern in verschiedenen Wörterbüchern. Gewisse Ähnlichkeiten lassen sich jedoch natürlich entdecken.

Die Aufnahme der Sprichwörter im phraseologischen Synonymwörterbuch von Schemann ist leichter einsehbar, da Sprichwörter im weiten Sinne phraseologische Einheiten sind. Sprichwörter werden allerdings in vielen phraseologischen Wörterbüchern ausgeklammert, was sich auch durch die theoretische Abgrenzung der Phraseologie von der Sprichwortforschung begründen läßt. Die Kodifikation von Sprichwörtern in Schemanns Wörterbuch wirft jedoch die gleichen Probleme auf wie in den allgemeinen onomasiologischen Wörterbüchern. Sprichwörter sind in ein Wortfeldsystem – wie Schemann seine Gliederung nennt – kaum einzuordnen, da Wortfelder Wörter und Redewendungen, aber wohl keine Sprichwörter enthalten können. Synonymität zwischen Redewendungen und Sprichwörtern ist unmöglich. Ähnlichkeit und eventuelle Synonymität von Sprichwörtern untereinander ist in Schemanns Wörterbuch zwar vereinzelt zu erkennen, aber Untersuchungen zu Sprichwörtern mit ähnlicher Thematik können viel größere Erfolgsaussichten in speziellen Sprichwort-Wörterbüchern (z.B. Müller-Hegemann/Otto) haben.

6 Literatur

FEILKE, Helmuth (1996): Sprache als soziale Gestalt. Ausdruck, Prägung und die Ordnung der sprachlichen Typik. Frankfurt am Main: Suhrkamp.

FLEISCHER, Wolfgang (1994): Phraseologismus und Sprichwort: lexikalische Einheit und Text. In: Sandig, B. (Hrsg.): Europhras 92. Tendenzen der Phraseologieforschung. Bochum: Brockmeyer (Studien zur Phraseologie und Parömiologie 1), 155-172.

HAUSMANN, Franz Josef (1985): Phraseologische Wörterbücher des Deutschen. In: Sprache und Literatur in Wissenschaft und Unterricht 56, 105-109.

HAUSMANN, F. J.; REICHMANN, O.; WIEGAND, H. E.; ZGUSTA. L. (Hrsg.) (1990): Wörterbücher. Dictionaries. Dictionnaires. Ein internationales Handbuch zur Lexikographie, 2. Teilband. Berlin – New York: de Gruyter.

HOSE, Susanne (1993): Die Systematisierung der sorbischen Sprichwörter für ein Sprichwörterlexikon. In: Letopis 40, 87-96.

KÜHN, Peter; Püschel, Ulrich (1990): Die deutsche Lexikographie von den Brüdern Grimm bis Trübner. In: Hausmann et al.: 2078-2100.

LUTZEIER, Peter Rolf (1996): Aufgaben der Lexikologie. In: Weigand, E.; Hundsnurscher, F. (Hrsg.): Lexical Structures and Language Use. Proceedings of the International Conference on Lexicology and Lexical Semantics. Münster, September 13-15, 1994. Vol. 1. Tübingen: Niemeyer, 119-131.

— (1995): Lexikologie. Ein Arbeitsbuch. Tübingen: Stauffenburg.

MÖHRING, Jörg (1992): Onomasiologische Verfahren in der Phraseologie. In: Földes, Cs. (Hrsg.): Deutsche Phraseologie in Sprachsystem und Sprachverwendung. Wien: Edition Praesens, 125-147.

PIIRAINEN, Elisabeth (1990): Rezension zu Schemann. In: Zeitschrift für Dialektologie und Linguistik 57, 215-217.

REICHMANN, Oskar (1990): Das onomasiologische Wörterbuch: Ein Überblick. In: Hausmann et al.: 1057-1067.

RÖHRICH, Lutz; Mieder, Wolfgang (1977): Sprichwort. Stuttgart: Metzler.

RUEF, Hans (1995): Sprichwort und Sprache. Am Beispiel des Sprichworts im Schweizerdeutschen. Berlin – New York: de Gruyter.

SCHINDLER, Wolfgang (1996): Mehrwortlexik in einer lexikologischen Beschreibung des Deutschen. In: Weigand, E.; Hundsnurscher, F. (Hrsg.): Lexical Structures and Language Use. Proceedings of the International Conference on Lexicology and Lexical Semantics. Münster, September 13-15, 1994. Vol. 2. Tübingen: Niemeyer, 119-128.

— (1993): Phraseologismen und Wortfeldtheorie. In: Lutzeier, P. R. (Hrsg.): Studien zur Wortfeldtheorie. Tübingen: Niemeyer, 87-106.

WIEGAND, Herbert Ernst (1990): Die deutsche Lexikographie der Gegenwart. In: Hausmann et al.: 2100-2246.

WOLSKI, Werner (1993): Zwei neue phraseologische Wörterbücher. In: Der Deutschunterricht 45, 94-96.

Wörterbücher

DORNSEIFF = Dornseiff, Franz (⁶1965/¹1933): Der deutsche Wortschatz nach Sachgruppen. Berlin: de Gruyter.

FRIEDERICH 1966 = Friederich, Wolf (1966): Moderne deutsche Idiomatik. Systematisches Wörterbuch mit Definitionen und Beispielen. München: Hueber.

FRIEDERICH 1976 = Friederich, Wolf (²1976): Moderne deutsche Idiomatik. Alphabetisches Wörterbuch mit Definitionen und Beispielen. München: Hueber.

GÖRNER = Herbert Görner (1979): Redensarten. Kleine Idiomatik der deutschen Sprache. Leipzig: Bibliographisches Institut.

MÜLLER-HEGEMANN/OTTO = Müller-Hegemann, Anneliese; Otto, Luise (1965): Das kleine Sprichwörterbuch. Leipzig: Bibliographisches Institut.

ROGET = Roget's Thesaurus of English Words and Phrases. New Edition prepared by Betty Kirkpatrick. Penguin Books 1988.

SANDERS = Sanders, Daniel (1985): Deutscher Sprachschatz geordnet nach Begriffen zur leichten Auffindung und Auswahl des passenden Ausdrucks. Ein stilistisches Hülfsbuch für jeden Deutsch Schreibenden. Nachdruck der Ausgabe Hamburg 1873-1877. Tübingen: Niemeyer.

SCHEMANN = Schemann, Hans (1989): Synonymwörterbuch der deutschen Redensarten. Unter Mitarbeit von Renate Birkenhauer. Straelen: Straelener Manuskripte Verlag; in unveränderter Fassung erschienen als: PONS Synonymwörterbuch der deutschen Redensarten. Stuttgart: Klett 1992.

WEHRLE/EGGERS = Deutscher Wortschatz (1993). Ein Wegweiser zum treffenden Ausdruck. Von Hugo Wehrle und Hans Eggers (Neubearbeitung d. 1. Aufl. 1961). Stuttgart – Dresden: Klett.

Variantenschreibung – die Hauptcrux/-krux der Orthographie-/Orthografiereform?!

Wilfried Kürschner

1 Bericht zur Lage Anfang September 1999

Vor wenigen Wochen, am 1. August 1999, haben die deutschsprachigen Nachrichten-agenturen die Neuregelung der Rechtschreibung des Deutschen übernommen. Nach ihrer Einführung in Schulen und Ämtern – vorerst mit Ausnahme Schleswig Holsteins – ist die Reform damit gewissermaßen flächendeckend sichtbar geworden, und zwar auch in solchen Presseorganen, die noch im Herbst 1996 anlässlich des Aufstandes der Dichter und Denks[1] geschworen hatten, nie und nimmer umzustellen, wie der „Spiegel", oder sich bis zuletzt als Kampfblatt gegen die Reform hervorgetan hatten, wie die „Frankfurter Allgemeine Zeitung". Sie schließen sich dabei den Konventio-nen und Sonderregelungen an, die von einer Arbeitsgruppe der deutschsprachigen Nachrichtenagenturen ausgearbeitet wurden (NA-1, 1999; NA-2, 1999). Wenn man das Erarbeitete näher betrachtet, kann man nicht anders als mit Lob äußerst zurück-haltend zu sein: Abgesehen davon, dass willentlich in drei großen Punkten von der amtlichen Neuregelung abgewichen wird – dies ist 1. bei den Eigennamenableitungen auf *-sch* vom Typ *Ohmsches† (Ohm'sches*, ohmsches*) Gesetz, Grimmsche† (Grimm'sche*, grimmsche*) Märchen* der Fall, 2. bei der Schreibung von semantisch isolierten Adjektiv-Substantiv-Verbindungen vom Typ *Erste† (erste*) Hilfe, Schwar-zes† (schwarzes*) Brett* und 3. bei der Schreibung von Anredepronomina der 2. Per-son in Briefen *(Du†, du*, Ihr†, ihr*)*[2], wo es jedes Mal beim Alten bleibt-, davon ab-gesehen also ist die der Sachdarstellung beigegebene Wörterliste „Die Rechtschreib-reform in Beispielen" gekennzeichnet von faktischen Irrtümern und Fehlern, die so-wohl die alte wie die neue Rechtschreibung betreffen, und von Inkonsequenzen, die aber zum Teil die Inkonsequenz und Unentschiedenheit bereits der Vorlage, des amt-lichen Regelwerks in seinen beiden Teilen, dem Regelteil und dem Wörterverzeichnis (aW 1996), widerspiegeln. Dies muss den Verantwortlichen selber bewusst geworden sein, denn die ursprünglich ins Internet gehängte Version vom Februar 1999 wurde im Juni 1999 durch eine andere ersetzt, die einen Teil der Fehler der ersten Fassung aus-merzte, dabei aber neue erzeugte. So wurde etwa richtigerweise der Irrtum korrigiert, das Wort *Negligé* sei früher, vor der Reform, mit zwei e am Ende geschrieben worden *(Negligee)*. Jetzt steht dort richtig *Negligé*, aber in der Neu-Spalte heißt es jetzt *Ne-glige*, hinten mit einfachem *e* und ohne Akzent. Dies ist nur ein Beispiel für viele. Zu allem Unglück ist das, was zunächst nur flüchtig und flüssig im Netz hing, auch in Papierform erschienen, und zwar Mitte Juli, kurz vor der Umstellung, in Form einer

---

[1] Vgl. dazu Zabel (1996:388-408).
[2] Das Kreuz kennzeichnet eine nicht mehr gültige Altschreibung, das Gradzeichen eine weiterhin gültige Altschreibung, das Sternchen eine Neuschreibung.

Broschüre mit dem kurz-bündigen Titel „Die Rechtschreibreform". Wieso „zum Unglück"? Man hat die erste Fassung vom Januar/Februar 1999 zugrunde gelegt und nicht die – wenigstens angestrebte – Korrektur vom Juni 1999. So stimmt zwar wieder oder noch die Neuschreibung von *Negligee* (man hat als empfohlene Schreibung die Neuschreibungsvariante mit Doppel-*e* am Ende gewählt zuungunsten der französischen Altschreibungsvariante mit akzentuiertem *é*), dafür stimmt aber, wie gesagt, die Angabe über die Altschreibung nicht.

Vor oder gleichzeitig mit der Liste der Nachrichtenagenturen und besonders um den Umstellungstermin herum sind weitere mehr oder minder umfangreiche Darstellungen und Wörterlisten erschienen. Von diesen „Hausorthografien" sind aufgrund ihres Umfangs zwei ernst zu nehmen: die der „Zeit" von Dieter E. Zimmer und die der „Woche", für deren Redaktion Ulrich Raschke verantwortlich zeichnet. Die der „Woche" war die erste, denn sie stellte ihre Schreibung bereits zum Jahreswechsel 1996/97 um. Diese Hausorthografien haben Gültigkeit nur für eine Zeitung, eine Zeitschrift oder eben für eine Gruppe von Zeitschriften und Zeitungen, die einen großen Teil ihrer Texte von den Nachrichtenagenturen beziehen. Jede Hausorthografie unterscheidet sich von der anderen, sie alle differieren von der amtlichen Regelung und stehen wie diese nicht in Übereinstimmung mit dem Nachfolgewerk des „Buchdruckerdudens" von 1903, das unter dem Titel „Duden: Praxiswörterbuch zur neuen Rechtschreibung" (PWb) erschienen ist, und zwar im Herbst 1998.

2   Variantenschreibung im amtlichen Regelwerk und ihre Verarbeitung in diversen Wörterverzeichnissen

Das Duden-Praxiswörterbuch ist eine Reaktion auf einen wichtigen Zug der Neuregelung der Orthografie: Sie lässt in vermehrtem Maße bei bestimmten Wörtern mehr als eine Schreibweise zu. Variantenschreibung war zwar auch vorher vorhanden, aber jetzt umfasst sie weitere Fälle (und streicht einige wenige alte wie etwa den *Schofför* und den *Tschardasch*). *So* war es schon vor der Reform möglich *Mayonnaise* oder *Majonäse* zu schreiben, *Nougat* oder *Nugat*, *Reineclaude* oder *Reneklode*. Nunmehr kommen, um im Bereich der Speisenbezeichnungen zu bleiben, zu *Chicorée Schikoree* hinzu, zu *Ketchup Ketschup* (*Catchup* muss weichen), zu *Soufflé Soufflee*, zu *Spaghetti Spagetti* und zu *Joghurt Jogurt* (auch hier muss eine alte Variante, *Yoghurt*, weichen). Was für den individuellen Schreiber eine angenehme Erleichterung ist, ist aber nicht immer nur von Vorteil. Denn für viele Berufszweige ist es, wie die Dudenredaktion im Vorwort des Praxiswörterbuchs feststellt, „wichtig, eine möglichst einheitliche Gestaltung von geschriebenen Texten zu bewahren. Wer schreibt oder Geschriebenes überarbeitet, soll sich nicht ständig neu entscheiden müssen, wer liest, soll nicht durch den häufigen Wechsel von Schreibweisen irritiert werden". Hier setzt nun das Praxiswörterbuch an: „Es ist für Zeitungen und Verlage, für Setzereien und Druckereien, für Firmen und Institutionen mit größeren Korrespondenzabteilungen und für alle anderen gedacht, die aus beruflichen oder sonstigen Gründen Empfehlungen für eine einheitliche Schreibung suchen." Somit könne das Praxiswörter-

buch „die oft mühevolle Ausarbeitung einer so genannten ‚Hausorthographie' erspa-
ren oder nützliche Anregungen dafür geben" (S. 5).

Ich glaube nach gründlicher Arbeit mit dem Verzeichnis nicht, dass das Praxiswörterbuch die selbst gesteckten Ziele erreichen kann. Ich beschränke mich bei meiner Kritik auf den Bereich der Erfassung und Darstellung der orthografischen Varianten, also von Wörtern, bei denen einer Lautung zwei, in seltenen Fällen sogar drei
Schreibungen entsprechen. Zum einen sind hierher gehörige Wörter überhaupt nicht
aufgenommen worden. Was die neuen Varianten-Wörter angeht, fällt auf Anhieb das
Fehlen von in der Reformdiskussion so häufig genannten Wörtern wie *Schenke°/
Schänke** und *Chicoreé°/Schikoree** auf. Natürlich fehlt auch *Stendel(wurz)°/Ständel-
(wurz)**. Diesem einen Extrem der Nulleinträge entspricht auf der anderen Seite das
der Doppeleinträge. Hierher gehören Fälle wie *Citrat°/Zitrat°, Nicotin°/Nikotin°* usw.,
wobei allerdings die Schreibungen mit c jeweils als „fachsprachliche" gekennzeichnet
sind, also offenbar in Fachtexten verwendet werden sollen. Ganz gelegentlich tritt
auch der Fall ein, dass eine frühere Variante statt der nunmehr allein gültigen notiert
ist, so etwa bei *Ayatollah†* mit y (statt jetzt nur noch *Ajatollah°*). Auf die Frage, nach
welchem Prinzip unter den Varianten eine Wahl getroffen wird, gehe ich gleich ein.

Das Praxiswörterbuch löst also seine Versprechen nicht ein. Dies ist von seinem
großen Bruder, dem Rechtschreibduden (in Form der 21. Auflage 1996), von vornherein nicht zu erwarten. Hier soll ja gerade der gesamte Wortschatz (in den bekannten Grenzen) mit allen zulässigen Varianten verzeichnet werden. Zwar wäre denkbar,
dass dort jeweils eine Variante zur Erstform oder Vorzugsvariante erklärt wird. Doch
gehen in diese Richtung zeigende Bemühungen in einem Chaos von unterschiedlichen
Auszeichnungs- und Verweisverfahren völlig unter. Dasselbe gilt für die Bertelsmann-
Rechtschreibung, zwar nicht im selben schlimmen Maß wie für den Rechtschreibduden, aber beide Bertelsmann-Versionen, die erste Ausgabe von 1996 mit ihren vielen variierenden Nachdrucken und die Neuausgabe von 1999, sind als Ersatz für ein
konsequentes Vereinheitlichungswörterbuch ungeeignet.[3] Noch viel mehr trifft dies
auf die angesprochenen Journalisten-Verzeichnisse zu, die ja keinerlei Vollständigkeit
bei der Variantenschreibung anstreben, sondern vor allen Dingen exemplarisch die
Fälle aufzählen wollen, in denen es zu Änderungen gegenüber der bisherigen Schreibung kommt, also Fälle wie *behände*, Gämse*, schnäuzen*, im Ganzen*, in Bezug
auf** und was einem so auf Anhieb einfällt. Zwar wird bei den beiden ernst zu
nehmenden, weil genügend umfangreichen Verzeichnissen, dem der „Zeit" und dem
der „Woche", im Falle von Variantenschreibungen jeweils eine zur bevorzugten erklärt, doch geschieht die Auswahl nicht immer nach durchschaubaren und nachvoll-
ziehbaren Grundsätzen. Dabei wäre ein solches Verfahren eigentlich durchaus denkbar. Es könnte folgendermaßen aussehen: Bezugspunkt ist das Wörterverzeichnis der
amtlichen Regelung, also das amtliche Wörterverzeichnis. Dort wird bei Variantenschreibung jeweils festgelegt, ob es sich um gleichgewichtige Varianten handelt oder
ob die Varianten ungleichgewichtig sind. Im letzteren Fall stellt die eine die Hauptform, die andere die Nebenform dar. In den Vereinheitlichungslisten könnte dann je-

---

[3] Vgl. dazu Kürschner (1997).

weils die amtliche Hauptform als Vorzugsvariante erscheinen. Dem stehen aber zwei Schwierigkeiten entgegen, eine handwerklich-zufällige und eine prinzipielle. Handwerklich-zufälliger Natur ist die leider vielfältig zu beobachtende Schlampigkeit der Ausführung des „amtlichen" Wörterverzeichnisses. So funktioniert das Verweisverfahren, aus dem sich Haupt- und Nebenformen ergeben, nicht durchgängig. Prinzipieller Art ist die Zulassung gleich gewichteter Varianten wie bei *Schenke°/Schänke**, *aufwendig°/aufwändig**. Hier könnte jeweils entweder die neu hinzugekommene oder aber gerade umgekehrt die ältere Schreibung zur Erstform erklärt werden, etwa im Sinn der Unterscheidung zwischen progressiver bzw. konservativer Wahl, wie sie in Konverterprogrammen vorgesehen ist. Sie funktioniert aber nur bei neuen Varianten, nicht bei alten gleichberechtigten Variantenschreibungen wie *Blässhuhn°/Blesshuhn°*, *Boutique°/Butike°*, *Maffia°/Mafia°*, *Vandalismus°/Wandalismus°*. Und es funktioniert schon gar nicht in all den vielen Fällen der im amtlichen Wörterverzeichnis nicht aufgenommenen einschlägigen Alt-Variantenwörter wie *glubschen°/glupschen°*, *Carabiniere°/Karabiniere°*, *Panaché°/Panaschee°*.

Bevor ich einen eigenen Lösungsvorschlag vorstelle, möchte ich an einigen Beispielen die desolate Situation, wie sie sich bei Durchsicht der umfangreicheren Vereinheitlichungsglossare ergibt, demonstrieren. Die Beispiele stammen aus den Bereichen Getrennt- und Zusammenschreibung einschließlich Bindestrichschreibung, Groß- und Kleinschreibung, Laut-Buchstaben-Zuordnungen vor allem bei Fremdwörtern. Dabei stehen die Kürzel „aW" für „amtliches Wörterverzeichnis", „NA" für das Verzeichnis der Nachrichtenagenturen („NA-1 „ für die im Januar 1999 ins Internet gehängte und der Broschürenfassung zugrunde gelegte Version, „NA-2" für die Internetversion Juni 1999), „PWb" für das Duden-Praxiswörterbuch, „W" für das Verzeichnis der „Woche", „Z" für Zimmers Verzeichnis der „Zeit". „Hf." und „Nf." stehen für Haupt- bzw. Nebenform im amtlichen Wörterverzeichnis. Die Tilde steht zwischen gleichberechtigten Varianten.

- *von Seiten** (aW, NA, W) ~ *vonseiten** (aW, PWb, Z)
- *Bigband** (aW, PWb, W) auch: *Big Band°* (aW, NA, Z)
- *Shortstory** (aW, W) auch: *Short Story** (aW, PWb, NA, Z)
- *Knock-out** (aW, PWb) auch: *Knockout°* (aW, NA, Z)
- *Know-how°* (aW, PWb, NA, Z) oder: *Knowhow**
- *Betttuch** (aW, PWb, NA, W) oder: *Bett-Tuch** (aW, NA-1, Z)
- *tausende** (aW) ~ *Tausende°* (aW, PWb, W, Z)
- *Bonbonniere°* (Hf. – aW, PWb) ‖ *Bonboniere** (Nf – aW, W)
- *Ordonnanz°* (Hf. – aW, PWb) ‖ *Ordonanz** (Nf.- aW, W)
- *Mayonnaise°* (Nf. – aW, PWb) ‖ *Majonäse°* (Hf. – aW)
- *Portemonnaie°* (Nf – aW, PWb, NA, W, Z) ‖ *Portmonee* (Hf. – aW)*
- *Nougat°* (Nf. – aW, NA) ‖ *Nugat°* (Hf. – aW, PWb)
- *Chicorée°* (Hf. – aW, NA, W, Z) ‖ *Schikoree** (Nf. – aW)
- *Ketchup°* (Nf. – aW, PWb, NA, W, Z) ‖ *Ketschup* (Hf. – aW)*
- *Credo°* (Nf. – aW, PWb) ‖ *Kredo°* (Hf. – aW)
- *Crux°* (aW) ~ *Krux°* (aW, PWb)

- *Geographie°* (Hf. – aW, PWb, NA) ‖ *Geografie** *(Nf.* – aW, W, Z)
- *Pornographie°* (Nf. – aW) ‖ *Pornografie** (Hf. – aW, PWb, NA, W, Z)

Mir fehlt der Platz, im Detail auszuführen, inwieweit innerhalb der einzelnen Listen konsistent verfahren wird oder aber keine Konsistenz festzustellen ist – dass in kaum einem Punkt alle Listen gleich verfahren, zeigt aber schon die flüchtige Betrachtung. Es dürfte auch klar sein, dass dies zu großen Behaltensproblemen führt, selbst wenn man innerhalb einer Liste bleibt. Dauerndes Nachschlagen ist notwendig und hinderlich beim Verfassen eines Textes. In vielen Situationen ist auch kein Nachschlagewerk zur Hand oder ein Nachschlagen nicht opportun, etwa im Unterricht, wenn ein Wort an die Tafel zu schreiben ist. Und es würde voraussetzen, dass man ständig Zugriff auf fünf Bücher oder Broschüren hätte:

- auf das Wörterverzeichnis im amtlichen Regelwerk, wenn man sich etwa vornähme, immer die dort genannte Hauptform zu verwenden (bei gleichberechtigten Varianten ist man allerdings hilfslos),
- auf das Duden-Praxiswörterbuch als das umfangreichste Verzeichnis, das aber nicht vollständig alle Variantenwörter verzeichnet, das nicht immer eindeutig ist, sondern gelegentlich beide Variante zulässt, und das nicht immer konsistent verfährt,
- auf die Liste der Nachrichtenagenturen, die aber in zwei Fassungen vorliegt,
- auf das Verzeichnis der „Woche", das es auch als Heyne-Mini im Handflächenformat gibt – nur sind dort im Gegensatz zur Zeitungsbeilage die von der „Woche" bevorzugten Variantenschreibungen nicht markiert,
- schließlich auf Zimmers „Zeit"-Orthographie, bei der die Zeitungs- und die Broschürenfassung sich geringfügig unterscheiden und der Zeitungsfassung die kumulierte alphabetische Wörterliste zum bequemen Nachschlagen fehlt.

3   (M)ein Lösungsvorschlag

In dieser Situation, die in ihrer ganzen Schärfe eigentlich erst im Sommer 1999 deutlich geworden ist, habe ich die Anlage meiner eigenen Darstellung der Neuregelung der deutschen Rechtschreibung im Gunter Narr Verlag Tübingen („Orthografie 2000") grundlegend geändert. Aus der zunächst geplanten kurzen, aber systematischen Darstellung der Neuerungen mit relativ wenigen Beispielwörtern ist nun ein Verzeichnis geworden, das größere Vollständigkeit im Bereich der Variantenwörter anstrebt und für jeden Einzelfall eine Erstform vorschlägt. Nun könnte man einwenden, dass damit das Chaos nur noch vergrößert würde, wenn jetzt eine sechste Zusammenstellung folgt. Dem soll jedoch nicht so sein, vielmehr folgt meine Variantenwahl einem einfachen und, wie ich glaube, leicht memorierbaren Schema. Dieses Schema umfasst acht Schreibverfahren, die hierarchisch aufeinander bezogen sind:

Zusammenschreibung >
Bindestrichschreibung >
Getrenntschreibung >

Großschreibung >
Kleinschreibung >

Stammschreibung >
Deutschschreibung >
Fremdschreibung

Wie leicht zu erkennen ist, sind das die drei großen Gebiete, auf denen sich unsere Orthografie, was die Domäne der Wortschreibung angeht, vollzieht: Wortgliederung, Wortauszeichnung, Buchstabenschreibung. Auf die andere Domäne, die der Zeichensetzung, gehe ich hier nicht ein. Das Verfahren ist nun folgendes: Bei Variantenwörtern ist zunächst zu entscheiden, welche Verfahren beteiligt sind. Beginnen wir mit dem ersten Beispiel: VONSEITEN kann getrennt oder zusammengeschrieben werden. Unsere Hierarchie gibt der Zusammenschreibung den Vorrang, also heißt es *vonseiten**. So auch bei BIGBAND und SHORTSTORY, wo, wie oben zu sehen, das Praxiswörterbuch und die Nachrichtenagenturen einmal so und einmal so schreiben.

Zusammenschreibung geht auch vor Bindestrichschreibung. Dies hat zur Folge, dass sowohl *Knockout°* als auch *Knowhow** empfohlen werden. Es hat allerdings auch zur Folge, dass *Roomingin**, *Goin** und *Sitin** gewöhnungsbedürftig werden. Nun könnte eingewendet werden, dass die Orthografiereform eigentlich der Getrenntschreibung vor der Zusammenschreibung mit ihren Spezialformen der Bindestrichschreibung und der Schreibung mit Apostroph im Wortinnern den Vorzug gibt. Doch ist dies nicht durchgängig so, ja es kommt sogar zu neuen Zusammenschreibungen wie bei *irgendetwas**, *irgendjemand**, bei *zurzeit** und in anderen Fällen. Bei neuer Getrenntschreibung wie bei *hier zu Lande**, *zu Schanden** *(machen)* oder *zu Tage** *(treten)* steht die alte Zusammenschreibung als gleichberechtigte Variante daneben und stimmt überein mit Fällen wie *zurzeit**, *zustatten° (kommen)*, *zuteil° (werden)*, *zuhanden° (sein)*. Aber es ist zuzugeben, dass unserer Bevorzugung der Zusammenschreibung ein Element von Willkür zu Eigen ist.

Zum zweiten Block: Großschreibung geht vor Kleinschreibung. Diese Festlegung steht in Übereinstimmung mit der Gesamttendenz der Reform, der Großschreibung ein größeres Gewicht gegenüber der Kleinschreibung einzuräumen. Die Zahl der Variantenwörter ist gering. Ein Beispiel ist etwa die alte Großschreibung *Tausende°*, an deren Seite die neue Kleinschreibung *tausende** getreten ist in Übereinstimmung mit der Festlegung, dass Zahlwörter kleingeschrieben werden. Nach unserer Hierarchie wird empfohlen, bei der alten Großschreibung zu bleiben.

Zum dritten Block: Hier ist zuerst einmal der Ausdruck ‚Deutschschreibung' zu erklären. Damit ist eine Schreibung gemeint, die Züge aufweist oder Elemente enthält, die typisch für das Deutsche sind, also beispielsweise die Umlautbuchstaben *ä, ö, ü*, die Verdoppelung von Konsonantenbuchstaben zur Kennzeichnung von Vokalkürze, die Vermeidung des Buchstabens *y*, aber auch des *x* (daher wird *Hachse°* mit der ‚deutschen' Konsonantenhäufung *chs* gegenüber *Haxe°* mit *x* bevorzugt). Die Reihenfolge „Stammschreibung geht vor Deutschschreibung" wird wichtig etwa beim Variantenpaar *Bonboniere** (mit einem *n*) und *Bonbonniere°* (mit zwei *n*). Die (neue) Form mit dem einen *n* erhält den Vorzug, weil es dazu das Wort, den Stamm *Bonbon*, ebenfalls mit einem *n*, gibt. Umgekehrt beim Paar *Ordonanz** (ebenfalls mit einem *n*) und *Ordonnanz°* (zwei *n*). Wegen des Fehlens eines Wortes, eines Stammes *Ordon* wird hier die typisch deutsche Schreibung mit dem doppelten Konsonantenbuchstaben bevorzugt. Das, was hier etwas locker ‚Deutschschreibung' genannt wird, hilft auch bei der Entscheidung zwischen *aufwendig°* mit *e* und *aufwändig** mit *ä*. Die Schreibung mit dem Umlautbuchstaben erhält den Zuschlag. Etwas anders verhält es sich bei der Wahl zwischen *Ständel(wurz)** mit *ä* und *Stendel(wurz)°* mit *e*. Das Ergebnis ist zwar dasselbe – es wird die Schreibung mit *ä* empfohlen –, doch hier gilt der Vorrang der Stammschreibung: *Ständel* (mit *ä*) steht neben *Ständer*.

Die letzte Hierarchieebene stellt der Vorrang der Deutschschreibung vor der Fremdschreibung dar. Damit komme ich auf das Titelwort *Krux* zurück. Das Wort hat gemäß dem amtlichen Wörterverzeichnis zwei gleichberechtigte Varianten, eine, die fremde, mit *c*, eine andere, die deutsche, mit *k*. Letztere wird nach meiner Hierarchie bevorzugt, wie auch etwa bei *Kredo*, das mit *k* und nicht mit *c* geschrieben wird. Hier kann man sich übrigens auch noch einmal von der Inkonsistenz der im amtlichen Wörterverzeichnis getroffenen Festlegungen überzeugen: *Crux°* und *Krux°* sind dort gleich gewichtete Varianten, *Credo°* und *Kredo°* sind nicht gleich gewichtet, vielmehr wird *Credo*, die fremde Schreibung, zur Hauptform erklärt. Nach welchem Prinzip dies geschieht, ist nicht ersichtlich. Interessant ist schließlich noch, dass im Praxiswörterbuch einmal, bei *Credo*, die fremde Schreibung mit *c*, einmal, bei *Krux*, die eindeutschende Schreibung mit *k* empfohlen wird. Auch hier ist ein System schwer zu erkennen. Ich beantworte die Titelfrage also mit einem Ja: Ja, die Variantenschreibung ist die Hauptkrux der Orthografiereform. Aber sie ist in den Griff zu bekommen, wenn man die Auswahl aus den jeweiligen Varianten der entsprechenden Wörter konsistent regelt. Dann braucht der Schreiber nur noch zweierlei zu beachten:

- Bei welchen Wörtern ist Variantenschreibung vorgesehen?
- Und er muss sich an unsere Hierarchie erinnern, vielleicht mithilfe des Merkspruchs

> Zusammenbinden die Getrennten,
> die Großen und Kleinen,
> die stämmigen Deutschen und Fremden![4]

---

[4] Mittlerweile hat sich herausgestellt, dass es wohl doch günstig wäre, in der obersten Hierarchieebene, der der Wortgliederung, eine Ausnahme von der Regel „Zusammenschreibung vor Bindestrichschreibung" vorzusehen. Um Schriftbilder wie *griechischlateinischdeutsches Wörterbuch* oder *angelsächsischanglonormannische Beziehungen zu* vermeiden, ist jetzt vorgesehen, gleichrangige Adjektive mit Bindestrichen zu versehen. Dies hat zur Folge, dass auch für *süß-sauer**, *blau-rot°* usw. Bindestrichschreibung empfohlen wird. Der Merkvers lautet daher jetzt:
Zusammenbinden die Getrennten,
bindet nur die Gleichen –
ihr Großen und Kleinen,
ihr stämmigen Deutschen und Fremden!

4   Literatur

AW (1996) = Deutsche Rechtschreibung. Regeln und Wörterverzeichnis. Text der amtlichen Regelung. Tübingen: Narr. – Zahlreiche Nachdrucke, darunter: Duden-Taschenbücher, Band 28.

BERTELSMANN-RECHTSCHREIBUNG (1996) = Die neue deutsche Rechtschreibung. Verfasst von Ursula Hermann. Völlig neu bearbeitet und erweitert von Lutz Götze. Mit einem Geleitwort von Klaus Heller. Gütersloh: Bertelsmann Lexikon-Verlag. – Neuausgabe 1999 unter dem Titel „Die deutsche Rechtschreibung. […]".

BUCHDRUCKERDUDEN (1903) = Rechtschreibung der Buchdruckereien deutscher Sprache. Auf Anregung und unter Mitwirkung des Deutschen Buchdruckervereins, des Reichsverbandes Österreichischer Buchdruckereibesitzer und des Vereins Schweizerischer Buchdruckereibesitzer herausgegeben vom Bibliographischen Institut, bearbeitet von Konrad Duden. Leipzig: Bibliographisches Institut. – [2] 1907.

KÜRSCHNER, Wilfried (1997): „Entspricht den neuen amtlichen Richtlinien … " – Zur Umsetzung der Orthografiereform in den Rechtschreib-Wörterbüchern von Bertelsmann und Duden (1996). In: Brinkmann, Th. et al. (Hrsg.): Vergleichende germanische Philologie und Skandinavistik. Festschrift für Otmar Werner. Tübingen: Niemeyer, 173-192.

NA-1 (1999) = Arbeitsgruppe der deutschsprachigen Nachrichtenagenturen: Beschluß zur Umsetzung der Rechtschreibreform [datiert: 1999-01-14], ca. 5 S.; dpa: Die Rechtschreibreform in Beispielen [datiert: 1999-02-08], ca. 22 S. 1999-06-01 <http://www.dpa.de/home1.html>. – Diese Texte sind Grundlage der Broschüre „Die Rechtschreibreform. Der Leitfaden für Journalisten. Gemeinsam erarbeitet von den Nachrichtenagenturen AFP, AP, dpa […]". Freilassing: Oberauer, 1999 [1999-06].

NA-2 (1999) = Arbeitsgruppe der deutschsprachigen Nachrichtenagenturen: Beschluß zur Umsetzung der Rechtschreibreform. (Mit ergänzendem Hinweis zur Einführung ab 31. Juli 1999) [datiert: 1999-06-21], ca. 7 S.; dpa: Die Rechtschreibreform in Beispielen […] Stand: 21.6.1999 [datiert: 1999-06-17], ca. 22 S.; Arbeitsgruppe der deutschsprachigen Nachrichtenagenturen: Rechtschreibreform: Feste Adjektiv-Substantiv-Fügungen, ca. 2 S.; Arbeitsgruppe der deutschsprachigen Nachrichtenagenturen: Rechtschreibreform: Feste Wendungen, Getrennt- und Zusammenschreibung, ca. 4 S. [beide datiert: 1999-06-21]. 1999-06-28 <http://www.dpa.de/info/rechtschr/rs_index.htm>.

PWB (1998) = Duden. Praxiswörterbuch zur neuen Rechtschreibung. Herausgegeben und bearbeitet von der Dudenredaktion. Mannheim: Dudenverlag.

RECHTSCHREIBDUDEN ([21] 1996) = Duden. Rechtschreibung der deutschen Sprache. 21., völlig neu bearbeitete und erweiterte Auflage. Hrsg. von der Dudenredaktion. Auf der Grundlage der neuen amtlichen Rechtschreibregeln. Mannheim: Dudenverlag.

W (1996) = Die Woche extra. Die neue Rechtschreibung. Redaktion: Ulrich Raschke. Beilage zu „Die Woche", Nr. 52, 1996-12-20, 4 S. – Auch als „Heyne MINI Nr. 33/1351" unter dem Titel: „Die neue Rechtschreibung. Die wichtigen neuen Regeln. Originalausgabe". München: Heyne, 1996. [Ohne Kennzeichnung der von der „Woche" bevorzugten Schreibungen]

Z (1999) = Neue Rechtschreibung in der ZEIT. Zusammengestellt und erläutert, kritisiert und vorsichtig repariert von Dieter E. Zimmer. In: Die Zeit, Nr. 24, 1999-06-10, 37-42. – Leicht redigiert auch als „ZEIT-Dokument 1/1999". Hamburg: Zeitverlag, 1999.

ZABEL, Hermann (1996): Keine Wüteriche am Werk. Berichte und Dokumente zur Neuregelung der deutschen Rechtschreibung. Hagen: Padligur.

Lexikographische Darstellung von Nomen aus dem Sachgebiet der Psyche

Željka Matulina, Josip Kolega

1 Einleitung

Gegenstand des vorliegenden Beitrags ist die lexikographische Darstellung deutscher Substantive, die auf das Sachgebiet des psychischen Lebens des Menschen referieren. Es wurden folgende Substantive berücksichtigt: *die Ambition, die Angst, der Ärger, die Begeisterung, der Eifer, die Eifersucht, die Enttäuschung, das Entzücken, die Freude, die Furcht, der Haß, die Hoffnung, der Kummer, die Langeweile, das Leid, die Liebe, die Überraschung, die Unruhe, die Wut, der Zorn.* Am ausgewählten Belegmaterial wird gezeigt, auf welche Art und Weise dieses Sach- und lexikalische Feld in der Makro- und Mikrostruktur verschiedenartiger Wörterbücher, die an kroatischen Schulen und Universitäten im DaF-Unterricht am häufigsten verwendet werden, präsentiert werden. Es handelt sich dabei sowohl um deutsche einsprachige als auch um deutschkroatische zweisprachige Wörterbücher (siehe Literaturverzeichnis). Bei der Analyse des hier erwähnten lexikographischen Materials sind wir von folgenden Fragen ausgegangen:

1) Sind alle zwanzig Substantive in die Makrostruktur der obengenannten Wörterbücher aufgenommen?
2) Wie sind die jeweiligen Mikrostrukturen in diesen Wörterbüchern aufgebaut?
3) Durch welche lexikographischen Mittel werden die morphologischen und die semantischen Eigenschaften der genannten Substantive beschrieben?

Aufgrund von in diesen Wörterbüchern inventarisierten lexikalischen Einheiten einerseits und in den jeweiligen Wörterbuchartikeln vorhandenen oder nicht-vorhandenen expliziten metasprachlichen Angaben andererseits hat sich eine Typologie lexikographischer Mittel ergeben, die uns als ein Kriterium für die Evaluierung der Wörterbücher und für die Bewertung ihrer Benutzerfreundlichkeit diente.

2 Makrostruktur

Im Deutschunterricht sind an den Schulen und Universitäten Kroatiens hauptsächlich die einsprachigen Wörterbücher von Duden, Langenscheidt und Wahrig und die zweisprachigen Wörterbücher von Hurm, Šamšalović und Medić/Bosner vorgesehen. Es handelt sich um Wörterbücher unterschiedlichen Umfangs und unterschiedlicher Ausstattung. Das umfangreichste unter ihnen, das *Universalwörterbuch A-Z* von Duden, enthält ca. 50.000 Einträge und das *Großwörterbuch Deutsch als Fremdsprache* von Langenscheidt ca. 40.000 Einträge. Wahrigs *Wörterbuch der deutschen Sprache* (dtv) zählt mit seinen ca. 16.000 Einträgen zu den kleinen Wörterbüchern, gilt jedoch auf der anderen Seite als Vorbild für den Aufbau der Wörterbuchartikel. Die größten zweisprachigen deutsch-kroatischen Wörterbücher sind Šamšalović mit ca. 70.000 Einträgen und Hurm mit ca. 50.000 Einträgen. Das Schulwörterbuch von Medić/Bosner enthält nur ca. 2.500 Einträge und ist somit das kleinste unter den zweisprachigen Wörterbüchern.

Die hier berücksichtigten Wörterbücher inventarisieren den deutschen gegenwärtigen standardsprachlichen Wortschatz und wenden sich an alle, die Deutsch erlernen wollen und „ihre Kenntnisse im Schreiben, Lesen, Sprechen und Hören deutscher Texte vertiefen und erweitern wollen" (*Großwörterbuch DaF*: VII). Sie geben Hinweise zu Rechtschreibung, Grammatik und Bedeutung eines Wortes sowie Beispiele zu seinem richtigen Gebrauch. In diesem Sinne sind die genannten Wörterbücher als ‚Lernwörterbücher' zu bezeichnen.

Dabei wird zwischen den ‚erklärenden' Wörterbüchern (einsprachige Wörterbücher) und den ‚übersetzenden' Wörterbüchern (zweisprachige Wörterbücher) unterschieden.

Bei der Analyse der lexikographischen Mikrostruktur in den obengenannten sechs Wörterbüchern sind wir von der Annahme ausgegangen, daß in einem benutzerfreundlichen Wörterbuch jeder Wörterbuchartikel dreigliedrig ist: im ersten Teil des Wörterbuchartikels werden die morphologisch-grammatischen Eigenschaften des Lemmas gegeben; es folgt darauf im zweiten Teil des Wörterbuchartikels die semantische Explikation des Lemmas (so in einsprachigen Wörterbüchern), bzw. es werden Übersetzungsäquivalente in der Zielsprache angeboten (so in zweisprachigen Wörterbüchern). Im dritten Teil des Wörterbuchartikels werden anhand von Beispielen die Regeln zum Gebrauch des Lemmas veranschaulicht. Hier sind auch Angaben zum Stil zu finden, d.h. alle relevanten Informationen über die möglichen diachronischen, diatopischen und diastratischen Besonderheiten des Lemmas. In Tabelle 1 sehen wir, wie dieser theoretische Ansatz in die konkreten lexikographischen Werke umgesetzt ist.

	Einsprachige Wörterbücher			Zweisprachige Wörterbücher			insgesamt
	Duden	Langensch.	Wahrig	Hurm	Šamšal.	Medić/Bosner	
dreigliedrige Mikrostruktur	20	18	17	13	13	5	85
zweigliedrige Mikrostruktur	0	1	0	7	7	3	18
nicht inventarisiert	0	1	3	0	0	12	16
insgesamt	20	19	7	20	19	8	

Tabelle 1: Integration von Korpuseinheiten in die Makro- und Mikrostruktur der einzelnen Wörterbücher

Die meisten Wörterbuchartikel in den einsprachigen Wörterbüchern weisen eine dreiteilige Struktur auf. In der Makrostruktur des Wörterbuchs von Wahrig fehlen drei Korpuseinheiten und im *Großwörterbuch DaF* fehlt eine Korpuseinheit. In den zweisprachigen Wörterbüchern ist die Integration der Korpuseinheiten in die Makro- bzw. Mikrostruktur von Wörterbuch zu Wörterbuch unterschiedlich. Im Wörterbuch von Hurm stehen dreizehn Lemmata innerhalb einer zweigliedrigen Mikrostruktur, wobei hier die Demonstration des Gebrauchs der jeweiligen Lexikoneinheit ausgeblieben ist. Bei Šamšalović sind dreizehn Lemmata innerhalb eines dreigliedrigen Wörterbuchartikels zu finden und sieben Lemmata innerhalb eines zweigliedrigen Wörterbuchartikels. Im Wörterbuch von Medić/Bosner sind nur fünf von insgesamt zwanzig Lemmata in einem dreigliedrigen Wörterbuchartikel integriert, drei Lemmata in einem zweigliedrigen Wörterbuchartikel, und die meisten Lemmata (insgesamt zwölf) sind in die Mikrostruktur des Wörterbuchs nicht aufgenommen. Allein diese einfache Statistik ermöglicht uns eine erste Evaluierung der ausgewählten Wörterbücher. Nur Duden lemmatisiert alle zwanzig Substantive aus unserem Korpus, wobei alle in einem dreiteiligen Wörterbuchartikel integriert sind. Auf der entgegengesetzten Seite steht das *Schulwörterbuch* von Medić/Bosner mit nur acht lemmatisierten Substantiven aus dem Korpus, von denen nur fünf in einem dreiteiligen Wörterbuchartikel integriert sind.

Was die Makrostruktur angeht, kann man das einsprachige Wörterbuch von Duden einerseits und das zweisprachige Wörterbuch von Hurm andererseits als die besten qualifizieren.

3 Mikrostruktur

3.1 Grammatische Angaben

Während die morphologischen Besonderheiten der lexikalischen Einheiten aus unserem Korpus im allgemeinen sehr deutlich präsentiert sind (d.h. entweder durch die Anführung des betreffenden bestimmten Artikels zum Lemma oder durch den expliziten metasprachlichen Hinweis ‚Femininum‘, ‚Maskulinum‘ oder ‚Neutrum‘), ist die lexikographische Darstellung des ‚Numerus‘ ziemlich problematisch, vor allem bei den polysemen lexikalischen Einheiten. Die meisten Substantive aus unserem lexikalischen Feld gehören in die morphologische Klasse der ‚Singulariatantum‘, weshalb sie keine Pluralform haben. Ausnahmen sind das Substantiv *die Angst*, das in der Bedeutung ‚seelische Empfindung‘ beide Numerusformen hat, und das Substantiv *die Ambition*, das zwar beide Numerusformen hat, aber im Bereich des ‚Seelischen‘ doch meist in der Pluralform auftritt.

Bei der Evaluierung von Wörterbüchern ging es uns vor allem um die Untersuchung der lexikographischen Mittel, durch die die einzelnen Wörterbücher die Besonderheiten des Numerus darstellen. Es haben sich vier Arten von lexikographischen Techniken herausgestellt:

a) nur explizite metasprachliche Angaben;
b) nur implizite Angaben;
c) explizite und implizite Angaben gleichzeitig und
d) keine Angaben (Nullangaben).

Unter den „expliziten" Angaben sind im grammatischen Teil der jeweiligen Mikrostruktur meist folgende anzutreffen: *ohne Plural* (Duden), *nur Singular* (Langenscheidt) und *unzählbar* (Wahrig). Dazu werden gelegentlich noch andere verwendet: meist Singular, *meist Plural, oft Plural* in Langenscheidt und *meist Singular, Plural selten* in Duden.

Als eine „implizite" grammatische Angabe bezeichnen wir das meistens gleich nach dem Lemma angegebene Flexionsmorphem oder die graphischen Zeichen, unter denen der vertikale Strich (-) am häufigsten verwendet wird.

Als Beispiel für nur explizite Mittel sei der grammatische Teil des Wörterbuchartikels die *Unruhe* aus dem *Universalwörterbuch* angeführt: *Unruhe, die; 4 /o.Pl./*. Als Beispiel für implizite Mittel können wir den grammatischen Teil des Wörterbuchartikels der Zorn aus dem *Universalwörterbuch* anführen: *Zorn, der; -(e)s*. In demselben Wörterbuchartikel findet man auch eine Nullangabe; die Stelle des möglichen Pluralmorphems ist leer – dem Benutzer des Wörterbuchs wird weder ein expliziter noch ein impliziter Hinweis auf die Abwesenheit des Plurals gegeben. Noch verwirrender für den Benutzer des Wörterbuchs ist das Fehlen irgendeiner morphologischen Angabe beim Lemma, wie dies z.B. im Wörterbuchartikel *die Unruhe* in Wahrig der Fall ist: *Unruhe (f.) 1. ∅*. Durch die hier vorgestellten vier Methoden der lexikographischen Darstellung von morphologischen Eigenschaften der Substantive aus unserem Korpus haben wir ein weiteres Kriterium zur Bewertung von Wörterbüchern gewonnen. Die Ergebnisse der Analyse sind den Tabellen 2a und 2b zu entnehmen.

	Duden Universal-wörterbuch	Langenscheidts Großwörterbuch DaF	Wahrig Wörterbuch (dtv)	insgesamt
a) explizite Angaben	Enttäuschung, Eifersucht, Freude, Liebe, Unruhe	Eifersucht, Enttäu-schung, Freude, Haß, Überraschung, Unruhe	Liebe, Überraschung	13
	(5)	(6)	(2)	
b) implizite Angaben	Angst, Ärger, Begeisterung, Eifer, Entzücken, Furcht, Haß, Kummer, Langeweile, Leid, Wut, Zorn	Angst, Hoffnung	Angst, Freude, Hoffnung	17
	(12)	(2)	(3)	
c) explizite u. implizite Angaben	Ambition, Hoffnung, Überraschung	Ambition, Ärger, Begeisterung, Eifer, Entzücken, Furcht, Kummer, Leid, Liebe, Wut, Zorn	Ärger, Begeisterung, Eifer, Eifersucht, Furcht, Haß, Kummer, Langeweile, Leid, Wut, Zorn	25
	(3)	(11)	(11)	
d) keine Angaben			Unruhe	
	(0)	(0)	(1)	1
Insgesamt	20	19	17	56

Tabelle 2a: Darstellung von morphologischen Eigenschaften der Einheiten aus dem lexikalischen Feld ‚menschliches Seelenleben' in einsprachigen Wörterbüchern

	Hurm Njemačko-hrvatski rječnik	Šamšalović Njemačko-hrvatski rječnik	Medić/Bosner Njemačko-hrvatski džepni rječnik	insgesamt
a) explizite Angaben				0
b) implizite Angaben	Ambition, Angst, Ärger, Begeisterung, Eifer, Eifersucht, Enttäuschung, Entzücken, Freude, Furcht, Haß, Hoffnung, Kummer, Langeweile, Leid, Liebe, Überraschung, Unruhe, Wut, Zorn	Ambition, Angst, Ärger, Begeisterung, Eifer, Eifersucht, Enttäuschung, Entzücken, Freude, Furcht, Haß, Hoffnung, Kummer, Leid, Liebe, Überraschung, Unruhe, Wut, Zorn	Angst, Freude, Furcht, Hoffnung, Leid, Liebe, Überraschung, Wut	47
c) explizite u. implizite Angaben				0
d) keine Angaben				0
Insgesamt	20	19	8	47

Tabelle 2b: Darstellung von morphologischen Eigenschaften der Einheiten aus dem lexikalischen Feld ‚menschliches Seelenleben' in zweisprachigen Wörterbüchern

Aus der Untersuchung geht also hervor, daß die meisten Angaben zum Numerus in den einsprachigen Wörterbüchern zu den kombinierten Mitteln gehören, d.h., es werden gleichzeitig explizite und implizite Mittel verwendet. Unter den drei einsprachigen Wörterbüchern macht das *Universalwörterbuch* von Duden am wenigsten von dieser redundanten Methode Gebrauch, während das *Großwörterbuch DaF* und das Wörterbuch von Wahrig gerade dieses lexikographische Mittel bevorzugen. Es hat sich weiter gezeigt, daß das *Großwörterbuch DaF* unter den einsprachigen Wörterbüchern am meisten auch die expliziten metasprachlichen Angaben verwendet und das *Universalwörterbuch* meistens die impliziten Angaben. Die zweisprachigen Wörterbücher verwenden nur implizite Mittel zur Darstellung von grammatischen Eigenschaften der von uns ausgewählten Substantive.

3.2 Semantische Angaben

Bei der Analyse des semantisch-explikativen Teils der lexikographischen Mikrostruktur haben wir uns an folgenden zwei Fragen orientiert:

1) Wird innerhalb der semantischen Explikation auf den Referenzbereich hingewiesen und wenn ja, durch welche Mittel?

2) Findet man innerhalb der Mikrostruktur Angaben zur Intensität bzw. zur Art des jeweiligen psychischen Gefühls?

Um die erste Frage beantworten zu können, haben wir drei Angabentypen berücksichtigt:

a) die expliziten metasprachlichen Angaben;
b) die impliziten Angaben und
c) die gleichzeitige Verwendung von expliziten und impliziten Angaben.

Als eine „explizite" semantische Angabe bezeichnen wir die Nennung des Oberbegriffs (Hyperonyms) zum jeweiligen Substantiv innerhalb der Explikation der Bedeutung (z.b. im Universalwörterbuch: *die Angst = ... undeutliches Gefühl des Bedrohtseins ...*). Als eine „implizite" semantische Angabe bezeichnen wir die Nennung eines Synonyms/Antonyms oder mehrerer Synonyme/Antonyme innerhalb der Explikation (z.b. im *Universalwörterbuch: das Entzücken = Begeisterung, Freude*). Wünschenswert ist das gleichzeitige Auftreten von expliziten und impliziten Hinweisen zur Bedeutung des Lemmas (z.b. im *Großwörterbuch: der Ärger = ein Gefühl starker Unzufriedenheit und leichten Zorns* oder im Wörterbuch von Wahrig: *das Leid = großer Kummer, seelischer Schmerz ...*). Welcher Typ von Angabe wie oft und in welchem Wörterbuch verwendet wird, zeigt Tabelle 3.

	Duden	Langenscheidt	Wahrig	insgesamt
a) explizite Angaben (Oberbegriff)	Gefühl: 5 Zustand: 2 Gemütszustand: 1 Stimmung: 1 seelisch: 1 (10)	Gefühl: 7 psych. Zustand: 1 Zustand: 1 psychisch: 1 seelisch: 1 empfinden: 1 (12)	Gefühl: 5 seelisch: 2 innerlich: 1 (8)	30
b) implizite Angaben (Synonyme und/oder Antonyme)	Synonyme: 10 (10)	Synonyme: 6 (6)	Synonyme: 10 (10)	26
c) explizite u. implizite Angaben	(6)	(13)	(6)	25
insgesamt	26	31	24	81

Tabelle 3: Semantische Hinweise auf den Referenzbereich (gilt nur für einsprachige Wörterbücher)

Die statistischen Angaben in dieser Tabelle zeigen, daß alle drei Typen von lexikographischen Mitteln in allen drei einsprachigen Wörterbüchern Verwendung finden und daß die expliziten Angaben zum Referenzbereich überwiegen. Als Hyperonyme werden meist die Substantive *Gefühl* und *(psychischer) Zustand* verwendet, daneben auch die aus demselben Feld stammenden attributiven Adjektive *psychisch, seelisch* und *innerlich*. Unter den einsprachigen Wörterbüchern nutzt auch hier das Großwörterbuch DaF am häufigsten diese lexikographische Methode. Ebenso oft wird in diesem Wörterbuch die kombinierte Methode verwendet, nämlich die gleichzeitige Anwendung von expliziten und impliziten semantischen Angaben. Bei der Erlernung des Deutschen als Fremdsprache haben kroatische Lerner meist Schwierigkeiten bei der Differenzierung der Intensität und der Qualität der psychischen Gefühle. Deshalb haben sie bei der Produktion von Texten in der Zielsprache Probleme bei der Auswahl des passenden Adjektivs. Diese Schwierigkeiten beruhen auf der unterschiedlichen Auffassung der außersprachlichen Realität und demnach auf intersprachlichen Unterschieden. Liebe kann im Kroatischen „groß" oder „klein", manchmal „schmerzhaft", auch „leidenschaftlich" sein; Haß kann „tief" oder „blind" sein, Unruhe „groß", Enttäuschung „tief" usw.

Anhand des ausgewählten Belegmaterials haben wir geprüft, ob dem Benutzer des Wörterbuches in der jeweiligen Mikrostruktur erforderliche Informationen über die Art des betreffenden psychischen Gefühls angeboten werden und wie. So hat sich herausgestellt, daß das Wörterbuch von Duden nur in neun von insgesamt zwanzig Wörterbuchartikeln solche Angaben zur Verfügung stellt, Wahrig in nur acht Wörterbuchartikeln und das Großwörterbuch DaF in dreizehn Wörterbuchartikeln. In zweisprachigen Wörterbüchern sind keine Hinweise zur Art bzw. Intensität der psychischen Gefühle zu finden, obwohl gerade in diesem Bereich die beiden Sprachen am stärksten differieren.

3 Schlußfolgerung

Es hat sich somit noch einmal bestätigt, daß das Großwörterbuch DaF stets den Benutzer im Auge hat. So können wir dieses Wörterbuch als das benutzerfreundlichste unter den einsprachigen Wörterbüchern bewerten. Die drei zweisprachigen Wörterbücher stehen in der Evaluierungsskala ganz unten, weil in ihnen kein einziger expliziter metasprachlicher Hinweis weder zu den morphologischen Besonderheiten noch zu den semantischen Eigenschaften von Nomen aus dem ausgewählten Sach- und lexikalischen Feld vorhanden ist.

4 Literatur

BRATANIĆ, Maja (1983): Osvrt na englesko-hrvatsku leksikografiju. In: Strani jezici 1–2, 37-46.
DUDEN (1989, 1996): Deutsches Universalwörterbuch A–Z. Mannheim: Dudenverlag.
GLOVACKI-BERNARDI, Zrinjka (1983): Gramatika u njemačko-hrvatskim ili srpskim rječnicima. In: Strani jezici 1-2, 34-36.
HURM, Antun (1958, 1982, 1993): Njemačko-hrvatski rječnik. Zagreb.
LANGENSCHEIDTS GROSSWÖRTERBUCH: Deutsch als Fremdsprache (1993). Berlin – München.
MEDIĆ, Ivo & Irena; BOSNER, Silvija (1992): Njemačko-hrvatski i hrvatsko-njemački džepni rječnik za osnovnu školu. Zagreb: Školska knjiga.
ŠAMŠALOVIĆ, Gustav (1964, 1978, 1995): Njemačko-hrvatski rječnik. Zagreb: Zora.
WAHRIG, Gerhard (1979): Wörterbuch der deutschen Sprache. München: dtv.

Wörterbuchbenutzung in Ungarn
Im Fokus: Wirtschaftsdeutsch und Fachübersetzungen

Judith Muráth

1 Einleitung

Untersuchungsgegenstand der vorliegenden Arbeit ist die Wörterbuchbenutzung von Wirtschaftsstudenten an der JPU Pécs/Ungarn in verschiedenen Wörterbuchbenutzungssituationen.

Obwohl die Wörterbuchbenutzungsforschung in der internationalen, so auch in der deutschen Fachliteratur als ein ziemlich junges Forschungsfeld gilt (Ripfel/Wiegand 1986:492), sind zahlreiche Untersuchungen in diesem Bereich der Lexikographie bekannt. Es handelt sich um empirische Arbeiten, die die Benutzungshandlung mittels verschiedener Verfahren (Befragung, Beobachtung, Test, Experiment und Inhaltsanalyse) aufzudecken versucht haben (Ripfel/Wiegand 1986:492).

In Ungarn zeichnen sich zwar die letzten vier Jahrzehnte durch eine rege lexikographische Tätigkeit aus (vgl. Hessky 1996b:1), doch würdigt Hessky, Leiterin des Wörterbuchprojektes[1] an der ELTE Budapest diese Tätigkeit wie folgt:

> „Insgesamt ist für diese Zeit jedoch eine gewisse Einseitigkeit kennzeichnend, da die lexikographische Theorie mit der Praxis keineswegs Schritt gehalten hat. Vereinzelte Arbeiten (Gáldi 1957; Országh 1966, 1968; Kelemen 1970; Magay 1979) können nicht darüber hinwegtäuschen, daß vor allem auf dem Gebiet der zweisprachigen Lexikographie kaum systematische Forschung betrieben wurde. Es gab auch keine wörterbuchkritischen Arbeiten, geschweige denn empirische Untersuchungen etwa zu Fragen der Wörterbuchbenutzung. Die einzige Ausnahme bildete eine Promotionsarbeit (Gáborján 1983), die auf fehleranalytischer Grundlage konzipiert war ..." (Hessky 1996b:1)

Die obigen Feststellungen zu Fragen der Wörterbuchbenutzung sind nicht nur für die zweisprachige Lexikographie der Allgemeinsprache, sondern auch für die zweisprachige Fachlexikographie gültig. In Ungarn sind keine Forschungsergebnisse bekannt, auf die man in diesem Bereich zurückgreifen könnte. Um überhaupt Kenntnisse zu erwerben, müssen empirische Forschungen durchgeführt werden. In dieser Arbeit soll über einige Ergebnisse einer sehr bescheidenen empirischen Untersuchung kurz referiert werden.

2 Die Erhebung

Im Frühjahr 1999 kam es an der Wirtschaftswissenschaftlichen Fakultät der Janus-Pannonius-Universität Pécs/Ungarn zu einer empirischen Datenerhebung. Die Unter-

---

[1] Es geht um „die gründliche Vorbereitung und Erstellung des deutsch-ungarischen Handwörterbuchs ... als erste Etappe eines größer angelegten Projektes ..." (Hessky 1996:6).

suchungen erfolgten im Bereich der Wirtschaftssprache, folglich beschränken sich alle Feststellungen auf diesen Bereich.

An unserer Fakultät studieren jedes Jahr etwa 400 bis 450 Studierende Deutsch als Fachsprache. Im 4. und 5. Studienjahr belegen etwa je 15 Studierende (in Deutsch) Fachübersetzungen als Nebenfach (Hauptfach: Wirtschaftswissenschaften). Diese Grundgesamtheit bildete den Ausgangspunkt für die Untersuchung.

2.1   Ziel und Hypothese

Zunächst einmal sollten Daten erhoben werden, deren Auswertung zu Kenntnissen darüber führt, wie Ökonomiestudenten Wörterbücher in konkreten Wörterbuchbenutzungssituationen benutzen.

In Kenntnis der Tatsache, daß die allgemeinen zweisprachigen Wörterbücher in Ungarn in vieler Hinsicht „einen überholten Sprachzustand widerspiegeln" (Hessky 1996b:5) und Fachtexte ohne Fachwörterbücher nicht bewältigt werden können, wurde von der Hypothese ausgegangen, daß Studierende unserer Fakultät sowohl einsprachige, d.h. deutsche: Duden, Wahrig und Langenscheidt (EW) als auch zweisprachige, d.h. deutsch-ungarische und ungarisch-deutsche Wörterbücher: Halász Hand- und Großwörterbuch, ev. Langenscheidt Taschenwörterbuch (ZW) und insbesondere zweisprachige deutsch-ungarische und ungarisch-deutsche Fachwörterbücher: Tefner, Hamblock/Wessels/Futász u.a. (FW) zu Rate ziehen würden.

Die parallele Benutzung von mehreren Wörterbüchern wurde von Fachübersetzern vor allem deswegen erwartet, da sie am Anfang ihrer Studien auf verschiedene Hilfsmittel beim Übersetzen aufmerksam gemacht wurden.

2.2   Die Versuchspersonen

Die Erhebung erstreckte sich auf insgesamt 140 Studierende, die sich auf zwei Gruppen aufteilen.

2.2.1 Gruppe 1: Studium der Fachsprache

Die Gruppe 1 bildeten 120 Studierende im 1. bis 5. Studienjahr, die darauf überprüft wurden, wie sie beim Studium der Fachsprache Hilfsmittel, v.a. Wörterbücher benutzten. Sie studierten entweder Landeskunde oder Geschäftsverhandlungen oder aber Geschäftskorrespondenz und Wirtschaftsdeutsch. Ihre Deutschkenntnisse waren als gut bis sehr gut einzuschätzen, viele von ihnen hatten eine Mittelstufen-, manche von ihnen eine Oberstufenprüfung in Deutsch bereits am Gymnasium oder am Anfang des Studiums bestanden, deswegen studierten sie die Fachsprache. Während der fünf Jahre werden in diesem Rahmen alle Fertigkeiten entwickelt: Lese- und Hörverstehen, mündlicher und schriftlicher Ausdruck sowie Übersetzen.

2.2.2 Gruppe 2: Übersetzen von Wirtschaftstexten

Die Versuchspersonen (VP) der Gruppe 2 waren Fachübersetzerstudenten, insgesamt 20 Personen. Sie studierten in zwei kleinen Gruppen, eine Gruppe im 4. und eine andere im 5. Studienjahr. Von ihnen wurde erwartet, daß sie kommunikativ äquivalente Texte produzierten. Vorausgesetzt wurden ausgezeichnete Sprach- und Fachkenntnisse sowie Übersetzungstechniken. Darüber hinaus mußten sie in der speziellen Terminologie eines Fachgebietes bewandert sein. Sie hatten bereits Sprachprüfungen bestanden, die meisten Oberstufe, einige Mittelstufe in Deutsch. Alle hatten Landeskunde, Geschäftsverhandlungen, Geschäftskorrespondenz und Wirtschaftsdeutsch studiert, außerdem noch eine Abschlußprüfung Mittel- oder Oberstufe in Wirtschaftsdeutsch abgelegt. Im 4. und 5. Studienjahr studierten sie Übersetzungstheorie, Übersetzungstechnik, ungarische Sprache und Stilistik sowie Wirtschaftsdeutsch für Fachübersetzer.

2.3 Die Methode

Als Methode wurde die schriftliche Befragung gewählt. Die VP füllten einen Fragebogen aus, der in ungarischer Sprache formuliert wurde.

Der Fragebogen für Wirtschaftsstudenten in der Gruppe 1 enthielt 19 Fragen und bestand aus zwei Frageeinheiten. Es wurde erstens danach gefragt, welche Hilfsmittel, v.a. Wörterbücher, die Studierenden besitzen und wie viele es insgesamt sind, zweitens wurde gefragt, wie häufig und in welchen Situationen Wörterbücher beim Studieren der Fachsprache (im weiteren Wirtschaftsdeutsch) benutzt wurden, sowie was nachgeschlagen wurde.

Der Fragebogen für Wirtschaftsstudenten in der Gruppe 2, die Fachübersetzungen als zweites Fach belegt haben, umfaßte 22 Fragen. Auch sie wurden gebeten, die eigenen Wörterbücher und andere Hilfsmittel aufzulisten. Die zweite Frageeinheit erkundigte sich nach den benutzten Hilfsmitteln v.a. nach den gebrauchten Wörterbüchern beim Übersetzen von Fachtexten (Fachübersetzungen) und auch danach, was nachgefragt wird.

Dabei wurde in beiden Gruppen auf die Rolle der Fachwörterbücher besonderer Wert gelegt. Die VP wurden gebeten, auch Gründe für die Benutzung der jeweiligen Wörterbücher anzugeben.

3 Die Auswertung der Fragebögen

Die Antworten der beiden Gruppen wurden zunächst einmal – voneinander getrennt – statistisch ausgewertet und die Gründe aufgelistet. Es ist leider nicht möglich, über die Ergebnisse eines vollständigen Fragebogens zu berichten. In diesem Bericht möchte ich lediglich über die Auswertung der Antworten auf die Frage *Wie oft benutzen Sie Wörterbücher?* eingehen.

3.1 Gruppe 1 Wirtschaftsdeutsch-Studium

3.1.1 Einsprachige (deutsche) Wörterbücher

Wie in Abbildung 1 veranschaulicht wird, benutzen 20% der Befragten EW, z.b. Duden oder Wahrig, aber auch davon nur 7% regelmäßig, 13% eher selten und die meisten nie. Auffallend war, daß 32% diese Frage nicht beantwortet haben.

3.1.2 Zweisprachige Wörterbücher

Die Frage wurde von jedem beantwortet. Die meisten, 80% der Befragten, benutzen oft ein ZW (Halász), 18% selten und 2% nie. 110 von ihnen (91,6%) besitzen ein Handwörterbuch und 40 Personen (30%) ein großes zweibändiges Wörterbuch, ebenfalls Halász, das sie oft benutzen (Abb. 2).

3.1.3 Fachwörterbücher

Obwohl alle Studierenden Wörterbücher beim Erlernen der Fachsprache zu Rate ziehen, benutzen nur 34% FW und davon auch nur 6% oft, 28% selten, 20% nie.Von 46% der VP wurde die Frage nicht beantwortet. Hier handelt es sich um deutsch-ungarische, ungarisch-deutsche Wörterbücher der Wirtschaft, die in Ungarn herausgegeben worden sind (Abb. 3).

Abb. 1: Die Benutzung von einsprachigen (deutschen) Wörterbüchern

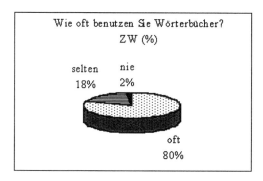

Abb. 2: Die Benutzung von zweisprachigen Wörterbüchern

Abb. 3: Die Benutzung von Fachwörterbüchern

3.2   Gruppe 2 Übersetzen von Fachtexten

3.2.1 Einsprachige (deutsche) Wörterbücher

95% der Befragten benutzen ein EW: Duden, Wahrig oder Langenscheidt, davon 80% oft und 15% selten. 5% allerdings verwenden kein EW (Abb. 4).

3.2.2 Zweisprachige Wörterbücher

Alle ohne Ausnahme besitzen mindestens ein ZW und halten es für angebracht, es auch zu Rate zu ziehen: 80% oft und 20% selten. 17 (85%) der VP besitzen das zweibändige große Wörterbuch (Halász), 14 (70%) ein Handwörterbuch (Abb. 5).

3.2.3 Fachwörterbücher

90% der VP benutzen zwar ein FW bzw. mehrere FW beim Übersetzen, aber nur 30% davon oft und 60% selten. 10% haben die Frage nicht beantwortet (Abb. 6).

Abb. 4: Die Benutzung von einsprachigen (deutschen) Wörterbüchern

Abb. 5: Die Benutzung von zweisprachigen Wörterbüchern

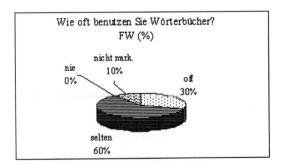

Abb. 6: Die Benutzung von Fachwörterbüchern

4 Vergleich der Daten

4.1 Zweisprachige Wörterbücher

Wenn wir die Wörterbuchbenutzung der Wirtschaftsstudenten mit denen von Fachüber-setzerstudenten vergleichen, kommen wir zum überraschenden Ergebnis, daß die Be-nutzung von ZW in beiden Gruppen eine fast 100%-ige Korrelation aufweist. In bei-den Gruppen benutzen 80% der VP ZW oft, 18% der Gruppe 1 und 20% der Gruppe 2 selten (Abb.7). Die überwiegende Mehrheit bezeichnete das ZW als das wichtigste Wörterbuch.

Die Hauptgründe für die Konsultation von ZW sind:

- die Tradition: die Eltern besitzen eben ZW, oder den VP-n wurden zum Geburts-tag oder zu Weihnachten ZW geschenkt, und diese stehen nun zu Hause zur Verfügung;
- Vertrautheit mit der Strukturierung eines ZW, seine Benutzung wird deswegen als praktisch empfunden, und
- meistens wird das Äquivalent eines Wortes oder einer Wendung gesucht.

4.1.2 Einsprachige (deutsche) Wörterbücher

Der erste große Unterschied wurde beim Gebrauch von EW verifiziert. Ein EW wird in der Gruppe 1 von 7% der VP oft, von 13% selten verwendet, während 80% der VP es entweder nie benutzen oder die Frage außer acht gelassen haben. Das Gegenteil wurde bei der Gruppe 2 beobachtet: genau 80% der VP schlagen im EW bei Fachübersetzungen oft und 15% von ihnen selten nach (Abb. 8).

EW werden als „Begleitwörterbücher" parallel zu ZW benutzt, nur einige Fachüber-setzerstudenten verwenden sie anstelle der ZW als Hauptinformationsquelle.

Gründe gegen die Benutzung von EW waren in der Gruppe 1:

- Verständnisschwierigkeiten bei den Erklärungen;
- da hauptsächlich das Äquivalent gesucht wird, ist das Nachschlagen im EW Zeitverschwendung.

Der Hauptgrund für die Benutzung eines EW in der Gruppe 2 war gerade, was in der Gruppe 1 als Nachteil empfunden wurde: Die Bedeutungserklärungen wurden als großer Vorteil erwähnt. Ein EW wurde oft herangezogen, wenn man sich für ein Äquivalent im ZW nicht entscheiden konnte, oder wenn man sich sicher war, daß kein Äquivalent im ZW vorhanden war. Auch der Kontext im EW erwies sich als hilfreich.

4.1.3 Fachwörterbücher

Bei der Benutzung von FW war ebenfalls ein gravierender Unterschied zwischen den beiden Gruppen feststellbar. FW wurden in der Gruppe 1 von 6% der VP oft, von

28% selten und von 64% entweder nie benutzt, oder die Frage wurde nicht beantwortet. In der Gruppe 2 wurde zwar von 30% der VP behauptet, FW oft und von 60% FW selten benutzt zu haben, wobei nur 10% der VP die Frage nicht beantworteten (Abb. 9), aber auch das kann als sehr bescheidenes Ergebnis betrachtet werden.

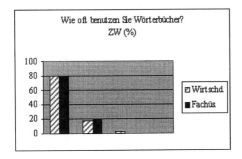

Abb. 7: Die Benutzung von zweisprachigen Wörterbüchern im Vergleich

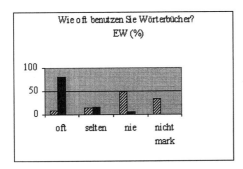

Abb. 8: Die Benutzung von einsprachigen deutschen Wörterbüchern im Vergleich

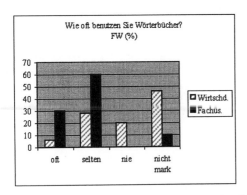

Abb. 9: Die Benutzung von Fachwörterbüchern im Vergleich

5   Schlußbetrachtungen

Zusammenfassend kann zur Wörterbuchbenutzung der beiden Gruppen folgendes gesagt werden: Wirtschaftsstudenten (Gruppe 1 und 2) gleichgültig, ob sie Wirtschaftsdeutsch studieren oder Fachübersetzungen anfertigen, konzentrieren sich beim Re-
cherchieren immer noch zu sehr auf ZW. Diese sind die allmächtigen Wörterbücher,
niemand zweifelt an deren Inhalt. Allerdings gehen Fachübersetzerstudenten (Gruppe
2) sorgfältiger beim Einsatz von Wörterbüchern vor als Studierende der Gruppe 1 und
nutzen eher die zur Verfügung stehenden Möglichkeiten. Sie ziehen darüber hinaus
alle möglichen Hilfsmittel heran. Einige kombinieren EW mit einem deutschen Wirt-
schaftslexikon (Gabler). Sie arbeiten auch mit anderen Medien, benutzen die Möglichkeiten der elektronischen Datenverarbeitung, übersetzen mit dem Computer und
verwenden Informationen aus dem Internet. Bei ihnen fällt vor allem auf, wie selten
sie FW benutzen.
     Der seltene Gebrauch von FW in beiden Gruppen muß auch an deren Mängeln lie-
gen. Die politische Wende von 1989 und der Übergang von der Planwirtschaft zur
Marktwirtschaft hatte zur Folge, daß das damalige Wirtschaftswörterbuch von heute
auf morgen an Aktualität verloren hatte. In der Zwischenzeit wurden in Ungarn mindestens ein Dutzend Wirtschaftswörterbücher herausgebracht, darunter viele, die auf
seriösen Forschungen basieren; Wörterbücher, die alle oder nur einzelne Bereiche der
Wirtschaft (Außenhandel, Bank- und Finanzwesen, Marketing, etc.) betreffen. Es
fehlt aber an Koordinierung und die FW widersprechen sich oft. Außerdem sind sie
meistens Glossare ohne Erklärungen, so bleibt es dem Benutzer überlassen, für welches Äquivalent er sich entscheidet. Auch eine Koordinierung der Terminologiearbeit
in Ungarn wäre angebracht.
     Konsequenzen aus dem oben Gesagten: Erstens sind ZW unerläßliche Hilfsmittel,
können aber FW nicht ersetzen. Das sollte Wirtschaftsstudenten bewußt gemacht werden. Zweitens soll für FW eine geeignete, didaktisierte Form ausgearbeitet werden, und
drittens sollten Arbeiten an FW koordiniert werden.

6   Literatur

HESSKY, Regina (Hrsg.) (1996a): Lexikographie zwischen Theorie und Praxis: das deutsch-ungari-
     sche Wörterbuchprojekt. Tübingen: Niemeyer.
— (1996b): Das neue deutsch-ungarische Handwörterbuch: Projektvorstellung. In: Hessky (1986a):
     5-20.
KÜHN, Peter (1983): Sprachkritik und Wörterbuchbenutzung. In: Wiegand, Herbert Ernst (Hrsg.):
     Studien zur neuhochdeutschen Lexikographie 3. Hildesheim – Zürich – New York: Olms (Ger-
     manistische Linguistik 1-4/1982), 157-177.
RIPFEL, Martha; WIEGAND, Herbert Ernst (1988): Empirische Wörterbuchbenutzungsforschung. Ein
     kritischer Bericht. In: Wiegand, Herbert Ernst (Hrsg.): Studien zur neuhochdeutschen Lexikogra-
     phie VI.2. Hildesheim – New York: Olms (Germanistische Linguistik 87-90/1988), 491-520.

Wörterbücher

Halász, Előd (1988): Magyar-német szótár. Budapest: Akadémia
— (1970): Német-magyar szótár. Budapest: Akadémia
Hamblock/Wessels/Futász (1995): Magyar-német üzleti nagyszótár. Budapest
— (1995): Német-magyar üzleti nagyszótár. Budapest
Tefner, Zoltán (1997): Német-magyar közgazdasági szótár. Budapest: Aula
— (1994): Magyar-német közgazdasági szótár. Budapest: Aula

Adjektive im bilingualen Wörterbuch[*]

Maurice Vliegen

1 Einleitung

In diesem Beitrag möchte ich auf die Behandlung von Adjektiven im bilingualen Wörterbuch eingehen. Diese erscheint mir ihrem Gegenstand nicht angemessen. Ich werde meine Bemerkungen am Beispiel der Adjektive *blij* und *bedroefd* im Niederländischen, *froh* und *traurig* im Deutschen sowie der ‚near synonyms' in beiden Sprachen machen. In Abschnitt 2 werde ich auf die gängige Praxis eingehen, in Abschnitt 3 auf einige allgemeine Bedeutungsaspekte, in Abschnitt 4 auf Synonymie und Antonymie. In diesem Abschnitt werden auch die Bedeutungsrepräsentationen in WordNet und GermaNet besprochen. In Abschnitt 5 behandele ich das von mir untersuchte Korpusmaterial, in Abschnitt 6 schließlich werde ich zusammenfassend einige Empfehlungen vorschlagen. Am Ende des Abschnitts werden diese auf das niederländische Adjektiv *blij* und dessen deutsche Entsprechungen angewendet.

2 Die Praxis

Das hier besprochene Lemma *bedroefd* stammt aus Van Dale Groot woordenboek Nederlands-Duits (Cox 1992:136). Es handelt sich um das zur Zeit beste Niederländisch-Deutsche Wörterbuch.

bedroefd I <bn.> 0.1 [verdrietig] *betrübt, traurig, bekümmert* 1.1 diep ~ *zu Tode betrübt* 6.1 ~zijn om, over iets *betrübt sein wegen einer Sache, über etwas* <4ᵉ nv.>
bedroefd II <bw.> [zeer] *erbärmlich, kümmerlich, jämmerlich* 2.1 een ~ klein beetje *eine erbärmlich kleine Menge, ein kümmerliches Häufchen*

Bei Einträgen von Adjektiven in bilingualen Wörterbüchern wie dem oben genannten fallen einige Aspekte besonders auf:

1) Der Versuch über konstruierte Bedeutungen oder Bedeutungsumschreibungen dem Benutzer behilflich zu sein. Eine Begründung für die einzelnen Bedeutungen findet sich nie. Hier in eckigen Klammern: [verdrietig] und [zeer]. Man bedenke die verschiedentlich gemachte Bemerkung (Miller 1978:102, Warren 1984: 46), dass Lexikographen dazu tendieren, bloß Impliziertes als zusätzliche Bedeutung festzuhalten, statt es dem Kotext zuzuschreiben.
2) Die weiter nicht differenzierte Angabe einer Reihe offenbar gleichberechtigter Übersetzungsäquivalente: *betrübt, traurig, bekümmert* und *erbärmlich, kümmerlich, jämmerlich*.
3) Das fast vollständige Fehlen relevanter ausgangs- und zielsprachlicher Kotexte. Das Fehlen ersterer ist besonders hervorzuheben, da vor allem der muttersprachliche Benutzer nur hier anknüpfen kann.

---

[*] Für hilfreiche Kommentare bedanke ich mich bei Lineke Oppentocht und Willy Martin.

4) Das Fehlen von Informationen zu den syntaktischen Eigenschaften des betreffenden Adjektivs. Im genannten Beispiel finden sich hier nur zwei Angaben in spitzen Klammern: bn.: bijvoeglijk naamwoord (Adjektiv); bw.: bijwoord: (Adverb).

Zum Teil lassen sich diese Unvollkommenheiten auf „Platzgründe" zurückführen. Sieht man sich übrigens die CD-ROM-Ausgabe an (Cox 1997), dann stellt man fest, dass der einzige Unterschied darin besteht, dass die Wortartbezeichnungen jetzt ausgeschrieben werden. Diese Bemerkungen lassen sich alle auf einen Nenner bringen. In diesem traditionellen Verfahren wird die paradigmatische Dimension gegenüber der syntagmatischen bevorzugt (Sinclair 1998:13). Im Folgenden werde ich zu zeigen versuchen, dass Bedeutungsumschreibungen auch aus theoretischer Sicht namentlich bei Adjektiven weniger sinnvoll sind, dass stattdessen eine repräsentative Auflistung ausgangssprachlicher Realisierungen mit deren Übersetzungsäquivalenten unter Angabe der entsprechenden syntaktischen Positionen erwünscht ist.

3   Die Bedeutung von Adjektiven

Adjektive charakterisieren Individuen, Gegenstände usw. Die Tatsache, dass Individuen, Objekte oder Ereignisse Qualitäten in geringerem oder größerem Umfang aufweisen können, macht Adjektive zu inhärent vagen Ausdrücken (Stechow/Wunderlich 1991:660). Die genauere Bedeutung von Adjektiven ist sehr stark von der Bedeutung der Kollokationspartner, meist Nomina aber auch Verben, abhängig, d.h., der Kotext ist entscheidend. Die hier besprochenen Adjektive gehören zur Gruppe der qualifizierenden Adjektive. Weis (1998:156-157) zeigt, dass es sich beim Gebrauch von Adjektiven im Bereich *Freude/Traurigkeit* nicht etwa um die Beschreibung einer Eigenschaft, sondern fast ausschließlich um die Beschreibung eines bestehenden Zustandes handelt. Zu typischen Adjektiven lassen sich bekanntlich antonyme Paare bilden: *richtig - falsch*. Diese Eigenschaft ist bei den hier genannten Adjektiven aber kaum vorhanden (s. weiter unten).

Bei dem Versuch, Adjektive der Bedeutung nach einzuteilen, lassen sich zwei Verfahren beobachten. In dem einen versucht man die Bedeutung wiederzugeben, indem man jedes einzelne Adjektiv mit Synonymen und Antonymen verbindet, wie etwa in WordNet (Gross/Miller:1990), im anderen verwendet man sog. Bedeutungsgruppen (Hundsnurscher/Splett 1982). Eine Mischform findet sich in Rachidi (1989) und der darauf basierenden Beschreibung von Adjektiven im GermaNet (1997, s. http://www. sfs.nphil.uni-tuebingen.de/lsd/Adj.html). Bevor ich auf diese Vorschläge eingehe, möchte ich zunächst einige Bemerkungen zu den wichtigsten Bedeutungsrelationen zwischen Adjektiven machen.

4 Synonymie and Antonymie

Der Begriff Synonymie ist ein schwieriger und vorhandene Definitionen sind meist nicht zufriedenstellend. Cruse (1986:278f) und auch Lyons (1981) unterscheiden mehrere Gradierungen der Synonymie. Eine ausführliche Besprechung an dieser Stelle würde jedoch zu weit führen. Bei Cruse ist ein Lexem eine aus lexikalischen Einheiten bestehende Familie. Cruse legt den Begriff der lexikalischen Einheit zugrunde. Diese setzt sich aus einer Bedeutung (‚sense‘) und einer lexikalischen Form zusammen. Auf dieser Ebene gibt es dann semantische Relationen wie Synonymie und Antonymie. Cruse meidet den Begriff Polysemie, weil dieser die Annahme einer Haupt- oder Grundbedeutung impliziere, die anderen Bedeutungen würden folglich als abgeleitet gelten. Synonyme werden in meinem Beitrag als ‚cognitive synonyms‘ im Sinne von Cruse aufgefasst. Sie weisen kollokationelle (‚co-occurrence‘-Restriktionen auf, die keinen Einfluss auf Wahrheitswerte nehmen. Entsprechende Beispiele aus unserer Sammlung (s. Tafel 1) sind: *froh* und *vergnügt*. In attributiver Verwendung beziehen sich beide auf Personen oder Abstrakta, nur *froh* dagegen auf Konkreta.

Die Definition von Antonymen ist ähnlich problematisch. Hier gibt es viele Gradierungen. Die Standardbeispiele am einen Ende einer imaginären Skala sind die dimensionalen Adjektive wie *kurz* und *lang* oder *dünn* und *dick*. Dimensionale Adjektive haben polaren Charakter. Es heißt *2 Meter lang* und nicht (!) *2 Meter kurz* (! semantisch merkwürdig). Diese Adjektive sind außerdem jeweils von einer impliziten Norm abhängig, *ein kleiner Elefant* ist im Allgemeinen größer als *eine große Mücke*. Relationale Adjektive wie *republikanisch* bilden das andere Ende: Sie haben keine Antonyme, sind also auch nicht polar und haben keinen Bezug zu einer (impliziten) Norm.

Cruse (1986:206) bezeichnet die Adjektive in einem Adjektivpaar wie *froh* und *traurig* als äquipollent. Nach Rachidi (1989:275) handelt es sich um zwei unabhängig protoypisch organisierte aber als Gegensatz aufgefasste komplexe Eigenschaften, die in viel geringerem Maße als etwa dimensionale Adjektive von einer impliziten Vergleichsform abhängig sind. Sie listet folgende Eigenschaften auf:

1) Äquipollente Adjektive sind konträr: *Er ist nicht froh* impliziert nicht *er ist traurig* und umgekehrt.

2) Äquipollente Adjektive sind graduierbar, aber nicht im Bereich von Grenzwerten: *Er ist sehr froh. Er ist ein bisschen traurig.* Nicht aber (!) *Er ist fast froh/traurig.*

3) Die Opposition ist nicht neutralisierbar (!): *Er ist genauso froh wie sie; sie sind beide traurig.* Oder (!): *Er ist froh, aber trauriger als sie.*

4) Der große Unterschied zu Gradadjektiven liegt darin, dass die Bedeutung sich kaum mit einer Paraphrase umschreiben läßt: Ein Gradadjektiv wie *langsam* lässt sich umschreiben als: ‚durch geringe Geschwindigkeit charakterisiert‘, *traurig* dagegen lässt sich so nicht paraphrasieren. Möglich ist allenfalls eine prototypische Umschreibung wie: ‚traurig ist wenn man …‘.

Die üblichen Verfahren, Bedeutungen von Adjektiven über Synonyme und Antonyme zu unterscheiden, greifen bei den hier besprochenen nicht. Dies bedeutet, dass man in diesen Fällen andere Verfahren anwenden muss. Es drängen sich zwei Fragen auf. Die Erste lautet: Welche anderen Möglichkeiten gibt es? Die Zweite: Ist es sinnvoll, innerhalb einer Wortart unterschiedliche Verfahren anzuwenden, bzw. sollte man nicht den Schluss ziehen, dass Synonyme und Antonyme generell nicht als Definitionsmittel taugen?

4.1   WordNet und GermaNet

In WordNet, einem umfangreichen Netzwerk mit Adjektiven, Substantiven und Verben (Gross et al. 1989, Gross und Miller 1990), sind die Bedeutungen prädikativer Adjektive im Englischen mit Hilfe der Synonymie- und der Antonymierelation gespeichert, also entlang der paradigmatischen Dimension. Die Basisstruktur sieht so aus, dass sich die (fast) synonymen Adjektive um die beiden Antonyme gruppieren. Jedes prädikative Adjektiv ist also entweder Glied eines antonymen Paares oder ein ‚near synonym' eines der beiden Antonyme. Die übrigen Adjektive sind also Synonyme der Antonyme. Bedeutungen gliedern sich so in ‚synsets', die aus einem Adjektiv, dessen Antonym und beider Synonymen bestehen.

In WordNet gibt es zwei Klassen von Adjektiven; qualifizierende (‚ascriptive') und relationale (‚nonascriptive'). Relationale Adjektive haben keine Antonyme und werden deshalb mit dem entsprechenden Substantiv versehen: {star | astral, stellar}. Bei jedem Adjektiv werden ebenfalls etwaige syntaktische Beschränkungen angegeben.

In einer kritischen Besprechung gehen Murphy und Andrew (1993) unter anderem auf die von Gross und Miller (1990) gestellte Frage ein, wieso Synonyme oft nicht die gleichen Antonyme haben. Murphy und Andrew weisen darauf hin, dass sich Antonyme nur in einer Dimension auf einer Skala voneinander unterscheiden, nämlich vom neutralen Punkt aus, in die andere Richtung. Dies sei graduell bestimmt. Es gibt also gute und weniger gute Antonyme. *Small* wäre ein gutes, oder gar das perfekte Antonym zu *big*, wenn es nicht *little* gäbe. Sie weisen außerdem darauf hin, dass in ihren eigenen Tests die Versuchspersonen nicht immer auf die ‚richtigen' Synonyme kommen. Oft werden Wörter als Synonym oder Antonym gewählt, weil dies zufälligerweise in der betreffenden Adjektiv-Substantiv-Verbindung der Fall ist. So ist *muscular* nur ein Antonym zu *frail* in Verbindung mit *shoulders*. Dieses Ergebnis legt meiner Meinung nach nahe, dass Wissen und Interesse von Versuchspersonen eher auf der lexikalischen Ebene, eben im Bereich der Kollokationen liegen. Ein weiteres Ergebnis zeigt, dass Wörter als Synonyme betrachtet werden, die eigentlich nur ursächlich zusammenhängen, wie etwa *polluted* und *dirty*. Auch in diesem Fall also ist der Kotext entscheidend.

Im deutschen Pendant GermaNet wird eine solche paradigmatische semantische Gruppierung aufgegeben. Stattdessen findet sich hier wie schon bei den Substantiven und Verben in WordNet eine hierarchische Ordnung. Der Preis dafür ist eine weitere semantische Relation im Bereich der Adjektive, nämlich die der Hyponymie (@):

{*toll*, *gut*, @}. Diese Relation war allerdings in WordNet bei Verba und Nomina ohnehin erforderlich. Es werden 14 Bedeutungsklassen angenommen. Diese stammen aus Hundsnurscher und Splett (1982), werden aber auch in Rachidi (1989) verwendet. Die Adjektive aus unserem Beitrag gehören zur Klasse der ‚mood-related Adjectives‘ und zwar zu den Subklassen ‚Empfindung/Gefühl‘ und ‚Reiz‘. Im Grunde ist das die Aufteilung, die auch schon in Dornseiff (1959) vorhanden ist (Dornseiffs Nummerierung):

11. Fühlen Affekte, Charaktereigenschaften: 9. Lust empfinden; 10. Lust verursachen; 13. Unlust empfinden; 14. Unlust verursachen.

Die Hyponymierelationen in der Klasse äquipollenter Adjektive festlegen zu müssen, scheint mir keine einfache Aufgabe zu sein. Man vergleiche etwa *fröhlich*, *froh*, *lustig* und *munter* (s. weiter unten und Tafel 1).

Justeson und Katz (1995) gehen von ‚lexical co-occurrences‘ aus. Sie benutzen ein Korpus mit 25 Millionen Wörtern. Sie gehen davon aus, dass das Verhältnis zwischen Adjektiven und Substantiven eher semantisch (inhaltsspezifisch, konzeptuell) als lexikalisch (wortspezifisch) ist. Sie wählen solche Sätze aus, worin sowohl das betreffende Adjektiv als auch dessen Antonym vorhanden ist: *Old men saw visions and young men dreamed dreams*. Es gelingt so, fünf Adjektive zu disambiguieren: *hard*, *light*, *old*, *right* und *short*. Justeson und Katz (1995) schließen, dass etwa drei Viertel der Adjektive entweder durch die Verbindungen mit Substantiven oder durch die syntaktischen Konstruktionen disambiguiert werden können. Schon einige wenige semantische Werte von Substantiven in Verbindung mit Antonymen würden bei der Disambiguierung von Adjektiven ausreichen: ‚human‘, ‚concrete‘, ‚body part‘, ‚color‘, ‚abstract‘ (‚text/utterance‘, ‚mental activity‘).

Die Substantive funktionieren als Indikatoren der Adjektivbedeutung. Es erübrigt sich dann ihrer Meinung nach, klassische, konstruierte Wortbedeutungen aufzustellen. Im Grunde handelt es sich um eine Mischung aus paradigmatischer und syntagmatischer Beschreibung. Die große Frage ist allerdings die, ob Sprecher mit solchen semantischen Werten umgehen können. Für semantische Werte wie ‚body part‘ oder ‚color‘ mag dies zutreffen, für ‚mental activity‘ erscheint dies fraglich. Die Ergebnisse in Murphy und Andrew 1993) sind in dieser Hinsicht nicht sehr positiv.

Welche Schlüsse lassen sich aus dem Vorangehenden für die Darstellung im (bilingualen) Wörterbuch ziehen? Im Rest dieses Beitrags hoffe ich, darauf eine Antwort zu formulieren.

5   Das Korpusmaterial

In diesem Beitrag werden die niederländischen Adjektive *blij* und *bedroefd* und deren deutsche Teiläquivalente *froh* und *traurig* besprochen. Es handelt sich dabei um Korpusmaterial aus zwei Korpora. Fürs Niederländische das 38 Millionen Wörter (‚tokens‘) umfassende Korpus des INL in Leiden, ein Korpus mit gemischten, meist schriftlichen Texten. Es wurden allerdings auch vorgelesene Texte aus der Tagesschau für Kinder aufgenommen. Diese Texte bewegen sich an der Grenze zur gesprochenen Standardsprache. Fürs Deutsche wurden einige Korpora des Instituts für deutsche Sprache in Mannheim benutzt. Die betreffenden Adjektive finden sich in den Tafeln 1 und 2.

Insgesamt fanden sich ungefähr 13 000 über beide Sprachen in etwa gleich verteilte Belege. Fast ausschließlich per Hand wurde diese Zahl auf 1900 zurückgebracht. Die Adjektive wurden ausgewählt , nachdem sowohl ein- als auch zweisprachige Wörterbücher zu Rate gezogen waren. Die wichtigste Beschränkung steckte darin, dass diese Adjektive nur insofern berücksichtigt wurden, als sie ‚near synonyms' von *bedroefd* und *blij* sind.

In den Tafeln 1 und 2 sind die untersuchten Adjektive nach semantischem Wert und syntaktischer Position angeordnet. In der ersten Zeile finden sich die syntaktischen Verwendungsmöglichkeiten: attributiv, prädikativ, adverbial (ad), modifizierend (mo) und satzeinleitend (in). Zu dieser Terminologie sind einige Bemerkungen erforderlich. Ich habe mich für folgende pragmatische Lösungen entschieden: Verwendungen mit Kopulae oder (semantisch) kopulaähnlichen Verben bzw. Verben mit Gleichsetzungsakkusativen gelten als prädikativ. Verbindungen mit anderen Verben als adverbial. Es handelt sich hier um ein graduelles Phänomen: Wenn ein besonderer Aspekt des Subjektsreferenten durch das Adjektiv modifiziert wird, erscheint ein semantisch spezifischeres Verb als *sein*: ... *ist schön* (prädikativ), ... *singt schön* (adverbial) (Bickes 1984:96). Der modifizierende Gebrauch von Adjektiven (mo) liegt dann vor, wenn ein solches Ajektiv ein weiteres Adjektiv näher bestimmt: *lustig gestreift*. Der satzeinleitende Gebrauch (in) liegt dann vor, wenn das Adjektiv in Kotexten wie: *es ist ...*, *dass ...* verwendet wird. Weis (1998:172) bezeichnet diesen Gebrauch als den Ausdruck eines ‚kategorischen Urteils'.

In der ersten Zeile findet sich eine grobe Einteilung nach Vorkommenshäufigkeit, in der zweiten finden sich die syntaktischen Positionen, in der dritten Zeile schließlich finden sich die aus Justeson und Katz (1995) übernommenen Begriffe.

Tafel 1	vielfach belegt			spärlich belegt				nicht belegt			
Lemma	attributiv				prädikativ				ad	mo	in
	Person	konkret	abstrakt	Zeit/Ort	Pe	ko	ab	Z/O			
blij											
opgewekt											
uitgelaten											
vrolijk											
freudig											
froh											
fröhlich											
heiter											
lustig											
munter											
unbekümmert											
vergnügt											

Tafel 2	vielfach belegt				spärlich belegt			nicht belegt			
Lemma	attributiv				prädikativ				ad	mo	in
	Person	konkret	abstrakt	Zeit/Ort	pe	co	ab	Z/O			
bedroefd											
droef											
droevig											
treurig											
triest											
triestig											
verdrietig											
bekümmert											
betrüblich											
betrübt											
schwermütig											
traurig											
trist											
trübe											
trübselig											

Im Allgemeinen gibt es keine großen Unterschiede zwischen den Ergebnissen in beiden Sprachen. Bei den Adjektiven in Tafel 1 fällt alllerdings auf, dass es im Deutschen mehr Adjektive gibt. Die Adjektive *fröhlich, heiter, lustig* und *munter* kommen in den gleichen syntaktischen Kotexten mit gleichen semantischen Werten vor. Vor allem hier muss also feiner differenziert werden. Anders gesagt: Es reicht hier nicht aus, ausschließlich nach den semantischen Werten von Substantiven (und Verben) zu unterscheiden, Einbeziehung des kollokationellen Bereichs ist erforderlich.

Der modifizierende Gebrauch ist im Deutschen viel geläufiger als im Niederländischen. Wenn schon im Niederländischen beobachtet, dann mit Konversen von Partizipien: *blij verrast* (*froh überrascht*). Verbindungen vom Typus *heiter nachdenklich* dagegen gibt es nicht (siehe Tafel 3).

Der introduzierende Gebrauch kommt im Niederländischen nur bei Verben der Tafel 2 vor, im Deutschen findet sich nur *lustig* in Tafel 1. Dieses Ergebnis deckt sich mit den Ergebnissen in Weis (1998:172, 176), die besagen, dass die Verben der Tafel 1 bei einer emotionalen Bewertung ein persönliches Verhältnis zum Ausdruck bringen, die Verben der Tafel 2 ein kategorisches Urteil. Die einzige Ausnahme bildet hier *lustig*. Dieses Adjektiv findet sich bei Weis allerdings nicht.

6   Empfehlungen

Wie immer man die Bedeutung von Adjektiven zu repräsentieren versucht, der Kotext spielt die entscheidende Rolle. In einem problematischen Fall wie bei den hier besprochenen äquipollenten Adjektiven bleibt einem sogar nur der Kotext, denn wirkliche Antonyme gibt es nicht und Bedeutungsangaben durch Synonyme sind nicht zuverlässig. Für die Aufnahme von Adjektiven in Wörterbücher heißt dies, dass es weniger sinnvoll erscheint, nach diesem Verfahren Adjektivbedeutungen herzustellen, oder zumindest, dass auch der ausgangssprachliche Kotext eine viel größere Rolle als bisher spielen muss. Dabei wäre es dann auch gleichzeitig möglich, die unterschiedlichen syntaktischen Verwendungsmöglichkeiten der betreffenden Adjektive zu berücksichtigen. Die Konsequenz ist möglicherweise, dass Adjektive aufgrund ihrer Eigenart anders als etwa Nomina oder Verben darzustellen sind. Martin (1988:9) plädiert dafür, lexikalische Wörter anders zu beschreiben als grammatische, und diese dann wieder anders als kollokationelle und pragmatische. Bei diesem Licht besehen handelt es sich bei meinem Vorschlag um eine weitere Differenzierung. Die vorrangige Aufgabe dabei ist nun, repräsentative Kotexte zusammenstellen. In Tafel 3 findet sich der Versuch, dies für das niederländische Adjektiv darzustellen.

Tafel 3	*blij*
attributief: *een blij persoon*; *persoon*: freudig, fröhlich, froh, heiter, lustig, munter, unbekümmert, vergnügt; *dier*: lustig, munter; *gezicht*: freudig, fröhlich, froh; *stemming*: freudig, fröhlich; *bericht, vooruitzicht*: freudig	
predicatief: *de persoon is/wordt blij*; *persoon*: fröhlich, froh, unbekümmert sein; fröhlich, froh werden; *lijken, zich tonen, voelen*: froh scheinen, s. froh fühlen, s. froh zeigen; *maken, stemmen*: jmdn. froh machen, stimmen; *blij over*: froh über(Akk); *blij met*: mit (Dat); *blij dat*: dass	
bijwoordelijk: *de vrienden vertrekken blij*; *lachen, praten, vertrekken*: fröhlich; *feest vieren, kijken, lachen*: froh; *begroeten, dansen, genieten, knikken*: freudig	
modificerend: *blij verrast*: freudig erregt/gerötet; froh überrascht; *blij (maar) weemoedig*: heiter wehmütig	

Das niederländische Adjektiv wird mit seinen Kollokationspartnern aufgelistet. In attributiver Verwendung handelt es sich dabei um Substantive. Wo besonders viele bedeutungsähnliche Kollokationspartner vorkommen, etwa bei Bezeichnungen für Personen, wurde übersichtlichkeitshalber ein stellvertretendes Substantiv gewählt. In prädikativer Verwendung gibt es zwei Kollokationspartner: ein Substantiv und ein Verb. Bei der adverbialen Verwendung handelt es sich beim Kollokationspartner um ein Verb und bei der modifizierenden schließlich um ein Adjektiv/Partizip. Weitere Angaben zur syntaktischen Kombinierbarkeit, etwa zu *dass*-Konstruktionen finden sich jeweils am Ende der betreffenden Gebrauchsweise.

7 Literatur

BICKES, Gerhard (1984): Das Adjektiv im Deutschen. Frankfurt a.M. – Bern: Peter Lang (Europäische Hochschulschriften, Reihe I: Deutsche Sprache und Literatur 774).

COX, Heinz (Hrsg.) (1997): Cd-romversie Van Dale Groot woordenboek Nederlands-Duits en Duits-Nederlands. Utrecht: Van Dale Lexicografie.

— (Hrsg.) (1992): Van Dale Groot woordenboek Nederlands-Duits. Utrecht: Van Dale Lexicografie.

CRUSE, David A. (1986): Lexical Semantics. Cambridge: Cambridge University Press.

DORNSEIFF, Franz (1959): Der deutsche Wortschatz nach Sachgruppen. Berlin: De Gruyter.

GROSS, Derek; FISCHER, Ute; MILLER, George A. (1989): The Organization of Adjectival Meanings. In: Journal of Memory and Language 28, 92-106.

GROSS, Derek; MILLER, Katherine J. (1990): Adjectives in WordNet. In: International Journal of Lexicography 3.4, 265-278.

HUNDSNURSCHER, Franz; SPLETT, Jochen (1982): Semantik der Adjektive des Deutschen. Analyse der semantischen Relationen. Opladen: Westdeutscher Verlag (Nordrhein-Westfalen: Forschungsberichte des Landes Nordrhein-Westfalen 3137: Fachgruppe Geisteswiss.).

JUSTESON, John S.; Katz, Slava M. (1995): Principled Disambiguation: Discriminating Adjective Senses with Modified Nouns. In: Computational Linguistics 21.1, 1-27.

LYONS, John (1981): Language Meaning and Context. Suffolk: Fontana Paperbacks.

MARTIN, Willy (1988): Een kwestie van woorden. Antrittsvorlesung. Amsterdam: Vrije Universiteit Amsterdam.

MILLER, George A. (1978): Semantic relations among words. In: Halle, M. et al. (Hrsg.): Linguistic Theory and Psychologic Reality. Cambridge Massachusetts, 60-117.

MURPHY, Gregory L. & Andrew, Jane M. (1993), The Conceptual Basis of Antonymy and Synonymy in Adjectives. In: Journal of Memory and Language 32, 301-319.

RACHIDI, Renate (1989): Gegensatzrelationen im Bereich deutscher Adjektive (Diss. Erlangen-Nürnberg). Tübingen: Niemeyer (Reihe germanistische Linguistik 98).

SINCLAIR, John (1998): The Lexical Item. In: Weigand, E. (Hg.): Contrastive Lexical Semantics. Amsterdam Studies in the Theory and History of Linguistic Science. Amsterdam: John Benjamins (Series IV: Current Issues in Linguistic Theory 171), 1-24.

STECHOW VON, Arnim; WUNDERLICH, Dieter (Hrsg.) (1991): Semantik. Ein internationales Handbuch der zeitgenössischen Forschung. Berlin – New York: De Gruyter.

WARREN, Beatrice (1984): Classifying Adjectives. Gothenburg: Acta Universitatis Gothoburgensis. (Göteborgs Universitet: Acta Universitatis Gothoburgensis / Gothenburg Studies in English 56).

WEIS, Elisabeth (1998): Der Sinnbereich *Freude/Traurigkeit* im Sprachenpaar Deutsch-Französisch. Eine kontrastive Studie zur Textsemantik. Frankfurt am Main – Bern: Peter Lang (Bonner romanistische Arbeiten 65).

Geschlossene Klassen?

Ulrich Hermann Waßner

1 Einleitung

Bei meiner Beschäftigung mit Konjunktionen bin ich häufig auf die Redeweise gestoßen, diese Wortart – wie auch benachbarte Wortarten – bildeten eine „geschlossene Klasse" oder „closed class" (vgl. etwa Bergenholtz/Schaeder 1977:42, 73, 192; Engel 1977:66; Schachter 1985:4-5 und 23ff; und mit Bezug darauf Brauße 1994:53-57).[1] Explizite Definitionen dieses Terminus sind jedoch äußerst selten[2], selbst in Lexika linguistischer Terminologie.[3] Und noch weniger findet man Reflexionen auf seine Anwendbarkeit in der Sprachbeschreibung.

Eigenartigerweise ist der Urheber dieses Begriffs kaum dingfest zu machen.[4] Zwei Anfragen in der LINGUIST List von 1995, wer die Ausdrücke *open/closed class* geprägt hat, brachten keinerlei Ergebnis (Slobin, prs. Mitteilung). Soweit mir bekannt, kommt einer Lösung am nächsten Klaus, die in ihrer Dissertation (1999) Martinet (1968:124ff, Orig. 1960) als Begriffsschöpfer vorschlägt (prs. Mitteilung). Sasse (1993: 652) weist zwar auf Fries (bereits 1952) hin, jedoch ohne Angabe von Seitenzahlen; eine Nachprüfung hat ergeben, daß bei Fries zwar das inhaltliche Konzept vorhanden ist, anscheinend aber nicht der Terminus.

Daß der Begriff der geschlossenen Klasse für relevant gehalten wird, und zwar auch für allgemeine wissenschaftstheoretische Erwägungen, zeigt sich unter anderem daran, daß mehr als die Hälfte des Eintrags von Norbert Fries zum Lemma *Klasse* im *Metzler Lexikon Sprache* von der Dichotomie geschlossen/offen handelt (vgl. Glück 1993: 308)[5]; hier finden wir auch die Anmerkung „Z.B. handelt es sich bei der Wortklasse der Konjunktionen im D[eu]t[schen] um eine geschlossene K[lasse]". Konjunktionen sollen also prototypische Vertreter dieses Typs von Klassen sein. Diese These soll in diesem Vortrag etwas näher untersucht werden – Bilden Konjunktionen eine ge-

---

[1] Auf das dichotomische Gegenstück *offene Klasse* (*open class*) gehe ich hier aus leicht verständlichen Gründen nicht weiter ein.

[2] Und von diesen raren Definitionen ist eine bezeichnenderweise nicht einmal in der gedruckten Fachliteratur, sondern im Internet zu finden, vgl. http://www.ucl.ac.uk/internet-grammar/glossary/c.htm.

[3] Meist taucht der Begriff nicht einmal als Lemma auf. Selbst in dem umfangreichen Terminologie- und Sachregister der Fachsystematik der Allgemeinen Sprachwissenschaft (Herbermann, Gröschel, Waßner 1997) kommen *offen vs. geschlossen* bzw. *open vs. closed* nur im Kontext der Phonologie (und Phonetik) vor. Als Arten von Wortklassen wären sie – wie auch *Hauptwortarten* und *Nebenwortarten* – etwa den Wortarten (8.2) oder der Lexikologie (10.1.7) zuzuordnen. Solche Nachträge werden in einer überarbeiteten Auflage berücksichtigt werden.

[4] Der *mengentheoretische* Begriff der geschlossenen Menge (was ja oft synonym mit *Klasse* verwendet wird) wurde auf Französisch 1884 von Cantor eingeführt und findet sich im Englischen seit 1902. Er hat aber mit dem linguistischen Begriff praktisch nichts gemein.

[5] Der Terminus kommt hier also nicht als eigener Eintrag, sondern „versteckt" im Rahmen der Erläuterung eines anderen Lemmas vor.

schlossene Klasse? Genereller: Was sind geschlossene Klassen und gibt es welche unter den Wortarten oder in anderen Bereichen der Sprachbeschreibung?

2   Definition von geschlossenen Klassen

Wenn entschieden werden soll, ob es x gibt, ist zuerst zu klären, was unter *x* zu verstehen wäre, d.h. wonach zu suchen ist. Was soll also unter *geschlossenen Klassen* im Kontext der Wortartentheorie verstanden werden? Versucht man, die communis opinio in Worte zu fassen, dürfte man etwa zu folgendem Ergebnis gelangen:[6]

- Geschlossene Klassen sind solche mit einer kleinen Anzahl[7] von Elementen (Kleinheit)[8]. Das ist zwar ein Indiz, aber begrifflich nicht hinreichend für *geschlossen*. Man könnte einfach von *kleinen Klassen* sprechen.

- Wesentlich für Geschlossenheit ist vielmehr darüber hinaus das Kriterium, daß keine neuen Elemente dazukommen können (Unvermehrbarkeit).

Zu dem zweiten Kriterium eine Anmerkung: Man könnte sagen, Unvermehrbarkeit (und damit wesentlich der Begriff der geschlossenen Klasse) sei eine Frage der Diachronie. Eine Entscheidung in dieser Sache hängt davon ab, wie eng oder wie weit man die Periode der Synchronie faßt. Wenn man aber die Ausdehnung der „synchronen" Zeitspanne gegen Null gehen läßt, fallen Satzbildung (Syntax) und Wortbildung (Komposition) aus dem Untersuchungsbereich einer synchronen Linguistik ganz weg. Will man das nicht – und es dürfte eine durchaus unerwünschte Konsequenz sein –, muß über Geschlossenheit oder Offenheit von Klassen auch in der synchronen Linguistik entschieden werden können. Mit einem ganz rigiden Verständnis von Synchronie (als auf einen ausdehnungslosen Zeit*punkt* bezogen) hingegen würde die Dichotomie *geschlossen/offen* überhaupt sinnlos, weil in diesem Sinn sich synchron nichts verändern kann und dürfte, also alle Klassen geschlossen wären. Vermehrbar muß etwas immer in der Zeit sein. Synchron daran ist die Fragestellung, ob die derzeitige Sprache, z.B. das Gegenwartsdeutsch, (produktive) Mechanismen bereitstellt, mittels derer neue Elemente zur Klasse hinzutreten können. In diesem Sinn meine ich also mit *Unvermehrbarkeit* synchrone Unvermehrbarkeit und, daß man *unvermehrbar* so verstehen *muß*.

---

[6]   Vgl.: Closed classes „consist of finite sets of words which can be exhaustively listed, and they do not admit new members", so die oben angesprochene Internet-Definition. „Ist die Menge von Elementen einer K[lasse] synchron nicht erweiterbar, spricht man von einer geschlossenen K., im anderen Fall von einer offenen" (Fries; in Glück 1993:308).

[7]   Das setzt Abzählbarkeit und damit wiederum diskrete, individuelle, gestalthafte – und erst somit zählbare – Elemente voraus. Dieses Merkmal ist bereits im Begriff der *Klasse* (im Gegensatz zum *Typ*) enthalten und wird daher nicht eigens herausgestellt.
      Insbesondere endliche Abzählbarkeit ist im Begriff der Kleinheit ebenfalls enthalten.

[8]   Faktisch scheint 100 als – wenn auch vager – Grenzwert angesehen zu werden, d.h., Klassen mit zweistelliger Mächtigkeit werden als klein betrachtet, solche mit deutlich mehr als einhundert Elementen als groß.

Die beiden genannten Kriterien zusammen führen dazu, daß man ein und für allemal angeben kann, aus wievielen Elementen eine geschlossene Klasse besteht. Dies wird hier und da in Bezug auf Konjunktionen auch tatsächlich gewagt – ich sage „gewagt", da solche Zahlenangaben sicherlich zu den am leichtesten falsifizierbaren wissenschaftlichen Aussagen gehören. Dabei will ich nicht einmal auf die Tatsache rekurrieren, daß natürlich jedes Zählen, jede Zahlenangabe abhängig ist von der Definition der Klasse, deren Elemente zu zählen sind, und nur für eine auf bestimmte Art definierte Menge überhaupt sinnvoll ist.

3   Sind Konjunktionen demnach eine geschlossene Klasse?

Geradezu überwältigend oft werden die Konjunktionen als eine geschlossene Klasse bezeichnet (vgl. etwa Bergenholtz/Schaeder 1977:118; Gasser 1984:47f; Kortmann 1992:429; sowie auch Engel 1977:66). Ist das berechtigt? Deklinieren wir die Bestimmungsfaktoren durch:

Eine Bestimmung der Konjunktionen als *Klasse*, also als Menge mit scharfen Außengrenzen, bestehend aus diskreten Elementen, ist – falls überhaupt möglich – erst noch zu leisten, so daß man schon deshalb zumindest beim derzeitigen Forschungsstand über die Geschlossenheit oder Offenheit der Konjunktionenklasse eigentlich gar nichts Definitives aussagen kann.

Daß Konjunktionen diskrete Elemente sind, dieser Behauptung kann man jedoch mit für die derzeitigen Zwecke hinreichend ruhigem Gewissen zustimmen. Dennoch gibt es gewisse Probleme mit der Ab- bzw. Aufzählbarkeit, wie sie in Bezug auf Worteinheiten weit verbreitet sind. Je nachdem, ob man token-Textwörter, type-Wortformen oder Lexeme zählt, kommt man in dem Satz *Er sah ihn und sah ihn doch nicht* zu drei verschiedenen Ergebnissen. Speziell bei Konjunktionen ergeben sich Probleme bei gewissen Schreibweisen, wenn nämlich gewisse tokens in Listen mit Schrägstrich oder Klammerung zusammengefaßt werden, wie *sowohl ... als/wie (auch), als ob/als wenn/wie wenn, wenn ... ø/dann/so, obwohl/-schon/-zwar/-gleich; (an)statt zu, (an)statt daß; insofern/-weit als, nichtsdestotrotz/-weniger/-minder*. Handelt es sich hier in einem relevanten Sinn je um ein Element mit Varianten oder um zwei oder mehr Elemente, sind sie als eine oder als zwei bzw. mehrere Konjunktionen zu zählen? Zählen, jede Zahlenangabe setzt ein klares Identitätskriterium voraus, wie diese Fälle zeigen. Glücklicherweise aber schwankt der Umfang der präsumtiven Konjunktionenklasse aufgrund dieses Effekts nicht in einem solchen Maß, daß es verhindern würde, zu einer Entscheidung bezüglich „groß" oder „klein" zu kommen.

Sind die Konjunktionen dann von geringer Anzahl? Das hängt natürlich außer von dem in einer Definition zu enthaltenden Identitätskriterium von der allerdings nebensächlichen Frage, was man unter *klein* in diesem Zusammenhang verstehen will. Jedenfalls gibt es im Deutschen und in vergleichbaren Sprachen weit mehr Konjunktionen als man auf den ersten Blick denken mag; ihre Zahl liegt deutlich im dreistelligen

Bereich.[9] Nichtsdestotrotz mag die Einstufung der Klasse als *klein* in Relation zu den sogenannten Hauptwortarten, also als *relativ* klein, durchgehen.

Wer aber exakte Zahlenangaben macht (wie fürs Deutsche Gasser[10]) oder „alle" Konjunktionen einer Sprache aufzählt (wie Engel 1988: vgl. 710 und 739) (beides vgl. Bergenholtz/Schaeder 1977: etwa 121), suggeriert damit Geschlossenheit, und nicht nur im Sinne von Kleinheit, sondern auch von (synchroner) Unvermehrbarkeit.

Dagegen jedoch, daß keine Konjunktionen mehr zu der Klasse stoßen *können*, sprechen diverse Fakten, insbesondere das Vorkommen von innereinzelsprachlichen Neubildungen (produktive Muster der Derivation und Komposition, Wortartwechsel) und Entlehnungen.

Die Konjunktionen wurden und werden faktisch vermehrt.[11] Das kann für die Vergangenheit nachgewiesen werden, man vergleiche nur den Zustand des Alt- und Mittel- mit dem des Neuhochdeutschen (vgl. etwa ...[12]).

Für die Zukunft ist einiges geradezu prognostizierbar,[13] wenn auch die Behauptung, daß sie immer noch jederzeit vermehrbar sind, natürlich Spekulation bleiben muß. Sie kann aber m.E. zumindest als plausibel gelten, schon als Extrapolation aus den genannten Erfahrungen mit der deutschen Sprachgeschichte. Nirgends findet sich ein Grund dafür, warum das irgendwann aufgehört haben sollte, und ich kann mir auch keinen vorstellen; insbesondere wird sicherlich niemand behaupten wollen, daß Geschlossenheit eine neu entstandene Eigenschaft dieser Klassen ist.

Auch in der Gegenwart werden Vermehrungstendenzen sichtbar, Neubildungen bei genauerem Hinsehen beobachtbar. So wird das Substantiv *Ursache* (und werden semantisch verwandte Substantive) in gewissen Zusammenhängen heute auch wie eine Konjunktion verwendet. Einige von vielen gesammelten echtsprachlichen Beispielen seien angeführt:

> „Zumal die Tabelle der Vorrundengruppe derzeit für ihn ‚zweifellos ein falsches Bild vermittelt und unsere Situation in Wirklichkeit viel besser ist.' Der Grund: Nach den gemeinsam

---

[9] Ich habe für das Deutsche ohne große Mühe, einfach durch Vereinigung der Listen der einschlägigen Literatur, also von Fachkollegen als Konjunktionen angebotene Sammlungen von Beispielen oder „vollständigen" Aufzählungen, je nach Zählung der Worteinheiten bis zu über 700 gefunden.

[10] Gasser schreibt: „Pronomina [...] dürfte es 150 geben, [...] Konjunktionen 58" (1984:48) (Die erste Zahl kann man noch als mit einem impliziten „etwa" versehen auffassen, nicht aber die zweite, wenn auch das „dürfte es geben" eine gewisse Vorsicht verrät, die jedoch durch die genaue Zahl konterkariert wird.) Die zweite Zahl resultiert nach Gassers eigener Angabe (48 n13) aus der Zählung der „Listen der Dudengrammatik [...] [³1973], von Helbig/Buscha (1979) [...] und Schulz/Griesbach (1980)". Es ist müßig, das nachzurechnen.

[11] Daß die Tendenz der Sprachentwicklung weg von Asyndesis, hin zu Syndesis verläuft, ist geradezu ein Gemeinplatz.

[12] Die Gesamttendenz der Sprachentwicklung nicht nur des Deutschen zeigt deutlich eine Zunahme der Anzahl der Konjunktionen wie auch der Häufigkeit ihres Gebrauchs. Für viele heute konjunktionenhaltige Sprachen wird sogar behauptet, daß sie ursprünglich gar keine Konjunktionen hatten.

[13] So könnte man annehmen, daß zusätzlich zu der Reihe *obwohl/obzwar/obgleich/obschon* auch analog Bildungen wie *obdóch oder *objá möglich wären (je länger man sie sich vorsagt, desto vertrauter und „normaler" kommen sie einem vor).

vereinbarten Terminen tritt die Türkei am Samstag zum vierten Mal hintereinander zu Hause an, während die Deutschen und Finnen nach ihrem Aufeinandertreffen am Mittwoch je ein Heim- und drei Auswärtsspiele bestritten haben." (*Frankfurter Rundschau*, 24. März 1999: 19)

„Dallinger am Dienstag in einer Rede ...: ‚Wir werden im Jänner eine Arbeitslosenzahl von 150.000 erreichen. Ich stelle zur Diskussion und plädiere dafür, das Konjunkturausgleichsbudget 1982 sofort freizugeben.' Begründung: Man könnte damit die Stimmung in der Wirtschaft insofern verbessern, als die Unternehmer sich ..." (*profil* 4/1982: 17; entnommen aus Ortner (1987), dort auch noch weitere Beispiele.)

„Verärgert zeigt sich die CDU-Ortsunion Gremmendorf. Grund: Im Ortsteil wurde Informationstafeln der Bürgerinitiative ‚Gegen Schulschließungen' überklebt; und zwar mit Plakaten der ‚Elterninitiative Reform Gesamtschule Münster'." (*Westfälische Nachrichten*, 15. November 1996: R MS 1).

Die konjunktionale Funktion des Wortes in diesem Kontext kann etwa durch einen Substitutionstest gezeigt werden: *Begründung* bzw. (*der*) *Grund* (und in anderen Fällen eben auch *Ursache*) ersetzen hier offenkundig von ihrer Funktion her die Konjunktionen *denn* (und gegebenenfalls *weil₂*), die stets an ihrer Stelle möglich wäre, und sind von diesen – sieht man von unseren Gewohnheiten ab, sie einfach als Substantiv anzusehen – kaum klassifikatorisch zu unterscheiden – weder semantisch noch syntaktisch. Dieses Schema scheint mir ein synchrones Beispiel für Neubildung zu sein. Es zeigt ein typisches Muster der Neubildung von Konjunktionen, hier aus Substantiven, zu zeigen (vgl. damit das sprachhistorische Faktum der Ableitung von *weil* aus *die Weile*). Vgl. nur ebenso:

A: ...
B: *Einwand!* ... (Es folgt der Einwand)

Hier scheint i.d.R. Substitution mit *aber* möglich. Ebenso bei *Moment!* oder *Augenblick!*

Für andere Sprachen gilt ähnliches, z.T. ist das Phänomen noch wesentlich deutlicher. Im Italienischen etwa gibt es ganze Reihen von Konjunktionen, die je nach demselben Schema gebaut sind, etwa solche mit der Form Partizip + *che* (‚daß'). Neubildungen scheinen eher die Regel als die Ausnahme.

Solange es aber offenkundig produktive Wortbildungsmechanismen gibt, kann von einer geschlossenen Klasse nicht die Rede sein.

Ein anderes Argument ist das Vorkommen von *Entlehnung*. Sogar in „strukturell asyndetischen" Sprachen, die (angeblich) ursprünglich ganz ohne Konjunktionen auskamen, denen Konjunktionalsätze geradezu strukturfremd sein sollen, wurden (und werden wohl) Konjunktionen neu eingeführt.[14] Bei anderen Sprachen wurde (und wird nach wie vor) die Anzahl der durchaus schon vorhandenen Konjunktionen auf diesem Weg vermehrt.[15]

---

[14] Als Beispiel sei vor allem das Türkische genannt (vgl. insbesondere Johanson 1996). Nach Boretzky (1977:177), hatte die türkische Umgangssprache früher keine konjunktionalen Nebensätze, entlehnte dann aber die persische „Allerweltskonjunktion" *ki*.

[15] Ich verweise auf eine ausführliche Untersuchung zur Entlehnung von Funktionswörtern aus dem Spanischen in die amerindischen Sprachen Mesoamerikas (Stolz/Stolz 1996).

Wir können festhalten: Konjunktionen sind eine relativ (im Verhältnis z.b. zu Verben oder Substantiven) kleine Wortart, die aber umfangreicher ist, als man spontan annehmen sollte. Vermehrung ihrer Mitglieder (ebenso wie Verlust von Mitgliedern, wie man an archaischen Restformen noch erkennen kann) durch innereinzelsprachliche Neuprägung ebenso wie durch Entlehnung findet – anscheinend in allen Sprachen – beständig statt. Sie bilden also keine geschlossene Klasse, wie Berry-Rogghe schon 1970 wußte: der Effekt der „traditionellen" Definition des angeblichen „„closed set'" der Konjunktionen[16] ist, „that it does not define a closed grammatical set but rather an open lexical set"[17] (5).

4   Erweiterung des Blickfelds über die Konjunktionen hinaus

Konjunktionen sind also keine geschlossene Klasse; ja es stellt sich die Frage – Gibt es überhaupt geschlossene Klassen in der Sprache? Angesichts der Begrenztheit des mir zur Verfügung stehenden Raumes kann ich die Perspektive allerdings nur andeutungsweise über die Konjunktionen hinaus ausweiten.

Zunächst will ich in exemplarischen Schlaglichtern auf Wortarten hinweisen, die zwar nicht im Deutschen, aber in gewissen anderen Sprachen Kandidaten für den Status einer geschlossenen Klasse sein könnten.

Generell könnte man schon in Frage stellen, ob sich der Begriff des Wortes überhaupt den Ansprüchen fügt, die an eine *Klasse* zu stellen sind. Dies aber einmal vorausgesetzt: Gehen wir kurz einige „Verdächtige" durch![18]

Die Hauptwortarten scheinen auf den ersten Blick sicher auszuscheiden, aber auch für sie gibt es Sprachen, wo sie als geschlossene Klasse behauptet werden. Zumindest gilt das für die Adjektive. Dixon etwa vertritt die Annahme, daß es in gewissen Sprachen eine geschlossene Adjektivklasse gibt (vgl. 1994). Seine diesbezüglichen Aussagen lassen aber aufmerken; es geht um „rekonstruierte" Stufen von Sprachen, um „Kerngebiete" der Adjektive etc. Und: sind diese in diesen Sprachen wirklich als eigene Klasse anzusehen? Oder nur eine kleine Unterart einer Klasse? Und selbst da stellte sich die Frage nach ihrer Unvermehrbarkeit.

Vor allem aber sind die sogenannten Nebenwortarten (*Synsemantika* bzw. *Synkategoremata*, auch *Partikeln* genannt) potentielle geschlossene Klassen:[19]

---

[16] Diese Definition beruht auf ihrer Funktion, nämlich „„linking two similar units (mostly two sentences)' and ‚expressing a relation between them'".

[17] Man beachte, daß hier die *Geschlossenheit* von Klassen mit der *Grammatik*, ihre *Offenheit* mit dem *Lexikon* in Verbindung gebracht wird.

[18] Darüber, welche Wortarten eigentlich universal oder auch einzelsprachbezogen anzusetzen sind, besteht bekanntlich keine Einigkeit.

[19] Nach Schachter (1985:4f), kommen in den Sprachen der Welt als „closed classes" vor: Pronomina; Kasus-, Diskursmarker und andere Adpositionen; Quantifier, Classifier, Artikel; Hilfsverben, Verbalpartikel; Konjunktionen, Klitika, Kopulas und Prädikatoren, Existenzmarker, Interjektionen, Modalia, Negatoren sowie Höflichkeitsmarker. In der in Fn. 2 angesprochenen Internet-Definition heißt es, daß zu den „Closed-class items" Hilfsverben, Präpositionen, Kon-

Für die Präpositionen wie für die Modalpartikeln gilt vergleichbares wie für die Konjunktionen. Die Geschlossenheit der Klasse der Interjektionen wage ich stark zu bezweifeln, ohne darauf näher eingehen zu können.

Numeralia sind einerseits in einem gewissen Sinn trivialerweise von unendlicher Anzahl (da sie jedes Element der ebenfalls nach oben unbegrenzten Menge der natürlichen Zahlen denotieren können), verstoßen also massiv gegen die Kleinheitsforderung; das aber kann sicher nicht gemeint sein, wenn es um die Frage ihrer Geschlossenheit geht, sondern diese muß sich auf die Bauelemente der Zahlwörter beziehen. Aber auch hier werden in Einzelsprachen ganze Klassen neu gebildet, wie die der Bildungsweise ‚x-mal‘ (lat. *semel, bis, ter* etc.); oder ‚-tel‘ (*halb! drittel* etc.); oder *je zwei* etc.; usw. Also müssen wir weiter einschränken – wenn, sind dann z.B. die „Kardinalia" geschlossen?! Man könnte ja – da ihr Bildungs-System gegeben ist – sagen, diese seien geradezu logisch unvermehrbar. Aber es ist zumindest möglich, daß neue Bezeichnung für 10^{3n}-Bereiche notwendig werden (in Fortsetzung von *Tausend, Million, Milliarde, Billion*); prinzipiell könnten auch neue einfache Kardinalia nach *elf/zwölf* neu aufkommen; und auch an neue Zahlennamen wie *pi, e* etc. ist zu denken. (Nirgends steht, daß Kardinalia notwendig auf die natürlichen Zahlen als ihr Denotat beschränkt sind.) Also scheinen auch die Numeralia nicht geschlossen zu sein.

Ein sehr verdächtiger Kandidat für Geschlossenheit sind die definiten und indefiniten Artikel (und besonders der „Nullartikel" als einelementige und per definitionem unvermehrbare Klasse ...). Aber in manchen Untersuchungen werden diese gar nicht als Wörter angesehen. Und: Es gibt Neubildung überhaupt dieser Wortart als Ganzer in gewissen Sprachen.

Kandidaten für geschlossene Klassen könnten vor allem solche Wortarten sein, die nur einelementige Mengen sind, z.B. die Kopula oder das Infinitiv-*zu* bzw. englisch *to*, sofern diese allerdings als eigene Wortart angesetzt werden, was eine wenig verbreitete Ansicht ist.[20]

Neben den Wortarten – und vielleicht eher als diese – kommen prinzipiell aber auch andere Kategorien der Sprachbeschreibung als geschlossene Klassen in Frage, etwa grammatische, genauer morphosyntaktische Kategorien (Genus, Kasus, Numerus etc.), deren Werte (Singular und Plural, etc.) sowie die sprachlichen Ausdrucksmittel für diese (die Menge der Grammeme oder Flexionsaffixe einer Sprache bzw. Untermengen für gewisse Wortarten oder Flexionsdimensionen).

Der Ausdruck *geschlossene Klasse* wird nicht nur bezüglich lexikalischer Einheiten („Word classes are of two types: OPEN-CLASS and closed-class", s. Fn. 2), son-

---

junktionen, „Determiner" und Pronomen gehören. Eine Diskussion der letztgenannten muß hier aus Platzmangel leider entfallen.

[20] Diese singulären Klassen deuten aber darauf hin, daß man möglicherweise in einer Klassifikationshierarchie einfach weit genug nach „unten" gehen muß. Demnach wären nicht die Großklassen etwa der traditionellen Schulgrammatik Kandidaten für Geschlossenheit, sondern sollten hinreichend kleine (Unter-)Klassen als Kandidaten erwogen werden, z.B. nicht die Pronomen als ganze, sondern etwa die Demonstrativpronomen, oder gar noch eine Teilklasse davon.

dern auch z.B. bezüglich nichtlexikalischer Morpheme gebraucht.[21] Aber auch Affixe werden bekanntermaßen neu gebildet. Und die Behauptung, eine Sprache habe ein und für allemal so-und-so-viele Kasus, ist bestenfalls unter Verzicht auf das „ein und für allemal", also für einen Zeitpunkt, unter synchroner Betrachtung, aufrechtzuerhalten. Selbst bei den grammatischen Kategorien schließlich halte ich Geschlossenheit nicht für gegeben; so gewinnt das Deutsche mit Formulierungen wie *Ich bin am arbeiten* offenkundig neu oder verstärkt die bisher in der Grammatikschreibung unserer Sprache wenig bemerkte Kategorie des *Aspekts* oder der *Aktionsart* hinzu. Andere Sprachen haben mit Artikeln auch explizite Ausdrucksmöglichkeiten für die Kategorie definit/indefinit hinzugewonnen.

5   Lösungsvorschlag

Trotz alledem scheint der Begriff der geschlossenen Klasse durchaus eine gewisse Intuition zu fassen. Ein Versuch, diese zu retten, könnte darin bestehen, Geschlossenheit als *Tendenz* anzusehen, d.h. nur von *relativer* Geschlossenheit auszugehen. Echt geschlossene Klassen würden dann einen – möglicherweise nur idealen – Grenzwert darstellen. Sind also closed classes nicht schlechthin klein und geschlossen, sondern klein*er*, geschlossen*er* als open classes? Aber eine solche Lösung würde zu begrifflichen Merkwürdigkeiten führen. Geschlossenheit ist nun einmal ein entweder-oder-Faktum; halb geschlossen ist eben offen. Möglich ist jedoch, nicht das Definiendum (*geschlossenere Klasse*), sondern das Definiens in die Komparativform zu bringen, m.a.W. zwar den Begriff der geschlossenen Klasse „absolut" zu lassen, aber ihn vorsichtiger und realitätsnäher zu bestimmen: nämlich als eine Klasse sprachlicher Einheiten mit *relativ* wenigen Elementen, die nur *schwerlich* (prinzipiell aber eben doch) neue Mitglieder zuläßt. Als mögliches Unterscheidungskriterium könnte die „Dauer" der Neubildung dienen: Substantivkomposita werden täglich häufig, schnell, ad hoc gebildet und ebenso schnell vergessen – Substantive sind eine offene Klasse. Die Neubildungen von Konjunktionen dagegen findet nicht ad hoc statt, dauert vielmehr ebenso wie ihr ‚Absterben' lange, in der Regel Jahrhunderte. Noch heute sind viele „archaische", selten gebrauchte durchaus präsent (etwa die bereits angesprochene *obzwar*-Gruppe, *alldieweil* etc.). Konjunktionen wären also in diesem vorsichtigen Sinn doch eine geschlossene Klasse.

Als Schlußbemerkung noch eine prinzipielle Erwägung. Die menschliche Sprache ist in ihrem Wesen durch Offenheit geprägt – sie ist ergänzbar, um neuen Ausdrucksbedürfnissen Rechnung zu tragen.

> „[I]n principle, deductive systems are closed and can absorb no new primitives […]. The human cognitive map as represented in language change, however, clearly attests to the open-endedness of the system" (Givón 1982:112f).

---

[21] Offenheit und Geschlossenheit werden auch geradezu als Unterscheidungsmerkmal für lexikalische gegenüber grammatischen Morphemen gebraucht: Geschlossene Klassen gehören danach in die Grammatik, offene ins Lexikon.

6   Literatur

BERGENHOLTZ, Henning; SCHAEDER, Burkhard (1977): Die Wortarten des Deutschen. Versuch einer syntaktisch orientierten Klassifikation. Stuttgart: Klett.

BERRY-ROGGHE, G. (1970): The 'Conjunction' as a Grammatical Category. In: Linguistics 63, 5-18.

BORETZKY, Norbert (1977): Einführung in die historische Linguistik. Reinbek bei Hamburg: Rowohlt.

BRAUSSE, Ursula (1994): Lexikalische Funktionen der Synsemantika. Tübingen: Narr.

DIXON, R. M. W. (1994): Adjectives. In: Asher, R. E. (Hrsg.): The Encyclopedia of Language and Linguistics, Vol. 1. Oxford – New York – Seoul – Tokyo: Pergamon, 29-35.

ENGEL, Ulrich (1988): Deutsche Grammatik. Heidelberg: Groos.

— (1977): Syntax der deutschen Gegenwartssprache. Berlin: E. Schmidt.

FRIES, Charles Carpenter (1973): The Structure of English. An Introduction to the Construction of English Sentences. New impression, London: Longman. Copyright 1952.

GASSER, Herbert (1984): Wortart oder Lexemklassen oder ...? Zu Fragen grammatischer Begriffsbildung. In: Deutsche Sprache 12, 41-53.

GIVÓN, Talmy (1982): Logic vs. Pragmatics, with human language as the Referee: Toward an Empirically Viable Epistemology. In: Journal of Pragmatics 6, 81-133.

GLÜCK, Helmut (Hrsg.) (1993): Metzler Lexikon Sprache. Stuttgart – Weimar: Metzler.

HERBERMANN, Clemens-Peter; GRÖSCHEL, Bernhard; WASSNER, Ulrich Hermann (1997): Sprache & Sprachen. Fachsystematik der Allgemeinen Sprachwissenschaft und Sprachensystematik. Wiesbaden: Harrassowitz.

JOHANSON, Lars (1996): Kopierte Satzjunktoren im Türkischen. In: Sprachtypologie und Universalienforschung 49, 39-49.

KLAUS, Cäcilia (1999): Grammatik der Präpositionen. Studien zur Grammatikographie mit einer thematischen Bibliographie. Frankfurt am Main u.a.: Lang.

KORTMANN, Bernd (1992): Reanalysis completed and in progress: Participles as source of prepositions and conjunctions. In: Kellermann , G.; Morrissey, M. D. (Hrsg.): Diachrony within Synchrony: Language History and Cognition. Frankfurt am Main etc.: Lang, 429-453.

MARTINET, André ([3]1968): Grundzüge der Allgemeinen Sprachwissenschaft. Stuttgart etc.: Kohlhammer. – [Frz. Orig. 1960.]

ORTNER, Hanspeter (1987): Über die Bedingungen der Möglichkeit des Ellipsengebrauchs. In: Kienpointner, M.; Schmeja, H. (Hrsg.): Sprache, Sprachen, Sprechen. Festschrift für Hermann M. Ölberg zum 65. Geburtstag am 14. Oktober 1987. Innsbruck: Institut für Germanistik, 103-119.

SASSE, Hans-Jürgen (1993): Syntactic Categories and Subcategories. In: Jacobs, J. et al. (Hrsg.): Syntax. Ein internationales Handbuch zeitgenössischer Forschung, 1. Halbband. Berlin – New York: de Gruyter, 646-686.

SCHACHTER, Paul (1985): Parts-of-speech systems. In: Shopen, T. (Hrsg.): Language typology and syntactic description, Vol. I: Clause structure. Cambridge etc.: Cambridge University Press, 3-61.

SLOBIN, Dan I. (1997): The Origins of Grammaticizable Notions: Beyond the Individual Mind. In: Slobin, D.I (Hrsg.): The Crosslinguistic Study of Language Acquisition, Vol. 5: Expanding the Contexts. Mahwah, New Jersey – London: Erlbaum, 265-323.

STOLZ, Christel; STOLZ, Thomas (1996): Funktionswortentlehnung in Mesoamerika. Spanisch-amerindischer Sprachkontakt (Hispanoindiana II). In: Sprachtypologie und Universalienforschung 49, 86-123.

Computerlinguistik

A Natural Language Processor for Physics Word Problems

Arunava Chatterjee, Lisa Barboun

1 Introduction

A model for natural language processing of physics word problems is presented. The model uses a language dependent phrase structure grammar (PSG) and a language independent case grammar (CG) to filter kinematics word problems for a physics engine. The physics engine is itself language independent and uses a match of knowns and unknowns to solve the word problem. Key features of the model are the ability to extend the PSG through plug-ins and a run-time interpreter, and the ability to extend the physics engine beyond one-dimensional kinematics problems through plug-in engines. This effort was inspired by the work of Bottner et al (1998) and is the initial phase of establishing a parsing framework using the Java programming language.

2 Background

In recent studies, the solving of physics word problems has come under interest from the perspective of neuroscience, artificial intelligence, and linguistics. In particular Suppes et al presented a grammar for physics word problems that successfully negotiates a range of kinematics problems. The model presented here extends this approach by allowing substantial load-time and run-time configuration using plug-ins, dictionary lookups, and a rules interpreter. While our original intention was to introduce extensibility through a neural net processor and a fuzzy logic filter, we have since abandoned this approach. Our finding was that in the absence of substantial hardware, and somewhat ad hoc approaches to filtering strategies, a fuzzy-neural system is inelegant and does not simulate the kind of problem solving used by physics students. In our view, the solving of physics problems involves the isolation of key numerical quantities and their respective interrelationships. Consequently, we did not use a frequency analysis of words in a corpus. Rather, the PSG has an understanding of sentence structure and can be augmented by plug-in filters and a rules interpreter for language specific cases.

3 Natural Language Processing

We start with the basic assumption that physics problems are language independent and can therefore be cast in a language independent manner. In particular, the equations of physics use mathematics which is human language independent.

3.1   Phrase Structure Grammar

Phrase Structure Grammars (PSG) present a means to incorporate contextual information while also encompassing information found in Context Free Grammars. A
typical PSG may involve the notion of a "sentence" which is comprised of "phrases."
Phrases in turn are composed of "words," which we take as an atomic lexical unit
along with characters for punctuation.

3.2   Case Grammar

Case Grammars (CG) are a language independent representation of concepts. Numerous attempts have been made to develop a complete CG that can be applied to parse
languages. While this is an ambitious task, the possibility of developing a CG for the
limited case of kinematics problems becomes much more feasible. The processor
constructs a PSG that is language dependent and uses it to construct a language independent CG for kinematics word problems.

4   Physics Processing

We limit ourselves to the realm of one dimensional kinematics problems. This reduces the complexity of the problems solved to those involving position, velocity, acceleration and time. These are related through the classical equations of kinematics. In
a subsequent publication we will discuss extending the physics processing beyond the
realm of kinematics. In this document, we present a sense of the overall architecture
and an example of the range of problems solved.

5   Design

The design of the processor emulates a series of filters that reduce the input into numerical values that are interpreted by the physics engine. Plug-ins can intercept the
input and output between each filter to introduce additional processing if necessary.

6   Implementation

A natural language processing framework was developed around the concepts of a
PSG and CG. The PSG was used to reduce the word problem from a collection of declarative and interrogative sentences to a collection of phrases that could be parsed in
terms of the CG. Lastly a table of knowns and unknowns was constructed from the
CG and fed to a physics engine to solve the problem.

6.1 Phrase Grammar

The parsing framework used an atomic unit called Word. Words were represented as a combination of symbols in accordance with the Unicode standard. Word boundaries default to Unicode white space, but can be set to some other symbol if desired. Each word is assigned a type. In particular, noun (N), verb (V), auxiliary verb (AV), adverb (ADV), adjective (ADJ), determiner (D), preposition (P) and conjunction (C) were used as Word types. A "Quantity" consisted of a 2 Word aggregate where the first Word was a number and the second Word represented the item to which the number referred, e.g. 10 meters/second represents a single Quantity but 2 Words. A Phrase was defined as one of the following 4 types of Word constructs:

- Noun Phrase (NP) → [D? ADJ* N]
- Verb Phrase (VP) → [AV? ADV* V]
- Adjective Phrase (AP) → [ADJ+ | ADV+]
- Preposition Phrase (PP) → [P NP]

where regular expression notation has been used i.e.

- ? = zero or one
- * = zero or more
- + = one or more.
- | = or.

For convenience the concept of a Sentence and Compound Sentence (CS) was also defined using Sentence Delimiters (SD) consisting of:

- Sentence → [(PP) NP VP SD].
- Compound Sentence (CS) → [Sentence C Sentence SD].

Sentences were categorized into interrogative and declarative types based on the presence of an interrogative indicator (e.g. "?") in the Sentence Delimiter position. Additionally, a subset of Words, called Question Words, was further used to identify interrogative sentences should interrogative indicators not be present.

The PSG parser was seeded with an initial dictionary of words associated with kinematics. All dictionaries are used for lookups at run-time, consequently, the dictionary can be extended while the processor is running.

The rules interpreter is configured using a simple scripting language which is limited to allow hints in identifying unknown words. For example, the language can be used to associate word types with respect to other word types. The scripting language allows the representation of pattern-heuristic pairs, such that given a pattern match, the associated heuristic is performed. A heuristic can be another pattern-heuristic pair (identified by name), a dictionary lookup, or a rule application on an associated Word. The result of the rule is true or false to indicate that a Word corresponds to a known Word type. The intention of the rule is the identification of words based on language specific constructs on the level of a word or a phrase e.g. "tion/sion" endings are indicative of nouns, or "es" indicates noun plurals or present tense verbs.

6.2   Case Grammar

In order to represent the word problem in a language independent form, a CG was devised based on the assumption that all kinematics problems to be solved could be represented in terms of 5 abstract constructs:

- Agent = The system that undergoes a transition from an initial state to a final state (e.g. a car).
- Action = The type of transition the system undergoes (e.g. acceleration, velocity).
- Duration = The time required for the transition.
- Initial State = The state of the system prior to the transition.
- Final State = The state of the system after the transition.

In practice an Agent is not necessary for the equations of kinematics. It is introduced for purposes of completeness and further extensions. The equations to which the above constructs are related are as follows. Let "x_0" represent start position, "v_0" represent start velocity, "t" represent time, "a" represent acceleration, "v" represent final velocity, and "x" represent final position. The equations of classical kinematics are:

- $x = x_0 + v_0t + \frac{1}{2}at^2$
- $v = v_0 + at$
- $v^2 = v_0^2 + 2ax$
- $v = dx/dt$
- $a = dv/dt,$

where the notation d/dt represents the derivative with respect to time as defined by the differential calculus.

6.3   Physics Engine

The physics engine matches known and unknown Quantities to the equations mentioned above, as well as matches based on algebraic manipulations of those equations. This engine has no knowledge of the language from which the problem is derived. Its only inputs are numbers as associated with the equations.

7   Result Set

Given the PSG, CG, and the Physics engine we were able to solve problems of the form (represented in terms of the Case Grammar):

- Given Initial State, Final State, Duration. Find Action.
- Given Final State, Action, Duration. Find Initial State.
- Given Initial State, Action, Duration. Find Final State.

- Given Initial State, Final State, Action. Find Duration.
- Given Initial State, Final State. Find Action (e.g. Given v, v_0, x and x_0 find a).

A set of sample word problems are as follows:

- "A car starts from rest and reaches 40 m/s in 4 s. What is the acceleration?"
- "If a boy travels 3000 m and reaches a final speed of 20 m/s, what is the acceleration?
- "Given that a car reaches a final position of 30000 m in 40 s, find the velocity."
- "How long does it take a man to run 32000 m at an average speed of 3 m/s?"

8 Extending the Processor

8.1 Generalization 1 – learning new language specific rules

As mentioned earlier the rules interpreter allows the PSG to be augmented through language specific rules. It is our intention to test the PSG and rules interpreter with multiple languages that can be represented in terms of the constructs discussed above. In addition to the rules interpreter, the PSG parser can have behavior extended through the use of plug-in modules which are invoked before and after the PSG parser runs. In this way language specific artifacts such as idiomatic expressions and contractions can be handled.

8.2 Generalization 2 – extending the physics engine

The current form of the physics engine allows only solutions of one-dimensional kinematics problems. However since the architecture of the system allows plug-in extensions, a second generalization is the addition of physics engines for other problem domains that can be resolved in terms of the CG. The classification of the problems is handled by each physics plug-in in terms of the known and unknown data and recognition of units.

9 Conclusion

Our efforts to develop a robust parsing machinery for physics word problems has met with some initial success. We note that the CG makes no assumptions about the type of physics problem to be solved. It only assumes that a physics word problem can be parameterized in terms of 5 quantities, namely, AGENT, ACTION, INITIAL_STATE, FINAL_STATE, and DURATION. This project represents the initial steps in establishing a dynamic parsing framework that can be extended at run-time to handle heuristics based word problems. While our initial efforts involved non-heuristic approaches with neural nets and fuzzy logic, for the class of problems we intend to address (i.e. those represented as mathematical equations), our studies of non-heuristic approaches have proved cumbersome and inelegant. We have therefore chosen an approach where the heuristics are extensible in order to simulate the addition of newly acquired strategies by the student.

10   References

BOTTNER, Michael; LIANG, Lin; SUPPES, Patrick (1998): In: Aliseda, A. (ed.): Computing Natural Languages. Stanford University: CSLI Publications, 141-154.

A Platform for the Integration and the Evaluation of Linguistic Formalisms: Formal Methods

Bilel Gargouri, Mohamed Jmaiel, Abdelmajid Ben Hamadou

Several formalisms have been proposed to describe and represent linguistic knowledge (i.e., Formal Grammars, Unification Grammars, Lexical Functional Grammars, HPSG, etc.). The diversity of formalisms arises a crucial problem of evaluating and choosing the appropriate formalisms needed to develop an application. In this paper, we present a platform that helps to solve these problems. This platform is based on formal methods.

Starting from a unified (or pivot) representation of the main linguistic formalisms, we develop an integration process of a variety of knowledge described initially by different formalisms. This process is very useful for the development of lingware that deals with different aspects of language (i.e., morphologic, syntactic, semantic, etc.). Moreover, it guides the selection process, based on formal evaluation, of the appropriate formalism needed to develop a lingware.

1   Introduction

Several formalisms have been proposed to describe and represent linguistic knowledge at different levels (i.e., morphologic, syntactic, semantic, etc.) (Miller & Torris 1990; Gérard 1989). Many of these formalisms are designed to specify linguistic knowledge at only one level. Others try to cover more than one level (i.e., HPSG, Unification Grammar, etc.). In addition, we can see that knowledge of the same level can be represented in different manners using different formalisms.

Besides the variation in nature of knowledge to describe, linguistic formalisms can be distinguished by the mechanisms and the tools of description that they use. Indeed, several formalisms describe the same knowledge in different manners.

This diversity arises a crucial problem of evaluating and choosing the appropriate formalisms needed to develop an application.

However, few studies have been entirely devoted to the comparison and the evaluation of linguistic formalisms. These studies are oriented, generally, to the evaluation of the newly proposed formalisms with respect to others. They insist, especially, on the advantages that these new formalisms provide without recourse to mathematical tools and formal proofs, which limits the credibility of the recommended results (Broker 1998; Kaplan 1994; Gérard 1989). Few are those who proposed a rigorous process to compare linguistic formalisms (Miller & Torris 1990). In addition, in the context of lingware development, the evaluation of formalisms has not been considered.

In the lingware development context, the formalism to use (eventually many) has to describe the required knowledge in the best manner, in order to improve the development process and to ensure the coherence between data and processing. Moreover, the formalism should provide all possibilities of extension or adaptation of the application. From another point of view, using several formalisms in the same application arises a problem of data coherence and integration: which formalisms can be integrated or substituted in the same lingware?

In this paper, we present a rigorous approach for the integration and the evaluation of linguistic formalisms using formal methods. This approach is treated in the context of lingware development. The first objective of this approach is to promote the integration of various linguistic knowledge, described initially by different formalisms (i.e., Formal Grammars, Unification Grammars, Lexical Functional Grammars, HPSG, etc.) in a unified representation. This allows to obtain a complete description of the needed linguistic knowledge when developing a lingware.

The second objective is the formal evaluation of the linguistic formalisms in the context of lingware development. This allows to offer formal arguments for the choice of the appropriate formalism for a lingware on the basis of some criteria such as: the adequacy to the problem, the expressive power, the facility of integration in a lingware, the complementarity, the possibility of extension, etc.

We begin by reminding the interests of using formal methods in lingware engineering (Gargouri, Jmaiel, Hamadou 1998a, 1998b). After that, we discuss the unified (or pivot) representation of linguistic formalisms. Thereafter, we present our approach to integrate a variety of linguistic knowledge, described initially by different formalisms. Then, we present some formal criteria for the choice of the appropriate formalism(s) to use in a lingware and we give some details of their use. Finally, we detail the basis components of the proposed platform. We illustrate our works by examples with the VDM formal method (Vienna Development Method) (Jones 1986).

2   The advantages of formal methods in the lingware development process

The study of the approaches used for the lingware development allowed us to observe some problems and difficulties such as:

- The absence of standardised and appropriate methodologies of lingware development that cover all of the life cycle;
- The diversity of linguistic models and knowledge representation methods that arises a selection problem;
- The dichotomy data-processing that is behind some incoherence problems;
- The quasi absence of a formal specification phase of needs;
- The absence of a formal validation of the lingware design before the implementation phase;
- The absence of integration methods for linguistic formalisms within a lingware that control the coherence and the complementarity of the knowledge described by these formalisms;

All these problems decrease the lingware quality i.e. the performance, the possibilities of maintenance, and extension, the reuse, etc.

To palliate these general problems, we propose the use of formal methods in the lingware development process (Gargouri, Jmaiel, Hamadou 1998b). It is well known that these methods have already been used in the development process of some critical applications such that real time and distributed systems (Barroca & McDermid 1992; Dick & Woods 1997). According to our investigations, the use of formal method in the Natural Language Processing area allows to consolidate the global advantages of these methods and to provide others which are specific to this area (Gargouri, Jmaiel, Hamadou 1998a).

Indeed, the use of formal methods in the lingware development process gives the possibility to detect the limits of the system to develop from the earliest phases of this process. Similarly, following the validation of the design with respect to needs, it allows to validate the choice of a linguistic reference model for the lingware to develop.

On the other hand, formal methods allow to realise a validated integration of data-processing, in a single language of specification, in order to well manage the dichotomy data-processing. This validation concerns the coherence between data and processing on the one hand, and between heterogeneous data on the other hand (especially various linguistic knowledge).

Finally, the validation of the lingware (or of its design) with respect to needs allows to avoid the use of some expensive techniques, in absence of formal validation tools, to test or evaluate the developed lingware. Indeed, these techniques, which are generally based on a specific corpus, can be applied only after the development phase. Moreover, they do not have a formal basis.

3   A unified representation of linguistic formalisms

The investigation of the main linguistic formalisms (i.e., Formal Grammars, Unification Grammars, Lexical Functional Grammars, HPSG, etc.),allowed us to observe that these formalisms use a common set of description elements. Indeed, despite the diversity of the used notation and the desired semantics, these formalisms use elementary constituents such as sets, functions, constraints, production rules, maps, features, etc. In order to describe a formalism, one has to specify its elementary constituents and their manner of arrangement (an appropriate structure for the represented linguistic knowledge).

Starting from these observations, we propose to represent the linguistic formalisms in a pivot language that considers all the elementary constituents and the manners of arrangement (for each formalism). In our approach, the representation of the generic definition of a linguistic formalism in the pivot language is accomplished in the following steps:

* Decomposition of the formalism in its elementary canonical components (i.e. sets, rules, etc.);
* Transformation of these constituents in the pivot language;
* put together the obtained constituents to obtain an equivalent representation to the initial one.

The pivot language that we propose, in this approach, is VDM-SL (Dawes 1991) (specification language associated to the formal method VDM; Jones 1986). This language, based on the first order logic of predicates, is expressive enough to cover the above linguistic formalisms. It allows, among other things, a simple representation of the elementary components (or constituents) and their round-up with respect to the initial formalism.

In our approach, we start from the standard definitions of the linguistic formalisms (Chomsky 1959; Haas 1989) which are, in general, described in a formal way. The transformations from the original definitions to the desired formal one should be realised in a rigorous way in order to ensure the equivalence of their meaning.

The example, given thereafter, illustrates the representation of some elementary constituents of linguistic formalisms in VDM-SL. For simplicity reasons, we present, in this example, the generic definition of the Context Free Grammar (Chomsky 1959).

Let: - $NTERM = \{A,B, ..., Z\}$ the set of non terminals letters
- $TERM = \{a,b, ...,z\}$: the set of terminals letters

A Context Free Grammar in VDM-SL corresponds to the following composed structure that we call *Formal-G2*:

Formal-G2::
 T: set of (TERM)
 N: set of (NTERM)
 S: NTERM
 P: set of (N → set of (seq of (TUN)))
 where inv-Formal-G2() ≜ ((T≠∅)∧(N≠∅)∧(T∩N=∅)∧(S∈N)∧(P≠∅)∧(S≠[]))

Example: The definition of the generic Context Free Grammar in VDM-SL.

In this example, we represent the generic definition of the Context Free Grammar as a composed structure called *Formal-G2*. The Constituents implied in this representation (in this composed structure) are:

- Sets: *TERM*, *NTERM*, *T* (set of terminals), *N* (set of non terminals), *P* (set of production rules);
- Sequences: the sequences of characters that represent some set elements;
- Rules: the production rules forming the *P* set;
- Constraints: that are imposed at the end of this definition by *where inv-Formal-G2()*;
- The composed structure: the Formal-G2 structure that translates the manner of grouping together the different elementary constituents of a Context Free Grammar.

Note that the specification of the *Formal-G2* composed structure is inspired from the initial definition of the Context Free Grammar.

4 The linguistic knowledge integration

The diversity of the linguistic knowledge useful for a lingware and the variety of the formalisms that describe and represent this knowledge arise some problems such as the redundancy of description and the diversity of processing styles. This last point causes some integration difficulties in the software engineering context.

The integration of linguistic knowledge, that we propose in this paper, is based on a pivot representation of the formalisms that describe them (generic representation in the same pivot language: see section 3). Indeed, we deal, in this context, with instances of these formalisms that describe and represent the required knowledge.

The integration approach of linguistic knowledge uses the following phases:

- Decomposition of the linguistic knowledge description (the instance of the formalism) in its elementary components;
- Transformation of these constituents in the pivot language using appropriate rules according to the generic pivot representation of the initial formalism;
- Round-up of the obtained elements according to the generic pivot representation of the initial formalism.

Although this integration is not optimised in term of redundancy at this stage of works, it provides, among others, the following advantages:

First of all, at the level of the knowledge representation, this integration allows to obtain a rigorous and complete description of natural languages in a unified representation, independent from the linguistic formalisms used.

In the context of lingware development, the pivot representation of the linguistic knowledge allows to combine the processing description and consequently to unify the development mechanisms. In this way, we never depend on particularities of the linguistic formalisms or on certain programming languages associated to these formalisms.

On the other hand, this aspect of unification of the linguistic knowledge description, the related processing and the development mechanisms, facilitates the integration of the lingware from the point of view of software engineering. This allows to construct a platform of standardised and reusable lingware.

The figure (cf. next page) given hereafter explains our approach for the integration of various linguistic knowledge in a unified representation in order to use it in a lingware.

In this figure, the linguistic knowledge described initially by different formalisms is transformed in the pivot language. The transformation of a formalism is done automatically by applying a set of rules.

Once such a description is obtained, the same mechanism of lingware development can be applied to the necessary restrictions of this knowledge in order to develop the intended application. The set of lingware developed in this standardised manner constitutes a platform of reusable lingware.

Finally, this approach of linguistic knowledge integration benefits from the global advantages of linguistic formalisms and preserves the advantages of using formal method for simplicity reasons.

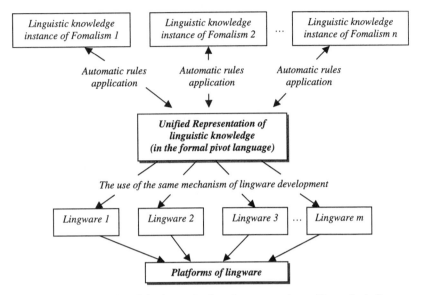

Figure 1: The linguistic knowledge integration in a pivot presentation and its use in the lingware development.

5   Evaluation criteria for the choice of linguistic formalisms

The evaluation of linguistic formalisms is very useful in order to choose an appropriate formalism for a lingware to develop. Indeed, the formalism has to satisfy the needs of the application to develop at the specification level. Also, it is desirable that the use of this formalism facilitates the development process and allows the possibility of extension and adaptation.

Actually, the choice of a formalism constitutes a crucial task that is increasingly difficult in the case of applications that process complex and various linguistic knowledge. Is it necessary, then, to use a single complex formalism or several which are single and complementary?

To solve this problem, we propose a formal evaluation approach that allows, among other things, to justify the choice of an appropriate formalism for an application. Based on this approach, we present the following evaluation criteria:

- *Possibility of integration in a lingware*: It concerns the possibility of using a particular formalism to describe and represent the needed linguistic knowledge for a lingware. It is based on the representation of the formalism in the formal language (used also to specify the processing part) which allows to promote the integration. Then, we validate the possibility of integration through the validation of the lingware design;

- *Facility of integration in a lingware*: It deals with the facility of the integration of a linguistic formalism with another. We quantify this facility by measuring the simplicity of their representation in the pivot language, notably of their canonical elementary components and their manners of combination. The measure of simplicity accounts for the number of elementary constituents, the nature of constituents (i.e., maps, functions, etc .), the depth of description, etc.
- *Adequacy to the problem*: It is necessary that the formalism used for lingware development allows to suitably describe all necessary linguistic knowledge for the processed problem. The validation of the appropriateness is insured through the validation of the lingware design with respect to needs;
- *Expressiveness*: This criterion can be studied in a general framework of comparison of formalisms. It concerns the power of a formalism to describe and represent the linguistic knowledge. To measure the expressive power, we propose to (formally) specify all generation functions associated with a formalism. This cam supplement the classical comparison techniques on the basis of generated language. In addition, based on the unified formalism representation, we propose to compare elementary constituents in the representation: to compare the cardinality of sets, the expressive power of relations and functions, etc.;
- *Complementarity*: It allows to know in which case two (or more) formalisms can be used together in the same lingware and if the one completes the other. The evaluation of this criterion profits from the unified representation of the linguistic formalisms in the formal language. Thus, the validation of the lingware design allows to validate the various data (or knowledge) described initially by different formalisms;
- *Extensibility*: It concerns the possibility offered by a formalism to extend a developed lingware, notably, by extending the linguistic knowledge that it describes. In this framework, the use of tools associated to formal methods (i.e., editors) allows to realise some needed adaptations of the specification. Thereafter, the validation of the obtained specification proves the properties of extensibility and adaptation.

The importance of one criterion with respect to another depends on the nature and objectives of the application to develop. Consequently, the attribution of weights to the different criteria and the choice of a classification method are left to the lingware developer.

Moreover, the evaluation approach that we present is applied jointly to the formal development process of a lingware (Gargouri, Jmaiel, Hamadou 1999). It is based on a unified representation of linguistic formalisms in a pivot language and on the formal validation associated to the formal method used. It allows to provide evaluation results before the implementation phase.

Actually, we concentrate our works to finalise the quantitative aspects of this evaluation approach; in particular for some criteria that necessitate particular measures (i.e., facility of integration, expressiveness, etc.).

6   The components of the platform

The platform that we propose in this paper, has two principles objectives. First, it favours the investigation of formal evaluation of linguistic formalisms. Second, it enables to integrate, in a pivot formal language, various linguistic knowledge described by different formalisms. This platform is based on formal methods and some associated tools.

The basic components of this platform are:

- A pivot language (i.e., the specification language of the formal method);
- A set of interfaces allowing the acquisition of linguistic knowledge descriptions according to the initial representations of the linguistic formalisms;
- A set of transformation rules (by formalism) to obtain the pivot representation;
- A library containing the generic descriptions of linguistic formalisms and the linguistic knowledge descriptions in the pivot language;
- Software and validation tools associated to the formal method (i.e., editors, theorem prover, checker, etc.);
- A set of procedures allowing the generation of reports according to the evaluation of formalisms.

7   Conclusion

In this paper, we presented an integration and evaluation platform for linguistic formalisms based on formal methods. Starting from the pivot representation of the linguistic formalisms, this platform allows to bring formal solutions to the problem of choosing the appropriate formalisms for a lingware development.

Also, the platform allows to integrate various linguistic knowledge, described initially by different formalisms, in a unified representation. This will be used for a standardised lingware development.

Besides finishing the implementation of the platform that we presented, the investigation of the elimination of the redundancy in the unified linguistic knowledge description remains to be realised. Moreover, in our future works, we are interested on the generalisation of the evaluation of formalisms in order to investigate their comparison.

8   References

BARROCA, L.M.; MCDERMID, J. A. (1992): Formal methods: use and relevance for the development of safety-critical systems. In: The Computer Journal 35.6.

BROKER, Norbert (1998): A Projection Architecture for Dependency Grammar and how it compares to LFG, Proceedings of the LFG'98 Conference, Brisbane, Austria.

CHOMSKY Noam (1959): Structures syntaxiques. Paris: Le Seuil.

JONES, Cliff B. (1986): Systematic software development using VDM. Prentice Hall. International.

DAWES, John (1991): The VDM-SL reference guide. London: Pitman publishing.

DICK J.; WOODS E. (1997): Lessons learned from rigorous system software development, In: Information and Software Technology 39, 551-560.

GARGOURI, B.; JMAIEL, M.; BEN HAMADOU, A. (1998a): Intérêts des Méthodes Formelles en Génie Linguistique, TALN 1998, 10-12 Juin 1998, Paris, FRANCE.

— (1998b): Vers l'utilisation des méthodes formelles pour le développement de linguiciels, CO-LING-ACL'98, 10-14 Août 1998, Montréal, Québec, Canada

— (1999): A formal approach to lingware development, IEA/AIE'99, May 31-June 03, 1999, Cairo, EGYPT (LNCS, Springer-Verlag Number 1611).

HAAS, Andrew (1989): A Parsing Algorithm for Unification Grammar. In: Computational Linguistics 15.4.

KAPLAN, Ronald M. (1994): The Formal Architecture of Lexical-Functional Grammar, Formal issues in Lexical-Functional Grammar. Stanford University.

MILLER, Philip; Torris Thérèse (1990): Formalismes syntaxiques pour le traitement automatique du langage naturel. Paris: Hermes.

SABAH, Gérard (1989): L'intelligence artificielle et le langage: volume 1 et 2. Paris: Hermès.

Conceptualization in Agents: The System RoAD

Karl Ulrich Goecke

1   Introduction

Typically, AI-oriented natural language generation (NLG) systems as well as psycholinguistic models of language production have as a starting point a more or less structured representation (SR) of the content to be verbalized. Generation is then thought of as a process comprising (at least) two steps: Selection of a propositional content (depending on context, partner model, and text structure rules) and linguistic realization (selection of syntactic frames, lexical selection, etc.).

Jackendoff has proposed a specific variant of SR, namely *Conceptual Semantics (CS)* (Jackendoff 1983; Jackendoff 1990). It has had a great impact on either psycholinguistics (cf. Levelt 1989) as well as on NLG, especially as intermediate representation for machine translation (Dorr 1993). Generating on the basis of CS is well-developed by now (see Rehm 1999).

But CS has not only the function to provide a starting point for language generation. In its original formulation, it is a variant of the "language of thought" (Fodor 1975) and therefore serves an interface function to many representational systems like vision, motor activity, and haptic representations (see Jackendoff 1996). However, the processes leading to the building-up of representations along the lines of CS *(CS representations, CSRs)* are investigated to a lesser extent than the use of CSRs for language generation. This is probably because the modularity of language generation facilitates the formulation of a corresponding model, whereas the multiple sources of information involved in the former process make the formulation of an appropriate model difficult.

In this paper, I propose the outline of an architecture for building up CSRs. However, I do not intend (and am not able) to provide a full model of human conceptualization processes. Instead, the focus of this paper lies in the investigation of the interface function of a representation format integrating non-linguistic and conceptual information as a basis for NLG. I am going to present recent work comprising an artificial system, namely a virtual assembly robot, that talks about its actions. To achieve this, it is necessary to

1) integrate multimodal information from within the system into appropriate CSRs.
2) select a CSR for generation.
3) generate utterances depending on the selected CSR.

The first two of these steps are the subject of this paper. They are modeled and implemented in the system *RoAD (Robot Action Description,* see also Goecke & Milde 1998a; Goecke & Milde 1998b). The third step is described in detail in Rehm (1999) where the parallel, incremental surface generator IPaGe is introduced. However, in principle it is possible to take any NL generator that is able to cope with the variant of CS used in RoAD.

The linguistically interesting issue about this approach is that a connection between linguistic entities (words, phrases, sentences), conceptual entities (CSRs) and
sensoric entities (visual, haptic) or internal parameters driving the actions of the robot
(joint values etc.) is made explicit. Thus, a closer investigation of the referential semantics of a specific kind of utterances is made possible.

Section 2 focuses on this specific kind of utterances *(situation-and-action descriptions, SADs)*. They are utterances of an agent that have a strong connection to the environmental and internal situation of agents and thus display some particularly interesting features with respect to my theoretical claims. In section 3, I discuss some
properties and difficulties of a system able to produce SADs. I propose a "meta-rep-
resentation" format *(interpretative schemata, ISM)* by which the connection between
sensoric[1] and CSRs is achieved. The implementation of a system using ISM as a conceptualization mechanism is described in section 4. Finally, a summary is given and
an outlook on directions for further research is outlined.

2   Situation-and-action descriptions

"SAD" denotes a type of utterance bearing a strong relation to the actual configuration of the environment and the internal state of an *agent*. There has been much debate about what should count as an agent; I do not want to participate actively in this
discussion. Rather, I follow the notion of "autonomous agent" as it is introduced by
Franklin & Graesser (1996):

> "An autonomous agent is a system situated within and a part of an environment that senses that
> environment and acts on it, over time, in pursuit of its own agenda and so as to effect what it
> senses in the future."

For the current purpose, the notion of "autonomy" is irrelevant. For the definition of
SADs, it is sufficient to capture that there is a sensing, acting entitiy within an envi-
ronment. RoAD is currently integrated into the architecture of such an agent, namely
CoRA (Communicating Reactive Agent, cf. Milde et al. 1997*).* CoRA controls the
actions of a simulated assembly robot that is able to manipulate small wooden
BAUFIX-parts like screws, cubes, and connection bars. It is instructable by a human
interactor. Due to its behavior based architecture (see e.g. Brooks 1991 or Sloman &
Logan 1999), it is possible not only to initiate an action by the robot, but also to in-
tervene an ongoing action. Additionally, the overall behavior is very robust such that
CoRA always has an option to act in an environment-adapted way. The sensoric
equipment of CoRA consists of a hand-mounted camera, telemetric and contact sensors.

Under these premises, it is now possible to give a definition of SADs and illustrate
it in the example domain. SADs are, unlike e.g. talks or poems, solely based on the

---

[1]   I am going to use the term *sensoric representation* as an abbreviation for all non-conceptual and
non-linguistic types of representation occuring in RoAD (sensoric, action control, and motor
control).

immediate perceptual context. In particular, the following characteristics apply to SADs :

- perceptual basis
  The concepts underlying SADs are activated by percepts delivered through sensoric representations. In CoRA, sensoric representations are: values for objects within the visual field like *cube* or *screw*, values for joint parameters like *1.3437*, values for contact sensors (*0* or *1*) etc.
- direct specification of parameters
  Sensoric parameters activate conceptual entities via a 1:1- or X:1-mapping. Thus, single percepts (like objects) as well as perceptual groups (like several joint parameters) map onto a single conceptual entity. 1:X-mappings are not intended; lexical selection is dealt with in the surface realization. For example, if the percept is a cube, then, for the time being, only the concept CUBE is activated. In a latter step, a possible word form for CUBE is selected, e.g. "cube" or "block".
- no additional knowledge bases
  SADs are independent from discourse context or motivational conditions. Though SADs can perform certain functions in a discourse, the corresponding CSR contains no information going beyond the perceptual context.

Typically, the perceptual context itself or an action of the agent establish the content of a SAD. Therefore, they result in utterances from the first-person perspective. Examples for SADs in the chosen domain are "I see the red block", "I am moving forward" or "I grasp the long screw".

3   Conceptualization

How can SADs be generated by an agent? This section outlines a possible solution which is not settled in a specific agent architecture or formalism. Instead, I am going to put forward some issues marking the boundary conditions for the formulation of a representation format that is developed in the following sections.

As mentioned in section 1, the representational basis of any natural language utterance is a SR. I have committed myself to a specific kind of SR, namely a variant of Conceptual Semantics because generation on these grounds is well-developed. The issue to be treated now is how a CSR is built up out of the sensoric information an agent has available.

I propose a schema-based way to represent sensoric information on the one hand and conceptual information on the other. Both types of information are included in so-called interpretative Schemata (ISM). They describe a situation or an action in their respective representation format. For example, if the sensoric information consists of the gripper being closed, then the dedicated CSR is (in abbreviated notation) EVENT: grasp, AGENT: i. The agent has a default value for this event meaning that it is a first-person conceptualization, i.e. the agent itself is grasping something.

In more complex cases, there are transition rules mediating between the two representation modes. In the case of an ISM like "see", the sensoric information consists of an object that is currently in the visual field. As it does not make sense to introduce an individual ISM for every possible object, there is a transition rule that propagates the information about the object from the visual system to an underspecified CSR. There it fills a certain slot to result in a complete CSR like EVENT: see, AGENT: i, OBJECT: cube. More complex transitions are necessary to gain the appropriate CSRs for the direction of movement where multiple joint values have to be considered (cf. example in section 4).

On this basis, a CSR can be seen as a label for a specific sensoric state. As can be seen from the examples, however, it is a structured label. Conceptual types have as values tokens instantiated by parts of the sensoric information available. At first sight, this organization seems rather arbitrary. But consider the following argument:

There is no use in representing an object without specifying the way in which this object is perceived as being the part of a state or an event the representing entity (the agent) is involved in. In this context, "state" and "event" are technical terms denoting the corresponding subclasses of the conceptual types as defined in Jackendoff (1990). In other words, we do not need (and possibly cannot) represent an object without making explicit the interrelation of the object and the perceiver. Such an explication is two-fold: First, the state or event the object is involved in has to be represented. An object may stand in various relations with respect to the perceiver: it may just be perceived as lying on the floor in front of the perceiver (e.g a stone) or it may be doing something (e.g. a bird flying in the skies). In the former case, the relation between perceiver and object is only the relation of perception in some sense modality by the perceiver (e.g. seeing). The latter case is more complex: It is the perception of an event the object is involved in. Second, the relation between the object and the state or event has to be represented. For example, it is necessary to specify the object as either "agent" or "patient" (not Jackendoffs terminology). This property of the conceptual label makes it plausible to use it as a starting point for NLG in a natural way.

To sum up, with ISM there is a powerful tool for representing multiple types of information, sensoric and conceptual. Transition rules play the role of interfaces, bridging the gap between the various representational systems within an agent. The benefit for linguistics lies in the possibility to correlate, via CS, the environmental situation with natural language utterances.

4   The system RoAD

The preceding considerations have been merged into an implementation of the conceptualization module of the agent CoRA called RoAD (Robot Action Description). In the next section, the central representation unit ISM (Interpretative Schema) is defined. Section 4.2 describes the hierarchical organization of multiple ISM, section 4.3 sketches the selection mechanism between the possible CS for surface realization. Lastly, section 4.4 highlights the difference in the conception of RoAD and other systems in the field.

4.1 Two example ISM

ISM are units representing a state or an event in a sensoric as well as a conceptual representation format. Transition rules mediate between these formats (cf. Section 3). A simple example is the ISM *move*. The following representations constitute this specific ISM:

- *sensoric representation*
  ((BS-ROB-OUT-velocity > 0) & ((BS-ROB-OUT-down > 0) | (BS-ROB-OUT-left > 0)
  | (BS-ROB-OUT-forward > 0))) & ((ACT-BM-MOVE 1) | (ACT-BM-MOVETODIR 1)
  | (ACT-BM-MOVETOOBJ 1))
- *transition rules*
  none
- *CSR*
  EVENT: move, AGENT: i

The various values for the attributes beginning with "BS-ROB-OUT" are control parameters of the robots' joints. The other attributes represent the state (active or inactive, 1 or 0) of the action-generating modules in the control architecture of the robot. "&" is the logical "and", "|" the logical "or". If the values of these attributes are present in the sensoric constellation of the robot, this particular ISM becomes active. The CSR is a candidate for being propagated to the surface generator (see section 4.3 for an explanation of the selection mechanism). A possible utterance is "Ich bewege mich" ("I am moving"). Note that in this case, no mediation between the two representations is necessary.

Another case is the ISM *move-to-dir*. Additional to the simple detection of an unspecific movement, one needs to specify the value of the CSR attribute DIRECTION. This is accomplished by the use of multiple transition rules. In this example, "not" denotes the logical "not" while "||" denotes "xor". Furthermore, an operator "X for Y cycles" is introduced, implying that the sensoric representation X is present for Y time spans, measured in cycles (approximately 0.4 sec in the current implementation). In this example, only two of the six possibilities for DIRECTION are displayed:

- *sensoric representation*
  (down not 0 | left not 0 | forward not 0) for 3 cycles
- *transition rules*
  ((down > 10) & not(left > 10 || left < -10) & not(forward > 10 || forward < -10))
  for 3 cycles → DIRECTION = down
  ((down < -10) & not(left >10 || left < -10) & not(forward > 10 || forward < -10))
  for 3 cycles → DIRECTION = up
- *CSR*
  EVENT: move, AGENT: i, DIRECTION: "specified by transition rule"

Thus, any relevant sensoric pattern is translated into CSRs. An utterance basing on this ISM might be "Ich bewege mich nach rechts" ("I am moving to the right"). In RoAD, ISM are not elements of an unstructured set. Rather, they constitute a hierarchy in which higher ISM feed upon the functionality of lower ones. For example, an ISM *move-to-obj* conceptualizing a movement of the robot in the direction of a reference object integrates the two lower ISM *move* and *see*. The former detects a movement of the robot, whereas the latter provides information about an object in the visual field. If, from the robots perspective, this object becomes larger over time, it is apparent that a movement towards the object is taking place. If no movement information is present, then it is the object rather than the robot that has to be moving. This leads to a different conceptualization.

Currently, the hierarchy has five levels of complextity. On the bottom are *move*, *see*, and *bump*. The most complex ISM is *place-obj-to-obj* conceptualizing an action of the robot consisting of the seizing of an object A, the carrying of A to an object B, and the placing of A near B. All this can be recognized solely on the grounds of sensoric information, without the need to falling back to a plan that might have led to this behavior. Of course, a post-hoc comparison of plan and actual event might help in explaining errors in the execution of action plans (cf. Längle et al. 1996).

4.3   Selection

In many NLG-systems, the mechanisms leading to a selection amongst one of the activated CSs for surface realization are well-studied (e.g. Hovy 1993). They include knowledge about the interlocutor (partner model), the discourse context, and general discourse strategies. None of these is present in the current version of RoAD. Instead, at a given time, the most complex ISM (i.e. the highest ISM of the hierarchy) presently activated is going to propagate its CS to the surface realization component. The logic behind this is that probably the most complex behavior of the agent is going to be most interesting for the interlocutor. Additionally, by this strategy the conceptualization performance of RoAD is demonstrated. It is clear, however, that the abovementioned knowledge bases have also to be considered in order to achieve a natural discourse behaviour of RoAD.

4.4   Related work

There are a number of systems dealing with language generation by real or simulated artificial agents. Herzog & Wazinski (1994) describe a systems connecting pattern recognition and language generation. Traffic and soccer scenes are analyzed and a natural language description is given. Längle et al. (1995) present the verbalization component KANTRA of the assembly robot KAMRO. In Torrance (1994), a template-based NLG system is shown explaining the movements of a robot on the basis of an internal map.

Unlike RoAD, all these systems have an internal, coherent model of the environment serving as basis for NLG as well as other tasks like planning. This can count as a drawback of their architectures (e.g. Brooks 1991). RoAD does not prevent the (possibly erroneous) conceptualization of contradictory information which, on theoretical grounds, is an advantage over said systems. On top of this, the modularity of RoAD and the use of a standard interface representation format (CS) make it a flexible tool for any conceptualization task. Additionally, by the close interrelation of sensoric and conceptual representations in ISM, the ISM hierarchy (see section 4.1) licenses predications about the complexity of a conceptualization and of the corresponding utterance.

5 Summary

In this paper, a model of conceptualization processes in an agent architecture leading to first-person descriptions of the agents´ actions (SADs) was presented. Thus, a step towards combining a NLG-system with a perceiving, acting entity is completed, enabling both NLG and, in a more remote future, psycholinguistics to be correlated to a broader technical or cognitive background, namely agent architectures.

This model has been implemented and tested in connection to CoRA, an instructable assembly robot. The inclusion of RoAD in CoRA's architecture leads to an improvement of the discourse ability and thus enhances the acceptance of this particular technical system on the part of the human interactor.

In part, possible improvements over the current version of RoAD are of a merely quantitative nature: Enlargement of the ISM-hierarchy to capture more "pieces of behaviour", inclusion of more sophisticated calculations of the trajectories of the robot arm. The main focus of future work in RoAD, however, is going to concern the inclusion of deliberative knowledge of the agent: Discourse context, partner model, and plans. To achieve this, an extension of the representation format "ISM" is possibly necessary to handle these kinds of structured information properly.

6 References

BROOKS, Rodney A. (1991): Intelligence without Representation. Artificial Intelligence 47, 139-159.

DORR, Bonnie Jean (1993): Machine translation: A view from the lexicon. Cambridge, Mass: MIT Press.

FODOR, Jerry A. (1975): The Language of Thought. New York: Crowell.

FRANKLIN, Stan; GRAESSER, Art (1996). Is It an Agent, or Just a Program?: A Taxonomy for Autonomous Agents. In: Müller, J. P.; Woolridge, M. J.; Jennings, N. R. (eds.): Intelligent Agents III. Agent Theories, Architectures, and Languages, Berlin: Springer, 21-35.

GOECKE, Karl Ulrich; MILDE, Jan-Torsten (1998a): Situations- und Aktionsbeschreibungen durch einen teilautonomen Montageroboter. In: Computers, Linguistics, and Phonetics between Language and Speech. Proceedings of the 4th Conference on Natural Language Processing – KONVENS 98. Frankfurt a. M.: Peter Lang, 331-335.

— (1998b): Talking About What I Do: Conceptualization and Robots. In: Hildebrandt, B; Moratz, R; Scheering, C. (eds.): Architectures in Cognitive Robotics. Report 98/13, SFB 360 "Situierte Künstliche Kommunikatoren", Universität Bielefeld, 11-18.

HERZOG, Gerd; WAZINSKI, Peter. (1994). VIsual TRAnslator: Linking Perceptions and Natural Language Descriptions. In: Artificial Intelligence Review 8.2, 175-187.

HOVY, Eduard H. (1993): Automated Discourse Generation Using Discourse Structure Relations. In: Artificial Intelligence 63, 341-386.

JACKENDOFF, Ray (1983): Semantics and Cognition. Cambridge, MA: MIT Press (Current studies in linguistics series 8).

— (1996): The Architecture of the Linguistic-Spatial Interface. In: Bloom, P.; Peterson, M.A.; Nadel, L.; Garrett, M.F. (eds.): Language and Space. Cambridge, MA: MIT Press.

JACKENDOFF, Ray (1990). Semantic Structures. Cambridge, MA: MIT Press.

LÄNGLE, Thomas; LÜTH, Tim C.; STOPP, Eva; HERZOG, Gerd (1996): Natural Language Access to Intelligent Robots: Explaining Automatic Error Recovery. In: Ramsay, A. M. (ed.): Artificial Intelligence: Methodology, Systems, Applications. Amsterdam: IOS, 259-267.

LÄNGLE, Thomas; LÜTH, Tim C.; STOPP, Eva; HERZOG, Gerd; KAMSTRUP, Gjertrud (1995): KANTRA – A Natural Language Interface for Intelligent Robots. In: Rembold, U.; Dillman, R.; Hertzberger, L. O.; Kanade, T. (eds.): Intelligent Autonomous Systems. Amsterdam: IOS (IAS 4), 357-364.

Levelt, Willem J.M. (1989). Speaking: From intention to articulation. Cambridge, MA: MIT Press.

MILDE, Jan-Torsten; STRIPPGEN, Simone; PETERS, Kornelia (1997): Situated Communication with Robots. In: Proceedings of the First international workshop on human-computer conversation. Bellagio, Italy.

REHM, Matthias (1999): IpaGe – An Incremental Parrallel Generator for Natural Language. This volume.

SLOMAN, Aaron; Logan, Brian (1999): Building Cognitively Rich Agents. Communications of the ACM. 42.3.

TORRANCE, Mark (1994). Natural Language Communication with Robots (Master's Thesis at the Department of Electrical Engineering and Computer Science, Massachusetts Institute of Technology).

The Potential of New Technologies:
Linguistic Education in the New Millennium[1]

Jürgen Handke

1 Introduction

There are only few inventions in the history of mankind that have had such an impact on so many aspects of human life like the digital computer. And this impact – both negative and positive – continues. Today, in many areas, such as administration, economy, entertainment, healthcare, military and scientific research, to name a few, it seems inconceivable to do without computers and other modern information technologies. A vast number of fields are being transformed at an enormously high speed leading to completely new approaches and a number of challenges.

This paper discusses the implications of the "digital revolution" for the teaching of linguistics. It will be shown that traditional methods will soon be obsolete in a society where education and training will become increasingly independent of place and time. Hence facilities that permit learning virtually everywhere and at any time have to be provided. Concepts such as "distance (or tele) learning" and "computer-based training" (CBT) are among the most frequently discussed approaches towards this issue. This paper shows the ease with which complex linguistic phenomena can be presented using such environments and discusses the consequences for linguistic education.

2 The use of computers in education

Educational applications of computer technology have been under development since the early 1960s. These applications have included scheduling courses, managing teaching aids, and grading tests (Barr/Feigenbaum 1982:225). The most important application in this field, however, has been to use the computer as a device that interacts with the student in the process of education. There have been three approaches to do this.

2.1 Approaches

The *environmental* approach allows the student a more or less free-style use of the computer. The best known realisation of it is the use of Papert's LOGO laboratory, a specific programming tool for students. The assumption is that a side-effect of computer programming is learning problem-solving strategies, especially when the pro-

---

[1] This essay is dedicated to my teacher, Ekkehard König, who celebrated his 60th birthday in January 2001.

gram suggests good problem-solving strategies to the student. Another approach uses *games and simulations* as instructional tools. Again, the student is involved in a computer-based activity, for example, in constructing syntactic trees, for which learning is a side effect. The third and most important application in education is *computer-assisted instruction* (CAI). Unlike the first two approaches, the goal of CAI is to instigate and control learning. The first instructional programs took many forms, but all adhered to essentially the same philosophy: The student was normally given some sort of instructional text and was asked some questions that required a brief answer. After the student's response he was told whether he was right or wrong. Depending on the type of CAI system, linear, branching or generative (O'Shea/Self: 1986:55ff), the response was sometimes used to determine the path through the curriculum, i.e. to determine the sequence of problems or questions.

2.2   The conception of ITS

In the 1970s, the growing field of Artificial Intelligence (AI) prompted CAI-researchers to integrate AI-techniques into educational programs. Early research on ICAI (Intelligent CAI) systems focused on the representation of the subject matter. A second phase in the development of ICAI tutors was characterised by the inclusion of additional expertise in the systems concerning the student's learning behaviour and the strategies of tutoring. These new approaches were subsumed under the heading of ITS (Intelligent Tutoring System).

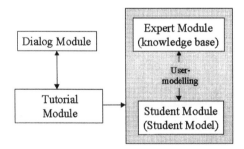

Figure 1: The theoretical conception of ITS

Figure 1 exhibits the main components of an ITS. The *dialogue* module is concerned with the interaction between man and machine, ideally in spoken natural language. The *tutorial* module integrates knowledge about teaching methods and the subject area. It communicates with the student, selects problems for him, monitors and criticises his performance, provides assistance upon request, and selects remedial material when necessary. The heart of an ITS is realised by the *expert* module on the one hand and the *student* module on the other. Together they constitute the *expertise* module or *expert* component (Barr/Feigenbaum: 1982, 229). Despite numerous attempts to develop ITS (see Swartz/Yazdani: 1992), true ITS have not yet become available. First, there is still a lot to understand about the characteristics of the learner and teaching practice before adequate expert and student modules can be built and implemented. Secondly, the principles of user-modelling highly depend on the subject matter. Nevertheless, the theoretical conception of an ITS constitutes an important guideline for any developer of an educational program.

2.3 Multimedia and CBT

Recent advances in graphical interface and multimedia technology have developed new, exciting tools for CAI. Sound, video, graphics, animation and text can now be combined resulting in powerful multimedia systems. Since the mid 1990s, the market has been flooded with multimedia systems of every kind: games, simulations, dictionaries, catalogues, etc. A number of these systems also involve some sort of tutorial component. However, they do not realise any of the ITS strategies discussed above and do not deserve the name. They are still behaviouristic, program-guided systems, which have not superseded the standard of the early 1970s. Their tutorial responses are mainly confined to yes-no/right-wrong responses and the path through the curriculum depends on the student's responses. ITS-strategies, such as assistance upon request, or the selection of remedial material based on the student's performance, are hardly used in today's CBT systems.

2.4 The new technologies in linguistic education

Despite the inadequacies discussed, there is no doubt that computer-based methods of presentation and learning will revolutionise education (Glotz 1997:19). The university of the not-so-distant future will present large amounts of its course material using the new technologies as online applications in the world-wide web, and as offline variants on external storage devices.

2.4.1 Online applications

The fundamental advantage of online applications is their constant availability. However, due to loading and streaming limitations, they are in most cases confined to mere text collections and are in their present form hardly superior to conventional methods of education. Furthermore, the degree of interactivity is very low. In most cases it is restricted to simple mouse-click actions. Nevertheless, the easy way to access these new environments has already influenced education, and it is only a question of a few years until a large number of standard courses will be presented online.

2.4.2 Offline applications

 Offline material uses storage devices, such as CD-ROMs or DVDs (digital versatile disks). Thus, the general limitations of the world-wide web do not exist. Course material presented in such a way exhibits previously unknown aspects of visualisation, i.e. of displaying and explaining scientific phenomena; it involves auditive support, spoken comments, explanations, etc. Often, certain scientific problems are supported by complex animations and, in some cases, even by video material. Over and above these new ways of presenting course material, many of these exciting new programs incorporate tutorial components which allow the evaluation of the student's performance.

3   The benefits of the new technologies

Whether and how the new technologies can actually benefit education has been a controversial issue for some time. Research and development have both their success stories and failures, providing believers and disbelievers in technology-based education alike with support for their positions. Over and above general didactic aspects such as individualised, self-controlled learning, today's key motivation can be seen in the multimedia capabilities of the new technologies and the resulting innovative methods of teaching complex scientific aspects.

In the following sections we will illustrate on the basis of some selected examples from "The Interactive Introduction to Linguistics" (Handke/Intemann 1999), how linguistic phenomena can be converted into screen representation using multimedia techniques. We will see that some of these phenomena cannot be explained in such elegant ways on the basis of traditional methods of teaching, such as face-to-face education or the use of the print media.[2]

3.1   Simple rollover effects

The most common technique in multimedia applications is the use of rollover effects. As soon as the cursor is over a specific object (text or graphic) the program responds in a predefined way. Figure 2 exhibits two rollover effects: textual information about the language family and a photo of a corresponding native speaker. Both aspects become visible as soon as the cursor is over the area "Niger-Congo". This technique enriches formerly static representations with some sort of dynamicness. Moreover, it combines textual with additional visual information, leading to a more interesting and vivid presentation of the subject material.

---

[2] *The Interactive Introduction to Linguistics* (short *Linguistics Interactive*) is a CBT-system seeking to realise the basic requirements of an ITS. At Marburg University it has replaced the obligatory introductory course to linguistics since summer 1998.

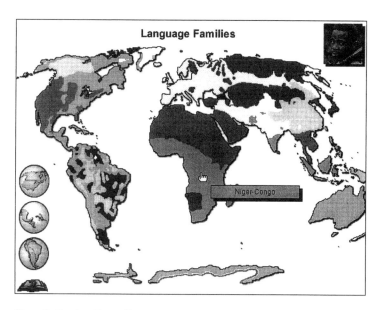

Figure 2: Simple rollover effects

Rollover effects of this kind belong to the basic repertoire of modern hypertext/ hypermedia systems and are familiar from the world-wide web. However, in contrast to the web, they can be used much more effectively in an offline application, since the format and the size of graphics is much less important, due to the absence of loading or streaming limitations imposed by the internet.

3.2 Complex visual aspects

Over and above the mere visual support, the teaching of complex scientific processes often involves more than just the presentation of a simple diagram or a highlighted part of a picture. The following example of the Great Vowel Shift (GVS), a phonetic change that affected the quality of the Middle English long vowels between 1350 and 1550 AD, may serve as an example. Figure 3 reduces this process to a static description of the situation before and after the GVS. The interpretation of this static representation involves some degree of phonetic understanding and fantasy. The shifting of the quality of each individual vowel can only be understood on the basis of additional explanations about phonetic principles. In a multimedia environment, however, two techniques suffice to represent a complex process such as the GVS: path-animation and fading. First, an animation sequence shows the path of each example and its respective vowel by moving them from their original to their target position. During the animation, the original vowel fades into the target vowel. This process is supported by changing colours, and, optionally, by spoken examples, which can be retrieved by a simple mouse click on each word.

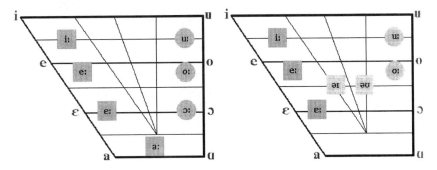

Figure 3: The Great Vowel Shift, before, on the left, after, on the right

The teaching of linguistics involves numerous problems of this kind, for example, all aspects of articulatory phonetics, e.g. place and manner of articulation, the dynamic building of tree representations, specific linguistic operations, e.g. transformations, or the unfolding of linguistic rules, e.g. phrase-structure rules.

In addition to these examples, there is a relatively large number of linguistic diagrams and models whose function can most adequately be explained using animation techniques (e.g. perception models, grammar models, etc.).

3.3   Auditive support

Using today's audio devices, we can choose from a variety of sound options: spoken comments, linguistic examples (words, dialogues, language samples), background music, jingles, sounds. Whereas all those sound options that involve music primarily serve as means of general support (invoking interest, changing attention, creating fun etc.), spoken comments and spoken linguistic examples are important means of explaining linguistic facts. Figure 4 displays a map of the Austroasiatic language family where each language serves as a sensitive area. As soon as the left mouse button is pressed, the respective area is highlighted and an example of the language associated with it can be heard. Simultaneously, various representations of the spoken passage and some additional options are represented in a specific window.

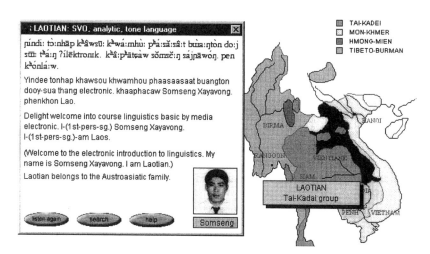

Figure 4: Language maps and audio support

A different method of using sound support presents single words or even individual sounds to the student. Figure 5 exhibits the British English (RP) diphthongs where the transitional paths for each diphthong can be retrieved via simple mouse click. At the same time, a spoken example is presented.

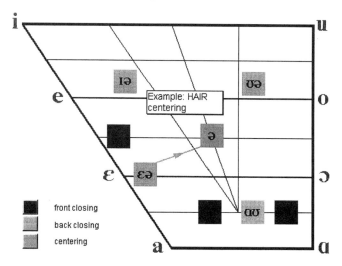

Figure 5: RP-diphthongs and their transitional paths on the vowel chart

Over and above the enormous advantage of having auditive support, this way of representing diphthongs is superior to conventional methods. In printed form it is impossible to present the transitional paths for all 8 RP-diphthongs in one diagram. Using 8 different diagrams, by contrast, would be too costly in book form.

3.4   Synchronisation

Aspects of synchronisation involve the presentation of specific elements (graphics, text, animation, etc.) in line with other multimedia events. The most common technique in this respect is the use of sound material and the simultaneous presentation of sequences of graphics or text. Figure 6 displays a simple example of this kind. It involves the spoken comment in example (1). By means of so-called "cue-points" (the items underlined) it can be subdivided into six parts:

1) a. Normally, in all vowels the
   b. velum is raised so that there is a
   c. velic closure and air does not flow out through the nose.
   d. However, if the velum is
   e. lowered to allow part of the airstream to fill the nasal cavity, vowels may be
   f. nasalised. In other words, the nasal cavity is used as a second resonance-chamber.

(The Interactive Introduction to Linguistics, Module: Phonetics/Cardinal Vowels)

As a default, a standard graphic, the vocal tract, is visible. As soon as the student retrieves the spoken comment via a specific button, additional objects are presented. In Figure 6 the objects are synchronised with the cue-points of example (1) from left to right.

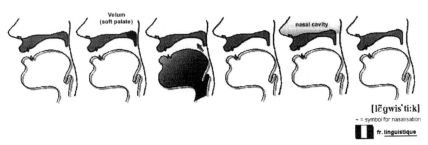

[lɛ̃gwisˈtiːk]
~ = symbol for nasalisation
  fr. linguistique

Figure 6: An example of synchronisation

Synchronisation effects are highly efficient means of multimedia representation, similar to video, TV, or movie. The advantage in a multimedia environment, however, is their interactive character: effects of this kind can be repeated, paused or stopped as often as desired.

3.5 Aspects of generation

A large number of linguistic phenomena can most adequately be illustrated by means of tree diagrams. Such structures are inherently procedural. This property, however, cannot be shown on paper; it can, with some care, be exhibited using chalk and blackboard. In a multimedia environment, however, the unfolding of the rules leading from a linguistic structure to a tree, or vice versa, is not problematic at all. It can either be represented as a continuous animation or as a structure which unfolds via button click.

Figure 7 displays an example from syntax, where the phases of generating and dismantling of a syntactic tree can be retrieved step-by-step.

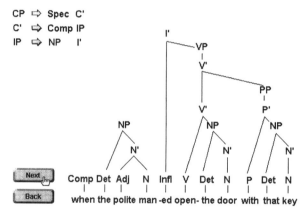

Figure 7: Syntactic rule application

Representations of this kind are primarily used in morphology and syntax, but also play a role in phonology, for example, in displaying syllable structures, or in non-linear representations. The use of multimedia techniques seems to be the best format to account for the dynamic character of this highly important means of linguistic description.

3.6 Elaborate CBT-methods

In addition to the simple representation of linguistic phenomena elaborate CBT-methods involve the use of an interactive tutorial component, which closely interacts with the student during the educational process. Standard teaching methods are by and large inferior to modern CBT. Exercises in linguistic textbooks, for example, do not allow any interaction, let alon any alternatives to their pregenerated answers (if there are any). In face-to-face teaching environments, interaction is often limited to an exchange of ideas between a handful of active students and the teacher. Thus, the necessity for interactive CBT-systems, especially in those areas where human teachers fail to evoke excitement among their students (e.g. in simple linguistic exercises), seems obvious. The following sections illustrate this on the basis of two examples, naming tasks and phonemic transcription tasks.

3.6.1 Naming tasks

Naming tasks involve the naming of objects, processes and other linguistic phenomena. The general procedure of these exercises is as follows: The CBT-component of an interactive system asks a question or displays a specific diagram or picture and the student has to type the required answer into a specific text field. Normally, the answers are one-word-answers. Figure 8 exhibits an example from phonology, where the student has to name the place of articulation to be associated with an animation.

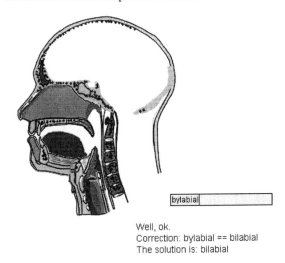

bylabial

Well, ok.
Correction: bylabial == bilabial
The solution is: bilabial

Figure 8: Naming Consonantal Articulation

In exercises of this type, one has to make sure that deviant input, for example, *bylabial* instead of *bilabial* is not simply rejected but analysed and accepted via internal routines, as illustrated in figure 8.

3.6.2 Transcription tasks

A completely different evaluation technique is used in a phonemic transcription task (figure 9). In order to decide whether the student's transcription, which he generates via a virtual keyboard, is correct or not, two mechanisms interact: a position mechanism and a character mechanism.

With CBT-techniques of this kind, it is possible to evaluate the student's perform-ance in such a way that mistakes do not lead to a rejection of the input but to a helpful correction. Moreover, those parts of the response that are correct will be positively reinforced. The human teacher will eventually be freed from the presentation and the correction of standard exercises of this kind.

Figure 9: Phonemic Transcription Tasks

4 The new scenario

There is no doubt that the multimedia capabilities of the new technologies will first supplement and eventually replace traditional methods of teaching. Despite some pre-sent limitations of man-machine interaction (e.g. the lack of natural language pro-cessing capabilities), we will soon be surrounded by computers that offer exciting new ways for education by serving students as virtual mentors and collaborators that provide them with individualised, qualified and engaging support in their learning. Consequently, the role of the human teacher will change, and, additionally, human interaction, i.e. discussions in class, will have to be redefined. Let us assume the fol-lowing scenario, which has partly been realised by the semi-online phonology semi-nar at Marburg University:

Course: Phonology
Number of course units: 14
Course requirements: worksheets, final examination
Example: Unit 4: RP-phonology

Questions (to be answered after unit 4):
a. What do you understand by Received Pronunciation ?
b. ....
    ....
g. Study the consonantal system of RP and describe each consonant articulatorily.

Virtual sessions and exercises for unit 4 (represented as hyperlinks):
Virtual Session: British English Phonology
Exercise 1: RP-vowels
...
Exercise 8: RP-phonemic transcription

Figure 10 shows the initial screen of the virtual session on British English Phonology. Using such a virtual environment, learning is now fully self-controlled allowing the student to access the material at any time from any place. By means of additional CBT-modules the student can test his educational progress. His results are saved in a local file and transferred to the course conductor for further examination.

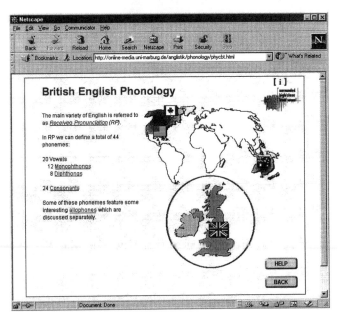

Figure 10: British English Phonology, an online session

4.1 The role of the human teacher

In addition to the online course material optional plenary meetings will be offered where the students can practice in groups and discuss additional issues. These meetings, however, will involve a passive teacher, who no longer has to present the course material but is available for discussion. His role can now most adequately be defined as that of a coach. Freed from the presentation of the basic material, in our example the presentation of the RP-sound-system, the teacher can now concentrate on those aspects which have previously been neglected: individual advising, problem solving, and tutoring (specific help on course assignments). Thus, teachers may eventually invest more time to establish more efficient relationships between themselves and their students, allowing more individualised problem solving and educational support.

4.2 The role of the student

A number of critics predict an educational scenario where the student will spend most of his time on his own separated from his fellow students and his teachers. According to this point of view, learning will be a self-contained but isolated activity where communication is restricted to the exchange of emails and computer-based chats. However, the actual integration of a CBT-system into the linguistic curriculum at Marburg University has developed a different reality. CBT seems to create a new type of group conscience where students favour learning in small groups: they gather around the computer to discuss the proposals and implications of the program. In other words, CBT does not block communication but may establish new forms of communication and – considering the crowded lecture halls and the resulting anonymity of the student – promotes a learning society where communication becomes more important than before.

5 Conclusion and further issues

The first and most important conclusion to be drawn is simply this: The new technologies make an enormous impact on education and training. Students will primarily access their course material online or via specific tools, such as CD-ROM or DVD. Traditional methods, such as textbooks, will not become obsolete, but they will be used as supplementary rather than as dominant knowledge sources. Furthermore, new ways of information interchange will be established. Learning in groups and new forms of communication between students and tutors will be used.

Apart from these consequences for teaching, the new technologies have a considerable effect on course work and scientific publication. Course work will increasingly involve the digital technologies, such as email and web-documents. Book publications, at least those with textbook character, will first be supplemented and eventually be superseded by the new technologies. Even today, there is no point in publishing a conventional textbook in linguistics without supplementary computerised material. A

CD-ROM combining textual information with graphics and audio material provides in many cases a much more informative solution.

At present, however, the acceptance of such new ways of publishing is still low. Virtual courses such as "Linguistics Interactive" are often considered as "nice little devices" with toy character.[3] Despite the fact that this system contains more than 400 pages of text-material, ca. 850 graphics, 200 animations, 12 videoclips and more than 500 spoken examples, it is still considered inferior to a comparable textbook (even though there is none of comparable complexity). However, this attitude is beginning to change. CD-ROMs as book supplements (Labov et al. 2000; Handke 2000) or independent offline-publications will soon dominate the "textbook-segment" of the linguistic market and it will only be a matter of time until the value of such publications will be properly acknowledged by the scientific community.

6   References

FARRINGTON, Gregory C. (1997): Das Hochschulstudium im Informationszeitalter. Eine amerikanische Perspektive. In: Hamm; Müller-Böling: 45-70.

GLOTZ, Peter. (1997): Hochschulentwicklung mit neuen Medien. Ein Appell an die Politik. In: Hamm; Müller-Böling: 19-24.

HAMM, Ingrid; Müller-Böling, Detlef (eds.) (1997): Hochschulentwicklung durch neue Medien. Erfahrungen – Projekte – Perspektiven; mit einer Bestandsaufnahme über Multimedia-Projekte an deutschen Hochschulen. Gütersloh: Verlag Bertelsmann Stiftung (Bildungswege in der Informationsgesellschaft).

HANDKE, Jürgen; INTEMANN, Frauke (1999): The Interactive Introduction to Linguistics. An interactive course for students of languages and linguistics (CD-ROM). München: Max Hueber Verlag.

HAUFF, Mechtild (ed.) (1998): media@uni-multi.media. Entwicklung – Gestaltung – Evaluation neuer Medien; [Fachtagung, 16. - 18. September 1997 in Hagen]. Münster: Waxmann Verlag (Medien in der Wissenschaft 6).

ISSING, Ludwig; KLIMSA, Paul (eds.) (1995): Information und Lernen mit Multimedia. Weinheim: Beltz.

KRAEMER, Wolfgang; MILIUS, Frank; SCHEER, August-Wilhelm (eds.) (1997): Virtuelles Lehren und Lernen an deutschen Universitäten. Eine Dokumentaation. Gütersloh: Bertelsmann (Initiative: BIG – Bildungswege in der InformationsGesellschaft).

LABOV, William; ASH, Sharon; BOBERG, Charles (2000): Atlas of North American English: phonetics, phonology and sound change. Berlin – New York: Mouton de Gruyter. CD-ROM supplement by Jürgen Handke.

O'SHEA, Tim; SELF, John. (1986): Lernen und Lehren mit Computern. Künstliche Intelligenz im Unterricht. Stuttgart: Birkhäuser.

SCHULMEISTER, Rolf (1996): Grundlagen hypermedialer Lernsysteme. Theorie – Didaktik – Design. Bonn: Addison-Wesley.

SIMON, Hartmut (ed.) (1997): Virtueller Campus: Forschung und Entwicklung für neues Lehren und Lernen. Münster: Waxmann Verlag (Medien in der Wissenschaft; 5. Jahrestagung / Gesellschaft für Medien in der Wissenschaft 1996).

---

[3]   *You can play around with it. Scientificly, however, it should not be taken too seriously!* was among the more polite comments at various conferences where the system was presented.

SWARTZ, Merryana; YAZDANI, Masoud (eds.) (1992): Intelligent Tutoring Systems for Foreign Language Learning. the bridge to international communication; [proceedings of the NATO Advanced Research Workshop "The Bridge to International Communication: Intelligent Tutoring Systems for Foreign Language Learning", held in Washington, DC, September 19 - 21, 1990]. Berlin: Springer Verlag (NATO ASI series : Series F, Computer and systems sciences 80).

Conceptual Cartography: A New Approach for Text Mining

Jacques Ladouceur, Arman Tajarobi, Frédérick Brault

1   Introduction

Numerous studies dealing with concept mapping and semantic networks have been carried out over the last few decades. Most of these studies have focused on the relationships between concepts out of context. In this paper, we present a new approach designed primarily to deal with the relationships of concepts inside a text for the purposes of text mining. The approach is based on *complex term*[1] extraction and manipulations allowing a contextual classification of terms used in a text. We will look at three methods developed so far for conceptual cartography, namely, formal proximity, combinational properties and syntactic structures.

2   Context

A textual document may be considered as a set of inter-related concepts[2]. Concepts are the building blocks of discourse. Language enables us to organize these building blocks in an infinite number of ways. Establishing appropriate links and relationships between concepts is an important part of *understanding* discourse.

Conceptual cartography is primarily based on establishing appropriate links and finding the relationships between concepts in predetermined and defined contexts, such as in a textual document. Theoretically, any concept can enter into a semantic relationship with any other concept in discourse because language and its use in discourse are not limited to objective reality. A classical example is the theory of sets which attributes zero membership to the set of dogs who can write computer programs. Although *programmer dogs* do not exist in the extra-mental reality, their conception in imagination and their production in discourse is easily achievable. Abstract thought, reporting of events and formulating new ideas often translate to empty sets from a referential point of view. For this reason, tools such as general and specialized dictionaries and thesauri often fall short of explaining a great quantity of relationships that exist in discourse. Seemingly unrelated concepts can, and are, associated in discourse regularly. These associations are only meaningful in given contexts.

Therefore, mapping of concepts according to the context in which they appear presents interesting possibilities for text mining applications such as content access, document classification, information retrieval, term extraction and term alignment.

---

[1] cf. section 3

[2] We adopt the general definition given for concept by Kocourek (1991) and Sager (1990): mental categories for objects, events, or ideas that have a common set of features

2.1   Concepts and terms

Terminologists such as Sager (1990) consider that terms are the linguistic representation of concepts. This is particularly true for special languages where a conscious effort is made to name concepts according to pre-specified rules. This property of terms can be used in a *conceptual reading system* to recognize and extract the concepts in a text, to organize and map the extracted concepts to show the existing relationships between them inside the text, and to make implicit and explicit information from the text more readily accessible.

Therefore, the first step of conceptual cartography involves the extraction of terms from a text. In the next section, a brief description of *Termplus*, a complex term extraction unit, will follow. We will then explore a few simple techniques of concept mapping.

3   Termplus: [3] A complex term extraction unit

The majority of terms in a specialized text are graphically complex; that is, they are composed of two or more words (i.e. *supreme court, bill of rights*, etc.). However, the automatic extraction of complex terms is a difficult problem which has not been completely resolved yet.

Generally speaking, two distinct approaches are used for the automatic recognition and extraction of complex terms: numerical and linguistic. Each of these approaches presents certain advantages and drawbacks which we will not elaborate here. It suffices to say that the technology of Termplus uses both of these approaches in its design in order to maximize the advantages and minimize the drawbacks of each approach.

Basically, a text analysed by Termplus goes through a series of numerical and linguistic analyses. The numerical analysis is assured by an independent module which works in conjunction with the linguistic module. The linguistic module is highly customizable and new languages can be added to enable Termplus to work in different languages. So far, the English, French and Portuguese language modules have been added.

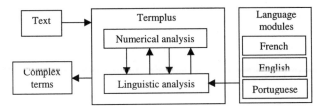

Figure 1

---

[3]   Termplus© was developed at Laval University by professor Ladouceur's research team.

The architecture of Termplus is designed to eliminate, or at least reduce to a minimum, the *silence* in the results. During the first phase of processing, all possible text segments that may be a complex term are extracted. A deductive process during which each segment is rated according to its probability of being a complex term follows this phase. Segments having zero probability of being a term are eliminated, and those with probabilities approaching 100% are sent to the top of the list. The final result is a list of segments sorted according to the probability of each segment being a term.

3.1 Some results

The English and French language modules have been tested on corpora of juridical texts. The English corpus contained 37 texts totalling approximately 533,000 words, and the French corpus contained 33 texts with over 510,000 words. The list of segments retained by Termplus for the English text contained 42% complex terms and 58% non-terms or noise. Similar results were obtained for the French (40% complex terms, 60% noise). For each segment, the context and strict terminological criteria were used to arrive at the above results. The overall silence was around 11%.

As mentioned above, one of the powerful features of Termplus is the classification of segments according to their probability of being a term. For the English corpus, the first and last 30 segments for each text were evaluated as well. On the average, 28 out of the first 30 segments (93%) were terms, whereas only 11 of the last 30 segments (36.6%) were terms (see Table 1).

First 15 segments	Middle 15 segments	Last 15 segments
supreme court	overall group mission	twisted rope
supra note	group defamation offence	night horror movie
court of canada	narrow 4	mentes reae
supreme court of canada	treaty party	robyn packard
principles of fundamental justice	extradition treaty	bloc québécois leader lucien bouchard
freedom of expression	federal transportation policy	marty friedland
court of appeal	justifying federal supremacy	chemical deoxyribonicleic acid
aboriginal rights	renewed federal interest	commanded wholehearted
charter of rights	equally subject	offically atheistic
judicial review	federal indian laws	vocal critic
democratic society	treaty agreements	terra incognita
fundamental justice	federal legislative powers	expendable desiderata
federal government	treaty commissioners	Tomey homma
constitution act	federal fishery regulations	chronic schizophrenia
freedom of religion	proposed federal regulations	saudi arabia

Table 1

The above results are based on a strict terminological evaluation. Many of the non-term segments (ex. *right of access to hunt, concept of fiduciary obligation, theories of extinguishments, standard of care,* etc.) retained by Termplus are not completely devoid of interest. In fact, as will be seen in the next section, over 80% of segments extracted by Termplus carry useful information about the text, and can therefore be used for purposes such as conceptual cartography.

4   Conceptual cartography

Table 1 contains a partial list of segments extracted by Termplus from a text of approximately 13,000 words[4]. A thematic definition or characterization of the text may be formulated from this list, which is organized in order of productivity ratio. However, this list is only a one dimensional and static view of the text. In the following sections, we will present three techniques which may be used to restructure this list in order to navigate through the terms and to carry out a conceptual reading of text. None of these techniques require any heavy databases or parsing. They can each be used independently or simultaneously.

4.1   Formal proximity

Formal proximity refers to semantic associations between complex terms that can be derived from their graphical form. Complex terms contain at least two words. Two complex terms sharing one or more similar words are most often, but not always, linked conceptually; that is, they refer to different realities that have something in common. For example, the four concepts represented by *aboriginal courts, aboriginal land, aboriginal language* and *aboriginal rights* refer to very different realities with a common denominator, which is *aboriginal.* We have used this property to develop a first technique for conceptual cartography. The technique uses each component of a term as an anchor to access other complex terms with the same components.

Starting from a first complex term, we can obtain a list of all the terms that share at least one word with that term. From there we can continue a navigation process that would allow us to run through a large number of related concepts in the text.

For example, if we are interested in finding the concepts related to *aboriginal rights* in the text, we can easily obtain a list of terms which contain the words *aboriginal* and *rights.*

aboriginal	rights
aboriginal constitution	aboriginal rights provisions
aboriginal courts	aboriginal rights to fish
aboriginal land	aboriginal rights to land
aboriginal language	canadian charter of rights
aboriginal laws	cree legislative rights
aboriginal peoples of Canada	indigenous rights
aboriginal rights to fish	fishing rights
aboriginal treaty	hunting rights

---

[4]   In all, 1254 segments were extracted out of which 620 were terms.

aboriginal	rights
distinct character of aboriginal peoples	indian rights
enforcement of aboriginal laws	indian territorial rights
exclusion of aboriginal issues	inuit aboriginal rights
exclusive aboriginal right	inuit hunting rights
musqueam aboriginal right to fish	native rights
paradigm of aboriginal policy	political rights
recognized aboriginal title	rights of indigenous peoples
	rights provisions
	rights to hunt
	united nations human rights
	usufructuary right

Table 2

Each term in these lists may be used in the same way to obtain other terms that would in theory bear a more distant relationship with the original term. For example, the component *treaty* in *aboriginal treaty* in the list above would yield a list of concepts each of which may be used to access other related concepts in the text:

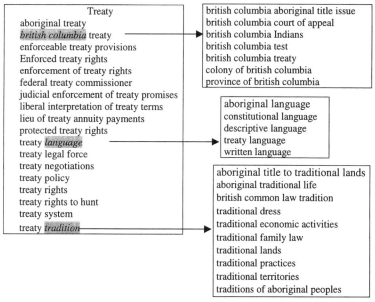

Figure 2

In addition, aligning the concepts having a number of components in common can be used to discover certain semantic relationships such as hyponymy. For example, *aboriginal rights to fish* and *aboriginal rights to land* are both subsets or hyponyms of *aboriginal rights*, and *Musqueam aboriginal right to fish* is a subset of both *aboriginal rights to fish* and *aboriginal rights*.

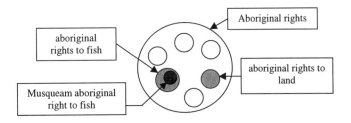

Figure 3

4.2   Combinational properties (co-occurrences)

A great number of studies on co-occurrences have shown the existence of semantic associations between words appearing near each other in a text. Position is an important criterion for concept association in the universe of discourse. Unrelated concepts are regularly combined in discourse to formulate specific thoughts and information. For example, normally, *Mohawk warriors* and *Canadian army* are not semantically associated, but once the idea of *armed confrontation* comes into the picture, these two seemingly unrelated concepts find a common link in context of a sentence such as:

> During the summer, an armed confrontation at Oka in Quebec involved Mohawk warriors on one side and the Canadian army on the other.

The paragraph from which the above sentence was extracted contained other terms such as *land claim* and *golf course*, other seemingly unrelated concepts. However, examining the context reveals that the text is referring to a *land claim* which led to an *armed confrontation* involving the *Canadian Army* and the *Mohawk warriors* over land which was to be transformed into a *golf course.*

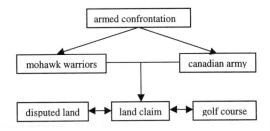

Figure 4

As with the first technique, this technique allows us to navigate through related concepts. The contextual combinational properties of terms as indicators of semantic association is exploited to restructure the list of Termplus and to navigate through the concepts appearing near each other in the text.

Distribution, or the rate of occurrence, is also an important indicator of semantic association. In the above text, *aboriginal rights* and *supreme court* occur together in seven different sentences. This is not surprising if we consider that this text is a report on several cases handled by the *supreme court* concerning *aboriginal rights*. But more importantly, by merely looking at this kind of data we can predict the content of a text, and how each concept is related to others.

supreme court	northwest territories	musqueam indian band
blanket extinguishments	aboriginal title	legal rights
supreme court of canada	treaty rights	reserve lands
guerin case	constitution act	musqueam people
hunting rights	aboriginal and treaty rights	community buildings

4.3 Syntactic structures

Certain syntactic structures are regularly used in discourse to establish semantic relationships such as hyponymy (inclusion relation) between concepts (Hearst 1992; Tajarobi 1998). The prototype structure for hyponymy is constructed around the phrase *is a kind of* as in BMW *is a kind of car* where *BMW is* a hyponym of *car.*

Hyponym	is a kind of	Hyperonyme

Such syntactic structures may be used to extract concepts which are in an inclusion relationship in a text. For example, in 1) and 2) below, the base structure *and other* reveals that *Guerin* and *Sparrow* refer to *cases*, and that *Gitksan* and *Wet'suwet'en* are *First Nations.*

1) Section 35 and the decisions in Guerin, Sparrow *and other* cases establish that some elements of the pre-contact aboriginal legal order are part of Canadian law.

2) The Gitksan and Wet'suwet'en *and a number of other* First Nations are proceeding within the process.

This type of information could also be used to enrich lexical databases such as thesauri. But more importantly, we can use this technique in the context of a text to extract concepts which are in a semantic relationship as in 3).

3) The parties have concentrated for too long on legal and constitutional questions *such as* ownership, sovereignty and rights, which are fascinating legal concepts.

The structure *such as* is used to establish an inclusion relationship between the concepts *ownership, sovereignty* and *rights* on the one hand, and *legal and constitutional questions* on the other.

5   Conclusion

Until recently, textual documents have been available only in paper format. This format has conditioned the way we read texts. That is, we have become accustomed to a left to right, top to bottom linear reading of texts. Today, with the increasing number of textual documents available in electronic format, we can consider new approaches of reading a text.

In designing the conceptual cartography system, we have favoured the use of simple techniques to arrive at a system that is light, rapid, independent of enormous databases and complicated parsing procedures, easy to implement and adapt to different environments and applications, and most importantly, a system that can be used to enhance and enrich existing databases by exploiting textual information and content, rather than relying on existing dictionaries and thesauri for its work.

The approach has been successfully tested in the development of a few applications such as conceptual summarization, cross text concept synthesis, and complex term alignment using non-parallel texts (Ladouceur and Tajarobi 1998). Beside these, the development of other applications such as *assisted textual content understanding* can be envisaged using the conceptual cartography approach.

6   References

ALLWOOD, Jens; ANDERSON, Lars-Gunnar; DAHL, Sten (1977): Logic in Linguistics. Cambridge: Cambridge University Press.

BATTY, David (1976): Knowledge and its Organization. College of Library and Information Services, University of Maryland.

BENVENISTE, Émile (1974): Problèmes de linguistique générale, t. 2. Paris: Gallimard.

BOLTON, Neil, 1977, Concept formation, New York – Toronto, Pergamon Press.

HEARST, Marti A. (1992): Automatic Acquisition of Hyponyms from Large Text Corpora. In: Proceedings of the Fifteenth International Conference on Computational Linguistics (Coling-92), Nantes, France, p. 539-545.

KOCOUREK, Rostislav (1991): La langue française de la technique et de la science; vers une linguistique de la langue savante. Wiesbaden: Oscar Brandstetter Verlag KG and Co.

LADOUCEUR, Jacques (1997): Une méthode pour l'alignement de termes complexes plurilingues dans des textes specializes. In: Actes des Journées Scientifiques et techniques du Réseau Francophone de l'ingénierie de la langue de l'AUPELF-UREF, Avignon, 493-500.

LADOUCEUR, Jacques; DROUIN, Patrick (1997): Une analyse terminométrique pour le repérage automatique des descripteurs complexes dans les textes de spécialité. In: Meta 42.1, 207-218.

LADOUCEUR, Jacques; TAJAROBI, Arman (1998): Computer-Assisted Plurilingual Reading System. In: Structures and Relations in the Organization of Knowledge. Würzburg.

OTMAN, Gabriel (1996): Représentations sémantiques en terminologie. Paris: Masson.

SAGER, Juan C. (1993): Language Engineering and Translation Consequences of Automation. Amsterdam – Philadelphia: John Benjamins.

— (1990): A Practical Course in Terminology Processing. Amsterdam – Philadelphia: John Benjamins.

TAJAROBI, Arman (1998): La reconnaissance automatique des hyponymes. Theses (M.A.). Québec: Université Laval.

Lexical Correspondence in a Logic Programming Implementation of Dependency-based Parsing

Tom B. Y. Lai, Changning Huang

1   Introduction

In Dependency Grammar (Tesnière 1959), words contract binary, asymmetrical governor-dependent relationships. Hays (1964) has proposed *dependency rules* to generate syntactic dependency structures in which dependency links do not cross one another and in which nodes do not have more than one governor. Gaifman (1965) has studied the affinity of this kind of *projective* syntactic dependency with context-free phrase-structure grammar, and Robinson (1970) has defined dependency structures in terms of constraining *axioms*.

We have added constraints to Hays' dependency rules (Lai and Huang 1994, 1995) and a logic programming implementation has been attempted (Lai and Huang 1998a). We have also tried to place, as far as possible, grammatical information in the lexicon and reduce dependency rules into binary-branching ones (Lai and Huang 1998b, 1999a, 1999c). *Non-projective* phenomena are handled by constraints defined in terms of dependency relations (Lai and Huang 1999b).

In this paper, we discuss the treatment of alternate usage patterns of the same lexical item in our approach.

2   Projective syntactic dependency

2.1   Dependency Grammar

In Dependency Grammar (Tesnière 1959), words contract binary, asymmetrical governor-dependent relationships. For example, in the English sentence *John saw Mary*, the word *saw* governs the two dependents *John* and *Mary*.

It is general practice that names are given to different kinds of dependency links between words. In the example given above, *John* is usually called the *subject* of *saw*, and *Mary* is its *object*. The dependency structure, with labeled dependency links, for this sentence is:

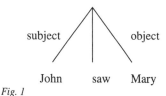

Fig. 1

2.2   Projective dependency

Merely identifying dependency relations between words does not in itself delimit the kind of syntactic structures allowed in language. In order to constrain syntactic structures, Robinson (1970) has posited four *axioms* of well-formedness:

1a) one and only one element is independent;
1b) all others depend directly on some element;
1c) no element depends directly on more than one other;
1d) if A depends directly on B and some element C intervenes between them (in linear order of string), then C depends directly on A or on B or some other intervening element.

These axioms disallow dependency structures like Fig. 2, in which branches cross one another (violating 1d). They also disallow a word depending on more than one governor (violating 1c). It is in this sense that dependency structures satisfying these axioms are *projective*.

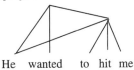

He   wanted   to hit me

Fig. 2

2.3   Dependency rules

Hays (1964) has suggested using *dependency rules* to generate dependency structures:

2a) X(A,B,C, ... ,H, * ,Y, ... ,Z)
2b) X(*)
2c) * (X)

Rule 2a) states that the governing *auxiliary alphabet* (i.e. *symbol* or *category*) X has dependents A, B, C, ..., H, Y, ..., Z (in this order) and that X itself (the governor, denoted by *) is situated between H and Y. Rule 2b) says that the *terminal alphabet* X occurs without any dependents. In 2c), X occurs without any governor. Hays calls this the *main* or *central* element.

Whereas Robinson's axioms do not put any requirement on word order except when projectivity is at stake, Hays' rules contain information about the linear order of dependents of a word. Gaifman (1965) has established that a *projective* Dependency Grammar obtained using Hays' dependency rules is 'equivalent' to a (context-free) phrase structure grammar in the sense that every structure attributed to a string by one grammar has a corresponding structure attributed by the other.

3   Constrained binary dependency rules in a lexicalist architecture

3.1   Non-projectivity

The approach to *projective* syntactic dependency described above requires that there should be no multiple governors, no mutual dependency and no crossing branches. Many computational linguists have based their work on projective syntactic dependency (e.g. Courtin and Genthial 1998; Nagao 1993; Yuan and Huang 1992).

It is however known that there are indeed non-projective grammatical phenomena in human languages. To account for these phenomena, followers of Dependency Grammar like Hudson (1982), Mel'cuk (1988), Starosta (1988) and Hajicova (1991), have allowed multiple-headedness and non-projectivity in their frameworks.

3.2   Constraints defined in terms of dependency relations

Computational linguists who base their work on a projective syntactic component have dealt with non-syntactic phenomena as constraints on other levels (e.g. semantic constraints in Bourdon et al. 1998). Working on Chinese, we (Lai and Huang 1994, 1995, 1998b) have tried to maintain single-headedness and projectivity in the syntactic component. Constraints defined in terms of syntactic dependency structures are introduced to deal with morphological processes and other non-projective grammatical phenomena.

We note that such functional information can be added to Hays' dependency rules (cf. *functional annotation* in Kaplan and Bresnan 1982):

   3a) $X(A(fa), B(fb), ..., * , ... Z(fz))$

or, in an equivalent notation:

   3b) $X(A, B, ..., X, ..., Z)$
   $X.fa = A$
   ....
   $X.fz = Z$"

Adapting the PATR formalism (Shieber 1986; Gazdar and Mellish 1989), we emulated these rules with re-write rules delimited by unification-based constraints. For the sentence *John saw Mary*, the following syntactic structure is produced:

   4) [tv, [[n, [john]], saw, [n, [mary]]]]

A functional structure accompanies the syntactic structure 4). It specifies that *John* and *Mary* are the *subject* and *object*, respectively, of the governor *saw* (cf. Fig. 1).

In rules 3a) and 3b), the X outside the brackets is like the left hand side of a re-write rule, and (A, B, ..., X, ..., Z) is like the right hand side. However, there is one important difference between the two kinds of rules. In a phrase-structure re-write rule, if two identical symbols are found on both sides of the rule, they are different *tokens* of the same *type*. For a Hays-style dependency rule, the two occurrences of X are the same *token*.

As a result, the *projection* of a word is the word itself and there are no *intermediate phrasal nodes* in the dependency structure 4). This is an important characteristic of our dependency-based approach as opposed to phrase-structure-based approaches.

3.3 Binary dependency rules in a lexicalist architecture

It has been noted above that Hays' dependency rules are different from Robinson's axioms in that linear word order of dependents of a governing word is stipulated. In principle, Robinson's approach, being more flexible, should be preferred. Stipulation on word order can be added to the axioms when necessary.

In order to reduce the effect of explicit word order stipulation in Hays' rules, we (Lai and Huang 1998b, 1999a) have made dependency rules *binary* as follows (with constraint annotations):

5a) X(X, Y)

    .....

H:subcat:right = = = List,

    .....

5b) X(Y, X)

    .....

H:subcat:left = = = List,

    .....

To work with these rules, lexical entries are equipped with subcategorization lists (cf. Pollard and Sag 1994). For example:

6) 'give'

subcat.left = [subj::n]

subcat.right = [iobj::n, obj::n]

Complements licensed by a governing word are divided between two subcategorization lists depending on whether they occur to the left or to the right of the word. In rules 5), an element is returned by a procedure from the left or right subcategorization list. It contains information on the syntactic category and grammatical function of the dependent. Details of our logic programming implementation are described in Lai and Huang (1998b, 1999c).

Elements in a subcategorization list are arranged so that for languages with relatively fixed word order like English, complements subcategorized by a governing word are generated by retrieving elements in the list one after another. For languages with free word order, the way in which the subcategorization lists are accessed can be manipulated (Lai and Huang 1999a).

Adjunct dependents are provided by global rules

7a) X(X, Y)
   X.adjunct = Y
7b) X(Y, X)
   X.adjunct = Y

which contain additional constraints to make sure that the adjuncts are of the correct syntactic categories.

3.4   Non-projectivity and movement

The non-projectivity in Fig. 2 is motivated by the fact that the word *he* answers both the subcategorization requirements of *wanted* and *hit* for a subject. Treatment of non-projectivity arising from this and from movement has been discussed in Lai and Huang (1999b). The result of this treatment is a projective syntactic dependency as in Fig. 3.

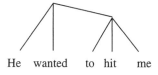

He   wanted   to   hit   me

Fig. 3

In the non-projective *functional* structure, a subject link between *he* and *hit* is added in accordance with the *control* information in the word *wanted*.

4   Lexical correspondences

4.1   Morphological variants

In our earlier work (e.g. Lai and Huang 1998b), we have not included morphology in our consideration. We required that *syntactic* dependency be projective, and consideration of morphology is left to another level. In particular, morphological variants of a word (e.g. the present and past forms of a verb) were encoded as separated entries in the dictionary, and their relationship was to be dealt with by other mechanisms.

In our present implementation, a lexical entry has a base form (the form of the word found in a dictionary) and a list of morphological variants indexed by a complex of relevant features (residing in the *category* feature). When the parser program *sees* a morphological variant of a lexical entry, in cases like English tensed verb forms, the value of an initially uninstantiated feature of the verb is assigned according to the verb form found in the input. In cases like number agreement between governing verb and subject noun, the process is triggered when a global dependency rule involving the governor (e.g. a verb) and a certain kind of dependency (e.g. subject) is applied. The governor and the dependent (e.g. the subject noun) are then required to *unify* (cf. Shieber 1986) with respect to a certain feature (e.g. *number*).

Our commitment to defining grammatical constraints in terms of dependency relations requires that a morphological process should either be triggered by a feature residing in the governor, or by a dependency rule involving the governor.

Regular morphological variation (e.g. conjugation of *weak* verbs in English) is implemented as rules. Irregular morphological forms are implemented by means of table look-up that takes precedence over the application of regular rules.

4.2   Multiple subcategorization frames

A word may have more than one usage pattern. For example, in English:

    8a) They give John a book.
    8b) They gave a book to John.
    8c) I know that he is coming.
    8d) I know.

The usage of *give* in 8a) can be accounted for by the subcategorization information given in 6). The usage in 8b) (apart from the morphological variation between the two morphological forms of *give* – see above) requires another *subcategorization frame*:

    9) 'give'
        subcat.left = [subj::n]
        subcat.right = [obj::n, pobj::p(to)]

The two usage patterns of *know* in 8c) and 8d) also involve two subcategorization frames in the lexical entry of the verb.

This kind of subcategorization property variation within the domain of a governor involves *movement*, but does not involve non-projectivity. In our implementation, multiple subcategorization lists are used to capture multiple subcategorization frames like this. These subcategorization lists are stored in a list (of lists), which is searched when subcategorization information is needed.

In our implementation, dependents of a governing word are generated by separate firings of dependency rules 5). It is thus essential that a subcategorization frame must be returned when a lexical entry is looked up. Thus, for example, the lexical entry of *give* is (in Prolog and PATR notations):

    10)   Word give :-
         .....
        return_frame(give, [Left, Right]),
        W:subcat:left = = = Left,
        W:subcat:right = = = Right,
        .....

where the procedure *return_frame* returns a subcategorization frame (consisting of lists of complement dependents on the left and on the right) of the word *give*. Alternate subcategorization frames are returned on *backtracking*.

4.3 Global usage pattern variation

Usage pattern variation is not always triggered by lexical properties. For example, the Chinese equivalent of 8d) should be attributed to the fact that transitive verbs in Chinese can in general also be used intransitively. We have a rule (for Chinese) that generates the intransitive frame (without the object) from the transitive frame (with the object). This rule is implemented as a sub-procedure of the *return_frame* procedure described above.

Complements of a governing word occupying different positions relative to one another in a language with relatively free word order is another example. This is a global phenomenon of the grammar of the language in question rather than a local lexical phenomenon. In our implementation, this is taken care of by the definition of the procedure that searches subcategorization lists for information of complements of a governor. In the extreme case of completely free word order, the procedure returns a random member in the list.

4.4 Subcategorization satisfaction outside domain of governor

Sometimes, the subcategorization requirements of a governor are satisfied by a word outside its immediate domain. For example, the subject *he* of the verb *hit* in Fig. 2 is not to be found in its immediate domain, but in the domain of its own governor. Like other cases involving *movement* and non-projectivity, this is not determined by the verb in question (but by the higher *control* verb). Such cases are discussed in Lai and Huang (1996b).

5 Conclusion

We have discussed how we, in a constrained dependency-based syntactic analysis model, deal with lexical correspondences arising from morphological variation, multiple lexical subcategorization frames and global syntactic phenomena. Though we have been working on Chinese, a language with relatively fixed word order like English, we would like our approach to be applicable not only to Chinese, but also to other languages in the world. So, we have also looked at some linguistic issues in several other languages. In this paper, the examples are mainly in English for the convenience of a wider audience.

6   References

BOURDON, Marie; DA SYLVA, Lyne; GAGNON, Michel; KHARRAT, Alma; KNOLL, Sonja; Maclachlan, Anna (1998): A Case Study in Implementing Dependency-Based Grammars. In: Proceedings of COLING-ACL'98 Workshop on Processing of Dependency-Based Grammars, Montreal, 15 August 1998, 78-87.

COURTIN, Jacques; GENTHIAL, Damien (1998): Parsing with Dependency Relations and Robust Parsing. In: Proceedings of COLING-ACL'98 Workshop on Processing of Dependency-Based Grammars, Montreal, 15 August 1998, 88-94.

COVINGTON, Michael A. (1990): Parsing Discontinuous Constituents in Dependency Grammar. In: Computational Linguistics 16.4, 234-236.

GAIFMAN, Haim (1965): Dependency Systems and Phrase-Structure Systems. In: Information and Control 8, 304-337.

GAZDAR, Gerald; MELLISH, Chris (1989): Natural Language Processing in Prolog. Wokingham, UK: Addison Wesley.

HAJICOVA, Eva (1991): Free Word Order Described without Unnecessary Complexity. In: Theoretical Linguistics 17, 99-106.

HAYS, David G. (1964): Dependency Theory: A Formalism and Some Observations. In: Language 40, 511-525.

HELLWIG, Peter (1986): Dependency Unification Grammar. In: Proceedings of COLING'86, 1986, 195-199.

HUANG, Changning; YUAN, Chunfa; PAN Shimei. (1992): Yuliaoku, Zhishi Huoqu He Jufa Fenxi (Corpora, Knowledge Acquisition and Syntactic Parsing). In: Journal of Chinese Information Processing 6.3, 1-6.

HUDSON, Richard (1994): Discontinuous Phrases in Dependency Grammar. In: University College London Working Papers in Linguistics, 6, 89-124.

— (1990): English Word Grammar. Oxford: Blackwell.

— (1984): Word Grammar. Oxford: Blackwell.

KAPLAN, Ronald; Bresnan Joan (1982): Lexical-Functional Grammar: A Formal System for Grammatical Representation. In: Bresnan, J. W. (ed.): The Mental Representation of Grammatical Relations. Cambridge, MA: MIT Press, 173-281.

LAI, Tom B. Y.; HUANG, Changning (1999a): Free Word Order in a Constraint-based Implementation of Dependency Grammar. In: Proceedings of PACLIC13, Taipei, 10-11 February 1999, 161-168.

— (1999b): Functional Constraints in Dependency Grammar. In: Multilinguale Corpora: Codierung, Strukturierung, Analyse – 11. Jahrestagung der Gesellschaft für Linguistische Daten Verarbeitung (GLDV'99), Frankfurt a. M, 8-10 July 1999. Prague: Enigma Corporation, 235-244. (Expected to appear in December 1999.)

— (1999c): Unification-based Parsing Using Annotated Dependency Rules. Proceedings of 5th Natural Language Processing Pacific Rim Symposium 1999 (NLPRS'99), Beijing, 5-7 November 1999, 102-107.

— (1998a): An Approach to Dependency Grammar for Chinese. In: Gu, Y. (ed.): Studies in Chinese Linguistics. Hong Kong: Linguistic Society of Hong Kong, 143-163.

— (1998b): Complements and Adjuncts in Dependency Grammar Parsing Emulated by a Constrained Context-Free Grammar. In: Proceedings of COLING-ACL'98 Workshop on Processing of Dependency-Based Grammars, Montreal, 15 August 1998, 102-108.

— (1995): Single-Headedness and Projectivity for Syntactic Dependency. Paper presented at Linguistics Association of Great Britain Spring Conference, University of Newcastle, 10-12 August, 1995.

— (1994): Dependency Grammar and the Parsing of Chinese Sentences. In: Proceedings of 1994 Kyoto Conference (Joint ACLIC8 and PACFoCoL2), Kyoto, 10-11 August 1994, 63-71.

MAXWELL, Dan (ms.): Unification Dependency Grammar.

MEL'CUK, Igor A. (1998): Dependency Syntax: Theory and Practice. New York: State University of New York Press.

NAGAO, Makoto (1993): Current Status and Further Trends of Natural Language Processing. In: Proceedings of KB&KS'93, Tokyo, December 1993, 31-40.

POLLARD, Carl; Sag, Ivan (1994): Head-Driven Phrase Structure Grammar. Chicago: University of Chicago Press.

ROBINYSON, Jane J. (1970): Dependency Structures and Transformation Rules. In: Language 46, 259-285.

SHIEBER, Stuart M. (1986): An Introduction to Unification-Based Approach to Grammar. Chicago: Chicago University Press.

STAROSTA, Stanley (1988): The Case for Lexicase. London: Pinter.

TESNIÈRE, Lucien (1959): Elements de syntaxe structurale. Paris: Klincksieck.

YUAN, Chunfa; HUANG, Changning (1992): Knowledge Acquisition and Chinese Parsing Based on Corpus. In: Proceedings of COLING'92, Nantes, France, 23-28 August 1992, 13000-13004.

ZHOU, Ming; HUANG, Changning (1994): An Efficient Syntactic Tagging Tool for Corpora. In: Proceedings of COLING'94, Kyoto, 5-9 August 1994, 949-955.

Boolean Constraint Grammars

Christoph Lehner

1   Motivation

BCG can be seen as a special purpose extension of Prolog. They combine Prolog's DCG[1] with Constraint Logic Programming (CLP). Systems based on BCG allow to directly encode feature structures that are the formal objects of choice in most applications of information-based linguistics. However, the feature structures are based on first order terms so that BCG benefits from the efficiency of Prolog's term unification. The systems written in BCG are highly expressive as well as lean and tractable. As BCG is based on DCG, its relation to Prolog is obvious. We can therefore take advantage of efficient implementations of Boolean constraint satisfaction techniques that are available with several high performance Prolog implementations such as Sicstus Prolog. Leading work in this context has been done by Carpenter (ALE, cf. Carpenter 1993) and Dörre and Eisele (CUF, Dörre/Dorna 1993[2]). ALE and CUF use typical CLP methods like typing and to some degree coroutining and delay techniques to achieve a more expressive and more efficient way to implement natural language systems. Both systems do however have important differences, i.e. CUF offers optional typing while ALE requires the type system to be fully type resolved and the syntax is different.

Another important system in this context is M. Covington's GULP (Covington 1994). Although the syntax chosen for BCG follows CUF, BCG is much more like GULP a tool for programming in Prolog rather than a programming language of its own. CUF and ALE on the other hand seem to be taken as programming languages by their authors (but, cf. König 1994:3).

The main advantage of BCG is their simplicity. The compilation step from BCG to Prolog is very simple. Therefore compiling BCG into Prolog is virtually almost as fast as compiling Prolog sources themselves. We use standard CLP techniques modelling natural language grammars that are more thoroughly described in Saint-Dizier (1994).

Our hypothesis now concerning BCG's theoretical suitability as a tool for implementing natural language grammars is that interesting linguistic generalizations can be captured simply by using a horn clause backbone providing means to encode feature value structures augmented by propositional calculus equations.

We show how to encode multifunctionality of lexical elements in an abstract way capturing the relevant generalizations. Furthermore, we will show how BCG naturally translate into a concrete programming language with a Boolean constraint solving

---

[1]   Pereira/Warren (1980), widely accepted in the Prolog programming community, not only for NLP applications, cf. O'Keefe (1990), 287ff.

[2]   Formal properties of CUF rely on work done by G. Smolka, e.g. Smolka (1989).

mechanism like Sicstus Prolog. The major test case we are going to present will be a lexicalist treatment of passive in German.[3]

2   Finite domains as sets of Boolean vectors

One of the central assumptions of BCG is that most of the disjunctive specifications in natural language grammars are specifications over finite domains. Almost all attributes used within syntax can be interpreted as finite domain attributes.

There are clear examples of finite domain attributes like *case, number, gender*. It seems, as if Pollard/Sag had exactly this idea in mind when describing a verb form like walk (cf. Pollard/Sag 1987:45).

The conclusions Pollard/Sag draw are only valid if the domains of the attributes, which make up the type *agr-value* representing the phenomenon of agreement, are interpreted as finite domains. So, in BCG a non-third-person-singular verb form could be described like in Prog. 1. Values of finite domain attributes are then interpreted as Boolean variables which can take the values 0 and 1.[4]

Prog. 1
lex : = cat : verb & orth : walk & semantics : (reln : walk(X) & arg1 : X) &
   subcat:[agr : (index : X & case: nom & pers: third : Third & number: sing : Sing)]
   (Sing * Third) = 0.

It is important to see that because of the fact that syntactic domains are finite we can represent the domain by mapping it into a set of Boolean vectors.[5] Boolean vectors themselves can be used to formulate Boolean constraints. The representation of *case* (and in a similar fashion for *person* and *gender* etc.) would be something like Prog. 2.

We can map the domain of an attribute like *case* and so forth to a finite set of Boolean vectors with four elements. Every element out of *{nom,acc,dat,gen}* (for German) can be represented by a specific pattern of 0 and 1. This mapping can of course be performed automatically. The consumption of memory will be fairly low (cf. Pulman 1994). The internal representation of a finite domain like *{nom,acc,dat, gen}* will be something like Prog. 2. which is a possible translation to Sicstus Prolog.[6]

Prog. 2
nom([B1,B2],B):- bool:sat(B =:= B1 * B2).
acc([B1,B2],B):- bool:sat(B =:= B1 * ~B2).
dat([B1,B2],B):- bool:sat(B =:= ~B1 * B2).
gen([B1,B2],B):- bool:sat(B =:= ~B1 * ~B2).

---

[3]   The examples presented here are taken from a larger grammar of German coping with free word order, adverbials, various sorts of subordinate clauses, dicontinuous phrases etc.

[4]   We are going to use the operators of the Boolean constraint solver of Sicstus Prolog. The system was developed using Sicstus Prolog. Hence, * denotes conjunction, + disjunction (inclusive OR), # exclusive OR and ~ negation.

[5]   The techniques for using a constraint logic programming language for modelling natural language phenomena have been described in full length in Saint Dizier (1994).

[6]   Cf. footnote 8.

So, unification of features with values being elements of finite domains becomes conjunction within propositional calculus. Likewise, generalization has its direct counterpart on the implementational side in disjunction. In addition, it is an empirical fact that no linguistic object can have two different values for a specific attribute at the same time. Therefore we can replace disjunction by the exclusive OR operation. Example 1 shows Prolog's (internal) version of the case assignment to the determiner *der* which must be either *nominative/masculinum/singular* or *genitive/plural*. This renders a set of blocked (delayed) constraints.

Example 1
```
?- orth(F,der), agr(F,A),case(A,C), nom(C,Nom), gen(C,Gen),
bool:sat(B=:=Nom#Gen).
A = [num(_A),gend(_B),case([_C,_D])|_E],
C = [_C,_D],
F = [orth(der),agr([num(_A),gend(_B),case([_C,_D])|_E])|_F],
bool:sat(Nom=:=(_G*B#B)),
bool:sat(_C=\=((_H*B#_G*B)#_H)),
bool:sat(_D=:=(((_H*B#_G*B)#_H)#B)),
bool:sat(Gen=:=_G*B) ?
```

The system keeps track of all constraints to be satisfied and resolves that the value has to be e.g. *genitive* as soon as more constraints are added. This may happen by combining *der* with let's say the German noun *Männer/men* which has to be plural.

3 Separating finite domains from atomic features

A remaining question is, how finite domain attributes can be separated from atomic attributes. A clear example is the difference between *orth : kinder* and *case : nom*. There are basically two simple solutions here:

1) Explicitly marking atomic values as e.g. orth : @ *kinder*
2) Providing the compiler with information which attributes have to be treated as finite domains

The first solution burdens the grammar writer with some coding work while writing the grammar. On the other hand, it always assures that the grammar writer keeps things clear, which attributes can be reasonably treated as finite domains and which cannot.

The second solution only demands that before compiling a grammar the compiler has to be provided with basic information which attributes and values have to be treated as finite domains. There is no need for such distinctions inside concrete specifications. The information to be provided to the compiler might be something like *finite_domain(case([nom,acc,dat,gen])*. This would be a way of simple type information as erroneous specifications like *case : pers1* or *case : akk* could be detected by the system. The simplest reaction would be to have a warning like *undefined predicate : acc* on the fly. A system fully automatically inferring which domains are to be taken as finite domains simply would blow up the intended domain *finite_domain (case([nom,acc,dat,gen])* to something like *finite_domain (case([nom,acc,dat,gen, akk, pers1])*. Of course one could have the system print out all sets found as domains of certain attributes and this would be an easy way to check if something went wrong (here, e.g. simply by detecting that *pers1* does not belong to the domain of *case*).

We rather take the personal point of view that it is not so irreasonable to have an extra small defnitional part where the grammar writer has to define explicitly which basic attributes and values exist. This keeps the system clear and avoids dynamic effects while writing a grammar where features and values may just be invented without good motivation.

However, we do not follow developments in strongly typed feature systems like ALE where the grammar writer has to define the complete type system before compiling the grammar. Fully type resolved systems seem to become very complicated in the definitional part of the type system (Meurer 1994:72ff).

4   Modelling multiple subcategorization frames

As in most natural languages, there are verbs in German that have more than one complementation pattern. Prog. 3 gives an example of such a verb *(sehen* which shows similar behaviour like *to see* in English):

a) subcategorizing for a nominative and a accusative complement:
   Der Lehrer sieht die Schüler. (The teacher sees the students.)

b) subcategorizing for a that-clause:
   Der Lehrer sieht, daß die Schüler einschlafen. (The teacher sees that the students are falling asleep.)

c) subcategorizing for a nominative complement and an infinitival complement without *zu*:
   Der Lehrer sieht die Schüler einschlafen. (The teacher sees the students falling asleep.)

One way to describe this is by assigning multiple subcategorization frames to the verbs in question. This is going to end up as multiple hornclauses:

Prog. 3
paradigma(sehen):= (subcat : [sem : var : X & agr : case : nom, sem : var : Y & agr : case : acc]
    & sem : reln : sehen(X,Y).
paradigma(sehen):= (subcat :[sem : var : X & agr : case : nom, sem : var : Y & agr : case : dass)]
    & sem : reln : sehen(X,Y).
paradigma(sehen):= subcat : [sem : var : X & agr : case : nom, sem : var : Y & agr : case : acc,
sem : var : Z & agr : case : zu_minus]
    & sem : reln : sehen(X,Y,Z).

There is, however, no need for leaving propositional calculus here as the formulation in Prog 4. demonstrates. The only drawback there is the cost of introducing an additional feature called *real* which may however be useful in a fully developed theory of syntax anyway.[7] *real* indicates whether a complement may, must or must not be realized. So, *real: 1* means that the complement may be realized, *real : 0* means that it must not be realized. If *real* is not specified at all, the complement in question has to be realized, i.e. it is obligatory. Our version of a subcat-principle is made sensitive towards this parameter. With that, we have a very clear and comfortable defaulting mechanism.[8] Most of the complements are not marked for *real : 1* or *real : 0* as most of them are obligatory.

Prog. 4
paradigma(sehen):= subcat : [sem : var : X & agr : case : nom, sem : var : Y & agr : case : (acc :
Acc & dass : Dass), real : Real & sem : var : Z & agr : case : zu_minus]
& sem : reln : sehen(X,Y,Z) & (Dass # Acc) * (Dass # Real) = 1.

Another argument made against this treatment may be that the semantic relation associated with the lexical entry has to be generalized to have at most three arguments where one argument will be left unbound in case there is no (optional) infinitival complement. But this can also be handled by assigning a variable number of arguments to the *reln*-attribute. On the other hand one is accustomed to unbound or implicit arguments in passive contructions anyway. So, this should not be taken as a serious drawback.

5   Treating passive in German

There are basically three forms of passive constructions in German. Typical sentences showing each type can be seen in 1) (brackets indicating optionality of constituents):

1)   a. Sam wird (von Joe) beobachtet. / Sam is (by Joe) watched / Sam is watched (by Joe).

b. Es wird geschlafen (während der Vorlesung) / It is slept (during the lecture) / There are people asleep (during the lecture).

c. Sam bekommt (von Joe) eine Belohnung übergeben. / Sam receives by Joe a reward given/Sam receives a reward (from Joe).

Papers in the context of HPSG (e.g. Kathol 1994) have shown how to treat passive in a lexicalist fashion, without lexical rules. Passive in German can be taken as a property of the lexical paradigm of the auxiliary *werden / to become* and of the verb *bekommen / to receive*. The latter also has the functionality of a passive inducing auxiliary in the context of 1c). A lexicalist's view that is strongly supported by HPSG allows one to treat auxiliaries and full verbs simply as two sorts of lexical items, i.e. they are not necessarily put into disjunctive classes on which different rules operate. This allows a uniform treatment of all verbal constructions, i.e. we can formulate abstract rule schemata that work for auxiliary verbs as well as for full verbs. Dealing

---

[7]   For similar ideas concerning the introduction of non-traditional features for the treatment of valency and subcategorization cf. Jacobs (1994).
[8]   Clearly, all variables introduced in Prolog are by default unbound.

with the constructions shown above it means that they work for active constructions as well as for passive constructions. HPSG emphasizes the view of treating multi-functionality in terms of disjunctive constraints rather than taking the approach of enumerating all different functions of fully fledged lexical forms. This has become known under the expression Constraint Based Grammar Development (CBGD) in contrast to Rule Based Grammar Development (RBGD). Note here that the German auxiliary *werden* functions not only as one form of passive constructor but as a potential indicator of future tense, as well.

2) Die Gauner werden Sam / The crooks will Sam admire. / The crooks are going to admire Sam.

Things become even more complicated when the bifunctional *werden* is combined with a bifunctional nonfinite verb. 2) is at least four times ambiguous. It can be either future/active or present/passive voice. More ambiguity is added by the proper names Joe and Sam which can be nominative and dative as well as accusative, of course. German is a partially free word order language and case isn't generally assigned structurally; in 3) all case properties may be possible, depending on certain contextual circumstances.

3) Sam wird Joe übergeben / Sam will / is Joe transfer / transferred / Sam will transfer Joe.
OR   Sam is being transferred to Joe.

In ths case both proper nouns can carry two cases, i.e. accusative and nominative. Therefore our system produces four different readings of 3), mapping the surface case values to more semantically motivated role values.[9]

Example 2
?- parse([sam,wird,joe,übergeben]).
fut(übergeben(agens:sam,recipient:A,patiens:joe)) solution:100 msec
fut(übergeben(agens:joe,recipient:A,patiens:sam)) solution:80 msec
übergeben(agens:A,recipient:joe,patiens:sam) solution:190 msec
übergeben(agens:A,recipient:sam,patiens:joe) solution:160 msec
Total: 760 msecs/Solutions: 4

In order to maintain the strict CBGD view, we do not only model both functions of the verb *werden* in one entry, i.e. as a passive auxiliary as well as a future tense indicator. We also have to model nonfinite forms with Boolean constraints, because we want to capture all possible functions by abstract constraints instead of enumerating all possible solutions which is done in a derivational approach.

The main advantages of using Boolean constraints to modell multifunctionality become apparent here. Firstly, it is a way to avoid redundancies as the grammar writer is not forced to multiply encode multifunctional elements inside the lexicon. Secondly, we claim that avoiding multiple encoding leads to a cognitively more adequate

---

[9]   All parse samples were performed on a Sparc 10 with Sicstus Prolog. Even on a small Macintosh platform, where most of the grammar was developed, the execution times are quite acceptable.

model as humans processing natural language might use a similar strategy, i.e. they keep in mind that e.g. a simple proper noun may not only have one possible case. Many lexical elements and even phrases receive their actual functionality by computing the constraints of a wider context. So the strategy is to check out which constraints may withstand in a more global context before enumerating costly hypotheses concerning structural poperties of phrases. It is the general idea of 'constrain and generate' instead of 'generate and test' which seems to be much more plausible from a psychological point of view.[10]

6 Modelling passive with lexical Boolean macros

6.1 Paradigmatic information on *werden*

The following entry shows paradigmatic information on *werden*. Paradigmatic information is used to assign general properties to individual word forms. All different functionalities of *werden* are treated in this declaration by the use of Boolean constraints. First, the subcategorization list is specified. It consists of three elements:

1. the raised subject (*Raised_Subject*)
2. the nonfinite verbal complement (*sem : reln : Y & ...*)
3. the optional complement in case of passive that is marked as a
   von-PP-Phrase (*agr : case : pp_von ...*)

Prog. 5
```
paradigma(werden):= subcat : [Raised_Subject, pass : Pass & sem : reln : Y & agr : case :
    (zu_minus : ZM & ge_hat : GH) & subcat : [ Raised_Subject | _] ,
    agr : case : pp_von & sem : var : X & opt : Opt & pass : Pass] &
    /* This is the part where the actual constraining takes place */
    nonfin(B) & (B =< Pass) = 1 & (ZM # GH) = 1 & (ZM =:= ~Pass) = 1
    & (GH =:= Pass) = 1 & (Opt =:= Pass) = 1 &
    /* The next constraints assure that in case of passive the von-marked constituent
    finds its right place, i.e. the place of the logical subject */
    verb_sem(P) & {select_binary(Pass,freeze(Y,Y =..[_,_:X|_]),true),
    select_binary(Pass,P = Y,P = fut(Y))}.
```

Then, at the end of Prog. 4 , the Boolean constraints are used to regulate the interaction of all individual complements. The value of the attribute *Pass* regulates whether the function of *werden* is either to transform the semantics of *Y* (this is done according to the type of verb that is to be passivized) or to apply the future tense marker to the verbal complement. The operation is executed by a special routine called *select_binary/3* performing a decision depending on the value of a binary parameter. The decision is delayed until the value of the binary parameter (here *Pass*) is

---

[10] Frühwirth (1993), iii: CLP "is a new class of programming languages combining the declarativity of logic programming with the efficiency of constraint solving. [...] The most important advantage is that these languages offer the short development time while exhibiting an efficiency comparable to imperative languages."

known. No enumeration of individual trees representig passive or future-tense functionality is necessary.

6.2   Different types of (full) verbs

The different types of verbs induce the different sorts of *werden*-passives. In the last section we gave a sketch of how the entry for *werden* works. The different functionalities of *werden* are triggered by different complement patterns of specific verb types. The question how exactly passivization influences the argument structure and semantico-logical behaviour of a certain verb is taken care of inside the specifications for the individual verbal definitions. They are actually macro specifications that will be useful for whole classes of verbs.

The first example in Prog. 6 shows a classical transitive verb (*treffen/to meet*). The crucial thing in this case is the exchange of semantic roles and syntactic surface cases. This is exactly what is performed by the special constraint *select_binary*. Furthermore the constraint *Pass* =< *~Opt* and *Real* =:= *~Pass* assures that there is no accusative object in case of passive voice. These two constraints also give the system some kind of help in solving the constraint system, and in this sense support the parsing process. *Real* =:= *~Pass* can be translated as: "If the accusative object is not realized then it must be passive voice and vice versa."

```
Prog. 6
lex:= cat : @ v & constr v_agr_3_sing & orth : @ trifft & paradigma(treffen).
paradigma(treffen):= constr lex_v2 & sem_name : @ treffen.
lex_v2 := subcat : [sem : var : X & agr : case : nom, sem : var : Y & agr : case : acc &
        real : Real & opt : Opt] & pass : Pass & agr : case : ge_hat : GH &
        ((Pass =< ~Opt) = 1) & ((Real =:= ~Pass) = 1) & ((~GH =< ~Pass) = 1) &
        {select_binary(Pass,(A = Y, B = X),(A = X , B = Y))}
        & verb_sem(P) & construct_reln([agens:A,patiens:B],P).
```

Things are a little different in case of a German dative transitive verb like *helfen / to help*. There is no change in surface case values. The only change in passive voice is that the nominative subject must not be realized *Pass* =< *~Opt1*. And, there is – syntactically speaking – only a third person singular version of this kind of passive (*Pass* =< *(P3 * Sing)*).

```
Prog. 7
lex:= cat : @ v & constr v_agr_2_plu & orth : @ helft & paradigma(helfen).
paradigma(helfen).– constr lex_v2_dat & sem_name; @ helfen.
lex_v2_dat := subcat : [sem : var : A & opt: Opt1 & agr : (case : nom & pers : pers3 : P3 & num .
        sing : Sing), sem : var : B & agr : case : dat & opt ] & pass : Pass & ((Pass =< ~Opt1) =
        1) & (Pass =< (P3 *  Sing)) = 1 & verb_sem(P) & construct_reln([agens:A,patiens:B],P).
```

It seems as if the classical impersonal passive shares important features with the dative transitive case (cf. 3). In Prog. 8 the nominative complement is blocked away and is restricted to third person singular in the case of passive. Impersonal passive only works for certain kinds of verbs so that the generalization is made inside the system of paradigmatic information.

Prog. 8
lex:= cat : @ inf & orth : @ schlafen & paradigma(schlafen).
paradigma(schlafen):= constr lex_v1 & sem_name : @ schlafen.
lex_v1 := subcat : [opt : Opt & sem : var : X & agr : (case : nom & pers : pers3 : P3 & num : sing : Sing)] & pass : Pass & (Pass =< (~ Opt * P3 * Sing)) = 1 & verb_sem(P) & construct_reln ([agens:X],P).

6.3   bekommen-Passive

So, the treatment of *bekommen* is strictly lexicalistic as well. It is no surprise that *bekommen* itself does not allow for passivization nor does it take a passivized verbal complement. This is assured by the constraint ~*pass*. The function of *bekommen* is somewhat similar to *werden* combined with a accusative transitive verb. The difference is, *bekommen* takes a dative transitive verb as its complement. The syntactic object of *bekommen* becomes the logical subject of the embedded complement and vice versa, represented by the shared variables *X* and *Y* in Prog. 9.

Prog. 9
paradigma(bekommen):= ~pass &
    subcat : [agr : case : nom & sem : var : X, opt & agr : case : pp_von & sem : var : Y & pass,
    sem : reln : P & agr : case : ge_hat & ~pass & subcat : [agr : case : nom & sem : var : Y,
    agr : case : dat & sem : var: X & ~real | _]] & verb_sem(P) .

7   Conclusion

BCG combines several achievements. The implementation plattform of a Constraint Logic Programming language provides the efficiency of an imperative language although the specifications can be made in a Feature Based Grammar Formalisms. Secondly certain aspects of logical and functional programming are combined in a way as to avoid unnecessary reference to variables thus relieving the programmer as well as the reader of overload that is typically encountered during the developement of large scale natural language grammars.

8   References

COVINGTON, Michael (1994): Natural Language Processing for Prolog Programmers.
CARPENTER, Robert (1993): ALE: Attribute Logic Engine. Users Guide. Technical Report, Carnegie Mellon University.
COLMERAUER, A. (1990): An Introduction to PrologIII. Communications of the ACM, 33;7.
DÖRRE, Jochen; DORNA, Michael (1993): CUF. A Formalism for linguistic Knowledge Representation. DYANA deliverable. Institut für maschinelle Sprachverarbeitung, Universität Stuttgart.

FRÜWIRTH, Thom et al. (1993): Constraint Logic Programming – An Informal Introduction. Munich 1993, Technical Report ECRC-93-5.

GAZDAR, Gerald; MELLISH, Chris (1989): Natural Language Processing in PROLOG. An Introduction to Computational Linguistics. Addison-Wesley.

JACOBS, Joachim: Kontravalenz. Opladen 1994.

KATHOL, Andreas (1995): Passive without Lexical Rules. In: Nerbonne; Netter; Pollard.

KÖNIG, Esther (1994): A Study in Grammar Design. Bericht Nr. 54. Stuttgart (Arbeitspapiere des Sonderforschungsbereichs 340).

MEURERS, Detmar: On implementing an HPSG theory – Aspects of the logical architecture, the formalization, and the implementation of head-driven phrase structure grammars. In: Hinrichs, Erhard et al.: Partial-VP and Split-NP Topicalization in German – An HPSG Analysis and its Implementation. Tübingen (Arbeitspapiere des Sonderforschungsbereichs 340, # 58)

NERBONNE, John; NETTER, Klaus; POLLARD, Carl (eds.): German in Head-Driven Phrase Structure Grammar. CSLI Publications 1995. Distributed by University of Chicago Press.

O'KEEFE, Richard (1990): The Craft of Prolog. MIT Press.

PEREIRA, Fernando C. N.; WARREN, David (1980): Definite clause grammars for language analysis – a survey of the formalism and a comparison with augmented transition networks. In: Artificial Intelligence 13, 231-278.

POLLARD, Carl; SAG, Ivan A. (1994): Head Driven Phrase Structure Grammar. Chicago University Press.

— (1987): Information Based Syntax and Semantics. Vol. 1. Fundamentals. CSLI Lecture Notes 13. Stanford.

PULMAN, Steven (1994): Expressivity of Lean Formalisms. In: Markantonaou, Stella; Sadler, Louisa: Grammatical Formalisms: Issues in Migration and Expressivity. Studies in machine translation and natural language processing, Vol. 4. Bruxelles – Luxembourg ECSC-EEC-EAEC (Studies in machine translation and natural language processing 4).

SAINT-Dizier, Patrick (1994): Advanced Logic Programming for Language Processing. Academic Press.

SMOLKA, Gert (1990): Feature Constraint Logics for Unification Grammars. IWBS Report 93, IWBS, IBM Deutschland, November 1989. Also in: Proceedings of the Workshop on Unification Formalisms – Syntax, Semantics and Implementation, Titisee, The MIT Press, 1990.

Automatische Extrahierung idiomatischer Bigramme aus Textkorpora[*]

Wolfgang Lezius

1 Einführung

Die Erkennung von Mehrwortausdrücken ist in der maschinellen Textanalyse von zentraler Bedeutung. Durch die Verwendung statistischer Methoden konnten Verfahren implementiert werden, die linguistisch signifikante Mehrwortgruppen zuverlässig ermitteln und damit in linguistischen Anwendungen nutzbar machen. Einen Überblick über die verwendeten statistischen Methoden geben Kilgariff (1996) und Manning/ Schütze (1999: Kapitel 5). Aus Texten extrahiertes Wissen über Mehrwortausdrücke ist insbesondere für die Lexikographie relevant (Church/Hanks 1990; Smadja 1993). Weitere Anwendungen liegen im Information Retrieval, z.B. bei der Bestimmung von Wort-Ähnlichkeiten (Lin 1998) oder der Berechnung von Wortassoziationen (Rapp 1996; Ruge 1995).

Im vorliegenden Papier werden 2-Wort-Kollokationen aufeinanderfolgender Wortformen (Bigramme) untersucht. Für linguistische Anwendungen, vor allem für Anwendungen im Bereich des Information Retrieval, sind dabei diejenigen Bigramme besonders interessant, die idiomatischen Charakter haben (vgl. Abschnitt 2). Beispiele sind *absolute Mehrheit, schwarze Zahlen*, aber auch Eigennamen wie *Boris Becker*. Sie spielen in Texten oftmals die Rolle von Schlüsselbegriffen, d.h., sie repräsentieren den Inhalt eines Textes in signifikantem Maße.

Eine manuelle Auflistung aller idiomatischen Bigramme ist schon aufgrund der Anzahl dieser speziellen Mehrwort-Ausdrücke nicht möglich. Im vorliegenden Papier wird ein Ansatz vorgestellt, der idiomatische Bigramme mit Hilfe statistischer Verfahren aus Textkorpora extrahiert (vgl. Abschnitt 3). Dabei wird zunächst diskutiert, ob sich die verwendeten Verfahren zur Extrahierung überhaupt eignen (vgl. 4.1). Anschließend wird der Einfluß der linguistischen Vorverarbeitung (kontextsensitive Wortartenbestimmung und Lemmatisierung) auf die Qualität der erzielten Ergebnisse untersucht (vgl. 4.2). Ein Vergleich der Extrahierung auf einem Textdokument, das in deutscher und englischer Sprache vorliegt, schließt die Diskussion des Ansatzes ab (vgl. 4.3).

2 Anwendungen

Aus dem Blickwinkel der Linguistik stellen idiomatische Bigramme einen ersten Schritt zur Extrahierung von Mehrwort-Ausdrücken dar. Erweitert man die Verfahren

---

[*] Diese Arbeit ist am Centrum für Informations- und Sprachverarbeitung (CIS) der LMU München in Zusammenarbeit mit Herrn Prof. Guenthner enstanden. Für die zahlreichen Anregungen bei der Ausweitung der Experimente möchte ich Herrn Dr. Ulrich Heid vom Institut für Maschinelle Sprachverarbeitung (IMS) der Universität Stuttgart danken.

auf die Erkennung von n-Grammen, können die Methoden zur Identifikation signifikanter Nominal- und Präpositionalphrasen beitragen. Beispiele sind *im vergangenen Jahr* oder *nach eigenen Angaben.*
Eine zentrale Aufgabe des Information Retrieval ist die Indexierung von Fließtext (vgl. Baeza-Yates/Ribeiro-Neto 1999). Als Suchterme werden dabei in der Regel einzelne Wortformen betrachtet. Doch stecken die zentralen Inhalte häufig in idiomatischen Bigrammen: *katholische Kirche, bosnische Serben, besetzte Gebiete.* Eine Berücksichtigung dieser Ausdrücke dürfte die Resultate der bekannten Retrieval-Verfahren daher nachhaltig verbessern.
Die unterschiedlichen Anwendungssichtweisen führen bei der Bewertung der Ergebnisse zu durchaus unterschiedlichen Beurteilungen. Für das Information Retrieval sind Eigennamen wie *Boris Becker* und idiomatische Wendungen wie *rote Zahlen* besonders relevant, Mehrwort-Adverbien wie *darüber hinaus* oder nicht-idiomatische Kollokationen wie *(im) vergangenen Jahr* dagegen zu vernachlässigen. Für den Linguisten hingegen können gerade diese den Kern der linguistischen Untersuchung darstellen, z.B. in der Lexikographie. Die Ergebnisbewertungen des Lesers mögen daher, abhängig vom jeweiligen Erkenntnisziel, von den Bewertungen in Abschnitt 4 abweichen.

3   Vorgehensweise

Als Datengrundlage werden in einem Textdokument alle Einzelwortformen A und Bigramme AB ermittelt und ihre Auftretenshäufigkeiten H(A) bzw. H(AB) ausgezählt.[1] Die Signifikanz eines Bigramms AB wird nun anhand der Korpushäufigkeit H(AB) und der Einzelhäufigkeiten H(A) und H(B) mit einem statistischen Signifikanztest gewichtet. Aus der Sicht der Statistik wird hier die Abhängigkeit von Ereignissen gemessen. Mit den Ereignissen *A* bzw. *B* sind dabei das Auftreten der jeweiligen Wortformen A bzw. B, mit dem Ereignis *AB* das Auftreten der Wortfolge AB gemeint. Ein Bigramm AB gilt als signifikant, wenn das Ereignis *AB* häufiger eintritt als es die Häufigkeiten der Ereignisse *A* und *B* erwarten lassen. Zur Bewertung der Signifikanz stehen die ausgezählten Merkmalsausprägungen H(A), H(B) und H(AB) zur Verfügung.
Verschiedene statistische Verfahren wurden für die Anwendung in der linguistischen Textanalyse evaluiert. Neben dem *chi-Quadrat-Test*, einem Standardtest zur Messung der Unabhängigkeit von Ereignissen (vgl. Manning/Schütze 1999: Kapitel 5.3), wurde in der Vergangenheit vor allem das Maß *mutual information* verwendet (vgl. Church/Hanks 1990). Doch werden bei diesen Maßen seltene Ereignisse bevorzugt, was auch durch die Einrichtung von Schwellwerten nicht eingedämmt werden kann (Dunning 1993). Aus diesem Grunde ist das *log-likelihood*-Maß sehr verbreitet.

---

[1]   Es sei darauf hingewiesen, daß aus der Menge der Korpus-Bigramme diejenigen herausgefiltert werden, die ein Stopwort (hier: Wortform der geschlossenen Klassen) enthalten. Damit wird zum einen der Rechenaufwand drastisch reduziert. Zum anderen hat sich gezeigt, daß sich ohne diese Filterung statt für das Information Retrieval relevante Bigramme eher Mehrwort-Adverbien wie *wie immer* oder beliebige Wortformen wie *aber auch* durchsetzen.

Es hängt kaum von der Voraussetzung einer Normalverteilung ab und bevorzugt weder häufige noch seltene Ereignisse (Dunning 1993). Daneben sei noch der *common birthday approach* genannt, der ähnliche statistische Eigenschaften wie der log-likelihood-Test aufweist und ebenfalls bereits erfolgreich eingesetzt wurde (Läuter/Quasthoff 1999).

In der hier beschriebenen Arbeit sind alle genannten Signifikanztests implementiert und in Hinblick auf die Problemstellung evaluiert worden. Die Ergebnisse lassen damit neben der Beantwortung der Frage nach der Extrahierbarkeit idiomatischer Bigramme auch einen Vergleich der Eignung für die Extrahierung von Kollokationen zu.

4 Ergebnisse

4.1 Vergleich der Signifikanzmaße

Die ersten durchgeführten Experimente sollten zum einen die Frage klären, ob sich idiomatische Bigramme überhaupt extrahieren lassen, zum anderen einen Vergleich der Eignung der Signifikanzmaße ermöglichen. Um Auswirkungen der Wahl der Textsorte auf die Resultate einschränken zu können, wurden mit einem Jahrgang der Süddeutschen Zeitung (Jahrgang 1993, 20 Mio. Wortformen) und einer Dissertation aus dem Umfeld der Computerlinguistik (42.000 Wortformen) zwei sehr unterschiedliche Textsorten ausgewählt.

4.1.1 Experiment 1: Zeitungskorpus

Das Korpus enthält 3,2 Mio. Bigramme, durch den Ausschluß von Bigrammen, die Stopwörter enthalten, reduziert sich die Anzahl der Kandidaten auf 677.000. Tabelle 1 zeigt die 20 am höchsten bewerteten Bigramme für die log-likelihood-Methode.

Da eine Referenzliste idiomatischer Bigramme nicht vorliegt, ist eine objektive Bewertung der Bigramm-Liste nicht möglich. Für die subjektive Bewertung haben drei Versuchspersonen unabhängig voneinander für jedes Bigramm unter den ersten 100[2] ermittelten entschieden, ob es idiomatisch ist oder nicht. In Tabelle 1 sind zur Veranschaulichung alle Bigramme markiert worden, die von mindestens zwei Versuchspersonen als idiomatisch gekennzeichnet wurden.

Tabelle 2 zeigt für jeden der Signifikanztests die Anzahl der durchschnittlich als idiomatisch gekennzeichneten Bigramme. Die letzte Spalte gibt an, wieviele Bigramme bei der Anordnung nach der absoluten Häufigkeit H(AB) als idiomatisch bezeichnet wurden.

---

[2] Man beachte, daß der *cut-off*-Punkt (d.h. die Position der Ausgabeliste, bis zu der die Ergebnisse ausgewertet werden) intellektuell bestimmt wurde.

Nr.	A	B	idiom
1	Mill	DM	
2	Eigener	Bericht	
3	Millionen	Mark	
4	New	York	
5	Mrd	DM	
6	Milliarden	DM	
7	Vereinten	Nationen	ja
8	vergangenen	Jahr	
9	darüber	hinaus	
10	IG	Metall	ja
11	Milliarden	Mark	
12	Christian	Ude	ja
13	Edmund	Stoiber	ja
14	Jahre	alt	
15	FC	Bayern	ja
16	neuen	Bundesländern	ja
17	Helmut	Kohl	ja
18	Theo	Waigel	ja
19	GmbH	Co	
20	Sachsen	Anhalt	ja

Tabelle 1: Top 20-Bigramme des SZ-Korpus (Jahrgang 1993)

Maß	log-likelihood	common birthday	chi-Quadrat-Test	mutual information	absolute Häufigkeit
idiomatisch (davon Eigennamen)	46 (30)	48 (35)	0 (0)	1 (0)	33 (26)

Tabelle 2: Bewertung der Top 100-Bigramme im Vergleich

4.1.2 Experiment 2: Fachtext

Beim verwendeten Fachtext handelt es sich um die Dissertation „Die Berechnung von Assoziationen – Ein korpuslinguistischer Ansatz" von Rapp (1996). Von 4.920 Bigrammen sind auch hier die 20 am höchsten bewerteten für die log-likelihood-Methode abgedruckt (Tabellen 3 und 4).

Als Fazit der ersten beiden Experimente ist zunächst festzustellen, daß die Ergebnisse plausibel sind. Zum Teil leiden sie unter Schwächen der Vorverarbeitung, vor allem der Tokenisierung (Beispiel: *Sachsen-Anhalt* in Tabelle 1; Bindestrich wird als Wortgrenze analysiert). Schwerwiegender ist jedoch die Tatsache, daß sich unter den ermittelten Bigrammen noch sehr viele befinden, die nicht signifikant idiomatisch sind (sog. *false positives*). Im Vergleich der beiden Experimente stellen sich die Ergebnisse für den Fachtext schlechter dar, was in erster Linie auf die geringeren Auftretenshäufigkeiten zurückzuführen sein dürfte.

Für die statistischen Tests läßt sich festhalten, daß die Tests log-likelihood und common birthday am besten abschneiden. Der Effekt, daß eine Sortierung der Bigramme nach ihrer absoluten Häufigkeit, d.h. ein Verzicht auf den statistischen Test, ebenfalls gute Ergebnisse liefert, ließ sich in weiteren Experimenten hingegen nicht durchgängig reproduzieren.

Nr	A	B
1	assoziativen	Antworten
2	Wettler	Rapp
3	Sparse	Data
4	Brown	Korpus
5	Tag	Liste
6	Wort	Tag
7	assoziative	Antwort
8	Data	Problem
9	Russell	Messeck
10	Rapp	Wettler
11	gemeinsamen	Auftretens
12	Russell	Jenckins
13	vergl	Kapitel
14	Tabelle	zeigt
15	gemeinsame	Auftreten
16	there	is
17	Kroeber	Riel
18	besteht	darin
19	ortographischen	Ähnlichkeit
20	Rangfolge	gebracht

Tabelle 3: Top 20-Bigramme für einen Fachtext

Maß	log-likelihood	common birthday	chi-Quadrat-Test	mutual information	absolute Häufigkeit
idiomatisch (davon Eigennamen)	24 (8)	34 (13)	0 (0)	15 (5)	26 (6)

Tabelle 4: Bewertung der Top 100-Bigramme im Vergleich

4.2 Einfluß der linguistischen Vorverarbeitung

Um die extrahierten Bigramme dem gewünschten Bigramm-Typ anzunähern, liegt es nahe, die Grundmenge der Bigramme anhand linguistischer Kriterien einzuschränken. In einem ersten Experiment ist für das Zeitungskorpus die Eingabemenge daher auf alle Adjektiv-Nomen-Bigramme beschränkt worden. Die Wortarten-Annotierung wurde mit Hilfe des CISLEX-Lexikons durchgeführt, einem nahezu vollständigen Lexikon des Deutschen (vgl. Langer/Maier/Oesterle 1996). Bei mehrdeutigen Wortformen wurde die wahrscheinlichste Lesart gewählt.

4.2.1 Experiment 3: Adjektiv-Nomen-Bigramme

Tabelle 5 zeigt die 20 am höchsten bewerteten Bigramme für die log-likelihood-Methode. Man betrachte die Ergebnisse auch im Vergleich mit Tabelle 1.

Nr	A	B
1	vergangenen	Jahr
2	bosnischen	Serben
3	besetzten	Gebieten
4	eigenen	Angaben
5	achtziger	Jahre
6	vergangenen	Woche
7	vergangenen	Jahres
8	kommenden	Jahr
9	lange	Zeit
10	unter	Druck
11	unter	Berufung
12	anderen	Seite
13	wenigen	Tagen
14	absolute	Mehrheit
15	roten	Zahlen
16	sechziger	Jahre
17	wenige	Tage
18	katholischen	Kirche
19	ganz	Deutschland
20	siebziger	Jahren

Tabelle 5: Top 20-Bigramme unter Adjektiv-Nomen-Bigrammen des SZ-Korpus (Jahrgang 1993)

Wie die Tabelle zeigt, werden die Ergebnisse nun deutlich signifikanter. Während ohne die linguistische Vorverarbeitung nur 16 Bigramme als brauchbar gekennzeichnet wurden (zuzüglich 30 Eigennamen, die in diesem Adjektiv-Nomen-Experiment herausfallen), werden nun 31 der 100 Bigramme als brauchbar bezeichnet. Die Ergebnisse der log-likelihood-Methode werden hier stellvertretend für die verschiedenen Signifikanzmaße reproduziert, vergleichbare Ergebnis-Verbesserungen zeigen sich auch bei den übrigen Tests.

4.2.2 Experiment 4: Lemmatisierte Adjektiv-Nomen-Bigramme

Ein weiteres Experiment schränkt die Grundmenge zusätzlich auf lemmatisierte Adjektiv-Nomen-Bigramme ein, d.h. Kombinationen mit verschiedenen Formen werden zusammengefaßt. Damit fallen z.b. die Frequenzdaten für *vergangenen Jahr* und *vergangenen Jahres* zusammen, die in Tabelle 5 noch zwei Ränge (Nr. 1 und 7) belegen.

Nr	A	B
1	vergangen	Jahr
2	vergangen	Woche
3	erst	Halbjahr
4	halb	Stunde
5	bosnisch	Serbe
6	erst	Linie
7	besetzt	Gebiet
8	kommend	Jahr
9	achtziger	Jahr
10	letzt	Jahr
11	siebziger	Jahr
12	katholisch	Kirche
13	eigen	Angabe
14	sechziger	Jahr
15	erst	Mal
16	wenig	Tag
17	unter	Berufung
18	unter	Druck
19	erst	Quartal
20	jung	Leute

Tabelle 6: Top 20-Bigramme unter lemmatisierten Adjektiv-Nomen-Bigrammen des SZ-Korpus (Jahrgang 1993)

Wieder werden die Resultate prägnanter, die Versuchspersonen bezeichnen 42 Bigramme von 100 als brauchbar. Als Fazit läßt sich festhalten, daß die Ergebnisse stark von einer linguistischen Vorverarbeitung profitieren, diese Qualitätssteigerung aber den Einsatz hochwertiger lexikalischer Ressourcen voraussetzt.

4.3 Sprachvergleich Deutsch-Englisch

Während im Deutschen viele Fachausdrücke durch Nominalkomposition gebildet werden, werden diese im Englischen fast ausschließlich durch Kookkurrenzen ausgedrückt: *compound noun, document retrieval, family planning.* Die Datengrundlage für die Extrahierung idiomatischer Bigramme wird dadurch gegenüber dem Deutschen deutlich breiter. Durch diese verbesserte statistische Ausgangslage sind daher auch bessere Ergebnisse zu erwarten. In einem abschließenden Experiment wurde daher ein Vergleich durchgeführt, der auf dem Wortlaut der FIFA-Fußballregeln beruht.[3]

Nr	A	B	A	B
1	Football	Association	opposing	team
2	Übertretung	ereignet	free	kick
3	Tor	geht	infringement	occured
4	Association	Board	see	page
5	gegnerische	Mannschaft	indirect	free
6	Stelle	verhängt	goal	line
7	International	Football	Annual	General
8	ins	Tor	direct	free
9	indirekter	Freistoß	penalty	area
10	anderer	Spieler	kick	taken
11	ihn	berührt	Infringement	Sanctions
12	Spieler	ihn	LAW	the
13	siehe	Wenn	fourth	official
14	Schiedsrichter	Assistenten	yellow	card
15	Hand	gespielt	Football	Association
16	Fuß	gestoßen	Business	Meeting
17	direkter	Freistoß	assistant	referees
18	technische	Zone	unsporting	behaviour
19	Karte	verwarnt	opponents	remain
20	gelben	Karte	current	year

Tabelle 7: Top 20-Bigramme für die deutsche und englische Version der FIFA-Fußballregeln

Unter den ersten 50 Bigrammen bezeichneten die Versuchspersonen 16 für das Deutsche und 28 für das Englische als idiomatisch. Es scheint also im Englischen deutlich mehr Bigramme zu geben, die als relevant und idiomatisch empfunden werden.

5   Zusammenfassung und Ausblick

Wir haben ein statistisches Verfahren vorgestellt, das idiomatische Bigramme aus Texten automatisch extrahiert. Die Ergebnisse zeigen, daß die Extrahierung grundsätzlich möglich ist, sie machen aber zugleich deutlich, daß die Ergebnislisten für (computer-) linguistische Anwendungen manuell nachbearbeitet werden müssen.

Die linguistische Vorverarbeitung macht sich bezahlt, setzt aber hochwertige lexikalische Ressourcen voraus. Hier scheinen Experimente mit Wortarten-Taggern vielversprechend, die mit maximal 3-4% Fehlern Voraussagen über die Wortarten der Wortformen treffen (vgl. z.B. Lezius/Rapp/Wettler 1998).

---

[3]   Dieser Text ist für die Sprachen Englisch, Deutsch, Französisch und Spanisch verfügbar unter der URL: http://www.fifa.com.

Vor allem die Ergebnisse für das Englische geben Anlaß zur Hoffnung, daß durch weitere Optimierungen der statistischen Tests und der Datengrundlage noch deutlich bessere Ergebnisse erzielt werden können.

6   Literatur

BAEZA-YATES, Ricardo; RIBEIRO-NETO, Berthier (1999): Modern Information Retrieval. Harlow: Addison-Wesley – New York: ACM Press.

CHURCH, Kenneth; Hanks, Patrick (1990): Word Association Norms, Mutual Information and Lexicography. In: Computational Linguistics 16.1, 22-29.

DUNNING, Ted (1993): Accurate Methods for the Statistics of Surprise and Coincidence. In: Computational Linguistics 19.1, 61-74.

KILGARIFF, Adam (1996): Which words are particularly characteristic of a text? A survey of statistical approaches. In: Proceedings of the AISB Workshop on Language Engineering for Document Analysis and Recognition, Sussex University, 33-40.

LANGER, Stefan; MAIER, Petra; OESTERLE, Jürgen (1996): CISLEX – An Electronic Dictionary for German: Its Structure and a Lexicographic Application. In: Proceedings of COMPLEX 1996, Budapest, 155-163.

LÄUTER, Martin; QUASTHOFF, Uwe (1999) Kollokationen und semantisches Clustering. In: Gippert, J.; Oliviér, P. (Hrsg.): Multilinguale Corpora – Codierung, Strukturierung, Analyse – 11. Jahrestagung der Gesellschaft für Linguistische Datenverarbeitung. Prag: Enigma Corporation.

LEZIUS, Wolfgang; RAPP, Reinhard; WETTLER, Manfred (1998): A Freely Available Morphological Analyzer, Disambiguator and Context Sensitive Lemmatizer for German. In: Proceedings of the COLING-ACL 1998, Montreal, 743-747.

LIN, Dekang (1998): Extracting Collocations from Corpora. In: Proceedings of the COLING-ACL 1998, Montreal, 57-63.

MANNING, Christopher D.; SCHÜTZE, Hinrich (1999): Foundations of Statistical Natural Language Processing. Cambridge: MIT Press.

RAPP, Reinhard (1996): Die Berechnung von Assoziationen: Ein korpuslinguistischer Ansatz (Diss. Konstanz 1995). Hildesheim – Zürich – New York: Olms (Sprache und Computer 16).

RUGE, Gerda (1995): Wortbedeutung und Termassoziation: Methoden zur automatischen semantischen Klassifikation (Diss. Tübingen 1994). Hildesheim: Olms (Sprache und Computer 14).

SMADJA, Frank (1993): Retrieving collocations from text: Xtract. In: Computational Linguistics 19.1, 143-178.

Cohesive Paths in Hypertext

Alexander Mehler

The following paper deals with hypertext from the perspective of structural text semantics. The view is taken that hypertexts represent linguistic units above the level of
texts. They manifest intertextual regularities which allow the application of the concept of *lexical cohesion* as a *linguistic criterion* in the process of text linkage. As a
consequence, not local contexts of immediately linked texts, but whole chains of texts
are evaluated as a basis for evaluating hypertext traversals. A formal model is outlined using *semantic spaces* as the underlying information structure of a two-level
hypertext system: based on the concept of meaning as usage, semantic spaces result
from explorative corpus analysis. They propose a uniform format for representing
meanings of signs belonging to different strata. As required in the framework of hypertext, semantic spaces permit the connection of signs of whatever stratum based on
their meaning representations. The model proposed is *procedural* in the sense that it
does not presuppose linguistic knowledge to link texts; rather, this knowledge is explored by analyzing the usage regularities of signs in the corpus to be converted into
hypertext.

1 Introduction

This paper deals with the problem of automatically creating hypertexts from corpora
of natural language texts. A central aspect of this problem relates to the flexibility of
information processing, according to which the same text can be interpreted differently dependent on a recipient's varying context. This context dependency underlies
the observation that text corpora do not have predefined hypertext structures. As a
consequence, the theoretical justification of the link criterion becomes crucial. In this
paper, a text semantic basis is chosen: the decision to link texts is based on the similarity of their meanings. This is done by means of an explorative corpus analysis. As
a consequence, the knowledge underlying text linkage is not presupposed but results
from automatically analysing the corpora to be converted into hypertext. In this context, implicit text relations are reflected. This means that texts may be connected with
each other even if they have only few or no constituents in common, but share *semantically similar* components. In accordance with Salton et al. (1994), a descriptive statistical approximation of hypertext construction is elaborated. But in contrast to Salton,
the statistical model outlined in the following is based on linguistic considerations:
the text semantic criterion is extended by applying the concept of cohesion to hypertext. As a consequence, the focus is changed from single text links to whole chains of
such links.

Semantic similarity of texts is approximated with the help of the concept of cohesion. According to Halliday/Hasan (1976), cohesion represents (besides coherence)
an aspect of *textuality*. As part of language, cohesion refers to a system of text-form-

ing resources used to connect text components so that texts are perceived as semantic wholes. Whereas coherence comprises situational, cognitive and social aspects of text processing, cohesion refers to the characteristics of a text as a linguistic unit. Halliday/ Hasan distinguish four types of cohesion: reference, ellipsis and substitutions, conjunction, and *lexical cohesion*, which is based on the repetition and co-occurrence of lexical items sharing *sense relations* or *paradigmatic usage regularities*. The latter kind of cohesion is based on the fact that words which tend to appear in similar contexts generate a cohesive force if they co-occur.

For the sake of applying the concept of cohesion to hypertext, the view is taken that any chain of interlinked texts or text segments forming a traversal in hypertext can be seen as a text which a reader possibly processes following the corresponding links. These texts can be qualified regarding their cohesiveness. In the following, only lexical cohesion is considered. Suppose a negative example, in which semantic similarity of text pairs is optimised so that only associative links are produced. As a result, the risk of thematic diversification arises. This situation is exemplified in figure 1, where underlined lexical anchors are used to link texts. Using the text sample about *economics* as a starting node, a text dealing with *weather system* is reached via texts about *information science* and *physics*. Comparing these texts, a strong change in topic is realised: the starting and end node of this traversal do not form a cohesive whole; they do not hang together on lexical means.[1] This *thematic diversification* results from *intransitive meaning relations*: two nodes A and B may be semantically similar for other reasons than B and C. Therefore, to connect A and C via B can lead to an incohesive traversal.

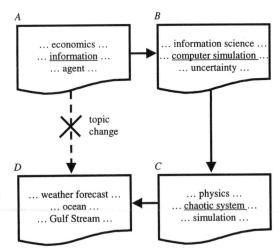

Figure 1: A thematic diversification resulting from associative links.

In order to reduce the risk of thematic diversification, the concept of cohesion is applied: any chain of interlinked texts can be described as a higher level text which can be evaluated regarding its cohesion. This is outlined in figure 2. Suppose that the text path $(R, ..., A, C)$ is more cohesive than path $(R, ..., B, C)$, while B and C are more semantically similar than A and C. From the perspective of optimising associativity of directly linked texts, the linkage of B and C is preferred. But to link the texts A and C allows to reduce the risk of incohesive topic change by producing the more *cohesive path* $(R, ..., A, C)$, since in this case semantic relationships of indirectly linked texts are reflected, too. As a consequence, only a weak change of topic is caused. To follow this premise means to optimise global aspects of cohesive paths instead of local, associative text-to-text similarities. Furthermore, two sorts of links can be distinguished: cohesive hierarchical links underlying cohesive paths and associative cross-reference links, as in the case of linking B and C.

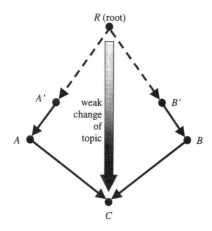

Figure 2: A lexically cohesive text (segment) path in hypertext

The semantic similarity of the lexical organisation of texts to be linked serves as a criterion for the evaluation of the cohesiveness of the resulting hypertext. Cohesion is a characteristic of complex linguistic signs, which in the case of hypertext controls the link process. This approach aims at using cohesion as a semantic source of text linkage for the sake of optimising the cohesiveness of whole hypertexts: two linked texts are seen to be cohesive to the extent that they comprise semantically similar lexemes. And the more lexically cohesive a set of texts, the more cohesive a path containing these units. In this context, a fish-eye-mechanism (see Furnas 1988) is applied: the shorter the distance of two nodes in a path, the more important their cohesiveness. Longer distance can be balanced by higher semantic similarity. As a consequence, a weak change of topic is allowed as the path grows. Now, the *link criterion* can be formulated as follows: Let H be a hypertext with the set of nodes N. Let x be a text to be inserted into the hypertext H. Find the node $n \in N$ as the end of a path (beginning with the root R of H) optimising cohesion when x is attached to that path.

2   Semantic Spaces

The question arises, how to explore lexical cohesion as a source for evaluating the cohesiveness of chains of whole texts? This is done with the help of semantic spaces. Semantic spaces are based on explorative corpus analysis. They propose a uniform representational format for the meanings of signs belonging to different levels. Semantic spaces do not invent any kind of predefined, atomic meaning constituents. On the contrary, their dimensions are defined by the lexical signs to be explored. Semantic spaces are based on the concept of meaning as usage: two words are seen to be semantically similar to the extent that they are used in semantically similar contexts. In order to be evaluated as being semantically similar, it is not necessary that the signs co-occur. Semantic spaces are computed in three steps (for a detailed description of semantic spaces see Rieger 1989 and Mehler 1998): in Rieger (1989) *syntagmatic* regularities of words $a_i, a_j \in V = \{a_1, ..., a_n\}$ are analysed with the help of a correlation coefficient:

$$\alpha(a_i, a_j) = \frac{\sum_{k=1}^{m}(h_{ik} - h_{ik}')(h_{jk} - h_{jk}')}{\sqrt{\sum_{k=1}^{m}(h_{ik} - h_{ik}')^2 \sum_{k=1}^{m}(h_{jk} - h_{jk}')^2}} \in [-1,1] \ ,$$

where $h_{ik}' = (H_i/L)l_k$ and $h_{jk}' = (H_j/L)l_k$. L is the length of corpus $C = \{x_1, ..., x_m\}$; l_k is the length of text x_k. h_{ik} is the frequency of word $a_i \in V$, and H_i is the overall frequency of a_i in C. With the help of α the *corpus space* $K \subseteq R^n$ is constructed. The corpus point of $a_i \in V$ is given by the vector $c_i = (\alpha(a_i, a_1), ..., \alpha(a_i, a_n)) \in K$. Rieger (1989) models similarities of syntagmatic regularities by means of a Euclidian metric:

$$\delta(c_i, c_j) = \left(\sum_{k=1}^{n}(\alpha(a_i, a_k) - \alpha(a_j, a_k))^2\right)^{\frac{1}{2}} \in [0, 2\sqrt{n}]$$

c_i, c_j are the corpus points of words a_i and a_j. These values are used to construct meaning points as elements of the *semantic space* $S \subseteq R^n$. The co-ordinate values of meaning point $m_i \in S$ of word a_i are defined as follows:

$$\forall j \in \{1, ..., n\} : m_{ij} = 1 - \frac{\delta(c_i, c_j)}{2\sqrt{n}} \in [0,1]$$

Finally, in Mehler (1998) meaning points of signs above the word level are integrated with the help of a weighted mean value reflecting different roles of lexemes in the process of meaning constitution. If $x_k \in C$ is a text, the meaning point $m(x_k) \in S$ is defined as:

$$m(x_k) = \sum_{a_i \in W(x_k)} w_{ik} m(a_i) \ ,$$

where $W(x_k)$ is the set of types occurring in x_k and $m(a_i)$ is the meaning point of type a_i. w_{ik} is a bias having the same function as the well known *tfidf*-score elaborated in information retrieval. After mapping the corpus C onto the space S, all texts can be compared regarding the similarity of their lexical organisation. Semantic spaces represent the signs' structural meanings as points of a high dimensional space. Meaning similarity is modelled by distances of meaning points: the more similar the signs' usage regularities the shorter the distances of their meaning representations. In other words, neighbourhoods of meaning points reflect similarity of paradigmatic usage regularities realised by the corresponding signs. Semantic spaces represent the kind of information structure needed for hypertext construction, because they allow to model *indirect* meaning relations:

- Words can be connected with each other even if they do not or only rarely co-occur, but realise similar paradigmatic usage regularities.
- Words and texts (or text segments) can be connected even if the words do not occur in these texts, but realise similar usage regularities as the texts' lexical components.
- Texts (or text segments) can be connected even if they do not share components at all.
- Finally, non-linguistic signs (e.g. images) can be connected with linguistic signs on the basis of their linguistic descriptions (e.g. captions).

In the literature, many models of semantic spaces are discussed: for example, Landauer et al. (1997) use factor analytic methods for *latent semantic analysis* of texts. Schütze (1997) builds context vectors for the sake of automatic disambiguation. The algorithm for automatic hypertext construction proposed in the following is designed in order to work on any of these models. It only assumes the possibility to build a complete undirected weighted graph based on the sign's vector representations.

3 Cohesive Trees

Because of space limits, the algorithm for hypertext construction can only be outlined. It comprises five steps:

i) First occurs the computation of the semantic space by assigning meaning points to all signs observed in the corpus C.

ii) Next, a text $z \in C$ is chosen as the root of the hypertext to be constructed out of C.

iii) Eventually, a subspace of the semantic space is activated dependent on a user's information demand.

iv) A *cohesive tree* based on cohesive paths is constructed using z as its root and the elements of the activated subspace as its successors.

v) Finally, cross-reference links or additional cohesive paths may be produced under the control of hypertext metrics.[2]

As a result, a *two level hypertext system* is realised: dependent on the same semantic space as the underlying information structure of a two-level hypertext system and varying roots and contexts, different hypertexts can be computed. The algorithm is based on a relational model called *dependency scheme*. It generalises *dispositional dependency structures* (see Rieger 1989) in the sense of reflecting path contexts. At the same time, it departs from *minimal spanning trees* which only model associativity. The edge set of any dependency scheme is defined as follows:

$$E(z) = \{\{x, y\} \mid x \leq_z^{(1)} y \wedge \neg \exists v \in N : v \leq_z^{(1)} y \wedge v \leq_z^{(2)} x\} \subset N^2 \ ,$$

where N is the set of nodes. The dependency scheme describes a *class* of hierarchical interpretation structures based on signs relation as represented in the semantic space. It is constructed with the help of two order relations having the following generalised interpretations:

- $\leq_z^{(1)}$ models root priming effects by defining the order in which the signs are inserted into the tree dependent on their distance to the root z.

- $\leq_z^{(2)}$ models context priming effects by determining the predecessor of a sign y to be inserted as the end of the path optimising path cohesion when y is attached to that path.

With the help of varying instantiations of $\leq_z^{(1)}$ and $\leq_z^{(2)}$, different interpretation structures can be derived from the same dependency scheme. As a result, a parameterised algebraic model for automatic hypertext construction can be described which allows the production of different hypertexts reflecting varying strengths of cohesiveness. In order to get a cohesive tree as an instance of the dependency scheme, path context needs to be reflected: let $D(z) = (V, E)$ be a tree, $P = (v_1, ..., v_k)$ be the unique path in $D(z)$ starting with root $z = v_1$, and x a node (sign) to be inserted into the tree, then path sensitive distance of P and x is defined as follows:

$$\delta^*(P, x) = \sum_{i=1}^{k} w_i \delta(m(x), m(v_i)) \in [0,1] \ ,$$

---

[2]   For the use of these metrics in the course of hypertext construction, see Smeaton (1996).

where $\sum_{vi \in V(P)} w_i \leq 1$. $V(P)$ is the set of nodes of path P. The metric δ measures the similarity of the meaning representations of x and v_i. The bias w_i has a threefold interpretation:

- *Order independence:* if w_i is constant for all $v_i \in V(P)$, then the position of a vertex in P is seen to be irrelevant.
- *Path sensitivity:* if w_i is monotonously increasing with path length, then the syntagmatic order of P is reflected in the sense that the shorter the distance of x to a vertex in the path, the more important their similarity. As a consequence, the descending impact of more distant units allows a weak change of topic as the path grows.
- *Path insensitivity:* if all w_i are set to 0, except w_k, then the path distance criterion degenerates to a dependency structure. In other words, dispositional dependency structures form a special case of more general cohesive trees.

The *cohesive dependency tree* $D(z)$ of sign z results from defining the relation $\leq_z^{(2)}$ with the help of the path distances $\vec{\delta}(P, x)$, whereas $\leq_z^{(1)}$ is defined on the basis of distances of the signs' meaning points with respect to the local centre z forming the infimum of $\leq_z^{(1)}$. The approach outlined so far has a fourfold *semiotic* interpretation:

1) *Denotation and connotation:* signs are mapped onto meaning points serving as distributed representations of their *meanings* – the *denotation* in Eco's (1991) sense. Relational representations of their *interpretations* result from analysing the environment of their positions in the semantic space – the signs' *connotations* in Eco's sense.

2) *Structural semantics:* signs are interpreted with the help of signs, and *not* by reference to a finite set of atomic, crisp semantic features (defined prior to any corpus analysis).

3) *Corpusanalytic reconstruction:* the lexical dependencies of lexemes are not presupposed, but result from automatic explorative corpus analysis.

4) *Applying the concept of cohesion:* the relational representations of the signs' interpretations do not rely on association, but take (lexical) cohesion into account. Instead of optimising associativity of immediately linked texts, chains of texts are considered.

4 Some Empirical Results

In this section, as short example of automatic hypertext construction is described. The experimental setting was the following: a corpus of 502 texts was mapped onto a semantic space. For this sake, 2,058 types were chosen as its dimensions by excluding stop words as well as words of low and high frequency. The text sample, serving as the root of the hypertext to be constructed, is given in table 1. Based on this text and the distances of meaning points represented in the semantic space, a hypertext was automatically built as outlined in figure 3.

> "In the Caucasus Republic striving for independence: Yeltsin orders the end of all battles in Chechnya/ negotiations with rebel leader Dudajew are announced.
> The peace plan of the Russian President includes the retreat of the army out of all 'peaceful regions' as well as the election of a Parliament. Acts of terrorism are further on answered with military means. An immediate end of the mission is impossible.
> tu Moscow (own report) – The Russian President Boris Yeltsin gave the Russian task forces in the Caucasus Republic Chechnya on Sunday the order to stop all actions from April, the 1st, midnight, on. Nevertheless, acts of terrorism of the Chechnyans are answered further on. ..."

Table 1: Süddeutsche Zeitung from 01.04.1996, p.1

In this hypertext, lexical anchors are used to link the dominating node with the dominated node as the link target. The introductory text chain of this hypertext forms a cohesive whole with respect to the topic of war in Chechnya. Next, two chains, realising different topic changes, follow. The one is dealing with foreign affairs of Russia, whereas the other handles border dispute in Korea (and civil war in Rwanda). In other words, following the links in this hypertext causes a weak change in topic controlled by cohesion relations of indirectly linked texts. This example supports the idea that it is possible to use text meaning relations as a source for text linkage under the control of cohesion relations.

Figure 3: A sample hypertext

5 Prospect

In this paper, lexical cohesion was used as a linguistic source for text linkage in hypertext. For this sake, the concept of cohesive path was introduced. Associative links, as traditionally produced in automatic hypertext authoring (see for example Salton et al. 1994) are not neglected, but may be generated as additional cross-reference links. In order to model sign relations, semantic spaces are used as a uniform representational format of a two-level hypertext system. Future work aims at three points: (i) The *elaboration of a formal framework of hypertext construction based on the linguistic concept of cohesion:* this formalism aims at representing hypertexts with the help of graph theory. It describes hypertexts as relations (graphs) which result from instantiating a finite set of linguistically interpretable parameters in order to produce different hypertexts of varying cohesiveness. (ii) *Incorporation of different types of cohesion:* so far, the construction algorithm only reflects lexical cohesion as modelled with the help of semantic spaces. Regarding the system of functional equivalents for producing cohesive textures, this approach is underdetermined. Therefore, it is planned to consider other types of cohesion relations as a source for text linkage. (iii) *Empirical evaluation:* in order to show the usefulness of the information structure proposed for hypertext construction, a more elaborated, comparative study is needed. This will be part of a study in preparation.

6 References

ECO, Umberto (1991): Einführung in die Semiotik. München: Fink (UTB 105).

FURNAS, George. W. (1988): Generalised Fisheye Views. In: Proceedings of the ACM CHI' 86 Conference on Human Factors in Computing Systems. Boston: ACM Press, 16-23.

HALLIDAY, Michael A. K.; HASAN, Ruqaiya (1976): Cohesion in English. London: Longman.

LANDAUER, Thomas K.; DUMAIS, Susan T. (1997): A Solution to Plato's Problem: The Latent Semantic Analysis Theory of Acquisition, Induction, and Representation of Knowledge. In: Psychological Review 104.2, 211-240.

MEHLER, Alexander (1998): Toward Computational Aspects of Text Semiotics. In: Proceedings of the 1998 IEEE ISIC/CIRA/ISAS Joint Conference on the Science and Technology of Intelligent Systems. Piscataway: IEEE/Omnipress, 807-813.

RIEGER, Burghard B. (1989): Unscharfe Semantik: die empirische Analyse, quantitative Beschreibung, formale Repräsentation und prozedurale Modellierung vager Wortbedeutungen in Texten (Habil.-Schr. Aachen 1986). Frankfurt a. Main: Lang.

SALTON, Gerald; ALLAN, James; BUCKLEY, Chris (1994): Automatic Structuring and Retrieval of Large Text Files. In: Communications of the ACM 37.2, 97-108.

SCHÜTZE, Hinrich (1997): Ambiguity Resolution in Language Learning: Computational and Cognitive Models. CSLI Lecture Notes 71. Stanford: CSLI Publications.

SMEATON, Alan F. (1996): Building Hypertext under the Influence of Topology Metrics. In: Fraisse, S.; Garzotto, F.; Isakowitz, T.; Nanard, J.; Nanard, M. (eds.): Proceedings of the International Workshop on Hypermedia Design 1995. Berlin: Springer, 105-106.

A Generic Multilingual Parser for Multiple NLP Applications[1]

Juri Mengon, Christopher Laenzlinger

1   Introduction

The IPS project (Interactive Parsing System, LATL, University of Geneva) aims at developing a parsing system for French, Italian, English, and German. The IPS system is conceived as the core engine in various NLP applications: tagging, speech processing, translation and computer assisted language learning. Most importantly, the parser is based on a well-defined linguistic theory, the Principles & Parameters model of Generative Grammar (Chomsky and Lasnik 1995). The IPS system focuses on robustness, genericity, and deep linguistic analyses. Robustness is required for reliable NLP tools. For instance, when a complete analysis fails, partial structures are still exploitable for NLP applications. Genericity is inherent to the Principles & Parameters Theory implemented here. The Principles correspond to operations common to all languages, while the Parameters refer to specific processes to each language. Like most grammar-based systems, IPS differs from shallow approaches in that it relies on detailed linguistic analyses from which specific information can be drawn depending on the intended application. It will be shown in this paper how this richness of information can be advantageously exploited in the field of automatic translation.

The paper is organized as follows. In section 2, we will address the issue of using a Principle & Parameters Theory in a parser and the way in which it differs from rule-based parsing. In section 3, we give a description of the IPS system developed at the LATL. We present its modular architecture, the parsing algorithm and we address the questions of robustness, genericity and deep linguistic analyses in language processing applications. In section 4, we will illustrate how these linguistic analyses are profitably exploited for large-scale automatic translation. In section 5, we will give a short overview of some other NLP applications developed at the LATL, which are based on the syntactic parser IPS.

2   On principle-based parsing

Government & Binding Theory (Chomsky 1981) presents a radical change in theoretical linguistics research. Within the Standard Theory of Transformational Grammar of the '60s, the notion of grammar refers to a set of sentences generated by phrase structure rules and (cyclic) transformations. Within the GB model, the grammar is conceived as a set of interactive principles of well-formedness, which hold cross-linguistically, and as a set of parameters, the values of which are language-specific.

[1]   The research presented in this paper has been supported in part by a grant from the Swiss National Science Foundation (grant n° 1214-053792.98). We would like to thank Paola Merlo for her comments and suggestions.

The architecture of many parsers relies either on a mainly rule-based grammar, as the context-free backbone of GPSG (Gazdar et al. 1985) or LFG (Bresnan 1982), or on constraint-based grammars using unification, as HPSG (Pollard and Sag 1994). Parsers relying on phrase structure rules have undeniable advantages due to their well-known mathematical and computational properties. These lead to a uniform description of the grammar and therefore make it easier to calculate their run-time complexity. Furthermore, there are several efficient parsing algorithms available for grammars expressed with phrase structure rules. Despite these advantages rule-based grammars often also have to face serious shortcomings. The most important limitations are due to the fact that phrase structure rules are used to describe the surface structure of the input sentences. Since these rules tend to be rather construction and language dependent, moving towards a multilingual implementation means that the rules in question need either to be expanded automatically or have to be multiplied by the number of languages treated by the system. Thus, several thousands of rules are needed to implement a large-scale multilingual parser with a reasonable coverage. In a principle-based approach, a small number of Principles & Parameters can cope with these difficulties (see also Berwick 1991).

3   The IPS system

The principle-based approach implemented in the IPS system (Wehrli 1997) differs from conventional rule-based parsers in two basic points. First, phrase structure rules are replaced by more generic modules. Second, a particular parsing algorithm is used that combines a bottom up process with an incremental interpretation. Basically, the IPS system focuses on robustness, genericity and rich/deep linguistic analyses.

3.1 The modularity of the IPS system

The modules of the IPS system constitute interacting components corresponding to some of the modules of the Principles & Parameters Theory. On the one hand, there are generic (or universal) modules, corresponding to Principles, which apply to all languages. On the other hand, there are language-specific modules that correspond to values of Parameters.

Among the generic modules, the X' module dictates the general schema of syntactic structures. The X'-format is simplified in the IPS system as 1) (see also Table 1 below).

1) $[\text{Specifier}_{\text{list}} \ X^0 \text{Complement}_{\text{list}}]_{XP}$

Generic modules	Parsing example	Language-specific modules
Step 1 : Lexical analysis	[$_D$ Hans] [$_I$ hat] [$_D$ einen] [$_N$ Brief] [$_V$ gelesen] [$_D$ Jean] [$_I$ a] [$_V$ lu] [$_D$ une] [$_N$ lettre]	
Step 2 : Phrasal structure projection (X'-theory)	XP Spec X^0 Compl X$^\circ$={P, N, V, Adv, Adj, D, I, C}	
Step 3 : Attachments	CP DP C^0 IP I^0 VP DP V^0 D^0 NP Hans hat$_i$ t$_i$ einen Brief gelesen.	CP IP DP I^0 VP V^0 DP D^0 NP Jean a lu une lettre.	German: – verb second position – OV order
Step 4: Chain formation	[*hat*, t]$_{chain}$	
Step 5: Thematic/Case module	Argument 1 : *Hans/Jean* = AGENT/nominative Argument 2 : *einen Brief/une lettre* = THEME/accusative	

Table 1: Parse example

There is no bar-level and Specifier and Complement are implemented as (possibly empty) lists of maximal projections. X^0 is a variable for a lexical (Adv, Adj, N, V, P) or functional (C, I, D, F) category[2] projecting a maximal projection XP. Since this geometry is category-independent, it provides the basis for the uniform nature of syntactic structures in the IPS parser. Even in German, where the complements often precede a verb, the Complement list is situated on the right of the head. In fact, some German verb complements can be attached to the Specifier list[3]. The attachment module contains information on which constituents can be attached in the Specifier and Complement lists of an XP. The attachment relations are determined by selectional properties of heads, and constrained by agreement relations. The chain-building module inserts traces into a syntactic structure and binds them to their antecedents. These modules are generating devices that easily lead to overgeneration. Therefore, the IPS

---

[2]   The following abbreviations are used to represent the constituents: Adj(ective), Adv(erb), N(oun), V(erb), P(reposition), D(eterminer), C(omplementizer), I(nflection) and F(unctional).

[3]   In this sense, the Specifier and Complement lists do not have an interpretative function as such. Thus, a true verb complement can occur in a Specifier list, while an adjunct (i.e. a specifier-like element) can occur in a Complement list.

system contains top-down filtering modules, such as the theta module and the case module, that filter out ungrammatical structures.

Among language-specific modules, there are for German those applying to the verb second configuration, the Object-Verb (OV) order, to constituent reordering possibilities ("scrambling"), to extraposition on the right of the predicate. The specific modules for French apply to pronominal chains, inversion configuration, verb placement, among others.

We will illustrate how the parsing mechanism works with the following examples.

2) a. Hans hat einen Brief gelesen.
   b. Jean a lu une lettre
      'John has read a letter'

The IPS system first undertakes a lexical analysis by segmenting the input sentence (in phonetic or orthographic form) into lexical units and inserts them as edges for all their possible readings into a chart. Thus, the lexical analysis of the input sentences in 2) gives rise to the set of maximal projections in Table 1, step 1, in accordance with the X'-module in Table 1, step 2. Every lexical unit X stored in the graph projects a maximal projection XP and lexical features are transferred to the syntactic level (XP) in accordance with the Projection Principle. Then, the attachment module checks all possible attachments to the Specifier and Complement positions of the various XPs.[4] The X'-module given in Table 1, step 2 (projection), defines the attachment options according to selectional rules and thematic relations. The backbone of the clause structure is CP > IP > VP, as shown in Table 1, step 3. The complementizer phrase (CP) functionally selects the inflectional phrase (IP), which in turn selects the verbal phrase (VP). In other words, IP functions as the right complement of CP, while VP is the right-complement of IP. Consider first the French sentence in 2b). Following Abney's (1987) DP-hypothesis, the nominal phrase *lettre* is the right-complement of the determiner phrase *une*. The entire DP is a subcategorized complement of the verb *lu*, hence is right-attached to V. The participial verb is the head ($V°$) of VP, while the auxiliary is the morphological spell-out of $I°$. The proper name *Jean* projects a determiner-less DP and is attached in Spec-IP, a typical subject position. Comparatively, the corresponding German sentence is parsed by means of the same generic modules. Only the attachment of some constituents is different given the configurational specificities of German. The verb second constraint is analyzed in configurational terms. In main clauses, the first constituent, here the DP subject *Hans*, is attached in Spec-CP, the first position of the clause.[5] The tensed verb is raised to $C°$, the second posi-

---

[4]   The IPS parser is a bottom up licensing parser that pursues all alternatives in parallel. Its parsing strategy is called "right-corner attachment" (Wehrli 1997:220) and proceeds in the following way: in an iteration, from left to right, every new element that is read from the input stream is combined with one of the (sub)structures of its left context. A more detailed description of the algorithm used in the IPS parser and the psycholinguistic evidence that supports it can be found in Wehrli (1997).

[5]   In fact, as illustrated in 4a), the subject is base-generated in Spec-VP in German and is attached in Spec-CP in a verb second configuration. Thus, a chain is formed between the raised subject and its base-position in Spec-VP.

tion of the clause. This is a simple way of analyzing the verb second (V2) constraint. The participial verb is placed in the same position as in French, namely V°. The OV configuration of German results from the attachment of the nominal complement *einen Brief* in Spec-VP. The chain formation module links the raised auxiliary in C° with a trace in I° (Table 1, step 4). The whole structure is given in Table 1, step 3, for the German and the French sentence. Finally, the filtering interpretative modules verify that each argument of the clause be assigned a thematic role from the verb (Thematic module), while every nominal phrase be in the right configuration to receive a Case (Case module).

3.2   Characteristics of the IPS system

Robustness is a crucial characteristic for any natural language parser to be used in a real world application. It includes the treatment of unknown words, the use of "micro-grammars" for idioms, parentheticals, temporal expressions, etc. Most importantly, when a complete analysis of a given sentence fails (for instance, in cases of complicated, marginal or simply incorrect constructions), partial parsing results are provided by the system, and can be used for specific applications.

Genericity is expressed at three distinct levels. First, as we have seen, the parsing procedure is generic, i.e. it holds for any language. Second, the architecture of the parser, as well as the implemented grammar, is generic in accordance with the modular conception of the Principles & Parameters Theory of grammar. Third, genericity is reflected within the parse trees of different languages. As in the case of German and French, two typologically distinct languages, we have seen that they are assigned the same clause architecture based on identical phrase structure composition mechanisms. Only the treatment of specific constructions (pronominalization, anteposition, verb placement, verb/complement order) bring out some structural differences between French and German.

The IPS system provides rich and deep linguistic information for a given input stream, unlike the results of shallow parsers. This means that the parse result is not adapted to a specific application. The IPS system is rather a domain independent, large-scale parser that provides as much linguistic information as possible. This contrasts with the quite wide-spread conception of using some kind of linguistic pre-processing devices developed exclusively for single applications. In our conception, a robust, generic parser should constitute an application independent tool providing rich linguistic information that can be intensively used by a large number of applications, for instance automatic translation.

4   Translation applications based on the IPS system

ITS (Interactive Translation System) is a translation tool developed at the LATL. The former version , ITS-2 (Wehrli and Ramluckum 1993), was an interactive translator (interacting with the user) based on the standard analysis-transfer-generation architecture. The mode of transfer is both lexical and structural. The system rapidly faced serious problems of translation, specially with complex and discontinuous structures. The new version, ITS-3 (Etchegoyhen and Wehrli 1998), is based on a more elaborate mode of transfer, oriented towards an *interlingua*, very close to abstract semantic structures.

In the ITS-3 translation system, the syntactic transfer component of the ITS-2 system is replaced by more abstract interface structures called *pseudo-semantic structures* (PSS). The PSS have a hybrid nature combining abstract semantic representations with lexical items, and constitute the entry to the syntactic generator GBGen (Etchegoyhen and Wehrle 1998). To understand how the entire translation procedure works, we will examine the pair of German and French equivalent sentences given in 3).

3) a. Hans hatte es diesem Mann gesagt.
   b. Hans l'avait dit à cet homme.
   'Hans had said it to this man'

IPS produces a phrase structure analysis of the German source sentence, as in 4a), enriched with lexico-semantic information. The subject is attached in Spec-CP, while the tensed auxiliary is placed in C° (verb second analysis). Both elements leave a trace in their base-position. The verb's complements are both attached in the left-hand list of specifier of V (the analysis of OV order): the order is specified as [Subject > Pronoun > DP].

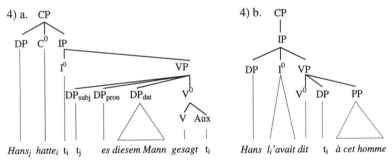

The next step consists of transferring the syntactic parse results to an interface structure and converting lexico-syntactic information into a lexico-semantic structure called *pseudo-semantic structure* (PSS). A PSS contains information about the clause, namely its mood (finite, indicative, conditional, subjunctive), its tense and aspect specifications. The tense values of a clause are determined in accordance with the continuum relationship between Reichenbach's (1947) Event time (E) value and Speech time (S) value (e.g. E<S, E=S, E>S), and also in accordance with aspectual values, such as progressive, perfective, imperfective. Information about voice, the utterance type of the clause and negation is also specified. The lexical transfer is restricted to open lexical categories such as verb, noun, adjectives, adverbs.[6] Thus, the predicate is specified as a lexical entry, associated with arguments. Non-clausal arguments are represented as DP-structures of operator-property type, specifying the determiner-noun relation. The lexical transfer applies to common nouns and proper names, but not to pronouns, which are specified abstractly as morpho-syntactic features. Thematic and agreement features are associated with each DP-structure. Finally, modifiers (adjuncts) are taken as satellites also associated with a pseudo-semantic structure containing values about their category, their function, their scope, etc. Thus, for 4a), a pseudo-semantic structure like 5) is derived, from which a corresponding French sentence is generated.

5) Pseudo-Semantic Structure

Information about the clause
Mood : real (= indicative)
Tense : E<S (= past)
Aspect : (non progressive, perfective)
Voice : active
Negation : not negated
Utterance type : declaration
Predicate : *sagen* / *dire*

Information about the arguments

Theta role : agent	**Theta role** : theme	**Theta role** : beneficiary
Property : *Hans* / *Jean*	**Property** : Δ	**Property** : *Mann* / *homme*
Operator : Δ[7]	**Operator** : Δ	**Operator** : demonstrative
	Gender : neutral	**Number** : singular
	Person : 3rd person	
	Number : singular	

On the basis of the above information, the sentence to be generated must be a declarative, active, non negated clause. The tense corresponds to the 'plus-que-parfait' (past perfect) in the indicative mood. The corresponding verbal predicate is *donner*, with three arguments. The external argument ('agent') is expressed as a proper name, a DP attached in the Spec of IP. The second argument is a direct object personal pronoun, which must be cliticized to the auxiliary in I°. A trace is posited in its base (thematic) position, namely Compl-VP. The third argument is a demonstrative common noun. As a 'dative' indirect object, it must be expressed as a PP introduced by the subcategorized preposition *à* and attached as Compl-VP. The resulting structure is given in 4b).

To conclude, the hybrid lexico-semantic transfer approach to large-scale automatic translation is a satisfying solution at present (see also Dorr 1997). On the one side, the lexico-structural approach encounters serious problems with complex and language-specific constructions, which often make the translation results, if there is any,

---

[6] The use of lexical transfer seems at present unavoidable in automatic translation, given that the assignment of abstract, lexically-independent, values to open lexical categories is too complex to be computed efficiently.

[7] The symbol Δ indicates that the values assigned here are left un(der)specified.

awkward and unnatural. On the other side, the use of purely abstract interface structures is not conceivable, mainly because they are too complex for domain-independent applications.

5   Other applications

The syntactic parser IPS is also the core engine for a series of NLP applications developed at the LATL of the University of Geneva, as represented in figure 1. First, the FIPSVox system (Gaudinat and Wehrli 1996) is a Text-to-Speech system for French using the IPS parser. The main theoretical concern of this project is to show the importance of a linguistic analysis for phonetisation and output phases in a Text-to-Speech system, as it is the case for the prosodic aspects of the output, the treatment of homographs, or, in particular for French, phenomena such as denasalisation and *liaison*. Second, FIPSTag is a part-of-speech tagger for French using the parse result of the IPS parser. The tagging consists of two phases. First, the parse results are transformed into morpho-syntactic categories. Second, the tags are rewritten according to contextual rules and heuristics. Finally, the SAFRAN project (*Système pour l'Apprentissage du FRANçais,* Hamel and Wehrli 1997) aims at the design of a computer assisted language learning system for French. In this project, NLP tools are used for didactic purposes within a multimedia environment. These tools are based on the IPS parser and the derived FIPSVox system.

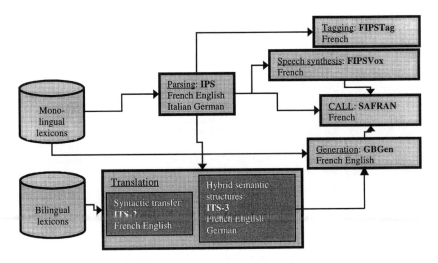

Fig. 1: NLP Applications based on the IPS parser

6 Conclusion

The use of the Principles & Parameters Theory to implement a generic parser is an interesting alternative to the use of rule-based systems. Even if both conceptions have their advantages and shortcomings, a generic parser that includes a steadily increasing number of languages might well take advantage of a principle-based approach. Implementing a large-scale, domain-independent parser provides us with a useful tool that can be used as the "core engine" for different NLP applications, particularly for large-scale automatic translation.

7 References

ABNEY, Steven. (1987): The English Noun Phrase in its Sentential Aspect (Ph.D. thesis). Cambridge, Mass: MIT.

BERWICK, Robert (1991): Principles of Principle-based Parsing. In: Berwick, R.; Abney, S.; Tenny, C. (ed.) (1991): Principle-Based Parsing: Computation and Psycholinguistics. Dordrecht: Kluwer Academic Press.

BRESNAN, Joan (ed.) (1982): The Mental Representation of Grammatical Relations. Cambridge, Mass.: MIT Press.

CHOMSKY, Noam (1981): Lectures on Government and Binding. Dordrecht: Foris Publications.

CHOMSKY, Noam; LASNIK, Howard (1995): The Theory of Principles and Parameters. In: Chomsky, Noam: The Minimalist Program. Cambridge, Mass.: MIT Press, 13-127.

DORR, Bonnie (1997): Large-Scale Dictionary Construction for Foreign Language Tutoring and Interlingual Machine Translation. Machine Translation 12, 271-322.

ETCHEGOYHEN, Thierry; WEHRLE, Thomas (1998a): Overview of GBGen : A Large-Scale Domain Independent Syntactic Generator. In. Proceedings of the 9th International Workshop on Natural Language Generation. Niagara Falls, 288-291.

— (1998b): Traduction automatique et structures d'interface. In: Actes de TALN'98, Paris, 2-11.

GAUDINAT, Arnaud; WEHRLI, Eric (1997): Analyse syntaxique et synthèse de la parole: le système FIPSVox. In: TA-Informations 38.1, 121-134.

GAZDAR, Gerald; KLEIN, Ewan; PULLUM, Geoffrey; SAG, Ivan (1985): Generalized Phrase Structure Grammar. Oxford: Blackwell.

HAMEL, Marie-Josée; WEHRLI, Eric (1997): Outils de TALN en EIAO: le projet SAFRAN. In: Actes des 1res JST 1997 FRANCIL de l'AUPELF-UREF, Avignon. 277-282.

POLLARD, Carl; SAG, Ivan (1994): Head-Driven Phrase Structure Grammar. Chicago: University Press of Chicago.

REICHENBACH, Hans (1947): Elements of Symbolic Logic. New York: Free Press.

WEHRLI, Eric (1997): L'analyse syntaxique des langues naturelles. Problèmes et methodes. Paris: Masson.

WEHRLI, Eric; RAMLUCKUM, Mira (1993): ITS-2 : an interactive personal translation System, In: Actes du colloque de l'EACL, 476-477.

Identifying Proper Names in Danish News Text for the Use in Information Extraction Systems

Mette Nelson

1 Introduction

The semantic problems of proper names, or more specifically the problem of reference of proper names, have occupied a great deal of philosophers, logicians and linguists since ancient times, cf. Frege (1892), Russell (1912), Searle (1969), Kripke (1972) and Lyons (1977) among others. Unlike the above mentioned, I will not discuss the problem of reference, nor the use of proper names. I will concentrate on what a proper name is and how it can be identified in order to make an Information Extraction system identify proper names automatically. I shall do this by first giving a short introduction to Information Extraction. I will then describe why computer applications have to pay special attention to proper names and describe in short the proper name in Danish. Finally, I will present an algorithm which identifies proper names in Danish news text on the basis of the initial capital letter and the syntactic structure of Danish proper names as well as a semantic ontology. I have used this algorithm in the NLP system NIF.

This paper addresses the issues above by examining proper names in Danish. I am focusing primarily on company names, and especially on analytic proper names, i.e. proper names that are constructed using words from other parts of speech, such as adjectives and common nouns. An example of an analytic proper name is *Den Danske Bank* (The Danish Bank).

While the automatic identification of proper names may not be a new task (see e.g. Coates-Stephens 1992, Ravin et al. 1997, Mani et al. 1993, and McDonald 1993), it has not been performed with a specific focus on Danish (see, however, Bredenkamp et al. 1996). Furthermore, the recognition of Danish analytic proper names has never been based on the internal structure of the proper names.

I will follow Allerton (1987) and Lehrer (1992) in making the distinction between proper nouns and proper names. I use the term proper noun as the name of a noun subclass. A proper noun is a string like *Peter* or *København* (Copenhagen), whereas a proper name is a phrase like *Den Danske Bank* (The Danish Bank) or *Peter Rasmussen*. As a deliberate choice, the paper emphasizes main ideas at the expense of technical data.

2 Information extraction

At the moment there exists a huge amount of news texts that is constantly expanding. Simply consider the Internet, where a vast amount of newspaper text can be found. In Denmark alone one finds 26 daily papers, 54 weekly papers, 16 online news agencies and 7 television news agencies on the Internet. It is almost impossible for a user to go through all the available articles in order to select the relevant ones. Even when the user can actually select the articles relevant to the topic of interest, the problem of selecting a small subset that the user can actually read in a limited time is still present. Therefore there is a need for search and selection services, and this is what Information Extraction can do.

Information Extraction (IE) is a term that has come to be applied to the activity of automatically extracting information about a pre-specified set of entities, relations or events from unrestricted, unedited text (typically newspaper articles) and of recording this information in database records or in so-called templates. For instance, it might be interesting for a company to monitor management succession events within competing companies. With an IE system the company could then scan business newspaper texts for announcements of management succession events (appointments, retirements, promotions, etc.), extract the names of the participating companies and individuals, the position involved, the vacancy reason, and so on. After having extracted this information, it could then be placed in templates. An example of information extraction from a text within the domain of management succession is shown in Figure 1.

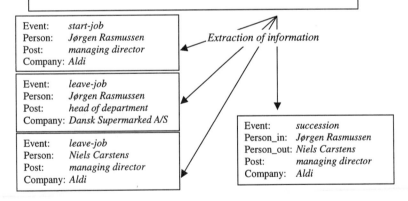

Figure 1

Using statistics or – as most often – using natural language processing techniques, the IE system fills out the slots in the templates in Figure 1. The templates consist of four or five slots – *event, person* (or *person_in* and *person_out*), *post, company* – making it possible to store information about a certain event (appointments, retirements, promotions, etc.), which has taken place for a certain person with a certain position in a certain company respectively. The template at the bottom right corner makes it possible to store information about the entire management succession event.

So, by using IE you can get specific information from huge document collections. The system is not looking for keywords, but for information that fits a predefined template pattern. This information is then stored in a template (typically structured by the use of SGML-markup), and the information can then e.g. be used for searching, using conventional database queries or for generating a summary.

3 The importance of proper name identification

The example in Figure 1 illustrates the importance of the identification of proper names. For every template in Figure 1 the IE system will need to identify at least two proper names (one proper name referring to the person in question and one referring to the company in question). On top of this, the system must identify that *Jørgen Rasmussen* and *Rasmussen* refer to the same entity to get the right information. The two strings, *Jørgen Rasmussen* and *Rasmussen*, are not identical and they form part of two different sentences. However, the two strings both refer to the entity with the full name *Jørgen Rasmussen*, who has just resigned as head of department as well as being named managing director. So not only does the IE system need to identify proper names, it also has to identify coreference between proper names in the input text.[1] An investigation I made shows that approximately 8.3 % of the words in Danish newspaper texts are proper names.[2] Since entities play a dominant part in most events described in newspaper articles, resulting in a high frequency of proper names that refer to these entities, it is of utmost importance that an IE system can automatically identify proper names, when dealing with newspaper texts as input.

The appropriate treatment of proper names is important not only in the development of IE systems, but also of systems for e.g. topic classification of text (proper names provide a good index for classification), machine translation (proper names are usually transferred unchanged to the target output text), alignment of corpora texts (proper names provide good anchors), spell checking, POS tagging, etc.

Consider for example applications for machine translation (MT). When an MT application encounters a proper name in the natural language input text, the MT application should not translate the proper name, but merely transfer the proper name unchanged to the output text[3]. Figure 2 shows an example of what might happen if the MT application does not disregard the proper names in the input text, but translates them.

---

[1] However, the automatic identification of coreference between proper names is not treated in this paper.

[2] A similar test performed for English shows that approximately 10% of words in English newspaper texts are proper names (Coates-Stephens 1992:3).

[3] There are, however, exceptions, such as *The Irish Republican Army*, which is often translated to the Danish equivalent *Den Irske Republikanske Hær*, unless the acronym *IRA* is used.

> Apple may have turned large deficits into surpluses. But Steve Jobs still has to prove that (...).

Translation

> *Nok har Æble vendt store underskud til overskud. Men Steve Arbejder har stadig at bevise (...).*

Figure 2

In Figure 2 the organisation name *Apple* and the surname *Jobs* have been translated into the Danish equivalent common nouns *æble* and *arbejder*, which was not intended, and thereby leaves the resulting text incomprehensible.

The crux of the matter is that most of the computer applications mentioned above, use lexicons to identify proper names, lexicons that are always incomplete and out of date as regards proper names – even when just created. This is due to the fact that proper names are classified as an open part of speech, i.e. the part of speech does not consist of a finite set of proper names, but new ones can be constructed when needed. An example is the invention of names for new companies or products. This holds in particular for proper names as opposed to e.g. verbs and common nouns which are also classified as open parts of speech. This is due to proper names being formed more frequently as referring to individual objects or entities, contrary to, for instance, nouns referring to general objects. Since proper names can be constructed so easily, lexicons will never be fully complete and therefore a method for automatically identifying proper names must be found.

Summing up, the main purpose of this paper is to report a method for making an IE system able to automatically identify proper names. The automatic identification of proper names is not only important while developing IE systems, but is also pertinent to the development of other kinds of computer applications. Before looking at how to identify proper names automatically, one might look at what kind of things we name. This will be the main topic for the next section.

4   Proper names in Danish

What kind of things can names be attached to? We actually name a large variety of entities such as concrete things, semiabstract entities, and events. For instance, we name persons (*Peter, Diane*), pets (*Plet, King*), ships (*Mette Mols, Fakarwee*), companies (*Den Danske Bank, McDonald's*), products (*Mega Salt Kodylguf, Citroën*), places (*København, Germersheim*), astronomical objects (*Jupiter, Castor*), meteorological objects (*Bonnie, Mitch*), rock bands (*666, Simply Red*), buildings and houses (*Slottet, Pax*), works of various kinds (*Hvad er proprier?* [What are proper names?], *Star Trek*), aeroplanes (*Memphis Belle*), wars (*Den Spanske Borgerkrig* [Spanish

Civil War]), computer files (*34cl.doc*), religious communities (*Jehovas Vidner* [Jehovah's Witnesses]), just to mention a few.

Some names may be said to be *namier* than others, that is, more prototypical than others. The most prototypical names are likely to be those which have lost their meaning and have become lexicalized – i.e. proper nouns. Less prototypical names are e.g. numbers used as names, like the proper name *666* for the German rock group or kinship terms like *Mor* (Mother).

As can be seen from the examples above, proper names can be made up of all kinds of constituents. However, in the following I will delimit the term *proper name* not to include VPs and sentences. This leaves us with four types of proper names in Danish, as illustrated in Figure 3.

Types of proper names		Examples
PURE	proper name phrases which contain one or more proper nouns	*Peter Rasmussen* *København*
MIXED	proper name phrases which contain both proper nouns and common nouns	*Erichsens Klinik* *Arkitektgruppe 83* *EKR Kreditforening*
COMMON BASED	proper name phrases which are made up entirely of constituents of a common noun phrase	*Den Danske Bank* *Institut for Datalingvistik* *Rock Uglen*
CODED	proper name phrases which are made up of initial letters and numbers, i.e. acronyms	*NESA* *KAD*

Figure 3

5 How to identify proper names?

How can one make a computer identify proper names automatically in natural language texts? Do proper names have a feature that makes them differ from other words in a text and can this feature be used as a criterion for automatic identification? The most common Danish dictionaries provide a description of proper names as words that are written with initial capital letters. However, capital letters as indicators for proper names are not sufficient in order to automatically identify them. This is illustrated by the examples in Figure 4.

A. *Blodprøver fra flere hundrede uskyldige danskere (...).*
   (Politiken 05/17/1998)
   Blood samples taken from several hundred innocent Danes (...).
B. *(...) hvor man finder det billigste tilbud på Beastie Boys' seneste CD.*
   (Morgenavisen Jyllands-Posten 08/05/1998)
   (...) where you find the cheapest sale on Beastie Boys' latest CD.
C. *(...) ved at tage fat på nedre ende af arbejdsmarkedets B-hold (...).*
   (Bergenholtz DK87-90 corpus, avis24.89)
   (...) by starting at the bottom level of the labour market (...).

Figure 4

In Figure 4A one finds the word *Blodprøver* (Blood samples) which is spelled with an initial capital letter, but it is not a proper name. The capital letter in *Blodprøver* marks the beginning of the sentence. The example in Figure 4B illustrates another problem in using capital letters as indicators for proper names. Here the word *CD* is found. The common noun *CD* is spelled with a capital letter. *CD* is one of a large number of words that are abbreviations, formed of the initials from several words or parts of words. In the case of *CD* it is the abbreviation of the common noun *compactdisk* (compact disc). Another type of word which is spelled with a capital letter is a word which begins with an initial capital letter that indicates e.g. form, sequence or quality, like *B-hold* (second place team) in Figure 4C, which indicates sequence. Other examples are *V-udskæring* (neck opening shaped like a V) indicating shape and *B-film* (second rate film) indicating quality.

The list of problems that arise when using capital letters as indicators for proper names can be further continued. However, the examples in Figure 4 clearly illustrate that capital letters are not a sufficient criterion on their own. However, by using the initial capital letters and combining this feature with other features that proper names in Danish have, it is possible to automatically identify them in Danish newspaper text.

The method that I have used for the automatic identification of proper names, is to reuse as much as possible from the modules that already exist in an Information Extraction system. Consider the sample grammar in Figure 5.

NP → DET ADJ N
NP → PROP PROP

DET → *den* (the)
ADJ → *danske* (Danish)
N → *bank$_{corp}$* (bank)
PROP → *Peter*
PROP → *Schumacher*
PROP → *Bill Clinton*

Figure 5

Even though an Information Extraction system with a grammar like the one in Figure 5 does not know the proper name *Den Danske Bank* (The Danish Bank), the grammar already contains the building blocks that make up the proper name. This means that the potential for knowing or identifying the proper name is already present in the grammar. The string *Den Danske Bank* consists of the determiner *Den* (The), the adjective *Danske* (Danish) and the common noun *Bank* (Bank), and these words are already in the grammar, only in a version with small letters. However, if one associates the words that have an initial capital letter with the feature *cap* (for capital letter) and converts the capital letters to small letters, then one can actually reuse the grammar in order to identify proper names that the system considers unknown. This means that if one associates the words in *Den Danske Bank* with the feature *cap* the proper name can then be viewed as the phrase *den danske bank*, or more precisely *den$_{[cap]}$*

danske[cap] *bank*[cap], which can then be identified by the grammar. The same holds for proper names that consist of personal names which are already in the grammar, but where the full form is unknown to the system. The proper name *Bill Clinton* is likely to be found in the grammar of an Information Extraction system, because it refers to a well known politician and therefore is likely to appear in newspaper articles. The proper name *Peter Schumacher*, on the other hand, does not refer to a well known or famous person and therefore the name in full is not likely to be found in the grammar of an Information Extraction system.

However, since one might find NPs that have the same structure as proper name phrases and which also have an initial capital letter, it is necessary to test whether the head in the phrase is a head that is acceptable for proper names. In order to test whether the head is an acceptable head, I use a semantic ontology that I have designed, based on the FUNES semantic hierarchy as shown in Coates-Stephens (1992:201). In the example with *Den Danske Bank*, the head *Bank* is of the semantic type *corp*. Common nouns of the type *corp* are acceptable as heads of proper names according to the semantic ontology, so therefore an Information Extraction system with the grammar in Figure 5 is able to identify *Den Danske Bank* as an acceptable proper name.

6   NIF (Names in FraCaS)

I have developed a system, called NIF (Names in FraCaS), which is based on the FraCaS III unification grammar system developed by Stephen Pulman at the University of Cambridge Computer Laboratory in England. The NIF system uses the features mentioned in section 5 – an initial capital letter, a syntactic structure and a semantic feature – in order to identify unknown phrases as proper names in Danish news text.

The procedure that the system uses in order to automatically identify proper names is shown schematically in Figure 6.

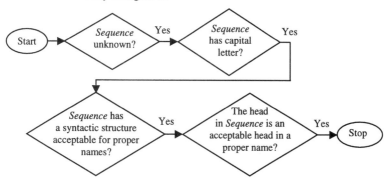

Figure 6

If the NIF system finds an unknown string of words, it examines the string to determine if it is a proper name. It does this by first checking if the unknown string of words is spelled with an initial capital letter. If this is so the system then changes the initial capital letters of the words (as well as associating the words with the feature *cap*) and then examines the string of words to determine whether it has a syntactic structure that is acceptable for proper names according to the grammar of the system. If this is the case the system then examines the head of the string of words to determine whether it is acceptable according to the semantic ontology. If this is so, the system considers the unknown string of words to be a proper name.

7   Evaluation

Most of the research in Information Extraction performed today is being performed with a reference to MUC, the Message Understanding Conferences. MUC is a continuous line of conferences where the distinguishing characteristics are not the conferences themselves, but the evaluations to which the participants must submit in order to be permitted to attend the conference (see MUC, 1999). I have made a small evaluation of the NIF system in accordance with the MUC instructions for evaluating Information Extraction systems. The result showed that NIF had a success-rate of 89.99% (P&R). The systems that participated in MUC-7, which was held in the spring of 1998, were for the largest part systems that take English texts as input. However, compared to the performance of the systems at MUC-7, only 3 of the 14 systems that participated had a better performance than NIF.

8   References

BOGURAEV, B.; PUSTEJOVSKY, J. (eds.) (1996): Corpus Processing for Lexical Acquisition, Cambridge: The MIT Press.

BREDENKAMP, Andrew; FOUVRY, Frederik; DECLARCK, Thierry; MUSIC, Bradley (1996): Efficient Integrated Tagging of Word Constructs. In: Proceedings of COLING-96, Copenhagen: Center for Sprogteknologi.

COATES-STEPHENS, Sam (1992): The Analysis and Acquisition of Proper Names for Robust Text Understanding (PhD Thesis London: City University).

FREGE, Gottlob (1892/⁶1986): Über Sinn und Bedeutung. In: Frege, G.: Funktion, Begriff, Bedeutung: Funf logische Studien, Göttingen: Vandenhoeck & Ruprecht (Kleine Vandenhoeck-Reihe 1144), 40-65.

KRIPKE, Saul (1972/1985): Naming and Necessity. In: Martinich, A. P. (ed.): The Philosophy of Language, New York-Oxford: Oxford University Press, 275-291.

LYONS, John (1977): Semantics, Cambridge: Cambridge University Press.

MANI, Inderjeet; MACMILLAN, T. Richard (1996): Identifying Unknown Proper Names in Newswire Text. In: Boguraev; Pustejovsky: 41-59.

MCDONALD, David D. (1996): Internal and External Evidence in the Identification and Semantic Categorization of Proper Names. In Boguraev; Pustejovsky: 21-39.

MUC (1999): MUC OnLine Home Page, http://www.muc.saic.com/.

NELSON, Mette (1999a): Information Extraction. En introduktion til systemer der uddrager information fra tekster, København: Institut for Datalingvistik, Handelshøjskolen i København.

NELSON, Mette (1999b): What are proper names and how do we identify them? In: Hansen, S. L. (ed.): World Knowledge and Natural Language Analysis. København: Samfundslitteratur (Copenhagen Studies in Language 23), 83-103.

RAVIN, Yael; WACHOLDER, Nina (1997): Extracting Names from Natural-Language Text. IBM Research Report, IBM Research Division.

RUSSELL, Bertrand (1905/1977): On Denoting. In: Logic and Knowledge, London: George Allen & Unwin Ltd, 39 - 56.

SEARLE, John (1969/1974): Speech Acts. Cambridge: Cambridge University Press.

Corpus Linguistics in the Analysis of Basic Color Terms[*]

Adam Pawłowski

1   Introduction

In 1969 Berlin and Kay published their famous study devoted to the analysis of color vocabulary in ninety eight different languages belonging to unrelated language families. They tried to challenge the hypothesis of "total semantic arbitrariness of the lexical coding of color" and consider colors as semantic universals: "Our feeling was that color words translate too easily among various pairs of unrelated languages for the extreme linguistic relativity thesis to be valid." (Berlin & Kay 1969:2). They have found eleven basic color categories which can be combined or modified to form complex color terms. They also noticed that in languages which encode fewer basic colors, color terms do not appear at random but in a certain order, as shown in the figure below (ibid.:4):[1]

$$
\begin{bmatrix} white \\ black \end{bmatrix} \rightarrow [red] \rightarrow \begin{bmatrix} green \\ yellow \end{bmatrix} \rightarrow [blue] \rightarrow [brown] \rightarrow \begin{bmatrix} purple \\ pink \\ orange \\ grey \end{bmatrix}
$$

Figure 1.

This well-known scheme should be read as follows: all languages contain terms for white and black; if a language contains three terms, it contains also *red*; if a language contains four terms, it contains either *green* or *yellow*; if a language contains five terms, it contains both *green* and *yellow* etc. The sequence of colors read from the left to the right also corresponds to the chronological order of their appearance and can be interpreted as a sequence of evolutionary stages on a diachronic axis.

2   Goal of the Study

In the following study, we analyse the frequencies of basic color terms in the multi-lingual language corpus, comprising data from eleven frequency dictionaries.[2] We

---

[*]   The extended version of this study was published in the Journal of Quantitative Linguistics 6, 1999.

[1]   Although physically *black, white* and *grey* are achromatic, in natural language they are considered as colors. This apparently unscientific and naive semantics reflects elementary human experience and is the main characteristic of the linguistic image of the world (see Berlin & Kay 1969; Wierzbicka 1990b; Tokarski 1995).

[2]   The analysed languages are Czech, Slovak, Russian, Polish, Ukrainian, Italian, English, French, Spanish and Rumanian (see the list in the *Appendix*). As far as English is concerned, the only

will not analyse in detail the semantics of particular color terms in different languages. We rely in this respect on the information from bilingual dictionaries verified by native speakers (see the list of color terms in the *Appendix*). We proceed in the following way:

1) We compare the order of colors based on the frequency of color terms in the lexical corpora of every language and the order of colors on the scheme of Berlin and Kay (further on B & K). The names of colors in various languages, arranged according to their frequency, will either remain in the same order as in Figure 1 or the frequency criterion would lead to different arrangements.

2) We analyse the independence of distributions of color terms in particular languages (by means of the *chi2* test). If the hypothesis of independence is confirmed, we will have good reasons to believe that in all analysed sub-corpora (thus irrespective of language) color terms follow exactly the same distribution. Indirectly, we will challenge the hypothesis of linguistic relativity in coding the spectrum of colors in different languages. In the contrary case, we will gain one more argument supporting the concept of particular conceptualisations of the world in different languages.

3   Previous Studies

Bibliographical record of quantitative studies in anthropological linguistics, especially those based on the data from linguistic corpora, is modest. If the frequencies of the use of a particular linguistic form appear in studies from the verge of linguistics and the anthropology of culture at all, they rather follow various surveys. An exception is the theoretical introduction to the frequency dictionary of Slovak, by Mistrík (1969). The author claims that quantitative data from the dictionary describe something more than the statistical structure of the vocabulary. Like a mirror, they reflect the image of the world cast in the collective memory of members of a given linguistic community.[3]

Another study from the field of ethnolinguistics, making occasional use of quantitative lexical data, is the paper of Wierzbicka (1990a) discussing the meaning of three Russian lexemes (*душа, тоска, судьба* – soul, sorrow, lot/fate) which, according to the author, well characterise Russian culture and mentality.[4]

---

accessible source was the frequency dictionary by Kučera and Francis (1967). Unfortunately, it contains non-parsed linguistic data, including many ambiguous items. Since in all the other dictionaries we analysed the frequencies of adjective forms only, the data from Kučera's and Francis' dictionary cannot be considered as fully reliable.

[3] "Frekvenčný slovník preto možno sledovať nielen ako inventár nesúvislých čísel, ale aj ako ukazovateľ systémov v jazyku a spoločenských 'zákonitostí' na území nositeľov jazyka." (The Frequency dictionary can be thus considered not as a set of independent numbers but as a manifestation of linguistic structures as well as of social relations on the territory of the linguistic community) (Mistrík 1969:128).

[4] More applications of data from large corpora can be found in the studies of Brunet (1981), Olsen (1993), Olsen and Harvey (1988), Biber et al (1998); Habert et al (1997).

4 Results

In the table below (Tab. 1), we present the results of our research. The list of analysed colors is based on B & K's list (*violet* has been added). If some parts of the spectrum are analysed differently in different languages, only the total frequency of relevant terms is given.[5] Color terms in the table are presented in the same order as on the B & K scheme. We can easily see that their frequency generally diminishes (Tab. 1, third row from the bottom) but some colors are displaced. It concerns *blue* which has on the average 11,3% of occurrences of all the color terms, much more than *yellow* (5%) and more than *green* (10,2%). It is also remarkable that *grey*, one of the least significant colors according to the results of B & K, turns out to be much more frequent than *purple*, *pink* and *orange*.

	white	black	red	green	yellow	blue	brown	purple	pink	orange	grey	violet	Total
Czech	604	519	416	205	96	206	127	3	158	4	146	16	2500
	24,2%	20,8%	16,6%	8,2%	3,8%	8,2%	5,1%	0,1%	6,3%	0,2%	5,8%	0,6%	1,00
English	365	203	197	116	55	143	176	13	48	23	12	7	1358
	28,6%	15,9%	15,5%	9,1%	4,3%	11,2%	13,8%	0,0%	0,0%	0,0%	0,9%	0,5%	1,00
French (Juilland)	136	113	74	35	7	58	17	0	0	0	20	0	460
	29,6%	24,6%	16,1%	7,6%	1,5%	12,6%	3,7%	0,0%	0,0%	0,0%	4,3%	0,0%	1,00
French (Engwall)	298	278	170	101	77	134	61	0	0	9	98	12	1238
	24,1%	22,5%	13,7%	8,2%	6,2%	10,8%	4,9%	0,0%	0,0%	0,7%	7,9%	1,0%	1,00
Italian	155	115	122	91	40	79	22	0	16	0	55	11	706
	22,0%	16,3%	17,3%	12,9%	5,7%	11,2%	3,1%	0,0%	2,3%	0,0%	7,8%	1,6%	1,00
Polish	87	93	52	39	19	36	24	0	8	2	29	2	391
	22,3%	23,8%	13,3%	10,0%	4,9%	9,2%	6,1%	0,0%	2,0%	0,5%	7,4%	0,5%	1,00
Romanian	165	104	75	78	64	60	18	0	0	0	0	0	564
	29,3%	18,4%	13,3%	13,8%	11,3%	10,6%	3,2%	0,0%	0,0%	0,0%	0,0%	0,0%	1,00
Russian	471	473	371	216	109	317	88	30	49	16	116	22	2278
	20,7%	20,8%	16,3%	9,5%	4,8%	13,9%	3,9%	1,3%	2,2%	0,7%	5,1%	1,0%	1,00
Slovak	461	473	315	275	104	181	43	7	71	19	58	19	2026
	22,8%	23,3%	15,5%	13,6	5,1%	8,9%	2,1%	0,3%	3,5%	0,9%	2,9%	0,9%	1,00
Spanish	141	102	44	51	21	71	6	0	0	3	41	6	486
	29,0%	21,0%	9,1%	10,5%	4,3%	14,6%	1,2%	0,0%	0,0%	0,6%	8,4%	1,2%	1,00
Ukrainian	282	310	193	118	50	175	23	4	36	0	114	10	1315
	21,4%	23,6%	14,7%	9,0%	3,8%	13,3%	1,7%	0,3%	2,7%	0,0%	8,7%	0,8%	1,00
Totals:	3165	2783	2029	1325	642	1460	605	57	386	76	689	105	13322
Mean (*m*):	24,7%	20,9%	14,6%	10,2%	5,0%	11,3%	4,4%	0,3%	2,1%	0,5%	5,4%	0,7%	1,00
σ:	0,032	0,030	0,022	0,022	0,023	0,020	0,031	0,004	0,019	0,005	0,029	0,005	
100*σ/m:	13%	14%	15%	21%	46%	18%	70%	155%	93%	104%	54%	62%	

Table 1: Absolute and proportional values of frequencies of color terms.
Notations: m – *mean percentage for each color;* σ – *standard deviation;* σ/m – *coefficient of variation.*

---

[5] Among the most common doublets or triplets there are terms for brown and blue (cf. *Appendix*).

The order of colors in particular languages and on B & K's scheme was compared by means of the Spearman's test. We notice in Table 2 that all the series are strongly correlated. Moreover, in spite of the differences concerning the positions of blue and grey, all the "national" lexical spectra are positively correlated with the order of B & K's scheme.

	English	French Juilland	French Engwall	Italian	Polish	Roumanian	Russian	Slovak	Spanish	Ukrainian	B & K
Czech	0,81	0,89	0,85	0,93	0,94	0,75	0,92	0,94	0,82	0,95	0,76
English		0,84	0,75	0,78	0,83	0,89	0,80	0,83	0,72	0,76	0,92
French AJ			0,93	0,94	0,94	0,84	0,97	0,87	0,91	0,93	0,85
French GE				0,94	0,93	0,77	0,93	0,86	0,98	0,92	0,78
Italian					0,95	0,81	0,96	0,92	0,90	0,96	0,82
Polish						0,80	0,91	0,94	0,91	0,95	0,81
Roumanian							0,82	0,86	0,76	0,78	0,99
Russian								0,93	0,91	0,99	0,84
Slovak									0,84	0,95	0,87
Spanish										0,89	0,75
Ukrainian											0,80

Table 2: Spearman's rank correlation coefficients for color terms.[6]

The positive result of the rank correlation test allows us to design a new diagram of colors, based on the average cross-linguistic frequencies of color terms (Fig. 2). It is noticeable that these frequencies, split into groups, largely coincide with B & K's scheme. The most distinctive and contrastive colors (*white, black, red, blue, green*) turn out to be the most frequent and the most important ones. They constitute the kernel of the structure of colors. Other colors (considered as mixed and derived from the former) can be regarded as peripheral. In spite of some differences concerning the position of *blue, yellow* and *grey*, the resemblance is striking. The scheme of color terms based on quantitative data from ten Indo-European languages, designed in the style of Berlin and Kay's scheme, would be then as follows:

$$[white\ 24,7\%] \rightarrow [black\ 20,9\%] \rightarrow [red\ 14,6\%] \rightarrow \begin{bmatrix} blue\ 11,3\% \\ green\ 10,2\% \end{bmatrix} \rightarrow \begin{bmatrix} grey\ 5,4\% \\ yellow\ 5,0\% \\ brown\ 4,4\% \end{bmatrix} \rightarrow \begin{bmatrix} pink\ 2,1\% \\ violet\ 0,7\% \\ orange\ 0,5\% \\ purple\ 0,3\% \end{bmatrix}$$

Figure 2.

The result displayed in Table 2 proves that in all the analysed languages, color terms arranged according to their frequency should appear in a similar order. But the new

---

[6]   The values of the rank coefficient cover the interval <–1; 1>; the more they approach –1 or 1, the stronger the correlation (respectively negative or positive) of the two compared series of items.

question arises whether or not the cross-linguistic frequencies of specific color terms in the lexical field of colors in every language remain stable. According to the neo-humboldtian theories, every language conceptualises reality in a particular way; hence, one should expect not only qualitative but also significant quantitative variations in coding of the semantic categories. But, on the other hand, the languages dealt with in the present study issue from a very similar – geographical, climatic, cultural – environment and stem from the common, Indo-European root. Considering these facts, as well as the significant rank correlation, we assume as a working hypothesis that the cross-linguistic distribution of color terms frequencies in the analysed corpora is stable, thus independent of the language, and that the differences observed are due to chance factors.

We start the verification of this hypothesis with two simple measures of variation: *standard deviation* (second row from the bottom) and *coefficient of variation* (first row from the bottom). Relatively small values of the latter (ranging up to 21%) appear only in the case of the most frequent colors (*white, black, red, blue* and *green*). Nothing can be said about the other color terms – they have very low cross-linguistic means (e.g. 0,3% for *purple* or 0,5% for *orange*) and their measures of variation cannot be considered reliable.

More satisfactory results can by obtained with the *chi2* test of independence. The advantage of this test is that it does not require any preliminary assumptions concerning the statistical distribution in the analysed population. The conditions of the experiment are defined in the following manner: From the corpus (population) of texts we draw n color terms. We admit that every term has two relevant qualitative features: language and color. We formulate the H_0 hypothesis of independence of these features.

We build the table of contingency containing the observed and theoretical frequencies of color terms in every language (Tab. 3). The value of the *chi2* statistics obtained from the data in table 3 is 1110. As the number of the degrees of freedom is greater than 30 ($v = 110$), we cannot use the tables of *chi2* distribution. However, it can be demonstrated that for $v \to \infty$, the random variable $X = \sqrt{2\chi^2}$ asymptotically approaches the normal distribution $N(\sqrt{2v-1}, 1)$. Consequently, instead of χ^2 we calculate the U-statistics $u = \sqrt{2\chi^2} - \sqrt{2v-1}$ which has a standardised normal distribution $N(0, 1)$ (Hammerl & Sambor 1990, 310). We easily find $u = 32,3$. As the critical interval of the U-statistics on the level $\alpha = 0,5$ is $[-1,96; 1,96]$, we **reject** the H_0 hypothesis and conclude that **the distribution of color terms is statistically different in the analysed corpora.**[7]

---

[7] This result, however, concerns the **global** quantitative structure of the data. A more detailed analysis of this structure, based on the so called *partial chi2*, can be found in Pawłowski 1999b.

		white	*black*	*red*	*green*	*yellow*	*blue*	*brown*	*purple*	*pink*	*orange*	*grey*	*violet*
Czech	obs.	604	519	416	205	96	206	127	3	158	4	146	16
	theor.	*594*	*522*	*381*	*249*	*120*	*274*	*114*	*11*	*72*	*14*	*129*	*20*
English	obs.	365	203	197	116	55	143	176	13	48	23	12	7
	theor.	*323*	*284*	*207*	*135*	*65*	*149*	*62*	*6*	*39*	*8*	*70*	*11*
French	obs.	136	113	74	35	7	58	17	0	0	0	20	0
(Juilland)	theor.	*109*	*96*	*70*	*46*	*22*	*50*	*21*	*2*	*13*	*3*	*24*	*4*
French	obs.	298	278	170	101	77	134	61	0	0	9	98	12
(Engwall)	theor.	*294*	*259*	*189*	*123*	*60*	*136*	*56*	*5*	*36*	*7*	*64*	*10*
Italian	obs.	155	115	122	91	40	79	22	0	16	0	55	11
	theor.	*168*	*147*	*108*	*70*	*34*	*77*	*32*	*3*	*20*	*4*	*37*	*6*
Polish	obs.	87	93	52	39	19	36	24	0	8	2	29	2
	theor.	*93*	*82*	*60*	*39*	*19*	*43*	*18*	*2*	*11*	*2*	*20*	*3*
Romanian	obs.	165	104	75	78	64	60	18	0	0	0	0	0
	theor.	*134*	*118*	*86*	*56*	*27*	*62*	*26*	*2*	*16*	*3*	*29*	*4*
Russian	obs.	471	473	371	216	109	317	88	30	49	16	116	22
	theor.	*541*	*476*	*347*	*227*	*110*	*250*	*103*	*10*	*66*	*13*	*118*	*18*
Slovak	obs.	461	473	315	275	104	181	43	7	71	19	58	19
	theor.	*481*	*423*	*309*	*202*	*98*	*222*	*92*	*9*	*59*	*12*	*105*	*16*
Spanish	obs.	141	102	44	51	21	71	6	0	0	3	41	6
	theor.	*115*	*102*	*74*	*48*	*23*	*53*	*22*	*2*	*14*	*3*	*25*	*4*
Ukrainian	obs.	282	310	193	118	50	175	23	4	36	0	114	10
	theor.	*312*	*275*	*200*	*131*	*63*	*144*	*60*	*6*	*38*	*8*	*68*	*10*

Table 3: Observed and theoretical frequencies of color terms.

Should this result be regarded as definite and conclusive for the question? We are still convinced that further verifications on greater and better corpora are necessary. No reliable conclusion can be based on the frequency of a word which occurs, say, 10 times per 500'000. Yet, rare colors, introducing to the model a great deal of random element, were treated together with the most frequent ones, as we did not find an argument to split the spectrum of colors in an arbitrary way. If the corpora were larger, the "gap" between the empirical and theoretical values would probably significantly diminish.

5 Conclusions

It was proved that no extreme hypothesis on the frequency and distribution of color terms in the linguistic corpora can be accepted. While the rank correlation tests yield a positive result (color terms, arranged according to their frequency of usage, appear in the same order, irrespective of language, and this order is coherent with that proposed by Berlin and Kay), the *chi2* test proves that the distribution of frequencies of color terms is statistically different in every language, the most frequent colors being significantly more balanced then the rare ones (Tab. 3). The result obtained is thus an argument in favour of a moderate relativity of coding color categories in language.

The difference between the scheme of B & K (Fig. 1) and ours (Fig. 2), although statistically insignificant, may result from the fact that our research was restrained to Indo-European languages. A similar, quantitative study, carried out on a greater and more diverse set of languages, representing other linguistic families as well as other cultural and climatic environments, would complete our conclusions and bring a satisfactory explanation to that incompatibility.

When analysing the result obtained in a more general perspective, one might ask the difficult but fundamental question: what real phenomenon do the proposed models describe? Distribution of color terms in the vocabulary is certainly related to the distribution of colors in the real, extra-linguistic world. Statistical structure of vocabulary could thus serve as a tool of indirect cognition of reality. But the quantitative structure of the lexical field of colors, described by means of a mathematical model (Pawłowski 1999b), could also be interpreted as a realisation of a human *cognitive scheme*.[8] If such a *cognitive scheme* or *frame* for colors exists – and according to Fillmore this is the case (Fillmore 1977, 55) – it must have been worked out in a feedback with the external world, the result of this process being a complex cognitive structure, roughly reflecting in the human brain the universe of colors.

6   References

ANDRÉ, J. (1949): Étude sur les termes de couleurs dans la langue latine. Paris: Klincksieck.

BERLIN, B.; KAY, P. (1969): Basic Color Terms. Berkeley: University of California Press.

BIBER, D.; CONRAD, S.; REPPEN, R. (1998): Corpus Linguistics. Oxford: CUP.

BRUNET, E. (1981): Le vocabulaire français. De 1789 à nos jours. Paris, Genève: Slatkine, Champion.

FILLMORE, Ch. J. (1977): Scenes-and-frames semantics. In: Zampolli, A. (ed.): Linguistic Structures. Amsterdam: North Holland Publishing Company.

HABERT, B.; NAZARENKO, A.; SALEM, A. (1997): Les linguistiques de corpus. Paris: Armand Colin.

HAMMERL, R.; SAMBOR, J. (1990): Statystyka dla językoznawców (Statistics for linguists). Warszawa: Wydawnictwo Uniwersytetu Warszawskiego.

HARDIN, C.L.; Maffi, L. (eds.) (1997): Color Categories in Thoughts and Language. Cambridge: CUP.

OLSEN, M. (1993): Quantitative Linguistics and *Histoire des mentalités*: Gender Representation in the *Trésor de la langue française* 1600-1950. In: Köhler, R; Rieger, B. (eds.): Contributions to Quantitative Linguistics. Dordrecht: Kluwer Academic Publishers, 361-371.

OLSEN, M.; HARVEY, L.-G. (1988), Computers in Intellectual History: Lexical Statistics and the Analysis of Political Discourse. In: Journal of Interdisciplinary History 18, 449-464.

PAWŁOWSKI, A. (1999a): Metodologiczne podstawy wykorzystania słowników frekwencyjnych w badaniu językowego obrazu świata (Methodological Principles of Application of Frequency Dictionaries in the Analysis of the Linguistic Image of the World). In: Pajdzińska, A.; Krzyżanowski, P. (eds.): Przeszłość w językowym obrazie świata (Past in the Linguistic Image of the World). Lublin: Wyd. UMCS, 81-98.

---

[8] A *cognitive scheme* can be defined as a sort of *filter* transforming (or deforming) the reality in the process of perception ("physiologically built-in predisposition in human being for perceiving or recognizing or categorizing certain hues" – Fillmore 1977:55). It is related to the notion of *cognitive frame*, used in psycholinguistics and cognitive semantics (*ibid*.:58-59).

PAWŁOWSKI, A. (1999b): The Quantitative Approach in Cultural Anthropology: Application of Linguistic Corpora in the Analysis of Basic Color Terms. In: Journal of Quantitative Linguistics 6, 1999.

PASTOUREAU, M. (1999): La révolution des couleurs ou le triomphe du bleu. In: L'Histoire 229, 62-67.

SAMBOR, J. (1972): Słowa i liczby (Words and numbers). Warszawa: Ossolineum.

TOKARSKI, R. (1995), Semantyka barwy we współczesnej polszczyźnie (The semantics of colors in contemporary Polish). Lublin: Wydawnictwo UMCS.

WIERZBICKA, A. (1990a): Duša (~soul), toska (~yearning), sud'ba (~fate): three key concepts in Russian language and Russian culture. In: Saloni, Z. (ed.): Metody formalne w opisie języków słowiańskich (Formal methods in the description of Slavic languages). Białystok: Wydawnictwo Uniwersytetu Warszawskiego, 13-32.

— (1990b): The Meaning of Color Terms: Semantics, Culture and Cognition. In: Cognitive Linguistics 1, 99-150.

Frequency dictionaries used in the study

BORTOLINI, U.; Tagliavini, C.; Zampolli, A. (1971): Lessico di frequenza della lingua italiana contemporanea. Milano: Garzanti.

ENGWALL, G (1984), Vocabulaire du roman français (1962-1968). Dictionnaire des fréquences. Stockholm: Almqvist & Wiksell International.

JELÍNEK, J.; Bečka, J.V.; Těšitelová, M. (1961): Frekvence slov, slovních druhů a tvarů v českém jazyce (Frequency of Words, Grammatical Classes and Linguistic Forms in Czech). Praha: Státní Pedagogické Nakladitelství.

JUILLAND, A.; BRODIN, D.; DAVIDOVITCH, C. (1971): Frequency Dictionary of French Words. The Hague: Mouton.

JUILLAND, A.; CHANG-RODRIGUEZ E. (1964), Frequency Dictionary of Spanish Words. The Hague: Mouton.

JUILLAND, A.; EDWARDS P.M.H.; JUILLAND I, (1965), Frequency Dictionary of Rumanian Words. The Hague: Mouton.

KURCZ, I.; LEWICKI, A.; SAMBOR, J.; SZAFRAN, K.; WORONCZAK, J. (1990): Słownik frekwencyjny polszczyzny współczesnej (Frequency Dictionary of Contemporary Polish). Kraków: Polska Akademia Nauk, Instytut Języka Polskiego.

KUČERA, H.; FRANCIS W. N. (1967): Computational Analysis of Present-Day American English. Providence: Brown University Press.

MISTRÍK, J. (1969): Frenvencia slov v slovenčine (Frequency of Words in Slovak). Bratislava: Vydavateľstvo Slovenskej Akadémie Vied.

ЗАСОРИНА, Л.Н. (eds.) (1977): Частотный Словарь Руского Языка (Frequency Dictionary of Russian Language). Москва: Издателство Русский Язык (Moskva: Izdatel'stvo Ruskij Jazyk).

ОРЛОВА, Л.В.; ПЕРЕБИЙНІС, В.С. (eds.): Частотний словник сучасної української художньої прози (Frequency Dictionary of Contemporary Ukrainian Artistic Prose). Київ: Видавництво Наукова Думка 1981 (Kiev: Vidavnictvo Naukova Dumka).

Appendix: color terms analysed in the study

Czech:

white – *bílý; black* – *černý*; red – *rudý, červený*; green – *zelený*; yellow – *žlutý*; blue – *blankytný, modrý, tmavomodrý*; brown – *bronzový,* hnědý; purple – purpuyrový; pink – růžoyvý; orange – oranyžový, grey – šedyý, šedivý, šeryý; violet – fialovyý.

French:

white – *blanc*; black – *noir*; red – *rouge*, green – *vert*; yellow – *jaune*; blue – *bleu*; brown – *brun, marron*; purple – *pourpre*; pink – *rose*; orange – *orange*; grey – *gris*; violet – *violet*.

Italian:

white – *bianco*; black – *nero*; red – *rosso*; green – *verde*; yellow – *giallo*; blue – *celeste, azzuro*; brown – *marrone, castano, bruno*; purple – *purpureo, scarlatto*; pink – *rosa*; orange – *arancio*; grey – *grigio, bigio*; violet – *viola*.

Polish:

white – *biały*; black – *czarny*; red – *czerwony*; green – *zielony*; yellow – *żółty*; blue – *niebieski, błękitny, granatowy*; brown – *brązowy, brunatny*; purple – *purpurowy*; pink – *różowy*; orange – *pomarańczowy*; grey – *szary*; violet – *fioletowy*.

Rumanian:

white – *alb*; black – *negru*; red – *roşu*; green – *verde*; yellow – *galben*; blue – *bleu, albastru, azuriu*; brown – *brun*; purple – *purpuriu*; pink – *trandafiriu*; orange – *oranj*; grey – *gri, inchis*; violet – *violet*.

Russian:

white – белый; black – чёрный; red – красный; green – зелёный; yellow – жёлтый; blue – голубой, синий, блакитний; brown – бронзовый, бурый, коричневой; purple – пурпуровый, багровый, алый; pink – розовый; orange – оранжевый; grey – серый; violet – фиолетовый.

Slovak:

white – *biely*; black – *čierny*; red – *červený*; green – *zelený*; yellow – *žltý*; blue – *belasý, modrý*; brown – *hnedý, bronzový*; purple – *purpurový*, pink – *ružový*; orange – *oranžový*, grey – *šedý, šedivý, šerý*; violet – *fialový*.

Spanish:

white – *blanco*; black – *negro*; red – *rojo*; green – *verde*; yellow – *amarillo*; blue – *azul*; brown – *castaño, marrón*; purple – *purpúreo*; pink – *rosa*; orange – *anaranjado*; grey – *gris*; violet – *violeta*.

Ukrainian:

white – білий; black – чорный; red – червоний; green – зелений; yellow – жовтий; blue – голубой, блакитний, синій; brown – бронзовий, бурый, коричневий; purple – пурпуровий багряний; pink – рожевий; orange – оранжовий; grey – сірий; violet – фіолетовий.

Die Berechnung syntagmatischer und paradigmatischer Wortassoziationen

Reinhard Rapp

1 Einführung

Nach Ferdinand de Saussure (1916) gibt es zwei grundlegende Beziehungen zwischen Wörtern, von denen er annimmt, daß sie Basisoperationen unseres Gehirns entsprechen: *syntagmatische* und *paradigmatische Assoziationen*. Um eine syntagmatische Beziehung handelt es sich, wenn zwei Wörter in gesprochener oder geschriebener Sprache häufiger als zufällig gemeinsam auftreten und wenn sie im jeweiligen Satz unterschiedliche grammatische Rollen einnehmen. Beispiele für syntagmatische Assoziationen sind etwa die Wortpaare *essen – Brot, Sonne – heiß* sowie *Lehrer – Schule*. Hingegen ist die Beziehung zwischen zwei Wörtern paradigmatisch, wenn das eine Wort durch das andere ersetzt werden kann, ohne daß dadurch die Grammatikalität oder Akzeptanz des Satzes beeinträchtigt wird. Beispiele sind etwa *essen – trinken, Schaf – Lamm* oder *schwarz – weiß*. Normalerweise handelt es sich bei paradigmatischen Assoziationen um Wörter derselben Wortart, während dies bei syntagmatischen Assoziationen zwar der Fall sein kann, aber nicht muß.

In der vorliegenden Arbeit wird gezeigt, daß die Produktion syntagmatischer und paradigmatischer Wortassoziationen mittels statistischer Methoden simuliert werden kann, die die Verteilung der Wörter in umfangreichen Textkorpora analysieren. Nach dem aus der Psychologie bekannten Kontiguitätsgesetz (Rapp 1996; Wettler et al. 1993) kann das Erlernen von Wortassoziationen durch die Hebb'sche Regel erklärt werden. Diese Regel besagt, daß die assoziative Verbindung zwischen zwei Nervenzellen genau dann gestärkt wird, wenn beide Zellen gleichzeitig aktiviert werden. Wörter, die in einem Text häufig gemeinsam auftreten, erfahren damit eine assoziative Verknüpfung. Es zeigt sich, daß mit einer solchen Statistik 1. Ordnung insbesondere die von Versuchspersonen genannten syntagmatischen Assoziationen vorausgesagt werden können. Für die Berechnung paradigmatischer Assoziationen sind hingegen Statistiken 2. Ordnung besser geeignet. Dabei wird nicht betrachtet, welche Wörter gemeinsam auftreten, sondern welche Wörter ähnliche Nachbarn haben. Beispielsweise kommen Synonyme in Texten nicht unbedingt gemeinsam vor, weisen aber eine ähnliche lexikalische Umgebung auf. Beide Ansätze werden verglichen und mittels empirischer Daten validiert. Es zeigt sich, daß sowohl für die Berechnung von Assoziationen 1. Ordnung als auch für die Berechnung von Assoziationen 2. Ordnung die Ergebnisse der Simulation den bei der Befragung von Versuchspersonen erhaltenen Ergebnissen gleichkommen oder sie sogar übertreffen.

2   Paradigmatische Assoziationen

Eine paradigmatische Beziehung besteht zwischen Wörtern mit hoher semantischer Ähnlichkeit. Nach Ruge (1992) kann die semantische Ähnlichkeit zweier Wörter dadurch berechnet werden, daß die Übereinstimmung ihrer lexikalischen Umgebungen bestimmt wird. Beispielsweise kann die semantische Ähnlichkeit der beiden Wörter *rot* und *blau* daraus abgeleitet werden, daß beide gleichermaßen mit Wörtern wie *Farbe, Blume, Kleid, Auto, hell, dunkel, schön* usw. überzufällig häufig gemeinsam auftreten. Wenn zu jedem Wort eines Korpus ein Kookkurrenzvektor bestimmt wird, dessen Einträge die Häufigkeiten des gemeinsamen Auftretens mit allen anderen Wörtern im Korpus sind, so können die semantischen Ähnlichkeiten zwischen Wörtern durch einfache Vektorvergleiche berechnet werden. Zur Bestimmung der zu einem vorgegebenen Wort ähnlichsten Wörter wird dessen Kookkurrenzvektor unter Verwendung eines der üblichen Vergleichsmaße (z.B. Cosinus-Maß) mit den Kookkurrenzvektoren aller anderen Wörter im Korpus verglichen. Diejenigen Wörter, für die sich die höchsten Werte ergeben, können als am bedeutungsähnlichsten betrachtet werden. Praktische Implementierungen solcher Algorithmen führten zu ausgezeichneten Ergebnissen (Ruge 1992; Schütze & Pedersen 1993; Grefenstette 1994; Agarwal 1995; Landauer & Dumais 1997; Schütze 1997; Lin 1998).

2.1   Experimentelle Vergleichsdaten

Zur quantitativen Evaluierung der Simulationsergebnisse ist es sinnvoll, diese mit experimentellen Daten zu vergleichen, die durch die Befragung von Versuchspersonen erhalten wurden. Hierfür verwendeten wir Daten des *Educational Testing Service*, die uns freundlicherweise von Thomas K. Landauer zur Verfügung gestellt wurden (Landauer & Dumais 1997). Die Daten entstammen dem Synonymteil des *Test of English as a Foreign Language* (TOEFL), einem Sprachtest, dem sich ausländische Studenten unterziehen müssen, die an einer englischsprachigen Universität studieren wollen.

Die Testdaten bestehen aus insgesamt 80 Fragen. Jede Frage besteht aus einem Satz, in dem ein einzelnes Wort unterstrichen ist, sowie aus vier Alternativwörtern für das hervorgehobene Wort. Die Aufgabe der Testteilnehmer besteht darin, unter den vier Wörtern dasjenige auszuwählen, das die Bedeutung des Satzes am wenigsten verändert, wenn es anstelle des unterstrichenen Wortes eingesetzt wird. Beispielsweise sollte in dem vorgegebenen Satz „Both boats and trains are used for transporting the materials" unter den vier Alternativwörtern *planes, ships, canoes* und *railroads* das hervorgehobene Wort *boats* durch das Alternativwort *ships* ersetzt werden, da zwischen diesen beiden Wörtern die größte Bedeutungsähnlichkeit besteht.

2.2 Textkorpus

Wie bereits erwähnt beruht unsere Simulationsmethode auf der Analyse statistischer
Regelmäßigkeiten in der Verteilung von Wörtern in Texten. Je umfangreicher und re-
präsentativer diese Texte, um so besser die zu erwartenden Ergebnisse. Ein englisch-
sprachiges Korpus, das diese Anforderungen in besonders guter Weise erfüllt, ist das
British National Corpus (BNC), das aus geschriebener und transkribierter gesprochener Sprache im Umfang von 100 Millionen Wörtern besteht und mit der Intention zusammengestellt wurde, einen repräsentativen Querschnitt durch das britische Englisch
zu geben.

   Um dieses umfangreiche Korpus sowohl in Bezug auf die Ausführungsgeschwin-
digkeit als auch den Speicherplatzbedarf effizient bearbeiten zu können, entschieden
wir uns dafür, alle Funktionswörter vorab aus dem Korpus zu entfernen. Dies geschah
auf der Basis einer etwa 200 Einträge umfassenden Funktionswortliste. Weiterhin
lemmatisierten wir sowohl das gesamte Korpus als auch die Testdaten (Karp et al.
1992; Lezius et al. 1998). Dadurch wird die Anzahl der zu bearbeitenden Wortformen
erheblich reduziert, was einerseits die statistische Absicherung der beobachteten Kookkurrenzhäufigkeiten verbessert (sparse data problem), andererseits auch die Größe
der zu berechnenden Kookkurrenzmatrix wesentlich vermindert.

2.3 Auszählen der Kookkurrenzhäufigkeiten

Die Bestimmung des gemeinsamen Auftretens von Wörtern beruht darauf, daß gezählt wird, wie häufig zwei Wörter in einem bestimmten Textfenster auftreten, das als
eine feste Anzahl benachbarter Wörter definiert wird. Das Festlegen einer bestimmten
Fenstergröße beinhaltet einen Kompromiß zwischen den Parametern Prägnanz und
statistischer Abgesichertheit. Eine kleine Fenstergröße läßt zwar deutlichere Assoziationen erwarten, da das eher zufällige Auftreten der Wörter in größerer Entfernung
nicht berücksichtigt wird. Andererseits können bei seltenen Wörtern die beobachteten
Kookkurrenzhäufigkeiten so klein sein, daß sie nicht mehr ausreichend statistisch abgesichert sind. Wir entschieden uns für eine Fenstergröße von nur ±1 Wort. Im Vergleich zu anderen Arbeiten erscheint diese Fenstergröße sehr klein. Allerdings kann
sie dadurch gerechtfertigt werden, daß wir das Problem der statistischen Absicherung
durch die Wahl eines sehr umfangreichen Textkorpus und durch die Lemmatisierung
reduziert haben. Außerdem entspricht eine Fenstergröße von ±1 nach Entfernung der
Funktionswörter in etwa einer Fenstergröße von ±2 ohne Entfernung der Funktionswörter (wenn angenommen, daß ungefähr jedes zweite Wort ein Funktionswort ist).

   Ausgehend von der Fenstergröße ±1 berechneten wir eine Kookkurrenzmatrix der
insgesamt etwa eine Million unterschiedlichen Wörter des lemmatisierten British National Corpus. Wegen der extremen Größe der entstehenden Matrix wurde bei der Implementierung auf sog. dünne Matrizen zurückgegriffen. Diese reduzieren den Speicherplatzbedarf wesentlich, indem nur solche Einträge gespeichert werden, deren Wert
ungleich Null ist.

2.4   Berechnung der Wortähnlichkeiten

Zur Bestimmung der zu einem vorgegebenen Wort ähnlichsten anderen Wörter wird der Kookkurrenzvektor dieses Wortes mit den Vektoren aller anderen Wörter verglichen und die berechneten Ähnlichkeitswerte werden in eine Rangfolge gebracht. Es wird erwartet, daß die ähnlichsten Wörter auf den ersten Rangplätzen erscheinen.

Zur Berechnung der Vektorähnlichkeiten werden in der Literatur eine Vielzahl von Ähnlichkeitsmaßen angegeben, u.a. der Kosinuskoeffizient, der Jaccard-Koeffizient, der Dice-Koeffizient, der Euklidische Abstand und die City Block Metrik (Salton & McGill 1983). Nach einer Anzahl von Simulationsläufen mit den genannten Maßen entschieden wir uns für die City Block Metrik, die mit weniger Rechenaufwand zu mindestens ebenso guten Ergebnissen führte wie die anderen Maße. Die City Block Metrik berechnet die Ähnlichkeit zweier Vektoren als die Summe der Beträge der Differenzen einander korrespondierender Vektorpositionen:

$$s = \sum_{i=1}^{n} |A_i - B_i|$$

2.5   Ergebnisse

Tabelle 1 zeigt die fünf stärksten paradigmatischen Assoziationen auf sechs Stimuluswörter. Mit Ausnahme von *drink* gehören alle berechneten Assoziationen derselben Wortart an wie das jeweilige Stimuluswort. Dies muß zwar so sein, denn unsere in der Einführung angegebene Definition des Begriffes *paradigmatisch* impliziert dies. Allerdings ist dieses Ergebnis dennoch erstaunlich, da während des Simulationsprozesses an keiner Stelle Wortarteninformationen einflossen. Dies bedeutet also, daß über die bloße Analyse von Wortkookkurrenzen die Gruppierung von Wörtern nach Wortarten möglich ist (s. auch Ruge 1995 und Rapp 1996).

blue	cold	fruit	green	tobacco	whiskey
red	hot	food	red	cigarette	whisky
green	warm	flower	blue	alcohol	brandy
grey	dry	fish	white	coal	champagne
yellow	drink	meat	yellow	import	lemonade
white	cool	vegetable	grey	textile	vodka

Tabelle 1· Berechnete paradigmatische Assoziationen zu sechs Stimuluswörtern.

Die Durchsicht der Tabelle ergibt, daß fast alle der berechneten Assoziationen, beispielsweise *blue – red*, *cold – hot* und *tobacco – cigarette*, intuitiv plausibel erscheinen. Allerdings wäre natürlich eine quantitative Evaluierung einer qualitativen vorzuziehen. Zu diesem Zweck betrachteten wir unser Simulationsprogramm als eine künstliche Versuchsperson, die die Testfragen des Synonymteils des *Test of English as a Foreign Language* (TOEFL) lösen sollte. Es wurde angenommen, daß eine Testfrage dann richtig gelöst sei, wenn in der vom Programm produzierten Rangliste das jeweils korrekte Lösungswort unter den vier vorgegebenen Alternativwörtern den höchsten Rangplatz belegte. Dies war bei 55 der insgesamt 80 Testfragen der Fall, was eine Trefferquote von 69% bedeutet. Diese Genauigkeit mag niedrig erscheinen. Allerdings ist zu bedenken, daß sich die Testfragen an angehende Studenten richten und deshalb eher schwierig sind. Dies zeigt sich daran, daß die Leistung der getesteten Studenten im Durchschnitt sogar schlechter war als die des Systems. Sie konnten im Mittel nur 51,6 der Testfragen lösen, was einer Trefferquote von 64,5% entspricht. Interessant ist, daß ein durchschnittliches Abschneiden beim TOEFL, der aber natürlich noch viele weitere sprachliche Leistungen überprüft, den Zugang zu fast allen Universitäten ermöglicht. Andererseits sind die Englischkenntnisse der TOEFL-Teilnehmer sicherlich nicht mit denen von Muttersprachlern vergleichbar, so daß von letzteren ein wesentlich besseres Abschneiden zu erwarten wäre. Eine Benachteiligung des Simulationsprogrammes ergibt sich allerdings in der Hinsicht, daß es ausschließlich für die Berechnung von Wortähnlichkeiten konzipiert wurde und den Kontext des jeweiligen Testwortes nicht berücksichtigen konnte. Einige Informationen, die für die Versuchspersonen möglicherweise hilfreich waren, wurden also gar nicht verwendet.

3   Syntagmatische Assoziationen

Eine syntagmatische Beziehung besteht zwischen solchen Wörtern, die häufiger als zufällig gemeinsam auftreten. Sie läßt sich dadurch überprüfen, daß die gemessene Kookkurrenzhäufigkeit zweier Wörter mittels eines statistischen Tests auf Signifikanz geprüft wird. Der bekannteste Signifikanztest ist der chi-Quadrat-Test. Allerdings zeigte Dunning (1993), daß sich für korpusstatistische Zwecke der sog. log-likelihood-Test besser eignet, da er für sehr niedrige beobachtete Häufigkeiten, wie sie bei seltenen Wörtern vorkommen, bessere Ergebnisse liefert. Demnach müßten sich die syntagmatischen Assoziationen zu einem vorgegebenen Wort also dadurch berechnen lassen, daß der zugehörige Kookkurrenzvektor ausgezählt und auf diesen der log-likelihood-Test angewandt wird. Die erhaltenen Signifikanzwerte werden anschließend in eine Rangfolge gebracht.

Zu bemerken ist, daß die angegebene Berechnungsmethode sehr viel weniger rechenaufwendig ist als die im vorigen Abschnitt angegebene für paradigmatische Assoziationen. Während zur Berechnung der syntagmatischen Assoziationen zu einem vorgegebenen Wort nur ein einziger Kookkurrenzvektor zu berücksichtigen ist, findet zur Berechnung der paradigmatischen Assoziationen ein Vergleich mit den Vektoren aller anderen Wörter des Vokabulares statt. Man spricht im einen Fall auch von Assoziationen 1. Ordnung (direkte Assoziationen), im anderen von Assoziationen 2. Ordnung (indirekte Assoziationen). Entsprechend unserer Annahmen müßte es sich bei den Assoziationen 1. Ordnung um syntagmatische, bei den Assoziationen 2. Ordnung um paradigmatische Assoziationen handeln. Es zeigt sich, daß dies zwar weitgehend, aber nicht vollständig der Fall ist. Insbesondere stellt es sich heraus, daß als Assoziationen 1. Ordnung nicht nur syntagmatische, sondern auch paradigmatische Assoziationen generiert werden. Darauf wird bei der Vorstellung der Simulationsergebnisse (Abschnitt 3.3) näher eingegangen.

3.1   Assoziationsnormen

Entsprechend der Vorgehensweise bei den paradigmatischen Assoziationen sollen die Simulationsergebnisse mit von Versuchspersonen erhaltenen Ergebnissen verglichen werden. Als Vergleichsdaten verwendeten wir den *Edinburgh Associative Thesaurus*, eine umfangreiche Sammlung von Assoziationsnormen, die von Kiss et al. (1973) erarbeitet wurde. Kiss legte Versuchspersonen Listen mit Stimuluswörtern vor und instruierte sie, zu jedem Stimuluswort dasjenige andere Wort anzugeben, das ihnen als erstes einfiel. Tabelle 2 zeigt einige von den Versuchspersonen genannte Assoziationen.

blue	cold	fruit	green	tobacco	whiskey
sky	hot	apple	grass	smoke	drink
black	ice	juice	blue	cigarette	gin
green	warm	orange	red	pipe	bottle
red	water	salad	yellow	poach	soda
white	freeze	machine	field	road	Scotch

Tabelle 2: Einige Beispielassoziationen aus dem Edinburgh Associative Thesaurus.

Wie man der Tabelle entnehmen kann, sind nicht alle von den Versuchspersonen angegebenen Assoziationen syntagmatisch. Beispielsweise handelt es sich bei *blue – black*, *whiskey – gin* oder *cold – hot* um paradigmatische Assoziationen.

3.2   Berechnung der Assoziationen 1. Ordnung

Wie bei den paradigmatischen Assoziationen so wurde auch hier als Textgrundlage das British National Corpus verwendet. In einem Vorabexperiment überprüften wir, ob es einen statistischen Zusammenhang zwischen der Auftretensposition eines Stimuluswortes und der Auftretensposition der zugehörigen von den Versuchspersonen meistgenannten assoziativen Antwort gibt. Hierzu erstellten wir ein Balkendiagramm mit den Auftretenshäufigkeiten der jeweiligen Response-Wörter in Abhängigkeit von ihrer Auftretensposition relativ zum Stimuluswort (s. Abb. 1). Die relativen Abstände ergeben sich dabei aus der Anzahl der Wörter, die sich zwischen Stimulus- und Response-Wort befinden (zuzüglich 1), wobei Inhalts- und Funktionswörter gleichermaßen gezählt werden.

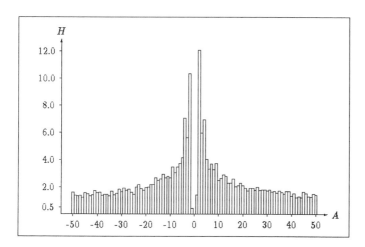

Abb. 1: Auftretenshäufigkeit H einer assoziativen Antwort im Abstand A
vom zugehörigen Stimuluswort (gemittelt über 100 Stimulus/Response-Paare).

Wie man dem Diagramm entnehmen kann, wird das Aufreten eines Response-Wortes um so wahrscheinlicher, je stärker wir uns dem Stimuluswort annähern. Eine Ausnahme bilden lediglich die beiden Positionen in unmittelbarer Nachbarschaft zum Stimuluswort, wo die Response-Wörter nur äußerst selten zu finden sind. Diese zunächst überraschende Beobachtung kann damit erklärt werden, daß es sich bei unseren 100 Stimulus- und Response-Wörtern durchweg um Inhaltswörter handelt. Inhaltswörter treten in normalen Texten aber meist nicht in direkter Aufeinanderfolge auf, sondern es befinden sich in der Regel Funktionswörter (z. B. Artikel) dazwischen.

Der von uns verwendete Algorithmus zur Berechnung von Assoziationen 1. Ordnung arbeitet wie folgt: Zunächst wird unter Verwendung einer Fenstergröße von ±20 Wörtern der Kookkurrenzvektor für ein vorgegebenes Stimuluswort berechnet. Da wir beobachtet haben, daß Versuchspersonen überwiegend häufige Wörter als assoziative Antworten nennen, werden in diesem Vektor alle Wörter mit einer Korpushäufigkeit von 100 oder weniger gelöscht. Anschließend wird der log-likelihood-Test auf die Einträge dieses Vektors angewandt. Nach Lawson & Belica[1] werden zur Berechnung des log-likelihood-ratios zwischen Wort W und Assoziation S vier Parameter A, B, C und D benötigt, die beschreiben, in wie vielen Fenstern W und S entweder gemeinsam, einzeln oder gar nicht vorkommen und die sich aus der folgenden Kontingenztabelle ergeben (N ist die Anzahl der Fenster bzw. die Anzahl der Wörter im Korpus):

	S	$\neg S$	gesamt
W	A	B	$A+B$
$\neg W$	C	D	$C+D$
gesamt	$A+C$	$B+D$	N

---

[1]   Handout bei der GLDV-Jahrestagung 1999 in Frankfurt.

Das log-likelihood-ratio wird dann wie folgt berechnet:

$$G = 2(A \log A + B \log B + C \log C + D \log D$$
$$+ N \log N - (A + B) \log(A + B)$$
$$- (A + C) \log(A + C) - (B + D)$$
$$\log(B + D) - (C + D) \log(C + D))$$

Schließlich wird das Vokabular nach absteigenden Werten von *G* sortiert. Bei den Wörtern auf den ersten Rangplätzen handelt es sich dann um die stärksten Assoziationen.

3.3   Ergebnisse

Tabelle 3 zeigt einige vom Simulationsprogramm generierte Assoziationen 1. Ordnung, die mit den Assoziationen der Versuchspersonen in Tabelle 2 verglichen werden können. Ein quantitativer Vergleich sollte in Betracht ziehen, daß von unterschiedlichen Versuchspersonen nicht immer dieselben Antworten gegeben werden. Die Frage ist also, ob die Antworten der künstlichen Versuchsperson „Simulationsprogramm" stärker von den Antworten der übrigen Versuchspersonen abweichen, als die Antworten der Versuchspersonen untereinander. Dies ist tatsächlich nur in geringem Maße der Fall. Für 27 der insgesamt 100 Stimuluswörter ist die berechnete Antwort des Programmes identisch mit der meistgenannten Antwort der Versuchspersonen. Der entsprechende Wert für eine durchschnittliche Versuchsperson ist hingegen 28, also nur geringfügig besser.

Blue	cold	fruit	green	tobacco	whiskey
Red	hot	vegetable	red	advertising	drink
Eyes	water	juice	blue	smoke	Jesse
Sky	warm	fresh	yellow	ban	bottle
White	weather	tree	leaves	cigarette	Irish
Green	winter	salad	colour	alcohol	pour

Tabelle 3: Simulationsergebnisse für Assoziationen 1. Ordnung.

Offensichtlich eignet sich die beschriebene Methode also gut dafür, menschliches Assoziationsverhalten zu simulieren. Wie die Versuchspersonen, so generiert auch das Programm eine Mischung aus syntagmatischen und paradigmatischen Assoziationen. Sollte es hingegen einmal erwünscht sein, ausschließlich syntagmatische Assoziationen zu generieren, so bietet es sich an, die beiden Methoden zur Berechnung von Assoziationen 1. und 2. Ordnung zu kombinieren. Naheliegend ist es, aus den Listen der Assoziationen 1. Ordnung die Assoziationen 2. Ordnung zu löschen, d. h. aus den gemischt syntagmatisch/paradigmatischen Assoziationen die paradigmatischen zu entfernen.

Tabelle 4 vergleicht für einige Stimuluswörter die jeweils stärksten fünf Assoziationen erster und zweiter Ordnung. In der Liste wurden jene Assoziationen 1. Ordnung fett gedruckt, die nicht unter den Top 5 der Assoziationen zweiter Ordnung auftreten. Die Durchsicht dieser hervorgehobenen Wörter zeigt, daß es sich durchweg um syntagmatische Assoziationen handelt. Die vorgeschlagene Methode scheint also zumindest im Ansatz zu funktionieren. Allerdings ergeben sich in der Praxis dennoch eine Anzahl von Schwierigkeiten: Zum einen müßten für eine quantitative Evaluierung die Begriffe syntagmatisch und paradigmatisch präziser definiert werden, als dies in der Einführung geschehen ist, da es immer wieder Zweifelsfälle gibt. Zum anderen müssen zur Generierung vollständigerer Listen der syntagmatischen Assoziationen längere Wortlisten betrachtet werden, als dies in der Tabelle geschehen ist. Je weiter wir uns aber in den sortierten Listen nach unten bewegen, um so weniger typisch für das jeweilige Paradigma sind die vorgefundenen Wörter, und mit um so schlechteren Ergebnissen muß demnach gerechnet werden.

Stimulus	1. Ordnung	2. Ordnung
blue	red ⟷	red
	eyes	green
	sky	grey
	white	yellow
	green	white
cold	hot ⟷	hot
	water	warm
	warm	dry
	weather	drink
	winter	cool
fruit	vegetable	food
	juice	flower
	fresh	fish
	tree	meat
	salad	vegetable
green	red ⟷	red
	blue ⟷	blue
	yellow	white
	leaves	yellow
	colour	grey
tobacco	**advertising**	cigarette
	smoke	alcohol
	ban	coal
	cigarette	import
	alcohol	textile
whiskey	**drink**	whisky
	Jesse	brandy
	bottle	champagne
	Irish	lemonade
	pour	vodka

Tabelle 4: Vergleich der berechneten Assoziationen 1. und 2. Ordnung.

4   Zusammenfassung und Diskussion

Es wurden Algorithmen zur Berechnung von Assoziationen 1. und 2. Ordnung vorgestellt, und es wurde gezeigt, daß diese in der Lage sind, das Verhalten von Versuchspersonen beim freien Assoziieren bzw. bei einem Synonymtest mit hoher Genauigkeit zu simulieren. Dabei ergab sich die Beobachtung, daß ein Zusammenhang zwischen den von Ferdinand de Saussure eingeführten Begriffen *syntagmatisch* und *paradigmatisch* und den beiden beschriebenen statistischen Rechenmethoden besteht. Durch unterschiedliche Kombination der beiden Rechenmethoden lassen sich sowohl ausschließlich paradigmatische, ausschließlich syntagmatische oder aber gemischt paradigmatisch/syntagmatische Assoziationen erzeugen.

Wir glauben, daß die Übereinstimmung zwischen dem Verhalten der Versuchspersonen und den Berechnungen unserer statistischen Modelle nicht zufällig ist. Den tieferen Grund für diese Beobachtung sehen wir darin, daß das menschliche Gedächtnis in einer Weise statistisch arbeitet, wie es etwa durch das aus der Psychologie bekannte Kontiguitätsgesetz ausgedrückt wird (Wettler et al. 1993). Letztendlich bedeutet dies, daß das Gedächtnis Operationen durchführt, die dem Auszählen von Kookkurrenzhäufigkeiten, der Durchführung von Signifikanztests oder der Berechnung von Vektorähnlichkeiten entsprechen. In weiteren Arbeiten soll untersucht werden, inwieweit solche statistischen Betrachtungen außer für die Produktion von Assoziationen auch für andere sprachliche Leistungen von Bedeutung sind.

5   Literatur

AGARWAL, R. (1995): Semantic Feature Extraction from Technical Texts with Limited Human Intervention (Diss. Mississippi State University).

DUNNING, T. (1993): Accurate methods for the statistics of surprise and coincidence. In: Computational Linguistics 19.11, 61-74.

GREFENSTETTE, G. (1994): Explorations in Automatic Thesaurus Discovery. Boston – Dordrecht: Kluwer (The Kluwer international series in engineering and computer science 278: Natural language processing and machine translation).

KARP, D.; SCHABES, Y.; ZAIDEL, M.; EGEDI, D. (1992): A freely available wide coverage morphological analyzer for English. In: Proceedings of the 14th International Conference on Computational Linguistics. Nantes, France, 950-955.

KISS, G.R., ARMSTRONG, C., MILROY, R., PIPER, J. (1973): An associative thesaurus of English and its computer analysis. In: Aitken, A.; Beiley, R.; Hamilton-Smith, N. (eds.): The Computer and Literary Studies. Edinburgh: University Press, 153 -165.

LANDAUER, T. K.; DUMAIS, S. T. (1997): A solution to Plato's problem: the latent semantic analysis theory of acquisition, induction, and representation of knowledge. In: Psychological Review 104.2, 211-240.

LEZIUS, W.; RAPP, R.; WETTLER, M. (1998): A freely available morphology system, part-of-speech tagger, and context-sensitive lemmatizer for German. In: Proceedings of COLING-ACL 1998, Montreal, Vol. 2, 743-748.

LIN, D. (1998): Automatic Retrieval and Clustering of Similar Words. In: Proceedings of COLING-ACL 1998, Montreal, Vol. 2, 768-773.

RAPP, R. (1996): Die Berechnung von Assoziationen. Ein korpuslinguistischer Ansatz (Diss. Konstanz 1995). Hildesheim: Olms (Sprache und Computer 16).

RUGE, G. (1995): Wortbedeutung und Termassoziation. Methoden zur automatischen semantischen Klassifikation (Diss. München 1994). Hildesheim: Olms (Sprache und Computer 14).

— (1992): Experiments on Linguistically Based Term Associations. In: Information Processing & Management 28.3, 317-332.

SALTON, G.; McGILL, M. J. (1983): Introduction to Modern Information Retrieval. New York: McGraw-Hill (McGraw-Hill computer science series).

SAUSSURE, F. de (1916/1996): Cours de linguistique générale. Paris: Payot.

SCHÜTZE, H. (1997): Ambiguity Resolution in Language Learning: Computational and Cognitive Models (Diss. Stanford 1995). Stanford, Calif.: CSLI Publications (Center for the Study of Language and Information <Stanford, Calif.>: CSLI lecture notes 71).

SCHÜTZE, H., PEDERSEN, J. (1993): A vector model for syntagmatic and paradigmatic relatedness. In: Proceedings of the 9th Annual Conference of the UW Centre for the New OED and Text Research, Oxford, England, 104-113.

WETTLER, M., RAPP, R., FERBER, R. (1993): Freie Assoziationen und Kontiguitäten von Wörtern in Texten. In: Zeitschrift für Psychologie 201, 99-108.

IPaGe – An Incremental Parallel Generation System for Natural Language

Matthias Rehm

1   Introduction

It is generally assumed that the production of natural language utterances can be split in two parts, the so called what-to-say and how-to-say parts. If such a modular build-up is embraced interesting questions arise concerning the take over of processing between these parts. One crucial aspect often stressed (e.g., Kempen and Hoenkamp 1987; Levelt 1989) is the necessity of an incremental processing behaviour. In this paper a system is described that realizes the how-to-say part of the generation process. The notion of flexibility will be used as a key to an incremental and parallel processing behaviour. It will be shown that splitting an input structure in different increments can yield the possibility to implement different levels of parallel processing. Thereby the role of the input structures to the generation process will be stressed. These constitute the interface between a possible application or – in production term – the what-to-say part of the generation process. The different levels of distributing the processing along with the characteristic features of the input structures used support a certain system architecture. Such an architecture will be described that was implemented as *IPaGe* (*I*ncremental *Pa*rallel *Ge*nerator).

2   Flexibility

In this section the two crucial aspects of *IPaGe* are introduced – incremental and parallel processing behavior. These two behaviours are summarized under the notion of flexibility. Flexibility as a key to incremental and parallel processing is understood here as a reactive behaviour to arbitrarily ordered input fragments. As *IPaGe* was developed as an application independent generation system such flexibility is necessary to not constrain the interface to possible applications too much. Conceptual structures constitute this interface. These structures support incremental and parallel processing in a natural way as will be exemplified below.

2.1   Incremental processing

An incremental processing behaviour is one of the crucial aspects of language generation as was already stressed by Kempen and Hoenkamp (1987). Incremental processing roughly means processing can start although only parts of the input structure are available. Every part of the input structure that can start processing is called an increment. Thus, one requirement posed to possible input structures is decomposability.

A given input structure should be decomposable in a number of input increments that can be processed independently of one another.

Finkler gives a formal definition of an incremental processing behaviour. I will cite here the three main conditions:

> „*Der inkrementelle Verarbeitungsmodus* in einem System S ist durch eine Kombination aus Konsumierung der Eingabe und Produktion der Ausgabe definiert, wobei die drei folgenden Bedingungen erfüllt sein müssen:
> 1. Die Verarbeitung startet, bevor die Eingabe komplett vorliegt (…)
> 2. Die Ausgabe des Ergebnisses wird gestartet, bevor die Verarbeitung der Aufgabenstellung abgeschlossen ist (…)
> 3. Die Ausgabe des Ergebnisses des Systems wird gestartet, bevor die Eingabe für die aktuelle Aufgabenstellung komplett vorliegt (…)
> Ein System heißt *inkrementelles System*, wenn es in der Lage ist, im inkrementellen Verarbeitungsmodus zu arbeiten." (Finkler 1997:22f).[1]

Conditions 1 and 2 are guaranteed to be met by *IPaGe*. As will be shown in section 2.3 complex conceptual structures that are used as input are composed of other conceptual structures. These can all serve as single input increments and carry enough information to start processing independently of one another. Whenever such an increment is supplied, processing of this increment starts (condition 1). The output structure of the system is a natural language sentence (German). This is composed of different constituents. At the moment a constituent which can start the sentence is supplied by the system's processes, the production of the output will start, regardless whether there are constituents missing yet (condition 2). Condition 3 poses a special problem to *IPaGe* because of the way the generation process is realized as a whole. Production of output is started when a relevant constituent is supplied. Whether the input structure is already completely given is irrelevant. All processes work autonomously with the structures available. Therefore the input increments can be supplied in arbitrary order. The order of the output is influenced by the order of the input increments but not determined by it. Thus, it cannot be guaranteed that condition 3 (start output before input is totally supplied) is met. This is no fundamental problem to the system. It is just irrelevant for processing. In fact, most of the time output starts before the whole input structure is supplied. So the third condition seems not be applicable here since it relates to systems with fixed input/output ordering. Another factor is the speed of the application *IPaGe* is attached to. The faster the increments are supplied the less probable it is that condition 3 is met.

As condition 3 is no problem of principle to the system, *IPaGe* can be seen as a system working in the incremental processing mode.

---

[1] "The *incremental processing mode* in a system S is defined by a combination of consuming the input and producing the output. Thereby the following three conditions have to be met:
1.Processing starts before the input is completely supplied (…)
2.The output of the result is started before processing of the whole task is finished (…)
3.The output of the system's result is started before the input for the current task is completely supplied (…)
A system is called *incremental system* if it is able to work in the incremental processing mode."
[my translation, MR]

2.2   Levels of parallel processing

If the input structures allow incremental processing, different levels of parallel processing can be implemented according to the characteristic features of these structures. First of all processing can be started by each input increment according to the idea of an incremental processing behaviour. This means the different increments can be processed independently of one another at least to a certain degree. Following this is the fact that the different increments can be processed simultaneously at least to a certain degree. This can be identified as the first level of parallel processing. If the different input structures moreover carry enough information to start different processes at the same time, a second level of parallel processing is realized. The first level of parallel processing is concerned with single processes and the distribution of these, whereas the second level also has implications concerning the architecture of the whole system.

To sum up, the first level is possible if incremental processing is possible at all. Different increments can be processed independently and simultaneously by the same process. The second level depends on the features of the input structure. A single input increment has to carry enough information to initiate different processes simultaneously.

In the next section it will be shown that the chosen input structures, namely conceptual structures, allow this naturally. Thereby a certain system architecture is supported as will be described afterwards.

2.3   Conceptual structures

Conceptual structures were already used successfully in natural language processing (e.g., Nogier and Zock 1992, Dorr 1993). Through their recursive buildup an incremental and parallel input behaviour is achievable. This kind of behaviour is suggested by psycholinguistically motivated language production models (e.g., Levelt 1989).

In this section the internal structure of conceptual structures will be described. With this information at hand, it will be shown how these structures allow parallel and incremental processing. As an example the structure shown in Figure 1 is used. This input will yield an output like *Die lange Leiste bewege ich zu dem Würfel* (I move the long bar to the cube) or *Zu dem Block bewege ich die Leiste* (To the block I move the bar).[2]

---

[2]   To develop a natural language generation system a context has to be established for the generation task. *IPaGe* is connected to a simulated assembly robot (Puma 260) that manipulates small toy construction *Baufix*-parts. The user is able to give natural language instructions to the robot, which it will interpret by integrating its perceptions, its actions and the language data (e.g., Milde, Strippgen, and Peters 1997, Goecke 2001). The goal of the generation process is a first person description of the robot's current actions.

2.3.1 Internal structure

The notion of conceptual structures used here is derived from Jackendoff's theory of conceptual semantics (e.g., Jackendoff 1990). A conceptual structure consists at least of a type and a logical head. In the example the types are given in capital letters. They serve two tasks. On the one hand they are needed to analyze the given heads, thus taking part in the lexical processing. On the other hand they impose restrictions on the choice of phrases that can be generated from the given structure. This is part of the syntactical processing. The type *PATH* e.g., is often realized as a prepositional phrase. Thus the *PATH*-argument in the example will yield s.th. like *zu dem Würfel* (to the cube).

The logical head is the value of a given structure, e.g. *block*. It is analysed by a conceptual lexicon according to its type, thus constraining the choice of possible lexemes. A structure like *[OBJECT block]* corresponds to nominal phrases like *Würfel, Bauklotz, Quader,* etc. (cube, buildung block, rectangular solid). Some structures require logical arguments to represent certain meanings. These arguments are themselves conceptual structures. In the *PATH*-structure e.g., the end point has to be specified (*[OBJECT block]*).

Logical modifiers further elaborate a given concept leading to the generation of adjectives or adverbs. *[OBJECT block]* is modified by the structure *[COLOR yellow]*, yielding e.g., *gelben Würfel* (yellow cube).

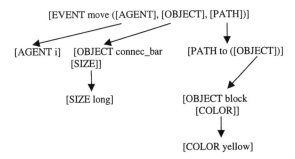

[EVENT move ([AGENT], [OBJECT], [PATH])]

[AGENT i]   [OBJECT connec_bar   [PATH to ([OBJECT])]
             [SIZE]]

[SIZE long]   [OBJECT block
                           [COLOR]]

[COLOR yellow]

Figure 1: A complex conceptual structure with its subparts. These can serve as input increments to the generation process. The relevant features to generate from conceptual structures are: the type of the logical head, the logical head itself, and the number and types of logical arguments.

2.3.2 From internal structure to incremental and parallel processing

As shown in figure 1 a complex conceptual structure is based on other conceptual structures. To clearly identify a structure at least two parameters are essential: The type and the head. If arguments are necessary to represent the intended meaning, number and types of these arguments are essential, too. Once this information is provided, it is possible to start processing the given structure without fully specifying it.

For the example the following underspecified structure is acceptable: *[EVENT move ([AGENT], [OBJECT], [PATH])]*.

The argument structures can be provided at any time. There are no restrictions on the order in which they have to arrive as input. The same holds true for modifiers of a given structure. Thus the internal structure of conceptual structures directly supports quantitative incremental processing (for a formal definition of different types of incrementality see Finkler 1997).

As mentioned above, conceptual structures carry information for lexical (type, head, arguments) as well as for syntactical processing (type). Nothing prevents the use of both kinds of information to speed up processing as will be shown in the next section.

To sum up, conceptual structures are an efficient choice as input. Complex structures are composed of other conceptual structures, which can serve as input increments. Thus, realization of incremental processing is directly supported by the input structures. Moreover they carry the information for the two different kinds of processing, which can be identified in the generation task: Lexical and syntactical processing. Because this information can be used independently the second level of parallel processing is possible.

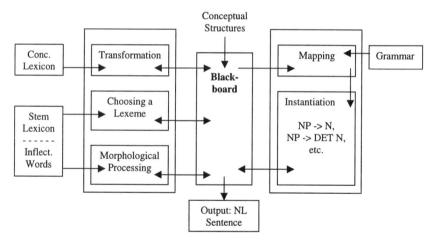

Figure 2: The architecture of IPaGe. Processing is initiated by a single input increment in both, the lexical and the syntactical unit. There, different processes can be distinguished that operate on different increments simultaneously. These communicate via a blackboard that serves as a central storing device.

3 System architecture

In this section a certain system architecture namely a blackboard architecture will be described that is supported by the input structures and the object-oriented paradigm of the chosen programming language. In such an architecture the blackboard is the central storing device from which all processes obtain their inputs and on which all processes write their outputs.

The blackboard architecture along with the characteristic features of the conceptual structures allows the realization of different levels of parallel processing as they were described above. The fundamental division in a lexical and a syntactical processing unit can be seen in Figure 2. This division is adapted from Levelt (1989) and is supported by the conceptual structures. Already the most simple conceptual structure (*[TYPE head]*) that is the most simple input increment carries enough information to initiate processing in both units. The type along with the logical head can start processing inside the lexical unit (*Transformation*, see Figure 3), the type initiates processing in the syntactical unit thereby using the type-phrase correspondence (*Mapping*, see Figure 4).

The second level of processing can be identified inside the fundamental units. Different processes can work on different inputs simultaneously. More interesting is the fact that the same process can work on different input structures (see figure 3 and figure 4). To distribute processing in a single process the relevant features of the input structures have to be identified. Choosing a programming language with an object-oriented paradigm leads to an elegant solution to the implementation problem. A closer look at figure 3 will reveal this fact.

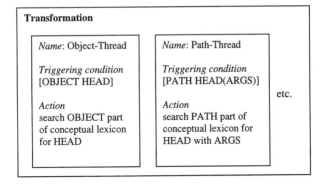

Figure 3: Distribution of processing inside a single process depends on the features of the input structures. The crucial aspect for the transformation process is the type of the conceptual structure along with the logical head. Thus a type-specific distribution is realized.

The first step of the lexical processing is the disambiguation of input structures. As conceptual structures describe meaning by a structural mechanism, the same head can have different meanings in combination with different types and even in combination with the same type but different arguments. This disambiguation process is implemented as a lookup process in a conceptual lexicon. The entries in this lexicon are sorted by different keys, first of all by the types of conceptual structure. Input increments to the lexical processing unit are typed conceptual structures. Thus a type specific distribution of processing seems natural here

The transformation process is basically the same for all types. Here the object-oriented paradigm comes into play. A transformation class was defined that implements the necessary processing behaviour. For every possible type an instance of this class was created and started as an independent thread that is triggered only by the given type (Figure 3).

This yields two obvious advantages: maintainability and adaptability. First, all necessary processes have to be defined only once. If modifications are necessary they have to be done only once. Second, an easy adaptability of the overall system is guaranteed. If new types are necessary in the domain of interest, only new instances of the relevant class have to be invoked.

By this way of distributing the processing a quantitative incremental processing behaviour as described by Finkler is implemented. Processing will start with any given increment and moreover different increments can get processed simultaneously. The instantiation process is the only exception to this kind of distributing the processing. Thereby a qualitative incremental processing behaviour is achieved.

An example will illustrate this point. When the input increment *[OBJECT con-nec_bar]* is written on the blackboard, processing is initiated in both processing units. In the lexical unit the *OBJECT*-thread of the transformation process is triggered. At the same time the *OBJECT*-thread of the mapping process starts working. As *OB-JECT*-structures are always realized as noun phrases in an utterance the noun phrase rules are selected (Figure 4).

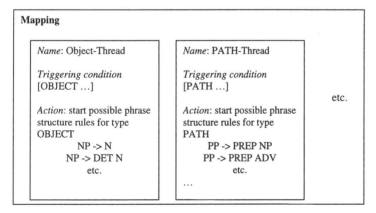

Figure 4: The crucial aspect to distribute the mapping process is the type of the conceptual structure as the type-phrase correspondence is used here. Thus a type-specific distribution is realized.

All possible rules given in the grammar are started as independent threads that try to substitute the non-terminal signs of their right hand sides by inflected lexemes. These threads constitute the instantiation process. Figure 5 depicts a snapshot of the instantiation process at a certain moment of time. Different rules that were selected for a given structure are coindexed. The degree of elaboration for a rule depends on the availability of the necessary constituents on the blackboard. The determiner is ready for the rules with index 43 and the adjective for those with index 57. So these constituents are already substituted.

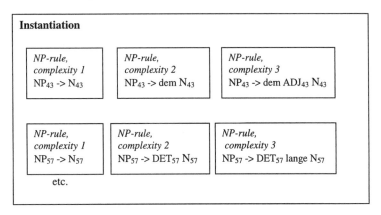

Instantiation

| NP-rule, complexity 1
$NP_{43} \rightarrow N_{43}$ | NP-rule, complexity 2
$NP_{43} \rightarrow$ dem N_{43} | NP-rule, complexity 3
$NP_{43} \rightarrow$ dem $ADJ_{43}\ N_{43}$ |

| NP-rule, complexity 1
$NP_{57} \rightarrow N_{57}$ | NP-rule, complexity 2
$NP_{57} \rightarrow DET_{57}\ N_{57}$ | NP-rule, complexity 3
$NP_{57} \rightarrow DET_{57}$ lange N_{57} |

etc.

Figure 5: *Distribution of the instantiation process is rule specific. Every possible phrase structure rule that can realize parts of the conceptual structure in the utterance is started as an independent thread. All concurrent threads for a given structure are coindexed.*

Let's have a closer look on one set of rules, namely the ones indexed 43. At the moment a noun with the right index is written on the blackboard two rules are fulfilled: $NP \rightarrow N$ (1) and $NP \rightarrow dem\ N$ (2). As thread (2) has a greater complexity value thread (1) will be stopped immediately and thread (2) will write its result structure on the blackboard: $NP \rightarrow dem\ W\ddot{u}rfel$. If the output process reaches the noun phrase constituent, at that moment of time *dem Würfel* would be the system output for this constituent of the utterance. Otherwise, if more time is left for further processing, the still active threads can try to finish their task. If an adjective, e.g., *yellow*, is supplied, the rule of thread (3) will be fulfilled and it will overwrite the former result on the blackboard. From that time on the system's output for the noun phrase constituent would be *dem gelben Würfel* (the yellow cube).

The way of distributing processing of the instantiation process yields an interesting effect. A first, simple result is supplied relatively fast. If there is more time to process further, this result will get more elaborated leading to more complex utterances.

4   Summary

The role of the input structures for the realization of an incremental and parallel processing behaviour was shown, as well as a system architecture that takes advantage of the characteristic behaviours of possible input structures to implement these behaviours. Thereby a flexible generation process becomes possible. Flexibility in this context is understood as a reactive behaviour to arbitrarily ordered input fragments. In a modular build-up of the overall production process such a flexible processing is necessary to amend taking over the processing between the two modules of what-to-say and how-to-say. Two main features of the input structures contribute to achieve the necessary flexibility. First of all they are decomposable in different increments. Moreover these increments carry enough information to make two different levels of parallel processing possible. Each increment can be processed independently of the others and each increment can initiate different processes simultaneously. Thus the chosen blackboard architecture and the distribution of single processes is directly supported.

5 References

DORR, Bonnie J. (1993): Machine Translation – A View from the Lexicon. Cambridge: MIT Press.

FINKLER, Wolfgang (1997): Automatische Selbstkorrektur bei der inkrementellen Generierung gesprochener Sprache unter Realzeitbedingungen: Ein empirisch-simulativer Ansatz unter Verwendung eines Begründungsverwaltungssystems. Bonn: infix.

GOECKE, Karl U. (2001): Conceptualization in agents: The System RoAD. In this Volume.

JACKENDOFF, Ray (1991): Semantic Structures. Cambridge: MIT Press.

KEMPEN, Gerard; HOENKAMP, E. (1987): An incremental procedural grammar for sentence formulation. In: Cognitive Science 11, 201-258.

Levelt, Willem J. M. (1989): Speaking. Cambridge: MIT Press.

MILDE, Jan T.; STRIPPGEN, Simone; PETERS, Kornelia: Situated communication with robots. In: First international workshop on human-computer conversation. Bellagio, Italien.

NOGIER, J.-F.; ZOCK, Michael (1992): Lexical choice as pattern matching. In: Knowledge Based Systems 5.3, 200-212.

REHM, Matthias (1998): Entwurf eines Systems zur Versprachlichung der Handlungssequenzen eines teilautonomen Roboters. Masters thesis, University of Bielefeld.

Zur automatisierten Inhaltserschließung von Nachrichtendokumenten

Ulfert Rist

1   Standardorientierte Dokumentation

Das Dokumentationsgut besteht aus einfachen Textmeldungen aus dem News-Bereich, die an einen automatisierten dokumentarischen Verarbeitungsprozess geleitet werden. Verschiedene Linguistikprogramme (u. a. Sprachenerkenner, Satzendeerkenner, Lemmatisierer, binäre Automaten, elektronisches Wörterbuch, NP-Grammatik) erzeugen Meta-Content wie automatische Inhaltserschließungen und Eigennamenqualifizierungen. Die semantische Interpretation folgt einer zugehörigen allgemeinsprachlich ausgerichteten, semantischen Struktur (siehe Langer 1996). Im Sinne einer wünschenswerten dokumentarischen Kompatibilität – sowohl die interne Dokumenterschließungen verschiedener Inhouse-Retrievalsysteme, als auch die Dokumentation externer Informationsanbieter und -abnehmer betreffend – wird die Unterstützung internationaler informationeller Standards bzw. eines übergreifend gültigen Metadatensystems als strategisches Ziel eingestuft. Dies betrifft geografische Standardkodierungen von Ländernamen nach ISO 3166-1,[1] die Themenerschließung nach IPTC (1997, 1999) (*International Press Telecommunication Council*), die formale und inhaltliche Kodierung von Bewegtbilddokumenten nach ETSI (1996) in bezug auf EPGs (*Electronic Programm Guide*), die DVB-Spezifikation (*Digital Video Broadcasting*) nach ETSI (1997) und im Aufbau befindliche internationale Standards wie die Kodierung von Kommunikationsangeboten nach SMPTE (*Society of Motion Picture and Television Engineers*).

1.1   Einsatz von IPTC/3

Als Standarddokumentationssystem bietet sich die aus dem Bereich der Nachrichtenagenturen und der Presse stammende Kodierung des Information Interchange Model (IIM) des International Press Telecommunication Council (IPTC) an. Das IPTC-NAA[2] IIM bietet sowohl *formale* Dokumentstrukturierungen z.B. für Textmarkierungen mit Überschriften und Absätzen an, die in XML gemäß News Interchange Text Format (NITF) notiert werden können, als auch eine *inhaltliche* Klassifikation. Das IPTC-Verschlagwortungssystem besteht derzeit aus ca. 450 auch numerisch kodierten Schlagwörtern, die in 17 unterschiedlich differenzierten Grobklassen, den sogenannten *Subjects*, Spezifizierungen (*Matters*) und thematischen Detailangaben (*Details*)

---

[1]   Vom 1.1.1997.
[2]   *News Association of America.*

eingeteilt sind. Ein Subject ist beispielsweise *01000000 Arts, Culture & Entertainment (general)* (siehe Anhang A).

1.1.1 IPTC-Evolution

Der dynamische Charakter der IPTC-Schlagwortstruktur schlägt sich in laufenden Aktualisierungen nieder. Neben einfachen inhaltlichen Differenzierungen, die durch Hinzufügen neuer Klassen in das bestehende IPTC-System bewerkstelligt werden, sind weitere Operationen beobachtbar. So wird in der gegenwärtig aktuellen Version IPTC/3 (1999) das Matter *01009000 Libraries & Museums* angeboten, eine Verschmelzung der früheren Klassen *01009000 Libraries* und *01023000 Museums*. Die Konjunktion wurde zugunsten der Klassenneudefinition *01023000 Nightclubs* vorgenommen.

Für die Dokumentation beziehungsweise für den Status eines elektronischen Archivsystems stellen derartige Änderungen der Dokumentationssprache ein Konsistenzproblem dar. Die syntaktische und inhaltliche Datennormalisierung erfolgt daher entweder bereits vor einem gegebenen Datenbankimport auf dem Inputstream, oder aber nachträglich auf den bereits getätigten Datenbankeintragungen, wobei hier zusätzlich mannigfache Abhängigkeiten von Feldern und Tabellen zu beachten sind. Bei semantischen Veränderungen nach Inhalt und Umfang von Klassen (Verallgemeinerung, Spezialisierung, Art der Inhaltsänderung) sind spezielle Methoden erforderlich

2   Wissenschaftliche Dokumentation in der Praxis

2.1   Klassifikationstypen

Um den Zusammenhang zwischen i. den *künstlich-sprachig basierten Klassifikationen*, wie sie im Bereich der Wissenschaftlichen Information und Dokumentation verwendet werden, und ii. *den natürlich-sprachig basierten Klassifikationen*, wie sie in der Linguistik verwendet werden, darstellen zu können, skizzieren wir beide *Ansätze* im Vergleich. Zu i.: Gemäß DIN 32705 (1987) und Ladewig (1997: 66ff) verstehen wir unter einer Klassifikation aus wissenschaftlich-dokumentarischer Sicht ein *Begriffssystem*, das begrifflich ordnend in bezug auf Gegenstände und Wissen zu Gegenständen angewendet wird. Ein solches System, das aus *Klassen* besteht, die zueinander in hierarchischer Beziehung stehen, setzt logischerweise die konstruktive Operation der *Klassenbildung* voraus. Eine Klasse vereint hierbei diejenigen Begriffe, die mindestens ein einziges gemeinsames *Merkmal*, bzw. einen gemeinsamen *Aspekt* oder *Unterscheidungsgesichtspunkt* aufweisen; dieses Merkmal wird *Klassem* genannt. Auf Grundlage dieser Vorgaben entstehen baumstrukturierte Gebilde. Unter einem *Klassifikat* verstehen wir hierbei die Gesamtheit von Klassen, z.B. Klassen zu einem Begriff wie ‚Kleidung'. Mit dem Vorgang des *Klassierens*, der den Klassen Elemente zuordnet, entsteht nun die Gesamtheit des Klassierten (Klassen und zugeordnete Elemente), das *Klassat*. Zu ii.: Nach Langer (1996) erfolgt die Gewinnung von natürlich-sprachig basierten Klassen durch die Anwendung von *Testrahmen*; die theoretischen

Überlegungen hierzu sind u. a. in Gross (1994) fundiert. Die sprachlich angewendeten Kriterien können demnach wie folgt grob eingeteilt werden:

    i.   Kontexte zum Testen von *Sinnrelationen*;

    ii. *Selektionskontexte* durch Operatoren (Verben, Adjektive, Nomina)[3];

    iii. *Spezielle Konstruktionen*, die ausschließlich oder typischerweise mit bestimmten semantischen Klassen auftreten, z.b. vokativische Kontexte für Schimpfwörter.

Es ist nicht ratsam und methodisch fragwürdig, diese beiden Klassifikationsansätze, bzw. deren klassifikatorische Produkte direkt zu vereinen. Zu ii. in bezug zu i. vermerkt Langer (1996:70) aus Sicht der Nominalkodierung des deutschen Wortschatzes:

> „Zur inhaltlichen Klassifizierung eines Textes auf Grundlage der themenspezifischen Nomina ist eine Klassifikation des Nominalwortschatzes in einem Thesaurus erforderlich. Thesauri im Information Retrieval sind ontologische Begriffshierarchien, deren Begriffen Lemmata zugeordnet sind; sie sind also eine auf thematischen Kriterien beruhende Einteilung des Wortschatzes oder eines Teilwortschatzes einer Sprache."

Der Ansatz von Langer (1999:176ff), thematische Klassen aus semantischen Klassen zu konstruieren, geht also dahin, zu sagen, ein bestimmtes Dokument, in dem beispielsweise genügend viele nominale Kandidaten aus den Klassen SEELSORGERISCHE BERUFE, RELIGIÖSE EREIGNISSE & RITEN und KIRCHLICHE GEBÄUDE sowie deren Unterklassen vorkommen, die ihrerseits zu der Bereichsklasse ‚Kirche und Klerus' zusammengefasst werden, habe thematisch mit einem Deskriptor „Kirche und Klerus" einer künstlich-sprachig basierten Dokumentationssprache zu tun.

> „Unser Ansatz zielt darauf ab, die linguistisch ermittelten semantischen Klassen durch die Bildung von sog. *Thematischen Klassen* in der automatischen Dokumentation zu verwenden. Insbesondere bei Einbezug von dokumentationssystemfremden Inhaltserschließungen sind Transformationen bereitzustellen, die auf einer tief angesiedelten semantischen Ebene die Konstruktion von Dokumentationssystemklassen, also z.B. *Deskriptoren*, ermöglichen. Der dokumentarische und der linguistische Ansatz werden durch diese methodische Verknüpfung sinnvoll kombiniert."

2.2   Allgemein- und Spezialklassifikation

Um den Bereich FERNSEHEN in IPTC/3 notieren zu können, steht die Klasse *01016000 Television* zur Verfügung. In konjunktiver Verbindung können Themenklassen zur Differenzierung zugeordnet werden. Um jedoch eine spezifische Fernsehthematik aus dem Bereich der *Fernsehsendungen* wie *Hauptabendnachrichten* bezeichnen zu können, sind thematische Detailklassen nötig, die ergänzend in einer ge-

---

[3] Langer (1996:85) erklärt: „Bei der Prüfung von Selektionskontexten handelt es sich darum, zu testen, ob ein Nomen als Kopf eines bestimmten Komplements des Verbs oder des Adjektivs auftreten kann; teilen verschiedene Nomina einen oder eine Menge von solchen Kontexten, konstituieren sie eine Selektionsklasse."

sonderten Dokumentationssprache[4] ausformuliert und die wiederum auf bestehende IPTC-Klassen abgebildet werden können.

3   Automatisierte Dokumentation

Über den erfolgreichen Einsatz linguistischer Methoden im Bibliothekenbereich berichtet etwa Lepsky (1999). Er führt aus, inwieweit die bzgl. der Schlagwortnormdatei (SWD) durchgeführte automatische Indexierung von bibliotekarisch erstellten Titeldaten mit Hilfe von linguistischen Verarbeitungen eingesetzt wurde (z.b. Grundformreduktion, Derivation, Dekomposition, Mehrwortlexemerkennung, Ergänzung von Wortbindestrichtilgungen, Präferenztermermittlung und Hyponymieverarbeitung).

Hierdurch wurden bestimmte bibliothekarische Aufgaben automatisiert und deutlich optimiert. Die hier vorgenommene direkte Verwendung eines dokumentarischen Klassifikationssystems in der linguistischen Informationsverarbeitung stellt Bezüge von Textwörtern zu Deskriptoren her; eine natürlichsprachliche Semantik wird anscheinend nicht benötigt. Inwieweit neben der automatischen Grobklassierung auch Spezialerfassungen möglich sind, z.B. die Ermittlung von geeigneten Stichwörtern und archivarisch akzeptable Erschließungen, zeigen aber die jeweils konkreten Ergebnisse. Unseres Erachtens ist das semantische System, das die Verarbeitung von Textsegmenten und Sinnrelationen auf Satzebene ermöglicht, hinsichtlich seiner Motivation und Struktur jedoch langfristig als Schlüsselkomponente im Bereich der Textklassifikation anzusehen.

3.1   Entitätenerkennung

Integrative Möglichkeiten bestehen in der Nutzung von Entitätenreferenzen (z.B. URNs (*Uniform Resource Names*) als Superset von URLs), DOIs (*Document Object Identifiers*) und universellen Medienidentifikationen (UMIDs) (vgl. a. Lehmann 1998; Lynch 1998). Es interessiert grundsätzlich jede Identifikation von Dokumenten, z.B. von Filmen, Fernsehprogrammen und anderen Medienangeboten, sowie deren Bestandteilen.

In bezug auf ein multimedial ausgelegtes Information Retrieval ist eine vernetzte Struktur denkbar, in qualifizierte *Entitäten* wie z.B. Personen auf andere Entitäten wie z.B. Dokumente referieren. Da eine umfassende und heterogene Standardisierung für ein derart umfassendes Thema vorläufig nicht absehbar ist, wird systemintern mit relativen Identifikationen gearbeitet, die ggf. durch absolute Identifikationen, also Standardzuordnungen, ersetzt werden können.

---

[4]   Bei der ProSieben Digital Media GmbH wird die Dokumentationssprache *PROLEX* eingesetzt, eine Entwicklung d. A.

3.1.1 Personenqualifikation

Die folgende Abbildung zeigt ein Zwischenergebnis der maschinellen Eigennamen-identifikation anhand grammatikalischer Muster.[5] Bestimmte Strukturen werden stabil erkannt, wie z.b. Nominalphrasen (NP) wie <det nomen name name>[6] oder Präpositionalphrasen (PP) wie <praep det nomen name name>.[7]

Muster	Instanz
name name	*Doris Schröder-Köpf*
name nomen	*Niedersachsens* Ministerpräsident
*name nomen	*Bernd Boehlendorf*
praep name	bei *Bonn*
praep name	um *Bitterfeld*
praep name name	mit *Monica Lewinsky*
praep det nomen name name	mit dem FDP-Vorsitzenden *Wolfgang Gerhard*
praep det nomen abk name name	durch den Wahlkampf: *Tobias Willmann*
praep det nomen name satzz num satzz	wegen ihrer Tochter *Klara* (7)
praep det adj nomen name	in der *mongolischen* Hauptstadt *Ulan-Bator*
det nomen name	der Ortschaft *Grüneck*
det nomen name	die Stadt *Frankfurt*
det nomen name name	der *CDU*-Generalsekretär *Peter Hintze*
det nomen name name	der *BdSt*-Präsident *Karl-Heinz Däke*
det nomen name name	ihr Finanzminister *Claus Möller*
det nomen det nomen name name	der Generalsekretär der *Liberalen Guido Westerwelle*
det nomen det nomen name name	der Vorsitzende der *FDP*-Fraktion *Wolfgang Kubicki*
det adj nomen name name	der *schleswig-holsteinische* Finanzminister *Claus Möller*
det adj nomen name name	dem *saarländischen* Landesvorsitzenden *Werner Klumpp*
det nomen praep det name praep name name	ein Jugendlicher mit der Maske von Bundeskanzler *Helmut Kohl*

Nach Auswahl eines syntaktischen Musters, das korrekte Analysen zulässt, erfolgt eine Informationsextraktion. Exploitative und zugleich hochfrequente Muster sind <*det nomen name name*> oder <*det adj nomen name name*> wie in „Der *baden-württembergische* Ministerpräsident *Erwin Teufel*" und „Der *bayerische* Landwirtschaftsminister *Reinhold Bocklet*".

Die temporalen (z.B. *bisherig, damalig, jetzig*), parteipolitisch-farbbezogenen (*rot, grün, gelb, schwarz, grau, braun, rosa*) und geografischen Nominaattributionen erlauben zusätzliche Analysen, die eine Auflösung der Phrasen in essentielle Informationen bzw. Felder in Verbund mit Kontextdaten wie dem Erscheinen eines Textes nahe legt,

---

[5] Gemeinsam mit der ELEXIR Sprach- und Informationstechnologie GmbH, München, einer Ausgründung des Centrums für Informations- und Sprachverarbeitung (CIS) der Universität München, wurden Strategien zur konkreten linguistischen Arbeit erarbeitet und umgesetzt.

[6] Kurzform für <*Determinator Nomen Eigenname Eigenname*>.

[7] Kurzform für <*Präposition Determinator Nomen Eigenname Eigenname*>.

wie in „Der *bisherige* Bundesaußenminister *Klaus Kinkel*", „Der *designierte* Bundes-
kanzler *Gerhard Schröder*", „Der *ehemalige* DDR-Gefängniswärter *Horst Jahn*" und
„Der *frühere* Filmschauspieler *Joseph Estrada*". Die folgende Tabelle demonstriert
das Vorgehen:

name	attr_adj	attr_nomen	sem
schröder gerhard	designiert	kanzler	MPT
möller claus	schleswig-holsteinisch	finanz|minister	MPT
stoiber edmund	bayerisch	minister|präsident	MPT,XNK
kinkel klaus	deutsch	amts|kollege	MVA
simonis heide	schleswig-holsteinisch	minister|präsidentin	FEM("Präsident")[8]
klima viktor	österreichisch	bundes|kanzler	MPT

Die semantische Klasse *MPT* bezeichnet „Ämtertitel in der Politik", *MVA* „Verwandt-
schaftsähnliche" und *XNK* „nicht klassifiziert, weil keine passende Oberklasse" (Langer 1999). Die semantischen Kodierungen beziehen sich hierbei nicht auf die vollständigen Komposita, sondern auf deren Basen[9].

Aus der Kombination der semantischen Klassen und den Attributionen lassen sich
automatisch Personenindices aufbauen, die personengebundene Funktionen beinhalten.
Eine Analyse z.B. der adjektivischen Nominalattributionen kann zur Erstellung hoch-
spezifischer Indices herangezogen werden. In Verbindung mit einer personenbezogenen Entitätenerkennung ist auf diesem Wege ein Personenfunktionsscanner konstruier-
bar, der über die Zeit personengebundene Beschreibungen aus Massedaten extrahiert
und automatisch Personenprofile erzeugt.

3.2   Multimedia-Dokumente

Multimedia-Dokumente wie Bild-, Audio- und Video-Dokumente und Verbunddoku-
mente werden als textlich annotierte Dokumente vorausgesetzt. Da der momentane
Stand der Echtweltbildverarbeitung zwar eine Segmentierung von Bildinhalten zuläßt,
nicht aber eine präzise Bezeichnung von Bildsegmenten (siehe Smeulders et al. 1998),
wird in unserem Fall der Weg beschritten, Annotationen linguistisch zu verarbeiten

3.3   Automatische Dokumentklassifikation

Anwendungsbereiche der automatischen Dokumentklassierung, die Methoden der Automatischen Textklassifikation[10] beinhaltet, sind

---

[8] Der Relator *FEM* gibt für ein gegebenes, in femininer Form stehendes Lexem die kanonische
   Grundform an.
[9] Die differenzierte Kompositakodierung kann momentan nicht auf automatische Weise erfolgen,
   sondern muß händisch oder teilautomatisiert durchgeführt werden, insbesondere in solchen Fällen, in denen keine oder nicht verwertbare Kodierungen wie *XNK* vorliegen.
[10] Wir verwenden hier den eingeführten Fachbegriff anstelle des präziseren Begriffs 'Textklassie-
   rung'.

i. die dokumentarische Inhaltserschließung für das Information Retrieval und
ii. die Bereitstellung von Meta-Content für ein Packaging-System.

Neben formalen Klassemen, z.b. den Medientyp betreffend, stehen an dieser Stelle textorientierte Klassierungen im Vordergrund. Zu i.: Eine flexible automatische Klassierung von Content erlaubt die dokumentationssystemspezifische Sicht auf Dokumente. Ziel ist ein Konvertmechanismus, der Content aus der Sicht von verschiedenen Inhaltserschließungen z.b. im Rahmen einer visuellen Suche auf Baumdarstellungen, abbildet. Zu ii.: Im Rahmen eines automatisierten Packaging-Systems, das Dokumente anhand formaler und inhaltlicher Vorgaben an Klienten verteilt, ist die thematisch zielgenaue automatische Zuordnung unerläßlich. Ein Packager weiß dank einer IPTC-genauen bzw. spezifischeren Verschlagwortung, wie ein Dokument adressiert werden muß. Die Contentvergabe auf der Basis von Metadaten im Rahmen eines Packaging-Systems geschieht darüber hinaus über mehrere Dokumentationssprachen hinweg, d. h. ggf. hinsichtlich Kundenwunsch gemäß klientenspezifischer Metadatenvorgabe.

4 Zusammenfassung und Ausblick

Um den Dokumentenverkehr zwischen verschiedenen Dokumentationssystemen kompatibel und einheitlich zu gestalten, bietet sich eine automatisierte standardisierte Dokumentation z.b. gemäß IPTC/3 und ergänzend eine spezialthematische Dokumentationssprache an. Der Einsatz linguistischer Technologien ist insbesondere dort zu motivieren, wo Massedaten aus Zeit- und Kostengründen nicht händisch erschließbar sind. Um hinsichtlich der automatischen Dokumentverbreitung etwa durch einen Packager in der B2B[11]-Kommunikation und bzgl. eCommerce kostenminimal agieren zu können, bietet sich der Einsatz eines natürlichsprachlich-basierten automatischen Klassierungssystems an.

Im Blick auf praxisorientierte Recherchemöglichkeiten werden Mechanismen benötigt, die eine automatische Identifizierung von Entitäten in Dokumenten ermöglichen. Durch den Zusammenschluß derartiger Metadaten sind automatische Ermittlungen von textbezogenen Lebensläufen, Image-Profilen und Kollokationen z.b. von bestimmten Personen recherchierbar, die in der Informationsvermarktung erfolgreich genutzt werden können.

5 Literatur

DIN 32705 (1987): Klassifikationssysteme. Erstellung und Weiterentwicklung von Klassifikationssystemen. Berlin: Beuth.
EUROPEAN TELECOMMUNICATIONS STANDARDS INSTITUTE (ETSI) ([2]1997): Digital Video Broadcasting (DVB); Specification for Service Information (SI) in DVB systems. ETS 300 468. CEDEX (FRANCE).

---

[11] *Business to Business.*

EUROPEAN TELECOMMUNICATIONS STANDARDS INSTITUTE (ETSI) (1996): Enhanced Teletext specification. – DRAFT EUROPEAN pr ETS 300 706. CEDEX (FRANCE).

GROSS, Gaston (1994): Classes d'objets et description des verbes. In: Giry-Schneider, Jacqueline: Sélection et sémantique: classes d'objets. complément appropriés, complément analysables. Paris: Larousse (Langage Nr. 115), 15-30.

INTERNATIONAL PRESS TELECOMMUNICATION COUNCIL (IPTC) (1999): IPTC-NAA News Industry Information Interchange Guideline 3. – Draft Oct 1999. Windsor.

INTERNATIONAL PRESS TELECOMMUNICATION COUNCIL (IPTC) (1997): IPTC-NAA News Industry Text Format. Version 2.0, http://www.iptc.org/iptc/Nitfdocnp2.pdf, 1999-03.

LADEWIG, Christa (1997): Grundlagen der inhaltlichen Erschließung. – Schriftenreihe des Instituts für Information und Dokumentation (IID) der Fachhochschule Potsdam. – Berlin:.

LANGER, Stefan (1999): Liste aller semantischen Beschreibungselemente für Nomina im CISLEX. München: Universität München, Centrum für Informations- und Sprachverarbeitung, http://www.cis.uni-muenchen.de/people/langer/semantik.html.

— (1996): Selektionsklassen und Hyponymie im Lexikon – CIS-Bericht-96-94 zur Inaugural-Dissertation an der Ludwig-Maximilians-Universität München.

LEHMANN, Klaus-Dieter (1998): Die Deutsche Bibliothek als digitale Depotbibliothek im europäischen Kontext. – Die Deutsche Bibliothek: Internet http://www.ddb.de/service/digit_depot.htm, 1999-03-14.

LEPSKY, Klaus (1999): Automatische Indexierung zur Erschließung deutschsprachiger Dokumente. – In: Nachrichten für Dokumentation (nfd) 50, 325- 330.

LYNCH, Clifford (1998): Identifiers and Their Role in Networked Information Applications. In: Information Technology column February 1998, http://magi.com/~mmelick/it98feb.htm, 1999-03-14.

SMEULDERS, Arnold W. M.; GEVERS, Theo; KERSTEN, Martin L. (Hrsg.) (1998): Computer vision and image search engines. In: Hiemstra, Djoerd; de Jong, Franciska; Netter, Klaus (Hrsg.): TWLT 14. Language Technology in Multimedia Information Retrieval. Proceedings of the Fourteenth Twente Workshop on Language Technology. December 7-8, 1998, Enschede, The Netherlands. Enschede: Universiteit Twente, Faculteit Informatica, 107-115.

Anhang A: IPTC/3 (1999) (Auszug)

01000000 Arts, Culture & Entertainment (general); 01001000 Archeology ; 01002000 Architecture; 01003000 Bull fighting; 01004000 Festive Events (incl. Carnivals); 01005000 Cinema; 01006000 Dance; 01007000 Fashion; 01008000 Language; 01009000 Libraries & Museums; 01010000 Literature; 01011000 Music; 01012000 Painting; 01013000 Photography; 01014000 Radio; 01015000 Sculpture; 01016000 Television; 01016013 Contracts; 01017000 Theatre; 01018000 Monuments & Heritage Sites; 01019000 Customs & Traditions; 01020000 Arts (general); 01021000 Entertainment (general); 01022000 Culture (general); 01023000 Nightclubs [...].

A German Parser and Error Checker[1]

Ruth H. Sanders, Alton F. Sanders

1   Introduction

Using an extensive grammatical lexicon and an 'error grammar' focused on typical student errors, a parser-based writing aid for German is being completed that will accept German input of any length and analyze its grammatical structure. Its intended users are American university students of German.

2   Description of the parser

Syncheck, our comprehensive syntactic parser for German,[2] can accept German input of any length and analyze its grammatical structure. It was written in Arity Prolog and runs under Windows. It is intended to identify syntactic structure only and does not handle semantics at the word, sentence or text level. The parser contains a compehensive grammar of sentence types of modern written German. It has a large inventory of noun phrase types, including those with premodifiers, complex verb constructions, and other sentence-level constituents. This completeness makes it likely that even complex sentence types written by advanced students will be parsable. While perfect completeness is an unachievable goal in a description of a natural language, we believe that Syncheck has come reasonably close to all-inclusiveness of the written language in both formal and informal registers (though doubtless it is defective in very casual registers such as that characteristic of comic-book captions, or in specialized ones such as that of instruction booklets; and it is not intended for use with sound files or written transcripts of spoken language).

2.1   Some examples of structures that are parsed as correct by Syncheck

Compound sentences with main clauses connected by punctuation:

- 'Das Essen war sehr gut; es gab jeden Morgen Schokolade.' (The food was very good; there was chocolate every morning)

Complex sentences, including those with clauses functioning as noun phrases within the sentence:

---

[1]   Our thanks for generous support of this project, pursued during a sabbatical leave in Helsinki during academic 1997-98, go to both Miami University of Oxford, Ohio, U.S.A., and the Department of General Linguistics at the University of Helsinki, Finland.

[2]   designed and implemented under a grant from the U.S. Department of Education International Research and Studies Program Grant No. GOO 8540767

- 'Ich weiß, dass sie krank sind' (I know that they are sick; dass-clause as object);
- 'Ich weiß nicht, wer das ist' (I know who that is; indirect question as object);
- 'Wer fremde Sprachen nicht kennt, kennt nicht seine eigene' (Whoever doesn't know foreign languages doesn't know his own; indirect question as subject);
- 'Das Buch ist nicht zu kaufen' (The book cannot to be bought; infinitive clause as complement)

Greetings and fixed phrases:

- 'Guten Tag! Vielen Dank!' (Good day!; Thank you!)

Imperatives:

- 'Trink deine Milch und geh ins Bett!' (Drink your milk and go to bed)

Tag questions:

- 'Das ist gut, nicht wahr?' (That's good, isn't it?)

Premodifiers:

- 'All mein bisschen Geld' (All my little bit of money)

Compound adverbial phrases:

- 'früh am Morgen vor der Heirat und nach dem Frühstück' (early in the morning before the wedding and after breakfast)

Compound verb structures in the second verb prong, in both main clause and dependent clause word orders:

- 'wird gesehen werden' (will be seen)
- 'hat sehen sollen' (should have seen)
- 'muss gesehen werden' (must be seen)
- 'hätte gesehen werden können' (should have been able to be seen)

Various types of compound noun phrases:

- 'Der Saft, das Bier, die Milch, und auch das Wasser' (the juice, the beer, the milk, and also the water)
- ' nicht alle der bisher lesbaren Texte' (not all of the formerly readable texts)

Subject-verb agreement after such compound subjects as:

- 'Sowohl der Kaffee als auch der Apfel sind ...' (the coffee as well as the apple are...)

- 'Nicht nur die Nilpferde, sondern auch ich bin ...' (Not only the hippopotamuses, but also I am ...)[3]

3 Analysis

Recognizing correct structures such as those above is only part of the job of an instructional writing aid. Much of the input will contain errors of one kind or another (a study of our corpus of student writing[4] yielded the statistic that 50% of its sentences contain at least one syntactic or morphological error). The difference between parsing of more or less normal or correct language in order to glean meaning from it (the goal of much work in parsing, but not our goal) and parsing the unreliable input of language learners in order to identify syntactic errors (which is our goal) needs to be kept in mind. The writing aid will identify for its users, with a fairly specific error message, the category of their errors, in order that they may correct these errors themselves. The program will not undertake to reformulate incorrect structures or to correct errors, as we believed this was both overambitious (because the parser cannot 'know' what was intended) and pedagogically unwise (because the parser should aid in the learning process, not write the essay for the student).

Admittedly, there will be some sentences in the input that have such global errors that the parser may not be able to give an effective error message. To illustrate, here is a sentence from our corpus of student writing:

- *'Flecken stehen wo das Papier bevor es wird krumm stehen sollte.'
  (Spots stand where the paper before it becomes crooked stand should)

Needless to say, neither the human instructor nor the parsing program will find it easy to produce a helpful error message here. The potential existence of such puzzling sentences should not, however, deter attempts to produce a writing aid that may be helpful in the largest portion of student writing.

4 The lexicon of Syncheck

The comprehensiveness in syntax is not matched in Syncheck's lexicon, which has a vocabulary of only 1,300 German words with their grammatical variants.[5] It has been tested on essays from our corpus of student writing, but because of its small vocabulary as well as its somewhat user-unfriendly interface, Syncheck has not been used by students directly.

---

[3] For grammar conundrums such as this one, representing the rule of hierarchy of person, we consulted a number of comprehensive grammar references, such as Hammer (1991) and Helbig/Buscha (1992).

[4] the Miami Corpus, approximately 220 essays written by Miami University students in second- and third-year German courses, collected in the 1980s for the purpose of analyzing student error types and testing the parser

[5] selected in part from Pfeffer (1964) and in part through language-teacher intuition

We are currently merging this parser with the very large (ca. one million entries) GERTWOL grammatical lexicon of German.[6] Doing so will provide us with a way to recognize not only many more German lexical items, but also proper nouns including both German and English/American place, personal, and family names.

The intention is to use this parser and enlarged lexicon as a writing aid for American college-level students of German language. Typically, second-, third-, and fourth-year students are required to write essays of from one to twenty pages, depending upon the course level, throughout every semester of their studies. (While first year students write essays also, they are typically very short and simple and we have chosen not to include them in our target user group.) Such a writing aid would be available in student computer laboratories to help students identify errors in morphology (case and gender agreement of noun phrases, subject-verb agreement; case assignment in prepositional phrases) and syntax (tensed verb in second position, word order in main and dependent clauses) in their early drafts of essays. These error types were shown by inspection of our corpus to be the most frequent in student writing (Sanders 1991). Content of the essays would of course continue to be graded by the instructor, as the parser has syntactic information only and does not represent natural-language 'understanding'. This means, however, that some common errors considered to be grammatical ones, such as case selection following two-way prepositions (which is meaning dependent), cannot be identified by the parser.

5   Enabling the parser to recognize specific incorrect forms

In its current form, the Syncheck parser recognizes grammatically correct sentences; in the case of incorrect ones, it does not provide the user with information about the nature of any error found. In fact, it merely tags incorrect sentences and provides a report summarizing how many and which sentences of an essay were found to be grammatically incorrect.

We have recognized from the beginning of the Syncheck project that students need more specific information about errors. However, computerized analysis of even straightforward errors in a form that is helpful to the user is notoriously difficult.

The parser's method is to read a sentence and build an internal tree structure, then to backtrack if at some point a correct tree cannot be built on the input, in order to search for an alternate tree structure. If none is ultimately found, the sentence is tagged as incorrect. But what kind of error information can this method provide to the user? Unfortunately, usually none, as this method is so different from human thought processes that information from failed tree formation is useless to the hapless student.

---

[6]   now marketed by Lingsoft Oy, Helsinki, Finland; originally developed at the Department of General Linguistics at the University of Helsinki by a team including Mariikka Haapalainen, Mikko Silvonen and Krister Linden, with Professors Kimmo Koskenniemi and Fred Karlsson as advisors (Koskenniemi and Haapalainen 1994); it includes both pre- and post-spelling reform variants.

5.1   An 'error grammar'

To address this problem we have designed an error grammar – a grammar of common error types. The input will first be analyzed by the error grammar, and if any sentences match a pattern from the error grammar, very precise information about the error can be provided to the user.

Examples of clauses in the error grammar (written as regular expressions, about which more later) include mistakes in gender-number-case agreement within noun phrases, strong-weak adjective endings, word order of verb placement, and about a dozen frequently misused idioms. Error types which the error grammar cannot identify are those that impact the structure of the sentence as a whole. These include as incorrect case selection for sentence constituents such as objects; or subject-verb agreement (a nontrivial problem in itself due to the difficulty of identifying the subject, which may appear virtually anywhere within a German sentence). These sentence-level errors will be rejected by the complete parser, but without helpful error messages.

The student user will have an opportunity to correct the errors found in this first scanning by the error grammar, and then the corrected input will be re-scanned by the full grammar of the parser.

5.1.1   Regular expressions in the error grammar

The error grammar defines common errors and categories of errors expected within German essays written by American students. Using the mathematical formalism regular expressions, we have defined these error types and an appropriate error message for each type. The error grammar includes, for example:

Fixed phrases: here are contained semantic errors that are not definable by morphology or syntax, but which are common in the writing of native English speakers, probably because of transference from English. For example, 'die erste/letzte Zeit' for 'das erste/letzte Mal' (the first/last time); 'zu schlecht' for 'schade'; failure to use article contractions after a preposition (in dem Haus for 'im Haus'); use of 'Mann' instead of the pronoun 'man' (identified by lack of an article before 'Mann'); use of 'meist' preceding an adjective instead of a superlative construction. Unfortunately, many typical semantic errors are not so easily defined for the computer and so will pass unnoticed by the program.

Common morphology errors, such as lack of gender-case concord in noun phrases, will (unlike the preceding category of fixed phrases) always be rejected by the full parser, though without any reason being given for the rejection. Since such errors are so characteristic of the writing of native speakers of English, we decided they deserve a place in the error grammar so that a specific error message can be generated.

The error grammar also recognizes an additional morphology error type, that is, the use of a form of 'sein' followed by an infinitive verb form (probably an attempt to duplicate in German the English continuous verb form be + ing), and produces a corresponding error message.

In like manner an error message is generated for certain word order errors, such as beginning a sentence with one or more adverbs, not followed by a conjugated verb; use of 'denn' or 'sondern' as the first word in a sentence; placement of the conjugated verb immediately after a subordinating conjunction instead of at the end of the clause, or immediately after a coordinating conjunction instead of following another sentence element, as is required by the rules of German syntax.

We also used regular expressions to define correct noun phrases in various cases, with and without definite and indefinite articles, because the permutations of strong/ weak adjective endings in such phrases are more efficiently parsed in regular expressions than in the Prolog of the full parser; the noun phrases may then be labeled as internally correct for a specified grammatical case (or a list of cases) and are sent to the full parser for insertion into expected slots as subjects, predicate nominatives, or direct or indirect objects.

5.1.2 Technical description of the error grammar

The 'grammar' is a set of rules, given as a pattern that represents some standard error and a message that is to be given when that pattern is found in a student's text. The pattern is expressed as a regular expression and the message is simply plain text. Each rule is numbered and optionally named. Names or numbers may be used for brevity for embedding a given regular expression inside of another one. Ultimately, the finite state automata representing the individual regular expressions are inter- sected into a single automaton that performs the match to the text.

Regular expressions are a well understood and familiar notation for specifying regular languages. Regular languages are very appealing since they can be recognized and parsed using finite state methods. However, for specifying natural languages, they suffer some disadvantages:

- Natural languages are probably not regular. Even if they are, it would appear that the complexity of the regular expression and the number of states in the un- derlying finite state automaton would be so large to make standard finite state methods, at best, highly inconvenient.
- Processing natural languages normally involves a lexicon wherein lexical ambi- guity is manifested by a number of alternate possibilities for a given entry. For example the appearance of the word 'der' in a text produces the following set of tokens from the GERTWOL lexicon:

< der ART DEF SG NOM MASK>
< die ART DEF SG DAT FEM>
< die ART DEF SG GEN FEM>
< die ART DEF PL GEN>
< der PRON DEM SG NOM MASK>
< die PRON DEM SG DAT FEM>
< die PRON DEM VERALTET SG GEN FEM>
< die PRON DEM VERALTET PL GEN>

< der PRON RELAT SG NOM MASK>
< die PRON RELAT SG DAT FEM>
< die PRON RELAT GESPROCHEN PL GEN>

The set of tokens indicate that the word 'der' could be a singular definite masculine article in the nominative case, or a singular feminine definite article in the dative case, or one of several other possibilities. The notation of the regular expression needs to be rich enough to allow matching the surface form of the word or to match some or all of the lexical features.

We have addressed these requirements in several ways:

- The alphabet has been extended to be arbitrary strings of characters. This, of course, means that the language specified is not truly regular. That fact, however, does not prohibit us from using finite state methods to recognize and parse strings in our application.

- The semantics of the regular expression are altered to account for the existence of a lexicon. Each regular expression represents a pattern that is to be matched to a target text. The notation allows the linguist to specify conveniently a match to a surface form and/or the presence or absence of lexical features. In particular, when a regular expression is matched to a given input, each word in the input is first looked up in the lexicon and replaced with a list of tokens. It is a list because of ambiguity; each token contains morphological information concerning the word, as illustrated above with the word 'der'. Hence, a match of a regular expression means that there exists a choice of one token within each list of tokens such that the regular expression matches the token sequence. For example, the pattern <*der*> *Buch* would represent any sequence of two words for which the following hold:

  1) The first word, when presented to the lexicon, produced a set of tokens that include at least one of the form <*der ... (perhaps some attributes)...*>
  2) The second word was the word 'Buch'.
  Note that <*der*> *Buch* and *der Buch* do not represent the same sequences of words. The former would include *die Buch* because it is possible to interpret *der* as a form of *die*. In this example, not all attributes are mentioned and so are not considered in the pattern.

- The usual regular expression notation is expanded to include extra key words and metasymbols that incorporate the patterns most commonly used by a linguist who is defining error patterns.

As an illustration of both the form and the nature of the two grammars, consider the following cases. The German preposition 'mit' (with) takes an object in the dative case. A simple common error would be to use the accusative case: *'mit seinen Freund' (with his [male] friend). The student has produced a correct noun accusative noun phrase; yet its context (as object of a dative preposition) makes it incorrect in use. In the phrase *'mit seinen Freundin' (with his [female] friend), the noun phrase is misformed (the ending on 'sein-' is in no case consistent with a following feminine singular noun) and so a different error message would be appropriate.

The error grammar, then, includes not only specific errors, but a large subset of descriptions of correct noun phrase types in order that it can identify for the student user whether an error is one of concord within a noun phrase, or in the case selected for a prepositional phrase. However, unlike the full definite clause grammar, it cannot identify whether a given noun phrase is in the correct case as a subject or object of a sentence. The regular expression error grammar is substantial, but it is less comprehensive than the full definite clause grammar.

6   Conclusions

Syncheck contains a very nearly complete syntactic characterization of German syntactic expressions, including extensive description of allowable noun phrases. The Syncheck grammar cannot claim absolute completeness, since allowable sentence types and allowable noun phrase types may be infinite or at least pliable (depending on the judgment of each interlocutor). As a practical matter we have chosen to aim at recognition of the commonest types of student-written errors at the highest possible level of accuracy. That is, we have described the grammar of correct sentences as widely as possible even at the cost of some possible overgeneration, while designing the error grammar as narrowly as possible to avoid at all cost any designation of a correct sentence as incorrect. The error grammar enumerates and recognizes the commonest errors we have found in our corpus: gender-number-case agreement within noun phrases, lack of concord in strong-weak adjective endings; word order in verb placement, and additionally a number of frequently misused idioms.

Currently the error grammar and the GERTWOL lexicon are being made compatible with the original Syncheck grammar; the resulting writing aid will be tested with Miami University students of German before being released to the profession.

7   References

HAMMER, Alfred Edward ([2]1991): German grammar and usage. London – New York: E. Arnold.
HELBIG, Gerhard; BUSCHA, Joachim ([7]1992). Leitfaden der deutschen Grammatik. Leipzig: Verlag Enzyklopädie.
KOSKENNIEMI, Kimmo; HAAPALAINEN, Marikka (1996): GERTWOL-Lingsoft Oy. Linguistische Verifikation: Documentation zur Ersten Morpholympics 1994. Tüblngen. Max Niemeyer Verlag.
SANDERS, Ruth H. (1991): Error analysis in purely syntactic parsing of free input: The example of German. CALICO Journal. Autumn; 72-89.

Inkrementelle minimale logische Formen für die Antwortextraktion

Gerold Schneider, Diego Mollá, Michael Hess

1   Einführung

1.1   Informationssuche in technischen Dokumenten

Ein Großteil der verfügbaren technischen Dokumente ist nach wie vor in natürlicher Sprache verfasst, was beim Auffinden relevanter Dokumente oder Textstellen große Probleme aufwirft und den Einsatz linguistischer Methoden nahelegt. Gerade im technischen Bereich hat sich in den letzten Jahrzehnten eine Vervielfachung an verfügbarem Textmaterial ergeben. Die zunehmende Komplexität der Technik spiegelt sich im Umfang der Dokumentation wieder. Handbücher für große industrielle Anlagen sind oft tausende, machmal zehntausende Seiten lang, was deren Handhabung für den menschlichen Benutzer auch dann schwer macht, wenn sie in maschinenlesbarer Form vorliegen. Abgesehen von ihrer großen Länge zeichnen sich technische Dokumente insbesondere dadurch aus, dass sie

- sehr viele Fachbegriffe enthalten, die häufig Komposita sind,
- nur wenig Redundanz enthalten,
- einen engen Bereich abdecken,
- eine technische Sprache, oft gar kontrollierte Sprache verwenden.

1.2   Traditionelle Ansätze zur Fragenbeantwortung

Das Auffinden von spezifischer Information in textuellen Dokumenten ist ein zentrales Problem der Informationswissenschaft. Üblicherweise werden Lösungsansätze verfolgt, die auf den folgenden Techniken beruhen:

1.2.1 Information Retrieval

Die Suchmethoden des Information Retrieval (IR) basieren in der Regel auf Schlüsselwörtern (Salton 1983). Diese Methoden sind zwar sehr schnell, aber doch häufig für das Fragebeantworten ungeeignet:

- Erstens kann dasselbe Wort verschiedene Typen von Objekten bezeichnen, wie auch derselbe Typ von Objekt durch mehrere verschiedene Wörter bezeichnet werden kann.
- Zweitens liegen die Wörter selten in ihrer Grundform im Text vor, sondern häufiger in einer flektierten Form. Die meisten IR-Verfahren verwenden zu wenig morphologische Informationen, was u.a. zu einem Verlust an *Ausbeute* führt (viele der relevanten Dokumente werden nicht gefunden).

- Drittens missachtet eine Schlüsselwortsuche jede Form der syntaktischen und letztlich semantischen Zusammenhänge innerhalb eines Satzes, die in der Wortreihenfolge, durch Kasus oder durch Funktionswörter ausgedrückt sind. Die Vernachlässigung dieser Zusammenhänge führt zu einem Verlust an *Präzision* (viele der gefundenen Dokumente sind nicht relevant).

- Viertens werden nur ganze Dokumente gefunden, oft in sehr großer Anzahl, sodass der Schritt bis zum Auffinden der Textstelle, die die Antwort auf eine Frage enthält, noch zeitaufwändiges manuelles Überlesen großer Textmengen mit sich bringt.

1.2.2 Informationsextraktion:

Informationsextraktion (IE) erlaubt das effiziente Absuchen großer Textmengen auf präzise, vordefinierte Fragestellungen hin, die einen Sachverhalt ausdrücken (Message Understanding Conference, http://www.muc.saic.com). Da dabei ein fixes, datenbankähnliches Informationsraster gefüllt wird, können nur sehr eng definierte thematische Bereiche abgedeckt werden. Für das Stellen natürlichsprachlicher Anfragen ist dieses Verfahren daher ungeeignet.

1.2.3 Textbasiertes Fragenbeantworten

Der ideale Lösungsansatz wäre zweifellos der Einsatz von Systemen zur automatischen Fragenbeantwortung über Texten. Die Erfahrungen bei der Entwicklung derartiger Systeme, z.B. LILOG (Herzog 1991) haben allerdings gezeigt, dass der Entwicklungsaufwand für derartige Systeme sehr groß ist.

1.3   Antwortextraktion

Antwortextraktion (AE) bietet einen realistischen Kompromiss zwischen den oben genannten Ansätzen (Hess 1997, 1998). Im Unterschied zum textbasierten Fragenbeantworten geht AE davon aus, dass man in den vorhandenen Texten oft Stellen lokalisieren kann, welche die Antwort auf eine Frage *explizit enthalten*. Dieses Verfahren ist rechnerisch durchaus beherrschbar und kann bis auf Texte von mehreren 100 MB skaliert werden (Mollá et al. 1999a).

Im Unterschied zum IR baut AE auf einer vollständigen morphologischen und syntaktischen Analyse auf. Auch wichtige Aspekte der Semantik wie thematische oder terminologische Relationen werden vollautomatisch analysiert. Im Unterschied zu IE erlaubt AE beliebige und unbeschränkte Benutzeranfragen. Die Anwendung des Abfragesystems auf neue Bereiche bedingt nur eine neue Textsammlung und die Aufbereitung der fachspezifischen Terminologie. Der neugeschaffene Q&A-Track der TREC-8 (1999) zeigt, dass AE heute als wichtiger Forschungsbereich des Information Management anerkannt ist.

2   Das Projekt ExtrAns

Das Projekt *ExtrAns* (Mollá et al. 1998) untersucht, ob AE in der Praxis relevante und schnelle Ergebnisse liefern kann. Dabei stand das theoretische Konzept der AE auf dem Prüfstand der praktischen Anwendbarkeit. Gegenwärtig wird der Bereich der UNIX Manpages verwendet.[1] Im anlaufenden Nachfolgeprojekt werden jetzt die Airbus Aircraft Maintenance Manuals verwendet.

Die zu befragende Textsammlung (z.b. UNIX Manpages) wird offline abgearbeitet, bevor ein Benutzer online natürlichsprachliche Anfragen (NL Query) stellt, die auf dieselbe Weise geparst und in logische Form überführt werden.

Die Textstellen, welche die Antwort auf eine Anfrage enthalten, werden lokalisiert und graphisch markiert ausgegeben, so z.B. für die Frage *How do I remove a directory?*

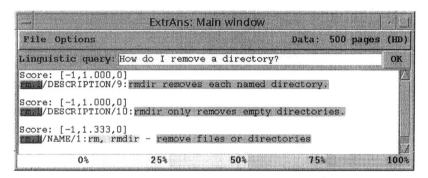

Fig. 1: Antworten auf die Frage How do I remove a directory? in ExtrAns' Hauptfenster

ExtrAns besteht aus einer Reihe von Modulen; die wichtigsten unter ihnen sind:

- *Der Link Grammar Parser:* Sleator und Temperley (1993) beschreiben den Link Grammar Parser. Er eignet sich für das Projekt ExtrAns aufgrund seiner sehr hohen Parsinggeschwindigkeit, seiner Robustheit und seiner mitgelieferten umfassenden englischen Grammatik, welche wir nur unwesentlich erweitern mussten. Da Link Grammar dependenzbasiert ist, sind gewisse funktionale Informationen (wie Subjekt, Objekt) oft einfacher als aus einer rein konfigurational orientierten Grammatiktheorie abzuleiten (Mollá et al. 1999b)

- *Der Desambiguator:* Brill und Resnik (1994) beschreiben eine Korpus-basierte Methode zur Desambiguierung von Präpositionalphrasenanbindung, die wir für unsere Zwecke erweitert haben. Ihr regelbasierter Ansatz bietet den Vorteil, dass vom statistischen Modul leicht verständliche und erweiterbare linguistische Regeln extrahiert werden.

---

[1]   Die UNIX Manpages bilden das textorientierte online Hilfesystem des UNIX Betriebssystems

- *Die Anaphernauflösung:* Wir verwenden eine leicht modifizierte Version von Lappin and Leass' (1994) syntaxbasiertem Resolutionsalgorithmus für die ebenfalls dependenzbasierte Slot Grammar (McCord 1992).
- *Die Syntax-Semantik-Übersetzung:* Die von der Link Grammar erzeugten Syntaxstrukturen werden in eine einfache Semantikrepräsentation überführt. Da sie das Kernstück des ganzen Systems sind, werden wir sie im Folgenden näher erläutern.

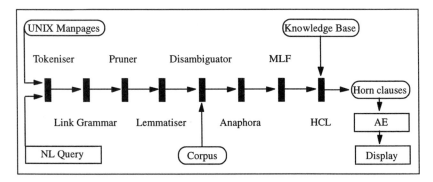

Fig. 2: Die Module des Antwortextraktionssystem ExtrAns

3   Minimale logische Formen

3.1   Anforderungen an eine Semantikrepräsentation

Unsere Erfahrungen haben gezeigt, dass eine Semantikrepräsentation für ein praxisorientiertes System mindestens den folgenden Anforderungen genügen sollte:

- Sie soll *einfach aus der Syntaxstrukur herzuleiten* sein.
- Sie soll *einfach zu verarbeiten* sein.
- Sie soll genügend *ausdrucksstark* sein: Die semantische Kernbedeutung (wie z.b. funktionale Relationen) soll in ihr problemlos ausgedrückt werden können.

Die im folgenden erläuterten *minimalen logischen Formen* (*Minimal Logical Forms,* MLF) erfüllen diese Voraussetzungen (Schwitter et al. 1999).

3.2   Flache existentiell geschlossene Formeln

Die MLFs basieren auf Hobbs' (1985) Vorschlag für eine nicht-intensionale Notation der Prädikatenlogik erster Stufe, die folgende Eigenschaften hat:

- Die Übersetzung der Syntax in die Semantik ist naiv kompositional.

- Die logische Form eines Satzes besteht aus einer Konjunktion einfacher Prädikate anstelle einer eingebetteten und komplexen Formel.
- Alle Variablen sind existentiell quantifiziert.

Eine erste vereinfachte Darstellung des Satzes *cp copies files* wird in dieser Notation wie folgt dargestellt:

object(cp,x1).
evt(copy,[x1,x2]).
object(file,x2).

Unter *object* verstehen wir dabei alles, worauf ein NP referieren kann und als *evt* bezeichnen wir alles, was ein Verb typischerweise beschreibt, d.h. Eventualitäten (Zustände, Prozesse und Ereignisse).

Wir verwenden drei Prädikatstypen: *object* (Objekte), *evt* (Eventualitäten) und zusätzlich *prop* (Eigenschaften). Die erste Argumentsposition kann dabei als Korrelat des Prädikates in einer ungetypten Darstellung betrachtet werden.

3.3   Reifikation

Während sich mit dieser Darstellung sehr einfache Sachverhalte darstellen lassen, kann man komplexere, aber in natürlichen Sprachen allgegenwärtige Phänomene wie Adverbien, Adjektive, Tempus, Aspekt, Implikation oder Proposition nicht ausdrücken.

Adverbien beispielsweise können eine modifizierende Aussage *über* eine Eventualität machen, was nur in einer logischen Notation ausgedrückt werden kann, in der auf die Eventualität zugegriffen werden kann. *Reifikation*, die wir nur auf unsere getypten Prädikate anwenden, ermöglicht diese Funktionalität.

Wir folgen dabei Davidson (1967), der vorschlägt, Eventualitäten als Individuen zu behandeln, um die Adverbialmodifikation zu erleichtern. Im Satz *cp copies files quickly* prädiziert das Adverb *quickly* über die ganze *copy*-Eventualität. Wenn man die *copy*-Eventualität als ein Individuum *e1* darstellt, so kann die Adverbialmodifikation trivial durch das Prädikat *quickly(e1)* ausgedrückt werden.

Zu diesem Zweck wird die Eventualität *e1* als zusätzliches Argument der *evt*-Prädikation eingeführt:

evt(copy,*e1*,[x1,x2]).

e1 bedeutet das Konzept, dass *x1 x2* kopiert. Somit lässt sich der Satz *cp copies files quickly* darstellen als:

object(cp,x1).
evt(copy,*e1*,[x1,x2]). % Verb-Reifikation e1
object(file,x2).
quickly(*e1*). % Modifikation von e1

Dieses Verfahren der Reifikation bedeutet also, dass abstrakte Konzepte, welche durch eine Prädikation beschrieben werden, konkretisiert werden. Über die so geschaffenen Entitäten kann man quantifizieren und prädizieren und man kann auf sie referieren (was wir im folgenden allgemein als *modifizieren* bezeichnen werden). Hobbs (1985: 62) beschreibt ein reifiziertes Konzept metaphorisch als einen *Haltegriff*, an dem eine Prädikation durch eine übergeordnete Prädikation gefasst werden kann. Ein anderer Fall, wo über Eventualitäten prädiziert wird, sind untergeordnete Sätze. Der Satz *cp refuses to copy files onto itself* lässt sich beispielsweise wie folgt darstellen:

object(cp,x1).
evt(copy,$e1$,[x1,x2]). % Verb-Reifikation e1
evt(refuse,$e2$,[x1,$e1$]). % Modifikation von e1; Verb-Reifikation e2
object(file,x2).
onto(e1,x2).

Die obige Darstellung einer Objektsprädikation *object(file,x2)* ist noch vereinfacht, da wir auch diese reifizieren müssen, um gewisse Arten von Adjektiven analysieren zu können: Während intersektive Adjektive die Extension eines Objektes modifizieren, modifizieren nicht-intersektive Adjektive (auch opake oder intensionale Adjektive genannt) wie *former* oder manche Verwendungen von *new* das Konzept eines Objektes. Die Repräsentation des Satzes *mkdir creates new directories* ist deshalb:

object(mkdir,o1,x1).
evt(create,e1,[x1,x2]).
object(directory,$o2$,x2).
prop(new,$o2$). % new modifiziert ein Konzept

o2 bedeutet: *Das Konzept, dass x2 ein Verzeichnis ist.* Intersektive Adjektive (z.B. *long files*) werden zum Vergleich wie folgt dargestellt:

object(file,o2,$x2$).
prop(long,$x2$).

Auch die Darstellung von Eigenschaften (*prop*), wie sie durch Adjektive und Adverbien ausgedrückt werden, muss in analoger Weise erweitert werden. Das Adverb *very* modifiziert beispielsweise die Eigenschaft *long* in *very long*. Reifikation von Eigenschaften erlaubt die Darstellung dieser Art von Modifikation.

prop(long,$p1$,x2).
prop(very,p2,$p1$).

4   Unterspezifikation und Inkrementalität

MLFs verfügen über zwei weitere Eigenschaften, die sich für die Antwortextraktion als sinnvoll erwiesen haben.

- Sie sind *unterspezifizierbar*: Auch partielle Aussagen ermöglichen das Ziehen sinnvoller Schlussfolgerungen.

- Sie sind *inkrementell erweiterbar*: Partielle Aussagen können jederzeit, je nach Verfügbarkeit, durch spezifischere ergänzt werden, ohne dass schon vorhandene Information überschrieben wird.

4.1 Unterspezifikation

Reifikation erlaubt auch explizite Aussagen über das Verhältnis zwischen dem Platonischen Universum (welches alle vorstellbaren Entitäten enthält) und dem realen (welches nur einen Ausschnitt des Platonischen enthält). Im Beispiel *cp refuses to copy a file onto itself* aus Kapitel 3.3 existiert nur die Eventualität *refuse* im realen Universum, was durch ein Zusatzprädikat *holds/1* ausgedrückt wird, während *copy* eben nicht in der Realität, sondern bloß im platonischen Universum existiert. In der MLF wird daher keine Aussage über den ontologischen Status der *copy*-Eventualität gemacht, sodass ihr Status in Bezug auf das reale Universum unterspezifiziert bleibt:

> holds(e2).   % Refuse existiert auch in der Realität.
> object(cp,x1).
> evt(refuse,*e2*,[x1,*e1*]).
> evt(copy,*e1*,[x1,x2]).
> object(file,x2).
> onto(e1,x2).

Die Verwendung des *holds/1*-Prädikates wie auch Reifikation sind Methoden, welche die Verwendung flacher und deshalb rechnerisch effizienter Strukturen erlauben. Sie bieten den Zusatzvorteil, dass schon aufgrund unterspezifizierter Strukturen sinnvolle Aussagen möglich sind.

Die Benutzeranfrage *Which command copies files?* wird genauso wie ein Satz aus dem Textkorpus in eine MLF überführt, wobei statt Konstanten Variablen verwendet werden:

> object(command, O1,X1),
> evt(copy,E1,[X1,X2]),
> object(file,O2,X2).

Der Prolog-Beweismechanismus findet drei Antworten auf diese Frage in den UNIX manpages.

- *cp copies files*. Die direkte Antwort.
- *cp refuses to copy a file onto itself.* Wir glauben, dass in einem AE-Umfeld dieser Satz eine wichtige Zusatzantwort auf die Frage darstellt. Die Verwendung flacher Strukturen belässt die *copy*-Prädikation uneingebettet, sodass sie im Satz durch ExtrAns ebenso als relevante Textstelle gefunden und dem Benutzer angezeigt wird, auch wenn der ontologische Status der *copy*-Prädikation unterspezifiziert bleibt und die *copy*-Prädikation der refuse-Prädikation untergeordnet ist.

- *If the user types y, then cp copies the files.* Das Antezedens *if the user types y* kann gar nicht evaluiert werden. Nur dank Unterspezifikation und der Verwendung flacher Prädikate in den MLFs wird diese Antwort gefunden. Die Verwendung einer voll ausgebauten Inferenzmaschinerie würde hier sogar schlechtere Ergebnisse liefern.

Obwohl mit entsprechendem Mehraufwand Tempus, Pluralität, Modalität und Quantifikation in MLFs behandelt werden kann (siehe z.b. Hobbs 1996), haben wir uns entschlossen, diese Aspekte der Sprache unterspezifiziert zu lassen, da sie im technischen Bereich der UNIX Handbücher selten relevant sind. Die Anfragen *Which command can copy files?* und *Which command will copy any file?* sind äquivalent zur obigen Anfrage *Which command copies files?* und erhalten dieselbe MLF.

4.2   Inkrementalität

Obwohl Tempus, Pluralität, Modalität und Quantifikation in ExtrAns zur Zeit nicht modelliert werden, sind entsprechende Erweiterungen in der Form zusätzlicher Aussagen über das Verhältnis zwischen dem platonischen und dem realen Universum möglich. Der Satz *cp can copy files* könnte wie folgt dargestellt werden:

object(cp,o1,x1).
evt(copy,e2,[x1,x2]).
object(file,o2,x2).
possible(e2).

Ohne dass schon gemachte Aussagen revidiert werden müssen, können so inkrementell zusätzliche Aussagen zu den bestehenden hinzugefügt werden.
  Ein weiteres Beispiel stellen Nominalkomposita dar. Sie sind in mindestens zweifacher Weise mehrdeutig. Erstens ist die Klammerung unklar. Soll z.B. *computer design system* als *((computer design) system)* oder als *(computer (design system))* gemeint sein? Zweitens sind die funktionalen Relationen zwischen den beteiligten Nomina unklar. Ist *computer design system* Entwurf *durch, mit, von* oder *wegen* eines Computers? Sehr häufig könnte nur extensives Weltwissen zur Desambiguierung beitragen. Wo dieses Wissen nicht vorhanden ist, kann man aber oft auch mit der unterspezifizierten Information sinnvoll arbeiten. *Computer design system* wird in ExtrAns in eine MLF überführt, die nur aussagt, welche Teilsegmente vorliegen und dass es sich um ein Kompositum handelt:

object(computer,o1,x1).
object(design,o2,x2).
object(system,o3,x3).
nominal_compound(i1,o1,o2,o3).

Wenn ExtrAns zu einem späteren Zeitpunkt zusätzliche Information erhält, welche dieses Nominalkompositum (teilweise) desambiguiert, so kann man diese jederzeit inkrementell hinzufügen, ohne dass die unterspezifizierte Teilinformation geändert werden müsste. Die Information nimmt also nur monoton zu. Folgendes Prädikat sagt beispielsweise in Ergänzung zu obigem Beispiel aus, dass der *computer* das Agens für das *design* ist.

agent(x1,x2).

Präpositionen schließlich werden in ExtrAns homomorph von der Syntax in die Semantik übernommen. Das Prädikat *on/2* in *the train arrives on track 12 on Monday* ist beispielsweise mehrdeutig zwischen einer lokalen Lesart (*on track 12*) und einer temporalen Lesart (*on Monday*), was in der MLF des Satzes zunächst unterspezifiziert bleibt:

object(train,o1,x1).
object(track_12,o2,x2). object(monday,o3,x3).
evt(arrive, e1,[x1]).
on(e1,x2). on(e1,x3).

Sobald verfügbar, können zusätzliche Informationen aber inkrementell hinzugefügt werden:

location(e1,x2).   % lokale Lesart für track_12
time(e1,x3).   % temporale Lesart für monday

5   Schlussfolgerungen

Wir haben das Format und die Funktionsweise der Minimalen logischen Formeln (MLF) vorgestellt und ihre Eignung für die Antwortextraktion illustriert. Wir haben gezeigt, wie sich mit MLFs einerseits semantisch komplexe Modifikationen durch Reifikation ausdrücken lassen, und wie andererseits die Information, die sie enthalten, jederzeit inkrementell erweitert werden kann.

6   Literatur

BRILL, Eric; RESNIK, Philipp (1994): A rule-based approach to prepositional phrase attachment disambiguation. In: Proceedings of COLING'94, 2. Kyoto, 998-1004.
DAVIDSON, Donald (1967): The Logical Form of Action Sentences. In: Rescher, N. (Hrsg.): The Logic of Decision and Action. Pittsburgh, Pennsylvania: University of Pittsburgh Press, 81-95.
HERZOG, O.; ROLLINGER, C. R. (Hrsg.) (1991): Text Understanding in LILOG. Berlin, Heidelberg, New York: Springer.
HESS, Michael (1998): Antwortextraktion über beschränkten Bereichen. In: Proceedings of KONVENS-98, Bonn, 337-346.
— (1997): Mixed-Level Knowledge Representations and Variable-Depth Inference in Natural Language Processing. In: International Journal on Artificial Intelligence Tools (IJAIT) 6.4, 481-509.
HOBBS, Jerry R. (1996): Monotone decreasing quantifiers in a scope-free logical form. In: van Deemter, K.; Peters, S. (Hrsg.): Semantic Ambiguity and Underspecification. Stanford, CA: CSLI publications, 55-76.
— (1985): Ontological promiscuity. In: Proceedings of ACL'85, University of Chicago, 61-69.

LAPPIN, Shalom; LEASS, Herbert J. (1994): An algorithm for pronominal anaphora resolution. Computational Linguistics 20.4, 535-561.

MOLLÁ, Diego; HESS, Michael (1999a): On the Scalability of the Answer Extraction System ExtrAns. In: Applications of Natural Language to Information Systems (NLDB'99), Klagenfurt, 219-224.

MOLLÁ, Diego; BERRI, Jawad; HESS, Michael (1998): A real world implementation of answer extraction. In: Proceedings of NLIS'98, Vienna, 143-148.

MOLLÁ, Diego; SCHNEIDER, Gerold; SCHWITTER, Rolf; HESS, Michael (1999b): Answer Extraction Using a Dependency Grammar in ExtrAns. Submitted to: Traitement Automatique de Langues (T.A.L.), Special Issue on Dependency Grammars.

SCHWITTER, Rolf; MOLLÁ, Diego; HESS, Michael (1999): ExtrAns – Answer Extraction from Technical Documents by Minimal Logical Forms and Selective Highlighting. Presented at: The Third International Tbilisi Symposium on Language, Logic and Computation, Batumi, Georgia.

SALTON, Gerard; MCGILL, Michael J. (1983): Introduction to Modern Information Retrieval. International Student Edition. Auckland: McGraw-Hill, Computer Science Series.

SLEATOR, Daniel D.; TEMPERLEY, David (1993): Parsing English With a Link Grammar. Technical Report, Carnegie Mellon University.

TREC-8 (1999): Call for participation Text Retrieval Conference 1999 (TREC-8), http://trec.nist.gov/cfp.html, http://www.research.att.com/~singhal/qa-track.html.

The Semantic Component of a Natural Language Parser

Jürg Strässler

In this paper I would like to show some features of a so-called semantic parser. The term as well as the method is based on Seuren's semantic syntax (Seuren 1996). The term might be misleading as we are not concerned with semantics but with syntax. The underlying idea of semantic parsing is that the output of the parser, or better of one of the parsers involved, is a semantic representation which is expressed in standard predicate calculus structure. I would like to show the different stages that lead from the syntactic surface structure to the respective semantic representation and then further on to the underlying discourse domain. As the generative transformational part of Seuren's system is language independent to a large degree the respective part of the parser will also be highly universal. The semantic component is not one which is treated in a specific stage of the process, but one which is present in the different stages and it is interesting to see what the function of this component is and where the power of a semantic parser lies.

The overall structure of the theory of semantic syntax is shown in the fig. 1 (Seuren 1996:22).

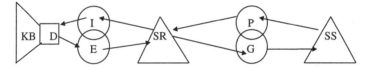

KB	= knowledge base	D	= discourse domain
SR	= semantic representation	SS	= surface structure
E	= expression procedure	G	= grammar
I	= incrementation	P	= parser

Figure 1: The overall structure of the theory of semantic syntax

It can be seen in fig.1 that the grammar and the parser, as well as the incrementation and expression procedure overlap to a certain degree but are not identical. The cognitive discourse domain serves as a working memory which has open access to the available contextual and background knowledge and which is incremented with every newly uttered sentence.

We have to distinguish quite distinct parts in the overall structure, the links between the discourse domain and the semantic representation (or analysis) on the one hand and the link between the semantic representation and the surface structure on the other. At a later stage we might also want to introduce the level of a shallow structure between the semantic representation and the surface structure.

The underlying idea is the belief that surface structures cannot be treated semantically in another way than via structural, non-semantic reduction to a semantic representation, which in turn represents a syntactic deep structure, or in other words that the transformational part does not change meaning.

Traditionally, the part which generates the deep structure, i.e. the phrase structure rules, is also considered to be part of the grammar and it might be a onomasiological inadequacy in the overall structure of semantic syntax that the term *grammar* is only applied to the transformational part. The same of course is true with respect to the parser.

Apart from this problem the division into two distinct parts, however, is of great value to natural language parsing. The semantic representation is a fix state, arrived at by a set of context-free rewrite rules, i.e. a type-2 grammar in the Chomsky hierarchy of grammars.[1] The link between the semantic representation and the surface structure, however, is made by cyclic and post-cyclic context-sensitive transformation rules, i.e. a type-1 grammar.

One prerequisite for a viable parser has been met, namely that type-0 grammars have to be avoided as they risk not being parsable, which would lead us to the conclusion that natural language may not be parsable. Furthermore, the parser can be divided into two independent parts, one of which is much easier to design.

Although the finite-state grammar leading to the semantic representation is language dependent and thus the output is so as well, the skeleton frame (fig. 2) (Seuren 1996:28) of the semantic representation seems to be highly universal. For example the only difference between VSO and SOV languages is, that for the former, the semantic representations are as given in fig. 2, whereas for the latter the structures are left-branching, i.e. their skeleton frame is but a mirror-image of fig. 2.

The same degree of universality is also present in the transformation rules that operate between the semantic representation and the surface structure. A parser based on such a grammar would then also be highly universal.

All lexical elements are derived from predicates in the SR-structure. Not only the logical operators (including negation, the quantifiers, *and* and *or*) but also the tenses, prepositions, and all kinds of adverbs and adverbials are treated as predicates, and it is the lexicon of each language which determines the surface category of these predicates. The respective category changes take place along with the transformational treatment.

The skeleton structure of the semantic representation is divided into the auxiliary system and the lexical nucleus. The former contains the tenses, the logical operators, and the adverbials, whereas the latter contains the main lexical predicates (verb, adjective, or NP) and the appropriate arguments. The shaded area in the auxiliary system represents the modal complex, which is optional. S" denotes a fully tensed sentence with the complete two-tense system: *past* or *present* / *simultaneous* or *preceding*. S' denotes a sentence which carries only the tense feature *simultaneous* or *preceding*, and S° denotes an untensed sentence (infinitive structures).

---

[1]   A brief outline of the Chomsky hierarchy of languages can be found in Strässler (1999:448-449).

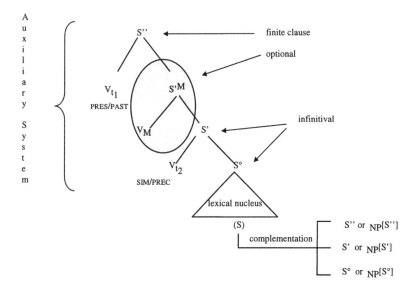

Figure 2: Skeleton Frame of Semantic Representations

In the following section I shall outline the development of the sentence: *The cat ate the mouse*. The expression procedure, i.e. the finite-state grammar, which links the discourse domain with the semantic representation can be stated in only three basic rewrite rules:

1) $S'' \rightarrow V_{t1} + S'$

2) $S' \rightarrow V_{t2} + S°$

3) $S° \rightarrow V_{lex} + $ <lexical argument frame>

which result in the skeleton frame of the semantic representation given in fig. 3 below.

The lexicon, which provides the fillers for the terminal nodes, does not only indicate the possible fillers, but it also gives information on the surface categories, the lexical argument frames, as well as the cyclic transformation rules which have to be applied in turn to get to the surface structure, or at least to the shallow structure of the sentence. In table 1 below we see the relevant information for the tense predicates, whereas the mini-lexicon given in table 2 gives the information for the lexical predicates. Both tables might of course be collapsed into one, but as the tense predicates are independent of argument frames, and as they are the same for all possible sentences, it seems to be better to deal with them separately.

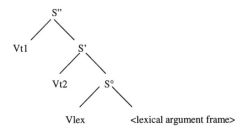

Figure 3: Skeleton frame of the sentence "The cat eat the mouse"

SR-Category	Fillers	Surface category	Cyclic rules
Vt1	PRES / PAST	Affix (affix handling → finite verb)	SR (subject raising), L (lowering)
Vt2	SIM	Verb	L
	PREC	Verb	PaP (Past Participle), L

Table 1: The lexicon for the tense predicates Vt1 and Vt2

V_{lex}	Fillers	argument frame	Surface category	Cyclic rules
V_{verb}	eat, read, drink, write, follow, ...	+ NP (+NP)	Verb	none
V_{nom}	house, cat, child, mouse, book, ...	+ NP	Noun	none

Table 2: A mini-lexicon for the lexical predicates

If we insert the predicates in the skeleton frame given in fig. 3 above, we get the semantic representation of the sentence *"The cat ate the mouse"* (fig. 4):

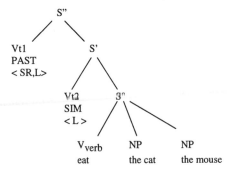

Figure 4: Semantic representation of the sentence "The cat ate the mouse"

As this stage is reached relatively easily by means of a simple phrase structure grammar it can be parsed for instance by means of a table-controlled shift-reduce parser. The disadvantage of such a parser is the fact that a new control table has to be constructed each time a change in the grammar is made. However, as the number of formation rules in the expression procedure phase is relatively small, this drawback might be accepted in face of the high efficiency of such a parser.

As mentioned above, the next stage in the generation process is a *highly universal* cyclic transformational one. Furthermore, the transformations that have to be applied are already indicated in the semantic representation, together with the order in which they have to be applied.

Fig. 5 to 7 show the different stages of the generative transformational process:

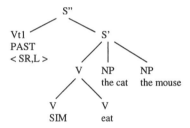

Figure 5: After lowering (L) indicated in the Vt2 predicate

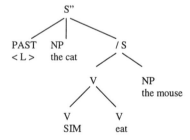

Figure 6: After subject raising (SR) indicated in Vt1

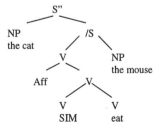

Figure 7: After lowering (L) indicated in Vt1

Based on these cyclic rules a new parser has to be found that projects the shallow structure onto the semantic representation. The big advantage of the transformational part of the underlying grammar is the fact that we know what the skeleton frame of the result looks like and by means of the lexicon we can look up which transformations have been applied. As we deal with a type-1 grammar, consisting of context-sensitive transformation rules, we might consider either an augmented transition network (ATN) or a slot-filler chart-parser.

ATN normally have the disadvantage that they have to be re-written for every new language from scratch, whereas the context-sensitive material in a slot-filler chart-parser has to be kept to a minimum.

However, as the part that has to be handled with this component of the parser is highly universal, the disadvantage of an augmented transition network might not be such a big one. At least within a language family many components might be transferred to another language and need not be re-written completely.

The next task within the project of semantic parsing will be to establish language specific type-2 parsers that can handle all the formation rules which lead to the semantic representation of the languages under consideration. In a further step we then hope to develop a highly universal parser for the context-sensitive generative transformational type-1 grammar to project the shallow structures onto the semantic representations.

So far we have not dealt with the post-cyclic rules, such as e.g. affix handling. Although these rules are again language specific, they seem to be a minor problem within the total framework.

We are just at the beginning of our project, but we trust that semantic syntax, as outlined in Seuren (1996) is a very good candidate for a grammar onto which a powerful, highly language independent parser can be based.

References

SEUREN, Pieter A. M. (1996): Semantic Syntax. Oxford: Blackwell.
STRÄSSLER, Jürg (1999): Semantic Parsing. In: Spillmann, Hans Otto; Warnke, Ingo (eds.): Internationale Tendenzen der Syntax, Semantik und Pragmatik. Akten des 32. Linguistischen Kolloquiums in Kassel 1997. Frankfurt a. M. etc.: Lang (Linguistik International 1), 447-455.

Design und formale, korpusbasierte Evaluation robuster Textanalyse-Technologie am Beispiel des Anaphernresolutions-Systems ROSANA

Roland Stuckardt

1   Einleitung

Im Zeitalter der neuen Medien kommt der textuellen Informationsvermittlung weiterhin eine zentrale Rolle zu. Bedingt u.a. durch die globale Vernetzung sieht sich das informationssuchende Individuum einer stetig wachsenden Menge potenziell inhaltsrelevanter Textdokumente gegenüber. Da viele Texte bereits in elektronischer Form vorliegen, ist das wirtschaftliche Potenzial einer Computerunterstützung für die Kernaufgaben der inhaltsorientierten Textverarbeitung enorm. Grundvoraussetzung für die Entwicklung entsprechender Anwendungssysteme ist die Verfügbarkeit einer *Basistechnologie* für die zentralen Teilprobleme der Textinhaltserschließung, die den Anforderungen einer *robusten Verarbeitung von Anwendungskorpora beliebiger Domänen* genügt.

Im vorliegenden Beitrag werden Möglichkeiten und Grenzen einer robusten, massendatentauglichen Textinhaltserschließung am Beispiel des textanalytischen Basisproblems der *Koreferenz-Resolution* untersucht. Dass es sich um ein Kernproblem der Textinhaltserschließung handelt, wird anhand von folgendem Beispiel deutlich:

1) *Peter Behrens* war ein berühmter Architekt. *Er* entwickelte eine neue architektonische Konzeption. *Seine* Arbeiten begründeten die moderne Architektur in Deutschland.

Eine inhaltliche Interpretation der Sätze 2 und 3 erscheint nur auf der Grundlage einer Identifikation der Referenzen der anaphorischen (hier: pronominalen) Ausdrücke „*Er*" bzw. „*Seine*" möglich. Erst auf der Grundlage einer *referentiellen Interpretation* erschließt sich somit etwa die durch Satz 3 kommunizierte Aussage, dass *Peter Behrens* aufgrund seiner Arbeiten als Begründer der modernen Architektur in Deutschland anzusehen ist. Vermöge Eingrenzung der Aufgabenstellung auf die Erschließung von Beziehungen *identischer* Referenz ergibt sich folgende erste, informelle Definition:

Die Aufgabe der computergestützten Koreferenz-Resolution besteht in der algorithmischen Bestimmung koreferenter Antezedensausdrücke für diejenigen sprachlichen Ausdrücke, die eine textuell bereits eingeführte Entität wiederaufgreifen.

Ohne auf die vielfältigen Probleme einzugehen, die mit dieser verkürzten Abgrenzung verbunden sind – für eine präzisere Abgrenzung vgl. etwa die MUC-7 Coreference Task Definition (1997) oder Stuckardt (1999) –, soll hervorgehoben werden, dass es sich um einen idealen Studiengegenstand handelt. Die Einfachheit der Aufgabenstellung täuscht darüber hinweg, dass es sich um ein *beliebig schwieriges* Sprachverarbeitungsproblem handelt, dessen algorithmische Lösung in einigen Fällen nur unter Rekurs auf außersprachliche Hintergrundinformation möglich erscheint. Andererseits bedingt gerade die gute kognitive Zugänglichkeit der Aufgabenstellung die mit Blick auf die Zielsetzung der formalen Evaluation essenzielle *hinreichend klare Definierbarkeit* des Interpretationsproblems.

Aufbauend auf der Identifikation einiger Grundstrategien der algorithmischen Koreferenz-Resolution sowie der Formulierung eines Rahmenalgorithmus in Abschnitt 2 wird in Abschnitt 3 die Aufgabenstellung der *robusten* Verarbeitung anhand eines wichtigen Teilproblems – *fragmentarische* syntaktische Beschreibungen – diskutiert und gelöst. Eine zentrale Rolle für die Entwicklung und Optimierung massendatentauglicher Texttechnologie spielt die formale Evaluation, deren Beiträge in Abschnitt 4 analysiert werden sollen.

2   Basisstrategien der algorithmischen Koreferenz-Resolution

Entsprechend dem von Carbonell und Brown (1988) vorgeschlagenen Analyseparadigma bietet es sich an, das Problem der computergestützten Koreferenz-Resolution durch eine *Kombination elementarer Interpretationsstrategien* anzugehen. Zu unterscheiden sei zwischen *Restriktionen* als (quasi-)stringenten Strategien und *Präferenzen*, die heuristischen Stellenwert haben. Bekannte Beispiele stringenter Strategien sind die *morphologische Kongruenzbedingung*, dergemäß in folgendem Beleg

2) Behrens sagte *seiner* Kollogin, dass *er sie* schätze.

die Antezedenten der drei Pronomen „*seiner*", „*er*" und „*sie*" – und damit indirekt deren Referenz – alleine auf der Grundlage der distinktiven Merkmale *grammatischer Genus und Numerus* bestimmt sind, sowie *syntaktisch-konfigurationale Bedingungen*, durch die der Bezug der Pronomen in den folgenden Belegen

3a) Behrens bemerkt, dass der Friseur *sich* rasiert.
3b) Behrens bemerkt, dass der Friseur *ihn* rasiert.

aufgrund der jeweiligen Ausdrucksform (*reflexiv* vs. *nichtreflexiv*) auf ein (in noch festzulegendem Sinne) *lokales* bzw. *nichtlokales* Antezedens eingegrenzt werden kann. Während den Restriktionen somit in Algorithmen zur Koreferenz-Resolution die Rolle eines A-Priori-Filters zur *Elimination* definitiv inkorrekter Antezedenskandidaten zukommt, bilden die Präferenzstrategien die Basis zur Auswahl unter den verbleibenden Kandidaten: Fokussierungstheoretisch gerechtfertigte und praktisch nutzbringende Heuristiken sind etwa die Regel der *Präferenz des syntaktischen Subjekts*, die in Beleg

4) Gropius betrat den Raum. Behrens wartete bereits auf *ihn*.

zur (richtigen) Auswahl „*Gropius*" (anstelle des ebenfalls möglichen Antezedens „*Raum*") führt, sowie die Regel der *syntaktischen Rollenträgheit*, die in Fällen wie etwa

5) Behrens besuchte Gropius in Dessau. Der Architekt bat *ihn* um Unterstützung.

zur (korrekten) Entscheidung für das (als transitives Objekt) *syntaktisch rollengleiche* Antezedens „*Gropius*" führt. Dass es sich hierbei nicht um stringente Kriterien, sondern um Heuristiken handelt, wird z.b. daran ersichtlich, dass die beiden genannten Präferenzstrategien in einigen Fällen zu gegensätzlichen Vorhersagen führen. Folgt man dem Mehrstrategieparadigma von Carbonell und Brown sowie deren Unterscheidung zwischen stringenten und nichtstringenten Kriterien, so gelangt man zu einem *dreiphasigen Rahmenalgorithmus*, der in die Schritte *Restriktionsanwendung, Präferenzbewertung* und *Antezedensauswahl* unterteilt ist. Speziell betreffend die Präferenzkriterien verbleibt festzulegen, auf welche *Typen* anaphorischer Ausdrücke die unterschiedlichen Heuristiken anzuwenden sind und mit welcher relativen *Gewichtung* deren Vorhersagen in die Gesamtbewertung einfließen.

Ein entsprechender Basisalgorithmus, der in die genannten drei Phasen zerfällt, liegt dem Anaphernresolutions-System ROSANA (*RObuste Syntaxbasierte ANApherninterpretation*) zugrunde (Stuckardt 1999:178ff). Durch die Beschränkung auf solche Strategien, die auf morphologischen bzw. syntaktischen Beschreibungen aufbauen, werden die Grundvoraussetzungen für dessen tatsächliche Operationalisierbarkeit geschaffen.

3 Robuste Koreferenz-Resolution

Wenn zuvor von einem Basis-„Algorithmus" gesprochen wurde, so wird nicht alleine die noch zu leistende Explikation sowohl der Typspezifität der Präferenzfaktoren als auch deren relativer Gewichtung außer Acht gelassen; bereits der mehr oder weniger stillschweigende Rekurs auf *vollständige* morphologische bzw. syntaktische Beschreibungen des referentiell zu interpretierenden Texts erweist sich als problematisch. In der folgenden Diskussion soll die offensichtliche Abhängigkeit von syntaktischen Analysen näher untersucht werden. Insbesondere scheint dies für die algorithmische Umsetzung der anhand der Belege 3a) und 3b) motivierten syntaktisch-konfigurationalen Bedingungen zu gelten.

Ein bekanntes theoretisches Modell, das derartige Restriktionen formal expliziert, ist die als Modul der Chomsky'schen GB-Theorie formulierte *Bindungstheorie* (vgl. Chomsky 1981). Durch die drei *Bindungsprinzipien A, B und C* für unterschiedliche Typen sprachlicher Ausdrücke werden folgende Bedingungen postuliert:

A) Reflexiva und Reziproka sind lokal gebunden.
B) (sonstige) Pronomen sind nicht lokal gebunden.
C) R-Ausdrücke (Nichtpronomen) sind weder lokal noch nichtlokal gebunden.

Was unter *lokal* bzw. *nichtlokal* sowie unter *Bindung* zu verstehen ist, wird unter Rekurs auf Konstrukte der GB-Theorie formal definiert. Ohne auf die theoretischen Feinheiten näher einzugehen, ist zunächst festzuhalten, dass die genannten Begriffe unter Rekurs auf Beschreibungen der *syntaktischen Oberflächenstruktur* formalisiert werden.

In Abbildung 1 ist die oberflächenstrukturelle Beschreibung des Belegs

6) Peter Behrens verlangt, dass der Friseur *sich / ihn / Peter Behrens* rasiert.

skizziert. Augenscheinlich ist die Wahl des Hauptsatzvorkommens von „*Peter Behrens*" als Antezedens des anaphorischen Ausdrucks im Objektsatz ausschließlich im Falle des nichtreflexiven Pronomens „*ihn*" grammatisch akzeptabel. In der Bindungstheorie wird dieser Sachverhalt per Postulierung eines Lokalitätsbegriffs modelliert, der (u.a.) an den durch finite Verben induzierten S-Knoten festmacht. Demnach kommt für das Reflexivum als (unmittelbares) Antezedens ausschließlich ein Vorkommen *innerhalb* des Komplementsatzes in Frage (Bindungsprinzip A, „*Friseur*" als *lokaler* Binder). Bindungsprinzip C schließt die Wahl des ausdrucksidentischen Hauptsatzvorkommens für die nichtpronominale Anapher „*Peter Behrens*" aus, da eine nichtlokale *Bindungsbeziehung* entstehen würde. Die formale Definition der Bindungsrelation rekurriert auf die GB-theoretisch zentrale, ebenfalls an der oberflächenstrukturellen Beschreibung *festmachende K-Herrschafts-Relation*. In dem betrachteten Syntaxbaum etwa besteht eine K-Herrschafts-Beziehung zwischen den Knoten NP_1 und NP_2 (hervorgehoben durch Pfeil).

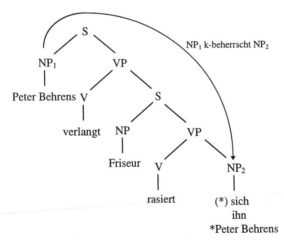

Abbildung 1: Bindungstheoretische Bedingungen und Oberflächenstruktur

Diverse Forschungsergebnisse belegen die vergleichsweise große Bedeutung der syntaktisch-konfigurationalen Bedingungen für die computergestützte Koreferenz-Reso-

lution (vgl. etwa Lappin; Leass 1994). Auf den ersten Blick scheint es allenfalls eine Fleißaufgabe darzustellen, diese Strategie in einem Computerprogramm umzusetzen. Dabei wird jedoch oftmals übersehen, dass die hiermit einher gehende stillschweigende *Annahme der Verfügbarkeit eindeutiger syntaktischer Beschreibungen* für die Sätze des zu interpretierenden Textes problematisch ist. Bekanntermaßen ist die Syntaxanalyse natürlichsprachiger Texte ein schwieriges Problem, das sich insbesondere in *strukturellen Ambiguitäten* in der Interpretation von Präpositionalphrasen, Adverbial- und Relativsätzen sowie der syntaktischen Funktion einzelner Konstituenten manifestiert. Im typischen Anwendungsszenario einer uneingeschränkt operationalen, massendatentauglichen Koreferenz-Resolution kann daher allenfalls von der Verfügbarkeit *fragmentarischer* syntaktischer Beschreibungen ausgegangen werden.
In Abbildung 2 sind die oberflächenstrukturellen Gegebenheiten im Falle einer aus Sicht des Syntaxanalysealgorithmus ambigen Präpositionalphrase skizziert. Anhand des folgenden Belegs lässt sich veranschaulichen, dass die algorithmische Verifikation der bindungstheoretischen Bedingungen durch die syntaktische Fragmentierung tangiert wird. Die referentielle Identifikation des in der PP enthaltenen Pronomens „*ihm*" mit dem Ausdruck „*Feldstecher*" – formal: die *Koindexierung* der entsprechenden NP-Knoten des Syntaxbaums – ist im Falle der (hier offenkundig intendierten) *adverbialen* Interpretation statthaft, bei einer attributiven Interpretation hingegen nicht, da eine unzulässige Konfiguration entstünde, die gegen eine weitere bindungstheoretische Bedingung, den sog. *i-über-i-Filter*, verstieße.

7) Peter Behrens beobachtet den Eigentümer des Feldstechers mit *ihm*.

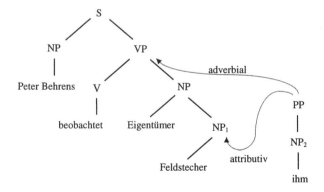

Abbildung 2: Fragmentarische oberflächenstrukturelle Beschreibung

Eine nähere theoretische Analyse zeigt auf, dass das beschriebene Problem im Allgemeinen nicht alleine auf fehlendes Weltwissen im Parsingvorgang zurückgeführt werden kann, sondern grundsätzlicherer Natur ist. Tatsächlich erweist sich das stillschweigend zugrunde gelegte *sequenzielle* Prozessmodell, derzufolge die referentielle Interpretation auf den Ergebnissen der syntaktischen Analyse aufbaut, als inadäquat:

In der Chomsky'schen GB-Theorie wird vielmehr eine *Interaktion* der bindungstheoretischen Prinzipien mit den übrigen Modulen der Theorie angenommen, die durch ein (quasi-)*paralleles* Verarbeitungsmodell einzulösen wäre. In einer solchen theoretisch adäquaten Verschränkung der Interpretationsprozesse ist es insbesondere möglich, dass auch umgekehrt die referentielle Interpretation einen Beitrag zur strukturellen Disambiguierung des Oberflächenstrukturbaums leistet.

Dass ein solches (anspruchsvolles) Programm einer im engeren Sinne Menzels (1995) *robusten Interpretation qua Interaktion von syntaktischer und referentieller Analyse* algorithmisch formalisiert werden kann, wurde in der Arbeit von Stuckardt (1997) nachgewiesen. Auch unter Beibehaltung eines programmiertechnisch einfacher umsetzbaren sequenziellen Verarbeitungsmodells ist jedoch im (Regel-)Falle fragmentarischer syntaktischer Beschreibungen oftmals mehr möglich als ein heuristisches Akzeptieren eines vorgeschlagenen, in einem anderen syntaktischen Fragment befindlichen Antezedens. Wenn beispielsweise die Syntaxanalyse für folgenden Beleg

8) Kohl ging, bevor der Präsident kam, weil das Staatsoberhaupt *sich* verspätete.

auf Anknüpfungsambiguität des Kausalsatzes befindet, so kann für das Reflexivpronomen „*sich*" dennoch definitiv entschieden werden, dass der Ausdruck „*das Staatsoberhaupt*" das bindungstheoretisch einzig zulässige Antezedens ist: Diese Beobachtung fußt u.a. auf dem Sachverhalt, dass der den Kausalsatz beschreibende Syntaxbaum lokal abgeschlossen in dem Sinne ist, dass dessen oberster (S-)Knoten *bindende Kategorie* des Reflexivums ist und somit eine lokale Bindungsdomäne konstituiert, innerhalb derer das Pronomen qua Bindungsprinzip A ein Antezedens haben muss; Aus ebendiesem Grund scheiden die weiteren Kandidaten „*Kohl*" und „*Präsident*" sowie ggf. zusätzliche intersentientielle Kandidaten aus. Dieses *Derivat von Bindungsprinzip A für fragmentarische Syntax* lässt sich durch folgende Regel operational explizieren (nvk = nächstverzweigender Knoten, bk = bindende Kategorie, k = Antezedenskandidat, a = zu resolvierende Anapher):

$$* \{ ... \quad Fi = [... nvk(k)(...k_{typ \ A/B/C} ...) ...], \quad Fj = [... bk(a)(...a_{typ \ A} ...) ...] ... \}$$

Analog lassen sich Regeln für weitere Bedingungen der Bindungstheorie angeben (Stuckardt 1999:196ff.).

Dass diese im Vergleich zum parallelen Verarbeitungsmodell in abgeschwächtem Sinne robuste Operationalisierung der syntaktisch-konfigurationalen Restriktionen in praktischen Anwendungen sehr gute Ergebnisse liefert, wurde durch Implementierung und formale Evaluation des Anaphernresolutions-Systems ROSANA auf einem Korpus von Nachrichtenagenturmeldungen nachgewiesen (ibd.:243ff). Unter Zugrundelegung eines äquivalenzklassenbezogenen Evaluationsmaßes, das sich in wesentlichen Punkten an der Vorarbeit von Vilain et al (1995) orientiert, wurden Precision- und Recall-Werte von 81 bzw. 68 % in der Disziplin der Ermittlung der Koreferenzrelation ermittelt. Für die aus der Anwendungssicht zentralen, da häufigsten und schwieriger zu resolvierenden Personal- und Possessivpronomen in dritter Person wurden korrekte Antezedenten in 71 bzw. 76 % aller Fälle bestimmt. Legt man die im Hinblick auf typische Anwendungsszenarien naheliegende verschärfte Zielsetzung der Ermittlung *nichtpronominaler* Antezedenten zugrunde, so erzielt ROSANA unter Anwendung eines entsprechend erweiterten Algorithmus Precision-Werte von 68 bzw. 66 %. Dass letzteres Problem schwieriger ist, lässt sich u.a. fokustheoretisch begründen (ibd.:266f). Der Nachweis der textgenre-übergreifenden Gültigkeit der verwendeten Interpretationsstrategien wurde durch einen zweiten Evaluationslauf auf einem Korpus von Operntexten erbracht, der die hohe Güte der Interpretationsergebnisse von ROSANA bestätigte.

Die Qualität der Ergebnisse reicht nahe an die im Rahmen der MUCs erzielte Interannotator-Übereinstimmung in der Schlüsselerstellung (81 %, Sundheim 1996) und damit an die Grenze des prinzipiell Messbaren heran. Als von zentraler Bedeutung für die Aussagekraft der Resultate ist zu bewerten, dass die Evaluationskorpora keiner vorherigen Korrektur etwaiger orthographischer und syntaktischer Fehler unterzogen wurden und die morphologischen und syntaktischen Voranalysen unter Rekurs auf verfügbare Software (z.B. Järvinen; Tapanainen 1997) vollständig computergestützt bewerkstelligt wurden.

4   Beiträge der formalen, korpusbasierten Evaluation

Die formale, korpusbasierte Evaluation erweist sich in mehrfacher Hinsicht als zentral für die Förderung der Entwicklung robuster Computersysteme zur Textinhaltserschließung. Zu den *Basisbeiträgen* sind die Formulierung *inhaltlich adäquater Rahmenvorgaben* sowie die Definition numerischer *Maße* zur Bewertung der Interpretationsleistung in *standardisierten Inhaltserschließungs-Disziplinen* zu sehen, wodurch überhaupt erst die Grundlage zum Leistungsvergleich unterschiedlicher Softwaresysteme geschaffen wird; dass es sich hierbei in aller Regel um eine nichttriviale Aufgabe handelt, wird anhand der Komplexität der zuvor zitierten *Coreference Task Definition* für eine auf den ersten Blick elementare Interpretationsdisziplin ersichtlich. Ein weiterer zentraler Beitrag der formalen, korpusbasierten Evaluation ist in der *Förderung der Entwicklung tatsächlich robuster, operationaler Textanalyse-Algorithmen* zu sehen, die durch die Eingrenzung der Betrachtungen auf implementierte und ohne intellektuelle Intervention lauffähige *Softwaresysteme* erreicht wird. Die große Bedeutung dieses Punkts erschließt sich mit Blick auf zahlreiche „Algorithmen" in der computerlinguistischen Literatur, die ihren Namen aufgrund von nichttrivialen Explikationslücken unter Anlegung informatischer Maßstäbe zu Unrecht tragen.

Weitere wichtige *sekundäre Einsatzgebiete* der formalen Evaluation ergeben sich im Rahmen von *Systementwicklung* und *Optimierung*. Erneut am Beispiel der Interpretationsdisziplin Koreferenz-Resolution kann gezeigt werden, dass es sich anbietet, in der Evaluation zwischen Teildisziplinen zu unterscheiden, die in der Regel durch unterschiedliche *Subalgorithmen* des Computersystems bearbeitet werden: Eine Differenzierung und evaluationstechnische Trennung in *Ermittlung vorkommensinduzierender (referenzierender) sprachlicher Ausdrücke* und eigentliche *Referenzresolution*

(Antezedenssuche) erscheint zweckmäßig, denn sie ermöglicht die gezielte Optimierung der Interpretationsstrategien der entsprechenden Softwaremodule (Stuckardt 1999:223ff). Im Rahmen der Teildisziplinen erweist sich ferner eine Aufschlüsselung nach unterschiedlichen Typen referenzierender Ausdrücke als sinnvoll, da in den Subalgorithmen i.d.R. ausdrucksspezifische Interpretationsstrategien zum Einsatz gelangen, die einer getrennten Optimierung bedürfen.

Zu den möglichen sekundären Beiträgen der formalen, korpusbasierten Evaluation zählt ferner die Bewertung der Basistechnologie unter der Maßgabe spezifischer Anforderungen in *Anwendungsszenarien*. Im Rahmen der Bewertung von Systemen zur Koreferenz-Resolution erweist es sich so z.b. als sinnvoll, den Disziplinenkanon um die Aufgabe der *Ermittlung nichtpronominaler Substitute* zu erweitern (vgl. o.). Ferner können *korpusbezogene Performanzunterschiede* ermittelt werden; auf dieser Grundlage ist es etwa möglich, eine Feinabstimmung der Interpretationsstrategien im Hinblick auf domänen- oder genrespezifische Gegebenheiten von Anwendungsszenarien vorzunehmen. Im Rahmen der Evaluation des Anaphernresolutions-Systems ROSANA wurden systematische Unterschiede in den Kohärenzstrukturen der beiden betrachteten Evaluationskorpora (Nachrichtenagenturmeldungen und Operntexte) aufgedeckt, die eine korpusspezifische Zuordnung bzw. Gewichtung der Präferenzkriterien in der Plausibilitätsbewertungs-Phase des Rahmenalgorithmus ermöglichen.

5   Schluss

Die obigen Ausführungen belegen die zentrale Rolle formaler, korpusbasierter Evaluationen als Motor der Entwicklung anwendungstauglicher Texttechnologie und verdeutlichen ferner die Leistungsfähigkeit gegenwärtig verfügbarer Softwaresysteme am Beispiel des Anaphernresolutions-Systems ROSANA. Auf dem Weg ins neue Jahrtausend hat sich die Computerlinguistik den Herausforderungen einer globalen, vernetzten Wissensgesellschaft zu stellen – ein Anspruch, der somit letztlich nur auf der Grundlage ingenieurwissenschaftlicher Herangehensweisen sowie durch konkrete Anwendungen einlösbar erscheint.

Mit der Etablierung der *„Message Understanding"*-Konferenzen wurde ein erster wesentlicher Schritt in den USA bzw. für die englische Sprache vollzogen (vgl. Grishman und Sundheim 1996; Hirschman 1998). Mit Blick auf den Erfolg der Institutionalisierung formaler, korpusbasierter Evaluationen in den *englischsprachigen Message Understanding Conferences* und unter Würdigung des wirtschaftlichen Potenzials der *„Information Extraction"*-Technologie wird somit für eine Verstärkung und Koordinierung entsprechender Forschungsanstrengungen in Kontinentaleuropa sowie speziell im deutschsprachigen Raum plädiert.

6 Literatur

CARBONELL, Jaime G.; BROWN, Ralf D. (1988): Anaphora Resolution: A Multi-Strategy Approach. In: Proceedings of the 12th International Conference on Computational Linguistics (COLING), Budapest, 96-101.

CHOMSKY, Noam (1981): Lectures on Government and Binding. Dordrecht: Foris Publications.

GRISHMAN, Ralph; SUNDHEIM, Beth (1996): Message Understanding Conference, vol 6: A Brief History. In: Proceedings of the 16th International Conference on Computational Linguistics (COLING), I, Kopenhagen, 466-471.

HIRSCHMAN, Lynette (1998): The Evolution of Evaluation. Lessons from the Message Understanding Conferences. In: Computer Speech and Language 12, 281-305.

JÄRVINEN, Timo; TAPANAINEN, Pasi (1997): A Dependency Grammar for English. Technical Report TR-1. Helsinki: Department of General Linguistics, University of Helsinki.

LAPPIN, Shalom; LEASS, Herbert J. (1994): An Algorithm for Pronominal Anaphora Resolution. In: Computational Linguistics 20.4, 535-561.

MENZEL, Wolfgang (1995): Robust Processing of Natural Language. Hamburg: Fachbereich Informatik, Universität Hamburg.

MUC-7 Coreference Task Definition, Version 3.0 (1997). In: Proceedings of the Seventh Message Understanding Conference (MUC-7), http://www.muc.saic.com/.

STUCKARDT, Roland (1999/[2000]): Qualitative Inhaltsanalyse durch Computer – ein uneinlösbarer Anspruch? – Untersuchungen zur algorithmischen Textinhaltserschließung am Beispiel der referentiellen Interpretation (Diss. Frankfurt a. M.). Berlin: Tenea [in diesem Beitrag als Diss. 1999 zitiert; Publikation Berlin 2000].

— (1997): Resolving Anaphoric References on Deficient Syntactic Descriptions. In: Proceedings of the ACL'97 / EACL'97 Workshop on Operational Factors in Practical, Robust Anaphora Resolution for Unrestricted Texts, Madrid, 30-37.

SUNDHEIM, Beth (1996): Overview of Results of the MUC-6 Evaluation. In: Proceedings of the Sixth Message Understanding Conference (MUC-6). San Francisco: Morgan Kaufmann, 13-31.

VILAIN, Marc; BURGER, John; ABERDEEN, John; CONNOLLY, Dennis; HIRSCHMAN, Lynette (1995): A Model-Theoretic Coreference Scoring Scheme. In: Proceedings of the Sixth Message Understanding Conference (MUC-6). San Francisco: Morgan Kaufmann.

Treating Polarity Sensitivity by Lexical Underspecification: Motivation from Semantic Scope

Judith Tonhauser

1   Introduction[1]

Polarity Sensitive Items (PSIs) come in two flavors, namely *Negative Polarity Items* (Npis) and *Positive Polarity Items* (Ppis). 1) exemplifies the Npis *a red cent* and *ever* and 2) presents the Ppis *rather* and *pretty*.

1) a. Chris didn't win *a red cent*.
    b. *Chris won *a red cent*.
    c. Sandy hasn't *ever* eaten cheese cake.
    d. *Sandy has *ever* eaten cheese cake.

2) a. *Chris isn't *rather* boring.
    b. Chris is *rather* boring.
    c. *Sandy isn't *pretty* clever.
    d. Sandy is *pretty* clever.

Whereas Npis may occur in negated propositions as in 1a) and 1c), they are not available in the positive propositions 1b) and d). Ppis, on the other hand, occur in positive propositions like 2b) and d. but are ungrammatical in the negated counterparts 2a) and c). In 1) and 2), the presence of negation constrains whether the environment is suitable for the particular PSI. In general, PSIs are sensitive to various environments: 3) presents several environments in which Npis may occur some of which are restricted for Ppis.[2] Further such environments are indirect questions, conditionals, comparatives and certain adverbs like, e.g., *rarely* (see Ladusaw 1979 for an overview).

3) a. I doubt that Chris will win *a red cent*. (adversative *doubt*).
    b. Sandy payed the bill without *ever* finishing her drink. (preposition *without*)
    c. Every person who *ever* walked this earth is guilty. (determiner *every*)
    d. Did Sandy *ever* read the newspaper? (question mode)

Analyses of the natural language phenomenon *Polarity Sensitivity* (PS) should provide intuitive answers to the following two problems around which the phenomenon centers, namely the Sensitivity Problem – *Why are PSIs sensitive to their context?* – and the Licensing Problem – *Which environments allow PSIs to occur and how do they do so?* In this paper, after introducing an underspecified approach to semantic scope (§2), I present PSIs as presuppositional elements in §3, and formalize intuitive answers to the Sensitivity and the Licensing Problem in an underspecified semantics. In §4, evidence for the interplay of structural and semantic licensing as formalized in

---

[1]   This research was partially supported by a Fulbright Scholarship taking me to Stanford University. I would like to thank the following people for helpful comments on various versions of this paper: Emily Bender, Dan Flickinger, Hans Kamp, Uwe Reyle, Ivan Sag, Michael Schiehlen and Peter Sells. Any remaining errors are my own.

[2]   I return to the distribution of Ppis and Npis in §3.

§3 is presented. Also, further motivation for the underspecified treatment of PS is provided by the interaction of PS and semantic scope. §5 concludes the paper.

2   Underspecification and Scope Ambiguities

Consider the proposition in 4) which is ambiguous due to the two possible scope relations of the two quantified noun phrases.

4) Every woodpecker claims a tree.

5) formalizes the two possible readings in Predicate Logic: there either is a specific tree which every woodpecker claims a) or every woodpecker claims some tree which is not necessarily the same as the others claim b).

5) a. $\exists$ x (tree(x) $\wedge$ $\forall$ y (woodpecker(y) $\rightarrow$ claim(y,x)))
   b. $\forall$ y (woodpecker(y) $\rightarrow$ $\exists$ x (tree(x) $\wedge$ claim(y,x)))

The intended reading of 4) is determined by context. Until sufficient context is provided for, further computations operate on compact, scopally underspecified representations. An underspecified semantics identifies semantic relations by labels. Certain labels may be left underspecified to represent various readings until context resolves the intended one. As an example, the underspecified representation for 4) is given in 6): here, the labels of the scope positions of the two quantifiers are left underspecified. The two possible instantiations in 7a) and b) correspond to the readings in 5a) and b), respectively.

6) $l1$:exists(x,$l2$,$l8$), $l2$:tree(x), $l3$:every(y,$l4$,$l9$), $l4$:woodpecker(y), $l5$:claim(e,y,x)
7) a. $l8$=$l3$ and $l9$=$l5$: $l1$:exists(x,$l2$,$l3$), $l2$:tree(x), $l3$:every(y,$l4$,$l5$), $l4$:woodpecker(y), $l5$:claim(e,y,x)
   b. $l8$=$l5$ and $l9$=$l1$: $l1$:exists(x,$l2$,$l5$), $l2$:tree(x), $l3$:every(y,$l4$,$l1$), $l4$:woodpecker(y), $l5$:claim(e,y,x)

The underspecified semantic formalism used in this paper is Minimal Recursion Semantics (MRS, see Copestake et al. 1997), a variant of the just presented Underspecified DRT (UDRT, see Reyle 1993). MRS represents semantic relations as feature structures and therefore is easily compatible with Head-driven Phrase Structure Grammar (HPSG, see Pollard & Sag 1994), the grammar framework in which the grammar of PS formalized here is presented (see also Tonhauser 1999). The underspecified representation in MRS corresponding to 6) is given in 8).[3] The H-CONS (handle constraints) feature encodes lexical and contextual constraints on possible resolutions of the underspecified structure. H-CONS in 8) encodes the constraints introduced by the quantifiers as in 7a) and b).

---

[3]   The feature LISZT encodes the list of semantic relations, HANDEL labels a semantic relation, the remaining feature names should be self-explanatory.

8)

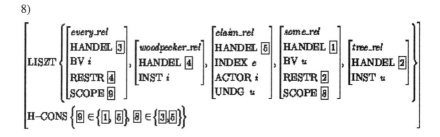

3   Polarity Sensitivity and Lexical Underspecification

Lexical semantic approaches to PS (see, e.g., Kadmon & Landmann 1993, Tovena 1996, Israel 1996) identify properties of (single or classes of) PSIs which are argued to provide for important insights to the sensitivity and distribution of PSIs. In this paper, I follow up on the analysis presented in Tonhauser (1999) in which the property *scale referring* is identified to account for the sensitivity and distribtion of PSIs: *PSIs refer to a point or range on a contextually specified scale.*[4] Consider 9) and 10), where the NPI *a red cent* and the PPI *rather* refer to a low point on a scale of winning and a high point on a scale of cleverness, respectively.

   9)   Chris didn't win *a red cent*.
  10)   Sandy is *rather* clever.

The scale to which a PSI refers is created by certain lexical items in the clause as well as contextual information. The idea of PSIs referring to a scale and certain environments evoking a scale isn't new (see, e.g., Fauconnier 1975; Ladusaw 1979) but has not yet been formally exploited to account for the sensitivity and distribution of PSIs.

Now what if the context doesn't provide for a scale? In this case, the PSI can't be interpreted because the property *scale referring* is not supported. In this analysis, I argue that PSIs are sensitive to the context because they require a scale in the context in order to be interpreted. This provides for an answer to the Sensitivity Problem. Formally, PSIs lexically impose a constraint on the context checking whether a scale is available. If a proposition fulfills the constraint imposed on it by the PSI, the proposition allows for the PSI to be interpreted.

So what are the appropriate scales for a particular PSI? Ladusaw (1979) presents a semantic approach to licensing which characterizes the environments suitable for NPIs by the semantic notion of *downward-entailingness*. PPIs under his approach are available in *upward-entailing* environments or downward-entailing ones without overt negation. Zwarts' (1993) findings further refine Ladusaw's analysis: some downward-entailing environments are also *anti-additive* and some are even *anti-mor-*

---

[4]   The property *scale referring* also characterizes other elements like, e.g., *very*. The lexical property erty uniquely singling out PSIs is yet to be found.

phic (the three types of environments stand in the subset relation). PSIs are found to be sensitive to the various strengths of environments, not only to downward- or upward-entailingness. See Table 1 for the mathematical definitions of the environments, the various kinds of PSIs and examples of both. The answer to the Licensing Problem under this analysis is the following: PSIs are licensed by operators which provide for an environment suitable for the particular PSI.

Summarizing, PSIs are identified as presuppositional items: they impose a constraint on the context which needs to ensure the availability of an appropriate (as defined by the particular PSI) scale for the PSI. Table 2 summarizes these lexical constraints. The remaining sections of §3 formalize the analysis of Polarity Sensitivity in HPSG/MRS.

operator f		example	(available) PSIs	example
1a.	downward-entailing (weak) $\alpha \le \beta \to f(\beta) \le f(\alpha)$	*at most n*	weak NPI weak PPI	*any* *rather*
1b.	anti-additive (strong) $f(\beta \vee \alpha) \leftrightarrow f(\beta) \wedge f(\alpha)$	*no one*	weak NPI strong NPI	*any* *yet*
1c.	anti-morphic (superstrong) $f(\beta \vee \alpha) \leftrightarrow f(\beta) \wedge f(\alpha)$ and $f(\beta \wedge \alpha) \leftrightarrow f(\beta) \vee f(\alpha)$	*not*	weak NPI strong NPI superstrong NPI	*any* *yet* *a bit*
2.	upward-entailing $\alpha \le \beta \to f(\alpha) \le f(\beta)$		weak PPI strict PPI	*rather* *some*

Table 1: Environments and PSIs

PSI	constraint on context
weak NPI	at least downward-entailing environment
strong NPI	at least anti-additive environment
superstrong NPI	anti-morphic environment
weak PPI	at most downward-entailing environment
strict PPI	only upward-entailing environments

Table 2: Contextual Constraints of PSIs

3.1   Lexical Entries

The type hierarchy in 11) encodes the possible strengths of the operators. It models the subset relation of the environments (cf. Table 1) and thereby allows PSIs to lexically express their minimal requirement on the strength of the environment (cf. Table 2).

11)

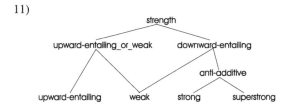

12a) presents the relevant part of a lexical entry of a PSI (here, NPI *ever*) and 12b) presents the relevant part of the operator *every* creating a superstrong environment.

12)

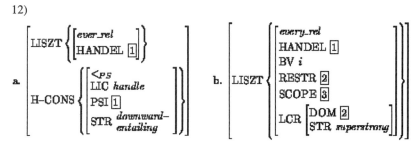

In 12a), the NPI *ever* lexically introduces a constraint on the context in the H-CONS feature. The constraint specifies that the PSI identifed by the handle ⊡ needs to stand in the $^{<PS}$-relation to the handle of some LIC(enser) which is underspecified in the lexical entry. (The $^{<PS}$-relation between handles and the resulting PS-chain are introduced in §3.2.) The constraint models the property *scale referring* of PSIs. *ever* also requires the strength (STR) of the licenser to be at least downward-entailing. The feature LCR in 12b) marks the lexical item *every* as a licensing operator which introduces a superstrong environment in its restriction. The domain feature DOM encodes semantic restrictions on licensing applying to, e.g., determiners and conditionals (see §4). In the formalization, PPIs impose a negative constraint on the context: strict (weak) PPIs impose a constraint on the context ensuring that no downward-entailing (anti-additive) environment is present.

3.2   Constructing the PS-chain

The PS-chain captures the relation in which PSIs and operators stand to each other in the proposition. The PS-chain of the representation of a proposition is the top level value of the feature PS which encodes the $^{<PS}$-relation. PSIs and operators are iden-tifed by the type *ps* which requires them to introduce their relevant handle to the $^{<PS}$-relation 13): PSIs introduce their handle a) whereas operators introduce the DOM handle b).

13)

$$\text{a.}\quad ps \longrightarrow \begin{bmatrix} \text{LISZT}\left\{ \begin{bmatrix} psi\_rel \\ \text{HANDEL}\ \boxed{1} \end{bmatrix} \right\} \\ \text{H CONS}\,|\,\text{PS}\left\{\boxed{1}\right\} \end{bmatrix} \quad\text{b.}\quad ps \longrightarrow \begin{bmatrix} \text{LISZT}\left\{ \begin{bmatrix} ps\_operator\_rel \\ \text{LCR}\,|\,\text{DOM}\ \boxed{1} \end{bmatrix} \right\} \\ \text{H CONS}\,|\,\text{PS}\left\{\boxed{1}\right\} \end{bmatrix}$$

The $^<$PS-relation and thereby the PS-chain for a proposition is created by the following rule: The PS-value of a mother is the $^<$PS-relation holding between the PS-value of the head daughter and the PS-value of the complement daughter.

As an example, consider the proposition *Sandy hasn't ever missed John* represented in 14). The NPI *ever* introduces an underspecified constraint on the context (*handle* $^<$PS$\boxed{1}$) which is propagated up to the top of the representation. Negation as well as the NPI introduce themselves to the PS-chain which at the top level is $\boxed{2}$ $^<$PS$\boxed{1}$. The resolution component finally needs to check whether the underspecified constraint can be resolved based on the relation encoded in the PS-chain. In 14), the underspecified handle in the constraint of *ever* can be unified with $\boxed{2}$, the handle of *not*, which stands to *ever* in the $^<$PS-relation as indicated by the PS-chain and lexically suits the requirements of *ever* by creating an at least downward-entailing scale. Additionally, resolution needs to adhere to the following constraint:

Constraint PS: Resolved PS-constraints and resolved scope constraints may not express contradicting relations between handles.

The interplay of structural and semantic licensing as formalized here by the PS-chain together with Constraint PS is empirically supported in §4. Furthermore, employing the resolution component in a treatment of PS is motivated by accounting for the interaction of PS and semantic scope.

14)

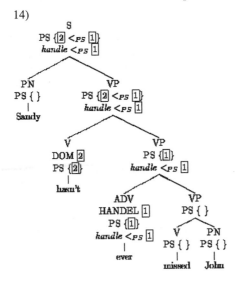

4   Polarity Sensitivity and Semantic Scope

The grammaticality judgements of the examples in 15) with the NPI *ever* are accounted for by *every* only being a licenser in its restriction which is easily captured in the lexicalist, semantic approach to PS by the lexical entry of *every* as given in 12) b.

15) a. *Every boy who went to school *ever* had apples for lunch.
   b. Every boy who *ever* went to school had apples for lunch.

15 a) and b) are analyzed as given in 16a) and b), respectively.

16)

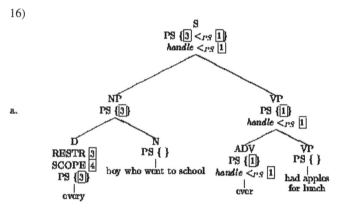

For both propositions, *ever* introduces an underspecified constraint and the PS-chain is ③ <PS①. However, 16) a. violates Constraint PS since semantically *ever* is in the scope of *every* and therefore 16) a. is ruled out. The interplay of structural and semantic licensing formalized here overcomes the problems these licensing proposals exhibit in isolation. The final examples in 17) concern the disambiguation of semantic scope by PS constraints.

17) a. Nobody talks to a friend who cheated at school.
    b. Nobody talks to a friend who *ever* cheated at school.

Whereas 17 a) is ambiguous between a specific and a non-specific reading for *a friend*, only the non-specific reading is available for b) due to the NPI *ever*. However, for both propositions, the constraints on quantifier scope allow either (i) *nobody* < *a friend* or (ii) *a friend* < *nobody* (notice that for 17b), *ever* always is in the restriction of *a friend*). In the analysis of 17b), given in 18), *ever* additionally introduces the constraint *handle* <PS①.

18)

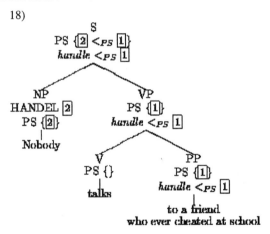

Based on the PS-chain, the underspecified constraint can be resolved by the handle of *nobody*. Due to Constraint PS, this is only possible under scope solution (i) thereby singling out the correct reading for 17b). The contextual constraint on resolution introduced by the NPI disambiguates 17b). This variant of interaction between PS and semantic scope, too, is accounted for by the formalization employing underspecification and resolution as presented here.

5   Conclusions

In this paper, I present the presuppositional nature of PSIs in an underspecified semantics. The grammar of Polarity Sensitivity formalizes the empirically motivated interplay between structural and semantic licensing and accounts for the interaction of Polarity Sensitivity and semantic scope. The interaction provides further motivation for the underspecified treatment of Polarity Sensitivity. Future research might integrate the lexical semantics of individual PSIs to this formalization as presented in, e.g., Kadmon & Landmann (1993) and Tovena (1996) and investigate further on the deiambiguating nature of PSIs.

6 References

COPESTAKE, Ann; Flickinger, Dan; Sag, Ivan (1997): Minimal Recursion Semantics. An Introduction, Manuscript, CSLI, Stanford University

FAUCONNIER, Gilles (1975): Pragmatic Scales and Logical Structure. In: Linguistic Inquiry 6.

ISRAEL, Michael (1996): Polarity Sensitivity as Lexical Semantics. In: Linguistics and Philosophy 19

KADMON, Nirit; LANDMANN, Fred (1993): Any. In: Linguistics and Philosophy 16.

LADUSAW, William (1979): Polarity Sensitivity as Inherent Scope Relations (PhD University of Texas). Austin.

POLLARD, Carl; SAG, Ivan (1994): Head-driven Phrase Structure Grammar. Chicago: Chicago University Press

REYLE, Uwe (1993): Dealing with Ambiguities by Underspecification: Construction, Representation, and Deduction. In: Journal of Semantics 10.

TONHAUSER, Judith (1999): Lexical Underspecification and Polarity Sensitivity (Minor Thesis University of Stuttgart).

TOVENA, Lucia (1996): Studies on Polarity Sensitivity (PhD University of Edinburgh).

ZWARTS, Frans (1993): Three Types of Polarity (Manuscript University of Groningen).

A Parallel Corpus as a Translation Aid: Exploring EU Terminology in the ELAN Slovene-English Parallel Corpus

Spela Vintar

A Slovene-English parallel corpus of 1 million words was compiled within the framework of the EU MLIS project ELAN. It consists of several subcorpora, the largest of which contains legal and other texts pertaining to the Slovenian accession to the EU. As the corpus is among the first such resources for Slovene, the paper briefly describes the process of corpus compilation and the tools used for sentence alignment, tokenization and annotation. We then focus on possible uses of the corpus for translation purposes, especially for parallel terminology extraction.

The concept of a parallel corpus is closely related to translation memories; the former can be converted into the latter or vice versa, depending on the method we chose for further studies of translation equivalence. In our case, a range of different tools were used to explore the possibilities of semi-automatic terminology extraction on a statistical basis. The aim is to show that translators, with some computational enthusiasm and some basic corpus-processing tools, can successfully exploit parallel corpora to create their own lexical resources.

1   Introduction

Over the past few years Slovenia has been undergoing deep political and economic changes, causing among other things a substantial increase in interlingual contacts. As a result of the process of transition as well as the trends towards globalisation and localisation, the need for translations is growing in almost all fields. An especially large portion of translation work derives from the government and political sector as part of Slovenian preparations for the accession to the EU. These documents are mainly legislation and other texts pertaining to Slovenian aspired membership in the EU, their total amount being estimated at over 200,000 pages.

The translation of these texts is already under way, managed by the Government Office of European Affairs, together with the implementation of translation technologies and tools to facilitate and speed up this enormous task. The tools chosen were those by Trados (Translator's Workbench, MultiTerm and WinAlign), in accordance with the recommendations of the European Commission. However, due to lack of qualified staff and work overload in the translation unit of this government office, few translators are actually using translation memories and the building of TM and terminological databases is lagging behind.

In translating legally binding texts from various fields, from agriculture to military affairs or economic agreements, terminological consistency and accuracy are of utmost importance. They can only be achieved through efficient terminology management which produces well-structured and up-to-date term banks. Although some tools for terminology management are already being used, most notably MultiTerm, the search for terms and their translation equivalents is still done manually. In the long run, the management of textual and terminological resources will have to be improved.

A parallel corpus is a useful linguistic resource for various purposes, especially for lexical and terminological studies. The ELAN Slovene-English corpus is the first step towards providing such a resource and presents a testbed for exploring possibilities of automatic or semi-automatic term extraction.

2   Making the ELAN parallel corpus

Although the compilation of the corpus served, in a broad sense, to develop multilingual technologies for the Slovene language, the primary motivation was terminological research, especially the exploration of different statistical or linguistic methods for term extraction. The making of the corpus was guided by practical principles – as the project was quite constrained as regards duration and financing, the primary aim was to collect as much textual data as possible covering a wide range of domains. Our criteria for text selection could thus be summed up as follows:

- terminological relevance
- "digital" availability – both original and translation could be easily obtained in digital form
- "loose copyright" – the texts either belong to public domain or the government; in some cases special copyright agreements were signed
- length – to save on processing time, only texts over 10,000 words were included.

The ELAN Slovene-English parallel corpus was compiled at the Jožef Stefan Institute in Ljubljana (Erjavec 1999) within the framework of the EU ELAN project (European Language Activity Network). It consists of 15 original texts and their translations, together amounting to 1 million words. The texts can be divided into the following groups:

- legislation, texts pertaining to the Slovenian accession to the EU (33%)
- political speeches of the Slovenian president Mr Kučan (6%)
- Slovenian Economic Mirror – a periodical (23%)
- Linux user's guide, and a glossary of computer terms (18%)
- "1984", novel by George Orwell (18%)
- Lek Vademecum – catalogue of medical products (2%)

These proportions clearly show that the texts come from various fields and adhere to different text types, but – with the exception of Orwell's novel – they nevertheless share one characteristic: both the original and the translation are recent – not older than 10 years, and all texts are terminologically relevant because they contain a large percentage of domain specific lexical items.

A further aim was to produce a basic resource that could be accessed and distributed freely on the Internet. For this purpose we prepared a special copyright agreement regulating the relationship between the text providers and ourselves that was signed if necessary.

2.1 Corpus processing and annotation

Each of the parallel texts was first converted into plain text format and "cleaned up", which also meant removing graphical elements such as pictures and tables from text, and then aligned. For the alignment two different tools were used – the Unix-based Vanilla aligner (Danielsson/Ridings) and the Windows-based aligner component of the Translation Memory System DejaVu by Atril; both require hand-validation of the results. The former was preferred by the more computationally oriented project collaborators, whereas the latter was selected chiefly on the grounds of its simple and flexible user interface and reasonable price and proved especially suitable for non-expert users.

The texts were then tokenised using *mtseg* and converted to SGML according to the TEI guidelines. The texts were kept in 15 separate files, with the header containing all administrative data about the text, e.g. title, source, length, provider, tools used for processing etc. The body of the text is constituted of translation units. Each translation unit contains two language segments, Slovene and English or vice versa, depending on which of the two was the source language.

The organisation of language segments into translation units is a feature related to the notion of a translation memory and was chosen deliberately so as to facilitate the conversion of the parallel text into a TM format. Some of our text providers, especially the Government Office of European Affairs, were very eager to benefit from this kind of exchange and we indeed returned all the texts we obtained from them in the TRADOS translation memory format .tmw.

The last step in corpus annotation was the lemmatisation of the Slovene part. For highly inflectional languages like Slovene this is a prerequisite for almost all further corpus studies and at the same time a very difficult operation due to the morphological complexity and ambiguity. The lemmatisation was kindly provided by Amebis d.o.o., a Slovene company specialised in language technologies. However, since we were dealing with terminologically rich texts, many words were unknown to the program and all ambiguities remained unresolved.

2.2 Lexical analysis of the corpus

After we had reached the limit desired – 1 million words – and the corpus had been annotated and encoded according to our intentions and purposes, the need appeared for an analysis of the data collected. As described above, the process of corpus compilation, particularly the text selection phase, was guided by ad hoc strategies and most decisions were made on the basis of what was available at that moment rather than what would have been ideal. Before any serious exploitation of the corpus could be undertaken it was therefore necessary to analyse the material gathered.

The analysis included the following phases (Vintar 1999):

- general corpus statistics – number of words, sentences, average word and sentence length, type/token ratio, comparison across all 15 texts
- word frequencies – producing frequency tables for the whole corpus as well as individual texts, producing lists of stopwords both for Slovene and English
- keywords – lists of domain specific words for each text, obtained by matching the text frequency lists against a reference (corpus) wordlist and extracting only those items where the relative frequency in the text is higher than the one in the corpus
- translation equivalents – a study of polysemous words and their various translation possibilities
- multi-word units – the collocational behaviour of eight highly frequent nouns was observed mainly to establish the ratio between occurrences of the word as a single-word item and occurrences of the word within a larger multi-word lexical unit

Several corpus tools were used for this task: Wordsmith, MonoConc, ParaConc and CQP. Through the process of analysing the corpus many interesting features were observed either due to general differences between the two languages or, more importantly, due to the lexical inventory of the texts. To exemplify the former we list a few general qunatitative differences between English and Slovene: The type/token ratio in Slovene is much higher (9.05) than in English (3.1) due to morphological variety, the average length of Slovene words is greater than in English, but on the other hand English sentences tend to contain more words (25.13) than Slovene sentences (19.88).

The lexical inventory of the texts can be represented very clearly through lists of keywords, moreover these can even be used as provisional lists of term candidates, since they contain mostly domain or field specific words that also constitute the core terminology of the text. As we inspected those lists we saw that most terms that could be of interest in translation-oriented terminographical work had indeed been identified through this simple procedure, however with the exception of hapaxes.

For the terminological analysis presented here, a subcorpus of EU-related texts was chosen comprising the following texts:

- <spor> Europe Agreement. Size: 589 KB, 34 kW
- <anx2> Europe Agreement – Annex II. Size: 483 KB, 25 kW
- <stra> National Strategy for Integration into EU. Size: 1511 KB, 89 kW
- <kmet> Slovenia's programme for accession to EU – agriculture. Size: 543 KB, 29 kW
- <ekon> Slovenia's programme for accession to EU – economy. Size: 394 KB, 23 kW
- <usta> Constitution of the Republic of Slovenia. Size: 364 KB, 20 kW
- <vino> EC Council Regulation No 3290/94 – agriculture. Size: 1182 KB, 69 kW

3 Towards a methodology for bilingual term extraction

The lists of keywords were taken as a starting point. If the keyword list for each individual text is combined with the list of words unknown to the lemmatizer (see Figure 1) a provisional list of (monolingual) term candidates is obtained. The next step required is the word-to-word alignment of parallel texts to extract translation equivalents, and for this we used the 21 software, a freely available statistical word alignment tool produced at the University of Twente (Hiemstra 1998). However, if Twente is run on Slovene-English texts as they are its output will be next to useless, so prior to the word alignment some pre-processing steps were necessary.

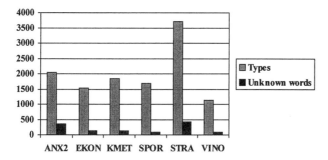

Figure 1: Words unknown to the lemmatizer

The first was removing stopwords from the corpus, i.e. functional words that tend to be highly frequent but carry little meaning. Lists of stopwords were obtained mostly on the basis of the general frequency list and supplemented according to grammatical rules. The second step was the replacement of wordforms by lemmas for the purpose of increasing their relative frequency in the corpus; this was performed only for the Slovene part.

Given such normalised input Twente produces much better results, however, with still far too much noise (see Figure 2). An analysis revealed that the results are only reliable for those items that occur more than 4 times in the corpus and are at the same time matched together as translation equivalents with a probability of over 0.50. We therefore implement a Perl filter over the initial term list that extracted only the word pairs matching these criteria. The result is a bilingual text-specific glossary of single-word terms (see Figure 3).

```
sprejeti              sprejetje             sprememba             spremeniti
---------------       ---------------       ---------------       ---------------
adopted      0.45     adoption      0.94    amendments    0.54    amended       0.38
approved     0.33     responsibilit 0.06    changes       0.21    will          0.17
adoption     0.11                           amendment     0.14    Health        0.16
approval     0.10                           Act           0.03    amending      0.03
                                            Harmonized    0.02    evidence      0.03
                                            devices       0.02    supplementing 0.03
                                            medical       0.02    short         0.03
                                            responsibilit 0.01    awaiting      0.03


spremljajocx          spremljanje           spricxevalo           sprostiti
---------------       ---------------       ---------------       ---------------
accompanying   0.47   monitoring    1.00    referral      0.16    adapted       0.27
responsibilit  0.16                         issue         0.11    equestrian    0.27
Institutions   0.16                         attached      0.11    events        0.27
800            0.07                         changed       0.11    there         0.18
regulates      0.05                         veterinarians 0.11    free          0.01
cost           0.03                         attestations  0.11
work           0.03                         appointed     0.11
begin          0.02                         emergency     0.08
```

Figure 2: Twente word alignment output

The majority of translation equivalents obtained through this multi-level filtering are correct – the precision was estimated to 98%. Taking a closer look at our sample text gives the following figures:

Sample text: National programme of the Republic of Slovenia for accession to the European Union – agriculture

Total words (Slovene): 13,383
Words after pre-processing: 10,902
Types: 1,837
Terms extracted: 304
Precision: 98%

Freq.	Slovene	English	Match
45	agencija	Agency	0.58
9	agraren	agrarian	0.78
9	akt	regulations	0.79
18	AKTRP	AAMRD	0.84
5	analiza	analysis	0.69
5	C	C	1.00
6	carinski	Tariff	0.83
8	celovit	integrated	1.00
5	cena	prices	0.96
15	center	Centre	0.57
10	časoven	Timescale	0.70
26	članica	Member	0.94
8	človek	persons	0.63
8	človeški	Staff	1.00
14	dejavnost	activities	0.80

Figure 3: Sample from the bilingual term glossary

4 Limitations, problems and possible solutions

Although this method allows us to automatically extract bilingual text specific terminological glossaries with a relatively high precision, it has, on the other hand, some severe limitations. First of all, not all extracted word pairs are terms, because neither the keyword list nor the list of unknown words can really guarantee that a text specific item is actually a term. Secondly, the accuracy of this method depends on the frequency of the item extracted in the corpus and works reliably only with words that occur over four times. For less frequent words and hapaxes alternative extraction methods should be devised. On the other hand, many terms may actually occur over four times, but if the lemmatizer does not know the word it is retained in its various wordforms and counts as several different types. Consequently, such items cannot be extracted.

Probably the greatest limitation of the methodology described is the fact that only single-word items are extracted. Although many terms consist of a single word, an even greater proportion of terms are composed of two or more words. By observing and extracting just single-word items we lose a significant part of the terminological and idiomatic inventory of the text. A brief (manual) analysis of 8 highly frequent words showed that in over 40 per cent of the cases the word appears as part of a larger – idiomatic – unit, i.e. the unit itself occurs more than once in the entire corpus. We can therefore conclude that such a bilingual glossary of terms can probably serve mainly as a basis for multi-word term extraction or as resource for bilingual corpus querying, while its use for translation purposes remains rather limited.

4.1 Improving the results

The results presented above could be improved in various ways, as none of the steps in the methodology proposed had really been developed to its optimum. In the corpus pre-processing phase, much could be gained by lemmatizing the English part as well and by improving the stoplists. This would render a "cleaner" corpus and would probably result in higher precision of the Twente raw output.

Another possibility to considerably improve the word-to-word alignment procedure would be the identification of cognates. Especially in legal texts, and more generally in the majority of terminologically rich texts, we encounter many internationalisms and words derived from a common (Latin or Greek) stem, so the implementation of a "fuzzy matching" module that would recognize such pairs could improve the precision and recall of the Twente software, apart from being a valuable aid in the sentence alignment process.

4.2 Identifying multi-word terms

For the identification of multi-word units several methods could be used. The first would be the identification of typical part-of-speech patterns of multi-word terms in

Slovene and English and establishing statistically significant correspondences (Heid 1999). For the legal domain, an existing database of legal terms containing over 10.000 entries is maintained at the Office of the Government of Slovenia for European Affairs, and it might serve as a basis for such an analysis. If we then retrieve such typical patterns and check for single-word terms, we might arrive at multi-word term units.

Another approach was taken by Dias et al (1999), where the identification of multi-word units is based solely on the statistical evaluation of relations between words in the corpus. Some preliminary tests have already been run also on the ELAN corpus which showed that purely statistical methods sometimes give very accurate results in detecting relevant collocations even in unprocessed (non-lemmatised) texts.

5   Conclusions

Terminology, sometimes regarded as a branch of applied science, but actually having a scope much wider that this, is a field developing at a pace that – at least theoretically – equals than of the most rapid developments in technology, society and science. It is therefore next to impossible that a person – say a terminologist – could effectively keep track of all these changes and developments, much less record and document them adequately, solely on the basis of "manual" observation and intuition. What is needed is a methodology (and technology) for efficient processing of large quantities of textual material, because these not only reflect the state-of-the-art within a certain domain but constitute it.

For this reason and the fact that terminology is nowadays no longer coined only by terminologists and standardising committees but increasingly by translators themselves, it is essential that technical, legal and/or scientific translators and interpreters understand their role and responsibility as term creators and therefore learn to use the appropriate tools that will facilitate this task. Extracting terms, relevant collocations, variants and contexts from parallel corpora is certainly an important step towards this goal, and building terminological databases on the basis of such resources is the next step towards which the methodology proposed here wishes to contribute.

The aim of this paper was to show firstly how an important resource for translators, interpreters and terminologists can be created and processed and, secondly, how significant terminological data can be automatically extracted, interpreted and used. Although the procedure described here is very basic compared to some existing methods of term identification and retrieval, it shows that a combination of available corpus processing tools and some self-devised filters can produce useful results. A bilingual text specific glossary of terms may not be highly relevant as a translator's resource, but it is certainly useful for further identification of terms, translation equivalents and translation-oriented text mining.

Apart from the ways of overcoming limitations described above, several other plans are included in our wishlist for the future. From the perspective of those involved in the training of translators and interpreters, more attention should be paid to developing the skills needed to exploit corpora for translation purposes in creative and innovative ways. This also means developing a methodology of how to teach corpus linguistics, how to encourage students to view language as a set of computer-analysable patterns and how to use the knowledge of such patterns in translation. Another area of future development is the provision of appropriate training for active translators and terminologists, who can also be included in the process of building multilingual databases and corpora. Although the present situation in translation technologies and especially terminography leaves a lot to hope for, things are beginning to change both on the technological and the "awareness" side. We hope that this process will eventually result in better translations and happier translators.

6 References

DIAS, Gael et al. (1999) Multilingual Aspects of Multiword Lexical Units. In: Proceedings of the Workshop Language Technologies – Multilingual Aspects. Ljubljana: Faculty of Arts.

ERJAVEC, Tomaž (1999) A TEI Encoding of Aligned Corpora as Translation Memories. In: Proceedings of the EACL Workshop on Linguistically Interpreted Corpora. Bergen: ACL.

HEID, Ulrich (1999) Extracting Terminologically Relevant Collocations from German Technical Texts. In: Sandrini, Peter (ed.) Terminology and Knowledge Engineering (TKE '99). Vienna: TermNet.

HIEMSTRA, Djoerd (1998) Multilingual Domain Modelling in Twenty-One: automatic creation of a bi-directional translation lexicon from a parallel corpus. In: Peter-Arno Coppen et al. (eds.) Proceedings of the eighth CLIN meeting, pp. 41-58.

VINTAR, Spela (1999) A Lexical Analysis of the IJS-ELAN Slovene-English Parallel Corpus. In: Proceedings of the Workshop Language Technologies – Multilingual Aspects. Ljubljana: Faculty of Arts.

Autorenverzeichnis

A

Agranat, Dr. Tatiana, Moscow Linguistics University, IV.Babushkina, 20-13, 11792 Moscow, Russland, agran@sosh.mccme.ru

Ahoua, Prof. Firmin, Departement de Linguistique, 08 BP 887 Abidjan 08, Abidjan 08, Elfenbeinküste (Westafrika), ega@africaonline.co.ci

Ahrens, Helga, Media Supervision Software Consulting GmbH, G. F. Händel-Straße 13, D-69214 Eppelheim, Deutschland, h-ahrens@t-online.de

Alake, Drs. Christopher Adegoke, Catholic University of Leuven, p.a. Raghorstgo, 6708 KP Wageningen, Niederlande, calake@hotmail.com

Al-Kharashi, Dr. Ibrahim, King Abdulaziz City for Science and Technology, P.O. Box 6086, Riyadh 11442, Saudi Arabien, kharashi@kacst.edu.sa

Alter, Dr. Kai, Max Planck Institute of Cognitive Neuroscience, Stefanstr. 1a, D-04103 Leipzig, Deutschland, alter@cns.mpg.de

Al-Zamil, Abdullah, King Abdulaziz City for Science and Technology, P.O. Box 6086, Riyadh 11442, Saudi Arabien, azamil@kacst.edu.sa

Andrzejewski, Prof. Dr. Bolesław, Uniwersytet im. A. Mickiewiecza, Szamarzewskiego 91, 61-674 Poznań, Polen

Anipa, Dr. Kormi, University of St Andrews, North Street, St Andrews KY16 9AL, Großbritannien, ka17@st-andrews.ac.uk

Antoni, Dr. Marie-Hélène, Université de Poitiers, Faculté des Lettres et Langues, 95, av. du recteur Pineau, 86000 Poitiers, Frankreich, Marie-Helene.Antoni@mshs.univ-poitiers.fr

Antrim, Dr. Nancy Mae, University of Texas at El Paso, 500 W. University, El Paso, Texas 79968-0531, USA, nantrim@utep.edu

B

Balanga, Panagiota, Universität Münster, Arbeitsbereich Linguistik, Hüfferstraße 27, 48149 Münster, Deutschland, balanga@marley.uni-muenster.de

Barboun, Prof. Lisa, Coastal Carolina University, P.O. Box 1954, Conway, S.C. 29526, USA

Bärenfänger, Olaf, M.A., Universität Bielefeld, Fakultät für Linguistik und Literaturwissenschaft, Postfach 10 01 31, 33501 Bielefeld, Deutschland, olaf.baerenfaenger@uni-bielefeld.de

Belluscio, Giovanni M. G., University of Calabria, Arcavacata di Rende (CS) 87036, Italien, gbelluscio@unical.it

Ben Hamadou, Prof. Abdelmajid, ISIM-Sfax, Route Mharza, 3000-Sfax, Tunesien, Abdelmajid. Benhamadou@fsegs.rnu.tn

Benndorf, Beate, State University of New York at Buffalo, Lärchenstr. 38, D-06179 Teutschenthal, Deutschland, Beate.Benndorf@verwaltung.uni-magdeburg.de

Bilut-Homplewicz, Prof. Dr. Zofia, Uniwersytet Rzeszowski, ul. Rejtana 16 B, 35-310 Rzeszów, Polen, zbilut@poczta.wp.pl

Birken-Silvermann, PD Dr. Gabriele, Universität Mannheim, D-68131 Mannheim, Deutschland, birkens@rumms.uni-mannheim.de

Boas, Prof. Hans Christian, Department of Germanic Studies, University of Texas at Austin, E.P.S. 3.102, Austin, TX 78712-1190, USA, hcb@mail.utexas.edu

Bondaruk, Dr. Anna, Catholic University of Lublin, al. Raclawickie 14, 20-950 Lublin, Polen, bondaruk@kul.lublin.pl

Borgonovo, Claudia, Université Laval, Cité universitaire, Québec G1K 7P4, Kanada, claudia.borgonovo@lli.ulaval.ca

Bračič, Prof. Dr. Stojan, Univerza v Ljubljani, Filozofska Fakulteta, Aškerčeva 2, 1001 Ljubljana, Slowenien, stojan.bracic@ff.uni-lj.si

Brault, Frédérick, Université Laval, Cité Universitaire, Sainte-Foy, Quebec G1K 7P4, Kanada, aba955@agora.ulaval.ca

Budde, Monika, Technische Universität Berlin, Institut für Sprache und Kommunikation, Sekr. TEL 16-1, Ernst-Reuter-Platz 7, D-10587 Berlin, Deutschland, monika.budde@tu-berlin.de

C

Can, Cem, Çukurova University, Egitim Fk. Balcali, 01330 Adana, Türkei, cem_can@hotmail.com

Candalija, Associated Prof. Dr. José Antonio, Universidad de Alicante, Spanien, JA.Candalija@ua.es

Canisius, Dr. Peter, Lehrstuhl für germanistische Sprachwissenschaft, Universität Pécs, Ifjúság útja 6, H-7624 Pécs, Ungarn, canisius@btk.pte.hu

Chatterjee, Dr. Arunava, Hyperdigm Research, Washington Technology Park, 15000 Conference Center Drive, Suite 1070 North, Chantilly, VA 20151, USA

Chirko, Dr. Tatyana, Voronezh State University, Universitetskaya Sq. 1, 394000, Voronezh, Russland, chirko@vmail.ru

Cifuentes-Honrubia, Prof. Dr. José Luis, Universidad de Alicante, Ap. Correos 99, E-03080 Alicante, Spanien, Cifu@ua.es

Collier-Sanuki, Dr. Yoko, The University of British Columbia, 1871 West Mall, Vancouver, BC V6T 1Z2, Kanada, yoko@interchange.ubc.ca

Cortez-Gomes, Ana Maria, Université Paris Nord-13, Faculté des Lettres, Av. J.B. Clément, F-93430 Villetaneuse, Frankreich, amcortez@magic.fr

Cummins, Sarah, Université Laval, Cité universitaire, Quebec G1K 7P4, Kanada, sarah.cummins@lli.ulaval.ca

Curell, Dr. Hortènsia, Universitat Autònoma de Barcelona, Edifici B, 08193 Bellaterra, Spanien, hortensia.curell@uab.es

D

Danilewicz, Dr. Tadeusz, Gdańsk University, Hallera 14, 80-401 Gdańsk, Polen

Darski, Prof. Dr. Józef, Uniwersytet im. Adama Mickiewicza, Instytut Filologii Germanskiey, al. Niepodleglosci 4, 61-295 Poznań, Polen, darski@main.amu.edu.pl

De Brabanter, Philippe, (CP 175) Université Libre de Bruxelles, 50, Av. F. Roosevelt, 1050 Brussels, Belgien, pdebraba@ulb.ac.be

De Echeandia, Diane, University at Albany, SUNY, Albany, New York, USA

Dettmer, Dr. Andrea, Universität Bielefeld, Oberbauerschafter Str. 45, 32278 Kirchlengern, Deutschland, adettmer@web.de

Dodane, Christelle, Laboratoire de phonétique de Besançon, 20 rue des Arènes, Place aux Fleurs, F-39 100 Dole, Frankreich, cdodane@granvelle.univ-fcomte.fr

E

Ebeling, Dr. phil. Karin, Otto-von-Guericke-Universität Magdeburg, Postfach 4120, D-39016 Magdeburg, Deutschland, karin.ebeling@gse-w.uni-magdeburg.de

Eckert, Prof. Dr. Hartwig, Universität Flensburg, Mürwiker Str. 77, D-24943 Flensburg, Deutschland, eckert@foni.net

Eizaga-Rebollar, Bárbara, Universidad de Cádiz, Facultad de Filosofía y Letras, Departamento de Filología Francesa e Inglesa, Avda. Gómez Ulla 1, 11003 Cádiz, Spanien, barbara.eizaga@uca.es

Ekmekci, Prof. F. Özden, Çukurova University, Yadim, Balcali, 01330 Adana, Türkei, oekmekci@cu.edu.tr

Elsen, Priv.-Doz. Dr. Hilke, Josef Maria Lutz-Straße 10a, D-85293 Reichertshausen, Deutschland, hilkee@lrz.uni-muenchen.de

Embarki, Dr. Mohamed, Université Paul-Valéry, Montpellier III, Route de Mende, 34 199 Montpellier Cedex 5, Frankreich, mohamed.embarki@univ-montp3.fr

Endo, Prof. Yuichi, Tohoku Gakuin University, 1-3-1 Tsuchitoi, Aoba-ku, Sendai 980-8511, Japan, endo@tscc.tohoku-gakuin.ac.jp

F

Ferrer Mora, Prof. Dr. Hang, University of Valencia, Blasco Ibanez 32, E-46010 Valencia, Spanien, hang.ferrer@uv.es

Feyrer, Dr. Cornelia, Universität Innsbruck, Institut für Translationswissenschaft, Herzog-Siegmund-Ufer 15/4, A-6020 Innsbruck, Österreich, cornelia.feyrer@uibk.ac.at

Filimonova, Dr. Elena, Universität Konstanz, Sprachwissenschaft, Fach D 185, D-78457 Konstanz, Deutschland

Fink, Dr. Gernot A., Universität Bielefeld, Technische Fakultät, Postfach 100 131, D-33501 Bielefeld, Deutschland, gernot@techfak.uni-bielefeld.de

Floricic, Franck, Université de Toulouse le Mirail, Frankreich, floricic@univ-tlse2.fr

Fögen, Dr. phil. Thorsten, Humboldt-Universität Berlin, Institut für Klassische Philologie, Unter den Linden 6, 10099 Berlin, Deutschland, thorsten.foegen@rz.hu-berlin.de

Franco, Jon, Ph.D., University of Deusto, Aptdo. 1, 48080 Bilbao, Spanien, franco@orion.deusto.es

Friederici, Prof. Angela D., Max Planck Institute of Cognitive Neuroscience, Stefanstr. 1a, D-04103 Leipzig, Deutschland

Frigeni, Chiara, M.A., University of Toronto, Department of Linguistics, 130 St. George Street, # 6076, Toronto M5S 3H1, Kanada, cfrigeni@chass.utoronto.ca

G

Gaca, Maciej, Ph.D., Adam Mickiewicz University, Poznań, ul. Miedzychodzka 5, 60-371 Poznań, Polen, gaca@amu.edu.pl

Gargouri, Dr. Bilel, FSEG-Sfax, Route de l'aéroport, 3018-Sfax, Tunesien, Bilel.Gargouri@sfsegs.rnu.tn

Godart-Wendling, Dr. Béatrice, CNRS - UMR 7597, 2 Place Jussieu, 75251 Paris Cedex 05, Frankreich, godart@ccr.jussieu.fr

Godglück, HD Dr. Peter, FR 4.1 Germanistik, Universität des Saarlandes, D-66123 Saarbrücken, Deutschland, sl11wheg@rz.uni-sb.de

Goecke, Karl-Ulrich, Universität Bielefeld, Fakultät für Linguistik und Literaturwissenschaft, Postfach 10 01 31, D-33501 Bielefeld, Deutschland, goecke@lili.uni-bielefeld.de

Göpferich, Prof. Dr. Susanne, Hochschule für Technik (FH) Karlsruhe, Moltkestraße 30, D-76133 Karlsruhe, Deutschland, susanne.goepferich@fh-karlsruhe.de

Grabowski, Prof. Dr. Joachim, University of Education Heidelberg, Psychology Department, Keplerstraße 87, D-69120 Heidelberg, Deutschland, grabowski@ph-heidelberg.de

Graham, Prof. Lisa J., Washington College, Department of Foreign Languages, Literatures and Cultures, 300 Washington Avenue, Chestertown, MD 21620, USA, lisa.graham@washcoll.edu

Grass, Dr. Thierry, Universität Tours, 3, rue des Taneurs, F-37041 Tours Cedex, Frankreich, grass@univ-tours.fr

Gross, Prof. Dr. Thomas Michael, Aichi University, Machihata-machi 1-1, 441-8522 Toyohashi, Japan, tmgross@vega.aichi-u.ac.jp

H

Hammer, Dr. Françoise, Universität Heidelberg, Institut für Übersetzen und Dolmetschen, Ploeck 57a, D-69117 Heidelberg, Deutschland, francoise.hammer@urz.uni-heidelberg.de

Handke, Prof. Dr. Jürgen, Institut für Anglistik u. Amerikanistik, Philipps-Universität Marburg, Wilhelm Röpke-Str. 6D, D-35032 Marburg, Deutschland, handke@mailer.uni-marburg.de

Hess, Prof. Dr. Michael, University of Zurich, Department of Information Technology, Computational Linguistics, Winterthurerstrasse 190, CH-8057 Zürich, Schweiz, hess@ifi.unizh.ch

Hokkanen, Dr. Tapio, University of Joensuu, Linguistics Department, P.O.Box 111, FIN-80101 Joensuu, Finnland, tapio.hokkanen@joensuu.fi

Horvat-Dronske, Renata, Gornji bukovac 11a, 10 000 Zagreb, Kroatien, udronske@inet.hr

Hsu, Assoc. Prof. Hui-chuan, National Chiao-Tung University, Department of Foreign Languages and Literatures, 1001 Ta Hsueh Road, Hsinchu 300, Taiwan, hchsu@cc.nctu.edu.tw

Huang, Prof. Changning, Microsoft Research China, Zhichun Road, 100080 / Beijing, China, cnhuang@microsoft.cn

I

Ikoma, Miki, Keio University, Seijo 7-35-36, Setagaya-ku, Tokyo 157-0066, Japan, m-ikoma@nifty.com

J

Järvikivi, Juhani, University of Joensuu, P.O. Box 111, FIN-80101 Joensuu, Finnland, juhani.jarvikivi@joensuu.fi

Jmaiel, Dr. Mohamed, ENIS-Sfax, Route Sokkra, 3018-Sfax, Tunesien, Mohamed.Jmaiel@enis.rnu.tn

K

Ka, Prof. Omar, University of Maryland, Baltimore County, 1000 Hilltop Circle, Baltimore, MD 21075, USA, ka@umbc.edu

Kakita, Prof. Kuniko, Toyama Prefectural University, 5180 Kurokawa, Kosugi, 939-0398, Japan, kkakita@pu-toyama.ac.jp

Kamwangamalu, Prof. Nkonko, Linguistics Program, University of Natal, King George V Avenue, Durban 4041, Südafrika, kamwanga@nu.ac.za

Kappa, Dr. Ioanna, University of Crete, Department of Philology / Linguistics, University Campus, 74100 Rethymno - Crete, Griechenland, kappa@phl.uoc.gr

Kappus, Martin, Ph.D., Marienstraße 110, D-72827 Wannweil, Deutschland, mkappus@t-online.de

Kawai, Prof. Dr. Michiya, University of Connecticut, Connecticut College, Box 5463, Connecticut College, New London, CT 06320, USA, mkaw@conncoll.edu

Kawamori, Dr. Masahito, NTT Communication Science Laboratories, Media Information Laboratory, Dialog Understaning Group, 3-1, Morinosato-Wakamiya, Atsugi-shi, Kanagawa 243-0198, Japan, kawamori@atom.brl.ntt.co.jp

King, Prof. Robert D., HRHRC 3.318, University of Texas, Austin, Texas 78713, USA, rking@mail.utexas.edu

Kispál, Tamás, Universität Szeged, Institut für Germanistik, Lehrstuhl für Germanistische Linguistik, Egyetem u. 2, H-6722 Szeged, Ungarn, kispal@lit.u-szeged.hu

Kleine, Ane, Universität Trier, Fachbereich 2, Jiddistik, D-54286 Trier, Deutschland, kleine@uni-trier.de

Kohlmayer, Prof. Dr. Rainer, Johannes Gutenberg Universität Mainz, Fachbereich Angewandte Sprach- und Kulturwissenschaft, An der Hochschule 2, D-76726 Germersheim, Deutschland, kohlmayer@mail.fask.uni-mainz.de

Koldau, Dipl.-Ing. Martin, Spessartstraße 2, D-64342 Seeheim, Deutschland, M.Koldau@t-online.de

Kreutz, Dr. Philippe, Université Libre de Bruxelles, Linguistic Department, CP 175, 50, av. F. Roosevelt, 1050 Bruxelles, Belgien, pkreutz@ulb.ac.be

Kummert, PD Dr. Franz, Universität Bielefeld, Technische Fakultät, Postfach 100 131, D-33501 Bielefeld, Deutschland, franz@techfak.uni-bielefeld.de

Künstler, Mieczyslaw J., University of Warsaw, ul. Rakowiecka 22a m. 37, Pl-02-591 Warszawa, Polen

Kürschner, Prof. Dr. Wilfried, Universität in Vechta, Driverstraße 22, D-49377 Vechta, Deutschland, wk@uni-vechta.de

Kuße, Dr. Holger, Goethe-Universität Frankfurt am Main, Slavische Philologie, Dantestraße 4-6, D-60325 Frankfurt am Main, Deutschland, kusse@em.uni-frankfurt.de

L

Ladouceur, Prof. Jacques, Université Laval, Cité Universitaire, Sainte-Foy, Québec G1K 7P4, Kanada, Jacques.Ladouceur@lli.ulaval.ca

Laenzlinger, Dr. Christopher, LATL, Université de Genève, 2 rue de Candolle, CH-1211 Genève-4, Schweiz, laenzlinger@latl.unige.ch

Lai, Assoc. Prof. Tom, City University of Hong Kong, Tat Chee Avenue, Hong Kong, China, cttomlai@cityu.edu.hk

Lehner, Dr. Christoph, Universität Hildesheim, Marienburger Platz 22, D-31141 Hildesheim, Deutschland, lehner@cl.uni-hildesheim.de

Lenz, PD Dr. Friedrich, Universität Passau, 94030 Passau, Deutschland, friedrich.lenz@uni-passau.de

Lezius, Wolfgang, IMS, University of Stuttgart, Azenbergstraße 12, D-70174 Stuttgart, Deutschland, lezius@ims.uni-stuttgart.de

Lomova, Dr. Tatiana, Voronezh State University, Universitetskaya Sq. 1, 394000, Voronezh, Russland

Lösener, Dr. Hans, Hochschule Vechta, Driverstraße 22, D-49377 Vechta, Deutschland, hans.loesener@uni-vechta.de

Lotfi, Dr. Ahmad R., Azad University at Khorasgan, Jay, Esfahan, Iran, lotfi@www.dci.co.ir

Lutjeharms, Prof. Dr. Madeline, Vrije Universiteit Brussel, Pleinlaan 2, B-1050 Brussel, Belgien, mlutjeha@vub.ac.be

M

Maddalon, Prof. Marta, University of Calabria, Arcavacata di Rende (CS) 87036, Italien, madmar@unical.it

Malinowska, Dr. Maria, Uniwersytet Jagielloński, IFRom Romance Languages Institute, Al. Mickiewicza 9/11, 31-120 Kraków, Polen, mmalinow@vela.filg.uj.edu.pl

Mańczyk, Prof. Dr. habil. Augustyn, Uniwersytet Zielonogórski, Institut für Germanistik, al.Wojska Polskiego 71a, 65-625 Zielona Góra, Polen

Mannewitz, Dr. phil. habil. Cornelia, Universität Rostock, Institut für Slawistik, August Bebel-Str. 28, D-18051 Rostock, Deutschland, cornelia.mannewitz@philfak.uni-rostock.de

Marinis, Dr. Theodore, University of Essex, Department of Language & Linguistics, Wivenhoe Park, Colchester, CO4 3SQ, Großbritannien, thodoris@essex.ac.uk

Matulina, Prof. Dr. Željka, Filozofski fakultet u Zadru, Obala kralja P. Krešimira IV, 2, HR-23000 Zadar, Kroatien, matulina@ffzd.hr

Méhes, Márton, Collegium Hungaricum Berlin, Karl Liebknecht-Straße 9, D-10178 Berlin, Deutschland, mehes@hungaricum.de

Mehler, Alexander, M.A., Universität Trier, Universitätsring 15, D-54286 Trier, Deutschland, mehler@uni-trier.de

Meinschaefer, Dr. Judith, Universität Konstanz, Fachgruppe Sprachwissenschaft, Fach D 185, D-78457 Konstanz, Deutschland, judith.meinschaefer@uni-konstanz.de

Mendicino, Antonio, University of Calabria, Arcavacata di Rende (CS) 87036, Italien

Mengon, Juri, LATL, Université de Genève, 2 rue de Candolle, CH-1211 Genève-4, Schweiz, mengon@latl.unige.ch

Meskill, Prof. Carla, University at Albany, SUNY, ED 115 University at Albany, Albany, New York, 12222, USA, meskill@cnsvax.albany.edu

Metoui, PD Dr. habil. Mongi, Johannes Gutenberg-Universität Mainz, Institut für Allgemeine und Vergleichende Sprachwissenschaft, Jakob Welder-Weg 18, D-55128 Mainz, Deutschland, metoui@mail.uni-mainz.de

Meyer, Dr. Martin, Centre for Functional Imaging Studies, Institute for Adaptive and Neural Computation, Division of Informatics, The University of Edinburgh, 5 Forrest Hill, Edinburgh EH1 2QL, Großbritannien, mmeyer@anc.ed.ac.uk

Mikołajczyk, Dr. Beata, Adam-Mickiewicz-Universität Poznań, Uminskiego 9A/7, 61-517 Poznań, Polen

Mitchell, Dr. Erika, Zayed University, P.O. Box 19282, Dubai, Vereinigte Arabische Emirate, em63@cornell.edu

Miyakoda, Dr. Haruko, Tokyo University of Agriculture and Technology, 2-24-16 Nakacho Koganei-shi, 184-8588 Tokyo, Japan, miyakoda@cc.tuat.ac.jp

Młodecki, Michał, Adam Mickiewicz Universität Poznań, 28 Czerwca 1956 nv 198, 61-485 Poznań, Polen, misza@main.amu.edu.pl

Mollá Aliod, Dr. Diego, Macquarie University, Division of Informaiton and Communication Sciences, Computing Department, Sydney, NSW, Australien, diego@ics.mq.edu.au

Müller, Priv.-Doz. Dr. Dr. Horst M., AG Experimentelle Neurolinguistik, Fakultät für Linguistik und Literaturwissenschaft, Universität Bielefeld, Universitätsstraße 25, 33615 Bielefeld, Deutschland, horst.mueller@uni-bielefeld.de

Muráth, Assoc. Prof. Dr. Judith, University of Pécs, Faculty of Business and Economics, Department of Business Communication and Foreign Languages, Rákóczi u. 80., H-7622 Pécs, Ungarn, murath@ktk.pte.hu

N

Nakamura, Wataru, Department of Information and Communication Engineering, The University of Electro-Communications, 4-17-11 Shakujii-machi, Nerima, Tokyo 177-0041, Japan, nakamura@e-one.uec.ac.jp

Nelson, Dr. Mette, University of Southern Denmark, Engstlen 1, DK-6000 Kolding, Dänemark, nelson@sitkom.sdu.dk

Nicol, Dr. Fabrice, University of Paris-III, Sorbonne Nouvelle, UFR du monde anglophone, rue de Santeuil, 75005 Paris, Frankreich, f.nicol@univ-paris3.fr, fabrni@aol.com

Niemi, Prof. Jussi, University of Joensuu, Linguistics, P.O. Box 111, FIN-80101 Joensuu, Finnland, jussi.niemi@joensuu.fi

Niemi, Sinikka, Ph.D., University of Joensuu, Linguistics, Department of Linguistics, Yliopistokatu 2, P.O. Box 111, FIN-80101 Joensuu, Finnland, sinikka.niemi@joensuu.fi

O

Okon, Prof. Dr. Luzian, Haute Ecole spécialisée, rue de la Source 21, CH-2501 Biel / Bienne, Schweiz

Opitz, Dr. phil. Kurt, Brahmsallee 75, 20144 Hamburg, Deutschland

P

Parada, Prof. Dr. Arturo, Universidade de Vigo, Lagoas-Marcosende, s/n, 36200 Vigo (Pontevedra), Spanien, aparada@uvigo.es

Pawłowski, Dr. Adam, Uniwersytet Wrocławski, Instytut Filologii Polskiej, pl. Nankiera 15, 50-140 Wrocław, Polen, apawlow@pwr.wroc.pl

Pekar, Dr. Viktor, BSPU, English Language Department, Okt. Revolutsii, 3a, 450097 Ufa, Russland, provp@mail.ru

Peña Pollastri, Ana Paulina, Universidad Nacional de la Rioja, Islas Shetland 2331, Bo. Antártida I, 5300 La Rioja, Argentinien, paulina@satlink.com

Petursson, Prof. Dr. Magnus, Universität Hamburg, Institut für Phonetik, Allgemeine Sprachwissenschaften, Bogenallee 11, D-20144 Hamburg, Deutschland

Pieciul, Eliza, Adam-Mickiewicz-Universität Poznań, b. Smialego 10/3, 60-682 Poznań, Polen, eliza@main.amu.edu.pl

Popova, Dr. Natalia, Universität Jakutsk, Belinskogo 58, 677000 Jakutsk, Russland

Prior, Dr. Martin H., London, Großbritannien, martinprior99@hotmail.com

R

Rangelova, Prof. Krassimira, Sofia University, Department of English and American Studies, 15 Tsar Osvoboditel Blvd, 1504 Sofia, Bulgarien

Rapp, Dr. Reinhard, Universität Mainz, Fachbereich Angewandte Sprach- und Kulturwissenschaft, An der Hochschule 2, D-76726 Germersheim, Deutschland, rapp@mail.fask.uni-mainz.de

Reder, Anna, Universität Pécs, Ifjúság 6., H-7624 Pécs, Ungarn, reder@btk.pte.hu

Rehm, Matthias, Faculty of Linguistics, University of Bielefeld, Postfach 10 01 31, D-33501 Bielefeld, Deutschland, rehm@coli.uni-bielefeld.de

Rengsirikul, Kesinee, Faculty of Humanities, Kasetsart University, 65 Kaset Village 2, Nakom Pathom, 73140, Thailand, kesinee@np.a-net.net.th

Rickheit, Prof. Dr. Gert, Fakultät für Linguistik und Literaturwissenschaft, Universität Bielefeld, Universitätsstraße 25, D-33615 Bielefeld, Deutschland, gert.rickheit@uni-bielefeld.de

Rist, Dr. Ulfert, Kirch Intermedia GmbH, Freisinger Landstraße 74, 80939 München, Deutschland, ulfert.rist@kirchintermedia.de

Romito, Dr. Luciano, University of Calabria, Department of Linguistics, 87036 Arcavacata di Rende (CS), Italien, luciano.romito@unical.it

Ronan, Patricia, Philipps Universität Marburg, Marburger Landstraße 22, D-35091 Cölbe, Deutschland, ronan@stud-mailer.uni-marburg.de

Rubio Cuenca, Prof. Francisco, Universidad de Cadiz, C/Barbate, 8, 11510 Puerto Real- Cadiz, Spanien, paco.rubio@uca.es

Rudolph, Dr. Elisabeth, Klaus Groth-Straße 47, D-22926 Ahrensburg, Deutschland

Ruiz de Zarobe, Dr. Yolanda, University of the Basque Country, Paseo de la Universidad, 5, 01006 Vitoria-Gasteiz, Spanien, fipruzay@vc.ehu.es

Ruprecht, Prof. Dr. Robert, Berner Fachhochschule, Hochschule für Technik und Architektur,
Quellgasse 21, CH 2500 Biel 1, Schweiz, robert.ruprecht@hta-bi.bfh.ch

S

Sacia, Laura, Department of Linguistics, University of Hawaii at Manoa, 1890 East-West Road,
Honolulu, Hawaii 96822, USA, sacia@hawaii.edu

Sagerer, Prof. Dr. Gerhard, Universität Bielefeld, Technische Fakultät, Postfach 100 131,
D-33501 Bielefeld, Deutschland, sagerer@techfak.uni-bielefeld.de

Sanders, Prof. Alton F., Miami University, Department of Computer Science and Systems Analysis,
Oxford, Ohio 45056, USA, sanderaf@muohio.edu

Sanders, Prof. Ruth H., Miami University, Department of German, Russian and East Asian
Languages, Oxford, Ohio 45056, USA, sanderrh@muohio.edu

Savtschenko, Veronika, Pedagogical University, Radischev Street 87/7, 15, 305006 Kursk, Russland,
kgpu@pub.sovtest.ru

Schaefer, Dr. Steven, E.S.C.O.M., 8, rue Alphonse Daudet, F-95600 Eaubonne, Frankreich,
steven.schaefer@libertysurf.fr

Schapansky, Dr. Nathalie, Chilliwack Street, New Westminster, BC V3L 4V5, Kanada,
nathalie_ schapansky@sfu.ca

Schlüter, Julia, Universität Paderborn, FB 3 - Anglistik / Sprachwissenschaft, Warburger Str. 100,
D-33098 Paderborn, Deutschland, schlueter@hrz.uni-paderborn.de

Schmalhofer, Prof. Dr. Franz, Institute of Cognitive Science, Katharinenstraße 24,
D-49069 Osnabrück, Deutschland, Franz.Schmalhofer@uos.de

Schneider, Gerold, Universität Zürich, Institut für Informatik, Winterthurerstrasse 190,
CH-8057 Zürich, Schweiz, gschneid@ifi.unizh.ch

Schöneborn, Thomas, Universität Konstanz, Fachbereich Sprachwissenschaft, D-8457 Konstanz,
Deutschland, thomas.schoeneborn@uni-konstanz.de

Sengani, Thomas M., University of South Africa, Department of African Languages, P.O. Box 392,
Pretoria 0003, Südafrika, sengatm@unisa.ac.za

Seong, Dr. Sang Hwan, Seminar für Orientalische Sprachen, Universität Bonn, Nassestraße 2,
D-53113 Bonn, Deutschland, sseong@uni-bonn.de

Shima, Norio, M.A., Sophia Universität (Tokyo), Center for the Teaching of Foreign Languages in
General Education, 7 1 Kioi-cho, Chiyoda-ku, 102-8554 Tokyo, Japan, shima-n@sophia.ac.jp

Sieradzka, Mag. Malgorzata, Universität Rzeszow, Rejtana 16 B, 35-310 Rzeszow, Polen,
masieradzka@up.pl

Sikorska, Mag. Malgorzata, Katholische Universität Lublin, Germanistisches Institut,
Al. Racławickie 14, 20-950 Lublin, Polen, malgorzata.sikorska@kul.lublin.pl

Simon, Bernd-Paul, Institut für Anglistische und Allgemeine Linguistik, Technische Universität
Berlin, Ernst Reuter-Platz 7, D-10587 Berlin, Deutschland, bps@pcangl.kgw.tu-berlin.de

Sokołowska, Dr. Olga, University of Gdańsk, Institute of English, ul. Wita Stwosza 55,
80-952 Gdańsk, Polen, angos@univ.gda.pl

Souleimanova, Prof. Dr. Olga A., Moscow Pedagogical University, Zelenograd 1504-230,
103683 Moscow, Russland

Sroka, Prof. Dr. Kazimierz A., University of Gdańsk, Pomorska 15 A 30, 80-333 Gdańsk-Oliwa, Polen, angkas@univ.gda.pl

Stanulewicz, Dr. Danuta, University of Gdańsk, Wita Stwosza 55, 80-952 Gdańsk, Polen, angds@univ.gda.pl

Steinhauer, Dr. Karsten, Georgetown University, Department of Neuroscience, GICCS, Brain and Language Lab, 3900 Reservoir Rd, NW, Washington DC 20007, USA

Stoel-Gammon, Prof. Dr. Carol, University of Washington, Department of Speech & Hearing Sciences, 1417 NE 42nd Street, Seattle, WA 98105, USA

Strässler, Dr. Jürg, Universität Bern, Institut für englische Sprachen und Literaturen, Länggass-strasse 49, CH-3000 Bern 9, Schweiz, strassler@bluewin.ch

Stromswold, Prof. Dr. Karin, Rutgers University, Department of Psychology and Center for Cognitive Science, New Brunswick, NJ 08903, USA, karin@ruccs.rutgers.edu

Stuckardt, Dipl.-Inf. Roland, INM GmbH, Im Mellsig 25, D-60433 Frankfurt am Main, Deutschland, stuckardt@compuserve.com

Świercz, Jacek, Institute of Oriental Studies, University of Warsaw, Ul. Krakowskie Przedm. 26/28, 00-927 Warszawa, Polen, swierczj@plearn.edu.pl

Szucsich, Dr. Luka, Universität Leipzig, Institut für Slavistik, Augustusplatz 10, 04109 Leipzig, Deutschland, szucsich@rz.uni-leipzig.de

T

Taborek, Dr. Janusz, Universität Poznań / Uniwersytet im A. Mickiewicza, Al. Niepodległości 4, 61-874 Poznań, Polen, taborek@amu.edu.pl

Tajarobi, Arman, Université Laval, Cité Universitaire, Sainte-Foy, Quebec G1K 7P4, Kanada, aac423@agora.ulaval.ca

Tanaka, Prof. Shin, Chiba University, Yayoicho 1-33, 263-8522 Chiba, Japan, shtanaka@cfl.f.chiba-u.ac.jp

Tęcza, Dr. Zygmunt, Lehrstuhl für Germanistik, Pädagogische Hochschule in Rzeszów, Rzeszów, Polen

ten Cate, Dr. Abraham P., Rijksuniversiteit Groningen, Germanistisches Institut, Postbus 716, 9700 AS Groningen, Niederlande, a.p.ten.cate@let.rug.nl

Thaiyanan, Orasa, Faculty of Humanities, Kasetsart University, Thailand, fhumort@ku.a.th

Tonhauser, Judith, Institut für Maschinelle Sprachverarbeitung, Universität Stuttgart, Azenbergstraße 12, D-70174 Stuttgart, Deutschland, tonhauser@ims.uni-stuttgart.de

Torras i Calvo, Maria-Carme, Universitat Autònoma de Barcelona, Edifici B, Facultat de Lletres, 08191 Bellaterra, Spanien, mctorras@hotmail.com

Trampe, Dr. Wilhelm, Institut für Informations- und Kommunikationsökologie (IKÖ), Im Osterfelde 1, D-31603 Diepenau, Deutschland, trampe.deutschland@t-online.de

Trumper, Prof. John B., University of Calabria, Department of Linguistics, 87036 Arcavacata di Rende (CS), Italien, trumper@unical.it

Tsiamita, Fanie, Aristotle University of Thessaloniki, P.O. Box 1553, 54006 Thessaloniki, Griechenland, tsiamita@otenet.gr

Tsujimoto, Tomoko, Osaka Institute of Technology, 5-16-1 Ohmiya, Asahiku, Osaka 535-8585, Japan, tomoko@ge.oit.ac.jp

Tumtavitikul, Apiluck, Faculty of Humanities, Kasetsart University, Bangkhen, BKK 10900, Thailand, oapiluck@ku.ac.th

U

Uesseler, Prof. Dr. habil. Manfred, Müritzstraße 18, D-10318 Berlin, Deutschland

V

Vassileva, Prof. Dr. Irena, Sprachlernzentrum der Universität Bonn, Am Hof 1, D-53113 Bonn, Deutschland, jvassile@slz.uni-bonn.de

Vinagre, Dr. Margarita, Universidad Europea de Madrid, Villaviciosa de Odón, 28670 Madrid, Spanien, marga.v@ing.fil.uem.es

Vintar, Spela, University of Ljubljana, Faculty of Arts, Department of Translation and Interpreting, Borstnikov trg 3, SI-1000 Ljubljana, Slowenien, spela.vintar@guest.arnes.si

Vliegen, Dr. Maurice, Faculteit der Letteren, Vrije Universiteit Amsterdam, De Boelelaan 1105, 1081 HV Amsterdam, Niederlande, m.vliegen@let.vu.nl

Vogt, Helmut, Universität-GH Paderborn, Otto Wels-Str. 42, D-33102 Paderborn, Deutschland, HelmutVogt@t-online.de

von Cramon, Prof. D. Yves, Max Planck Institute of Cognitive Neuroscience, Stefanstr. 1a, D-04103 Leipzig, Deutschland

W

Wanner, Dr. Anja, English Department, University of Göttingen, Käte Hamburger-Weg, D-37073 Göttingen, Deutschland, awanner@gwdg.de

Waßner, Dr. Ulrich Hermann, Institut für Deutsche Sprache, R5, 6-13, D-68161 Mannheim, Deutschland, wassner@ids-mannheim.de

Weber, Prof. Dr. Heinrich, Universität Tübingen, Deutsches Seminar, Wilhelmstraße 50, D-72074 Tübingen, Deutschland, heinrich.weber@uni-tuebingen.de

Wei, Jennifer M., English Department, Soochow University, 11102 Taipei, Taiwan, wei@mail.scu.edu.tw

Wong, Andrew, Stanford University, Margaret Jacks Hall, Bldg. 460, Stanford, CA 94305, USA

Wrede, Britta, M.A., Universität Bielefeld, Technische Fakultät, Universitätsstraße 25, D-33615 Bielefeld, Deutschland, bwrede@techfak.uni-bielefeld.de

Y

Yamaguchi, Dr. Toshiko, National University of Singapore, Department of Japanese Studies, BLK AS4, 9 Arts Link, 117570 Singapore, Republic of Singapore, jpsyt@nus.edu.sg

Z

Zajdo, Krisztina, University of Washington, Department of Speech & Hearing Sciences, 1417 NE 42nd Street, Seattle, WA 98105, USA, zajdo@u.washington.edu

Zimmermann, Dr. Kai, Rutgers University, Department of Psychology and Center for Cognitive Science, New Brunswick, NJ 08903, USA, kaiz@ruccs.rutgers.edu

Zinken, Jörg, M.A., Universität Bielefeld, Universitätsstraße, D-33615 Bielefeld, Deutschland, joerg.zinken@uni-bielefeld.de

Zitzen, Michaela, Universität Düsseldorf, Anglistik III, Universitätsstr. 1, D-40225 Düsseldorf, Deutschland, zitzen@phil-fak.uni-duesseldorf.de

Zybatow, Prof. Dr. Lew, Universität Innsbruck, Institut für Translationswissenschaft, Herzog-Siegmund-Ufer 15, A-6020 Innsbruck, Österreich, Lew.Zybatow@uibk.ac.at

Zybatow, Tatjana, Universität Leipzig, Institut für Linguistik, Brühl 34-50, D-04109 Leipzig, Deutschland, zybatov@rz.uni-leipzig.de

Zydek-Bednarczuk, Prof. Dr hab. Urszula, Uniwersytet Slaski, Plac Sejmu Slaskiego 1, 40-032 Katowice, Polen, zydek@homer.fil.us.edu.pl

Linguistik International

Herausgegeben von Heinrich Weber, Susanne Beckmann,
Abraham P. ten Cate, Wilfried Kürschner, Kazimierz Sroka, Ingo Warnke und Lew Zybatow

Band 1   Hans Otto Spillmann / Ingo Warnke (Hrsg.): Internationale Tendenzen der Syntaktik, Semantik und Pragmatik. Akten des 32. Linguistischen Kolloquiums in Kassel 1997. 1999.

Band 2   Cäcilia Klaus: Grammatik der Präpositionen. Studien zur Grammatikographie. Mit einer
thematischen Bibliographie. 1999.

Band 3   Käthi Dorfmüller-Karpusa / Ekaterini Vretta-Panidou (Hrsg.): Thessaloniker Interkulturelle
Analysen. Akten des 33. Linguistischen Kolloquiums in Thessaloniki 1998. 2000.

Band 4   Lew N. Zybatow (Hrsg.): Sprachwandel in der Slavia. Die slavischen Sprachen an der
Schwelle zum 21. Jahrhundert. Teil 1 und 2. 2000.

Band 5   Gerhild Zybatow / Uwe Junghanns / Grit Mehlhorn / Luka Szucsich (eds.): Current Issues
in Formal Slavic Linguistics. 2001.

Band 6   Christoph Küper (ed.): Meter, Rhythm and Performance – Metrum, Rhythmus, Performanz.
Proceedings of the International Conference on Meter, Rhythm and Performance, held in
May 1999 at Vechta. 2002.

Band 7   Reinhard Rapp (Hrsg.): Sprachwissenschaft auf dem Weg in das dritte Jahrtausend. Akten
des 34. Linguistischen Kolloquiums in Germersheim 1999. Teil I: Text, Bedeutung, Kommunikation. Linguistics on the Way into the Third Millennium. Proceedings of the 34th Linguistics Colloquium, Germersheim 1999. Part I: Text, Meaning, and Communication. 2002.

Band 8   Reinhard Rapp (Hrsg.): Sprachwissenschaft auf dem Weg in das dritte Jahrtausend. Akten
des 34. Linguistischen Kolloquiums in Germersheim 1999. Teil II: Sprache, Computer, Gesellschaft. Linguistics on the Way into the Third Millennium. Proceedings of the 34th Linguistics Colloquium, Germersheim 1999. Part II: Language, Computer, and Society. 2002.

Peter Lang · Europäischer Verlag der Wissenschaften

Ulla Fix / Hannelore Poethe / Gabriele Yos

Textlinguistik und Stilistik für Einsteiger

Ein Lehr- und Arbeitsbuch
Unter Mitarbeit von Ruth Geier

Frankfurt/M., Berlin, Bern, Bruxelles, New York, Oxford, Wien, 2001.
236 S., zahlr. Abb., 3 Tab., 1 Graf.
Leipziger Skripten. Einführungs- und Übungsbücher aus dem Institut für Germanistik. Bd. 1
Herausgegeben von Irmhild Barz, Ulla Fix und Marianne Schröder.
ISBN 3-631-38162-X · br. € 24.50*

Mit diesem Lehr- und Arbeitsbuch sollen Studierende in die beiden linguistischen Teilgebiete eingeführt werden, die den Text zum Gegenstand haben. Dabei sollen sowohl die engen Beziehungen zwischen beiden Disziplinen als auch ihre jeweils eigenständigen Untersuchungsinteressen zum Ausdruck kommen. Das Buch vermittelt Grundzüge von Text- und Stilauffassungen und führt in die methodischen Grundlagen der Text- und Stilanalyse ein. An ausgewählten Texten verschiedener Kommunikationsbereiche werden unterschiedliche Ansätze für Text- und Stilanalysen musterhaft vorgeführt. An praktischen Bedürfnissen der Textproduktion und -rezeption orientiert ist ein abschließendes Kapitel zum Umgang mit sprachlich-kommunikativen Normen.

Frankfurt/M · Berlin · Bern · Bruxelles · New York · Oxford · Wien
Auslieferung: Verlag Peter Lang AG
Jupiterstr. 15, CH-3000 Bern 15
Telefax (004131) 9402131

*inklusive der in Deutschland gültigen Mehrwertsteuer
Preisänderungen vorbehalten
Homepage http://www.peterlang.de